FOOTBALL OUTSIDERS™
ALMANAC 2021

THE ESSENTIAL GUIDE TO THE 2021 NFL AND COLLEGE FOOTBALL SEASONS

Edited by Aaron Schatz

With

Thomas Bassinger • Ian Boyd • Parker Fleming • Brian Fremeau
Derrik Klassen • Bryan Knowles • Rivers McCown • Dan Pizzuta • Andrew Potter
Scott Spratt • Mike Tanier • Vincent Verhei • Robert Weintraub • Carl Yedor

Copyright 2021 EdjSports, LLC

ISBN: 9798534032932
All rights reserved

Table of Contents

NFL PLAYERS

COLLEGE FOOTBALL

FURTHER RESEARCH

Introduction

Are you ready for the biggest NFL season ever?

That is, of course, the NFL's ostentatious come-on advertising the upcoming 2021 season. They are reminding you of this year's expansion of the schedule to 17 regular-season games. But why shouldn't the biggest NFL season ever follow the weirdest NFL season ever?

A year ago, we didn't know what the COVID-19 pandemic would mean for the 2020 NFL season. But things ended up running rather smoothly, considering. Yes, there were plenty of things different about last season: players randomly disappearing onto the COVID list for a week or two, bye weeks changed at midseason, games played on Tuesdays and Wednesdays, even whole units (like the Denver quarterback room) being wiped out for a week. Yet every NFL team played its entire regular-season schedule. We had the new ex-panded playoffs with 14 teams, and we ended up with Tom Brady winning the Super Bowl. So in some ways, it was the same as it ever was.

With COVID, there was more roster turnover in 2020 than ever before. Including COVID opt-outs, the average team had a record 83.6 adjusted games lost according to our injury metric. (The previous record was 82.2 AGL in 2016.) New rules allowed players to move on and off the injured list easily, or to be activated from the practice squad and then sent back without going through waivers. In 2019, 70.4 players per team appeared on an active roster for at least one week during the regular season. In 2020, that number rose to 74.4 players per team, led by the San Francisco 49ers using 88 different active players during the season. Most of last year's COVID-related changes to the roster rules are expected to be kept for 2021, though nothing has officially been announced as of July 1.

With the year of COVID came the year of offense. NFL teams averaged 24.8 points per game, more than a point higher than the previous high of 23.4 points in 2013. Completion rates hit an all-time high while both interceptions and fumbles hit an all-time low. Even rushing averages were the highest they've ever been, at 4.41 yards per carry.

Were the offensive levels of 2020 related to COVID, and the reduced opportunity for de-fenses to practice together? It's hard to tell, especially since offenses had the same reduced opportunity to practice together. Was there more offense because the defense couldn't count on loud home crowds? The numbers weren't particularly different for home teams com-pared to road teams. And COVID was not the only possible explanation for the increase in scoring last season.

First of all, the gradual rise of offense has been a theme in the NFL for two decades now. It speeded up a little last year, but this was not a new phenomenon. There was also a major change in the way the game was officiated in 2020, at the direction of the NFL league office. Officials called a much looser game, particularly when it came to offensive penalties. In 2018 and 2019, the average team was flagged for 3.6 offensive penalties per game, including declined and offsetting penalties. In 2020, that dropped to 2.6 offensive penalties per game. The biggest change came in offensive holding, which was down from 725 total flags in 2019 to just 430 in 2020 (not including special teams). But other offensive penal-ties were down as well, including false starts, illegal blocks, and offensive pass interfer-ence. If we assume that the game will be called similarly in 2021, then the offensive levels should stay as high or perhaps rise even a little bit higher.

However, there are plenty of things we don't know about the 2021 season, hangovers left from last year's COVID-affected campaign. What will happen to second-year players who are only just getting their first proper offseason now? Will players who opted out of last season return with the same production we last saw from them in 2019? Are there lingering effects on the health of players who contracted COVID last season? What will happen in the upcoming season with non-vaccinated players who still have to observe last year's COVID protocols?

Then, of course, there are the financial effects of the COVID year. NFL teams claimed to have lost between $3 billion and $4 billion due to the effects of COVID. The salary cap for 2021 went down for the first time in a decade, dropping from $198.2 million to $182.5 mil-lion. That drop is balanced out by the expectation of a new broadcast agreement coming in the near future which will dramatically increase the cap in the coming seasons. Teams worked hard to structure contracts in such a way that cap charges would be avoided in 2021 in favor of higher charges in future years when everyone in the league expects a fi-nancial windfall and a much higher cap.

So while 2021 may be the biggest NFL season ever in terms of a 17-game schedule, the financials will pale in comparison to what we're going to see in 2023 and 2024. The real biggest NFL seasons ever are just around the corner.

Even with a higher salary cap, teams are still going to have to efficiently make their finan-cial decisions. A 17-game season brings up questions about player rest, making roster deci-sions more complicated. Teams will continue to make in-game deci-sions, from how often to run play-action to how often to go for it on fourth downs. In each of these areas, football analytics are going to continue to play an ever-increasing role in the NFL.

Football analytics have come a very long away since Football Outsiders first pioneered ana-lytical writing about the National Football League back in 2003. ESPN sports analytics writer Seth Walder maintains a list of analytics staffers for each NFL team. The only team that currently has nobody on the list, the Tennes-see Titans, posted a job opening for a data analyst in June.

More NFL teams are following more of the precepts of football analytics. Teams are more aggressive on fourth downs than ever before. Teams are passing more than ever before. Teams are us-ing play-action more than ever before. And teams are spreading out defenses more than ever before.

Analysts working for the NFL have developed new metrics (a.k.a. "Next Gen Stats") using the tracking systems that are now installed in every player's pads and in every football used on the field. The NFL now provides some of that data to the public to create new analytics in their annual Big Data Bowl. Those who don't have access to this tracking data have cre-ated their own new metrics using game charting data, such as the data collected by our part-ners at Sports Info Solutions. And a whole community of analysts has sprouted up on Twitter, developing new ways to look at the game and debating the great questions of cur-rent NFL fandom.

At its heart, the football analytics revolution is about learning more about the game. It's about not accepting the idea that certain players "just win." It's about gaining insight into the complexity behind the modern offense. It's about understanding the dramatic way that strength of schedule affects the way we see a team's performance. It's about figuring out which player skills translate from college to the pros. And it's about accepting that the pass dominates the run in the National Football League, and it has for at least 30 years.

As the original football analytics website, Football Outsiders is still doing its part to chal-lenge conventional wisdom and look deeper inside the numbers. Yes, there are a lot of ta-bles of numbers in this book, but words are the meat of our analysis; numbers are just the spice. There's a rumor that stat analysts don't watch game tape. In reality, stat analysts watch more tape than most beat writers or national Internet columnists, and *a lot* more tape than the average fan. We take everything we learn off the tape, synthesize it with the statistics, and deliver it to you.

Everybody who writes about football uses both statistics (whether they be basic yardage totals or more advanced stats like ours) and scouting (whether scouting reports by profes-sionals or just their own eyes). The same goes for us, except that the statistics portion of our analysis is far more accurate than what you normally see from football coverage. Those numbers are based on three ideas:

1) Conventional football statistics are heavily dependent on context. Down and dis-tance, field position, the current score, time left on the clock, the quality of the opponent—all of these elements influence the objective of the play and/or its outcome. Yet, the official NFL stats add together all yardage gained by a specific team or player without considering the impact of that particular yardage on wins and losses. In addition, filtering out bits of luck and random chance can help us figure out which teams are really more likely to play better for the rest of the season, or even in the following season.

2) On any one play, the majority of the important action is not tracked by the con-ventional NFL play-by-play. We now partner with both ESPN Stats & Info and Sports Info Solutions to collect data on every single NFL regular-season and postseason play. We know how many pass-rushers teams send on each pass, how often teams go three-wide or use two tight ends, how often teams use a play-action fake, and which defensive backs are in coverage, even when they don't get a tackle in the standard play-by-play.

3) A player's production in one year does not necessarily equal his production the next year. This also applies to teams, of course. Even when stats are accurate, they're often extremely variable from year to year and subject to heavy forces of regres-sion to the mean. Field goal percentage, red zone performance, third-down performance on defense, intercep-tions and fumble recoveries—these are but a few examples. In addition, the age curves for football players are much steeper than in other sports. Old players break down faster, and young players often improve faster. Many football analysts concentrate on looking at what players did last year. We'll talk about that as well, but we're more interested in what players are going to do *this* year. Which performances from a year ago are flukes, and which ones represent long-term improvement or decline? What will one more year of expe-rience do to this player's production? And how will a player's role change this year, and what does it mean for the team?

As with past books, *Football Outsiders Almanac 2021* starts off with "Pregame Show" (reviewing the most important research we've done in past books) and "Statistical Toolbox" (explaining all our stats). Once again, we preserve the ridiculousness of the foot-ball season for posterity with another version of "The Year in Quotes" and we introduce you to some of the more promising (and lesser-known) young bench players with our 15th annual list of Top 25 Prospects chosen in the third round or later.

Each NFL team gets a full chapter covering what happened in 2020 and our projections for the upcoming season. Are there rea-sons to believe that the team was inherently better or worse than its record last year? What did the team do in the offseason, and what does that mean for the team's chances to win in 2021? Each chapter also includes all kinds of ad-vanced statistics covering 2020 performance and strategic tendencies, plus detailed com-mentary on each of the major units of the team: offensive line, defensive front seven, defen-sive secondary, and special teams.

"Skill players" (by which we mean "players who get counted in fantasy football") get their own section in the back of the book. We list the major players at each position alphabetical-ly, along with commentary and a 2021 KUBIAK projection that will help you win your fantasy football league.

Next comes our preview of the college football season. We go in-depth with the top 50 pro-jected teams in the nation. Just like with our NFL coverage, the goal of our college pre-views is to focus as much as possible on "why" and how," not just "which team is better." We're not just here to rank the Football Bowl Subdivision teams from 1 to 130. We break things down to look at offense and defense, to consider returning talent levels, and to ana-lyze passes and runs in specific situations.

We hope our book helps you raise your level of football ex-pertise, win arguments with your friends, and win your fantasy football league. Occasionally, there are also jokes. Just don't ex-pect all of our predictions to be right. The unexpected is part of the fun. And given the unknown impact of COVID in its second year, there's likely to be more unexpected than usual. Just not quite as much as last year.

Aaron Schatz
Auburn, Mass.
July 12, 2021

P.S. Don't forget to visit FootballOutsiders.com every day for fresh coverage of the NFL and college football, plus the most intelligent football discussion threads on the Internet.

Pregame Show

It has now been 18 years since we launched Football Outsiders. In that time, we've done a lot of primary research on the National Football League, and we reference that research in many of the articles and comments in *Football Outsiders Almanac 2021*. New readers may come across an offhand comment in a team chapter about, for example, the idea that fumble recovery is not a skill, and wonder what in the heck we are talking about. We can't repeat all our research in every new edition of *Football Outsiders Almanac*, so we start each year with a basic look at some of the most important precepts that have emerged from Football Outsiders research. You will see these issues come up again and again throughout the book.

You can also find this introduction online at http://www.footballoutsiders.com/info/FO-basics, along with links to the original research in the cases in which that research appeared online instead of (or as well as) in print.

Our various methods for projecting NFL success for college prospects are not listed below but are referenced at times during the book. Those methods are detailed in an essay on page 447.

You run when you win, not win when you run.

If we could only share one piece of anti-conventional wisdom with you before you read the rest of our book, this would be it. The first article ever written for Football Outsiders was devoted to debunking the myth of "establishing the run." There is no correlation whatsoever between giving your running backs a lot of carries early in the game and winning the game. Just running the ball is not going to help a team score; it has to run successfully.

There is also no evidence that running the ball more early in the game creates the opportunity for longer gains late in the game, i.e., the so-called "body blows" thesis. And there is no evidence that passing the ball too frequently puts the defense on the field too much and tires it out.

Why does nearly every beat writer and television analyst still repeat the tired old school mantra that "establishing the run" is the secret to winning football games? The biggest issue is confusing cause and effect. There are exceptions, but for the most part, winning teams have a lot of carries because their running backs are running out the clock at the end of wins, not because they are running wild early in games.

A sister statement to "you have to establish the run" is "team X is 8-1 when running back John Doe runs for at least 100 yards." Unless John Doe is possessed by otherworldly spirits the way Adrian Peterson was a couple years ago, the team isn't winning because of his 100-yard games. He's putting up 100-yard games because his team is winning.

At this point, it's hard to figure out why so many commentators and fans still overrate the importance of the running game. One problem has always been history. Older NFL analysts and fans came of age during the 1970s, when the rules favored the running game much more than those in the modern NFL. We used to have to explain that optimal strategies from 1974 are not optimal strategies for today. But this would seem to be a smaller problem now than it was 10 years ago; most current NFL analysts played the game in the 1990s or beyond, when the game was heavily pass-centric.

Another issue may be a confusion of professional football with other levels. As you go down the football pyramid, from NFL teams to FBS to FCS to Division II and so on, all the way down to high school, at every level further down the running game becomes more important. Strategies that win on Saturday do not necessarily win on Sunday.

A great defense against the run is nothing without a good pass defense.

This is a corollary to the absurdity of "establish the run." With rare exceptions, teams win or lose with the passing game more than the running game—and by stopping the passing game more than the running game. Ron Jaworski puts it best: "The pass gives you the lead, and the run solidifies it." The reason why teams need a strong run defense in the playoffs is not to shut the run down early; it's to keep the other team from icing the clock if they get a lead. You can't mount a comeback if you can't stop the run.

Running on third-and-short is more likely to convert than passing on third-and-short.

On average, passing will always gain more yardage than running, with one very important exception: when a team is just 1 or 2 yards away from a new set of downs or the goal line. On third-and-1, a run will convert for a new set of downs 36% more often than a pass. Expand that to all third or fourth downs with 1 or 2 yards to go and the run is successful 40% more often. With these percentages, the possibility of a long gain with a pass is not worth the tradeoff of an incompletion that kills a drive.

This is one reason why teams have to be able to both run and pass. The offense also has to keep some semblance of balance so they can use their play-action fakes—you can't run a play-fake from an empty set—and so the defense doesn't just run their nickel and dime packages all game. Balance also means that teams do need to pass occasionally in short-yardage situations; they just need to do it less than they do now. Teams pass roughly 60% of the time on third-and-2 even though runs in that situation convert 20% more often than passes. They pass 68% of the time on fourth-and-2 even though runs in that situation convert twice as often as passes.

You don't need to run a lot to set up play-action.

Of course, the idea that you have to run a little bit so play-action will work doesn't mean you have to run as often as NFL teams currently do. There's no correlation between a team's rushing frequency or success rate rushing and its play-action effectiveness over the course of either a single game or an entire season. That doesn't mean there wouldn't be a correlation at an extreme run/pass ratio, but we have yet to see an NFL team that even comes close to what that extreme might be.

Standard team rankings based on total yardage are inherently flawed.

Check out the schedule page on NFL.com, and you will find that each game is listed with league rankings based on total yardage. That is still how the NFL "officially" ranks teams, but these rankings rarely match up with common sense. That is because total team yardage may be the most context-dependent number in football.

It starts with the basic concept that rate stats are generally more valuable than cumulative stats. Yards per carry says more about a running back's quality than total yardage, completion percentage says more than just a quarterback's total number of completions. The same thing is true for teams; in fact, it is even more important because of the way football strategy influences the number of runs and passes in the game plan. Poor teams will give up fewer passing yards and more rushing yards because opponents will stop passing once they have a late-game lead and will run out the clock instead. For winning teams, the opposite is true. For example, which team had a better pass defense last year: Cincinnati or Tampa Bay? According to the official NFL rankings, Cincinnati (3,859 yards allowed on 558 passes and sacks, 6.9 net yards per pass) was a better pass defense than Tampa Bay (3,945 net yards allowed on 665 passes and sacks, 5.9 net yards per pass).

Total yardage rankings are also skewed because some teams play at a faster pace than other teams. For example, last year Arizona (6,153) had more yardage than Cleveland (5,913). However, the Browns were the superior offense and much more efficient; they gained those yards on only 159 drives while the Cardinals needed 176 drives.

A team will score more when playing a bad defense and will give up more points when playing a good offense.

This sounds absurdly basic, but when people consider team and player stats without looking at strength of schedule, they are ignoring this. In 2012, for example, rookie Russell Wilson had a higher DVOA rating than fellow rookie Robert Griffin III because he faced a more difficult schedule, even though Griffin had slightly better standard stats. A more recent example: In 2019, Seattle and Houston both had 5.7 yards per play on offense. Seattle was the better offense by DVOA in part because Seattle played the third-hardest schedule of opposing defenses in the league while Houston played an average schedule of opposing defenses.

If their overall yards per carry are equal, a running back who consistently gains yardage on every play is more valuable than a boom-and-bust running back who is frequently stuffed at the line but occasionally breaks a long highlight-worthy run.

Our brethren in the baseball analytics world believe that the most precious commodity in baseball is outs. Teams only get 27 of them per game, and you can't afford to give one up for very little return. So imagine if there was a new rule in baseball that gave a team a way to earn another three outs in the middle of the inning. That would be pretty useful, right?

That's the way football works. You may start a drive 80 yards away from scoring, but as long as you can earn 10 yards in four chances, you get another four chances. Long gains have plenty of value, but if those long gains are mixed with a lot of short gains, you are going to put the quarterback in a lot of difficult third-and-long situations. That means more punts and more giving the ball back to the other team rather than moving the chains and giving the offense four more plays to work with.

The running back who gains consistent yardage is also going to do a lot more for you late in the game, when the goal of running the ball is not just to gain yardage but to eat clock time. If you are a Giants fan watching your team with a late lead, you don't want to see three straight Saquon Barkley stuffs at the line followed by a punt. You want to see a game-icing first down.

A common historical misconception is that our preference for consistent running backs means that "Football Outsiders believes that Barry Sanders was overrated." Sanders wasn't just any boom-and-bust running back, though; he was the greatest boom-and-bust runner of all time, with bigger booms and fewer busts. Sanders ranked in the top five in DYAR five times (third in 1989, first in 1990, and second in 1994, 1996, and 1997).

Rushing is more dependent on the offensive line than people realize, but pass protection is more dependent on the quarterback himself than people realize.

Some readers complain that this idea contradicts the previous one. Aren't those consistent running backs just the product of good offensive lines? The truth is somewhere in between. There are certainly good running backs who suffer because their offensive lines cannot create consistent holes, but most boom-and-bust running backs contribute to their own problems by hesitating behind the line whenever the hole is unclear, looking for the home run instead of charging forward for the 4-yard gain that keeps the offense moving.

Further research has shown that rushing success is also heavily dependent on scheme as well as how the defense sets up against the play, in particular how many men the defense puts in the box (i.e., in between the offensive tackles). Research from 2019's NFL Big Data Bowl suggests that the results of a running play can be almost entirely predicted using the movement of the blockers and defenders, without needing to consider the identity of the running back at all. It's research like this that has given birth to the popular Twitter saying that "running backs don't matter." That's a bit of an extreme; it's more likely that running backs matter a little bit, but much less than NFL wisdom has historically believed, and most of the differentiation between different backs comes from their skills in the passing game.

In addition, "running backs don't matter" is sometimes mistaken for the idea that the running game doesn't matter. The latter is a bit of an analytical strawman, even if analytics has shown that the running game is less important than the passing game.

As for pass protection, some quarterbacks have better instincts for the rush than others and are thus better at getting out of trouble by moving around in the pocket or throwing the ball away. Others will hesitate, hold onto the ball too long, and lose yardage over and over.

Note that "moving around in the pocket" does not necessarily mean "scrambling." In fact, a scrambling quarterback will often take more sacks than a pocket quarterback, because while he's running around trying to make something happen, a defensive lineman will catch up with him.

Shotgun formations are generally more efficient than formations with the quarterback under center.

From 2013 to 2017, offenses averaged roughly 5.9 yards per play from shotgun (or pistol), but just 5.1 yards per play with the quarterback under center. Since 2018 that gap has closed a bit, but offenses still averaged 5.9 yards per play from shotgun or pistol over the last three seasons compared to 5.4 yards per play with the quarterback under center. This wide split exists even if you analyze the data to try to weed out biases like teams using shotgun more often on third-and-long, or against prevent defenses in the fourth quarter. Shotgun offense is more efficient if you only look at the first half, on every down, and even if you only look at running back carries rather than passes and scrambles.

It's hard to think of a Football Outsiders axiom that has been better assimilated by the people running NFL teams since we started doing this a decade ago. In 2001, NFL teams only used shotgun on 14% of plays. Five years later, in 2006, that had increased slightly, to 20% of plays. By 2012, shotgun was used on a 47.5% of plays (including the pistol, but not counting the Wildcat or other direct snaps to non-quarterbacks). In 2016, the league as a whole was up to an average of 64.4% of plays from shotgun or pistol. Last year, that average was at 66.3%.

There's an interesting corollary here which we are just starting to study, because there does seem to be one split where offenses are *less* efficient from shotgun: play-action. In 2019, offenses averaged 8.1 yards per play when using play-action from an under-center formation compared to 7.0 yards per play when using play-action from a shotgun formation. In 2020, that gap was smaller, but still 7.6 yards per play with play-action under center compared to 7.1 yards per play with play-action from shotgun. A number of teams that are near the top of the league in play-action usage, such as the Rams and Titans, are also near the bottom of the league in using shotgun.

Wide receivers must be judged on both complete and incomplete passes.

Here's an example from 2019: Stefon Diggs had 1,130 receiving yards while Robby Anderson had 779 receiving yards, even though the two receivers were just one target apart. Each receiver ran his average route roughly 15 yards downfield. But there was a big reason why Diggs had a much better season than Anderson: Diggs caught 67% of intended passes and Anderson caught just 54%.

Some work has been done on splitting responsibility for incomplete passes between quarterbacks and receivers, but not enough that we can incorporate this into our advanced stats at this time. We know that wide receiver catch rates are almost as consistent from year to year as quarterback completion percentages, but it is also important to look at catch rate in the context of the types of routes each receiver runs. A few years ago, we expanded on this idea with a new plus-minus metric, which is explained in the introduction to the chapter on wide receivers and tight ends.

The total quality of an NFL team is four parts offense, three parts defense, and one part special teams.

There are three units on a football team, but they are not of equal importance. Work by Chase Stuart, Neil Paine, and Brian Burke suggests a split between offense and defense of roughly 58-42, without considering special teams. Our research suggests that special teams contributes about 13% to total performance; if you measure the remaining 87% with a 58-42 ratio, you get roughly 4:3:1. When we compare the range of offense, defense, and special teams DVOA ratings, we get the same results, with the best and worst offenses roughly 130% stronger than the best and worst defenses, and roughly four times stronger than the best and worst special teams.

Offense is more consistent from year to year than defense, and offensive performance is easier to project than defensive performance. Special teams are less consistent than either.

Nobody in the NFL understood this concept better than former Indianapolis Colts general manager Bill Polian. Both the Super Bowl champion Colts and the four-time AFC champion Buffalo Bills of the early 1990s were built around the idea that if you put together an offense that can dominate the league year after year, eventually you will luck into a year where good health and a few smart decisions will give you a defense good enough to win a championship. (As the Colts learned in 2006, you don't even need a year, just four weeks.) Even the New England Patriots, who are led by a defense-first head coach in Bill Belichick, have been more consistent on offense than on defense since they began their run of success in 2001.

Field goal percentage is almost entirely random from season to season, while kickoff distance is one of the most consistent statistics in football.

This theory, which originally appeared in the *New York Times* in October 2006, is one of our most controversial, but it is hard to argue against the evidence. Measuring every kicker from 2012 to 2018 who had at least 10 field goal attempts in each of two consecutive years, the year-to-year correlation coefficient for field goal percentage was an insignificant .06. Jason Myers of Seattle is a great example. He was below 80% in both 2016 and 2017. In 2018, he had a Pro Bowl season and connected on 92% of field goals, which got him a big contract in Seattle. In 2019, he declined to just 82%. Then in 2020, he rebounded and hit all 24 of his field goal attempts with no misses.

On the other hand, the year-to-year correlation coefficient for touchback percentage from 2012 to 2018, with a minimum of 10 kickoffs in each of two consecutive years, was .62. The same players consistently lead the league in kickoff distance. In recent years, that group includes Justin Tucker, Dustin Hopkins, and Myers.

Teams with more offensive penalties generally lose more games, but there is no correlation between defensive penalties and losses.

Specific defensive penalties of course lose games; we've all sworn at the television when the cornerback on our favorite team gets flagged for a 50-yard pass interference penalty. Yet overall, there is no correlation between losses and the total of defensive penalties or even the total yardage on defensive penalties. One reason is that defensive penalties often represent *good* play, not bad. Cornerbacks who play tight coverage may be just on the edge of a penalty on most plays, only occasionally earning a flag. Defensive ends who get a good jump on rushing the passer will gladly trade an encroachment penalty or two for 10 snaps where they get off the blocks a split-second before the linemen trying to block them.

In addition, offensive penalties have a higher correlation from year to year than defensive penalties. The penalty that correlates highest with losses is the false start, and the penalty that teams will have called most consistently from year to year is also the false start.

Recovery of a fumble, despite being the product of hard work, is almost entirely random.

Stripping the ball is a skill. Holding onto the ball is a skill. Pouncing on the ball as it is bouncing all over the place is not a skill. There is no correlation whatsoever between the percentage of fumbles recovered by a team in one year and the percentage they recover in the next year. The odds of recovery are based solely on the type of play involved, not the teams or any of their players.

The Minnesota Vikings are a good example. In 2019, the Vikings recovered 13 of 19 fumbles by opponents (68%). The next year, the same defense recovered just four of 13 fumbles by opponents (31%).

Fumble recovery is equally erratic on offense. In 2019, the Oakland Raiders recovered 11 of 18 fumbles on offense (61%). In 2020, the Raiders recovered only five of 20 fumbles on offense (25%).

Fumble recovery is a major reason why the general public overestimates or underestimates some teams. Fumbles are huge, turning-point plays that dramatically impact wins and losses in the past, while fumble recovery percentage says absolutely nothing about a team's chances of winning games in the future. With this in mind, Football Outsiders stats treat all fumbles as equal, penalizing them based on the likelihood of each type of fumble (run, pass, sack, etc.) being recovered by the defense.

Other plays that qualify as "non-predictive events" include two-point conversions, blocked kicks, and touchdowns during turnover returns. These plays are not "lucky," per se, but they have no value whatsoever for predicting future performance.

Field position is fluid.

As discussed in the Statistical Toolbox, every yard line on the field has a value based on how likely a team is to score from that location on the field as opposed to from a yard further back. The change in value from one yard to the next is the same whether the team has the ball or not. The goal of a defense is not just to prevent scoring, but to hold the opposition so that the offense can get the ball back in the best possible field position. A bad offense will score as many points as a good offense if it starts each drive 5 yards closer to the goal line.

A corollary to this precept: the most underrated aspect of an NFL team's performance is the field position gained or lost on kickoffs and punts. This is part of why players such as Cordarrelle Patterson can have such an impact on the game, even when they aren't taking a kickoff or punt all the way back for a touchdown.

The red zone is the most important place on the field to play well, but performance in the red zone from year to year is much less consistent than overall performance.

Although play in the red zone has a disproportionately high importance to the outcome of games relative to plays on the rest of the field, NFL teams do not exhibit a level of performance in the red zone that is consistently better or worse than their performance elsewhere, year after year. The simplest explanation why is a small(er) sample size and the inherent variance of football, with contributing factors like injuries and changes in personnel.

Injuries regress to the mean on the seasonal level, and teams that avoid injuries in a given season tend to win more games.

There are no doubt teams with streaks of good or bad health over multiple years, and we have found some correlation from year-to-year in each team's level of injuries. However, teams who were especially healthy or especially unhealthy, as measured by our adjusted games lost (AGL) metric, almost always head towards league average in the subsequent season. Furthermore, injury—or the absence thereof—has a huge correlation with wins and a significant impact on a team's success. There's no doubt that a few high-profile teams have resisted this trend in recent years. The Patriots often deal with a high number of injuries, and the 2017 Eagles obviously overcame a number of important injuries to win the championship. Last year, though, Tampa Bay finished No. 1 with the fewest AGL and won the Super Bowl. Meanwhile, out of the 10 teams with the highest overall AGL, only Washington made the playoffs.

By and large, a team built on depth is better than a team built on stars and scrubs.

Connected to the previous statement, because teams need to go into the season expecting that they will suffer an average number of injuries no matter how healthy they were the previous year. You cannot concentrate your salaries on a handful of star players because there is no such thing as avoiding injuries in the NFL. The game is too fast and the players too strong to build a team based around the idea that "if we can avoid all injuries this year, we'll win."

Running backs usually decline after age 28, tight ends after age 29, wide receivers after age 30, and quarterbacks after age 32.

This research was originally done by Doug Drinen (former editor of Pro Football Reference) in 2000. A few players have had huge seasons above these general age limits, particularly at the quarterback position, but the peak ages Drinen found still apply to the majority of players.

As for "non-skill players," research we did in 2007 for *ESPN The Magazine* suggested that defensive ends and defensive backs generally begin to decline after age 29, linebackers and offensive linemen after age 30, and defensive tackles after age 31. However, because we still have so few statistics to use to study linemen and defensive players, this research should not be considered definitive.

The strongest indicator of how a college football team will perform in the upcoming season is their performance in recent seasons.

It may seem strange because graduation enforces constant player turnover, but college football teams are actually much more consistent from year to year than NFL teams. Thanks in large part to consistency in recruiting, teams can be expected to play within a reasonable range of their baseline program expectations each season. Our Program F/+ ratings, which represent a rolling five-year period of play-by-play and drive efficiency data, have an extremely strong (.76) correlation with the next year's F/+ rating.

Championship teams are generally defined by their ability to dominate inferior opponents, not their ability to win close games.

Football games are often decided by just one or two plays: a missed field goal, a bouncing fumble, the subjective spot of an official on fourth-and-1. One missed assignment by a cornerback or one slightly askew pass that bounces off a receiver's hands and into those of a defensive back 5 yards away and the game could be over. In a blowout, however, one lucky bounce isn't going to change things. Championship teams—in both professional and college football—typically beat their good opponents convincingly and destroy the cupcakes on the schedule.

Aaron Schatz

Statistical Toolbox

After 18 years of Football Outsiders, some of our readers are as comfortable with DVOA and ALY as they are with touchdowns and tackles. Yet to most fans, including our newer readers, it still looks like a lot of alphabet soup. That's what this chapter is for. The next few pages define and explain all of all the unique NFL statistics you'll find in this book: how we calculate them, what the numbers mean, and what they tell us about why teams win or lose football games. We'll go through the information in each of the tables that appear in each team chapter, pointing out whether those stats come from advanced mathematical manipulation of the standard play-by-play or tracking what we see on television with Sports Info Solutions game charting. This chapter covers NFL statistics only. College metrics such as FEI are explained in the introduction to the college football section on page 397.

We've done our best to present these numbers in a way that makes them easy to understand. This explanation is long, so feel free to read some of it, flip around the rest of the book, and then come back. It will still be here.

Defense-Adjusted Value Over Average (DVOA)

One running back runs for 3 yards. Another running back runs for 3 yards. Which is the better run?

This sounds like a stupid question, but it isn't. In fact, this question is at the heart of nearly all of the analysis in this book.

Several factors can differentiate one 3-yard run from another. What is the down and distance? Is it third-and-2, or second-and-15? Where on the field is the ball? Does the player get only 3 yards because he hits the goal line and scores? Is the player's team up by two touchdowns in the fourth quarter and thus running out the clock, or down by two touchdowns and thus facing a defense that is playing purely against the pass? Is the running back playing against the porous defense of the Panthers, or the stalwart defense of the Vikings?

Conventional NFL statistics value plays based solely on their net yardage. The NFL determines the best players by adding up all their yards no matter what situations they came in or how many plays it took to get them. Now, why would they do that? Football has one objective—to get to the end zone—and two ways to achieve that, by gaining yards and achieving first downs. These two goals need to be balanced to determine a player's value or a team's performance. All the yards in the world won't help a team win if they all come in 6-yard chunks on third-and-10.

The popularity of fantasy football only exacerbates the problem. Fans have gotten used to judging players based on how much they help fantasy teams win and lose, not how much they help *real* teams win and lose. Typical fantasy scoring further skews things by counting the yard between the one and the goal line as 61 times more important than all the other yards on the field (each yard worth 0.1 points, a touchdown worth 6.0). Let's say Julio Jones catches a pass on third-and-15 and goes 50 yards but gets tackled 2 yards from the goal line, and then Derrick Henry takes the ball on first-and-goal from the 2-yard line and plunges in for the score. Has Henry done something special? Not really. When an offense gets the ball on first-and-goal at the 2-yard line, they are going to score a touchdown five out of six times. Henry is getting credit for the work done by the passing game.

Doing a better job of distributing credit for scoring points and winning games is the goal of **DVOA**, or Defense-adjusted Value Over Average. DVOA breaks down every single play of the NFL season, assigning each play a value based on both total yards and yards towards a first down, based on work done by Pete Palmer, Bob Carroll, and John Thorn in their seminal book, *The Hidden Game of Football*. On first down, a play is considered a success if it gains 45% of needed yards; on second down, a play needs to gain 60% of needed yards; on third or fourth down, only gaining a new first down is considered success.

We then expand upon that basic idea with a more complicated system of "success points," improved over the past four years with a lot of mathematics and a bit of trial and error. A successful play is worth one point, an unsuccessful play zero points with fractional points in between (for example, 8 yards on third-and-10 is worth 0.54 "success points"). Extra points are awarded for big plays, gradually increasing to three points for 10 yards (assuming those yards result in a first down), four points for 20 yards, and five points for 40 yards or more. Losing three or more yards is -1 point. Interceptions average -6 points, with an adjustment for the length of the pass and the location of the interception (since an interception tipped at the line is more likely to produce a long return than an interception on a 40-yard pass). A fumble is worth anywhere from -1.7 to -4.0 points depending on how often a fumble in that situation is lost to the defense—no matter who actually recovers the fumble. Red zone plays get a bonus: 20% for team offense, 5% for team defense, and 10% for individual players. There is a bonus given for a touchdown that acknowledges that the goal line is significantly more difficult to cross than the previous 99 yards (although this bonus is nowhere near as large as the one used in fantasy football).

(Our system is a bit more complex than the one in *Hidden Game* thanks to our subsequent research, which added larger penalty for turnovers, the fractional points, and a slightly higher baseline for success on first down. The reason why all fumbles are counted, no matter whether they are recovered by the offense or defense, is explained in the essay "Pregame Show.")

Every single play run in the NFL gets a "success value" based on this system, and then that number gets compared to the average success values of plays in similar situations for all players, adjusted for a number of variables. These include down and distance, field location, time remaining in game, and the team's lead or deficit in the game score. Teams are always compared to the overall offensive average, as the team made its own choice whether to pass or rush. When it comes to individual players, however, rushing plays are compared to other rushing plays, passing plays to other passing plays, tight ends to tight ends, wideouts to wideouts, and so on.

Going back to our example of the 3-yard rush, if Player A gains 3 yards under a set of circumstances in which the average NFL running back gains only one yard, then Player A has a certain amount of value above others at his position. Likewise, if Player B gains 3 yards on a play on which, under similar circumstances, an average NFL back gains 4 yards, that Player B has negative value relative to others at his position. Once we make all our adjustments, we can evaluate the difference between this player's rate of success and the expected success rate of an average running back in the same situation (or between the opposing defense and the average defense in the same situation, etc.). Add up every play by a certain team or player, divide by the total of the various baselines for success in all those situations, and you get VOA, or Value Over Average.

Of course, the biggest variable in football is the fact that each team plays a different schedule against teams of disparate quality. By adjusting each play based on the opposing defense's average success in stopping that type of play over the course of a season, we get DVOA, or Defense-adjusted Value Over Average. Rushing and passing plays are adjusted based on down and location on the field; passing plays are also adjusted based on how the defense performs against passes to running backs, tight ends, or wide receivers. Defenses are adjusted based on the average success of the *offenses* they are facing. (Yes, technically the defensive stats are "offense-adjusted." If it seems weird, think of the "D" in "DVOA" as standing for "opponent-Dependent" or something.)

The biggest advantage of DVOA is the ability to break teams and players down to find strengths and weaknesses in a variety of situations. DVOA can be separated not only by player, but also by down, or by week, or by distance needed for a first down. This can give us a better idea of not just which team is better, but why, and what a team has to do in order to improve itself in the future. You will find DVOA used in this book in a lot of different ways—because it takes every single play into account, it can be used to measure a player or a team's performance in any situation. All Pittsburgh third downs can be compared to how an average team does on third down. Derek Carr and Marcus Mariota can each be compared to how an average quarterback performs in the red zone, or with a lead, or in the second half of the game.

Since it compares each play only to plays with similar circumstances, it gives a more accurate picture of how much better a team really is compared to the league as a whole. The list of top DVOA offenses on third down, for example, is more accurate than the conventional NFL conversion statistic because it takes into account that converting third-and-long is more difficult than converting third-and-short, and that a turnover

is worse than an incomplete pass because it eliminates the opportunity to move the other team back with a punt on fourth down.

One of the hardest parts of understanding a new statistic is interpreting its scale, or what numbers represent good performance or bad performance. We've made that easy with DVOA. For each season, ratings are normalized so that 0% represents league average. A positive DVOA represents a situation that favors the offense, while a negative DVOA represents a situation that favors the defense. This is why the best offenses have positive DVOA ratings (last year, Green Bay led the NFL at 29.1%) and the best defenses have negative DVOA ratings (with Pittsburgh on top at -20.2%).

The scale of offensive ratings is wider than the scale of defensive ratings. In most years, the best and worst offenses tend to rate around +/- 30%, while the best and worst defenses tend to rate around +/- 20%. For starting players, the scale tends to reach roughly +/- 40% for passing and receiving, and +/- 30% for rushing. As you might imagine, some players with fewer attempts will surpass both extremes.

Team DVOA totals combine offense and defense by subtracting the latter from the former because the better defenses will have negative DVOA ratings. (Special teams performance is also added, as described later in this essay.) Certain plays are counted in DVOA for offense and not for defense, leading to separate baselines on each side of the ball. In addition, although the league ratings for offense and defense are always 0%, the league averages for passing and rushing separately are *not* 0%. Because passing is more efficient than rushing, the average for team passing is always positive and the average for team rushing is always negative. However, ratings for individual players only compare passes to other passes and runs to other runs, so the league average for individual passing is 0%, as are the league averages for rushing and the three separate league averages for receiving by wide receivers, tight ends, and running backs.

Some other important notes about DVOA:

- We began using a new version of DVOA in September 2020 which now counts scrambles as passing plays instead of rushing plays. It also corrected an error regarding defensive adjustments for playing indoors. DVOA numbers in this book will differ slightly from DVOA numbers in our past books because of these changes.
- Only four penalties are included in DVOA. Two penalties count as pass plays on both sides of the ball: intentional grounding and defensive pass interference. The other two penalties are included for offense only: false starts and delay of game. Because the inclusion of these penalties means a group of negative plays that don't count as either passes or runs, the league averages for pass offense and run offense are higher than the league averages for pass defense and run defense.
- Aborted snaps and incomplete backwards lateral passes are only penalized on offense, not rewarded on defense.
- Adjustments for playing from behind or with a lead in

the fourth quarter are different for offense and defense, as are adjustments for the final two minutes of the first half when the offense is not near field goal range.

- Offense gets a slight penalty and defense gets a slight bonus for games indoors.

How well does DVOA work? Using correlation coefficients, we can show that only actual points scored are better than DVOA at indicating how many games a team has won (Table 1) and DVOA more stable from year to year than either wins or points scored (Table 2).

(Correlation coefficient is a statistical tool that measures how two variables are related by using a number between 1 and -1. The closer to -1 or 1, the stronger the relationship, but the closer to 0, the weaker the relationship.)

Table 1. Correlation of Various Stats to Wins, 2006-2020

Stat	Offense	Defense	Total
Points Scored/Allowed	0.752	-0.671	0.915
VOA (no opponent adjustment)	0.740	-0.562	0.892
DVOA	0.716	-0.501	0.872
Yards Gained/Allowed per Play	0.528	-0.356	0.704
Yards Gained/Allowed	0.535	-0.387	0.677

Table 2. Correlation of Various Stats from Year to Year, 2006-2020

Stat	Correlation
Yardage Differential	0.467
DVOA	0.458
Point Differential	0.426
Pythagorean Wins	0.416
Yards per Play Differential	0.407
Wins	0.344

Special Teams

The problem with a system based on measuring both yardage and yardage towards a first down is what to do with plays that don't have the possibility of a first down. Special teams are an important part of football and we needed a way to add that performance to the team DVOA rankings. Our special teams metric includes five separate measurements: field goals and extra points, net punting, punt returns, net kickoffs, and kick returns.

The foundation of most of these special teams ratings is the concept that each yard line has a different expected points value based on the likelihood of scoring from that position on the field. In *Hidden Game*, the authors suggested that the each additional yard for the offense had equal value, with a team's own goal line being worth -2 points, the 50-yard line 2 points, and the opposing goal line 6 points. (-2 points is not only the value of a safety, but also reflects the fact that when a team is backed up in its own territory, it is likely that its drive will stall, forcing a punt that will give the ball to the other team in good field position. Thus, the negative point value reflects the fact that the defense is more likely to score next.) Our studies have updated this concept to reflect the actual likelihood that the offense or defense will have the next score from a given position on the field based on actual results from the past few seasons. The line that represents the value of field position is not straight, but curved, with the value of each yard increasing as teams approach either goal line.

Our special teams ratings compare each kick or punt to league average based on the point value of the position of the kick, catch, and return. We've determined a league average for how far a kick goes based on the line of scrimmage for each kick (almost always the 35-yard line for kickoffs, variable for punts) and a league average for how far a return goes based on both the yard line where the ball is caught and the distance that it traveled in the air.

The kicking or punting team is rated based on net points compared to average, taking into account both the kick and the return if there is one. Because the average return is always positive, punts that are not returnable (touchbacks, out of bounds, fair catches, and punts downed by the coverage unit) will rate higher than punts of the same distance which are returnable. (This is also true of touchbacks on kickoffs.) There are also separate individual ratings for kickers and punters that are based on distance and whether the kick is returnable, assuming an average return in order to judge the kicker separate from the coverage.

For the return team, the rating is based on how many points the return is worth compared to average, based on the location of the catch and the distance the ball traveled in the air. Return teams are not judged on the distance of kicks, nor are they judged on kicks that cannot be returned. As explained below, blocked kicks are so rare as to be statistically insignificant as predictors for future performance and are thus ignored. For the kicking team they simply count as missed field goals, for the defense they are gathered with their opponents' other missed field goals in Hidden value (also explained below).

Field goal kicking is measured differently. Measuring kickers by field goal percentage is a bit absurd, as it assumes that all field goals are of equal difficulty. In our metric, each field goal is compared to the average number of points scored on all field goal attempts from that distance over the past 15 years. The value of a field goal increases as distance from the goal line increases. Kickoffs, punts, and field goals are then adjusted based on weather and altitude. It will surprise no one to learn that it is easier to kick the ball in Denver or a dome than it is to kick the ball in Buffalo in December. Because we do not yet have enough data to tailor our adjustments specifically to each stadium, each one is assigned to one of four categories: Cold, Warm, Dome, and Denver. There is also an additional adjustment dropping the value of field goals in Florida (because the warm temperatures allow the ball to carry better).

The baselines for special teams are adjusted in each year for rule changes such as the introduction of the special teams-only "k-ball" in 1999, movement of the kickoff line, and the

2016 change in kickoff touchbacks. Baselines have also been adjusted each year to make up for the gradual improvement of kickers over the last two decades.

Once we've totaled how many points above or below average can be attributed to special teams, we translate those points into DVOA so the ratings can be added to offense and defense to get total team DVOA.

There are three aspects of special teams that have an impact on wins and losses, but don't show up in the standard special teams rating because a team has little or no influence on them. The first is the length of kickoffs by the opposing team, with an asterisk. Obviously, there are no defenders standing on the 35-yard line, ready to block a kickoff after the whistle blows. However, over the past few years, some teams have deliberately kicked short in order to avoid certain top return men, such as Devin Hester and Cordarrelle Patterson. Therefore, the special teams formula includes adjustments to give teams extra credit for field position on kick returns if kickers are deliberately trying to avoid a return.

The other two items that special teams have little control over are field goals against your team, and punt distance against your team. Research shows no indication that teams can influence the accuracy or strength of field goal kickers and punters, except for blocks. As mentioned above, although blocked field goals and punts are definitely skillful plays, they are so rare that they have no correlation to how well teams have played in the past or will play in the future, thus they are included here as if they were any other missed field goal or botched punt, giving the defense no additional credit for their efforts. The value of these three elements is listed separately as "Hidden" value.

Special teams ratings also do not include two-point conversions or onside kick attempts, both of which, like blocks, are so infrequent as to be statistically insignificant in judging future performance.

Defense-Adjusted Yards Above Replacement (DYAR)

DVOA is a good stat, but of course it is not a perfect one. One problem is that DVOA, by virtue of being a percentage or rate statistic, doesn't take into account the cumulative value of having a player producing at a league-average level over the course of an above-average number of plays. By definition, an average level of performance is better than that provided by half of the league and the ability to maintain that level of performance while carrying a heavy workload is very valuable indeed. In addition, a player who is involved in a high number of plays can draw the defense's attention away from other parts of the offense, and, if that player is a running back, he can take time off the clock with repeated runs.

Let's say you have a running back who carries the ball 250 times in a season. What would happen if you were to remove this player from his team's offense? What would happen to those 250 plays? Those plays don't disappear with the player, though some might be lost to the defense because of the asso-

ciated loss of first downs. Rather those plays would have to be distributed among the remaining players in the offense, with the bulk of them being given to a replacement running back. This is where we arrive at the concept of replacement level, borrowed from our friends at Baseball Prospectus. When a player is removed from an offense, he is usually not replaced by a player of similar ability. Nearly every starting player in the NFL is a starter because he is better than the alternative. Those 250 plays will typically be given to a significantly worse player, someone who is the backup because he doesn't have as much experience and/or talent. A player's true value can then be measured by the level of performance he provides above that replacement level baseline, totaled over all of his run or pass attempts.

Of course, the *real* replacement player is different for each team in the NFL. Last year, the player who was originally the third-string running back in Baltimore (Gus Edwards) ended up as the starter with a higher DVOA than original starter Mark Ingram. Sometimes a player such as Raheem Mostert will be cut by one team and turn into a star for another. On other teams, the drop from the starter to the backup can be even greater than the general drop to replacement level. (The 2011 Indianapolis Colts will be the hallmark example of this until the end of time.) The choice to start an inferior player or to employ a sub-replacement level backup, however, falls to the team, not the starter being evaluated. Thus we generalize replacement level for the league as a whole as the ultimate goal is to evaluate players independent of the quality of their teammates.

Our estimates of replacement level are computed differently for each position. For quarterbacks, we analyzed situations where two or more quarterbacks had played meaningful snaps for a team in the same season, then compared the overall DVOA of the original starters to the overall DVOA of the replacements. We did not include situations where the backup was actually a top prospect waiting his turn on the bench, since a first-round pick is by no means a "replacement-level" player.

At other positions, there is no easy way to separate players into "starters" and "replacements," since unlike at quarterback, being the starter doesn't make you the only guy who gets in the game. Instead, we used a simpler method, ranking players at each position in each season by attempts. The players who made up the final 10% of passes or runs were split out as "replacement players" and then compared to the players making up the other 90% of plays at that position. This took care of the fact that not every non-starter is a freely available talent.

As noted earlier, the challenge of any new stat is to present it on a scale that's meaningful to those attempting to use it. Saying that Justin Herbert's passes were worth 228 success value points over replacement in 2020 has very little value without a context to tell us if 228 is good total or a bad one. Therefore, we translate these success values into a number called "Defense-adjusted Yards Above Replacement, or DYAR. Thus, Rodgers was eighth among quarterbacks with 861 passing DYAR. It is our estimate that a generic replacement-level quarterback, throwing in the same situations as Rodgers, would have been worth 861 fewer yards. Note that this doesn't mean the replacement level quarterback would have gained exactly 861 fewer yards. First downs, touchdowns, and turnovers all have an estimated yardage value in this system, so what we are saying is that a generic replacement-level quarterback would have fewer yards and touchdowns (and more turnovers) that would total up to be equivalent to the value of 861 yards.

Problems with DVOA and DYAR

Football is a game in which nearly every action requires the work of two or more teammates—in fact, usually 11 teammates all working in unison. Unfortunately, when it comes to individual player ratings, we are still far from the point at which we can determine the value of a player independent from the performance of his teammates. That means that when we say, "In 2020, Aaron Jones had rushing DVOA of 20.3%," what we really are saying is, "In 2020, Aaron Jones, playing in Matt LaFleur's offensive system with the Green Bay offensive line blocking for him and Aaron Rodgers selling the fake when necessary, had a DVOA of 20.3%."

DVOA is limited by what's included in the official NFL play-by-play or tracked by our game charting partners (explained below). Because we need to have the entire play-by-play of a season in order to compute DVOA and DYAR, these metrics are not yet ready to compare players of today to players throughout the league's history. As of this writing, we have processed 38 seasons, 1983 through 2020, and we add seasons at a rate of roughly two per year (the most recent season, plus one season back into history.)

In addition, because we need to turn around DVOA and DYAR quickly during the season before charting can be completed, we do not have charting data such as dropped passes incorporated into these advanced metrics.

Pythagorean Projection

The Pythagorean projection is an approximation of each team's wins based solely on their points scored and allowed. This basic concept was introduced by baseball analyst Bill James, who discovered that the record of a baseball team could be very closely approximated by taking the square of team runs scored and dividing it by the sum of the squares of team runs scored and allowed. Statistician Daryl Morey, now general manager of the Houston Rockets, later extended this theorem to professional football, refining the exponent to 2.37 rather than 2.

The problem with that exponent is the same problem we've had with DVOA in recent years: the changing offensive levels in the NFL. 2.37 worked great based on the league 20 years ago, but in the current NFL it ends up slightly underprojecting teams that play high-scoring games. The most accurate method is actually to adjust the exponent based on the scor-

ing environment of each individual team. Kansas City games have a lot of points. Pittsburgh games feature fewer points.

This became known as Pythagenport when Clay Davenport of Baseball Prospectus started doing it with baseball teams. In the middle of the 2011 season, we switched our measurement of Pythagorean wins to a Pythagenport-style equation, modified for the NFL.[1] The improvement is slight, but noticeable due to the high-scoring teams that have dominated the last few years.

Pythagorean wins are useful as a predictor of year-to-year improvement. Teams that win a minimum of one full game more than their Pythagorean projection tend to regress the following year; teams that win a minimum of one full game less than their Pythagorean projection tend to improve the following year, particularly if they were at or above .500 despite their underachieving. The Atlanta Falcons had the worst Pythagorean luck in 2020, going 4-12 despite 7.6 Pythagorean wins. In fact, this was the third-worst Pythagorean luck of any team since the 1970 merger, trailing only the 1981 Patriots (2-14, 6.6 Pythagorean wins) and the 1971 Cincinnati Bengals (4-10, 7.6 Pythagorean wins). Jacksonville and Houston also underperformed their Pythagorean expectations by more than two wins apiece.

On the other side, the Kansas City Chiefs went 14-2 despite having only 10.5 Pythagorean wins. Cleveland went 11-5 despite having only 7.7 Pythagorean wins. Both the Chiefs and Browns rank among the top seven teams with the most Pythagorean luck since the 1970 merger. Buffalo, Seattle, and Green Bay also outperformed their Pythagorean expectations by more than two wins apiece.

Adjusted Line Yards

One of the most difficult goals of statistical analysis in football is isolating the degree to which each of the 22 men on the field is responsible for the result of a given play. Nowhere is this as significant as the running game, in which one player runs while up to nine other players—including not just linemen but also wideouts and tight ends—block in different directions. None of the statistics we use for measuring rushing—yards, touchdowns, yards per carry—differentiate between the contribution of the running back and the contribution of the offensive line. Neither do our advanced metrics DVOA and DYAR.

We do, however, have enough play-by-play data amassed that we can try to separate the effect that the running back has on a particular play from the effects of the offensive line (and other offensive blockers) and the opposing defense. A team might have two running backs in its stable: RB A, who averages 3.0 yards per carry, and RB B, who averages 3.5 yards per carry. Who is the better back? Imagine that RB A doesn't just average 3.0 yards per carry, but gets exactly 3 yards on every single carry, while RB B has a highly variable yardage output: sometimes 5 yards, sometimes -2 yards, sometimes 20 yards. The difference in variability between the runners can

---

[1] The equation, for those curious, is 1.5 x log ((PF+PA)/G).

be exploited not only to determine the difference between the runners, but the effect the offensive line has on every running play.

At some point in every long running play, the running back passes all of his offensive line blocks as well as additional blocking backs or receivers. From there on, the rest of the play is dependent on the runner's own speed and elusiveness and the speed and tackling ability of the opposing defense. If Nick Chubb breaks through the line for 50 yards, avoiding tacklers all the way to the goal line, his offensive line has done a great job—but they aren't responsible for the majority of the yards gained. The trick is figuring out exactly how much they *are* responsible for.

For each running back carry, we calculated the probability that the back involved would run for the specific yardage on that play based on that back's average yardage per carry and the variability of their yardage from play to play. We also calculated the probability that the offense would get the yardage based on the team's rushing average and variability using all backs *other* than the one involved in the given play, and the probability that the defense would give up the specific amount of yardage based on its average rushing yards allowed per carry and variability.

A regression analysis breaks the value for rushing yardage into the following categories: losses, 0-4 yards, 5-10 yards, and 11+ yards. In general, the offensive line is 20% more responsible for lost yardage than it is for positive gains up to 4 yards, but 50% less responsible for additional yardage gained between 5 and 10 yards, and not at all responsible for additional yardage past 10 yards.

By applying those percentages to every running back carry, we were able to create **adjusted line yards (ALY)**, a statistic that measured offensive line performance. (We don't include carries by receivers, which are usually based on deception rather than straight blocking, or carries by quarterbacks, although we may need to reconsider that given the recent use of the read option in the NFL.) Those numbers are then adjusted based on down, distance, situation, opponent and whether or not a team is in the shotgun. (Because defenses are generally playing pass when the quarterback is in shotgun, the average running back carry from shotgun last year gained 4.57 yards, compared to just 4.26 yards on other carries.) The adjusted numbers are then normalized so that the league average for adjusted line yards per carry is the same as the league average for RB yards per carry. Adjusted line yards numbers are normalized differently in each season, so that normalization is based on that year's average for RB yards per carry rather than a historical average.

The NFL distinguishes between runs made to seven different locations on the line: left/right end, left/right tackle, left/right guard, and middle. Further research showed no statistically significant difference between how well a team performed on runs listed as having gone up the middle or past a guard, so we separated runs into just five different directions (left/right end, left/right tackle, and middle). Note that there may not be a statistically significant difference between right tackle and middle/guard either but pending further research (and for the

sake of symmetry) we still list runs behind the right tackle separately. These splits allow us to evaluate subsections of a team's offensive line, but not necessarily individual linesmen, as we can't account for blocking assignments or guards who pull towards the opposite side of the line after the snap.

Success Rate

Success rate is a statistic for running backs that measures how consistently they achieve the yardage necessary for a play to be deemed successful. Some running backs will mix a few long runs with a lot of failed runs of 1 or 2 yards, while others with similar yards-per-carry averages will consistently gain 5 yards on first down, or as many yards as necessary on third down. This statistic helps us differentiate between the two.

Since success rate compares rush attempts to other rush attempts, without consideration of passing, the standard for success on first down is slightly lower than those described above for DVOA. In addition, the standard for success changes slightly in the fourth quarter when running backs are used to run out the clock. A team with the lead is satisfied with a shorter run as long as it stays in bounds. Conversely, for a team down by a couple of touchdowns in the fourth quarter, 4 yards on first down isn't going to be a big help.

The formula for running back success rate is as follows:

- A successful play must gain 40% of needed yards on first down, 60% of needed yards on second down, and 100% of needed yards on third or fourth down.
- If the offense is behind by more than a touchdown in the fourth quarter, the benchmarks switch to 50%, 65%, and 100%.
- If the offense is ahead by any amount in the fourth quarter, the benchmarks switch to 30%, 50%, and 100%.

The league-average success rate in 2020 was 50.8%. Success Rate is not adjusted based on defenses faced and is not calculated for quarterbacks and wide receivers who occasionally carry the ball. Note gain that our calculation of success rate for running backs is different from the success rate we use as a basis for DVOA, and other success rate calculations you may find across the Internet.

Approximate Value

Approximate Value is a system created by Doug Drinen of Pro Football Reference. The goal is to put a single number on every season of every NFL player since 1950, using a very broad set of guidelines. The goal is not to make judgments on individual seasons, but rather to have a format for studying groups of seasons that is more accurate than measuring players with a very broad brush such as "games started" or "number of Pro Bowls." Skill players are rated primarily using basic stats, while offensive linemen and defensive players are rated in large part based on team performance as well as individual accolades and games started. Advanced stats from

Football Outsiders play-by-play breakdown are not part of this system. It is obviously imperfect—"approximate" is right there in the name—but it's valuable for studying groups of draft picks, groups of players by age, and so on. The system is introduced and explained at https://www.pro-football-reference.com/blog/index37a8.html

Expected Points Added

Expected Points Added (EPA) seeks to measure the value of individual plays in terms of points. This is done by calculating the expected average next score before and after each play based on a number of variables including down, distance, field position, and remaining timeouts. This is similar to the system of expected points that underlies our special teams methodology. A freely available model for EPA has become popular in football analysis on the Internet over the last couple seasons, and that model is used a few places in this book.

KUBIAK Projection System

"Skill position" players whom we expect to play a role this season receive a projection of their standard 2021 NFL statistics using the KUBIAK projection system, designed by Scott Spratt.

The new KUBIAK combines two things:

- Projected player efficiencies based on their regressed per-play production from recent seasons and that of players with similar roles and combine measurements; and
- Workload projections based on team and player tendencies and the anticipated effect of projected team qualities on their teams' run-pass ratios.

KUBIAK then adjusts those projections for expected team context each week, capturing the typical changes players in similar roles see because of factors including the venue, weather, and opponent. These preseason projections are an extension of the weekly fantasy projections available as part of our premium FO+ package on FootballOutsiders.com.[2] The KUBIAK system accounts each week for the possibility of injuries, and therefore overall projections are less than what we would expect from playing a full season. The exception comes in the Quarterbacks chapter, where each quarterback is still given a 17-game projection to help readers understand the expectations if circumstances force a backup quarterback to start for an extended period.

Each player with a KUBIAK projection also comes with a Risk variable for fantasy football, which measures the likelihood of the player hitting his projection. The default rating for each player is Green. As the risk of a player failing to hit his projection rises, he's given a rating of Yellow or, in the worst cases, Red. The Risk variable is based not only on age and injury probability, but also how a player's projection compares to his recent performance as well as our confidence (or lack thereof) in his offensive teammates. A few players with the strongest chances of surpassing their projections are given a Blue rating. Most players marked Blue will be backups with low projections, but a handful are starters or situational players who can be considered slightly better breakout candidates.

When we named our system KUBIAK, it was a play on the PECOTA system used by our partners at Baseball Prospectus—if they were going to name their system after a long-time eighties backup, we would name our system after a long-time eighties backup. Little did we know that Gary Kubiak would finally get a head coaching job the very next season. After some debate, we decided to keep the name, although discussing projections for Denver players was a bit awkward for a while.

To clear up a common misconception among our readers, KUBIAK projects individual player performances only, not teams.

2020 Win Projection System

In this book, each of the 32 NFL teams receives a **2021 Mean Projection** at the beginning of its chapter. These projections stem from three equations that forecast 2021 DVOA for offense, defense, and special teams based on a number of different factors. The system starts by considering the team's DVOA over the past three seasons and, on offense, a separate projection for the starting quarterback. We also incorporate a measure that's based on the net personnel change in DYAR among non-quarterbacks (for offense) and the net change in Approximate Value above replacement level (for defense). Other factors include coaching experience, recent draft history, certain players returning from injury, and combined tenure on the offensive line.

These three equations produce precise numbers representing the most likely outcome, but also produce a range of possibilities, used to determine the probability of each possible offensive, defensive, and special teams DVOA for each team. This is particularly important when projecting football teams, because with only 17 games in a season, a team's performance may vary wildly from its actual talent level due to a couple of random bounces of the ball or badly timed injuries. In addition, the economic structure of the NFL allows teams to make sudden jumps or drops in overall ability more often than in other sports.

This projection system was built using the years 2003-2014. For the six years following, 2015-2020, the mean DVOA forecast by this new projection system had a correlation coefficient with actual wins of .509. By comparison, previous year's point differential had a correlation of .407, and previous year's wins had a correlation of just .354.

The next step in our forecast involves simulating the season one million times. We use the projected range of DVOA possibilities to produce 1,000 different simulated seasons with 32 sets of DVOA ratings. We then plug those season-long DVOA

---

2 https://www.footballoutsiders.com/subscribe

ratings into the same equation we use during the season to determine each team's likely remaining wins for our Playoff Odds Report. The simulation takes each season game-by-game, determining the home or road team's chance of winning each game based on the DVOA ratings of each team as well as home-field advantage. A random number between 0 and 100 determines whether the home or road team has won that game. We ran 1,000 simulations with each of the 1,000 sets of DVOA ratings, creating a million different simulations. The simulation was programmed by Mike Harris.

We use a system we call a "dynamic simulation" to better approximate the true distribution of wins in the NFL. When simulating the season, each team had 2.0% DVOA added or subtracted after a win or loss, reflecting the fact that a win or loss tends to tell us whether a team is truly better or worse than whatever their mean projection had been before the season. Using this method, a team projected with 20.0% DVOA which goes 13-4 will have a 38.0% DVOA entering the play-offs, which is much more realistic. This change gave us more projected seasons at the margins, with fewer seasons at 8-9 or 9-8 and more seasons at 14-3 or 3-14. The dynamic simulation also meant a slight increase in projected wins for the best teams, and a slight decrease for the worst teams. However, the conservative nature of our projection system still means the distribution of mean projected wins has a much smaller spread than the actual win-loss records we will see by the end of December. We will continue to experiment with changes to the simulation in order to produce the most accurate possible forecast of the NFL season in future years.

Game Charting Data

Each of the formulas listed above relies primarily on the play-by-play data published by the NFL. When we began to analyze the NFL, this was all that we had to work with. Just as a television broadcast has a color commentator who gives more detail to the facts related by the play-by-play announcer, so too do we need some color commentary to provide contextual information that breathes life into these plain lines of numbers and text. We added this color commentary with game charting.

Beginning in 2005, Football Outsiders began using a number of volunteers to chart every single play of every regular-season and postseason NFL game. To put it into perspective, there were over 54,000 lines of play-by-play information in each NFL season and our goal is to add several layers of detail to nearly all of them.

It gradually became clear that attempting to chart so much football with a crew of volunteers was simply not feasible, especially given our financial resources compared to those of our competitors. Over the past few years, we have partnered with larger companies to take on the responsibilities of game charting so that we can devote more time to analysis.

In 2015, Football Outsiders reached an agreement with Sports Info Solutions to begin a large charting project that would replace our use of volunteers. We also have a partnership with ESPN Stats & Info and use their data to check

against the data collected by Sports Info Solutions. All charting data for the 2020 season is provided by one of these two companies.

Game charting is significantly easier now that the NFL makes coaches' film available through NFL Game Rewind. This tape, which was not publicly available when we began charting with volunteers in 2005, includes sideline and end zone perspectives for each play, and shows all 22 players at all times, making it easier to see the cause-and-effect of certain actions taken on the field. Nonetheless, all game charting is still imperfect. You often cannot tell which players did their jobs particularly well or made mistakes without knowing the play call and each player's assignment, particularly when it comes to zone coverage or pass rushers who reach the quarterback without being blocked. Therefore, the goal of game charting from both ESPN Stats & Info and Sports Info Solutions is *not* to "grade" players, but rather to attempt to mark specific events: a pass pressure, a blown block, a dropped interception, and so on.

We emphasize that all data from game charting is unofficial. Other sources for football statistics may keep their own measurements of yards after catch or how teams perform against the blitz. Our data will not necessarily match theirs. Even ESPN Stats & Info and Sports Info Solutions have a number of disagreements, marking different events on the same play because it can be difficult to determine the definition of a "pressure" or a "dropped pass." However, any other group that is publicly tracking this data is also working off the same footage, and thus will run into the same issues of difficulty and subjectivity.

There are lots of things we would like to do with all-22 film that we simply haven't been able to do yet, such as charting coverage by cornerbacks when they aren't the target of a given pass, or even when pass pressure prevents the pass from getting into the air. Unfortunately, we are limited by what our partners are able to chart given time constraints.

In the description of data below, we have tried to designate which data from 2020 comes from ESPN Stats & Info group (ESPN S&I), which data comes from Sports Info Solutions (SIS), and where we have combined data from both companies with our own analysis.

Formation/Personnel

For each play, we have the number of running backs, wide receivers, and tight ends on the field courtesy of SIS. Players were marked based on their designation on the roster, not based on where they lined up on the field. Obviously, this could be difficult with some hybrid players or players changing positions in 2020, but we did our best to keep things as consistent as possible. SIS also marks when a team uses six (or seven) offensive linemen, and they mark the backfield formation as empty back, single back, I formation, offset I, split backs, full house, or "other." These notations of backfield formation were recorded directly before the snap and do not account for positions before pre-snap motion. The exception comes when a running back motions out of the backfield before the snap but does not set in a receiver position; we count that player as being in the backfield, not on the line of scrimmage.

SIS then marked defensive formations by listing the number of linemen, linebackers, and defensive backs. There will be mistakes—a box safety may occasionally be confused for a linebacker, for example—but for the most part the data for defensive backs will be accurate. Figuring out how to mark whether a player is a defensive end or a linebacker is a different story. The rise of hybrid defenses has led to a lot of confusion. Edge rushers in a 4-3 defense may play standing up because they used to play for a 3-4 defense and that's what they are used to. A player who is usually considered an outside linebacker for a 3-4 defense may put his hand on the ground on third down (thus looking like a 4-3 defensive end), but the tackle next to him is still two-gapping (which is generally a 3-4 principle). SIS marked personnel in a simplified fashion by designating any front seven player in a standing position as a linebacker and designating any front seven player in a crouching position as a defensive lineman.

We also have data from SIS on where receivers lined up before each of their pass targets (wide, slot, tight, or backfield) and what routes they ran, as well as the play design on running plays.

Rushers and Blockers

ESPN Stats & Info provided us with two data points regarding the pass rush: the number of pass rushers on a given play, and the number defensive backs blitzing on a given play. SIS also tracked this data for comparison purposes and then added a count of blockers. Counting blockers is an art as much as a science. Offenses base their blocking schemes on how many rushers they expect. A running back or tight end's assignment may depend on how many pass-rushers cross the line at the snap. Therefore, an offensive player was deemed to be a blocker if he engaged in an actual block, or there was some hesitation before running a route. A running back that immediately heads out into the flat is not a blocker, but one that waits to verify that the blocking scheme is working and then goes out to the flat would, in fact, be considered a blocker.

Pass Play Details

Both companies recorded the following data for all pass plays:

- Did the play begin with a play-action fake, including read-option fakes that developed into pass plays instead of being handed to a running back?
- Was the quarterback in or out of the pocket?
- Was the quarterback under pressure in making his pass?
- Was this a screen pass?

SIS game charting also marks the name of the defender who caused the pass pressure. Charters were allowed to list two names if necessary, and could also attribute a hurry to "overall pressure." No defender was given a hurry and a sack on the same play, but defenders were given hurries if they helped force a quarterback into a sack that was finished by another player. SIS also identified which defender(s) caused the pass

pressure which forced a quarterback to scramble for yardage. If the quarterback wasn't under pressure but ran anyway, the play could be marked either as "coverage scramble" (if the quarterback ran because there were no open receivers) or "hole opens up" (if the quarterback ran because he knew he could gain significant yardage). All pressure data in this book is based on SIS data.

Some places in this book, we divide pass yardage into two numbers: distance in the air and yards after catch. This information is tracked by the NFL, but the official scorers often make errors, so we corrected the original data based on input from both ESPN S&I and SIS. Distance in the air is based on the distance from the line of scrimmage to the place where the receiver either caught or was supposed to catch the pass. We do not count how far the quarterback was behind the line or horizontal yardage if the quarterback threw across the field. All touchdowns are counted to the goal line, so that distance in the air added to yards after catch always equals the official yardage total kept by the league.

Incomplete Passes

Quarterbacks are evaluated based on their ability to complete passes. However, not all incompletes should have the same weight. Throwing a ball away to avoid a sack is actually a valuable incomplete, and a receiver dropping an otherwise quality pass is hardly a reflection on the quarterback.

Our evaluation of incomplete passes began with ESPN Stats & Info, which marked passes as Overthrown, Underthrown, Thrown Away, Batted Down at the Line, Defensed, or Dropped. We then compared this data to similar data from SIS and made some changes. We also changed some plays to reflect a couple of additional categories we have kept in past years for Football Outsiders: Hit in Motion (indicating the quarterback was hit as his arm was coming forward to make a pass), Caught Out of Bounds, and Hail Mary.

ESPN S&I and SIS also marked when a defender dropped an interception; Football Outsiders volunteers then analyzed plays where the two companies disagreed to come up with a final total. When a play is close, we tend to err on the side of not marking a dropped interception, as we don't want to blame a defender who, for example, jumps high for a ball and has it tip off his fingers. We also counted a few "defensed" interceptions, when a quarterback threw a pass that would have been picked off if not for the receiver playing defense on the ball. These passes counted as dropped interceptions for quarterbacks but not for the defensive players.

Defenders

The NFL play-by-play lists tackles and, occasionally, tipped balls, but it does not definitively list the defender on the play. SIS charters attempted to determine which defender was primarily responsible for covering either the receiver at the time of the throw or the location to which the pass was thrown, regardless of whether the pass was complete or not.

Every defense in the league plays zone coverage at times, some more than others, which leaves us with the question of how to handle plays without a clear man assigned to that receiver. Charters (SIS employees in 2015-2020, and FO volunteers in previous seasons) had three alternatives:

- We asked charters to mark passes that found the holes in zone coverage as Hole in Zone, rather than straining to assign that pass to an individual defender. We asked the charter to also note the player who appeared to be responsible for that zone, and these defenders are assigned half credit for those passes. Some holes were so large that no defender could be listed along with the Hole in Zone designation.

- Charters were free to list two defenders instead of one. This could be used for actual double coverage, or for zone coverage in which the receiver was right between two close defenders rather than sitting in a gaping hole. When two defenders are listed, ratings assign each with half credit.

- Screen passes and dumpoffs are marked as Uncovered unless a defender (normally a linebacker) is obviously shadowing that specific receiver on the other side of the line of scrimmage.

Since we began the charting project in 2005, nothing has changed our analysis more than this information on pass coverage. However, even now with the ability to view all-22 film, it can be difficult to identify the responsible defender except when there is strict man-to-man coverage.

Additional Details

All draw plays were marked, whether by halfbacks or quarterbacks. Option runs and zone reads were also marked.

Both SIS and ESPN S&I when the formation was pistol as opposed to shotgun; the official play-by-play simply marks these plays all as shotgun.

Both SIS and ESPN S&I track yards after contact for each play.

SIS marks when a play uses pre-snap motion and when the play design is a run-pass option (RPO).

SIS charters marked each quarterback sack with one of the following terms: Blown Block, Coverage Sack, QB Fault, Failed Scramble, or Blitz/Overall Pressure. Blown Blocks were listed with the name of a specific offensive player who allowed the defender to come through. (Some blown block sacks are listed with two blockers, who each get a half-sack.) Coverage Sack denotes when the quarterback has plenty of time to throw but cannot find an open receiver. QB Fault represents "self sacks" listed without a defender, such as when the quarterback drops back, only to find the ball slip out of his hands with no pass-rusher touching him. Failed Scramble represents plays where a quarterback began to run without major pass pressure because he thought he could get a positive gain, only to be tackled before he passed the line of scrimmage.

SIS tracked "broken tackles" on all runs or pass plays. We define a "broken tackle" as one of two events: Either the ballcarrier escapes from the grasp of the defender, or the defender is in good position for a tackle but the ballcarrier jukes him out of his shoes. If the ballcarrier sped by a slow defender who dived and missed, that did not count as a broken tackle. If the defender couldn't bring the ballcarrier down because he is being blocked out of the play by another offensive player, this did not count as a broken tackle. It was possible to mark multiple broken tackles on the same play. Broken tackles are not marked for special teams.

How to Read the Team Summary Box

Here is a rundown of all the tables and stats that appear in the 32 team chapters. Each team chapter begins with a box in the upper-right hand corner that gives a summary of our statistics for that team, as follows:

2020 Record gives each team's actual win-loss record. **Pythagorean Wins** gives the approximate number of wins expected last year based on this team's raw totals of points scored and allowed, along with their NFL rank. **Snap-Weighted Age** gives the average age of the team in 2020, weighted based on how many snaps each player was on the field and ranked from oldest (New Orleans, first at 27.3) to youngest (Jacksonville, 32nd at 25.4). **Average Opponent** gives a ranking of last year's schedule strength based on the average DVOA of all 16 opponents faced during the regular season. Teams are ranked from the hardest schedule of 2020 (Atlanta) to the easiest (Indianapolis).

Total DVOA gives the team's total DVOA rating, with rank. **Offense, Defense**, and **Special Teams** list the team's DVOA rating in each category, along with NFL rank. Remember that good offenses and special teams have positive DVOA numbers, while a negative DVOA means better defense, so the lowest defensive DVOA is ranked No. 1 (last year, Pittsburgh).

2021 Mean Projection gives the average number of wins for this team based on the 2021 Win Projection System described earlier in this chapter. Please note that we do not expect any teams to win the exact number of games in their mean projection. First of all, no team can win 0.8 of a game. Second, because these projections represent a whole range of possible values, the averages naturally tend to drift towards 8.5 wins. Obviously, we're not expecting a season where no team goes 4-13 or 13-4. For a better way to look at the projections, we offer **Postseason Odds**, which give each team's chance of making the postseason based on our simulation, and **Super Bowl Appearance** odds, which give each team's chance of representing its conference in Super Bowl LVI. The average team will make the playoffs in 43.8% of simulations (now a higher number due to the expansion to seven playoff teams per conference), and the Super Bowl in 6.3% of simulations.

Projected Average Opponent gives the team's strength of schedule for 2021; like the listing for last year's schedule strength in the first column of the box, this number is based not on last year's record but on the mean projected DVOA for each opponent (now 17 opponents instead of 16). A positive schedule is harder, a negative schedule easier. Teams are ranked from the hardest projected schedule (Chicago, first) to the easiest (New England, 32nd). This strength of schedule projection does not take into account which games are home or away, or the timing of the bye week.

The final column of the box gives the team's chances of finishing in four different basic categories of success:

- On the Clock (0-5 wins; NFL average 17%)
- Mediocrity (6-8 wins; NFL average 33%)
- Playoff Contender (9-11 wins; NFL average 33%)
- Super Bowl Contender (12+ wins; NFL average 17%)

The percentage given for each category is dependent not only on how good we project the team to be in 2021, but the level of variation possible in that projection, and the expected performance of the teams on the schedule.

You'll also find a table with the team's 2021 schedule placed within each chapter, along with a graph showing each team's 2020 week-to-week performance by single-game DVOA. Black dots represent wins, white dots represent losses, and the shaded dot for Cincinnati and Philadelphia represents a tie. The second, dotted line on the graph represents a five-week moving average of each team's performance, in order to show a longer-term view of when they were improving and declining. After the essays come statistical tables and comments related to that team and its specific units.

Weekly Performance

The first table gives a quick look at the team's week-to-week performance in 2020. (Table 3) This includes the playoffs for those teams that made the postseason, with the four weeks of playoffs numbered 18 (wild card) through 21 (Super Bowl). All other tables in the team chapters represent regular-season performance only unless otherwise noted.

Table 3. 2020 Cardinals Stats by Week

Wk	vs.	W-L	PF	PA	YDF	YDA	TO	Total	Off	Def	ST
1	at SF	W	24	20	404	366	-1	0.4%	10.2%	3.9%	-5.8%
2	WAS	W	30	15	438	316	1	10.8%	10.0%	0.3%	1.1%
3	DET	L	23	26	377	322	-3	-23.2%	-23.3%	-3.6%	-3.5%
4	at CAR	L	21	31	262	444	0	-37.9%	-6.2%	32.2%	0.6%
5	at NYJ	W	30	10	496	285	-1	40.7%	46.6%	9.7%	3.8%
6	at DAL	W	38	10	438	344	4	57.1%	16.4%	-38.8%	1.9%
7	SEA	W	37	34	519	572	1	11.7%	6.7%	-6.6%	-1.6%
8	BYE										
9	MIA	L	31	34	442	312	-1	-4.9%	26.2%	15.5%	-15.6%
10	BUF	W	32	30	453	369	0	45.1%	8.3%	-34.0%	2.7%
11	at SEA	L	21	28	314	347	0	-24.9%	1.7%	23.8%	-2.8%
12	at NE	L	17	20	298	179	1	9.3%	-23.6%	-52.3%	-19.4%
13	LAR	L	28	38	232	463	-1	-27.4%	-15.1%	14.3%	1.9%
14	at NYG	W	26	7	390	159	3	63.8%	-17.2%	-58.1%	22.9%
15	PHI	W	33	26	526	422	-3	-4.3%	-8.5%	-1.3%	2.9%
16	SF	L	12	20	350	398	-1	-64.9%	-43.7%	27.5%	6.4%
17	at LAR	L	7	18	214	333	1	21.4%	-13.8%	-40.1%	-4.9%

Looking at the first week for the Arizona Cardinals in 2020, the first five columns are fairly obvious: Arizona opened the season with a 24-20 win on the road in San Francisco. **YDF** and **YDA** are net yards on offense and net yards against the defense. These numbers do not include penalty yardage or special teams yardage. **TO** represents the turnover margin. Unlike other parts of the book in which we consider all fumbles as equal, this only represents actual turnovers: fumbles lost and interceptions. So, for example, the Cardinals forced one more turnover than Washington in Week 2 but had three more turnovers than Detroit in Week 3.

Finally, you'll see DVOA ratings for this game: Total **DVOA** first, then offense (**Off**), defense (**Def**), and special teams (**ST**). Note that these are DVOA ratings, adjusted for opponent, so a loss to a good team will often be listed with a higher rating than a close win over a bad team. For example, the Cardinals have a positive DVOA for their Week 17 loss to the Los Angeles Rams, but a negative DVOA for their Week 15 win over Philadelphia.

Trends and Splits

Next to the week-to-week performance is a table giving DVOA for different portions of a team's performance, on both offense and defense (Table 4). Each split is listed with the team's rank among the 32 NFL teams. These numbers represent regular season performance only.

Table 4. Falcons Trends and Splits

	Offense	Rank	Defense	Rank
Total DVOA	-3.1%	21	-0.1%	14
Unadjusted VOA	-4.3%	22	3.6%	20
Weighted Trend	-4.3%	16	-4.4%	12
Variance	3.3%	4	8.4%	29
Average Opponent	-0.8%	11	6.1%	2
Passing	15.8%	13	11.6%	19
Rushing	-25.9%	29	-20.7%	6
First Down	4.5%	14	-5.7%	13
Second Down	-23.9%	29	8.0%	24
Third Down	12.5%	9	-1.6%	16
First Half	-1.1%	17	-3.3%	13
Second Half	-5.5%	20	2.8%	15
Red Zone	-24.0%	28	6.2%	21
Late and Close	-24.3%	30	-0.8%	18

Total DVOA gives total offensive, and defensive DVOA in all situations. **Unadjusted VOA** represents the breakdown of play-by-play considering situation but not opponent. A team whose offensive DVOA is higher than its offensive VOA played a harder-than-average schedule of opposing defenses; a team with a lower defensive DVOA than defensive VOA player a harder-than-average schedule of opposing offenses.

Weighted Trend lowers the importance of earlier games to give a better idea of how the team was playing at the end of the regular season. The final four weeks of the season are full strength; moving backwards through the season, each week is given less and less weight until the first three weeks of the season, which are not included at all. **Variance** is the same as noted above, with a higher percentage representing less consistency. This is true for both offense and defense: Atlanta, for example, was very consistent on defense (3.3%, fourth) but inconsistent on offense (8.4%, 29th). **Average Opponent** is that the same thing that appears in the box to open each chapter, except split in half: the average DVOA of all opposing defenses (for offense) or the average DVOA of all opposing offenses (for defense).

Passing and **Rushing** are fairly self-explanatory. As noted earlier, passing DVOA now includes quarterback scrambles. Rushing DVOA still includes designed runs by quarterbacks as well as handoffs and broken plays.

The next three lines split out DVOA on **First Down**, **Second Down**, and **Third Down**. Third Down here includes fourth downs on which a team runs a regular offensive play instead of punting or attempting a field goal. **First Half** and **Second Half** represent the first two quarters and last two quarters (plus overtime), not the first eight and last eight games of the regular season. Next comes DVOA in the **Red Zone**, which is any offensive play starting from the defense's 20-yard line through the goal line. The final split is **Late and Close**, which includes any play in the second half or overtime when the teams are within eight points of each other in either direction. (Eight points, of course, is the biggest deficit that can be made up with a single score, a touchdown and two-point conversion.)

Five-Year Performance

This table gives each team's performance over the past five seasons. (Table 5) It includes win-loss record, Pythagorean Wins, **Estimated Wins**, points scored and allowed, and turnover margin. Estimated wins are based on a formula that estimates how many games a team would have been expected to win based on 2020 performance in specific situations, normalized to eliminate luck (fumble recoveries, opponents' missed field goals, etc.) and assuming average schedule strength. The formula emphasizes consistency and overall DVOA as well as DVOA in a few specifically important situations. The next columns of this table give total DVOA along with DVOA for offense, defense, and special teams, and the rank for each

among that season's 32 NFL teams.

The next four columns give the adjusted games lost (AGL) for starters on both offense and defense, along with rank. (Our total for starters here includes players who take over as starters due to another injury and then get injured themselves, such as Andy Dalton and Mike Davis last year. It also includes important situational players who may not necessarily start, such as pass-rush specialists and slot receivers.) Adjusted games lost was introduced in *Pro Football Prospectus 2008*; it gives a weighted estimate of the probability that players would miss games based on how they are listed on the injury report. Unlike a count of "starter games missed," this accounts for the fact that a player listed as questionable who does in fact play is not playing at 100% capability. Teams are ranked from the fewest injuries (2020: Tampa Bay on offense, Kansas City on defense) to the most (2020: Philadelphia on offense, San Francisco on defense).

Individual Offensive Statistics

Each team chapter contains a table giving passing and receiving numbers for any player who either threw five passes or was thrown five passes, along with rushing numbers for any players who carried the ball at least five times. These numbers also appear in the player comments at the end of the book (except for runs by wide receivers). By putting them together in the team chapters we hope we make it easier to compare the performances of different players on the same team.

Players who are no longer on the team are marked with an asterisk. New players who were on a different team in 2020 are in italics. Changes should be accurate as of June 21. Rookies are not included.

All players are listed with DYAR and DVOA. Passing statistics then list total pass plays (**Plays**), net yardage (**NtYds**), and net yards per pass (**Avg**). These numbers include not just passes (and the positive yardage from them) but aborted snaps and sacks (and the negative yardage from them). Then comes average yards after catch (**YAC**) based on charted receptions, not total pass attempts. The final three numbers are completion percentage (**C%**), passing touchdowns (**TD**), and interceptions (**Int**).

It is important to note that the tables in the team chapters contain Football Outsiders stats, while the tables in the player comments later in the book contain official NFL totals, at least when it comes to standard numbers like receptions and yardage. This results in a number of differences between the two:

Table 5. Ravens Five-Year Performance

Year	W-L	Pyth W	Est W	PF	PA	TO	Total	Rk	Off	Rk	Def	Rk	ST	Rk	Off AGL	Rk	Def AGL	Rk	Off Age	Rk	Def Age	Rk	ST Age	Rk
2016	8-8	8.6	9.1	343	321	+5	7.2%	12	-7.2%	23	-9.5%	6	4.9%	4	29.5	12	31.2	11	28.0	3	27.2	5	26.1	18
2017	9-7	10.5	10.3	395	303	+17	17.9%	7	-4.6%	21	-13.4%	4	9.2%	1	62.1	28	42.9	22	27.3	10	27.0	6	25.7	22
2018	10-6	10.8	10.8	389	287	-5	15.8%	6	1.2%	13	-11.7%	4	3.0%	6	17.1	5	11.5	2	26.3	20	27.6	2	25.7	21
2019	14-2	13.4	12.9	531	282	+10	41.2%	1	28.2%	1	-11.5%	5	1.5%	9	9.7	1	59.1	31	25.7	31	27.3	3	26.7	4
2020	11-5	12.0	9.5	468	303	+4	18.5%	7	4.3%	11	-6.9%	9	7.4%	2	37.4	16	22.2	6	25.0	32	26.5	12	26.8	4

- Net yardage for quarterbacks in the team chapter tables includes the lost yardage from sacks and intentional grounding penalties. Aborted snaps are considered as run plays.
- Football Outsiders stats omit kneeldowns from run totals and clock-stopping spikes from pass totals.
- "Skill players" who played for multiple teams in 2020 are only listed in team chapters with stats from that specific team; combined stats are listed in the player comments section.

Table 6. Bills Passing

Player	DYAR	DVOA	Plays	NtYds	Avg	YAC	C%	TD	Int
J.Allen	1460	25.9%	598	4385	7.3	4.7	69.2%	37	10
M.Barkley*	21	4.5%	22	190	8.6	5.0	52.4%	1	1
M.Trubisky	79	-7.5%	315	1930	6.1	5.0	67.0%	16	8

Rushing statistics start with DYAR and DVOA, then list rushing plays and net yards along with average yards per carry and rushing touchdowns. The final two columns are fumbles (Fum)—both those lost to the defense and those recovered by the offense—and Success Rate (Suc), explained earlier in this chapter. Fumbles listed in the rushing table include all quarterback fumbles on sacks and aborted snaps, as well as running back fumbles on receptions, but not wide receiver fumbles.

Table 7. Bears Rushing

Player	DYAR	DVOA	Plays	Yds	Avg	TD	Fum	Suc
M.Davis*	37	-3.5%	165	642	3.9	6	1	50%
C.McCaffrey	37	5.0%	59	225	3.8	5	0	56%
T.Bridgewater*	43	6.6%	45	279	6.2	5	4	--
R.Smith	16	-0.8%	41	156	3.8	1	1	61%
C.Samuel*	99	3.1%	41	200	4.9	2	0	--
R.Bonnafon	9	12.8%	12	69	5.8	0	0	33%
T.Cannon	-10	-33.7%	10	33	3.3	0	0	40%
A.Armah*	2	-4.0%	6	9	1.5	0	0	83%
S.Darnold	72	35.3%	30	224	7.5	2	0	--
Da.Moore	47	57.6%	8	61	7.6	0	0	--

Receiving statistics start with DYAR and DVOA and then list the number of passes thrown to this receiver (**Plays**), the number of passes caught (**Catch**) and the total receiving yards (**Yds**). Yards per catch (**Y/C**) includes total yardage per reception, based on standard play-by-play, while yards after catch (**YAC**) is based on information from our game charting project. Finally we list total receiving touchdowns, and catch percentage (**C%**), which is the percentage of passes intended for this receiver which were caught. Wide receivers, tight ends, and running backs are separated on the table by horizontal lines.

Table 8. Bengals Receiving

Player	DYAR	DVOA	Plays	Ctch	Yds	Y/C	YAC	TD	C%
T.Boyd	56	-6.2%	110	79	841	10.6	4.4	4	72%
T.Higgins	142	3.9%	108	67	908	13.6	4.6	6	62%
A.J.Green*	-172	-33.0%	104	47	523	11.1	1.8	2	45%
A.Tate	-9	-17.8%	22	14	150	10.7	4.1	0	64%
M.Thomas	-34	-33.5%	21	13	132	10.2	2.2	1	62%
A.Erickson*	6	-7.9%	17	12	139	11.6	5.6	0	71%
J.Ross*	-29	-67.5%	7	2	17	8.5	1.5	0	29%
T.Taylor	-82	-58.7%	21	10	86	8.6	4.3	0	48%
D.Sample	-12	-10.8%	53	40	349	8.7	5.0	1	75%
C.J.Uzomah	21	21.5%	11	8	87	10.9	3.8	1	73%
C.Carter*	-5	-18.5%	7	5	53	10.6	2.0	0	71%
G.Bernard*	40	-1.7%	59	47	355	7.6	7.4	3	80%
J.Mixon	13	-4.8%	26	21	138	6.6	8.1	1	81%
S.Perine	17	11.8%	12	11	66	6.0	8.1	0	92%

Performance Based on Personnel

These tables provide a look at performance in 2020 based on personnel packages, as defined above in the section on marking formation/personnel as part of Sports Info Solutions charting. There are four different tables, representing:

- Offense based on personnel
- Offense based on opponent's defensive personnel
- Defense based on personnel
- Defense based on opponent's offensive personnel

Most of these tables feature the top five personnel groupings for each team. Occasionally, we will list the personnel group which ranks sixth if the sixth group is either particularly interesting or nearly as common as the fifth group. Each personnel group is listed with its frequency among 2020 plays, yards per play, and DVOA. Offensive personnel are also listed with how often the team in question called a running play instead of a pass play from given personnel. (Quarterback scrambles are included as pass plays, not runs.)

Offensive personnel are given in the standard two-digit format where the first digit is running backs and the second digit is tight ends. You can figure out wide receivers by subtracting that total from five, with a couple of exceptions. Plays with six or seven offensive linemen will have a three-digit listing such as "611" or "622." Any play with a non-quarterback taking a direct snap from the quarterback position was counted as "Wildcat." This personnel group only appears on the table for Denver, listed as "WC."

When defensive players come in to play offense, defensive backs are counted as wide receivers and linebackers as tight ends. Defensive linemen who come in as offensive linemen are counted as offensive linemen; if they come in as blocking fullbacks, we count them as running backs. Taysom Hill (and any other quarterback who lines up at another position) is counted as a wide receiver.

We no longer give giving personnel data based on the number of defensive linemen and linebackers. This is because of the difficulty in separating between the two, especially with our simplified designation of players as defensive linemen or linebackers based simply on who has a hand on the ground. There are just too many hybrid defensive schemes in today's game: 4-3 schemes where one or both ends rush the passer from a standing position, or hybrid schemes that one-gap on one side of the nose tackle and two-gap on the other. Therefore, defensive personnel is listed in only five categories:

- Base (four defensive backs)
- Nickel (five defensive backs)
- Dime+ (six or more defensive backs)
- Big (either 4-4-3 or 3-5-3)
- Goal Line (all other personnel groups with fewer than four defensive backs)

11, or three-wide personnel, was by far the most common grouping in the NFL last year, used on 59% of plays. After 11 personnel came the standard two-tight end set 12 personnel (19% of plays) and the more traditional 21 personnel (7.3%). Defenses lined up in Base on 24% of plays, Nickel on 60% of plays, Dime+ on 15% of plays, and either Big or Goal Line on 1.6% of plays. Table 9 lists the average performance from the ten most common personnel groups in 2020. Note that because we don't track personnel grouping on penalties, those negative plays are all missing from this analysis, so the average offensive DVOA for this table is 3.7% rather than 0.0%. On Table 10, which shows the same numbers from the defensive perspective, the average DVOA is still 0.0%.

Strategic Tendencies

The Strategic Tendencies table presents a mix of information garnered from the standard play-by-play a well as charting from both Sports Info Solutions and ESPN Stats & Information. It gives you an idea of what kind of plays teams run in what situations and with what personnel. Each category is given a league-wide **Rank** from most often (1) to least often (32) except as noted below. The sample table shown here lists the NFL average in each category for 2020.

The first column of strategic tendencies lists how often teams ran in different situations. These ratios are based on the type of play, not the actual result, so quarterback scrambles count as "passes" while quarterback sneaks, draws and option plays count as "runs."

Runs, first half and **Runs, first down** should be self-evident. **Runs, second-and-long** is the percentage of runs on second down with seven or more yards to go, giving you an idea of how teams follow up a failed first down. **Runs, power situations** is the percentage of runs on third or fourth down with 1-2 yards to go, or at the goal line with 1-2 yards to go. **Runs, behind 2H** tells you how often teams ran when they were behind in the second half, generally a passing situation. **Pass, ahead 2H** tells you how often teams passed when they had the lead in the second half, generally a running situation.

In each case, you can determine the percentage of plays that were passes by subtracting the run percentage from 100 (the reverse being true for "Pass, ahead 2H," of course).

The final entry in the first column gives the percentage of each offense's plays that were coded as **Run-Pass Options** by SIS charters.

The second column gives information about offensive formations and personnel, as tracked by Sports Info Solutions.

The first three entries detail formation, i.e. where players were lined up on the field. **Form: Single Back** lists how often the team lined up with only one player in the backfield, **Form: Empty Back** lists how often the team lined up with no players in the backfield, and **Form: Multi Back** lists how often the team lined up with two or three players in the backfield.

The next three entries are based on personnel, no matter where players were lined up in the formation. **Pers: 3+ WR** marks how often the team plays with three or more wide receivers. **Pers: 2+ TE/6+ OL** marks how often the team plays with either more than one tight end or more than five offensive linemen. **Pers: 6+ OL** marks just plays with more than five offensive linemen. Finally, we give the percentage of plays where a team used **Shotgun or Pistol** in 2020. This does not count "Wildcat" or direct snap plays involving a non-quarterback.

The third column shows how the defensive **Pass Rush** worked in 2020.

Rush 3/Rush 4/Rush 5/Rush 6+: The percentage of pass plays (including quarterback scrambles) on which Sports Info Solutions recorded this team rushing the passer with three or fewer defenders, four defenders, five defenders, and six or

Table 9. NFL Offensive Performance by Personnel Group, 2020

Pers.	Plays	Pct	Yds	DVOA
11	19,418	59.3%	5.9	4.8%
12	6,253	19.1%	5.8	2.2%
21	2,403	7.3%	5.8	-0.1%
13	1,114	3.4%	4.9	-2.6%
22	940	2.9%	5.0	-3.2%
10	671	2.1%	6.4	12.7%
01	347	1.1%	6.2	21.8%
612	263	0.8%	3.9	-17.9%
02	247	0.8%	6.7	14.5%
20	229	0.7%	5.0	3.9%

Table 10. NFL Defensive Performance by Personnel Group, 2020

Pers.	Plays	Pct	Yds	DVOA
Nickel	19,522	59.7%	5.9	1.5%
Base	7,789	23.8%	5.4	-5.6%
Dime+	4,863	14.9%	6.2	2.9%
Goal Line	285	0.9%	1.2	7.8%
Big	231	0.7%	4.7	-11.0%
10 Men	29	0.1%	9.0	94.4%

more defenders.

Edge Rusher Sacks/Interior DL Sacks/Second Level Sacks: These numbers list how often sacks came from each level of the defense. Second-level sacks are those that come from linebackers who are not edge rushers, plus sacks from defensive backs.

The fourth column has more data on the use of defensive backs.

4 DB/5DB/6+ DB: The percentage of plays where this defense lined up with four, five, and six or more defensive backs, according to Sports Info Solutions.

Man Coverage: The percentage of passes where this defense was in some sort of man coverage, according to Sports Info Solutions.

CB by Sides: One of the most important lessons from game charting is that each team's best cornerback does not necessarily match up against the opponent's best receiver. Most cornerbacks play a particular side of the field and in fact cover a wider range of receivers than we assumed before we saw the charting data. This metric looks at which teams prefer to leave their starting cornerbacks on specific sides of the field.

To figure CB by Sides, we took the top two cornerbacks from each team and looked at the percentage of passes where that cornerback was in coverage on the left or right side of the field, ignoring passes marked as "middle." For each of the two cornerbacks, we took the higher number, right or left, and then we averaged the two cornerbacks to get the final CB by Sides rating. Teams which preferred to leave their cornerbacks in the same place last season, such as Chicago and Seattle, will have high ratings. Teams that did more to move their best cornerback around to cover the opponent's top targets, such as New England and Miami, will have low ratings.

S/CB Cover Ratio: This is our attempt to track which teams like to use their safeties as hybrid safety/corners and put them in man coverage on wide receivers. This ratio takes all pass targets with a defensive back in coverage, and then gives what percentage of those targets belonged to a player who is rostered as a safety, ranging from New Orleans, which used safety Chauncey Gardner-Johnson as a nickelback (40%) to Minnesota, who had very defined roles for their two starting safeties (15%).

DB Blitz: We have data on how often the defense used at least one defensive back in the pass rush courtesy of ESPN Stats & Info.

Finally, in the final column, we have some elements of game strategy.

Play action: The percentage of pass plays (including quarterback scrambles) which began with a play-action fake to the running back. This percentage does not include fake end-arounds unless there was also a fake handoff. It does include flea flickers.

Offensive motion: The percentage of offensive plays which began with a man in motion before the snap.

Average Box: These items list the average number of men in the box faced by each team's offense and the average number of men in the box used by this team's defense, according to Sports Info Solutions.

Offensive Pace: Situation-neutral pace represents the seconds of game clock per offensive play, with the following restrictions: no drives are included if they start in the fourth quarter or final five minutes of the first half, and drives are only included if the score is within six points or less. Teams are ranked from quickest pace (Arizona, 27.1 seconds) to slowest pace (Green Bay, 32.8 seconds).

Defensive Pace: Situation-neutral pace based on seconds of game clock per defensive play. This is a representation of how a defense was approached by its opponents, not the strategy of the defense itself. Teams are ranked from quickest pace (San Francisco, 28.8 seconds) to slowest pace (Houston, 31.8 seconds).

Go for it on fourth: This is the aggressiveness index (AI) introduced by Jim Armstrong in *Pro Football Prospectus 2006*, which measures how often a team goes for a first down in various fourth down situations compared to the league average. A coach over 1.00 is more aggressive, and one below 1.00 is less aggressive. Coaches are ranked from most aggressive to least aggressive.

You may notice on the Strategic Tendencies sample table that the average Aggressiveness Index for 2020 was 1.62, far above the multi-year average of 1.00. There is no question that NFL coaches, some following the example of the Super Bowl LII Champion Philadelphia Eagles, have been more aggressive on fourth downs in the past three seasons than in the 30 years that came before. Thirty-three out of 35 head coaches (including those who coached partial seasons) had an Aggressiveness Index above 1.00 in 2020.

Following each strategic tendencies table, you'll find a series of comments highlighting interesting data from that team's charting numbers. This includes DVOA ratings split for things like different formations, draw plays, or play-action passing. Please note that all DVOA ratings given in these comments are standard DVOA with no adjustments for the

Table 11. NFL Strategic Tendencies, 2020

Run/Pass		Rk	Formation		Rk	Pass Rush		Rk	Secondary		Rk	Strategy		Rk
Runs, first half	38%	--	Form: Single Back	80%	--	Rush 3	7.7%	--	4 DB	24%	--	Play Action	27%	--
Runs, first down	47%	--	Form: Empty Back	9%	--	Rush 4	66.2%	--	5 DB	60%	--	Offensive Motion	46%	--
Runs, second-long	27%	--	Form: Multi Back	11%	--	Rush 5	20.8%	--	6+ DB	15%	--	Avg Box (Off)	6.56	--
Runs, power sit.	60%	--	Pers: 3+ WR	64%	--	Rush 6+	5.4%	--	Man Coverage	31%	--	Avg Box (Def)	6.56	--
Runs, behind 2H	28%	--	Pers: 2+ TE/6+ OL	29%	--	Edge Rusher Sacks	50.1%	--	CB by Sides	75%	--	Offensive Pace	30.31	--
Pass, ahead 2H	48%	--	Pers: 6+ OL	3%	--	Interior DL Sacks	25.7%	--	S/CB Cover Ratio	28%	--	Defensive Pace	30.30	--
Run-Pass Options	8%	--	Shotgun/Pistol	66%	--	Second Level Sacks	24.2%	--	DB Blitz	13%	--	Go for it on 4th	1.62	--

specific situation being analyzed. The average DVOA for a specific situation will not necessarily be 0%, and it won't necessarily be the same for offense and defense. For example, the average offensive DVOA on play-action passes in 2020 was 19.4%, while the average defensive DVOA was 13.5%.

How to Read the
Offensive Line Tables

All offensive linemen who had at least 160 snaps in 2020 (not including special teams) are listed in the offensive line tables along with the position they played most often and their **Age** as of the 2021 season, listed simply as the difference between birth year and 2021. Players born in January and December of the same year will have the same listed age.

Then we list games, games started, snaps, and offensive penalties (**Pen**) for each lineman. The penalty total includes declined and offsetting penalties. Finally, there are three numbers for blown blocks in 2020.

- Blown blocks leading directly to sacks
- All blown blocks on pass plays, not only including those that lead to sacks but also those that lead to hurries, hits, or offensive holding penalties
- All blown blocks on run plays; generally, this means plays where the running back is tackled for a loss or no gain, but it also includes a handful of plays where the running back would have been tackled for a loss if not for a broken tackle, as well as offensive holding penalties on running plays

SIS charters mark blown blocks not just on sacks but also on hurries, hits, and runs stuffed at the line. However, while we have blown blocks to mark bad plays, we still don't have a metric that consistently marks good plays, so blown blocks should not be taken as the end all and be all of judging individual linemen. It's simply one measurement that goes into the conversation.

As with all player tables in the team chapters, players who are no longer on the team have an asterisk and those new to the team in 2020 are in italics.

The second offensive line table lists the last three years of our various line stats.

The first column gives standard yards per carry by each team's running backs (**Yds**). The next two columns give adjusted line yards (**ALY**) followed by rank among the 32 teams.

Power gives the percentage of runs in short-yardage "power situations" that achieved a first down or touchdown. Those situations include any third or fourth down with 1 or 2 yards to go, and any runs in goal-to-go situations from the 2-yard line or closer. Unlike the other rushing numbers on the Offensive Line table, Power includes quarterbacks.

Stuff gives the percentage of runs that are stuffed for zero or negative gain. Since being stuffed is bad, teams are ranked from stuffed least often (1) to most often (32).

Second-Level (**2Lev**) Yards and Open-Field (**OpFld**) Yards represent yardage where the running back has the most power over the amount of the gain. Second-level yards represent the number of yards per carry that come 5 to 10 yards past the line of scrimmage. Open-field yards represent the number of yards per carry that come 11 or more yards past the line of scrimmage. A team with a low ranking in adjusted line yards but a high ranking in open-field yards is heavily dependent on its running back breaking long runs to make the running game work, and therefore tends to have a less consistent running attack. Second-level yards fall somewhere in between.

New for 2021 is blown block rate (**BB Rt**), which is simply this team's total of blown blocks on running plays divided by the total number of running plays, along with rank among the 32 teams. Only blown blocks by the offensive line are included, not blown blocks by skill players.

The next seven columns give information about pass protection. That starts with total sacks, followed by adjusted sack rate (**ASR**) and its rank among the 32 teams. Some teams allow a lot of sacks because they throw a lot of passes; adjusted sack rate accounts for this by dividing sacks and intentional grounding by total pass plays. It is also adjusted for situation (sacks are much more common on third down, particularly third-and-long) and opponent, all of which makes it a better measurement than raw sacks totals. Remember that quarterbacks share responsibility for sacks, and two different quarterbacks behind the same line can have very different adjusted sack rates.

Next comes **pressure rate**: this is the percentage of pass plays where we have marked pass pressure, based on Sports Info Solutions charting. Sacks or scrambles due to coverage are not counted as passes with pressure. Pressure rates around

Table 12. Browns Offensive Line

Player	Pos	Age	GS	Snaps	Pen	Sk	Pass	Run	Player	Pos	Age	GS	Snaps	Pen	Sk	Pass	Run
J.C. Tretter	C	30	16/16	1061	4	0.5	5	12	Jedrick Wills	LT	22	15/15	957	11	4.5	16	7
Joel Bitonio	LG	30	16/16	1061	3	1.5	5	7	Wyatt Teller	RG	27	11/11	694	5	3	8	7
Jack Conklin	RT	27	15/15	999	2	2	9	9	Christopher Hubbard	RG	30	11/5	290	0	0	3	2

Year	Yards	ALY	Rk	Power	Rk	Stuff	Rk	2Lev	Rk	OpFld	Rk	BB Rt	Rk	Sacks	ASR	Rk	Press	Rk	BB Rt	Rk	Cont
2018	4.61	4.24	18	50%	32	23%	29	1.27	16	1.16	4	7.6%	24	38	6.7%	16	27.7%	11	5.9%	6	38
2019	4.85	4.46	10	53%	29	18%	14	1.34	5	1.17	2	8.9%	10	41	7.2%	18	28.1%	7	11.6%	7	26
2020	4.91	4.79	6	56%	28	18%	24	1.45	1	1.10	4	10.3%	18	26	6.5%	16	24.8%	16	9.9%	6	27

| 2020 ALY by direction: | Left End: 4.71 (8) | Left Tackle: 5.50 (2) | Mid/Guard: 4.50 (14) | Right Tackle: 4.60 (12) | Right End: 6.49 (1) |

the league were down in 2020, five percentage points lower than in 2019. So a team may have a lower pressure rate in 2020 but be ranked worse because the pass protection declined in comparison to the rest of the league. Quarterbacks also share responsibility for pressure rates. And just as with runs, we've listed blown block rate (**BB Rt**) for pass plays.

Finally, continuity score (**Cont.**) tells you how much continuity each offensive line had from game-to-game in that season. It was introduced in the Cleveland chapter of *Pro Football Prospectus 2007*. Continuity score starts with 48 and then subtracts:

- The number of players over five who started at least one game on the offensive line;
- The number of times the team started at least one different lineman compared to the game before; and
- The difference between 16 and that team's longest streak where the same line started consecutive games.

The Giants and Rams led the NFL with a continuity score of 36 last season, while the lowest score belonged to Philadelphia at 15.

Finally, underneath the table in italics we give 2020 adjusted line yards in each of the five directions with rank among the 32 teams. The league average was 4.40 on left end runs (**LE**), 4.24 on left tackle runs (**LT**), 4.41 on runs up the middle (**MID**), 4.40 on right tackle runs (**RT**), and 4.57 on right end runs (**RE**).

How to Read the Defensive Front Tables

Defensive players make plays. Plays aren't just tackles—interceptions and pass deflections change the course of the game, and so does the act of forcing a fumble or beating the offensive players to a fumbled ball. While some plays stop a team on third down and force a punt, others merely stop a

receiver after he's caught a 30-yard pass. We can measure opportunities in pass coverage thanks to our charting partners at Sports Info Solutions.

Defensive players are listed in these tables if they meet one of three baselines:

1) at least 20 plays during the 2020 season
2) at least eight games with 25% of the team's defensive snaps in those games
3) at least five games with 80% of the team's defensive snaps in those games

Defensive players who were with two teams last year are only listed with the final team they played with.

Defensive Linemen/Edge Rushers

As we've noted earlier in this toolbox: as hybrid defenses become more popular, it becomes more and more difficult to tell the difference between a defensive end and an outside linebacker. What we do know is that there are certain players whose job is to rush the passer, even if they occasionally drop into coverage. We also know that the defensive ends in a two-gapping 3-4 system have a lot more in common with run-stuffing 4-3 tackles than with smaller 4-3 defensive ends.

Therefore, we have separated defensive front players into three tables rather than two. All defensive tackles and defensive ends from 3-4 teams are listed as **Defensive Linemen**, and all ranked together. Defensive ends from 4-3 teams and outside linebackers from 3-4 teams are listed as **Edge Rushers**, and all ranked together. Most 4-3 linebackers are ranked along with 3-4 inside linebackers and listed simply as **Linebackers**. For the most part this categorization puts players with similar roles together. Some players who have hybrid roles are ranked at the position more appropriate to their role, such as J.J. Watt as an edge rusher despite playing defensive end in a nominally 3-4 scheme.

The tables for defensive linemen and edge rushers are the same, although the players are ranked in two separate categories. Players are listed with the following numbers:

Age in 2021, determined by 2021 minus birth year, plus

Table 13. Cowboys Defensive Line and Edge Rushers

Defensive Line	Age	Pos	G	Snaps	Plays	Overall TmPct	Rk	Stop	Dfts	BTkl	vs. Run Runs	St%	Rk	RuYd	Rk	Pass Rush Sack	Hit	Hur	Dsrpt
Antwaun Woods*	28	DT	14	456	23	3.2%	80	16	1	3	22	68%	67	3.4	92	1.0	1	2	0
Neville Gallimore	24	DT	14	416	29	4.0%	66	22	8	2	25	80%	26	2.0	27	0.5	3	7	1
Justin Hamilton	28	DT	10	236	10	1.9%	--	8	2	0	10	80%	--	2.0	--	0.0	1	6	1
Carlos Watkins	28	DE	16	542	30	3.5%	75	21	6	2	24	67%	69	2.5	49	2.0	1	4	3
Brent Urban	30	DE	16	369	37	4.5%	--	33	6	2	32	88%	--	1.8	--	2.5	1	6	2

Edge Rushers	Age	Pos	G	Snaps	Plays	Overall TmPct	Rk	Stop	Dfts	BTkl	vs. Run Runs	St%	Rk	RuYd	Rk	Pass Rush Sack	Hit	Hur	Dsrpt
Aldon Smith*	32	DE	16	808	50	6.0%	25	40	10	8	42	76%	31	2.9	63	5.0	9	37	5
Demarcus Lawrence	29	DE	16	666	60	7.2%	10	46	25	6	47	72%	46	1.5	9	6.5	4	37	3
Tyrone Crawford*	32	DE	16	443	14	1.7%	95	9	3	0	11	55%	91	5.5	97	2.0	2	14	1
Dorance Armstrong	24	DE	16	367	32	3.9%	--	16	3	2	25	56%	--	3.7	--	0.0	1	8	0
Randy Gregory	29	DE	10	270	22	4.2%	59	18	11	1	17	76%	30	1.8	22	3.5	10	9	2
Tarell Basham	27	OLB	16	734	34	3.9%	67	26	13	8	23	78%	21	1.9	24	3.5	9	19	0

position (**Pos**) and the number of defensive **Snaps** played in 2020.

Plays (**Plays**): The total defensive plays including tackles, assists, pass deflections, interceptions, fumbles forced, and fumble recoveries. This number comes from the official NFL gamebooks and therefore does not include plays on which the player is listed by Sports Info Solutions in coverage but does not appear in the standard play-by-play. Special teams tackles are also not included.

Percentage of team plays (**TmPct**): The percentage of total team plays involving this defender. The sum of the percentages of team plays for all defenders on a given team will exceed 100%, primarily due to shared tackles. This number is adjusted based on games played, so an injured player may be fifth on his team in plays but third in **TmPct**.

Stops (**Stop**): The total number of plays which prevent a "success" by the offense (45% of needed yards on first down, 60% on second down, 100% on third or fourth down).

Defeats (**Dfts**): The total number of plays which stop the offense from gaining first down yardage on third or fourth down, stop the offense behind the line of scrimmage, or result in a fumble (regardless of which team recovers) or interception.

Broken tackles (**BTkl**): The number of broken tackles recorded by SIS game charters.

The next five columns represent runs only, starting with the number of plays each player made on **Runs**. Stop rate (**St%**) gives the percentage of these run plays which were stops. Average yards (**AvYd**) gives the average number of yards gained by the runner when this player is credited with making the play.

Finally, we have pass rush numbers, starting with standard NFL **Sack** totals.

Hit: To qualify as a quarterback hit, the defender must knock the quarterback to the ground in the act of throwing or after the pass is thrown. We have listed hits on all plays, including those nullified by penalties. (After all, many of the hardest hits come on plays cancelled because the hit itself draws a roughing the passer penalty.) Our count of hits does not add in sacks; that count is referred to elsewhere as "knockdowns."

Hurries (**Hur**): The number of quarterback hurries recorded by Sports Info Solutions game charters. This includes both hurries on standard plays and hurries that force an offensive holding penalty that cancels the play and costs the offense yardage.

Disruptions (**Dsprt**): This stat combines two different but similar types of plays. First, plays where a pass-rusher forced an incomplete pass or interception by hitting the quarterback as he was throwing the ball. These plays are generally not counted as passes defended, so we wanted a way to count

them. Second, plays where the pass-rusher batted the ball down at the line of scrimmage or tipped it in the air. These plays are usually incomplete, but occasionally they lead to interceptions, and even more rarely they fall into the hands of offensive receivers. As with the "hit in motion" disruptions, some plays counted as tips by Football Outsiders were not counted as passes defended by the NFL.

Defensive linemen and edge rushers are both ranked by percentage of team plays, run stop rate, and average yards per run tackle. The lowest number of average yards earns the top rank (negative numbers indicate the average play ending behind the line of scrimmage). Defensive linemen and edge rushers are ranked if they played at least 40% of defensive snaps in the games they were active. There are 97 defensive linemen and 97 edge rushers ranked.

Linebackers

Most of the stats for linebackers are the same as those for defensive linemen. Linebackers are ranked in percentage of team plays, and also in stop rate and average yards for running plays specifically. Linebackers are ranked in these stats if they played at least 35% of defensive snaps in the games they were active, with 87 linebackers ranked.

The final six columns in the linebacker stats come from Sports Info Solutions game charting.

Targets (**Tgts**): The number of pass players on which game charters listed this player in coverage.

Success rate (**Suc%**): The percentage plays of targeting this player on which the offense did not have a successful play. This means not only incomplete passes and interceptions, but also short completions which do not meet our baselines for success (45% of needed yards on first down, 60% on second down, 100% on third or fourth down).

Yards per pass (**Yd/P**): The average number of yards gained on plays on which this defender was the listed target.

Passes defended (**PD**) and interceptions (**Int**) come from the NFL totals.

These stats are explained in more detail in the section on secondary tables. There are 75 linebackers are ranked in the charting stats, based on hitting one of two minimums: 16 charted passes with fewer than eight games started, or 12 charted passes with eight or more games started (but a minimum of five games). As a result of the different thresholds, some linebackers are ranked in standard stats but not charting stats.

Further Details

Just as in the offensive tables, players who are no longer on the team are marked with asterisks, and players who were

Table 14. Broncos Defensive Line and Edge Rushers

Linebackers	Age	Pos	Overall								vs. Run					Pass Rush			vs. Pass					
			G	Snaps	Plays	TmPct	Rk	Stop	Dfts	BTkl	Runs	St%	Rk	RuYd	Rk	Sack	Hit	Hur	Tgts	Suc%	Rk	Yd/P	Rk	PD	Int
A.J. Johnson	30	ILB	16	1063	126	14.9%	22	74	13	12	80	66%	14	3.7	29	1.0	5	14	39	64%	9	4.8	15	2	0
Josey Jewell	27	ILB	16	1011	118	14.0%	33	60	20	6	66	61%	27	3.7	33	2.0	3	5	41	61%	11	5.1	19	5	0

on other teams last year are in italics. Defensive front player statistics are not adjusted for opponent.

Numbers for defensive linemen and linebackers unfortunately do not reflect all of the opportunities a player had to make a play, but they do show us which players were most active on the field. A large number of plays could mean a strong defensive performance, or it could mean that the linebacker in question plays behind a poor part of the line. In general, defensive numbers should be taken as information that tells us what happened on the field in 2020, but not as a strict, unassailable judgment of which players are better than others—particularly when the difference between two players is small (for example, players ranked 20th and 30th) instead of large (players ranked 20th and 70th).

After the individual statistics for linemen and linebackers, the Defensive Front section contains a table that looks exactly like the table in the Offensive Line section, with two differences:

- Blown block rates are based on blown blocks forced by each defense, and include all blown blocks including those by both offensive linemen and skill players.
- Rushing numbers are for all opposing running backs against this team's defensive front. As we're on the opposite side of the ball, teams are now ranked in the opposite order, so the No. 1 defensive front is the one that allows the fewest adjusted line yards, the lowest percentage in Power situations, and has the highest adjusted sack rate. Directions for adjusted line yards are given from the offense's perspective, so runs left end and left tackle are aimed at the right defensive end and (assuming the tight end is on the other side) weakside linebacker.

As noted earlier, charted pressure rates around the league were down five percentage points in 2020, so a defense may have a lower pressure rate in 2020 but a higher rank than it had in 2019.

How to Read the Defensive Secondary Tables

The first few columns in the secondary tables are based on standard play-by-play, not game charting, with the exception of broken tackles. Age, total plays, percentage of team plays, stops, and defeats are computed the same way they are for other defensive players, so that the secondary can be compared to the defensive line and linebackers. That means that total plays here includes passes defensed, sacks, tackles after receptions, tipped passes, and interceptions, but not pass plays on which this player was in coverage but was not given a tackle or passed defense by the NFL's official scorer.

The middle five columns address each defensive back's role in stopping the run. Average yardage and stop rate for running plays is computed in the same manner as for defensive linemen and linebackers.

The third section of statistics represents data from Sports Info Solutions game charting. We do not count pass plays on which this player was in coverage, but the incomplete was listed as Thrown Away, Batted Down, or Hit in Motion. Hail Mary passes are also not included.

Targets (**Tgts**): The number of pass plays on which game charters listed this player in coverage.

Target percentage (**Tgt%**): The number of plays on which this player was targeted divided by the total number of charted passes against his defense, not including plays listed as Uncovered. Like percentage of team plays, this metric is adjusted based on number of games played.

Average depth of target (**aDOT**): The average distance in the air beyond the line of scrimmage of all passes targeted at this defender. It does not include yards after catch and is useful for seeing which defenders were covering receivers deeper or shorter. This is also often referred to as "Air Yards."

Success rate (**Suc%**): The percentage plays of targeting this player on which the offense did not have a successful play. This means not only incomplete passes and interceptions, but also short completions which do not meet our baselines for success (45% of needed yards on first down, 60% on second down, 100% on third or fourth down). Defensive pass interference is counted as a failure for the defensive player similar

Table 15. Lions Defensive Secondary

Secondary	Age	Pos	G	Snaps	Plays	TmPct	Rk	Stop	Dfts	BTkl	Runs	St%	Rk	RuYd	Rk	Tgts	Tgt%	Rk	aDOT	Suc%	Rk	Yd/P	Rk	PD	Int
Duron Harmon*	30	FS	16	1102	77	9.2%	57	9	5	11	35	6%	70	11.6	67	18	4.3%	66	12.5	39%	65	15.6	70	5	2
Amani Oruwariye	25	CB	16	1028	60	7.2%	70	23	7	11	11	55%	15	3.9	8	75	19.1%	46	14.6	52%	38	9.6	73	7	1
Tracy Walker	26	SS	15	755	84	10.7%	37	30	10	11	40	48%	16	4.9	12	36	12.5%	13	10.5	42%	58	8.9	51	4	0
Jayron Kearse*	27	FS	11	503	59	10.2%	42	22	4	4	35	46%	22	4.4	6	24	12.5%	12	6.4	54%	22	4.0	2	2	0
Justin Coleman*	28	CB	11	470	30	5.2%	--	11	7	9	3	33%	--	6.7	--	29	16.1%	--	9.2	45%	--	9.3	--	1	0
Darryl Roberts*	31	CB	11	469	45	7.8%	--	16	6	5	7	29%	--	7.9	--	40	22.3%	--	10.4	45%	--	6.8	--	6	1
Jeff Okudah	22	CB	9	460	49	10.4%	--	20	9	7	19	63%	--	3.0	--	45	25.5%	--	11.2	36%	--	11.9	--	2	1
Desmond Trufant*	31	CB	6	324	23	7.3%	--	9	5	5	6	17%	--	6.5	--	28	22.6%	--	11.1	46%	--	8.4	--	4	1
Will Harris	26	SS	16	312	34	4.1%	--	3	3	4	15	7%	--	9.3	--	14	11.7%	--	6.9	57%	--	5.9	--	1	0
Corn Elder	27	CB	16	411	40	4.9%	--	13	5	3	8	38%	--	6.1	--	26	15.5%	--	10.0	42%	--	7.8	--	3	0
Quinton Dunbar	29	CB	6	397	35	10.5%	--	12	4	3	8	50%	--	4.5	--	39	22.3%	--	12.1	46%	--	8.7	--	5	1

Table 16. Packers Secondary Team Stats

Year	Pass D Rank	vs. #1 WR	Rk	vs. #2 WR	Rk	vs. Other WR	Rk	WR Wide	Rk	WR Slot	Rk	vs. TE	Rk	vs. RB	Rk
2018	28	9.0%	22	14.9%	25	-4.1%	13	4.1%	22	13.6%	25	20.8%	27	25.1%	32
2019	9	1.4%	15	-29.7%	3	-12.8%	9	-12.6%	12	-13.0%	6	9.8%	26	-17.0%	4
2020	15	-11.1%	10	10.6%	24	-20.0%	6	-2.4%	15	-8.4%	7	-12.0%	8	15.3%	27

to a completion of equal yardage (and a new first down).

Yards per pass (**Yd/P**): The average number of yards gained on plays on which this defender was the listed target.

Passes defensed (**PD**) and Interceptions (**Int**) represent the standard NFL count for both stats.

Cornerbacks need 50 charted passes or eight games started to be ranked in the defensive stats, with 80 cornerbacks ranked in total. Safeties require 20 charted passes or eight games started, with 71 safeties ranked in total. Strong and free safeties are ranked together.

Just like the defensive front, the defensive secondary has a table of team statistics following the individual numbers. This table gives DVOA figured against different types of receivers. Each offense's wide receivers have had one receiver designated as No. 1, and another as No. 2. (Occasionally this is difficult, due to injury or a situation with "co-No. 1 receivers," but it's usually pretty obvious.) The other receivers form a third category, with tight ends and running backs as fourth and fifth categories. The defense is then judged on the performance of each receiver based on the standard DVOA method, with each rating adjusted based on strength of schedule. (Obviously, it's a lot harder to cover the No. 1 receiver of the Buffalo Bills than to cover the No. 1 receiver of the Detroit Lions.) **Pass D Rank** is the total ranking of the pass defense, as seen before in the Trends and Splits table, and combines all five categories plus sacks and passes with no intended target.

The "defense vs. types of receivers" table should be used to analyze the defense as a whole rather than individual players. The ratings against types of receivers are generally based on defensive schemes, not specific cornerbacks, except for certain defenses that really do move one cornerback around to cover the opponent's top weapon (i.e., New England). The ratings against tight ends and running backs are in large part due to the performance of linebackers.

In addition, we list each team's numbers covering receivers based on where they lined up before the snap, either wide or in the slot. The "vs. Other WR" number has sometimes been misrepresented as measuring coverage of slot receivers, but in the modern NFL, the team's No. 1 or No. 2 receiver will often be working predominantly out of the slot, while other receivers will switch back and forth between the two positions. The listing of coverage of wide receivers in the slot also includes wide receivers lined up tight in a tight end position.

How to Read the Special Teams Tables

The special teams tables list the last three years of kick, punt, and return numbers for each team.

The first two columns list total special teams DVOA and rank among the 32 teams. The next two columns list the value in actual points of field goals and extra points (**FG/XP**) when compared to how a league average kicker would do from the same distances, adjusted for weather and altitude, and rank among the 32 teams. Next, we list the estimated value in actual points of field position over or under the league average based on net kickoffs (**Net Kick**) and rank that value among the 32 teams. That is followed by the estimated point values of field position for kick returns (**Kick Ret**), net punting (**Net Punt**), and punt returns (**Punt Ret**) and their respective ranks.

The final two columns represent the value of "**Hidden**" special teams, plays which throughout the past decade have usually been based on the performance of opponents without this team being able to control the outcome. We combine the opposing team's value on field goals, kickoff distance, and punt distance, adjusted for weather and altitude, and then switch the sign to represent that good special teams by the opponent will cost the listed team points, and bad special teams will effectively hand them points. We have to give the qualifier of "usually" because, as explained earlier, certain returners such as Cordarrelle Patterson will affect opposing special teams strategy, and a handful of the missed field goals are blocked. Nonetheless, the "hidden" value is still "hidden" for most teams, and they are ranked from the most hidden value gained (Detroit, 19.4 points) to the most value lost (Philadelphia, -18.0 points).

We also have methods for measuring the gross value of kickoffs and punts. These measures assume that all kickoffs or punts will have average returns unless they are touchbacks or kicked out of bounds, then judge the kicker or punter on the value with those assumed returns. We also count special teams tackles; these include both tackles and assists, but do not include tackles on two-point conversions, tackles after onside kicks, or tackles of the player who recovers a fumble after the punt or kick returner loses the ball. The best and worst individual values for kickers, punters, returners, and kick gunners (i.e. tackle totals) are listed in the statistical appendix at the end of the book.

Table 17. Texans Special Teams

Year	DVOA	Rank	FG/XP	Rank	Net Kick	Rank	Kick Ret	Rank	Net Punt	Rank	Punt Ret	Rank	Hidden	Rank
2018	3.5%	5	4.4	8	7.8	1	0.5	11	4.5	11	0.5	14	-2.5	19
2019	2.9%	5	-1.9	20	4.7	8	0.1	14	10.5	2	1.0	13	-7.6	28
2020	-1.0%	21	-2.5	20	1.9	13	-4.7	30	2.1	15	-1.8	20	10.9	6

Administrative Minutia

Receiving statistics include all passes intended for the receiver in question, including those that are incomplete or intercepted. The word passes refers to both complete and incomplete pass attempts. When rating receivers, interceptions are treated as incomplete passes with no penalty.

For the computation of DVOA and DYAR, passing statistics include sacks as well as fumbles on aborted snaps. We do not include kneeldown plays or spikes for the purpose of stopping the clock. Some interceptions which we have determined to be "Hail Mary" plays that end the first half or game are counted as regular incomplete passes, not turnovers.

All statistics generated by ESPN Stats & Info or Sports Info Solutions game charting, or our combination of the two sources, may be different from totals compiled by other sources.

Unless we say otherwise, when we refer to third-down performance in this book we are referring to a combination of third down and the handful of rushing and passing plays that take place on fourth down (primarily fourth-and-1).

Aaron Schatz

The Year In Quotes

'HIT BIRDS, WE'VE LOST THRUST, WE MAY END UP IN THE HUDSON'

"[The loss of Jamal Adams] really doesn't [affect how the Jets use safeties]. We're very multiple with how we do those things anyway. Jamal may get bored there because they don't use their safety-type things with all the complexities. ... maybe not showing what they're doing as much as we do."

—New York Jets defensive coordinator Gregg Williams threw a jab at the Seahawks after the Jamal Adams trade. Yeah, Earl Thomas and Kam Chancellor always looked pretty bored out there, coach.

"We don't make as many mistakes as he does. ... He's not bringing Gregg Williams with him, that's for sure."

—Seattle Seahawks head coach Pete Carroll responded to Williams from the top rope. (New York Post)

FROM THE COACHING MIND OF JOE JUDGE

"There are consequences for making mistakes."

—New York Giants head coach Joe Judge made both players and coaches run laps for mistakes during practice. (Pro-FootballTalk)

"We're not going to accept penalties. So we'll find any little trick we can to teach them."

—Judge also had Giants defensive backs tape tennis balls to their palms in order to mitigate holding penalties in pass coverage. (Dan Duggan, The Athletic via Twitter)

"I've got the strength staff downstairs right now putting bars of soap in socks and we're just going to take him out back and wail on him for a while."

—Judge later took heat for suggesting that that the Giants might expose Daniel Jones to contact during practices. This quote was meant as sarcasm. Probably. (Art Stapleton, The Record Sports via Twitter)

MILE-HIGH MISSES

"I just kind of know. It's like it's been red 10 times on roulette so I'm going to bet black this time. Doesn't work that way."

—Tennessee Titans head coach Mike Vrabel wasn't afraid to put kicker Stephen Gostkowski in a position to win after he had missed three field goals and an extra point on Monday Night Football. Gostkowski hit a 25-yarder in the final seconds to beat the Broncos. (Kyle Tucker, The Athletic via Twitter)

"I would have taken my pants off to make that last kick."

—Gostkowski, when asked why he was seen on the sideline with the sock and shoe removed from his kicking foot before the game-winner. (Jim Wyatt, Titans Online via Twitter)

THE YEAR IN ANDY REID

"I'm one happy guy. I put on my best Tommy Bahama for all you guys to celebrate this."

—Floral pattern aficionado Andy Reid dressed to his comfort level to celebrate Patrick Mahomes' contract extension. (Field Yates, ESPN via Twitter)

"You wear it for special occasions, or if you want a free cheeseburger, you just point right there and show 'em that ring and you might get one."

—Reid, on the awesome power of a Super Bowl ring. Let's be real, though: who's not going to recognize Andy freakin' Reid in Kansas City? (Andy Teicher, NFL Nation via Twitter)

CUE THE IMPERIAL MARCH

"I think it's a cool name for our stadium. I don't give a damn about Star Wars. That's what we're calling our stadium and I don't care what anybody else thinks. It's a cool stadium, it's a great name, and we just have to play good when we're in there."

—Jon Gruden loves the "Death Star" nickname for the Raiders' new stadium in Las Vegas but wants to reassure you that he is a real Football Guy, not one of those geekity-geeks who likes space movies and nerd stuff. (Las Vegas Review-Journal)

The Year in a Global Pandemic

COACHES REACT

"The Raiders players [logged] onto a Zoom call last week expecting to see Jon Gruden. Instead they saw Rich Bisaccia, the special teams coach and the assistant head coach. Bisaccia told them, 'Guys, Coach Gruden has COVID, and he's at the hospital now and he's being taken care of.' And the players were taken aback, woah. They shortly thereafter told them, 'Y'know what, we're just putting you on a little bit.' And it wasn't a joke. What it was was the team illustrating to the players that this could happen at any moment to anybody. ... The point to the players was 'You've gotta stay ready, you've gotta stay ready, everybody's gotta stay ready' because this virus that Gruden himself said they want to 'crush' could pop up, and it doesn't discriminate."

—The Las Vegas Raiders' coaching staff put their players through a mental rollercoaster in training camp by pretending that head coach Jon Gruden had tested positive for COVID-19. (Mike Garafolo, NFL Network via Twitter)

WHO ARE WE TRADING WITH? SQUIRRELS?

"I'm not trading for peanuts. If they make a substantial of-fer, then we will consider it."

—Houston Texans interim head coach Romeo Crennel, before the trade deadline.

"Nobody really came through with a Deluxe Nut Package. If there had been some Deluxe Nuts laid out on the table, it could have been a different deal."

—Crennel after the trade deadline.

"Most of them come in a mixed variety, you know, they're mixed in a can, so I like them all."

—Crennel's response when asked for his "Deluxe Nut of choice." Meanwhile, somewhere in America, Bill O'Brien was munching on shells. (Beaumont Enterprise)

WE'RE ON TO ITALIAN B.M.T.'S

"When Subway reached out, shared the Footlong Season campaign objectives and the ideas for the commercial, I de-cided the timing was right to have some fun and enjoy some sandwiches."

—New England Patriots head coach Bill Belichick going full Belichick when explaining his role as a Subway pitchman. (CBS Boston)

The Year in a Global Pandemic

PLAYERS REACT

"Did not contract the virus. It took one look at me and ran the other way. Probably in its best interest."

—Jacksonville Jaguars quarterback Gardner Min-shew was listed as a false positive during pre-camp COVID testing. When pressed on the result, Minshew answered in the most Gardner Minshew way possible. (Barstool Sports)

"Tell me why they pull me from warming up so I can go get tested... my s**t come back positive... I tested positive for Covid WTF"

"The crazy thing is I have the same damn routine.... this s**t do not make sense to me."

"Yea I'm going to go ahead and call it a quit for the rest of the season... I can't deal with this."

"Since I tested positive for Covid before the game do the game stop or go on? @NFL"

"I'm about to drink some wine and cope...."

—Baltimore Ravens wide receiver Dez Bryant sent off several tweets after being pulled from a Week 13 game for a positive test minutes before kickoff. It would have been Bryant's opportunity to face off against the Cowboys, his former team. Bryant later asked fans to post pictures of their glasses of wine in solidarity. (Dez Bryant via Twitter)

CAN'T QUESTION HIS LOGIC

"I don't know. I've been telling them we can't start winning until we stop losing and right now we are doing things to beat ourselves with the turnovers and sacks and safeties and penal-ties on third downs on defense. I'm just not going to deal with it anymore."

—Minnesota Vikings head coach Mike Zimmer made it clear to his 0-2 team that they, in fact, could not win games while they were losing them. (ESPN)

THE YEAR IN CAM NEWTON

"One thing I did, kind of from walking in Day 1—there's an aura that you get when you play as a member of the New England Patriots, and that aura can sometimes be like 'grrr,' you know what I'm saying? The Patriot Way, to a degree, from the outside looking in. But from the inside looking out, these guys really enjoy the process, as well as myself. And me being a member, I'm just lucky to be here. Any time I can lighten the mood in some way, shape, or form, I hesitate not."

—New England Patriots quarterback Cam Newton tried to bring a lighter atmosphere to the notoriously dour Foxbor-ough locker room. One Newton innovation: giving everyone a nickname. (NESN)

"Highway 11"
"Doughboy"
"Dirty Dave"
"Smokin' Joe"
"Winnie the Pooh"
"Free Mason"
"Buzzo"
"Burky"
"Twin No. 1"
"Twin No. 2"
"Bo Diddly"
"Crazy Legs"
"Bent Dog"
"Stiddy"
"The Hoyster"

—Newton rattled off several of those nicknames during the press conference. When asked if head coach Bill Belichick had a nickname, Newton revealed that the coach is "Dolla Dolla Bill." Belichick's likely reaction was "grrr." (Zack Cox, NESN)

"I'm beginning to think he either has like a Staples easy button or a Buffalo Wild Wings button or just a straight direct line to the football gods because he's like a football whisperer when it comes to anticipating what the game's going to be like."

—Newton gave us better metaphors for understanding Belichick in just one season than Tom Brady gave us in two decades. (Jeff Howe, The Athletic via Twitter)

THE YEAR IN MOMS

"My mom called me before the game. ... The first thing she told me was, 'I'm your mom and everything, but are you going to hit some holes today?' I was like, 'You know what? I got you, mom.' It just really hit home when your own mom is not liking what she sees out there."

—Arizona Cardinals running back Kenyan Drake received some coaching points from his mom before running for 164 yards and two touchdowns on 20 carries during Arizona's 38-10 win over Dallas in Week 6. (Arizona Cardinals via Twitter)

"She said that I'm not leading the league in sacks."

—Washington Football Team rookie defensive end Chase Young also received some pretty poor reviews from his mom. She gave him a C+ through his first six NFL games. (Nicki Jhabvala, Washington Post via Twitter)

"My mom found out I put my Xbox Live account on her credit card. She been paying since I was in sixth grade"

—Baltimore Ravens wide receiver Miles Boykin, despite cashing NFL checks for a full year, still made his mother pay about $60 for his annual Xbox Live subscription last year. Boykin followed up with "Before y'all get mad I tried to start paying today and she said she been paying this long she might as well continue." Chase Young's mother would NOT put up with this sort of tomfoolery. (Miles Boykin via Twitter)

Question: *"At what point in your football career did you decide no one can guard you?"*

DK Metcalf: *"When my mom had me."*

—Seattle Seahawks wide receiver DK Metcalf was unguardable out of the womb, though his results in the 3-cone APGAR were disappointing. (KJR reporter Curtis Crabtree via Twitter)

REALEST IN THE COMMONWEALTH

*"I'M THE REALEST, TOUGHEST, BADDEST MOTHERF***ER IN THE STATE OF VIRGINIA!"*

—The mantra former Virginia Commonwealth basketball coach Shaka Smart made Colts tight end Mo Alie-Cox shout at the top of his lungs in the mirror of his dorm room every night. Smart claimed Alie-Cox had a "sluggish vibe" coming into college, but that "a blind man could've seen the potential" in the future football player. (The Athletic)

JUST TRYING TO FIT IN

"I'm going to have a fake Heisman made so all four of us can have them."

—Pittsburgh Steelers quarterback Ben Roethlisberger wanted to join fellow AFC North quarterbacks Lamar Jackson, Baker Mayfield, and Joe Burrow as part of the Heisman Trophy-winners club. (Brooke Pryor, ESPN NFL Nation via Twitter)

ALWAYS HAVE A BACKUP PLAN

Reporter #1: *"Teddy why are you wearing that?"*

Teddy Bridgewater, wearing referee stripes: *"I'm here to throw a flag on any question I don't want to answer. Nah, I'm just playing. I just came from work, my other job. Foot Locker."*

Reporter #2: *"Is there a reason that you are working at Foot Locker?"*

Bridgewater: *"Well, when you've got a punter who's 100% on the season completing passes, man, he makes it tough on you. So I'm trying to find another way to generate some income."*

—Carolina Panthers quarterback Teddy Bridgewater after punter Joseph Charlton completed a 28-yard pass on fourth-and-7 against the Kansas City Chiefs. Bridgewater was right to be a little worried about his long-term job security. (Carolina Panthers via Twitter)

INSIDE THE AVERAGE LOOSE BALL PILE

"They are gross. Guys smell bro. Them dirty linemen, dirty O-line and D-line that don't put deodorant on and they don't brush their teeth."

—Miami Dolphins linebacker Kyle Van Noy on what it's like to go for a fumble in the NFL. Hint: it's gross. (Pat McAfee via Twitter)

SCRAMBLING FOR COMPLIMENTS

"That's a very good football team. People forget that because they haven't won a game."

—Kansas City Chiefs defensive tackle Chris Jones tried his best to play the humble card by complimenting his upcoming opponent, but praise for the New York Jets only comes off as confusing. (Adam Teicher, NFL via Twitter)

The Year in a Global Pandemic

THEY SHOULD HAVE CREATED A LAUGH TRACK FOR JETS GAMES

"NFL Films sound engineers have developed club specific audio pallets (crowd noise) for each NFL club. A trained audio engineer hired by the League office will work collaboratively with network personnel to incorporate the audio into the in-game broadcast feed.

"In addition to music and established club audio prompts, the League office will provide your club with an audio file that contains a loop of pre-recorded crowd noise ('curated audio') that is specific to your stadium."

—From an official NFL memo announcing pumped-in stadium and broadcast crowd noise amidst COVID attendance restrictions. (Tom Pelissero, NFL Network via Twitter)

REVENGE OF THE JOURNEYMAN

"Every week is a 'revenge game' for me, because I've played on every dang team in the NFL."

—Former Rams, Bengals, Bills, Titans, Texans, Jets, Buccaneers, and Dolphins quarterback Ryan Fitzpatrick, who officially signed with his ninth team this offseason, the Washington Football Team, when asked if he has any 'I'll show you' left in the tank at age 38. (David Aldridge, The Athletic via Twitter)

MASCOTS: THE MOST UNDERRATED ASPECT OF FREE AGENCY DECISIONS

*"I like the warm weather I like being here. I like being a Jaguar, I'd rather be a Jaguar than a Falcon or like a bird or some s***"*

—If Jacksonville Jaguars wide receiver Keelan Cole was deciding between two teams, the tiebreaker would be which team had the cooler mascot. (Ben Murphy via Twitter)

The Year in a Global Pandemic

LIFE WITHOUT FANS

"My first four years in the league there weren't many fans in the stadium anyway."

—Green Bay Packers linebacker Preston Smith wasn't worried about playing in empty stadiums, because he had been drafted by the Washington Redskins in 2015. (Zach Kruse, The Packers Wire via Twitter)

"It felt like we were at a Tampa Bay game."

—New Orleans Saints defensive end Cam Jordan wasn't used to empty stadiums. This quip, as you might imagine, came early in the season. (Katherine Terrell, The Athletic NOLA via Twitter)

Question: *"What was the atmosphere like in the stadium without fans there? Can you compare it to anything else that you've experienced in your football life?"*

Bill Belichick: *"Practice."*

—New England Patriots head coach Bill Belichick wasn't used to empty stadiums, either. (Whistle Sports via Twitter)

"Usually I would try at key points to get the crowd involved, but now I'm literally playing music directly to the players and specifically for them. Even without fans, I still have to be that 12th man and be that extra person to give them an advantage."

—Los Angeles Rams in-house DJ Jamal McCoy, otherwise known as DJ Mal-Ski, on how he did his job without fans. McCoy took personal requests from players, playing "Surf" by Young Thug for linebacker Leonard Floyd and Gucci Mane songs for tight end Tyler Higbee. (Los Angeles Times)

'NO ONE KNOWS WHAT IT MEANS, BUT IT'S PROVOCATIVE. IT GETS THE PEOPLE GOING!'

*"Steve... we're gonna f***ing kill everyone. Full speed. We're gonna kill everyone. ... And we're gonna get a Super Bowl ring so f***ing big on our finger that a f***ing show dog wouldn't be able to jump over it."*

—Arizona Cardinals linebacker Zaven Collins sounded pretty fired up on his phone call with general manager Steve Keim after finding out he was being drafted 16th overall. (Arizona Cardinals via Twitter)

WHAT'S SCARIER: HARRY POTTER OR AN UNBLOCKED T.J. WATT?

"[I was] a little scared of everything growing up. I still don't like scary movies, I don't like haunted houses or anything like that. I couldn't watch Harry Potter, Lord of the Rings, House. I was strictly a SpongeBob, Disney Channel, Nickelodeon kinda guy."

—Cincinnati Bengals quarterback Joe Burrow, in a moment of vulnerability and openness during a press conference, revealed he was a complete scaredy-cat growing up. (Ben Baby, ESPN via Twitter)

THE POWER OF THE BROADCAST BOOTH

Joe Buck: *"Justin Tucker since 2016 has made 70 straight inside 40 yards."*

Troy Aikman: *"It's nice when you've got a kicker like that that you can depend on, and now we'll see if he keeps that streak alive."*

Buck: *"I'm just gonna say he is. There's no announcer's jinx, come on."*

Buck: *"Aaaaaaaaand he yanked it. No good. Who gets blamed for that?"*

—Fox Sports broadcasters Joe Buck and Troy Aikman as Baltimore Ravens kicker Justin Tucker missed a 36-yard field goal attempt in a Tuesday night game against the Dallas Cowboys.

"There are few things I relish more than affecting the outcome of kicks, no-hitters, wins, and losses from the broadcast booth. It's fun. It's power that cannot fall into the wrong hands. Think about it—had I not said what I said, Justin would have made the kick. There is zero doubt. I have sent a letter of apology to Tucker, the Ravens, their fans and Kim Jong-Un (just to be safe). I'm most fun at parties. All I have to do is say it and it the opposite happens. Please, Jimmy, don't let this secret get out. I beg you. People's lives and careers are at stake and I'm tired of being asked to parties."

—Buck's statement to *Sports Illustrated*'s Jimmy Traina after "jinxing" Tucker. (Sports Illustrated)

THE YEAR IN DAN CAMPBELL

"Here's what I do know, is that this team is going to take on the identity of this city. This city has been down and it found a way to get up. It has found a way to overcome adversity. So this team's going to be built on: we're going to kick you in the teeth, and when you punch us back, we're going to smile at you, and when you knock us down, we're gonna get up and on the way up, we're gonna bite a kneecap off, alright, and we're going to stand up and then it's gonna take two more shots to knock us down, alright, and on the way up, we're going to take your other kneecap and we're going to get up and then it's going to take three shots to get us down, and when we do, we're gonna take another hunk out of you. Before long, we're going to be the last one standing."

—Newly hired Detroit Lions head coach Dan Campbell used his introductory press conference to establish a culture, emphasizing toughness, resilience, and some light cannibalism. (Will Burchfield, 97.1 The Ticket via Twitter)

"I said this to Chris [Spielman] the other day, I was like, 'I love the fact we're only known as meatheads.' I'm a meathead? I have limited brain capacity? I like that. I'm good with that, you know what I mean? I have zero problem with it."

—Campbell, reveling in his public persona. (MLive)

"I'd say this about [Michael] Brockers, he's probably one of the few in this league that can wield the hammer of Thor. We're real excited about that."

—Campbell comparing free agent acquisition Michael Brockers to a Norse god, or at least to [watches 50-plus hours of Marvel movies] Captain America or Vision. (Field Yates, ESPN via Twitter)

"I don't think we're going to be able to do it, but I would love to literally just have a pet lion. Just a legit pet lion on a chain, a big-ass chain, and he really is my pet. We just walk around the building, we go out to practice, we're at seven-on-seven, we're behind the kicker when he's kicking. ... On command, you could train him, like if one of your groups isn't doing well you could just take him over to their section and just have it take a dump right there in the middle of where their section is at and then bring him on back. I mean, think about it. It'd be outstanding. ... We're going somewhere. The problem, I don't know if PETA's going to allow that. Even though we would take great care of it. It would be fed well, it would be petted, it would be manicured. I might end up losing an arm because of it, but that would be even better because it would validate what, this is a freaking, this a creature now. This is an animal. This thing, this is from the wild."

—Campbell jokingly suggested the team get him a pet lion to bring to practice as a motivational tool during training camp. Campbell was also partial to the idea of placing a stuffed sheep in front of the Lions' practice facility and ordering players not to look at it, because "lions do not concern themselves with the opinions of sheep." Just your typical tough guy discussing stuffed animals and manicured pets. (USA Today)

COMBINES ARE FLEETING, BUT WEIRD SCOUTING COLLOQUIALISMS ARE FOREVER

"I don't even know what ['He can spin it'] means. It's the equivalent of a guy who looks good on the driving range. There's a lot of guys who can spin it. Not as many who can actually play quarterback."

—Peyton Manning hates the expression "he can spin it" when evaluating quarterback passing. He's not alone. (Sam Farmer, Los Angeles Times via Twitter)

HORSES, PIRATES, THEY ALL LOOK THE SAME

"We've just got to finish strong. I mean, hats off to the Raiders. They've done an unbelievable job the past two games of presenting a challenge on third downs and in the red zone."

—Kansas City Chiefs tight end Travis Kelce referenced the wrong team in a Sunday Night Football on-field interview following his team's win over the Broncos. (NFL Update via Twitter)

"Playas mess up too."

—Kelce's response to ESPN's Sarah Spain after she posted the clip to Twitter. (Travis Kelce via Twitter)

COOKIN' WITH GAS

"In their beginning years, they're like a fart in a skillet. They're just bouncing around everywhere. Like popcorn. You don't know where they're gonna be."

—Pittsburgh Steelers offensive coordinator Randy Fichtner on the unpredictable nature of young wide receivers. (Brooke Pryor, ESPN via Twitter)

'SORRY, I'M NEW HERE'

Buccaneers personnel: *"Ceremony is down there."*
Mike Evans: *"It's a ceremony?"*
Personnel: *"Yeah."*
Evans: *"Ceremony? I'm new to this, bruh."*

—Tampa Bay Buccaneers wide receiver Mike Evans had no idea there was a ceremony to commemorate his first-ever NFC championship. You learn something new every day. (The Checkdown via Twitter)

The Year in a Global Pandemic

SOCIALLY DISTANCED SECONDARY

Instagram Commenter: *"Why u guys playing too far away from the WR?"*
Sean Murphy-Bunting: *"COVID"*

—Tampa Bay Buccaneers cornerback Sean Murphy-Bunting on the lack of press coverage by the Bucs secondary. (Greg Auman, The Athletic via Twitter)

THE YEAR IN GRONK

"Karen, hello! Where are you, Boston? This is crazy, you're Zooming into our press conferences. This is nuts."

—Tampa Bay Buccaneers tight end Rob Gronkowski, despite living in a socially distanced world for nearly a year, was still baffled by the concept of video conference calls in 2021. (Ryan Hannable, WEEI via Twitter)

Gronk: *"We're going to the AFC Championship Game!"*
Devin White: *"We ain't in no AFC!"*

—Gronk hopped in a video with linebacker Devin White and reverted to muscle memory when celebrating a Buccaneers playoff win. (Ian Steele, ABC 6 via Twitter)

"Alright, you gotta go. You gotta turn up, dawg. Yo, he's gotta turn up!"

—Gronk, in the background of wide receiver Mike Evans' Super Bowl postgame press conference, telling Evans it was time to party. Evans responded by telling the NFL Network team he "ain't never did this." Now that's what experienced Super Bowl leadership is all about. (NFL Network via Twitter)

"It's actually at an aquarium, our afterparty. So there's gonna be fishes. Hopefully there's some sharks, some whales. I'll go swimming with them. Why not? I'm a tank! I belong in that fish tank! 'Cause I'm a tank!"

—Gronk, in his own postgame press conference, making perfect sense. (NFL via TikTok)

ONE OF LIFE'S GREATEST PLEASURES

"I'll miss holding a football and running into a human being as hard as I possibly can."

—Pittsburgh Steelers tight end Vance McDonald after announcing his retirement. McDonald said he sometimes looks at walls and objects around his farm and thinks "If only this were a defender and I could run through it." (Brooke Pryor, ESPN via Twitter)

The Year in a Global Pandemic

PUTTING THE NBA'S DISNEY BUBBLE TO SHAME

"I brought up the idea of testing 50,000 people and quarantining them in a hotel and having the most safest Superdome known to man, scientifically. Bus them, they've tested every day, and you've got a COVID-free facility."

—New Orleans Saints head coach Sean Payton jokingly (we think) floated the idea of turning the Superdome into a bubble for the playoffs in order to create home-field advantage. (Luke Johnson, New Orleans Advocate via Twitter)

YOU GOT YOUR CHOCOLATE IN MY PEANUT BUTTER

"You know, when you're at the Reese's Senior Bowl, there's—by the end of the week, you've probably had enough. There's bags in your room, there's Reese's Pieces on your door handle, it's everywhere. I just felt like I had enough. It's been a long week—a lot of meetings, a lot of walkthroughs, a lot of practice, a lot of meetings with players. I've probably gained a few pounds, so I'm trying to head in the right direction starting today."

—Miami Dolphins head coach Brian Flores, who coached at the Reese's Senior Bowl, has had enough candy. (Josh Houtz, The Phinsider via Twitter)

DECISIONS, DECISIONS

Twitter User: *"You wanna sign somewhere or nah?"*
J.J. Watt: *"I scroll through DoorDash for like an hour before I pick a restaurant man... You're gonna have to give me a second to choose a new team and city."*

—Then-free agent defensive end J.J. Watt took his time selecting his new employer after leaving the Houston Texans. Then he picked the Cardinals, the Chipotle taco salad of football teams. (J.J. Watt via Twitter)

SPORTS MEDIA HAS REACHED ITS LOGICAL CONCLUSION

"Almost 100%, [wife Emily Wilkinson] and I just saw a UFO drop straight out of the sky on our way home from dinner. ... we stopped and looked at each other and asked if either of us saw it. ... Very bright ball of light going straight down out of the sky towards Lake Travis. Anybody else witness this?"

—Cleveland Browns quarterback Baker Mayfield reporting a potential close encounter near Lake Travis, Texas. (Baker Mayfield via Twitter)

"Last night on Twitter, Baker Mayfield saw a UFO. ... To that, I would say I would prefer, of all the qualities of a franchise quarterback—I want to know your arm, are you good pre-snap, are you mobile—the ability to see UFOs in the offseason is nowhere near my top 10 qualifications. Joe Montana, Troy Aikman, Terry Bradshaw, and Tom Brady have never seen aliens. I would prefer my guys don't talk about it. In fairness, Aaron Rodgers also admits he has seen a UFO and he did win a Super Bowl."

—Fox Sports personality and sometime-Mayfield antagonist Colin Cowherd, working hard to remain on-brand.

"How do you know I've never seen aliens, Colin?"

—Tampa Bay Buccaneers quarterback Tom Brady, blasting a hole into Cowherd's airtight theory. (Tom Brady via Twitter)

ADVICE FOR ALL THE KIDS AT HOME

"Punch it in the face. Punch it straight in the mouth."

—San Francisco 49ers defensive tackle Javon Kinlaw, who survived a brutal childhood, on dealing with adversity. (Chris Biderman, The Sacramento Bee via Twitter)

QUOTE OF THE YEAR

Robby Anderson: *"What's that bear doing?"*

DJ Moore: *"The bear?"*

Anderson: *"Panther."*

Moore: *"That's Sir Purr, bro."*

Anderson: *"Who?"*

Moore: *"Sir Purr."*

Anderson: *"How you say that?"*

Curtis Samuel: *"Sir Purr."*

Anderson: *"Sir Purr. Oh, Sir Purr? Wow. You call him that?"*

Samuel: *"Yeah, that's his name."*

Anderson: *"So you be like, 'What's up Sir Purr?'" (looks away, shakes head)*

—Carolina Panthers wide receivers DJ Moore and Curtis Samuel explaining to Robby Anderson who that big anthropomorphic panther in the stands is. Anderson had spent his entire NFL career up to that point with the New York Jets, one of only four teams in the NFL without a mascot. That said, he probably should have been familiar with the general concept. (Carolina Blitz via Twitter)

compiled by Cale Clinton

The Year in a Global Pandemic

THERE'S A TOMLIN-ISM FOR EVERYTHING

"That was the Jell-O we couldn't get back in the box."

—Pittsburgh Steelers head coach Mike Tomlin on the physical conditioning of players entering Steelers training camp after weeks of quarantines and virtual OTAs. We can't tell if this is a good thing, a bad thing, or something in between, but it sure is a quote. (Missi Matthews, Pittsburgh Steelers via Twitter)

Full 2021 Projections

The following table lists the mean DVOA projections for all 32 NFL teams. We also list the average number of wins for each team in our one million simulations, along with how often each team made the playoffs, reached the Super Bowl, and won the NFL Championship.

Full 2021 Projections

Team	Avg Wins	Postseason Odds			Mean DVOA Projections								Schedule	
		Make Playoffs	Reach Super Bowl	Win Super Bowl	Total DVOA	Rk	Off DVOA	Rk	Def DVOA	Rk	ST DVOA	Rk	Average Opponent	Rk
TB	11.1	79.8%	22.6%	13.1%	20.1%	1	14.8%	3	-6.2%	6	-0.9%	27	-2.6%	30
BAL	10.6	72.7%	18.8%	10.3%	17.6%	2	9.5%	5	-4.5%	8	3.6%	2	1.1%	10
KC	10.5	71.5%	17.2%	9.2%	15.5%	3	17.9%	1	3.5%	22	1.1%	5	-0.1%	18
BUF	10.2	67.6%	13.1%	6.7%	11.3%	5	4.2%	11	-7.1%	4	-0.1%	15	-2.4%	29
NE	9.8	62.4%	9.9%	4.8%	6.5%	11	-4.0%	20	-6.5%	5	4.0%	1	-3.0%	32
SEA	9.7	59.9%	10.3%	5.4%	11.1%	6	11.6%	4	0.9%	16	0.4%	10	0.2%	14
SF	9.7	58.7%	8.7%	4.4%	8.2%	8	1.1%	13	-7.8%	2	-0.7%	23	-2.0%	25
GB	9.6	61.7%	11.8%	6.3%	13.9%	4	15.0%	2	-0.6%	15	-1.7%	31	2.9%	3
NO	9.5	57.6%	9.0%	4.6%	8.6%	7	0.3%	15	-7.4%	3	1.0%	6	-0.2%	19
DAL	9.2	56.4%	7.4%	3.5%	5.0%	12	6.5%	8	1.6%	18	0.1%	13	-1.3%	24
MIN	9.1	52.3%	7.3%	3.6%	7.0%	10	7.9%	6	-0.7%	14	-1.6%	30	1.6%	7
LAR	9.1	50.4%	7.0%	3.5%	7.1%	9	6.4%	9	-2.2%	12	-1.5%	29	1.7%	6
MIA	9.0	49.3%	6.0%	2.7%	2.2%	14	0.9%	14	-1.7%	13	-0.5%	19	-2.0%	26
DEN	8.8	45.6%	4.9%	2.1%	0.2%	16	-3.3%	19	-4.4%	9	-0.9%	26	-2.1%	27
PIT	8.8	46.0%	6.2%	2.9%	4.9%	13	-4.0%	21	-9.0%	1	-0.1%	16	3.2%	2
IND	8.7	50.5%	5.4%	2.4%	-0.6%	17	-4.7%	22	-3.7%	11	0.4%	11	-1.3%	23
CLE	8.6	42.8%	5.0%	2.2%	1.9%	15	7.0%	7	4.5%	26	-0.6%	22	1.5%	8
LV	8.2	37.5%	3.6%	1.5%	-2.1%	18	1.5%	12	3.3%	21	-0.3%	17	0.6%	13
TEN	8.2	42.1%	3.6%	1.5%	-4.8%	22	5.1%	10	8.7%	32	-1.2%	28	-1.2%	21
WAS	8.1	39.4%	3.6%	1.6%	-2.1%	19	-8.2%	28	-5.4%	7	0.8%	7	1.0%	11
ARI	7.9	31.9%	2.6%	1.2%	-3.7%	20	-0.8%	16	2.3%	19	-0.7%	24	1.0%	12
CIN	7.5	27.0%	1.9%	0.8%	-8.2%	24	-5.7%	23	4.5%	25	2.0%	3	1.9%	5
NYG	7.4	28.3%	1.8%	0.7%	-8.7%	26	-7.0%	25	1.4%	17	-0.3%	18	0.0%	17
CHI	7.3	27.1%	2.1%	0.9%	-4.8%	21	-8.1%	27	-3.9%	10	-0.5%	21	4.4%	1
LAC	7.3	25.6%	1.8%	0.7%	-8.6%	25	-1.7%	17	4.2%	23	-2.8%	32	1.3%	9
PHI	7.3	27.6%	1.7%	0.6%	-11.1%	27	-5.8%	24	4.5%	27	-0.8%	25	-1.3%	22
DET	7.2	24.9%	1.7%	0.7%	-7.8%	23	-2.5%	18	6.5%	30	1.2%	4	2.9%	4
CAR	7.1	22.2%	1.2%	0.5%	-11.2%	28	-8.7%	29	2.4%	20	0.0%	14	0.1%	16
ATL	7.1	21.9%	1.2%	0.5%	-11.4%	29	-7.1%	26	4.4%	24	0.1%	12	0.1%	15
JAX	7.0	25.5%	1.3%	0.5%	-16.0%	30	-9.7%	30	7.0%	31	0.7%	8	-2.7%	31
HOU	6.7	21.0%	0.9%	0.3%	-18.5%	31	-12.9%	31	6.0%	29	0.4%	9	-2.3%	28
NYJ	6.1	13.0%	0.5%	0.1%	-21.6%	32	-15.6%	32	5.5%	28	-0.5%	20	-0.8%	20

Arizona Cardinals

They say the sun sets quickly out west. That was certainly true for the Arizona Cardinals last year. A season that once looked bright and full of promise quickly turned as dark as midnight in the Sonoran Desert, leaving the team, its coach, and its quarterback suddenly facing an uncertain future. The Cardinals' miracle win over the Bills in November moved them into a tie for the division lead, but seven weeks later they had fallen out of the playoff field entirely as their offense disintegrated late in the year. That collapse did more than torpedo Arizona's playoff hopes in 2020—it raised the stakes for everyone involved heading into 2021.

After this season, the Cardinals will need to make a decision on Kyler Murray's fifth-year option, adding another year to his contract at a value of $20 million or more. They may also face a difficult choice concerning head coach Kliff Kingsbury—coaches who fail to make the playoffs in any of their first three seasons rarely get there in later years either. If this regime is going to last, Murray will have to prove that he is more than just a scrambler with a big arm, that he can develop the touch and process to deliver in obvious passing situations. And Kingsbury must show that his offense can work at the pro level, because in the final third of last season it looked decidedly minor league.

To show the depth of Arizona's late-year offensive collapse, we must first go back to the beginnings of the Kingsbury-Murray regime. The pair of them arrived in Glendale in 2019, the coach with his Ryan Gosling haircut and an Air Raid playbook that had ravaged the defenses of the Big 12, and the quarterback with a Heisman Trophy and hours of YouTube highlights in football and baseball alike. They took over an Arizona offense that had posted a DVOA of -41.8% in 2018 (the second-worst mark on record, ahead of only the expansion Texans in 2002) and raised that to 3.2% in 2019. They built on that success in the first half of 2020 as comeback wins over Seattle and Buffalo moved them to a 6-3 record that left them tied with the Seahawks and Rams atop the NFC West. They followed that up with a disappointing loss in Seattle, but even after that setback, the Arizona offense looked like one of the better units in the league.

Through Week 11, the Cards led the NFL with 4,143 yards of total offense and were averaging more than 28 points per game. Their advanced numbers weren't quite that impressive, but they still ranked 11th or better in passing, rushing, and overall DVOA. Murray was threatening to set quarterback rushing records, while DeAndre Hopkins (stolen from Houston in one of the best moves of that offseason) led the league in receiving yards.

Then came a Week 12 game against the Patriots, and everything went to hell. The Cardinals ran a whopping 70 plays against New England and still scored only 17 points, and that includes a short-field touchdown set up by a Markus Golden interception deep in Patriots territory. Arizona averaged 4.3 yards per play overall and only 4.4 yards per passing play. The defense performed well enough that the Cardinals still should have won, but a number of big mistakes on offense (a failed fourth-and-goal play at the end of the first half, an interception that set up a New England touchdown) and special teams (a 58-yard punt return allowed to Gunner Olszewski, a missed field goal in the fourth quarter) led to a 20-17 defeat instead. The Cardinals finished the day with an offensive DVOA of -23.6%, their worst of the year up to that point.

Given what Arizona had done to opposing defenses all season, the Patriots game felt like a fluke. Instead, it proved to be a grim harbinger of things to come. The Cardinals offense had a positive DVOA in eight of their first 10 games (Weeks 3 and 4 against Detroit and Carolina being the exceptions), but after that Patriots loss they never had a positive DVOA again. They only won two more games, and those came against moribund Giants and Eagles franchises. Arizona finished 8-8 and out of the postseason entirely. The same team that had moved into playoff position with wins over Russell Wilson and Josh Allen found themselves at home in January after back-to-back losses to C.J. Beathard and John Wolford.

Technically, the losses started to pile up with that Week 11 28-21 defeat to the Seahawks, but even then the offense played well. It was New England that exposed the weaknesses in the Cardinals attack and laid out the blueprint for others to follow … which is funny, because the Patriots defense didn't really play any differently against Arizona than they did against anyone else. They went ultra-small, going with five-plus defensive backs on 69 of 70 plays. And they used those defensive backs to replace linemen, not linebackers, using two or fewer linemen 48 times. With all that speed on the field, Arizona's Air Raid passing attack and Murray's option run game were both effectively neutered.

Other defenses took New England's game plan and went

2021 Cardinals Schedule

Week	Opp.	Week	Opp.	Week	Opp.
1	at TEN	7	HOU	13	at CHI
2	MIN	8	GB (Thu.)	14	LAR (Mon.)
3	at JAX	9	at SF	15	at DET
4	at LAR	10	CAR	16	IND (Sat./Xmas)
5	SF	11	at SEA	17	at DAL
6	at CLE	12	BYE	18	SEA

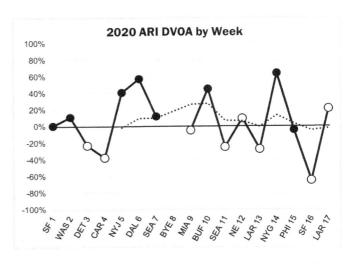

2020 ARI DVOA by Week

even farther with it. The Cardinals offense saw more two-lineman sets (115) and dime formations (98) in their last six games than they had in their first 10 (111 and 76). And it's not as if those small defenders were crowding the line of scrimmage, either. Arizona saw a light box (six or fewer defenders) on 56% of plays in their first 10 games, a number that jumped to 69% over the last six contests.

The results were catastrophic for Arizona (Table 1). Defenders were able to drop into zone coverage to keep receivers blanketed downfield or come up to fill any available running lane. Murray was suddenly useless on designed runs—through 10 games he was averaging 6.2 yards per carry with an 18.1% DVOA on those plays, figures that fell to 3.6 and -47.5% from the New England game onwards. The Air Raid was limited to short throws with few yards after the catch, and only four quarterbacks finished the year with more failed completions[1] than Murray.

Kingsbury seemed unable to adapt to these defensive changes and incapable of dictating anything to the opposition. Though he runs one of pro football's most creative rushing attacks, his passing scheme can be repetitive, dull, and ineffectual. On any given running play, the Cardinals are liable to mix up formations and personnel (single-back shotgun, six-lineman I-formations, two backs to one side of the quarterback in a Go-Go set, etc.) and give the ball to any player on the field (quarterback, running back, or wideout) in an endless variety of play designs (zone read, speed option, power, duo, counters, reverses, sweeps, pitches, and many more). But when it comes time to pass, it often seems like Kingsbury's route tree hasn't branched out to an NFL level yet (Figure 1).

The Cardinals threw a curl on 18.1% of all throws, the highest rate in the league. They were also in the top five in rates of comebacks and go/fly throws. Wide receiver screens aren't often listed on the standard route tree, but the Cardinals loved those plays too, finishing second behind Green Bay in that category.

Meanwhile, the Cardinals had the NFL's lowest rate of both dig and post routes, the in-breaking patterns that let receivers find seams in zone coverage and make big catches downfield. They were also in the bottom 10 in both flat and corner routes, while ranking about average in slant and out patterns. These are some of the most basic routes—Arizona didn't use many of the deep cross or drag routes that can be so effective against zone coverage either. In short, Kingsbury loved to call low-risk, low-reward passes that made life easy for his offensive line and quarterback while rarely pushing the ball downfield. The Cardinals basically only threw deep when they had one-on-one opportunities down the sideline. The lack of those zone-breaking routes to the interior—digs, posts, crosses, and drags—is critical for Arizona, because defenses rely on zone coverage to contain Murray's scrambles. In each of his first two seasons, Murray has faced man coverage on just 23% of his passes, ranking him next to last each year.

How does Kingsbury expect to win with such a limited passing attack? With tempo. The Cardinals had the league's fastest offense in neutral situations, and they rarely took their foot off the gas—they were also fastest when leading by seven points or more. There was no secret to what Arizona was doing: get to the line, call a run or a short pass, then get back to the line and do it again as fast as they could. Their pace was so frantic that they rarely used motion, doing so only 29% of the time, the lowest rate in the league. But Kingsbury didn't care about confusing the defense or giving Murray an easy pre-snap read—he just wanted his quarterback to check down to receivers underneath the coverage and make defenses execute over and over again, hoping they eventually wore down and blew an assignment or missed a tackle. It led to

Table 1. Arizona's Offensive Collapse

Weeks	Overall					Passing						Rushing			
	W-L	Pts/G	Yd/G	Yd/Play	DVOA	C%	Yd/Att	TD-INT	Sk-Yds	aDOT	DVOA	Yd/Run	TD	Stuff%	DVOA
Weeks 1-11	6-4	28.7	414.3	6.1	9.3%	68.3%	7.5	19-8	16-78	8.31	26.7%	5.2	16	15%	3.4%
Weeks 12-17	2-4	20.5	335.0	4.9	-21.8%	65.8%	6.6	8-5	13-108	7.69	-3.2%	3.8	6	24%	-33.0%

[1] Failed completions are completions that still don't reach our baselines for success: 45% of needed yards on first down, 60% on second down, and 100% on third or fourth down.

an aerial attack that made life frustrating for Cardinals fans, simple for defensive coordinators, and maddeningly dull for everyone else.

This scheme may work fine in college, against defenses staffed by economics majors who are squeezing a couple of hours of daily practice in between morning classes and evening studies. But this is not the Big 12. This is the NFL, where players use every waking hour to prepare for the game and defenders who beat themselves don't often make it out of training camp. If anything, it was the Cardinals making the sloppy mistakes. They were flagged for a league-high 65 offensive penalties, including 29 false starts—five more than anyone else and more than double the average team (14.1). No center had more penalties than Mason Cole, no guard had more penalties than Justin Pugh, and Kelvin Beachum and D.J. Humphries were both in the top 10 among tackles. The Cardinals were also in the top five in fumbles, including a league-high 11 loose balls in the last six weeks of the year.

How can Arizona reverse these trends and rebound in 2021? There's room for Murray to improve, specifically by taking care of the ball; only Carson Wentz threw more adjusted interceptions. He also needs to play better in obvious passing situations; the Cardinals were 29th in DVOA on third-and-long plays. Quarterbacks who can't deliver on third-and-long don't typically stick around—of the three teams below Arizona, Dallas and Washington will definitely have new primary quarterbacks in 2021, and New England could as well. New receivers A.J. Green (signed from Cincinnati in free agency) and Rondale Moore (a second-round draft pick out of Purdue) can only help, but the receivers were rarely the problem last year—the Cardinals dropped only 16 passes, fewest in the NFL.

Arizona's running attack also badly needed a talent infusion—the easiest way to attack an undersized defense is to run right over them, and the Cardinals' inability to do so at the end of the year was a critical failure. General manager Steve Keim tried to build a more powerful run game by replacing Kenyan Drake with a more physical runner in James Conner. He also made upgrades on the interior offensive line, trading for former Pro Bowl center Rodney Hudson and signing guard Brian Winters in free agency.

The offense will need to make progress, because the defense may well regress. Vance Joseph worked some miracles after Chandler Jones went down, leading a unit with just one Pro Bowler (safety Budda Baker) to a top-10 finish in DVOA. He mainly did so with aggressive blitz packages, as Arizona ranked eighth or higher in blitz rate, big blitzes of six or more pass-rushers, and DB blitzes. As a result, the Cardinals used man coverage more than anyone except New Orleans. So if it worked last year, why are we skeptical it can work again? The unit is built around edge rushers J.J. Watt and Chandler Jones, two Hall of Fame-caliber players who are now both in their early thirties with some troubling injury history. The inside linebackers (first-round draftee Zaven Collins and 2020 first-rounder Isaiah Simmons) have plenty of talent but precious little experience, with Simmons playing fewer than 400 snaps on defense last year despite appearing in all 16 games. And

Figure 1: NFL Route Trees

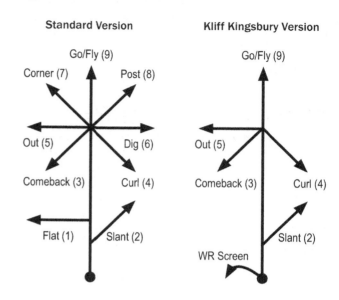

the secondary consists of Baker and a long series of question marks. If Joseph calls for blitzes and man coverage as often as he did last year, opposing receivers should have little trouble getting open.

Mostly, the burden here is on Kingsbury to grow into a better coach. It's plain that he needs to diversify his passing game to scheme receivers open rather than relying on them to win one-on-one battles on every single snap, but he also badly mismanaged several critical end-of-half scenarios last year. He led the league in Aggressiveness Index because he loves to go for it on fourth-and-medium near midfield, but he tended to get conservative at the worst possible times. Per EdjSports' Game-Winning Chance, his call to kick a field goal on fourth-and-1 from the 31-yard line while trailing by three with 1:58 left against Miami was the worst coaching decision of the year; his call to try for three on fourth-and-1 in a tie game against New England was the second-worst decision of the year. That's not even counting the time Arizona settled for a 41-yard field goal try on second down in overtime against Seattle … which almost became a 46-yard try before Kingsbury used a timeout to avoid a delay of game penalty. (The Football Gods punished Kingsbury for his cowardice as Zane Gonzalez missed all three of those kicks.)

Further, Kingsbury was erratically passive-aggressive with his timeout usage. In Week 13, he failed to stop the clock when the Rams picked up a first-and-goal inside the two-minute warning in the first half, letting L.A. kill 27 seconds before snapping the ball; the Cardinals did get a possession after the Rams scored, but had to settle for a 48-yard field goal try on second down with eight seconds to go (Gonzalez, naturally, missed the kick). A week later, when Murray tweaked his hamstring on a red zone incompletion against the Giants, Kingsbury called a timeout so his quarterback could stay in the game … then called a handoff and a screen pass to set up a kick on fourth-and-15 (at least Mike Nugent nailed that one).

One way or another, the Cardinals will need to improve,

because they can't expect to play like they did last year and reach the postseason from the NFC West. The Seahawks, Rams, and 49ers all look like strong playoff contenders. Even with an average overall schedule and a third wild-card berth up for grabs, it's hard to make the playoffs when you finish last in your own division.

Like they say, the sun sets quickly in the desert. And if Kingsbury and Murray want to see many more of those orange skies on the horizon, they'll need to deliver in a big way this fall.

Vincent Verhei

2020 Cardinals Stats by Week

Wk	vs.	W-L	PF	PA	YDF	YDA	TO	Total	Off	Def	ST
1	at SF	W	24	20	404	366	-1	0.4%	10.2%	3.9%	-5.8%
2	WAS	W	30	15	438	316	1	10.8%	10.0%	0.3%	1.1%
3	DET	L	23	26	377	322	-3	-23.2%	-23.3%	-3.6%	-3.5%
4	at CAR	L	21	31	262	444	0	-37.9%	-6.2%	32.2%	0.6%
5	at NYJ	W	30	10	496	285	-1	40.7%	46.6%	9.7%	3.8%
6	at DAL	W	38	10	438	344	4	57.1%	16.4%	-38.8%	1.9%
7	SEA	W	37	34	519	572	1	11.7%	6.7%	-6.6%	-1.6%
8	BYE										
9	MIA	L	31	34	442	312	-1	-4.9%	26.2%	15.5%	-15.6%
10	BUF	W	32	30	453	369	0	45.1%	8.3%	-34.0%	2.7%
11	at SEA	L	21	28	314	347	0	-24.9%	1.7%	23.8%	-2.8%
12	at NE	L	17	20	298	179	1	9.3%	-23.6%	-52.3%	-19.4%
13	LAR	L	28	38	232	463	-1	-27.4%	-15.1%	14.3%	1.9%
14	at NYG	W	26	7	390	159	3	63.8%	-17.2%	-58.1%	22.9%
15	PHI	W	33	26	526	422	-3	-4.3%	-8.5%	-1.3%	2.9%
16	SF	L	12	20	350	398	-1	-64.9%	-43.7%	27.5%	6.4%
17	at LAR	L	7	18	214	333	1	21.4%	-13.8%	-40.1%	-4.9%

Trends and Splits

	Offense	Rank	Defense	Rank
Total DVOA	-2.4%	19	-6.6%	10
Unadjusted VOA	-2.2%	18	-8.1%	7
Weighted Trend	-8.1%	23	-9.1%	7
Variance	4.8%	12	8.4%	30
Average Opponent	-1.8%	8	-2.6%	23
Passing	15.0%	14	0.1%	9
Rushing	-9.7%	17	-16.3%	14
First Down	-0.2%	18	-9.8%	7
Second Down	6.1%	12	-6.4%	10
Third Down	-19.4%	28	-0.2%	17
First Half	-5.5%	22	-7.9%	8
Second Half	0.5%	15	-5.1%	9
Red Zone	8.9%	14	-16.7%	6
Late and Close	-13.0%	24	-6.8%	11

Five-Year Performance

Year	W-L	Pyth W	Est W	PF	PA	TO	Total	Rk	Off	Rk	Def	Rk	ST	Rk	Off AGL	Rk	Def AGL	Rk	Off Age	Rk	Def Age	Rk	ST Age	Rk
2016	7-8-1	9.4	8.1	418	362	0	4.6%	13	-6.2%	22	-17.1%	2	-6.3%	30	45.5	22	49.8	21	28.3	1	25.9	29	25.5	27
2017	8-8	6.1	6.0	295	361	-4	-8.2%	19	-18.1%	29	-15.4%	3	-5.5%	28	73.6	32	34.5	15	28.6	1	28.1	2	26.5	6
2018	3-13	2.8	2.7	225	425	-12	-38.4%	32	-41.8%	32	-2.4%	12	1.0%	11	59.8	29	32.5	15	26.1	25	27.2	4	26.2	9
2019	5-10-1	6.0	7.3	361	442	-1	-3.1%	17	3.2%	13	4.0%	20	-2.4%	26	45.6	19	39.4	20	27.3	6	26.7	9	26.0	10
2020	8-8	9.1	8.0	410	367	0	3.6%	13	-2.4%	19	-6.6%	10	-0.6%	19	34.8	15	60.9	28	27.2	10	26.9	6	26.5	6

2020 Performance Based on Most Common Personnel Groups

ARI Offense					ARI Offense vs. Opponents					ARi Defense				ARI Defense vs. Opponents			
Pers	Freq	Yds	DVOA	Run%	Pers	Freq	Yds	DVOA	Run%	Pers	Freq	Yds	DVOA	Pers	Freq	Yds	DVOA
11	44%	5.7	0.0%	32%	Base	18%	5.4	-0.2%	59%	Base	36%	5.5	-0.4%	11	52%	5.6	-10.5%
12	25%	6.0	-2.3%	55%	Nickel	65%	5.9	1.9%	38%	Nickel	54%	5.7	-10.9%	12	30%	5.4	-3.9%
10	20%	6.4	18.7%	22%	Dime+	16%	6.1	19.8%	21%	Dime+	1%	4.1	-29.2%	21	11%	6.2	6.9%
612	4%	3.5	-22.6%	80%	Goal Line	0%	3.0	-47.3%	100%	Goal Line	2%	1.0	-22.4%	13	3%	2.2	-52.7%
21	2%	8.7	103.3%	47%						Big	7%	5.4	-1.4%	22	2%	7.2	42.6%
611	2%	7.1	-16.7%	76%										10	1%	8.1	29.2%

Strategic Tendencies

Run/Pass		Rk	Formation		Rk	Pass Rush		Rk	Secondary		Rk	Strategy		Rk
Runs, first half	37%	21	Form: Single Back	82%	14	Rush 3	4.2%	22	4 DB	36%	3	Play Action	32%	8
Runs, first down	51%	8	Form: Empty Back	11%	8	Rush 4	58.0%	26	5 DB	54%	23	Offensive Motion	29%	32
Runs, second-long	17%	32	Form: Multi Back	7%	22	Rush 5	28.3%	4	6+ DB	1%	26	Avg Box (Off)	6.32	31
Runs, power sit.	67%	7	Pers: 3+ WR	66%	17	Rush 6+	9.5%	2	Man Coverage	44%	2	Avg Box (Def)	6.70	10
Runs, behind 2H	33%	7	Pers: 2+ TE/6+ OL	32%	12	Edge Rusher Sacks	55.2%	13	CB by Sides	72%	17	Offensive Pace	27.14	1
Pass, ahead 2H	47%	18	Pers: 6+ OL	5%	5	Interior DL Sacks	26.0%	14	S/CB Cover Ratio	23%	22	Defensive Pace	31.34	30
Run-Pass Options	14%	3	Shotgun/Pistol	92%	2	Second Level Sacks	18.8%	23	DB Blitz	16%	8	Go for it on 4th	3.12	1

The Cardinals led the NFL with 131 total penalties, though they were only ninth with 868 yards. Arizona was No. 1 in offensive penalties, as noted earlier in the chapter, but also No. 5 in defensive penalties. ✎ For the second straight season, the Cardinals led the league in using four-wide 10 personnel, although the frequency dropped from 33% in 2019 to 20% last season. Arizona had an above-average 6.4 yards per play with 18.7% DVOA on these plays. ✎ The Cardinals were phenomenal with empty backfields, averaging 7.5 yards with 49.5% DVOA. About 40% of these plays cross over with the 10 personnel numbers listed above, but the empty backfield plays with 11 personnel were just as successful. ✎ Arizona used pistol on 9.5% of plays, third in the league behind Baltimore and Miami. The Cardinals had just -12.0% DVOA and 5.1 yards per play, far behind the 21.2% DVOA and 7.1 yards per play they had from the pistol the year before. ✎ Arizona dropped from seventh to dead-last in the frequency of runs on second-and-long, but they improved from 26th to seventh in frequency of runs in short-yardage power situations. ✎ It wasn't as large as the year before, but once again Arizona had one of the league's biggest gaps between defensive DVOA with pass pressure (-89.7%, fifth, with 1.7 yards/play) and defensive DVOA without pass pressure (30.9%, 13th, with 7.7 yards/play). ✎ The Arizona defense loves its big blitzes of six or more pass-rushers. The Cardinals were No. 1 in sending six in 2019, then second behind Kansas City last year. The Cardinals are consistently good on these plays as well. Last year, they allowed -21.3% DVOA and 4.0 yards per play with six or more pass-rushers.

Passing

Player	DYAR	DVOA	Plays	NtYds	Avg	YAC	C%	TD	Int
K.Murray	590	4.6%	577	3760	6.5	4.7	68.7%	26	12
C.Streveler	-39	-45.9%	18	95	5.3	8.9	68.8%	1	1
C.McCoy	-132	-40.7%	71	351	4.9	3.2	60.6%	1	1

Rushing

Player	DYAR	DVOA	Plays	Yds	Avg	TD	Fum	Suc
K.Drake*	57	-3.4%	239	955	4.0	10	3	50%
K.Murray	186	15.8%	124	834	6.7	11	5	--
C.Edmonds	42	1.8%	97	448	4.6	1	1	49%
J.Conner	8	-7.5%	169	721	4.3	6	2	49%
C.McCoy	-14	-71.2%	5	16	3.2	0	0	--

Receiving

Player	DYAR	DVOA	Plays	Ctch	Yds	Y/C	YAC	TD	C%
D.Hopkins	207	3.4%	160	115	1407	12.2	4.5	6	72%
C.Kirk	46	-5.5%	79	48	621	12.9	3.6	6	61%
L.Fitzgerald*	-30	-18.1%	72	54	409	7.6	3.4	1	75%
A.Isabella	-31	-24.4%	35	21	224	10.7	3.9	2	60%
K.Johnson	-15	-20.8%	23	15	173	11.5	3.3	0	65%
T.Sherfield	1	-11.2%	7	5	50	10.0	5.4	0	71%
A.J.Green	-172	-33.0%	104	47	523	11.1	1.8	2	45%
D.Arnold*	101	26.7%	45	31	438	14.1	5.6	4	69%
D.Daniels	26	27.1%	11	8	92	11.5	7.1	1	73%
M.Williams	27	29.5%	10	8	102	12.8	8.3	1	80%
C.Edmonds	135	24.0%	67	53	402	7.6	6.2	4	79%
K.Drake*	10	-8.1%	31	25	137	5.5	6.6	0	81%
J.Conner	-23	-23.5%	43	35	215	6.1	6.7	0	81%

Offensive Line

Player	Pos	Age	GS	Snaps	Pen	Sk	Pass	Run	Player	Pos	Age	GS	Snaps	Pen	Sk	Pass	Run
D.J. Humphries	LT	28	16/16	1130	6	4.0	17	5	Justin Murray	RG	28	13/7	602	1	0.5	7	4
Kelvin Beachum	RT	32	16/16	1127	5	4.0	17	3	Lamont Gaillard	C	25	13/2	217	2	1.0	2	1
Justin Pugh	LG	31	15/15	958	9	0.5	7	4	Rodney Hudson	C	32	16/16	1082	0	1.0	9	6
Mason Cole*	C	25	14/14	914	6	2.0	10	9	Brian Winters	RG	30	16/9	616	7	2.0	18	5
J.R. Sweezy*	RG	32	13/10	644	3	1.0	10	3									

Year	Yards	ALY	Rk	Power	Rk	Stuff	Rk	2Lev	Rk	OpFld	Rk	BB Rt	Rk	Sacks	ASR	Rk	Press	Rk	BB Rt	Rk	Cont
2018	3.58	4.00	25	69%	10	16%	6	0.98	30	0.36	31	5.2%	9	52	9.2%	26	35.4%	29	13.4%	30	17
2019	4.61	4.12	22	74%	4	18%	8	1.30	8	0.97	9	8.8%	9	50	8.4%	26	27.7%	6	15.0%	27	31
2020	4.16	3.91	30	66%	16	19%	25	1.08	27	0.74	16	7.4%	4	29	5.4%	8	24.7%	15	10.8%	11	27

2020 ALY by direction:	Left End: 1.60 (32)	Left Tackle: 3.53 (25)	Mid/Guard: 4.32 (18)	Right Tackle: 3.26 (31)	Right End: 4.33 (20)

Context is important even when looking at advanced numbers, and the context surrounding Arizona's offensive line does them no favors. The Cardinals got to play with a great runner at quarterback, which typically makes life easier on offensive linemen because the threat of a bootleg or option keeper prevents defenses from clogging the line to stop running backs. Since 1997, there have been 43 teams (including the Cardinals, Patriots, Ravens, and Seahawks last year) with a quarterback who ran for at least 500 yards. Nearly two-thirds of those teams (28, to be precise) finished in the top half of the NFL in adjusted line yards; 20 made the top 10. Only one—the 2017 Seahawks—ranked lower than Arizona did last year. ● Murray's one-of-a-kind escapability also bailed out his line more often than not. Murray scrambled for a positive gain 50 times while taking only 27 sacks; that plus-23 differential was the best in the league. ● Tackles Kelvin Beachum and D.J. Humphries and left guard Justin Pugh will all return this year. The Cardinals made a big upgrade at center, trading a third-round pick to Las Vegas for Rodney Hudson (getting a seventh-rounder back in the deal) and then signing him to a two-year contract extension that lasts through 2023. Hudson, 32, has played in three Pro Bowls. In the last four years, he has committed only seven penalties and missed just one start, and the Raiders have perennially been of the best teams in football on runs up the middle. ● Brian Winters started 88 games for the Jets, but he is now in the journeyman phase in his career, spending one year with the Bills before signing with Arizona in free agency. That one year in Buffalo was no good—he made the top 10 guards in blown blocks in barely 600 snaps—but he's the favorite to start at right guard in place of J.R. Sweezy (still unsigned as of press time). Other candidates include Justin Murray, who made a dozen starts for Arizona at right tackle in 2019, and Josh Jones, a third-round rookie last year who saw spot duty as a sixth lineman. ● Not available: Marcus Gilbert. The Cardinals traded for Gilbert to start at right tackle in 2019, but he never played a down for them, missing all of that season with a torn ACL, opting out of 2020 due to COVID, and then retiring this year.

Defensive Front

Defensive Line	Age	Pos	G	Snaps	Plays	TmPct	Rk	Stop	Dfts	BTkl	Runs	St%	Rk	RuYd	Rk	Sack	Hit	Hur	Dsrpt
						Overall						vs. Run					Pass Rush		
Zach Allen	24	DE	13	504	38	5.5%	37	34	10	1	30	87%	5	1.8	20	2.0	5	6	3
Corey Peters*	33	DT	9	380	16	3.4%	77	11	5	1	12	67%	69	3.2	84	2.0	2	8	1
Angelo Blackson*	29	DE	16	552	24	2.8%	87	17	5	7	20	70%	60	1.8	18	2.5	5	11	0
Jordan Phillips	29	DT	9	267	12	2.5%	92	9	3	1	8	75%	47	3.3	87	2.0	2	4	1
Leki Fotu	23	DT	11	286	11	1.9%	--	11	6	2	10	100%	--	0.6	--	1.0	2	3	0
Rashard Lawrence	23	DT	9	167	9	1.9%	--	7	1	1	9	78%	--	1.7	--	0.0	0	0	0
Xavier Williams	29	DT	12	318	24	3.9%	69	19	2	2	22	82%	19	2.8	66	1.0	0	6	0

Edge Rushers	Age	Pos	G	Snaps	Plays	TmPct	Rk	Stop	Dfts	BTkl	Runs	St%	Rk	RuYd	Rk	Sack	Hit	Hur	Dsrpt
						Overall						vs. Run					Pass Rush		
Haason Reddick*	27	OLB	16	875	65	7.7%	6	42	28	7	34	56%	89	3.6	84	12.5	5	24	2
Markus Golden	30	OLB	16	590	35	4.1%	63	29	12	6	22	77%	26	0.6	3	4.5	15	32	4
Devon Kennard	30	OLB	13	364	19	2.8%	86	16	8	1	15	80%	13	2.2	33	3.0	6	11	1
Chandler Jones	31	OLB	5	288	11	4.2%	--	9	1	2	9	89%	--	1.3	--	1.0	8	6	0
J.J. Watt	32	DE	16	1013	59	6.8%	15	43	23	4	45	64%	74	1.5	10	5.0	13	28	9

Linebackers	Age	Pos	G	Snaps	Plays	TmPct	Rk	Stop	Dfts	BTkl	Runs	St%	Rk	RuYd	Rk	Sack	Hit	Hur	Tgts	Suc%	Rk	Yd/P	Rk	PD	Int
						Overall						vs. Run				Pass Rush					vs. Pass				
Jordan Hicks	29	ILB	16	1026	122	14.4%	29	57	19	8	76	54%	52	4.1	51	0.0	1	9	37	51%	33	6.3	36	4	1
De'Vondre Campbell*	28	ILB	16	883	102	12.1%	45	44	12	14	57	51%	62	4.5	65	2.0	0	4	41	49%	44	5.5	25	3	0
Isaiah Simmons	23	ILB	16	377	48	5.7%	--	24	11	5	19	63%	--	5.0	--	2.0	1	9	21	48%	49	7.4	61	2	1

Year	Yards	ALY	Rk	Power	Rk	Stuff	Rk	2Lev	Rk	OpFld	Rk	BB Rt	Rk	Sacks	ASR	Rk	Press	Rk	BB Rt	Rk
2018	4.92	4.32	14	80%	32	20%	12	1.46	30	1.28	30	6.1%	24	49	8.8%	3	28.8%	22	8.3%	22
2019	4.22	4.17	14	57%	4	22%	5	1.29	24	0.74	16	22.4%	1	40	7.0%	16	30.5%	15	15.4%	15
2020	4.39	4.44	18	58%	3	20%	9	1.38	27	0.71	16	12.5%	17	48	7.5%	8	25.5%	14	14.6%	12

2020 ALY by direction:	Left End: 3.78 (7)	Left Tackle: 3.14 (4)	Mid/Guard: 4.67 (24)	Right Tackle: 5.00 (23)	Right End: 4.50 (14)

Arizona's defense is built around two young first-round picks, rookie Zaven Collins and sophomore Isaiah Simmons, at inside linebacker. Kingsbury dubbed them the league's "prettiest linebacker duo" at rookie minicamp, calling them "two big, long, athletic cats" at 6-foot-4 each. (He also called them "two really fast trees," which sounds like terrible news for the residents of Isengard.) 🦅 Simmons' playing time wavered last season, peaking at 75% of Arizona's defensive snaps in Week 15 against Philadelphia but then dropping below 40% in the two games after that. He killed the Seahawks, with a critical overtime interception in Week 7 and a team-high 10 tackles in the Week 11 rematch. His pass coverage numbers are badly skewed by one play in his NFL debut: a 76-yard Raheem Mostert catch in Week 1 that made up nearly half the yardage he surrendered on the year. He didn't give up another catch longer than 12 yards all season. 🦅 Collins is an absolute load at 260 pounds, perhaps the biggest off-ball linebacker in the league. And he can move, running a 4.66s 40 at Tulsa's pro day. There is concern about his athleticism (it's hard to change direction at that size and speed) and he's a bit of a gamble coming out of a 3-3-5 scheme that limited his responsibilities compared to what he'll be asked to do in the NFL. 🦅 Jordan Hicks remains on the roster, but that seems temporary—he was given permission to seek a trade after Collins was drafted. 🦅 Pass rush off the edge will be supplied by a pair of All-Pros with plenty of question marks between them. J.J. Watt's 101.0 career sacks are third among active players, but he had 5.0 or fewer in four of the last five seasons, missing 32 games over that stretch due to injury. Chandler Jones is sixth among active players with 97.0 sacks, but he missed 11 games last year with a torn biceps, and he was largely a non-factor in the five games he did play, with one sack against San Francisco and none against Carolina, Detroit, Washington, or the Jets, four teams that all ranked in the league's bottom half in adjusted sack rate. There's a good chance that both Watt and Chandler will post double-digit sacks and lead Arizona back to the playoffs. There's also a good chance that age and injuries will render both non-factors. 🦅 Additional pass rush will be provided by Markus Golden, who started each of Arizona's last eight games after they re-acquired him via trade in October, and Dennis Gardeck, a career special-teamer who got 94 defensive snaps last year and somehow produced 7.0 sacks in that sliver of time. Gardeck tore his ACL in Week 15 and may not be ready for the start of the 2021 season, but he signed a one-year, $3.4-million contract in March that more than doubled his career earnings. 🦅 Watt is the only lineman on the roster of any note. Zach Allen, a 2019 third-rounder, will take the other end spot. At nose tackle, Leki Fotu and Rashard Lawrence (both drafted in the fourth round in 2020) will battle veteran Jordan Phillips for the starting role, though all figure to get playing time in Arizona's rotation.

Defensive Secondary

Secondary	Age	Pos	G	Snaps	Plays	Overall TmPct	Rk	Stop	Dfts	BTkl	Runs	vs. Run St%	Rk	RuYd	Rk	Tgts	vs. Pass Tgt%	Rk	aDOT	Suc%	Rk	Yd/P	Rk	PD	Int
Patrick Peterson*	31	CB	16	1098	69	8.2%	51	21	10	9	20	30%	60	10.3	73	67	15.7%	72	12.5	43%	67	8.6	61	8	3
Budda Baker	25	SS	15	1007	124	15.6%	2	52	26	15	69	46%	19	5.7	24	25	6.4%	50	11.7	60%	8	5.3	7	6	2
Byron Murphy	23	CB	15	796	59	7.4%	65	21	11	11	9	44%	35	8.3	62	58	18.7%	47	12.9	47%	60	7.1	31	8	0
Dre Kirkpatrick*	32	CB	14	752	63	8.5%	43	18	6	12	14	36%	53	8.7	66	79	27.0%	3	10.2	48%	55	6.8	25	7	3
Chris Banjo	31	FS	13	436	48	7.0%	--	17	5	6	24	50%	--	6.0	--	12	7.1%	--	7.3	58%	--	6.3	--	1	0
Deionte Thompson	24	SS	13	333	26	3.8%	--	11	3	5	13	46%	--	5.8	--	17	13.1%	--	9.6	53%	--	4.3	--	3	0
Jalen Thompson	23	FS	5	232	20	7.6%	--	4	1	1	9	11%	--	10.6	--	7	7.8%	--	7.0	57%	--	2.7	--	1	0
Malcolm Butler	31	CB	16	1085	114	13.1%	1	40	10	10	34	32%	59	8.8	67	111	24.7%	8	11.1	49%	51	7.5	37	14	4
Darqueze Dennard	30	CB	8	437	41	10.0%	--	18	8	3	7	71%	--	4.7	--	39	21.2%	--	11.8	59%	--	4.7	--	5	1

Year	Pass D Rank	vs. #1 WR	Rk	vs. #2 WR	Rk	vs. Other WR	Rk	WR Wide	Rk	WR Slot	Rk	vs. TE	Rk	vs. RB	Rk
2018	8	-0.7%	14	13.6%	23	-6.7%	12	-9.8%	12	11.0%	24	3.0%	17	-3.1%	14
2019	27	15.3%	27	-3.3%	12	30.2%	31	7.7%	23	19.2%	27	28.2%	32	31.7%	29
2020	9	4.1%	20	10.3%	23	-7.7%	10	19.6%	29	3.8%	22	0.2%	15	17.5%	30

This wasn't an especially strong secondary to begin with, and it was left in tatters by the departures of starting corners Patrick Peterson and Dre Kirkpatrick this offseason. 🦅 We'll start with the positives: Budda Baker is one of the best big-play safeties in the league, ranking first or second at the position in defeats in each of the past three seasons. His pass coverage numbers haven't always been great, but they were exceptional last year. And … that's it, that's the end of the positives. 🦅 Jalen Thompson, a supplemental draft pick in 2019, was supposed to start at free safety in 2020, but missed 11 games due to ankle injuries. With only 13 starts in his career, he remains very much an unknown. 🦅 At cornerback, Malcolm Butler came over from Tennessee, but he has been steadily declining for years now. From 2017 to 2019, he failed to make the top 40 cornerbacks in either success rate or yards allowed per target in coverage. Last year, he gave up 829 yards on 111 targets, both the highest totals in the league. 🦅 Robert Alford, the other penciled-in starter, missed all of 2020 with a torn pec after missing all of 2019 with a broken leg. His last healthy season was 2018 … when he ranked next to last in both success rate and yards per target. He also turns 33 on Halloween. 🦅 Nickelback Byron Murphy has failed to rank higher than 60th in success rate in either of his two pro seasons. He started 16 games as a rookie before being (deservedly) demoted last year. ❧ If the starters here are comically bad, the depth is tragic. The top corner beyond those three is either Darqueze Dennard (a 30-year-old journeyman with a long injury history signed very late in free agency), Tae Hayes (a former undrafted free agent who has played in all of three NFL games and is on his fourth team in three years), Marco Wilson (a fourth-round rookie out of Florida), or Tay Gowan (sixth round, Central Florida).

Special Teams

Year	DVOA	Rank	FG/XP	Rank	Net Kick	Rank	Kick Ret	Rank	Net Punt	Rank	Punt Ret	Rank	Hidden	Rank
2018	1.0%	11	-5.1	25	2.6	11	-1.5	19	6.5	5	2.3	12	9.5	7
2019	-2.4%	26	0.4	17	0.6	14	-4.5	30	-9.8	30	1.4	10	1.9	15
2020	-0.6%	19	-5.8	26	6.5	3	-4.0	23	3.2	10	-2.8	22	11.8	5

The coverage teams were the strength here, as Arizona led the league with 60 combined stops (tackles that stopped a return short of the league average) on kickoff and punt returns. The kickoff coverage was particularly dominant, whether it was Zane Gonzalez or Mike Nugent doing the kicking. And it was a team effort—Isaiah Simmons, Ezekiel Turner, and Jonathan Ward were all in the top 20 with seven kickoff stops apiece; Tanner Vallejo was right behind them with six. The punt coverage (led by Trent Sherfield and Charles Washington) also shined, and it's hard to believe that nine teams played better than Arizona most weeks. But they did give up that 58-yarder against New England, and, well, it was a big year for punting. ❧ Andy Lee led all players in gross punt value in 2018 but has been close to average in each of the two years since. He'll return this fall at age 39. ❧ Matt Prater, a 15-year veteran for Atlanta, Denver, and Detroit, will assume placekicking duties. Prater's Lions teams finished in the top half of the league in kicking for points every year from 2015 to 2019, but they tumbled to 23rd place last year as Prater hit just 10 of 17 kicks from 40 yards or more. Prater also saw sporadic duty on kickoffs and didn't do anything to earn more than that. ❧ Christian Kirk needs to stop giving up ground on punt returns—he led the NFL with four punt returns that lost yardage, including three that lost at least 4 yards (nobody else had more than one). His 8-yard loss against Buffalo was the worst of any player all season. ❧ Chase Edmonds was the primary man on kickoff returns in 2020 and should be again in 2021 as he splits backfield duties with John Conner. ❧ Rondale Moore, Arizona's second-round draft choice, returned both kickoffs and punts at Purdue, though he wasn't particularly effective at either one.

Atlanta Falcons

2020 Record: 4-12	**Total DVOA:** -3.6% (15)	**2021 Mean Projection:** 7.1 wins	**On the Clock (0-5):** 30%
Pythagorean Wins: 7.5 (18)	**Offense:** -3.1% (21)	**Postseason Odds:** 21.9%	**Mediocrity (6-8):** 42%
Snap-Weighted Age: 26.9 (6)	**Defense:** -0.1% (14)	**Super Bowl Odds:** 1.2%	**Playoff Contender (9-11):** 23%
Average Opponent: 6.6% (1)	**Special Teams:** -0.7% (20)	**Proj. Avg. Opponent:** 0.1% (15)	**Super Bowl Contender (12+):** 6%

2020: Think the Super Bowl collapse was bad? Watch this!

2021: We're not trying to win Super Bowl LI anymore.

The best place to start is Week 2. Less than two minutes left in the fourth quarter. Falcons 39, Cowboys 37. It had once been 20-0. Then 29-10. Then 39-26.

The Cowboys line up for an onside kick. Dallas is out of timeouts, so if Atlanta recovers, the game is over. Greg Zuerlein places the ball on the ground, laces up, at a 45-degree angle. He kicks the right side of the ball, sending it spinning like blades on a helicopter.

As it spins, the Falcons watch. And watch. And watch. They're frozen, unsure whether to attack the ball or assume it will sputter out of bounds before it travels the required 10 yards. You scream at your television, "Someone do something!"

The ball takes an unexpected turn and stays in bounds. The Falcons lunge for it, but they're too late. The Cowboys have boxed them out. They pounce. It's Dallas' ball.

Two plays later, Falcons cornerback Darqueze Dennard stumbles, leaving CeeDee Lamb open for a 24-yard gain. The completion sets the stage for a 46-yard game-winning field goal. Zuerlein's kick sails through the uprights as time expires.

The truth is time had run out on the Falcons long ago. For a while, you could understand owner Arthur Blank's reluctance to make sweeping changes. His patience had been rewarded before. In 2015, the Falcons started 5-0 but lost eight of their final 11 games to miss the playoffs for the third straight season. General manager Thomas Dimitroff and offensive coordinator Kyle Shanahan received the largest share of the blame. Blank chose not to fire either. The next season, Atlanta went 11-5 and reached the Super Bowl. Vindication. And then soul-crushing heartbreak.

The week after the Falcons collapsed against the Cowboys last year, they did it again, blowing a 16-point fourth-quarter lead against the Bears. Back-to-back chokes. Somehow, the Falcons out-Falconed the Falcons.

Someone do something!

It took two more losses to finally extinguish the false hope Atlanta had been clinging to for years. Hours after the team fell to 0-5, Blank, at last, did something, dismissing both Dimitroff and head coach Dan Quinn. It was more than a firing. It was a clear-eyed admission that the Falcons would not be returning to the Super Bowl, that they needed to start over. In the interim, Raheem Morris filled in as coach. Atlanta kept collapsing, blowing three more fourth-quarter leads en route to a 4-12 record, the team's worst since 2013. "I think the team is better than a 4-12 record, there's no question about that," Blank said at his end-of-season news conference. "But it's probably not better than 7-9 or 8-8, and that puts us back where we were the last two years. We can't fool ourselves."

Indeed, the Falcons were better than their record suggested. They finished 17th in DVOA, becoming the first 12-loss team to rank that high since the 2012 Lions. By Pythagorean wins, it was an all-time underperformance. They fell short of expectations by 3.5 wins, the third-largest deficit since the 1970 AFL-NFL merger (Table 1).

But to paraphrase Blank: So what? Say Atlanta had gotten to seven or eight wins. That wasn't the goal. Some teams are unlucky. But these Falcons? They just weren't good enough—and they weren't getting better. The 4-12 record might have been a blessing. It forced the organization to face reality.

Table 1. Largest Gap Between Wins and Pythagorean Wins, 1970-2020

Team	Year	W-L	Pct	PF	PA	Pyth	Pyth Wins	Dif	W-L Y+1
NE	1981	2-14	0.125	322	370	0.416	6.6	-0.291	5-4
CIN	1971	4-10	0.286	284	265	0.541	7.6	-0.256	8-6
ATL	**2020**	**4-12**	**0.250**	**396**	**414**	**0.472**	**7.5**	**-0.222**	**--**
SD	2001	5-11	0.313	332	321	0.520	8.3	-0.208	8-8
CLE	2017	0-16	0.000	234	410	0.206	3.3	-0.206	7-8-1
CIN	1989	8-8	0.500	404	285	0.702	11.2	-0.202	9-7
SF	1979	2-14	0.125	308	416	0.322	5.1	-0.197	6-10
SD	1990	6-10	0.375	315	281	0.567	9.1	-0.192	4-12
LARD	1987	5-10	0.333	301	289	0.524	7.9	-0.191	7-9
GB	2008	6-10	0.375	419	380	0.562	9.0	-0.187	11-5

2021 Falcons Schedule

Week	Opp.	Week	Opp.	Week	Opp.
1	PHI	7	at MIA	13	TB
2	at TB	8	CAR	14	at CAR
3	at NYG	9	at NO	15	at SF
4	WAS	10	at DAL	16	DET
5	NYJ (U.K.)	11	NE (Thu.)	17	at BUF
6	BYE	12	at JAX	18	NO

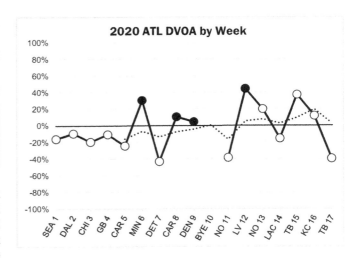

2020 ATL DVOA by Week

To take Atlanta in a new direction this offseason, Blank hired Arthur Smith as coach and Terry Fontenot as general manager. You know Smith best for putting Ryan Tannehill back together after Adam Gase broke him. He spent the past 10 seasons in Tennessee, the past two as the coordinator of one of the NFL's most efficient offenses (sixth in DVOA in 2019 and fourth in 2020). Fontenot comes over from New Orleans, where he started as a marketing intern in 2003 and worked his way up the ranks to vice president/assistant general manager of pro personnel.

Smith has said that his expectation is to win now, telling Peter King, "They hired the wrong guys if they thought we were going to lower expectations, take our time, and rebuild. That's just not who we are." Fontenot was more measured during his introductory news conference. "We understand the salary cap," he said. "We're going to make decisions to have sustained success. We're not going to be prisoners of the moment. We're not going to make decisions that are going to help us in 2021 but they're going to hurt us in 2022 and 2023."

Fontenot's most pressing order of business was to figure out what to do about his two biggest stars. Combined, Matt Ryan's and Julio Jones' contracts were set to eat up a third of the Falcons' salary cap. Even if Fontenot wanted to tear it down Sam Hinkie-style, Ryan's contract effectively made him untradeable. The resulting dead-money charge from a trade would have been larger than his 2021 cap hit ($40.9 million). And so Fontenot preserved what has become an annual tradition in Atlanta and restructured Ryan's contract, reducing his 2021 cap hit by $14 million while all but ensuring his 2022 return. If the Falcons were to cut him after this season, they would incur a record-setting $40.5-million dead-money charge.

As we have come to learn, keeping Jones was never an option. He wanted out. His agent requested a trade in March, and the Falcons eventually fulfilled that request, sending Jones and a 2023 sixth-round draft pick to the Titans for a 2022 second-round pick and a 2023 fourth-round pick.

Jones' departure stings. He's a franchise icon, a future Hall of Famer. But he's also a banged-up 32-year-old wide receiver. The $38.3 million left on his contract was a luxury Atlanta could not afford. Jones might very well go on to have another productive season or two, but expecting much more isn't realistic. The list of wide receivers age 32 or older to post three 1,000-yard seasons is a short one.[1] It contains 16 names. Only two—Jerry Rice and Joey Galloway—did so after suffering a late-career injury that cost them a chunk of games.

At the moment, Ryan might not be regarded as one of the league's best quarterbacks, but we should be wary of placing too much weight on the past couple of seasons. The playcaller and the offensive line bear at least some responsibility for his decline from very good (and sometimes great) to ordinary. From his rookie season in 2008 through 2018, he finished in the top eight in DVOA nine times. He's 36, but we're seeing quarterbacks play at a high level into their late thirties and even forties. Plus, he doesn't have an extensive injury history, missing only three games (two in 2009 because of turf toe and one in 2019 because of an ankle sprain) in 13 seasons.

The offensive line remains a concern—it will feature at least two new starters—but Smith is an upgrade over Dirk Koetter as the playcaller. His offense very much resembles Shanahan's, which helped elevate Ryan to league MVP in 2016. He's going to run the ball. A lot. Early in the game. Late in the game. On first down. On second-and-long. When the Falcons are ahead. When they're behind. More handoffs, fewer dropbacks—that's one way to keep Ryan upright.

Mike Davis, who gained 1,015 yards from scrimmage and scored eight touchdowns for the Panthers while filling in for Christian McCaffrey last season, will be Smith's primary running back. By now you've probably heard "he's no Derrick Henry." And he's not. Henry is 6-foot-3 and 247 pounds. Davis is 5-foot-9 and 221 pounds. But Derrick Henry wasn't even Derrick Henry until Matt LaFleur (the Titans offensive coordinator in 2018) and Smith started calling plays. Not to dismiss Henry's prolificacy, but it's worth noting that wide zone run schemes don't require freaks of nature. Consider some of the running backs that have had success under Shanahan: Steve Slaton. Alfred Morris. Devonta Freeman. Tevin Coleman. Matt Breida. Raheem Mostert. Jeff Wilson. Simply put, Smith doesn't need Davis to be Henry. He does need him, however, to be a factor as a receiver, something Henry has not been. Davis caught 59 passes last season; Henry has caught 76 *over five seasons.* Smith frequently uses multi-back formations, so 2019 fifth-rounder Qadree Ollison and free-agent signee Cordarrelle Patterson could see substantial snaps as well.

[1] https://stathead.com/tiny/ocX6y

In addition to a greater commitment to the run, the Falcons offense will feature a heavy amount of play-action and pre-snap motion, concepts they have gotten away from in recent seasons, even as the rest of the NFL has used them more than ever. Under Smith, the Titans last season ranked third in play-action rate (35.9%) and fourth in motion rate (57.0%). The Falcons were about league average in both.

History tells us Ryan will benefit from the greater frequency of play-action (Table 2), but his performance on pass plays that use motion bears watching. We assume that motion gives a quarterback an edge, either by helping him dissect a defense's coverage or by creating favorable matchups for his receivers. It has been a devastating weapon for Patrick Mahomes, Tom Brady, and Aaron Rodgers. But it hasn't been for Ryan. And that has been true regardless of his coordinator. It was true under Koetter. It was true under Steve Sarkisian. And it was true under Shanahan. Ryan gains more yards per pass on non-motion plays than motion plays (Table 3).

That doesn't mean the Falcons should abandon motion on pass plays, but it could mean that motion might be a more powerful weapon in the run game than the pass game. After all, the Titans gained a healthy 5.5 yards per carry on motion plays last season (excluding quarterback kneels and scrambles), second to only the Ravens.

Atlanta will miss Jones, but two things might soften the blow: the addition of Kyle Pitts, possibly the most highly regarded rookie tight end ever, and Smith's personnel tendencies, which will take full advantage of Pitts' athleticism and versatility. The Falcons skewed heavily toward 11 personnel last season, using the grouping more than 60% of the time. Expect that to fall this season to about 40% as Smith shifts toward 12 and 13 personnel groupings. In 2020, only the Browns (52.0%) used formations featuring multiple tight ends (and/or six offensive linemen) more often than Smith's Titans.

The defense is much more of an unknown. It's a situation that would drive most coordinators into retirement. But not 71-year-old Dean Pees—it actually brought him *out* of retirement. The Falcons didn't even have to sell him on the idea. Pees, who was the defensive coordinator in Tennessee in 2018 and 2019, was eager to get back in the game and reunite with his former Titans colleague.

Pees has what the Falcons do not—a track record of defensive success. With nearly five decades of coaching experience, he has been around football longer than anyone on the roster has been alive. In addition to the Titans, he has been a coordinator for the Patriots and Ravens, winning a Super Bowl with Baltimore in 2012 despite losing Ray Lewis and Terrell Suggs for significant stretches of the season. He has never presided over a truly great defense, but he's not responsible for any dumpster fires, either. In his 12 seasons as a coordinator, he has led his defenses to six top-10 finishes in DVOA.

The challenges ahead won't surprise him. The Titans, too, were short on talent on defense, particularly at edge rusher. Yet Pees managed to keep them competitive thanks to pre-snap subterfuge and simulated pressure. That makes him a logical fit in Atlanta, where the most dependable pass-rusher is defensive tackle Grady Jarrett. When Pees met Falcons media members in March, he vowed to do whatever is necessary to disrupt offenses. "Every position will blitz," he said. "Every position. Not just the safeties. Not just the linebackers. It's corners. It's everybody. … I want the offense to know we're coming from everywhere."

Though the Falcons have talked a lot this offseason about preparing for the future, they might harbor some hope for a faster-than-expected turnaround. The Buccaneers are far and away the best team in the NFC South, but the Saints and Panthers also are teams in transition. The schedule is full of beatable teams. Maybe, just maybe, Smith and Pees can scheme this team to a wild-card berth.

Our projections don't see it happening, docking Atlanta for the Jones trade and the coaching changes. The Falcons also lost a home game to London, which means they're on the road for 10 games this season. They will rank second in net travel miles (the 49ers will log the most), according to ESPN's Brian Burke.

Losing is never fun, but if Atlanta is trading a couple of wins now for more wins later, a sub-.500 finish isn't such a bad thing. The Falcons aren't stuck anymore, and that's progress. Finally, they're thinking about what can be instead of chasing what could have been.

Thomas Bassinger

Table 2. Matt Ryan, Arthur Smith, and Play-Action Passes, 2016-2020

Matt Ryan						
Team	Years	Coordinator	Rate	PA Yd/Pass	Non-PA Yd/Pass	Yd/Pass Diff
ATL	2016	Kyle Shanahan	25.9%	11.5	8.4	+3.1
ATL	2017-2018	Steve Sarkisian	23.8%	9.1	7.6	+1.5
ATL	2019-2020	Dirk Koetter	23.7%	8.2	7.0	+1.2
Arthur Smith						
Team	Years	Coordinator	Rate	PA Yd/Pass	Non-PA Yd/Pass	Yd/Pass Diff
TEN	2019-2020	Arthur Smith	31.5%	10.9	7.0	+3.9

Table 3. Matt Ryan, Arthur Smith, and Motion, 2016-2020

Matt Ryan						
Tm	Season	Coordinator	Rate	Motion Yd/Pass	Non-Motion Yd/Pass	Yd/Pass Diff
ATL	2016	Kyle Shanahan	53.7%	8.2	10.5	-2.3
ATL	2017-2018	Steve Sarkisian	48.5%	7.9	8.0	-0.1
ATL	2019-2020	Dirk Koetter	39.2%	6.7	7.7	-1.0
Arthur Smith						
Tm	Season	Coordinator	Rate	Motion Yd/Pass	Non-Motion Yd/Pass	Yd/Pass Diff
TEN	2019-2020	Arthur Smith	55.4%	8.7	8.0	+0.7

2020 Falcons by Week

Wk	vs.	W-L	PF	PA	YDF	YDA	TO	Total	Off	Def	ST
1	SEA	L	25	38	506	383	-2	-16.1%	10.8%	26.6%	-0.4%
2	at DAL	L	39	40	380	570	3	-9.6%	-2.7%	9.6%	2.7%
3	CHI	L	26	30	371	437	1	-19.7%	-8.3%	-6.9%	-18.3%
4	at GB	L	16	30	327	403	0	-10.8%	12.1%	17.3%	-5.6%
5	CAR	L	16	23	373	437	-1	-24.4%	-8.1%	23.2%	6.9%
6	at MIN	W	40	23	462	365	2	30.3%	-4.6%	-34.7%	0.2%
7	DET	L	22	23	388	386	-1	-43.0%	-25.9%	18.0%	0.9%
8	at CAR	W	25	17	401	304	0	10.5%	8.6%	-1.1%	0.8%
9	DEN	W	34	27	363	405	0	4.6%	15.6%	8.8%	-2.3%
10	BYE										
11	at NO	L	9	24	248	376	-1	-38.4%	-34.4%	7.0%	3.0%
12	LV	W	43	6	304	243	4	44.4%	-35.0%	-80.3%	-0.9%
13	NO	L	16	21	332	424	0	20.0%	5.7%	-11.9%	2.4%
14	at LAC	L	17	20	319	345	-2	-15.5%	-19.4%	-8.9%	-4.9%
15	TB	L	27	31	369	416	0	37.3%	29.4%	-2.2%	5.7%
16	at KC	L	14	17	367	395	1	11.8%	-0.4%	-15.3%	-3.0%
17	at TB	L	27	44	385	485	-1	-39.4%	6.6%	48.4%	2.4%

Trends and Splits

	Offense	Rank	Defense	Rank
Total DVOA	-3.1%	21	-0.1%	14
Unadjusted VOA	-4.3%	22	3.6%	20
Weighted Trend	-4.3%	16	-4.4%	12
Variance	3.3%	4	8.4%	29
Average Opponent	-0.8%	11	6.1%	2
Passing	15.8%	13	11.6%	19
Rushing	-25.9%	29	-20.7%	6
First Down	4.5%	14	-5.7%	13
Second Down	-23.9%	29	8.0%	24
Third Down	12.5%	9	-1.6%	16
First Half	-1.1%	17	-3.3%	13
Second Half	-5.5%	20	2.8%	15
Red Zone	-24.0%	28	6.2%	21
Late and Close	-24.3%	30	-0.8%	18

Five-Year Performance

Year	W-L	Pyth W	Est W	PF	PA	TO	Total	Rk	Off	Rk	Def	Rk	ST	Rk	Off AGL	Rk	Def AGL	Rk	Off Age	Rk	Def Age	Rk	ST Age	Rk
2016	11-5	10.9	12.3	540	406	+11	23.9%	3	25.1%	1	3.6%	19	2.5%	7	18.5	2	32.3	12	27.8	5	26.0	25	27.3	2
2017	10-6	9.1	9.0	353	315	-2	5.0%	14	8.5%	9	2.3%	17	-1.2%	19	10.4	4	4.5	2	27.4	8	25.7	25	26.5	5
2018	7-9	7.8	7.7	414	423	+1	-2.2%	17	8.9%	9	12.5%	30	1.4%	10	32.2	13	43.7	26	28.1	4	26.4	13	26.7	3
2019	7-9	7.5	7.9	381	399	-5	-1.9%	15	2.3%	15	1.4%	17	-2.9%	28	15.5	5	37.7	19	27.7	4	26.4	13	26.3	8
2020	4-12	7.5	6.7	396	414	+3	-3.6%	17	-3.1%	21	-0.1%	14	-0.7%	20	13.1	2	35.0	15	27.8	2	26.1	22	26.4	9

2020 Performance Based on Most Common Personnel Groups

ATL Offense					ATL Offense vs. Opponents					ATL Defense					ATL Defense vs. Opponents			
Pers	Freq	Yds	DVOA	Run%	Pers	Freq	Yds	DVOA	Run%	Pers	Freq	Yds	DVOA		Pers	Freq	Yds	DVOA
11	60%	5.8	5.9%	26%	Base	24%	5.2	-10.4%	53%	Base	24%	5.2	-24.0%		11	62%	6.5	3.1%
12	14%	5.8	-1.1%	43%	Nickel	53%	5.8	5.3%	36%	Nickel	75%	6.8	8.3%		12	15%	6.7	7.0%
21	12%	5.5	-12.6%	59%	Dime+	22%	5.5	-6.9%	11%	Dime+	0%	17.0	150.3%		21	6%	3.9	-31.7%
22	4%	5.9	20.4%	59%	Goal Line	1%	3.8	17.7%	64%	Goal Line	1%	1.2	-5.4%		13	3%	7.1	27.1%
01	3%	4.8	10.3%	4%											611	3%	8.1	35.1%
13	3%	3.4	-25.7%	44%											22	2%	3.6	-97.4%

Strategic Tendencies

Run/Pass		Rk	Formation		Rk	Pass Rush		Rk	Secondary		Rk	Strategy		Rk
Runs, first half	34%	25	Form: Single Back	77%	23	Rush 3	9.6%	10	4 DB	24%	16	Play Action	26%	18
Runs, first down	45%	21	Form: Empty Back	6%	26	Rush 4	61.0%	22	5 DB	75%	4	Offensive Motion	45%	15
Runs, second-long	25%	22	Form: Multi Back	17%	8	Rush 5	25.7%	7	6+ DB	0%	32	Avg Box (Off)	6.47	19
Runs, power sit.	54%	26	Pers: 3+ WR	65%	20	Rush 6+	3.6%	22	Man Coverage	36%	13	Avg Box (Def)	6.58	19
Runs, behind 2H	28%	15	Pers: 2+ TE/6+ OL	23%	23	Edge Rusher Sacks	43.1%	24	CB by Sides	70%	23	Offensive Pace	29.58	8
Pass, ahead 2H	54%	6	Pers: 6+ OL	3%	8	Interior DL Sacks	19.0%	20	S/CB Cover Ratio	21%	29	Defensive Pace	30.66	21
Run-Pass Options	6%	19	Shotgun/Pistol	54%	27	Second Level Sacks	37.9%	2	DB Blitz	10%	24	Go for it on 4th	1.90	9

Compared to the year before, Atlanta ran much more often with three or more wide receivers in the game. But the Falcons still weren't very good at it, with -15.5% DVOA (25th). 🖐 The Falcons had a league-low -35.5% DVOA with just 2.4 yards per carry against heavy boxes of eight or more defenders. 🖐 Atlanta was 27th in the league with -35.4% DVOA on targets at or behind the line of scrimmage, a slightly improvement over being dead last in 2019. 🖐 After four strong years from an empty backfield, the Falcons had a below-average 4.3 yards per play with -12.8% DVOA in 2020. 🖐 On defense, the Falcons had just one coverage sack, with 90% of their sacks attributed to pressure. 🖐 For the second straight year, Atlanta's defense faced the smallest rate of passes thrown to the middle of the field: 18% compared to a league average of 24%. 🖐 The listed Aggressiveness Index combines both Dan Quinn and Raheem Morris. Quinn was very aggressive (2.80 AI) in the limited time before he was fired, going for it on five out of six fourth-and-2s (including both a fake punt and a play where Atlanta was flagged for too many men on the field).

Passing

Player	DYAR	DVOA	Plays	NtYds	Avg	YAC	C%	TD	Int
M.Ryan	817	7.6%	666	4303	6.5	4.0	65.3%	26	10

Rushing

Player	DYAR	DVOA	Plays	Yds	Avg	TD	Fum	Suc
T.Gurley*	-54	-14.9%	194	677	3.5	9	1	46%
B.Hill*	0	-8.6%	100	465	4.7	1	1	48%
I.Smith	21	0.0%	63	268	4.3	1	0	60%
M.Ryan	-21	-30.3%	20	98	4.9	2	2	--
C.Ridley	-8	-77.7%	5	1	0.2	0	0	--
K.Smith	5	8.9%	4	7	1.8	0	0	100%
M.Davis	37	-3.5%	165	642	3.9	6	1	50%
C.Patterson	67	-20.6%	64	232	3.6	1	0	--

Receiving

Player	DYAR	DVOA	Plays	Ctch	Yds	Y/C	YAC	TD	C%
C.Ridley	230	6.7%	143	90	1374	15.3	3.1	9	63%
R.Gage	93	-1.7%	109	72	786	10.9	3.9	4	66%
J.Jones*	231	29.8%	68	51	771	15.1	4.5	3	75%
O.Zaccheaus	51	8.5%	32	20	274	13.7	3.2	1	63%
C.Blake	7	-7.8%	18	13	141	10.8	2.0	0	72%
B.Powell*	-40	-41.2%	18	12	69	5.8	2.8	2	67%
L.Treadwell*	34	46.6%	7	6	49	8.2	2.2	2	86%
C.Patterson	-39	-33.2%	25	21	132	6.3	5.4	0	84%
H.Hurst	13	-5.2%	88	56	571	10.2	4.4	6	64%
L.Stocker*	-19	-31.6%	11	7	63	9.0	7.4	0	64%
L.Smith	8	6.9%	6	4	35	8.8	5.0	2	67%
T.Gurley*	-29	-28.6%	35	25	164	6.6	4.9	0	71%
B.Hill*	29	3.7%	30	25	199	8.0	6.5	0	83%
I.Smith	-77	-62.1%	26	17	75	4.4	4.8	0	65%
K.Smith	-10	-25.5%	15	11	59	5.4	4.0	0	73%
M.Davis	55	0.2%	70	59	373	6.3	7.2	2	84%

Offensive Line

Player	Pos	Age	GS	Snaps	Pen	Sk	Pass	Run	Player	Pos	Age	GS	Snaps	Pen	Sk	Pass	Run
Chris Lindstrom	RG	24	16/16	1122	1	3.5	14	9	James Carpenter*	LG	32	13/13	826	0	1.5	10	8
Jake Matthews	LT	29	16/16	1113	3	2.5	16	8	Matt Gono	RT/LG	25	16/4	336	0	0	12	3
Alex Mack*	C	36	14/14	972	2	0.5	14	8	Matt Hennessy	C	24	13/2	225	4	1	6	2
Kaleb McGary	RT	26	14/13	890	2	1.5	20	9	Josh Andrews	RG	30	15/4	311	1	0	8	3

Year	Yards	ALY	Rk	Power	Rk	Stuff	Rk	2Lev	Rk	OpFld	Rk	BB Rt	Rk	Sacks	ASR	Rk	Press	Rk	BB Rt	Rk	Cont
2018	4.59	4.08	24	60%	27	25%	31	1.29	13	1.30	2	4.0%	3	42	6.6%	14	28.2%	12	6.4%	7	28
2019	3.73	3.98	24	65%	16	21%	27	1.08	25	0.52	27	11.9%	27	50	6.6%	13	32.1%	24	15.0%	26	27
2020	3.90	4.12	26	57%	26	17%	16	1.02	30	0.55	26	12.6%	29	41	6.7%	18	26.0%	19	14.0%	22	30

2020 ALY by direction: Left End: 3.60 (27)   Left Tackle: 3.88 (22)   Mid/Guard: 4.14 (27)   Right Tackle: 3.78 (27)   Right End: 5.42 (8)

Matt Ryan has taken a beating of late. Over the past two seasons, he has been sacked 89 times (third-most) and hit 165 times (most). The offensive line is only partly to blame. Atlanta went from having the fourth-lowest rate of non-pressure sacks (10.7%) in 2019 to the fourth-highest rate (39.0%) in 2020. An NFL-high 14 coverage sacks drove the increase. 🖐 Since 2019, the Falcons have drafted five offensive linemen in the first four rounds, a total matched by only the Dolphins and Vikings. It's possible that four of the five will be starters this season alongside left tackle Jake Matthews, who hasn't missed a game since Week 2 in 2014. 🖐 At left guard, third-round pick Jalen Mayfield, who played mostly right tackle at Michigan, will try to beat out journeyman Josh Andrews. Andrews got the bulk of the reps with the first-team offense during OTAs. 🖐 At center, fourth-round pick Drew Dalman (son of former 49ers lineman Chris) will challenge Matt Hennessy. When the Falcons drafted Hennessy out of Temple in the third round last year, it seemed as if he eventually would replace Alex Mack. In limited snaps, however, he scuffled, particularly in pass-protection. Dalman started 22 games in Stanford's pro-style offense and excelled in the pass and run games. He had the third-best overall blown block rate among drafted centers. ❧ Offensive line coach Dwayne Ledford has said he intends to start his five best linemen, so Hennessy and Dalman could join the competition at left guard too. Willie Wright is also in the mix. ❧ Atlanta placed a second-round tender on Matt Gono, but the swing tackle could miss significant time as he recovers from surgery on an undisclosed injury. ❧ Both of the Falcons' 2019 first-round picks took steps forward. Chris Lindstrom, who had missed 11 games his rookie season because of a broken foot, looked like the plug-and-play starter Atlanta thought it was getting when it drafted him 14th overall: tough (he led all right guards in snaps) and reliable (he posted the team's best blown block rate). Right tackle Kaleb McGary, drafted 17 picks after Lindstrom, recovered from an ugly debut season, cutting his sacks allowed from 13.5 to 1.5. There remains much room for improvement, however. His blown block rate was fourth highest among right tackles.

Defensive Front

Defensive Line	Age	Pos	G	Snaps	Plays	TmPct	Rk	Stop	Dfts	BTkl	Runs	St%	Rk	RuYd	Rk	Sack	Hit	Hur	Dsrpt
						Overall						vs. Run				Pass Rush			
Grady Jarrett	28	DT	16	851	52	6.4%	21	40	20	8	42	76%	44	2.1	37	4.0	18	26	1
Tyeler Davison	29	DT	16	519	36	4.4%	59	22	6	3	33	61%	86	2.8	69	0.5	1	5	0
Jacob Tuioti-Mariner	25	DT	16	373	22	2.7%	--	13	5	2	14	64%	--	2.6	--	1.0	4	16	2

Edge Rushers	Age	Pos	G	Snaps	Plays	TmPct	Rk	Stop	Dfts	BTkl	Runs	St%	Rk	RuYd	Rk	Sack	Hit	Hur	Dsrpt
						Overall						vs. Run				Pass Rush			
Steven Means	31	DE	16	643	38	4.7%	50	25	7	5	28	68%	59	3.1	75	3.0	3	19	0
Dante Fowler	27	DE	14	601	24	3.4%	77	18	12	8	17	65%	73	1.7	18	3.0	5	21	0
Allen Bailey*	32	DE	16	424	15	1.8%	--	13	3	4	12	83%	--	3.0	--	1.5	3	6	1
John Cominsky	26	DE	13	397	28	4.2%	62	19	5	2	23	70%	55	3.9	90	1.0	2	9	2
Charles Harris*	26	DE	13	289	19	2.9%	--	12	4	2	8	88%	--	3.1	--	3.0	2	8	1

Linebackers	Age	Pos	G	Snaps	Plays	TmPct	Rk	Stop	Dfts	BTkl	Runs	St%	Rk	RuYd	Rk	Sack	Hit	Hur	Tgts	Suc%	Rk	Yd/P	Rk	PD	Int
						Overall						vs. Run				Pass Rush				vs. Pass				
Deion Jones	27	MLB	16	1040	112	13.7%	36	55	26	14	69	51%	65	4.4	63	4.5	6	12	27	41%	60	7.4	59	6	2
Foyesade Oluokun	26	MLB	15	895	121	15.8%	14	62	25	14	60	58%	34	4.1	46	3.0	6	18	35	49%	46	6.6	45	4	2
Mykal Walker	24	OLB	16	385	40	4.9%	86	19	2	1	20	50%	66	4.6	66	0.0	2	4	9	56%	--	4.2	--	1	0

Year	Yards	ALY	Rk	Power	Rk	Stuff	Rk	2Lev	Rk	OpFld	Rk	BB Rt	Rk	Sacks	ASR	Rk	Press	Rk	BB Rt	Rk
2018	4.66	5.07	31	74%	27	14%	32	1.25	18	0.80	15	5.9%	26	37	6.6%	25	25.7%	30	7.4%	27
2019	4.25	4.29	19	64%	15	22%	6	1.24	22	0.77	18	15.4%	8	28	5.8%	28	27.0%	27	13.8%	22
2020	3.87	4.16	9	63%	10	22%	3	1.31	22	0.39	4	16.6%	3	29	5.5%	23	24.7%	18	10.7%	27
2020 ALY by direction:		Left End: 2.40 (1)			Left Tackle: 4.16 (15)			Mid/Guard: 4.68 (25)				Right Tackle: 3.91 (10)				Right End: 3.60 (5)			

Grady Jarrett wasn't as productive as he was in 2019, but his 20 defeats still led all defensive tackles. Though he didn't miss any games, he played through hip, back, and groin injuries. ❧ We never got an extended look at 2020 second-round pick Marlon Davidson. The defensive tackle's rookie season was marred by a knee injury and a stint on the COVID list. ❧ Atlanta's pass rush was a bit underrated. To be clear, we're not arguing it was good; we're pointing out it was more mediocre than bad. For the first time since 2016, the Falcons cracked the top 20 in pressure rate. ❧ From a talent standpoint, there's little reason to think Atlanta will build upon that mild improvement. After a disappointing first season with the Falcons, edge rusher Dante Fowler Jr. is back on a reworked deal heavy on incentives. His monster 2019 season—11.5 sacks and 39 hurries for the Rams—is looking more and more like an outlier that had much to do with playing alongside Aaron Donald. Besides Fowler, Atlanta has a collection of rotational players—Steven Means, Jacob Tuioti-Mariner, and fifth-round pick Adetokunbo Ogundeji (Notre Dame). ❧ While much of the defense is in flux, Atlanta is set at inside linebacker with Deion Jones and Foye Oluokun. Jones regressed in coverage but was disruptive in the backfield, recording a team-high 4.5 sacks. Oluokun, a sixth-round pick in 2018, validated the Falcons' decision to let De'Vondre Campbell walk. His 62 stops were most on the team and his four forced fumbles were tied for third-most in the NFL. Fourth-round rookie Mykal Walker also stood out, particularly in coverage, and could be in line for a larger role.

Defensive Secondary

Secondary	Age	Pos	G	Snaps	Plays	Overall TmPct	Rk	Stop	Dfts	BTkl	vs. Run Runs	St%	Rk	RuYd	Rk	vs. Pass Tgts	Tgt%	Rk	aDOT	Suc%	Rk	Yd/P	Rk	PD	Int
Keanu Neal*	26	SS	15	917	99	12.9%	10	33	15	13	34	38%	33	5.9	26	43	11.2%	17	7.2	49%	38	8.7	48	2	1
A.J. Terrell	23	CB	14	908	81	11.3%	7	32	12	17	14	43%	38	9.5	70	84	22.0%	22	13.8	49%	48	8.4	55	7	1
Isaiah Oliver	25	CB	16	830	76	9.3%	26	35	14	8	20	50%	24	3.6	5	65	18.6%	49	11.7	55%	24	9.6	71	6	0
Ricardo Allen*	30	FS	12	604	30	4.9%	71	7	6	1	8	13%	68	12.8	69	13	5.1%	59	17.5	54%	25	11.1	66	5	2
Kendall Sheffield	25	CB	13	524	53	8.0%	56	10	6	6	6	17%	77	8.0	58	53	24.1%	11	12.7	40%	73	10.8	80	3	0
Darqueze Dennard*	30	CB	8	437	41	10.0%	--	18	8	3	7	71%	--	4.7	--	39	21.2%	--	11.8	59%	--	4.7	--	5	1
Sharrod Neasman*	30	SS	16	289	20	2.5%	--	5	2	2	7	43%	--	7.9	--	4	3.3%	--	14.5	25%	--	13.3	--	0	0
Duron Harmon	30	SS	16	1102	77	9.2%	57	9	5	11	35	6%	70	11.6	67	18	4.3%	66	12.5	39%	65	15.6	70	5	2
Erik Harris	31	FS	14	724	61	8.4%	61	15	6	14	27	26%	56	8.9	56	23	7.9%	40	13.2	43%	53	10.7	64	5	0

Year	Pass D Rank	vs. #1 WR	Rk	vs. #2 WR	Rk	vs. Other WR	Rk	WR Wide	Rk	WR Slot	Rk	vs. TE	Rk	vs. RB	Rk
2018	29	15.8%	27	-6.3%	11	16.7%	27	14.7%	28	5.6%	21	0.9%	15	13.5%	28
2019	25	4.0%	18	29.4%	30	20.7%	27	15.2%	27	16.4%	25	-11.0%	6	-7.9%	13
2020	19	13.8%	26	13.2%	26	-5.4%	11	14.6%	28	6.9%	24	10.7%	23	-4.8%	13

Cornerback Isaiah Oliver started the season on the outside opposite first-round pick A.J. Terrell but moved inside in Week 5. Though he went on to post the best success rate of his three-year career, he struggled to limit chunk plays. 🏈 Kendall Sheffield wasn't an upgrade. His success rate ranked among the eight worst qualifying cornerbacks, and he allowed the highest yards per pass average. He'll have to hold off free-agent signing Fabian Moreau, who lined up outside during OTAs. 🏈 The Falcons surrendered at least 20 yards on 66 pass plays, tied with the Lions for most in the NFL. There was no single culprit. Terrell was the primary man in coverage on 10 plays, as was Oliver. Sheffield was the primary man on nine plays. 🏈 At safety, Atlanta is pretty much starting from scratch. Jaylinn Hawkins, a fourth-round pick in 2020, remains, but Keanu Neal, Ricardo Allen, Sharrod Neasman, and Damontae Kazee—that's nearly 2,500 snaps—are gone. 🏈 The Falcons drafted Richie Grant, a hard-hitting ballhawk out of UCF, in the second round this year. His versatility—he can cover the slot and defend the run—will help his cause as he pushes for a starting spot. 🏈 Figuring it might be a good idea to have at least a couple of safeties with some meaningful NFL experience, Atlanta signed Duron Harmon and Erik Harris to one-year deals.

Special Teams

Year	DVOA	Rank	FG/XP	Rank	Net Kick	Rank	Kick Ret	Rank	Net Punt	Rank	Punt Ret	Rank	Hidden	Rank
2018	1.4%	10	12.0	1	-0.7	18	-2.4	22	1.0	16	-2.7	21	-11.3	28
2019	-2.9%	28	-4.8	25	1.6	13	-1.1	16	-5.6	24	-4.3	27	5.9	8
2020	-0.7%	20	5.7	8	-4.1	23	-4.2	25	-2.1	23	1.5	11	-6.6	23

In his first full season as the Falcons' placekicker, Younghoe Koo impressed, converting 37 of his 39 field goal kicks, including all eight of his attempts from 50 yards and beyond. His 37 field goals led the NFL and set a new team record. 🏈 Atlanta's punting situation, however, is very much up in the air. After finishing 31st in gross punting value, Sean Hofrichter's job is on the line. The Falcons' first acquisition this offseason was Wake Forest product Dom Maggio, who signed with the Ravens after the 2020 draft but did not make the team. 🏈 Atlanta hasn't had a decent kick return game since 2015, when Eric Weems filled in for an injured Devin Hester for most of the season. With Cordarrelle Patterson in the fold, that should change. His 9.1 points of return value last season led the NFL, extending his streak of top-five finishes to three. After signing Patterson, the Bears went from last in average line of scrimmage after kickoffs in 2018 to the top 10 in 2019 and 2020. 🏈 Rookie cornerback Avery Williams is the favorite for the punt return job. During his four seasons at Boise State, he returned six punts for touchdowns (and three kickoffs for touchdowns). Second-year wide receiver Chris Rowland also is an option.

Baltimore Ravens

2020 Record: 11-5	**Total DVOA:** 18.5% (1)	**2021 Mean Projection:** 10.6 wins	**On the Clock (0-5):** 4%
Pythagorean Wins: 12 (1)	**Offense:** 4.3% (11)	**Postseason Odds:** 72.7%	**Mediocrity (6-8):** 17%
Snap-Weighted Age: 25.9 (26)	**Defense:** -6.9% (9)	**Super Bowl Odds:** 18.8%	**Playoff Contender (9-11):** 40%
Average Opponent: -5.3% (29)	**Special Teams:** 7.4% (2)	**Proj. Avg. Opponent:** 1.1% (10)	**Super Bowl Contender (12+):** 39%

2020: Lamar Jackson cleared another set of goalposts. Time to move the goalposts.

2021: Super Bowl or Bust for a player, a franchise, and a philosophy.

The 2021 season will be a final, binding referendum on the whole Lamar Jackson option-heavy offensive experiment, and perhaps on Jackson himself.

Don't shoot the messenger! *Football Outsiders Almanac* didn't make the rules, and we don't have to like them. But we're obligated to acknowledge them. The NFL establishment is ready to pass judgment on the Ravens' radical offense, and the old guard is itching to render a guilty verdict.

Josh Allen stumbled around like a newborn fawn for two years before breaking out, and the Bills are now hailed as a model organization for patiently nurturing him. Baker Mayfield had half a really good season after riding the Drama Express for two-and-a-half years, and it has been interpreted as vindication of the entire Browns organizational paradigm. And of course, quarterbacks on the Derek Carr-Kirk Cousins spectrum can be flawed in traditional ways for years but get rewarded with opportunity after opportunity.

But Jackson? He can be a late-season sensation as a rookie and an MVP as a sophomore, then lead his team to a third-straight playoff appearance and a postseason victory in his third season, yet still face questions about his viability as a long-term franchise quarterback and the sustainability of the unique offense tailored to his talents.

Now, to paraphrase the great Darin Gantt's famous expression about Cam Newton, Lamar Jackson makes people stupid. Criticism of Jackson generally follows a lazy, perfunctory, crotchety father-in-law formula. Support for Jackson can also be partisan and shrill. Every Jackson wibble-wobbler or Ravens playoff loss is not proof that he would be better off playing wide receiver for a *reliable pocket passer and decision-maker™* such as Joe Flacco. At the same time, pointing out Jackson's severe November slump, noting his deficiencies when throwing toward the sidelines, or worrying that a 212-pound quarterback who runs 11 times per game might not survive to see the back half of a nine-figure contract is not the equivalent of lobbying to preserve the Confederate statue in the town square.

There's no denying that Jackson's ultimate fate will be determined by folks who think more like Facebook father-in-laws than Twitter #activists. The fact that no team has rushed to copy the Ravens' success is a clear tell about which way the NFL is leaning when it comes to the Jackson option experiment. They want it to fail so they can go back to using slightly tweaked versions of offensive playbooks handed down from Bill Walsh and Don Coryell and the defensive schemes designed to counter them. So either the Ravens reach the Super Bowl this year or their offense will be written off as too gimmicky to beat quality opponents, and Jackson's "can't win the big game" label will get written with a permanent marker.

Jackson, therefore, needs to take another step forward as (you guessed it) a traditional dropback passer, particularly when throwing to the outside.

The Ravens rarely attempt passes outside the numbers. Just 36.2% of Ravens attempts last season were marked as passes to the far left or right (as opposed to left-middle, middle, or right-middle) by Sports Info Solutions. That was the third-lowest rate in the league, ahead of only the Patriots and 49ers.

Even that low 36.2% rate was inflated a bit. Many of those passes along the sideline came at the end of Jackson scrambles: close your eyes and you can probably picture Jackson tossing the ball over a defender's arms just as he's about to step out of bounds. Just 25.4% of Ravens attempts last season were sideline passes from the pocket, by far the lowest rate in the league and well below the league average of 35.0%.

Keep in mind that the Ravens attempted just 406 passes last season, the lowest figure in the NFL. That means that sideline passes from the pocket were a true rarity in their offense, occurring 6.4 times per game. The average NFL team attempted 12.3 such passes per game. The league-leading Buccaneers attempted 16.3. And yes, it's worth noting that Jackson did something reluctantly/poorly that Tom Brady did eagerly/well, because the hive mind has surely noted it.

When the Ravens did throw from the pocket to the sidelines, they weren't very good at it. Jackson's completion rate of 59.3% on such passes ranked 35th in the NFL in 2020 (among quarterbacks with at least 50 such attempts). Jackson's yards per attempt on such passes ranked 26th, while four interceptions on just 91 throws resulted in the fourth-highest interception rate in the category.

We can make lots of chicken-or-egg arguments about Jackson's issues as a sideline passer. Greg Roman's option offense may simply not be built to accommodate lots of 10-yard outs. The Ravens wide receivers are a convenient target for criticism, even though most of them arrived in Baltimore as draftnik favorites (as does first-round pick Rashod Bateman, one of six receivers drafted by the Ravens in the last three years).

2021 Ravens Schedule

Week	Opp.	Week	Opp.	Week	Opp.
1	at LV (Mon.)	7	CIN	13	at PIT
2	KC	8	BYE	14	at CLE
3	at DET	9	MIN	15	GB
4	at DEN	10	at MIA (Thu.)	16	at CIN
5	IND (Mon.)	11	at CHI	17	LAR
6	LAC	12	CLE	18	PIT

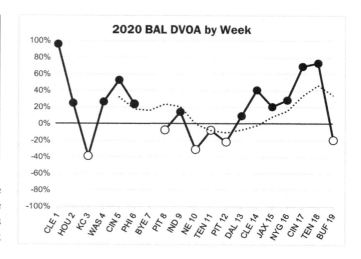

2020 BAL DVOA by Week

Jackson looks uncomfortable resetting his feet for sideline throws and reluctant to pull the trigger on quick-out type plays, particularly when he's pressing or struggling. Perhaps Roman or the receivers are to blame for his discomfort. But whatever the issue, it's a real issue.

All of the harping on Jackson's sideline passing can come across as special pleading: go through any quarterback's splits and you'll find some shortcomings. But sideline passing directly impacts the Ravens' biggest problem over the last two seasons: an inability to come from behind against a quality opponent.

The Ravens offense ranked 22nd in the league when losing by more than a touchdown in 2020. They also ranked 30th in the NFL in situation-neutral pace and last in offensive pace when trailing by a touchdown or more. Crisp sideline passes are a fundamental component of up-tempo tactics and a nutritious part of any comeback effort. Right now, the Ravens are terrible at playing catch-up when an opponent takes the lead. That's not a flaw they can allow to remain baked into their offensive philosophy.

The Ravens wouldn't have to worry much about comebacks if they were still shattering rushing records. But their rushing offense fell from a league-leading 16.9% DVOA in 2019 to a merely very good 6.0% in 2020.

Some inevitable "figuring out" of Roman's offense, particularly the lack of sideline throws, was one likely cause of the decline; cornerbacks and slot defenders knew they could cheat into the option lanes a little bit. Losses along the offensive line were another culprit. Marshal Yanda retired before the 2020 season, Ronnie Stanley suffered a season-ending injury against the Steelers in Week 8, and Matt Skura declined suddenly and shockingly from a quality starter to a guy who could barely execute a shotgun snap without incident.

Stanley will be back, but Orlando Brown played so well after sliding over to replace Stanley that he forced a trade to the Chiefs so he could get paid left-tackle bucks. Veteran guard Kevin Zeitler and tackle Alejandro Villanueva were imported to stabilize the right side of the line, with third-round pick Ben Cleveland in the mix and Bradley Bozeman moving over from left guard as Skura's replacement. It's a good line but not a dominant one. Jackson's talent and Roman's scheme will make the Ravens a formidable rushing team, but probably not a record-breaker.

It's business as usual on the other side of the ball. The Ravens defense has finished among the NFL's top 10 in DVOA 22 times in the last 24 years. The 2021 season should be no exception. Top edge rusher Matt Judon left via free agency, but the Ravens have plenty of veterans such as Tyus Bowser, Calais Campbell, and Pernell McPhee on hand, and they have been playing the draft-and-develop game successfully along the front seven for decades. Rookie linebacker Patrick Queen finished tied for second in the league with 18 broken tackles and often needed a GPS in coverage but displayed gobs of speed, hustle, and big-play potential. The Ravens, of course, know how to develop inside linebackers. The secondary is deep, talented, and experienced.

The Ravens special teams have also finished in the top 10 in DVOA for nine consecutive years and 11 out of the last 12, which is remarkable because special teams DVOA fluctuates so wildly from year to year. Then again, All-Galaxy kicker Justin Tucker missed two field goals in blustery conditions in Buffalo in the playoffs. That served as a reminder that a team with the reigning MVP at quarterback and a groundbreaking offense shouldn't have to rely on its kicker when holding an opponent to 17 points.

Fairly or unfairly, everything circles back to Jackson and the fact that he and the Ravens offense do things differently, especially when the defense and special teams are holding up their ends of the bargain. When a team does things differently, they need to get results, especially in playoff games. And they absolutely cannot afford to reveal a fundamental flaw—that lack of comeback ability, fueled by a passing game that only uses the middle third of the field—that is obvious to both casual fans and folks scouring the advanced metrics.

Jackson's contract extension is looming, and it's easy to pound the table and insist he will earn every dime of a $125-million deal when it's not our money, cap space, or reputation on the line. Jackson was knocked out of the playoff loss to the Bills with a concussion, and Baltimore's robust analytics department is surely doing research on whether Jackson's style of play comes with increased injury risk. The Ravens have also watched other perennial contenders such as the Rams and Eagles suffer buyer's remorse after pulling the nine-figure quarterback contract trigger. A little hesitancy by the Ravens would be understandable, as would an expectation that a huge extension would come bundled with some offensive changes that expose Jackson to fewer hits.

Ultimately, Jackson will likely get the Jared Goff-, Carson Wentz-, Dak Prescott-sized contract he has earned. But if Jackson backslides, the Ravens will be less likely to find a market for him than the Rams and Eagles found for Goff and Wentz. He's more likely to get Newton's second chance: one-year deals with successors waiting in the wings.

And of course, teams will offer the keys to their franchises to Goff- and Wentz-types until the end of time, no matter how many of them fail. But should Jackson be less than spectacular this year, we'll hear the usual condescending proclamations about read-option tactics from old-fogey insiders and their media heralds, followed by new job opportunities for "proven" offensive minds such as Adam Gase and Brian Schottenheimer.

Our projections place the Ravens side-by-side with the Chiefs in the AFC's Super Bowl conversation, slightly ahead of the Bills and well ahead of the fashionable Browns. The Ravens have known nothing but regular-season success, not to mention excitement and relevance, since Jackson became their starter. The fact that television personalities can straight-facedly talk about waiting for him to "graduate" says a great deal about the NFL, the sports media, and society at large. But it remains a fact.

Jackson will be held to an almost impossibly high standard this year. It's a testament to what he has already accomplished that the analytics suggest he has a chance of meeting it.

Mike Tanier

2020 Ravens Stats by Week

Wk	vs.	W-L	PF	PA	YDF	YDA	TO	Total	Off	Def	ST
1	CLE	W	38	6	381	306	2	95.9%	39.0%	-47.9%	8.9%
2	at HOU	W	33	16	407	304	2	25.0%	2.1%	-20.8%	2.0%
3	KC	L	20	34	228	517	0	-38.9%	-43.6%	23.0%	27.7%
4	at WAS	W	31	17	350	343	-1	26.6%	27.4%	10.1%	9.4%
5	CIN	W	27	3	332	205	2	52.8%	-15.7%	-65.7%	2.9%
6	at PHI	W	30	28	355	364	1	23.8%	-5.0%	-9.3%	19.4%
7	BYE										
8	PIT	L	24	28	457	221	-3	-7.3%	-8.1%	6.4%	7.1%
9	at IND	W	24	10	266	339	1	14.6%	-5.5%	-19.4%	0.7%
10	at NE	L	17	23	357	308	-1	-30.8%	-9.7%	28.3%	7.2%
11	TEN	L	24	30	306	423	0	-7.5%	-15.6%	-1.1%	7.1%
12	at PIT	L	14	19	219	334	0	-21.6%	-36.2%	-3.0%	11.6%
13	DAL	W	34	17	401	388	0	9.8%	20.5%	-1.1%	-11.8%
14	at CLE	W	47	42	385	493	1	40.9%	40.1%	7.7%	8.6%
15	JAX	W	40	14	409	267	0	20.8%	21.7%	5.3%	4.3%
16	NYG	W	27	13	432	269	-1	28.8%	32.6%	12.5%	8.6%
17	at CIN	W	38	3	525	195	1	69.6%	19.4%	-46.2%	4.0%
18	at TEN	W	20	13	401	209	0	73.5%	19.3%	-51.4%	2.8%
19	at BUF	L	3	17	340	220	-1	-19.3%	-47.5%	-42.9%	-14.6%

Trends and Splits

	Offense	Rank	Defense	Rank
Total DVOA	4.3%	11	-6.9%	9
Unadjusted VOA	8.7%	8	-7.9%	9
Weighted Trend	7.2%	9	-2.6%	15
Variance	6.6%	16	7.0%	26
Average Opponent	1.8%	23	-4.1%	26
Passing	13.9%	17	0.4%	10
Rushing	6.0%	3	-18.4%	12
First Down	3.5%	16	-8.9%	8
Second Down	-6.5%	23	6.8%	22
Third Down	21.9%	6	-24.5%	4
First Half	1.1%	16	-17.9%	2
Second Half	8.0%	10	3.1%	17
Red Zone	21.3%	8	-2.0%	13
Late and Close	5.0%	13	22.7%	31

Five-Year Performance

Year	W-L	Pyth W	Est W	PF	PA	TO	Total	Rk	Off	Rk	Def	Rk	ST	Rk	Off AGL	Rk	Def AGL	Rk	Off Age	Rk	Def Age	Rk	ST Age	Rk
2016	8-8	8.6	9.1	343	321	+5	7.2%	12	-7.2%	23	-9.5%	6	4.9%	4	29.5	12	31.2	11	28.0	3	27.2	5	26.1	18
2017	9-7	10.5	10.3	395	303	+17	17.9%	7	-4.6%	21	-13.4%	4	9.2%	1	62.1	28	42.9	22	27.3	10	27.0	6	25.7	22
2018	10-6	10.8	10.8	389	287	-5	15.8%	6	1.2%	13	-11.7%	4	3.0%	6	17.1	5	11.5	2	26.3	20	27.6	2	25.7	21
2019	14-2	13.4	12.9	531	282	+10	41.2%	1	28.2%	1	-11.5%	5	1.5%	9	9.7	1	59.1	31	25.7	31	27.3	3	26.7	4
2020	11-5	12.0	9.5	468	303	+4	18.5%	7	4.3%	11	-6.9%	9	7.4%	2	37.4	16	22.2	6	25.0	32	26.5	12	26.8	4

2020 Performance Based on Most Common Personnel Groups

BAL Offense					BAL Offense vs. Opponents					BAL Defense				BAL Defense vs. Opponents			
Pers	Freq	Yds	DVOA	Run%	Pers	Freq	Yds	DVOA	Run%	Pers	Freq	Yds	DVOA	Pers	Freq	Yds	DVOA
11	48%	6.4	9.9%	36%	Base	36%	5.7	0.1%	66%	Base	21%	5.4	-4.4%	11	64%	5.3	-9.1%
22	13%	5.6	13.5%	71%	Nickel	45%	6.5	22.4%	46%	Nickel	62%	5.2	-9.3%	12	16%	5.5	-13.0%
21	11%	6.7	0.3%	55%	Dime+	14%	5.8	-5.1%	16%	Dime+	16%	6.1	2.6%	21	7%	5.5	8.5%
12	9%	5.4	4.6%	38%	Goal Line	1%	3.9	50.9%	92%	Goal Line	0%	0.3	19.4%	13	3%	6.7	26.7%
20	7%	5.0	23.2%	79%	Big	4%	4.6	-22.4%	66%					01	3%	8.6	59.1%
621	5%	4.8	3.3%	80%										22	2%	4.6	-32.3%

Strategic Tendencies

Run/Pass		Rk	Formation		Rk	Pass Rush		Rk	Secondary		Rk	Strategy		Rk
Runs, first half	47%	2	Form: Single Back	65%	29	Rush 3	5.8%	18	4 DB	21%	20	Play Action	34%	7
Runs, first down	61%	2	Form: Empty Back	10%	11	Rush 4	54.3%	32	5 DB	62%	15	Offensive Motion	68%	2
Runs, second-long	32%	9	Form: Multi Back	25%	4	Rush 5	33.2%	1	6+ DB	16%	13	Avg Box (Off)	6.70	8
Runs, power sit.	88%	1	Pers: 3+ WR	56%	24	Rush 6+	6.6%	9	Man Coverage	37%	9	Avg Box (Def)	6.71	9
Runs, behind 2H	44%	1	Pers: 2+ TE/6+ OL	32%	14	Edge Rusher Sacks	41.0%	26	CB by Sides	88%	7	Offensive Pace	32.63	30
Pass, ahead 2H	40%	26	Pers: 6+ OL	9%	2	Interior DL Sacks	23.1%	16	S/CB Cover Ratio	22%	26	Defensive Pace	28.86	2
Run-Pass Options	6%	21	Shotgun/Pistol	97%	1	Second Level Sacks	35.9%	4	DB Blitz	18%	4	Go for it on 4th	2.28	4

Baltimore was once again far past the rest of the league, using pistol on 44% of plays while no other offense was above 13%. The Ravens had 5.4 yards per play with -1.3% DVOA from the pistol. 🏈 No surprise, the Ravens were the team most likely to run from shotgun/pistol (36% of plays) or with three or more wide receivers on the field (41% of plays). In the latter category, they led the league with 6.1 yards per carry and were second with 15.5% DVOA. 🏈 Two years ago, the Ravens had a league-best 82.9% DVOA with 8.2 yards per play from an empty backfield. Last year, the Ravens somehow cratered to a horrendous -92.8% DVOA and 4.4 yards per play from an empty backfield, with four interceptions and five fumbles on just 98 plays. 🏈 Ravens receivers had just 27 drops, slightly below the NFL average of 28. But because the Ravens run so much, that actually worked out to the fourth-highest rate at 7.2%. 🏈 Baltimore was tied for seventh in broken tackles on offense, but second in the percentage of plays that had at least one broken tackle. 🏈 In 2019, the Ravens offense allowed the lowest pressure rate on third downs. In 2020, they allowed one of the 10 highest pressure rates on third downs at 35.5%. 🏈 Not a surprise given his propensity for scrambling, but Lamar Jackson faced man coverage on a lower rate of passes (22%) than anyone else. 🏈 The Ravens offense actually used a faster pace last year when leading (one play every 28.7 seconds) than when trailing (29.2 seconds). In the last six years, this has only been true of one other team, the 2018 Arizona Cardinals. 🏈 Baltimore's use of dime defense dropped by more than half, from 44% in 2019 (second) to 16% last season (13th). 🏈 The Ravens aren't just high in the rate of defensive back blitzes, they're excellent at them. Their -42.2% DVOA on these plays ranked fourth in the league. In 2019, the Ravens ranked second in DVOA on defensive back blitzes. 🏈 Baltimore's defense went from second in DVOA in the first quarter of games to seventh in the second quarter, 10th in the third quarter, and then 23rd in the fourth quarter or overtime. 🏈 Baltimore's offense recovered 16 of 23 fumbles, although the defense recovered only 11 of 27 fumbles.

Passing

Player	DYAR	DVOA	Plays	NtYds	Avg	YAC	C%	TD	Int
L.Jackson	265	-0.7%	402	2597	6.5	4.8	64.9%	26	9
R.Griffin*	-127	-147.5%	17	22	1.3	4.3	57.1%	0	2
T.McSorley	15	14.0%	10	90	9.0	17.7	30.0%	1	0

Rushing

Player	DYAR	DVOA	Plays	Yds	Avg	TD	Fum	Suc
L.Jackson	69	-3.6%	151	1003	6.6	7	5	--
G.Edwards	177	17.4%	144	723	5.0	6	1	63%
J.K.Dobbins	196	26.1%	134	805	6.0	9	2	59%
M.Ingram*	5	-6.8%	71	299	4.2	2	0	51%
J.Hill	13	28.4%	12	60	5.0	0	0	33%
R.Griffin*	16	27.1%	8	73	9.1	0	1	--
T.Huntley	-28	-83.3%	7	24	3.4	0	0	--
T.McSorley	-1	-14.2%	5	17	3.4	0	0	--

Receiving

Player	DYAR	DVOA	Plays	Ctch	Yds	Y/C	YAC	TD	C%
M.Brown	48	-6.5%	100	58	769	13.3	4.7	8	58%
W.Snead*	81	10.1%	48	33	432	13.1	5.7	3	69%
M.Boykin	45	5.7%	33	19	266	14.0	4.2	4	58%
D.Duvernay	-2	-14.0%	26	20	201	10.1	5.9	0	77%
D.Bryant*	-3	-15.9%	11	6	47	7.8	5.7	2	55%
S.Watkins	57	-0.4%	55	37	421	11.4	4.2	2	67%
M.Andrews	52	1.6%	88	58	701	12.1	3.1	7	66%
N.Boyle	25	14.5%	17	14	113	8.1	2.4	2	82%
J.K.Dobbins	-9	-20.0%	24	18	120	6.7	7.2	0	75%
G.Edwards	35	46.3%	13	9	129	14.3	10.3	0	69%
P.Ricard	7	-5.3%	12	9	45	5.0	5.0	1	75%
M.Ingram*	1	-10.9%	8	6	50	8.3	8.2	0	75%

Offensive Line

Player	Pos	Age	GS	Snaps	Pen	Sk	Pass	Run	Player	Pos	Age	GS	Snaps	Pen	Sk	Pass	Run
Orlando Brown*	LT/RT	25	16/16	1027	5	2.5	12	3	Tyre Phillips	RG/RT	24	12/8	419	1	2	9	5
Bradley Bozeman	LG	27	16/16	1017	2	1.5	8	5	Ronnie Stanley	LT	27	6/6	312	5	1.5	2	1
Matt Skura*	C	28	15/12	661	3	0	5	8	Alejandro Villanueva	LT	33	16/16	1098	4	1.5	21	5
Patrick Mekari	C	24	14/8	553	3	2	3	4	Kevin Zeitler	RG	31	16/16	1001	4	2	6	4
D.J. Fluker*	RT	30	16/8	531	9	1.5	9	4	Michael Schofield	LG/LT	31	11/3	270	3	2.5	7	4
Ben Powers	RG	25	16/7	513	4	1	3	0									

Year	Yards	ALY	Rk	Power	Rk	Stuff	Rk	2Lev	Rk	OpFld	Rk	BB Rt	Rk	Sacks	ASR	Rk	Press	Rk	BB Rt	Rk	Cont
2018	4.53	4.59	9	78%	1	15%	3	1.33	7	0.67	24	2.6%	1	32	6.1%	8	28.5%	14	5.8%	5	29
2019	4.97	4.73	3	61%	23	13%	2	1.37	2	0.95	11	5.6%	1	28	6.0%	8	28.2%	8	7.5%	1	36
2020	5.21	4.58	8	75%	5	14%	5	1.30	9	1.24	1	6.7%	3	32	7.5%	23	30.8%	29	10.7%	10	22

2020 ALY by direction:	Left End: 4.68 (10)	Left Tackle: 4.54 (12)	Mid/Guard: 4.45 (16)	Right Tackle: 4.00 (22)	Right End: 5.99 (2)

The Ravens offensive line continuity score of 22 last year tied for 26th in the NFL. They were forced to use nine different starters, and their longest stretch with the same five linemen lasted just three weeks. The Ravens made multiple additions to add depth and versatility on the line in the wake of last season's problems and Orlando Brown's departure, including a few veteran free agents who arrived after the draft. ◆ Alejandro Villanueva, a 33-year-old Steelers cap casualty who hasn't missed a start at left tackle since 2016, joined the Ravens in early May. Villaneueva is penciled in at right tackle, though John Harbaugh said in OTAs that Villanueva could still move to the left side if needed. Villanueva told reporters that linemen really enjoy the Ravens' run-heavy philosophy. "I'm assuming it's not as much fun for the receivers because they're not getting all of the catches," he said. "They're making the TikToks and they're having fun on their social media." JuJu fatigue is real, everyone. ◆ Tackle Ja'Wuan James also signed with the Ravens around the same time he filed a grievance with the Broncos, who cut him after he suffered an Achilles injury away from team facilities. Harbaugh suggested that James could return and play a role this season, but that seems like a longshot. ◆ Finally, the Ravens signed Michael Schofield in early June. Schofield's most natural position is right guard, where former Giants and Bengals starter Kevin Zeitler is penciled in. Schofield may compete with third-round pick Ben Cleveland, your typical cement mixer from Georgia, at left guard. Ben Powers is also in the mix. ◆ Bradley Bozeman, a left guard for the last two seasons but a center at Alabama, was designated the starting center in OTAs. Bozeman told the Ravens website in June that he already had a strong bond with Jackson but was working to make it stronger. "I've always had a close relationship with all my quarterbacks," Bozeman said. "It's very important to have that open line of communication, for him to be able to come to me and say, 'Your snap was off high left.' And I can come to him and say, 'Your hand placement needs to be more to your right, you need to be more firm.' It's huge to be able to communicate those things." Jackson spent too much time communicating "That snap was 6 feet over my head" to Patrick Mekari and Matt Skura last season.

Defensive Front

Defensive Line	Age	Pos	G	Snaps	Plays	TmPct	Rk	Stop	Dfts	BTkl	Runs	St%	Rk	RuYd	Rk	Sack	Hit	Hur	Dsrpt
Derek Wolfe	31	DE	14	621	53	7.4%	10	40	13	1	45	80%	26	1.9	24	1.0	4	4	2
Calais Campbell	35	DE	12	410	34	5.5%	36	32	15	5	21	90%	1	1.6	9	4.0	7	14	6
Brandon Williams	32	DT	13	354	35	5.3%	45	28	7	1	32	81%	21	2.4	47	0.0	2	5	2
Justin Madubuike	24	DT	10	259	19	3.7%	72	12	4	0	14	57%	92	2.6	52	1.0	1	5	0
Jihad Ward*	27	DE	10	271	18	3.5%	--	14	5	3	12	67%	--	4.1	--	3.0	6	6	2
Justin Ellis	31	DT	13	358	18	2.7%	--	13	0	2	17	71%	--	2.9	--	0.0	0	2	1
Broderick Washington	25	DT	8	161	2	0.5%	--	2	0	1	2	100%	--	1.0	--	0.0	0	1	0

Edge Rushers	Age	Pos	G	Snaps	Plays	TmPct	Rk	Stop	Dfts	BTkl	Runs	St%	Rk	RuYd	Rk	Sack	Hit	Hur	Dsrpt
Matt Judon*	29	OLB	14	563	52	7.2%	9	35	18	2	26	81%	11	2.8	56	6.0	15	26	3
Tyus Bowser	26	OLB	16	539	39	4.8%	48	29	12	7	20	85%	6	2.4	42	2.0	13	22	3
Pernell McPhee	33	OLB	15	458	35	4.6%	53	25	6	7	28	71%	48	3.2	76	3.0	13	17	4
Yannick Ngakoue*	26	DE	15	657	24	3.1%	82	19	13	4	12	75%	33	2.6	46	8.0	8	28	1
Jaylon Ferguson	26	OLB	14	301	31	4.3%	--	19	8	5	24	58%	--	3.6	--	2.0	4	9	2

Linebackers	Age	Pos	G	Snaps	Plays	TmPct	Rk	Stop	Dfts	BTkl	Runs	St%	Rk	RuYd	Rk	Sack	Hit	Hur	Tgts	Suc%	Rk	Yd/P	Rk	PD	Int
Patrick Queen	22	ILB	16	858	107	13.0%	41	55	20	18	67	58%	35	4.1	47	3.0	7	12	26	50%	41	6.9	51	2	1
L.J. Fort	31	ILB	14	380	48	6.7%	76	26	7	5	27	63%	20	3.8	35	0.0	2	5	11	55%	--	4.8	--	2	0
Malik Harrison	23	ILB	16	263	37	4.5%	--	17	2	2	25	56%	--	4.3	--	0.0	0	1	10	50%	--	3.4	--	1	0
Chris Board	26	ILB	16	261	25	3.0%	--	12	8	7	9	44%	--	6.7	--	2.5	3	5	10	40%	--	5.4	--	1	0

Year	Yards	ALY	Rk	Power	Rk	Stuff	Rk	2Lev	Rk	OpFld	Rk	BB Rt	Rk	Sacks	ASR	Rk	Press	Rk	BB Rt	Rk
2018	3.52	3.90	5	72%	25	19%	16	1.07	5	0.29	2	9.8%	9	43	8.1%	6	32.8%	7	11.6%	11
2019	4.41	4.11	10	68%	24	19%	16	1.16	16	1.01	29	14.1%	12	37	7.1%	15	35.0%	3	13.5%	23
2020	4.50	4.16	10	55%	2	15%	22	1.20	16	0.91	25	11.9%	20	39	6.8%	13	26.7%	11	12.3%	21

2020 ALY by direction:	Left End: 4.25 (12)	Left Tackle: 3.83 (12)	Mid/Guard: 4.46 (17)	Right Tackle: 4.23 (14)	Right End: 3.18 (3)

Brandon Williams missed the Eagles, Titans, and second Steelers game plus most of the Patriots game with a midseason ankle injury in 2020. The Eagles rushed for 194 yards, the Titans and Patriots 173 yards each; the Steelers managed just 68 rushing yards but posted a positive rushing DVOA, as did the Patriots, against a defense that's usually stingy against the run. Williams recorded 28 tackles for a loss against the run on just 341 snaps, the highest figure for any defensive lineman with fewer than 400 snaps. Williams looked like a potential cap casualty in the offseason, but the Ravens elected to retain him and his $12.9-million cap figure. Three of Calais Campbell's four sacks came against the Eagles in Week 6 last year, and he spent much of the second half of the season dealing with an ankle injury. Campbell turns 35 in September, and while he still looks sharp when healthy, he appears to be entering the twilight of his career. Derek Wolfe's 38 tackles short of a first down ranked 17th in the NFL. The Ravens pass rush led the NFL with 15 forced quarterback fumbles and 12 batted passes, per Sports info Solutions charting. First-round pick Odafe Oweh will be one of several players asked to fill the pass-rush void left by Matt Judon. Oweh produced an impressive SackSEER projection of 24.5 sacks in his first five seasons and a fine 90.9% rating, thanks to a reported 4.37s 40-yard dash at 257 pounds and other metahuman pro day workout results. But Oweh produced exactly zero sacks in seven games for a weak Penn State defense as a senior, and while he's athletic as heck on film, 2021 pro day results were a wee bit fishy. The Ravens like to slow-cook their edge rushers, so Oweh will likely ease into the role by rotating with fifth-year vet Tyus Bowser, who intercepted three passes and registered 22 hurries while playing mostly on passing downs last year, and Jaylen Ferguson, another former draftnik darling who showed promise in 2020. Pernell McPhee is also still around to provide his customary three sacks per year. Patrick Queen admitted during OTAs that he was out of shape due to COVID restrictions at the start of his rookie season. "I came in around 240 [pounds] or something," he said. "Couldn't catch my breath when we were running. It's just so hard when you're not doing any football activity outside of working out. … It took me like five games to get in shape." Queen didn't look out of shape last season, but he did look lost in coverage and allowed too many ballcarriers to plow through him. Queen improved as the season wore on and produced enough big plays to suggest that he can make a huge leap in his second season. Third-round pick Malik Harrison also struggled in coverage early last year. He's expected to challenge sturdy veteran L.J. Fort on the weak side.

Defensive Secondary

Secondary	Age	Pos	G	Snaps	Plays	Overall TmPct	Rk	Stop	Dfts	BTkl	vs. Run Runs	St%	Rk	RuYd	Rk	vs. Pass Tgts	Tgt%	Rk	aDOT	Suc%	Rk	Yd/P	Rk	PD	Int
Chuck Clark	26	SS	16	1063	100	12.2%	20	37	13	6	53	38%	34	6.9	37	38	8.8%	30	8.9	58%	13	5.9	12	4	1
DeShon Elliott	24	FS	16	1044	84	10.2%	41	23	9	12	33	30%	49	10.0	64	30	7.1%	46	13.4	60%	10	8.9	50	4	0
Marlon Humphrey	25	CB	15	972	92	12.0%	3	40	17	14	15	33%	56	9.3	69	93	23.6%	13	9.6	57%	13	5.8	6	11	1
Marcus Peters	28	CB	14	912	61	8.5%	44	26	13	13	9	67%	3	5.4	28	65	17.6%	59	12.5	48%	56	7.8	46	9	4
Jimmy Smith	33	CB	11	454	28	5.0%	--	9	4	4	6	17%	--	8.0	--	28	15.2%	--	12.8	71%	--	3.0	--	1	0
Anthony Averett	27	CB	10	354	34	6.6%	--	11	4	4	1	0%	--	14.0	--	39	27.2%	--	8.7	33%	--	8.0	--	7	0

Year	Pass D Rank	vs. #1 WR	Rk	vs. #2 WR	Rk	vs. Other WR	Rk	WR Wide	Rk	WR Slot	Rk	vs. TE	Rk	vs. RB	Rk
2018	3	-9.7%	8	-26.2%	2	-11.6%	8	-32.5%	2	-4.4%	12	16.1%	22	-44.7%	1
2019	4	-16.1%	6	3.1%	19	-31.6%	2	-15.8%	9	-13.9%	5	-5.6%	10	-10.8%	8
2020	10	-22.8%	3	-0.6%	16	-20.9%	5	-29.3%	2	-13.4%	1	6.8%	22	3.8%	21

With four interceptions last year, Marcus Peters ended the season ranked third on the active leaderboard with 31 interceptions; Richard Sherman leads all active players with 36, with Jonathan Joseph (who retired in June) second with 32. Peters' six career interception return touchdowns tie him with Malcolm Jenkins for second on the active list, third if you count Joseph with seven. Janoris Jenkins (eight) is the active leader. ❧ Marlon Humphrey finished second in the NFL to Tennessee's Malcolm Butler with 93 targets, but his 5.8 yards allowed per attempt ranked sixth among qualifying cornerbacks. ❧ Safeties Chuck Clark and DeShon Elliott barely missed a snap last season and were a big reason why the Ravens finished sixth in DVOA against both deep passes and over-the-middle passes. Clark and Elliott are both former sixth-round picks whom the Ravens slowly developed. ❧ Slot cornerback Tavon Young missed 2017 with an ACL injury, 2019 with a neck injury, and most of last season with another ACL injury. The Ravens are hoping he can finally stay healthy so Humphrey can spend more time outside. If you ever see Young and Jason Verrett in the same place, get as far away as you can before a tornado touches down upon them. ❧ Third-round pick Brandon Stephens started his college career as a UCLA running back, then transferred to SMU, moved to cornerback, and became a two-year starter and team captain for the Mustangs. He's the kind of player the Ravens have been drafting in middle rounds and developing into useful starters since about the turn of the century. ❧ Fifth-round pick Shaun Wade could step into the slot role if/when Young gets injured. Wade excelled in the slot early in his Ohio State career before struggling with the transition to outside cornerback in 2020. ❧ Jimmy Smith is back for his 11th season. A holdover (along with McPhee) from the Ray Lewis/Ed Reed era, Smith slides from free safety to cornerback as needed. According to *The Washington Post*, Smith and Lamar Jackson spent some of their time during OTAs trying to dodge cicadas between drills. They should have been protecting Tavon Young from getting carried away and buried in the forest for 17 years.

Special Teams

Year	DVOA	Rank	FG/XP	Rank	Net Kick	Rank	Kick Ret	Rank	Net Punt	Rank	Punt Ret	Rank	Hidden	Rank
2018	2.9%	6	11.0	3	0.9	15	-1.3	18	-3.4	25	7.5	2	8.3	9
2019	1.5%	9	14.1	1	0.5	17	-1.4	21	-6.4	25	0.5	14	-3.7	23
2020	7.4%	2	10.6	4	6.4	4	8.9	1	9.4	5	1.5	12	12.5	4

Justin Tucker missed three field goals in the 2020 playoffs after going 12-of-13 in his prior postseason career. In the windy playoff loss to Buffalo, he missed two field goals in one game for the first time since December of 2018, when he missed 56- and 65-yarders against the Chargers; it was just the fourth two-miss game of his career. Tucker attempts fewer 50-plus-yarders than he did earlier in his career because the Ravens offense no longer stalls at the opponents' 35-yard line like clockwork. Chalk Tucker's bad playoff game to the wind and random fluctuations in a kicker's performance until there is reason to believe otherwise. Tucker is just 31 and could easily remain the NFL's best kicker for another decade. ❧ With Adam Vinatieri retired, punter Sam Koch is now the NFL's oldest kicking specialist; he turns 39 in September. Johnny Townsend replaced Koch briefly during a COVID quarantine in late December and remains on the roster but is likely just a camp leg. ❧ Devin Duvernay was excellent on kickoff returns, with a touchdown against the Chiefs and 35-plus-yarders against the Browns, Eagles, and Titans. Duvernay also took over punt returns from James Proche late in the season. He may handle both chores this year if Proche is caught in a numbers game on the wide receiver depth chart. ❧ Regression watch for 2021: Opposing field goal kickers were worth an estimated 14.7 points worse than average against Baltimore, by far the worst figure in the league last season. Remarkably, this was despite Baltimore being quite low in how many field goal attempts were tried by their opponents: only 24, when the NFL average is 30. Opposing kickers hit just 16 of those 24 attempts, including three misses by Greg Zuerlein in one Week 13 game (won by the Ravens 34-17). Opposing kickers also shanked five extra points against Baltimore.

Buffalo Bills

2020 Record: 13-3	**Total DVOA:** 23.8% (13)	**2021 Mean Projection:** 10.2 wins	**On the Clock (0-5):** 5%
Pythagorean Wins: 10.9 (5)	**Offense:** 15.6% (5)	**Postseason Odds:** 67.6%	**Mediocrity (6-8):** 21%
Snap-Weighted Age: 26.6 (13)	**Defense:** -2.2% (12)	**Super Bowl Odds:** 13.1%	**Playoff Contender (9-11):** 42%
Average Opponent: -1.6% (22)	**Special Teams:** 5.9% (4)	**Proj. Avg. Opponent:** -2.4% (29)	**Super Bowl Contender (12+):** 33%

2020: You analyze me, tend to despise me / There may come a day when I'll dance on your grave.

2021: At last it's the real thing (or close enough to pretend).

So. Let's all agree this is a little bit awkward. But the only way out is through.

When Josh Allen was coming out of school, the analytics community as a whole responded very, very negatively—and we here at Football Outsiders were no exception. In *Football Outsiders Almanac 2018*, Allen was called a "parody of an NFL quarterback prospect," referencing a QBASE projection that gave Allen a 65% chance of busting and just a 5% chance of developing into an elite passer. With horrendous accuracy at Wyoming, Allen's comparables were players such as C.J. Beathard, Connor Cook, and Christian Hackenberg. "A lot of belief has to be invested to get to the point where the Bills have a good offense *two seasons from now*," we wrote. Or, in other words, in 2020.

Bills fans had that belief from the start. It took stats-minded writers a little longer to come on board. I wrote the 2019 chapter covering Allen's rookie year, and while I found plenty of praise for Allen's legs, improvement over the course of the year, and flashes of highlight-play potential, I had *strong* negative words to say about Allen's accuracy, decision-making, and ability to handle pressure—"so many negative things he needs to overcome." All of those improved some from Year 1 to Year 2, but last year's chapter (written by Derrik Klassen) said that Allen was "unlikely to take a massive leap from Year 2 to Year 3," and that Allen would need to have a massive improvement to be "an average NFL quarterback, let alone a good one."

All of this was backed up by thoroughly researched stats and historical evidence. All of the stats and evidence were laid out in perfectly good tables. And we all know what Bills fans do to perfectly good tables.

Josh Allen's explosion into an elite passer has shifted the balance of power in the AFC. Allen blasted right past average with the third-highest passing DVOA and fourth-highest passing DYAR in the league. Those stats alone don't even scratch just how important Allen was to the Bills. Buffalo passed the ball 64% of the time in neutral situations[1], second in the

league behind only Patrick Mahomes and the Chiefs. And when you add in Allen's rushes, both scrambles and designed, his share of those situation-neutral plays rises to a very nice 69%, highest in the league. If you would have told us three years ago that no offense in football would rely more on their quarterback than Josh Allen and the Bills, we would have assumed disaster, destruction, and dismay, not the fifth-best offense in the league.

What we saw last year from Allen was unprecedented. From 1983 to 2020, 87 different quarterbacks have qualified for our main leaderboards in both their second and third NFL seasons. Allen put up the biggest increase in passing DYAR we have ever seen, and the second-biggest increase in DVOA, the second-biggest increase in completion percentage, and the second-biggest increase in yards per attempt (Table 1).[2]

Table 1. Biggest Year 3 Improvements by Passing DYAR, 1983-2020

Year	Player	Team	DYAR+	DVOA+	Y/A+	CMP%+
2020	Josh Allen	BUF	1,453	37.7%	1.64	9.8%
2005	Carson Palmer	CIN	1,134	30.8%	1.05	5.5%
1985	Ken O'Brien	NYJ	1,097	27.4%	0.78	3.4%
1991	Troy Aikman	DAL	1,049	44.0%	1.26	8.7%
1988	Jim Everett	LAR	1,023	21.4%	0.88	5.9%
1986	Jay Schroeder	WAS	825	11.9%	0.80	-2.6%
2012	Sam Bradford	STL	780	23.3%	1.20	6.8%
1994	Craig Erickson	TB	771	28.5%	0.87	5.2%
2000	Brian Griese	DEN	743	35.3%	1.39	5.7%
1996	Gus Frerotte	WAS	713	20.6%	0.47	6.8%

Minimum 200 pass attempts in Year 2 and Year 3.

Allen also had the second biggest improvement we've ever seen between Year 1 and Year 3, sandwiched between Jared Goff and Matthew Stafford. In just three seasons, Allen has

---

[1] Defined here as games with the scoring margin within 10 points in the first half or eight points in the third quarter, the same guidelines we use for situation-neutral pace.

[2] The largest Year 3 increase in yards per attempt belonged to Randall Cunningham in 1987. The largest Year 3 increase in completion percentage belonged to, of all people, former Bills quarterback J.P. Losman in 2006.

2021 Bills Schedule

Week	Opp.	Week	Opp.	Week	Opp.
1	PIT	7	BYE	13	NE (Mon.)
2	at MIA	8	MIA	14	at TB
3	WAS	9	at JAX	15	CAR
4	HOU	10	at NYJ	16	at NE
5	at KC	11	IND	17	ATL
6	at TEN (Mon.)	12	at NO (Thu.)	18	NYJ

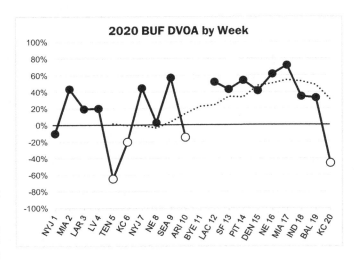

2020 BUF DVOA by Week

transformed himself from on-field liability to one of the most valuable players in football.

The point of these essays is to look forward, not backward, and to predict how the team will do in 2021, not to dwell on predictions of years past. And yet, it feels a bit disingenuous not to emphasize just how much better Allen has done than *any* analytically based projection system had him coming out of college; how he and the Bills are doing better than any of us thought possible a few seasons ago. We gave Allen a 5% chance of developing into an elite player, sure, and 5% chances do occasionally happen ... roughly 5% of the time if everything's calibrated properly. We're nerds; we know that sometimes you roll a 20 and have a critical success. But we're human, too. We see something with a very low probability, and we tend to dismiss it as impossible, or at least unlikely enough to not be worth considering. You didn't need sodium pentothal to know that we felt the Bills made a mistake by trading up for Allen.

Are the Bills fortunate that Allen developed better than expected? Yes, but let's not pretend this was all luck. Endless amounts of credit have to go to Allen for tremendous improvement in his mechanics and his ability to read the field, and to Sean McDermott, Brian Daboll, and the rest of the offensive staff for crafting an offense that not only plays to Allen's strengths, but is designed around putting their passer in advantageous situations as frequently as possible. We may be eating humble pie, but if the end result is one of the more entertaining and analytically sound offenses in the league, well, our compliments to the chefs.

So, with all that being said, the question is—can the Bills do it again?

Vegas lines tend to have Buffalo as co-favorites in the AFC, or at least a clear second place behind Kansas City. Our projections are a little less rosy—still AFC East champs, but more in the range of good rather than great. That's not to say that they don't come out as contenders by any stretch of the imagination, but our numbers are clearly a bit lower on Buffalo than the general consensus.

What the Bills are running into here, at least in part, is the Plexiglass Principle, which states that teams that significantly improve (or decline) in one season have a tendency to relapse (or bounce back) in the next. The Bills jumped from a 1.6% DVOA in 2019 to 23.8% in 2020. They were one of six teams to have a jump of at least 20 percentage points, and the only one to do it without a head coaching or quarterback change to explain the increase.

Teams that improve by that much in one season tend to regress back towards the mean the year afterwards (Table 2). Progress in the NFL is typically more gradual; personnel changes and standard player development generally don't produce huge year-to-year fluctuations. A jump of that magnitude is usually a combination of an improvement in skill *and* an improvement in luck—in a 16-game sample size, sometimes a team is simply going to go on a hot streak due to sheer randomness. That's not to say the underlying team isn't better, or that they won't continue to get better the next season, but luck isn't a reliable skill. Buffalo now finds itself part of the 20/20 club—teams with at least a 20.0% DVOA and a 20-point improvement from the year before. Last year's inductees were the 49ers and the Ravens; both fell significantly in 2020, as has most every other team to find itself in that situation. There have been 58 20/20 club members since 1983; only six improved their DVOA in the following season, and the average drop was 18.5%.

Table 2. Plexiglass Bounces, 1984-2019

DVOA Change	Teams	DVOA Change Y+1	Win Change Y+1	Pct of Teams Improving	Pct of Teams Decreasing
+30% or Better	63	-9.5%	-1.5	23.8%	76.2%
+20% to +30%	95	-10.3%	-1.5	26.3%	73.7%
+10% to +20%	178	-6.0%	-1.0	36.5%	63.5%
+0% to +10%	198	-0.7%	+0.0	46.5%	53.5%
-10% to 0%	228	1.6%	+0.3	51.8%	48.2%
-20% to -10%	179	3.5%	+0.1	58.1%	41.9%
-30% to -20%	95	10.3%	+2.0	74.7%	25.3%
-30% or worse	57	15.2%	+2.2	78.9%	21.1%

Now, Plexiglass isn't gospel—Buffalo themselves improved by 20.2% between 2018 and 2019 and kept improving last year, though there's no evidence that beating projections one year means anything going forward. And a slight decline isn't the end of the world—the 2019 Chiefs were one of those 20/20 clubs that slid slightly in the regular season, and they ended up winning the Super Bowl. But there is certainly enough of a trend there, above and beyond simple regression to the mean, to be at least a concern for Plexiglass teams.

Every team that finds itself in this position thinks it will be different; it will be one of the 25% that pushes through and keeps getting better. And we have, in past years, found some situations which do tend to temper Plexiglass bounces. Teams with an obvious external reason for improvement—specifically, a new head coach or new starting quarterback—do tend to experience less of a Plexiglass bounce than average, though they still tend to cede some ground. The Bills don't fall into that category; they're banking on Josh Allen's development being the factor that helps them beat the odds. Supporters argue that the Bills weren't fortunate to have their first positive offensive DVOA since 2016 and their best mark since 1998; this was the culmination of a dedicated plan, and everything will keep firing on all cylinders going forwards.

And you know what? I think they're right. Or mostly right, at the very least.

First things first: Allen's improvement didn't come out of nowhere. We're highlighting Allen's improvement from 2019 to 2020, but Allen actually had one of the top 25 improvements we have ever seen between his rookie and sophomore seasons as well, jumping by over 400 combined DYAR to reach replacement level. In many ways, it was a miniature version of what we saw in 2020. A significant upgrade at receiver, going from Zay Jones and Kelvin Benjamin to John Brown and Cole Beasley, coupled with a year of experience in the system, led to Allen increasing his completion percentage over expected (CPOE) by five percentage points, going from a league-worst -8.3% to a simply bad -2.4%. He still couldn't hit the broad side of a barn, but he could at least hit the farm on a regular basis. That was the 11th-biggest year-to-year CPOE improvement we have seen (since 2006), somewhat foreshadowing 2020's seventh-biggest jump. Had he just repeated that sort of improvement, Allen would have ranked 16th in DYAR last season, right next to Baker Mayfield and Philip Rivers. That alone would likely have been enough to make Buffalo a playoff contender.

There's not a lot of history of players improving their DYAR after both their first and second seasons; Allen is just the 15th to do so while qualifying for the leaderboards all three years. The players that *did* pull that feat off, however, are quite impressive—Peyton Manning, Troy Aikman, and John Elway are all Hall of Famers; Derek Carr, Andrew Luck, and Ryan Tannehill are all Pro Bowlers. Even after the top tier, you get players who ended up with long careers as a starter such as Bernie Kosar and Joe Flacco.

Now, it should be noted that players who saw their DYAR improve two years in a row do tend to do a little worse the next season. You have probably just had a pretty good season if you keep improving, and at some point, you hit a ceiling. Players in their twenties who just had back-to-back improvements drop, on average, by -298 DYAR the following season, compared to -125 for players who are coming off of just one

year of better play. That's simple regression to the mean. But double-improvers end up with an average of 665 DYAR, compared to 439 for single-improvers. It's quite possible that 2020 ends up being Allen's career-best season; everyone has to hit a high-water mark at some point. Only 12 other players have had multiple years as good as Allen's 2020, and 10 are or will be Hall of Famers.[3] Still, even if 2021 ends up not being quite as sharp, Allen's continual improvement helps set him apart from the Matt Cassels and Nick Foleses of the word. He's not a one-year wonder riding high on a lucky year.

The headline for Allen's improvement in 2020 was his accuracy. One of the major reasons that models were so dubious of Allen's potential was the scattershot nature of his throws; he had never completed even 60% of his passes at Wyoming, or at Reedley College, or even in high school. And while a player can work on their technique and footwork and improve their accuracy in a vacuum, doing so in game positions, while on the move and throwing from different platforms, is another matter entirely. Allen's completion percentage was always going to be lower than average thanks to his penchant for the deep ball, but even in 2019 his CPOE on passes 16 or more yards downfield was -6.3%, fourth worst among qualified passers. A full 42% of his deep shots two years ago were charted as either under- or overthrown, including 26 miscues from a clean pocket. And then all of a sudden, last year Allen becomes the third-most accurate passer in all of football. His 7.6% CPOE on deep shots was eighth best in the league (and his 8.1 completions over expectation third most in the league) and his inaccurate passes dropped to 34%. 2020 was the year Allen's howitzer gained a targeting system.

Allen credits this improvement to working on his mechanics, digitally mapping his throwing motion, and making tweaks to his sequencing. It jumps out on film—his lower body isn't hopping around as much as it was, helping his balance and weight transfer, and his throwing angle is more consistent. All that helps, but equally important is Allen's comfort in the system. Two years ago, it felt like alarm bells started flashing at the slightest sign of pressure. Allen would abandon the play and try to make something happen with his legs or with a heroball throw. It was sandlot ball which occasionally worked out thanks to Allen's athleticism. Things improved a little bit in 2019, but Allen was still just 22nd out of 34 in DVOA when pressured; if things weren't going well, you could see him getting antsy. In 2020, it clicked. Allen was third best in the league with a -11.3% DVOA when pressured and displayed a calmness and understanding of the offense that simply wasn't there in previous seasons. It's the combination of having the offense internalized and the mechanics to pull it off that has turned Allen's talent into production. That's not to say things were perfect—Allen still tends to hold on to the ball a bit too long and has a tendency to miss high when on the move. But throws that were uncatchable ducks in 2019 became catchable balls in 2020.

And when you throw a catchable ball, Stefon Diggs is going to catch it; it's kind of his thing. Diggs replacing John

---

[3] The two exceptions here are Daunte Culpepper, who won't make the Hall of Fame, and Philip Rivers, who might.

Brown as Allen's most targeted receiver opened everything else up. Not only did Diggs set franchise records and nearly top our leaderboards when targeted, but the attention and respect given to him opened defenses up for everyone beneath him, giving them easier cornerbacks to work against and more space in which to work. Opposing defenses gave Diggs an extra yard of cushion compared to what they had given Brown the year before, and as Diggs is a more complete route-runner compared to Browns' skill set, he averaged an extra 0.6 yards of separation compared to 2019 Brown—even if Allen hadn't become more accurate, more of those near-catchable balls would have come down in Diggs' hands. The extra attention Diggs drew freed up Cole Beasley to have a career year, and let Gabriel Davis have plenty of room to break out. By adding Diggs to the top and letting the other receivers take one step down on the ladder, Buffalo essentially improved every spot in their receiving corps. If anything, they had too many quality receivers—only the Cardinals ran more four-wide sets than Buffalo did last year.

Bills fans should trust in Brian Daboll's offense, which is built out of positive throwing situations. Run down a checklist of Repeated Analytical Talking Points and the Bills tick pretty much every box. Passing more efficient than running? As previously mentioned, no team passed more in neutral situations than Buffalo did. Play-action successful even without a running game? The Bills led the league by using play-action 36% of the time, with the third-highest DVOA, despite running the ball a bare minimum of the time. Pre-snap motion forcing the defense to show their hand early and disrupt their coverages? While the Bills were middle-of-the-pack in overall offensive motion, they were in the top five when it came to having someone in motion as the ball was snapped. Don't run into stacked boxes? 41% of Buffalo's rushing attempts came with six or fewer defenders by the line of scrimmage, fourth most in the league. Tick, tick, tick, tick, tick. You could identify Buffalo's offense as one of the soundest in the league before watching a second of film, though then you would miss out on all the finer points of Daboll's play calling; his adjustments to take advantage of defensive tendencies and the like which helped turn a solid plan on paper into the best offense Buffalo has seen since the K-Gun era. Buffalo's passing attack was ruthless last season, taking full advantage of Allen's exceptional development and the new toys they had to work with in the receiving game. All young quarterbacks should be so lucky as to have this kind of system to develop in.

We're not saying Buffalo's offense is perfect, by any means. The interior line was shaky for most of last season and didn't gel until the last month and a half of the year. The Bills weren't particularly efficient when they did run the ball, and the duo of Zack Moss and Devin Singletary needs to perform better (if not actually run *more*) in 2021 to help the Bills get better at situational football—running out the clock and holding onto leads and things of that nature. The Bills essentially abandoned running inside by the end of the year; they only had 31 rushes listed as "middle" or "guard" between the 20s after their bye, less than two a game and by far the fewest in the league. You can see why McDermott would highlight the

running game as the first area where Buffalo has to do better going forward; it's not good when the other teams knows you just can't do something. The overarching point, however, is that the optimism Bills fans have about their offense can be supported by the film and the analytics. After a few years at sixes and sevens, it's nice to be back on the same page.

And, of course, the Plexiglass bends both ways. Our projections have McDemott and Leslie Frazier's defense rebounding to very good status after some early-season struggles last year. There were injuries to deal with, with Matt Milano, Tremaine Edmunds, Tre'Davious White, Levi Wallace, and Josh Norman, among others, all missing time. There were also growing pains along the defensive line as Buffalo worked out a new rotation replacing Shaq Lawson and Jordan Phillips. Before their bye, the Bills ranked 17th with a 2.1% DVOA, a far cry from what we had come to expect. But those problems quieted down as the year went along; the team got healthier and players settled into their new roles; Buffalo's defense was sixth in the league over the final weeks of the season. The model sees a defense that was top-10 two years in a row and then stumbled for a season, and assumes the latter was the outlier, bouncing it back toward its historical averages.

Buffalo also wisely spent draft day bolstering the defensive line. The Bills only generated pressure on 25.3% of pass plays in 2020—that's league average, which isn't where you want to be if you're contending for Super Bowls and having to chase down Patrick Mahomes. Jerry Hughes did have 31 hurries, but no one else on the team topped 20, and there was a distinct lack of depth on the edge. After flirting with the idea of bringing in J.J. Watt through free agency, the Bills instead used their first two draft picks on the fourth- and fifth-best edge rusher prospects according to SackSEER, Gregory Rousseau and Boogie Basham. That won't produce as big of an immediate impact as bringing in a high-priced free agent, with both picks likely playing more rotational roles to start with—and, in fact, second-round pick Basham might be more game-ready than first-rounder Rousseau—but it's a wiser long-term strategy than going out and splurging on high-priced free agents. The Bills aren't necessarily trying to go all in on winning a Super Bowl this season; they're trying to solidify their position so they can compete for an extended period of time.

The Bills' pass rush in 2021 would likely have been better if they had, say, passed on re-signing Matt Milano and used the cap room to bring in Watt or Carl Lawson or Jadeveon Clowney. But that would have put the team in a bind when it came to extending Allen and other key players; the sustainable way to build a team is through savvy draft picks and finding value. You could make an argument that the Bills were in a position last offseason where they needed a big player such as Stefon Diggs to help propel the offense over the top, to turn it into a top unit that could be legitimately considered a contender. But now, the Bills are *there*. Even if they just ran back everyone they had last year, they would be serious Super Bowl contenders, and they didn't need another superstar to help put them over the top. The goal now is to stay in that position for as long as possible, to get the most bites at the apple while both the offense and defense are playing at a high level. And if those rookie defenders develop faster than expected, so much the better—but it's something that would be nice to have, as opposed to a necessity if the Bills are going to compete for a title.

And we do believe the Bills are going to be serious contenders. Last season, we ended the chapter by noting that Buffalo's roster had been built up as successfully as any coach and general manager duo could ask for, and there was little to suggest

a poor season other than the development of Allen. We close by saying the exact same thing this year, only now with plenty more reasons to be bullish about the passer. The parody of an NFL quarterback prospect has become a legitimate superstar, and the Bills will be near the top of our projections for as long as that holds true.

Bryan Knowles

2020 Bills Stats by Week

Wk	vs.	W-L	PF	PA	YDF	YDA	TO	Total	Off	Def	ST
1	NYJ	W	27	17	404	254	0	-9.9%	-0.7%	2.7%	-6.5%
2	at MIA	W	31	28	523	410	-1	43.9%	52.5%	9.1%	0.5%
3	LAR	W	35	32	375	478	0	19.5%	36.3%	28.5%	11.7%
4	at LV	W	30	23	337	383	2	20.3%	21.9%	2.3%	0.6%
5	at TEN	L	16	42	370	334	-3	-64.4%	-32.4%	19.7%	-12.4%
6	KC	L	17	26	206	466	0	-20.1%	-12.7%	15.3%	7.9%
7	at NYJ	W	18	10	422	191	1	44.9%	7.6%	-35.1%	2.1%
8	NE	W	24	21	339	349	0	3.0%	11.5%	8.1%	-0.4%
9	SEA	W	44	34	420	419	4	57.3%	31.4%	-14.6%	11.3%
10	at ARI	L	30	32	369	453	0	-14.5%	-11.3%	6.7%	3.6%
11	BYE										
12	LAC	W	27	17	332	367	-2	52.2%	8.1%	-28.8%	15.2%
13	at SF	W	34	24	449	402	1	43.4%	35.3%	-4.0%	4.1%
14	PIT	W	26	15	334	224	0	54.2%	13.6%	-33.2%	7.4%
15	at DEN	W	48	19	534	255	0	41.6%	40.6%	5.7%	6.8%
16	at NE	W	38	9	474	201	0	61.8%	33.5%	-15.7%	12.7%
17	MIA	W	56	26	455	454	2	72.2%	27.4%	-15.1%	29.7%
18	IND	W	27	24	397	472	0	34.8%	43.6%	14.4%	5.6%
19	BAL	W	17	3	220	340	1	33.1%	-7.1%	-50.7%	-10.5%
20	at KC	L	24	38	363	439	0	-45.5%	-26.5%	30.8%	11.9%

Trends and Splits

	Offense	Rank	Defense	Rank
Total DVOA	15.6%	5	-2.2%	12
Unadjusted VOA	15.1%	5	-3.9%	11
Weighted Trend	17.8%	5	-8.0%	8
Variance	5.2%	13	3.6%	9
Average Opponent	-0.3%	14	-1.6%	20
Passing	43.3%	3	2.2%	12
Rushing	-15.1%	22	-8.3%	17
First Down	18.8%	4	9.7%	25
Second Down	9.4%	8	-4.9%	11
Third Down	19.2%	7	-20.3%	5
First Half	20.6%	3	-3.4%	12
Second Half	9.9%	9	-1.1%	11
Red Zone	20.8%	9	-3.8%	11
Late and Close	24.3%	5	-17.5%	6

Five-Year Performance

Year	W-L	Pyth W	Est W	PF	PA	TO	Total	Rk	Off	Rk	Def	Rk	ST	Rk	Off AGL	Rk	Def AGL	Rk	Off Age	Rk	Def Age	Rk	ST Age	Rk
2016	7-9	8.5	7.2	399	378	+6	-0.7%	19	10.5%	10	9.4%	27	-1.9%	22	37.6	18	60.8	28	26.6	19	27.2	6	27.3	1
2017	9-7	6.3	6.8	302	359	+9	-10.7%	22	-11.1%	26	2.5%	18	2.9%	10	28.9	12	18.0	8	27.8	2	26.8	11	27.5	1
2018	6-10	5.0	6.4	269	374	-5	-18.6%	28	-27.5%	31	-14.0%	2	-5.1%	32	15.3	4	15.7	6	26.2	24	26.6	10	27.1	2
2019	10-6	9.8	7.6	314	259	+4	1.6%	13	-7.1%	21	-9.9%	7	-1.2%	21	46.5	20	18.1	3	26.7	16	26.4	14	27.2	2
2020	13-3	10.9	12.1	501	375	+4	23.8%	4	15.6%	5	-2.2%	12	5.9%	4	28.9	8	34.2	13	26.4	22	26.8	7	26.5	7

2020 Performance Based on Most Common Personnel Groups

BUF Offense					BUF Offense vs. Opponents					BUF Defense					BUF Defense vs. Opponents			
Pers	Freq	Yds	DVOA	Run%	Pers	Freq	Yds	DVOA	Run%	Pers	Freq	Yds	DVOA	Pers	Freq	Yds	DVOA
11	73%	6.5	19.5%	33%	Base	8%	6.9	-14.7%	53%	Base	7%	5.8	15.2%	11	68%	5.9	0.1%
10	15%	7.0	39.1%	24%	Nickel	73%	6.3	16.8%	34%	Nickel	91%	5.6	-4.6%	12	18%	5.4	-9.1%
12	8%	6.8	-8.4%	61%	Dime+	18%	7.1	45.8%	31%	Dime+	1%	10.8	90.9%	21	7%	5.5	-4.5%
20	1%	6.8	73.6%	25%	Goal Line	1%	1.1	92.1%	38%	Goal Line	1%	0.9	7.5%	13	2%	3.3	-18.3%
613	1%	0.4	52.3%	38%										20	2%	4.4	-0.3%

Strategic Tendencies

Run/Pass		Rk	Formation		Rk	Pass Rush		Rk	Secondary		Rk	Strategy		Rk
Runs, first half	31%	30	Form: Single Back	80%	19	Rush 3	1.2%	31	4 DB	7%	30	Play Action	36%	1
Runs, first down	36%	31	Form: Empty Back	11%	10	Rush 4	67.5%	12	5 DB	91%	1	Offensive Motion	41%	21
Runs, second-long	30%	11	Form: Multi Back	9%	16	Rush 5	23.1%	10	6+ DB	1%	28	Avg Box (Off)	6.46	20
Runs, power sit.	69%	6	Pers: 3+ WR	90%	1	Rush 6+	8.2%	5	Man Coverage	27%	22	Avg Box (Def)	6.64	12
Runs, behind 2H	21%	31	Pers: 2+ TE/6+ OL	10%	31	Edge Rusher Sacks	35.5%	30	CB by Sides	61%	28	Offensive Pace	29.78	11
Pass, ahead 2H	57%	3	Pers: 6+ OL	2%	17	Interior DL Sacks	18.4%	22	S/CB Cover Ratio	23%	25	Defensive Pace	29.65	5
Run-Pass Options	9%	12	Shotgun/Pistol	71%	11	Second Level Sacks	46.1%	1	DB Blitz	19%	2	Go for it on 4th	1.49	18

Josh Allen faced a defensive back blitz on a league-leading 21% of pass plays. It was the third straight year he was near the top of the league. He didn't struggle against these blitzes like he did in his first two years, although Buffalo's 7.8% DVOA on these plays was lower than the Bills' passing DVOA otherwise. ✎ The Bills went with four-wide 10 personnel on 15% of plays, second in the league behind Arizona. They were phenomenal on these plays, averaging 7.0 yards with 39.1% DVOA. ✎ Buffalo used the pistol on 5% of plays, fourth in the league, and had an excellent 36.4% DVOA on these plays with an average of 5.7 yards. Overall, Buffalo had the league's largest gap in DVOA between plays from shotgun or pistol and plays with the quarterback under center. ✎ The Bills offense climbed from below average to top of the league in frequency of using play-action. ✎ Buffalo receivers dropped just 4.0% of passes (fourth), a year after dropping 7.1% of passes (31st in 2019). ✎ Sean McDermott defenses have always shown very strong personnel tendencies: near the top of the league in nickel with no dime. ✎ Buffalo had the smallest gap in the league between defensive DVOA with and without pass pressure. With pressure, Buffalo had -36.5% defensive DVOA, 30th in the league. Without pressure, Buffalo had 15.7% defensive DVOA, sixth in the league. ✎ Compared with 2019, Buffalo's rate of interior line sacks dropped by more than half while the rate of second-level sacks more than doubled. ✎ For the second straight year, Buffalo opponents threw the lowest rate of passes deep, with just 13% of attempts going 16 or more air yards. After they were second in the league against these passes in 2019, the Bills declined to league average in 2020. ✎ The Bills were strong against wide receiver screens for the third straight year (-10.9% DVOA) but struggled against running back screens (26.0% DVOA).

Passing

Player	DYAR	DVOA	Plays	NtYds	Avg	YAC	C%	TD	Int
J.Allen	1460	25.9%	598	4385	7.3	4.7	69.2%	37	10
M.Barkley*	21	4.5%	22	190	8.6	5.0	52.4%	1	1
M.Trubisky	79	-7.5%	315	1930	6.1	5.0	67.0%	16	8

Rushing

Player	DYAR	DVOA	Plays	Yds	Avg	TD	Fum	Suc
D.Singletary	-20	-11.5%	156	687	4.4	2	1	49%
Z.Moss	23	-4.1%	112	481	4.3	4	0	53%
J.Allen	74	3.0%	80	441	5.5	8	4	--
A.Williams	20	33.1%	12	63	5.3	2	0	58%
T.J.Yeldon*	13	16.1%	10	70	7.0	0	1	60%
I.McKenzie	-22	-77.3%	10	9	0.9	0	0	--
M.Breida	-8	-11.8%	59	254	4.3	0	2	56%
M.Trubisky	9	-7.0%	33	195	5.9	1	1	--

Receiving

Player	DYAR	DVOA	Plays	Ctch	Yds	Y/C	YAC	TD	C%
S.Diggs	377	15.8%	166	127	1535	12.1	3.7	8	77%
C.Beasley	267	19.9%	107	82	967	11.8	4.3	4	77%
G.Davis	115	10.7%	62	35	599	17.1	3.7	7	56%
J.Brown*	99	11.4%	52	33	458	13.9	5.4	3	63%
I.McKenzie	99	25.1%	34	30	282	9.4	6.3	5	88%
E.Sanders	150	9.6%	82	61	726	11.9	2.8	5	74%
B.Powell	-40	-41.2%	18	12	69	5.8	2.8	2	67%
D.Knox	-13	-11.6%	44	24	288	12.0	6.7	3	55%
T.Kroft*	42	29.2%	16	12	119	9.9	3.7	3	75%
L.Smith*	8	6.9%	6	4	35	8.8	5.0	2	67%
J.Hollister	-11	-11.5%	40	25	209	8.4	3.2	3	63%
D.Singletary	32	-2.2%	50	38	269	7.1	7.1	0	76%
Z.Moss	29	13.4%	18	14	95	6.8	6.2	1	78%
M.Breida	42	49.9%	10	9	96	10.7	10.7	0	90%

Offensive Line

Player	Pos	Age	GS	Snaps	Pen	Sk	Pass	Run	Player	Pos	Age	GS	Snaps	Pen	Sk	Pass	Run
Daryl Williams	RT	29	16/16	1048	8	2.5	12	5	Jon Feliciano	RG	29	9/9	571	2	0.5	9	7
Dion Dawkins	LT	27	16/16	1032	4	4.5	27	6	Cody Ford	LG	25	7/7	383	3	0.5	6	6
Mitch Morse	C	29	14/14	878	5	1	6	6	Forrest Lamp	LG	27	16/16	1173	1	1.0	21	14
Ike Boettger	LG	27	12/7	622	4	0	13	6	Bobby Hart	RT	27	14/13	871	3	4.5	23	5
Brian Winters*	RG	30	16/9	616	7	2	18	5									

Year	Yards	ALY	Rk	Power	Rk	Stuff	Rk	2Lev	Rk	OpFld	Rk	BB Rt	Rk	Sacks	ASR	Rk	Press	Rk	BB Rt	Rk	Cont
2018	3.53	3.89	30	68%	14	21%	23	0.92	32	0.43	30	4.3%	5	41	8.0%	23	35.3%	28	9.6%	18	32
2019	4.26	4.32	15	58%	24	22%	28	1.27	10	0.78	17	8.6%	8	40	7.8%	23	31.6%	23	11.5%	6	37
2020	4.49	4.36	15	66%	17	17%	15	1.26	13	0.87	9	12.1%	27	27	4.8%	5	30.5%	27	14.1%	23	27

2020 ALY by direction:	Left End: 4.75 (7)	Left Tackle: 4.47 (14)	Mid/Guard: 4.17 (23)	Right Tackle: 3.80 (26)	Right End: 5.96 (3)

While Dion Dawkins and Daryl Williams started every game at tackle, the interior of the line saw a good amount of turmoil. Buffalo had seven different starting lineup combinations, with five different combos at guard alone. A combination of injuries (Mitch Morse, Cody Ford) and poor play (Quinton Spain, Brian Winters) kept the line in flux until the last eight games of the season. Once the interior stopped shuffling every other game, however, the performance of the line as a whole increased. Over that final stretch of the season, the Bills ranked second in adjusted sack rate and 10th in adjusted line yards. Continuity on your line is good for your offense! ⬤ Dawkins' 27 blown blocks in the passing game were a career high and seventh most in the league. Of course, that's because Dawkins was pass-blocking more than ever before in Buffalo's new offense; it may well have been his best year to date. ⬤ Williams also had his best season. The ex-Panther had career bests in blown blocks, sacks allowed, run stuffs, you name it—except for penalties, where he was whistled for five false starts last year after having just one in his career before 2020. ⬤ Mitch Morse is one of the league's better pass-blockers, but his work in the running game has never overly impressed. In Buffalo, Morse has blown a pass block once every 75 snaps and whiffed on a run block once every 40. All five of his holding flags have been in the run game, too. ⬤ Guard remains the weak point on the line. Jon Feliciano is a decent run-blocker but not great at pass protection; Cody Ford's lack of lateral movement means he looked better at guard than tackle, but that's not saying too much. Forrest Lamp (ex-Chargers) and Jamil Douglas (in Tennessee the last three seasons) should provide some competition there, though the Bills hope Feliciano and Ford will win those battles. ⬤ Northern Iowa's Spencer Brown is a bit of a developmental project. Buffalo's third-round pick is agile with good hand and foot speed, making him dangerous in space. He's also 6-foot-8 and plays like it; there are issues with his high center of gravity and getting his pad level low enough to win leverage battles. Those are issues that could get fixed with some experience and coaching, but at the moment he's a swing tackle with some potential to be more rather than a Day 1 starter. ⬤ Fifth-round tackle Tommy Doyle is tall (6-foot-7, 315 pounds) and athletic (a 7.57s 3-cone), but not technically sound—toolsy rather than polished.

Defensive Front

Defensive Line	Age	Pos	G	Snaps	Plays	TmPct	Rk	Stop	Dfts	BTkl	Runs	St%	Rk	RuYd	Rk	Sack	Hit	Hur	Dsrpt
						Overall						vs. Run				Pass Rush			
Ed Oliver	24	DT	16	578	36	4.3%	61	27	13	3	28	68%	68	2.4	45	3.0	5	20	3
Quinton Jefferson*	28	DT	16	534	24	2.9%	85	16	9	2	19	58%	91	2.6	53	3.0	9	10	2
Vernon Butler	27	DT	14	428	19	2.6%	90	16	6	0	17	82%	16	1.1	3	0.0	2	9	3
Harrison Phillips	25	DT	12	332	18	2.9%	86	15	1	0	18	83%	13	2.1	36	0.0	4	7	1
Justin Zimmer	29	DT	12	275	21	3.3%	--	15	6	3	19	68%	--	1.8	--	1.0	6	9	0

Edge Rushers	Age	Pos	G	Snaps	Plays	TmPct	Rk	Stop	Dfts	BTkl	Runs	St%	Rk	RuYd	Rk	Sack	Hit	Hur	Dsrpt
						Overall						vs. Run				Pass Rush			
Jerry Hughes	33	DE	15	629	32	4.1%	64	25	12	6	21	76%	31	2.9	60	4.5	8	31	5
Mario Addison	34	DE	15	606	34	4.3%	58	23	9	7	17	71%	53	2.3	36	5.0	3	20	6
Trent Murphy*	31	DE	10	343	19	3.6%	73	10	4	2	10	40%	96	2.3	37	2.0	4	6	0
A.J. Epenesa	23	DE	14	291	15	2.0%	--	13	5	1	12	83%	--	1.0	--	1.0	4	7	1
Efe Obada	29	DE	16	415	18	2.2%	--	16	9	2	11	82%	--	2.5	--	5.5	8	10	0

Linebackers	Age	Pos	G	Snaps	Plays	TmPct	Rk	Stop	Dfts	BTkl	Runs	St%	Rk	RuYd	Rk	Sack	Hit	Hur	Tgts	Suc%	Rk	Yd/P	Rk	PD	Int
						Overall						vs. Run				Pass Rush				vs. Pass					
Tremaine Edmunds	23	MLB	15	911	122	15.5%	17	52	17	14	71	49%	69	4.2	52	2.0	1	4	43	49%	43	6.7	49	3	0
A.J. Klein	30	OLB	16	652	77	9.1%	65	44	14	14	37	62%	22	3.3	18	5.0	3	9	26	54%	25	4.9	16	4	0
Matt Milano	27	OLB	10	335	48	9.1%	66	26	13	3	20	45%	76	5.2	82	3.5	6	11	22	73%	2	4.1	7	3	1
Tyrel Dodson	23	MLB	10	172	22	4.2%	--	9	4	3	6	50%	--	3.5	--	1.0	0	0	5	60%	--	5.4	--	2	0
Tyrell Adams	29	ILB	16	812	126	14.5%	28	53	18	14	66	47%	73	4.0	43	2.0	1	3	39	41%	59	7.2	57	4	0

Year	Yards	ALY	Rk	Power	Rk	Stuff	Rk	2Lev	Rk	OpFld	Rk	BB Rt	Rk	Sacks	ASR	Rk	Press	Rk	BB Rt	Rk
2018	4.14	4.15	10	62%	9	26%	1	1.33	24	0.76	13	8.5%	16	36	6.9%	19	33.3%	4	10.8%	15
2019	4.37	4.15	12	59%	8	25%	4	1.32	26	0.90	26	10.2%	27	44	7.2%	13	31.1%	12	16.2%	7
2020	4.51	4.48	19	61%	7	19%	11	1.48	32	0.71	18	12.6%	16	38	6.8%	14	25.3%	15	12.8%	19

2020 ALY by direction:	Left End: 5.62 (31)	Left Tackle: 3.97 (13)	Mid/Guard: 4.56 (20)	Right Tackle: 3.60 (4)	Right End: 3.99 (7)

It's not too difficult to see why the Bills spent their first two picks on pass-rushers. While Buffalo's total of 38 sacks last season was middle-of-the-pack, nearly half those sacks were of the "non-pressure" varieties. They had nine coverage sacks and a league-high nine sacks on failed scrambles—five from Sam Darnold alone. A 47% non-pressure sack rate was third highest in the league; if the front seven could generate more sacks on their own, that would make life much easier for the secondary. ❧ Jerry Hughes was second in ESPN's Pass Rush Win Rate despite only recording 4.5 sacks; adding more talent around him will hopefully translate more of those pressures into big plays. ❧ Mario Addison was floated as a potential cap casualty after his worst season in sacks, hurries, QB hits, and knockdowns since 2013. He's still here, but expect A.J. Epenesa to see more work, like he did down the stretch last year. ❧ The Bills are still waiting for that Ed Oliver breakout season, and 2021 may be his last chance. While his athleticism still flashes on film, his run stop rate was just 40th out of 57 interior linemen, and frankly and even that probably overstates his effectiveness. ❧ Star Lotulelei is returning after opting out of 2020; he should provide stouter run defense than Vernon Butler did a year ago. ❧ Matt Milano has now ranked third, second, and second in pass coverage success rate over the past three years; he's a big reason Buffalo can play so much nickel instead of dime. ❧ Tremaine Edmunds had his fifth-year option picked up. He regressed in pass coverage last year and hasn't really lived up to his draft position, but he's still only 23 years old, younger than half of this year's draft class. ❧ Re-signing Milano and reupping Edmunds makes more sense when you note that A.J. Klein had 14 broken tackles. His 25% broken-tackle rate was second worst in the league for linebackers with at least 40 tackles. ❧ First-round pick Gregory Rousseau (Miami) was underwhelming in SackSEER, only ninth in rating and fourth in sack projections. Poor workout results, especially in the vertical and broad jumps, raise questions about his explosion potential, and he struggled when lined up as a true edge rusher in college. He had more success as an inside rusher, and that may be where he starts his career. With only seven games of starting experience, he still is plenty raw. ❧ Even though he was drafted a round later, SackSEER likes Carlos "Boogie" Basham (Wake Forest) nearly as much as Rousseau, with both projected around 21 sacks in their first five years. Basham may be a bit bulkier than ideal at 285 pounds, but he plays with an explosiveness that belies that size.

Defensive Secondary

Secondary	Age	Pos	G	Snaps	Plays	TmPct	Rk	Stop	Dfts	BTkl	Runs	St%	Rk	RuYd	Rk	Tgts	Tgt%	Rk	aDOT	Suc%	Rk	Yd/P	Rk	PD	Int
								Overall					vs. Run							vs. Pass					
Jordan Poyer	30	SS	16	1010	123	14.6%	4	45	17	10	63	37%	35	7.7	46	34	8.4%	37	7.0	53%	27	4.9	6	5	2
Micah Hyde	31	FS	15	938	75	9.5%	49	21	6	9	39	31%	46	7.5	43	12	3.2%	69	10.0	58%	11	6.5	19	5	1
Tre'Davious White	26	CB	14	878	68	9.2%	27	27	12	6	21	43%	38	4.2	12	55	15.6%	73	10.0	55%	26	7.0	30	11	3
Taron Johnson	25	CB	16	825	100	11.9%	4	46	16	10	38	58%	11	4.1	11	61	18.4%	52	7.8	54%	28	7.4	36	7	1
Levi Wallace	26	CB	12	612	56	8.9%	35	16	7	3	13	15%	78	8.0	58	56	22.7%	17	12.0	46%	61	7.7	44	8	2
Josh Norman*	34	CB	9	344	28	5.9%	--	11	8	5	8	50%	--	4.5	--	30	21.7%	--	9.6	37%	--	7.8	--	4	1
Dane Jackson	25	CB	5	193	20	7.6%	--	8	4	3	7	29%	--	7.1	--	14	18.0%	--	8.9	50%	--	4.5	--	5	1

Year	Pass D Rank	vs. #1 WR	Rk	vs. #2 WR	Rk	vs. Other WR	Rk	WR Wide	Rk	WR Slot	Rk	vs. TE	Rk	vs. RB	Rk
2018	2	-11.2%	7	14.9%	24	-33.0%	2	-15.1%	6	-7.4%	8	-40.0%	2	-10.2%	9
2019	5	-32.8%	2	-20.7%	4	-8.1%	12	-24.4%	6	-16.7%	3	-0.3%	14	-5.8%	14
2020	12	13.0%	23	-22.8%	3	-21.7%	4	-4.4%	10	-8.9%	6	-2.6%	13	-3.5%	15

Seeing that Buffalo ranked third and fourth against second and third wideouts, but only 23rd against top receivers, is a bit counterintuitive at first. Buffalo generally has their cornerbacks match up with specific receivers, with Tre'Davious White shadowing most top wideouts around the field. Evidence that White is overrated? Well, no, it's selection bias—top wideouts actually had more targets against Levi Wallace than White, and Josh Norman nearly matched White's total as well. You can't have a bad play against White if you never throw the ball his way! ❧ Wallace was still in the bottom 20 in cornerback success rate, but his numbers took a tick up from 2019. His tackling also improved, with a 9% broken tackle rate compared to 17% two years ago. ❧ When White was targeted, all his numbers (success rate, yards per target, pass defenses) were down from two years ago—but he also had 23 fewer targets. Teams just don't throw at him anymore; he had the eighth-lowest target rate among qualifying corners last year. ❧ With an average depth of just 7.8 yards, no cornerback with at least 50 targets faced shorter passes than Taron Johnson did last season. That, coupled with solid tackling, explains how he has a solid success rate despite allowing a career-worst 62.3% completion rate. 🏈 Jordan Poyer and Micah Hyde are one of the best safety duos in the league, but there's precious little behind them—every other safety on the training camp roster has combined for 102 career defensive snaps.

Special Teams

Year	DVOA	Rank	FG/XP	Rank	Net Kick	Rank	Kick Ret	Rank	Net Punt	Rank	Punt Ret	Rank	Hidden	Rank
2018	-5.1%	32	-5.4	26	-1.6	25	-2.3	21	-9.1	27	-7.3	31	-5.2	22
2019	-1.2%	21	3.2	12	-5.1	29	4.1	6	-9.4	29	1.2	12	15.5	1
2020	5.9%	4	1.2	14	10.0	1	6.5	5	3.8	9	8.0	2	-7.2	25

Buffalo was one of just three teams to be above average in all five areas of special teams, having vastly improved both their kickoff and punt units from two seasons ago. The Bills hadn't managed that feat since 2014. 🏈 Tyler Bass' field goal value was below Steven Hauschka's from 2019 because he missed three field goals from under 40 yards. Two of those were in Week 1 against the Jets, however, and from then on, he was a top-10 kicker. He also gave Buffalo the most kickoff value since Jordan Gay in 2015. 🏈 The departed Corey Bojorquez outperformed replacement Matt Haack last season by our numbers, but Haack has the superior career averages. Buffalo itself did the most damage to Haack's 2020 numbers, with Isaiah McKenzie's Week 17 punt return touchdown coming out as the fourth-worst punt of the year. 🏈 That one McKenzie return technically gave him the fourth-most punt return value in the league last year, with exactly one opportunity. He'll battle rookie Marquez Stevenson to replace Andre Roberts as the team's primary returner in 2021. 🏈 Tyler Matakevich is the Bills' top gunner, and all eight of his tackles on kickoffs stopped the opponent short of an average return.

Carolina Panthers

2020 Record: 5-11	**Total DVOA:** -6.7% (29)	**2021 Mean Projection:** 7.1 wins	**On the Clock (0-5):** 29%
Pythagorean Wins: 6.6 (23)	**Offense:** -0.2% (17)	**Postseason Odds:** 22.2%	**Mediocrity (6-8):** 42%
Snap-Weighted Age: 26 (23)	**Defense:** 7.3% (24)	**Super Bowl Odds:** 1.2%	**Playoff Contender (9-11):** 23%
Average Opponent: 6.5% (2)	**Special Teams:** 0.8% (16)	**Proj. Avg. Opponent:** 0.1% (16)	**Super Bowl Contender (12+):** 6%

2020: Potential for better days ahead.

2021: What good is unrealized potential?

Most football fans, even the most blinkered die-hards, recognize a looming rebuild when they see one. Eighteen months ago, as the 2019 Carolina Panthers fell off again from a winning start to finish with a losing record, everybody could see a change coming. Quarterback Cam Newton was injured again, no longer the talisman he had been since the start of the decade. The front seven, for so long the key to the team's defensive success, allowed a run defense DVOA that ranked fifth worst all-time. Head coach Ron Rivera was unable to arrest the team's slide and departed at the start of December. Even shiny new rookie quarterback Will Grier, drafted in the third round as a contingency plan for Newton, went 1-for-8 with a pick-six in the final game before he, too, got hurt. Finishing a disappointing 5-11 after opening 4-2, a third straight year with a declining record, and with 12 of 22 preferred starters turning 29 or older, the Panthers were in obvious need of a reboot.

Fast forward a year, and once again, the Panthers finished 5-11 after a winning start. Again, a star offensive player lost most of the season to injury. Again, they earned a pick in the top eight of the draft. However, this time the mood is different. Newton is now in New England, replaced initially by former Vikings first-round pick Teddy Bridgewater, and now by 24-year-old former Jets No. 3 overall pick Sam Darnold. Rivera is now in Washington, replaced by Matt Rhule, an experienced former college head coach with a reputation for rebuilding struggling football programs. The defense went from the second-oldest by snap-weighted age in 2019 to second-youngest in 2020. This time, only three of their 22 primary starters were more than 29 years old, and of those three only center Matt Paradis returns for 2021.

This was not just youth for youth's sake, either. Under Rhule, Carolina's efficiency improved in all three major phases: offense, defense, and special teams. Despite the poor record, the team was competitive throughout the season. Their only defeats by more than eight points came twice against the eventual champion Buccaneers and in the meaningless season finale against playoff-bound New Orleans. Compared with the end of the previous year, when the Panthers lost by 20 or more points four times in just the final seven games, this was clear progress. They may have lost the same number of games, but the 2020 Panthers threaded the needle of getting younger and better even if the standings didn't show it.

Joe Brady's offense made the biggest impression, leaping from No. 27 in DVOA in 2019 to almost exactly league average (-0.2% DVOA, 17th) despite the loss of star running back Christian McCaffrey after only three games. Teddy Bridgewater had his most productive season yet, setting personal bests in completion percentage, net yards per attempt, and DYAR in the first 500-attempt season of his professional career. Four different Panthers players had over 1,000 yards from scrimmage, including all three starting wideouts plus 27-year-old career backup halfback Mike Davis. Brady earned plaudits for how creatively he deployed his array of receiving talent, exemplified by Curtis Samuel leading all receivers in rushing DYAR, and by both Robby Anderson and DJ Moore excelling in what many observers had presumed to be the other's role before the season started.

For all its creativity, however, the offense's efficiency fell the further downfield it advanced the ball. Behind their own 40-yard line, Carolina had the No. 2 offense in the league by DVOA, trailing only Kansas City. The Panthers then fell to 14th between the 40s, 24th between the opposition 40- and 20-yard lines, and 27th in the red zone. They ranked 30th in goal-to-go situations. Passing efficiency was the big problem: the running game was roughly league average in the red zone, but Bridgewater's -53.7% DVOA was third-worst of any player with at least 20 red zone pass attempts, and P.J. Walker's -221.0% on nine attempts was the worst of any player with at least four such throws.

Conceptually, it makes sense that an offense predicated on getting playmakers in space would find success tougher as that space naturally condenses. Anderson's DVOA plunged to -62.0% in the red zone, second-worst of any receiver with at least 10 red zone targets, as he caught just 47% of his passes for a paltry 2.8 yards per reception. Moore fared even worse: his nine red zone targets resulted in more interceptions (three) than receptions (two) and averaged a tiny 0.78 yards per target, good for -80.1% DVOA. Bridgewater's completion rate dropped by 12.3% inside the opposition 20, nearly double the league average difference (-6.6%), and he threw a quarter of his interceptions there on just 12% of his attempts. Even his completed passes were subpar: among quarterbacks with at least 10 attempts, only Daniel Jones posted a lower DVOA than Bridgewater on red zone completions. This fits the general impression of Bridgewater as an efficient but limited passer

2021 Panthers Schedule

Week	Opp.	Week	Opp.	Week	Opp.
1	NYJ	7	at NYG	13	BYE
2	NO	8	at ATL	14	ATL
3	at HOU (Thu.)	9	NE	15	at BUF
4	at DAL	10	at ARI	16	TB
5	PHI	11	WAS	17	at NO
6	MIN	12	at MIA	18	at TB

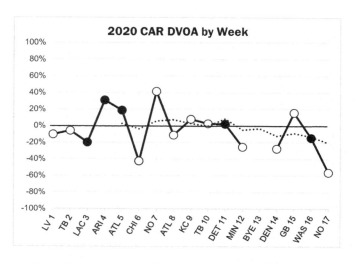

2020 CAR DVOA by Week

whose biggest weakness—his lack of arm strength—impacts these most crucial game situations. Although he finished exactly middle of the pack among the 36 qualifying passers in both DYAR (18th) and DVOA (19th), it's easy to see why the Panthers felt that they needed an upgrade.

Whether they *got* an upgrade is highly debatable. They certainly tried. Throughout the early portion of the offseason, as the Panthers were aggressively clearing cap space, reputable rumors abounded that they were trying to put together an offer to pry the unsettled Deshaun Watson from the Texans. After Watson's legal problems lay that idea to rest, most observers suspected they would turn to the draft, perhaps trading up to snag their quarterback of the future. Instead, San Francisco leapt into the third overall spot, trading so much for the privilege that their selection could only possibly be a quarterback. Within days, the Panthers traded second-, fourth-, and sixth-round picks to the Jets for Sam Darnold, with Bridgewater offloaded to Denver shortly thereafter.

On the surface, that decision is mystifying. We know from pre-draft footage[1] that the Panthers had a very accurate idea of who every team above them would draft. They knew, absent further trades, that at least two first-round quarterback prospects—Justin Fields and either Trey Lance or Mac Jones—would be available with the eighth overall pick. Either player would be younger than Darnold, on a full rookie contract rather than just a year plus the fifth-year option remaining, giving time to sit them for a season behind an adequate starter if needed. Neither would have Darnold's track record of both failure and decline, nor his impending contract negotiations if they were to succeed. To not only trade for Darnold instead of drafting one of the incoming rookies, but also trade Bridgewater to make way for him, the Panthers must be very confident that he is the right piece to fit their specific puzzle.

The chance of that being the case is slender, at best. Only a disastrous season from Carson Wentz kept Darnold out of bottom spot in overall DYAR last season, and only Wentz and the two-headed Alex Smith/Dwayne Haskins monstrosity in Washington joined Darnold below -30.0% DVOA. There was a gap of almost 1,000 DYAR from Darnold's -540 to Bridgewater's 446. And using a cutoff of 20 attempts, Darnold was the worst red zone passer in the league, one of only two passers who were *less* efficient than Bridgewater. Darnold is still just 24 years old—the three-year veteran is younger than a couple of his rookie teammates—and has flashed potential,

but his efficiency has declined every year and he has yet to stay healthy for even 14 games. In New York, he was the kind of bust who doesn't usually recover, which is why the Jets were happy to accept a smaller return for a player they chose No. 3 overall just three seasons ago. The outlook for quarterbacks with Darnold's history is grim: Alex Smith, a player who spent a third of his career in the bottom 10 of DVOA, is among the *best*-case comparisons.

For once, the reason to be optimistic about a young quarterback's prospects is Adam Gase. Before Darnold, the last quarterback that Gase was hired specifically to develop was Ryan Tannehill. Like Darnold, Gase asked Tannehill to play a conservative, short-passing game ill-suited to his attributes. Like Darnold, Tannehill lost games to injury in every year under Gase, including a disastrous mishandling of an ACL injury that cost Tannehill the entire 2017 season. Like Darnold, Tannehill's net yards per attempt declined and his sack rate increased from one season to the next. Consequently, like Darnold, Tannehill's DVOA declined every year under Gase, culminating in a 32nd-place finish that led to Gase being fired and the quarterback being traded. Tannehill landed with a team that was much more willing to let him play in an offense suited to his skills. Joe Brady certainly seems smart enough to do the same with Darnold. If Darnold comes out of this trade looking anything remotely like Titans Ryan Tannehill, the Panthers got a great deal—the kind of great deal that defines careers.

On the other hand, Tannehill never had a year as bad as the one Darnold just waded through. With the lone exception of his final season in Miami, which immediately followed his ACL recovery, every season of Tannehill's Dolphins career was more effective than anything Darnold has achieved so far. If Darnold comes out of this trade looking anything remotely like Jets Sam Darnold, the Panthers made a huge mistake—the kind of huge mistake that also defines careers.

To improve the likelihood of the former scenario, it's vital that the Panthers get the best out of the pieces around their new quarterback. Moore is a half-step away from being a star in his own right, a genuine No. 1 receiver with over 1,200

---

[1] Panthers Confidential, https://www.youtube.com/watch?v=JMtSvMy5Vdo

scrimmage yards in each of the past two seasons, whose only blot in his production copybook is a relative lack of touchdowns. Anderson is already familiar with Darnold from their time in New York: Anderson had over 750 yards and at least five touchdowns in both of their seasons together before finally breaking the 1,000-yard mark in Carolina. McCaffrey should be back at full strength after the team justifiably kept him out last season while he battled a high-ankle sprain. Only Samuel, now in Washington, does not return from last season's four preferred primary targets.

In Samuel's stead, general manager Scott Fitterer brought in not one, but three players already known to him and his staff. From his own former employers in Seattle, Fitterer signed David Moore, a 6-foot deep threat with 4.42s speed who scored 13 touchdowns in three years catching passes from Russell Wilson. From Joe Brady's former college employer, they drafted Terrace Marshall, a physical outside receiver with first-round talent and star potential who was overshadowed at LSU by Justin Jefferson and Ja'Marr Chase. From Brady's former NFL employer, albeit via a year in Arizona, they brought in receiver-turned-tight-end Dan Arnold, who started his professional career in New Orleans while Brady was an offensive assistant. Arnold should immediately improve the receiving potential of a tight end corps that was simply not a factor in 2020, while Moore and Marshall add even more size and speed to a receiver group already brimming with both. If Darnold struggles again this season, the quality of his targets should certainly not be the reason.

The offensive line is more of a question. Unless free agent Russell Okung unexpectedly rejoins the team by opening day, Carolina will begin the season with their eighth different starting left tackle in as many years. The intended long-term solution, 2019 second-round pick Greg Little, was such a disappointment that he ended up a game-day inactive, with former Chargers backup Trent Scott starting ahead of him while Okung struggled (and ultimately failed) to stay healthy. With the chaos at the left end of the line, bringing back free-agent right tackle Taylor Moton was imperative, and Moton is the one Panthers lineman who appears to have his spot locked down for the long term.

Following the draft, the team has a new intended long-term solution in third-rounder Brady Christensen (BYU), with Scott, Little, and former Browns first-round pick Cameron Erving also in the mix. Rhule described Christensen as "a third-round tackle and a second-round guard" during the team's draft discussions, suggesting that he will make the lineup at one spot or the other. Erving also has experience at both tackle and guard, and fellow free-agent addition Pat Elflein can contribute along the interior. The Panthers tried nine different starters in a variety of configurations last year, never starting the same five in more than two consecutive games, so they will move players around until they are satisfied with the fit. However, offensive line play is as much about cohesion as it is about talent, and with the third-worst continuity score in 2020, the Panthers line can hardly be described as cohesive.

In New York, Darnold was pressured on 33.0% of his dropbacks last year, throwing up a -70.8% DVOA. Take out sacks and scrambles and the Jets' offensive DVOA dropped 38 percentage points when Darnold was forced to throw outside the pocket. If the Panthers can form a line cohesive enough to make Darnold comfortable, his targets are good enough that at least *some* success on offense should follow. If not, we've seen the results, and they are not pretty.

The path to success on defense is more straightforward, if not necessarily more assured. The run defense made huge strides last year, going from a running joke throughout 2019 to league average by the end of 2020, gradually improving as the season went along and even posting a dominant stretch ahead of the team's Week 13 bye. Top pick Derrick Brown started slowly but took over as the primary force in the defensive line rotation after Kawann Short was lost for the season in Week 5. That, along with increased playing time for sixth-round rookie Bravvion Roy, coincided with an eight-game stretch where the Panthers averaged -26.6% DVOA against the run, a figure that would have ranked second in the league over the full season. They fell off a bit in December, thanks mainly to a difficult afternoon in Green Bay, but the addition of a strong veteran in DaQuan Jones and another couple of Day 3 picks should help solidify the interior rotation and keep the core contributors fresh throughout the winter. Former Rams defensive end Morgan Fox has the size and versatility to be a large end on running downs and an interior rusher against the pass, and former Chargers linebacker Denzel Perryman can be an upgrade on Tahir Whitehead as a three-down contributor at the second level. More of the pieces are in place for the run defense to at least sustain its improved level of play.

Assuming it can do so, the pass defense will make or break the unit. There are plenty of reasons to be optimistic: although it declined after losing veterans such as Luke Kuechly, Mario Addison, and Eric Reid, the Panthers defense went from the second-oldest in 2019 to third-*youngest* in 2020. No team gave more defensive snaps to rookies. A callow cornerback group was thrown into the deep end against the strongest group of opposing receivers in any division in the league, and just about held their own: the list of players with over 100 yards in a game against them may as well be a list of the best veteran receivers in the sport.[2] To improve their chances against those elite opponents, the team spent the eighth overall pick on the top cornerback prospect, South Carolina's Jaycee Horn, who should be an opening-day starter in the secondary. They also brought in a couple of veteran free agents to fill out their back seven, including A.J. Bouye and Rashaan Melvin.

Perhaps more importantly, they also completely restocked the edge rusher rotation behind Brian Burns. Out go disappointing veteran Stephen Weatherly and former British American Football Association prospect Efe Obada. In comes former Cardinals first-round pick Haason Reddick, coming off a 12.5-sack breakout season, along with the aforementioned Fox and former Jets rotational edge rusher Frankie Luvu. With last year's second-round pick, Yetur Gross-Matos, finally getting

---

[2] Outside the division, only Travis Kelce, Tyreek Hill, and Keenan Allen put up 100-yard games against Carolina.

a proper offseason, and 2018 fourth-rounder Marquis Haynes also still in the mix, Carolina has its deepest stable of edge rushers since the front seven's heyday under Rivera. Burns and Reddick alone combined for 21.5 sacks in 2020, which would have been three quarters of Carolina's team-wide total. Though there are reasons to be skeptical that Reddick can repeat his career year, in theory the improved depth should help keep everybody fresh and productive, and a productive pass rush would be a great help to what is still a very young back end.

Ultimately, that youth is what determines the team's outlook, not only in the secondary but throughout the roster. With Darnold at quarterback instead of Bridgewater; McCaffrey at running back instead of Davis; and Kawann Short, Tahir Whitehead, Efe Obada, and Tre Boston all now off the roster, the Panthers got younger again at a number of key positions. With that youth comes potential, but at some point, potential must translate to results.

On defense, we project a modest improvement thanks to improved depth, young players maturing, and the addition of a potential cornerstone player in the draft. On offense, even our heartless computer looks at Darnold's history and winces. During the pre-draft process in 2018, FO guest columnist Seth Galina described Darnold as the most tantalizing quarterback of his class[3], while QBASE projected him with almost a 60% bust chance. That is Darnold in a nutshell: the personification of the old coaching quip "Son, your potential is gonna get me fired." Subjectively, we can look at the state of the Adam Gase Jets and mentally adjust for context. Objectively, Darnold has been getting worse, not better, and we have yet to devise a formula for Gase-adjusted VOA.

If the Panthers are to be anything more than a makeweight in a tough division, the offense will have to carry its weight. That's a dicey proposition unless you are absolutely convinced that Gase was the sole reason for Darnold's struggles in New York over the past two years. In Joe Brady's Panthers offense, we should have a clear idea by the end of the season who Darnold is, and what he's likely to achieve in Carolina. All our projections can go on is Darnold's past results, and that makes them very, very skeptical that he will be worth the price. Stranger things have happened than a young player improving significantly with better coaching, but that doesn't mean we can expect it to work like that every time.

Factor in the tough division, and it looks like another season of building in Carolina, mostly spent looking for reasons to be optimistic about 2022. That's fine, as long as those reasons are found. One of the lessons of the past 18 months that transcends football is that people can endure anything as long as they have hope. It's when the hope ends that the trouble starts—for Darnold, and for the rest of us as well.

Andrew Potter

[3] https://www.footballoutsiders.com/futures/2018/futures-sam-darnold

2020 Panthers by Week

Wk	vs.	W-L	PF	PA	YDF	YDA	TO	Total	Off	Def	ST
1	LV	L	30	34	388	372	0	-10.4%	14.1%	26.2%	1.7%
2	at TB	L	17	31	427	339	-2	-5.9%	2.3%	2.3%	-5.9%
3	at LAC	W	21	16	302	436	4	-20.0%	-9.4%	12.1%	1.5%
4	ARI	W	31	21	444	262	0	30.9%	35.5%	-4.2%	-8.8%
5	at ATL	W	23	16	437	373	1	18.7%	23.8%	3.4%	-1.6%
6	CHI	L	16	23	303	261	-2	-42.6%	-43.9%	1.1%	2.4%
7	at NO	L	24	27	283	415	1	41.7%	52.3%	12.6%	2.1%
8	ATL	L	17	25	304	401	0	-11.1%	7.0%	20.9%	2.8%
9	at KC	L	31	33	435	397	1	8.1%	23.0%	9.4%	-5.5%
10	TB	L	23	46	187	544	0	2.8%	-5.9%	17.8%	26.6%
11	DET	W	20	0	374	185	-1	2.2%	-37.0%	-35.6%	3.6%
12	at MIN	L	27	28	374	387	2	-25.3%	-12.8%	-0.9%	-13.4%
13	BYE										
14	DEN	L	27	32	370	365	1	-27.4%	26.8%	37.7%	-16.5%
15	at GB	L	16	24	364	291	-1	16.1%	-8.0%	-17.2%	6.9%
16	at WAS	W	20	13	280	386	2	-14.4%	-18.8%	11.8%	16.2%
17	NO	L	7	33	320	347	-5	-56.0%	-48.5%	8.7%	1.3%

Trends and Splits

	Offense	Rank	Defense	Rank
Total DVOA	-0.2%	17	7.3%	24
Unadjusted VOA	-3.5%	19	7.5%	24
Weighted Trend	-5.7%	19	5.8%	22
Variance	8.3%	21	2.9%	3
Average Opponent	-3.7%	6	3.9%	6
Passing	12.3%	20	15.5%	23
Rushing	-8.8%	16	-4.5%	20
First Down	-6.8%	22	-2.0%	16
Second Down	7.9%	9	6.1%	21
Third Down	0.1%	15	29.2%	31
First Half	1.9%	15	3.8%	22
Second Half	-2.4%	18	11.1%	26
Red Zone	-22.8%	27	11.1%	26
Late and Close	-13.7%	25	12.2%	25

Five-Year Performance

Year	W-L	Pyth W	Est W	PF	PA	TO	Total	Rk	Off	Rk	Def	Rk	ST	Rk	Off AGL	Rk	Def AGL	Rk	Off Age	Rk	Def Age	Rk	ST Age	Rk
2016	6-10	7.1	6.6	369	402	-2	-6.3%	24	-8.3%	25	-4.4%	10	-2.5%	25	36.8	17	37.2	15	27.0	12	26.2	23	26.6	6
2017	11-5	9.0	10.3	363	327	-1	12.6%	9	-0.1%	17	-8.0%	8	4.7%	6	30.1	14	10.3	5	26.3	25	28.4	1	26.6	4
2018	7-9	7.8	7.7	376	382	+1	0.3%	14	6.0%	11	5.5%	23	-0.2%	18	51.1	25	51.5	27	26.7	16	28.9	1	26.6	5
2019	5-11	4.9	4.0	340	470	-14	-26.5%	29	-14.4%	27	8.0%	26	-4.1%	31	36.5	14	29.7	14	26.1	27	27.4	2	26.0	12
2020	5-11	6.6	6.4	350	402	+1	-6.7%	21	-0.2%	17	7.3%	24	0.8%	16	34.1	14	38.9	16	26.8	13	25.2	30	25.9	18

2020 Performance Based on Most Common Personnel Groups

CAR Offense					CAR Offense vs. Opponents					CAR Defense				CAR Defense vs. Opponents			
Pers	Freq	Yds	DVOA	Run%	Pers	Freq	Yds	DVOA	Run%	Pers	Freq	Yds	DVOA	Pers	Freq	Yds	DVOA
11	56%	6.4	9.0%	24%	Base	26%	5.2	1.3%	59%	Base	5%	5.3	14.3%	11	57%	5.8	7.8%
12	18%	5.1	-11.9%	50%	Nickel	60%	6.2	6.4%	30%	Nickel	53%	5.6	-1.9%	12	21%	6.3	15.4%
21	8%	5.6	2.7%	54%	Dime+	12%	5.1	-26.7%	14%	Dime+	41%	6.2	19.7%	21	5%	5.3	-14.9%
01	6%	4.9	-2.3%	32%	Goal Line	1%	0.9	57.3%	82%	Goal Line	0%	1.0	29.9%	22	3%	3.4	-35.4%
22	4%	3.8	-19.8%	81%	Big	1%	4.1	20.9%	64%	Big	1%	2.4	12.5%	13	3%	6.3	-22.5%
13	4%	4.8	14.8%	65%										10	2%	5.8	19.3%

Strategic Tendencies

Run/Pass		Rk	Formation		Rk	Pass Rush		Rk	Secondary		Rk	Strategy		Rk
Runs, first half	38%	17	Form: Single Back	81%	17	Rush 3	20.0%	2	4 DB	5%	32	Play Action	22%	26
Runs, first down	48%	18	Form: Empty Back	9%	16	Rush 4	61.1%	21	5 DB	54%	24	Offensive Motion	53%	7
Runs, second-long	19%	29	Form: Multi Back	11%	13	Rush 5	15.5%	27	6+ DB	41%	3	Avg Box (Off)	6.54	16
Runs, power sit.	61%	13	Pers: 3+ WR	65%	19	Rush 6+	3.5%	24	Man Coverage	17%	32	Avg Box (Def)	6.32	27
Runs, behind 2H	29%	14	Pers: 2+ TE/6+ OL	28%	18	Edge Rusher Sacks	72.4%	1	CB by Sides	56%	30	Offensive Pace	31.86	29
Pass, ahead 2H	54%	8	Pers: 6+ OL	0%	25	Interior DL Sacks	17.2%	26	S/CB Cover Ratio	38%	5	Defensive Pace	30.00	13
Run-Pass Options	7%	18	Shotgun/Pistol	62%	20	Second Level Sacks	10.3%	31	DB Blitz	14%	12	Go for it on 4th	1.89	10

Carolina threw a league-leading 45% of passes to the left side and ranked fourth in DVOA on passes to the left. But the Panthers were only 26th in DVOA on passes up the middle and 27th in DVOA on passes to the right side. ✎ The Panthers threw only 8% of passes to tight ends, tied with New England for the lowest figure in the league. ✎ Carolina averaged just 3.6 yards per play on RPOs, the lowest figure among teams that used RPOs on at least 5% of plays. ✎ The Panthers surprisingly finished tied for second in the league with 141 broken tackles and had at least one broken tackle on a league-best 12.8% of plays. Mike Davis was tied for fifth in the league with 56 broken tackles, while the Panthers had three players among the 30 wide receivers in the league who had at least a dozen broken tackles: Curtis Samuel with 15, Robby Anderson with 14, and DJ Moore with 12. ✎ Under new defensive coordinator Phil Snow, the Panthers went from 31st to second in frequency of sending just three pass-rushers and from 30th to third in frequency of using dime personnel. One thing that stayed the same: the Panthers were near the top of the league in using zone coverage both seasons. ✎ Carolina had the best fumble recovery luck in the league last season, recovering 69% of all fumbles. They recovered more than half of fumbles on both offense (seven of 12) and defense (13 of 18). They also recovered two out of three kicks muffed by their opponents; leaguewide, these plays were recovered by the kicking team only 21% of the time.

Passing

Player	DYAR	DVOA	Plays	NtYds	Avg	YAC	C%	TD	Int
T.Bridgewater*	446	2.0%	521	3508	6.7	5.5	69.7%	15	11
P.J.Walker	-217	-71.1%	60	337	5.6	4.4	57.1%	1	5
S.Darnold	-540	-32.2%	396	1974	5.0	5.3	60.1%	9	11

Rushing

Player	DYAR	DVOA	Plays	Yds	Avg	TD	Fum	Suc
M.Davis*	37	-3.5%	165	642	3.9	6	1	50%
C.McCaffrey	37	5.0%	59	225	3.8	5	0	56%
T.Bridgewater*	43	6.6%	45	279	6.2	5	4	--
R.Smith	16	-0.8%	41	156	3.8	1	1	61%
C.Samuel*	99	3.1%	41	200	4.9	2	0	--
R.Bonnafon	9	12.8%	12	69	5.8	0	0	33%
T.Cannon	-10	-33.7%	10	33	3.3	0	0	40%
A.Armah*	2	-4.0%	6	9	1.5	0	0	83%
S.Darnold	72	35.3%	30	224	7.5	2	0	--
Da.Moore	47	57.6%	8	61	7.6	0	0	--

Receiving

Player	DYAR	DVOA	Plays	Ctch	Yds	Y/C	YAC	TD	C%
R.Anderson	19	-10.9%	137	95	1099	11.5	5.2	3	70%
D.J.Moore	191	7.9%	118	66	1193	18.1	5.8	4	56%
C.Samuel*	95	0.1%	97	77	851	11.1	4.2	3	79%
P.Cooper*	13	9.6%	8	5	73	14.6	7.0	0	63%
S.Roberts*	-14	-42.4%	6	4	31	7.8	5.5	0	67%
Da.Moore	76	7.0%	47	35	417	11.9	4.8	6	74%
I.Thomas	-48	-30.1%	31	20	145	7.3	3.9	1	65%
C.Manhertz*	-8	-22.8%	8	6	52	8.7	5.5	0	75%
D.Arnold	101	26.7%	45	31	438	14.1	5.6	4	69%
M.Davis*	55	0.2%	70	59	373	6.3	7.2	2	84%
C.McCaffrey	60	42.5%	20	17	149	8.3	6.8	1	89%
R.Smith	3	-8.0%	11	9	59	6.6	5.1	0	82%
A.Armah*	-30	-64.3%	9	5	18	3.6	4.0	0	56%

Offensive Line

Player	Pos	Age	GS	Snaps	Pen	Sk	Pass	Run	Player	Pos	Age	GS	Snaps	Pen	Sk	Pass	Run
Taylor Moton	RT	27	16/16	1034	2	2	10	6	Trenton Scott	LT	27	14/4	348	3	2.5	10	1
Matt Paradis	C	32	16/16	1031	1	3.5	11	14	Michael Schofield*	LG/LT	31	11/3	270	3	2.5	7	4
John Miller	RG	28	14/14	912	6	3	13	7	Pat Elflein	LG	27	7/7	419	2	0.5	9	7
Chris Reed	LG	29	14/14	894	3	1.5	11	9	Cameron Erving	LT	29	6/5	278	2	1	4	2
Russell Okung*	LT	33	7/7	406	4	1	5	3									

Year	Yards	ALY	Rk	Power	Rk	Stuff	Rk	2Lev	Rk	OpFld	Rk	BB Rt	Rk	Sacks	ASR	Rk	Press	Rk	BB Rt	Rk	Cont
2018	4.62	4.55	11	67%	18	17%	7	1.27	17	0.97	12	5.1%	8	32	6.1%	10	28.9%	15	9.5%	17	34
2019	4.84	4.30	17	43%	32	18%	10	1.20	15	1.26	1	10.2%	16	58	8.6%	29	30.4%	20	13.6%	18	28
2020	3.85	4.43	13	73%	6	16%	13	1.17	19	0.32	32	12.6%	28	36	6.6%	17	24.0%	12	12.4%	16	20

2020 ALY by direction: Left End: 4.46 (15)　Left Tackle: 5.18 (3)　Mid/Guard: 4.24 (21)　Right Tackle: 4.14 (20)　Right End: 5.07 (13)

Carolina had the third-worst offensive line continuity score in 2020, ahead of only the disastrous Eagles and the Chargers. They made 10 different lineup changes in 16 games, using nine different starters, and never started the same five players for more than two consecutive games. This despite the offensive line being almost exactly league average in our injury metric, adjusted games lost. Left tackle was the biggest problem area: three different players started at least three games there, but none of them started more than three in a row. ● Taylor Moton was the pick of the linemen, starting all 16 games at right tackle for the third successive season. Moton was also the only Panthers offensive lineman who averaged better than 50 snaps per blown block or ranked better than No. 20 at his position in that statistic. ● Center Matt Paradis also started all 16 games for the second straight year. His performance improved from his disappointing 2019 season, but the oldest starter on the team enters the final year of his $29-million contract having yet to justify the price tag. ● Third-round pick Brady Christensen (BYU) was a three-year starter at left tackle in college, but some teams had concerns about his age (he will be 25 in September, older than many multi-year veterans) and his relatively short arms by NFL tackle standards. ● In addition to Christensen, the Panthers brought in veteran free agents Pat Elflein and Cameron Erving. Though valuable veteran depth, neither is much more than a solid backup and spot starter. ● Sixth-round pick Deonte Brown is one of the few human beings who might be too big to play offensive line in the NFL, tipping the scales at 344 pounds. He did not allow a single sack during this career at Alabama, where he was a first-team All-SEC guard as a senior. If he can trim some weight, and his mobility and balance improve accordingly, he has the frame and technique to become a very effective interior lineman.

Defensive Front

Defensive Line	Age	Pos	G	Snaps	Plays	TmPct	Rk	Stop	Dfts	BTkl	Runs	St%	Rk	RuYd	Rk	Sack	Hit	Hur	Dsrpt
						Overall						vs. Run				Pass Rush			
Derrick Brown	23	DT	16	742	37	4.6%	57	32	12	3	28	82%	18	1.8	17	2.0	10	18	4
Bravvion Roy	25	DT	15	419	29	3.8%	70	15	4	3	27	52%	96	3.6	96	1.0	4	10	0
Zach Kerr*	31	DT	13	390	34	5.1%	50	29	7	2	29	83%	15	2.1	34	2.0	6	12	1
DaQuan Jones	30	DT	16	704	49	5.7%	34	32	9	3	43	65%	75	2.2	40	2.0	3	11	0
Morgan Fox	27	DE	16	403	28	3.5%	--	20	10	2	19	58%	--	2.6	--	6.0	3	11	2

Edge Rushers	Age	Pos	G	Snaps	Plays	TmPct	Rk	Stop	Dfts	BTkl	Runs	St%	Rk	RuYd	Rk	Sack	Hit	Hur	Dsrpt
						Overall						vs. Run				Pass Rush			
Brian Burns	23	DE	15	750	62	8.1%	4	39	20	3	33	58%	86	3.3	78	9.0	15	32	4
Efe Obada*	29	DE	16	415	18	2.2%	--	16	9	2	11	82%	--	2.5	--	5.5	8	10	0
Marquis Haynes	28	DE	15	390	19	2.5%	--	13	6	2	10	60%	--	7.3	--	4.0	2	9	1
Yetur Gross-Matos	23	DE	12	377	24	3.9%	66	19	8	0	16	88%	4	2.1	31	2.5	4	13	0
Stephen Weatherly*	27	DE	9	358	17	3.7%	70	11	3	5	15	67%	60	1.1	4	0.0	3	10	0
Haason Reddick	27	OLB	16	875	65	7.7%	6	42	28	7	34	56%	89	3.6	84	12.5	5	24	2
Frankie Luvu	25	OLB	13	257	21	3.0%	--	14	7	5	8	88%	--	0.1	--	2.0	2	8	2

Linebackers	Age	Pos	G	Snaps	Plays	TmPct	Rk	Stop	Dfts	BTkl	Runs	St%	Rk	RuYd	Rk	Sack	Hit	Hur	Tgts	Suc%	Rk	Yd/P	Rk	PD	Int
						Overall						vs. Run				Pass Rush				vs. Pass					
Shaq Thompson	27	OLB	16	1031	119	14.6%	25	60	21	9	55	56%	40	4.0	42	0.0	3	7	50	50%	38	6.5	43	5	0
Tahir Whitehead*	31	MLB	14	398	52	7.3%	72	23	2	6	33	61%	27	3.1	11	0.0	1	3	11	27%	--	6.6	--	1	1
Jermaine Carter	26	MLB	16	284	44	5.4%	--	23	3	7	28	57%	--	3.5	--	0.0	0	1	11	55%	--	4.3	--	1	0
Denzel Perryman	29	MLB	13	317	49	7.7%	69	28	6	4	29	69%	9	2.9	7	1.0	1	3	13	62%	--	2.5	--	1	0

Year	Yards	ALY	Rk	Power	Rk	Stuff	Rk	2Lev	Rk	OpFld	Rk	BB Rt	Rk	Sacks	ASR	Rk	Press	Rk	BB Rt	Rk
2018	4.71	3.97	8	78%	31	24%	7	1.40	27	1.32	31	8.7%	14	35	6.8%	20	31.6%	10	7.6%	26
2019	5.32	4.89	30	74%	29	17%	22	1.49	32	1.41	31	15.0%	9	53	8.8%	3	28.6%	22	15.5%	12
2020	4.92	4.72	26	70%	22	17%	19	1.34	26	1.10	29	12.3%	18	29	5.8%	21	24.9%	17	14.7%	11

2020 ALY by direction:	Left End: 5.51 (30)	Left Tackle: 4.78 (24)	Mid/Guard: 4.46 (18)	Right Tackle: 4.77 (20)	Right End: 4.93 (23)

One offseason priority was to replace the oft-injured Kawann Short on the defensive line. Former Titans defensive end DaQuan Jones is mostly likely to start alongside Derrick Brown. His 43 run tackles were among the top dozen on the defensive interior. Last year's second interior lineman, Bravvion Roy, is a true nose tackle who will mostly feature on run-friendly downs. Fifth-round pick Daviyon Nixon (Iowa) is an agile, penetrating 3-technique tackle who was named first-team All-America in 2020 as a redshirt junior. He projects as a situational interior pass-rusher. Finally, seventh-round pick Phil Hoskins (Kentucky) is a developmental gap-filling nose tackle who spent most of his college career as a backup, and whose most likely destination in 2020 is the practice squad. ✎ Brian Burns' 32 hurries were more than 10 of the 13 players ahead of him on the sack leaderboard, including new teammate Haason Reddick. That's a strong indicator for another high-sack year in 2021. ✎ Reddick broke out in his fourth season with 12.5 sacks for the Cardinals. However, he more than doubled his career total in one season by recording a sack on more than 70% of his quarterback knockdowns, a rate that has historically proven unsustainable. His one-year contract reflects that: $8 million is roughly the going rate for edge rusher prove-it deals. Reddick was not a one-trick pony, however: he added nine run defeats. Only T.J. Watt had more total defeats among edge rushers. ✎ Yetur Gross-Matos started slowly as a rookie, playing just 78 snaps through Week 5 before missing most of October with a high-ankle sprain. He returned to start each of the final seven games.

Defensive Secondary

Secondary	Age	Pos	G	Snaps	Plays	Overall TmPct	Rk	Stop	Dfts	BTkl	vs. Run Runs	St%	Rk	RuYd	Rk	vs. Pass Tgts	Tgt%	Rk	aDOT	Suc%	Rk	Yd/P	Rk	PD	Int
Tre Boston*	29	FS	16	1037	98	12.1%	21	32	7	15	53	36%	37	6.3	32	37	8.8%	31	7.3	49%	39	5.8	11	4	1
Jeremy Chinn	23	FS/LB	15	967	121	15.9%	1	40	9	15	59	31%	47	7.6	45	40	10.2%	24	8.9	55%	18	5.7	10	5	1
Rasul Douglas*	26	CB	14	821	71	10.0%	19	25	6	9	12	50%	24	6.3	34	71	21.2%	30	10.9	49%	44	8.1	52	9	0
Juston Burris	28	SS	13	790	57	8.6%	60	20	8	10	19	32%	44	6.2	29	23	7.2%	45	8.3	39%	64	7.7	32	4	1
Donte Jackson	26	CB	14	599	45	6.3%	75	25	5	7	12	58%	9	4.8	18	54	22.2%	20	13.3	56%	23	6.1	9	11	3
Troy Pride	23	CB	14	529	43	6.0%	76	14	5	4	16	44%	37	5.7	30	26	12.1%	79	11.7	46%	62	8.6	58	2	0
Corn Elder*	27	CB	16	411	40	4.9%	--	13	5	3	8	38%	--	6.1	--	26	15.5%	--	10.0	42%	--	7.8	--	3	0
Sam Franklin	25	SS	14	248	23	3.2%	--	8	4	5	10	30%	--	9.6	--	9	8.9%	--	11.1	56%	--	4.0	--	1	0
A.J. Bouye	30	CB	7	410	30	8.1%	--	8	2	8	6	17%	--	9.7	--	33	20.9%	--	11.9	42%	--	7.5	--	6	0

Year	Pass D Rank	vs. #1 WR	Rk	vs. #2 WR	Rk	vs. Other WR	Rk	WR Wide	Rk	WR Slot	Rk	vs. TE	Rk	vs. RB	Rk
2018	24	-15.0%	5	29.5%	32	-2.9%	15	-4.2%	20	5.4%	19	17.2%	24	-15.1%	5
2019	11	-10.7%	8	8.0%	23	-22.6%	4	-28.0%	4	7.7%	19	7.4%	22	-3.0%	17
2020	23	-10.1%	12	1.1%	20	13.3%	24	-4.2%	11	-0.6%	18	2.2%	16	16.3%	29

Only one team, Houston, had fewer interceptions than the Panthers, though Detroit and Philadelphia also had a lower rate of interceptions per drive. ◥ Carolina ranked a mediocre No. 18 in zone defense DVOA, but allowed 52.3% DVOA in man defense, 28th in the NFL. Out of a stated desire to play better man defense, they brought in two press-man corners through the draft. Eighth overall pick Jaycee Horn (South Carolina) is the headline act, a potential shutdown cornerback in the mold of Jalen Ramsey or Darrelle Revis who is likely to start from opening day. Less-heralded fifth-round pick Keith Taylor (Washington) is a 6-foot-2 press-man corner who also shows the physicality and mentality to contribute in run defense. He is likely to begin as a backup outside corner for sub packages. ◥ The arrival of Horn likely bumps Donte Jackson back down to No. 2 cornerback, but Jackson held his own as the No. 1: he allowed 10.5 yards per target in 2019 but just 6.1 yards per target in 2020, a top-10 figure at the position. This was not due to his teammates being picked on, either, as Jackson saw almost the exact same number of targets in both seasons. His starting role should be secure across from Horn. ◥ Although Carolina listed Jeremy Chinn at outside linebacker on the Pro Bowl ballot, Chinn alternated between linebacker and safety depending on the situation. On passing downs, he was often deployed alongside Shaq Thompson at linebacker. On more neutral or run-friendly downs, he would play safety. Although no player we listed at safety was involved in more defensive plays, this is likely at least partially a result of his involvement at linebacker. Following the release of Tre Boston, and with Denzel Perryman considered a more effective coverage linebacker than Tahir Whitehead, Chinn is likely to be more of a full-time safety this season. ◥ A.J. Bouye and Rashaan Melvin bring veteran experience to a young position group, but both are on the downside of their careers. Bouye still has two games to serve of the PED suspension that ended his 2020 season; he allowed 7.5 yards per target and missed 25% of his tackle attempts for the Broncos. Melvin opted out in 2020 but allowed at least 8.7 yards per target on bad defenses in 2018 with the Raiders and 2019 with the Lions. Both players had their best season in 2017, an eternity ago in NFL terms.

Special Teams

Year	DVOA	Rank	FG/XP	Rank	Net Kick	Rank	Kick Ret	Rank	Net Punt	Rank	Punt Ret	Rank	Hidden	Rank
2018	-0.2%	18	3.4	10	-1.2	20	-3.6	27	3.6	12	-3.1	24	-11.6	30
2019	-4.1%	31	1.9	13	3.0	10	-2.9	26	-17.3	32	-5.4	30	6.1	7
2020	0.8%	16	-3.9	22	5.0	7	4.2	8	2.6	12	-3.7	26	-9.2	27

Joey Slye converted just 80.6% of his field goal attempts, a bottom-10 figure among kickers with at least 20 attempts. However, that raw figure is slightly misleading: his misses included a 65-yard attempt that fell short in New Orleans and a 67-yarder wide right as the clock ran out in Kansas City. A 29-for-34 performance from realistic range sounds much more reasonable, though Slye was just 1-for-6 from 50-plus yards. ◥ Whatever his limitations on field goals, Slye is a master of the booming kickoff. Although his 62.9-yard average distance ranked just 21st among players with at least 20 kickoffs, Carolina's kick coverage allowed just seven returns all year, for a league-best 87.7% touchback rate. That was somehow a *decline* from the previous year, when 94.3% of Slye's kickoffs resulted in touchbacks. ◥ Despite being one of only six teams to allow a punt return touchdown, coverage was also the strength of the punt unit. Joseph Charlton's gross and net punt averages were middle-of-the-pack, but the Panthers allowed only 18 returns, seventh fewest, and only the Patriots and Seahawks pinned opponents inside the 20 at a higher rate. That one touchdown accounted for 45% of return yards against them; without it, the Panthers would have leapt from 12th to fifth in our net punting metric. Even with it, this was a massive improvement over their runaway last-place finish in 2019. ◗ With last year's primary kick and punt returner, Pharoh Cooper, now in Jacksonville, the question of his replacement(s) is unresolved heading into training camp. Trenton Cannon led the team in average kick return distance during 2020, but most of that was the result of a single 98-yard non-scoring return; he averaged just 22.2 yards across his other nine attempts. Former Edmonton Eskimos and Minnesota Vikings receiver Brandon Zylstra and former Seahawks receiver David Moore both have experience as returners, and rookie Shi Smith returned both kicks and punts at South Carolina, so both spots will probably see an open competition during the summer. ◗ Those cultured few who love a good long-snapper battle should keep an eye on Panthers news: incumbent J.J. Jansen is the longest-tenured player on the roster, but he will compete against sixth-round pick Thomas Fletcher VII (Alabama) for the job.

Chicago Bears

2020 Record: 8-8	**Total DVOA:** -0.6% (18)	**2021 Mean Projection:** 7.3 wins	**On the Clock (0-5):** 26%
Pythagorean Wins: 8.1 (15)	**Offense:** -10.6% (25)	**Postseason Odds:** 27.1%	**Mediocrity (6-8):** 41%
Snap-Weighted Age: 27.1 (2)	**Defense:** -7.5% (8)	**Super Bowl Odds:** 2.1%	**Playoff Contender (9-11):** 26%
Average Opponent: 2.5% (9)	**Special Teams:** 2.6% (8)	**Proj. Avg. Opponent:** 4.4% (1)	**Super Bowl Contender (12+):** 7%

2020: Too little, too late for Trubisky.

2021: Fields will fix everything, right?

There wasn't the same exhibitionism as there was in 2020. That year, COVID turned general manager Ryan Pace's dining room into the Bears draft room. And if you could tear your eyes away from his massive spherical chandelier and the intimidating four-monitor, multi-computer setup on his dining table, you could stare at Pace and try to infer his state of mind. This year, the Bears were back in their typical draft room in Halas Hall, and Pace was one of 10 similar-looking suited men whose masks hid their countenances as much as they promoted safe social practices. But you could hear, as Adam Jahns of The Athletic reported, head coach Matt Nagy scream in happiness and excitement. And even if Pace was more stoic in his delivery of the news that they were getting Justin Fields, you could vividly picture how he must have looked and felt in the 90 minutes between when the draft started and when he landed the team's coveted next franchise quarterback.

In some ways, that selection was predictable. A year before it, Pace had declined former franchise quarterback Mitchell Trubisky's fifth-year option, a vote of non-confidence that has almost always foreshadowed a player's departure from his drafting team. But by many measures, Trubisky enjoyed something of a renaissance in 2020. His 67.0% completion rate and 6.9 yards per attempt echoed his 66.6% and 7.4 rates from his fan-forgotten 2018 Pro Bowl season. And his 6-3 record as the starter—even if aided by backup Nick Foles' comeback efforts in Week 3 in Atlanta—propelled the team to a playoff berth. Trubisky produced meager passing statistics in a 21-9 wild-card loss to the Saints, but teams have talked themselves into another year with the same core roster for less than his 3-1 December finish and a dropped 40-yard would-be touchdown that changed the complexion of an eventual playoff loss. Especially teams with a possible lame-duck general manager.

Pace deserves credit for his proper reading of Trubisky's apparent rebound and stewardship of the Bears franchise. Because while traditional statistics paint an optimistic picture of Trubisky's development, peripheral and advanced metrics suggest the quarterback improved in 2020 because of improved circumstances. Trubisky netted close to an extra yard per pass attempt last season than he did the year before, but that boost owes more to a 33% increase in yards after the catch (YAC) than it does any improvement in his accuracy or decision-making (Table 1). Trubisky declined to an average depth of target of 8.0 yards in 2020, close to the career low of his rookie season. His completion rate spiked because he attempted easier throws—likely the only ones Nagy trusted him to make—that couldn't keep the offense ahead of the sticks. His -7.5% passing DVOA fell dramatically short of his 3.6% rate from his standout sophomore season. In fact, it barely beat his -11.0% rate from 2019 and did not far outpace Foles' -16.3% rate last year from what were mostly losses in the latter's time as the starter.

Table 1. Mitchell Trubisky's Career Passing Statistics

Year	W-L	C%	YPA	CPOE	aDOT*	YAC	YAC+	Pass DVOA	SOS**
2017	4-8	59.4%	6.6	-3.7%	7.9	3.0	-0.4	-16.8%	-4.7% (1)
2018	11-3	66.6%	7.4	+0.7%	9.3	3.3	-0.4	3.6%	1.8% (27)
2019	8-7	63.2%	6.1	-3.7%	8.2	2.7	-1.3	-11.0%	0.0% (17)
2020	6-3	67.0%	6.9	-1.5%	8.0	3.6	+0.2	-7.5%	8.1% (32)

*Average depth of target does not include passes marked as thrown away, batted down, or hit in motion.
**Strength of schedule: average defensive DVOA of Trubisky opponents. Rank is compared the other 31 offenses.

It is difficult to look at Foles' and Trubisky's traditional 2020 passing statistics and see anything close to the similar efficiency that DVOA suggests. Foles lost five of his seven starts, threw nearly as many interceptions (eight) as touchdowns (10), and averaged a full yard less per pass attempt (5.9) than Trubisky did. But Foles and Trubisky faced dramatically different levels of competition. The former drew top-seven defenses—the Colts, Bucs, Rams, Saints—in four of his seven starts and pulled just one bottom-seven opponent, the Titans. In contrast, Trubisky bookended his Week 3 benching and Foles' Week 11 hip injury with four starts against teams in the bottom seven of defensive DVOA: the Texans, Jaguars, and Lions twice. And he never faced a better defense than the Falcons' No. 14-rated unit that spurred his midseason benching. In aggregate, Foles faced opponents with an average of a -5.5% defensive DVOA, stronger than all but one other team's collective quarterbacks faced. Meanwhile, Trubisky enjoyed an average opponent with an 8.1% defensive DVOA, the easi-

2021 Bears Schedule

Week	Opp.	Week	Opp.	Week	Opp.
1	at LAR	7	at TB	13	ARI
2	CIN	8	SF	14	at GB
3	at CLE	9	at PIT (Mon.)	15	MIN (Mon.)
4	DET	10	BYE	16	at SEA
5	at LV	11	BAL	17	NYG
6	GB	12	at DET (Thu.)	18	at MIN

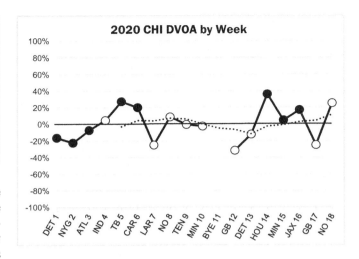

2020 CHI DVOA by Week

est in football. He metaphorically faced the Bengals defense every week. He would almost certainly regress with the more balanced schedule another year as a starter would undoubtedly bring him. Just look at his annual trends (Table 1). Trubisky performed markedly better in 2018 and 2020, the two seasons when he lucked into easy schedules.

That may have needed two paragraphs to be properly explained, but Trubisky's shortcomings remain easier to understand than to address—at least on any timetable that Pace could survive. Pace became the Bears' general manager in 2015. He could shrug off his modest totals of six and three wins in his first two seasons because they came mostly with an inherited quarterback in Jay Cutler. But when he traded up to draft Trubisky in 2017, Pace flipped an hourglass of owner Virginia McCaskey's patience. For most owners, that would have run out of sand about when Pace declined Trubisky's fifth-year option. Broadly speaking, 28 wins and two playoff berths in the past three seasons do not typify failure. But those wins progressed and plateaued from 12 in 2018 to eight in 2019 and 2020. Those postseason appearances netted just 24 points and two losses. Unrelated to Pace's results, the deep 2021 quarterback class offered an opportunity for a new coach and front office to rebuild the team with a passer to match their vision. That's an opportunity an 8-8 team seldom has. McCaskey's decision to keep Pace could have delayed the fruits of an eventual rebuild for several years. Even if she fired Pace after the 2021 season, the Bears might have to wait a few more years for the draft to break their way again.

By draft night, Pace may have escaped the concerns of competing personal and team interests. With the hope for a trade for one of the league's unhappy superstar quarterbacks such as Russell Wilson seemingly dashed, Pace signed Andy Dalton and announced him as the Bears starter. Dalton was underrated for much of his career, but the now-33-year-old suffered his two worst passing DVOA seasons in 2019 and 2020, the latter despite the Cowboys' skill talent that seems better than what his new team plans to provide him. Expectations couldn't be high, so Pace presumably realized his best chance for the short-term success he needs for his job security came from the draft.

That wouldn't stop him from sweating. After the draft started with three quarterback selections, Pace had to balance the concerns that other teams would beat him to Justin Fields or Mac Jones with worries that teams in the top 10 would demand a king's ransom in a trade-up. He could take a breath when the Falcons forestalled their rebuild with a selection of tight end

Kyle Pitts. He could take a breath when the Bengals' reunited quarterback Joe Burrow with his favorite college receiver Ja'Marr Chase, leaving top left tackle prospect Penei Sewell for a Lions team that might have otherwise traded back. He could take a couple more breaths when the quarterback-needy Panthers and Broncos selected cornerbacks Jaycee Horn and Patrick Surtain II. But he couldn't breathe freely until infamous trade-back-averse Giants GM Dave Gettleman called in the trade that landed the Bears their quarterback, Fields.

Pace walked a delicate tightrope in those 90 minutes, and if that were the full measure of his fitness to remain the Bears' GM, then he most certainly would deserve the role. The problem is that Pace's great triumph belies a pattern of forfeiting traded draft pick value in his tenure with the team. Fields may well be worth the haul it took to get him. Football Outsiders draft analyst Derrik Klassen believes him to be the second-best quarterback in the class and a player archetypically worthy of a No. 1 draft pick in a year without a Trevor Lawrence-quality prospect. But Pace believed the same when he traded up for Trubisky. And whether you trust the results that show that Pace has been one of the worst drafters in the league or trust the broader research that suggests that no team can consistently draft better than any other, Pace has handicapped the Bears with his willingness to shed pick value to land his preferred players.

Even for a disciple of the "can't beat the market" doctrine, draft-pick valuation is tricky. Since former Cowboys head coach Jimmy Johnson introduced the public to relative pick value in his trade value chart from the early 1990s, other researchers have tried to answer the trade value question in different ways and come up with meaningfully different conclusions. Chase Stuart of *Football Perspective* focused on on-field player value in the first five years of their careers— a proxy for the duration of their rookie contracts. Rich Hill of *Pats Pulpit* looked instead at actual trades for picks and only those since the 2012 collective bargaining agreement that installed a first-round rookie wage scale and allowed compensatory picks to be traded. Jason Fitzgerald and Brad Spielberger of *Over the Cap* used second contracts to retroactively estimate the value of players on their rookie deals. And those different approaches led to disparate opinions on some of the most important draft considerations, like whether a No. 1 overall pick is dramatically better than other picks in the top 10 and whether an average first-round pick is 50% more valuable than an average second-round pick, twice as valuable, or somewhere in between.

The different trade value charts can agree on one thing: Pace has hemorrhaged draft pick value in his time with the Bears (Table 2). He ranks in the bottom four of net pick value in all four charts. And using each chart to estimate its own projection of that loss, Pace has sacrificed between 1.9 and 3.5 average first-round picks with his various pick-involved trades since 2015.

Table 2. Net Value of Traded Bears Draft Picks in the Ryan Pace era (2015-2021)

Value Chart	Net Value	Rank	1st-Rounder Equiv.
Jimmy Johnson	-2,292.3	29	-2.0
Chase Stuart	-59.0	30	-3.2
Rich Hill	-666.9	29	-1.9
Fitzgerald-Spielberger	-5,929.6	30	-3.5

The Johnson and Hill charts are more forgiving of Pace's imbalanced trades because they reflect the market. In practice, teams demand more for top-10 picks and picks that net quarterbacks than the performance-based Stuart chart estimates they are worth. And there are justifications for those surpluses that likely make this analysis too critical of Pace—Trubisky and Fields sold and will sell tickets and merchandise before they ever took or take an NFL snap. But Pace's employment will likely depend on the Bears' performance on the field the next season or two. And while teams' net value of traded draft picks from recent seasons do not predict their projected 2021 DVOA, they do visually correlate with their roster depth, a critical component of sustained success if secondary to having an elite quarterback (Table 3).

The Rams are a fascinating experiment. Their recent loss of pick value has rendered the Bears' and Texans' otherwise outlier totals modest, and they have climbed to the bottom of this table with eyes wide open. Reporters such as Jourdan Rodrigue of The Athletic have pulled back the curtain on the team's unique perspective on the draft and willingness to move on from the perceived best scouting practices that every other team employs if experience tells the Rams they do not improve their ability to hit on their draft picks. Clearly, the Rams are comfortable trading away first-round picks for proven star players. They have done this in five of the last six drafts.

And maybe the Bears deserve some of the same benefit of the doubt the public offers the Rams for their trade practices. After all, the Khalil Mack trade created a big chunk of the Bears' draft value deficit, and he has excelled for his new team and pushed Chicago's defense to historic heights in his first year with them in 2018. But I can't help but wonder if a Super Bowl berth and standout Sean McVay coaching have to

Table 3. Net Value of Traded Draft Picks per Chase Stuart's Chart (2015-present)

Tm	Trades	Net Value	Rk	1st-Rounder Equiv.	Tm	Trades	Net Value	Rk	1st-Rounder Equiv.
MIA	46	+60.9	1	+3.3	NE	68	-3.1	17	-0.2
CLE	47	+59.3	2	+3.2	PHI	42	-3.5	18	-0.2
LV	42	+55.1	3	+3.0	ATL	17	-5.2	19	-0.3
JAX	21	+51.8	4	+2.8	LAC	4	-8.7	20	-0.5
BAL	32	+48.8	5	+2.7	NO	21	-11.6	21	-0.6
NYJ	36	+43.5	6	+2.4	CAR	24	-16.0	22	-0.9
DET	28	+40.6	7	+2.2	PIT	19	-18.6	23	-1.0
NYG	18	+37.7	8	+2.0	DAL	17	-18.6	23	-1.0
MIN	39	+23.1	9	+1.3	BUF	28	-19.2	25	-1.0
TEN	25	+16.0	10	+0.9	KC	28	-26.5	26	-1.4
CIN	12	+11.7	11	+0.6	SF	35	-32.4	27	-1.8
IND	23	+11.5	12	+0.6	SEA	42	-34.2	28	-1.9
DEN	34	+10.3	13	+0.6	ARI	21	-34.7	29	-1.9
TB	18	+5.1	14	+0.3	CHI	24	-59.0	30	-3.2
GB	18	+2.4	15	+0.1	HOU	30	-78.6	31	-4.3
WAS	22	+1.3	16	+0.1	LAR	41	-109.2	32	-5.9

date covered up the financial mistakes Rams GM Les Snead has made that may have the 2021 Rams in the same situation as the 2021 Bears: needing their new quarterback to hide the holes those mistakes have dug.

Pace may not see those holes after draft trade-ups filled the two biggest ones with Fields at quarterback and Teven Jenkins at offensive tackle. The Bears have at least a promising plan at every starter position. Jenkins will join an offensive line that retains James Daniels, Cody Whitehair, and Germain Ifedi with 2020 blown block rates below 2.0%. Allen Robinson is back on a franchise tag, and he will likely have better support from receiver Darnell Mooney and tight end Cole Kmet in their sophomore seasons. David Montgomery owes much of his late-season outburst to the same schedule imbalance that benefited Trubisky, but he has nevertheless outplayed his basic statistics in his career, finishing in the top 20 of backs with 80 or more touches with 19.9% and 23.9% broken-tackle rates the last two years.

Defensively, Akiem Hicks rebounded from an injury-shortened 2019 season with 25 hurries, ranking in the top 10 among interior defensive linemen. He'll have the All-Pro Mack and free-agent additions from last offseason Robert Quinn and Mario Edwards (once the latter returns from his two-week PED suspension) to help him rush the passer. Middle linebacker Roquan Smith allowed just a 10.9% broken-tackle rate, fourth best—behind Demario Davis, Bobby Wagner, and Jaylon Smith—among linebackers with 75 or more attempted tackles. Eddie Jackson is an All-Pro safety. And cornerback Jaylon Johnson had a top-10 58% coverage success rate in his rookie season.

But the NFL has a way of testing depth, and the Bears may be unable to pass that test after trading away their first-

and second-round draft picks from 2018; their first-, third-, and fourth-round draft picks from 2019; and their third- and fourth-round draft picks from 2020. They have staved off regression with top-10 defensive DVOA rates each of the last three seasons. But what happens if their adjusted games lost on an aging defense continues to descend after falling from fourth-fewest in 2018 to 12th-fewest in 2019 to 13th-most in 2020? Without the boon of extra contributors on inexpensive rookie contracts that more picks from the draft tend to provide, the Bears lack the financial flexibility to fight any adversity. They have less than $6 million of available cap space, a bottom-10 total in the league.

Pace may never have been able to be Ravens GM Eric DeCosta. There is an inertia to team-building through the draft, and Pace didn't inherit Ozzie Newsome's enviable machine. But Pace pushed all-in on a Trubisky-fronted roster. And when Trubisky didn't become Patrick Mahomes or Russell Wilson, Pace borrowed more from the Bears' future to push all-in again. He couldn't have played his cards any better in the trade-up for Fields. But with the debt he has amassed for his team, Pace has nothing left to do but hope that Fields and his supporting 2021 roster doesn't flop.

Scott Spratt

2020 Bears Stats by Week

Wk	vs.	W-L	PF	PA	YDF	YDA	TO	Total	Off	Def	ST
1	at DET	W	27	23	363	426	1	-16.2%	-11.2%	3.2%	-1.7%
2	NYG	W	17	13	304	295	0	-22.2%	-29.4%	-13.3%	-6.0%
3	at ATL	W	30	26	437	371	-1	-7.1%	-16.2%	-12.6%	-3.4%
4	IND	L	11	19	269	289	-1	4.9%	4.7%	-10.8%	-10.7%
5	TB	W	20	19	243	339	0	27.4%	-2.2%	-23.0%	6.7%
6	at CAR	W	23	16	261	303	2	20.1%	-20.6%	-42.2%	-1.4%
7	at LAR	L	10	24	279	371	-1	-25.1%	-30.2%	0.1%	5.2%
8	NO	L	23	26	329	394	-1	8.7%	1.4%	-15.3%	-8.0%
9	at TEN	L	17	24	375	228	-2	-0.4%	-35.8%	-34.8%	0.6%
10	MIN	L	13	19	149	385	0	-2.3%	-56.4%	-23.2%	30.9%
11	BYE										
12	at GB	L	25	41	350	393	-3	-31.5%	-9.3%	21.5%	-0.7%
13	DET	L	30	34	389	460	0	-12.2%	11.7%	28.7%	4.9%
14	HOU	W	36	7	410	263	2	36.3%	3.9%	-23.8%	8.6%
15	at MIN	W	33	27	397	407	0	4.8%	2.4%	3.5%	5.8%
16	at JAX	W	41	17	391	279	1	17.1%	0.8%	-15.5%	0.8%
17	GB	L	16	35	356	316	-1	-24.8%	1.4%	35.7%	9.4%
18	at NO	L	9	21	239	385	1	25.4%	16.7%	-10.9%	-2.3%

Trends and Splits

	Offense	Rank	Defense	Rank
Total DVOA	-10.6%	25	-7.5%	8
Unadjusted VOA	-8.2%	24	-3.3%	12
Weighted Trend	-6.7%	21	-3.8%	13
Variance	3.5%	6	4.8%	16
Average Opponent	2.2%	27	6.4%	1
Passing	1.6%	23	3.4%	13
Rushing	-18.3%	25	-22.5%	4
First Down	-3.1%	21	-5.8%	12
Second Down	-6.1%	22	-15.8%	6
Third Down	-31.4%	32	1.5%	18
First Half	3.0%	14	-5.8%	11
Second Half	-24.1%	31	-9.2%	7
Red Zone	-10.4%	21	11.3%	27
Late and Close	-23.2%	28	-15.7%	7

Five-Year Performance

Year	W-L	Pyth W	Est W	PF	PA	TO	Total	Rk	Off	Rk	Def	Rk	ST	Rk	Off AGL	Rk	Def AGL	Rk	Off Age	Rk	Def Age	Rk	ST Age	Rk
2016	3-13	4.7	6.1	279	399	-20	-8.8%	25	-2.8%	17	5.4%	22	-0.6%	18	84.0	31	87.5	32	26.7	16	26.0	24	26.2	11
2017	5-11	6.2	5.7	264	320	0	-17.0%	25	-15.0%	28	-0.4%	14	-2.4%	23	56.4	25	68.1	30	26.6	20	26.1	17	26.0	10
2018	12-4	11.6	10.6	421	283	+14	19.1%	5	-3.1%	20	-25.4%	1	-3.2%	26	20.3	6	14.2	4	26.1	26	26.0	22	26.1	11
2019	8-8	7.4	7.6	280	298	0	-3.1%	18	-9.9%	25	-5.8%	10	0.9%	13	36.9	15	28.5	13	26.0	29	26.9	6	26.4	7
2020	8-8	8.1	7.9	372	370	-4	-0.6%	15	-10.6%	25	-7.5%	8	2.6%	8	40.2	18	46.9	20	26.6	20	27.5	2	27.2	3

2020 Performance Based on Most Common Personnel Groups

CHI Offense					CHI Offense vs. Opponents					CHI Defense					CHI Defense vs. Opponents			
Pers	Freq	Yds	DVOA	Run%	Pers	Freq	Yds	DVOA	Run%	Pers	Freq	Yds	DVOA		Pers	Freq	Yds	DVOA
11	56%	5.3	-7.0%	25%	Base	18%	5.1	-5.5%	57%	Base	33%	4.9	-20.3%		11	58%	5.9	-2.9%
12	19%	5.2	5.2%	51%	Nickel	56%	5.2	-7.4%	37%	Nickel	53%	5.9	5.2%		12	21%	5.5	-15.7%
01	8%	5.3	-18.1%	32%	Dime+	26%	5.4	-2.6%	13%	Dime+	13%	6.2	-33.3%		21	10%	5.5	-12.6%
13	6%	4.2	-45.3%	62%	Goal Line	0%	-1.0	-143.3%	67%	Goal Line	0%	0.6	11.7%		13	4%	4.1	-11.8%
02	5%	6.1	20.7%	45%											02	2%	6.7	40.1%
03	3%	3.6	-22.8%	37%											22	2%	4.9	-26.4%

Strategic Tendencies

Run/Pass		Rk	Formation		Rk	Pass Rush		Rk	Secondary		Rk	Strategy		Rk
Runs, first half	38%	15	Form: Single Back	84%	10	Rush 3	4.2%	21	4 DB	33%	8	Play Action	31%	9
Runs, first down	43%	24	Form: Empty Back	8%	19	Rush 4	76.1%	5	5 DB	53%	25	Offensive Motion	38%	26
Runs, second-long	29%	15	Form: Multi Back	7%	20	Rush 5	17.5%	23	6+ DB	13%	15	Avg Box (Off)	6.37	29
Runs, power sit.	56%	22	Pers: 3+ WR	70%	10	Rush 6+	2.1%	29	Man Coverage	27%	20	Avg Box (Def)	6.46	24
Runs, behind 2H	23%	26	Pers: 2+ TE/6+ OL	34%	10	Edge Rusher Sacks	42.9%	25	CB by Sides	96%	1	Offensive Pace	31.50	27
Pass, ahead 2H	51%	10	Pers: 6+ OL	0%	26	Interior DL Sacks	42.9%	4	S/CB Cover Ratio	27%	15	Defensive Pace	30.35	18
Run-Pass Options	10%	9	Shotgun/Pistol	65%	18	Second Level Sacks	14.3%	29	DB Blitz	6%	32	Go for it on 4th	1.42	21

The Bears went with two tight ends twice as often as they did the year before. ◔ The Bears are listed as running 32% of the time from 01 personnel (no backs) because this includes plays with Cordarrelle Patterson lined up in the backfield. ◔ Chicago receivers dropped just 18 passes, ranking them second in drop rate (3.1%) behind Arizona. ◔ Chicago receivers were also excellent at breaking tackles. Thirty wide receivers had at least 12 broken tackles last season and three of them were Bears: Darnell Mooney (14), Allen Robinson (13), and Patterson (13). Overall, the Bears finished sixth with 134 broken tackles. ◔ This was the third straight year Chicago's defense was No. 1 in "CB by Sides." ◔ Chicago opponents threw 36% of passes in the middle of the field, the highest figure in the NFL. Chicago's DVOA on these plays matched the league average. ◔ Matt Nagy was less aggressive on fourth downs than he was the prior season; he finished second in Aggressiveness Index at 2.26 in 2019.

Passing

Player	DYAR	DVOA	Plays	NtYds	Avg	YAC	C%	TD	Int
N.Foles	-112	-16.3%	329	1688	5.1	3.5	65.2%	10	8
M.Trubisky*	79	-7.5%	315	1930	6.1	5.0	67.0%	16	8
A.Dalton	-136	-16.7%	357	1976	5.5	4.8	65.1%	14	8

Rushing

Player	DYAR	DVOA	Plays	Yds	Avg	TD	Fum	Suc
D.Montgomery	57	-3.4%	247	1070	4.3	8	0	47%
C.Patterson*	67	-20.6%	64	232	3.6	1	0	--
M.Trubisky*	9	-7.0%	33	195	5.9	1	1	--
T.Cohen	13	16.4%	14	74	5.3	0	0	50%
A.Pierce	6	9.8%	6	34	5.7	1	0	67%
N.Foles	-7	-31.8%	5	12	2.4	1	0	--
A.Dalton	24	5.2%	24	116	4.8	0	1	--

Receiving

Player	DYAR	DVOA	Plays	Ctch	Yds	Y/C	YAC	TD	C%
A.Robinson	175	1.4%	151	102	1250	12.3	3.1	6	68%
D.Mooney	-60	-20.3%	98	61	623	10.2	4.2	4	62%
A.Miller	-80	-26.4%	76	49	485	9.9	3.0	2	64%
C.Patterson*	-39	-33.2%	25	21	132	6.3	5.4	0	84%
J.Wims	-1	-13.3%	12	6	48	8.0	0.7	1	50%
T.Ginn*	-13	-41.2%	6	3	40	13.3	3.3	0	50%
D.Byrd	2	-12.3%	77	47	604	12.9	3.7	1	61%
J.Graham	8	-5.8%	76	50	456	9.1	4.0	8	66%
C.Kmet	-63	-29.0%	44	28	243	8.7	4.9	2	64%
D.Harris*	-51	-58.3%	14	7	45	6.4	3.6	0	50%
D.Montgomery	113	14.1%	68	54	438	8.1	7.3	2	79%
R.Nall	32	54.5%	9	8	67	8.4	5.9	1	89%
T.Cohen	-12	-38.8%	9	6	41	6.8	10.2	0	67%

Offensive Line

Player	Pos	Age	GS	Snaps	Pen	Sk	Pass	Run	Player	Pos	Age	GS	Snaps	Pen	Sk	Pass	Run
Charles Leno*	LT	30	16/16	1066	7	3.5	19	4	Bobby Massie*	RT	32	8/8	470	1	3.5	12	1
Germain Ifedi	RG/RT	27	16/16	1066	4	1.5	9	9	Rashaad Coward	LG	27	16/5	333	2	1.5	8	4
Cody Whitehair	C/LG	29	14/14	893	0	1	7	3	James Daniels	LG	24	5/5	305	1	0	3	2
Alex Bars	RG	26	16/8	568	2	1	3	6	Elijah Wilkinson	RT	26	9/7	502	1	2	9	5
Sam Mustipher	C	25	9/7	504	0	1	4	10									

Year	Yards	ALY	Rk	Power	Rk	Stuff	Rk	2Lev	Rk	OpFld	Rk	BB Rt	Rk	Sacks	ASR	Rk	Press	Rk	BB Rt	Rk	Cont
2018	3.83	3.92	28	67%	18	21%	22	0.96	31	0.63	26	7.8%	26	33	6.0%	7	26.4%	8	10.6%	22	33
2019	3.56	3.86	29	50%	31	18%	16	0.89	31	0.39	30	10.7%	19	45	7.3%	21	29.5%	14	12.8%	13	26
2020	4.39	4.16	25	61%	25	19%	29	1.16	20	0.84	10	11.6%	22	36	6.2%	15	26.3%	20	10.3%	7	29

2020 ALY by direction:	Left End: 3.84 (26)	Left Tackle: 4.48 (13)	Mid/Guard: 4.05 (29)	Right Tackle: 4.26 (17)	Right End: 4.38 (19)

With little offensive line investment prior to 2021, the Bears' run-blocking plateaued at poor figures of 3.92, 3.86, and 3.97 adjusted line yards in 2018, 2019, and Weeks 1 to 10 of 2020. The team shuffled its lineup during their Week 11 bye and enjoyed improved rushing, jumping from -27.8% to -6.7% in DVOA. But that improvement owes a lot to open-field yards on breakaway carries. The team's adjusted line yards only improved to 4.40 (20th) after the bye. ❧ As the 39th overall pick in 2018, James Daniels was the team's biggest recent blocking investment. And he teased a junior-year breakout, cutting his blown block rate from 2.8% in 2019 to 1.7% in 2020 before a Week 5 pectoral injury. Meanwhile, the team traded up in 2021 and chose another lineman 39th overall: Oklahoma State tackle Teven Jenkins. The Bears' subsequent release of incumbent left tackle Charles Leno suggests a plan to play Jenkins in that spot as a rookie, but some scouts are skeptical of Jenkins' fit on the blind side since he sometimes struggled with speed off the edge in college. ❧ Cody Whitehair is an anchor on the interior but without a locked-in position. He shifted between center and guard in 2020 to accommodate other injuries and available substitutes, but he was his typical excellent self. He has never blown more than 1.5% of his blocks in five seasons with the Bears. ❧ With Bobby Massie and Rashaad Coward gone, some combination of Germain Ifedi, Elijah Wilkinson, Alex Bars, and Sam Mustipher should round out the starting line. The former first-rounder Ifedi underwhelmed in four seasons with the Seahawks, but he produced a career-best 1.7% blown block rate and allowed just two sacks in his first season with the Bears. He did so despite a midseason shift from an easier right guard position back to right tackle where he had played in Seattle. Perhaps Russell Wilson inflated his previous numbers. Offensive line coach Juan Castillo told reporters in June he thinks Ifedi could make the Pro Bowl this year. ❧ Wilkinson's one-year, $1.3-million contract suggests he is a backup. But the former undrafted Broncos tackle started 26 games in Denver and could start on the right side in Chicago if the team opts to bring Ifedi inside again. ❧ Bars and Mustipher were Notre Dame teammates the Bears signed after they went undrafted in 2019, and they showed promise in 2020 with 2.8% and 1.7% blown block rates as second-half starters at center and right guard. Perhaps the hour-and-40-minute drive from Soldier Field to South Bend allowed the Bears some extra scouting opportunities.

Defensive Front

Defensive Line	Age	Pos	G	Snaps	Plays	Overall TmPct	Rk	Stop	Dfts	BTkl	vs. Run Runs	St%	Rk	RuYd	Rk	Pass Rush Sack	Hit	Hur	Dsrpt
Akiem Hicks	32	DE	15	795	50	6.5%	18	42	13	3	44	82%	19	1.9	22	3.5	18	24	2
Bilal Nichols	25	DT	16	617	43	5.2%	49	37	11	6	32	84%	10	2.1	33	5.0	8	16	2
Brent Urban*	30	DE	16	369	37	4.5%	--	33	6	2	32	88%	--	1.8	--	2.5	1	6	2
Mario Edwards	27	DE	15	255	18	2.3%	--	16	6	1	10	90%	--	2.3	--	4.0	3	11	1
Roy Robertson-Harris*	28	DE	8	245	10	2.4%	93	7	1	1	9	67%	69	3.3	90	0.0	5	6	1
John Jenkins*	32	DT	11	223	22	3.9%	--	18	1	1	20	80%	--	2.4	--	0.0	1	2	1
Angelo Blackson	29	DE	16	552	24	2.8%	87	17	5	7	20	70%	60	1.8	18	2.5	5	11	0
Mike Pennel	30	DT	14	320	29	4.1%	--	20	1	0	26	73%	--	3.2	--	0.0	1	1	0

Edge Rushers	Age	Pos	G	Snaps	Plays	Overall TmPct	Rk	Stop	Dfts	BTkl	Runs	St%	vs. Run Rk	RuYd	Rk	Sack	Pass Rush Hit	Hur	Dsrpt
Khalil Mack	30	OLB	16	894	53	6.4%	19	45	23	3	38	79%	17	1.8	21	9.0	6	25	2
Robert Quinn	31	OLB	15	548	20	2.6%	90	10	7	3	15	53%	92	3.9	89	2.0	6	18	2
Barkevious Mingo*	31	OLB	16	389	31	3.8%	--	19	6	5	21	62%	--	3.2	--	2.5	2	8	1
James Vaughters	28	OLB	14	243	19	2.6%	--	14	3	1	15	73%	--	3.1	--	1.5	0	2	0

Linebackers	Age	Pos	G	Snaps	Plays	Overall TmPct	Rk	Stop	Dfts	BTkl	Runs	St%	vs. Run Rk	RuYd	Rk	Sack	Pass Rush Hit	Hur	Tgts	vs. Pass Suc%	Rk	Yd/P	Rk	PD	Int
Roquan Smith	24	ILB	16	1016	145	17.6%	8	90	33	12	85	59%	31	4.6	67	4.0	2	7	49	76%	1	3.9	6	7	2
Danny Trevathan	31	ILB	16	831	118	14.3%	30	54	14	10	68	60%	29	4.4	62	1.0	1	4	40	30%	72	11.0	75	5	0
Christian Jones	30	OLB	16	510	51	6.1%	81	28	4	6	38	55%	45	4.1	48	0.0	1	9	4	100%	--	2.8	--	1	0

Year	Yards	ALY	Rk	Power	Rk	Stuff	Rk	2Lev	Rk	OpFld	Rk	BB Rt	Rk	Sacks	ASR	Rk	Press	Rk	BB Rt	Rk
2018	3.63	3.97	9	58%	4	20%	14	0.98	4	0.45	4	15.0%	1	50	7.5%	12	33.4%	3	15.2%	1
2019	3.89	4.26	17	66%	19	14%	29	0.93	2	0.54	6	10.7%	26	32	6.6%	22	29.6%	20	14.4%	20
2020	4.15	4.17	11	60%	6	18%	15	1.21	17	0.63	11	13.2%	15	35	6.6%	15	22.8%	27	15.0%	9

2020 ALY by direction:	Left End: 4.65 (20)	Left Tackle: 4.35 (18)	Mid/Guard: 3.95 (5)	Right Tackle: 4.05 (11)	Right End: 4.76 (20)

The Bears saw their defensive pressure rate decline from 33.4% to 29.6% to 22.8% over the last three seasons. They'll hope to bounce back with their full lineup in 2020. In 2019, Akiem Hicks missed 11 games with an elbow injury. He returned to health and to form in 2020 with 24 hurries—he had 28 in one extra game in his Pro Bowl 2018 season. But he lost his running mate and 2019 Pro Bowl alternate Eddie Goldman to a COVID opt-out. ✎ Goldman will restore some line depth in a rotation with Hicks and 2020 breakout Bilal Nichols, who improved his run stop rate from 72% in his sophomore season to 84% last year, a top-10 rate among defensive tackles. And the Bears need Goldman now that they lost incumbent tackle Roy Robertson-Harris to a big-money deal with the Jaguars. ✎ Edge rushers Khalil Mack and Robert Quinn each saw their hurry totals decline more than 50% from their 2018/2019 standards, and they are both now on the wrong side of 30. The Bears will have to hope new defensive coordinator Sean Desai—a Vic Fangio disciple who was a defensive quality control coach for Fangio's full run with the team—can breathe new life into them. ✎ 2020 fifth-rounder Trevis Gipson and undrafted rookie Charles Snowden bring young potential on the edge. The latter's six sacks in eight starts as a senior at Virginia Tech gave him Day 2 draft potential, so perhaps his ankle surgery scared teams away in a difficult year for medical evaluation. ✎ If Mack has slipped, then linebacker Roquan Smith is ready to assume the mantle of the best Bears defender. Smith tied Super Bowl champion Devin White for the NFL lead with 33 defeats in 2020, and he nearly doubled White's coverage success rate 76% to 41%, leading the position there too. That latter piece is critical for the Bears since Smith's off-ball running mate Danny Trevathan has declined from 47% to 35% to 30% coverage success rate the last three seasons as he has entered his early thirties.

Defensive Secondary

Secondary	Age	Pos	G	Snaps	Plays	Overall TmPct	Rk	Stop	Dfts	BTkl	Runs	St%	vs. Run Rk	RuYd	Rk	Tgts	Tgt%	Rk	vs. Pass aDOT	Suc%	Rk	Yd/P	Rk	PD	Int
Kyle Fuller*	29	CB	16	1059	73	8.8%	36	29	12	18	19	37%	51	6.5	36	67	15.7%	71	13.1	58%	10	6.4	14	8	1
Eddie Jackson	28	SS	16	1059	87	10.5%	38	22	7	15	40	28%	54	8.9	55	35	8.2%	39	14.0	46%	48	9.4	56	5	0
Tashaun Gipson	31	FS	16	1054	73	8.8%	59	33	4	10	35	54%	8	5.1	17	30	7.1%	47	11.0	50%	36	8.3	45	7	2
Jaylon Johnson	22	CB	13	867	59	8.8%	39	29	14	7	14	57%	13	4.5	13	65	18.7%	48	13.4	57%	14	7.8	47	15	0
Buster Skrine*	32	CB	12	556	69	11.2%	12	25	11	9	21	52%	21	4.8	19	53	23.7%	12	10.4	40%	72	8.4	53	3	0
Duke Shelley	25	CB	11	208	16	2.8%	--	7	2	1	4	75%	--	5.0	--	13	15.6%	--	10.5	38%	--	6.0	--	1	0
Desmond Trufant	31	CB	6	324	23	7.3%	--	9	5	5	6	17%	--	6.5	--	28	22.6%	--	11.1	46%	--	8.4	--	4	1

Year	Pass D Rank	vs. #1 WR	Rk	vs. #2 WR	Rk	vs. Other WR	Rk	WR Wide	Rk	WR Slot	Rk	vs. TE	Rk	vs. RB	Rk
2018	1	-30.4%	1	-24.2%	3	-20.3%	4	-19.6%	3	-31.2%	1	-33.6%	3	-9.5%	10
2019	8	-17.3%	5	2.1%	17	-29.4%	3	2.1%	21	-27.1%	2	2.9%	16	-9.1%	12
2020	13	-24.1%	2	-10.1%	10	30.1%	32	2.9%	17	-4.0%	14	5.3%	19	-34.7%	2

Jaylon Johnson made good on his pre-draft scouting report as an excellent press man corner with a 57% coverage success rate, better than the five rookie corners taken ahead of him. But he also missed four games (including the team's playoff loss) with a shoulder injury like those that plagued him in college and spurred his fall to the second round. The Bears are hoping for a healthy second season since Kyle Fuller's departure for Denver promotes Johnson to No. 1 corner. ◦ Free-agent addition Desmond Trufant gives the Bears another corner with injury issues. He has managed just 15 total games the last two seasons thanks to various hamstring, toe, and arm injuries, but he also brings the experience of 103 career starts. He was effective in his last full season in 2018, allowing just 6.2 yards per target (14th), but struggled with 10.3 and 8.4 yards per target over the last two injury-riddled seasons. ◦ The Bears got it right in their second attempt to replace strong safety Adrian Amos. Veteran Tashaun Gipson produced a top-10 run stop rate of 54% in his first year with the team and earned another one-year deal and modest pay raise. ◦ Having confidence in Gipson in run defense will hopefully help 2018 All-Pro Eddie Jackson rebound from his worst season, which the Bears were undoubtedly disappointed to see in the first year of a four-year, $58.4-million extension. Jackson has done his best work with deeper starting alignments. He spent more time near the line of scrimmage in 2020 and failed to intercept a pass for the first time in his career. ◦ After releasing Buster Skrine to clear $2 million in cap space, the Bears ignored their nickel corner position in free agency. Perhaps that suggests some confidence in incumbent options Duke Shelley and Artie Burns, but the former has just two starts in two professional seasons and the latter missed his first Bears season with a torn ACL. It's also possible the team will look to sixth-round rookie Thomas Graham Jr. (Oregon), whose instincts and strong tackling may make a better fit in the slot than outside.

Special Teams

Year	DVOA	Rank	FG/XP	Rank	Net Kick	Rank	Kick Ret	Rank	Net Punt	Rank	Punt Ret	Rank	Hidden	Rank
2018	-3.2%	26	-10.2	29	-1.5	22	-6.2	31	-2.5	22	4.4	9	-17.1	32
2019	0.9%	13	-4.6	23	-3.5	24	7.5	2	2.0	16	3.3	6	2.2	13
2020	2.6%	8	7.0	6	2.7	11	7.9	3	-1.8	21	-2.9	23	5.3	10

After Cody Parkey doinked the Bears out of the playoffs in 2018, Chicago suffered so heavy a mental crisis that fans lined up in the snow to try (and fail) to make their own 43-yard field goals at a local brewery. It's not surprising then that the team traded a draft pick for Eddy Piñeiro and had a three-kicker camp battle that offseason. It is surprising and definitely funny that the Bears enjoyed dramatic improvement and a top-six placekicking unit in 2020 after Piñeiro suffered a preseason groin injury and the team added Cairo Santos, available for any team, in late August. Santos went on to convert 30 of 32 field goals, good for a 93.8% rate that was easily the best of his career. And yes, the Bears did re-sign Santos to a five-year, $16-million contract. How did you guess? ◦ Cordarrelle Patterson transformed the Bears' kick return game with two All-Pro seasons. His departure leaves a hole that the team may tab sixth-round rookie running back Khalil Herbert to try to fill. Herbert averaged 26.9 yards on 16 returns in his one year with Virginia Tech after transferring from Kansas. ◦ Bookend seasons of 9.4 and 9.2 yards per punt return may identify Tarik Cohen's 12.5-yard average in his All-Pro 2018 season as an anomaly, but even his lesser seasons landed him among the best punt returners in football. The Bears missed Cohen on special teams when he tore his ACL in 2020 and are a good bet to bounce back from their 23rd-ranked punt return point value with him back in 2021. ◦ Punter Pat O'Donnell is consistently close to league average.

Cincinnati Bengals

2020 Record: 4-11-1	**Total DVOA:** -24.7% (31)	**2021 Mean Projection:** 7.5 wins	**On the Clock (0-5):** 25%
Pythagorean Wins: 5.1 (28)	**Offense:** -18.2% (29)	**Postseason Odds:** 27.0%	**Mediocrity (6-8):** 41%
Snap-Weighted Age: 26 (24)	**Defense:** 9.1% (27)	**Super Bowl Odds:** 1.9%	**Playoff Contender (9-11):** 27%
Average Opponent: -1.3% (20)	**Special Teams:** 2.6% (9)	**Proj. Avg. Opponent:** 1.9% (5)	**Super Bowl Contender (12+):** 8%

2020: The Bengals break Joe Burrow moments after taking him out of the box.

2021: Look upon Marvin Lewis' works, ye Mighty, and despair. Nothing, not even Giovani Bernard, remains.

Writing about the Cincinnati Bengals in 2021 is like performing an autopsy on a skeleton unearthed from a burial mound near Stonehenge. The Jets and Jaguars are annual crime scenes requiring forensic scientists, but the Bengals are an archeological site. To figure out what annihilated their briefly thriving civilization, we need to scrape away layers of dust and neglect and piece together the pottery shards found in nearby middens.

Other teams are bad because their coaches or general managers made critical mistakes in the last two or three years. The Bengals are bad because of events that took place in playoff games during the Obama administration. The Bengals do not collapse or tank like other teams. They erode.

The Bengals are mired in a decline phase that began in 2016. It took them three miserable seasons to finally move on from Marvin Lewis and a fourth to finally get around to replacing Andy Dalton. The Eagles rose and began to fall in that period. The Browns went through two or three mini-epochs, depending on who's counting. But the Bengals operate on paleontological time. They don't get around to solving problems until those problems become crises. Then they jerry-rig temporary solutions. When those fail, they jerry-rig something else. And so forth, until a half-decade has passed and they have been duct-taping the duct tape together for so long that they honestly believe that's how it's supposed to be done.

The Bengals didn't feel the need to replace Dalton until Joe Burrow fell into their lap in the 2020 draft. Burrow was so obviously overqualified to be the first overall pick that even an organization operating on autopilot was bound to select him, and sure enough one did. The Bengals then installed Burrow behind an offensive line which had finished with adjusted sack rates higher than 7.0% in every season since 2016 and 22nd or lower in adjusted line yards in every season since 2017. The resulting devastating knee injury to Burrow was sadly inevitable.

In this year's draft, the Bengals faced a choice between Penei Sewell, one of the top tackle prospects of the last decade, and Ja'Marr Chase, the best of a typically stacked class at wide receiver—one of the few positions at which the Bengals boast a pair of capable starters in Tyler Boyd and 2020 rookie Tee Higgins. Naturally, the organization which fielded patchwork lines for half a decade and just subjected its budding franchise quarterback to a Mortal Kombat fatality chose Chase.

The Sewell/Chase scenario was much debated before and after the draft. It's easy to construct a plausible justification for selecting Chase. Left tackle Jonah Williams, when healthy, is currently the best player on the Bengals line; he or Sewell would have to switch positions, and Sewell later voiced his difficulties when sliding to right tackle in Lions camp. The Bengals signed veteran Riley Reiff to solidify right tackle before the draft; Reiff played left tackle for the Vikings, but let's put a pin in that for now. They also added rookies Jackson Carman, D'Ante Smith, and Trey Hill after selecting Chase, so the Bengals hardly ignored their offensive line. And Chase joins Tyler Boyd and Tee Higgins to give Burrow one of the league's best young receiving corps. Zac Taylor deployed 11 personnel on 76% of offensive plays last season and four wide receivers on an additional 5%, so the third receiver in the Bengals offense (even more so than in most NFL offenses) is essentially another starter.

To understand why shunning Sewell for Chase was such a bad idea, we need to head to the dig site with our shovels and tiny brushes.

The Bengals have been trying, in their half-baked way, to repair their offensive line for years. Way back in 2015, when they were still quasi-contenders with a set starting lineup, they drafted tackles Cedric Ogbuehi and Jake Fisher with their first- and second-round picks as developmental replacements for Andrew Whitworth and Andre Smith. It would have been a sound plan if the Bengals had chosen better prospects. But Ogbuehi was a first-round reach coming off an ACL tear at the end of his college career while Fisher was a combine hero who didn't quite fit at either left or right tackle.

Both Ogbuehi and Fisher suffered multiple injuries and other ailments early in their careers (heart arrhythmia, in Fisher's case) and flopped as starters. So what did the Bengals do? They let Whitworth go but kept running Andre Smith and Eric Winston onto the field well beyond their expiration dates whenever Ogbuehi, Fisher, or others were ineffective or unavailable. It goes without saying that Whitworth was still playing at a high level for the Rams at age 39 before getting injured last year.

The Bengals finally figured out that their prospects-and-old-timers platoon at tackle wasn't working after the 2017 season, so they traded for Cordy Glenn and signed Bobby Hart to a three-year deal. Glenn was available from the Bills because of

2021 Bengals Schedule

Week	Opp.	Week	Opp.	Week	Opp.
1	MIN	7	at BAL	13	LAC
2	at CHI	8	at NYJ	14	SF
3	at PIT	9	CLE	15	at DEN
4	JAX (Thu.)	10	BYE	16	BAL
5	GB	11	at LV	17	KC
6	at DET	12	PIT	18	at CLE

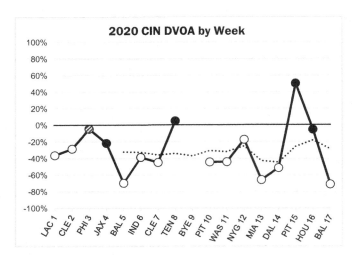

2020 CIN DVOA by Week

his persistent injuries; sure enough, he was rarely healthy in Cincinnati and squabbled with the organization about his concussion status for many weeks in 2019. Hart was every bit as terrible in Cincy as he had been with the Giants, so of course he was still starting at right tackle last season.

Center Billy Price came aboard with the 21st overall pick in 2018, then Jonah Williams with the 11th overall pick in 2019. Price, an Ohio State stalwart who tore a pectoral muscle at the combine, has been a glorified medical redshirt for three years. Williams promptly suffered a shoulder injury in rookie OTAs and missed all of 2019. He performed capably at left tackle last season in between a neck injury that sidelined him early in the season and a knee injury which knocked him out for the year in Week 13.

To restack your scorecard: the Bengals spent five years overdrafting offensive linemen who arrived on Day 1 as damaged goods (Ogbuehi, Price, Fisher), drafted some tackles whom many experts believed were better suited to guard (Williams, Fisher), acquired other teams' unwanted veterans (Glenn, Hart) and held onto just about everyone at least a year too long except for the possible Hall of Famer (Whitworth). They also had plenty of bad luck, but an organization makes its own luck when it keeps drafting and trading for the already injured.

So instead of selecting Sewell, the Bengals spent the 2021 offseason trying to upgrade their offensive line using the same tactics that have been failing for years. Reiff, while a fine acquisition on paper and an upgrade over Bobby and the Turnstiles if he starts at right tackle, is this year's Glenn: a 32-year-old available because his previous team (Vikings) was tired of paying him. Second-round pick Carman is a college tackle projected to move to guard because he's not quick enough to play tackle, checking off the "not quite a tackle" box. Fourth-round pick D'Ante Smith missed most of his senior season with an undisclosed injury, checking off the "damaged goods prospect" box. Sixth-round center Trey Hill has a reputation for wild snaps, checking off the Michael Jordan box: "major program center likely to move to guard." Factor in another cross-your-fingers season for Williams and another scholarship year for Price and Jordan and this year's makeover looks too much like the last five makeovers. That makes it tempting to pencil in Sewell as another Whitworth that got away.

The rickety line won't get much help from Zac Taylor's system. The Bengals attempted to pass from an empty backfield

146 times last season, the third-highest total in the NFL. With Burrow at quarterback, they had an exceptional 42.6% DVOA and averaged 6.4 yards per play from empty backfields. So the operation was a success, except that the patient nearly died: Bengals quarterbacks were sacked a league-high 13 times on empty-backfield attempts.

Meanwhile, Taylor did not use play-action as often or as effectively as his fellow Mini-McVays around the NFL. The Bengals dropped back for play-action passes just 151 times last year, 22nd in the NFL. They averaged just 6.5 yards per play on play-action passes, 25th in the NFL. That's right: the Bengals used empty backfields almost exactly as often as they used play-action!

The coach who called almost 10 empty-backfield plays per week for rookie/backup quarterbacks behind a revolving cast of potato sacks on the offensive line didn't draft Chase to join Boyd and Higgins because he's planning to go max protect this year. Burrow will spend 2021 hoping his receivers are enough of a deterrent to keep the defense from blitzing much, and that those receivers can get open before the pass rush arrives.

That's not an utterly foolish tactic: Derrik Klassen's film study for Football Outsiders[1] suggests that empty-backfield concepts mesh well with Burrow's strengths as a passer, and the Boyd-Chase-Higgins trio will keep some defenses on their heels. But the Bengals had gobs of cap space, a top-five draft pick, and no need at quarterback: the Holy Trinity of NFL rebuilding. They could have added Sewell AND Reiff AND a top guard such as Gabe Jackson or Joe Thuney AND drafted a center who can actually snap from a very deep class, with enough cash and draft capital left over for a third wide receiver and some defensive help. Taylor could then safely empty the backfield 60 times per game if that's what he's really into. Instead, the Bengals made changes that should upgrade their offensive line from 24th in adjusted sack rate to maybe 19th or 20th, their ranking from 2017 through 2019. From a risk/reward and investment/protection standpoint, the Bengals are really tempting fate.

The gingerbread improvements along the offensive line

---

[1] https://www.footballoutsiders.com/film-room/2020/film-room-joe-burrow

would be forgivable if the Bengals spent their cap space and draft picks improving a defense which finished 28th, 30th, and 27th in the league over the last three years. They opted instead to make a series of strange lateral defensive acquisitions. Edge rusher Carl Lawson signed with the Jets after an excellent season; the slightly cheaper Trey Hendrickson arrived from the Saints as a replacement. Young veteran cornerback William Jackson left for Washington; Chidi Awuzie of the Cowboys takes his place. Farewell, fading longtime starter Shawn Williams! Hello, oft-injured Falcons disappointment Ricardo Allen!

After all the shuffling, the 2021 Bengals defense will consist of All Pro-caliber free safety Jessie Bates, his sidekick Vonn Bell, and an odd assortment of journeymen and "where are they now?" cases. If you like failed prospects at cornerback, the Bengals have Eli Apple and Trey Waynes. If you prefer reclamation projects along the defensive line, Mike Daniels is somehow lurking on the back of the roster. If you like pass-rushers, well, sorry: Hendrickson and newcomer Larry Ogunjobi are the only guys on the roster with more than two sacks last year, and Ogunjobi had 2.5 for the Browns. And while Hendrickson's 13.5 sacks for the Saints in 2020 are more impressive than Lawson's 5.5, Hendrickson benefitted from playing for one of the league's deepest defensive line rotations.

Overall, the Bengals will likely enjoy a very modest net gain from the arrivals of Reiff, Hendrickson, Awuzie, and others. They also finally parted ways with A.J. Green, Gio Bernard, Geno Atkins, and Williams, which was progress in a way: the Bengals4Life from the early 2010s were becoming more of an anchor each season, all of them playing just well enough to eat cap space and forestall a real youth movement. It's just shocking to see a team in the Bengals' situation purposely settle for "very modest net gains." It's Year 3 of the Taylor era, Year 6 since the Bengals last reached the playoffs. Where have the money, resources, and time gone?

The lack of urgency and vision is the inevitable result of the Bengals' notoriously rickety power structure. The Bengals personnel department appears to consist of Taylor, Duke Tobin, Stevie Budd from *Schitt's Creek*, and one copier/fax/printer/scanner.

Tobin, officially Director of Player Personnel but unofficially owner/president Mike Brown's showrunner, was a hot general manager candidate in the early 2010s but has cooled after five seasons of wandering in the wilderness. Tobin has been part of the Bengals banana stand in various capacities since 1999; whatever his talents when helping build the wild-card teams of the early 2010s, he has clearly grown a tad myopic. His skeletal staff includes scouting directors who have been with the organization for years and never held executive roles outside the organization, with the notable exception of his father Bill, a general manager from the 1990s. The Bengals front office isn't exactly an idea factory, but they make up for it by being shorthanded.

Meanwhile, Taylor is supported by the most anonymous coaching staff in the NFL. Lou Anarumo has been a defensive coordinator for two years, yet could walk through the High Velocity sports bar at the Indianapolis J.W. Marriott on the first night of the scouting combine without being recognized. He has done nothing to keep his job, but in fairness, he did nothing to earn his job, either.

Several of Taylor's coaches are former scouts, including quarterback coach Dan Pitcher. There may be some benefits to cross-training scouts as coaches, but the fact remains that Burrow's development is currently in the hands of someone whose sole qualification is that he supervised Dalton's decline phase. Offensive coordinator Brian Callahan is a 36-year-old who "rose through the ranks" as the quarterback coach for veterans such as Matthew Stafford and Derek Carr while working for his dad's old pals.

The one semi-famous Bengals assistant from 2020 was actually infamous: offensive line coach Jim Turner, known for his role in the Dolphins Bullygate scandal and his sexist comments at a Texas A&M football clinic. Turner reportedly was up to his old tricks in Cincy, using abusive language that was too coarse for even NFL guys and playing favorites among the linemen. Turner was fired after last season's disaster and replaced by Frank Pollack, the former Dallas Ploughboys line coach who spent 2018 with the Bengals but left "by mutual decision" when Taylor was hired.

Taylor's staff, in other words, is full of guys who pose no professional threat to Taylor, who has also demonstrated a habit of clashing with veterans (he squabbled with Carlos Dunlap, leading to the edge rusher's trade to the Seahawks) and earned a reputation for not relating to his players. Taylor wields personnel control on par with Tobin, meaning that the Bengals are run by an overpromoted, overtaxed, over-his-head would-be wunderkind; his yes-man staff; an under-staffed company man of a general manager; and an ownership masthead populated by a failson and his family. No wonder both the short-term and long-term plans are a wee bit fuzzy.

The 2021 Bengals will look a lot like the 2020 model, with Chase replacing the 2012 version of A.J. Green who still existed in the minds and hearts of fans and the organization. They will also look a little like the New York Giants: great receiver corps, a defense lightly dusted with talent, lots of wishes and hopes on the offensive line, and a quarterback who may or may not be the future. Off the field, the Bengals resemble a small-market version of the Giants with their slow-cooked, keep-it-in-the-family management structure. There's a key difference: when the Giants promote from within or bring back old faces, they draw from folks who worked for Bill Parcells or Tom Coughlin, not holdovers from a glorious era of wild-card berths. Otherwise, the Tobin/Taylor/Brown Family Council shares with Dave Gettleman and the Giants a very vague sense of modern roster building and playoff/Super Bowl timetables.

It's clear to just about everyone outside the Bengals organization what's at stake. We have seen potential franchise quarterbacks ruined by early-career injuries too many times. We have watched bad organizations, including the Bengals, putter along for years without a plan.

The only thing that's unique about the Bengals is their level of lethargy. They'll get around to a serious rebuild around

Burrow eventually, or maybe he'll take too many hits (or already has) and they'll end up replacing him in, say, 2027. They'll attract some real front-office and coaching talent and modernize their operation someday, but what's the hurry? The Bengals appear satisfied to huddle beneath the ruins of their semi-great quasi-dynasty of the early 2010s, when Lewis led a crackerjack staff (Mike Zimmer, Jay Gruden, etc.), Tobin

enjoyed a draft hot streak, and the Bengals could fool themselves into thinking they were a model organization.

When Marvin Lewis is your Ozymandias, perhaps it's best that your empire gets buried in the sand so that someone else can come along and start over.

Mike Tanier

2020 Bengals Stats by Week

Wk	vs.	W-L	PF	PA	YDF	YDA	TO	Total	Off	Def	ST
1	LAC	L	13	16	295	362	-2	-36.3%	-35.6%	-4.1%	-4.8%
2	at CLE	L	30	35	353	434	0	-28.3%	-12.8%	25.7%	10.2%
3	at PHI	T	23	23	304	378	2	-4.4%	-21.8%	-13.4%	4.0%
4	JAX	W	33	25	505	429	0	-21.6%	14.1%	36.2%	0.4%
5	at BAL	L	3	27	205	332	-2	-69.5%	-83.3%	-15.2%	-1.5%
6	at IND	L	27	31	398	430	1	-38.7%	-14.0%	17.6%	-7.1%
7	CLE	L	34	37	468	398	-1	-44.7%	3.0%	51.3%	3.6%
8	TEN	W	31	20	367	441	1	5.2%	17.6%	18.6%	6.2%
9	BYE										
10	at PIT	L	10	36	324	377	-2	-44.2%	-17.1%	19.8%	-7.3%
11	at WAS	L	9	20	272	325	-1	-44.1%	-22.5%	15.5%	-6.1%
12	NYG	L	17	19	155	386	-2	-17.1%	-64.4%	-8.6%	38.8%
13	at MIA	L	7	19	196	406	-1	-65.7%	-54.1%	11.7%	0.2%
14	DAL	L	7	30	309	272	-3	-51.4%	-39.2%	8.2%	-3.9%
15	PIT	W	27	17	230	244	3	50.6%	8.7%	-40.7%	1.1%
16	at HOU	W	37	31	540	488	1	-4.9%	29.8%	32.3%	-2.4%
17	BAL	L	3	38	195	525	-1	-70.9%	-65.4%	15.0%	9.5%

Trends and Splits

	Offense	Rank	Defense	Rank
Total DVOA	-18.2%	29	9.1%	27
Unadjusted VOA	-20.4%	31	8.6%	25
Weighted Trend	-17.9%	28	8.9%	27
Variance	10.8%	30	5.1%	19
Average Opponent	-1.0%	10	-2.4%	22
Passing	-4.9%	25	18.6%	27
Rushing	-24.3%	28	-2.9%	21
First Down	-28.4%	32	8.3%	24
Second Down	-6.7%	24	22.6%	31
Third Down	-16.3%	25	-8.3%	12
First Half	-16.1%	29	-0.2%	17
Second Half	-20.4%	30	18.6%	32
Red Zone	-39.2%	32	7.0%	22
Late and Close	-2.0%	18	17.6%	29

Five-Year Performance

Year	W-L	Pyth W	Est W	PF	PA	TO	Total	Rk	Off	Rk	Def	Rk	ST	Rk	Off AGL	Rk	Def AGL	Rk	Off Age	Rk	Def Age	Rk	ST Age	Rk
2016	6-9-1	8.3	7.8	325	315	+3	3.2%	14	7.3%	11	1.4%	18	-2.7%	28	23.8	7	26.1	8	26.7	17	28.2	1	26.4	7
2017	7-9	6.2	6.5	290	349	-9	-14.3%	24	-6.9%	22	5.0%	21	-2.4%	21	42.0	21	37.0	18	26.6	19	26.4	14	25.1	29
2018	6-10	5.9	7.1	368	455	+1	-10.8%	24	-3.7%	21	9.7%	28	2.6%	7	55.3	27	42.6	23	25.6	29	25.8	25	25.6	23
2019	2-14	4.3	4.0	279	420	-14	-27.6%	31	-16.6%	29	15.6%	30	4.6%	1	55.9	28	27.3	11	26.1	26	26.3	15	25.9	15
2020	4-11-1	5.1	4.4	311	424	-7	-24.7%	30	-18.2%	29	9.1%	27	2.6%	9	39.0	17	49.9	21	25.6	27	26.3	18	26.2	13

2020 Performance Based on Most Common Personnel Groups

CIN Offense					CIN Offense vs. Opponents					CIN Defense				CIN Defense vs. Opponents			
Pers	Freq	Yds	DVOA	Run%	Pers	Freq	Yds	DVOA	Run%	Pers	Freq	Yds	DVOA	Pers	Freq	Yds	DVOA
11	76%	5.1	-13.8%	34%	Base	14%	4.9	4.3%	59%	Base	23%	5.4	-8.0%	11	61%	6.8	19.0%
12	14%	4.8	-10.5%	59%	Nickel	74%	5.2	-10.1%	37%	Nickel	63%	6.5	20.9%	12	18%	5.7	2.6%
10	4%	3.7	-15.7%	9%	Dime+	11%	3.7	-61.3%	7%	Dime+	13%	6.9	-14.7%	22	6%	5.8	3.4%
00	1%	4.9	43.2%	20%	Goal Line	0%	-0.2	-186.3%	60%	Goal Line	1%	0.7	-53.3%	21	5%	7.7	22.2%
13	1%	3.5	14.2%	36%										13	4%	4.3	-23.8%

Strategic Tendencies

Run/Pass		Rk	Formation		Rk	Pass Rush		Rk	Secondary		Rk	Strategy		Rk
Runs, first half	36%	23	Form: Single Back	83%	11	Rush 3	7.3%	12	4 DB	23%	17	Play Action	24%	23
Runs, first down	46%	20	Form: Empty Back	15%	3	Rush 4	66.2%	18	5 DB	63%	13	Offensive Motion	40%	23
Runs, second-long	26%	20	Form: Multi Back	2%	29	Rush 5	19.4%	19	6+ DB	13%	16	Avg Box (Off)	6.45	22
Runs, power sit.	53%	28	Pers: 3+ WR	83%	2	Rush 6+	7.1%	7	Man Coverage	41%	5	Avg Box (Def)	6.81	5
Runs, behind 2H	31%	11	Pers: 2+ TE/6+ OL	17%	30	Edge Rusher Sacks	55.9%	11	CB by Sides	75%	13	Offensive Pace	30.31	16
Pass, ahead 2H	50%	14	Pers: 6+ OL	1%	19	Interior DL Sacks	17.6%	25	S/CB Cover Ratio	26%	17	Defensive Pace	29.01	3
Run-Pass Options	5%	25	Shotgun/Pistol	77%	8	Second Level Sacks	26.5%	11	DB Blitz	14%	13	Go for it on 4th	1.41	22

We'll start with the same question we asked in last year's book: if Zac Taylor is trying to run a Rams-influenced offense, why isn't there more play-action? ● Cincinnati led the league by throwing 30% of passes to players we designated as "other wide receivers," i.e., not the No. 1 or No. 2 options (usually Tyler Boyd and A.J. Green). ● The Bengals finished second in the league in defensive DVOA against passes in the middle of the field, but 27th against passes to the offensive left and 24th against passes to the offensive right. ● Cincinnati allowed a league-worst 5.8 yards per carry with 11.1% DVOA when opponents ran with three or more wide receivers on the field. ● The Bengals started strong on defense, ranked fourth in DVOA in the first quarter, but then they ranked 31st in DVOA from the second quarter onward. ● Cincinnati was the only defense in the league that had a lower pressure rate on third and fourth down (19.5%) than on first and second down (20.1%). ● The Bengals faced the best performance by opposing field goal kickers, 6.25 points above average.

Passing

Player	DYAR	DVOA	Plays	NtYds	Avg	YAC	C%	TD	Int
J.Burrow	108	-7.3%	433	2457	5.7	4.3	65.8%	13	5
B.Allen	-125	-23.8%	149	860	5.8	6.2	63.8%	5	4
R.Finley*	-167	-82.9%	41	101	2.5	4.2	53.1%	1	2

Rushing

Player	DYAR	DVOA	Plays	Yds	Avg	TD	Fum	Suc
G.Bernard*	-29	-13.9%	124	416	3.4	3	1	48%
J.Mixon	-16	-11.6%	119	428	3.6	3	1	46%
S.Perine	35	4.4%	63	301	4.8	3	0	43%
J.Burrow	-43	-31.8%	33	119	3.6	3	4	--
T.Williams	5	-4.1%	26	157	6.0	0	1	46%
B.Allen	-14	-31.8%	11	29	2.6	0	0	--
R.Finley*	20	23.0%	10	68	6.8	1	0	--
T.Boyd	31	66.0%	5	49	9.8	0	0	--
T.Higgins	19	32.3%	5	28	5.6	0	0	--
A.Erickson*	-15	-85.4%	5	7	1.4	0	1	--

Receiving

Player	DYAR	DVOA	Plays	Ctch	Yds	Y/C	YAC	TD	C%
T.Boyd	56	-6.2%	110	79	841	10.6	4.4	4	72%
T.Higgins	142	3.9%	108	67	908	13.6	4.6	6	62%
A.J.Green*	-172	-33.0%	104	47	523	11.1	1.8	2	45%
A.Tate	-9	-17.8%	22	14	150	10.7	4.1	0	64%
M.Thomas	-34	-33.5%	21	13	132	10.2	2.2	1	62%
A.Erickson*	6	-7.9%	17	12	139	11.6	5.6	0	71%
J.Ross*	-29	-67.5%	7	2	17	8.5	1.5	0	29%
T.Taylor	-82	-58.7%	21	10	86	8.6	4.3	0	48%
D.Sample	-12	-10.8%	53	40	349	8.7	5.0	1	75%
C.J.Uzomah	21	21.5%	11	8	87	10.9	3.8	1	73%
C.Carter*	-5	-18.5%	7	5	53	10.6	2.0	0	71%
G.Bernard*	40	-1.7%	59	47	355	7.6	7.4	3	80%
J.Mixon	13	-4.8%	26	21	138	6.6	8.1	1	81%
S.Perine	17	11.8%	12	11	66	6.0	8.1	0	92%

Offensive Line

Player	Pos	Age	GS	Snaps	Pen	Sk	Pass	Run	Player	Pos	Age	GS	Snaps	Pen	Sk	Pass	Run
Trey Hopkins	C	29	15/15	937	3	1.5	3	7	Alex Redmond*	RG	26	9/7	448	5	3	7	2
Bobby Hart*	RT	27	14/13	871	3	4.5	23	5	Xavier Su'a-Filo	LG	30	6/5	293	1	1.5	2	6
Michael Jordan	LG	23	14/10	730	1	2	14	2	Hakeem Adeniji	LT/RT	24	15/5	232	2	3.5	9	2
Quinton Spain	RG	30	13/10	720	4	1.5	7	6	Billy Price	C	27	16/1	207	4	1	6	0
Jonah Williams	LT	24	10/10	633	2	5.5	13	10	Riley Reiff	LT	33	15/15	1002	1	2	10	10
Fred Johnson	LT/RG	24	12/6	491	3	3	11	4									

Year	Yards	ALY	Rk	Power	Rk	Stuff	Rk	2Lev	Rk	OpFld	Rk	BB Rt	Rk	Sacks	ASR	Rk	Press	Rk	BB Rt	Rk	Cont
2018	4.61	4.10	22	71%	7	20%	20	1.30	11	1.19	3	9.2%	30	37	7.0%	19	27.6%	10	9.5%	16	30
2019	3.95	3.90	26	67%	13	22%	29	1.10	23	0.70	19	15.8%	32	48	7.3%	20	24.8%	3	15.6%	29	21
2020	3.92	3.88	31	61%	24	19%	26	1.13	22	0.56	25	11.0%	20	48	7.6%	24	22.2%	9	14.6%	28	21
2020 ALY by direction:			Left End: 4.16 (23)			Left Tackle: 3.01 (30)			Mid/Guard: 4.30 (20)			Right Tackle: 4.08 (21)				Right End: 2.19 (32)				

The Bengals opened OTAs with Jonah Williams, Quinton Spain, Billy Price, Xavier Su'a-Filo, and Riley Reiff, left to right, as their first-team line. If they were to start the season with that lineup, Joe Burrow's cause of death would be listed as "interior pressure." Second-round rookie Jackson Carman (Clemson) and center Trey Hopkins, who suffered an ACL tear in the season finale, are expected to win two of the interior spots. ◥ Cincinnati's offense had the highest percentage of sacks due to pressure, with 87% of their sacks listed as blown block, rusher untouched, or overall pressure. ◥ Reiff's blown block rate has gone down in each of the last four seasons, from 4.3% in 2017 to 3.1% in 2018, 2.8% in 2019, and 2.1% last year. The only Bengals regular with a blown block rate below 2.1% last year was Hopkins. ◥ Here's returning offensive line coach Frank Pollack talking about his unit, while throwing some shade at Jim Turner, the toxic ferret who replaced him for two seasons: "We've got a lot of good players still developing. I can't wait to get them out on the grass and [start] teaching guys different techniques that maybe they haven't been exposed to in the last two years." Pollack coached the Cowboys line from 2013 through 2017 and is not Turner, so he should get the most out of the Bengals offensive line. But remember that he coached the Bengals line in 2018 and the Jets lines for the last two years: no coach can get more out of a unit than it actually has to offer.

Defensive Front

Defensive Line	Age	Pos	G	Snaps	Plays	Overall TmPct	Rk	Stop	Dfts	BTkl	vs. Run Runs	St%	Rk	RuYd	Rk	Pass Rush Sack	Hit	Hur	Dsrpt
Christian Covington*	28	DT	16	557	39	4.7%	55	29	4	3	38	76%	43	3.0	81	0.0	1	9	0
Mike Daniels	32	DT	11	354	17	3.0%	84	11	3	0	17	65%	78	3.4	94	0.0	1	2	1
Margus Hunt*	34	DT	13	385	12	1.8%	97	10	4	1	6	83%	13	1.7	10	1.0	3	7	5
Xavier Williams*	29	DT	12	318	24	3.9%	69	19	2	2	22	82%	19	2.8	66	1.0	0	6	0
D.J. Reader	27	DT	5	259	21	8.2%	1	18	5	1	17	88%	2	3.0	77	0.0	1	5	2
Larry Ogunjobi	27	DT	15	643	46	6.0%	30	30	9	4	41	63%	81	2.7	57	2.5	2	10	0

Edge Rushers	Age	Pos	G	Snaps	Plays	Overall TmPct	Rk	Stop	Dfts	BTkl	vs. Run Runs	St%	Rk	RuYd	Rk	Pass Rush Sack	Hit	Hur	Dsrpt
Carl Lawson*	26	DE	16	723	36	4.4%	56	26	8	4	28	64%	75	2.7	53	5.5	27	25	1
Sam Hubbard	26	DE	13	664	64	9.6%	2	49	13	5	54	78%	23	2.6	48	2.0	10	23	3
Amani Bledsoe	23	DE	14	311	19	2.6%	--	10	1	4	14	50%	--	3.6	--	0.0	0	5	2
Trey Hendrickson	27	DE	15	558	26	3.5%	76	24	17	2	10	90%	2	2.0	27	13.5	13	23	3

Linebackers	Age	Pos	G	Snaps	Plays	Overall TmPct	Rk	Stop	Dfts	BTkl	vs. Run Runs	St%	Rk	RuYd	Rk	Pass Rush Sack	Hit	Hur	vs. Pass Tgts	Suc%	Rk	Yd/P	Rk	PD	Int
Josh Bynes*	32	MLB	16	759	101	12.3%	44	55	8	16	74	61%	24	4.4	60	1.0	1	4	22	50%	37	6.5	42	2	0
Germaine Pratt	25	OLB	16	686	90	10.9%	54	41	9	14	60	48%	70	5.1	81	0.0	0	1	24	38%	67	7.4	60	2	0
Logan Wilson	25	MLB	12	343	30	4.9%	87	14	9	3	15	47%	74	4.9	78	1.0	1	3	14	50%	--	6.1	--	3	2
Akeem Davis-Gaither	24	OLB	16	314	29	3.5%	--	13	5	5	11	45%	--	4.5	--	0.5	1	4	18	44%	53	7.8	62	3	1

Year	Yards	ALY	Rk	Power	Rk	Stuff	Rk	2Lev	Rk	OpFld	Rk	BB Rt	Rk	Sacks	ASR	Rk	Press	Rk	BB Rt	Rk
2018	4.94	4.99	30	77%	29	14%	30	1.41	28	1.01	21	6.0%	25	34	7.1%	16	26.5%	28	10.2%	19
2019	4.58	4.55	24	66%	20	21%	9	1.36	28	0.88	24	13.5%	13	31	6.3%	24	31.4%	11	14.7%	19
2020	5.34	4.83	27	59%	5	13%	27	1.44	30	1.29	31	9.7%	25	17	3.7%	32	19.9%	31	9.8%	30
2020 ALY by direction:			Left End: 5.32 (28)			Left Tackle: 5.23 (29)			Mid/Guard: 4.73 (27)			Right Tackle: 4.46 (19)				Right End: 5.08 (24)			

Trey Hendrickson finished tied for second in the NFL in sacks in 2020 but tied for 49th in hurries. He finished third on the Saints in hurries behind Cameron Jordan and David Onyemata but ahead of Marcus Davenport and Carl Granderson in a deep pass-rushing rotation. If those numbers don't make your "product of the system" senses tingle, you must work in the Bengals pro personnel department! Hendrickson is a quick, relentless pass-rusher, but he shared many of his sacks with Jordan, Granderson, and others against quarterbacks with no means of escaping the pocket. ◥ Third-round edge rusher Joseph Ossai is a potential sacks-in-bunches type who took over a few games for Texas last year. That said, the Longhorns schemed to get

Ossai unblocked or matched up against slowpoke guards and centers on stunts. Both Hendrickson and Ossai look like 30- to 40-snap rotational defenders, which will be a problem for the Bengals, who have no one to rotate them with. ◕ OK, that last wisecrack was unfair to third-year defensive end Sam Hubbard, who told a Bengals podcast during OTAs that he is assuming a leadership role with the team. "There's no example to follow but ours, because we are the old guys now," he said. "It's on us to do everything right and get everyone else to do things the way we want them to be done, the way we have been trying to get them to be done for years." Sounds more fatalist than inspiring, but these are the Bengals, after all. ◕ Defensive tackle D.J. Reader arrived on a reported four-year, $53-million contract last year, played fairly well for five games, then suffered a quad injury which ended his season. Reader was limited at the start of OTAs. "I'll be ready to go when it's time to go," he told reporters in late May. ◕ Adequate run-plugger Larry Ogunjobi rounds out the interior defensive line, with Mike Daniels in the mix because the Bengals ran out of homegrown players who had their best seasons five years ago and had to import some from Green Bay. ◕ The Bengals linebackers stink, but at least they are young. Logan Wilson was a tackle machine at Wyoming, so maybe he will enjoy the linebacker equivalent of a Josh Allen Leap in his second season. Tiny, speedy Akeem Davis-Gaither just ran around out there while trying to transition from Appalachian State to the NFL. He could develop into an adequate nickel defender. Germaine Pratt has two years of coverage metrics ranking near the bottom of the league, then supplemented that last year by making his average run tackle after a long gain. Journeyman Josh Bynes, who started in the middle for the Bengals last season, was unsigned at press time.

Defensive Secondary

Secondary	Age	Pos	G	Snaps	Plays	TmPct	Rk	Stop	Dfts	BTkl	Runs	St%	Rk	RuYd	Rk	Tgts	Tgt%	Rk	aDOT	Suc%	Rk	Yd/P	Rk	PD	Int
Vonn Bell	27	SS	16	1059	119	14.5%	5	47	13	6	79	43%	26	6.3	30	47	10.9%	19	9.4	51%	33	7.6	30	5	0
Jessie Bates	24	FS	16	1050	122	14.8%	3	39	15	16	61	33%	42	10.2	65	31	7.3%	44	10.0	55%	19	6.2	14	15	3
William Jackson*	29	CB	14	886	56	7.8%	61	27	13	3	9	56%	14	4.7	17	67	18.6%	51	14.4	63%	5	7.1	33	11	1
Mackensie Alexander*	28	CB	13	642	53	7.9%	59	29	8	8	12	67%	3	5.8	31	47	18.0%	56	9.2	53%	31	7.6	40	6	1
LeShaun Sims*	28	CB	13	605	56	8.4%	46	14	2	10	11	64%	6	5.1	24	62	25.2%	6	11.1	26%	80	9.5	70	4	1
Darius Phillips	26	CB	12	593	48	7.8%	61	23	10	5	14	36%	53	11.7	78	50	20.7%	34	13.1	58%	11	6.2	10	12	1
Ricardo Allen	30	FS	12	604	30	4.9%	71	7	6	1	8	13%	68	12.8	69	13	5.1%	59	17.5	54%	25	11.1	66	5	2
Mike Hilton	27	CB	12	463	57	9.5%	--	36	22	13	23	61%	--	3.7	--	31	16.8%	--	14.7	55%	--	5.8	--	7	3
Chidobe Awuzie	26	CB	8	452	43	10.4%	--	15	6	3	16	25%	--	6.2	--	35	22.2%	--	13.7	54%	--	10.8	--	5	1

Year	Pass D Rank	vs. #1 WR	Rk	vs. #2 WR	Rk	vs. Other WR	Rk	WR Wide	Rk	WR Slot	Rk	vs. TE	Rk	vs. RB	Rk
2018	25	-2.6%	13	21.7%	28	-14.5%	7	7.9%	24	-3.8%	13	2.7%	16	22.0%	31
2019	28	22.3%	30	-2.5%	14	21.5%	28	30.1%	32	4.6%	14	10.9%	28	34.3%	31
2020	27	-2.5%	16	-14.7%	6	16.9%	27	9.7%	24	0.4%	20	-6.3%	12	8.0%	24

The secondary is the Bengals' second-greatest strength, after their wide receiver corps. ◕ Jessie Bates was the 2020 winner of the Adrian Wilson Trophy, given each year to an outstanding safety who is one of the few decent players on a terrible team. (Other recent winners included Jamal Adams and Kevin Byard before the Titans turned things around). Bates led all safeties with 15 passes defensed and might have earned All-Pro recognition if he had not dropped four potential interceptions. Or, you know, if the Bengals weren't the football equivalent of a crumbling farmhouse in a forgotten wilderness hollow. ◕ Bates' average depth of tackle on running plays was 10.2 yards, the highest in the NFL among players with at least 40 run tackles. Bates finished fifth among safeties in run tackles, while Vonn Bell was No. 1. When a team's two leading tacklers are its safeties, it's often a sign the safeties are really good but always a sign that the rest of the defense is terrible. ◕ Chidi Awuzie was solid-if-unspectacular at left cornerback for the Cowboys in 2018 and 2019. Defensive coordinator Mike Nolan then began flipping Awuzie to the right side last season for unclear reasons. Nolan's inestimable brilliance, plus a hamstring injury and a COVID stint, resulted in Awuzie's worst season as a pro. Awuzie is expected to replace William Jackson, who lined up mostly on the right, but such things are not hard to sort out given a full training camp. ◕ Darius Phillips registered seven passes defensed and two forced fumbles in the Bengals final four games. He's built like a tuff 'n' tiny slot cornerback, but he was most effective playing outside last season. ◕ Trey Waynes tore a pectoral muscle lifting weights last preseason. Eli Apple missed nearly all of last season with hamstring, ankle, and foot injuries. Both are gifted but unreliable former first-round picks; the Bengals should consider platooning them based on their horoscopes and biorhythms. ◕ Ricardo Allen played mostly free safety for the Falcons but is expected to compete for a slot corner role in Cincy with fellow free-agent acquisition Mike Hilton, who has more experience in such a role but is a horrendous tackler.

Special Teams

Year	DVOA	Rank	FG/XP	Rank	Net Kick	Rank	Kick Ret	Rank	Net Punt	Rank	Punt Ret	Rank	Hidden	Rank
2018	2.6%	7	1.0	14	2.9	8	8.6	3	-1.2	18	1.6	13	-10.8	27
2019	4.6%	1	8.1	6	5.1	6	8.7	1	4.2	12	-3.2	25	-10.3	29
2020	2.6%	9	-2.0	19	0.6	17	6.4	6	7.6	7	0.2	16	-9.5	28

Austin Seibert replaced Randy Bullock for the final four games of last season after Bullock suffered a series of ugly misses which were exacerbated by what was reported as either a calf injury or a "calf injury." (Some observers accused Bullock of limping like Gabby Hayes to avoid embarrassment after the shanks.) Siebert, the Browns' fifth-round pick in 2019, was cut by Cleveland after missing an extra point and a 40-yarder in the season opener but went 6-of-8 down the stretch. The Bengals drafted Florida's Evan McPherson in the fifth round to battle Seibert, because the Bengals are so wildly successful and stacked along the offensive line and defensive front seven that they can afford to waste draft picks on kickers to challenge other teams' former wasted draft picks. ❧ Kevin Huber is one of the league's most consistent punters, with yet another year of being slightly above average in gross punt value. ❧ Darius Phillips returned five kickoffs, one punt, and five interceptions for touchdowns at Western Michigan. He has returned a total of five punts and 17 kickoffs in three seasons for the Bengals. Phillips appears to have the inside track to replace Alex Erickson on punt returns. Brandon Wilson, who has a return touchdown in each of the last two seasons, will handle kickoffs, though Trent Taylor and undrafted rookie Pooka Williams may also be in the mix.

Cleveland Browns

2020 Record: 11-5	**Total DVOA:** -5.7% (24)	**2021 Mean Projection:** 8.6 wins	**On the Clock (0-5):** 13%
Pythagorean Wins: 7.7 (16)	**Offense:** 5.4% (9)	**Postseason Odds:** 42.8%	**Mediocrity (6-8):** 35%
Snap-Weighted Age: 26.2 (21)	**Defense:** 7.4% (25)	**Super Bowl Odds:** 5.0%	**Playoff Contender (9-11):** 37%
Average Opponent: -5.3% (30)	**Special Teams:** -3.7% (27)	**Proj. Avg. Opponent:** 1.5% (8)	**Super Bowl Contender (12+):** 15%

2020: At last, an actual NFL coach.

2021: Dreams and data collide again in Cleveland.

There is generally precious little to be gleaned from those half-speed practices known generically as offseason team activities, or OTAs. But in Berea, Ohio, where the Browns gathered early in the summer to run laps and hit the pads, there was a clear goal coming out of camp: Beat the Chiefs. That's right, the team that has been a laughingstock for basically the entirety of the 21st century no longer feels that the likes of the Ravens or Steelers are its direct competition. The Browns have their eyes set firmly on the two-time AFC champs who defeated them in the divisional round en route to the Super Bowl, a game that apparently was just the opening salvo in a larger, "Michael Jordan had to lose to the Pistons before he could beat them" war.

Even the practices themselves were fodder for the budding "rivalry," at least on the Browns' end of things. When asked if he was surprised that the Chiefs started OTAs earlier and had more players attend, Cleveland's star defensive end Myles Garrett snapped, "When we get to Game 1, we'll see who's been jelling better and who's got the upper hand."

By the by, said Game 1 will take place in Kansas City. Browns vs Chiefs—this time it's personal! This is probably as good a place as any to note that Cleveland hasn't won on opening Sunday since 2004.

Now, there is nothing wrong with a little offseason optimism. And it is certainly true that the 2020 Browns had a heck of a season under first-year coach Kevin Stefanski. They won 11 games, made the playoffs for the first time since 2002, and got the first postseason win since the team was rebooted in 1999—over the hated Steelers, no less. And they did give the Chiefs a scare in that divisional playoff game, although the fact that Patrick Mahomes watched most of the second half from the sideline seems particularly relevant to the tightness of the score. The folks in the Browns sales department surely didn't care much, hiking the cost of season tickets while calculating their starved fan base would pay any price to witness their immense patience rewarded at last.

It is also true that Cleveland was outscored 419-408 on the season, a Pythagorean ratio that should have seen the team go 8-8 rather than 11-5. It is also true that that first playoff win was gift-wrapped by a crumbling Steelers team that committed four turnovers in the opening 20 minutes, including a wayward snap into the end zone on the game's first play. And it is also true that, like orange juice and Listerine, the Browns and high expectations simply don't go well together.

We are dubious about the Browns' chances to dethrone Kansas City as AFC champs, or the Ravens as AFC North champs for that matter, because we have been down this road many times before. Just two years ago, for example, I wrote in these very pages that I was "forced to temper enthusiasm and dump cold analytical water on Cleveland's dreams" often over the years. As they did before the 2019 season, and several others that brimmed with high hopes before that, the numbers continue to view the Browns as … average.

We forecast the 2021 Browns to have a strong offense, a poor if not terrible defense, a tricky schedule, and a mean wins projection that has Cleveland closer to the rival Bengals than the Chiefs or the Ravens. Just as the data refused to believe that "This time, we're turning it around!" until it actually happened, we will have to see the Browns put together another winning season—one that has much better underlying statistics to gird the won-loss record—to buy in to what the franchise is selling.

There is at least some good news hidden in the numbers, however. The 2020 Browns were the second-worst 11-5 team of all time by DVOA (Table 1). Sounds like a candidate for decline, right? Not necessarily. Plenty of teams have had hollow 11-win campaigns and followed them up with better or as-good seasons the next year. Only two of the nine worst 11-5 teams since 1985 fell under .500 the following season. Four of these teams made the postseason (and that's before the advent of the seven-teams-per-conference playoff extravaganza). The 2006 Bears and 1986 Broncos even made the Super Bowl following their pyrite 11-5 seasons.

We can look even deeper to note that Cleveland's DVOA was weighed down in part by a pair of hideous losses early in the season—a 38-6 thumping by the Ravens in the first game of the year, which produced a -99.3% DVOA, and a 38-7 loss to Pittsburgh in Week 6 that was only slightly better at -94.4% (at least they made the PAT in that one). The Browns' third-worst showing (a 23-16 loss to the Jets late in the year) was a product of the COVID protocols that wiped out the entirety of Cleveland's wide receiver corps, making the -44.9% showing something of an achievement.

Only eight teams since 2001 have had two losses with DVOA worse than -80.0% and no others worse than -50.0%, as the Browns did in 2020. Cleveland won the most games of any of those teams, and as their two terrible performances

2021 Browns Schedule

Week	Opp.	Week	Opp.	Week	Opp.
1	at KC	7	DEN (Thu.)	13	BYE
2	HOU	8	PIT	14	BAL
3	CHI	9	at CIN	15	LV
4	at MIN	10	at NE	16	at GB (Sat./Xmas)
5	at LAC	11	DET	17	at PIT (Mon.)
6	ARI	12	at BAL	18	CIN

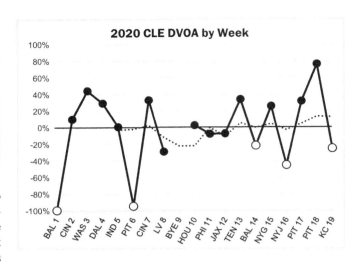

came earlier in the season than the others, it is reasonable to write off those spankings as beta tests rather than actual indicators of the Browns' quality going forward. (In fairness, we also might want to write off the 32.2% DVOA the Browns put up in the regular-season finale, playing Pittsburgh's reserves in a meaningless affair.)

All this is to say that for those inclined to think our projection system is unfairly smearing the Browns thanks to a couple of "burn the game tape" showings, there is evidence to back that up. And there are two far more compelling factors in their corner: the strength of the team's roster and the sudden professionalism of the coaching staff and front office.

First and foremost, Stefanski's hiring ended a dizzying run of sad-sack coaches hired and fired with Steinbrenner-esque frequency by owner Jimmy Haslem. This time, it appears the felonious truck-stop magnate may have at last stumbled into someone not clearly way out over his skis (Freddie Kitchens) or clearly suffering from Belichick Separation Anxiety (Romeo Crennel, Eric Mangini) or clearly being Hue Jackson. Stefanski immediately brought a workmanlike calm to the job, starkly contrasting with Kitchens, who wore t-shirts with anti-Steelers propaganda to press conferences, or Jackson, who spent most of his time pointing the finger at the easy-to-blame analytics types in the front office for all the failings under his watch.

As analytics types ourselves, we applaud Stefanski's more nuanced approach to data. Of course, we wouldn't be true

Table 1. Worst 11-5 Teams by DVOA, 1985-2020

Team	Year	DVOA	Rk	Y+1 W-L	Y+1 DVOA	Y+1 Rk
IND	2012	-16.2%	26	11-5	2.7%	14
CLE	**2020**	**-5.7%**	**18**	--	--	--
ARI	2014	-2.5%	20	13-3	30.2%	2
CHI	2005	-1.8%	17	13-3	24.0%	5
ATL	2004	-1.7%	15	8-8	-1.0%	16
MIN	2000	-1.3%	20	5-11	-24.3%	30
CAR	2003	-0.2%	16	7-9	-0.3%	14
DEN	1985	2.1%	15	11-5	19.0%	5
CHI	2010	2.2%	14	8-8	1.0%	15
TB	2005	2.3%	14	4-12	-21.5%	31
TEN	**2020**	**2.5%**	**14**	--	--	--
IND	2013	2.7%	14	11-5	4.5%	14

to ourselves if we didn't also point out that Stefanski's supposed schematic transformation didn't really take place. His Vikings offense was a play-action machine, using the concept to turn Kirk Cousins into a quarterback worthy of his enormous contract. The idea was that a similar series of play-fakes to the stud Cleveland backs would enable quarterback Baker Mayfield to improve in the same fashion, but the Browns' play-action rate only increased from 28% to 30%. There was also a thought that Stefanski would install a large number of RPOs, which Mayfield used to great effect at Oklahoma, but instead they were practically eliminated in the attack, with the Browns dropping from fifth to 31st in RPO rate. Instead, Stefanski and offensive coordinator Alex Van Pelt brought in a ton of pre-snap motion; the Browns increased usage from 31% of the time (28th overall) in 2019 to 55% (fifth) in 2020. Motion wasn't a big part of the 2019 Vikings attack, so give Stefanski credit for adapting to different tendencies.

Maybe it didn't come from his usual bag of tricks, but Stefanski's presence had a beneficial effect on Mayfield, who bounced back after a severely disappointing 2019. The quarterback improved from 25th to 16th in DYAR, and 25th to 17th in DVOA. Stefanski and general manager Andrew Berry were at least partially if not outright responsible. Mayfield struggled with his decision-making in 2019, partly because poor play at tackle made him jittery in the pocket. The signing of Jack Conklin (who turned in an All-Pro season) and drafting of Jerrick Wills in the first round shored up the edges of the line. Meanwhile, Stefanski sized up Mayfield's ability to be accurate while outside the pocket and featured more bootlegs and designed rollouts. (Mayfield went from 19% of plays outside the pocket to 28%, second behind Lamar Jackson.) The combination allowed the slight quarterback to have more clean sightlines and comfortable progressions, and the difference showed. The Browns also led the NFL in two-tight end sets and in max protect blocking on pass plays, all designed to make Mayfield feel as cozy and "dangerous" as possible.

The Browns also leaned heavily on the run game, especially on first downs, when they ran 60% of the time—good for fifth in the league and up from 51% in 2019. And in the second half of games, Cleveland ranked dead last in passes while ahead and fifth in runs while trailing. Stefanski wasn't conservative, in the way we usually think of it—indeed, he was third in Aggressiveness Index on fourth downs. But he coached as though determined not to let Mayfield get into negative situations and leeched the swashbuckling nature from his game unless there was no other option.

It helped mightily that Cleveland possesses the best one-two running back combo in the NFL. Hearts caught in throats across Ohio when Nick Chubb went down in Week 4 with an apparently serious knee injury. But Chubb, who tore an ACL while at Georgia, missed only a month with a sprained MCL and tore up the NFL in the second half of the year. Meanwhile, Kareem Hunt not only backed up Chubb with aplomb when he was sidelined but also was the third highest-rated back in the passing game by DYAR.

While the offensive line certainly improved, the Browns were top of the league in second-level yards and fourth in open-field yards, suggesting that it was really the backs powering the offense. No offense broke more tackles than Cleveland's 143, and Chubb (56) and Hunt (50) were both in the top 10 in that stat. They did this despite the fact that no team faced more defenders in the box, on average, than Cleveland did. Defenses knew the Browns were going to run it, and by and large couldn't do much about it.

This overall strategy was also affected by the loss of Odell Beckham Jr. to a torn ACL in Week 7, which had the ironic effect of allowing the offense to hum. That's a bit of correlation without causation that has led many to speculate Beckham could be expendable, as Mayfield appeared loosened without having to defer to his volatile star wideout. Maybe Baker felt free to cook (ouch), but the Browns lacked explosion with OBJ sidelined, which showed up in that playoff game against the Chiefs. When the game was there to be stolen late, Kansas City stacked up the running game and dared Mayfield to beat them deep, which he couldn't do. A small sample, to be sure, but if the Browns are going to match their preseason expectations, trading away their best receiver probably won't help.

The defense was the Browns' weak spot, and the front office took a blowtorch to the unit. Cleveland could see up to nine new starters on defense, with a complete renewal around building blocks Garrett and cornerback Denzel Ward. The newbies include free-agent signings John Johnson and Troy Hill, a pair of secondary players who were part of the Rams' fourth-rat-

ed pass defense; highly drafted cornerback Greg Newsome (Northwestern) and linebacker Jeremiah Owusu-Koramoah (Notre Dame), two high-octane athletes who should juice up the back seven; and edge rushers Jadeveon Clowney and Takkarist McKinley, two buy-low signings who could well prove useful in new surroundings. Defensive coordinator Joe Woods might have to put in a few 100-hour workweeks in order to blend all the new faces into a cohesive unit, but there's no doubt the talent has upgraded.

Nonetheless, the defense is where the Browns really run into problems in our projection system. Yes, defense is harder to project than offense, and more volatile from year to year. But Cleveland is coming off two seasons ranked in the bottom 10 of defensive DVOA. The Browns ranked 25th last year despite the fact that they were above average in turnovers per drive, a stat that is likely to regress for them in the wrong direction. Since 2008, 17 teams have ranked in the bottom 10 of defensive DVOA but the top 10 of turnovers per drive; these teams averaged 6.2% DVOA and a rank of 21st the following season. Only three of these 17 teams became top-10 defenses the next year. And while the Browns added a ton of defensive talent this offseason, many departing players were solid too, including defensive tackles Larry Ogunjobi and Sheldon Richardson as well as edge rusher Olivier Vernon. So their bonus for net additional/returning talent isn't as large as the bonus for other defenses such as Denver and New England. Even if we removed the Week 1 and Week 6 blowouts from Cleveland's 2020 ratings, their 2021 mean defensive projection would only move from 26th in the league to 23rd.

But enough with the inner workings of our algorithms. No less an analytical expert than Chiefs tight end Travis Kelce admitted in June that his squad and the Browns were "neck and neck," and the preponderance of NFL onlookers agree that Cleveland is on the short list of AFC favorites. With competent people running the show and the best roster Northeast Ohio has seen since the days of Kosar, Byner, and Slaughter, there is every reason to believe the team can outperform this projection, at least. That might not be as satisfying a goal as making a Super Bowl run, but with a franchise so accustomed to pratfalls, baby steps are in order.

Robert Weintraub

2020 Browns by Week

Wk	vs.	W-L	PF	PA	YDF	YDA	TO	Total	Off	Def	ST
1	at BAL	L	6	38	306	381	-2	-99.3%	-48.3%	33.8%	-17.2%
2	CIN	W	35	30	434	353	0	10.3%	27.1%	10.2%	-6.6%
3	WAS	W	34	20	300	309	5	44.7%	19.9%	-20.1%	4.7%
4	at DAL	W	49	38	508	566	3	29.6%	47.0%	17.0%	-0.4%
5	IND	W	32	23	385	308	0	1.1%	-2.3%	-20.8%	-17.4%
6	at PIT	L	7	38	220	277	-2	-94.4%	-64.0%	22.8%	-7.5%
7	at CIN	W	37	34	398	468	1	33.4%	63.8%	27.1%	-3.4%
8	LV	L	6	16	223	309	-1	-28.9%	-27.9%	-5.8%	-6.8%
9	BYE										
10	HOU	W	10	7	356	243	0	2.8%	-4.0%	-11.7%	-4.9%
11	PHI	W	22	17	324	315	2	-7.5%	-29.4%	-21.6%	0.3%
12	at JAX	W	27	25	459	375	-1	-7.0%	23.7%	38.7%	8.0%
13	at TEN	W	41	35	458	431	2	34.4%	13.7%	-19.4%	1.3%
14	BAL	L	42	47	493	385	-1	-21.5%	25.2%	37.0%	-9.7%
15	at NYG	W	20	6	392	288	0	26.1%	37.1%	5.3%	-5.7%
16	at NYJ	L	16	23	299	333	-2	-44.9%	-30.5%	18.9%	4.4%
17	PIT	W	24	22	358	394	1	32.2%	30.9%	1.0%	2.3%
18	at PIT	W	48	37	390	553	5	76.5%	76.8%	10.8%	10.5%
19	at KC	L	17	22	308	438	-1	-24.9%	-18.1%	12.4%	5.7%

Trends and Splits

	Offense	Rank	Defense	Rank
Total DVOA	5.4%	9	7.4%	25
Unadjusted VOA	7.6%	10	1.9%	17
Weighted Trend	8.1%	8	7.0%	25
Variance	13.2%	31	4.7%	15
Average Opponent	0.1%	18	-6.5%	32
Passing	20.9%	10	16.4%	25
Rushing	-0.8%	7	-5.4%	19
First Down	11.9%	5	3.9%	21
Second Down	6.3%	11	0.7%	15
Third Down	-8.5%	17	24.6%	28
First Half	7.0%	12	7.2%	26
Second Half	3.6%	12	7.6%	21
Red Zone	21.9%	7	-3.0%	12
Late and Close	29.3%	3	7.3%	23

Five-Year Performance

Year	W-L	Pyth W	Est W	PF	PA	TO	Total	Rk	Off	Rk	Def	Rk	ST	Rk	Off AGL	Rk	Def AGL	Rk	Off Age	Rk	Def Age	Rk	ST Age	Rk
2016	1-15	3.3	1.3	264	452	-12	-32.5%	31	-13.6%	29	16.4%	32	-2.5%	26	45.2	21	50.0	22	26.7	15	25.1	32	24.5	32
2017	0-16	3.3	3.1	234	410	-28	-28.7%	32	-20.1%	32	3.4%	20	-5.1%	27	19.9	7	35.9	16	24.9	32	24.5	32	24.1	32
2018	7-8-1	7.1	7.5	359	392	+7	-3.3%	19	-0.7%	17	-1.6%	13	-4.2%	30	9.1	1	38.8	22	25.6	30	24.9	31	25.4	27
2019	6-10	6.4	6.1	335	393	-8	-10.6%	24	-4.8%	20	6.6%	24	0.8%	15	15.4	4	41.4	23	26.3	22	25.4	30	25.0	32
2020	11-5	7.7	7.7	408	419	+5	-5.7%	18	5.4%	9	7.4%	25	-3.7%	27	31.4	11	58.3	27	25.8	26	27.1	4	25.4	26

2020 Performance Based on Most Common Personnel Groups

CLE Offense					CLE Offense vs. Opponents					CLE Defense					CLE Defense vs. Opponents			
Pers	Freq	Yds	DVOA	Run%	Pers	Freq	Yds	DVOA	Run%	Pers	Freq	Yds	DVOA	Pers	Freq	Yds	DVOA
11	41%	6.1	21.3%	39%	Base	43%	5.7	9.2%	59%	Base	27%	5.6	5.7%	11	68%	5.8	11.0%
12	28%	6.4	17.9%	33%	Nickel	44%	6.0	14.4%	36%	Nickel	68%	5.6	6.7%	12	18%	6.1	-1.8%
13	14%	6.2	2.9%	61%	Dime+	8%	7.0	6.9%	12%	Dime+	4%	8.6	51.2%	22	4%	3.6	-0.9%
21	7%	4.2	-27.3%	53%	Goal Line	2%	0.9	-5.2%	63%	Goal Line	1%	0.2	-7.9%	21	3%	6.5	18.6%
22	7%	5.1	-16.1%	81%	Big	3%	7.4	17.5%	70%					13	2%	5.7	38.7%

Strategic Tendencies

Run/Pass		Rk	Formation		Rk	Pass Rush		Rk	Secondary		Rk	Strategy		Rk
Runs, first half	39%	12	Form: Single Back	72%	28	Rush 3	2.9%	27	4 DB	27%	11	Play Action	30%	10
Runs, first down	60%	3	Form: Empty Back	9%	18	Rush 4	80.2%	4	5 DB	68%	7	Offensive Motion	55%	5
Runs, second-long	28%	17	Form: Multi Back	20%	5	Rush 5	14.5%	28	6+ DB	4%	22	Avg Box (Off)	6.95	1
Runs, power sit.	56%	21	Pers: 3+ WR	41%	31	Rush 6+	2.4%	28	Man Coverage	22%	27	Avg Box (Def)	6.58	20
Runs, behind 2H	35%	5	Pers: 2+ TE/6+ OL	52%	1	Edge Rusher Sacks	64.5%	3	CB by Sides	71%	21	Offensive Pace	30.61	21
Pass, ahead 2H	36%	32	Pers: 6+ OL	1%	20	Interior DL Sacks	18.4%	22	S/CB Cover Ratio	28%	14	Defensive Pace	30.69	23
Run-Pass Options	1%	31	Shotgun/Pistol	43%	29	Second Level Sacks	17.1%	26	DB Blitz	12%	19	Go for it on 4th	2.38	3

For the second straight year, Baker Mayfield excelled when opponents blitzed a defensive back. The Browns led the NFL with 9.4 yards per pass on these plays and ranked second behind Kansas City with 43.8% DVOA. ❧ With a rise in two-tight end sets came a rise in box count, as the Browns went from facing an average of 6.52 men in the box (21st in 2019) to a league-leading average of 6.95 in 2020. ❧ Although they averaged fewer yards per carry, the Browns had a slightly higher DVOA against boxes of eight or more (4.5 yards, 3.6% DVOA) than against boxes of seven or less (5.2 yards, 0.5% DVOA). This was a big change from 2019, when the Browns gained just 2.4 yards per carry with -37.2% DVOA when facing a heavy box of eight or more. ❧ The Browns finally fixed their tackling on defense last season, with fewer broken tackles than the league average after finishing as the second worst and worst defense in the previous two seasons. ❧ Joe Woods blitzed much less than Steve Wilks, as the Browns went from fifth in rushing five and sixth in rushing six to 28th in both. They also fell from second to 19th in the rate of defensive back blitzes. And Cleveland struggled when it did blitz: 13.4% defensive DVOA (6.3 yards per pass) when sending four pass-rushers but 53.2% DVOA (8.0 yards per pass) with five or more. ❧ Cleveland ranked 26th in pressure rate on first and second downs but improved to ninth on third and fourth downs. ❧ The Browns had the worst defense in the league when they were on the road. They ranked 12th in defensive DVOA when playing at home.

Passing

Player	DYAR	DVOA	Plays	NtYds	Avg	YAC	C%	TD	Int
B.Mayfield	545	5.1%	507	3326	6.6	4.5	64.2%	26	8
C.Keenum	-16	-32.9%	10	46	4.6	5.6	50.0%	0	0

Rushing

Player	DYAR	DVOA	Plays	Yds	Avg	TD	Fum	Suc
K.Hunt	64	-0.6%	198	841	4.2	6	1	51%
N.Chubb	276	25.5%	191	1067	5.6	12	1	52%
B.Mayfield	13	-6.8%	39	174	4.5	1	3	--
D.Johnson	1	-7.9%	33	166	5.0	0	1	42%
D.Hilliard*	9	11.3%	9	48	5.3	0	0	67%

Receiving

Player	DYAR	DVOA	Plays	Ctch	Yds	Y/C	YAC	TD	C%
J.Landry	130	4.0%	101	72	840	11.7	4.8	3	71%
R.Higgins	176	29.4%	52	37	599	16.2	2.1	4	71%
O.Beckham	13	-8.8%	43	23	319	13.9	2.0	3	53%
D.Peoples-Jones	95	51.9%	20	14	304	21.7	5.5	2	70%
K.Hodge	50	22.9%	17	11	180	16.4	2.1	0	65%
J.Bradley	-25	-44.2%	11	5	60	12.0	2.2	0	45%
A.Hooper	-10	-9.4%	70	46	435	9.5	3.7	4	66%
H.Bryant	-33	-18.8%	38	24	238	9.9	4.9	3	63%
D.Njoku	21	3.0%	29	19	213	11.2	4.6	2	66%
K.Hunt	148	35.1%	51	38	304	8.0	7.4	6	75%
N.Chubb	63	52.7%	18	16	150	9.4	8.3	0	89%

Offensive Line

Player	Pos	Age	GS	Snaps	Pen	Sk	Pass	Run	Player	Pos	Age	GS	Snaps	Pen	Sk	Pass	Run
J.C. Tretter	C	30	16/16	1061	4	0.5	5	12	Jedrick Wills	LT	22	15/15	957	11	4.5	16	7
Joel Bitonio	LG	30	16/16	1061	3	1.5	5	7	Wyatt Teller	RG	27	11/11	694	5	3	8	7
Jack Conklin	RT	27	15/15	999	2	2	9	9	Christopher Hubbard	RG	30	11/5	290	0	0	3	2

Year	Yards	ALY	Rk	Power	Rk	Stuff	Rk	2Lev	Rk	OpFld	Rk	BB Rt	Rk	Sacks	ASR	Rk	Press	Rk	BB Rt	Rk	Cont
2018	4.61	4.24	18	50%	32	23%	29	1.27	16	1.16	4	7.6%	24	38	6.7%	16	27.7%	11	5.9%	6	38
2019	4.85	4.46	10	53%	29	18%	14	1.34	5	1.17	2	8.9%	10	41	7.2%	18	28.1%	7	11.6%	7	26
2020	4.91	4.79	6	56%	28	18%	24	1.45	1	1.10	4	10.3%	18	26	6.5%	16	24.8%	16	9.9%	6	27

2020 ALY by direction:	Left End: 4.71 (8)	Left Tackle: 5.50 (2)	Mid/Guard: 4.50 (14)	Right Tackle: 4.60 (12)	Right End: 6.49 (1)

The conventional wisdom nationally was that the Browns fixed what was an awful line in 2019 by bringing a new set of tackles in free agent Jack Conklin and drafting Jerrick Wills and significantly upgrading their coaching with Bill Callahan and Kevin Stefanski developing otherwise talented underachievers into stars. The numbers did show improvement, but only slightly—from 10th to sixth in adjusted line yards, 18th to 16th in adjusted sack rate, and a one-slot jump in power success rate, all the way to 28th from 29th. ❧ For years the Browns ran counter to the classic precept that a team should build from the line out—even with Canton-bound Joe Thomas and Alex Mack up front, the team's skill personnel was too weak to take advantage. At last, the playmakers, especially the running backs, are better, and are arguably more responsible for the quality of the offense than the line. ❧ Conklin was seen by some as a creation of the play-action-heavy system in Tennessee, and only an average athlete, but he looked plenty spry in Cleveland, improving his pass-blocking significantly while maintaining a nasty edge in the run game. ❧ Given the practice limitations necessitated by COVID, Wills turned in a very good rookie year at left tackle. While he unsurprisingly struggled at times with his drops and control of enemy pass-rushers, he used his size to hammer away in the ground game. The Browns weren't shy about running his way, with the second-most runs over left tackle in the NFL. ❧ The guard combo, Joel Bitonio and Wyatt Teller, was probably the league's best. Nothing new for

Bitonio, but Teller was a revelation, a Bills castoff who played at an All-Pro level. Finally getting comfortable on the right side after playing only left guard in his college and pro career, Teller at last mastered his hand placement and footwork and could concentrate on pounding opponents, living up to his nickname, "IHOP" (for his pancake blocks, you see…). ⬧ JC Tretter, the center, is still an extremely effective pass-blocker, though he can get overpowered in the run game. If he seems distracted, cut him some slack—Tretter is the head of the NFL Players Association. ⬧ The unit's effectiveness was greatly helped by unusual health—they collectively played 73 of 80 games, with Teller accounting for five of the missed seven. Ironically, it was top reserve Chris Hubbard who suffered a debilitating injury in 2020 and is still recovering from December knee surgery. Depth is a concern should that run of injury luck not continue. ⬧ Cleveland used a fourth-round pick on athletic but raw James Hudson from Cincinnati as a developmental backup to play inside or outside. With Callahan as his position coach, the smart money is on Hudson to become a worthy player.

Defensive Front

Defensive Line	Age	Pos	G	Snaps	Plays	TmPct	Rk	Stop	Dfts	BTkl	Runs	St%	Rk	RuYd	Rk	Sack	Hit	Hur	Dsrpt
						Overall						vs. Run				Pass Rush			
Sheldon Richardson*	31	DT	16	799	66	8.0%	4	39	16	3	51	55%	94	3.3	90	4.5	5	24	3
Larry Ogunjobi*	27	DT	15	643	46	6.0%	30	30	9	4	41	63%	81	2.7	57	2.5	2	10	0
Jordan Elliott	24	DT	16	308	15	1.8%	--	4	1	0	13	31%	--	3.9	--	0.0	0	2	0
Malik Jackson	31	DT	15	537	30	3.8%	71	26	10	2	21	86%	7	1.5	8	2.5	10	14	2
Damion Square	32	DT	16	252	20	2.6%	--	15	3	1	18	72%	--	2.9	--	1.0	1	4	0

Edge Rushers	Age	Pos	G	Snaps	Plays	TmPct	Rk	Stop	Dfts	BTkl	Runs	St%	Rk	RuYd	Rk	Sack	Hit	Hur	Dsrpt
						Overall						vs. Run				Pass Rush			
Olivier Vernon*	31	DE	14	804	39	5.4%	34	33	16	10	27	78%	23	1.6	11	9.0	7	25	3
Myles Garrett	26	DE	14	758	50	7.0%	12	37	19	2	33	64%	77	2.9	64	12.0	9	25	1
Adrian Clayborn*	33	DE	15	404	13	1.7%	96	11	7	1	7	71%	48	1.4	8	3.5	4	15	1
Porter Gustin	24	DE	14	327	28	3.9%	--	18	4	2	26	65%	--	2.8	--	0.0	1	4	0
Jadeveon Clowney	28	OLB	8	425	22	5.1%	42	14	5	2	16	56%	88	2.3	40	0.0	6	17	4

Linebackers	Age	Pos	G	Snaps	Plays	TmPct	Rk	Stop	Dfts	BTkl	Runs	St%	Rk	RuYd	Rk	Sack	Hit	Hur	Tgts	Suc%	Rk	Yd/P	Rk	PD	Int
						Overall						vs. Run				Pass Rush				vs. Pass					
B.J. Goodson*	28	MLB	14	848	97	13.5%	38	45	17	5	42	55%	50	4.0	41	0.5	2	4	35	51%	32	6.3	35	6	2
Malcolm Smith	32	OLB	15	559	74	9.6%	61	34	13	6	36	44%	78	5.8	87	1.0	0	1	23	57%	20	4.9	17	2	1
Sione Takitaki	26	OLB	15	434	56	7.3%	73	35	7	5	43	70%	7	3.6	26	1.0	1	2	13	54%	26	6.5	40	1	1
Mack Wilson	23	OLB	13	372	40	6.0%	83	18	1	11	25	44%	80	3.9	38	0.0	0	1	18	61%	10	5.4	24	2	0
Jacob Phillips	22	OLB	9	169	24	5.2%	--	18	5	2	14	79%	--	3.6	--	0.0	1	2	5	40%	--	10.6	--	1	0
Anthony Walker	26	MLB	16	697	96	11.8%	47	47	6	9	51	59%	31	3.7	30	0.0	1	3	33	33%	70	7.3	58	5	1

Year	Yards	ALY	Rk	Power	Rk	Stuff	Rk	2Lev	Rk	OpFld	Rk	BB Rt	Rk	Sacks	ASR	Rk	Press	Rk	BB Rt	Rk
2018	4.75	4.21	11	63%	10	23%	9	1.51	31	1.16	28	12.3%	3	37	6.7%	23	27.1%	27	8.5%	21
2019	4.96	4.62	26	76%	30	18%	19	1.38	30	1.13	30	8.9%	30	38	7.0%	18	32.2%	9	13.0%	24
2020	4.08	4.61	23	66%	14	13%	26	1.19	15	0.33	2	9.4%	28	38	6.1%	19	23.9%	21	13.1%	17

| 2020 ALY by direction: | Left End: 2.86 (4) | Left Tackle: 4.25 (17) | Mid/Guard: 4.73 (26) | Right Tackle: 4.30 (15) | Right End: 6.06 (32) |

Other than Myles Garrett, the Browns could well replace the entirety of their 2019 starting front seven with new blood. ⬧ Injuries blunted Olivier Vernon's impact in Cleveland in much the same way they did in New York. In his place the team hopes a pair of underachievers can match his influence. Jadeveon Clowney can set the edge effectively, though has never rushed the passer in a way that could justify his lofty draft status back in 2014. Former Falcons first-rounder Takk McKinley battled injuries in college and unsurprisingly did so in Atlanta too. Cleveland hopes a change of scenery brings more luck—with 17.5 sacks in 41 games, McKinley does bring some juice off the edge. And his name does rhyme with "sack." ⬧ The Browns flushed out both tackles as well. Sheldon Richardson's presence forced natural 3-technique Larry Ogunjobi to play out of position as a true nose, and the run defense suffered. Ogunjobi is now in Cincinnati, and Richardson was a surprising cut before the draft. Replacement candidates include 2019 third-rounder Jordan Elliott; nose tackle (and COVID opt-out) Andrew Billings, formerly of the Bengals; veteran Malik Jackson; and a pair of rookies, fourth-round choice Tommy Togiai from Ohio State and undrafted free agent Marvin Wilson of Florida State. The wild card is Wilson, once upon a time the nation's top recruit who sagged badly amid friction with his coaches in Tallahassee. ❧ Cleveland struggled to cover tight ends (28th) and running backs (23rd) last year, so Anthony Walker was imported from Indianapolis to play middle linebacker. However, Walker's 33% success rate in coverage last season belies his reputation as a pass defender. ❧ Sione Takitaki played well against the run (70% success rate), as did rookie Jacob Phillips (79%) in limited snaps. Neither were much to talk about against the pass, however. ❧ Malcolm Smith won the MVP of Super Bowl XLVIII, but that was VIII years ago, and what have you done for me lately? In Smith's case, not much, but he is around for veteran depth. ❧ Smith may be reduced to mentor status after Jeremiah Owusu-Koramoah fell to the Browns in the second round of the draft. A hugely athletic, sideline-to-sideline playmaker at Notre Dame, the JOKer slid due to health concerns (a heart issue that he insists is overblown) and some thought that he is a tweener—too small at 215 pounds to hold up at linebacker in the pros, while not disciplined or experienced enough to play safety. He's a smaller Isaiah Simmons in that respect. Much will depend on defensive coordinator Joe Woods' ability to harness Owusu-Koramoah's unique set of skills.

Defensive Secondary

Secondary	Age	Pos	G	Snaps	Plays	TmPct	Rk	Stop	Dfts	BTkl	Runs	St%	Rk	RuYd	Rk	Tgts	Tgt%	Rk	aDOT	Suc%	Rk	Yd/P	Rk	PD	Int
						Overall						**vs. Run**						**vs. Pass**							
Terrance Mitchell*	29	CB	16	1071	78	9.5%	23	23	6	6	16	13%	79	8.1	60	82	18.6%	50	14.0	49%	49	8.4	54	13	0
Andrew Sendejo*	34	FS	14	919	68	9.5%	50	13	5	15	24	21%	64	7.7	47	35	9.2%	29	16.5	46%	47	9.1	53	2	0
Denzel Ward	24	CB	12	775	64	10.4%	17	24	9	4	13	23%	69	8.5	64	69	21.6%	26	11.8	55%	25	5.9	7	18	2
Karl Joseph*	28	SS	14	660	68	9.5%	50	24	7	10	37	41%	29	5.3	19	26	9.6%	27	9.9	35%	68	10.2	60	4	1
Kevin Johnson*	29	CB	13	576	37	5.5%	--	11	6	9	9	11%	--	8.9	--	32	13.5%	--	9.6	50%	--	7.3	--	3	0
Ronnie Harrison	24	SS	11	326	44	7.8%	--	21	8	5	17	53%	--	3.7	--	17	12.7%	--	12.2	47%	--	7.5	--	7	1
Sheldrick Redwine	25	FS	15	275	23	3.0%	--	6	3	5	7	43%	--	7.4	--	9	7.9%	--	12.2	33%	--	7.0	--	1	1
M.J. Stewart	26	CB	16	229	20	2.4%	--	11	7	0	6	67%	--	4.3	--	16	17.0%	--	9.5	44%	--	9.1	--	3	2
Tavierre Thomas*	25	CB	16	203	20	2.4%	--	8	3	2	3	67%	--	4.0	--	18	21.5%	--	8.1	33%	--	7.2	--	0	0
John Johnson	26	FS	16	1024	113	14.0%	6	48	13	12	36	47%	17	5.4	21	40	10.3%	22	7.7	63%	5	4.4	4	8	1
Troy Hill	30	CB	16	972	87	10.8%	13	40	18	18	23	52%	23	5.1	23	61	16.5%	68	9.4	52%	36	6.4	15	10	3

Year	Pass D Rank	vs. #1 WR	Rk	vs. #2 WR	Rk	vs. Other WR	Rk	WR Wide	Rk	WR Slot	Rk	vs. TE	Rk	vs. RB	Rk
2018	7	-3.6%	12	-15.8%	8	-25.4%	3	-7.9%	15	-21.3%	2	-12.5%	9	4.4%	17
2019	17	10.2%	25	14.7%	25	-5.0%	13	10.4%	25	1.0%	10	-6.4%	9	13.4%	25
2020	25	-18.8%	4	0.8%	18	20.0%	30	-7.4%	9	-0.6%	19	18.3%	28	7.6%	23

The Browns 25th-ranked pass defense got the lion's share of attention in the offseason, mainly courtesy of the Rams (whose ancestral home was in Cleveland, conspiracy theorists!). Safety John Johnson was one of our faves around FO HQ last season, in large part due to his role in helping to prevent big plays. He fills a gaping need in the Browns defensive backfield, which hasn't had a valuable back-end playmaker since T.J. Ward. ❧ Another ex-Ram, Troy Hill, will take over the slot corner position, where he evinced a knack for making plays, including 18 defeats and 10 passes defensed. But he also tied for the lead among defensive backs with 18 broken tackles. ❧ No. 1 cornerback Denzel Ward generally misses a quarter of the season (he has started a dozen games in each of his three campaigns), and he has yet to match his stalwart rookie year, but he isn't the problem—the Browns were fourth in the league in stopping opposing No. 1 wideouts. Enemy passers feasted on the other guys. ❧ In order to prevent this imbalance, Cleveland used its top draft choice on Greg Newsome of Northwestern, a long, scheme-diverse corner who has elite traits but is raw. He committed 15 penalties in his 18 college starts, the latter number being low due to a number of injuries sustained in Evanston. ❧ On the subject of injury, the secondary might truly transform if the "Broken Bayou Bengals" can recover and contribute. Cornerback Greedy Williams, a 2019 second-round pick from LSU, has battled injuries since arriving in Cleveland, including a training camp nerve injury in his shoulder last year. Fellow ex-Tiger Grant Delpit, a 2020 second-round pick at safety, tore his Achilles tendon on the same day Williams was hurt. Both players were first-round talents who slipped due to long stretches of slack play during their final seasons in Baton Rouge, not wanting to risk the awaiting paycheck, so the fact neither have been able to go due to injuries is cruelly ironic. Delpit is being counted on to return and start at free safety; Greedy may need another Browns corner to get hurt to get his long belated shot at the field. ❧ If Delpit needs more time, Ronnie Harrison, who was average overall but had some good moments at strong safety in 2020, could move over to free safety; ideally, the Browns could employ some three-safety looks, which may well include the aforementioned Owusu-Koramoah.

Special Teams

Year	DVOA	Rank	FG/XP	Rank	Net Kick	Rank	Kick Ret	Rank	Net Punt	Rank	Punt Ret	Rank	Hidden	Rank
2018	-4.2%	30	-9.8	28	0.8	16	-5.3	30	-10.8	30	4.2	10	0.4	15
2019	0.8%	15	0.7	16	6.2	2	-1.4	20	1.4	17	-3.0	23	3.5	11
2020	-3.7%	27	-5.8	25	-6.8	29	-0.4	15	-1.7	20	-3.6	25	-3.0	18

The third phase was a clear weakness of the 2020 Browns, a sign that while the front-line talent was good, Cleveland lacked depth. The coverage and return units consistently put the Browns at a disadvantage in starting field position, which ranked 22nd on offense and 26th on defense. ◆ Cody Parkey was reasonable in gross kickoff value, but the Browns dropped from second to 29th in net kickoff value because they went from allowing an estimated -6.0 points of field position value on returns in 2019 to allowing 6.8 points worth of returns in 2020. Parkey also missed four kicks (including three extra points) during the crucial stretch from Weeks 14 to 16 as Cleveland pushed for the postseason. Nonetheless, Cleveland re-signed Parkey to a one-year extension, and as of this moment he seems likely to kick again for the Browns in 2021. ◆ Only two qualifying players (at least 50 punts) dropped fewer boots inside the 20-yard line than Jamie Gillan, who had just 14. But at press time there was no other punter on the Browns roster. ◆ Likewise, the Browns appear set to utilize Donovan Peoples-Jones (punts) and D'Ernest Johnson (kickoffs) as return men; their numbers were perfectly mediocre in 2020.

Dallas Cowboys

2020 Record: 6-10	**Total DVOA:** -11.1% (6)	**2021 Mean Projection:** 9.2 wins	**On the Clock (0-5):** 9%
Pythagorean Wins: 6.2 (24)	**Offense:** -8.5% (24)	**Postseason Odds:** 56.4%	**Mediocrity (6-8):** 30%
Snap-Weighted Age: 25.8 (28)	**Defense:** 6% (23)	**Super Bowl Odds:** 7.4%	**Playoff Contender (9-11):** 40%
Average Opponent: -1.9% (24)	**Special Teams:** 3.3% (7)	**Proj. Avg. Opponent:** -1.3% (24)	**Super Bowl Contender (12+):** 21%

2020: Like many of us, the Cowboys barely managed to put on their pants for most of last year.

2021: "Back to normal" may really mean "back to better."

Despite the best efforts of the folks in charge, the Dallas Cowboys are likely to be very good this year.

Jerry Jones' contract melodramas and random spending splurges won't stop them. Mike McCarthy's "Hardest Working Man in the NFL (source: Mike McCarthy)" routine won't slow them down (much). Bumbling, cantankerous defensive coordinator Mike Nolan is gone. The pandemic has retreated to the point that "you can't teach entirely new systems on Zoom" will no longer be a stumbling block/excuse.

The Cowboys, as only they can, walked away from a disastrous 2020 season in better shape than they entered it.

The Dak Prescott situation is a fine example of how the Cowboys somehow manage to strike oil by accident while trying to shoot themselves in the foot. Just before the world went through the Black Mirror last March, Jerry franchise-tagged Prescott after months of bickering and posturing over the size and shape of the quarterback's long-term contract. The two parties appeared determined to walk the path Washington walked with Kirk Cousins: multiple years of expensive, mutually unsatisfactory friend-zoning, followed by a parting of ways that leaves the unprepared organization (the Cowboys, like Washington, weren't clever enough to draft or sign any feasible leverage/insurance) without a quarterback.

Then fate played its hand. Prescott suffered a compound fracture/dislocation of his right ankle, giving him extra motivation to seek the security of a long-term deal. Andy Dalton and others were terrible in relief, pouring ice water on any pipe dreams Team Jerry might have had that they could plug 'n' play a scrappy veteran replacement. And empty stadiums caused revenues to tank and the salary cap to shrink, creating a short-term cash-flow situation that would have caused a real problem for a team that, say, signed someone to a franchise-quarterback contract in 2019 or 2020 that backloaded the cap hit into 2021.

In other words, Jerry accidentally helped himself by handling the Prescott situation poorly. Prescott got the four-year deal he wanted this offseason, though it's really the five-year deal that Jerry wanted once the franchise year is tacked on. Team Jerry structured the contract so the big cap hits arrive in 2023 and 2024, when the salary cap should be booming again. Prescott's deal is relatively team-friendly this year and next, which allowed the Cowboys to keep much of their core roster intact at a time when potential rivals within the NFC East (Eagles) and around the conference (Saints, Rams) were forced to shed veterans.

Speaking of that core roster, it looks excellent on paper. Amari Cooper, CeeDee Lamb, and Michael Gallup form one of the league's best receiver corps. The remnants of a once-dominant offensive line are still around and excellent when healthy.

Jerry does most of his prospect-speculating and budget-pruning on defense, and it showed last year. But the Cowboys defense improved from a DVOA of 8.8% (24th in the NFL) over the first half of last season to 2.3% (19th) in the second half, when the egregious and obvious blown assignments mostly subsided. Linebacker Micah Parsons was one of five defensive reinforcements drafted in the first three rounds, while new additions Brent Urban and Keanu Neal offset the latest round of defections. Factor in the coordinator change and the Cowboys should be able to hold most opponents under 27 points, which is all their offense will need. The special teams, coached by the great John "Bones" Fassel, also overcame some early-season bloopers last year and performed well by season's end.

And of course, the Cowboys are coached by Super Bowl-winner, offensive guru, and purported analytics supporter Mike McCarthy!

Yeah … about that last guy.

Even when Prescott was healthy at the start of last season, the Cowboys played like a bunch of guys who met in the parking lot for a pickup game. Defenders blew simple assignments. Ballcarriers, particularly Ezekiel Elliott, fumbled at an alarming rate. Coaching decisions, including some ill-advised fake punts, were downright loopy at times. Thirty years ago, we might have made an edgy joke about the Cowboys' extracurricular activities. In 2020, the more likely culprit was a pandemic that turned much of the offseason and many elements of weekly planning into the type of conference call that most of us "attend" with our cameras off.

COVID restrictions were hard on every NFL team, as well as most humans, of course. But some teams were better equipped to roll with the pandemic's punches than others. The Cowboys were not one of those teams. They are run by an owner with Texas-sized skepticism about government/union protocols. Nolan has always considered himself an heir to Tom Landry's legacy, making him an unlikely candidate to adapt willingly and effectively to virtual learning. Most critically, the head

2021 Cowboys Schedule

Week	Opp.	Week	Opp.	Week	Opp.
1	at TB (Thu.)	7	BYE	13	at NO (Thu.)
2	at LAC	8	at MIN	14	at WAS
3	PHI (Mon.)	9	DEN	15	at NYG
4	CAR	10	ATL	16	WAS
5	NYG	11	at KC	17	ARI
6	at NE	12	LV (Thu.)	18	at PHI

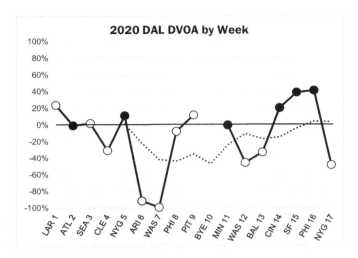

2020 DAL DVOA by Week

coach might have been hosting some of those Zoom meetings from the mineral baths at the Serenity Now Day Spa.

McCarthy, according to Ty Dunne's 2019 Bleacher Report expose of the Green Bay Packers, had a reputation at his last job for mid-workday retreats to his private office for massages; it was one of the many things which rankled America's Model Employee Aaron Rodgers. Upon dismissal from the Packers, McCarthy spent a year in a backyard cabin watching film of every single 2019 game, at least according to a Peter King profile. McCarthy then attended an in-service of sorts with the folks at Pro Football Focus, leaving with a Letter of Marque that provided him safe harbor and immunity from interrogation in some ports along the analytics archipelago. The King profile and analytics summit were remarkable feats of image rehabilitation, helped along by the growing awareness that Rodgers is the kind of guy who screams at the barista for not pumping enough caramel into his latte.

After getting the Cowboys job, however, McCarthy chuckled to reporters that he had not watched quite as much film as he claimed. There were no signs on the field of any revitalized Playbook from Big Pink game-planning. McCarthy's receivers ran many of the same "go straight, then turn around" patterns that made Rodgers want to speak to the manager, and it showed in the charting stats: Cowboys receivers were targeted for 199 passes listed as curl, out, or comeback by Sports Info Solutions, the highest figure in the league.

There was also little evidence that McCarthy experienced some sort of analytical epiphany during his cabin meditations. McCarthy's Aggressiveness Index of 1.68 ranked 12th in the league on fourth downs, and it wasn't far off his career AI of 1.22 once we adjust for changing tactics across the league over the last three years. Elliott still earned twice as many touches as Tony Pollard, despite fumbles and diminishing returns, though Elliott's workload might fall under Jerry's jurisdiction.

To sum things up politely, McCarthy may have focused more on self-promotion than self-improvement during his year off, then leaned into the Netflix-and-sweatpants 2020 lifestyle a smidge more last year than his hyper-motivated peers did. Whatever the cause, the whole Cowboys team didn't look all that focused or motivated when they were spotting opponents 29-10 and 31-14 halftime leads early in the season.

Not every fault with the 2020 Cowboys can be attributed to the coaching staff or the loss of Prescott. The Cowboys finished second to the Eagles with 46.4 adjusted games lost on the offensive line. They burned through nine starters and nine

different lineups. Tyron Smith missed all but two games, Zach Martin missed half the year, and La'el Collins missed the entire year. Bill Walsh in his prime could only do so much with guys such as Terence Steele and Brandon Knight protecting a banged-up, COVID-afflicted Dalton. Jerry's overspending on offense left Nolan with no front-line defensive talent beyond DeMarcus Lawrence, leaving lots of fading prospects (Leighton Vander Esch, Trysten Hill, Randy Gregory) and aging reclamation projects (Dontari Poe, Everson Griffin, a surprisingly spry Aldon Smith) among the starting rotation.

It's also worth mentioning that McCarthy coached the Packers to nine playoff appearances and 13-3 and 15-1 records, plus the Super Bowl. Rodgers had lots and lots to do with that, of course, but McCarthy must still have something to offer. Last year's pratfall may have chastened him and/or raised Jerry's ire. McCarthy stated before the draft that he was seeking "speed and energy," hinting that he noticed some players going through the motions last year. More importantly, McCarthy made much-needed changes on the defensive staff at season's end, firing old buddy Nolan and defensive line coach Jim Tomsula (Nolan's old buddy) and hiring defensive coordinator Dan Quinn.

Quinn's Falcons defenses had their problems—Lordy, did they have their problems—but they always gave 100%. Furthermore, Quinn's Seahawks-scented defense will be similar to what Kris Richard used when he was the Cowboys' de facto defensive coordinator in 2018 and 2019, meaning veterans should be more comfortable with it than they were with whatever the heck Nolan was trying to do last season.

Well-regarded offensive coordinator Kellen Moore is also still in the Cowboys fold and enjoying the shield from criticism that comes from working under McCarthy and Jason Garrett. (Note that all of the elements of the Cowboys offense that have worked well for the last two years, including their use of pre-snap motion, are attributed to Moore, while all the bad stuff was blamed on the head coaches.) Even if McCarthy puts cucumber slices over his eyes and allows Quinn, Moore, and Bones to run the Cowboys, the team will still be in pretty good hands.

In addition to fielding one of the most talented offenses in the NFC, the Cowboys promise to be one of most drama-free teams in the conference. That's a mild surprise, considering they're the Cowboys. It's also not something that DVOA is designed to measure, though organizational tumult can seep into the statistics in a variety of ways.

The Cowboys aren't in quarterback denial like the Saints. They don't have to cope with Rodgers, who may be gearing up for a long second career of berating game show production assistants, or Russell Wilson, who may be watching Rodgers and taking notes. They are not rebooting at quarterback like the Rams, 49ers, and Bears. They are not a team without a quarterback like Washington, a curmudgeon's vanity project like the Giants, or an impact crater like the Eagles. The Cowboys pass the eyeball test of a Super Bowl contender because so many would-be challengers simply don't. DVOA reassures us that our eyes are not deceiving us and that many of the bad things that turned the Cowboys into a slapstick comedy last year are unlikely to repeat themselves in 2021.

Jerry Jones' team management tactics will never be featured in a best-practices seminar. His Cowboys have whiffed on Super Bowl opportunities since Tony Romo sprang from nowhere to solve the team's quarterback problem in 2006. At the same time, the Cowboys keep stumbling into additional opportunities because quarterbacks keep plopping into their laps, and because Team Jerry's brute force approach—draft big college names, spend lavishly for established stars, worry about the salary cap the day after tomorrow—typically results in a competitive roster, if not an optimized roster.

The Cowboys would be a better team in 2021 if they were spending more money in the secondary and less at running back. The Prescott situation could have been handled much more elegantly. But Cowboys problems have a way of solving themselves, and after a year in which everything went wrong, the team appears poised for one of those seasons like 2014 and 2016 in which lots of things go their way, the front-line talent carries them into the playoffs, and Jerry convinces himself that his way of doing business really is the best way.

Mike Tanier

2020 Cowboys Stats by Week

Wk	vs.	W-L	PF	PA	YDF	YDA	TO	Total	Off	Def	ST
1	at LAR	L	17	20	380	422	1	23.6%	28.5%	-0.9%	-5.8%
2	ATL	W	40	39	570	380	-3	-0.9%	10.6%	8.5%	-3.0%
3	at SEA	L	31	38	522	412	-2	1.8%	-1.5%	-3.8%	-0.5%
4	CLE	L	38	49	566	508	-3	-30.9%	7.9%	35.6%	-3.3%
5	NYG	W	37	34	402	300	-1	11.0%	4.5%	-6.5%	0.0%
6	ARI	L	10	38	344	438	-4	-91.7%	-55.8%	28.3%	-7.6%
7	at WAS	L	3	25	142	397	-1	-99.5%	-77.4%	33.3%	11.2%
8	at PHI	L	9	23	265	222	2	-7.9%	-35.5%	-25.4%	2.2%
9	PIT	L	19	24	364	355	-2	11.8%	-5.7%	4.5%	21.9%
10	BYE										
11	at MIN	W	31	28	376	430	1	-0.2%	6.5%	10.7%	4.0%
12	WAS	L	16	41	247	338	-1	-45.7%	-30.4%	14.0%	-1.3%
13	at BAL	L	17	34	388	401	0	-32.8%	3.1%	27.0%	-8.9%
14	at CIN	W	30	7	272	309	3	20.3%	-12.2%	-17.9%	14.6%
15	SF	W	41	33	291	458	4	38.8%	12.6%	-13.3%	12.9%
16	PHI	W	37	17	513	477	2	41.1%	23.0%	-11.3%	6.8%
17	at NYG	L	19	23	307	336	1	-48.0%	-30.9%	27.1%	10.0%

Trends and Splits

	Offense	Rank	Defense	Rank
Total DVOA	-8.5%	24	6.0%	23
Unadjusted VOA	-14.1%	26	2.0%	18
Weighted Trend	-11.3%	25	4.9%	20
Variance	8.5%	22	3.7%	10
Average Opponent	-4.3%	3	-6.1%	31
Passing	-0.9%	24	13.1%	21
Rushing	-12.6%	20	-2.1%	23
First Down	-12.0%	25	11.2%	27
Second Down	2.3%	14	5.2%	20
Third Down	-18.3%	26	-2.0%	15
First Half	-8.6%	23	11.2%	29
Second Half	-8.4%	22	-0.4%	12
Red Zone	-31.5%	31	2.3%	15
Late and Close	-8.6%	22	-0.6%	19

Five-Year Performance

Year	W-L	Pyth W	Est W	PF	PA	TO	Total	Rk	Off	Rk	Def	Rk	ST	Rk	Off AGL	Rk	Def AGL	Rk	Off Age	Rk	Def Age	Rk	ST Age	Rk
2016	13-3	11	12.3	421	306	+5	24.0%	2	20.2%	3	-2.2%	14	1.6%	9	37.9	19	39.2	16	26.6	20	26.3	20	26.1	16
2017	9-7	8.6	9.4	354	332	-1	9.3%	11	6.6%	10	1.9%	16	4.6%	7	8.0	2	26.4	10	26.8	18	25.1	30	25.9	15
2018	10-6	8.4	7.3	339	324	+2	-2.3%	18	-6.3%	24	-6.0%	9	-2.1%	23	42.0	20	33.2	16	25.5	31	24.7	32	25.8	14
2019	8-8	10.9	11.4	434	321	-1	19.9%	6	24.5%	2	0.7%	16	-3.9%	30	11.3	2	24.5	7	27.0	13	26.2	18	26.9	3
2020	6-10	6.2	6.5	395	473	-3	-11.1%	23	-8.5%	24	6.0%	23	3.3%	7	75.6	29	42.9	18	25.2	31	26.3	15	26.2	11

2020 Performance Based on Most Common Personnel Groups

DAL Offense					DAL Offense vs. Opponents					DAL Defense				DAL Defense vs. Opponents			
Pers	Freq	Yds	DVOA	Run%	Pers	Freq	Yds	DVOA	Run%	Pers	Freq	Yds	DVOA	Pers	Freq	Yds	DVOA
11	72%	5.8	-1.3%	27%	Base	22%	4.7	-7.0%	60%	Base	18%	7.0	27.2%	11	55%	5.8	0.1%
12	21%	4.8	-13.3%	62%	Nickel	68%	5.9	-4.4%	29%	Nickel	70%	5.9	2.5%	12	20%	6.1	9.6%
10	2%	6.6	-19.5%	5%	Dime+	8%	4.7	-12.0%	10%	Dime+	9%	5.9	2.1%	21	11%	6.5	9.2%
13	1%	3.2	-13.8%	75%	Goal Line	1%	0.5	-5.0%	64%	Goal Line	2%	2.1	-60.1%	13	4%	6.7	41.8%
21	1%	1.3	-104.5%	20%	Big	1%	4.3	-22.7%	75%	Big	1%	6.1	-16.0%	22	3%	6.3	2.0%

Strategic Tendencies

Run/Pass		Rk	Formation		Rk	Pass Rush		Rk	Secondary		Rk	Strategy		Rk
Runs, first half	38%	16	Form: Single Back	88%	6	Rush 3	12.3%	6	4 DB	18%	26	Play Action	22%	27
Runs, first down	43%	23	Form: Empty Back	9%	15	Rush 4	67.3%	15	5 DB	70%	5	Offensive Motion	47%	13
Runs, second-long	25%	24	Form: Multi Back	3%	26	Rush 5	18.3%	21	6+ DB	9%	19	Avg Box (Off)	6.43	25
Runs, power sit.	59%	15	Pers: 3+ WR	75%	6	Rush 6+	2.1%	30	Man Coverage	28%	19	Avg Box (Def)	6.91	2
Runs, behind 2H	27%	17	Pers: 2+ TE/6+ OL	24%	22	Edge Rusher Sacks	62.9%	4	CB by Sides	69%	25	Offensive Pace	27.48	2
Pass, ahead 2H	43%	23	Pers: 6+ OL	1%	24	Interior DL Sacks	4.8%	32	S/CB Cover Ratio	18%	31	Defensive Pace	30.27	16
Run-Pass Options	10%	11	Shotgun/Pistol	66%	15	Second Level Sacks	32.3%	7	DB Blitz	6%	31	Go for it on 4th	1.68	13

Even without a healthy Dak Prescott, the Cowboys kept up the pace, ranking second in situation-neutral pace for the second straight year. ◕ Dallas ranked fifth rushing the ball on third or fourth down but 29th passing the ball. ◕ Dallas went from the lowest rate of passes thrown at or behind the line of scrimmage (11.8%) in 2019 to an above-average rate (19.4%) in 2020. They went from a league-low nine wide receiver screens in 2019 to an above-average 49 in 2020. They were also terrible on those wide receiver screens, with just 4.7 yards per pass and -28.8% DVOA. ◕ On the other side, the Dallas defense was terrible against wide receiver screens for the second straight year: 6.5 yards per pass, 43.4% DVOA. Good thing they faced just 27 compared to an NFL average of 35. ◕ Cowboys opponents went from the lowest rate of dropped passes in 2019 (3.6%) to the second-highest rate in 2020 (7.4%). ◕ Dallas dropped from fifth to 25th in "CB by Sides" as injuries forced them to mix, match, and move around their cornerbacks. ◕ Dallas recovered only four of 17 fumbles on offense but also recovered 12 of 17 fumbles on defense.

Passing

Player	DYAR	DVOA	Plays	NtYds	Avg	YAC	C%	TD	Int
A.Dalton*	-136	-16.7%	357	1976	5.5	4.8	65.1%	14	8
D.Prescott	399	14.0%	231	1790	7.7	5.4	68.3%	9	4
B.DiNucci	-199	-78.0%	49	146	3.0	5.8	54.8%	0	0
G.Gilbert	25	-0.5%	39	220	5.6	2.5	56.8%	1	1

Rushing

Player	DYAR	DVOA	Plays	Yds	Avg	TD	Fum	Suc
E.Elliott	87	-0.9%	244	979	4.0	7	5	50%
T.Pollard	91	13.0%	101	435	4.3	4	0	47%
A.Dalton*	24	5.2%	24	116	4.8	0	1	--
D.Prescott	46	33.3%	17	94	5.5	3	0	--
C.Lamb	62	66.2%	10	82	8.2	1	0	--
R.Dowdle	7	16.3%	7	24	3.4	0	0	43%
A.Cooper	3	-27.6%	6	14	2.3	0	0	--
B.DiNucci	-7	-32.9%	6	13	2.2	0	1	--

Receiving

Player	DYAR	DVOA	Plays	Ctch	Yds	Y/C	YAC	TD	C%
A.Cooper	184	4.7%	130	92	1114	12.1	4.5	5	71%
C.Lamb	78	-3.8%	111	74	935	12.6	4.2	5	67%
M.Gallup	58	-5.7%	105	59	843	14.3	4.3	5	56%
C.Wilson	4	-11.1%	28	17	189	11.1	6.6	2	61%
N.Brown	0	-12.6%	24	14	154	11.0	3.4	0	58%
D.Schultz	-8	-8.5%	89	63	615	9.8	4.4	4	71%
B.Bell*	-6	-13.0%	15	11	110	10.0	4.4	0	73%
E.Elliott	35	-5.2%	71	52	338	6.5	6.9	2	73%
T.Pollard	12	-8.3%	40	28	193	6.9	8.3	1	70%

Offensive Line

Player	Pos	Age	GS	Snaps	Pen	Sk	Pass	Run	Player	Pos	Age	GS	Snaps	Pen	Sk	Pass	Run
Connor Williams	LG	24	16/16	1144	5	3.5	17	11	Zack Martin	RG	31	10/10	618	1	0.5	3	0
Terence Steele	RT	24	16/14	968	7	9	33	4	Connor McGovern	RG	24	14/8	604	1	2	9	2
Brandon Knight	LT	24	13/9	773	1	7	21	8	Tyler Biadasz	C	24	12/4	426	2	1	4	1
Joe Looney*	C	31	13/12	763	1	0.5	3	10	Cameron Erving*	LT	29	6/5	278	2	1	4	2

Year	Yards	ALY	Rk	Power	Rk	Stuff	Rk	2Lev	Rk	OpFld	Rk	BB Rt	Rk	Sacks	ASR	Rk	Press	Rk	BB Rt	Rk	Cont
2018	4.46	4.61	8	75%	3	18%	11	1.31	9	0.87	14	5.9%	14	56	9.7%	28	34.1%	26	9.1%	14	32
2019	4.68	4.91	2	76%	2	13%	1	1.42	1	0.72	18	7.9%	4	23	4.3%	2	29.6%	15	9.4%	2	25
2020	4.09	4.48	12	71%	11	18%	23	1.12	23	0.54	27	9.5%	15	44	6.1%	14	24.5%	14	13.3%	19	24

2020 ALY by direction:	Left End: 4.68 (9)	Left Tackle: 4.96 (6)	Mid/Guard: 4.32 (19)	Right Tackle: 4.50 (14)	Right End: 4.04 (23)

Need evidence for how much the Cowboys missed their injured offensive linemen? Dallas allowed 24 sacks on blown blocks, tied for the most in the league. ✎ Left tackle Tyron Smith has not played a full 16-game season since 2015. Neck injuries have been the primary issue since 2018, and Smith underwent neck surgery last October in the hope of fixing the problem once and for all. Smith was limited at the start of OTAs, but the team website reported that he was in high spirits, and Smith gave himself a Best Shape of His Life bill of health: "I mean my strength is back—or probably better than it was, since I've just been sitting here working out." ✎ La'el Collins underwent hip surgery in October. Like Smith, he was limited at the start of OTAs for precautionary reasons but is expected to be a full participant at training camp. Collins also plans to shed weight and play in the 308-pound range after reportedly weighing in at around 323 pounds before the surgery. ✎ Zack Martin ended last season on the IR after a Thanksgiving calf injury. There were no reports of lingering issues at OTAs. Martin was charged with just three blown blocks on 598 offensive snaps last season. Only Jaguars center Brandon Linder had fewer blown blocks among linemen with 500-plus snaps. ✎ Center Tyler Biadasz started just four games and played significant roles in two others as a rookie. He struggled, but there was a lot of that going around on the Cowboys line once Smith and Collins went down. As of OTAs, Biadasz was the only player on the Cowboys roster who had ever snapped a football in the NFL. ✎ Left guard Connor Williams played all 16 games last season, the poor guy. Williams still gets pushed around by the Fletcher Cox-Aaron Donald class of interior defender but holds his own against mere mortals. He looks much more capable when he's the fourth-best player on the line than when he's the best. ✎ In case of another injury crisis, the Cowboys signed Ty Nsekhe, the greatest career backup tackle in NFL history. Nsekhe backed up Trent Williams in Washington for several years before backing up Dion Dawkins and others for two years in Buffalo, always playing just enough to demonstrate that he could get the job done. The Cowboys also spent a fourth-round pick on tackle Josh Ball, who was suspended by Florida State for what was reported as a "dating violence" incident and finished his career at Marshall.

Defensive Front

Defensive Line	Age	Pos	G	Snaps	Plays	Overall TmPct	Rk	Stop	Dfts	BTkl	Runs	vs. Run St%	Rk	RuYd	Rk	Pass Rush Sack	Hit	Hur	Dsrpt
Antwaun Woods*	28	DT	14	456	23	3.2%	80	16	1	3	22	68%	67	3.4	92	1.0	1	2	0
Neville Gallimore	24	DT	14	416	29	4.0%	66	22	8	2	25	80%	26	2.0	27	0.5	3	7	1
Justin Hamilton	28	DT	10	236	10	1.9%	--	8	2	0	10	80%	--	2.0	--	0.0	1	6	1
Carlos Watkins	28	DE	16	542	30	3.5%	75	21	6	2	24	67%	69	2.5	49	2.0	1	4	3
Brent Urban	30	DE	16	369	37	4.5%	--	33	6	2	32	88%	--	1.8	--	2.5	1	6	2

Edge Rushers	Age	Pos	G	Snaps	Plays	Overall TmPct	Rk	Stop	Dfts	BTkl	Runs	vs. Run St%	Rk	RuYd	Rk	Pass Rush Sack	Hit	Hur	Dsrpt
Aldon Smith*	32	DE	16	808	50	6.0%	25	40	10	8	42	76%	31	2.9	63	5.0	9	37	5
Demarcus Lawrence	29	DE	16	666	60	7.2%	10	46	25	6	47	72%	46	1.5	9	6.5	4	37	3
Tyrone Crawford*	32	DE	16	443	14	1.7%	95	9	3	0	11	55%	91	5.5	97	2.0	2	14	1
Dorance Armstrong	24	DE	16	367	32	3.9%	--	16	3	2	25	56%	--	3.7	--	0.0	1	8	0
Randy Gregory	29	DE	10	270	22	4.2%	59	18	11	1	17	76%	30	1.8	22	3.5	10	9	2
Tarell Basham	27	OLB	16	734	34	3.9%	67	26	13	8	23	78%	21	1.9	24	3.5	9	19	0

Linebackers	Age	Pos	G	Snaps	Plays	TmPct	Rk	Stop	Dfts	BTkl	Runs	St%	Rk	RuYd	Rk	Sack	Hit	Hur	Tgts	Suc%	Rk	Yd/P	Rk	PD	Int
						Overall						vs. Run				Pass Rush				vs. Pass					
Jaylon Smith	26	OLB	16	1081	159	19.2%	3	67	19	10	106	40%	83	4.9	79	1.5	5	9	36	50%	40	6.6	48	5	1
Leighton Vander Esch	25	MLB	10	459	60	11.6%	51	27	5	8	41	51%	61	4.3	55	1.0	0	0	11	27%	--	8.1	--	0	0
Joe Thomas*	30	MLB	15	408	47	6.0%	82	22	7	4	29	48%	71	4.4	64	0.0	2	5	11	55%	--	9.3	--	2	0
Sean Lee*	35	MLB	9	180	20	4.3%	--	7	0	5	15	40%	--	4.9	--	0.0	1	1	7	43%	--	6.4	--	0	0

Year	Yards	ALY	Rk	Power	Rk	Stuff	Rk	2Lev	Rk	OpFld	Rk	BB Rt	Rk	Sacks	ASR	Rk	Press	Rk	BB Rt	Rk
2018	3.88	3.87	3	67%	20	25%	5	1.16	10	0.76	14	11.4%	6	39	6.5%	27	32.2%	8	10.6%	16
2019	4.05	4.05	8	66%	20	21%	10	1.16	15	0.78	19	16.9%	6	39	6.8%	19	33.9%	6	19.8%	1
2020	4.87	4.98	30	65%	13	13%	28	1.41	29	0.83	23	9.1%	29	31	5.2%	25	27.0%	10	12.2%	22

2020 ALY by direction:	Left End: 4.81 (21)	Left Tackle: 4.69 (22)	Mid/Guard: 4.88 (30)	Right Tackle: 4.86 (22)	Right End: 5.85 (30)

The Dallas front seven consists of troubled mega-talents, gifted throwback linebackers, hustling newcomers expected to push the troubled mega-talents, and Tank Lawrence. These are their stories.

Trouble Mega-Talents: Randy Gregory, who turns 29 in November, missed all of the 2019 season and the first six games of 2020 due to a substance abuse suspension. He then performed very well over the back half of the season as a situational edge rusher. Defensive coordinator Dan Quinn gushed during OTAs about having been impressed with Gregory since scouting him at Nebraska. It's generally a discouraging sign when coaches have to keep harkening back to a player's college accomplishments to praise a player seven years later. (Think of it as The Sam Bradford Rule.) ❧ Defensive tackle Trysten Hill played just five games before tearing an ACL in 2020. Hill was a healthy scratch for much of his rookie 2019 campaign. He's now two defensive coordinators removed from the staff that was excited to work with him, so he's out of redshirts, medical and otherwise. ❧ Aldon Smith, the ultimate troubled mega-talent for the 2020 Cowboys, signed with the Seahawks as a free agent after an impressive comeback year.

Gifted Throwback Linebackers: First-round pick Micah Parsons has Bobby Wagner-level talent. He recorded six sacks, four forced fumbles, 14 tackles for a loss, and six pass breakups for Penn State in 2019 before opting out last year. Parsons earned glowing reviews in rookie camp and OTAs. He's likely to play a hybrid middle linebacker/edge rusher role as a rookie. ❧ Jaylon Smith has grown into a serviceable starter, though many Cowboys fans consider him a disappointment due to: A) his expectations before getting hurt at the end of his Notre Dame career; B) his huge contract, which is mostly the result of those expectations; and C) the fact that none of the defenders in front of him could be bothered to take on blocks last year. Smith is the Cowboys' best incumbent coverage linebacker, though he may be challenged for playing time by some of the newcomers. ❧ Smith will also be changing his uniform number from 54 to 9 this season. Perhaps he assumes that if he wears Tony Romo's old jersey, he can trick Jerry Jones into overpaying him. As mentioned, Smith is in the midst of a $63.8-million contract, so he really has no need for such trickery. ❧ Leighton Vander Esch left Boise State as a hustling athletic marvel in 2018 but looked baffled by routine assignments last year. He missed half of 2019 with a neck stinger, then missed six games last year with a broken collarbone followed by an ankle injury. Vander Esch may be the odd man out of a deep linebacker corps, and the Cowboys already declined his fifth-year option for 2022.

Hustling Newcomers: Third-round pick Osa Odighizuwa was a Senior Bowl standout who earned a reputation as a stout run defender while playing 3-4 defensive end at UCLA. He's likely to rotate with Hill and Carlos Watkins on the interior but may also play some end as Quinn (like every other defensive coordinator on earth) mixes one-gap and two-gap concepts. ❧ Fellow third-round pick Chauncey Golden was an edge rusher at Iowa but may be a better fit as a run-stopping end in the NFL. He could end up in a rotation with Gregory. ❧ Watkins, a Texans castoff, and Brent Urban, a former Ravens role player who started eight games for the Bears last season, add beef and experience to a young tackle rotation. ❧ Keanu Neal played safety for Quinn's Falcons but is now expected to compete for a nickel linebacker role. Experience should give him an edge over toolsy fifth-round pick Jabril Cox (LSU, by way of North Dakota State), a converted high school quarterback with the body of an edge rusher but the style of an in-space linebacker. ❧ Former Jets edge rusher Tarell Basham, another veteran the Cowboys picked up in the free-agent discount bin, summed up during OTAs what the team was looking for from their new arrivals: "They want somebody to cause some chaos for the back, cause some chaos in the run game. They want somebody with a whole lot of energy, and that's me." Basham also summed up the experience of playing for the Adam Gase Jets: "I feel like I've done enough losing in my past."

Tank Lawrence: He's still really, really good.

Defensive Secondary

Secondary	Age	Pos	G	Snaps	Plays	Overall TmPct	Rk	Stop	Dfts	BTkl	vs. Run Runs	St%	Rk	RuYd	Rk	vs. Pass Tgts	Tgt%	Rk	aDOT	Suc%	Rk	Yd/P	Rk	PD	Int
Xavier Woods*	26	FS	15	989	73	9.4%	52	26	7	10	42	43%	27	7.1	39	18	5.2%	58	6.7	61%	7	5.4	9	1	0
Jourdan Lewis	26	CB	15	816	61	7.8%	60	34	12	7	26	58%	12	3.7	6	49	17.2%	64	7.5	61%	6	6.3	13	2	0
Trevon Diggs	23	CB	12	757	72	11.6%	6	28	10	5	24	29%	61	6.7	41	74	28.0%	2	14.8	49%	50	8.6	59	14	3
Donovan Wilson	26	SS	14	671	68	9.4%	53	25	9	7	36	28%	52	7.8	48	11	4.7%	63	10.2	64%	4	7.0	25	3	2
Anthony Brown	28	CB	10	533	42	8.1%	54	13	4	5	11	55%	15	6.6	40	40	21.5%	29	12.9	35%	78	9.2	66	3	2
Darian Thompson	28	FS	15	477	42	5.4%	--	13	5	5	16	31%	--	10.5	--	17	10.2%	--	10.1	47%	--	9.5	--	1	1
Chidobe Awuzie*	26	CB	8	452	43	10.4%	--	15	6	3	16	25%	--	6.2	--	35	22.2%	--	13.7	54%	--	10.8	--	5	1
Rashard Robinson	26	CB	4	186	20	9.7%	--	7	2	1	8	38%	--	3.9	--	12	18.5%	--	10.1	42%	--	7.0	--	0	0
Keanu Neal	26	SS	15	917	99	12.9%	10	33	15	13	34	38%	33	5.9	26	43	11.2%	17	7.2	49%	38	8.7	48	2	1
Jayron Kearse	27	FS	11	503	59	10.2%	42	22	4	4	35	46%	22	4.4	6	24	12.5%	12	6.4	54%	22	4.0	2	2	0

Year	Pass D Rank	vs. #1 WR	Rk	vs. #2 WR	Rk	vs. Other WR	Rk	WR Wide	Rk	WR Slot	Rk	vs. TE	Rk	vs. RB	Rk
2018	16	-11.7%	6	-24.1%	4	6.9%	22	-4.6%	19	-8.1%	7	4.7%	19	12.5%	26
2019	23	4.8%	20	16.0%	26	5.7%	21	-10.1%	13	22.7%	30	8.3%	23	-1.5%	20
2020	21	13.5%	25	38.8%	32	5.8%	18	19.7%	30	19.8%	30	21.8%	29	-15.9%	6

Trevon Diggs was one of many Cowboys defenders who consistently blew rudimentary assignments in the first half of the season. He looked much better after returning from a foot injury for the final three games of the year, allowing just seven catches with an interception and three breakups in 14 targets in those games. Diggs played for Alabama and learned his craft from trying to cover much-older brother Stefon Diggs, so last year's extended mental fog was likely a combination of rookie lumps and the Mike Nolan Effect. Second-round pick Kelvin Joseph has the inside track to win the left cornerback job, but Anthony Brown is also in the mix. Joseph, an LSU-to-Kentucky transfer, is a size-speed prototype who played just 15 collegiate games. Brown is a veteran coming off his worst season (The Mike Nolan Effect) but is considered a locker room leader. Just ask Diggs. "That's like my big brother," he said of Brown. "I go over to his house. He's a really good influence on my career. I ask him questions all the time." Jourdain Lewis returns for another year in the slot after (sigh) suffering the worst season of his career in 2020. Donovan Wilson racked up four sacks despite rarely rushing the passer and playing deep more often than a typical strong safety. Look for him to play near the box and earn more pass-rushing opportunities in more of a Kam Chancellor-type of role this year. Falcons import Damontae Kazee is the favorite to win the free safety job. Kazee led the NFL with seven interceptions in 2018 but suffered an Achilles injury in Week 4 last year. Kazee was running at full speed in OTAs. Reggie Robinson, a 2020 combine marvel who somehow ended up in the Nolan doghouse, is also in the mix for a role in the dime package.

Special Teams

Year	DVOA	Rank	FG/XP	Rank	Net Kick	Rank	Kick Ret	Rank	Net Punt	Rank	Punt Ret	Rank	Hidden	Rank
2018	-2.1%	23	-2.6	23	-3.4	26	-0.8	15	-2.5	21	-1.1	18	-4.1	21
2019	-3.9%	30	1.7	14	-4.9	28	-7.1	32	-7.6	26	-1.8	21	2.6	12
2020	3.3%	7	3.7	13	4.3	9	4.4	7	3.0	11	1.2	13	4.3	11

John Fassel is one of the most respected special teams coaches in the NFL, and he dared to do things differently last year. Sometimes, the results were ridiculous, like on a handful of botched fake punts. Other times, they were sublime, like on a Music City Miracle-like punt return that went for 73 yards against the Steelers. When he coached the Rams special teams, Fassel helped turn Johnny Hekker into the most successful fake-punt passer in modern NFL history, so opponents should keep expecting the unexpected. Greg Zuerlein, who followed Fassel from the Rams, was 3-of-9 from beyond 50 yards but 31-of-32 otherwise. He led the NFL with 41 field goal attempts. Punter Hunter Niswander spent two years out of football after leaving Northwestern. Then he punted for the XFL's DC Defenders for five games before COVID descended. Niswander replaced injured Chris Jones in November of last season and proved to be an immediate upgrade, winning the full-time job for this season. Tony Pollard's kick return average improved from 17.5 yards per return as a rookie to 23.5 yards last season. Punt returner CeeDee Lamb mixed great returns (six over 15 yards) with returns that went nowhere (six for a loss or no gain). With only so many balls to go around on offense, return chores will be a fine way to get Pollard and Lamb a few more touches.

Denver Broncos

2020 Record: 5-11	Total DVOA: -21.9% (23)	2021 Mean Projection: 8.8 wins	On the Clock (0-5): 12%
Pythagorean Wins: 4.9 (29)	Offense: -20% (30)	Postseason Odds: 45.6%	Mediocrity (6-8): 33%
Snap-Weighted Age: 25.9 (27)	Defense: -0.2% (13)	Super Bowl Odds: 4.9%	Playoff Contender (9-11): 38%
Average Opponent: 3.9% (5)	Special Teams: -2.1% (24)	Proj. Avg. Opponent: -2.1% (27)	Super Bowl Contender (12+): 17%

2020: The Broncos fail to unlock Drew Lock.

2021: Trying to upgrade from bad offense, mediocre defense to great defense, mediocre offense.

Another season, another post-Peyton Manning quarterback dilemma in Denver. The Broncos have turned over every rock under the sun trying to solve the position since a decrepit Manning brought them a Lombardi Trophy in 2015, but they have failed time and time again. Last year's quarterback turmoil was a special brand of misery, though. The universe dug deep to make sure that everything that could go wrong, did go wrong in the Broncos quarterback room.

The Broncos cycled through a number of backup quarterbacks at both ends of the season. Some of that quarterback juggling was run-of-the-mill injury stuff. Drew Lock injured his hand early in the season, giving way to Jeff Driskel playing out most of the Week 2 match against Pittsburgh and starting the following week against Tampa Bay. Then Driskel suffered an injury late against Tampa Bay, giving the keys to Brett Rypien for the next five or so quarters. Rypien won his start against the Jets despite throwing more interceptions than touchdowns, though that still left Denver at 1-3 to start the year. Lock returned by Week 5, but that was not the end of Denver's quarterback woes. As it turns out, a bad quarterback is still better than no quarterback at all.

Late in November, Driskel tested positive for COVID. Due to failure to follow mask protocols, the entire quarterback depth chart was deemed ineligible just one day before hosting the New Orleans Saints. The Broncos were left scrambling for anything that even sort of resembled a passer. They found practice squad wideout Kendall Hinton, who played quarterback at Wake Forest for three seasons before transitioning to wide receiver. Hinton's start went about as poorly as everyone assumed it would—he finished 1-of-9 for 13 yards with two interceptions in a 31-3 loss. Hinton only even played about half of the team's snaps, leaving the other half to be Wildcat snaps to running back Phillip Lindsay.

On the frustration meter, however, one game where an emergency quarterback lives down to expectations doesn't quite match an entire season where a potential franchise quarterback fails to live up to expectations. A second-round pick in 2019, Lock looked every bit of the highly talented, yet incomplete prospect he was billed to be during his rookie season. His arm strength shined, allowing him to fit the ball into some of the smallest crevices around defenders. Lock's first-quarter touchdown pass to tight end Noah Fant over the heart of the end zone against the Houston Texans was the best example

of what he could do at his peak thanks to his arm talent and aggressive nature. He rifled in that throw right past a linebacker's frame and into Fant's outstretched arms on third-and-12, giving the Broncos an early lead in a 38-24 win. As mediocre as his efficiency numbers were, in addition to how remedial the offense was for most of his time as the starter, Lock's potential ceiling was exciting. Rose-colored glasses or not, the Broncos saw enough from Lock to give him another whirl in 2020, this time as the Week 1 starter.

Lock's first season as the big man on campus did not go as planned. While his five starts in 2019 were a small sample and largely upheld by an unsustainably fortunate performance against the Texans, Lock took a step back across the board in 2020. Lock's completion percentage over expected (CPOE), DVOA, net yards per play, and interception rate all got worse (Table 1). Even Lock's rushing stats were less impressive, falling from a -10.9% DVOA as a rookie to -16.0% in 2020. Middling rookie quarterbacks such as Lock tend to take some sort of leap in their second season, but that was far from the case here.

Table 1. Drew Lock Stats, 2019-2020

Metric	2019	2020
Starts	5	13
CPOE	-1.3%	-6.3%
DVOA	2.2%	-16.2%
Net Yd/Play	6.14	6.05
Int. Rate	1.9%	3.4%

While Lock was wholly uninspiring last season, there were some uphill battles he had to face that were largely out of his control. For one, ascending star wide receiver Courtland Sutton suffered a season-ending injury right off the bat in Week 1. The rest of the Broncos receiving corps was plenty talented thanks to Fant, rookie wide receivers Jerry Jeudy and KJ Hamler, and a mini-breakout season from Tim Patrick, but losing a pass-catcher of Sutton's talent, especially given he was the receiver Lock likely had the best connection with, was crushing.

Along those same lines, an already unremarkable Denver

2021 Broncos Schedule

Week	Opp.	Week	Opp.	Week	Opp.
1	at NYG	7	at CLE (Thu.)	13	at KC
2	at JAX	8	WAS	14	DET
3	NYJ	9	at DAL	15	CIN
4	BAL	10	PHI	16	at LV
5	at PIT	11	BYE	17	at LAC
6	LV	12	LAC	18	KC

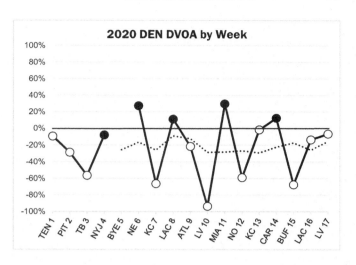

offensive line suffered the eighth-most adjusted games lost in the league. Right tackle Ja'Wuan James opted out of the season and his replacement, Demar Dotson, also missed some time. The right tackle spot was never solidified and there was a cascade effect caused by smaller injuries here and there at other spots. It's nothing close to what the Eagles had to deal with up front, for example, but it still hurts to lose so many pieces in the trenches during a fragile prospect's first real year as the starting quarterback. Denver's line also had a struggling rookie center in Lloyd Cushenberry. Between him and Lock, there was no stability and consistency in pass protection the way some of the league's more veteran quarterback-center duos have.

Lock had to learn a new offense under Pat Shurmur as well. Seeing as the Rich Scangarello offense in 2019 was stripped down once Lock took the job, it's not as though this should have been a major destabilizer for Lock's development as a player, but it was an added layer nonetheless and something he was seemingly incapable of handling.

Oddly enough, the Shurmur offense moved closer to what Lock was used to at Missouri. The offense's formations opened up from the under-center, heavy-personnel sets that Scangarello was using. Denver moved from 67% to 88% in single-back formations (thanks in part to losing fullback Andy Janovich in free agency) while also jumping up from 55% to 66% in shotgun/pistol formations. The offense also implemented motion at a higher rate, going from 39% to 47%. One might imagine that having the field expanded pre-snap would have made Lock feel more at home, but that is not how things turned out.

Lock is in danger of joining Brock Osweiler, Paxton Lynch, and others in John Elway's Club of Failed Quarterback Draft Picks. That litany of busts is a big reason Elway stepped away from general manager duties this year, surrendering the player personnel authority he had wielded since 2011 and accepting an "elevated" management role. The Broncos replaced him as GM with George Paton, who has been in the Vikings' front office for 14 seasons, working as assistant GM since 2012.

Paton made headlines the night before the draft when he traded a sixth-round pick to the Panthers in exchange for Teddy Bridgewater. It was a surprising bit of bargain shopping that looked even more curious the next day when Denver passed on both Justin Fields and Mac Jones with the ninth overall pick. By now Bridgewater's history is well known. The rookie of the year with Minnesota in 2014, he led the Vikings to the playoffs in his second season before a 2016 knee

injury threatened to end his career. He spent the next three years as a little-used backup for the Vikings, Jets, and Saints, then won all five of his starts for New Orleans in 2019, making the top 10 in DVOA in the process. That was enough for Carolina to sign him as a starter last year, but he finished the season just 19th in DVOA as the Panthers went 5-11. Bridgewater's unexceptional Panthers season juxtaposed against his undefeated Saints run serves to show that he is exactly as useful as the team around him.

There is certainly value in that, especially for a team that looks to have the other 50 roster spots sorted out the way Denver does. Bridgewater has proven able to handle any number of offenses from a mental standpoint, ranging from Norv Turner's scheme in Minnesota to Sean Payton's in New Orleans to Joe Brady's in Carolina, and delivers the ball with accuracy in a way that Lock has yet to master. The floor for the offense is much higher with Bridgewater than it would be with Lock.

Bridgewater's mental stability and decision-making are the critical factors here. Shurmur's offense tried to open things up pre-snap and give the quarterback a clear picture to work with, thanks in part to the use of motion, but Lock never quite got things to click. Bridgewater is coming over from a Carolina offense that used motion on 53% of snaps, just a bit higher than Shurmur's rate, and ran a full three-course meal worth of passing concepts. Though he did show more interception trouble in that Panthers offense than he historically has, Bridgewater proved he could keep the floor of the offense high, completing 3.4% of his passes over expectation according to our model.

That floor of play quality and freedom to open up the playbook with confidence is not something Lock has shown. During both of his pro seasons, Lock has seldom looked comfortable operating any concept beyond the offense's staple, Day 1-install type plays. There have been flashes here and there beyond that, but Lock has yet to string together a stretch of games where it was clear he consistently knew what he was looking at. Bridgewater, on the other hand, sees the field clearly to a fault, often resulting in him taking guaranteed yet inefficient gains underneath. At this point in the Lock experiment, Bridgewater's low-volatility play style may be a welcomed change.

Simple, reliable quarterback play should be all this Denver offense needs to be competent anyway, assuming the offensive line is not as in shambles as it was a year ago. The pass-catching corps, though young and somewhat unproven, is a playoff-caliber bunch. Sutton and Jeudy make for one of the more exciting one-two punches in the league, while the organization was confident enough in Hamler's ability out of the slot to try to shop DaeSean Hamilton prior to the draft before ultimately cutting him. Even Patrick, who had previously been a borderline practice-squad player, blossomed in 2020 and can provide some inside-outside flexibility for the Broncos' lineup.

At tight end, Fant ties the whole group together. As things stand now, the NFL tight end pantheon has a clear-cut top four with Travis Kelce, George Kittle, Darren Waller, and Rob Gronkowski. Among those on the outside looking in, Fant has the best chance to emerge as one of the league's elite. Fant's athleticism is as impressive as any and he improved on both his route-running and shaky hands last season.

Getting the most out of these skill players is still but a pipe dream. A third-year leap from Lock could creep up out of nowhere or Bridgewater may beat him out to provide more stable play, but the Broncos are likely to be testing the free-agent or draft market again next year. The best they can hope for is that the offense is competent in spite of its unexciting quarterback play.

On defense, however, Denver has reason for real optimism. The Broncos lost nobody of consequence, while they either returned or brought in key starters at the most valuable positions. The Broncos will have one of the biggest gains since 2003 in net Approximate Value over replacement on defense (see New England chapter, page 167). Having already finished a respectable 13th in DVOA last season, Denver's net upgrades across the board give reason to believe they have more in store than their middle-of-the-pack projection suggests.

Denver's secondary is the point of interest on defense this year. Justin Simmons (who earned a blockbuster extension this offseason) and Kareem Jackson are known quantities at the safety spot, but the cornerback room is chock-full of new talent. Though Bryce Callahan returns to handle nickel responsibilities, everything about the outside cornerback position was shaken up. The team signed Kyle Fuller (one of head coach Vic Fangio's old stars from Chicago) and Ronald Darby in free agency and drafted Patrick Surtain II in the first round.

On the surface, Denver's heavy investment at cornerback may be a response to the passing prowess in the division. It's a passing league to begin with, but the AFC West features the league's best quarterback in Patrick Mahomes, a budding star in Justin Herbert, and the ever-consistent Derek Carr. Making sure they have the top-end talent as well as the depth to be equipped to handle those passing attacks was imperative for the Broncos.

The particular way in which the Broncos went about their bolstering of the secondary very clearly has Fangio's fingerprints all over it. Denver is not just taking a few swings on talent and hoping enough of them work out. Fangio wants to recreate something similar to what he had going with the

Bears back in 2017 and 2018. Bringing over Callahan years ago was the first step, but signing Fuller and drafting Surtain completes Fangio's version of Exodia in the secondary.

Back in Chicago, Fangio often deployed his cornerbacks in a particular way. Fuller would align as the cornerback to one side in a deeper alignment, about 8 or so yards off the ball, and play from depth. He was and is one of the best zone cornerbacks in the league, so being able to play from depth with his quick feet and trigger was a recipe for success. Opposite Fuller would be Prince Amukamara, who was quietly one of the league's best press cornerbacks on film, jammed right up on the line of scrimmage. Callahan then handled the slot. Not every coverage call followed this rule, of course, but it was a common thread throughout Fangio's game plans that made his defense somewhat unique.

Fangio has not had the pieces for that scheme since coming to Denver. Callahan was a good player in 2020 after missing 2019, make no mistake, but he was forced into an outside role rather than slot duty, and nobody during Fangio's time in Denver has been close to what Amukamara was as a press piece. All of that has been solved. With Fuller and Callahan reconnected, all Fangio needed in the draft was the Amukamara role. That is where Surtain comes in.

Surtain's skill set branches beyond being a press coverage savant, but that is where he will make his money in the NFL. For one, Surtain is about as big as cornerbacks get. The ninth overall pick out of Alabama is 6-foot-2 and 208 pounds with a 90th-percentile wingspan and 95th-percentile hands. Surtain stands apart from most other big press corners with how disciplined he is at the line of scrimmage. He is not the type of press corner to aimlessly punch at a receiver's chest and hope to overwhelm them. The young cornerback does exceptionally well to play light on his toes and even over the receiver until they are forced to declare their route stem; only then will he pounce with his overwhelming length and bully receivers. Sprinkle that on top of his sharp route-recognition and smooth hips for a player his size, and you have a cornerback with all the tools to be as or more suffocating than Amukamara was at his peak.

Mind you, Denver is making all of these upgrades at cornerback after having already finished 11th in pass defense DVOA last season. Fangio held that unit together with third-round rookie Michael Ojemudia as one starting outside cornerback and Callahan playing somewhat out of position on the other side. With Callahan back inside and two upgrades on the outside, on top of the added depth with Darby, Denver has a strong opportunity to be one of the NFL's top pass defenses.

Better yet, very little is changing up front that could jeopardize what the Broncos have going in the secondary. The only notable move is the return of Von Miller from injury. When healthy, Miller remains one of the league's best pass-rushers. Even if Miller takes a slight step back, the three-headed attack of Miller, Bradley Chubb, and Malik Reed is still comfortably above average and will give the Broncos a faster and fuller pass-rush rotation than they had a year ago.

Beyond Miller, things look the same as they did in 2020. Shelby Harris, Dre'mont Jones, and Mike Purcell return along the defensive line. Though it's not a star-studded unit, Harris is capable as both a run defender and pass-rusher, while a healthy Purcell is a force against the run. The Broncos did finish 25th in run defense last season, but Purcell was only healthy for six games and the rest of the front battled other injuries here and there, including Jurrell Casey, who missed most of last season and is no longer on the roster. Depth is a concern, but if the Broncos can stay a bit healthier up front than last season, the unit should be capable enough to allow the rest of the defense to shine.

Alexander Johnson and Josey Jewell will again be starting at linebacker. The team did draft Baron Browning (Ohio State) in the third round, but the Broncos seldom ran with three linebackers last season and there is no reason to force Browning into the lineup over either Johnson or Jewell, each of whom fared well in both run defense and coverage last season. Drafting Browning could allow Denver to sprinkle in more three-linebacker sets, but there is no reason to worry about them trying to become the Seahawks.

All of that potential on defense may still not be enough to save Fangio from the quarterback situation he has been handcuffed to. With some of the draft trade rumors and poking around at Aaron Rodgers, it is clear the organization wants to move in a different direction at quarterback. The Broncos may give Fangio some breathing room for that reason, but the team needs to show signs of improvement outside the quarterback position, particularly on defense, for him to earn that safety net.

Fangio's reputation as a defensive mind gives reason to believe the defense can take flight now that he really has his guys in place. However, anything short of a top-eight unit, assuming the offense is as ordinary as it projects to be, could be the end of this coaching regime in Denver. The Broncos need their defense to be elite in order to overcome a depressing quarterback situation if they want any chance of scraping into the postseason.

Derrik Klassen

2020 Broncos by Week

Wk	vs.	W-L	PF	PA	YDF	YDA	TO	Total	Off	Def	ST
1	TEN	L	14	16	323	377	-1	-9.4%	-20.6%	-10.9%	0.3%
2	at PIT	L	21	26	319	410	0	-28.7%	-3.2%	7.1%	-18.4%
3	TB	L	10	28	226	353	-2	-56.3%	-43.0%	0.5%	-12.7%
4	at NYJ	W	37	28	359	321	-3	-7.9%	-22.3%	0.3%	14.7%
5	BYE										
6	at NE	W	18	12	299	288	1	27.3%	-35.3%	-50.5%	12.1%
7	KC	L	16	43	411	286	-3	-66.3%	-46.0%	-10.1%	-30.3%
8	LAC	W	31	30	351	485	1	11.1%	25.8%	10.8%	-3.8%
9	at ATL	L	27	34	405	363	0	-21.6%	-5.1%	18.9%	2.4%
10	at LV	L	12	37	313	357	-5	-93.6%	-81.9%	15.2%	3.5%
11	MIA	W	20	13	459	223	-1	29.7%	1.2%	-26.4%	2.1%
12	NO	L	3	31	112	292	-2	-58.8%	-88.4%	-23.3%	6.3%
13	at KC	L	16	22	330	447	-2	-1.5%	-0.1%	4.3%	2.9%
14	at CAR	W	32	27	365	370	-1	12.4%	19.1%	22.6%	15.9%
15	BUF	L	19	48	255	534	0	-67.4%	-19.6%	33.6%	-14.3%
16	at LAC	L	16	19	396	316	-2	-13.4%	-11.2%	-4.8%	-7.0%
17	LV	L	31	32	446	465	4	-6.4%	-1.2%	-1.7%	-6.9%

Trends and Splits

	Offense	Rank	Defense	Rank
Total DVOA	-20.0%	30	-0.2%	13
Unadjusted VOA	-19.0%	30	3.8%	22
Weighted Trend	-18.0%	29	1.6%	18
Variance	10.2%	29	4.3%	13
Average Opponent	0.6%	20	5.1%	3
Passing	-12.9%	31	0.6%	11
Rushing	-22.2%	26	-1.3%	25
First Down	-20.8%	30	1.5%	19
Second Down	-24.1%	30	7.9%	23
Third Down	-11.2%	20	-14.9%	9
First Half	-24.3%	31	3.0%	20
Second Half	-15.7%	27	-3.4%	10
Red Zone	3.6%	17	-21.9%	2
Late and Close	2.6%	16	-2.7%	15

Five-Year Performance

Year	W-L	Pyth W	Est W	PF	PA	TO	Total	Rk	Off	Rk	Def	Rk	ST	Rk	Off AGL	Rk	Def AGL	Rk	Off Age	Rk	Def Age	Rk	ST Age	Rk
2016	9-7	9.1	8.4	333	297	+2	2.9%	15	-12.0%	28	-17.2%	1	-2.3%	24	25.2	8	34.0	13	26.6	18	26.7	12	25.1	30
2017	5-11	5.4	5.5	289	382	-17	-22.4%	29	-18.7%	31	-3.8%	11	-7.4%	30	26.4	10	38.1	19	27.1	14	26.7	12	25.0	30
2018	6-10	7.4	8.6	329	349	+7	5.5%	13	0.8%	15	-8.9%	6	-4.2%	31	47.5	24	26.0	11	26.6	18	26.9	7	25.4	28
2019	7-9	6.9	6.4	282	316	+1	-10.4%	23	-11.3%	26	-2.8%	13	-1.9%	24	52.0	25	48.3	27	25.8	30	26.9	7	25.1	31
2020	5-11	4.9	5.5	323	446	-16	-21.9%	29	-20.0%	30	-0.2%	13	-2.1%	24	50.2	23	58.2	26	25.3	30	26.8	8	25.4	27

2020 Performance Based on Most Common Personnel Groups

DEN Offense					DEN Offense vs. Opponents					DEN Defense				DEN Defense vs. Opponents			
Pers	Freq	Yds	DVOA	Run%	Pers	Freq	Yds	DVOA	Run%	Pers	Freq	Yds	DVOA	Pers	Freq	Yds	DVOA
11	67%	5.6	-13.3%	32%	Base	17%	4.2	-30.3%	55%	Base	24%	6.0	-0.9%	11	66%	6.0	2.0%
12	21%	5.2	-17.4%	49%	Nickel	65%	5.3	-13.6%	40%	Nickel	66%	5.6	1.3%	12	17%	5.9	-11.2%
21	4%	3.1	-69.2%	43%	Dime+	17%	6.8	-16.7%	19%	Dime+	9%	6.7	-35.6%	21	5%	3.6	-34.6%
22	3%	5.2	-7.2%	76%	Goal Line	1%	0.8	41.3%	50%	Goal Line	0%	0.5	49.6%	13	5%	4.3	12.3%
13	3%	4.4	-43.8%	64%	Big	0%	0.2	-124.5%	60%	Big	1%	4.3	90.5%	22	2%	6.3	9.9%
WC	2%	3.4	-46.9%	100%										612	1%	7.9	25.3%

Strategic Tendencies

Run/Pass		Rk	Formation		Rk	Pass Rush		Rk	Secondary		Rk	Strategy		Rk
Runs, first half	41%	9	Form: Single Back	88%	5	Rush 3	4.2%	23	4 DB	24%	14	Play Action	24%	24
Runs, first down	49%	15	Form: Empty Back	3%	31	Rush 4	69.0%	10	5 DB	66%	10	Offensive Motion	39%	24
Runs, second-long	36%	2	Form: Multi Back	7%	21	Rush 5	21.1%	16	6+ DB	9%	18	Avg Box (Off)	6.69	9
Runs, power sit.	54%	27	Pers: 3+ WR	68%	12	Rush 6+	5.7%	13	Man Coverage	36%	11	Avg Box (Def)	6.00	32
Runs, behind 2H	33%	6	Pers: 2+ TE/6+ OL	28%	17	Edge Rusher Sacks	51.2%	17	CB by Sides	87%	8	Offensive Pace	29.75	10
Pass, ahead 2H	46%	20	Pers: 6+ OL	0%	28	Interior DL Sacks	39.3%	5	S/CB Cover Ratio	29%	11	Defensive Pace	29.98	12
Run-Pass Options	5%	26	Shotgun/Pistol	66%	17	Second Level Sacks	9.5%	32	DB Blitz	7%	30	Go for it on 4th	0.54	32

Denver's offense was tied for second with 39 drops and led the NFL in drop rate. ● Drew Lock threw 48% of passes to the right, the highest figure in the NFL, and only 31% of passes to his left. In 2019, however, those percentages were roughly even. ● Denver had the best pass defense in the league in the red zone but ranked 29th against red zone runs. ● Denver had the best DVOA in the league against passes down the middle of the field. They were below average against deep middle passes but excelled against passes in the short middle (15 air yards or fewer). ● The Broncos had a significant split in favor of playing man defense in 2020, with -2.0% DVOA in man coverage compared to 28.6% DVOA in zone coverage.

Passing

Player	DYAR	DVOA	Plays	NtYds	Avg	YAC	C%	TD	Int
D.Lock	-151	-16.2%	460	2781	6.0	5.4	58.0%	16	14
J.Driskel*	-36	-18.9%	75	334	4.5	3.7	54.7%	3	2
B.Rypien	-143	-63.0%	41	285	7.0	3.0	69.2%	2	4
K.Hinton	-98	-222.2%	10	12	1.2	16.0	11.1%	0	2
T.Bridgewater	446	2.0%	521	3508	6.7	5.5	69.7%	15	11

Rushing

Player	DYAR	DVOA	Plays	Yds	Avg	TD	Fum	Suc
M.Gordon	59	-1.8%	214	965	4.5	9	2	44%
P.Lindsay*	-70	-24.2%	118	508	4.3	1	0	40%
D.Lock	-8	-16.0%	36	167	4.6	3	4	--
R.Freeman	30	12.4%	35	170	4.9	0	0	43%
KJ Hamler	15	-10.4%	9	40	4.4	0	0	--
J.Driskel*	14	24.8%	6	28	4.7	0	0	--
L.Bellamy	-10	-67.2%	4	11	2.8	0	0	25%
T.Bridgewater	43	6.6%	45	279	6.2	5	4	--
M.Boone	14	14.5%	11	59	5.4	1	0	73%

Receiving

Player	DYAR	DVOA	Plays	Ctch	Yds	Y/C	YAC	TD	C%
J.Jeudy	-92	-22.9%	113	52	856	16.5	5.0	3	46%
T.Patrick	183	16.1%	79	51	742	14.5	4.7	6	65%
KJ Hamler	-33	-20.3%	56	30	381	12.7	4.1	3	54%
D.Hamilton*	-27	-20.3%	44	23	293	12.7	4.1	2	52%
T.Cleveland	-5	-18.9%	9	6	63	10.5	3.0	0	67%
C.Sutton	6	1.3%	6	3	66	22.0	2.3	0	50%
D.Spencer	-14	-40.1%	6	3	26	8.7	4.0	0	50%
N.Fant	37	-1.0%	93	62	673	10.9	6.1	3	67%
N.Vannett*	-35	-28.3%	21	14	95	6.8	4.6	1	67%
A.Okwuegbunam	29	17.9%	15	11	121	11.0	6.6	1	73%
T.Fumagalli*	-6	-13.0%	15	8	80	10.0	7.5	1	53%
M.Gordon	-93	-51.9%	44	32	158	4.9	5.1	1	73%
P.Lindsay*	-38	-62.3%	14	7	28	4.0	5.6	0	50%
R.Freeman	11	2.1%	13	12	81	6.8	5.3	0	92%

Offensive Line

Player	Pos	Age	GS	Snaps	Pen	Sk	Pass	Run	Player	Pos	Age	GS	Snaps	Pen	Sk	Pass	Run
Lloyd Cushenberry	C	24	16/16	1075	2	5	18	15	Demar Dotson*	RT	36	8/8	451	3	0.5	4	3
Garett Bolles	LT	29	15/15	1014	7	0	7	2	Austin Schlottmann	RG	26	16/2	268	0	1	10	4
Dalton Risner	LG	26	16/16	999	0	0	16	7	Cameron Fleming	RT	29	16/16	911	7	4.0	22	4
Graham Glasgow	RG	29	13/13	764	5	1	7	8	Bobby Massie	RT	32	8/8	470	1	3.5	12	1
Elijah Wilkinson*	RT	26	9/7	502	1	2	9	5									

Year	Yards	ALY	Rk	Power	Rk	Stuff	Rk	2Lev	Rk	OpFld	Rk	BB Rt	Rk	Sacks	ASR	Rk	Press	Rk	BB Rt	Rk	Cont
2018	4.88	4.75	6	71%	7	18%	14	1.42	5	1.01	10	8.4%	27	34	6.3%	11	32.1%	20	12.3%	26	31
2019	4.24	4.45	11	69%	8	15%	3	1.17	17	0.61	23	8.5%	7	41	8.1%	25	32.2%	25	12.3%	9	29
2020	4.46	4.02	28	78%	3	21%	32	1.26	14	0.87	8	11.9%	25	32	6.8%	19	29.4%	24	12.8%	18	25

2020 ALY by direction:	Left End: 4.07 (24)	Left Tackle: 3.40 (28)	Mid/Guard: 3.67 (32)	Right Tackle: 5.16 (5)	Right End: 5.22 (12)

Left tackle Garett Bolles had previously earned 13 and 17 penalties in 2018 and 2019, respectively, but finally came in below the double-digit mark for 2020. More specifically, Bolles had a whopping 13 holding calls in 2019, yet had just four in 2020. Penalties (and particularly offensive holding) were down league-wide, but at least Bolles fell in line with that trend. More impressive was the improvement in Bolles' blocking; for example, he fell from 23 blown blocks to just nine. 🏈 Denver's dramatic downfall in the run game is not solely because they replaced a quality veteran (Connor McGovern) with a third-round rookie, but it sure did not help. Lloyd Cushenberry was second-to-last in snaps per blown block among centers last season. The Broncos also fell from 13th to dead last in adjusted line yards right up the middle. 🏈 The Broncos were one of four teams to fall below average in adjusted line yards while still producing above average on yards per carry by running backs. Chicago, Indianapolis, and Philadelphia were the other three. 🏈 The Broncos are scrambling to solve their Ja'Wuan James-sized hole at right tackle. The team signed Cameron Fleming and Bobby Massie, both of whom finished outside the top 20 in snaps per blown block at that position. Fleming offers more on the ground but is among the worst pass-protectors in the league, which is why he had never started more than seven games in a season until 2020. 🏈 Third-round pick Quinn Meinerz started at guard at Wisconsin-Whitewater, but many expect his 6-foot-3, 320-pound frame to kick him inside to center. Meinerz shined at the Senior Bowl despite coming in with zero 2020 tape due to COVID, then blew up his pro day by clearing the 75th percentile in the 3-cone, broad jump, long jump, 40-yard dash, and 10-yard split. Meinerz is an athletic, mean interior player who could stand to clean up his footwork before becoming a good starter in the league.

Defensive Front

Defensive Line	Age	Pos	G	Snaps	Plays	Overall TmPct	Rk	Stop	Dfts	BTkl	Runs	vs. Run St%	Rk	RuYd	Rk	Pass Rush Sack	Hit	Hur	Dsrpt
Dre'Mont Jones	24	DE	13	560	42	6.1%	27	30	11	3	30	67%	69	3.0	75	6.5	5	13	2
Shelby Harris	30	DE	11	441	38	6.6%	17	33	14	4	25	84%	12	3.0	74	2.5	8	14	8
DeShawn Williams	29	DT	14	436	40	5.4%	39	26	6	2	31	65%	79	3.0	76	2.0	5	11	2
DeMarcus Walker	27	DE	13	384	18	2.6%	89	12	5	2	11	64%	80	3.0	77	4.5	1	8	0
Sylvester Williams	33	DT	8	173	11	2.6%	--	8	0	2	9	67%	--	3.6	--	0.0	0	0	2
Shamar Stephen	30	DT	16	663	34	4.1%	65	21	4	0	30	63%	82	3.1	83	0.5	2	6	1

Edge Rushers	Age	Pos	G	Snaps	Plays	Overall TmPct	Rk	Stop	Dfts	BTkl	Runs	vs. Run St%	Rk	RuYd	Rk	Pass Rush Sack	Hit	Hur	Dsrpt
Malik Reed	25	OLB	16	785	52	6.2%	23	39	14	6	32	78%	22	3.1	73	8.0	9	20	1
Bradley Chubb	25	OLB	14	741	42	5.7%	31	34	16	7	31	74%	36	2.6	45	7.5	11	28	0
Jeremiah Attaochu	28	OLB	13	414	29	4.2%	61	21	9	2	20	70%	54	3.3	77	5.0	6	13	0

Linebackers	Age	Pos	G	Snaps	Plays	Overall TmPct	Rk	Stop	Dfts	BTkl	Runs	vs. Run St%	Rk	RuYd	Rk	Pass Rush Sack	Hit	Hur	vs. Pass Tgts	Suc%	Rk	Yd/P	Rk	PD	Int
A.J. Johnson	30	ILB	16	1063	126	14.9%	22	74	13	12	80	66%	14	3.7	29	1.0	5	14	39	64%	9	4.8	15	2	0
Josey Jewell	27	ILB	16	1011	118	14.0%	33	60	20	6	66	61%	27	3.7	33	2.0	3	5	41	61%	11	5.1	19	5	0

Year	Yards	ALY	Rk	Power	Rk	Stuff	Rk	2Lev	Rk	OpFld	Rk	BB Rt	Rk	Sacks	ASR	Rk	Press	Rk	BB Rt	Rk
2018	4.78	4.58	23	73%	26	14%	30	1.14	8	1.16	29	6.4%	23	44	8.0%	9	30.2%	17	11.9%	9
2019	4.00	4.28	18	58%	6	18%	21	1.08	10	0.56	8	13.1%	15	40	7.6%	11	28.3%	24	15.4%	13
2020	4.56	4.51	20	73%	28	14%	24	1.11	9	0.92	26	11.3%	22	42	8.0%	5	24.0%	19	13.1%	18

2020 ALY by direction:	Left End: 5.20 (26)	Left Tackle: 4.76 (23)	Mid/Guard: 4.44 (16)	Right Tackle: 4.22 (13)	Right End: 4.72 (18)

Denver's issues up front last year had more to do with injuries than anything. This was not the strongest bunch in the league to begin with, but the Broncos also suffered the third-most adjusted games lost along the defensive line. Much of that had to do with Jurrell Casey missing a majority of the season with a bicep tear, while the unsung hero of run defense, Mike Purcell, missed more than half the season with a foot issue. ✎ Casey was cut this offseason, but Purcell is returning and could bolster the run defense. Purcell ranked seventh in rush yards allowed per tackle in 2019, often serving as a space-eater in the middle. Getting Purcell back would make life easier for linebackers Alexander Johnson and Josey Jewell, which could be explosive given that they both took steps forward in their own right last season. ✎ Denver's linebackers also took a step forward in coverage. The Broncos were one of just three teams with two qualifying linebackers to finish above a 60% coverage success rate. The Saints and Steelers were the other two, and only the Saints and Broncos had both of their 60%-or-better coverage defenders be their starters. ✎ Malik Reed was a good fill-in for Von Miller last season, but make no mistake, getting Miller back will do wonders for Denver's pass rush. Miller's 52 hurries in 2019 ranked seventh in the league that season—and were nearly double the number of hurries Chubb posted without Miller playing last season (28). ✎ There's probably no need to rush third-round linebacker Baron Browning (Ohio State) onto the field. Johnson and Jewell played almost every off-ball line-backer snap for the Broncos, and Denver played with the lightest average defensive box in the league last year. Browning is a phenomenal athlete who could use time on the bench to develop. He has all the athletic gifts necessary but does not see the run game consistently and has not shown he can reliably work through the muck. Browning may be a coverage piece early on who will rarely see the field on base downs.

Defensive Secondary

Secondary	Age	Pos	G	Snaps	Plays	TmPct	Rk	Stop	Dfts	BTkl	Runs	St%	Rk	RuYd	Rk	Tgts	Tgt%	Rk	aDOT	Suc%	Rk	Yd/P	Rk	PD	Int
Justin Simmons	28	FS	16	1088	105	12.5%	16	42	14	13	39	41%	28	8.2	51	40	9.6%	26	9.9	50%	35	7.8	36	9	5
Kareem Jackson	33	SS	16	1083	93	11.0%	33	34	7	14	47	36%	36	8.3	52	28	6.7%	48	8.8	57%	16	6.9	23	4	1
Michael Ojemudia	24	CB	16	852	67	7.9%	58	27	10	17	13	69%	2	7.8	56	68	20.8%	33	12.9	53%	32	9.6	75	6	0
Bryce Callahan	30	CB	10	655	47	8.9%	32	20	10	4	9	44%	35	5.3	27	44	17.5%	61	12.0	66%	1	4.0	1	5	2
A.J. Bouye*	30	CB	7	410	30	8.1%	--	8	2	8	6	17%	--	9.7	--	33	20.9%	--	11.9	42%	--	7.5	--	6	0
Essang Bassey	23	CB	12	382	24	3.8%	--	9	5	4	8	63%	--	2.9	--	19	12.9%	--	9.4	42%	--	7.4	--	2	1
Will Parks*	27	FS	10	314	29	5.5%	--	14	6	3	8	75%	--	1.3	--	17	14.2%	--	9.2	53%	--	8.1	--	0	0
De'Vante Bausby*	28	CB	11	277	25	4.3%	--	11	3	5	1	100%	--	12.0	--	33	31.0%	--	11.9	48%	--	8.0	--	5	0
Kyle Fuller	29	CB	16	1059	73	8.8%	36	29	12	18	19	37%	51	6.5	36	67	15.7%	71	13.1	58%	10	6.4	14	8	1
Ronald Darby	27	CB	16	1001	71	8.9%	34	34	10	4	17	53%	19	6.2	33	85	23.3%	14	14.0	58%	12	7.0	29	16	0

Year	Pass D Rank	vs. #1 WR	Rk	vs. #2 WR	Rk	vs. Other WR	Rk	WR Wide	Rk	WR Slot	Rk	vs. TE	Rk	vs. RB	Rk
2018	4	-5.8%	11	0.1%	17	-36.4%	1	-7.7%	16	-14.2%	3	-9.3%	12	5.4%	18
2019	14	11.2%	26	-9.0%	8	-20.7%	5	13.3%	26	-14.5%	4	-11.9%	5	-11.5%	6
2020	11	-13.2%	8	-2.7%	15	7.4%	21	10.6%	25	-4.2%	13	4.7%	18	-16.7%	4

Among the reasons Denver is making Justin Simmons one of the highest-paid safeties in the league: since entering the NFL in 2016, Simmons' 16 interceptions are tied for second behind Kevin Byard. ✎ Cornerback production is prone to instability. Ronald Darby is a good example. Darby posted a putrid 47% coverage success rate as the fourth-most frequently targeted corner in the NFL in 2019, yet in 2018 and 2020, Darby put up 57% and 58% coverage success rates, respectively. Denver is hoping Darby doesn't take a dip back down the production roller coaster. ✎ Kyle Fuller also showed some year-to-year ebb and flow, but that can more easily be explained by his dip in 2019 coinciding with the Bears playing their first year with Chuck Pagano as the defensive coordinator after Fangio left. Now that Fuller is reunited with Fangio, he should once again excel as one of the league's best off-zone cornerbacks. ✎ Drafting both Jamar Johnson (Indiana) and Caden Sterns (Texas) in the fifth round feels like Denver trying to get ahead of their safety depth problem. Starter Kareem Jackson is 33 years old and in the last year of his contract, while the team also had no depth to speak of before the draft. Johnson is more of a rangy (albeit volatile) coverage piece, while Sterns is best working from two-high or a bit closer to the box. ✎ Denver's real draft star is first-round cornerback Patrick Surtain II. Surtain started for most of his three seasons at Alabama, showing off some of the smoothest movement you'll see out of a 6-foot-2, 202-pound cornerback. Surtain also plays with great eye discipline and leverage, not to mention the ball skills that enabled him to break up 25 passes throughout his college career. The Broncos have a lot of talented cornerbacks, but Surtain should still see the field early and often.

Special Teams

Year	DVOA	Rank	FG/XP	Rank	Net Kick	Rank	Kick Ret	Rank	Net Punt	Rank	Punt Ret	Rank	Hidden	Rank
2018	-4.2%	31	0.3	15	-1.4	21	-6.4	32	-9.3	28	-4.3	27	11.4	4
2019	-1.9%	24	4.5	8	-4.0	26	3.3	8	-11.9	31	-1.4	17	-0.5	18
2020	-2.1%	24	5.1	10	-10.9	32	-4.3	27	-6.3	27	5.9	4	-3.2	19

Denver was one of two teams to hold the exact spot in special teams DVOA in both 2019 and 2020. The other team was the Chargers, who finished dead last both seasons. ● Diontae Spencer's fortunes flipped with respect to kick and punt returns. In 2019, Spencer was strong on kick returns and average on punt returns. In 2020, Spencer was near the bottom on kick returns, second worst in individual value ahead of only Brandon Powell of Atlanta. But he was one of the league's top punt returners, finishing second in individual value behind Gunner Olszewski of New England. Spencer should continue to hold both jobs in 2021, sharing kick returns with receiver Tyrie Cleveland. ● Kicker Brandon McManus has long been one of the worst in the league at kickoffs after adjusting for the Denver altitude, but he bounced up to average for 2020. He has been relatively consistent and good, not great, on field goals. ● The Broncos have had three different punters over the last three seasons and none of them have proved useful. Both of Denver's qualifying punters in 2018 were below average in gross punt value, and Colby Wadman ranked below average in 2019. The Broncos tried former Lions punter Sam Martin in 2020, but he finished 30th out of 34 qualifying punters in gross punt value. Martin is set to be the man again in 2021, though the team did sign Max Duffy (Kentucky) as an undrafted free agent to provide competition.

Detroit Lions

2020 Record: 5-11	Total DVOA: -15.7% (21)	2021 Mean Projection: 7.2 wins	On the Clock (0-5): 28%
Pythagorean Wins: 4.8 (30)	Offense: 0% (16)	Postseason Odds: 24.9%	Mediocrity (6-8): 42%
Snap-Weighted Age: 26.6 (12)	Defense: 17.7% (32)	Super Bowl Odds: 1.7%	Playoff Contender (9-11): 24%
Average Opponent: 4.3% (4)	Special Teams: 1.9% (11)	Proj. Avg. Opponent: 2.9% (4)	Super Bowl Contender (12+): 6%

2020: Matt Patricia's version of the Patriot Way was way off.

2021: Is the new Lions coach a crazy person?

We're going to kick you in the teeth. And when you punch us back, we're going to smile at you. And when you knock us down, we're going to get up. And on the way up, we're going to bite a kneecap off. And we're going to stand up, and it's going to take two more shots to knock us down. And on the way up, we're going to take your other kneecap. And we're going to get up. And then it's going to take three shots to get us down. And when we do, we're going to take another hunk out of you.

New Lions head coach Dan Campbell had a compelling introductory press conference. He dwarfed the podium with his massive 6-foot-5, 265-pound frame. He spoke with a deep bass voice that matched his build, his goatee, and the literal blue collar of his Lions-colored dress shirt. His 20-minute soliloquy sounded like a single run-on sentence, punctuated with more *ands*, *ums*, and *alrights* than periods. He darted from topic to topic, seemingly bursting with ideas and the energy of the gallon of coffee he drinks each day. He was animated. He was sweating. And as he hit his climax with the vivid, now viral metaphor of how his players would bite the kneecaps off their opponents to demonstrate their toughness, I couldn't help but picture his interview for the job and ponder the Lions coaches that came before him.

Campbell was not a top head coaching prospect in the public eye. Those names included new Jaguars hire Urban Meyer, a three-time national title winner at Florida and Ohio State. They included new Jets hire Robert Saleh, coordinator of the 49ers Super Bowl defense from 2019. They included new Falcons hire Arthur Smith, the Ryan Tannehill whisperer. They included new Chargers hire Brandon Staley, a Sean McVay disciple. And they included the unhired Eric Bieniemy, Patrick Mahomes' sometimes playcaller and the embodiment of the lack of diversity at the top of the NFL.

Campbell was not even the top head coaching prospect with his last name. That was Iowa State Cyclones head coach Matt Campbell. And whether you believe CBS Sports' Dennis Dodd's report that he turned down the team's $68.5-million contract offer or *Sports Illustrated*'s Albert Breer's subsequent report that discussions never made it to contract terms, the Lions had clear interest in the other Campbell. Dan even joked about it to kick off that infamous introductory press conference.

I told my agent Rick Smith make sure they think I'm Matt Campbell, so I think that's how this really worked out great for me.

Dan Campbell was never a college head coach. He was never an NFL coordinator. He spent the last five years with the Saints as Sean Payton's assistant head coach, a foreign title to most outsiders that therefore fails to imbue him with the allure of Payton's former play-calling assistants such as Doug Marrone and Joe Brady. Campbell was an interim head coach for the 2015 Dolphins after the team fired Joe Philbin. And while Campbell sparked some life in a then-1-3 team, the high of his initial 38-10 and 44-26 wins over the Titans and Texans—the latter a playoff team—faded with the team's 3-7 record down the stretch. A pessimist could read the trajectory of that Dolphins team as a metaphor for Campbell as a head coach. He has style in his rah-rah intensity that offers his players a temporary boost, but he may lack the substance of innovative college coaches and NFL coordinators, substance that can affect real change in the fortunes of a franchise.

Style was likely at the top of Dolphins owner Stephen Ross' wish list when he named Campbell his team's interim head coach. Philbin may have cut his teeth as an offensive line coach, but his monotone delivery and terse responses seemed to infect his players with listlessness rather than toughness. Campbell was the medicine Ross prescribed to try to cure that one team of that one specific sickness.

Lions fans no doubt fear that team owner Sheila Ford Hamp prioritized style in her new head coach for a team that needs a lot more than motivation to return to relevance. It would be understandable because, like those Dolphins, the Lions came to resent the style of their former head coach when it failed to win him many games.

Matt Patricia had style that masqueraded as substance. He stalked the sidelines of his games with an unkempt beard, wearing hoodies, and with a pencil on his ear that couldn't possibly write anything on his laminated play sheet. He would have looked disorderly if he didn't look like his former head coach Bill Belichick. But he did look like Belichick, and he is smart like Belichick—he has an aeronautical engineering degree from Rensselaer Polytechnic Institute, which makes him a literal rocket scientist. He seemed like the perfect coach to make over the Lions culture in the Patriot Way.

2021 Lions Schedule

Week	Opp.	Week	Opp.	Week	Opp.
1	SF	7	at LAR	13	MIN
2	at GB (Mon.)	8	PHI	14	at DEN
3	BAL	9	BYE	15	ARI
4	at CHI	10	at PIT	16	at ATL
5	at MIN	11	at CLE	17	at SEA
6	CIN	12	CHI (Thu.)	18	GB

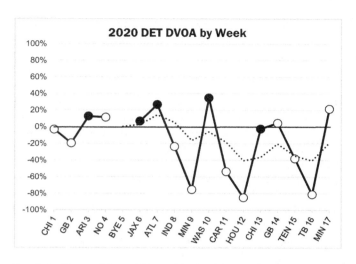

But Patricia failed to embrace the analytical wisdom of the best modern teams. His 2020 offense ranked 22nd in play-action percentage, 23rd in RPO rate, and 28th in fourth-down aggressiveness. And he failed to do what the Patriots often do the best: adapt his scheme to fit his personnel. The Lions played man coverage at consistent top-five rates of 49%, 55%, and 42% in Patricia's three seasons even though they finished with consistent bottom-10 defensive DVOAs of 55.1%, 46.7%, and 59.9% when playing man coverage.

Patricia did bring the less enjoyable elements of the Patriot Way to Detroit such as physically demanding practices, post-practice conditioning, profanity-laced tirades, and an expectation that players would fall in line without complaint and without much self-expression of any kind. That "my way or the highway" ethos drove some of the team's best players out of town. Three-time Pro Bowl cornerback Darius Slay went public with a trade demand on social media and the team shipped him to Philadelphia last March. Safety and team captain Quandre Diggs didn't ask for his trade to Seattle, but his outspoken nature clashed with his authoritarian head coach. And even returning Lions players were happy to escape Patricia's rule, if only for the offseason. Bleacher Report's Kalyn Kahler reported that 10 to 15 players celebrated their impending time away from Patricia with a mimosa party in the locker room before the final team meeting of their 6-10 2018 season.

Campbell won't foster that same resentment. His Dolphins players clearly loved him. But the Lions players loved Jim Caldwell, too. And while Caldwell (36-28) dramatically outperformed his replacement Patricia (13-29-1), he made it to just one playoff game in four seasons (and lost). Caldwell's Lions never cracked the top 10 in overall DVOA to spur confidence that he would be the man to finally win a playoff game for a franchise that hasn't been able to since 1991.

I don't blame you fans one bit. I get it. There's no telling how many of these press conferences you've seen. I'm not going to stand up here and give you coach speak. I'm going to tell you this. This team is going to take on your identity. There have been hard times here, and you've always found a way back up. And this team is going to do the same thing.

For all the outside ridicule, Campbell struck the proper chord for the immediate audience of his introductory press conference—and presumably also for Hamp in his interview for the job. He didn't just position himself as different from Patricia. He positioned himself as a citizen of Detroit returning home. And it is difficult to claim he wasn't earnest. Not only did he play a city-appropriate blue-collar tight end position with more seasons played (10) than catches per season (9.1), but Campbell actually played for the Lions his final three years.

That may make Campbell a covert political mastermind. Or it may simply express his world view. Regardless, that determination to build toughness is a better blueprint for a Lions rebuild than the one Patricia used because it places more value on unflashy offensive line and front-seven defensive positions, the same ones that analytically savvy teams such as the Colts, Browns, Ravens, and Bills have demonstrated they value over skill positions with their recent cap spending (Table 1).

Table 1. Positional Cap Spending, 2020

Rk	Tm	OL/DL/LB	RB/FB/WR	Diff	Rk	Tm	OL/DL/LB	RB/FB/WR	Diff
1	WAS	58.8%	6.0%	+52.8%	17	MIA	42.9%	11.6%	+31.4%
2	JAX	65.9%	13.3%	+52.6%	18	LAC	47.9%	19.4%	+28.5%
3	TB	58.3%	10.9%	+47.4%	19	DEN	41.4%	13.6%	+27.8%
4	PIT	53.2%	7.5%	+45.7%	20	ATL	48.5%	22.0%	+26.5%
5	LV	47.1%	7.0%	+40.1%	21	KC	48.5%	22.7%	+25.8%
6	IND	47.3%	11.1%	+36.2%	22	**DET**	**40.7%**	**15.3%**	**+25.5%**
7	HOU	53.9%	18.3%	+35.7%	23	CAR	48.6%	23.3%	+25.3%
8	GB	50.6%	15.0%	+35.7%	24	NYJ	47.7%	24.3%	+23.4%
9	NYG	50.9%	16.1%	+34.8%	25	DAL	50.6%	27.8%	+22.8%
10	NE	49.3%	15.9%	+33.5%	26	NO	37.0%	15.3%	+21.7%
11	CLE	50.3%	17.3%	+33.0%	27	ARI	44.6%	24.8%	+19.8%
12	CHI	49.1%	16.4%	+32.7%	28	TEN	33.8%	14.8%	+19.0%
13	LAR	45.3%	12.6%	+32.7%	29	PHI	38.2%	23.8%	+14.4%
14	BAL	49.4%	16.8%	+32.6%	30	SF	31.9%	24.3%	+7.6%
15	BUF	51.8%	19.7%	+32.0%	31	MIN	27.3%	23.7%	+3.5%
16	SEA	46.5%	15.0%	+31.5%	32	CIN	30.8%	32.2%	-1.4%

There's no secret. You've got to get good people around you who are all pulled in the same direction. It's team. It's all about team. There's no ego.

Campbell's philosophy would only go so far without front office support, but he and new general manager Brad Holmes appear to share a vision for the team. That unity is apparent in the latter's words—Campbell claims that he and Holmes finished a few of each other's sentences in their first meeting. And it is apparent in his actions this offseason. The Lions had clear holes at running back and especially wide receiver. They lost six of the seven wideouts that caught passes for the team in 2020 to free agency. But Holmes did not pander to the Lions' precedent that had them select wide receivers Charles Rogers, Roy Williams, Mike Williams, and Calvin Johnson with top-10 picks in consecutive drafts early in the new century. Instead, he used his team's first three draft picks on offensive tackle Penei Sewell and defensive tackles Levi Onwuzurike and Alim McNeill. And he spent the bulk of his free-agent dollars to extend 25-year-old center Frank Ragnow ($54 million) and retain 26-year-old edge rusher Romeo Okwara ($37 million). At the skill positions, Holmes made just modest expenditures of $6 million for Jamaal Williams, $4 million for Tyrell Williams, and $2.5 million for Breshad Perriman. After just one offseason, the Lions are up from 22nd to third in that cap-spending differential. Their new difference of +44.5% there may even undersell their line investments since players such as Sewell and Onwuzurike have inexpensive rookie contracts.

Every team-building philosophy agrees on the importance of the quarterback. Holmes may have needed to deal away Matthew Stafford, who requested a trade and at 33 years old may not fit with the Lions' plan to rebuild in any case. And it is easy to question Holmes' trade of Stafford for Jared Goff, a player whose -74.8% rookie passing DVOA the year before the Rams hired Sean McVay makes one wonder if he can succeed without his former coach. As the Rams former scouting director, however, Holmes likely realizes that Goff is an unexpectedly good fit for his new team. Goff suffered the biggest decline at his position from a 55.8% passing DVOA without pressure to a -126.8% DVOA with pressure in 2020, and the Lions allowed the eighth-lowest offensive pressure rate (21.6%) even before they added Sewell at right tackle. Holmes likely also realizes that Goff does not have to succeed to balance the trade. The new GM coaxed future first- and third-round draft picks in the deal that mirror the Browns' returns in their 2017 trade for Brock Osweiler, a truly distressed asset who never took a snap for his new team.

I'm going to put the right coordinators in place. I'm going to put the right staff together with those coordinators. They are going to be the right mix, the right balance, to complement who I am and know how to deliver the message.

Campbell may not be a schematic savant like Arthur Smith or Brandon Staley, but he doesn't have to be. Campbell can run the Lions like a CEO if he hires the right people and properly delegates responsibilities. And his offensive and defensive coordinators Anthony Lynn and Aaron Glenn look the part. Lynn drew the Chargers' ire with his poor strategic decision-making and subsequent 7-16 record in one-score games the last two seasons, but he won't have to make those fourth-down and fourth-quarter calls for the Lions. Instead, he can focus on the installation of an offensive scheme to fit his talent. When he had a quarterback in Philip Rivers with a quick release, he relied on West Coast passing concepts. When he had a quarterback in Tyrod Taylor that could run, he shifted to more spread concepts. And when he had a quarterback in Justin Herbert with a big and accurate arm, he added more vertical passing concepts. He may be the perfect coordinator to scheme around Goff's obvious strengths and limitations.

Glenn already has chemistry with Campbell from their time together in New Orleans. His shift to a base 3-4 scheme with split safeties will allow the team's best defenders such as Okwara, Trey Flowers, and Tracy Walker to keep their eyes on the quarterback and take chances to try to create turnovers. The Lions forced a turnover on just 7.3% of their defensive possessions in 2020, the second-worst rate in football. That philosophical change should mesh with Campbell's push for doggedness and should be more fun for defenders than Patricia's reactive man-heavy scheme. And Glenn is almost certainly a better messenger. Veteran tackle Michael Brockers told reporters this summer that Glenn is the best communicator he's ever had in a coach.

When it starts at the top and it's right, it'll go down. It'll trickle down to where it's supposed to. And those guys are going to have pride in where they're at, who they play for, and how they're going to play. And more times than not, that leads to success. There's only one way to do it, and that's the right way.

Campbell and Holmes have approached this offseason with a patience that suggests they understand the Lions need more than a quick fix. And more than any specific philosophy, that offers fans of the team hope that this time could be different.

The Lions need to add talent. They need to develop that talent. And Campbell and his coaching staff complement that priority with their constructive coaching and contemporary upbringing. It isn't just the 45-year-old Campbell and 49-year-old Glenn, both of whom played as recently as 2008. Quarterbacks coach Mark Brunell (50) played as recently as 2011. Running backs coach Duce Staley (46) played as recently as 2006. And wide receivers coach Antwaan Randle El (41) played as recently as 2010. They all can match Campbell's energy and offer specific technical advice that makes sense for present-day players.

I wanted this job. I wanted to be here. I think this is a special place. Because when we bring a winner to this city, it's going to be something we can all be proud of.

Campbell may never escape the media fixation with the kneecap-biting metaphor that introduced him, but if his subsequent press conference appearance in a motorcycle helmet is any indication, Campbell doesn't care what the broader public thinks. He cares what his players think and what his city thinks. And for a franchise that needs to follow its city out of its former depression, it's difficult to envision a better wheelman.

Scott Spratt

2020 Lions by Week

Wk	vs.	W-L	PF	PA	YDF	YDA	TO	Total	Off	Def	ST
1	CHI	L	23	27	426	363	-1	-3.0%	11.2%	14.3%	0.0%
2	at GB	L	21	42	307	488	-1	-19.5%	6.7%	29.5%	3.3%
3	at ARI	W	26	23	322	377	3	12.7%	-6.1%	-9.9%	8.8%
4	NO	L	29	35	281	392	0	11.5%	17.6%	8.2%	2.0%
5	BYE										
6	at JAX	W	34	16	403	275	1	7.0%	2.2%	-10.4%	-5.7%
7	at ATL	W	23	22	386	388	1	26.9%	18.8%	-4.3%	3.8%
8	IND	L	21	41	326	366	-2	-23.4%	-6.8%	6.3%	-10.4%
9	at MIN	L	20	34	421	487	-3	-75.2%	-17.7%	47.5%	-10.0%
10	WAS	W	30	27	372	464	1	34.9%	48.1%	22.0%	8.8%
11	at CAR	L	0	20	185	374	1	-53.5%	-55.2%	-6.1%	-4.4%
12	HOU	L	25	41	388	384	-2	-84.8%	-37.9%	42.8%	-4.0%
13	at CHI	W	34	30	460	389	0	-2.2%	35.2%	35.7%	-1.6%
14	GB	L	24	31	293	410	0	4.7%	13.7%	18.1%	9.1%
15	at TEN	L	25	46	430	463	-3	-37.9%	-0.5%	43.8%	6.4%
16	TB	L	7	47	186	588	-2	-81.0%	-60.9%	42.9%	22.8%
17	MIN	L	35	37	417	508	-2	21.8%	33.7%	13.8%	1.9%

Trends and Splits

	Offense	Rank	Defense	Rank
Total DVOA	0.0%	16	17.7%	32
Unadjusted VOA	-3.7%	20	21.4%	32
Weighted Trend	-2.3%	14	21.3%	32
Variance	9.5%	25	4.1%	12
Average Opponent	-1.7%	9	4.0%	5
Passing	14.8%	15	32.5%	32
Rushing	-13.8%	21	-0.5%	27
First Down	6.3%	12	23.0%	32
Second Down	2.0%	15	14.6%	29
Third Down	-16.1%	24	11.6%	24
First Half	9.0%	9	19.5%	32
Second Half	-9.3%	23	15.6%	29
Red Zone	9.3%	13	15.1%	30
Late and Close	3.2%	15	16.5%	27

Five-Year Performance

Year	W-L	Pyth W	Est W	PF	PA	TO	Total	Rk	Off	Rk	Def	Rk	ST	Rk	Off AGL	Rk	Def AGL	Rk	Off Age	Rk	Def Age	Rk	ST Age	Rk
2016	9-7	7.7	6.0	346	358	-1	-11.2%	26	-0.7%	15	14.0%	31	3.5%	6	54.5	27	35.6	14	26.2	25	26.4	18	25.9	21
2017	9-7	8.9	8.9	410	376	+10	9.0%	12	4.1%	12	0.1%	15	4.9%	5	27.0	11	44.3	23	26.6	21	26.0	21	26.0	9
2018	6-10	7.0	6.6	324	360	-5	-10.5%	23	-5.2%	22	4.4%	21	-0.9%	20	40.9	19	33.9	17	26.8	15	26.2	17	26.5	8
2019	3-12-1	5.9	6.6	341	423	-5	-8.1%	21	-3.0%	18	6.5%	23	1.4%	10	56.5	29	31.3	17	26.6	20	26.3	16	25.9	14
2020	5-11	4.8	6.2	377	519	-9	-15.7%	27	0.0%	16	17.7%	32	1.9%	11	32.5	12	51.1	22	26.8	14	26.6	10	26.1	16

2020 Performance Based on Most Common Personnel Groups

DET Offense					DET Offense vs. Opponents					DET Defense				DET Defense vs. Opponents			
Pers	Freq	Yds	DVOA	Run%	Pers	Freq	Yds	DVOA	Run%	Pers	Freq	Yds	DVOA	Pers	Freq	Yds	DVOA
11	66%	5.8	4.6%	25%	Base	25%	6.0	-1.2%	59%	Base	19%	6.1	9.3%	11	53%	6.5	18.8%
12	15%	6.6	10.1%	44%	Nickel	55%	5.9	5.3%	30%	Nickel	61%	6.9	22.5%	12	19%	6.3	17.1%
21	7%	4.8	-24.0%	63%	Dime+	18%	6.0	7.9%	9%	Dime+	20%	6.1	11.3%	21	11%	7.7	24.2%
22	3%	7.0	30.6%	84%	Goal Line	2%	1.5	-2.7%	78%	Goal Line	1%	1.5	-32.9%	22	4%	7.2	2.3%
13	3%	4.3	-51.3%	56%	Big	1%	3.6	-4.5%	40%					13	3%	5.8	22.6%

Strategic Tendencies

Run/Pass		Rk	Formation		Rk	Pass Rush		Rk	Secondary		Rk	Strategy		Rk
Runs, first half	40%	11	Form: Single Back	79%	20	Rush 3	12.5%	5	4 DB	19%	24	Play Action	24%	22
Runs, first down	42%	25	Form: Empty Back	9%	17	Rush 4	66.7%	16	5 DB	61%	16	Offensive Motion	43%	17
Runs, second-long	31%	10	Form: Multi Back	12%	11	Rush 5	16.3%	25	6+ DB	20%	12	Avg Box (Off)	6.43	26
Runs, power sit.	56%	20	Pers: 3+ WR	69%	11	Rush 6+	4.5%	20	Man Coverage	42%	4	Avg Box (Def)	6.62	15
Runs, behind 2H	24%	21	Pers: 2+ TE/6+ OL	24%	20	Edge Rusher Sacks	64.6%	2	CB by Sides	72%	18	Offensive Pace	29.65	9
Pass, ahead 2H	51%	11	Pers: 6+ OL	2%	10	Interior DL Sacks	16.7%	27	S/CB Cover Ratio	28%	13	Defensive Pace	30.78	24
Run-Pass Options	5%	23	Shotgun/Pistol	62%	19	Second Level Sacks	18.8%	23	DB Blitz	8%	27	Go for it on 4th	1.17	28

Only Tampa Bay had a bigger advantage than Detroit when it came to using play-action in 2020. The Lions averaged 9.1 yards per play with 41.4% DVOA with play-action, compared to 6.1 yards per play with 4.3% DVOA on passes without play-action. ◐ The Detroit offense needs to break more tackles. The Lions finished 30th with 78 broken tackles, a year after they ranked dead last. ◐ The Lions' top two safeties (Duron Harmon and Tracy Walker) had the league's second-largest gap between where safeties made their average plays, demonstrating a clear split between free and strong safety responsibilities. ◐ The Lions started the year moving their cornerbacks around a lot; by the end of the season, Amani Oruwariye was consistently on the offensive right with Darryl Roberts on the offensive left. ◐ Detroit had one of the league's worst fumble recovery records last season, with just four of 11 fumbles on offense and five of 17 fumbles on defense. ◐ The listed Aggressiveness Index combines Matt Patricia (1.10) and Darrell Bevell (1.29).

Passing

Player	DYAR	DVOA	Plays	NtYds	Avg	YAC	C%	TD	Int
M.Stafford*	684	7.7%	559	3820	6.8	5.1	65.2%	26	10
C.Daniel*	-36	-23.5%	45	235	5.2	4.1	69.0%	1	2
D.Blough	-60	-111.0%	11	39	3.5	4.5	60.0%	0	1
J.Goff	385	-1.1%	573	3761	6.6	5.8	67.6%	20	13

Rushing

Player	DYAR	DVOA	Plays	Yds	Avg	TD	Fum	Suc
A.Peterson*	64	0.9%	156	604	3.9	7	0	46%
D.Swift	106	13.0%	114	521	4.6	8	2	54%
K.Johnson*	-7	-11.7%	52	181	3.5	2	1	56%
M.Stafford*	42	23.0%	21	122	5.8	0	0	--
J.Agnew*	26	34.7%	6	33	5.5	0	0	--
J.Williams	60	2.8%	119	505	4.2	2	0	58%
J.Goff	-6	-14.8%	34	115	3.4	4	2	--

Receiving

Player	DYAR	DVOA	Plays	Ctch	Yds	Y/C	YAC	TD	C%
M.Jones*	235	12.3%	115	76	978	12.9	2.6	9	66%
D.Amendola*	62	-1.0%	69	46	602	13.1	6.4	0	67%
Q.Cephus	66	10.6%	35	20	349	17.5	4.3	2	57%
K.Golladay*	90	22.0%	32	20	338	16.9	1.9	2	63%
M.Hall*	40	5.0%	30	17	290	17.1	3.4	2	57%
M.Sanu*	44	12.2%	23	16	178	11.1	2.1	1	70%
J.Agnew*	-38	-36.2%	20	13	89	6.8	7.8	0	65%
B.Perriman	41	-4.4%	60	30	505	16.8	5.3	3	50%
K.Raymond	34	16.2%	15	9	187	20.8	4.2	0	60%
T.J.Hockenson	7	-6.2%	101	67	723	10.8	4.9	6	66%
J.James*	-26	-23.8%	22	14	129	9.2	5.4	2	64%
D.Fells	90	38.6%	28	21	312	14.9	8.4	4	75%
D.Swift	94	17.1%	57	46	357	7.8	7.6	2	81%
K.Johnson*	72	37.1%	26	19	187	9.8	9.6	1	73%
A.Peterson*	22	9.0%	18	12	101	8.4	8.6	0	67%
J.Williams	58	14.0%	35	31	236	7.6	7.1	1	89%

Offensive Line

Player	Pos	Age	GS	Snaps	Pen	Sk	Pass	Run	Player	Pos	Age	GS	Snaps	Pen	Sk	Pass	Run
Taylor Decker	LT	28	16/16	1049	6	1	12	3	Oday Aboushi*	RG	30	16/8	622	4	1	3	4
Jonah Jackson	LG	24	16/16	1007	5	1.5	17	8	Halapoulivaati Vaitai	RG	28	10/10	451	1	6	12	4
Frank Ragnow	C	25	14/14	931	3	0	4	6	Joe Dahl*	C/LG	28	9/4	263	1	1	3	1
Tyrell Crosby	RT	26	12/11	658	3	3	11	2	Matt Nelson	RT	26	16/1	242	2	0	4	0

Year	Yards	ALY	Rk	Power	Rk	Stuff	Rk	2Lev	Rk	OpFld	Rk	BB Rt	Rk	Sacks	ASR	Rk	Press	Rk	BB Rt	Rk	Cont
2018	4.10	4.14	20	68%	14	22%	27	1.18	22	0.74	23	7.7%	25	41	6.3%	12	27.0%	9	7.2%	10	28
2019	3.94	4.21	20	64%	19	18%	12	1.12	22	0.54	25	11.8%	26	43	7.2%	19	30.2%	18	14.6%	23	25
2020	4.07	4.30	19	67%	14	17%	18	1.06	29	0.62	20	8.2%	7	42	7.2%	21	20.8%	5	10.4%	8	23

2020 ALY by direction:	Left End: 4.32 (21)	Left Tackle: 4.09 (20)	Mid/Guard: 4.59 (10)	Right Tackle: 3.89 (24)	Right End: 3.78 (24)

The Lions are one of three NFC North teams to make their first-round 2021 draft selection a new offensive tackle, and they added the consensus best one in Penei Sewell out of Oregon. Sewell's size, quickness, and athleticism offer him the best chance to excel in the NFL at left tackle, but surprisingly for a team coming off three straight fourth-place division finishes, the Lions have the line depth to start Sewell at right tackle as a rookie. ◐ Taylor Decker should open the season at left tackle, and he has earned the role with a low 2.3% blown block rate in five seasons with the Lions. Decker endured a mild slump in the years after 2017 shoulder surgery, but he bounced back in 2020 with career bests in blown block rate (1.5%), sacks allowed (one), and holding penalties (one). ◐ 2018 first-round center Frank Ragnow has steadily improved from 2.4% to 2.0% to 1.1% blown block rates in his three seasons. The latter effort earned him his first trip to the Pro Bowl and the biggest ever contract extension for a center with $42 million in guarantees. ◐ Relative to his draft position, third-round guard Jonah Jackson was a pleasant surprise with a 2.8% blown block rate in his rookie season. That performance allowed the Lions to comfortably release veteran Joe Dahl—who missed time in each of the last three seasons with various leg and groin injuries—and save $2.9 million in cap space. ◐ The Lions would likely have preferred to release Halapoulivaati Vaitai after his 4.0% blown block rate in his first year with the team, but Vaitai's five-year, $45-million contract would have left them with an untenable $14.6-million dead cap hit if they had cut him this offseason. Expect him to start at right guard for one more year, after which that dead cap hit shrinks to $4.2 million. ❧ Tyrell Crosby looks like the odd man out with Decker and Sewell entrenched at the tackle spots, but his improvement from a 5.3% blown block rate in 2019 to 2.2% last year makes him starter-worthy. For now, he is one of the best backup plans in the NFL. But he could also find himself as a trade chip for a Lions team with plenty of holes left to fill.

Defensive Front

Defensive Line	Age	Pos	G	Snaps	Plays	TmPct	Rk	Stop	Dfts	BTkl	Runs	St%	Rk	RuYd	Rk	Sack	Hit	Hur	Dsrpt
John Penisini	24	DT	16	576	35	4.2%	63	29	4	6	32	81%	21	2.6	51	1.0	0	0	0
Nicholas Williams	31	DT	14	537	25	3.4%	76	19	3	0	22	73%	52	2.8	61	1.0	3	6	4
Danny Shelton*	28	DT	12	498	38	6.0%	28	25	5	3	33	70%	64	2.7	55	1.0	3	7	3
Michael Brockers	31	DE	15	624	51	6.7%	13	37	9	0	40	78%	37	1.9	25	5.0	4	11	0

Edge Rushers	Age	Pos	G	Snaps	Plays	TmPct	Rk	Stop	Dfts	BTkl	Runs	St%	Rk	RuYd	Rk	Sack	Hit	Hur	Dsrpt
Romeo Okwara	26	DE	16	748	45	5.4%	36	33	18	11	30	67%	60	3.0	66	10.0	11	28	1
Everson Griffen*	34	DE	14	527	37	5.1%	40	27	14	5	25	60%	81	3.5	82	6.0	7	17	4
Da'Shawn Hand	26	DE	10	353	19	3.6%	72	15	1	0	19	79%	17	1.9	26	0.0	0	4	0
Trey Flowers	28	DE	7	309	22	6.0%	27	16	5	1	15	80%	13	2.5	44	2.0	2	6	0
Charles Harris	26	DE	13	289	19	2.9%	--	12	4	2	8	88%	--	3.1	--	3.0	2	8	1

Linebackers	Age	Pos	G	Snaps	Plays	TmPct	Rk	Stop	Dfts	BTkl	Runs	St%	Rk	RuYd	Rk	Sack	Hit	Hur	Tgts	Suc%	Rk	Yd/P	Rk	PD	Int
Jamie Collins	32	OLB	14	829	107	14.6%	27	46	14	12	71	45%	75	4.4	58	1.0	2	7	28	50%	42	8.3	67	6	1
Jahlani Tavai	25	MLB	16	624	56	6.7%	77	25	5	8	38	55%	45	4.4	61	0.0	2	7	15	53%	29	6.6	46	0	0
Reggie Ragland*	28	MLB	16	562	52	6.2%	80	28	9	2	40	58%	37	3.6	25	1.0	2	9	10	50%	--	4.8	--	1	0
Christian Jones*	30	OLB	16	510	51	6.1%	81	28	4	6	38	55%	45	4.1	48	0.0	1	9	4	100%	--	2.8	--	1	0
Jarrad Davis*	27	MLB	14	329	41	5.6%	--	18	5	9	27	52%	--	4.7	--	0.5	3	9	6	33%	--	5.8	--	0	0
Alex Anzalone	27	ILB	16	525	40	5.1%	85	19	7	4	23	70%	8	2.5	2	0.0	0	5	14	50%	35	5.1	21	0	0
Shaun Dion Hamilton	26	OLB	14	109	20	2.9%	--	10	3	2	14	57%	--	3.1	--	0.0	1	0	5	60%	--	6.4	--	0	0

Year	Yards	ALY	Rk	Power	Rk	Stuff	Rk	2Lev	Rk	OpFld	Rk	BB Rt	Rk	Sacks	ASR	Rk	Press	Rk	BB Rt	Rk
2018	4.68	4.47	20	52%	1	15%	28	1.20	14	1.10	26	8.4%	17	43	8.1%	5	26.3%	29	7.8%	25
2019	4.09	4.55	23	74%	28	12%	32	1.07	9	0.48	3	9.5%	29	28	5.0%	31	26.8%	28	12.4%	25
2020	4.63	4.94	29	67%	17	12%	29	1.32	24	0.68	15	9.7%	26	24	4.9%	27	21.0%	28	9.7%	31

2020 ALY by direction:	Left End: 3.81 (8)	Left Tackle: 5.33 (31)	Mid/Guard: 5.09 (31)	Right Tackle: 5.02 (24)	Right End: 4.73 (19)

The change from a base 4-3 defense to a base 3-4 may not mean what it used to, but the Lions should still show some dramatic changes under new defensive coordinator Aaron Glenn. Romeo Okwara and Trey Flowers—likely the team's two best defenders—will now rush the passer as stand-up outside linebackers. Okwara clearly bought into the change for a price of three years and $37 million, an aggressive contract for a player whose 28 hurries in 2020 were a career-high but still not enough to crack the top 35 in football. But Okwara makes sense as a re-signing for the rebuilding Lions since he's unusually young entering his sixth NFL season, and since his brother Julian is a developmental prospect with the team. ❧ Flowers and interior linebacker Jamie Collins let down their old Patriots coach Matt Patricia in 2020, the former with a forearm fracture that cost him half the season and the latter with a poor performance both in defending the run and in pass coverage. Four years younger, Flowers may be the better bet to bounce back. But Glenn has made a point to talk up Collins' versatility to reporters this offseason and could be hinting at the latter's return to his role with the Patriots, which had him more frequently lining up near the line of scrimmage and blitzing. ❧ GM Brad Holmes brought veteran lineman Michael Brockers in from his old Rams teams. Brockers declined from 21 hurries in 2019 to 11 last year and may be a poor bet to rebound now in his thirties and without Aaron Donald drawing double-teams. But Brockers' most important role with his new team will be to mentor the prospects. That's because the Lions continued their inside-out rebuild with selections of defensive tackles Levi Onwuzurike and Alim McNeill from Washington and North Carolina State in the second and third rounds, as well as linebacker Derrick Barnes from Purdue in the fourth round. Onwuzurike sparks the most excitement with the best of his college plays, but he likely fell from the first to the second round because of a lack of consistent fundamentals and production.

Defensive Secondary

Secondary	Age	Pos	G	Snaps	Plays	TmPct	Rk	Stop	Dfts	BTkl	Runs	St%	Rk	RuYd	Rk	Tgts	Tgt%	Rk	aDOT	Suc%	Rk	Yd/P	Rk	PD	Int
Duron Harmon*	30	FS	16	1102	77	9.2%	57	9	5	11	35	6%	70	11.6	67	18	4.3%	66	12.5	39%	65	15.6	70	5	2
Amani Oruwariye	25	CB	16	1028	60	7.2%	70	23	7	11	11	55%	15	3.9	8	75	19.1%	46	14.6	52%	38	9.6	73	7	1
Tracy Walker	26	SS	15	755	84	10.7%	37	30	10	11	40	48%	16	4.9	12	36	12.5%	13	10.5	42%	58	8.9	51	4	0
Jayron Kearse*	27	FS	11	503	59	10.2%	42	22	4	4	35	46%	22	4.4	6	24	12.5%	12	6.4	54%	22	4.0	2	2	0
Justin Coleman*	28	CB	11	470	30	5.2%	--	11	7	9	3	33%	--	6.7	--	29	16.1%	--	9.2	45%	--	9.3	--	1	0
Darryl Roberts*	31	CB	11	469	45	7.8%	--	16	6	5	7	29%	--	7.9	--	40	22.3%	--	10.4	45%	--	6.8	--	6	1
Jeff Okudah	22	CB	9	460	49	10.4%	--	20	9	7	19	63%	--	3.0	--	45	25.5%	--	11.2	36%	--	11.9	--	2	1
Desmond Trufant*	31	CB	6	324	23	7.3%	--	9	5	5	6	17%	--	6.5	--	28	22.6%	--	11.1	46%	--	8.4	--	4	1
Will Harris	26	SS	16	312	34	4.1%	--	3	3	4	15	7%	--	9.3	--	14	11.7%	--	6.9	57%	--	5.9	--	1	0
Corn Elder	27	CB	16	411	40	4.9%	--	13	5	3	8	38%	--	6.1	--	26	15.5%	--	10.0	42%	--	7.8	--	3	0
Quinton Dunbar	29	CB	6	397	35	10.5%	--	12	4	3	8	50%	--	4.5	--	39	22.3%	--	12.1	46%	--	8.7	--	5	1

Year	Pass D Rank	vs. #1 WR	Rk	vs. #2 WR	Rk	vs. Other WR	Rk	WR Wide	Rk	WR Slot	Rk	vs. TE	Rk	vs. RB	Rk
2018	31	21.5%	32	19.4%	27	39.5%	32	19.3%	31	34.0%	31	19.4%	26	-6.6%	11
2019	29	-2.3%	13	22.0%	29	3.3%	19	-6.0%	17	13.2%	22	8.7%	24	24.6%	27
2020	32	21.2%	30	19.4%	28	6.2%	19	12.0%	27	16.3%	28	6.2%	21	46.2%	32

Jeff Okudah, the third overall draft selection in 2020, underwhelmed as a rookie with a 36% coverage success rate and 11.9 yards allowed per target, rates that would have landed him in the bottom five at his position if he hadn't missed half the season with a groin injury and failed to qualify. Okudah missed Week 1 and played through that injury in road games in Green Bay and Arizona. He saw 10 of his first 17 NFL targets in coverage of superstars Davante Adams and DeAndre Hopkins. ✎ With Desmond Trufant joining the division-rival Bears, Quinton Dunbar, Amani Oruwariye, and third-round rookie Ifeatu Melifonwu (Syracuse) will compete for the second corner job. Dunbar accepted a one-year, $1.1-million contract that does not look like starter money, but he endured a rocky 2020 that included a trade to Seattle, an arrest in an armed robbery case, and a knee injury. He was much better in an uneventful 2019 season with a top-20 59% success rate. A former fifth-rounder, Oruwariye started 15 games in his sophomore season and easily paced the Lions corners in coverage success rate in 2020. He may start on his own merits, and even if he doesn't, he is a good bet to play regularly with Dunbar's health history. Melifonwu is a physical and aggressive prospect whose traits offer him the flexibility to play at nickel or possibly free safety (his brother Obi's position with the Raiders and Patriots) despite a 6-foot-3 frame that should eventually push him outside. ✎ Tracy Walker figures to hold the starting free safety position at least in name. After a breakout year in the role in 2019, he transitioned to strong safety in 2020 and struggled. He also had to contend with the murder of cousin Ahmaud Arbery. He will aim for a fresh start in 2021 in a new split-safety scheme that will more frequently have him and Will Harris in zones with their eyes on the quarterback.

Special Teams

Year	DVOA	Rank	FG/XP	Rank	Net Kick	Rank	Kick Ret	Rank	Net Punt	Rank	Punt Ret	Rank	Hidden	Rank
2018	-0.9%	20	0.2	16	2.6	10	-0.7	14	-3.1	24	-3.5	25	20.0	2
2019	1.4%	10	4.5	9	-14.0	32	4.5	4	8.3	5	4.0	5	9.2	3
2020	1.9%	11	-5.4	23	-5.7	27	3.6	9	12.2	4	4.9	5	19.4	1

Special teams was one of the few Lions bright spots in 2020, but they won't enjoy stability there with kicker Matt Prater leaving for Arizona after seven years with the team. Veteran Randy Bullock comes over from Cincinnati and will battle second-year kicker Matthew Wright for the job. Bullock had slightly more value than Prater in each of the last three seasons and has comparable leg strength, at least outside Prater's former home in Denver. ✎ Rookie punter Jack Fox replaced another seven-year incumbent in Sam Martin and accomplished something the veteran never has: he made a Pro Bowl. Fox's 49.1 net yards per punt was third highest in 2020 (behind just Buffalo's Corey Bojorquez at 50.8 and Seattle's Michael Dickson at 49.6) and tied for 13th best in NFL history. Fox also held for kicks as a rookie, and he has worked to close his stance on those attempts this offseason, believing he may have contributed to Prater's struggles. ✎ With Jamal Agnew joining the Jaguars this offseason, the Lions will have to find a new returner on both punts and kickoffs. Rookie receiver Amon-Ra St. Brown did both in his time at USC, but speedy former Titans receiver Kalif Raymond seems like the more likely choice to earn that returner role. ✎ The Lions accumulated a staggering 19.4 points of "hidden" special teams value thanks to three blocked punts and their opponents shanking nine extra points. We shouldn't expect that to repeat in 2021, although somehow Detroit has ranked in the top three for hidden value in three straight seasons.

Green Bay Packers

2020 Record: 13-3	Total DVOA: 25.8% (9)	2021 Mean Projection: 9.6 wins	On the Clock (0-5): 7%
Pythagorean Wins: 11.2 (4)	Offense: 29.1% (1)	Postseason Odds: 61.7%	Mediocrity (6-8): 26%
Snap-Weighted Age: 26.4 (16)	Defense: 0.5% (17)	Super Bowl Odds: 11.8%	Playoff Contender (9-11): 41%
Average Opponent: -1.8% (23)	Special Teams: -2.7% (25)	Proj. Avg. Opponent: 2.9% (3)	Super Bowl Contender (12+): 26%

2020: Ridicule the Jordan Love pick all you want. We had the last laugh because it lit a fire under Aaron Rodgers.

2021: Rodgers said what now?

Congratulations, Packers fans! You have been chosen by the football gods to usher in the NFL player empowerment era!

[Pauses for the screaming.]

I know, I'm excited, too. Even with the expansion to 17 games, the NFL regular and postseasons fill just 22 of the 52 weeks in a year. Add in the eventized draft, combine, schedule release, and, inevitably, new team uniform fashion show weeks, and we're barely at half the year. But with the player empowerment era, you can have 365 days of NFL content if you closely follow the Instagram accounts of celebrities such as Shailene Woodley and Miles Teller and comb through country club membership records.

[That screaming gives way to a barrage of profanity with a barely audible "NBA" mixed in.]

What was that? You thought the NFL was too stuck in its ways to devolve into a reality show soap opera? Heavens no! Haven't you heard about us Millennials? We live on social media! And we're entitled! Always complaining about our silly little problems like "mental health" and "crippling student debt." And with a December 1983 birthday, Aaron Rodgers is the tip of an iceberg of Millennial and Gen Z quarterbacks in the league. Soon enough, every team's future Hall-of-Fame signal-caller will be demanding a trade for the tiniest of perceived grievances—like when his team, which is an upgrade or two away from winning a Super Bowl, trades up and drafts his replacement in the first round without first consulting him.

[That tirade turns to silence with some vigorous head-shaking.]

You still aren't convinced? You think Rodgers' situation with the Packers is different from the ones that James Harden had with the Rockets, Anthony Davis had with the Pelicans, Paul George had with the Thunder, Jimmy Butler had with the Timberwolves, Kawhi Leonard had with the Spurs, Kyrie Irving had with the Cavaliers, Dwight Howard had with the Magic, and Chris Paul had with the Hornets? OK, let's talk it through.

Objection: NFL players lack leverage because they don't play for enough years or make enough money to sit out a season and sacrifice income.

Debunked by: Tom Brady, Drew Brees, Philip Rivers, and Ben Roethlisberger.

Players at other positions may not have the same leverage (although Le'Veon Bell would likely disagree), but the best pocket passers can reasonably expect to play into their late thirties or early forties now that quarterbacks such as Brady, Brees, and Rivers from the previous generation have done so. At 38 years old and with the current MVP trophy to refute any suspicion that his play has slipped, Rodgers seems poised to play through all of teammate Jordan Love's rookie contract. And if Rodgers does so for the Packers, it would sabotage a major potential benefit of the Love selection, which is the cost savings of a rookie wage scale that, without Rodgers, would allow the team to bolster the rest of its roster in free agency.

As for salaries, quarterbacks are doing just fine. Rodgers' 2018 extension has an average annual value of $33.5 million. That isn't quite Harden ($42.8 million) or Davis ($38.0 million) money, but it easily clears the sub-$20-million standard of players such as Paul and Irving when they started this trend a decade ago. It's a lot of money, but star quarterbacks, like star NBA players, can risk it since they are likely to cross into the triple digits of millions made over the course of their careers.

Objection: NFL players lack leverage because they are too likely to get hurt to turn down guaranteed money.

Debunked by: Dak Prescott.

That is another one that likely means more for players at other positions. Quarterbacks do get hurt. But in his compound ankle fracture last year, Prescott suffered as serious an injury as a quarterback can while still reasonably expecting a return to play. And without having played a game in between, he has since signed a $160-million extension, the second highest ever by average annual value. The best quarterbacks are worth more to their teams' competitive chances than those teams can pay them in a salary-capped league, so even full-year injuries cannot depress their future earnings too far.

Yes, quarterbacks can suffer injuries that end their careers. But so too can NBA players. And at their similar income brackets, these players can and typically do protect themselves from debilitating potential injuries with insurance policies.

2021 Packers Schedule

Week	Opp.	Week	Opp.	Week	Opp.
1	at NO	7	WAS	13	BYE
2	DET (Mon.)	8	at ARI (Thu.)	14	CHI
3	at SF	9	at KC	15	at BAL
4	PIT	10	SEA	16	CLE (Sat./Xmas)
5	at CIN	11	at MIN	17	MIN
6	at CHI	12	LAR	18	at DET

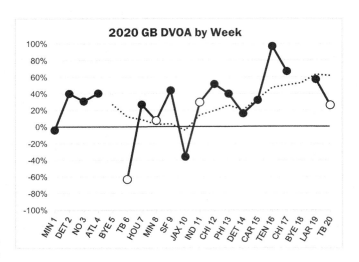

Objection: NFL players lack leverage because teams can extend their control of them with instruments like franchise tags.

Debunked by: Eli Manning and Carson Palmer.

It can be difficult for NFL players to fight their way to true free agency. Just ask Kirk Cousins, who had to traverse four years of a rookie contract and two franchise tags from Washington to hit the open market. But Cousins lacked leverage for the same reason Washington was reluctant to offer him a big extension: teams weren't convinced he was a real difference-maker. It isn't open, but signed quarterbacks still have a market. And if they are good enough, they can entice their teams to trade them because 1) their holdouts would cost their current teams more expected value than lesser players could with theirs, and 2) other teams will pay a steeper price to acquire them.

With only his potential as a prospect, Manning had the leverage to entice the Chargers to trade him to New York. Pro Bowler Carson Palmer convinced the Bengals to trade him to Oakland with a threat of retirement. They may not want to, but Justin Herbert and Joe Burrow could make the same requests today. And while the Chargers and Bengals would have the ultimate power to make those trade decisions, the bounty of future draft picks other teams would undoubtedly offer them would be difficult to turn down if they believed that, if retained, Herbert and Burrow would hold out and leave them with nothing.

Rodgers does not match Herbert or Burrow for value to his current team—his MVP trophy is evidence only of the 2020 season, and Herbert and Burrow could potentially outproduce their cap figures for their teams for the next decade or more. But Rodgers has three years left on his current contract that would give him time to aid another team's Super Bowl push like Peyton Manning did for Denver and Tom Brady did and continues to do for Tampa Bay.

Other teams are making trade offers. KFAN FM 100.3's Paul Allen reported the 49ers offered a number of picks (including No. 3 overall) plus Jimmy Garoppolo for Rodgers before this year's draft. The Packers turned that down, but similar packages will look better the longer Rodgers holds out.

Objection: NFL players lack leverage because the nature of football and financial nature of the NFL make it impractical to stack multiple star quarterbacks on a single team or trade them at all.

Debunked by: Jameis Winston and Taysom Hill.

That was a joke! You have me on this one. But as I see things, that limits the pool of options. It doesn't dry them up.

Rodgers may entice the Packers to try to trade him. But for a trade to work and fulfill the promise of a player empowerment era, it needs to appease Rodgers, satisfy a trade partner that cannot play him next to a star incumbent quarterback, and fit within both teams' financial constraints.

If my social media sleuthing can be trusted, then Rodgers is a bit of an enigma. His pre-draft list of preferred trade partners—the 49ers, Broncos, and Raiders, per Pro Football Talk—may suggest a desire to relocate to the West Coast, near where he grew up (Northern California) and where his fiancée Woodley works (Southern and Northern California, the latter as a filming location for the show *Big Little Lies*). But to broaden this exercise, I'll hypothesize that Rodgers has two simpler goals in his trade demand. First, he wants to leave the Packers and general manager Brian Gutekunst. And second, he wants to join a team with a chance to win the Super Bowl.

That second desire offers the most hope of a reconciliation. The Packers led the league in 2020 in Approximate Value (AV), Pro Football Reference's estimate of player value that applies to players at every position. And while Rodgers increased that lead with the 17 AV from his MVP season, the Packers also led the league in non-quarterback AV (Table 1). One could argue that Green Bay has the best supporting cast in the NFL.

The Packers may not have the best wide receiver depth, but Davante Adams can make a strong case he's the best No. 1 receiver in football after he led the position with 395 DYAR last year. Meanwhile, the rest of the team is stacked with All-Pro candidates at every position group. David Bakhtiari led all tackles with 300 or more snaps with a 0.6% blown block rate in 2020. Robert Tonyan and Aaron Jones finished second and fourth at their positions with 242 receiving and 254 rushing DYAR, respectively. Za'Darius Smith was tied for 19th among all defenders with 30 hurries and tied for fourth with 12.5 sacks. Darnell Savage finished second among safeties with 12 defensed passes. And Jaire Alexander was first among qualified corners with a 65.2% coverage success rate and second with 4.4 yards allowed per target. And even if second cornerback was the hole that the Love pick could have filled and pushed the 2020 team to a Super Bowl berth—and it certainly seemed that way after Kevin King lost Scotty Miller on a 39-

yard touchdown as time expired in the first half of the NFC Championship Game and then pulled Tyler Johnson's jersey to draw a pass interference penalty to seal their loss—the Packers tried to fill that hole this offseason with a first-round draft selection of cornerback Eric Stokes from Georgia.

The bad news is that Tom Brady provides very recent precedent of a quarterback leaving the league's best supporting cast and winning a Super Bowl with a group that looked worse the year before he arrived. The Patriots led the NFL with 254 non-quarterback AV with Brady in 2019, while the Buccaneers ranked 15th with 193 non-quarterback AV. Few people would weigh the Patriots and Bucs that way with hindsight. But the former team looked much better before they suffered an early postseason upset to the Titans, lost a bunch of defensive talent to free agency and COVID opt-outs, and failed to return to the playoffs in 2020. They led the league in defensive DVOA in 2019.

Table 1. Non-QB Approximate Value Leaders, 2020

Rk	Team	Total	QB	Other	Rk	Team	Total	QB	Other
1	GB	251	17	234	17	NE	203	14	189
3	TB	244	16	228	18	WAS	189	1	188
2	BAL	247	19	228	18	ATL	201	13	188
4	PIT	232	10	222	20	LAC	200	14	186
5	IND	233	12	221	21	LV	198	15	183
6	LAR	226	10	216	22	MIN	196	14	182
6	NO	231	15	216	23	CAR	194	13	181
6	KC	234	18	216	24	NYG	186	10	176
9	BUF	235	21	214	25	DEN	181	7	174
10	MIA	218	12	206	26	PHI	181	8	173
10	SEA	224	18	206	27	DAL	185	13	172
12	SF	210	11	199	28	HOU	185	16	169
12	ARI	216	17	199	29	CIN	177	10	167
12	TEN	216	17	199	30	DET	169	12	157
15	CLE	205	11	194	31	JAX	156	7	149
16	CHI	202	10	192	32	NYJ	148	5	143

But I won't quibble with differing opinions on the quality of Brady's help in New England. Because like Brady was, Rodgers seems finished with his former team. He's likely more interested in the how the Bucs looked in 2019 so he can make a similarly shrewd jump to a Super Bowl contender, whether the public sees them as one or not.

That's where this gets tricky. Football may be more volatile than basketball with its shorter regular season and single-elimination playoffs. But that shows itself in last-place-to-playoff-berth transformations more than it does in last-place-to-conference-title ones. Since Rodgers joined the league in 2005, 32 teams have made it to a Super Bowl. Almost three-quarters of those teams (23) reached 230 cumulative AV in their prior season, and all but one of them—the 2019 49ers (179 AV)—reached 195 AV.

If Rodgers joined the Giants, Broncos, Eagles, Cowboys, Texans, Bengals, Lions, Jaguars, or Jets and took them to Super Bowl LVI, it would be an outlier of an accomplishment in the modern game. And with some caveats I'll return to, that likely rules out a quarter of potential trade partners for Rodgers before even considering their interest in and capacity to make a trade for him.

As for interest, 15 teams—with some overlap with the previous list—seem likely to prefer to stick with their incumbent with consideration of their proximity to contention and their quarterbacks' talent, age, and cost. The Bucs have Brady. The Chiefs have Patrick Mahomes. The Seahawks have Russell Wilson. The Ravens have Lamar Jackson. The Bills have Josh Allen. The Rams have Matthew Stafford. The Cowboys have Dak Prescott. The Cardinals have Kyler Murray. The Chargers have Justin Herbert. The Bengals have Joe Burrow. The Jaguars have Trevor Lawrence. The Jets have Zach Wilson. The 49ers have Trey Lance. The Bears have Justin Fields. And the Patriots have Mac Jones.

And finally for capacity, teams are handicapped the most by their incumbent quarterbacks' dead cap figures because those remain on their books after a trade or release. That likely eliminates the Vikings, Titans, Texans, Falcons, Colts, Lions, Steelers, and Saints. Or at least, it does this deep into the offseason when none of these teams has more than $17 million in available cap space. Each team would take on roughly $20 million to $75 million in dead money by moving on from their current quarterbacks (including both Hill and Winston in New Orleans). It does not eliminate the Bills, Bengals, Dolphins, Chargers, or Cardinals, because their quarterbacks are on rookie contracts and are still cheap enough to retain as backups, but most of those teams would take their current starters over Rodgers anyway. The exception might be Miami, but only if they are pessimistic that Tua Tagovailoa will improve after an up-and-down rookie season.

All told, the Dolphins, Browns, Raiders, Panthers, and Washington Football Team are the only teams that could trade for Rodgers, that might plausibly want to trade for Rodgers, and that Rodgers could reasonably consider to be contenders for his services based on recent statistical precedent. I subjectively would add the Giants and Broncos to that list. Neither is ruled out by interest or capacity, and the "approximate" in Approximate Value may refer to the metric's inability to account for details like those teams' bottom-eight totals of adjusted games lost or COVID protocols forcing the latter team to start a wide receiver at quarterback last season. The outlier 2019 49ers bounced back from similar misfortune in adjusted games lost the year before their Super Bowl run. But that still leaves just seven teams.

That isn't many. But it is enough. Frankly, it is enough for disgruntled superstar trades to happen much more frequently than they have in recent years. The slow pace likely has less to do with the feasibility of the trades and more to do with the star quarterbacks' desires for them. More so than their NBA counterparts, those star quarterbacks tend to be good enough to make their teams competitive even with poorly built supporting casts, and that competitiveness has so far seemed enough to satisfy most of them.

And that's the irony of all of this. By that AV measure, the

Packers had the best supporting cast in football in 2020. And unlike the prior year's Patriots, whose cap circumstances forced them to jettison some of their best defensive players as they hit free agency, the Packers are poised to match their previous standard or at least come close. Our 2021 season projections see the team with Rodgers as a leading Super Bowl contender.

[The objections die with a drop of the head.]

Cheer up. That's the real reason for hope. Rodgers may have the leverage to force his way out of Green Bay, but player empowerment swings both ways. If Love isn't ready to lead the Packers or isn't good enough to ever do so—QBASE was skeptical with its 64% projected bust rate—then Green Bay could instantly become the top trade destination for the next unhappy star quarterback. Those might not come as frequently as they have in the NBA in recent years, but the conditions are there for the NFL to have at least a modest player empowerment era of its own. You'll just have to hope that, if a trade ever brings a Russell Wilson or Joe Burrow to Green Bay, Gutekunst will call him every once in a while to consult him on a draft or free-agent decision. Or rather, he'll text them. We Millennials never answer the phone.

Scott Spratt

2020 Packers by Week

Wk	vs.	W-L	PF	PA	YDF	YDA	TO	Total	Off	Def	ST
1	at MIN	W	43	34	522	382	1	-3.7%	23.7%	26.6%	-0.9%
2	DET	W	42	21	488	307	1	40.4%	41.7%	2.8%	1.4%
3	at NO	W	37	30	369	397	1	31.1%	30.1%	6.0%	7.0%
4	ATL	W	30	16	403	327	0	40.7%	51.7%	11.1%	0.1%
5	BYE										
6	at TB	L	10	38	201	324	-2	-62.9%	-53.5%	9.6%	0.1%
7	at HOU	W	35	20	379	365	1	27.1%	20.7%	-13.8%	-7.5%
8	MIN	L	22	28	400	324	-1	7.7%	40.9%	37.5%	4.3%
9	at SF	W	34	17	405	337	2	44.3%	40.2%	-7.9%	-3.8%
10	JAX	W	24	20	395	260	-1	-35.8%	-20.8%	-9.3%	-24.3%
11	at IND	L	31	34	367	420	-2	29.7%	34.2%	-4.4%	-9.0%
12	CHI	W	41	25	393	350	3	51.8%	62.9%	13.9%	2.7%
13	PHI	W	30	16	437	278	1	40.1%	38.0%	-11.8%	-9.8%
14	at DET	W	31	24	410	293	0	16.2%	27.4%	6.3%	-4.8%
15	CAR	W	24	16	291	364	1	32.3%	8.5%	-13.2%	10.6%
16	TEN	W	40	14	448	260	1	97.0%	51.1%	-52.0%	-6.0%
17	at CHI	W	35	16	316	356	1	66.9%	75.4%	4.6%	-3.9%
18	BYE										
19	LAR	W	32	18	484	244	0	57.4%	60.8%	6.8%	3.4%
20	TB	L	26	31	381	351	1	26.2%	7.8%	-17.3%	1.0%

Trends and Splits

	Offense	Rank	Defense	Rank
Total DVOA	29.1%	1	0.5%	17
Unadjusted VOA	29.9%	1	-1.0%	15
Weighted Trend	31.6%	1	-3.5%	14
Variance	9.8%	27	4.0%	11
Average Opponent	1.4%	22	0.7%	14
Passing	52.0%	1	4.9%	15
Rushing	2.9%	5	-5.4%	18
First Down	22.6%	2	-8.0%	9
Second Down	27.5%	1	4.8%	19
Third Down	44.4%	2	10.1%	23
First Half	31.9%	1	-8.5%	5
Second Half	25.4%	1	8.9%	23
Red Zone	55.2%	1	13.9%	28
Late and Close	24.6%	4	0.4%	20

Five-Year Performance

Year	W-L	Pyth W	Est W	PF	PA	TO	Total	Rk	Off	Rk	Def	Rk	ST	Rk	Off AGL	Rk	Def AGL	Rk	Off Age	Rk	Def Age	Rk	ST Age	Rk
2016	10-6	9.1	9.6	432	388	+8	11.0%	7	16.6%	4	3.8%	21	-1.9%	21	34.8	16	42.5	17	26.8	14	25.8	30	25.4	28
2017	7-9	6.2	7.6	320	384	-3	-4.5%	17	0.0%	16	5.8%	24	1.3%	14	45.1	23	39.4	21	27.0	16	25.5	28	25.2	28
2018	6-9-1	7.4	7.8	376	400	0	-4.4%	20	11.2%	7	11.6%	29	-4.1%	29	26.2	8	63.5	30	27.6	8	25.8	24	25.2	31
2019	13-3	9.8	9.9	376	313	+12	7.7%	9	6.6%	8	-0.9%	15	0.1%	18	39.5	17	26.2	9	28.1	2	25.5	29	25.5	24
2020	13-3	11.2	11.4	509	369	+7	25.8%	3	29.1%	1	0.5%	17	-2.7%	25	52.1	26	21.0	4	28.1	1	25.2	31	25.3	29

2020 Performance Based on Most Common Personnel Groups

GB Offense					GB Offense vs. Opponents					GB Defense				GB Defense vs. Opponents			
Pers	Freq	Yds	DVOA	Run%	Pers	Freq	Yds	DVOA	Run%	Pers	Freq	Yds	DVOA	Pers	Freq	Yds	DVOA
11	55%	6.7	40.2%	33%	Base	25%	5.6	16.8%	52%	Base	22%	4.9	-8.1%	11	62%	5.7	2.7%
12	23%	6.4	23.0%	55%	Nickel	63%	6.9	36.5%	41%	Nickel	27%	5.3	-2.8%	12	16%	4.7	-12.7%
21	17%	6.1	15.5%	42%	Dime+	11%	7.0	28.9%	16%	Dime+	50%	6.0	5.0%	21	7%	5.8	-14.5%
13	2%	5.2	7.8%	50%	Goal Line	0%	1.0	117.8%	0%	Goal Line	0%	1.0	99.4%	13	4%	7.0	3.0%
22	2%	10.1	74.0%	27%						Big	1%	1.6	20.4%	22	3%	6.1	33.8%
20	1%	8.2	23.6%	80%										02	2%	7.4	16.4%

Strategic Tendencies

Run/Pass		Rk	Formation		Rk	Pass Rush		Rk	Secondary		Rk	Strategy		Rk
Runs, first half	39%	13	Form: Single Back	82%	15	Rush 3	7.0%	13	4 DB	22%	19	Play Action	36%	2
Runs, first down	50%	9	Form: Empty Back	9%	12	Rush 4	71.1%	7	5 DB	27%	32	Offensive Motion	54%	6
Runs, second-long	34%	5	Form: Multi Back	9%	18	Rush 5	20.0%	18	6+ DB	50%	1	Avg Box (Off)	6.62	12
Runs, power sit.	45%	31	Pers: 3+ WR	56%	27	Rush 6+	2.0%	31	Man Coverage	20%	30	Avg Box (Def)	6.28	28
Runs, behind 2H	23%	25	Pers: 2+ TE/6+ OL	28%	19	Edge Rusher Sacks	52.4%	15	CB by Sides	81%	10	Offensive Pace	32.83	32
Pass, ahead 2H	49%	17	Pers: 6+ OL	1%	22	Interior DL Sacks	22.0%	17	S/CB Cover Ratio	34%	7	Defensive Pace	31.31	29
Run-Pass Options	14%	2	Shotgun/Pistol	60%	22	Second Level Sacks	25.6%	13	DB Blitz	10%	25	Go for it on 4th	2.08	5

Matt LaFleur's second season saw an increase in use of both play-action (from 27% to 36%) and motion (from 44% to 54%). ✎ Green Bay led the league by throwing 28.3% of passes behind the line of scrimmage. That was five percentage points ahead of every other offense except Washington's. ✎ The Packers led the league in DVOA on passes down the middle of the field but also threw only 18% of passes down the middle, the lowest figure in the league. ✎ Green Bay had a league-best 13.6% DVOA when handing the ball off on second-and-long. Only three offenses had positive DVOA on these plays: Green Bay, Indianapolis, and Chicago. ✎ This was the fifth straight year the Packers ranked first or second in using dime defensive personnel. Green Bay was the only defense to use dime significantly more often than nickel. (New England also used dime more often but only by two plays.) ✎ After struggling on blitzes in 2019, the Packers improved substantially last season. Green Bay went from allowing 6.3% DVOA with four pass-rushers to -11.6% DVOA with five or more. They actually averaged a loss of 0.2 yards on big blitzes of six or more, although that's a tiny sample with just 11 plays.

Passing

Player	DYAR	DVOA	Plays	NtYds	Avg	YAC	C%	TD	Int
A.Rodgers	1649	33.7%	543	4104	7.6	6.0	71.3%	48	5

Rushing

Player	DYAR	DVOA	Plays	Yds	Avg	TD	Fum	Suc
A.Jones	254	20.3%	201	1104	5.5	9	1	59%
J.Williams*	60	2.8%	119	505	4.2	2	0	58%
AJ Dillon	56	21.6%	46	242	5.3	2	0	54%
A.Rodgers	24	2.9%	29	144	5.0	3	3	--
T.Ervin*	25	32.6%	13	67	5.2	0	0	62%

Receiving

Player	DYAR	DVOA	Plays	Ctch	Yds	Y/C	YAC	TD	C%
D.Adams	395	19.7%	149	115	1374	11.9	5.2	18	77%
M.Valdes-Scantling	112	8.5%	63	33	690	20.9	7.3	6	52%
A.Lazard	153	28.3%	46	33	451	13.7	5.9	3	72%
E.St. Brown	27	14.5%	13	7	117	16.7	8.4	1	54%
D.Shepherd*	-18	-46.7%	8	5	46	9.2	3.6	0	63%
M.Taylor	36	63.9%	6	5	66	13.2	9.4	1	83%
R.Tonyan	242	51.7%	59	52	586	11.3	4.3	11	88%
M.Lewis	13	3.0%	17	10	107	10.7	5.7	3	59%
J.Sternberger	7	0.5%	15	12	114	9.5	5.5	1	80%
A.Jones	30	-5.6%	63	47	355	7.6	7.8	2	75%
J.Williams*	58	14.0%	35	31	236	7.6	7.1	1	89%
T.Ervin*	31	17.0%	15	11	84	7.6	7.6	0	73%

Offensive Line

Player	Pos	Age	GS	Snaps	Pen	Sk	Pass	Run	Player	Pos	Age	GS	Snaps	Pen	Sk	Pass	Run
Elgton Jenkins	LG	26	16/16	1038	5	0.5	5	9	Corey Linsley*	C	30	13/13	735	0	0	1	4
Lucas Patrick	RG	28	16/15	940	3	4	10	5	Rick Wagner*	RT	32	16/9	611	0	0.5	6	4
Billy Turner	OT/RG	30	14/14	885	3	2.5	11	14	Jon Runyan	LG	24	16/0	160	0	0	0	0
David Bakhtiari	LT	30	12/12	758	4	1.5	4	0									

Year	Yards	ALY	Rk	Power	Rk	Stuff	Rk	2Lev	Rk	OpFld	Rk	BB Rt	Rk	Sacks	ASR	Rk	Press	Rk	BB Rt	Rk	Cont
2018	4.70	4.71	7	65%	21	18%	12	1.49	2	0.80	20	5.5%	10	53	7.9%	21	29.0%	16	9.3%	15	33
2019	4.47	4.63	5	54%	27	17%	6	1.28	9	0.69	20	10.8%	22	36	6.4%	10	29.2%	12	12.3%	10	44
2020	5.03	4.85	5	66%	19	14%	1	1.37	5	1.04	5	9.1%	14	21	5.0%	6	22.2%	8	6.5%	1	26

2020 ALY by direction:	Left End: 5.02 (5)	Left Tackle: 4.88 (8)	Mid/Guard: 4.87 (5)	Right Tackle: 4.96 (8)	Right End: 4.43 (18)

Center Corey Linsley followed his former teammate Bryan Bulaga to Los Angeles with a big-money free agent contract this offseason. Fortunately for Green Bay, they still have their best blocker, left tackle David Bakhtiari. Bakhtiari somehow improved on his 1.4% blown block rate from the previous half-decade with a 0.6% rate in 2020 and earned his second All-Pro distinction. The question will be if he can make it back from his early-January ACL tear in time for Week 1. ● The Packers can afford the losses of linemen such as Linsley and Bulaga because of their exceptional developmental track record. Linsley and Bakhtiari were fifth- and fourth-round draft picks, respectively. Next in that line are guards Jon Runyan and Lucas Patrick. The former was a sixth-rounder in 2020 and blew just one block on 146 rookie snaps. The latter was undrafted in 2017 and blew just 1.7% of his blocks in his first year as a regular starter in 2020. Both players could start in Week 1 if the Packers prefer Pro Bowl left guard Elgton Jenkins to shift to center or left tackle to replace Linsley or Bakhtiari. Offensive line coach Adam Stenavich has even suggested Ben Braden could have a chance to start; the undrafted veteran bounced on and off the Packers practice squad last season. ● The team responded to its recent free-agent losses with 2021 draft selections of center Josh Myers (Ohio State) and guards Royce Newman (Ole Miss) and Cole Van Lanen (Wisconsin) in the second, fourth, and sixth rounds. Assuming Eagles draft pick Landon Dickerson plays guard at the next level, Myers was the first center off the board. He would offer incredible value as the 62nd overall pick if he could start at center as a rookie. ● Billy Turner has underwhelmed with 3.5% and 3.2% blown block rates in two seasons since signing a four-year, $28-million contract with the Packers and was one of the major reasons the team lost to the Bucs in the NFC Championship Game, allowing two sacks to Jason Pierre-Paul. But it was a tall order for Turner to step in for Bakhtiari against the No. 6 pressure-rate defense. He should be more comfortable back at right tackle in 2021, and he seems locked into that starting job after he restructured his contract and the team released veteran tackle Rick Wagner for cap space.

Defensive Front

Defensive Line	Age	Pos	G	Snaps	Plays	Overall TmPct	Rk	Stop	Dfts	BTkl	Runs	vs. Run St%	Rk	RuYd	Rk	Pass Rush Sack	Hit	Hur	Dsrpt
Dean Lowry	27	DE	16	602	38	4.7%	56	24	4	0	31	58%	90	3.0	77	3.0	1	8	2
Kenny Clark	26	DT	13	597	42	6.4%	20	27	5	2	37	65%	77	2.9	72	2.0	4	18	2
Kingsley Keke	25	DE	15	416	23	3.0%	83	18	8	4	17	71%	57	2.8	60	4.0	4	9	2
Tyler Lancaster	27	DT	15	353	24	3.2%	--	15	0	2	21	67%	--	2.0	--	0.0	0	3	1
Montravius Adams*	26	DE	8	130	11	2.7%	--	9	2	1	11	82%	--	1.7	--	0.0	0	2	0

Edge Rushers	Age	Pos	G	Snaps	Plays	Overall TmPct	Rk	Stop	Dfts	BTkl	Runs	vs. Run St%	Rk	RuYd	Rk	Pass Rush Sack	Hit	Hur	Dsrpt
Za'Darius Smith	29	OLB	16	860	54	6.7%	16	46	22	7	37	78%	19	2.7	52	12.5	12	30	2
Preston Smith	29	OLB	16	817	45	5.6%	32	34	12	4	31	71%	52	2.9	62	4.0	6	11	4
Rashan Gary	24	OLB	15	455	36	4.8%	47	29	12	5	25	80%	13	2.7	50	5.0	5	19	1

Linebackers	Age	Pos	G	Snaps	Plays	TmPct	Rk	Stop	Dfts	BTkl	Runs	St%	Rk	RuYd	Rk	Sack	Hit	Hur	Tgts	Suc%	Rk	Yd/P	Rk	PD	Int
					Overall							**vs. Run**				**Pass Rush**				**vs. Pass**					
Christian Kirksey*	29	ILB	11	548	81	14.6%	26	30	11	11	46	37%	85	5.3	83	2.0	0	3	23	48%	47	6.3	38	4	2
Krys Barnes	23	ILB	13	423	78	11.9%	46	37	12	8	48	56%	41	3.4	21	1.0	0	3	16	38%	66	7.1	56	0	0
Kamal Martin	23	LB	10	189	23	4.6%	--	12	3	5	15	53%	--	3.7	--	1.0	1	4	1	0%	--	13.0	--	0	0
Ty Summers	26	ILB	16	176	28	3.5%	--	11	3	5	13	38%	--	4.1	--	0.0	0	0	16	38%	65	6.4	39	1	0
De'Vondre Campbell	28	ILB	16	883	102	12.1%	45	44	12	14	57	51%	62	4.5	65	2.0	0	4	41	49%	44	5.5	25	3	0

Year	Yards	ALY	Rk	Power	Rk	Stuff	Rk	2Lev	Rk	OpFld	Rk	BB Rt	Rk	Sacks	ASR	Rk	Press	Rk	BB Rt	Rk
2018	4.32	4.78	27	63%	10	15%	29	1.15	9	0.62	7	8.6%	15	44	7.7%	10	30.8%	14	8.1%	24
2019	4.87	4.96	31	71%	27	13%	31	1.32	27	0.84	22	12.4%	19	41	7.5%	12	34.8%	4	15.8%	9
2020	4.39	4.61	24	70%	24	13%	25	1.10	8	0.68	14	10.5%	23	41	7.5%	10	22.8%	25	13.7%	14

2020 ALY by direction:	Left End: 5.10 (25)	Left Tackle: 4.49 (19)	Mid/Guard: 4.63 (22)	Right Tackle: 4.33 (17)	Right End: 4.65 (17)

The Smith (not) brothers Za'Darius and Preston suffered relative slumps in their sophomore seasons with the Packers, declining from 66 and 35 hurries in 2019 to just 30 and 11 last year. Of course, Za'Darius' 2020 total still landed him in the top 20 in football, and he had 12.5 sacks and continued to excel in run defense. But don't be fooled by the team's streak of top-12 finishes in adjusted sack rate. The Packers fell from fourth (34.8%) to 25th (22.8%) in defensive pressure rate and would have a dramatically worse pass defense if they had a lesser secondary. ● Preston Smith has slimmed down this offseason and no doubt hopes improved conditioning will spur a rebound and the recovery of a pay cut he accepted to return to the team. He has $4.4 million in incentives tied to his 2021 sack production. But Preston will have to fend off 2019 first-rounder Rashan Gary, who bested him with 19 hurries as a part-time player last year. ● The Packers have options in their efforts to rush the passer, but their run defense puts it all on tackle Kenny Clark's broad shoulders. Clark suffered a Week 1 groin injury last year, and while he stayed on the field for 597 defensive snaps, his run stop rate fell from 83% and 81% in 2018 and 2019 to 65% in 2020. He's still just 25 years old, so expect better production with better health in 2021. And keep an eye on fifth-round rookie tackle Tedarrell Slaton from Florida to see if the Packers finally found Clark a running mate. Slaton is strong with a high motor but was very inconsistent in Gainesville. ● Notorious non-spenders, the Packers eschewed an expensive replacement for departing free agent Christian Kirksey at inside linebacker. They could rely on any number of players in 2021, starting with veteran June addition De'Vondre Campbell, a five-year starter in Atlanta and Arizona. They also have a couple of second-year linebackers (fifth-rounder Kamal Martin and undrafted Krys Barnes) as well as a sixth-round rookie (Boston College's Isaiah McDuffie). Barnes is the least pedigreed of the trio but surprised in his rookie year with a 56% run-stop rate over 423 defensive snaps and is likely the starter opposite Campbell, at least when the team isn't in its preferred dime defensive alignments.

Defensive Secondary

Secondary	Age	Pos	G	Snaps	Plays	TmPct	Rk	Stop	Dfts	BTkl	Runs	St%	Rk	RuYd	Rk	Tgts	Tgt%	Rk	aDOT	Suc%	Rk	Yd/P	Rk	PD	Int
					Overall							**vs. Run**						**vs. Pass**							
Adrian Amos	28	FS	16	1010	92	11.4%	30	36	12	10	40	40%	31	6.5	34	33	8.5%	35	10.5	55%	20	6.2	13	9	2
Jaire Alexander	24	CB	15	902	64	8.5%	45	32	16	4	11	45%	34	10.8	75	70	20.2%	37	11.4	64%	3	4.5	2	13	1
Darnell Savage	24	SS	15	877	87	11.5%	28	31	16	10	39	33%	41	5.9	27	21	6.2%	52	17.3	48%	42	11.0	65	12	4
Chandon Sullivan	25	CB	16	731	46	5.7%	79	23	8	6	16	63%	7	3.4	4	50	17.8%	58	8.3	56%	18	6.0	8	6	1
Kevin King	26	CB	11	665	62	11.2%	10	15	3	12	22	23%	71	8.9	68	41	16.0%	69	11.5	44%	64	8.8	63	5	0
Will Redmond	28	SS	13	342	25	3.8%	--	9	3	9	7	29%	--	6.6	--	18	13.7%	--	5.7	44%	--	8.4	--	1	0
Josh Jackson	25	CB	12	332	26	4.3%	--	8	5	6	9	33%	--	10.7	--	25	19.6%	--	10.8	40%	--	7.0	--	2	0
Raven Greene*	26	FS	10	326	46	9.1%	58	21	13	6	10	70%	2	4.5	7	29	23.1%	1	7.1	31%	69	7.4	29	5	1

Year	Pass D Rank	vs. #1 WR	Rk	vs. #2 WR	Rk	vs. Other WR	Rk	WR Wide	Rk	WR Slot	Rk	vs. TE	Rk	vs. RB	Rk
2018	28	9.0%	22	14.9%	25	-4.1%	13	4.1%	22	13.6%	25	20.8%	27	25.1%	32
2019	9	1.4%	15	-29.7%	3	-12.8%	9	-12.6%	12	-13.0%	6	9.8%	26	-17.0%	4
2020	15	-11.1%	10	10.6%	24	-20.0%	6	-2.4%	15	-8.4%	7	-12.0%	8	15.3%	27

Cornerback Kevin King provided the lasting memory of the 2020 Packers season when he pulled on Tyler Johnson's jersey and was flagged for interference, netting the Bucs a new first down so they could kneel and advance to the Super Bowl. Many corners were overmatched against that offense, but King underwhelmed all season falling outside the top 60 in both coverage success rate and yards allowed per target. He's back on a one-year deal, but it's not a coincidence the Packers drafted cornerback Eric Stokes in the first round. Nicknamed "Dirty Red" because of his hair color, Stokes is big (6-foot-1) and fast and can play both man and zone. But he really struggled against the run at Georgia. ❦ The Packers took a break from their run of Round 1 and 2 defensive back picks to select Jordan Love in 2020. But since 2017, they've invested early in King, Josh Jones, Jaire Alexander, Josh Jackson, Darnell Savage, and now Stokes. Alexander and Savage make compelling cases to be the best corner and best safety in the league under 25 years old. Alexander was among the top three corners in both success rate and yards allowed per target, and according to Next Gen Stats, he led the league with a 42.3% tight-window rate. And while Savage had more pedestrian coverage rates in 2020, he was majorly disruptive with four interceptions and 12 defensed passes, both top-five totals among safeties. ❦ Adrian Amos rounds out the team's big three defensive backs. The Bears import rebounded from a down first season with the Packers to produce top-20 success and yards per target rates like he had in 2018. He is the perfect complement for a disrupter and run-stopper like Savage. ❦ Slot corner Chandon Sullivan more than doubled his previous career high with 729 defensive snaps in his third season and acquitted himself nicely with 6.0 yards allowed per target. He should continue to play frequently with the Packers' heavy reliance on dime, but he may face some long-term competition from fifth-round Appalachian State product Shemar Jean-Charles, a productive outside college corner whose 5-foot-10, 184-pound stature may force him into the slot at the next level.

Special Teams

Year	DVOA	Rank	FG/XP	Rank	Net Kick	Rank	Kick Ret	Rank	Net Punt	Rank	Punt Ret	Rank	Hidden	Rank
2018	-4.1%	29	-0.1	18	-4.5	28	-4.5	29	-2.1	19	-9.2	32	1.1	13
2019	0.1%	18	6.9	7	-0.4	19	-1.2	17	0.2	18	-4.8	28	-6.1	26
2020	-2.7%	25	8.8	5	-2.7	22	-4.6	28	-11.8	29	-3.3	24	-3.8	20

Mason Crosby has kicked for the Packers for 14 seasons, but 2020 was his first perfect season for making field goals. It helps that he only attempted 16 of them. With Aaron Rodgers playing like an MVP, the Packers gave Crosby many more extra-point opportunities—he led the league in both point-after attempts (63) and makes (59). ❦ Punter JK Scott improved his gross yards per punt from 44.7 and 44.0 yards his first two seasons to 45.5 yards last year, but his teammates gave away that advantage with the second-worst punt coverage in football. ❦ The Packers never found a satisfactory answer for their own returns. They tried six players at either punt and kick returner, and none of them had positive return value. ❦ Third-round rookie receiver Amari Rodgers may take the first crack at the former job this season. He returned 68 punts in four seasons at Clemson and averaged 7.8 yards per return. He also returned a punt for a touchdown, something the Packers haven't done since 2014 but their opponents did twice in 2020. ❦ The Packers don't have a clear solution at kick returner. Safety Christian Uphoff, an undrafted free agent out of Illinois State, was an All-Missouri Valley Football Conference honorable mention as a kick returner in 2018. ❦ Despite a decline from 77 punts in 2019 to 47 last year, Oren Burks and Ty Summers were two of just 23 players with 10 or more special teams tackles. That utility could be critical for their job security as unheralded linebackers Krys Barnes and Kamal Martin have passed them on the defensive depth chart.

Houston Texans

2020 Record: 4-12	**Total DVOA:** -12.6% (16)	**2021 Mean Projection:** 6.7 wins	**On the Clock (0-5):** 35%
Pythagorean Wins: 6.1 (25)	**Offense:** 2.7% (13)	**Postseason Odds:** 21.0%	**Mediocrity (6-8):** 41%
Snap-Weighted Age: 26.5 (15)	**Defense:** 14.3% (30)	**Super Bowl Odds:** 0.9%	**Playoff Contender (9-11):** 19%
Average Opponent: -0.1% (18)	**Special Teams:** -1% (21)	**Proj. Avg. Opponent:** -2.3% (28)	**Super Bowl Contender (12+):** 4%

2020: Bill O'Brien's Texans finally go up in flames.

2021: This is perhaps the most depressing franchise in the Big 4 sports.

The most important thing to know about 21st-century America is how late-stage capitalism works from a sales perspective. Instead of a marketplace of ideas where theories will naturally compete, many people now make a living by getting data on specific customers, targeting them directly, then offering ideas to them. Sometimes that's fairly innocent—buy our book, you love football and want in-depth knowledge—and more often it leads to a grifter class of Nigerian 401 scam-level comforting ideas masquerading as solutions. The phone calls you get about your extended warranty expiring or wanting to buy your house, the idea that bleach could cure COVID, the fact that you are pre-approved for a loan from a bank or payday operation for practically anything at onerous terms of repayment. We've long ago given up on the people who monitor fraud as a country—the phrase "red tape" killed them—and instead we simply live surrounded by it and judge those who fall for it.

Often, the NFL is a respite from that. Teams have incentives to win and the people in front offices are generally quite smart. The football cocoon, as Establish The Run's Evan Silva has called it, protects those within it and gives short shrift to outsiders. Even outsiders with good ideas! It took years and an Eagles championship before fourth-down goes started to gain more widespread acceptance.

Enter Jack Easterby, a man whose religious connection with Texans acting owner and CEO Cal McNair has put this franchise to the torch. Nobody in an NFL front office has turned more into less over the last two seasons. And nobody is as unimpeachably locked into his spot via the oldest trick of the 21st century: all you have to do is fool one person with power.

The 2020 Texans played less of a season and more of a dramatic opera. The curtain finally fell for Bill O'Brien after an 0-4 start, one where behind-the-scenes tensions reportedly led to shouting matches on the practice field between O'Brien and defensive coordinator Anthony Weaver as well as star end J.J. Watt. The epitaph for O'Brien doesn't make him look good, but it's not extremely complex. O'Brien was given the keys to several terrific players by Texans general manager Rick Smith and put in a division with two franchises struggling to overcome Jake Locker and Blaine Gabbert eras. He wasn't a bad X's and O's coach in every game, but he was lazy enough in many of them to cost his team. Thankfully, winning one of the weakest divisions in the NFL took the spotlight off of that. When the Texans hired Easterby, O'Brien was soon convinced to fire general manager

Brian Gaine, and the Texans' awkwardly failed pursuit of Nick Caserio made O'Brien the general manager even though he repeatedly referred to "decisions we make as a group."

And, well, the group was completely over their heads at making player personnel decisions. Like, historically out of their depth! In just two offseasons the team shepherded in one of the worst trades in NFL history by trading DeAndre Hopkins for David Johnson and a second-round pick, got rid of Jadeveon Clowney at the nadir of his worth because they didn't understand the NFL's trade value cycles, and overpaid for Laremy Tunsil in a preposterous enough way that even Tunsil is on record as saying "I'd trade me for that." Those are only the hits. They traded a third-round pick for Duke Johnson, then cut him this offseason. They traded the Clowney third-round pick for Gareon Conley, who never recovered from injury and played zero snaps in 2020. They signed Whitney Mercilus and Randall Cobb to contracts that continue to haunt their salary cap to this day with no understanding why those players were likely to regress or give up their starting roles to younger players with some upside. The catalogue of destruction that the O'Brien/Easterby power couple created with this roster reads like an oral history of Spinal Tap drummers. They turned what had been a 2017/2018 core of six or seven franchise-level stars into a team that managed to lose 12 games despite Deshaun Watson's breakout season. The defense forced only nine turnovers, the fewest of any team since 2002 except for the 2018 49ers. The running game finished dead-last in DVOA and David Johnson looked exactly as plodding and slow to process as he did when the Cardinals benched him in 2019. Still, Watson shined.

There are only five quarterbacks in the history of Football Outsiders stats to finish with 1,200 or more DYAR and have a losing record, and Watson is the only one of those to not finish at least 6-10 (Table 1). What he did last year was transcendent stuff, the kind of thing that would have him being talked about behind Patrick Mahomes as building block 1A of the NFL if not for, you know, the troubling sexual assault allegations from massage therapists that have cascaded into a number of lawsuits that threaten his career.

With Watson's breakthrough, along with the Texans' solid DVOA and 2-8 record in one-score games, there would have been reason to be encouraged about the 2021 Texans if the offseason had gone a certain way. The Texans were going to

2021 Texans Schedule

Week	Opp.	Week	Opp.	Week	Opp.
1	JAX	7	at ARI	13	IND
2	at CLE	8	LAR	14	SEA
3	CAR (Thu.)	9	at MIA	15	at JAX
4	at BUF	10	BYE	16	LAC
5	NE	11	at TEN	17	at SF
6	at IND	12	NYJ	18	TEN

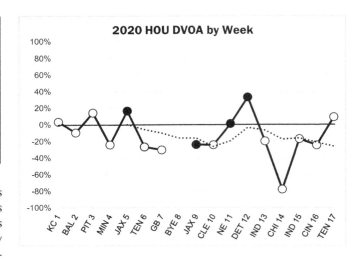

have some salary-cap issues with the reduced cap regardless of who took over, but putting Watson into an offense that was proven to generate open receivers à la Eric Bienemy's Chiefs or Joe Brady's Panthers would have produced an extremely promising unit. The Texans interviewed both of those coaches! A better-coached defense—preferably one that didn't switch from 3-4 to 4-3 in the middle of the season under an interim coach—meant that there was plenty of space to forecast upside. Additionally, the Easterby situation had started to become a very public problem as *Sports Illustrated* came out with two damning articles about his involvement with the team that sourced several people in the organization. Among the most concerning indictments made in the article were that Easterby had players followed during the 2020 season, that he spear-headed the Hopkins trade, that he forbade team employees from wearing sunglasses because he wanted to look them in the eyes, and that 85% to 90% of team employees did not trust Easterby. The initial article compared Easterby to the *Game of Thrones* character Littlefinger, a guy who knew how to play politics and left several corpses in his wake. It seemed very likely at the time that any new power players would simply flush Easterby from the equation.

Last year's *Football Outsiders Almanac* forecasted a committee search for a head coach and general manager if O'Brien were ever deposed, and indeed, that is what happened. What we did not predict was that Easterby, who survived the O'Brien purge with an interim tag, would manipulate the levers of power to stay. The way it is told by NFL.com's Lance Zierlein, a Houston institution, is that the Texans internally had settled on Steelers executive Omar Khan to be their next general manager, but when Easterby caught wind of

Table 1. Quarterbacks with 1,200 or More Passing DYAR and a Losing Record, 1983-2020

Player	Team	Year	Record	Passing DYAR
Deshaun Watson	HOU	2020	4-12	1,234
Matt Ryan	ATL	2018	7-9	1,232
Drew Brees	NO	2016	7-9	1,599
Drew Brees	NO	2014	7-9	1,225
Drew Brees	NO	2012	7-9	1,441
Trent Green	KC	2004	7-9	1,418
Jeff Garcia	SF	2000	6-10	1,642

this and the fact that Khan would likely not need Easterby's services, he stopped at McNair's house and held a prayer session about the job before steering McNair on a secret flight to New England to snag Caserio. (For reals, this time!) Caserio was able to barter a reported six-year, $36-million contract even though he had no other team actively bidding for him, and even though the search firm the Texans used didn't have him as a candidate. The move—retaining Easterby more than anything, as Watson had spoken about how the team needed new culture at his season-ending presser—led to Watson going AWOL on the Texans and requesting a trade. The Texans responded by pretending that this never happened.

In a divisive 42-minute session with the media, McNair and Caserio were both confronted by a press corps that couldn't begin to understand why either of them valued Easterby and saw McNair come up with a grand defense of "he took a lot of heat for being interim general manager." It also saw McNair launch an incredibly tone-deaf description of what the Texans are doing as "building a wall." A few weeks later, the Texans would introduce neither Brady nor Bienemy (who reportedly wanted some personnel control) but instead brought out David Culley, the Ravens wideouts coach whom nobody else in the NFL had even interviewed for a head coaching position.

Anybody with the power to flee from this situation then did so. Watt, the best player in franchise history, asked for and was granted his release, and received $23 million in guarantees from Arizona. Will Fuller, who had finally managed a fully healthy season before missing the last five games because of a PED suspension, signed with the Dolphins. Benardrick McKinney was traded to the Dolphins for Shaq Lawson to replace Watt. Former Texans wideout Andre Johnson, who worked with the team in a front office role while Easterby was in the building, has publicly trashed the organization for the decision to keep him and alienate Watson.

It's hard to talk about what has happened in Houston without referring to the power dynamics, and that is what this off-season was for the Texans. The Texans did not hire a head coach who nobody else had even interviewed on accident. They had narrowed it down to Culley and Leslie Frazier, who had already failed a stint as Vikings head coach and who was nobody's hot candidate. Everybody in the building now owes their jobs to Easterby and marches to the tune of his fife. The Texans likewise turned over the roster to an extent that defies reality, signing 37 free agents before the draft alone. The Texans didn't spend more than $4.3 million guaranteed on any of them, and that was on retaining David Johnson in the first sign that, spiritually, this may be Caserio's roster, but he's an underling. (When asked about the re-signing in a local press interview, Caserio referred to Johnson as someone who has "had production at points," which barely even qualifies as praise.) Easterby's no dummy and has likely ruminated on who is and isn't loyal to him. The fact that this team signed as many veteran free agents as they did, and then continued to seed the roster with Jeff Driskels and Rex Burkheads as we got deeper towards our publishing deadline, was no accident. More than anything else, they needed to make sure that there were players in place that believed in the fact that this wasn't a disaster, and nothing speaks louder than money and a crack at the roster for those desperate to stay in the league.

Hanging over the future of the franchise right now is the Watson "situation," one that the Texans steadfastly refuse to talk about any time it is mentioned. Caserio has brought that charming "we don't talk about anything" schtick from New England to the point where even in-house radio is left talking about Sam Houston State's FBS football championships or the 1996 NBA Draft as OTAs are happening so as not to "divulge state secrets." Watson stands accused of some heinous things and, until those are cleared up via settlement and NFL punishment or an actual verdict at a deposition currently scheduled for next February, it's hard for him to play and/or the Texans to trade him. He hasn't shown up for OTAs, and outside of reporting to toll a contract or to save some money in the event that he's suspended by the NFL, nobody believes that Watson will show up at all this year. All freezing Watson's status in carbonite does is further shine a light on the disaster of the roster without him.

Defensive coordinator Lovie Smith is the closest thing this team has to a reason for optimism. He's in a role as a pure defensive mind for the first time since 2003, which should lighten his plate and maybe get him deeper into the disguises and change-ups that his recent schemes have been lacking. Smith has a track record of great defenses in the NFL but was already going south in that area with Tampa Bay in the mid-2010s. His Illinois teams, it's true, didn't have much talent relative to the rest of the Big Ten. They also lacked any ability stop spread attacks to save their lives. There can be some modest belief that Lovie, without the responsibility of captaining the whole ship, can make improvements on the turnoverless 2020 defense, but his public comments about "the quarterback running more in college" were kind of a tell about where he's at. Meanwhile, Tim Kelly was kept on at offensive coordinator after doing almost nothing to help Watson out last season, in a role that he only had in the first place because he was an O'Brien lackey. Culley has a lot of character and a lot of optimism, but he either doesn't want to talk strategy because of the Caserio Veil or just flat-out isn't interested in discussing it beyond turnovers and vague generalities.

Listen, the Texans are going to play 17 games of football this year. That's a threat. We have a projection system that says so. They won't be favored in any of them in Vegas, even against a Jaguars team that won one game last season. Peter King and other well-sourced football minds have been all but saying the Texans are an expansion team. Frankly, it's hard to believe any of these games matter in a grander sense. Not only does this team have little in the way of young talent, but they barely are even pretending to acquire or develop it. They signed a three-player UDFA class to pair with a five-player draft headlined by Stanford quarterback Davis Mills. They got fewer snaps from their 2020 rookies than any team in the NFL. They preach competition and how the best player will play no matter what, but this team looks like a Madden franchise free-agency pool that plays games.

Now, was this ever likely to be a quick-fix situation given where the team ended 2020? Probably not. But new management could have inspired the team's best players to want to stay, and as sullied as Watson's name is right now, he was a superstar quarterback in 2020 and is signed to a long-term contract. If you hit on a head coach with 2020 Watson, you have a strong enough core to reload.

What this management team has done instead to a fan base that has watched them build the Springfield Monorail for two seasons and leave Lyle Lanley with major power, is ask them to believe in the people in charge. The direct quote from McNair during Caserio's introductory press conference was: "We believe you can't go wrong by doing what's right and ask our fans to trust that we know what's right." That's a non-starter based on any logical reading of how this has gone, but this team is post-logic.

The Texans may or may not eventually get a lot of picks for Watson. Caserio may hit on some of them given his pedigree. But we're talking about rookies playing for this particular brand of management. If the team can't create a major paradigm shift in how they are viewed league-wide, and can only win players with money, they are two years away from being two years away. Even if some of these veteran free agents work out, they're not signed to long-term contracts. If Desmond King has a great season as a Texan, he's about to get a chance to play somewhere where he can actually win or the Texans are going to have to pay him a ton of money.

At the center of all of this is a team that feels entitled to more of your respect than you're giving. A team that feels like having McNair show up places and donate money to charity is going to change the fact that they are selling a football product that conceptually won't exist for some time. It's not just that they're bad, it's that they've hit that particular point on the continuum where persecution complexes and "drowning out the noise" means that they are only digging in further on how good they think they are. The team handles it in a really haphazard way that suggests they truly don't engage with anything outside of the building. There's motivational wall signage displayed during one of their videos that merely says "Get Better." Easterby's stated job—everyone's very careful to say he doesn't have final say in personnel, though his opinion obviously matters—is to build this team's culture. "Get Better" is a testament to how good he is at that job, as are the *Sports Illustrated* reports about Easterby asking players to think about "playing ball with Ray-

Ray and Ki-Ki and them." He has never played, so he can't really speak from knowing; he has never had anywhere near this amount of power before; and he's as inspiring as a soggy Eggo to anybody not in the McNair family. McNair inadvertently revealed in one of these charity videos that donating a jersey to a firehouse was done because "One of their chief operators sent us an email." The PR jumps off the screen. Every bit of the making of the sausage that we are allowed to see paints this as a team that is stuffing casings with Play-Doh.

The Texans are a distressed asset, kept afloat because owning a football team is a license to print money and to be as dense as you want. They are Blockbuster tweeting about how bad Netflix is on the corporate account. It's hard to give any-

one a reason to be optimistic that Texans football will be more than this plus some highly drafted players fighting against the tide in the near future. McNair has succumbed to the whims of an unemployable grifter and they just live in that magical world of the out-of-touch rich now, where all they can see is themselves reflected in the best possible light. Both on and off the field, the only thing this team is building is a fantasy world where the socially awkward McNair is an affable gadabout who helps the whole city of Houston run with his philanthropy—preferably one where nobody asks him about how the team is actually doing.

Rivers McCown

2020 Texans Stats by Week

Wk	vs.	W-L	PF	PA	YDF	YDA	TO	Total	Off	Def	ST
1	at KC	L	20	34	360	369	-1	3.4%	11.2%	3.5%	-4.3%
2	BAL	L	16	33	304	407	-2	-9.7%	-10.3%	2.9%	3.5%
3	at PIT	L	21	28	260	387	-1	14.2%	26.8%	12.8%	0.1%
4	MIN	L	23	31	386	410	-1	-24.1%	-3.3%	21.0%	0.2%
5	JAX	W	30	14	486	364	0	16.5%	7.8%	-8.6%	0.1%
6	at TEN	L	36	42	412	607	2	-26.7%	20.4%	43.4%	-3.8%
7	GB	L	20	35	365	379	-1	-30.4%	-15.1%	8.0%	-7.2%
8	BYE										
9	at JAX	W	27	25	374	403	0	-24.0%	-7.7%	18.0%	1.7%
10	at CLE	L	7	10	243	356	0	-24.2%	-23.0%	2.7%	1.4%
11	NE	W	27	20	399	435	0	1.1%	23.5%	25.4%	3.0%
12	at DET	W	41	25	384	388	2	33.1%	23.0%	-15.3%	-5.1%
13	IND	L	20	26	398	371	-2	-19.8%	-3.1%	10.7%	-5.9%
14	at CHI	L	7	36	263	410	-2	-77.9%	-29.3%	45.9%	-2.7%
15	at IND	L	20	27	425	350	-2	-17.1%	2.4%	19.3%	-0.2%
16	CIN	L	31	37	488	540	-1	-24.6%	22.6%	47.0%	-0.2%
17	TEN	L	38	41	457	492	0	9.2%	10.4%	4.1%	3.0%

Trends and Splits

	Offense	Rank	Defense	Rank
Total DVOA	2.7%	13	14.3%	30
Unadjusted VOA	4.8%	13	14.9%	30
Weighted Trend	2.5%	12	17.0%	31
Variance	3.1%	3	3.4%	6
Average Opponent	3.2%	31	2.8%	9
Passing	24.1%	8	25.2%	29
Rushing	-28.0%	32	1.6%	29
First Down	7.5%	11	16.2%	30
Second Down	4.9%	13	10.5%	26
Third Down	-9.3%	19	16.2%	27
First Half	4.0%	13	17.9%	30
Second Half	1.4%	14	10.7%	25
Red Zone	-12.7%	22	14.5%	29
Late and Close	-7.5%	19	18.1%	30

Five-Year Performance

Year	W-L	Pyth W	Est W	PF	PA	TO	Total	Rk	Off	Rk	Def	Rk	ST	Rk	Off AGL	Rk	Def AGL	Rk	Off Age	Rk	Def Age	Rk	ST Age	Rk
2016	9-7	6.5	5.1	279	328	-7	-19.5%	28	-21.1%	30	-8.0%	8	-6.5%	31	50.7	24	51.4	23	25.7	30	26.5	17	26.2	12
2017	4-12	5.5	5.4	338	436	-12	-18.0%	26	-10.1%	24	3.4%	19	-4.5%	26	60.7	27	45.6	25	26.1	30	26.0	18	26.1	8
2018	11-5	10.3	9.5	402	316	+13	10.4%	11	-2.8%	19	-9.7%	5	3.5%	5	42.5	21	42.8	24	25.5	32	26.7	9	25.7	20
2019	10-6	7.8	7.7	378	385	0	-2.2%	16	0.6%	17	5.6%	22	2.9%	5	50.5	23	27.7	12	26.3	21	26.6	11	26.0	11
2020	4-12	6.1	5.2	384	464	-9	-12.6%	24	2.7%	13	14.3%	30	-1.0%	21	15.5	3	42.7	17	26.9	12	26.3	14	26.1	15

2020 Performance Based on Most Common Personnel Groups

HOU Offense					HOU Offense vs. Opponents					HOU Defense				HOU Defense vs. Opponents			
Pers	Freq	Yds	DVOA	Run%	Pers	Freq	Yds	DVOA	Run%	Pers	Freq	Yds	DVOA	Pers	Freq	Yds	DVOA
11	62%	6.8	9.5%	23%	Base	14%	5.8	8.3%	50%	Base	36%	5.8	2.7%	11	54%	6.8	24.2%
12	29%	6.2	2.9%	40%	Nickel	63%	6.8	6.9%	31%	Nickel	42%	6.7	19.6%	12	19%	6.3	2.4%
21	2%	6.9	9.8%	43%	Dime+	23%	6.3	7.4%	11%	Dime+	21%	6.9	28.4%	21	10%	6.0	-0.3%
10	2%	5.8	-67.8%	5%	Goal Line	0%	1.0	31.5%	100%	Goal Line	1%	4.4	15.4%	13	6%	5.5	2.7%
612	2%	5.1	20.8%	100%						Big	0%	12.4	-63.3%	22	4%	4.8	-4.6%

Strategic Tendencies

Run/Pass		Rk	Formation		Rk	Pass Rush		Rk	Secondary		Rk	Strategy		Rk
Runs, first half	29%	31	Form: Single Back	76%	25	Rush 3	12.0%	7	4 DB	36%	5	Play Action	22%	29
Runs, first down	35%	32	Form: Empty Back	14%	4	Rush 4	55.6%	30	5 DB	42%	29	Offensive Motion	38%	25
Runs, second-long	21%	26	Form: Multi Back	10%	15	Rush 5	27.1%	6	6+ DB	21%	10	Avg Box (Off)	6.51	17
Runs, power sit.	54%	25	Pers: 3+ WR	66%	16	Rush 6+	5.3%	15	Man Coverage	34%	14	Avg Box (Def)	6.91	1
Runs, behind 2H	27%	19	Pers: 2+ TE/6+ OL	31%	15	Edge Rusher Sacks	51.5%	16	CB by Sides	72%	20	Offensive Pace	30.27	15
Pass, ahead 2H	64%	1	Pers: 6+ OL	2%	15	Interior DL Sacks	12.1%	31	S/CB Cover Ratio	39%	2	Defensive Pace	31.81	32
Run-Pass Options	11%	6	Shotgun/Pistol	83%	3	Second Level Sacks	36.4%	3	DB Blitz	18%	5	Go for it on 4th	1.57	15

Houston's abysmal running game made no sense. First of all, the Texans were actually pretty good when running against a large box count. Against eight or men in the box, Houston averaged a league-high 5.2 yards per carry and finished second at 14.9% DVOA. Against seven or fewer men in the box, Houston averaged 3.6 yards per carry with a ridiculously bad -41.7% DVOA. Further confusing things, the best team in the league on RPOs was… the Houston Texans? Yes, the Texans averaged 6.6 yards on RPO plays, the highest figure in the league among teams that used RPOs at least 5% of the time. Those RPOs were a lot better when they turned out to be passes: 8.7 yards per attempt on RPO passes and 4.4 yards per carry on RPO runs. Still, that split is very strange when combined with the box stats, since the quarterback will normally hand off the ball on an RPO when there's a light box count. After two years at the bottom of the league running just a handful of running back screens, the Texans suddenly became screen fiends in 2020. They ran 29 running back screens, tied for third in the league, and had an awesome 63.6% DVOA with 9.3 yards per pass on these plays. One way around the bad running game was to just go empty backfield, and in fact Houston's 51.2% DVOA and 8.6 yards per play were the highest figures of the 11 teams that went empty backfield on at least 10% of plays. The Texans were once again killed by short middle passes, ranking 31st in defensive DVOA against these passes after ranking 32nd in 2019. Last year, Houston also ranked 31st in DVOA against deep middle passes (16 or more air yards). Houston was dead-last with just an 18% pressure rate when sending the standard four pass-rushers. The listed Aggressiveness Index combines Bill O'Brien (1.86) and Romeo Crennel (1.54).

Passing

Player	DYAR	DVOA	Plays	NtYds	Avg	YAC	C%	TD	Int
D.Watson	1234	20.2%	591	4530	7.7	5.2	70.5%	33	7
J.Driskel	-36	-18.9%	75	334	4.5	3.7	54.7%	3	2
T.Taylor	20	-0.7%	32	207	6.5	5.0	53.3%	0	0

Rushing

Player	DYAR	DVOA	Plays	Yds	Avg	TD	Fum	Suc
Da.Johnson	71	2.2%	147	691	4.7	6	0	46%
D.Watson	-12	-14.9%	80	439	5.5	3	4	--
Du.Johnson*	-117	-45.1%	77	235	3.1	1	2	43%
B.Howell	27	34.7%	16	64	4.0	0	0	56%
C.J.Prosise	-49	-120.1%	10	19	1.9	0	1	30%
P.Lindsay	-70	-24.2%	118	508	4.3	1	0	40%
M.Ingram	5	-6.8%	71	299	4.2	2	0	51%
R.Burkhead	60	12.9%	67	274	4.1	3	0	55%
J.Driskel	14	24.8%	6	28	4.7	0	0	--
T.Taylor	-14	-61.4%	5	8	1.6	0	0	--
A.Erickson	-15	-85.4%	5	7	1.4	0	1	--

Receiving

Player	DYAR	DVOA	Plays	Ctch	Yds	Y/C	YAC	TD	C%
B.Cooks	207	8.9%	119	81	1143	14.1	4.2	6	68%
W.Fuller*	326	41.2%	75	53	879	16.6	5.5	8	71%
R.Cobb	107	15.8%	48	38	441	11.6	4.5	3	79%
K.Coutee	85	14.6%	40	33	400	12.1	4.5	3	83%
C.Hansen*	49	12.5%	24	17	236	13.9	2.3	1	71%
K.Stills*	35	10.8%	19	11	144	13.1	1.5	1	58%
S.Mitchell*	6	-2.7%	8	5	60	12.0	2.0	0	63%
C.Conley	18	-9.0%	63	40	471	11.8	4.5	2	63%
A.Erickson	6	-7.9%	17	12	139	11.6	5.6	0	71%
J.Akins	65	12.4%	49	37	403	10.9	4.6	1	76%
D.Fells*	90	38.6%	28	21	312	14.9	8.4	4	75%
P.Brown	49	37.4%	16	14	163	11.6	5.4	2	88%
K.Warring	-14	-36.5%	7	3	35	11.7	2.7	0	43%
R.Izzo	8	-1.8%	20	13	199	15.3	5.2	0	65%
Da.Johnson	39	0.1%	46	33	314	9.5	7.1	2	72%
Du.Johnson*	30	1.4%	35	28	249	8.9	7.9	1	80%
R.Burkhead	42	8.4%	33	25	192	7.7	8.0	3	76%
P.Lindsay	-38	-62.3%	14	7	28	4.0	5.6	0	50%
M.Ingram	1	-10.9%	8	6	50	8.3	8.2	0	75%

Offensive Line

Player	Pos	Age	GS	Snaps	Pen	Sk	Pass	Run	Player	Pos	Age	GS	Snaps	Pen	Sk	Pass	Run
Nick Martin*	C	28	16/16	979	4	0	9	10	Senio Kelemete*	LG	31	14/5	366	2	2	10	2
Zach Fulton*	RG	30	16/16	952	3	6.5	19	2	Roderick Johnson	LT	26	12/3	245	2	0.5	6	1
Laremy Tunsil	LT	27	14/14	816	7	1	15	1	Brent Qvale*	LG	30	14/3	189	1	0	3	2
Tytus Howard	RT	25	14/14	810	9	1.5	19	6	Geron Christian	LT	25	6/6	399	1	4.5	9	1
Max Scharping	LG	25	15/8	454	2	2	7	5	Cole Toner	RG	27	10/3	294	0	0	4	1

Year	Yards	ALY	Rk	Power	Rk	Stuff	Rk	2Lev	Rk	OpFld	Rk	BB Rt	Rk	Sacks	ASR	Rk	Press	Rk	BB Rt	Rk	Cont
2018	4.01	3.93	27	63%	23	20%	21	1.09	26	0.83	17	5.7%	11	62	11.6%	32	38.5%	32	12.4%	27	23
2019	4.52	4.13	21	81%	1	18%	11	1.26	12	0.93	12	14.0%	29	49	8.4%	27	34.2%	28	13.1%	15	21
2020	4.04	4.02	27	67%	14	15%	8	0.94	32	0.68	18	10.7%	19	50	9.5%	32	30.0%	26	14.2%	24	26

2020 ALY by direction:	Left End: 3.50 (29)	Left Tackle: 4.89 (7)	Mid/Guard: 4.16 (24)	Right Tackle: 2.12 (32)	Right End: 5.55 (6)

The good news is that Laremy Tunsil took a big step towards undoing his bad 2019 season, cutting his penalties from 18 to seven. The bad news is that the team looked notably improved in the run game when Tunsil missed the last two games of the season and the Texans were forced to use Roderick Johnson out there. ◕ Tytus Howard has shown that he can create a highlight reel—there's a great video of him taking a Jaguars defender all the way off the field in Week 5—but he's still fighting to find consistency. The Texans are hopeful that firing Bill O'Brien confidant Mike Devlin, who had some utterly incoherent press availabilities, will help the line take a major step forward. ◕ The major question with the unit appears to be where Marcus Cannon will start. Cannon comes back from a COVID opt-out year at age 33 but was regarded as a stellar right tackle with the Patriots as of 2019. It would seem to make more sense to put Howard at guard than Cannon given Cannon's past struggles at that position, but it's all open to interpretation right now. ◕ Center sticks out as the major position battle. There's no doubting that Justin Britt has the most talent on paper, but we have no idea how much his 2019 ACL injury sapped that talent, and Britt went unsigned for the entirety of the 2020 season. There has been some talk about Max Scharping, who struggled enough at guard to get benched last year, taking over at center. A Scharping move probably leads to ex-Packer Lane Taylor joining the starting lineup at guard, though as always with this iteration of this team, there are like five extra layers of depth that could play with the right injuries—your Justin McCrays and Cole Toners.

Defensive Front

Defensive Line	Age	Pos	G	Snaps	Plays	Overall TmPct	Rk	Stop	Dfts	BTkl	vs. Run Runs	St%	Rk	RuYd	Rk	Pass Rush Sack	Hit	Hur	Dsrpt
Carlos Watkins*	28	DE	16	542	30	3.5%	75	21	6	2	24	67%	69	2.5	49	2.0	1	4	3
Brandon Dunn	29	DT	13	451	26	3.7%	73	19	1	0	24	75%	47	3.4	93	0.0	3	2	0
P.J. Hall*	26	DT	10	343	34	6.3%	23	26	3	2	31	81%	24	2.6	54	1.0	1	4	0
Jaleel Johnson	27	DT	16	655	44	5.3%	43	24	5	4	39	54%	95	3.9	97	1.5	0	1	0
Maliek Collins	26	DT	12	503	15	2.4%	94	10	2	2	13	77%	40	1.7	11	0.0	2	8	0

Edge Rushers	Age	Pos	G	Snaps	Plays	Overall TmPct	Rk	Stop	Dfts	BTkl	vs. Run Runs	St%	Rk	RuYd	Rk	Pass Rush Sack	Hit	Hur	Dsrpt
J.J. Watt*	32	DE	16	1013	59	6.8%	15	43	23	4	45	64%	74	1.5	10	5.0	13	28	9
Whitney Mercilus	31	OLB	13	614	22	3.1%	81	17	8	7	15	67%	60	3.7	85	4.0	3	9	0
Charles Omenihu	24	DE	15	546	19	2.3%	92	15	6	1	13	69%	57	2.2	32	4.0	12	14	4
Jacob Martin	26	OLB	14	375	21	2.8%	--	17	10	6	10	80%	--	2.9	--	3.0	0	14	0
Brennan Scarlett*	28	OLB	11	286	24	4.0%	--	13	2	5	19	58%	--	3.9	--	0.0	1	4	0
Jonathan Greenard	24	OLB	13	265	19	2.7%	--	8	3	5	12	42%	--	4.4	--	1.0	2	3	1
Shaq Lawson	27	OLB	14	571	33	4.7%	49	26	13	2	22	77%	26	1.6	12	4.0	16	27	1
Jordan Jenkins	27	OLB	12	528	33	5.0%	43	24	10	3	23	83%	10	1.7	14	2.0	5	19	2

Linebackers	Age	Pos	G	Snaps	Plays	TmPct	Rk	Stop	Dfts	BTkl	Runs	St%	Rk	RuYd	Rk	Sack	Hit	Hur	Tgts	Suc%	Rk	Yd/P	Rk	PD	Int
						Overall						**vs. Run**					**Pass Rush**			**vs. Pass**					
Zach Cunningham	27	ILB	16	944	165	19.0%	4	93	14	21	128	63%	21	3.7	31	3.0	1	5	23	35%	69	9.7	73	2	0
Tyrell Adams	29	ILB	16	812	126	14.5%	28	53	18	14	66	47%	73	4.0	43	2.0	1	3	39	41%	59	7.2	57	4	0
Benardrick McKinney*	29	ILB	4	234	38	17.5%	9	22	5	8	29	66%	16	2.8	4	0.0	0	2	4	75%	--	1.5	--	1	0
Neville Hewitt	28	ILB	16	1130	135	15.5%	16	64	16	16	77	58%	33	4.7	68	2.0	3	8	36	44%	54	8.4	68	4	0
Christian Kirksey	29	ILB	11	548	81	14.6%	26	30	11	11	46	37%	85	5.3	83	2.0	0	3	23	48%	47	6.3	38	4	2
Kevin Pierre-Louis	30	OLB	13	505	58	8.9%	67	29	6	7	26	58%	36	4.7	72	1.0	1	6	21	52%	31	7.1	55	2	0
Joe Thomas	30	MLB	15	408	47	6.0%	82	22	7	4	29	48%	71	4.4	64	0.0	2	5	11	55%	--	9.3	--	2	0
Kamu Grugier-Hill	27	ILB	15	207	23	3.1%	--	5	3	4	6	50%	--	6.2	--	1.0	1	2	9	0%	--	10.1	--	0	0

Year	Yards	ALY	Rk	Power	Rk	Stuff	Rk	2Lev	Rk	OpFld	Rk	BB Rt	Rk	Sacks	ASR	Rk	Press	Rk	BB Rt	Rk
2018	3.11	3.56	1	67%	18	25%	3	0.88	2	0.21	1	11.7%	4	43	7.4%	13	29.0%	20	11.4%	13
2019	4.62	4.50	22	59%	7	14%	27	1.14	13	1.00	28	11.1%	24	30	5.2%	29	28.3%	25	15.3%	16
2020	5.55	4.84	28	58%	4	16%	21	1.46	31	1.52	32	14.7%	8	34	6.9%	11	20.0%	30	10.5%	28

2020 ALY by direction:	Left End: 4.64 (19)	Left Tackle: 4.85 (25)	Mid/Guard: 4.77 (28)	Right Tackle: 5.49 (30)	Right End: 4.40 (12)

The Texans made out pretty well on the Benardrick McKinnney-Shaq Lawson swap. Lawson is nobody's No. 1 edge player, but he is a quality No. 2 for a team that didn't project to have anyone above a No. 3 after J.J. Watt was released. Lawson should pencil in at end for Lovie Smith's 4-3, but the Texans won't have a true No.1 barring something wild in July or August. 🏈 Who starts on the other end? Probably Charles Omeinhu. Omenihu led all non-Watt players in hurries and hits last year, but he had a rough time in run support as a 3-4 end. His run-down effectiveness will be the key to him staying on the field. 🏈 Behind those two, Whitney Mercilus is burnt toast but had such a brutal contract that the Texans restructured it to get it off the books sooner this offseason. Jacob Martin has had promising snaps and shows a real edge presence, but the Texans seem to have typecast him as someone who is too small to anchor in a 4-3. Jordan Jenkins has more success than either of them but is coming off a lost year with the Jets, missing four games with a torn labrum and generating just two sacks. 🏈 Speaking of lost seasons, Maliek Collins comes off a zero-sack year in Las Vegas to compete with Ross Blacklock for the starting 3-technique spot. Blacklock's rookie season was nothing short of disastrous, with Blacklock telling Texans in-house reporters that he called his dad after Week 6's loss to the Titans upset with his playing time, and the team continually refusing to increase his role. In fairness to the team, Blacklock looked lost two-gapping. 🏈 Brandon Dunn likely will take nose tackle unless Vincent Taylor can unseat him in training camp. Neither player has shown anything in an expanded role yet, though Taylor did have some decent run-stuff stats in smaller samples with the Dolphins. Rookie sixth-rounder Roy Lopez (Arizona) is probably looking at a redshirt year before he can join the nose tackle conversation. 🏈 Houston finished next to last with 142 broken tackles on defense, and the biggest problem was Zach Cunningham, who led the league with 21. Cunningham also keyed on the wrong gap on several of the defense's biggest runs allowed, got lost in coverage, and was a primary reason the team was destroyed in play-action. The team is all smiles and very positive, and Cunningham certainly has a lot of tackles, but projecting the player we saw last year into playing the middle on his own is certainly a little scary. 🏈 Next to Cunningham, the team has brought in no fewer than seven new off-ball linebackers as well as rookie fifth-rounder Garret Wallow (TCU). The presumed competition winners are probably Christian Kirksey and Kevin Pierre-Louis, but nothing would surprise us.

Defensive Secondary

Secondary	Age	Pos	G	Snaps	Plays	TmPct	Rk	Stop	Dfts	BTkl	Runs	St%	Rk	RuYd	Rk	Tgts	Tgt%	Rk	aDOT	Suc%	Rk	Yd/P	Rk	PD	Int
						Overall						**vs. Run**					**vs. Pass**								
Vernon Hargreaves	26	CB	16	981	79	9.1%	29	23	9	10	12	25%	67	10.9	76	86	24.4%	9	10.8	37%	76	9.0	65	7	1
Eric Murray	27	FS/CB	14	941	73	9.6%	47	18	8	10	25	24%	59	8.7	54	43	12.7%	8	11.7	40%	63	9.3	55	2	0
Justin Reid	24	SS	13	888	85	12.1%	22	27	13	16	40	35%	39	7.2	40	27	8.5%	36	9.1	52%	32	6.8	21	4	0
Lonnie Johnson	26	SS/CB	16	702	70	8.1%	64	18	7	10	30	23%	60	9.4	60	32	12.7%	9	10.3	50%	37	9.7	57	0	0
Bradley Roby	29	CB	10	613	44	8.1%	53	17	8	4	8	50%	24	7.5	47	34	15.5%	74	13.2	56%	21	5.5	4	7	1
A.J. Moore	26	FS	11	355	32	5.4%	--	10	7	3	14	21%	--	10.8	--	10	7.9%	--	7.8	50%	--	7.4	--	1	0
Keion Crossen	25	CB	16	307	39	4.5%	--	9	5	6	11	9%	--	6.9	--	26	23.6%	--	15.5	54%	--	8.1	--	5	0
Phillip Gaines*	30	CB	12	262	25	3.8%	--	7	2	2	8	38%	--	4.8	--	28	29.8%	--	11.1	43%	--	9.6	--	1	0
Terrance Mitchell	29	CB	16	1071	78	9.5%	23	23	6	6	16	13%	79	8.1	60	82	18.6%	50	14.0	49%	49	8.4	54	13	0
Desmond King	27	CB	15	708	56	6.9%	72	26	7	4	17	53%	19	4.8	20	38	12.6%	78	7.7	53%	33	6.8	24	2	0
Terrence Brooks	29	SS	14	254	20	2.8%	--	5	3	3	10	30%	--	5.5	--	11	11.7%	--	15.0	27%	--	12.5	--	0	0
Tavierre Thomas	25	CB	16	203	20	2.4%	--	8	3	2	3	67%	--	4.0	--	18	21.5%	--	8.1	33%	--	7.2	--	0	0

Year	Pass D Rank	vs. #1 WR	Rk	vs. #2 WR	Rk	vs. Other WR	Rk	WR Wide	Rk	WR Slot	Rk	vs. TE	Rk	vs. RB	Rk
2018	18	19.6%	31	0.9%	18	3.8%	20	-6.3%	18	25.9%	28	16.3%	23	-21.3%	3
2019	26	-1.1%	14	11.4%	24	-10.0%	10	-2.6%	20	6.4%	18	0.0%	15	21.7%	26
2020	29	23.6%	31	23.8%	30	14.7%	26	8.0%	23	22.4%	32	25.8%	31	10.1%	25

On paper, this looks like the best unit the Texans have on their team. Bradley Roby had a quietly impressive season while being asked to frequently check the opposing No. 1 receiver. Over the first five weeks he helped hold Tyreek Hill to 5/46/1 and DJ Chark to 3/16/0, only really allowing Adam Thielen (8/114/1) to go off. From there, he missed the Packers game for injury reasons, missed the second Jaguars game because of "personal reasons," and was suspended for PEDs as part of the same ring that Will Fuller was in. Clearly a good player, but he was also a rumored cut because of the PEDs and inability to stay on the field. ✎ Justin Reid had a rough time in run support last year, memorably getting shed by Nick Chubb on the long gain that ended a loss to the Browns. He's also clearly an upper-echelon, rangy free safety when healthy—which he hasn't been since 2018—and enters the final year of his rookie deal without an extension. ✎ Lonnie Johnson played much better at safety down the stretch after the Texans moved him there in the middle of the season for reasons that nobody could ever properly explain. He's one of the few young players the Texans have to be optimistic about as he tries to build on that in his third season. ✎ Houston scooped up Desmond King a couple of days into free agency as his market dried up. It's really hard to explain why he fell out of favor with the Chargers and why a Titans team that seemed to need corners badly let him walk, but King has had above-average success rates in two of the last three years, has a nose for the ball, and isn't afraid to hit. He'll look to rebuild this value here. ✎ The other starting corner job probably slides over to Terrance Mitchell, who has carved out a nice journey-man niche for himself and didn't have a bad year with the Browns. An interesting quirk of the statistics is that 17 of Mitchell's targets were against the Bengals, and he allowed just five completions on those targets, stymying A.J. Green. Was that about Green, or about Mitchell? And if you like draft busts who continually get snaps for no discernible reason, Vernon Hargreaves is a primary backup! ✎ Depth here comes from Keion Crossen, who showed himself to be a little out of his depth as a main corner during the end of last season, and free-agent bust Eric Murray, who will likely be the primary backup and dime option at safety coming off a disastrous year as the team's nickel corner.

Special Teams

Year	DVOA	Rank	FG/XP	Rank	Net Kick	Rank	Kick Ret	Rank	Net Punt	Rank	Punt Ret	Rank	Hidden	Rank
2018	3.5%	5	4.4	8	7.8	1	0.5	11	4.5	11	0.5	14	-2.5	19
2019	2.9%	5	-1.9	20	4.7	8	0.1	14	10.5	2	1.0	13	-7.6	28
2020	-1.0%	21	-2.5	20	1.9	13	-4.7	30	2.1	15	-1.8	20	10.9	6

The Texans invested heavily here in the offseason, signing Andre Roberts away from the Bills after three straight Pro Bowl appearances as a returner. Roberts is 33, so the step could disappear at any moment, but he led the NFL in kickoff return average last year and averaged 9.9 yards per punt return. ✎ New punter Cameron Johnston combined for 6.1 points of gross punting value in 2018 and 2019 but was worth -3.0 points last year. The Texans seemed to be in better shape with Bryan Anger. ✎ Ka'imi Fairbairn is being paid like a top-five kicker, but he has been below average in gross kickoff value for three straight seasons. He has also been below average on field goals the last two years, hitting just 65% of his kicks over 40 yards between 2019 and 2020. ✎ Among the many special teams-capable players that the Texans reeled in this offseason, Tavierre Thomas probably had the best 2020 season—he had 10 special teams tackles and an 80% stop rate on those tackles.

Indianapolis Colts

2020 Record: 11-5	**Total DVOA:** 14.2% (20)	**2021 Mean Projection:** 8.7 wins	**On the Clock (0-5):** 13%
Pythagorean Wins: 10.2 (8)	**Offense:** 2.7% (12)	**Postseason Odds:** 50.5%	**Mediocrity (6-8):** 34%
Snap-Weighted Age: 26.6 (11)	**Defense:** -9.5% (7)	**Super Bowl Odds:** 5.4%	**Playoff Contender (9-11):** 37%
Average Opponent: -6.6% (32)	**Special Teams:** 2% (10)	**Proj. Avg. Opponent:** -1.3% (23)	**Super Bowl Contender (12+):** 16%

2020: The last year of Philip Rivers rekindled visions of Chad Pennington.

2021: Frank Reich will attempt to defuse the ticking Carson Wentz time bomb every week.

I t's worth pointing out that while the Colts struggled to become everything they hoped that they would be in 2020, they are a team that is still trying to overcome the surprise Andrew Luck retirement in 2019. There's not really a "sorry your franchise quarterback instantly disappeared" gift basket to bail out teams in this situation. There are many, many teams who have lost a star quarterback and immediately crumbled. That the Colts were able to reload as quickly as they did under general manager Chris Ballard and head coach Frank Reich to compete for a division championship is laudable.

The problem is that Luck's retirement has inadvertently placed the Colts in a situation where they have to be hopeful about quarterbacks because they are simply too well-constructed to have a passer slide anywhere near where they pick in the draft. At the same time, the Colts are skittish of giving up a first-round pick in a trade and also are good enough that they aren't accumulating much extra draft capital from trading, say, their equivalent of a Laremy Tunsil or Jamal Adams. They managed to make some hay off trading Sam Darnold's pick to the Jets. But when it came time to compete for the quarterback falling in the draft (this time played by Justin Fields) or the best quarterback on the market (this time played by Matthew Stafford), the Colts seemed reluctant to pay the price from a team-building perspective. That isn't to say that they never will—the DeForest Buckner trade clearly marked a willingness to deal first-round picks for proven production. But clearly they didn't value the top of the available market the same way that other teams did.

After Philip Rivers' retirement was announced, Ballard met the media in January and gave a well-considered statement: "Go back and look at first-round quarterbacks drafted over the past 10 years. Everyone just thinks you take one, and you're going to fix the problem. ... Look, taking one will get y'all off my (butt) for a little bit, but the second that guy doesn't play well, I'm gonna be the first one run out the building. ... That position never leaves my mind. It's something we want to get fixed. But there's got to be a little timing and luck come into play when you get it."

Ballard was honest and forthright. The emphasis on timing and luck betray a lot about the willingness that the Colts have to play at the high-stakes table for a quarterback. And that's a big part of the reason that Carson Wentz is the solution that the Colts landed on—he checks familiarity boxes (Reich was his offensive coordinator), but he also came at a discount compared to Stafford and Fields, each of whom cost multiple future first-round picks. The Colts may not surrender a first-round pick at all if Wentz doesn't meet playing time requirements—75% of their snaps or 70% of their snaps and a playoff appearance.

Wentz himself is an extremely vague narrator of his story. His first media availability with the Colts was downright sheltered, with Philadelphia reporters having to complain publicly to get media access. Wentz took no real responsibility for how things went down beyond a generic "I watch the tape and know there are things that I must improve on" boilerplate, and he refused to directly answer questions about whether he demanded a trade. Ballard deferred to Reich on the official Colts podcast after the trade: "Reuniting him back with Frank, who has shown and proven that any time he gets his hands on a quarterback that he's already had a relationship with, there's a good chance it's going to be a good marriage and we're going to have success. So I thought it was a good risk for us to take." Reich told *Sports Illustrated*'s Albert Breer that Wentz's 2019 tape proved to Reich that Wentz still "has it," and noted that before Wentz became available, the plan was to draft a quarterback: "Honestly, I think Chris and I were thinking, somehow we were going to figure out how we were going to be able to draft the quarterback of our future. And then this thing came with Carson and it fell into our laps. And that's the great thing about it, when it works that way, it almost makes you feel like it's more meant to be because you can't make this stuff up and you can't manufacture it." At OTAs, Reich responded to a question about how he knows he'll be wearing the result of the trade by saying, "I love sticking my neck out for people I believe in. ... I believe in Carson. ... I do know that his play will reflect the work that he does. ... but I don't mind being the point person on that."

We're not going to post-mortem the Wentz Eagles here (you can go to p. 200 for that) but it's important to note how messy the Wentz exit was. The Philadelphia media is notably detailed about the team's failings or lack thereof. Reporting from Jeff McLane of *The Philadelphia Inquirer* had Wentz audibling out of Doug Pederson's play calls and noted that some Eagles staffers saw physical decline in Wentz during training camp. There was a story that got planted with both Breer and NBC's Peter King that Wentz couldn't handle hard

2021 Colts Schedule

Week	Opp.	Week	Opp.	Week	Opp.
1	SEA	7	at SF	13	at HOU
2	LAR	8	TEN	14	BYE
3	at TEN	9	NYJ (Thu.)	15	NE
4	at MIA	10	JAX	16	at ARI (Sat./Xmas)
5	at BAL (Mon.)	11	at BUF	17	LV
6	HOU	12	TB	18	at JAX

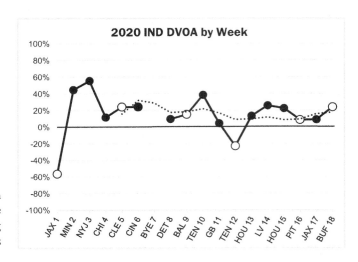

2020 IND DVOA by Week

coaching—and the Colts did coincidentally happen to sign former Eagles quarterbacks coach Press Taylor as an offensive assistant in January. There have been reports of Wentz being perceived as a bad teammate and selfish by his teammates as early as January 2019.

The Colts are trying to fix a player who was sacked on an NFL-high 10.3% of his dropbacks, who tied for the league lead in interceptions, and who was 0.1 percentage points away from the lowest completion rate among qualifying quarterbacks (behind Drew Lock). He was leading the league in fumbles at the time he was deservedly benched for the last four games of the season, and while there was no real book on Jalen Hurts, Hurts roundly outplayed Wentz with the same supporting cast. (And with Hurts having a -17.6% DVOA, that's not exactly a ringing endorsement of Hurts' future.) The recent history of a quarterback with Wentz's numbers is essentially unprecedented. No quarterback has been sacked 50 times, thrown 15 interceptions, and kept a sub-58% completion rate since David Carr for the expansion Texans in 2002 (Table 1).

Table 1. Carson Wentz and Similar Seasons

Player	Team	Year	Sacks	C%	INT	DVOA
Carson Wentz	**PHI**	**2020**	**50**	**57.4%**	**15**	**-35.9%**
David Carr	HOU	2002	76	52.4%	15	-47.4%
Aaron Brooks	NO	2001	50	55.9%	22	-5.1%
Drew Bledsoe	NE	1999	55	56.5%	21	-3.8%
Jake Plummer	ARI	1997	52	53.0%	15	-17.7%

Quarterbacks with 50+ sacks, 15+ interceptions, and completion rate below 58% since 1990.

Wentz was playing a turn-of-the century NFL quarterback game in a setting where that is wildly outdated, as a check of the DVOA tells us. Players that played like Wentz did in 2020 don't usually get to start as many games as he did without challenge. It says a lot about how Wentz's physical talents and franchise quarterback status were perceived that he was able to get to 12 games started playing like that. The only quarterbacks in the last 10 years to post a -30.0% DVOA one year and later post a top-15 DVOA as a full-time starter were rookie Josh Allen and rookie Jared Goff. (Blake Bortles got up to 16th with a barely positive DVOA in Jacksonville's run to the AFC Championship Game.) Wentz wasn't supposed to be

an overwhelmed rookie, but the hopes of his rebounding are pretty much pinned to that idea. The list of quarterbacks who have had a DVOA decline as major as the one Wentz had and went spiraling into the ugliest section of the DVOA charts is similarly not promising (Table 2).

The young players on that list do not bring the optimism you're looking for as a Colts fan. Jay Cutler essentially hovered between bad and mediocre for the rest of his career. Matt Cassel had a quick rebound in 2010 with a dominant run game and then disappeared into backup purgatory. Most of the list filters into those two major areas: mediocre or backup. The notable exception to the rule? Jake Plummer's effective Mike Shanahan years (he moved to Denver in 2003).

Now, were the Eagles also complicit in that statistical output? Sure. They started a 38-year-old Jason Peters at left tackle and their top two wide receivers by targets were Greg Ward and Travis Fulgham. All their alleged depth either never developed or wound up on injured reserve. At the same time, Wentz was described by Reich as a "dominant physical specimen" at OTAs, but he has never really been a dual-threat player as advertised. He attempted just 13 designed runs all season per Sports Info Solutions' charting, with some quarterback sneaks and scrambles mixed in to inflate his rushing figures. Eagles pundits have pointed out that Wentz looks a lot bulkier than he did in 2017, but he only had eight designed runs in his 13 starts that year, which is right about in line with 2020. It's possible that the extra bulk hurt him most with regards to his sack rate, but the "dominant physical specimen" thing is eye-test mumbo jumbo when you try to match it up against the results.

What Wentz did in his near-MVP season in 2017 was otherworldly stuff led by a ridiculous performance in the red zone and on third downs. Wentz's 94.9% red zone DVOA that year was almost double that of second-place Case Keenum among quarterbacks with at least 50 red zone attempts. His third-down DVOA of 90.7% almost doubled up second-place Jared Goff among quarterbacks with 100 third-down attempts. That Wentz, it's clear, was a historical outlier à la Lamar Jackson's 2019.

The Colts don't necessarily need that version of Wentz to win games. The problem is that splitting the difference between 2018-2019 Wentz and 2020 Wentz creates a situation where Wentz is not a franchise-caliber quarterback, but also isn't bad enough to outright get benched. The Colts lose their first-round pick if that happens. So to "win" the trade, they need Wentz to go to one of the polar extremes rather than the median outcome. If Wentz can rebound to 2019 levels, then the Colts are likely going to cruise to a playoff spot. But something in between 2019 and 2020 is much more likely.

The team around Wentz is well-considered, as most things Ballard touches are. The offensive line had another surprise retirement in stalwart left tackle Anthony Castonzo, but the Colts were able to rebound after the draft by signing former Chiefs left tackle Eric Fisher, a solid option. Fisher may take a bit to recover from the torn Achilles that kept him out of the Super Bowl, but it's a nice stab at a solution and that was the only egregious position of need for Indianapolis. The rest of the offensive line is extremely talented. The Colts have a deep backfield with strong complementary parts. Jonathan Taylor managed to piss off every fantasy owner in the nation for two months but also finished the year with a 5.0 yards per carry average. Michael Pittman came into his own after his mid-season injury and had a 90-yard receiving game in the playoffs. Parris Campbell will be back from injury. T.Y. Hilton is still a pretty stellar deep receiver. If Wentz can't find a way to make the talent on this unit work for him, that's a pretty bad look for his prospects of remaining an NFL starter

Defensively, the Colts are undergoing a bit of a transition on the edge, having spent their first two picks on edge rushers Kwity Paye (Michigan) and Dayo Odeyingbo (Vanderbilt). Jim Irsay, an unbridled master of optimism, told Odeyingbo on his draft call that "You know, we had Mathis and Freeney here and you guys are going to come in and wreak some havoc."

The Colts did a lot of what they did defensively last year without a top-tier pass-rush presence outside of Buckner. Justin Houston and Denico Autry had 8.0 and 7.5 sacks respectively, but didn't add much in the way of hurries. The Colts likely aren't going to be a heavy pressure team as a whole anyway without a dominant pass rush on the line—they rarely blitz under conservative defensive coordinator Matt Eberflus and play as much zone defense as anyone in the NFL. Last year the Colts finished 20th in pressure rate, and that was with

Buckner finishing fourth in quarterback hurries among interior defenders. Houston is still a free agent, so the Colts might turn back there if they get to training camp and don't like what they see. But turning over the pass rush to the youth is about the only area where you can see the Colts taking a clear hit without a regression (maybe linebacker if you consider Bobby Okereke a clear downgrade from Anthony Walker). "We've never had this depth before," said Eberflus at OTAs. "We are excited about where that is, because that's only going to elevate the play of the entire unit."

Our forecast has the Colts, narrowly, as division favorites. The offensive projection does not suffer much at all from last season's numbers with Wentz subbed in for Rivers. But they're also not a particularly good team, just as they weren't last year in DVOA's eyes, when their record was bolstered by the easiest schedule in the NFL. They are an ordinary team blessed to be in a division with a one-sided Titans squad, the beginning of the Trevor Lawrence era, and the smoldering remains of what used to be Deshaun Watson's Texans.

It feels weird to say this about a team that has been blessed with Peyton Manning and Luck for most of our adult lives, but the Colts are on a quarterback mediocrity treadmill. If they break one to the house with a fixed Wentz, they will absolutely have every right to lord it over the rest of the NFL. The more likely scenario is that Wentz is just a stopgap while we wait for the correct answer, and that what Reich does to try to make him the Wentz of the past amounts to trying to hammer a nail into a moving fan. The Colts don't have to wear the decision to trade for Wentz as a scarlet letter—even if they give up a first-round pick—because it's not like Jacoby Brissett was a real answer either. They continue to be active in the late-round quarterback market. There's no way to trade for a quarterback with this perceived value and not have some amount of fawning media attention. The terms of the trade and the terms of his contract—$12 million that can still come off the books with a release after the season—tell a tale that isn't exactly brimming with unbridled optimism for Wentz's return to the status of "franchise quarterback." That's the tale where there's every chance the Colts are searching for a new quarterback in 2022.

Rivers McCown

Table 2. Carson Wentz and Major QB Declines

Player	Year	Team	Drop	Exp	DVOA Y-1	Pass Y-1	DVOA	Pass	DVOA Y+1	Pass Y+1
Jay Cutler	2009	CHI	-38.4%	4	17.0%	626	-21.4%	589	-8.5%	484
Carson Wentz	**2020**	**PHI**	**-36.0%**	**5**	**0.1%**	**645**	**-35.9%**	**486**	--	--
Matt Cassel	2009	KC	-30.4%	5	1.1%	564	-29.3%	541	8.4%	471
Jake Plummer	2002	ARI	-29.6%	6	9.5%	556	-20.1%	569	25.8%	313
Eli Manning	2013	NYG	-29.2%	10	9.0%	555	-20.2%	590	4.6%	628
Ryan Fitzpatrick	2016	NYJ	-26.1%	12	3.5%	583	-22.6%	423	17.3%	170
David Carr	2005	HOU	-26.0%	4	-3.2%	519	-29.2%	491	-8.2%	484
Kordell Stewart	1998	PIT	-25.4%	4	4.9%	458	-20.4%	491	-31.4%	297
Boomer Esiason	1995	NYJ	-22.5%	12	-5.5%	460	-28.0%	420	7.7%	356
Jake Plummer	1999	ARI	-18.1%	3	-8.4%	595	-26.5%	407	-12.2%	496

Biggest year-to-year drops in pass DVOA with a resulting DVOA below -20%, minimum 400 passes in each season, since 1983.

2020 Colts by Week

Wk	vs.	W-L	PF	PA	YDF	YDA	TO	Total	Off	Def	ST
1	at JAX	L	20	27	445	241	-2	-56.3%	-10.2%	41.1%	-4.9%
2	MIN	W	28	11	354	175	2	44.9%	-15.7%	-54.4%	6.2%
3	NYJ	W	36	7	353	260	3	55.6%	13.3%	-38.4%	3.9%
4	at CHI	W	19	11	289	269	1	11.9%	1.0%	-2.8%	8.1%
5	at CLE	L	23	32	308	385	0	24.3%	-25.4%	-25.2%	24.4%
6	CIN	W	31	27	430	398	-1	24.4%	14.2%	-8.8%	1.4%
7	BYE										
8	at DET	W	41	21	366	326	2	9.6%	-5.7%	-23.7%	-8.3%
9	BAL	L	10	24	339	266	-1	15.1%	-9.6%	-26.1%	-1.4%
10	at TEN	W	34	17	430	294	0	38.6%	19.6%	-17.7%	1.3%
11	GB	W	34	31	420	367	2	4.6%	1.6%	1.0%	4.0%
12	TEN	L	26	45	336	449	-1	-22.9%	1.1%	18.5%	-5.5%
13	at HOU	W	26	20	371	398	2	13.4%	-5.4%	-17.5%	1.3%
14	at LV	W	44	27	456	424	3	25.8%	18.2%	-5.4%	2.2%
15	HOU	W	27	20	350	425	2	22.4%	12.9%	-5.5%	4.0%
16	at PIT	L	24	28	365	354	-2	8.5%	21.5%	20.2%	7.3%
17	JAX	W	28	14	437	283	0	9.1%	10.5%	-11.2%	-12.7%
18	at BUF	L	24	27	472	397	0	24.1%	26.6%	5.1%	2.6%

Trends and Splits

	Offense	Rank	Defense	Rank
Total DVOA	2.7%	12	-9.5%	7
Unadjusted VOA	8.0%	9	-9.0%	6
Weighted Trend	6.4%	10	-6.0%	10
Variance	1.9%	1	5.4%	21
Average Opponent	6.2%	32	0.6%	15
Passing	14.3%	16	-2.9%	8
Rushing	-5.4%	12	-19.7%	9
First Down	2.3%	17	-6.7%	11
Second Down	7.3%	10	-2.3%	12
Third Down	-3.0%	16	-25.1%	3
First Half	17.1%	6	0.5%	19
Second Half	-13.1%	25	-19.7%	5
Red Zone	-3.1%	19	-4.6%	9
Late and Close	-19.9%	27	-17.7%	5

Five-Year Performance

Year	W-L	Pyth W	Est W	PF	PA	TO	Total	Rk	Off	Rk	Def	Rk	ST	Rk	Off AGL	Rk	Def AGL	Rk	Off Age	Rk	Def Age	Rk	ST Age	Rk
2016	8-8	8.5	6.8	411	392	-5	-5.6%	23	3.3%	12	13.0%	29	4.1%	5	26.8	9	60.4	26	25.8	27	28.0	2	25.9	20
2017	4-12	4.2	4.2	263	404	+5	-23.9%	30	-18.3%	30	9.3%	27	3.7%	8	65.7	30	45.2	24	26.4	24	25.7	24	25.3	27
2018	10-6	10.3	10.0	433	344	+2	12.4%	8	7.9%	10	-3.5%	11	0.9%	12	57.0	28	51.6	28	25.8	28	25.3	28	25.7	19
2019	7-9	7.7	7.2	361	373	+2	-6.0%	20	-3.4%	19	3.0%	19	0.4%	16	38.6	16	26.7	10	26.0	28	25.6	25	25.1	29
2020	11-5	10.2	10.0	451	362	+10	14.2%	10	2.7%	12	-9.5%	7	2.0%	10	46.3	21	26.6	8	27.6	4	26.0	25	25.7	22

2020 Performance Based on Most Common Personnel Groups

IND Offense					IND Offense vs. Opponents					IND Defense				IND Defense vs. Opponents			
Pers	Freq	Yds	DVOA	Run%	Pers	Freq	Yds	DVOA	Run%	Pers	Freq	Yds	DVOA	Pers	Freq	Yds	DVOA
11	70%	6.7	12.4%	33%	Base	23%	4.9	1.3%	68%	Base	21%	4.8	-17.1%	11	62%	6.1	-3.5%
12	20%	4.7	-14.3%	68%	Nickel	62%	6.4	4.8%	40%	Nickel	78%	5.8	-8.3%	12	19%	5.4	-13.5%
13	7%	5.7	21.6%	65%	Dime+	15%	7.0	18.0%	15%	Dime+	0%	14.3	51.7%	21	6%	6.7	9.4%
21	1%	8.3	24.3%	11%	Goal Line	0%	-0.5	-75.4%	50%	Goal Line	1%	2.2	34.8%	22	5%	4.4	-30.7%
612	1%	4.0	-66.0%	75%										13	4%	2.2	-49.1%

Strategic Tendencies

Run/Pass		Rk	Formation		Rk	Pass Rush		Rk	Secondary		Rk	Strategy		Rk
Runs, first half	41%	10	Form: Single Back	91%	2	Rush 3	2.2%	30	4 DB	21%	23	Play Action	25%	21
Runs, first down	49%	14	Form: Empty Back	7%	23	Rush 4	82.4%	3	5 DB	78%	3	Offensive Motion	37%	27
Runs, second-long	32%	6	Form: Multi Back	2%	31	Rush 5	11.1%	30	6+ DB	0%	31	Avg Box (Off)	6.57	14
Runs, power sit.	70%	5	Pers: 3+ WR	71%	8	Rush 6+	4.3%	21	Man Coverage	20%	29	Avg Box (Def)	6.56	21
Runs, behind 2H	31%	12	Pers: 2+ TE/6+ OL	29%	16	Edge Rusher Sacks	56.3%	9	CB by Sides	86%	9	Offensive Pace	30.55	18
Pass, ahead 2H	45%	21	Pers: 6+ OL	1%	18	Interior DL Sacks	26.3%	12	S/CB Cover Ratio	21%	28	Defensive Pace	31.18	27
Run-Pass Options	8%	15	Shotgun/Pistol	75%	10	Second Level Sacks	17.5%	25	DB Blitz	8%	28	Go for it on 4th	1.36	23

The Colts had one of the league's biggest reverse splits on play-action. They had roughly the same yardage (7.4 yards with, 7.2 yards without) but a significant difference in DVOA: -5.0% DVOA with play-action, 21.6% DVOA without it. In-dianapolis ran a league-high 68% of the time when using 12 personnel. A league-high 43% of sacks for the Colts offense were "non-pressure" sacks, with seven listed as coverage sacks and two as failed scrambles. Indianapolis ranked dead last in max protect blocking (defined as seven or more blockers with at least two more blockers than pass-rushers), using it on just 3.9% of pass plays. Matt Eberflus put away his dime personnel, as the Colts almost never used six defensive backs in 2020 after they had ranked 11th with dime personnel on 20% of plays in 2019. Indianapolis had the biggest split in the league when it came to how frequently opponents threw on each side of the field: a league-low 28% of passes went on the offensive left (generally where Xavier Rhodes started), while 41% of passes went on the offensive right (Rock Ya-Sin or T.J. Carrie). The Colts ranked 15th in pressure rate on defense on first and second down but dropped to 30th on third and fourth down. The Colts and Rams were the only two teams whose opponents never missed an extra point all season. Frank Reich's low rank in Aggressiveness Index is quite a surprise, especially since the Colts tied for third with 18 goes in qualifying situations. The issue here is that the Colts were expected to go for it more than any other team, with 13.2 expected fourth-down goes according to the historical AI baselines. Pittsburgh was the only other offense above 11 expected goes. So while the Colts went for it on a league-leading 14 fourth-and-1s, that was out of 21 opportunities, a 67% rate not much different from the leaguewide rate of 63%. Reich also had a preference for trying long field goals instead of going for it in "no man's land" between the 31- and 37-yard lines.

Passing

Player	DYAR	DVOA	Plays	NtYds	Avg	YAC	C%	TD	Int
P.Rivers*	765	9.9%	559	4047	7.2	6.0	68.5%	24	11
J.Brissett*	-68	-135.2%	10	2	0.2	9.0	28.6%	0	0
C.Wentz	-780	-35.9%	486	2278	4.7	4.0	57.7%	16	15

Rushing

Player	DYAR	DVOA	Plays	Yds	Avg	TD	Fum	Suc
J.Taylor	127	3.8%	232	1169	5.0	11	1	52%
N.Hines	22	-2.5%	89	380	4.3	3	0	44%
J.Wilkins	-34	-18.0%	84	308	3.7	1	0	45%
J.Brissett*	27	18.0%	11	23	2.1	3	0	--
D.Harris	15	3.2%	6	46	7.7	0	0	--
M.Mack	6	23.5%	4	26	6.5	0	0	75%
C.Wentz	62	9.2%	50	261	5.2	5	3	--

Receiving

Player	DYAR	DVOA	Plays	Ctch	Yds	Y/C	YAC	TD	C%
T.Y.Hilton	138	5.7%	93	56	762	13.6	3.5	5	60%
Z.Pascal	99	5.5%	71	44	629	14.3	5.3	5	62%
M.Pittman	32	-5.8%	61	40	503	12.6	7.3	1	66%
M.Johnson	4	-10.9%	28	14	255	18.2	3.5	0	50%
D.Harris	11	3.0%	10	10	79	7.9	6.3	0	100%
P.Campbell	-7	-21.3%	9	6	71	11.8	3.0	0	67%
A.Dulin	-10	-30.0%	6	3	53	17.7	9.3	0	50%
T.Burton*	-47	-22.2%	47	28	250	8.9	3.1	3	60%
M.Alie-Cox	57	14.7%	39	31	394	12.7	5.9	2	79%
J.Doyle	27	4.9%	33	23	251	10.9	4.0	3	70%
N.Hines	158	23.7%	76	63	482	7.7	7.5	4	83%
J.Taylor	76	22.2%	39	36	299	8.3	10.1	1	92%
J.Wilkins	-6	-21.1%	16	12	105	8.8	11.9	0	75%

Offensive Line

Player	Pos	Age	GS	Snaps	Pen	Sk	Pass	Run	Player	Pos	Age	GS	Snaps	Pen	Sk	Pass	Run
Mark Glowinski	RG	29	16/16	1091	3	2.5	17	6	Chaz Green*	LT	29	15/1	210	3	3.5	5	0
Quenton Nelson	LG	25	16/16	1082	8	1	8	10	Eric Fisher	LT	30	15/15	1049	3	4	32	5
Ryan Kelly	C	28	15/15	1007	1	0	7	6	Sam Tevi	LT	27	14/14	1024	4	1.5	20	7
Braden Smith	RT	25	14/14	938	3	0	8	8	Chris Reed	LG	29	14/14	894	3	1.5	11	9
Anthony Castonzo*	LT	33	12/12	749	2	2	9	3									

Year	Yards	ALY	Rk	Power	Rk	Stuff	Rk	2Lev	Rk	OpFld	Rk	BB Rt	Rk	Sacks	ASR	Rk	Press	Rk	BB Rt	Rk	Cont
2018	4.55	4.83	4	59%	28	18%	9	1.34	6	0.74	22	5.0%	6	18	4.1%	2	25.9%	6	6.6%	8	24
2019	4.58	4.41	12	69%	7	20%	22	1.35	4	0.97	10	9.0%	11	32	6.0%	7	34.8%	29	17.0%	30	48
2020	4.60	4.23	20	66%	17	18%	22	1.31	8	0.97	7	8.3%	8	21	5.2%	7	18.5%	3	11.7%	14	23

2020 ALY by direction: Left End: 4.56 (14) Left Tackle: 4.23 (15) Mid/Guard: 4.19 (22) Right Tackle: 4.60 (11) Right End: 3.71 (25)

With Eric Fisher's Achilles still likely to keep him sidelined through training camp, and perhaps some of the regular season, the initial spotlight at left tackle will fall on Julién Davenport and Sam Tevi. You see the Tevi blown block numbers above— those numbers are an improvement on what he did in 2019, when he allowed seven sacks and blew 26 more blocks in just 794 snaps. Davenport allowed 3.5 sacks in 2019 and 24 blocked blocks in just eight starts, and in 2018, he allowed eight sacks, blew

30 blocks, and had 14 penalties as a full-time starter. You may be surprised to see Fisher also charted with a lot of blown blocks in 2020, but he hasn't blown more than 24 blocks in any other season of his career and hasn't allowed more than five sacks in a season since 2017. ● Quenton Nelson is by far one of the nastiest block-finishers in the business and a true anchor on the line who has been worth the price of admission of a first-round pick. Heading into his fifth-year option in 2022, it would not be surprising if the Colts started extension talks sooner rather than later. "It was a good year," Nelson said in his typical understated fashion at OTAs. ● Fellow class of 2018 member Braden Smith is coming off his finest season as a pro, cutting his blown block total by more than 20 from a down 2019. Without an extension, Smith will hit free agency after the year, and at OTAs he told reporters that he's "letting his agent handle it." Guard Mark Glowinski, a successful reclamation project mauler with a successful beard, is also a free agent after 2021. ● Ryan Kelly got the bag after we went to press last year, getting a four-year, $49.7-million contract with $34 million in guarantees. It has an interesting structure because his cap numbers are highest in 2020 and 2021, and his cap figure will only be $7.5 million in 2022. Kelly has not exactly been an iron man for the Colts, but he's a good enough center to play up to that deal. ● The only other lineman with 100 snaps to return is 2020 fifth-rounder Danny Pinter, who should again be in the mix as the top backup on the interior and has shown some tackle flexibility in his past. Chris Reed started 14 games for the Panthers last year and did some solid work in the run game. 2020 seventh-rounder Will Fries (Penn State) doesn't offer a ton of athleticism, but worked at both guard and tackle in college, with his strength in the run game probably profiling well at guard in the NFL. Fries' girlfriend made him a viral TikTok star by profiling his draft day waiting. When asked about it at OTAs, Fries made it very clear he is not on TikTok.

Defensive Front

Defensive Line	Age	Pos	G	Snaps	Plays	TmPct	Rk	Stop	Dfts	BTkl	Runs	St%	Rk	RuYd	Rk	Sack	Hit	Hur	Dsrpt
							Overall						**vs. Run**				**Pass Rush**		
DeForest Buckner	27	DT	15	751	61	8.0%	5	46	18	6	43	70%	63	2.8	65	9.5	17	30	4
Grover Stewart	28	DT	16	581	54	6.7%	15	37	9	3	48	71%	54	2.3	41	0.5	5	13	0
Antwaun Woods	28	DT	14	456	23	3.2%	80	16	1	3	22	68%	67	3.4	92	1.0	1	2	0

Edge Rushers	Age	Pos	G	Snaps	Plays	TmPct	Rk	Stop	Dfts	BTkl	Runs	St%	Rk	RuYd	Rk	Sack	Hit	Hur	Dsrpt
							Overall						**vs. Run**				**Pass Rush**		
Denico Autry*	31	DE	14	631	33	4.6%	51	26	12	5	23	74%	37	2.3	38	7.5	2	22	1
Justin Houston*	32	DE	16	608	25	3.1%	83	20	12	6	15	67%	60	2.3	41	8.0	3	17	3
Al-Quadin Muhammad	26	DE	16	579	22	2.7%	88	14	5	2	19	58%	85	3.1	74	2.0	4	22	0
Tyquan Lewis	26	DE	16	415	26	3.2%	80	23	13	2	18	89%	3	0.3	1	4.0	1	12	2
Isaac Rochell	26	DE	16	437	28	3.6%	74	19	4	2	21	67%	60	3.0	65	2.5	2	9	2

Linebackers	Age	Pos	G	Snaps	Plays	TmPct	Rk	Stop	Dfts	BTkl	Runs	St%	Rk	RuYd	Rk	Sack	Hit	Hur	Tgts	Suc%	Rk	Yd/P	Rk	PD	Int
							Overall						**vs. Run**				**Pass Rush**				**vs. Pass**				
Darius Leonard	26	OLB	14	825	139	19.6%	2	63	19	11	67	51%	64	4.2	53	3.0	0	6	35	29%	74	8.7	69	7	0
Anthony Walker*	26	MLB	16	697	96	11.8%	47	47	6	9	51	59%	31	3.7	30	0.0	1	3	33	33%	70	7.3	58	5	1
Bobby Okereke	25	OLB	14	685	78	11.0%	53	32	15	7	30	50%	66	3.0	9	0.0	1	6	33	55%	24	5.0	18	6	1

Year	Yards	ALY	Rk	Power	Rk	Stuff	Rk	2Lev	Rk	OpFld	Rk	BB Rt	Rk	Sacks	ASR	Rk	Press	Rk	BB Rt	Rk
2018	3.84	3.96	7	65%	14	25%	4	1.10	7	0.69	10	9.5%	11	38	5.3%	29	28.0%	25	6.6%	30
2019	4.11	4.24	15	83%	32	20%	13	1.18	18	0.65	11	12.6%	18	41	6.6%	21	30.1%	18	17.5%	4
2020	3.76	4.00	6	67%	18	17%	18	1.14	12	0.37	3	15.1%	6	40	6.8%	12	24.0%	20	13.6%	15
2020 ALY by direction:			Left End: 3.96 (9)			Left Tackle: 3.54 (9)				Mid/Guard: 3.94 (4)				Right Tackle: 4.77 (21)				Right End: 4.22 (10)		

While the Colts are of course wildly optimistic about their first two picks, SackSEER is not quite as sanguine. With only 11.5 sacks in 28 college games, Kwity Paye's production was extremely low, and he only had one pass defensed in his entire college career. The end result is a projection that is buoyed only by his high draft stock. Dayo Odeyingbo's SackSEER rating of 25.9% was one of the six worst in the draft, though it's hard to judge the athleticism of someone who couldn't work out at a pro day because of a torn Achilles. Odeyingbo finished his career with just eight college sacks—though he did add an additional 26.5 tackles for loss. Odeyingbo said the goal is to be back playing this year, though he admitted at rookie minicamp that he wasn't sure what that looked like yet. ● If neither of those two are up for early production, the Colts are probably looking at major roles early for Kemoko Turay, Al-Quadin Muhammad, and Tyquan Lewis. Lewis finally took a step forward in his third season, and Muhammad was re-signed after a solid 600-snap season as a backup. The Colts are also hoping for a step forward from 2019 second-rounder Ben Banogu. At OTAs, Banogu dodged questions about last year by saying he was focused on this year, and when continually questioned about what he learned, said "I learned a lot of things last year, and the years before that, and when I was five years old. You learn everything every day, and every year." Words to live by. ✎ Next to Buckner on the interior, the Colts saw a step forward from Grover Stewart, who had his best season yet as a nose tackle and was rewarded with a three-year extension after Thanksgiving. Stewart worked plenty on passing downs as well. ✎ Rounding out the collection of Colts stars aiming for a new contract is linebacker Darius Leonard, who has been rock solid in pretty much all facets. He contributes as a pass-rusher, and if you look at that poor success rate number, please note that many of those targets are in zone coverage and that has a strong influence. ✎ With Anthony Walker gone to Cleveland, the other off-ball linebacker spot should be occupied by one of last year's FO sleeper prospects, Bobby Okereke. Okereke was a guesser in run defense last year—he either blew the play up for the offense or for the defense. Zaire Franklin profiles as the primary backup/third linebacker, and while there aren't a lot of snaps to judge him on, he appears to be making steady progress from his first two starts in 2018.

Defensive Secondary

Secondary	Age	Pos	G	Snaps	Plays	Overall TmPct	Rk	Stop	Dfts	BTkl	vs. Run Runs	St%	Rk	RuYd	Rk	vs. Pass Tgts	Tgt%	Rk	aDOT	Suc%	Rk	Yd/P	Rk	PD	Int
Kenny Moore	26	CB	16	952	92	11.3%	8	48	17	13	21	67%	3	3.3	3	59	14.9%	75	9.1	53%	34	6.8	26	13	4
Julian Blackmon	23	FS	15	916	48	6.3%	69	12	10	7	20	25%	57	9.3	59	19	5.0%	61	20.6	37%	67	17.9	71	6	2
Xavier Rhodes	31	CB	16	902	54	6.7%	74	18	7	5	11	18%	75	8.3	61	67	17.9%	57	12.3	60%	9	6.9	27	12	2
Khari Willis	25	SS	14	842	88	12.4%	17	37	8	5	47	51%	14	5.4	20	30	8.6%	34	7.8	47%	45	6.3	15	6	2
Rock Ya-Sin	25	CB	13	550	51	7.7%	63	17	6	4	7	43%	38	4.6	15	53	23.2%	15	11.1	47%	58	8.0	50	7	1
T.J. Carrie	31	CB	15	396	35	4.6%	--	19	7	4	8	75%	--	1.8	--	35	21.3%	--	11.5	57%	--	6.9	--	8	2
Tavon Wilson*	31	SS	15	219	21	2.8%	--	10	4	1	6	83%	--	3.0	--	9	9.9%	--	12.2	56%	--	7.8	--	1	0

Year	Pass D Rank	vs. #1 WR	Rk	vs. #2 WR	Rk	vs. Other WR	Rk	WR Wide	Rk	WR Slot	Rk	vs. TE	Rk	vs. RB	Rk
2018	20	1.8%	17	-27.9%	1	-3.8%	14	-12.1%	8	-8.4%	6	21.2%	29	12.3%	25
2019	19	7.7%	22	7.2%	22	24.9%	29	7.4%	22	19.3%	28	4.1%	18	-11.1%	7
2020	8	1.4%	18	-11.2%	8	4.0%	17	-13.5%	7	-1.0%	17	-18.0%	4	1.5%	18

The Colts found a solid starter in free agency with former Vikings star Xavier Rhodes. The team's Cover-2/zone-heavy role was a natural fit for Rhodes' aging skill set, and he played almost all of his snaps wide. Facing a tough market, Rhodes signed another one-year deal with the Colts this offseason to try to replicate the results. ✎ The other outside corner role was essentially split down the middle between veteran T.J. Carrie and 2019 second-rounder Rock Ya-Sin. Ya-Sin had a rough season when he was healthy enough to get on the field—between Week 10 and Week 12 he was called for three separate DPIs and allowed 207 additional passing yards to Ryan Tannehill and Aaron Rodgers. Ya-Sin did pick off Rodgers, but between a knee injury and a few concussions, much of his year was lost. Carrie played fairly well, allowing only a lone touchdown to Laviska Shenault in Week 17. Marvell Tell, a 2019 fifth-round pick, is back after an opt-out year and could also make a run at a starting spot. ✎ It's hard to think of a better nickel corner than Kenny Moore over the past three years. The Colts don't have any guaranteed money left on his contract after this season but it wouldn't be a surprise to see him re-sign. Moore has good coverage metrics and teams clearly shy away from targeting him; he churned through a season of games against good quarterbacks where he put up something like five targets, one 20-yard catch allowed, and at least one pick or deflection. ✎ The replacement for Malik Hooker at free safety was 2020 third-rounder Julian Blackmon, a willing tackler who showcased big speed and nice change-of-direction in his first year. When teams were able to target Blackmon, though, he allowed more than two more yards per pass than any other qualifying safety. Another year learning the mental side of the game and another season removed from an ACL tear in the 2019 Pac-12 Championship Game should help tone down some of those mistakes. ✎ Khari Willis has been an impact run defender who draws a lot of underneath zone coverage as a box safety. Willis was better in run defense last year but had a lower success rate in coverage than he did in his 2019 rookie campaign. 2021 fifth-rounder Shawn Davis (Florida) profiles as Willis' direct backup; he's a thumper who needs some work on instincts and in coverage.

Special Teams

Year	DVOA	Rank	FG/XP	Rank	Net Kick	Rank	Kick Ret	Rank	Net Punt	Rank	Punt Ret	Rank	Hidden	Rank
2018	0.9%	12	-1.9	22	-1.5	24	-1.1	17	9.1	3	0.1	15	-8.6	26
2019	0.4%	16	-13.3	31	-1.3	21	-2.8	25	2.4	14	17.0	1	-11.7	31
2020	2.0%	10	-3.9	21	2.0	12	8.0	2	-0.7	18	4.5	7	9.9	7

Indy's first year after the Adam Vinatieri Era was a return to the pre-washed Vinatieri Era, with rookie kicker Rodrigo Blankenship coming close to 2018 Vinatieri's production. Blankenship made 9-of-11 field goals within 40 to 49 yards, but also missed a 33-yarder in the playoffs. Indianapolis brought in ex-Bears kicker Eddy Piñeiro to provide some camp competition. ◗ The Colts continue to employ Rigoberto Sanchez as a kickoff specialist, but his kickoffs have provided a grand total of -3.7 points of gross field position over the last three years. His punts are fairly average, though he did have the notable excuse of getting a cancerous tumor removed in November. ◗ George Odum was voted first-team All-Pro as a special teams ace for a reason—his 20 tackles and 16 return stops both led the league, and other than Seattle's Cody Barton, he had six more tackles than every other special teamer in the NFL. (Barton had 16.) ◗ Between Nyheim Hines (punts) and Isaiah Rodgers (kickoffs), the Colts have two excellent returners that each finished in the top five of return value at their respective spots.

Jacksonville Jaguars

2020 Record: 1-15	**Total DVOA:** -28% (28)	**2021 Mean Projection:** 7 wins	**On the Clock (0-5):** 31%
Pythagorean Wins: 3.7 (31)	**Offense:** -12.6% (27)	**Postseason Odds:** 25.5%	**Mediocrity (6-8):** 41%
Snap-Weighted Age: 25.4 (32)	**Defense:** 15.2% (31)	**Super Bowl Odds:** 1.3%	**Playoff Contender (9-11):** 22%
Average Opponent: 0.4% (16)	**Special Teams:** -0.1% (18)	**Proj. Avg. Opponent:** -2.7% (31)	**Super Bowl Contender (12+):** 6%

2020: One last bologna sandwich for the road.

2021: The table is set for Urban Meyer to perform an Urban Shocker.

A few words on the 2020 Jacksonville Jaguars: they were terrible. They started Jake Luton on purpose. They gave Mike Glennon five starts. They finished dead last in defensive DVOA, and outside of a pleasant James Robinson UDFA breakout season, almost nothing good came of them suiting up last year outside of securing the No. 1 overall pick. It was a culmination of the Sacksonville Jaguars slowly losing big players over the last few years and the disastrous decision to take Leonard Fournette No. 4 overall in 2017 while franchise quarterbacks were still on the board out of deference to Blake Bortles. Bortles will live on through *The Good Place* re-runs and the NFL's dedication to making sure any former first-round pick who is 6-foot-5 or taller gets at least five chances to become a credible backup. The era of Bortles being thought of as a good quarterback was ultimately as short-lived as that 2017 team. He was lightning in a bottle that fizzled away, and that fizzling took place before that 2017 team even took the field. Sadly, one of the few people who didn't recognize that in real time was ex-general manager David Caldwell, who didn't even survive the 2020 season.

Now, on to happier times. The Jacksonville Jaguars managed to land the No. 1 overall pick in the draft, and with it the rights to select Trevor Lawrence. Lawrence has been seen as the future No. 1 overall pick since his freshman season at Clemson, and it was hard to find an evaluator who didn't see him as a slam-dunk franchise quarterback. New head coach Urban Meyer, who we'll get to in a bit, said after the draft that the selection was decided in February. A video the Jaguars released in their "The Hunt" series in May had general manager Trent Baalke noting that the NFL made them wait at least seven minutes before turning in the card. This isn't just a transformational moment for the franchise in terms of talent—depending on how you felt about Mark Brunell, this is arguably the first time the Jaguars have ever had someone you could *expect* to be a franchise quarterback.

QBASE, our projection model for quarterbacks, had Lawrence as the best quarterback in this class. His 0.73 total DYAR per attempt projection is ninth among all quarterbacks selected since 2004. While Lawrence played with many impressive teammates—Tee Higgins, Travis Etienne, etc.—he also performed at a high level for all three years at Clemson, lessening the odds of him being a bust in the system's eyes.

From a scouting perspective, Lawrence has an arm that can truly hit any throw on the field plus an ability to throw off-platform and win with his legs late in the down. He has experience with pre-snap adjustments at Clemson and has thrown players open and demonstrated hitting his later reads often. There is an easy and telling comparison to Andrew Luck, who was the last quarterback prospect that was regarded as this flawless. Lawrence is probably even a more complete prospect than Luck was, but he heads into a situation that feels incredibly similar. The Jaguars are a rebuild from the ground up, but the division that they are in feels like it has taken a step towards being the AFC South of old after a promising 2020. The Colts in Luck's first year, it should be noted, made the playoffs even though he only completed 55.8% of his passes with a -5.1% DVOA. His highs were that high, and Lawrence immediately elevates the Jaguars into that sort of ceiling. Yes, this season.

Those mid-2010s Colts wasted Luck on Chuck Pagano and Ryan Grigson, making a series of idiotic draft selections, free-agent signings, and ill-fated Trent Richardson trades. In a way you could argue that the Colts did not deliver on the promise that Luck gave them more than Luck failed to deliver on his franchise quarterback status. It ended with Luck's abrupt retirement from the NFL before the 2019 season. This isn't to paint a picture that the Jaguars are absolutely the kind of organization that is going to do that to a quarterback, but to point out that the onus is now on them to grow up to what having Lawrence means. The era of athlete empowerment is here. The Jaguars are going to need to live up to what Lawrence gives them on the chalkboard and in the front office. That means that, in a reversal of how it usually goes, the major pressure is not on Lawrence, but on owner Shad Khan and his selection to steward Lawrence's progress, Meyer. If you want an example of what happens when you don't create that kind of atmosphere for a quarterback who is trying to lift all tides, look no further than the in-division implosion of the Houston Texans.

Khan, who has been described by Jacksonville institution Vito Stellino as an "absentee owner" in the face of how the Jaguars were allowed to stagnate these past few years, took a much more up-front position in Jacksonville's 2021 offseason. He was live in the draft room, talking to prospects as they were picked. His media statement to open the offseason with the firing of Doug Marrone was joined with a call for

2021 Jaguars Schedule

Week	Opp.	Week	Opp.	Week	Opp.
1	at HOU	7	BYE	13	at LAR
2	DEN	8	at SEA	14	at TEN
3	ARI	9	BUF	15	HOU
4	at CIN (Thu.)	10	at IND	16	at NYJ
5	TEN	11	SF	17	at NE
6	MIA (U.K.)	12	ATL	18	IND

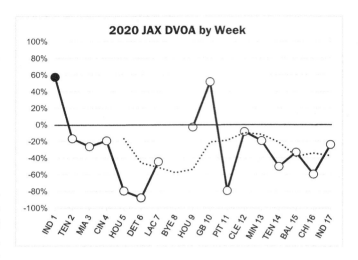

2020 JAX DVOA by Week

ambition: "The quest begins to find a head coach who shares my ambition for the Jacksonville Jaguars and our fans, whose loyalty and faith are overdue to be rewarded." Khan was a part of four different press conferences this offseason, sat in on Zoom meetings with prospects, and was showing, if not less stubbornness, perhaps a little willingness to be more involved.

Khan, with his Illinois ties and thus his focus on the Big Ten, had a lot of familiarity with Meyer, and Meyer was such a presumed candidate to take the job that the rumors were spreading before Khan's end-of-season presser happened. Khan noted at Meyer's introductory presser that "Really, last Monday when the opportunity came, he was one of the people I kind of reached out [to]. I think the more important thing was, I think it has been addressed, his health, but really the commitment, the fire in the belly. He has achieved a lot in college coaching. I'm sensitive to the legacy he has, and this is a very different challenge. I was just absolutely blown away [with] how he can help us and really reinvigorate the Jacksonville Jaguars."

Meyer's charisma and results more than qualify him for a try at NFL life. He talks the talk as far as "owning it" and realizing these are grown adult men rather than children, trying to accentuate every player's strengths and being hands-off in the right areas while being hands-on where it will matter most. Turning Ohio State back into a consistent year-in and year-out one- or two-loss team didn't hurt either as far as the reputa-

tion he carries with fans and players. There's a mythos around Meyer's accomplishments that is hard to ignore.

The flipside to this is that, when two people hold the cards (or as Khan noted in the introductory presser: "we're going to be carrying out Urban's vision of the team and the kind of players we want."), the old-boy network can start with aplomb. Baalke washed out of San Francisco having squandered Jim Harbaugh's roster down to the nubs, and Khan vouched to keep him on board as general manager. ("I mean, you can Google him, you can see what Trent has done in football and especially his track record as a GM in the NFL," Khan told reporters before introducing Baalke, as if that was going to enforce some strong positive opinions.) Meyer's defensive coordinator pick, Joe Cullen, has not coordinated a defense since the mid-aughts, when he led the mighty Indiana Hoosiers to allow 31.2 points per game in 2004 as a one-and-done. Fans of the Detroit Lions may remember Cullen from his arrests as their defensive line coach in 2006, where he pre-created the foundation for the "Sir, this is a Wendy's" meme by pulling up to the drive-in window naked. Tim Tebow, the best-known outfielder in the history of the Binghamton Rumble Ponies, is

Table 1. College Coaches Taking Over NFL Franchises for the First Time in the 2000s

Coach	Year	Tm	Yrs	Prev Yr DVOA	Y1 DVOA	Y2 DVOA	Y3 DVOA	Y4 DVOA	W-L
Butch Davis	2001	CLE	4	-41.5%	-8.0%	0.8%	-8.6%	-19.6%	24-35
Steve Spurrier	2002	WAS	2	-0.8%	-10.8%	-13.9%			12-20
Nick Saban	2005	MIA	2	-14.4%	1.2%	-1.6%			15-17
Bobby Petrino	2007	ATL	1	-5.2%	-23.1%				3-10
Lane Kiffin	2007	OAK	2	-34.7%	-30.8%	-24.1%			5-15
Jim Harbaugh	2011	SF	4	-12.4%	18.4%	30.2%	16.8%	6.3%	44-19
Chip Kelly	2013	PHI	3	-24.9%	13.5%	12.5%	-24.9%		26-21
Doug Marrone	2013	BUF	2	-12.4%	-3.9%	10.7%			15-17
Greg Schiano	2013	TB	2	-7.2%	-5.2%	-29.4%			11-21
Bill O'Brien	2014	HOU	7	-25.4%	-1.0%	-7.1%	-15.9%	-18.0%	52-48
Kliff Kingsbury	2019	ARI	2	-38.4%	-3.1%	3.6%			13-18-1
Matt Rhule	2020	CAR	1	-26.5%	-6.7%				5-11
Urban Meyer	2021	JAX	--	-28.0%	--				--
	AVERAGE			-20.9%	-5.0%	-1.8%	-8.2%	-10.4%	

here to play tight end because he's Meyer's guy.

The recent history of college head coaches in the NFL has not been kind, but it has generally led with a first-season upside (Table 1). Chip Kelly was a hit until he gained personnel control. Matt Rhule didn't shake anybody up in Carolina this year, but it was a big improvement over where the Panthers had been in 2019. The most successful coaches who came from the college ranks over the past two decades were Bill O'Brien and Harbaugh, and only Harbaugh had an empirically impressive career. The first-year bump sure seems nice, but the power struggles that O'Brien and Harbaugh created—as Baalke knows—were less fun. That doesn't mean that Meyer fits squarely into that box; he's someone with a much longer track record of success than most of those guys. But it is a bit eye-catching that you can't find much in the way of a success story for that subset of coach hire outside of Harbaugh.

High draft picks aside, Baalke didn't go wild improving the team in the offseason. Maybe that's a good thing. The history of free agency in Jacksonville has more often been led by the Jags overpaying Julius Thomas and Toby Gerhart rather than convincing quality players such as Calais Campbell to join up with bad teams. "We're looking at a lot of different positions and a lot of different players and the key word there was value. We're looking for value. That isn't always the most expensive player," Baalke would say in a pre-free agency presser. Jacksonville brought in just five outside free agents with more than $7.5 million guaranteed in their contracts. The only one of those who got more than $20 million was ex-Seahawks corner and UCF product Shaquill Griffin, who got what was essentially a two-year, $22-million deal. Griffin allowed six touchdowns in coverage last year per Sports Info Solutions' charting and hasn't had a notably good season for the Seahawks since his debut in 2016. Rayshawn Jenkins was the other major investment, another ex-Florida college product who had far and away his best season for the Chargers last year and has played several different middle-of-field positions as a nickel/safety. To add to those two, the Jags reeled in wideout Marvin Jones via his connection with offensive coordinator Darrell Bevell and put two big bodies up front in Malcom Brown and Roy Robertson-Harris.

After the layup first overall pick, the Jaguars went heavily against traditional analytics wisdom in taking Lawrence's college teammate Etienne 25th overall. (Reportedly they had their hearts set on Florida wideout Kadarius Toney, who went to the Giants a few picks earlier.) Baalke addressed that decision by saying "I don't know who questions it I guess, if there's other GM's that feel the same way, take a back, don't take a back. Our job is to take the best football players available and when you have a chance to add an explosive, dynamic player to your team, I don't think that's a roll of the dice. I think that's an educated decision that we were willing to make." Etienne is certainly a different kind of back in the sense that the Jaguars view him as a hybrid back/receiver, and they have plans to put him in a variety of roles and even mentioned putting him in two-back sets with Robinson. But that archetype of player is not exactly such an NFL commodity that you have to spend a first-round pick to find him. James

White signed a one-year, $2.4-million deal. Giovani Bernard signed a one-year, $1-million deal off a solid season. Duke Johnson is still a free agent after one bad season in that role with the Texans. The Jaguars finished the offseason with a league-high $39 million in cap space as of the end of May, almost $14 million more than the second-place Jets. And while they do get to roll cap space over, it's not exactly helping them this year while they have accumulated value free agents.

Cullen gave exactly one interview to the assembled media since being hired and it A) wasn't really informative, and B) is old enough that he still hasn't publicly spoken about a lot of changes made since. There were, of course, the old lines about having an attacking defense and stopping the run. The general tenor of the media conversation is that Cullen is going to run something Baltimore-ish based on his five-year apprenticeship under Ravens coordinator Wink Martindale, with the ability to be multiple as far as 4-3 versus 3-4. Most of the public emphasis per Meyer has been on getting the defensive front fixed first, both run defense and pass rush. They even traded up for edge rusher Jordan Smith on Day 3 to make sure to get one of the last guys on their board that sort of fit that intersection of board value and position.

The Jaguars were given an extremely precious gift this season by virtue of their last-place finish: one of the easiest projected schedules in the NFL by our numbers. Even though they have bottom-10 projections in offense and defense, they still hang around mediocrity in the win forecast. So what happens if Lawrence is just that good, that fast? What if he's already the best quarterback in the AFC South? (And we say that with no disrespect to Ryan Tannehill.) What if Jacksonville's defense actually does take a major step forward with a healthy Josh Allen and a second-year leap from K'Lavon Chaisson? Things could get very interesting for the Jaguars in a hurry. Meyer is certainly used to winning, and much as there are some solid football teams in the division, they won't share that Jaguars schedule.

It's hard, but not far-fetched, to create the story of a Jaguars playoff appearance in 2021. If you believe in Meyer's systems and the flags that he has planted to produce instant improvement on a roster that had no prayer in winning with the quarterbacks they used in 2020, everything is in reach. It's also possible that the Jaguars just don't have enough talent to begin with and this is a consolation year before they are truly able to stack the deck around Lawrence. That's what DVOA is betting on.

Ultimately the most important thing to watch will be how Meyer's first picks work out and how quickly he's prone to tinker with things that are going wrong. Meyer's health has led him to take a step back from being the all-involved coach that he once was, as well as forced retirements at each of his last two stops. For all the whitewashing of Meyer's image, his past has many red flags (ignoring spousal abuse allegations against assistant coach Zach Smith, a big *Sporting News* exposé called "How Urban Meyer broke Florida football" that detailed a bleak culture), and he started off his Jaguars career with an unforced error by hiring and firing strength coach Chris Doyle within the span of a day. Doyle had a history of mistreatment of Black players, and Meyer hopefully noted in introducing Doyle that "We did a very good job vetting that one." Well, not so much.

You can't argue with Meyer's results on the football field. He has generally been a good head coach that has gotten a lot out of his teams, even at high-profile college programs. How

that sausage was made is less appealing. And in trying to create a football team that can live up to the promise that Lawrence has, how that sausage is made in Jacksonville is going to be paramount to the tale we tell about the Jaguars in five years.

Rivers McCown

2020 Jaguars Stats by Week

Wk	vs.	W-L	PF	PA	YDF	YDA	TO	Total	Off	Def	ST
1	IND	W	27	20	241	445	2	57.4%	56.5%	0.9%	1.9%
2	at TEN	L	30	33	480	354	-2	-16.7%	11.6%	17.6%	-10.6%
3	MIA	L	13	31	318	294	-2	-26.1%	3.1%	22.7%	-6.5%
4	at CIN	L	25	33	429	505	0	-19.1%	17.6%	39.1%	2.4%
5	at HOU	L	14	30	364	486	0	-79.5%	-41.2%	27.1%	-11.2%
6	DET	L	16	34	275	403	-1	-87.8%	-58.6%	16.4%	-12.7%
7	at LAC	L	29	39	294	484	-1	-44.4%	-9.5%	33.9%	-1.0%
8	BYE										
9	HOU	L	25	27	403	374	0	-3.0%	-2.6%	9.3%	8.9%
10	at GB	L	20	24	260	395	1	51.8%	-15.3%	-32.0%	35.1%
11	PIT	L	3	27	206	373	-3	-79.2%	-66.1%	16.4%	3.3%
12	CLE	L	25	27	375	459	1	-8.3%	16.9%	20.9%	-4.2%
13	at MIN	L	24	27	390	420	-2	-19.1%	-29.6%	-14.6%	-4.1%
14	TEN	L	10	31	354	454	0	-50.1%	-22.6%	21.1%	-6.4%
15	at BAL	L	14	40	267	409	0	-33.0%	-8.1%	23.2%	-1.7%
16	CHI	L	17	41	279	391	-1	-59.3%	-37.5%	28.8%	7.0%
17	at IND	L	14	28	283	437	0	-23.6%	-4.3%	17.2%	-2.1%

Trends and Splits

	Offense	Rank	Defense	Rank
Total DVOA	-12.6%	27	15.2%	31
Unadjusted VOA	-11.0%	25	17.9%	31
Weighted Trend	-19.3%	30	14.4%	30
Variance	9.6%	26	3.2%	5
Average Opponent	2.3%	28	3.7%	7
Passing	-8.1%	26	30.1%	31
Rushing	-11.1%	19	-1.4%	24
First Down	-2.4%	20	13.2%	28
Second Down	-17.6%	27	23.5%	32
Third Down	-24.0%	31	6.9%	21
First Half	-10.1%	24	18.3%	31
Second Half	-15.2%	26	12.0%	27
Red Zone	6.3%	16	16.2%	31
Late and Close	-24.3%	29	4.7%	21

Five-Year Performance

Year	W-L	Pyth W	Est W	PF	PA	TO	Total	Rk	Off	Rk	Def	Rk	ST	Rk	Off AGL	Rk	Def AGL	Rk	Off Age	Rk	Def Age	Rk	ST Age	Rk
2016	3-13	5.8	5.2	318	400	-16	-11.7%	27	-11.5%	27	-2.1%	15	-2.3%	23	52.0	26	24.3	6	25.6	31	25.9	28	25.5	26
2017	10-6	11.9	9.0	417	268	+10	13.8%	8	0.4%	15	-15.9%	2	-2.5%	24	31.5	15	4.1	1	26.1	28	25.9	22	26.0	11
2018	5-11	5.7	6.0	245	316	-12	-8.5%	22	-21.7%	30	-8.8%	7	4.4%	4	87.1	32	15.4	5	26.3	21	26.2	16	25.6	24
2019	6-10	5.3	6.4	300	397	-1	-19.4%	28	-9.9%	24	12.3%	29	2.7%	6	55.4	27	44.8	25	25.3	32	25.6	26	25.8	17
2020	1-15	3.7	4.1	306	492	-8	-28.0%	31	-12.6%	27	15.2%	31	-0.1%	18	18.9	6	44.4	19	26.1	24	24.9	32	25.0	31

2020 Performance Based on Most Common Personnel Groups

JAX Offense					JAX Offense vs. Opponents					JAX Defense				JAX Defense vs. Opponents			
Pers	Freq	Yds	DVOA	Run%	Pers	Freq	Yds	DVOA	Run%	Pers	Freq	Yds	DVOA	Pers	Freq	Yds	DVOA
11	72%	5.5	-3.4%	21%	Base	21%	4.4	-21.5%	61%	Base	39%	6.7	10.6%	11	51%	6.8	23.8%
12	11%	5.1	-12.0%	57%	Nickel	57%	5.5	-3.6%	29%	Nickel	57%	6.8	23.5%	12	21%	7.4	17.7%
13	6%	3.1	-53.0%	56%	Dime+	22%	5.8	-9.2%	5%	Dime+	3%	6.1	-18.4%	21	9%	7.3	-4.3%
21	4%	5.7	-48.9%	58%	Goal Line	0%	1.0	110.8%	100%	Goal Line	1%	0.0	-74.0%	13	4%	5.5	21.1%
10	2%	8.3	107.0%	15%										22	4%	3.5	-9.3%

Strategic Tendencies

Run/Pass		Rk	Formation		Rk	Pass Rush		Rk	Secondary		Rk	Strategy		Rk
Runs, first half	36%	22	Form: Single Back	82%	12	Rush 3	2.9%	28	4 DB	39%	1	Play Action	19%	31
Runs, first down	46%	19	Form: Empty Back	8%	21	Rush 4	66.3%	17	5 DB	57%	19	Offensive Motion	35%	30
Runs, second-long	17%	30	Form: Multi Back	10%	14	Rush 5	24.5%	9	6+ DB	3%	23	Avg Box (Off)	6.37	28
Runs, power sit.	42%	32	Pers: 3+ WR	77%	5	Rush 6+	6.4%	10	Man Coverage	41%	6	Avg Box (Def)	6.72	8
Runs, behind 2H	24%	23	Pers: 2+ TE/6+ OL	20%	28	Edge Rusher Sacks	55.6%	12	CB by Sides	70%	22	Offensive Pace	31.08	24
Pass, ahead 2H	50%	14	Pers: 6+ OL	1%	21	Interior DL Sacks	13.9%	29	S/CB Cover Ratio	24%	18	Defensive Pace	30.14	15
Run-Pass Options	9%	13	Shotgun/Pistol	70%	13	Second Level Sacks	30.6%	8	DB Blitz	13%	16	Go for it on 4th	1.96	6

Most teams are better at running against light boxes, but the Jaguars took it to an extreme last season. Against six or fewer men in the box, handoffs went for 6.3 yards per carry and 13.1% DVOA. Against seven men, 4.1 yards per carry and -14.7% DVOA. Against eight or more, Jacksonville fell to 2.8 yards per carry and -26.3% DVOA. ◥ Something the Jaguars did well? RPOs. Jacksonville averaged 6.2 yards per play on RPOs, near the top of the league. ◥ Jacksonville was also good at running back screens, leading the league with 33 and gaining 8.2 yards per play with 55.4% DVOA. ◥ This was the third straight year the Jaguars ranked in the bottom five in frequency of using play-action, even though they were pretty good at it. The Jaguars gained 7.0 yards per play and 20.6% DVOA with play-action compared to 5.4 yards per play and -16.2% DVOA without it. ◥ Jacksonville opponents threw a league-high 28% of passes to their No. 1 receivers for the second straight season. ◥ Because their opponents were constantly running out the clock, Jacksonville used base defense on a league-high 39% of plays. ◥ Once again, the Jaguars defense was near the bottom of the league in broken tackles (135, fifth-most) and average yards allowed after the catch (5.8, 29th).

Passing

Player	DYAR	DVOA	Plays	NtYds	Avg	YAC	C%	TD	Int
G.Minshew	4	-11.0%	353	2112	6.0	4.7	66.3%	16	5
M.Glennon*	-105	-19.8%	186	988	5.3	3.6	63.4%	7	5
J.Luton	-287	-48.6%	117	572	4.9	4.6	54.5%	2	6
C.J.Beathard	75	-1.0%	112	716	6.4	5.2	64.1%	6	0

Rushing

Player	DYAR	DVOA	Plays	Yds	Avg	TD	Fum	Suc
J.Robinson	76	-0.8%	240	1070	4.5	7	1	49%
D.Ogunbowale	33	17.8%	32	145	4.5	0	0	38%
G.Minshew	11	-4.2%	27	156	5.8	1	1	--
L.Shenault	45	4.6%	18	91	5.1	0	0	--
C.Thompson*	-6	-30.2%	7	20	2.9	0	0	43%
M.Glennon*	-28	-85.3%	6	17	2.8	0	1	--
C.Hyde	46	4.7%	81	356	4.4	4	0	49%
C.J.Beathard	3	1.3%	5	29	5.8	0	0	--

Receiving

Player	DYAR	DVOA	Plays	Ctch	Yds	Y/C	YAC	TD	C%
DJ Chark	26	-9.1%	93	53	706	13.3	3.1	5	57%
K.Cole*	82	-1.7%	88	55	642	11.7	3.2	5	63%
L.Shenault	56	-4.0%	79	58	600	10.3	5.1	5	73%
C.Conley*	18	-9.0%	63	40	471	11.8	4.5	2	63%
C.Johnson	19	-5.0%	31	18	272	15.1	3.6	2	58%
T.Godwin	-8	-30.6%	6	3	32	10.7	1.0	0	50%
M.Jones	235	12.3%	115	76	978	12.9	2.6	9	66%
J.Agnew	-38	-36.2%	20	13	89	6.8	7.8	0	65%
P.Cooper	13	9.6%	8	5	73	14.6	7.0	0	63%
L.Treadwell	34	46.6%	7	6	49	8.2	2.2	2	86%
T.Eifert*	-56	-20.7%	60	36	349	9.7	2.8	2	60%
J.O'Shaughnessy	-10	-11.0%	38	28	262	9.4	3.4	0	74%
C.Manhertz	-8	-22.8%	8	6	52	8.7	5.5	0	75%
J.Robinson	50	1.2%	60	49	344	7.0	7.8	3	82%
C.Thompson*	35	16.7%	23	20	146	7.3	5.4	1	87%
D.Ogunbowale	-36	-50.3%	20	10	54	5.4	6.3	0	50%
D.Ozigbo	-1	-15.3%	9	9	42	4.7	4.3	0	100%
C.Hyde	-19	-33.6%	20	16	93	5.8	6.8	0	80%

Offensive Line

Player	Pos	Age	GS	Snaps	Pen	Sk	Pass	Run	Player	Pos	Age	GS	Snaps	Pen	Sk	Pass	Run
Jawaan Taylor	RT	24	16/16	1037	7	8	37	5	Tyler Shatley	C	30	16/10	642	1	1.5	8	5
Cam Robinson	LT	26	16/16	973	4	7	32	10	Brandon Linder	C	29	9/9	530	1	0	0	1
A.J.Cann	RG	30	15/15	919	4	1	11	5	Ben Bartch	RG/LG	23	13/1	219	0	0	4	1
Andrew Norwell	LG	30	13/13	801	1	2	8	4									

Year	Yards	ALY	Rk	Power	Rk	Stuff	Rk	2Lev	Rk	OpFld	Rk	BB Rt	Rk	Sacks	ASR	Rk	Press	Rk	BB Rt	Rk	Cont
2018	3.47	4.12	21	69%	12	19%	19	0.98	29	0.29	32	7.4%	22	53	9.3%	27	33.6%	25	12.7%	28	22
2019	4.17	3.88	27	63%	20	20%	23	1.02	27	1.09	4	11.4%	25	41	7.0%	16	29.4%	13	12.2%	8	44
2020	4.41	4.48	11	73%	7	15%	7	1.22	15	0.68	19	10.1%	17	44	7.6%	25	24.8%	17	15.7%	30	24

2020 ALY by direction:	Left End: 4.58 (12)	Left Tackle: 5.74 (1)	Mid/Guard: 4.61 (8)	Right Tackle: 5.15 (6)	Right End: 2.54 (31)

Franchise-tagging Cam Robinson has the look of a move with an eye towards this season rather than a move with an eye towards a long-term contract. Robinson allowed 8.5 sacks in 2019. Only six linemen allowed seven or more sacks last season, and two of them were on this roster. Robinson has not demonstrated a lot of growth since his rookie season, and though the Jaguars said they might look at extending him, there has been no noise about that since. ● Jawaan Taylor was said to be a second-round steal but has consistently been brutal on the stat sheet in each of his first two seasons. Urban Meyer said that "the two tackles are going to get better" in a March presser. "They're young players. That's an area that has got to play better than it did a year ago." Then he drafted Stanford's Walker Little in the second round. ● There's no doubting Little's pedigree, and he was definitely bandied about as a future first-round pick at a young age. But after suffering a season-ending knee injury in his junior year, Little opted out of his senior season. He hasn't played football in two years. Trent Baalke was never shy about drafting players with major injuries in their past. ● The Jaguars have an interior line foundation piece in place with Brandon Linder, one of the best in the business when healthy. Sports Info Solutions charting has him with just 10 blown blocks in the last two seasons combined. ● Guard Andrew Norwell hasn't quite been the stud the Jaguars thought they were getting when he was one of 2018's top free agents. He restructured this offseason with a one-year deal that pays him $9 million guaranteed and up to $12 million total coming off his best season in Jacksonville. ● A name in search of an old The Smiths song it can fit into, Tyler Shatley had a solid season as a fill-in starter for Linder and figures to again be the primary interior line depth piece. A.J. Cann is coming off his best season since the Gus Bradley administration, but if he falls back to earth in 2021, it wouldn't be surprising if flatly, Mr. Shatley got some run at guard.

Defensive Front

Defensive Line	Age	Pos	G	Snaps	Plays	TmPct	Rk	Stop	Dfts	BTkl	Runs	St%	Rk	RuYd	Rk	Sack	Hit	Hur	Dsrpt
						Overall						vs. Run				Pass Rush			
Taven Bryan	25	DT	16	511	18	2.1%	96	15	4	1	17	82%	16	3.0	77	0.5	5	3	0
Doug Costin	24	DT	12	455	34	5.3%	46	26	3	0	28	79%	32	3.0	82	0.0	1	5	2
Davon Hamilton	24	DT	11	407	31	5.2%	47	19	4	4	28	61%	85	2.1	35	1.0	4	7	2
Daniel Ekuale	27	DT	9	290	13	2.7%	88	7	1	2	12	50%	97	3.4	95	1.0	0	4	1
Malcom Brown	27	DT	13	345	27	4.2%	62	23	6	1	24	88%	4	1.1	2	1.0	2	7	0
Jihad Ward	27	DE	10	271	18	3.5%	--	14	5	3	12	67%	--	4.1	--	3.0	6	6	2
Roy Robertson-Harris	28	DE	8	245	10	2.4%	93	7	1	1	9	67%	69	3.3	90	0.0	5	6	1

Edge Rushers	Age	Pos	G	Snaps	Plays	TmPct	Rk	Stop	Dfts	BTkl	Runs	St%	Rk	RuYd	Rk	Sack	Hit	Hur	Dsrpt
						Overall						vs. Run				Pass Rush			
Dawuane Smoot	26	DE	16	665	25	2.9%	84	20	8	8	16	75%	33	2.7	51	5.5	11	16	1
Adam Gotsis	29	DE	16	579	40	4.6%	52	30	7	6	37	73%	45	2.1	30	0.0	4	5	3
K'Lavon Chaisson	22	DE	16	568	20	2.3%	93	16	4	4	15	73%	40	2.6	47	1.0	8	19	2
Josh Allen	24	DE	8	397	14	3.2%	79	11	4	3	9	78%	23	1.3	5	2.5	10	16	1
Kamalei Correa*	27	OLB	9	197	10	2.1%	--	6	0	2	8	63%	--	3.5	--	0.0	2	1	0
Aaron Lynch*	28	DE	8	152	7	1.6%	--	5	2	3	5	60%	--	3.4	--	1.0	3	8	1

Linebackers	Age	Pos	G	Snaps	Plays	TmPct	Rk	Stop	Dfts	BTkl	Runs	St%	Rk	RuYd	Rk	Sack	Hit	Hur	Tgts	Suc%	Rk	Yd/P	Rk	PD	Int
						Overall						vs. Run				Pass Rush				vs. Pass					
Joe Schobert	28	MLB	16	1109	145	16.8%	10	80	21	17	87	67%	13	3.2	15	2.5	3	6	42	57%	18	7.0	53	4	3
Myles Jack	26	OLB	14	931	123	16.3%	13	78	27	10	80	69%	10	3.7	32	1.0	1	5	34	59%	14	5.6	28	5	1
Joe Giles-Harris	24	OLB	9	204	18	3.7%	--	11	3	1	14	64%	--	3.8	--	1.0	4	4	1	0%	--	7.0	--	0	0
Damien Wilson	28	OLB	13	528	71	10.7%	57	32	7	5	47	55%	44	3.5	24	0.0	0	3	15	40%	62	8.0	65	1	0

Year	Yards	ALY	Rk	Power	Rk	Stuff	Rk	2Lev	Rk	OpFld	Rk	BB Rt	Rk	Sacks	ASR	Rk	Press	Rk	BB Rt	Rk
2018	4.07	3.87	4	61%	7	21%	11	0.90	3	1.03	22	8.1%	18	37	7.1%	15	33.2%	5	11.1%	14
2019	5.31	4.62	27	64%	17	18%	17	1.38	29	1.60	32	12.9%	16	47	8.1%	6	31.8%	10	14.8%	18
2020	4.84	4.42	17	66%	15	19%	12	1.30	20	1.19	30	16.5%	4	18	4.2%	30	20.2%	29	9.9%	29

2020 ALY by direction:	Left End: 4.92 (22)	Left Tackle: 4.92 (26)	Mid/Guard: 4.32 (13)	Right Tackle: 3.68 (7)	Right End: 4.50 (13)

Each of the top 10 front seven defenders by snap count returns, with Roy Robertson-Harris, Jihad Ward, and Malcom Brown joining them. Brown, acquired from the Saints in a salary-dump trade, has become a bit of a journeyman nose but he has been rock solid in that role and helped the Saints finish second in run defense DVOA. 🏈 Joe Cullen was heavily involved in the decision to pick up Ward, as Ward explained in his post-signing media availability: "We go way back and it's a strong connection back there with me and him when he was getting me right for the combine. He worked me out every time. It's just some stuff that's just really not explainable. He's just a good guy to me. I trust him. I give my all to that guy because he always gives his all to me, so that's my dog." Ward has been a solid rotational hybrid player and was with Cullen on the Ravens last year. 🏈 Robertson-Harris flashed some pass-rush ability in 2018 when he finished with three sacks and 23 hurries next to Akiem Hicks. He could wind up pushing former first-round pick Taven Bryan, who has not had his fifth-year option picked up yet and saw a massive decline from 17 hurries in 2019 to just three last season. 🏈 With Joe Schobert signed from the Browns last year, Myles Jack was freed from the Mike responsibilities that led to his lost 2019. Jack responded with a stellar season that was more up to his standards. Schobert is not someone you want on an island in man-to-man coverage, and of Schobert's three interceptions, two came in zone coverage and the other was tipped. Jack has generally been good in coverage outside of that year in the middle. 🏈 Josh Allen will be looking to make the third-year Josh Allen leap that we've come to expect of Josh Allens. This Allen was actually explosive in 2019 but fought through an injury-riddled 2020. K'Lavon Chaisson, the other first-round edge rusher, demonstrated how raw he was last year after collecting just 7.5 sacks in a year and a game at LSU. (He tore his ACL in the season opener of his sophomore year.) Chaisson isn't a natural edge-bender and his one sack was past Rodger Saffold on the interior. This is a huge offseason for his growth if he's going to be a real piece of the rebuild. 🏈 The Jags traded up for Jordan Smith in the fourth round, of which Meyer said: "So we're sitting there and we have our defensive coordinator sitting with us and here's this really raw, talented guy who can rush the passer. Very raw, has a long way to go, but that's why we did it." Smith was a Florida transfer to Alabama-Birmingham following an involvement in credit card fraud and was the first UAB player drafted since 2015. He's got length and displayed a good array of techniques but will probably need a full season in NFL weight rooms before he's ready to make a real impact.

Defensive Secondary

Secondary	Age	Pos	G	Snaps	Plays	Overall TmPct	Rk	Stop	Dfts	BTkl	vs. Run Runs	St%	Rk	RuYd	Rk	vs. Pass Tgts	Tgt%	Rk	aDOT	Suc%	Rk	Yd/P	Rk	PD	Int
Tre Herndon	25	CB	16	1016	81	9.4%	25	31	9	11	31	42%	44	7.7	54	56	14.9%	76	13.2	43%	68	9.2	67	5	0
Jarrod Wilson	27	FS	12	764	71	11.0%	34	23	9	11	41	29%	51	9.1	57	18	6.3%	51	9.5	44%	50	9.0	52	3	1
Josh Jones	27	SS	13	700	84	12.0%	23	29	4	9	48	44%	25	7.3	41	30	11.5%	15	8.4	40%	60	7.7	33	1	1
CJ Henderson	23	CB	8	474	42	9.7%	21	17	6	6	9	33%	56	7.6	49	45	25.6%	5	11.5	49%	46	8.6	60	6	1
Andrew Wingard	25	FS	13	461	47	6.7%	--	20	9	5	26	54%	--	4.5	--	18	10.5%	--	11.0	39%	--	8.3	--	5	2
Chris Claybrooks	24	CB	13	374	41	5.8%	--	11	3	3	14	29%	--	9.3	--	31	22.3%	--	12.4	39%	--	9.2	--	3	0
Sidney Jones	25	CB	9	302	34	7.0%	--	15	5	3	11	27%	--	6.6	--	32	28.6%	--	15.5	63%	--	10.6	--	9	2
Greg Mabin*	27	CB	5	248	24	8.9%	--	8	3	2	8	50%	--	7.1	--	24	26.1%	--	11.2	46%	--	7.2	--	3	0
Rayshawn Jenkins	27	SS	15	859	85	11.6%	26	44	19	12	40	53%	10	5.1	14	45	13.4%	6	8.6	53%	26	7.4	28	4	2
Shaquill Griffin	26	CB	12	812	75	11.3%	9	30	11	5	15	47%	31	5.2	26	75	21.0%	31	12.8	47%	59	7.9	48	12	3

Year	Pass D Rank	vs. #1 WR	Rk	vs. #2 WR	Rk	vs. Other WR	Rk	WR Wide	Rk	WR Slot	Rk	vs. TE	Rk	vs. RB	Rk
2018	6	-15.9%	4	-1.6%	16	-8.3%	11	-8.0%	14	-9.1%	5	-5.9%	13	-12.9%	8
2019	22	-11.4%	7	6.2%	20	18.2%	25	-3.1%	19	5.6%	15	23.0%	30	25.8%	28
2020	31	3.1%	19	-15.8%	5	19.7%	28	4.1%	18	1.7%	21	25.5%	30	-3.2%	16

The self-scouting that the Jaguars worked on this offseason led them to believe they needed to be much better in man coverage, and as Baalke pointed out in one of his post-draft calls, they have three "6-foot-tall corners who have a lot of versatility" between Shaq Griffin, 2020 first-rounder CJ Henderson, and 2021 second-rounder Tyson Campbell. 🏈 Henderson picked Philip Rivers in his first career start but had an uneven rookie year overall as he was largely thrown into the fire. The Colts targeted him 11 times in the opener. The Chargers picked up five first downs in nine targets with Keenan Allen. Henderson is recovering from offseason labrum surgery but should be ready for the season. 🏈 With the first pick of the second round spent on Campbell, the Jaguars picked up someone with 4.4s 40-yard speed at his Georgia pro day and good height and length. Footwork was an on-again/off-again issue for him in coverage, but he should profile as a slot corner this year at the very least. 🏈 The Jags hit the secondary again in the third-round with Andre Cisco who—shocker, as a Baalke pick—only played in two games in 2020 due to injury. Meyer said that he considered Cisco the best overhang player in the draft, comparing him to Malik Hooker and Reggie Nelson. Cisco picked off 12 passes and defensed another 28 in his two seasons before the injury, so it's hard to argue that he doesn't have plus talent. 🏈 Given those four major additions, last year's non-Henderson players are going to be fighting for their jobs. Sidney Jones had a nice couple of games while healthy, picking off Deshaun Watson in a highlight-reel play. Andrew Wingard was visually compared to Kid Rock by a CBS broadcast. Jarrod Wilson is the incumbent overhang safety; only seven of his 18 targets last year came in man coverage. Tre Herndon has made a nice little career for himself out of being a UDFA from Vanderbilt but would seem to be one of the main guys the Jaguars are trying to keep from starting games with their offseason moves.

Special Teams

Year	DVOA	Rank	FG/XP	Rank	Net Kick	Rank	Kick Ret	Rank	Net Punt	Rank	Punt Ret	Rank	Hidden	Rank
2018	4.4%	4	3.7	9	4.0	5	-0.9	16	10.7	1	4.5	8	0.2	16
2019	2.7%	6	8.5	3	0.5	15	-2.4	24	12.2	1	-5.1	29	2.1	14
2020	-0.1%	18	-8.2	29	0.7	16	-5.3	32	6.2	8	6.1	3	15.4	3

Signing Jamal Agnew away from the Lions should be a boon for the return game, which was disastrous on kickoffs and rode Keelan Cole's 91-yard touchdown against the Packers to a good ranking on punt returns. ◖ The Jaguars had six different placekickers last season, four of whom had negative value. Josh Lambo has hit over 90% of his field goals in every season in Jacksonville, including going an incredible 13-of-14 on field-goal attempts over 50 yards, but he's somehow the rarest of things: an injury-prone kicker. Lambo has missed games in three of his four years in Jacksonville, and Aldrick Rosas was carried on the roster throughout the offseason in response. Lambo also has a surprisingly high $4.4-million cap figure. ◖ The Jaguars extended punter Logan Cooke this offseason with a deal that averages $3 million a season. The Jaguars have finished in the top 10 of net punting in each of the last three years with Cooke.

Kansas City Chiefs

2020 Record: 14-2	**Total DVOA:** 19.6% (4)	**2021 Mean Projection:** 10.5 wins	**On the Clock (0-5):** 4%
Pythagorean Wins: 10.7 (7)	**Offense:** 23.9% (2)	**Postseason Odds:** 71.5%	**Mediocrity (6-8):** 18%
Snap-Weighted Age: 26.4 (17)	**Defense:** 4.9% (22)	**Super Bowl Odds:** 17.2%	**Playoff Contender (9-11):** 41%
Average Opponent: -2.2% (25)	**Special Teams:** 0.5% (17)	**Proj. Avg. Opponent:** -0.1% (18)	**Super Bowl Contender (12+):** 37%

2020: They were able to turn on the switch when it mattered, until suddenly in the Super Bowl they weren't.

2021: All the offensive linemen are belong to us.

E motions get the best of all of us. NFL decision-makers are not exempt from that. Everyone in the Kansas City Chiefs organization saw what the collapse of their offensive line cost them on the biggest stage and vowed to make sure that is not the reason they fail in 2021 and beyond, no matter the cost.

The Chiefs went into their second consecutive Super Bowl appearance with an XFL-caliber offensive line. From left to right, the Chiefs started Mike Remmers, Nick Allegretti, Austin Reiter, Stefen Wisniewski, and Andrew Wylie. Reiter was the only player of the bunch slotted to start before the season kicked off, and he was arguably the worst of the five intended starters to begin with. The two bookends—Remmers and Wylie—played about as poorly as possible, which was to be expected given the "better" of the two was a backup right tackle who got kicked to left tackle in the biggest game of the year.

Kansas City's Super Bowl offensive line would have been in trouble versus even an average front seven but was instead on the receiving end of one of the most disproportionate unit-versus-unit butt-whoopings in recent memory courtesy of the Tampa Bay Buccaneers' defensive front. Quarterback Patrick Mahomes had no choice but to scramble around like a chicken with its head cut off on nearly every play in that game.

Almost all of Kansas City's major resources this offseason were pumped into ensuring that Mahomes will be comfier in the pocket than he was in early February. Part of the all-in approach is an overreaction to how helpless the Super Bowl must have felt. It would be difficult to not get wrapped up in feeling as though you gave the best quarterback in the league no chance to win. It's not like the Chiefs' intended 2020 offensive line was particularly stellar when healthy, though. Even in 2019, without the opt-out of Laurent Duvernay-Tardif, the offensive line was firmly mediocre.

In each of the past two seasons, Kansas City finished with the second-highest blown block rate in pass protection. They finished 26th and 23rd in pressure rate in 2019 and 2020, respectively. Many of the Chiefs' issues up front were circumvented by Mahomes' Houdini act, as evidenced by their top-five finishes in adjusted sack rate through both seasons, but the life of the league's best quarterback should not have to be so chaotic, even if he does invite some of it through his own creation from time to time.

Kansas City's assumed improvement in pass protection should only be bolstered by some of the non-scrambling advantages Mahomes creates. Seeing as he is the best quarterback in the league throwing to two of the most dangerous pass-catchers in the league (Tyreek Hill, Travis Kelce), it tracks that opponents would want to keep defenders in coverage. Mahomes can also beat the blitz quite handily with his mind and quick trigger just the same as with his legs, so why try? Mahomes has been better against masses of pass-rushers for three years now. Last season, the Chiefs had 37.1% DVOA against four pass-rushers (6.8 yards per play) and 81.5% DVOA against five or more (9.3 yards per play).

The Chiefs tied for the fewest amount of five-plus-man rushes faced last season (19%) after having tied for the fourth-lowest mark in 2019. Likewise, the Chiefs tied for the most three-man rushes faced in 2020 (12%) while having finished tied for third the season before. Now, it's more than fair to say Mahomes' affinity for holding the ball and scrambling played a hand in the team's pressure rates despite these conservative pass-rush groupings, but it is not like it was a special offensive line, especially last season. It's also reasonable to explain that tendency to hold the ball, at least in part, as Mahomes knowing he is getting these conservative rushes and taking advantage of them accordingly. Assuming these pass-rush frequencies remain about the same, the Chiefs' new and improved offensive line may look as complete as it ever has in the Mahomes era.

Pampering the $400-million quarterback is hardly a storyline, though. Any team paying their signal-caller that much money should be doing the same (paging Brian Gutekunst). The real interest in Kansas City's all-out approach to the offensive line is not that they did it but how they went about it. The signings and draft picks the Chiefs made signal as much a desire to shake things up in the run game as they do a need for improved pass protection.

Schematic changes are often only assumed through the lens of a new quarterback, pass-catchers, or offensive coordinator, but Andy Reid seems to be making it a point to give his run game a makeover by bringing in different archetypes along the offensive line. For years, Reid's offense has been zone-oriented, as much of the NFL is. The Chiefs have run inside zone, outside zone, or stretch zone on 414 of their 630 handoffs over the past two seasons, which accounted for 66% of their run calls (Table 1). Conversely, the Chiefs called power, counter, or duo on just 129 of their 630 handoffs, good for about 20%.

2021 Chiefs Schedule

Week	Opp.	Week	Opp.	Week	Opp.
1	CLE	7	at TEN	13	DEN
2	at BAL	8	NYG (Mon.)	14	LV
3	LAC	9	GB	15	at LAC (Thu.)
4	at PHI	10	at LV	16	PIT
5	BUF	11	DAL	17	at CIN
6	at WAS	12	BYE	18	at DEN

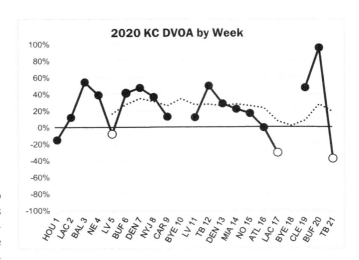

2020 KC DVOA by Week

The new pieces up front suggest Reid wants to lean into more gap/pulling schemes than before, perhaps as a means to counter the NFL's adoption of Tite/Mint odd-spacing defensive fronts. That has been the evolution of the game at the college level, and nobody has proven more capable of implementing college trends at the pro level than Reid. Reid is always among the first (and best) at making adjustments to his scheme to keep things fresh. Be it zone-read, pistol formations, option, shovel passes, RPOs, etc., Reid is always fishing for inspiration from the college game. Gap/pulling schemes are by no means a "college scheme," but they have become predominant at that level. It makes sense that Reid would be quick to recognize that.

Left tackle Orlando Brown, who joined the Chiefs from Baltimore at the cost of a first-round pick and change, is a hefty 6-foot-8, 355-pound lad with overwhelming power and surprising movement skills for his size. Former New England guard Joe Thuney is a sound, strong interior offensive lineman with plenty of experience as a puller. Rookie center Creed Humphrey (Oklahoma), who may or may not start Week 1, comes from a college offense that lived in the run game through various pulling concepts, most notably GT Counter. Not only will Humphrey be experienced in running these schemes, but he can probably help Reid incorporate them more easily.

Zone runs will probably still be the primary call in the offense. They are easier to install, rep, and marry to most play-action passing concepts, hence why they are the base for just about every team in the league. The Chiefs will almost surely call power, counter, and duo at a higher rate than their previ-

Table 1. Chiefs Play Design on Handoffs, 2019-2020

Run Type	2019	2020	Both	Rate
Inside Zone	90	72	162	25.7%
Outside Zone	65	84	149	23.7%
Stretch	55	48	103	16.3%
Power	34	50	84	13.3%
Zone-Counter	16	10	26	4.1%
Pitch	16	7	23	3.7%
Duo	6	17	23	3.7%
Counter	10	12	22	3.5%
Option	12	2	14	2.2%
Other	12	12	24	3.8%

ous 20%, though. We can also expect the Chiefs to incorporate these pulling plays into their RPO game. The Chiefs already led the league in RPO calls last season, after all. Sports Info Solutions marked 20% of their plays as RPOs; no other offense was above 14%.

Former Alabama offensive coordinator Steve Sarkisian (now at Texas) has harped on how difficult it can be for linebackers to read a pulling guard while still having coverage responsibilities, even more so than against zone-based RPOs. These pulling runs are often married with the "glance" route (a 10- to 15-yard dig/skinny post) behind them, which is something Alabama majored in over the last couple of years. The Carolina Panthers also did some of this with Cam Newton towards the end of his stint there, demonstrating that this concept can transfer from the college game to the NFL.

The only minor complication with Kansas City's offense comes from the Chiefs allowing Sammy Watkins to walk in free agency. Watkins has become something of a forgotten man relative to his days in Buffalo, but he was still a useful No. 3 option for the Chiefs as of late. Watkins' receptions were split almost evenly between the slot and wide alignments, providing a stable presence in the intermediate area from both spots. His touches were seldom wasted, either. Watkins earned just one failed completion on 37 catches last season. The days of old where Watkins could completely take the top off a defense are no more, but he would have been a good fit for some of the pulling-play RPOs the Chiefs aim to install.

It is hard to imagine the loss of Watkins will completely derail the Chiefs' offense, though. Mecole Hardman, Demarcus Robinson, and fifth-round rookie Cornell Powell should provide a flexible blend of talents to complement Hill and Kelce. Having Mahomes behind center helps make any receiving corps better anyway, which should be especially true in 2021 with the cleaner, more consistent pockets he will be working with. The Chiefs are still projected to have the best offense in the NFL.

The wide receiver room is not the only section of the roster that may have suffered a net loss in talent at the expense of improving the offensive line. With the majority of the Chiefs' resources getting thrown at protecting Mahomes, the Chiefs' middling defense was almost entirely ignored. They lost more likely contributors this offseason than they added, which is bad news for a defense that finished just 22nd in DVOA a year ago despite having the fewest adjusted games lost to injury on that side of the ball (14.5). The Chiefs defense is projected right around the same place next season, but a reversal in injury luck could certainly bring them in lower than that.

Most of the concern lies with the front seven. Kansas City finished 26th in run defense DVOA in 2019 and 31st in 2020. Defensive tackle Derrick Nnadi is competent, and Chris Jones' boom/bust play style can be valuable with how often he booms. But the rest of the front around them has been hopeless as of late. Kansas City's best run defender off the edge is Mike Danna, who was a fifth-round rookie last season. Danna plays sound, strong run defense for a rotational player, but he is not a starting-quality edge rusher.

The Chiefs' other "best" (an unbelievably generous phrase here) run defenders off the edge from last season are no longer with the team. Alex Okafor and Tanoh Kpassagnon were both allowed to walk in free agency. Neither were stars in run defense, but they were not the complete trainwreck that Frank Clark is on the opposite end. Clark's abysmal ranks in stop rate (90th) and average yards on run tackles (88th) brought down the unit as a whole, but the Chiefs were left with little option but to keep him on the field seeing as he was clearly their best pass-rusher off the edge. The same will be true in 2021. Taco Charlton, who was only slightly less embarrassing in run defense than Clark when he played a bigger role for the Dolphins in 2019, is not changing that; neither is fourth-round rookie Joshua Kaindoh.

That leaves only the linebackers to pick up the pieces, which could either be a saving grace or the nail in the coffin. Kansas City's linebacker group leaves the most room for volatility seeing as they will be relying on two recent second-round picks to get the job done: Willie Gay Jr. (2020) and Nick Bolton (2021). Anthony Hitchens will also remain in the mix, but he's a fairly known quantity as a replacement-level starter. It's up to the young guns to make or break the unit.

Kansas City's linebacker dilemma is two-pronged. First, the Chiefs need to figure out how good each player is sooner rather than later and find ways to keep them in comfortable assignments. Gay and Bolton are completely different players, which should ease some of the burden in that sense, but assessing and accommodating young players is seldom an easy task. Second, there remains an overarching question about how much good linebacker play actually affects the quality of a defense and in what ways.

The question of Gay's quality of play is half-answered. Gay was the Chiefs' best run defender last season. Though he technically did not cross the qualifying snaps threshold, Gay finished with the highest run stop rate (70%) and fewest average rushing yards on tackles (1.9) on the team. The film shows him as a quick-to-trigger linebacker with plenty of gusto when taking on blocks. His sideline-to-sideline speed is phenomenal, too, and a clear tier above his peers in the Chiefs linebacker room. Moving Gay to a full-time role should help the Chiefs defense clean up the leaks their defensive line is prone to allowing.

Defensive coordinator Steve Spagnuolo clearly did not trust him in coverage as a rookie, though. Gay's target sample is too small to make much of, but he was regularly taken off the field when the Chiefs played just one or two linebackers as opposed to three. There were flashes of Gay being able to roll-and-run to pick up crossers against play-action, as well as the range to play top-down and prevent YAC in zone, but there must have been something Spagnuolo knew about him that we did not that made him want to keep Gay off the field.

Bolton enters the league having few solutions for the vacancies in Gay's skill set. Missouri had zero hesitation with unleashing Bolton as a downhill player given his straight-line speed and willingness to take the fight to offensive linemen. The strength Bolton showed in taking on those blocks ran hot and cold in college, but his willingness to try to blow blockers away is a good start. His speed and high-intensity play style also made him a tackle machine, both near the line of scrimmage and when cleaning up the mess for others as a run-and-chase type.

The concerns with Bolton's NFL transition, not unlike Gay's, root in how he can handle third downs. At Missouri, Bolton showed quality zone spacing and discipline. Rarely did he run himself away from plays too early, and he did well to trigger on time when the quarterback threw the ball. However, Bolton turns like a 2-by-4 plank of wood on film, and his poor agility testing at the Missouri pro day backs that up. Bolton clocked a 7.40s 3-cone drill and a 4.50s short-shuttle, which places him in the 14th and 11th percentiles, respectively, among linebackers since 1999. In turn, Bolton's transitions when triggering on the ball in zone coverage can be clunky, as are his movements in man coverage assignments that take him anywhere but to the flat. Those issues will only be accentuated in the league, especially early on. Bolton being something along the lines of Will Compton is a more reasonable rookie outlook than expecting him to be an instant full-time starter that alters the makeup of the defense.

The combination of Gay and Bolton seeing increased reps will partly be in replacement of Damien Wilson, who was arguably the Chiefs' best (or at least most trusted) linebacker over the past two seasons. That is faint praise, to be clear, but Wilson did provide run support that was not completely disastrous while not being the unit's biggest liability in coverage. That is where the bar is at for Kansas City's two young linebackers.

Now, the second prong to the Chiefs' linebacker situation is how much we can reasonably expect them to swing the quality of the defense. Barring a complete collapse from Gay and Bolton, the linebackers probably will not be any worse and should not hinder the defense any more than they already has in the past. Slotting Gay into more of a full-time role should bolster the run defense to some degree, but until the defensive line is sorted out, it probably will not be enough to move the needle.

Massive improvement of the Chiefs defense through the linebacker unit would have to come through coverage, specifically against running backs. The Chiefs defense finished 31st in the league in DVOA against running back targets, which is almost directly a result of their poor linebacker play. Gay was the only good run-and-chase linebacker on the team last year, but he was not trusted in other coverage situations, which meant he was regularly off the field on passing downs. Bolton, to his credit, is best at stacking his zones effectively and playing down to prevent yards after the catch, so long as his stiff hips do not get in the way. Putting both Gay and Bolton on the field should limit some of the easier gains that teams try to make against the Chiefs, even if they may still provide close to nothing on tougher coverage assignments.

As such, we can probably expect the Chiefs to remain one of the biggest proponents of playing six defensive backs. The Chiefs ranked fourth in use of dime formations last year, which was both a reflection of their weakness at linebacker and strength in the secondary. Part of that may also have to do with game script and teams having to constantly chase the Chiefs offense with points through the air, but the reflection of roster strengths and weaknesses rings true nonetheless.

And thankfully for Kansas City, almost all of last year's secondary is returning. Seven defensive backs earned at least 35% of the team's defensive snaps last year. The only one not returning is Bashaud Breeland. Four of them (Tyrann Mathieu, Charvarius Ward, Daniel Sorenson, Juan Thornhill) recorded success rates of 52% or better in coverage in each of the past two seasons, and both L'Jarius Sneed and Rashad Fenton cleared the same mark in 2020.

Spagnuolo runs a heavy helping of man coverage. Kansas City's 40% man-coverage rate ranked eighth in the league last season, up slightly from their 36% man-coverage rate from 2019. The Chiefs' secondary is aided to some degree by Spagnuolo's blitz-happy nature (15% of plays with six-plus rushers), but that style still requires defensive backs to hold up in one-on-one coverage with no help anywhere for at least a couple of seconds. A defense has to have the horses in the secondary to get away with that like the Chiefs and Ravens do. The Bengals, who ranked seventh in big blitzes of six or more pass-rushers and fifth in man coverage rate last season, are what it looks like when a defense doesn't have the coverage guys to get away with it. With as many pieces returning to the Chiefs secondary, they should be able to stick to their same old formula again in 2021.

Sticking to much of the same is the general theme for the Chiefs' 2021 season, and for good reason. The Chiefs have looked like one of the strongest teams in the league in each of the past three seasons, only failing to capture the Lombardi Trophy in two of those years because the sport's most accomplished quarterback refuses to pass the torch yet.

Overhauling the offensive line will have some implications of change, particularly with how the Chiefs could spice up their run game, but their run-pass splits likely will not change, nor will the core of their passing concepts. The defense should come into the season with a similar formula as before and, to little surprise, net similar results. Elite offense and middling defense has been a functional formula in the Mahomes era, and there is little reason to believe 2021 should be any different.

Derrik Klassen

2020 Chiefs Stats by Week

Wk	vs.	W-L	PF	PA	YDF	YDA	TO	Total	Off	Def	ST
1	HOU	W	34	20	369	360	1	-14.9%	5.5%	19.7%	-0.7%
2	at LAC	W	23	20	414	479	1	12.2%	16.2%	12.3%	8.3%
3	at BAL	W	34	20	517	228	0	54.6%	54.0%	-36.7%	-36.0%
4	NE	W	26	10	323	357	3	39.2%	16.2%	-27.6%	-4.6%
5	LV	L	32	40	413	490	0	-7.9%	22.7%	34.0%	3.4%
6	at BUF	W	26	17	466	206	0	41.5%	31.6%	-18.7%	-8.8%
7	at DEN	W	43	16	286	411	3	47.7%	19.8%	-6.7%	21.2%
8	NYJ	W	35	9	496	221	1	36.8%	25.5%	-12.7%	-1.5%
9	CAR	W	33	31	397	435	-1	13.0%	37.1%	26.7%	2.6%
10	BYE										
11	at LV	W	35	31	460	364	0	12.2%	32.3%	17.3%	-2.7%
12	at TB	W	27	24	543	417	1	50.1%	49.5%	-3.8%	-3.2%
13	DEN	W	22	16	447	330	2	28.8%	33.4%	12.7%	8.2%
14	at MIA	W	33	27	448	367	-3	22.3%	-3.3%	3.0%	28.6%
15	at NO	W	32	29	411	285	0	17.1%	22.9%	-13.3%	-19.1%
16	ATL	W	17	14	395	367	-1	-0.2%	2.8%	11.4%	8.3%
17	LAC	L	21	38	268	416	-1	-30.5%	5.9%	40.7%	4.4%
18	BYE										
19	CLE	W	22	17	438	308	1	47.7%	28.8%	-20.3%	-1.5%
20	BUF	W	38	24	439	363	0	95.6%	60.3%	-32.4%	3.0%
21	TB	L	9	31	350	340	-2	-37.5%	-26.1%	12.5%	1.0%

Trends and Splits

	Offense	Rank	Defense	Rank
Total DVOA	23.9%	2	4.9%	22
Unadjusted VOA	22.5%	2	3.5%	19
Weighted Trend	23.4%	3	6.6%	24
Variance	2.6%	2	4.9%	17
Average Opponent	1.0%	21	-0.8%	19
Passing	49.0%	2	6.7%	16
Rushing	-5.7%	13	2.5%	31
First Down	10.9%	6	0.5%	18
Second Down	27.4%	2	10.6%	27
Third Down	46.2%	1	3.8%	19
First Half	25.7%	2	4.5%	24
Second Half	22.0%	3	5.3%	19
Red Zone	19.2%	10	35.8%	32
Late and Close	35.9%	1	-6.2%	12

Five-Year Performance

Year	W-L	Pyth W	Est W	PF	PA	TO	Total	Rk	Off	Rk	Def	Rk	ST	Rk	Off AGL	Rk	Def AGL	Rk	Off Age	Rk	Def Age	Rk	ST Age	Rk
2016	12-4	10.1	9.7	389	311	+16	13.5%	5	3.1%	13	-2.6%	13	7.8%	1	32.9	13	66.9	30	25.9	26	26.5	16	25.1	31
2017	10-6	10.0	10.0	415	339	+15	10.9%	10	16.4%	4	10.8%	29	5.3%	4	42.1	22	38.7	20	26.3	26	27.1	5	25.9	16
2018	12-4	11.0	13.0	565	421	+11	33.2%	1	35.4%	1	7.7%	27	5.6%	2	35.3	16	24.8	10	26.0	27	26.2	15	25.7	18
2019	12-4	11.6	12.0	451	308	+8	30.1%	4	23.5%	3	-2.6%	14	4.1%	2	32.2	13	43.6	24	27.0	12	25.6	27	26.2	9
2020	14-2	10.7	11.9	473	362	+6	19.6%	6	23.9%	2	4.9%	22	0.5%	17	50.7	24	14.5	1	27.1	11	25.9	26	25.8	20

2020 Performance Based on Most Common Personnel Groups

KC Offense					KC Offense vs. Opponents					KC Defense				KC Defense vs. Opponents			
Pers	Freq	Yds	DVOA	Run%	Pers	Freq	Yds	DVOA	Run%	Pers	Freq	Yds	DVOA	Pers	Freq	Yds	DVOA
11	73%	6.5	29.2%	26%	Base	11%	6.0	14.7%	54%	Base	22%	5.1	3.6%	11	57%	6.0	4.0%
12	19%	6.9	34.6%	48%	Nickel	72%	6.2	25.7%	35%	Nickel	42%	5.6	-3.4%	12	14%	6.2	1.8%
13	3%	4.5	-17.2%	61%	Dime+	15%	8.2	63.7%	11%	Dime+	35%	6.6	12.3%	21	12%	6.1	12.2%
21	3%	7.0	45.6%	70%	Goal Line	0%	1.5	-87.8%	25%	Goal Line	1%	1.1	46.6%	22	5%	4.4	-8.4%
22	1%	4.1	2.6%	73%										13	5%	3.5	-4.7%
														10	3%	6.5	23.6%

Strategic Tendencies

Run/Pass		Rk	Formation		Rk	Pass Rush		Rk	Secondary		Rk	Strategy		Rk
Runs, first half	28%	32	Form: Single Back	89%	4	Rush 3	4.0%	24	4 DB	22%	18	Play Action	35%	5
Runs, first down	43%	22	Form: Empty Back	4%	29	Rush 4	60.8%	23	5 DB	42%	30	Offensive Motion	60%	3
Runs, second-long	17%	30	Form: Multi Back	6%	24	Rush 5	20.2%	17	6+ DB	35%	4	Avg Box (Off)	6.36	30
Runs, power sit.	57%	17	Pers: 3+ WR	73%	7	Rush 6+	15.0%	1	Man Coverage	40%	8	Avg Box (Def)	6.59	18
Runs, behind 2H	27%	18	Pers: 2+ TE/6+ OL	24%	21	Edge Rusher Sacks	48.4%	20	CB by Sides	93%	4	Offensive Pace	29.37	7
Pass, ahead 2H	55%	5	Pers: 6+ OL	1%	23	Interior DL Sacks	29.7%	9	S/CB Cover Ratio	36%	6	Defensive Pace	30.69	22
Run-Pass Options	20%	1	Shotgun/Pistol	81%	6	Second Level Sacks	21.9%	18	DB Blitz	18%	3	Go for it on 4th	1.62	14

Most teams are better at running against light boxes, but the Chiefs took it to an extreme last season. Against six or fewer men in the box, handoffs went for 5.2 yards per carry and 12.6% DVOA. Against seven men, handoffs went for 4.0 yards per carry and -7.6% DVOA. Against eight or more, Kansas City fell to 2.9 yards per carry and -33.8% DVOA. 🏈 Kansas City led the league with 80.2% DVOA on wide receiver screens and were tied for third at 7.5 yards per pass. 🏈 The Chiefs were tied for second in broken tackles on offense, the third straight year they have ranked in the top four. 🏈 Kansas City's offense was No. 1 in DVOA passing the ball on third and fourth down but only 23rd running the ball. 🏈 The Chiefs were the strongest defense in the league against short middle passes in 2019, but last year they declined to rank 27th against short middle passes. 🏈 Kansas City led the league with 12 coverage sacks on defense, and more than half their sacks were "non-pressure sacks" (either coverage sacks or failed scrambles). 🏈 Kansas City's opponents dropped 6.9% of their passes, fourth highest in the league. 🏈 Penalties continue to be a problem for this Chiefs team, as they have finished in the top six of penalties for three straight seasons.

Passing

Player	DYAR	DVOA	Plays	NtYds	Avg	YAC	C%	TD	Int
P.Mahomes	1720	31.7%	609	4593	7.5	5.7	66.4%	38	6
C.Henne	89	22.3%	40	244	6.1	7.1	73.7%	2	0

Rushing

Player	DYAR	DVOA	Plays	Yds	Avg	TD	Fum	Suc
C.Edwards-Helaire	13	-6.9%	181	803	4.4	4	0	56%
L.Bell*	45	6.8%	64	255	4.0	2	0	55%
P.Mahomes	44	6.0%	47	314	6.7	2	2	--
D.Williams	22	2.7%	39	169	4.3	1	0	59%
D.Thompson	-10	-17.8%	27	97	3.6	1	1	44%
T.Hill	73	53.6%	13	123	9.5	2	0	--
M.Burton	4	-1.5%	7	18	2.6	0	0	86%

Receiving

Player	DYAR	DVOA	Plays	Ctch	Yds	Y/C	YAC	TD	C%
T.Hill	322	17.3%	135	87	1276	14.7	5.0	15	64%
M.Hardman	90	6.4%	62	41	560	13.7	7.0	4	66%
D.Robinson	81	5.2%	59	45	466	10.4	3.8	3	76%
S.Watkins*	57	-0.4%	55	37	421	11.4	4.2	2	67%
B.Pringle	47	18.3%	17	13	160	12.3	5.2	1	76%
D.Shepherd	-18	-46.7%	8	5	46	9.2	3.6	0	63%
T.Kelce	415	35.7%	145	105	1416	13.5	5.6	11	72%
D.Yelder*	-30	-47.6%	11	7	36	5.1	4.3	0	64%
N.Keizer	-21	-45.9%	9	6	63	10.5	6.7	0	67%
B.Bell	-6	-13.0%	15	11	110	10.0	4.4	0	73%
C.Edwards-Helaire	2	-13.2%	54	36	297	8.3	8.2	1	67%
D.Williams	8	-8.4%	26	18	116	6.4	8.7	0	69%
L.Bell*	-3	-17.0%	17	13	99	7.6	9.1	0	76%
D.Thompson	4	-6.1%	11	7	65	9.3	12.6	1	64%

Offensive Line

Player	Pos	Age	GS	Snaps	Pen	Sk	Pass	Run	Player	Pos	Age	GS	Snaps	Pen	Sk	Pass	Run
Eric Fisher*	LT	30	15/15	1049	3	4	32	5	Kelechi Osemele*	LG	32	5/5	282	5	0	0	0
Andrew Wylie	RG	27	14/14	972	3	2.5	18	9	Daniel Kilgore*	C	34	7/4	236	0	0	2	4
Austin Reiter*	C	30	15/12	867	0	0	4	1	Stefen Wisniewski	RG	32	5/3	209	1	0	6	4
Mike Remmers	RT	32	13/10	709	4	1	16	6	Austin Blythe	C	29	16/16	1120	1	2.5	12	11
Nick Allegretti	LG	25	16/9	694	4	0	12	5	Orlando Brown	LT	25	16/16	1027	5	2.5	12	3
Mitchell Schwartz*	RT	32	6/6	357	1	2	14	1	Joe Thuney	LG	29	16/16	979	3	1	6	3

Year	Yards	ALY	Rk	Power	Rk	Stuff	Rk	2Lev	Rk	OpFld	Rk	BB Rt	Rk	Sacks	ASR	Rk	Press	Rk	BB Rt	Rk	Cont
2018	4.66	4.37	16	72%	4	18%	13	1.27	18	1.01	11	5.8%	12	26	5.4%	5	33.2%	24	10.1%	20	28
2019	4.15	3.88	28	63%	21	19%	18	0.92	29	1.02	7	10.1%	15	25	4.9%	4	32.5%	26	17.1%	31	28
2020	4.22	4.38	14	51%	32	18%	20	1.32	7	0.48	30	11.8%	24	24	4.5%	4	28.4%	23	16.0%	31	22

2020 ALY by direction:	Left End: 4.82 (6)	Left Tackle: 2.71 (31)	Mid/Guard: 4.56 (12)	Right Tackle: 4.20 (18)	Right End: 4.32 (21)

Kansas City led the league by starting 12 different offensive linemen for at least one game. That does not even take into account the fact that starting guard Laurent Duvernay-Tardif opted out before the season. ✎ New left tackle Orlando Brown is as big an upgrade as it gets. Former left tackle Fisher finished 61st (out of 76) and 63rd (out of 71) among tackles in snaps per blown block in 2019 and 2020, respectively. Brown, on the other hand, finished third among all tackles as Baltimore's right tackle in 2019, then ninth in 2020 as he spent time at both bookend spots. ✎ Likewise, Joe Thuney finished first among left guards and seventh among all interior offensive linemen in snaps per blown block last season. Neither of Kansas City's qualifying guards finished higher than 88th place among interior offensive linemen. ✎ Former Bears guard Kyle Long is the wild card for this unit. Long sat out last year and has not finished a full 16-game season since 2015. The last time Long qualified with enough snaps for blown-block rankings was 2018, when he finished 40th of 107 interior offensive linemen. ✎ Second-round pick Creed Humphrey (Oklahoma) will have to earn the starting job over free-agent signing Austin Blythe (ex-Rams). Humphrey comes from an offense that ran a myriad of gap/power/pulling concepts from spread formations, which accentuated his strength and violence as a blocker. Though not the smoothest athlete, Humphrey should be excellent on down blocks for gap concepts and brings all the knowledge of protections and fronts expected of a top-64 pick. ✎ Blythe has starting experience at both center and guard but handled the center spot for Los Angeles last year. Blythe has been middling the past two years, sitting outside the top 20 in snaps per blown block at each position, but he brings a veteran presence with the flexibility to kick over to guard. ✎ Sixth-round pick Trey Smith fell in the draft more for medical reasons than quality of play. A stout, powerful 6-foot-5 and 312 pounds, Smith was diagnosed with blood clots in his lungs in 2018. Smith still started the following two years at Tennessee, but long-term health is the real concern. ✎ The Chiefs have steadily gotten worse in short-yardage "power" situations since 2018, going from fourth to 21st to dead-last by 2020. Bringing in bullies such as Brown, Thuney, and Humphrey is a signal that the team wants to turn things around on that front.

Defensive Front

Defensive Line	Age	Pos	G	Snaps	Plays	TmPct	Rk	Stop	Dfts	BTkl	Runs	St%	Rk	RuYd	Rk	Sack	Hit	Hur	Dsrpt
						Overall						**vs. Run**					**Pass Rush**		
Chris Jones	27	DT	15	693	40	5.2%	48	29	8	11	27	59%	88	2.9	70	7.5	24	41	8
Tershawn Wharton	23	DT	16	517	27	3.3%	78	16	7	1	22	59%	89	3.0	73	2.0	3	14	0
Derrick Nnadi	25	DT	15	459	47	6.1%	25	32	1	4	42	71%	53	2.5	48	0.0	1	7	0
Mike Pennel*	30	DT	14	320	29	4.1%	--	20	1	0	26	73%	--	3.2	--	0.0	1	1	0
Jarran Reed	29	DT	16	847	38	4.3%	60	28	11	2	27	70%	58	2.9	70	6.5	8	17	1

Edge Rushers	Age	Pos	G	Snaps	Plays	TmPct	Rk	Stop	Dfts	BTkl	Runs	St%	Rk	RuYd	Rk	Sack	Hit	Hur	Dsrpt
						Overall						**vs. Run**					**Pass Rush**		
Frank Clark	28	DE	15	756	31	4.0%	65	21	9	5	18	56%	90	3.8	88	6.0	11	27	4
Tanoh Kpassagnon*	27	DE	16	717	31	3.8%	68	25	7	9	23	74%	37	2.8	57	1.0	3	16	4
Michael Danna	24	DE	13	333	25	3.8%	--	19	6	3	19	74%	--	2.3	--	2.5	3	9	0
Alex Okafor*	30	DE	11	281	16	2.8%	--	13	5	2	11	82%	--	2.5	--	3.0	6	8	1
Kamalei Correa	27	OLB	9	197	10	2.1%	--	6	0	2	8	63%	--	3.5	--	0.0	2	1	0

Linebackers	Age	Pos	G	Snaps	Plays	TmPct	Rk	Stop	Dfts	BTkl	Runs	St%	Rk	RuYd	Rk	Sack	Hit	Hur	Tgts	Suc%	Rk	Yd/P	Rk	PD	Int
						Overall						**vs. Run**				**Pass Rush**				**vs. Pass**					
Anthony Hitchens	29	MLB	14	601	79	11.1%	52	32	5	6	54	50%	66	3.9	40	0.0	4	7	14	43%	56	6.2	34	1	0
Damien Wilson*	28	OLB	13	528	71	10.7%	57	32	7	5	47	55%	44	3.5	24	0.0	0	3	15	40%	62	8.0	65	1	0
Ben Niemann	26	MLB	15	466	43	5.6%	84	11	5	5	20	35%	87	5.7	85	1.0	2	9	19	32%	71	9.7	72	0	0
Willie Gay	23	OLB	16	267	40	4.9%	--	26	7	7	27	70%	--	1.9	--	1.0	0	4	7	43%	--	4.3	--	3	0

Year	Yards	ALY	Rk	Power	Rk	Stuff	Rk	2Lev	Rk	OpFld	Rk	BB Rt	Rk	Sacks	ASR	Rk	Press	Rk	BB Rt	Rk
2018	4.97	5.28	32	78%	30	15%	27	1.57	32	0.72	12	9.5%	10	52	8.0%	7	31.5%	11	13.4%	4
2019	4.89	4.81	28	71%	26	14%	30	1.45	31	0.89	25	12.0%	20	45	7.7%	10	30.0%	19	17.3%	5
2020	4.47	4.66	25	78%	32	11%	30	1.13	11	0.72	20	7.4%	32	32	6.2%	18	29.8%	4	16.7%	4

| 2020 ALY by direction: | Left End: 4.55 (17) | Left Tackle: 3.19 (5) | Mid/Guard: 4.62 (21) | Right Tackle: 5.59 (31) | Right End: 5.13 (25) |

Kansas City is the only defense to finish 25th or worse in run defense DVOA for the last three seasons, and free-agent addition Jarran Reed won't help solve that issue. In each of the past two seasons, Reed finished outside the top 45 interior linemen in stop rate and outside the top 65 in the average depth of his run tackles. Instead, Reed further leans into Kansas City's interior pass-rush plan (27 hurries since 2019). ◕ The Chiefs tried to manufacture pressure by sending more big blitzes (six or more pass-rushers) than any other team. Kansas City was at 15% and no other defense was over 10%. And the Chiefs allowed … 6.7 yards per play with a big blitz, slightly higher than their average yards allowed on pass plays overall. Kansas City did manage a 48% pressure rate on all blitzes (five or more pass-rushers), compared to just 25% with four pass-rushers. That was the largest such gap in the league, twice the average team's gap. ◕ The Chiefs have hemorrhaged edge talent since 2018, and the drain continues this year as both Alex Okafor and Tanoh Kpassagnon left without really being replaced. Expect the Chiefs to be very blitz-heavy again. ◕ Joshua Kaindoh, a fourth-round pick out of Florida State, is the only notable move the Chiefs made on the edge. Kaindoh is a former five-star recruit who showed great promise with 6.5 tackles for loss and four sacks as a true freshman in 2017, but a slew of injuries over the following three seasons, including a 2019 season-ending ankle injury, derailed things. When healthy, Kaindoh wins with length and strength over raw athleticism. ◕ Tershawn Wharton was a valuable UDFA pick up for the Chiefs last year. Wharton came out of college as more of a defensive end and had to bulk up to 280 pounds to play inside with the Chiefs. As such, it tracks that Wharton is lacking as an interior run defender, but he's got the quickness and violent hands to be a useful pass-rusher. ◕ The Chiefs were one of just three teams that had all of their qualifying linebackers (Damien Wilson, Anthony Hitchens, Ben Niemann) fall below a 45% coverage success rate. The other two were the Texans (Zach Cunningham, Tyrell Adams) and the Giants (where only Blake Martinez qualified). ◕ Willie Gay Jr. is expected to step into a larger role, but one issue that needs cleaning up is his tackling. Gay's 21.9% missed tackle rate ranked 92nd out of 112 linebackers in the NFL (minimum 20 solo tackles).

Defensive Secondary

Secondary	Age	Pos	G	Snaps	Plays	TmPct	Rk	Stop	Dfts	BTkl	Runs	St%	Rk	RuYd	Rk	Tgts	Tgt%	Rk	aDOT	Suc%	Rk	Yd/P	Rk	PD	Int
Tyrann Mathieu	29	SS	15	979	71	9.3%	55	22	12	12	29	28%	53	7.1	38	38	10.2%	23	13.1	58%	14	6.7	20	9	6
Daniel Sorensen	31	FS/SS	15	879	96	12.5%	15	31	11	16	42	36%	38	5.1	15	42	12.5%	10	9.9	57%	15	6.4	18	5	3
Charvarius Ward	25	CB	14	779	57	8.0%	57	20	9	3	18	22%	72	7.9	57	52	17.5%	60	9.6	52%	39	7.1	32	6	0
Juan Thornhill	26	FS	16	761	44	5.4%	70	11	3	8	19	32%	44	15.5	71	19	6.6%	49	14.3	53%	28	7.8	37	3	1
Bashaud Breeland*	29	CB	11	688	47	8.4%	47	20	11	11	14	29%	62	4.5	13	50	19.1%	45	13.1	56%	17	6.5	18	9	2
Rashad Fenton	24	CB	16	524	41	5.0%	--	17	10	4	9	33%	--	5.9	--	42	21.0%	--	13.2	60%	--	5.9	--	7	1
L'Jarius Sneed	24	CB	9	410	48	10.4%	--	22	8	4	11	45%	--	5.5	--	39	25.0%	--	9.7	56%	--	5.1	--	7	3
Will Parks	27	FS	10	314	29	5.5%	--	14	6	3	8	75%	--	1.3	--	17	14.2%	--	9.2	53%	--	8.1	--	0	0

Year	Pass D Rank	vs. #1 WR	Rk	vs. #2 WR	Rk	vs. Other WR	Rk	WR Wide	Rk	WR Slot	Rk	vs. TE	Rk	vs. RB	Rk
2018	12	-9.2%	9	-23.8%	5	21.6%	29	-9.8%	13	-0.1%	16	19.1%	25	7.3%	21
2019	6	-32.3%	3	-10.4%	7	5.1%	20	-48.4%	1	4.3%	12	-19.5%	4	-2.0%	18
2020	16	-11.2%	9	-2.8%	13	-18.1%	7	-15.6%	6	-12.7%	2	-2.1%	14	33.3%	31

The Chiefs were one of just four teams where all qualifying defensive backs finished above a 50% coverage success rate. Denver, Pittsburgh, and Washington were the others. ● Only the Chiefs, Texans, and Dolphins ranked top-10 in both S/CB cover ratio and DB blitz percentage. Spagnuolo had his defensive backs wearing a ton of different hats. ● The Chiefs were one of just three teams to not select a single defensive back in the 2021 NFL draft. The Bengals and Texans were the others. ● New cornerback Mike Hughes hardly played in 2020 due to a neck injury. In 2019, he saw the highest target rate in the NFL (30.0%). Hughes held a 47% coverage success rate (66th) and 7.2 yards per target (37th), which was not the worst, but becomes problematic at the volume he was targeted. ● Former Giants first-round pick DeAndre Baker could replace Bashaud Breeland. Baker was cut by the Giants following a criminal investigation but was picked up late last year by the Chiefs. As a rookie in 2019, Baker posted a 52% success rate (46th) and 9.1 yards per target (70th), which tracks for a player who was decent overall but occasionally got burned downfield. ● The Chiefs ranked fourth, fifth, and 10th in interceptions per drive over each of the past three seasons. Generally turnover-heavy defenses can be expected to regress some, but the Chiefs have consistently remained near the top here, which makes sense given their high-risk, high-reward brand of defense. ● Last year's rookie cornerback L'Jarius Sneed was an unexpected stud when healthy. Sneed posted a 56% coverage success rate and team-best 5.1 yards per target, though he did not qualify for our rankings. Sneed could use work in how fluidly he matches route breaks, but he's a bully at the line of scrimmage and has a real knack for finding the ball in the air even with his back turned to the quarterback.

Special Teams

Year	DVOA	Rank	FG/XP	Rank	Net Kick	Rank	Kick Ret	Rank	Net Punt	Rank	Punt Ret	Rank	Hidden	Rank
2018	5.6%	2	3.1	11	5.3	3	6.8	4	7.0	4	6.0	3	10.9	5
2019	4.1%	2	8.1	5	6.1	3	4.2	5	-0.6	19	2.6	7	5.5	9
2020	0.5%	17	3.9	12	-4.4	24	7.6	4	0.8	17	-5.2	29	0.1	15

2020 was the first season in which the Chiefs ranked outside the top 10 in special teams DVOA since head coach Andy Reid and special teams coach Dave Toub were hired before the 2013 season. The Chiefs have ranked in the top four in six out of Toub's eight years. ● Kansas City's kickoff coverage unit did kicker Harrison Butker no favors. Butker ranked a solid 10th in gross kickoff value, but the Chiefs coverage unit gave up the third-worst value on returns. ● Between 2016 and 2019, the Chiefs had their top punt returner rank in the top eight for return value. Tyreek Hill completed the feat from 2016 to 2018, while Mecole Hardman did so in 2019. Hardman was slightly below average as the main punt returner in 2020; most of Kansas City's negative value on punt returns came from Hill muffing his only punt return chance of the season and Demarcus Robinson fumbling a punt return against the Saints. ● Hardman split kick return duties with Byron Pringle, who had a 102-yard return touchdown against Denver in Week 7. ● Tommy Townsend returns as the punter after a very average rookie season in 2020.

Las Vegas Raiders

2020 Record: 8-8	**Total DVOA:** -6.2% (25)	**2021 Mean Projection:** 8.2 wins	**On the Clock (O-5):** 17%
Pythagorean Wins: 7 (20)	**Offense:** 1.8% (14)	**Postseason Odds:** 37.5%	**Mediocrity (6-8):** 38%
Snap-Weighted Age: 26.6 (10)	**Defense:** 9.6% (28)	**Super Bowl Odds:** 3.6%	**Playoff Contender (9-11):** 33%
Average Opponent: 1.2% (13)	**Special Teams:** 1.5% (13)	**Proj. Avg. Opponent:** 0.6% (13)	**Super Bowl Contender (12+):** 12%

2020: Another inch closer to the postseason, but still no cigar.

2021: It's not enough for Jon Gruden to keep treading water, or at least it shouldn't be.

The pressure is building for this Raiders regime to finally push the team over the hump. Entering Year 4 of the Jon Gruden and Mike Mayock era, the television duo has little to show for their reign besides returning the franchise to an uninspiring level of competitiveness. Shipping off Khalil Mack and Amari Cooper for blockbuster trade hauls in 2018 was supposed to be the catalyst for a grand rebuild, but the team has not drafted nearly well enough with its surplus of picks to make up for losing those star players.

That is no criticism of making those trades in the first place. Gruden signed a 10-year contract upon arrival. It makes perfect sense that he would be comfortable sacking Year 1 in favor of picking up an abundance of long-term assets. In total, the Raiders received three first-round picks and a third-round pick in exchange for Mack, Cooper, and a second-round pick. Some Day 3 picks also got shuffled around, but nothing that swings the quality of the deals one way or another. The Raiders also saved cap space by not having to pay those players, both of whom signed major deals almost immediately after leaving town.

Now three years out from those trades, it's fair to examine how well the Raiders have done with those picks to replace the stars they gave up. Las Vegas' approach to the first round since 2018 has netted them a handful of competent starters without much star power. Left tackle Kolton Miller was horrendous early in his career but has blossomed into a competent bookend. The 2019 trio of Clelin Ferrell, Josh Jacobs, and Johnathan Abram produced a decent run-first defensive end, a good running back, and a disaster of a strong safety. The jury is still out on the 2020 duo of Henry Ruggs and Damon Arnette, but Arnette was among the league's worst cornerbacks when healthy and Ruggs was reduced to mainly being a field-stretching role player last season. In all, the Raiders could have done worse, but there is not a single first-rounder in that bunch that comes anywhere near the firepower Mack or Cooper provided.

Day 2 drafting has not been a whole lot better, even with some of the added picks. From the class of 2018, Brandon Parker is a rosterable but ineffective tackle, and both P.J. Hall and Arden Key have been cut. To the Raiders' credit, cornerback Trayvon Mullen was a nice get in the second round of 2019, but it has been hard for him to look like a value given how bad the rest of the Raiders' secondary around him has

been as of late. The Day 2 picks of 2020 produced Bryan Edwards, who may become a competent bully-ball receiver in the short area, but that is offset by the selection of Lynn Bowden Jr., who was traded for Day 3 picks before the season even started. The Raiders' only real home run on Day 3 over that span has been defensive end Maxx Crosby.

It's not like the Raiders made great use of the cap space they afforded themselves, either. Since 2018, they have signed seven players—all defenders—to deals worth $5 million or more per season: Tahir Whitehead (2018), Rashaan Melvin (2018), Lamarcus Joyner (2019), Cory Littleton (2020), Nick Kwiatkowski (2020), Carl Nassib (2020), and Maliek Collins (2020). Joyner was decent enough, while both Littleton and Kwiatkowski shored up the linebacker group last season, but again, there is no bona fide star here that changes the complexion of the team.

What complicates Gruden's portion of blame here is that the team's failures in drafting and spending have mostly been on defense. Offensively, many of the Raiders' picks turned out at least OK, with Parker being the only clear failure in the top 100. The Raiders offense has also done well with finding cheaper free-agent contributors. Darren Waller, scooped off the Ravens' practice squad in 2018, is the obvious diamond in the rough, but moves like resuscitating Nelson Agholor's career on a one-year deal in 2020 have also helped keep the Raiders offense rolling.

Gruden, an offensive coach by nature, can take some credit for keeping the offense at a good, stable level despite a lot of the team's resources turning into defensive flops. He still deserves some portion of the blame for overall team failures since he does get final say on who makes the roster and who is coordinating his defenses, but not unlike Vic Fangio for the rival Broncos, Gruden has done his part on "his side" of the ball.

Gruden should continue to keep the train on the tracks in 2021. The Raiders offense has placed in the top half of the league in DVOA in each of the past two seasons and we project them to end up in that range again. Losses on the offensive line, particularly center Rodney Hudson, are going to leave a mark, but they may serve more as reasons that the Raiders offense will not improve rather than reasons they will see a decline.

As milquetoast as he may be perceived, quarterback Derek Carr plays a major role in the offense's consistency. Carr is a

2021 Raiders Schedule

Week	Opp.	Week	Opp.	Week	Opp.
1	BAL (Mon.)	7	PHI	13	WAS
2	at PIT	8	BYE	14	at KC
3	MIA	9	at NYG	15	at CLE
4	at LAC (Mon.)	10	KC	16	DEN
5	CHI	11	CIN	17	at IND
6	at DEN	12	at DAL (Thu.)	18	LAC

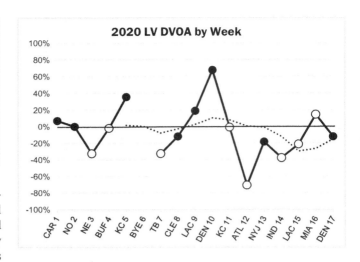

2020 LV DVOA by Week

sharp quarterback, both pre- and post-snap, and has historically centered his entire game around taking guaranteed small victories. If Carr's pre-snap read is there, he will take it and deliver an accurate ball, and you can count on him to quickly find the checkdown if not. He is as reliable a quarterback as any in that regard.

Carr's ability to protect the football is admirable as well. Everyone wants Carr to be more aggressive—and he really should be with his kind of arm talent—but it's hard to chastise him when he has been efficient for a good portion of his career while seldom turning over the ball. Carr's low turnover rate is not a matter of luck, either. Carr finished with the fifth-lowest adjusted interception rate in 2019 (1.8%) followed by the lowest rate in 2020 (1.9%). Carr's style of play also makes the life of a playcaller much easier, letting him easily envision how each play will be successful and feel less stressed about the quarterback single-handedly ruining a drive with a poor throw.

All that being said about Carr's high-floor play style, the quarterback has quietly been more aggressive than his past self over the last couple years. It's still fair to bin Carr in with the conservative passers rather than the aggressive ones, particularly due to some of his hesitancy to throw to the intermediate area or to play off-schedule, but he has opened himself up down the field as of late. The Raiders attempted 20% of their passes as deep throws last season (16 or more yards downfield), just above the 18% league average.

At first glance, losing Agholor this offseason could hurt Carr in that regard. Agholor was a good deep weapon for the Raiders last year in tandem with Ruggs. It's not unreasonable for the Raiders to be shy on paying Agholor market value after one seemingly random season of production, though, and they should have the pieces in place now to replace him.

The team signed former Bills receiver John Brown, who was as productive as usual last year when healthy. Brown finished just 38th in DYAR last year, but that's more a product of missing some games due to an ankle injury and COVID protocols than anything, seeing as he finished 19th in DVOA among wide receivers. Granted, Agholor was fourth in DVOA and earned the second-most defensive pass interference yards (155) of any wide receiver last year, but Brown is not a dramatic fall from that. It's not like Agholor has a long, reliable history of being this productive anyway. Blend the Brown signing together with Ruggs likely taking some form of a Year 2 jump, and it's not very difficult to see how the Raiders' receiving corps lands on their feet.

The real worry for the Raiders offense is the aforementioned loss of Hudson along the interior. Though Hudson's blown-block figures are well short of elite, the film tells a different story. Hudson plays with urgency and smooth movement in the run game, regularly beating defensive linemen to their landmarks and locking them out of plays with superior leverage. He may no longer be the pile-mover he was at his peak, but make no mistake, he is no pushover either. Hudson is also widely heralded as one of the smartest centers in the league, and the relationship between him and Carr made it easy for the Raiders offense to consistently limit mistakes and sniff out opposing pressures. The 32-year-old center will surely bring that same dynamic with him to Arizona, while the Raiders will be hoping former Texans center Nick Martin can be a competent replacement.

Carr is also sharp and experienced enough in his own right and Gruden is a quality offensive mind. The offense should be able to pick up the pieces just fine, even if they struggle to build on their progress and reach new heights without Hudson giving the offensive line as much stability as before.

The offense's inability to climb beyond "slightly above average" also has to do with how little they spent on getting better on that side of the ball. They did sign Brown to replace Agholor and drafted offensive tackle Alex Leatherwood to take over for Trent Brown, but the Raiders did not make any moves on offense to get better, they just tried to stabilize from their losses. Many of the Raiders' resources this offseason instead went to the defense. That was also true in 2020, but one offseason of moves was never going to be enough to fully turn around a historically terrible defense. Perhaps the Raiders' 2020 and 2021 efforts combined can get that job done.

Following the Leatherwood pick in the first round, the Raiders selected five straight defensive players in this year's draft. TCU safety Trevon Moehrig, Buffalo defensive end Malcom Koonce, and linebacker/safety Divine Deablo were the team's final three top-100 picks after Leatherwood. Moehrig is the most likely to start and the most likely to be a notable upgrade at his position.

For the past two seasons, Erik Harris (now with the Falcons) was manning the deep centerfield for the Raiders. Harris dropped to a 43% coverage success rate last year, which is not too surprising given his late eyes and trigger in coverage.

Harris has neither the top-end instincts nor the range to be anything more than a clean-up act over the middle of the field. Even that was a bridge too far for Harris in 2020, however. Of the 201 defensive backs with at least 10 solo tackles last season, Harris posted the fourth-worst broken-tackle rate (28%). All three of the players worse than him last season were cornerbacks, including teammate Arnette.

Moehrig should waltz right in and be an instant upgrade over Harris in both coverage and as a tackler. Moehrig's 4.52s 40-yard dash is above average for a safety prospect. More importantly, Moehrig has the eyes and quick trigger to get the ball rolling early in plays and maximize his speed. The TCU defense often asked Moehrig to play a deep half or quarter rather than a true centerfield position like Gus Bradley will ask of him, but his instincts and athletic ability should transition just fine to a true single-high position. Moreover, Moehrig still has the flexibility to roam all around the defense, be that as a box player or as a man coverage defender over the slot. Not only is he a tough enough tackler for the job, but the leverage and typewriter-speed footwork Moehrig showed in college makes it easy for him to keep up with all sorts of pass-catchers in coverage. If anything, Moehrig may get burned a time or two with how aggressive his trigger can be, but the idea is that the pros outweigh the cons and he will find the right degree of aggression with a season or two under his belt.

Sorting out the cornerback position is a bit trickier. The Raiders are at a crossroads where their cornerback room may be as talented as it has ever been in the Gruden era, yet completely unprepared for life beyond 2021.

On the bright side, the Raiders made the smart choice to pursue veteran cornerback Casey Hayward and reunite him with defensive coordinator Gus Bradley. The Raiders pulled Hayward on a cheap contract, too. Hayward, who has been an outside cornerback since leaving the Packers after the 2015 season, signed with Las Vegas on a one-year, $2.5-million deal. It's a low-risk, high-reward signing that immediately upgrades the Raiders' outside cornerback situation, even if only for a season.

The downside is that Hayward is an immediate upgrade in large part because the team already seems to be giving up on Arnette. The Athletic's Vic Tafur wrote in mid-June that Arnette's job opposite Mullen has effectively been given right to Hayward. Technically, either Hayward or Arnette could wind up in the slot, but neither of those seem likely. Hayward probably signed with Bradley's defense on the cheap on the condition that he could stay outside, while Arnette never showed the route recognition or controlled footwork to function from the slot very well, never mind his aforementioned tackling woes.

The team already has an answer at slot cornerback, too. With Lamarcus Joyner out of the picture, Nevin Lawson can fully slide back inside after mostly playing outside as a fill-in for an injured Arnette last year. Truthfully, Lawson has regularly shown he is better suited for slot work despite playing both inside and out for most of his career. In 2019, Lawson posted a 57% success rate on 21 targets while splitting equal time both outside and in the slot. That is a small sample, but Lawson was similarly successful in a split-time role with the Lions in 2018,

producing a 53% success rate over a much more representative 60-target sample. It was only in 2020, when he played outside most of the time, that Lawson's coverage success rate plummeted down to 43%. Moving Lawson to a full-time nickel position puts him in his most comfortable coverage position and also takes advantage of his tough, willing tackling.

It's not so much that Lawson is a clear winner at the slot position, it's that he's a sensible band-aid while Arnette offers very little potential there. Rookie fifth-round pick Nate Hobbs (Illinois) is not an immediate threat to Lawson either, so this is probably just what Las Vegas has to settle on for the year.

With Arnette potentially booted from the starting lineup and both Hayward and Lawson on one-year deals, the long-term outlook of the Raiders' cornerback room seems dire, even if some of the veteran presences on the roster may add some much-needed stability this season.

Las Vegas' front seven is a bit more promising, however, and offers a healthier blend between immediate production and long-term answers. The Raiders' 2021 front is not going to suddenly erupt into one of the league's best, but they did finally add some legitimate firepower to go along with some of the younger pieces they already had on the roster. Most importantly, the Raiders finally spent big on a real playmaker on defense: defensive end Yannick Ngakoue.

The book on Ngakoue is out by now. He is not a particularly strong or willing run defender, but he's a pass-rusher who knows what he gets paid for. Ngakoue can pin his ears back and get to the passer as well as anyone outside the small handful of truly elite quarterback hunters. He has earned at least 8.0 sacks in all four years that he has been in the league. Over that same span, only Aaron Donald and Khalil Mack can say the same. Sure, Ngakoue is only a one-dimensional player compared to those two All-Pros, but it's clear the kind of pass-rushing consistency Ngakoue provides.

A pass-rush specialist such as Ngakoue is best served when protected by run defenders who can take the field on early downs instead of him, at least part of the time. While the Raiders' two other defensive ends, Ferrell and Crosby, may not be stars, defending the run is no issue for them. Both ranked in the top 10 in run stop rate and average yards per run tackle, cementing them in elite territory for run defense despite how poor the team's interior defensive line made the rest of the front seven look. How exactly the Raiders plan on sorting their edge rotation out to accommodate Ngakoue is unclear, but they should have very little issue making him the designated pass-rusher that he should be.

Ngakoue is not a Mack-level star, nor is he enough to propel the Raiders defense into being a force to reckon with. But his prowess as a pass-rusher just might give the defense enough of a playmaking spark to go along with some of their other pieces up front, such as Littleton and Crosby, as well as some of the cheap free-agent swings the team took along the interior, including Quinton Jefferson from the Bills and Solomon Thomas from the 49ers.

If Ngakoue—the Gruden-era Raiders' first free-agent home-run swing at an impact defensive position—can at least help push the defense out of the abyss, which our projections suggest he should be able to do, perhaps Las Vegas can be convinced to take another swing when the cap goes back up next offseason.

But next year's spending is next year's problem. This year's Raiders are going to need their defense to outperform their projections if this team is going to reach new heights. While always possible, that is asking for a lot seeing as how much their projections are already a step or two above what they have been for the past three years. It's not likely a bad defensive squad is going to flip the switch overnight, especially not with a middling retread defensive coordinator in his first season with the team.

Barring a mini-miracle in which the defense does flip the switch, the Gruden Raiders look like they will continue treading water. Gruden's leash has to become shorter at some point, you would think. It's not a stretch to believe anything short of a playoff appearance, perhaps even a wild-card win, is going to begin turning up the temperature on Gruden's $100-million seat. There is something to be said about fielding a competitive football team year-in, year-out, but the calls for real success are only going to grow louder if the Gruden Grinders cannot find an extra gear.

Derrik Klassen

2020 Raiders by Week

Wk	vs.	W-L	PF	PA	YDF	YDA	TO	Total	Off	Def	ST
1	at CAR	W	34	30	372	388	0	7.4%	29.0%	19.2%	-2.4%
2	NO	W	34	24	377	424	0	0.4%	20.5%	20.2%	0.1%
3	at NE	L	20	36	375	406	-2	-32.5%	-2.6%	21.1%	-8.7%
4	BUF	L	23	30	383	337	-2	-1.9%	12.7%	10.0%	-4.6%
5	at KC	W	40	32	490	413	0	35.9%	30.0%	-0.5%	5.3%
6	BYE										
7	TB	L	20	45	347	454	-1	-32.6%	-12.6%	18.4%	-1.7%
8	at CLE	W	16	6	309	223	1	-12.0%	-19.3%	-13.9%	-6.6%
9	at LAC	W	31	26	320	440	0	19.1%	24.5%	15.2%	9.8%
10	DEN	W	37	12	357	313	5	67.6%	18.5%	-40.4%	8.8%
11	KC	L	31	35	364	460	0	-0.8%	14.9%	16.8%	1.1%
12	at ATL	L	6	43	243	304	-4	-70.6%	-85.6%	-10.1%	4.9%
13	at NYJ	W	31	28	440	376	1	-18.5%	-9.8%	18.5%	9.8%
14	IND	L	27	44	424	456	-3	-37.7%	-0.6%	37.1%	-0.1%
15	LAC	L	27	30	449	402	-1	-21.4%	-5.6%	13.8%	-2.1%
16	MIA	L	25	26	418	383	-1	14.6%	11.1%	-2.2%	1.2%
17	at DEN	W	32	31	465	446	-4	-12.1%	3.3%	25.3%	9.9%

Trends and Splits

	Offense	Rank	Defense	Rank
Total DVOA	1.8%	14	9.6%	28
Unadjusted VOA	-1.0%	17	10.7%	29
Weighted Trend	-3.9%	15	8.9%	28
Variance	7.7%	20	3.5%	7
Average Opponent	-0.2%	16	2.0%	11
Passing	21.3%	9	16.5%	26
Rushing	-17.7%	24	0.3%	28
First Down	-8.4%	24	-7.4%	10
Second Down	-0.6%	17	9.8%	25
Third Down	23.7%	5	42.2%	32
First Half	12.7%	8	3.1%	21
Second Half	-7.4%	21	17.6%	31
Red Zone	-7.5%	20	2.8%	16
Late and Close	1.9%	17	16.7%	28

Five-Year Performance

Year	W-L	Pyth W	Est W	PF	PA	TO	Total	Rk	Off	Rk	Def	Rk	ST	Rk	Off AGL	Rk	Def AGL	Rk	Off Age	Rk	Def Age	Rk	ST Age	Rk
2016	12-4	8.8	8.7	416	385	+16	7.6%	10	12.8%	7	5.6%	24	0.3%	14	32.9	14	48.5	19	26.5	21	26.6	13	26.9	5
2017	6-10	6.0	7.4	301	373	-14	-8.6%	20	3.6%	13	12.0%	30	-0.2%	17	10.1	3	33.4	14	27.6	4	26.6	13	25.8	17
2018	4-12	3.7	4.3	290	467	-7	-23.4%	31	-7.7%	25	14.2%	31	-1.6%	22	39.3	17	38.0	21	27.6	9	27.1	6	26.7	4
2019	7-9	5.2	7.2	313	419	-2	-12.7%	25	5.4%	9	15.8%	31	-2.3%	25	52.4	26	41.1	22	26.8	15	25.8	22	25.8	18
2020	8-8	7.0	6.9	434	478	-11	-6.2%	19	1.8%	14	9.6%	28	1.5%	13	54.3	27	32.6	11	27.4	9	26.0	24	26.5	8

2020 Performance Based on Most Common Personnel Groups

LV Offense					LV Offense vs. Opponents					LV Defense				LV Defense vs. Opponents			
Pers	Freq	Yds	DVOA	Run%	Pers	Freq	Yds	DVOA	Run%	Pers	Freq	Yds	DVOA	Pers	Freq	Yds	DVOA
11	50%	7.1	12.3%	29%	Base	27%	4.7	-16.4%	57%	Base	24%	5.3	-11.9%	11	66%	6.6	19.4%
12	19%	6.1	3.3%	44%	Nickel	60%	6.5	4.5%	37%	Nickel	70%	6.3	15.0%	12	16%	4.8	-20.6%
22	12%	4.1	-19.1%	62%	Dime+	12%	8.8	47.5%	18%	Dime+	5%	9.5	54.6%	21	5%	6.4	-6.8%
13	9%	5.5	6.9%	48%	Goal Line	2%	1.0	30.2%	59%	Goal Line	1%	0.8	-4.8%	13	4%	5.3	-16.3%
21	8%	6.1	-8.6%	57%										10	3%	6.3	-3.7%
23	2%	0.9	22.2%	63%										22	1%	5.4	18.0%

Strategic Tendencies

Run/Pass		Rk	Formation		Rk	Pass Rush		Rk	Secondary		Rk	Strategy		Rk
Runs, first half	37%	18	Form: Single Back	75%	27	Rush 3	6.4%	15	4 DB	24%	15	Play Action	26%	20
Runs, first down	54%	5	Form: Empty Back	5%	28	Rush 4	74.4%	6	5 DB	70%	6	Offensive Motion	52%	9
Runs, second-long	25%	23	Form: Multi Back	19%	7	Rush 5	16.4%	24	6+ DB	5%	21	Avg Box (Off)	6.81	5
Runs, power sit.	57%	18	Pers: 3+ WR	50%	28	Rush 6+	2.8%	25	Man Coverage	31%	16	Avg Box (Def)	6.37	26
Runs, behind 2H	32%	9	Pers: 2+ TE/6+ OL	42%	5	Edge Rusher Sacks	59.5%	7	CB by Sides	77%	11	Offensive Pace	30.99	23
Pass, ahead 2H	40%	27	Pers: 6+ OL	0%	30	Interior DL Sacks	16.7%	27	S/CB Cover Ratio	38%	3	Defensive Pace	29.30	4
Run-Pass Options	6%	20	Shotgun/Pistol	59%	24	Second Level Sacks	23.8%	15	DB Blitz	12%	21	Go for it on 4th	1.93	8

The Raiders had the league's biggest reverse play-action split when it came to yards per play. They had 6.4 yards per play with 12.6% DVOA using play-action but 7.9 yards per play with 24.8% DVOA on pass plays without play-action. ✇ Las Vegas threw only 11% of passes to the player we designated as the No. 1 wide receiver, usually Henry Ruggs. Every other offense was at 17% or greater. But the Raiders led the league with 33% of passes thrown to tight ends. ✇ Las Vegas recovered only five of 20 fumbles on offense. ✇ Las Vegas never used six offensive linemen. ✇ The Raiders did not blitz much but were very good when they did, tied with Washington for the largest DVOA difference between plays with four pass-rushers (28.0% DVOA, 7.5 yards per pass) and plays with five or more pass-rushers (-19.4% DVOA, 6.8 yards per pass). ✇ The Las Vegas defense was 30th in yards allowed per drive but 13th in three-and-outs forced per drive. ✇ The Raiders benefited from 39 dropped passes by opponents, second in the league. ✇ Las Vegas allowed a league-worst 13.8% DVOA with 5.1 yards per carry when opponents ran with three or more wide receivers on the field. ✇ Las Vegas was tied for a league-leading average of 13:54 of game time each week. ✇ Jon Gruden has historically been very conservative on fourth downs but had his most aggressive season ever in 2020, finishing ninth in Aggressiveness Index. This was the first time Gruden finished in the top half of the league since 2006.

Passing

Player	DYAR	DVOA	Plays	NtYds	Avg	YAC	C%	TD	Int
D.Carr	925	14.0%	539	3943	7.3	5.6	68.0%	27	9
M.Mariota	45	13.0%	27	226	8.4	4.5	63.0%	1	1
N.Peterman	-41	-104.5%	7	9	1.3	7.0	60.0%	0	0

Rushing

Player	DYAR	DVOA	Plays	Yds	Avg	TD	Fum	Suc
J.Jacobs	-54	-12.9%	273	1065	3.9	12	2	51%
D.Booker*	26	-1.8%	93	423	4.5	3	1	46%
D.Carr	3	-10.8%	31	144	4.6	3	3	--
J.Richard	46	46.8%	22	123	5.6	1	1	50%
H.Ruggs	1	-36.6%	9	49	5.4	0	1	--
M.Mariota	48	76.2%	9	88	9.8	1	0	--
T.Riddick	-7	-38.7%	6	14	2.3	0	0	17%
K.Drake	*57*	*-3.4%*	*239*	*955*	*4.0*	*10*	*3*	*50%*

Receiving

Player	DYAR	DVOA	Plays	Ctch	Yds	Y/C	YAC	TD	C%
N.Agholor*	277	28.0%	82	48	896	18.7	4.8	8	59%
H.Renfrow	59	-3.2%	77	56	656	11.7	6.0	2	73%
H.Ruggs	38	-2.4%	43	26	452	17.4	5.6	2	60%
Z.Jones	4	-9.9%	20	14	154	11.0	4.6	1	70%
B.Edwards	64	36.6%	15	11	193	17.5	7.3	1	73%
J.Brown	*99*	*11.4%*	*52*	*33*	*458*	*13.9*	*5.4*	*3*	*63%*
W.Snead	*81*	*10.1%*	*48*	*33*	*432*	*13.1*	*5.7*	*3*	*69%*
D.Waller	190	11.4%	145	107	1196	11.2	5.3	9	74%
J.Witten*	-13	-16.5%	17	13	69	5.3	1.5	2	76%
F.Moreau	55	78.5%	9	7	140	20.0	7.3	2	78%
J.Jacobs	20	-5.2%	45	33	238	7.2	7.2	0	73%
J.Richard	19	1.5%	23	19	138	7.3	5.1	0	83%
D.Booker*	-26	-37.5%	21	17	84	4.9	4.8	0	81%
A.Ingold	41	26.3%	17	12	110	9.2	7.3	1	71%
T.Riddick	12	25.0%	6	5	43	8.6	6.6	0	83%
K.Drake	*10*	*-8.1%*	*31*	*25*	*137*	*5.5*	*6.6*	*0*	*81%*

Offensive Line

Player	Pos	Age	GS	Snaps	Pen	Sk	Pass	Run	Player	Pos	Age	GS	Snaps	Pen	Sk	Pass	Run
Rodney Hudson*	C	32	16/16	1082	0	1	9	6	Brandon Parker	LT/RT	26	11/4	345	2	1.5	8	1
Gabe Jackson*	RG	30	16/16	1061	3	1	13	10	Trenton Brown*	RT	28	5/5	281	1	0	5	3
Kolton Miller	LT	26	14/14	960	5	1.5	9	8	John Simpson	LG	24	7/2	252	4	0	6	0
Denzelle Good	LG	30	15/14	957	5	1	14	4	*Nick Martin*	*C*	*28*	*16/16*	*979*	*4*	*0*	*9*	*10*
Sam Young	RT	34	11/7	381	2	3.5	12	0									

Year	Yards	ALY	Rk	Power	Rk	Stuff	Rk	2Lev	Rk	OpFld	Rk	BB Rt	Rk	Sacks	ASR	Rk	Press	Rk	BB Rt	Rk	Cont
2018	4.24	4.49	13	53%	31	18%	10	1.31	8	0.60	28	6.3%	17	52	8.7%	25	28.3%	13	11.2%	24	28
2019	4.26	4.63	6	58%	24	17%	7	1.14	21	0.67	22	10.4%	17	29	5.9%	6	25.7%	4	13.2%	16	22
2020	4.10	4.32	18	63%	21	17%	19	1.18	18	0.61	21	7.6%	5	28	5.5%	10	21.4%	6	12.6%	17	21

2020 ALY by direction:	Left End: 6.57 (1)	Left Tackle: 2.45 (32)	Mid/Guard: 4.58 (11)	Right Tackle: 3.50 (29)	Right End: 3.45 (27)

The Raiders' No. 5 finish in blown block rate in the run game was their best mark in the last three years, yet their No. 18 finish in adjusted line yards was their worst over that span. Many of the team's fill-in starters (Denzelle Good, Brandon Parker, Sam Young) hardly blew any blocks in the run game, but were not helpful in getting any push, either. ◗ There were 100 offensive linemen who saw the field for fewer than 400 snaps last season. Of those 100, only two of them were credited with more sacks allowed than Young. ◗ Now-departed center Rodney Hudson had been slowly blowing more blocks each season. Over the last three years, he slid from 10th to 12th to 17th in snaps per blown block among centers. He is still one of the best in the league, but perhaps a bit more volatile than assumed. ◗ That said, former Texans center Nick Martin, who is set to replace Hudson, has been no better over that span. Martin has never ranked higher than 14th in snaps per blown block and bottomed out at 25th place in 2020. Up until 2020, most of Martin's blown blocks were in the run game, and he was known for being a good pass-protector. Martin's nine blown pass blocks in 2020 were more than the previous two seasons combined (six). Hopefully for the Raiders, Martin's lapse in pass pro last year was a fluke. ◗ Returning guard Richie Incognito to the lineup could help offset the loss of Gabe Jackson. In 2019, Incognito blew just seven total blocks and was credited for zero sacks allowed, both the lowest marks among the team's starters. Granted, he did lead the bunch with eight penalties, but that comes with his nasty demeanor in the run game. ◗ First-round rookie Alex Leatherwood (Alabama) slots in at right tackle for Trent Brown. The pick was billed as one of the biggest reaches on draft night, but it's easy to see why Las Vegas bought Leatherwood in. Leatherwood has a wingspan in the 90th percentile among tackles while also clearing the 85th percentile in the 3-cone, broad jump, vertical jump, and 40-yard dash. The three-year college starter (two at left tackle) could stand to be lighter on his feet, but all the athletic gifts and years of SEC experience are there.

Defensive Front

Defensive Line	Age	Pos	G	Snaps	Plays	TmPct	Rk	Stop	Dfts	BTkl	Runs	St%	Rk	RuYd	Rk	Sack	Hit	Hur	Dsrpt
							Overall					vs. Run				Pass Rush			
Johnathan Hankins	29	DT	16	665	48	5.8%	31	41	3	6	43	86%	6	1.9	21	1.0	3	7	0
Maliek Collins*	26	DT	12	503	15	2.4%	94	10	2	2	13	77%	40	1.7	11	0.0	2	8	0
Kendal Vickers	26	DT	15	315	10	1.3%	--	7	3	2	8	63%	--	2.8	--	2.0	1	7	0
Maurice Hurst*	26	DT	11	277	28	4.9%	--	18	5	2	22	59%	--	3.0	--	0.5	5	6	1
Quinton Jefferson	28	DT	16	534	24	2.9%	85	16	9	2	19	58%	91	2.6	53	3.0	9	10	2
Matt Dickerson	26	DT	10	196	10	1.8%	--	6	1	0	8	63%	--	2.4	--	0.0	1	0	0

Edge Rushers	Age	Pos	G	Snaps	Plays	TmPct	Rk	Stop	Dfts	BTkl	Runs	St%	Rk	RuYd	Rk	Sack	Hit	Hur	Dsrpt
							Overall					vs. Run				Pass Rush			
Maxx Crosby	24	DE	16	904	40	4.8%	46	34	18	5	29	83%	9	1.4	7	7.0	8	32	1
Carl Nassib	28	DE	14	463	33	4.5%	54	25	10	5	22	77%	26	1.8	20	2.5	6	18	5
Clelin Ferrell	24	DE	11	461	30	5.3%	38	26	6	3	24	83%	7	1.4	6	2.0	9	18	3
Arden Key*	25	DE	14	433	17	2.3%	91	13	3	3	14	71%	48	2.0	27	0.0	11	16	3
Vic Beasley*	29	DE	10	198	4	0.8%	--	3	2	2	3	67%	--	2.0	--	0.0	0	2	0
Yannick Ngakoue	26	DE	15	657	24	3.1%	82	19	13	4	12	75%	33	2.6	46	8.0	8	28	1

Linebackers	Age	Pos	G	Snaps	Plays	TmPct	Rk	Stop	Dfts	BTkl	Runs	St%	Rk	RuYd	Rk	Sack	Hit	Hur	Tgts	Suc%	Rk	Yd/P	Rk	PD	Int
							Overall					vs. Run				Pass Rush				vs. Pass					
Cory Littleton	28	OLB	14	847	79	10.9%	55	41	12	9	42	62%	23	3.1	10	0.0	0	5	39	54%	27	7.8	63	0	0
Nicholas Morrow	26	OLB	14	722	85	11.7%	48	42	15	10	42	52%	57	5.4	84	3.0	3	7	29	72%	3	3.5	3	9	1
Nick Kwiatkoski	28	MLB	12	651	85	13.7%	37	41	9	9	48	56%	41	3.6	28	1.0	1	5	25	56%	22	4.7	14	4	1
Raekwon McMillan*	26	MLB	16	169	24	2.9%	--	12	2	6	18	61%	--	7.2	--	0.0	0	0	3	67%	--	10.3	--	1	0

Year	Yards	ALY	Rk	Power	Rk	Stuff	Rk	2Lev	Rk	OpFld	Rk	BB Rt	Rk	Sacks	ASR	Rk	Press	Rk	BB Rt	Rk
2018	4.76	4.63	25	65%	16	17%	20	1.29	22	1.05	25	5.3%	30	13	3.5%	32	22.0%	32	3.6%	32
2019	3.82	3.89	4	70%	25	22%	7	1.12	11	0.56	9	14.2%	11	32	6.1%	27	29.6%	21	11.1%	30
2020	4.82	4.55	21	70%	22	19%	13	1.40	28	1.02	28	15.8%	5	21	4.5%	29	22.8%	26	11.3%	23

2020 ALY by direction:	Left End: 5.22 (27)	Left Tackle: 5.73 (32)	Mid/Guard: 4.02 (8)	Right Tackle: 5.07 (26)	Right End: 3.72 (6)

Interior pass rush played a hand in Las Vegas' drop in pressure rate. Three qualifying interior defensive linemen combined for 50 hurries in 2019 (1,776 total snaps), while the Raiders' four qualifying interior defensive linemen in 2020 combined for just 28 hurries (1,760 snaps). ✎ The decline of Maurice Hurst, specifically, was critical. Hurst went from 26 snaps per hurry in 2019 to a putrid 46 snaps per hurry in 2020, nearly cutting his effectiveness in half thanks in part to a nagging ankle injury. Hurst was waived after the end of the season. ✎ On the surface, the opposite seems true with their edge defenders. Raiders edge defenders scored 86 hurries in 2020 (2,459) after just 73 hurries in 2019 (2,028 total snaps). However, the group of 2020 players combined for roughly 400 more snaps. Las Vegas' 2020 edge rushers earned a hurry for every 28.6 combined snaps in 2020, yet their 2019 qualifiers trailed just slightly behind at 27.8 combined snaps per hurry. ✎ Each of the Raiders' three qualifying linebackers had a coverage success rate over 50%. Corey Littleton was the only linebacker in the NFL credited with over 25 targets and a coverage success rate over 50% without recording a single pass defensed. That's good zone spacing and leverage right there. ✎ In Littleton's final two years with the Rams, he never ranked higher than 49th in either stop rate or yards allowed on tackles. Littleton skyrocketed inside the top 25 in both areas in his lone year with the Raiders, perhaps because he felt more comfortable in an even front defense as opposed to Wade Phillips' odd fronts.

Defensive Secondary

Secondary	Age	Pos	G	Snaps	Plays	Overall TmPct	Rk	Stop	Dfts	BTkl	vs. Run Runs	St%	Rk	RuYd	Rk	vs. Pass Tgts	Tgt%	Rk	aDOT	Suc%	Rk	Yd/P	Rk	PD	Int
Trayvon Mullen	24	CB	16	932	75	9.0%	31	32	11	15	17	47%	30	6.1	32	68	18.2%	54	10.9	49%	53	7.5	38	14	2
Johnathan Abram	25	SS	13	855	85	12.6%	14	32	7	17	41	46%	20	7.8	49	25	7.3%	43	16.5	40%	62	12.9	67	6	2
Nevin Lawson	30	CB	14	735	64	8.8%	38	20	8	5	16	19%	73	10.4	74	49	16.6%	66	12.9	43%	69	7.7	43	4	0
Erik Harris*	31	FS	14	724	61	8.4%	61	15	6	14	27	26%	56	8.9	56	23	7.9%	40	13.2	43%	53	10.7	64	5	0
Lamarcus Joyner*	31	FS/CB	14	669	71	9.8%	45	24	9	3	28	46%	18	4.5	7	48	17.9%	4	8.5	50%	34	7.0	24	5	0
Jeff Heath*	30	SS	13	414	38	5.6%	--	14	7	8	18	44%	--	6.3	--	13	7.8%	--	8.5	54%	--	6.3	--	4	3
Daryl Worley*	26	CB	10	344	25	4.8%	--	10	3	4	13	46%	--	7.8	--	16	11.7%	--	11.1	31%	--	11.6	--	3	0
Damon Arnette	25	CB	9	343	27	5.8%	--	12	4	13	9	56%	--	5.1	--	25	18.2%	--	11.6	36%	--	11.8	--	2	0
Rasul Douglas	26	CB	14	821	71	10.0%	19	25	6	9	12	50%	24	6.3	34	71	21.2%	30	10.9	49%	44	8.1	52	9	0
Casey Hayward	32	CB	14	788	50	7.3%	66	22	7	9	7	43%	38	5.0	22	68	22.1%	21	14.6	56%	20	8.7	62	9	1
Karl Joseph	28	SS	14	660	68	9.5%	50	24	7	10	37	41%	29	5.3	19	26	9.6%	27	9.9	35%	68	10.2	60	4	1
De'Vante Bausby	28	CB	11	277	25	4.3%	--	11	3	5	1	100%	--	12.0	--	33	31.0%	--	11.9	48%	--	8.0	--	5	0

Year	Pass D Rank	vs. #1 WR	Rk	vs. #2 WR	Rk	vs. Other WR	Rk	WR Wide	Rk	WR Slot	Rk	vs. TE	Rk	vs. RB	Rk
2018	32	-27.0%	2	-5.3%	13	27.8%	30	-16.0%	5	0.1%	17	39.7%	32	7.2%	20
2019	30	18.4%	28	32.0%	31	-4.7%	14	16.9%	29	15.4%	24	9.3%	25	34.0%	30
2020	26	20.4%	29	11.9%	25	19.7%	29	24.1%	31	17.6%	29	-15.4%	5	2.5%	20

From tackling to coverage, this unit was a major problem last season. First, tackling: Las Vegas ranked dead last in the league with 149 broken tackles on defense, and the biggest issue was in the secondary. The four worst Raiders in broken tackles were defensive backs: Johnathan Abram led the team with 17, while Trayvon Mullen, Erik Harris, and Damon Arnette each added more than a dozen. ✎ Next, coverage: only the Raiders and Jaguars failed to have a single qualifying defensive back post a success rate over 50% last season. ✎ Likewise, the Raiders were one of just two teams to rank in the bottom 10 in the league in pass defense DVOA against both outside and slot receivers. The Falcons were the other. ✎ Mullen, a 2019 second-round pick, is probably a good No. 2 who has been stuck as the Raiders' No. 1. ✎ 2020 first-round cornerback Arnette was billed as a reach on draft night and it proved true during his rookie season. Among the 128 cornerbacks to see at least 20 targets last year, Arnette ranked 119th in coverage success rate. The rookie played far too loose with his technique and footwork and often struggled to feel out routes as they were developing. While the wrist and concussion issues that kept him off the field for seven games played a factor, all of Arnette's issues still showed up just the same early in the year before the injury. ✎ Las Vegas signed Rasul Douglas, who spent three years in Philly and last season in Carolina. Douglas is a big press cornerback who lacks deep speed. He handles himself well at the line of scrimmage and when able to work back to throws breaking in front of him, but he has allowed over 8.0 yards per attempt in each of the last three seasons in large part because he cannot keep up down the field. ✎ Jeff Heath was the only safety in the league with three or more interceptions while also not seeing enough starts/targets to qualify for our coverage rankings. The only other two players in the league to match the bizarre feat were cornerbacks (Pittsburgh's Mike Hilton and Kansas City's L'Jarius Sneed). ✎ Returning Karl Joseph, who spent the 2020 season with Cleveland, is consistently one of the least productive safeties in football. In each of the past three seasons, Joseph has earned a coverage success rate of 40% or worse. ✎ 2019 first-round pick Johnathan Abram has not lived up to his draft billing. He gets a pass for his 2019 rookie season, most of which he missed with a groin injury, but Abram's 2020 season was a mess.

Abram too frequently plays like a hot head when hunting for ballcarriers, against both the run and underneath throws. Abram also struggled in coverage due to his slow feet and questionable discipline, resulting in teams constantly beating him over the top. ●, Fourth-round rookie safety Tyree Gillespie (Missouri) is better the more he can just play what is in front of him. The range to play as a single-high safety in the NFL is not really there, but Gillespie does well to trigger downhill against the run and to routes breaking in front of him, be they in-breakers over the middle or quick screen passes to the perimeter.

Special Teams

Year	DVOA	Rank	FG/XP	Rank	Net Kick	Rank	Kick Ret	Rank	Net Punt	Rank	Punt Ret	Rank	Hidden	Rank
2018	-1.6%	22	2.8	12	-4.4	27	0.1	12	-12.0	32	5.3	6	2.2	11
2019	-2.3%	25	-7.8	28	2.5	12	0.7	11	-5.5	23	-1.6	18	-6.0	25
2020	1.5%	13	4.0	11	0.0	18	-1.2	17	2.1	14	2.9	10	7.7	8

AJ Cole is the NFL's most average punter. Cole finished 17th out of 32 qualifiers in gross punt value in 2019, followed up by a 16th-out-of-34 finish in 2020. Considering Johnny Townsend was the worst punter in the league with the Raiders in 2018, the Raiders are probably happy with perfectly average play from Cole. He looked better last year because the Raiders' punt coverage team improved. ●, Kicker Daniel Carlson's work from long range has not been consistent year-to-year. Carlson went 11-of-12 beyond 40 yards in 10 games with the Raiders in 2018, then stumbled to just 6-of-12 in 2019. He then bounced back in 2020 with a 7-of-9 showing. ●, First-round pick Henry Ruggs saw seven kick returns last season, but do not expect him to take over the job any time soon. Three of Ruggs' returns were during Weeks 11 and 12, which starting kick returner Jalen Richard missed due to injury. Richard was kept off special teams entirely for the two weeks following his return, and Ruggs earned another one of his returns during that span. Richard probably returns to the role in 2021, and Hunter Renfrow will return as punt returner after a good performance last season.

Los Angeles Chargers

2020 Record: 7-9	**Total DVOA:** -14.7% (22)	**2021 Mean Projection:** 7.3 wins	**On the Clock (0-5):** 26%
Pythagorean Wins: 6.9 (22)	**Offense:** 1.5% (15)	**Postseason Odds:** 25.6%	**Mediocrity (6-8):** 41%
Snap-Weighted Age: 25.8 (29)	**Defense:** 4.4% (20)	**Super Bowl Odds:** 1.8%	**Playoff Contender (9-11):** 25%
Average Opponent: -1.5% (21)	**Special Teams:** -11.8% (32)	**Proj. Avg. Opponent:** 1.3% (9)	**Super Bowl Contender (12+):** 7%

2020: Only the Chargers could stumble into a stud rookie quarterback because a team doctor punctured the starter's lungs.

2021: The future in Los Angeles is as bright as ever, but 2021 hype may be a year too soon.

The Chargers are the football community's favorite trick to fall for. Year after year, fans and media alike rally behind the Bolts for one reason or another, usually because of everyone's infatuation with Philip Rivers and his many bolo ties. Though there is a new quarterback behind center now, the same old Chargers charm remains. The Chargers are almost universally expected to be among this year's rising stars.

It is easy to see why many think this may be the year Lucy lets Charlie Brown kick the football, too. The majority of recent teams to suddenly shoot into elite territory have done so off the back of top-class play from their quarterbacks in Year 2. Patrick Mahomes and Lamar Jackson are the most obvious and recent examples, but the 2017 Eagles and Rams with Carson Wentz and Jared Goff fall into the same bin. Justin Herbert, at least more so than his peers in the 2020 quarterback class, is an exciting candidate to make that second-year leap.

Herbert was the third quarterback selected in the 2020 draft but played like the first overall pick as a rookie. After sitting on the bench for the season opener, he took over the starting job in Week 2 under extremely Charger-esque conditions: starting quarterback Tyrod Taylor had his lung accidentally punctured by a team doctor right before kickoff.

Few expected Herbert to be ready, both in a broader sense and on such short notice, but he went 22-of-33 for 311 yards with one touchdown and an interception. He even tacked on a rushing touchdown as evidence of his dual-threat ability. The Chargers lost that Week 2 game against the Chiefs, as well as

the following three matches, but it became clear pretty quickly that Herbert was an NFL player. Eventually, Herbert finished the season with one of the top 10 passing DYAR totals ever put up by a rookie quarterback (Table 1).

Herbert's sudden success then raised the question of why he fell in the draft the way he did. Granted, he was still a top-10 pick and not even the last quarterback selected in Round 1, but he performed better than the two quarterbacks who were drafted before him and has far superior physical tools than both. Perhaps health was a factor. Herbert had a length injury history in college, though nothing quite as severe as Tua Tagovailoa's bum hip. Herbert missed six weeks as a sophomore with a clavicle facture, suffered another shoulder injury near the end of his junior year, and then tweaked his knee early in his senior year, although he finished out the remainder of the season just fine.

The Oregon offense did not help Herbert the way their reputation may suggest, either. Oregon is known for having speed, speed, and more speed at the skill positions, but by Herbert's final season, the cupboard was mostly bare as far as pass-catchers go. The offense was also completely unimaginative, often resorting to RPO bubble screens and similarly thoughtless tactics as a means to compensate for wide receivers who could not get open consistently. Herbert's execution of Oregon's more standard dropback and play-action scheme was far from perfect, to be fair, but he was not getting the same amount of help that the likes of Joe Burrow and Tagovailoa were.

Table 1. Top Rookies by Passing DYAR, 1983-2020

Name	Year	Team	Passes	DYAR	DVOA	Passes Y+1	DYAR Y+1	DVOA Y+1
Dak Prescott	2016	DAL	483	1302	31.6%	520	375	-0.2%
Matt Ryan	2008	ATL	451	1012	25.3%	465	702	12.4%
Ben Roethlisberger	2004	PIT	326	908	31.7%	292	885	35.8%
Dan Marino	1983	MIA	310	885	33.8%	579	2437	53.0%
Russell Wilson	2012	SEA	432	872	19.7%	453	770	15.6%
Justen Herbert	**2020**	**LAC**	**623**	**861**	**10.2%**	--	--	--
Robert Griffin	2012	WAS	425	727	16.6%	495	-60	-13.1%
Peyton Manning	1998	IND	592	697	7.7%	548	1581	34.0%
Baker Mayfield	2018	CLE	509	628	8.1%	573	48	-9.8%
Andy Dalton	2011	CIN	540	573	5.6%	571	194	-5.9%
Deshaun Watson	2017	HOU	221	497	23.1%	562	737	9.5%
Jameis Winston	2015	TB	560	467	2.1%	603	556	3.6%

2021 Chargers Schedule

Week	Opp.	Week	Opp.	Week	Opp.
1	at WAS	7	BYE	13	at CIN
2	DAL	8	NE	14	NYG
3	at KC	9	at PHI	15	KC (Thu.)
4	LV (Mon.)	10	MIN	16	at HOU
5	CLE	11	PIT	17	DEN
6	at BAL	12	at DEN	18	at LV

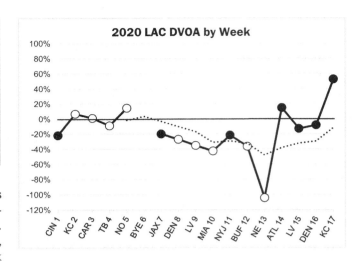

2020 LAC DVOA by Week

The disconnect between Herbert's pre-draft expectations and his play as a rookie can also be explained by how productive he was in unsustainable areas in his first season. Herbert finished sixth in DVOA on third and fourth downs, trailing only Tom Brady, Aaron Rodgers, Josh Allen, Patrick Mahomes, and Derek Carr—pretty good company. Likewise, Herbert finished with the fourth-highest DVOA while under pressure.

Herbert was plenty impressive for a rookie in more stable situations. Herbert posted a 45.0% DVOA without pressure, putting him a few percentage points above the NFL average in 2020. That is far from special and not quite the 70.0%-plus numbers both Deshaun Watson and Dak Prescott posted as rookies, but it is a good place to start. Herbert also earned a 34.3% passing DVOA from inside the pocket, good for just over double the NFL average and sixth in the league. It is more than fair to assume Herbert's play under pressure and on third down will regress some, but the floor for his game is sneaky-high and open to raising even further if he takes the second-year leap all young quarterbacks are expected to make.

However, that improvement may not be in the cards for Herbert, at least not statistically. Quarterbacks often take a leap in their second season not necessarily because they improve in such a dramatic way that suddenly makes them great, but because most rookie quarterbacks are simply bad. It's easier to go from bad to competent than to go from good to great in Year 2. Since 2005, there have only been 11 quarterbacks to throw 100 passes in both Year 1 and Year 2 while having a positive DVOA as rookies. They averaged a -12.1% *drop* in passing DVOA during Year 2, be that due to poorer injury luck, defenses figuring them out a bit, loss in surrounding talent during the offseason, or coaching changes. Quarterbacks with -10.0% DVOA or worse as rookies, however, improved by an average of 19.8% in their second seasons, which is mostly a reflection of bad rookie quarterbacks climbing into respectable territory. Herbert falls comfortably into the first tier of rookie quarterbacks who already produced well.

Los Angeles did everything it could to help Herbert take another step forward in his second season. The Chargers front office made it a point to ensure Herbert could play more comfortably in structure, which is where he could stand to improve most. The bulk of Los Angeles' resources this offseason was poured into reconstructing the offensive line. Signing center Corey Linsley from the Packers was the first domino to fall. Linsley replaces Dan Feeney, who converted from guard to center last season out of necessity. Feeney ranked 32nd out of 36 qualifying centers in snaps per blown block, while Linsley finished third. Linsley blew just one block in pass protection all of last season.

A center like Linsley brings more than just his own blocking ability, too. Having a sharp, well-rounded center who can help out in calling pass protections and identifying defensive fronts can go a long way in taking a weight off the quarterback's shoulders and further strengthening how good a given offense is pre-snap. The Dallas Cowboys' relationship between Travis Frederick and Dak Prescott is the best recent example, but Alex Mack and Matt Ryan's work in Atlanta, especially during the Kyle Shanahan era, falls into the same bin. The same goes for Derek Carr and Rodney Hudson, who was initially signed by the Raiders before Carr's second pro season.

In addition to Linsley, the Chargers also signed guard Oday Aboushi and tackle Matt Feiler. Though Feiler played tackle in Pittsburgh, the expectation is for him to kick inside to guard while Bryan Bulaga remains at right tackle. Granted, Bulaga has struggled to stay healthy as of late, but Feiler should remain inside until Bulaga gets hurt. None of these moves are game-changing, but they should bring the Chargers offensive line closer to competent than the trainwreck it has been of late.

To bring the unit home, Los Angeles spent its first-round pick on Northwestern tackle Rashawn Slater. Short arms be damned, Slater was widely viewed as the No. 2 tackle prospect behind Oregon's Penei Sewell, who went a handful of picks beforehand to the Lions. Whether or not Slater can be a Pro Bowl-caliber blindside tackle out of the gate is less important than if he can simply be an upgrade over Sam Tevi. While Tevi's blown-block numbers were merely below average over the past two seasons, he is anecdotally one of the worst tackles on film over the past decade, at least relative to the number of games he has started. There have been worse tackles, no doubt, but not many who were intentionally named the Week 1 starter for two years in a row.

All of those renovations up front should soften the blow of losing tight end Hunter Henry. The Chargers did bring in veteran Jared Cook, best-known for his field-stretching presence and shaky hands, but that is not exactly a 1:1 with Henry's skill set. Henry was more of a sure-handed short-to-intermediate threat with above-average blocking skills like a true in-line Y. Cook is more of an athlete and pure pass-catcher. At least Cook also has the added benefit of being familiar with new offensive coordinator Joe Lombardi, who was the quarterbacks coach in New Orleans during Cook's two seasons there.

In its totality, the Chargers offense is worth a healthy portion of the hype they are being showered with. The offensive line will be miles better and there is reason to be bullish on Herbert, even if he could regress some in volatile areas. The wide receiver corps may be top-heavy, but Keenan Allen and Mike Williams are as good a one-two punch at wide receiver as there is. Cook is a quality role player from the tight end spot and Austin Ekeler is among the league's best pass-catching backs in the league. If Herbert plays even halfway to the expectations people have thrust upon him, this should be a firmly above-average unit.

The bigger reason to be skeptical of Chargers hype is the defense. The shine of a new, exciting, defensive-minded head coach along with stars such as Joey Bosa and Derwin James has blinded the masses to what is an otherwise volatile roster. A 30,000-foot view of the defensive personnel makes it clear that the Chargers lost more contributors than they brought in.

Outside linebacker Melvin Ingram, cornerback Casey Hayward, safety Rayshawn Jenkins, and linebacker Denzel Perryman all left the team this offseason. Ingram was third on the team in pressures after playing just seven games, while Hayward held the team's best coverage success rate (56%). Jenkins, a solid box defender, could have been the third safety Staley's defense needs. Even losing Perryman, despite Staley's light use of linebackers with the Rams, could hurt considering he was far and away the Chargers' best run defender at the position.

It's unlikely that anyone the Chargers brought in will match the production of the players they are replacing. Former Packers and Giants pass-rusher Kyle Fackrell was signed on the cheap, but he is little more than a third or fourth edge rusher, not a bona fide starter like Ingram. Fourth-round rookie Chris Rumph is not replacing Ingram in Year 1, either. Los Angeles' effort to replace Hayward at cornerback was to draft the 5-foot-10, 180-pound Asante Samuel Jr. (Florida State) in the second round. While Samuel's aggressive play style is exciting, non-first-round cornerbacks are a coin flip to produce well as rookies.

The rest of the Chargers "additions" are returns from injury. Star safety Derwin James is returning from a bum knee and linebacker Drue Tranquill is coming back from a broken fibula. Getting James back in the lineup should do wonders for the defense if he is somewhere close to 100%, but Tranquill likely does not move the needle. Tranquill, while a decent player, does not make for a good direct replacement for Perryman's hard-nosed run defense, never mind how little Staley wants to do with his off-ball linebackers anyway.

And that brings us to the next question with the Chargers defense. Staley, while clearly brilliant in his one season with the Rams, brings a polar-opposite approach to that of former defensive coordinator Gus Bradley. The Rams' success in Staley's first year there was an exception that gives a mistak-

en impression of how easy it is to switch defensive schemes. In general, these transitions tend to be turbulent, especially considering how different Bradley's scheme was from what Staley is theoretically bringing to town.

To oversimplify the differences between Staley and Bradley's defenses, Staley runs a two-high safety structure while Bradley was a believer in one-high safety looks. The two coaches almost literally could not have been on further ends of the spectrum in this regard. Last season, Staley's Rams defense operated from one-high shells just 15.9% of the time (31st in the NFL), whereas Bradley did so 68.7% of the time (second). Conversely, Staley spent 78.6% of his snaps out of two-high shells (second), while Bradley only called two-high shells 26.3% of the time (30th).

Simple coverage preferences play a part in this. Bradley has been a faithful servant to the Cover-3 religion since his days with the Seattle Seahawks. It's what he has always done and will always do. Staley, on the other hand, is a believer in quarters (Cover-4) and Cover-6 (Cover-2 on one side, Cover-4 on the other)—at least as much as any team can be in a league that is oriented to play Cover-1 and Cover-3 across the board. Staley's style of defense has become more prevalent at the college level as an answer to RPOs, since the split-field safeties can "cap" any wide receivers breaking over the middle of the field. It's more than just coverage, though. Coverage is tied to how a team aligns up front and how they fit the run.

In short, single-high defenses generally fall into the bin of being "gapped out" in the run fit. Because one safety is rolled down, a defense can have one player per gap in the run game (unless the quarterback is added into the mix). This sacrifices numbers down the field in the passing game in exchange for advantageous numbers against the run. The point of these fits is to funnel plays back inside because that is where the help is.

Two-high defenses, on the other hand, are generally going to be out-gapped or have players late in the fit. With both safeties sitting high and playing pass-first, the defense is outnumbered in the run game, even without accounting for the quarterback potentially adding on. A defense then has to "steal" gaps one way or another, which is best achieved with either two-gapping defensive linemen or playing games up front with a stud athlete, à la Aaron Donald. Two-high fits will often ask players to "spill" when possible, which means forcing the play outside to the safeties who are coming down to play the run late.

It is worth wondering if any of what Staley did with the Rams is even feasible with the Chargers. The Chargers roster is very much built like the one-gap team Bradley wanted it to be. That presents issues in the context of what Staley's scheme looked like last season. One of the hot selling points with Staley was his adaptability, so it's entirely possible he sees this roster and does not try to force his Rams' scheme onto this Chargers roster.

The defensive line may be the biggest issue. The 2020 Rams not only had arguably the greatest defensive tackle of all time, but also deployed a handful of other capable two-gap defensive linemen. Michael Brockers, though not the name he once was, handled all of the two-gap, one-gap (TGOG; a

Nick Saban technique) and legit two-gap principles well from his defensive end spot. Nose tackle Sebastian Joseph-Day was also a force in the middle. His production numbers do not reflect it, but that's because his primary responsibility was to eat space and force plays outside, not to have plays forced back inside to him. Even the Rams' rotational pieces such as Morgan Fox and Greg Gaines handled those responsibilities well. The Rams had a defensive line built for what Staley wanted to do.

The Chargers have some question marks in that department. They were middling enough trying to defend the run from one-high last season, finishing 22nd in adjusted line yards and 26th in run defense DVOA. It's hard to imagine their pieces would somehow be better with more two-gap responsibilities. Linval Joseph, while competent, is no longer the run defense force he once was. 2019 first-round pick Jerry Tillery was repeatedly abused in run defense last season, evidenced by his 60% stop rate (87th) and his average run tackle coming after 3.3 yards (89th). That man is not two-gapping effectively. Justin Jones has been an effective 3-technique for the Chargers, but he is generally more of a quick one-gap player, not someone who wants to be handling two gaps. Joseph is probably not as good as Joseph-Day at this point, and neither Jones nor Tillery is Brockers.

Even Bosa is in an awkward spot with respect to Staley's defense. Staley often deployed two stand-up outside linebackers with defensive ends in 4i alignments inside of them. Bosa, at 6-foot-5 and roughly 275 pounds, is not really an every-down stand-up player, but imagining him as a 4i in Staley's Rams scheme does not add up, either. He could probably do it because a player of his caliber will be effective from anywhere, but it likely will not look as effective as when Bosa is in a more traditional defensive end spot from even-front spacing, and certainly not as effective as Donald from that spot.

Staley is only really left with two middling options. He can either force his Rams scheme with ill-fitting parts or he can lean on what the defense did previously despite having suffered a net-loss in talent from an already modest defensive front. It's possible Staley is sharp enough to get the unit to overachieve either way, but it's a stretch to believe this Chargers unit, as it stands now, can be anything close to the top-five front the Rams had.

The secondary is in a better, though still imperfect, position. Sorting out Los Angeles' defensive backfield is less about whether or not the players fit and more about what we can reasonably expect from most of them. Aside from cornerback Michael Davis, the Chargers secondary is filled with question marks, even from previously successful players.

Safety Derwin James is the crux of everything. Like John Johnson III with the Rams, James can be a do-it-all safety who plays centerfield, from the slot, and in the box all in the same drive. It was Johnson's versatility, as well as the assuredness of cornerback Jalen Ramsey handling his side of the field, that allowed Staley to do whatever he wanted to with the Rams secondary. James can certainly add that same value, but he is coming off a season-ending right knee injury after having already suffered a season-ending left knee injury back in col-

lege. He also missed a good portion of the 2019 season with a foot injury that required surgery. While the idealized version of James is certainly a difference-maker, it's optimistic to assume he is going to be right back to 100% as all these injuries pile up.

Also, there is no clear third safety the way the Rams had. The Rams used three-safety looks more than most of the rest of the league, and it's not a stretch to assume Staley would like to bring that to the Chargers. For now, the only two safeties on the roster beyond James and Nasir Adderley are Alohi Gilman (2020 sixth-round pick), Mark Webb (2021 seventh-round pick), and Ben DeLuca (2021 UDFA). The Rams had Johnson, Taylor Rapp, and Jordan Fuller as their top three guys, not to mention some of the contributions they got from Terrell Burgess. Fuller was a sixth-round pick for the Rams, so perhaps Staley can work some magic again, but betting on Day 3 picks hitting is not an ideal position to be in.

As hinted at earlier, the way in which Staley and Bradley use their safeties is entirely different. The Chargers' starting safeties last season (Nasir Adderley and Rayshawn Jenkins) had the largest gap in the NFL between where each of them made their average plays. Jenkins was the low player, Adderley was the high player, and the Chargers seldom strayed from that formula, whereas John Johnson III and Jordan Fuller's figures were much closer. James' return should make it easier for Staley to stick closer to what he wants to do, but it's still something to keep an eye on.

The cornerback room also has the glaring weakness of not having a Jalen Ramsey. Granted, precious few teams have a cornerback of that caliber, but the Chargers are not in that small handful. The sneaky good news is that all their veteran corners are useful, willing run defenders, which is absolutely necessary in Staley's defense (or at least what it looked like with the Rams). Michael Davis and Chris Harris Jr. each ranked in the top 25 in both stop rate and run yards allowed, while Tevaughn Campbell posted similar numbers despite not qualifying for the rankings. That's not the most exciting thing to hear about a cornerback unit, but it will be valuable.

Parsing the quality of the Chargers defense ultimately comes down to whether or not star power (James, Bosa, maybe Kenneth Murray) can outweigh an otherwise mediocre roster that suffered a net loss in talent and does not comfortably fit into the new head coach's defensive vision. A healthy Bosa and James alone will probably prevent the Chargers from being as bad as our mean defensive projection, but all the other hurdles make it difficult to see how they put it together this year.

That is not to say Staley is automatically a bad hire, either. Nobody should be writing off Staley long-term based on what he does with this current roster. The Chargers spent far more of their resources on offense year, which could mean next offseason will be focused on allowing Staley to fill out the defensive roster to fit his vision. Assuming that is the case, solidifying Staley's defense while Herbert leads the way on offense would give the Chargers a future worth getting excited about.

There is good football ahead of the Chargers. They should be a fun, scrappy team this season, and the duo of Staley and Herbert is one worth betting on long-term. Almost everything would need to hit just right for the defense to be any good in 2021, though, and it is optimistic to assume Herbert can lead a top-three offense right now in order to make up for the defense. There is no need to rush expectations on a first-year head coach and 23-year-old quarterback. Any and all excite-

ment for this iteration of the Chargers should be for 2022 and beyond.

Derrik Klassen

2020 Chargers Stats by Week

Wk	vs.	W-L	PF	PA	YDF	YDA	TO	Total	Off	Def	ST
1	at CIN	W	16	13	362	295	2	-21.7%	-16.8%	-5.1%	-9.9%
2	KC	L	20	23	479	414	-1	7.0%	4.0%	-6.6%	-3.6%
3	CAR	L	16	21	436	302	-4	1.2%	3.6%	1.8%	-0.6%
4	at TB	L	31	38	324	484	-1	-8.8%	18.0%	17.9%	-8.8%
5	at NO	L	27	30	350	408	1	14.7%	16.1%	-18.2%	-19.6%
6	BYE										
7	JAX	W	39	29	484	294	1	-19.8%	23.7%	9.7%	-33.8%
8	at DEN	L	30	31	485	351	-1	-27.1%	16.2%	43.9%	0.6%
9	LV	L	26	31	440	320	0	-35.0%	3.7%	22.1%	-16.6%
10	at MIA	L	21	29	273	280	0	-42.4%	4.6%	21.6%	-25.5%
11	NYJ	W	34	28	376	292	0	-21.5%	2.5%	13.4%	-10.6%
12	at BUF	L	17	27	367	332	2	-36.4%	-21.9%	-0.5%	-15.1%
13	NE	L	0	45	258	291	-2	-104.3%	-51.6%	6.9%	-45.7%
14	ATL	W	20	17	345	319	2	14.8%	-7.2%	-13.4%	8.6%
15	at LV	W	30	27	402	449	1	-12.9%	-0.8%	-4.3%	-16.4%
16	DEN	W	19	16	316	396	2	-8.1%	-4.7%	11.3%	7.9%
17	at KC	W	38	21	416	268	1	52.7%	40.5%	-11.8%	0.3%

Trends and Splits

	Offense	Rank	Defense	Rank
Total DVOA	1.5%	15	4.4%	20
Unadjusted VOA	5.1%	12	3.7%	21
Weighted Trend	0.0%	13	5.0%	21
Variance	4.4%	9	2.6%	2
Average Opponent	2.1%	26	-0.4%	17
Passing	27.5%	7	8.2%	17
Rushing	-26.7%	31	-0.7%	26
First Down	-17.0%	28	-3.9%	14
Second Down	13.2%	6	0.4%	14
Third Down	17.5%	8	25.9%	30
First Half	7.9%	10	-6.6%	10
Second Half	-5.2%	19	14.3%	28
Red Zone	-1.3%	18	9.8%	23
Late and Close	-8.6%	21	9.8%	24

Five-Year Performance

Year	W-L	Pyth W	Est W	PF	PA	TO	Total	Rk	Off	Rk	Def	Rk	ST	Rk	Off AGL	Rk	Def AGL	Rk	Off Age	Rk	Def Age	Rk	ST Age	Rk
2016	5-11	7.7	6.8	410	423	-7	-1.9%	21	-3.3%	18	-6.3%	9	-4.8%	29	61.7	28	65.7	29	27.9	4	25.7	31	25.7	24
2017	9-7	10.5	8.2	355	272	+12	6.8%	13	10.3%	8	-3.9%	10	-7.5%	31	35.4	17	31.9	13	27.6	5	25.7	26	25.4	25
2018	12-4	10.6	10.9	428	329	+1	22.1%	4	20.8%	3	-4.1%	10	-2.8%	25	30.7	11	52.2	29	27.8	7	25.7	26	25.4	29
2019	5-11	7.8	5.5	337	345	-17	-8.9%	22	3.5%	12	7.2%	25	-5.1%	32	51.7	24	40.3	21	27.3	7	26.7	10	25.5	23
2020	7-9	6.9	5.1	384	426	+3	-14.7%	26	1.5%	15	4.4%	20	-11.8%	32	45.6	20	63.4	29	25.6	28	26.3	16	25.2	30

2020 Performance Based on Most Common Personnel Groups

LAC Offense					LAC Offense vs. Opponents					LAC Defense					LAC Defense vs. Opponents			
Pers	Freq	Yds	DVOA	Run%	Pers	Freq	Yds	DVOA	Run%	Pers	Freq	Yds	DVOA	Pers	Freq	Yds	DVOA	
11	70%	5.8	6.2%	32%	Base	17%	5.6	-1.5%	56%	Base	21%	4.0	-19.8%	11	66%	6.0	6.1%	
12	12%	6.3	7.7%	47%	Nickel	65%	5.6	4.3%	39%	Nickel	66%	5.9	8.5%	12	12%	5.4	13.3%	
21	9%	4.5	-9.2%	56%	Dime+	15%	6.1	10.9%	9%	Dime+	13%	7.3	24.8%	21	6%	3.7	-30.2%	
13	3%	5.8	10.9%	32%	Goal Line	2%	0.5	-11.0%	65%	Goal Line	1%	1.2	76.0%	22	5%	4.2	-13.7%	
22	3%	3.5	-17.9%	71%										13	4%	4.1	-36.1%	

Strategic Tendencies

Run/Pass		Rk	Formation		Rk	Pass Rush		Rk	Secondary		Rk	Strategy		Rk
Runs, first half	37%	19	Form: Single Back	79%	21	Rush 3	3.5%	26	4 DB	21%	22	Play Action	28%	14
Runs, first down	51%	7	Form: Empty Back	9%	14	Rush 4	83.3%	2	5 DB	66%	9	Offensive Motion	37%	28
Runs, second-long	24%	25	Form: Multi Back	12%	10	Rush 5	10.7%	31	6+ DB	13%	17	Avg Box (Off)	6.38	27
Runs, power sit.	56%	19	Pers: 3+ WR	71%	9	Rush 6+	2.4%	27	Man Coverage	26%	23	Avg Box (Def)	6.72	7
Runs, behind 2H	30%	13	Pers: 2+ TE/6+ OL	20%	27	Edge Rusher Sacks	53.7%	14	CB by Sides	72%	19	Offensive Pace	29.14	5
Pass, ahead 2H	51%	12	Pers: 6+ OL	4%	7	Interior DL Sacks	18.5%	21	S/CB Cover Ratio	24%	20	Defensive Pace	30.79	25
Run-Pass Options	10%	10	Shotgun/Pistol	66%	15	Second Level Sacks	27.8%	10	DB Blitz	9%	26	Go for it on 4th	1.28	24

Los Angeles ranked 24th in DVOA passing the ball on first down but fourth on second down and sixth on third down. 🏈 The Chargers were strong in the screen game, with 30.3% DVOA on wide receiver screens and 46.8% DVOA on running back screens. 🏈 The Chargers blitzed less often than any other defense in the NFL but their performance was the same whether they blitzed or not: 6.6 yards allowed per play with a tiny DVOA difference between four pass-rushers (7.7%) and five or more (9.2%). 🏈 The Chargers started strong on defense, ranked seventh in DVOA in the first quarter, but then they ranked 26th in DVOA from the second quarter onward. 🏈 Los Angeles had one of the league's biggest gaps between defense against runs from shotgun (5.3 yards, 7.1% DVOA) and runs from under center (4.0 yards, -15.5% DVOA).

Passing

Player	DYAR	DVOA	Plays	NtYds	Avg	YAC	C%	TD	Int
J.Herbert	861	10.2%	623	4118	6.6	5.6	67.0%	31	10
T.Taylor*	20	-0.7%	32	207	6.5	5.0	53.3%	0	0
C.Daniel	-36	-23.5%	45	235	5.2	4.1	69.0%	1	2

Rushing

Player	DYAR	DVOA	Plays	Yds	Avg	TD	Fum	Suc
A.Ekeler	-23	-13.4%	116	530	4.6	1	1	43%
J.Kelley	-141	-36.4%	111	354	3.2	2	2	42%
K.Ballage*	-56	-21.1%	88	290	3.3	3	1	57%
J.Jackson	40	9.2%	59	270	4.6	0	0	46%
J.Herbert	-29	-23.2%	45	223	5.0	5	4	--
T.Pope	-2	-12.2%	15	76	5.1	0	0	60%
J.Reed	22	29.6%	5	29	5.8	1	0	--
T.Taylor*	-14	-61.4%	5	8	1.6	0	0	--

Receiving

Player	DYAR	DVOA	Plays	Ctch	Yds	Y/C	YAC	TD	C%
K.Allen	53	-8.1%	147	100	992	9.9	4.4	8	68%
M.Williams	117	4.5%	85	48	756	15.8	3.4	5	56%
J.Guyton	39	-3.7%	55	28	511	18.3	6.4	3	51%
T.Johnson	139	61.5%	26	20	398	19.9	3.0	3	77%
K.J.Hill	-7	-20.9%	11	7	73	10.4	2.6	0	64%
H.Henry*	27	-2.8%	93	60	613	10.2	3.8	4	65%
D.Parham	18	5.3%	20	10	159	15.9	5.6	3	50%
S.Anderson	21	25.2%	11	8	106	13.3	10.0	0	73%
V.Green*	3	1.1%	6	3	50	16.7	7.7	1	50%
J.Cook	88	13.9%	60	37	504	13.6	3.4	7	62%
A.Ekeler	111	16.6%	65	54	403	7.5	8.8	2	83%
K.Ballage*	-30	-32.6%	27	20	99	5.0	6.5	0	74%
J.Jackson	50	23.1%	24	19	173	9.1	11.6	0	79%
J.Kelley	27	7.3%	23	23	148	6.4	7.5	0	100%
T.Pope	-3	-18.0%	10	8	42	5.3	5.5	0	80%
G.Nabers	12	7.8%	7	5	25	5.0	4.6	2	71%

Offensive Line

Player	Pos	Age	GS	Snaps	Pen	Sk	Pass	Run	Player	Pos	Age	GS	Snaps	Pen	Sk	Pass	Run
Dan Feeney*	C	27	16/16	1173	2	2.5	14	16	Storm Norton	LT	27	6/3	308	1	0	9	3
Forrest Lamp*	LG	27	16/16	1173	1	1	21	14	Cole Toner*	RG	27	10/3	294	0	0	4	1
Sam Tevi*	LT	27	14/14	1024	4	1.5	20	7	Ryan Groy*	RG	31	4/3	271	1	0	2	1
Trey Pipkins	RT	25	13/5	570	3	3.5	16	4	Matt Feiler	LG	29	13/13	848	2	1.5	6	4
Trai Turner*	RG	28	9/9	536	2	1	6	8	Corey Linsley	C	30	13/13	735	0	0	1	4
Bryan Bulaga	RT	32	10/10	444	0	2	6	3	Oday Aboushi	RG	30	16/8	622	4	1	3	4

Year	Yards	ALY	Rk	Power	Rk	Stuff	Rk	2Lev	Rk	OpFld	Rk	BB Rt	Rk	Sacks	ASR	Rk	Press	Rk	BB Rt	Rk	Cont
2018	4.91	4.80	5	67%	18	18%	16	1.46	4	1.05	7	5.8%	13	34	6.4%	13	32.4%	22	13.8%	31	38
2019	4.13	4.37	13	68%	12	20%	21	1.16	19	0.68	21	13.2%	28	34	6.2%	9	30.3%	19	14.7%	24	27
2020	3.91	4.00	29	54%	31	19%	27	1.07	28	0.57	24	14.5%	32	34	6.1%	12	26.5%	21	14.5%	27	19

2020 ALY by direction: Left End: 4.35 (20)   Left Tackle: 4.18 (18)   Mid/Guard: 4.00 (30)   Right Tackle: 3.88 (25)   Right End: 3.63 (26)

The Chargers' offensive line has struggled for two years, but four of last year's top five linemen by snap count are now gone. ◉ Guard Trai Turner was not the addition the Chargers hoped he would be. Turner missed parts of the season with a groin injury and blew 14 blocks in just 536 snaps when healthy, good for a 38.3 snaps per blown block rate that ranked 96th among all interior offensive linemen. ◉ Guard Oday Aboushi was brought in to help replace Turner after coming off a career year in Detroit. Aboushi finished just 91st in snaps per blown block with the Cardinals in 2018 and did not qualify with just two starts for the Lions in 2019. But he stepped up last year and ranked 17th in blown block rate among interior offensive linemen. Aboushi committed just four penalties in 2020, only two of which were holding calls. ◉ Guard/tackle Matt Feiler was one of Pittsburgh's last remnants of capable offensive line play. A right tackle in 2019 and left guard in 2020, Feiler finished top-10 in snaps per blown block in both seasons. Feiler's flexibility could come in handy in the event that right tackle Bryan Bulaga suffers an injury and the line needs to be shuffled around. ◉ Northwestern tackle Rashawn Slater is the Chargers' only first-round pick at tackle since D.J. Fluker in 2013. Slater's short arms (28th-percentile among offensive linemen since 1999) give some reason for concern, but he has quick feet, a strong base, and fundamentals as clean as one could ask for. A move inside to guard is possible, but there's a good chance Slater makes it work as a bookend and he should be allowed to fail there first.

Defensive Front

Defensive Line	Age	Pos	G	Snaps	Plays	Overall TmPct	Rk	Stop	Dfts	BTkl	Runs	vs. Run St%	Rk	RuYd	Rk	Pass Rush Sack	Hit	Hur	Dsrpt
Jerry Tillery	25	DT	16	746	32	4.1%	64	22	5	5	25	60%	87	3.3	89	3.0	13	17	2
Linval Joseph	33	DT	16	725	62	7.9%	6	38	5	6	57	65%	76	3.2	86	0.0	2	13	0
Justin Jones	25	DT	13	526	34	5.4%	42	27	8	0	31	81%	24	2.5	50	1.0	3	10	0
Damion Square*	32	DT	16	252	20	2.6%	--	15	3	1	18	72%	--	2.9	--	1.0	1	4	0
Christian Covington	28	DT	16	557	39	4.7%	55	29	4	3	38	76%	43	3.0	81	0.0	1	9	0

Edge Rushers	Age	Pos	G	Snaps	Plays	Overall TmPct	Rk	Stop	Dfts	BTkl	Runs	vs. Run St%	Rk	RuYd	Rk	Pass Rush Sack	Hit	Hur	Dsrpt
Joey Bosa	26	DE	12	549	39	6.7%	17	33	18	2	30	80%	13	1.7	16	7.5	20	27	4
Isaac Rochell*	26	DE	16	437	28	3.6%	74	19	4	2	21	67%	60	3.0	65	2.5	2	9	2
Melvin Ingram*	32	DE	7	361	12	3.5%	--	9	2	3	8	63%	--	2.8	--	0.0	5	16	1
Uchenna Nwosu	25	DE	13	356	32	5.0%	44	22	9	4	23	65%	70	3.3	79	4.5	6	15	3
Kyler Fackrell	30	OLB	12	607	36	5.6%	33	24	12	9	23	65%	70	3.4	80	4.0	6	12	2

Linebackers	Age	Pos	G	Snaps	Plays	Overall TmPct	Rk	Stop	Dfts	BTkl	Runs	vs. Run St%	Rk	RuYd	Rk	Pass Rush Sack	Hit	Hur	Tgts	vs. Pass Suc%	Rk	Yd/P	Rk	PD	Int
Kenneth Murray	23	OLB	16	958	109	14.0%	34	50	12	8	68	53%	55	3.9	39	1.0	0	2	33	36%	68	8.8	70	3	0
Kyzir White	25	OLB	11	538	80	14.9%	23	31	10	8	43	37%	84	4.8	75	0.5	2	2	30	47%	50	6.6	44	3	0
Denzel Perryman*	29	MLB	13	317	49	7.7%	69	28	6	4	29	69%	9	2.9	7	1.0	1	3	13	62%	--	2.5	--	1	0
Nick Vigil*	28	OLB	15	312	43	5.9%	--	22	5	3	25	44%	--	5.8	--	2.0	0	0	12	58%	--	4.6	--	1	0

Year	Yards	ALY	Rk	Power	Rk	Stuff	Rk	2Lev	Rk	OpFld	Rk	BB Rt	Rk	Sacks	ASR	Rk	Press	Rk	BB Rt	Rk
2018	4.38	4.37	17	71%	23	19%	18	1.21	15	0.83	16	7.0%	21	38	6.7%	24	30.8%	15	11.5%	12
2019	4.29	4.35	20	63%	14	17%	23	1.06	8	0.78	20	15.5%	7	30	6.2%	25	28.2%	26	16.0%	8
2020	4.58	4.60	22	63%	11	18%	14	1.32	23	0.73	21	14.0%	13	27	5.8%	22	23.1%	23	15.1%	8

2020 ALY by direction:	Left End: 2.79 (3)	Left Tackle: 4.56 (21)	Mid/Guard: 4.80 (29)	Right Tackle: 4.11 (12)	Right End: 5.29 (29)

Former Bengals defensive tackle Christian Covington is a cheap gamble to try and fix the run defense. Though Covington struggled last season, he was previously a quality rotational run defender for Dallas and Houston. Covington ranked 18th in run stop rate with the Cowboys in 2019. ◉ The Chargers lost their only stud run defender at linebacker. Denzel Perryman, though mainly a two-down player, ranked in the top 15 in both run stop rate and average run tackle distance in each of the past two seasons. No linebacker left on the roster has ever ranked higher than 39th in either category over that same span. ◉ 2020 first-round pick Kenneth Murray was not the coverage star his speed suggests he should be. He often looked out-of-place when dropping into zones. ◉ That said, Murray was the high-quality run-and-chase player he was billed to be. Murray surrendered a broken tackle just 11.4% of the time, which was good for 26th out of 112 linebackers to record at least 10 solo tackles. ◉ Uchena Nwosu is likely stepping into a starting outside linebacker role, which he had already assumed for half of last season with Melvin Ingram out due to injury. Nwosu has never recorded more than 400 snaps or earned more than 16 hurries in a season since being drafted in 2018. ◉ Fourth-round pick Chris Rumph (Duke) enters the league a bit light for an edge defender, even a stand-up outside linebacker. Rumph is 6-foot-2 and 235 pounds, about 15 pounds lighter than Nwosu. He has passable athletic skills, but mostly gets by on sound hand placement and a hot motor.

Defensive Secondary

Secondary	Age	Pos	G	Snaps	Plays	TmPct	Rk	Stop	Dfts	BTkl	Runs	St%	Rk	RuYd	Rk	Tgts	Tgt%	Rk	aDOT	Suc%	Rk	Yd/P	Rk	PD	Int
						Overall						**vs. Run**							**vs. Pass**						
Michael Davis	26	CB	16	957	77	9.9%	20	33	10	8	22	55%	15	3.8	7	90	24.1%	10	13.1	50%	42	7.2	34	14	3
Nasir Adderley	24	FS	15	886	72	9.8%	44	11	4	13	35	11%	69	11.7	68	14	4.1%	67	12.9	43%	55	10.6	63	3	1
Rayshawn Jenkins*	27	SS	15	859	85	11.6%	26	44	19	12	40	53%	10	5.1	14	45	13.4%	6	8.6	53%	26	7.4	28	4	2
Casey Hayward*	32	CB	14	788	50	7.3%	66	22	7	9	7	43%	38	5.0	22	68	22.1%	21	14.6	56%	20	8.7	62	9	1
Chris Harris	32	CB	9	568	39	8.9%	33	17	10	6	18	50%	24	4.1	10	26	11.7%	80	10.3	54%	29	9.9	77	2	1
Tevaughn Campbell	28	CB	14	325	22	3.2%	--	8	4	4	6	67%	--	4.2	--	20	15.8%	--	12.8	50%	--	7.1	--	3	1
Jahleel Addae*	31	FS	11	210	19	3.5%	--	6	4	4	7	29%	--	3.7	--	7	8.5%	--	8.1	57%	--	7.4	--	2	1

Year	Pass D Rank	vs. #1 WR	Rk	vs. #2 WR	Rk	vs. Other WR	Rk	WR Wide	Rk	WR Slot	Rk	vs. TE	Rk	vs. RB	Rk
2018	10	10.3%	23	-2.6%	15	3.1%	19	7.2%	23	4.6%	18	-52.4%	1	9.7%	23
2019	20	7.7%	23	0.1%	16	-13.3%	8	-14.5%	10	11.9%	21	-1.7%	13	-1.9%	19
2020	17	-17.1%	5	15.4%	27	1.1%	16	-4.0%	13	-1.9%	16	5.4%	20	-0.3%	17

The Chargers' coverage of tight ends has declined from first in 2018 to 20th last year. Seeing as Derwin James played a full 16 games in 2018, five games in 2019, and zero games in 2020, it tracks that their quality of tight end coverage pretty directly matches with James' availability. ◗ Safety Nasir Adderley has not yet proved to be the answer at free safety the Chargers needed upon Eric Weddle's departure a few years ago. Adderley missed the 2019 season with a hamstring injury, then looked rough in 2020. Adderley's 43% coverage success rate was the worst on the team. He also had an 18.8% missed-tackle rate, 139th out of 201 defensive backs last year (minimum 10 solo tackles). ◗ Former cornerback Casey Hayward held the sixth-best coverage success rate among cornerbacks who switched teams this offseason, making him one of most damaging losses of the year to any secondary. ◗ Second-round pick Asante Samuel Jr. (Florida State) is the expected replacement for Hayward. Samuel is on the smaller side (5-foot-10 and 180 pounds at FSU pro day), but he plays with a chippy mentality and sees the ball in the air well in order to play it aggressively. Samuel's sloppy footwork matching route breaks and lack of muscle will likely make his rookie transition tough, though. ◗ Seventh-round pick Mark Webb (Georgia) is a cheap attempt to find someone who may be a sort of nickel/safety hybrid. Webb mostly played over the slot receiver at Georgia, though sometimes from a deeper alignment like a safety. Unfortunately, Webb posted horrid short-shuttle and 3-cone drills (both in the fifth percentile or worse).

Special Teams

Year	DVOA	Rank	FG/XP	Rank	Net Kick	Rank	Kick Ret	Rank	Net Punt	Rank	Punt Ret	Rank	Hidden	Rank
2018	-2.8%	25	-5.9	27	1.5	13	-3.2	26	-11.3	31	4.8	7	-3.4	20
2019	-5.1%	32	-5.6	26	-6.7	30	-3.3	28	-7.6	27	-2.5	22	13.3	2
2020	-11.8%	32	-12.4	31	-4.5	25	0.0	14	-37.8	32	-4.2	28	0.1	16

Los Angeles was the first team in DVOA history (since 1983) to put up back-to-back last-place finishes in special teams DVOA. Only Buffalo in 2000 (-15.4%) and Washington in 2013 (-12.0%) had lower special teams ratings than last year's Chargers. This unit hasn't ranked in the top 20 since a 15th-place finish in 2013. ◗ The Chargers punt unit was unfathomably bad. Not only did punter Ty Long post the worst gross punt value in the league, but the Chargers' punt coverage unit was the worst coverage unit in the league. We estimate that the Chargers lost -37.8 points of field position on net punting, the worst figure in DVOA history. Only four other teams since 1983 had even cleared -30 points. The good news here is that punt performance this bad rarely repeats itself. The 19 teams before last season that were worth below -20 points on net punting then averaged -3.0 points the following year. ◗ Michael Badgley was perfect on shorter field goals but went 10-for-19 on kicks of 40 or more yards. The Chargers brought back both Long and Badgley despite their poor 2020 performances. ◗ Not even the Chargers' best kickoff coverage tackler had a good season. Among the 40 players with at least nine tackles on kickoff coverage, Brandon Facyson's 44% stop rate was fourth lowest in the league. ◗ The only special teams area in which the Chargers did not produce negative value was on kick returns. Nasir Adderley finished with 4.1 points of estimated field position on just 11 kick returns, while Joe Reed finished with a subpar -1.7 points on a team-high 21 returns. ◗ On top of their other problems with the unit, the Chargers also tied for the NFL lead with 20 special teams penalties.

Los Angeles Rams

2020 Record: 10-6	**Total DVOA:** 15.4% (12)	**2021 Mean Projection:** 9.1 wins	**On the Clock (0-5):** 10%
Pythagorean Wins: 10.2 (9)	**Offense:** 4.4% (10)	**Postseason Odds:** 50.4%	**Mediocrity (6-8):** 31%
Snap-Weighted Age: 26.1 (22)	**Defense:** -17% (4)	**Super Bowl Odds:** 7.0%	**Playoff Contender (9-11):** 39%
Average Opponent: 2.1% (10)	**Special Teams:** -6% (30)	**Proj. Avg. Opponent:** 1.7% (6)	**Super Bowl Contender (12+):** 20%

2020: Defense powers a winning season as the offense stagnates.

2021: The Rams go all in on a new quarterback, but will the defense decline while the offense improves?

Los Angeles entered 2020 with a lot of questions on both sides of the ball. Although the core pieces of Aaron Donald, Jalen Ramsey, Jared Goff, Cooper Kupp, and Robert Woods were still around, there was a ton of uncertainty on the roster. The Rams ate massive dead money hits to get rid of Todd Gurley and Brandin Cooks, and they were relying on a large number of unproven or underwhelming defensive players to fill in holes left by free-agency departures. They also had to find a new defensive coordinator after firing the legendary Wade Phillips.

The Rams' replacement for Phillips was Brandon Staley, a relatively unknown Vic Fangio disciple, and while there was a great deal of uncertainty surrounding it initially, the hire was an absolute home run. Staley's understanding of how to defend modern offenses helped the Rams' defensive talent beyond Donald and Ramsey play at a high level. Many defenses are built to defend the run first, but Staley has employed the opposite approach, focusing on stopping the pass with increased numbers on the back end while fielding linebackers and secondary players that can fly up to the box once they determine that the offense is running the ball.

It sure helps having two superstars to build around when you want to take that approach. Staley typically started each week's defensive plan with which assignment to give Ramsey and then filled in the rest of the secondary's roles from there. And if you want to devote bodies to coverage, it helps to have a generationally talented defensive tackle like Donald holding the fort up front. Both Ramsey and Darnold are under contract through 2024, which means this dynamic duo will form the backbone of the Los Angeles defense for years to come.

The strong individual defensive performances didn't stop there. Cornerback Darious Williams broke out in his first year as a starter, and the combination of Williams, fellow cornerback Troy Hill, and safety John Johnson provided key complements to Ramsey throughout the defensive backfield. After all, if a defense only has one strong coverage player, teams can simply avoid throwing in his direction. Offenses trying to attack the Rams through the air had no such respite. Los Angeles was above average at defending receivers at all positions, and with no weak links, there were limited places to turn. With quarterbacks unable to find safe harbor, Donald and company had free rein to get after it rushing the passer, resulting in the league's second-best adjusted sack rate.

Donald wasn't doing it alone—Leonard Floyd enjoyed a breakout of his own as a supporting pass-rusher. After spending four years with the Bears, the former first-round pick joined the Rams on a one-year deal. Expectations for Floyd entering the season were not particularly high, but he ended up in a great situation and set a career high in sacks, parlaying his success into a long-term deal with Los Angeles for big money this past offseason. The Rams are hoping Floyd has fully tapped into the potential that made him a top-10 pick back in 2016.

Add it all up and the Rams ended the year with the No. 4 defense by DVOA, ranking in the top four against the run and the pass. They even finished first in weighted defensive DVOA, which meant that they were playing their best ball heading into the playoffs. Sounds like the recipe for a Super Bowl run when combined with a Sean McVay-coached offense, right?

Well, not exactly. While the combination of Goff, Kupp, and Woods led an offensive juggernaut as recently as 2018, the 2020 iteration was not nearly as good. Most of that can be blamed on the Rams' struggles throwing the football, as they finished in the bottom half of the league in pass offense DVOA. Goff managed to lead the Rams to a wild-card victory over the rival Seahawks despite playing through injury, but heading into the offseason, it became clear that Sean McVay was hoping for better play from the quarterback position.

Goff finished 2020 ranked 20th in passing DYAR and 22nd in passing DVOA out of 36 qualifying quarterbacks. That's not the worst in the league, but it is definitely not what the Rams thought they were getting when they signed Goff to an extension in September of 2019. Los Angeles tried to jump ahead of the next round of quarterback contract inflation when they got that extension done prior to Goff's fourth season in the league, and it is easy to see why the Rams felt they had a keeper. Heading into 2019, Goff was coming off back-to-back seasons where he finished sixth in the league in passing DYAR and fifth in passing DVOA.

However, Goff's numbers started to decline almost immediately after signing that contract, partially because McVay's previously pristine offensive ecosystem started to crumble around him. When the offense needed him to take the next step to maintain its excellent level of performance, the opposite happened, and that early extension started looking like

2021 Rams Schedule

Week	Opp.	Week	Opp.	Week	Opp.
1	BAL (Mon.)	7	PHI	13	WAS
2	at PIT	8	BYE	14	at KC
3	MIA	9	at NYG	15	at CLE
4	at LAC (Mon.)	10	KC	16	DEN
5	CHI	11	CIN	17	at IND
6	at DEN	12	at DAL (Thu.)	18	LAC

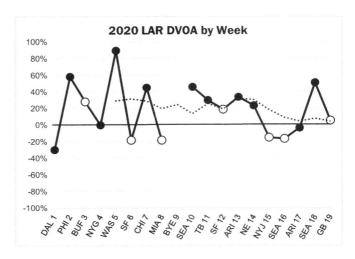

2020 LAR DVOA by Week

a massive mistake. Goff could have theoretically played 2020 on his fifth-year option had the Rams not signed him to an extension, leaving the team with much more flexibility. Instead, they were stuck with a contract that looked like an albatross even though the real extension years had not even kicked in yet.

It seemed unlikely that Los Angeles would be able to offload Goff's contract, but it is important to remember that these are the Rams we are talking about. They do not value first-round picks similarly to the rest of the league and are much more willing to trade them to acquire an impactful veteran, such as when they sent their 2020 and 2021 first-rounders to Jacksonville in exchange for Ramsey. Los Angeles has not made a first-round pick since they used the first overall selection in 2016 to draft Goff in the first place, and barring a trade that goes against the team's projected intention to contend, that streak will continue through at least 2023 thanks to their biggest move of the offseason.

The Rams were able to upgrade their quarterback situation and move on from Goff's contract in one fell swoop courtesy of the Detroit Lions, who agreed to take Goff (along with first-round picks in 2022 and 2023) in exchange for veteran quarterback Matthew Stafford. After years of frustrating seasons in Detroit, Stafford expressed interest in leaving town this offseason rather than continuing to play through a rebuild at age 33, and the Rams pounced on the opportunity. Los Angeles is hoping that upgrading from Goff to Stafford will turn the offense back into the unstoppable force that recently powered a Super Bowl run.

When you pair the quarterback change with the strength of the Rams' defense in 2020, it is easy to see why some are excited about the team's chances for a deep playoff run in 2021. Stafford has long been seen as an incredibly talented player with a cannon of an arm, and the hope is that he can help unlock a piece of the Los Angeles passing offense that has gone missing in recent years by making more plays outside the basic structure of the offense and pushing the ball down the field. He certainly has the potential to make that happen, but the Rams may want to hold off on planning out the parade route just a bit. Over the past two seasons, Stafford has been a better quarterback than Goff. That does not necessarily mean that the change from Goff to Stafford will cause a return to the halcyon days of 2018 for the Rams.

It is tough to make an apples-to-apples comparison between Goff and Stafford simply based on statistics because their surrounding situations have been so different recently.

While Stafford had some help in the receiving corps courtesy of Kenny Golladay, Golden Tate, and Marvin Jones, Detroit's offensive lines have not been on the same level as the ones that Goff was blessed with during the Rams' offensive heyday. Much of the narrative that Stafford has not had enough help on offense has centered around Detroit's struggles to run the ball effectively, and the Rams should serve as a good test case for this theory given that they finished fourth in rushing offense DVOA in 2020.

Stafford was off to an excellent start in 2019 prior to going down with an injury halfway through the season, managing to finish ninth in passing DYAR despite only starting eight games, and he has been at least above average in five of the past six seasons, excluding 2018. In Los Angeles, there will be less pressure on him to carry the offense by himself because of the better offensive infrastructure the Rams have assembled, and he has shown the potential to play at a high level even without an ideal assortment of talent around him relatively recently. His willingness to throw deep will also make the Rams offense less reliant on Kupp and Woods earning yards after the catch to grind out first downs, which should help Los Angeles sustain drives. Without someone like Sammy Watkins or Brandin Cooks stretching the field, it became a struggle for the Rams to generate explosive passing plays in 2020 that did not involve the receivers and tight ends squeezing every last yard out of a play post-reception.

However, it is important to note that those eight games in 2019 represented the best passing DVOA of Stafford's career at 28.8%, and he has not come close to equaling that mark in any full season he has played, with his next best year in that metric coming all the way back in 2011 when he hit 15.0%. He has not led an offense to a top-10 finish by DVOA since 2012, when Calvin Johnson set the single-season receiving yards record, and Detroit's best full-season pass offense DVOA since that record-breaking Johnson season came when they ranked No. 12 in 2017.

There is no doubting Stafford's talent, but after 12 years in the league, you would expect better results on the field if he was truly the kind of player that could turn a good offense into a dominant one. To be clear, even if Stafford is just comfortably above average, that would still represent an upgrade over what we saw from Goff in 2019 and 2020, and it should result in the passing offense improving. We just don't see that upgrade as one that turns the Rams offense back into a world-beating group that takes the league by storm like it did a few short years ago.

The defense has its own concerns. The Rams lost a substantial number of the pieces around Donald and Ramsey during the offseason. Hill and Johnson both signed with the Browns in free agency, and the Rams traded Brockers to Detroit to save cap space. Complementary pass-rushers Samson Ebukam and Morgan Fox took another 16 quarterback hits out the door with them when they departed as free agents.

While the Rams managed to overcome personnel turnover last season to build a dominant defense that carried them to the playoffs, we cannot just assume it will happen again. The Rams appear to have stumbled on a gem in 2020 sixth-round safety Jordan Fuller, who started 12 games as a rookie, but it is going to take more finds like that to keep replenishing the defensive talent that has been departing in recent years.

Making matters worse, Staley became a hot head coaching candidate as a result of the Rams' stingy defense and found a new home without needing to buy a new home. He will still be coaching home games at SoFi Stadium, but in 2021 that will be as head coach of the Chargers, meaning that the Rams will have turnover at defensive coordinator for the second year in a row. Raheem Morris, who most recently served as Atlanta's defensive coordinator and interim head coach, takes over for Staley and will be tasked with keeping Los Angeles' defensive unit playing at a high level.

Morris started his coaching career in the Tampa-2 system, but Los Angeles will not be making any drastic scheme changes heading into 2021. Morris' focus is going to be finding ways to get Donald matched up one-on-one in pass-rush situations and deploying Ramsey however each week's matchup dictates, much like Staley before him. There should be enough talent here for the Rams to remain a good unit, but they most likely will not be the dominant force we saw last year. Defensive performance tends to vary year to year even when the underlying talent is similar, and losing valuable players hurts a good amount.

All told, there is enough uncertainty that we are not convinced the Rams are clear Super Bowl contenders. To be clear, they're still a likely playoff team, but Los Angeles swung for the fences this offseason and expectations are certainly higher than that. If Stafford lives up to his billing and vaults the offense into the top five, they could easily outperform their projections and challenge for a Super Bowl. But if the defense cannot keep up its impressive level of play and Stafford cannot make up for that decline on his own, the Rams will likely find themselves no closer to that elusive championship.

Carl Yedor

2020 Rams by Week

Wk	vs.	W-L	PF	PA	YDF	YDA	TO	Total	Off	Def	ST
1	DAL	W	20	17	422	380	-1	-29.9%	-2.1%	16.8%	-11.0%
2	at PHI	W	37	19	449	363	2	58.5%	65.2%	1.5%	-5.3%
3	at BUF	L	32	35	478	375	0	28.0%	42.7%	4.2%	-10.5%
4	NYG	W	17	9	240	295	0	-0.2%	-17.1%	-19.9%	-3.0%
5	at WAS	W	30	10	429	108	-1	89.5%	41.3%	-44.7%	3.5%
6	at SF	L	16	24	311	390	-1	-18.3%	2.0%	21.5%	1.2%
7	CHI	W	24	10	371	279	1	45.0%	21.3%	-23.1%	0.6%
8	at MIA	L	17	28	471	145	-2	-18.4%	-9.1%	-30.9%	-40.2%
9	BYE										
10	SEA	W	23	16	389	333	2	46.0%	23.3%	-28.1%	-5.5%
11	at TB	W	27	24	413	251	0	29.9%	6.0%	-30.0%	-6.1%
12	SF	L	20	23	308	345	-1	18.6%	-21.8%	-39.8%	0.6%
13	at ARI	W	38	28	463	232	1	33.7%	27.0%	-25.2%	-18.4%
14	NE	W	24	3	318	220	0	23.2%	-21.2%	-52.1%	-7.8%
15	NYJ	L	20	23	303	289	-1	-15.3%	-8.5%	6.3%	-0.4%
16	at SEA	L	9	20	334	292	-1	-16.7%	-36.8%	-20.1%	0.0%
17	ARI	W	18	7	333	214	-1	-3.6%	-45.4%	-34.9%	6.9%
18	at SEA	W	30	20	333	278	2	51.1%	-3.9%	-43.9%	11.2%
19	at GB	L	18	32	244	484	0	5.2%	13.4%	18.3%	10.1%

Trends and Splits

	Offense	Rank	Defense	Rank
Total DVOA	4.4%	10	-17.0%	4
Unadjusted VOA	0.5%	15	-18.6%	3
Weighted Trend	-4.8%	17	-24.2%	1
Variance	9.4%	24	4.9%	18
Average Opponent	-3.5%	7	-2.9%	25
Passing	12.4%	19	-12.0%	4
Rushing	3.5%	4	-24.1%	3
First Down	9.0%	10	-11.2%	5
Second Down	-4.9%	20	-28.9%	1
Third Down	9.9%	10	-9.4%	11
First Half	-4.2%	20	-7.0%	9
Second Half	14.7%	5	-26.9%	3
Red Zone	10.5%	12	-6.9%	8
Late and Close	5.6%	12	-14.6%	8

Five-Year Performance

Year	W-L	Pyth W	Est W	PF	PA	TO	Total	Rk	Off	Rk	Def	Rk	ST	Rk	Off AGL	Rk	Def AGL	Rk	Off Age	Rk	Def Age	Rk	ST Age	Rk
2016	4-12	3.3	4.6	224	394	-11	-29.5%	30	-38.1%	32	-1.5%	17	7.1%	3	7.6	1	21.9	5	25.5	32	26.0	26	25.4	29
2017	11-5	11.6	11.3	478	329	+7	27.6%	3	11.3%	6	-9.5%	7	6.8%	2	3.3	1	27.4	12	26.0	31	26.0	19	25.0	31
2018	13-3	11.2	12.5	527	384	+11	23.9%	3	25.0%	2	1.0%	16	-0.2%	17	11.0	2	27.0	13	27.1	12	26.5	11	25.8	15
2019	9-7	8.8	9.1	394	364	0	5.3%	12	0.6%	16	-6.1%	9	-1.5%	23	29.8	9	30.8	16	26.3	24	26.8	8	25.4	25
2020	10-6	10.2	9.9	372	296	-3	15.4%	9	4.4%	10	-17.0%	4	-6.0%	30	17.3	4	28.3	9	26.6	19	26.1	20	24.9	32

2020 Performance Based on Most Common Personnel Groups

LAR Offense					LAR Offense vs. Opponents					LAR Defense				LAR Defense vs. Opponents			
Pers	Freq	Yds	DVOA	Run%	Pers	Freq	Yds	DVOA	Run%	Pers	Freq	Yds	DVOA	Pers	Freq	Yds	DVOA
11	65%	6.1	15.3%	29%	Base	26%	4.5	-2.4%	56%	Base	15%	3.7	-36.2%	11	58%	5.0	-12.3%
12	30%	5.1	-0.6%	60%	Nickel	64%	6.4	15.1%	37%	Nickel	59%	5.1	-8.6%	12	22%	4.9	-17.6%
13	4%	2.7	-5.8%	73%	Dime+	8%	4.3	-12.1%	8%	Dime+	26%	4.6	-30.8%	21	7%	4.3	-32.8%
					Goal Line	0%	1.4	3.5%	60%	Goal Line	0%	1.0	84.9%	10	6%	4.9	-25.0%
					Big	1%	3.6	11.9%	93%					13	1%	4.2	12.9%
														01	1%	3.8	-26.0%

Strategic Tendencies

Run/Pass		Rk	Formation		Rk	Pass Rush		Rk	Secondary		Rk	Strategy		Rk
Runs, first half	37%	20	Form: Single Back	81%	16	Rush 3	3.9%	25	4 DB	15%	28	Play Action	35%	6
Runs, first down	48%	17	Form: Empty Back	16%	1	Rush 4	71.1%	8	5 DB	59%	18	Offensive Motion	49%	12
Runs, second-long	27%	18	Form: Multi Back	2%	28	Rush 5	22.4%	12	6+ DB	26%	8	Avg Box (Off)	6.80	6
Runs, power sit.	65%	9	Pers: 3+ WR	66%	18	Rush 6+	2.5%	26	Man Coverage	21%	28	Avg Box (Def)	6.01	31
Runs, behind 2H	36%	4	Pers: 2+ TE/6+ OL	35%	9	Edge Rusher Sacks	35.8%	29	CB by Sides	60%	29	Offensive Pace	29.80	12
Pass, ahead 2H	49%	16	Pers: 6+ OL	0%	30	Interior DL Sacks	50.9%	3	S/CB Cover Ratio	33%	9	Defensive Pace	29.66	6
Run-Pass Options	0%	32	Shotgun/Pistol	43%	30	Second Level Sacks	13.2%	30	DB Blitz	7%	29	Go for it on 4th	1.46	20

Los Angeles dramatically changed its run/pass ratio when losing late in games. In 2019, the Rams had ranked 30th, running on 21% of downs in these situations. Last year, they ranked fourth, running on 36% of downs when losing in the second half. ✎ The Rams never run out of shotgun, or almost never. Last season, only 7% of shotgun plays were runs out the backfield compared to a league average of 21%. ✎ The Rams' move towards using more two-tight end sets (they climbed from 23rd to ninth) also led to their running game facing stronger defensive boxes. The Rams faced only six men in the box on 16% of handoffs, the lowest figure in the league. They faced eight or more on 43% of handoffs, second behind New England. In 2019, these same numbers had been 23% and 30%. The Rams' running game declined depending on the number of men in the box, but not by as much as you might expect: 5.1 yards and 9.5% DVOA against six or fewer, 4.6 yards and -0.1% DVOA against seven, and 3.8 yards and -5.4% DVOA against eight or more. ✎ For the fourth straight year, the Rams didn't run a single play with six offensive linemen. However, they find other players to block, and ranked third in the league with 12.3% of passes classified as max protect (seven or more blockers with at least two more blockers than pass-rushers). ✎ It wasn't as impressive as some past seasons—the Rams had 21.2% DVOA, which ranked ninth—but the Rams are above average on wide receiver screens pretty much every year. ✎ The Rams ranked 30th in the percentage of targets thrown to running backs. ✎ Los Angeles had a crazy home/road split, ranking 25th with -8.6% offensive DVOA at SoFi Stadium but fifth with 15.8% DVOA on the road. This is just for curiosity, as odd home/road splits like this have no history of carrying over from year to year. ✎ Los Angeles had 85% of its sacks attributed to pressure, the second-highest rate in the league. The Rams led the league with 26 sacks attributed to blown blocks and 14 sacks attributed to "overall pressure." ✎ The Rams were one of four defenses with a league-high 31% pressure rate when bringing just the standard four pass-rushers. ✎ The Rams' defense was not only stalwart, it was also disciplined, finishing last in the league with 26 defensive penalties. ✎ Los Angeles played base defense less than half as often as it had the year before (34% in 2019, third). ✎ The Rams and Colts were the only two teams whose opponents never missed an extra point all season.

Passing

Player	DYAR	DVOA	Plays	NtYds	Avg	YAC	C%	TD	Int
J.Goff*	385	-1.1%	573	3761	6.6	5.8	67.6%	20	13
J.Wolford	-63	-35.9%	40	223	5.6	4.2	57.9%	0	1
M.Stafford	684	7.7%	559	3820	6.8	5.1	65.2%	26	10

Rushing

Player	DYAR	DVOA	Plays	Yds	Avg	TD	Fum	Suc
C.Akers	-33	-13.7%	145	625	4.3	2	1	48%
D.Henderson	185	21.4%	138	624	4.5	5	0	55%
M.Brown*	89	11.7%	101	419	4.1	5	0	49%
J.Goff*	-6	-14.8%	34	115	3.4	4	2	--
R.Woods	94	32.3%	24	155	6.5	2	1	--
J.Wolford	14	25.6%	6	56	9.3	0	0	--
M.Stafford	42	23.0%	21	122	5.8	0	0	--

Receiving

Player	DYAR	DVOA	Plays	Ctch	Yds	Y/C	YAC	TD	C%
R.Woods	18	-10.9%	129	90	936	10.4	5.5	6	70%
C.Kupp	118	-0.8%	124	92	974	10.6	5.7	3	74%
J.Reynolds*	13	-10.6%	81	52	618	11.9	4.3	2	64%
V.Jefferson	-1	-12.9%	31	19	220	11.6	2.4	1	61%
D.Jackson	12	-6.9%	26	14	236	16.9	4.6	1	54%
G.Everett*	0	-7.3%	62	41	417	10.2	5.9	1	66%
T.Higbee	112	19.6%	60	44	521	11.8	5.4	5	73%
M.Brown*	-7	-17.5%	33	23	162	7.0	7.7	0	70%
D.Henderson	43	17.2%	25	16	159	9.5	9.4	1	67%
C.Akers	46	37.0%	14	11	123	11.2	8.3	1	79%

Offensive Line

Player	Pos	Age	GS	Snaps	Pen	Sk	Pass	Run	Player	Pos	Age	GS	Snaps	Pen	Sk	Pass	Run
Austin Corbett	RG	26	16/16	1120	4	1	13	7	David Edwards	LG	24	16/14	1006	1	1	10	4
Austin Blythe*	C	29	16/16	1120	1	2.5	12	11	Joseph Noteboom	LT/LG	26	10/9	634	3	1.5	11	3
Rob Havenstein	RT	29	16/16	1117	4	3	12	10	Andrew Whitworth	LT	40	9/9	599	5	1	3	1

Year	Yards	ALY	Rk	Power	Rk	Stuff	Rk	2Lev	Rk	OpFld	Rk	BB Rt	Rk	Sacks	ASR	Rk	Press	Rk	BB Rt	Rk	Cont
2018	5.00	5.49	1	68%	13	15%	2	1.58	1	0.84	16	5.1%	7	33	5.4%	6	25.2%	4	5.6%	3	48
2019	3.80	4.27	19	65%	18	21%	26	1.23	14	0.44	29	14.1%	30	22	3.7%	1	31.5%	22	13.0%	14	30
2020	4.34	4.66	7	69%	12	19%	30	1.18	17	0.78	15	8.3%	10	25	4.2%	2	24.4%	13	9.6%	5	36
	2020 ALY by direction:			Left End: 5.08 (4)			Left Tackle: 4.18 (17)			Mid/Guard: 4.59 (9)				Right Tackle: 5.13 (7)				Right End: 4.45 (17)			

Los Angeles enjoyed pretty good health along the offensive line, with their top six linemen accounting for all but four of the offensive snaps in 2020. ● Veteran left tackle Andrew Whitworth tore his MCL and PCL at midseason, but somewhat miraculously, he was able to return for the Rams' playoff run. He will be back at left tackle in 2021 at the ripe old age of 40. After ranking second in the league among qualifying left tackles in 2020 snaps per blown block (behind only Green Bay's David Bakhtiari), it sure looks like Whitworth still has gas in the tank. ● Whitworth's primary replacement during his absence was Joseph Noteboom, who held up OK while Whitworth recovered. Noteboom's path to 2021 playing time is at guard, but it seems likely that he starts out the year as a backup. A calf injury to Noteboom early in 2020 opened the door for former Wisconsin tackle David Edwards, who had an excellent season ranking ninth at left guard in snaps per blown block. ● On the right side, Austin Corbett and Rob Havenstein held down the fort, but both exceeded 20 blown blocks on the season, finishing around the middle of the pack at right guard and right tackle, respectively. ● The key question for the 2021 Rams line revolves around the center position. Last year's starter Austin Blythe is off to Kansas City, and the Rams are still sorting out how to replace him. Brian Allen spent the first half of 2019 at center before suffering a serious knee injury that allowed Blythe to take the job and run with it. However, based on what we saw from OTAs, Corbett may be the one taking the reins after sliding over from guard. ● If Corbett moves to center, it opens the door for third-year lineman Bobby Evans to earn the starting spot at right guard. Another tackle-to-guard conversion, Evans has only been a backup/injury fill-in at this point in his career, but he was drafted two rounds before Edwards in 2019.

Defensive Front

Defensive Line	Age	Pos	G	Snaps	Plays	TmPct	Rk	Stop	Dfts	BTkl	Runs	St%	Rk	RuYd	Rk	Sack	Hit	Hur	Dsrpt
						Overall					vs. Run					Pass Rush			
Aaron Donald	30	DE	16	865	46	5.7%	33	41	24	2	28	86%	7	1.2	4	13.5	16	44	4
Michael Brockers*	31	DE	15	624	51	6.7%	13	37	9	0	40	78%	37	1.9	25	5.0	4	11	0
Sebastian Joseph-Day	26	DT	16	412	58	7.2%	12	40	7	2	53	66%	73	2.8	62	1.0	3	5	2
Morgan Fox*	27	DE	16	403	28	3.5%	--	20	10	2	19	58%	--	2.6	--	6.0	3	11	2

Edge Rushers	Age	Pos	G	Snaps	Plays	TmPct	Rk	Stop	Dfts	BTkl	Runs	St%	Rk	RuYd	Rk	Sack	Hit	Hur	Dsrpt
						Overall					vs. Run					Pass Rush			
Leonard Floyd	29	OLB	16	916	56	6.9%	13	41	15	5	35	66%	68	2.9	60	10.5	8	34	1
Samson Ebukam*	26	OLB	16	363	27	3.3%	--	22	7	5	19	74%	--	2.7	--	4.5	4	13	1
Justin Hollins	25	OLB	16	349	26	3.2%	--	15	5	3	19	58%	--	3.5	--	3.0	2	3	1
Ogbonnia Okoronkwo	26	OLB	10	158	11	2.2%	--	8	6	1	6	67%	--	4.7	--	1.0	3	15	2
Terrell Lewis	23	OLB	8	124	5	1.2%	--	4	3	1	3	67%	--	2.0	--	2.0	2	8	1

Linebackers	Age	Pos	G	Snaps	Plays	TmPct	Rk	Stop	Dfts	BTkl	Runs	St%	Rk	RuYd	Rk	Sack	Hit	Hur	Tgts	Suc%	Rk	Yd/P	Rk	PD	Int
						Overall					vs. Run					Pass Rush			vs. Pass						
Micah Kiser	26	ILB	9	558	80	17.6%	7	43	7	8	49	63%	19	3.2	13	0.0	1	5	35	60%	13	4.5	9	3	0
Kenny Young	27	ILB	16	471	53	6.6%	78	28	7	6	28	54%	53	4.1	50	1.0	1	4	12	42%	--	5.3	--	2	1
Troy Reeder	27	ILB	16	423	74	9.2%	64	36	9	7	38	53%	56	3.4	20	3.0	1	2	23	43%	55	5.2	22	2	0

Year	Yards	ALY	Rk	Power	Rk	Stuff	Rk	2Lev	Rk	OpFld	Rk	BB Rt	Rk	Sacks	ASR	Rk	Press	Rk	BB Rt	Rk
2018	4.91	4.49	21	68%	21	16%	22	1.36	25	1.12	27	11.5%	5	41	7.0%	17	36.0%	1	13.8%	3
2019	4.16	4.26	16	62%	12	16%	24	1.18	18	0.61	10	14.8%	10	50	8.1%	7	32.7%	8	15.7%	11
2020	3.78	4.34	15	68%	20	14%	23	0.96	2	0.29	1	9.6%	27	53	8.6%	2	30.2%	2	17.3%	2
2020 ALY by direction:		Left End: 4.41 (14)			Left Tackle: 3.98 (14)			Mid/Guard: 4.39 (15)			Right Tackle: 4.32 (16)				Right End: 4.59 (16)					

It was another stellar year for Aaron Donald, as he finished second in the league in both sacks and hurries while racking up 41 stops and 24 defeats. ◗ Michael Brockers and Morgan Fox had some juice rotating alongside Donald, providing a combined 11 sacks, but Los Angeles will have to replace both. It opens up more playing time for A'Shawn Robinson, Sebastian Joseph-Day, and Greg Gaines in the interior. ◗ Donald was on the field for about 85% of the team's snaps, and the rest of the Rams' interior linemen played on a more rotational basis. Brockers was the only other player to be on the field more than half the time. They should have plenty of bodies up front to maintain that approach this year. Los Angeles added to the rotation on draft day by selecting nose tackle Bobby Brown III (Texas A&M) in the fourth round and defensive end Earnest Brown IV (Northwestern) in the fifth round. ◗ Leonard Floyd's breakout 2020 season has him penciled in at one outside linebacker spot but replacing the departed Samson Ebukam will involve some competition. 2020 third-round pick Terrell Lewis and 2018 draftee Ogbonnia Okoronkwo did not see the field much, but Okoronkwo was a bit more disruptive in that limited time, registering the third-most hurries on the team. Justin Hollins also has a rotational role as a hybrid who plays both inside and on the edge. ◗ The Rams have not devoted a ton of resources to inside linebacker in recent years. Micah Kiser, Kenny Young, and Troy Reeder are the primary inside linebackers; none of them were drafted higher than the fourth round. Kiser in particular is constantly around the ball, leading the team in run stops. He was also the Rams' best coverage linebacker but missed about half the season with a knee injury. ◗ The incumbent linebackers will have to contend with third-round rookie Ernest Jones of South Carolina, though he seems likely to start the season on the bench. Jones profiles best as a run-stuffer and his athletic profile may make it hard for him to stay on the field on passing downs.

Defensive Secondary

Secondary	Age	Pos	G	Snaps	Plays	TmPct	Rk	Stop	Dfts	BTkl	Runs	St%	Rk	RuYd	Rk	Tgts	Tgt%	Rk	aDOT	Suc%	Rk	Yd/P	Rk	PD	Int
John Johnson*	26	FS	16	1024	113	14.0%	6	48	13	12	36	47%	17	5.4	21	40	10.3%	22	7.7	63%	5	4.4	4	8	1
Troy Hill*	30	CB	16	972	87	10.8%	13	40	18	18	23	52%	23	5.1	23	61	16.5%	68	9.4	52%	36	6.4	15	10	3
Jalen Ramsey	27	CB	15	953	53	7.0%	71	18	9	7	8	50%	24	7.1	45	60	16.6%	67	11.8	57%	16	4.8	3	9	1
Darious Williams	28	CB	16	824	58	7.2%	69	26	12	7	12	42%	45	7.0	43	62	19.8%	39	17.0	65%	2	6.8	23	14	4
Jordan Fuller	23	SS	12	707	65	10.7%	36	16	6	7	24	25%	57	6.8	36	29	10.8%	20	10.2	38%	66	7.9	39	5	3
Taylor Rapp	24	SS	9	365	43	9.5%	--	16	7	5	17	47%	--	7.4	--	12	8.7%	--	6.6	58%	--	6.5	--	3	1

Year	Pass D Rank	vs. #1 WR	Rk	vs. #2 WR	Rk	vs. Other WR	Rk	WR Wide	Rk	WR Slot	Rk	vs. TE	Rk	vs. RB	Rk
2018	9	15.9%	28	-12.2%	9	9.9%	24	3.0%	21	10.2%	23	-22.1%	5	-18.1%	4
2019	10	-18.0%	4	-5.9%	9	-2.6%	16	-22.3%	7	6.4%	17	6.6%	21	9.3%	22
2020	4	-4.6%	13	-33.5%	1	-1.8%	14	-33.0%	1	-11.0%	4	-11.1%	10	-10.9%	7

While one would think that having Jalen Ramsey around would scare teams into throwing elsewhere, the cornerback trio of Ramsey, Troy Hill, and Darious Williams faced a very similar target volume, at 60, 61, and 62, respectively. Hill and Williams actually both outperformed Ramsey in passes defensed and interceptions, but Ramsey finished third in the league in yards allowed per pass. Overall, the Rams were the No. 1 defense against wide receivers lined out wide and against deep passes (16 or more air yards). 🏈 Hill departed for Cleveland alongside free safety John Johnson III, who bounced back from an injury-shortened 2019 to rank in the top five in both success rate and yards per pass allowed. 🏈 Rounding out the starting five was 2020 sixth-round pick Jordan Fuller from Ohio State, who took advantage of an early knee injury sustained by projected starter Taylor Rapp and never let go of the job. Fuller was objectively the weak link of the Rams secondary, with a fairly poor success rate despite not being targeted much, but with all the talent around him, he was in more of a supporting role. 🏈 Fuller and Rapp appear to be the likely safety duo with Johnson gone. Rapp has mostly played strong safety as a pro, so Fuller may slide to free safety to allow the two to start in tandem. 🏈 Third-year player David Long has the inside track for the nickel spot based largely on his draft pedigree (third round in 2019) and impressive change-of-direction ability. Long has barely been able to get on the field to this point in his career, largely due to the players in front of him. 🏈 Physically, fourth-round rookie Robert Rochell of Central Arkansas profiles as an outside press corner, but he may need a year behind Williams to develop before he is ready for prime time.

Special Teams

Year	DVOA	Rank	FG/XP	Rank	Net Kick	Rank	Kick Ret	Rank	Net Punt	Rank	Punt Ret	Rank	Hidden	Rank
2018	-0.2%	17	-4.9	24	1.1	14	-3.0	25	3.4	13	2.6	11	10.4	6
2019	-1.5%	23	-2.9	21	-4.3	27	-1.3	18	2.2	15	-1.0	16	-6.4	27
2020	-6.0%	30	-7.5	27	-5.9	28	-2.7	21	-5.4	25	-8.3	31	-11.0	29

The Rams' special teams unit has steadily declined since Sean McVay's first season, when they finished second overall in special teams DVOA. 🏈 Los Angeles cycled through three kickers in 2020, going from Sam Sloman to Kai Forbath to Matt Gay. Sloman was a seventh-round rookie but only lasted until October. Forbath played two games before getting hurt, forcing Los Angeles to sign Gay off of the Indianapolis practice squad. Gay made 30 out of 32 regular season kicks and will be the kicker entering 2021. 🏈 Four-time All-Pro punter Johnny Hekker had a poor 2020, which does not align with his career track record. With cap numbers above $4.6 million through 2023, he may need a serious rebound this year to keep his spot. 🏈 Los Angeles tried both wide receiver Nsimba Webster and running back Raymond Calais at kick returner and got negative value out of both of them. The Rams' punt returns handled by Webster and Cooper Kupp were even worse. Webster in particular was second worst in the league by estimated field position on punt returns. While Webster may enter camp with a shot to hold onto the starting returner job, don't be surprised if a rookie—either second-round wide receiver Tutu Atwell or seventh-round running back Jake Funk—wrests the role away from him.

Miami Dolphins

2020 Record: 10-6	Total DVOA: 4.6% (32)	2021 Mean Projection: 9 wins	On the Clock (0-5): 11%
Pythagorean Wins: 9.8 (11)	Offense: -2.1% (18)	Postseason Odds: 49.3%	Mediocrity (6-8): 31%
Snap-Weighted Age: 25.6 (31)	Defense: -3.3% (11)	Super Bowl Odds: 6.0%	Playoff Contender (9-11): 39%
Average Opponent: -3.7% (27)	Special Teams: 3.3% (6)	Proj. Avg. Opponent: -2% (26)	Super Bowl Contender (12+): 19%

2020: Hey, feel that Fitzmagic in the air?

2021: Everybody's counting on you, Alabama and me.

ebuilds are supposed to take time, right? That was Brian Flores' remit when he took the Dolphins job in 2019—to rebuild the team from the mismanagement of Adam Gase and a decade of institutional turmoil before that. That was the idea behind the Fish Tank. Flores and company were to jettison anyone of value who was not going to be part of the team's picture two or three years down the line. They would be hoarding draft picks and trying out new quarterbacks and instilling culture and philosophy. That's not something that happens overnight. In this chapter last year, we gushed about the culture Flores was installing and the philosophy Chris Grier was bringing to the front office—and we said that it wouldn't be reasonable for the Dolphins to go from having a top-five pick to reaching for the playoffs.

And yet, that's exactly where Miami found themselves at the end of last season: unfortunate to miss the playoffs at 10-6. It was the best record for the Dolphins since 2016, the first better-than-average defense since 2012, and their best overall DVOA since 2008. Beating Buffalo's backups in Week 17 would have seen Miami make the playoffs, but you can even paint that loss with a silver lining; maybe it was better to improve draft position to help build a long-term competitive team as the rebuild continues. We knew Flores had the Dolphins pointed in the right direction, but 10-6 in the second season? Even the most optimistic Miami fan would have had trouble imagining that while Tank for Tua was still all the rage.

We do need to splash a little bit of cold water on the 2020 Dolphins before turning the page entirely. They were a bit lucky to be in playoff contention at the end of the season, as their record slightly outpaced their underlying performance. Miami had 8.2 estimated wins, which takes into account things such as consistency and strength of schedule and performance with the score close. That's not a huge gap between expected and actual wins; it was only the sixth-largest of last season. But it does help show the reality that the 2020 Dolphins were an above-average team that also had some above-average luck. Let Zane Gonzalez make a 49-yard field goal in Week 9 and turn Fitzmagic mortal late against the Raiders and you have a slightly more realistic impression of how good the Dolphins actually were.

But even if you accept that, the Dolphins' year-over-year improvement was nearly unheard of. Their 4.6% DVOA was the second highest we've ever recorded for a team that was below

-35.0% the year before, and it's the seventh-greatest improvement in DVOA history, stretching back to 1983 (Table 1).

Table 1. Outhouse to the Penthouse, 1983-2020

Year	Team	Year N-1		Year N			Year N+1	
		DVOA	Record	DVOA	Diff	Record	DVOA	Record
2013	KC	-43.5%	2-14	16.0%	59.5%	11-5	9.8%	9-7
2020	MIA	-38.8%	5-11	4.6%	43.5%	10-6	--	--
2000	NO	-36.9%	3-13	2.1%	39.1%	10-6	-5.5%	7-9
2010	DET	-48.6%	2-14	2.1%	50.7%	6-10	13.1%	10-6
1991	CLE	-39.1%	3-13	-0.1%	39.0%	6-10	-1.4%	7-9
2019	ARI	-38.4%	3-13	-3.1%	35.3%	5-10-1	3.6%	8-8
2011	CAR	-38.2%	2-14	-4.3%	33.9%	6-10	4.2%	7-9
2010	OAK	-35.7%	5-11	-4.8%	30.9%	8-8	-8.5%	8-8
1986	HOIL	-37.2%	5-11	-7.4%	29.8%	5-11	-2.0%	9-6
2001	CLE	-41.5%	3-13	-8.0%	33.5%	7-9	0.8%	9-7

According to Paragraph 3, Subsection 72 of the Official *Football Outsiders Almanac* Chapter Handbook, this is normally where we start talking about regression and the Plexiglass Principle. Teams that make a huge jump from one year to the next tend to see their numbers fall back towards the mean the next year. A massive improvement from year to year is typically the result of both improved performance and improved luck, and while the former is something you can build on and repeat, the latter isn't. And yes, you can see some of that regression baked into Miami's DVOA projections—we have them pretty much bang-on average, which would be a slight step down from 2020.

At the same time, though, plexiglass doesn't feel like the right lens to use to try to predict how the Dolphins will do in 2021. Take another look at those teams from Table 1—while there's a decent amount of individual fluctuation, they were, on the whole, even better the next season, if only by a percentage point or two. The average team to improve by at least 30.0% in DVOA from one year to the next drops by 10 percentage points the following year, but the *worst* drop on Table 1 was just 6.2%. These aren't your average massively improved teams. These are colossal reclamation projects.

Nine of the 10 teams featured head coaches in their first or

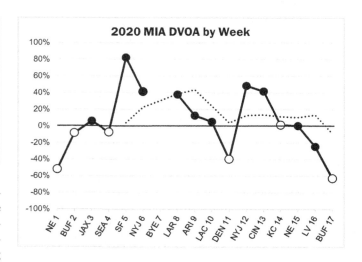

2021 Dolphins Schedule

Week	Opp.	Week	Opp.	Week	Opp.
1	at NE	7	ATL	13	NYG
2	BUF	8	at BUF	14	BYE
3	at LV	9	HOU	15	NYJ
4	IND	10	BAL (Thu.)	16	at NO (Mon.)
5	at TB	11	at NYJ	17	at TEN
6	at JAX (U.K.)	12	CAR	18	NE

second year with their new club, including Andy Reid in Kansas City and Bill Belichick in Cleveland. Seven of the 10 were recovering from not just one terrible season, but double-digit-negative DVOAs in at least four of their last five years, including mopping up the debris from an 0-16 squad or trading an entire draft class for Ricky Williams. What we have here is a collection of coaches coming into some of the worst situations in recent league history, mismanaged franchises with overpriced veterans and bare cupboards of prospects. Every new head coach comes into a situation like this saying that he will bring in a new culture and a new foundation, not to mention new players who are actually good at playing football. These are the teams that succeeded and set a new baseline for their franchises going forwards.

But there are some other similarities on this table which don't bode as well for Miami. Seven of the 10 teams on the table had better defensive DVOAs than offensive, and two of the others were within a couple of percentage points. This makes sense when you consider that seven of the 10 new head coaches were defensive minds—they bulked up the side of the ball they specialized in, to immediate results. The problem, however, is that defense is far less predictive from year to year than offense is; it's not as reliable of a base to build a long-term contender on. In general, offensive DVOA is about twice as good at forecasting future performance than defensive DVOA, and teams that rely heavily on interceptions and fumble recoveries regress far harder than those who rely on touchdown passes and chain-moving first downs.

Brian Flores' Dolphins led the league last year by forcing a turnover on 16% of opponents' drives, in case you were wondering.

Only three of our outhouse-to-penthouse teams turned their

one-year jump into sustained contention, defined as multiple double-digit-positive DVOA seasons over the next five years. Those were the three that developed productive offenses: Andy Reid, Alex Smith, and the Chiefs; Ron Rivera and Cam Newton's Panthers; and the run 'n' shoot Warren Moon Oilers. Everyone else, the teams which couldn't take the next step forward offensively, ended up either withering again or getting stuck in 8-8 purgatory.

We can confidently predict the Dolphins won't go 8-8 this year, but the point we're making is that in order for the team to take that next step forward, Miami's offense needs to carry more of the load. Which means it's time for Tua Tagovailoa to enter the conversation.

All things considered, Tagovailoa's rookie season was fine. He was 26th out of qualifying quarterbacks in both passing DYAR and DVOA—the worst of the three first-round passers, but not worryingly so. His DVOA ranked 30th of the 81 rookie quarterbacks to qualify for our main tables since 1983; his 74 combined passing and rushing DYAR ranked 26th. Of course, that includes a bunch of late-round players being forced into action, but even just looking at first-round picks, Tua's numbers aren't that bad—20th in DVOA and 18th in DYAR out of 54 qualified first-round passers. We've been spoiled some in recent years by top-five picks coming in and immediately having great success, but Tagovailoa is already better than you'd expect an average top-five pick to be (Table 2).

And yet, it never felt like Tagovailoa had the trust of the

Table 2. Rookie Seasons, Last 10 Top-Five Quarterbacks

Year	Player	Team	Pass Yds	Cmp%	TD	INT	Pass DVOA	Pass DYAR	Rush DYAR
2020	Tua Tagovailoa	MIA	1814	64.1%	11	5	-8.5%	56	18
2020	Joe Burrow	CIN	2688	65.3%	13	5	-7.3%	108	-43
2019	Kyler Murray	ARI	3722	64.4%	20	12	-3.1%	305	87
2018	Baker Mayfield	CLE	3725	63.8%	27	14	8.1%	628	-20
2018	Sam Darnold	NYJ	2865	57.7%	17	15	-15.2%	-110	23
2017	Mitchell Trubisky	CHI	2193	59.4%	7	7	-16.8%	-119	32
2016	Jared Goff	LAR	1089	54.6%	5	7	-74.8%	-881	-3
2016	Carson Wentz	PHI	3782	62.4%	16	14	-12.0%	-36	16
2015	Jameis Winston	TB	4042	58.3%	22	15	2.1%	467	42
2015	Marcus Mariota	TEN	2818	62.2%	19	10	-13.2%	-53	20

coaching staff. He was clearly outperformed by Ryan Fitzpatrick, although that's not altogether uncommon as a rookie finds his footing. What is uncommon is the rookie being pulled for the veteran multiple times late in games, leading to comebacks and opening the Pandora's Box of quarterback controversy. The play calling was also very different when the two quarterbacks were in the game, with Chan Gailey opening his playbook much wider for Fitzpatrick. There were plays designed with more quarterback agency; quick reads and checks for the quarterback with more experience. While Flores never wavered from keeping Tua as his starter once he made the switch, his quick hook had some whispering about the possibility of drafting *another* first-round quarterback at the top of the 2021 draft—not cutting bait on Tagovailoa just yet but creating an open competition at the most important position on the roster.

The "two first-round quarterbacks" strategy was a popular one in analytics circles. The idea is that finding a solid starter at the quarterback position is so important that it's worth throwing as many resources as possible at the problem until you feel comfortable with the results. There's also a strong argument against the strategy. Taking that second first-round quarterback will take away some of your opportunity to draft talent you can put around your young quarterback to help him develop. It would be one thing if Tagovailoa had a disaster of a rookie season, like Josh Rosen had in 2018 in Arizona. But Tagovailoa had a very reasonable rookie campaign, with plenty of promise shown on the field, especially when we consider the strange offseason he suffered through. Yes, he still has plenty that he needs to improve if he's going to be a long-term answer at the position, but the prospects that come out of college without flaws to be hammered out are few and far between. There's a reason why Tagovailoa was the presumed top quarterback in the draft before 2019 started, and quite a bit of what made him a highly touted prospect was visible from the moment he stepped onto the field. Tagovailoa showed more than enough promise to hold on to the starting passer job in 2021, even if Miami hadn't been offered a king's ransom to trade down in the draft.

Any discussion of Tagovailoa's development has to begin with his recovery from a dislocated hip and continue through the pandemic-altered 2020 offseason. That left Tua with plenty of classwork and tape review, but precious little time actually working on the field. It's not fair to call Tagovailoa's rookie season an extended redshirt year or anything, but you can view it through a more forgiving lens than most standard years; every rep is crucial for developing players, and those reps were simply not available. It's no surprise that a veteran like Fitzpatrick—already familiar with the offense, his receivers, and the NFL in general—would be notably better than a rookie in those sorts of situations. So we'll try to be a bit kind when reviewing where Tagovailoa stood out last season.

Tagovailoa's accuracy was stellar in college, but that didn't always translate to his rookie NFL season. His -3.5% completion percentage over expected (CPOE) was fifth-worst in the league, although that number is predicated on his receivers actually making receptions. According to SIS charting, 79.3%

of Tagovailoa's passes were catchable, fifth best in the league. But only 66.9% were charted as *on target*, seventh worst, and that 12.4% gap was the biggest in the league last year. Tua wasn't sailing passes or driving them into the ground, but he was only really getting them into the general vicinity of his receivers. At Alabama, that was alright; the likes of Jerry Jeudy, DeVonta Smith, and Henry Ruggs were talented enough to make plays over college defenders as long as the ball was in their zip code. That's not going to fly as well with DeVante Parker, Mike Gesicki, and Jakeem Grant lining up against NFL corners.

The Dolphins' plan to fix that was pretty clear in the offseason—massively upgrade the receiving corps around Tagovailoa. Will Fuller led the league in receiving DVOA last season and was on his way to possibly doing the same in DYAR before a suspension ended his season; he'll bring a deep threat on every snap that will open things up for Parker and Gesicki underneath. The Dolphins could have stopped there and called it a day, but they went ahead and used the sixth overall pick to draft Jaylen Waddle, who offers explosive athletic potential (even if Playmaker Score discounts him a bit due to a lack of big-time college production). In theory, adding these new weapons should have a similar effect to what happened in Buffalo in 2020. Stefon Diggs' arrival let everyone else step down one rung on the depth chart, facing easier matchups and more room in which to work. The same concept applies here. Parker as a third receiver is a heck of a better fit than Parker as the centerpiece of the passing game. That can help turn more of those catchable passes into receptions and keep drives moving.

Still, close isn't good enough in the NFL, and having your receivers be forced to make mid-route adjustments an eighth of the time isn't going to help an offense get out of neutral. Matters get worse when you consider that Tua only averaged 7.7 air yards per attempt and 5.3 air yards per completion, both well below average. It's one thing to be a little off target on a go route 30 yards down the field; having Fuller play centerfield on those balls is a fairly decent strategy. Being a step out of synch with your receiver on slants and digs, on the other hand, is going to limit YAC opportunities. Plus, 20.3% of Tagovailoa's pass attempts were "aggressive," per Next Gen Stats—throwing the ball into windows where there was a defender within 1 yard of the receiver. That's more of a receiver problem than a Tagovailoa problem (Fitzpatrick was at 21.7%, second-most in the league), but when receivers aren't getting open, it makes accuracy that much more important; it's hard to turn an off-target but catchable ball into a reception when there's a safety on your back.

That low air yards total is going to have to come up as well. The deep post and corner targets basically disappeared when Tagovailoa was on the field. Fitzpatrick would get four or five of those a game, often to Mike Gesicki about 15 yards down the field. Tua averaged just one or two of those shots a game. Instead, his passing profile was filled with throws to the flat or beneath routes to receivers maybe 3 yards downfield, upping his completion percentage but lowering his air yards. Fitz certainly had a better rapport with some of his receivers, and the coaching staff clearly trusted him more in situations where the ball had to go deep, but those opportunities were there for Tagovailoa as well. He just didn't *take* them as often, not trusting his receivers to go up and make a play and instead going for the safer option time and again. Or worse, he would hold the ball indecisively and take a sack; it's not a coincidence that he was sacked 6.5% of the time to Fitzpatrick's 5.0%.

Maybe that changes with a regular offseason as the clear-cut starter, allowing him to develop a rapport with his targets. Or maybe it changes with receivers who can actually create separation. It's clear from the film that Tagovailoa has the arm to make these big-time plays. Johnny Kinsley's Deep Ball Project had him as the second-most accurate deep passer out of clean pockets. There just needs be more confidence and chemistry, and a willingness to take risks that was not there in 2020. New offensive coordinators Eric Studesville and George Godsey at least offer something different from the departed Chan Gailey, but selecting a tight ends coach and a run-game coordinator to call the shots promises more two-tight end looks and ball control offense.

Giving Tua more clean pockets would help as well. Both Tagovailoa and Fitzpatrick were among the quickest quarterbacks to throw the ball in 2020. Not because Miami had a cutting-edge quick-fire passing attack, mind you, but because the offensive line simply wasn't up to par. The line ranked firmly below average in both adjusted line yards and adjusted sack rate. They were a little above average in pressure rate, but they ranked 27th in ESPN's pass block win rate. Opposing defenses didn't always have time to get pressure, as Miami's offense was designed around getting the ball out of their quarterbacks' hands as quickly as possible; the coaching staff did not trust the line to hold their blocks against talented opposition. Here's where drafting Waddle in the first round might be an issue, as it cost the Dolphins the opportunity to take consensus top lineman Penei Sewell instead.

At the very least, Miami has a clear plan and is sticking to it. The Dolphins' offensive line was the third-youngest in the league last season, so they're counting on recent draft picks such as Austin Jackson, Robert Hunt, and Michael Dieter to take steps forward, improving the line without spending any more capital on it and freeing them up to bring in weapons such as Waddle and Fuller. They want to surround Tagovailoa with as much skill position talent as possible and create the best possible environment for him to develop in. If you consider 2020 as Tagovailoa's Season Zero, forgiving him a bit for being a step behind the curve thanks to his injuries and the strange offseason, then 2021 would be the debut of what this new offense looks like with actual talent behind the wheel.

As far as gambles go, it's a logical one, though it's important to remember that subpar young players sometimes simply become subpar older players. Maybe everyone does take a step forward, and second-round pick Liam Eichenberg develops faster than expected. Maybe the line starts to provide holes for the bargain-basement running back corps and gives the high-priced receivers time to work their way open downfield. Or maybe it will be mediocre like last year, and any hope of the Tua-powered offense working more than 5 yards downfield at

a time is a pipe dream. The development of Tagovailoa may be the most important thing for the Dolphins' offense going forward, but the offensive line is a bigger question mark at this point in time.

Of course, the offense doesn't have to do everything on its own. Miami's success last year was built on its defensive performance, and the creativity and schematic ingenuity of Brian Flores should give Miami fans confidence that it won't just be a one-year wonder.

Here's a question for you: just how often did Miami actually blitz last season? Try to answer without looking at our strategic tendencies table; it's a tougher question than you might think. It's no secret that the Belichick coaching tree loves rushing only three, and Flores certainly lived up to that stereotype; the Dolphins came in fourth in the league at 16%. But sending five or six? Different charters have wildly different numbers here, with some having the Dolphins in the top two or three teams in the league. Our charting comes from Sports Info Solutions and has Miami firmly in the middle of the pack, sending five or more rushers on 29% of passing plays, 14th in the league. There are always a few discrepancies whenever you're charting something; judgment calls will be made differently by different people. But this is a pretty massive disagreement—what's going on?

The answer comes from Flores' creative play-calling style. Flores' defense relies heavily on confusion and misdirection. There are plenty of plays where essentially the entire front seven is standing within a yard of the line; edge rushers, linebackers, and interior linemen all more or less interchangeable. On the snap, some will rush, some will drop into coverage, and some will feint, taking a step or two in before dropping back themselves. Apart from Emmanuel Ogbah, most of Miami's sacks and pressures came from the second level of their defense, rather than from someone lining up at the 5-technique and beating a tackle. The question when going against Flores' defense was always both how many people would be rushing and *which* people would be rushing. If experienced charters with the benefit of high-def footage and a pause button have trouble figuring it out, good luck to an offensive lineman trying to shift his protection in a split second.

If you want to split the difference, you can think of Flores' defense as *committing* players to the pass rush more than nearly any other team in the league, while actually *using* players in the pass rush at a more average rate. Those players who drop back into coverage are a step or two behind someone who lined up in coverage, with the defense sacrificing some immediacy in exchange for confusion and disruption over the snap. It worked, too—Miami generated the fifth-most pressure in the league despite lacking a true world-beater edge rusher. We're not saying the Dolphins have no talent on defense or that adding Ogbah or Kyle Van Noy didn't play a role in Miami's defensive improvement last year, but Flores' scheme produces pressure above and beyond the résumés of the players actively involved. This separates him from some of the other Belichick disciples who have floundered and failed when they've tried to set out on their own; it's hard to believe Flores and Matt Patricia even learned the same sport, much less came out of the same system.

Of course, having so many of your defenders involved in the pass rush (or appearance thereof) leaves your secondary out on an island. The Dolphins used the third-most man-to-man coverage last season and ranked ninth in defensive back blitzes. Having Xavien Howard and Byron Jones on the outside frees a coordinator up to do a lot more with his safeties and linebackers towards the line of scrimmage, and Flores took good advantage of the athleticism of his front seven, trusting his linebackers to be able to drop back in time. But devoting so many players to the defensive front is always a gamble, even with the trust the Dolphins have in their secondary. Drafting Jaelan Phillips might help Miami generate more pressure without necessarily devoting so much personnel to creating it.

It's a good thing that Phillips and Jevon Holland fit very well with what Miami wants to do defensively, because we're not overly impressed with the veterans Miami has added this offseason. Waiving Van Noy was a surprise, and trading Shaq Lawson for Benardrick McKinney is a head-scratcher as well—both moves save Miami some cap space, but Van Noy and Lawson were useful players for Miami last season. The Dolphins certainly had a need at inside linebacker considering their 22nd-ranked run defense, and McKinney is in the big banger mold that fits what Miami does. But he's coming off a major shoulder injury and isn't a significant improvement over Elandon Roberts. And he's the big addition; neither Duke Riley (a coverage linebacker with middling success) nor

Justin Coleman (a reclamation project after several bad years in Detroit) really moves the needle much. While Flores has earned some benefit of the doubt that he'll get more out of these players than your average coach, the pressure is really on the returning defenders to improve to fight against historical regression.

As noted earlier, Miami led the league with takeaways on 16.0% of drives last season. Miami was a more pedestrian 15th in yards allowed per drive and three-and-outs forced per drive. They were also fourth in red zone points allowed per drive and first in DVOA on third/fourth downs. The Dolphins tended to have their best results on plays which had an outsized effect on their performance. Miami could be exactly as skilled in 2021 as they were in 2020 and still have a worse defensive performance simply due to random variation.

The Dolphins took a significant step forward last season, and fans have every reason to be optimistic about the future of their franchise for the first time in years. Miami should be right in the thick of the playoff hunt in 2021, even if they probably haven't arrived at true contender status just yet. It's important to realize, however, that 2020 was just one step, and that more work needs to be done if the Dolphins are going to have their first sustained run of success since the Dave Wannstedt era. Especially on offense, Miami needs to take another stride this year if we're going to start considering the Dolphins divisional title contenders in the near future.

Bryan Knowles

2020 Dolphins by Week

Wk	vs.	W-L	PF	PA	YDF	YDA	TO	Total	Off	Def	ST
1	at NE	L	11	21	269	357	-2	-52.1%	-26.7%	27.5%	2.1%
2	BUF	L	28	31	410	523	1	-8.4%	12.1%	29.6%	9.1%
3	at JAX	W	31	13	294	318	2	6.0%	12.9%	8.1%	1.2%
4	SEA	L	23	31	415	441	-1	-7.0%	-2.9%	12.7%	8.5%
5	at SF	W	43	17	436	259	3	82.4%	51.3%	-34.6%	-3.5%
6	NYJ	W	24	0	302	263	-1	41.5%	-5.6%	-34.3%	12.8%
7	BYE										
8	LAR	W	28	17	145	471	2	38.2%	-18.6%	-20.3%	36.5%
9	at ARI	W	34	31	312	442	1	12.8%	23.2%	21.9%	11.5%
10	LAC	W	29	21	280	273	0	5.4%	-8.0%	-1.9%	11.5%
11	at DEN	L	13	20	223	459	1	-39.5%	-28.3%	16.3%	5.0%
12	at NYJ	W	20	3	345	260	0	48.7%	-10.1%	-47.3%	11.5%
13	CIN	W	19	7	406	196	1	42.0%	-0.2%	-45.1%	-2.9%
14	KC	L	27	33	367	448	3	1.7%	3.9%	-22.2%	-24.4%
15	NE	W	22	12	383	303	0	0.7%	5.5%	-4.4%	-9.3%
16	at LV	W	26	25	383	418	1	-24.4%	-14.1%	7.9%	-2.3%
17	at BUF	L	26	56	454	455	-2	-62.7%	-30.3%	18.3%	-14.1%

Trends and Splits

	Offense	Rank	Defense	Rank
Total DVOA	-2.1%	18	-3.3%	11
Unadjusted VOA	-0.5%	16	-5.4%	10
Weighted Trend	-5.2%	18	-8.0%	9
Variance	4.4%	10	6.9%	25
Average Opponent	1.9%	24	-2.2%	21
Passing	12.8%	18	-4.1%	6
Rushing	-17.5%	23	-2.3%	22
First Down	5.9%	13	20.7%	31
Second Down	-5.6%	21	-11.3%	9
Third Down	-12.0%	21	-38.5%	1
First Half	-3.0%	19	-8.0%	7
Second Half	-1.2%	17	2.0%	14
Red Zone	-17.5%	26	-1.4%	14
Late and Close	13.3%	8	22.8%	32

Five-Year Performance

Year	W-L	Pyth W	Est W	PF	PA	TO	Total	Rk	Off	Rk	Def	Rk	ST	Rk	Off AGL	Rk	Def AGL	Rk	Off Age	Rk	Def Age	Rk	ST Age	Rk
2016	10-6	7.5	8.6	363	380	+2	-1.4%	20	1.5%	14	3.8%	20	0.8%	12	46.9	23	60.6	27	26.3	23	26.9	10	25.6	25
2017	6-10	4.9	5.4	281	393	-14	-21.7%	28	-13.6%	27	10.7%	28	2.6%	12	65.3	29	60.8	28	27.3	11	27.1	4	25.8	19
2018	7-9	5.1	5.0	319	433	+5	-17.7%	27	-9.5%	26	7.1%	26	-1.1%	21	66.3	30	26.8	12	27.3	10	26.1	20	25.8	17
2019	5-11	3.6	3.0	306	494	-10	-38.8%	32	-14.5%	28	23.0%	32	-1.3%	22	43.0	18	57.0	30	26.6	19	25.1	32	25.3	27
2020	10-6	9.8	8.2	404	338	+9	4.6%	12	-2.1%	18	-3.3%	11	3.3%	6	43.6	19	22.1	5	25.5	29	25.9	27	25.3	28

2020 Performance Based on Most Common Personnel Groups

MIA Offense					MIA Offense vs. Opponents					MIA Defense				MIA Defense vs. Opponents			
Pers	Freq	Yds	DVOA	Run%	Pers	Freq	Yds	DVOA	Run%	Pers	Freq	Yds	DVOA	Pers	Freq	Yds	DVOA
11	55%	6.0	2.4%	25%	Base	23%	4.5	-9.0%	55%	Base	27%	6.2	4.8%	11	64%	6.1	-8.2%
12	26%	5.5	0.1%	44%	Nickel	62%	6.0	2.5%	33%	Nickel	48%	6.4	4.4%	12	17%	6.1	-4.0%
21	4%	6.0	7.8%	51%	Dime+	13%	6.2	2.6%	17%	Dime+	24%	5.4	-33.4%	21	9%	6.2	22.8%
13	3%	3.8	-5.1%	47%	Goal Line	2%	0.7	21.0%	77%	Goal Line	1%	1.4	66.3%	10	3%	6.3	-0.8%
22	3%	3.3	-34.6%	89%						Big	1%	0.2	-107.5%	13	2%	7.1	-11.1%

Strategic Tendencies

Run/Pass		Rk	Formation		Rk	Pass Rush		Rk	Secondary		Rk	Strategy		Rk
Runs, first half	34%	27	Form: Single Back	76%	26	Rush 3	16.4%	4	4 DB	27%	12	Play Action	26%	19
Runs, first down	41%	28	Form: Empty Back	11%	7	Rush 4	54.9%	31	5 DB	48%	27	Offensive Motion	43%	18
Runs, second-long	29%	14	Form: Multi Back	12%	12	Rush 5	21.7%	13	6+ DB	24%	9	Avg Box (Off)	6.55	15
Runs, power sit.	64%	11	Pers: 3+ WR	60%	22	Rush 6+	6.9%	8	Man Coverage	43%	3	Avg Box (Def)	6.82	4
Runs, behind 2H	27%	16	Pers: 2+ TE/6+ OL	36%	7	Edge Rusher Sacks	59.8%	6	CB by Sides	54%	32	Offensive Pace	31.34	25
Pass, ahead 2H	43%	24	Pers: 6+ OL	4%	6	Interior DL Sacks	12.2%	30	S/CB Cover Ratio	31%	10	Defensive Pace	29.84	10
Run-Pass Options	11%	8	Shotgun/Pistol	81%	7	Second Level Sacks	28.0%	9	DB Blitz	16%	9	Go for it on 4th	0.86	31

Miami faced more man coverage than any offense in the league, with Ryan Fitzpatrick (39%) and Tua Tagovailoa (38%) ranking one-two in the NFL in their rate of facing man coverage. ✎ Miami used pistol on 13% of plays, second in the league behind Baltimore. The Dolphins averaged 5.5 yards on these plays with -2.8% DVOA. ✎ It wasn't quite 2019, when they averaged 8.6 yards per play, but the Dolphins were once again excellent from empty backfields: 6.8 yards per play and 32.1% DVOA. ✎ Miami ranked 21st in pressure allowed on first and second down but improved to fourth on third and fourth down. Miami and Tennessee were the only two teams to allow less pressure on third downs than first and second; leaguewide, pressure rate went up about 7.5% on third downs. ✎ Miami's defense had a remarkable split in the red zone: third against the pass but the worst defense in the league against the run. ✎ Miami opponents dropped only 19 passes, 31st in the league. ✎ The Dolphins had the league's third-highest gap between where the strong safety (Eric Rowe) and free safety (Bobby McCain) made their average plays. ✎ Brian Flores was dramatically conservative compared to his first season in Miami. He was one of only two head coaches (along with Vic Fangio) with an Aggressiveness Index below the historical average of 1.0. In 2019, Flores had ranked ninth at 1.75.

Passing

Player	DYAR	DVOA	Plays	NtYds	Avg	YAC	C%	TD	Int
T.Tagovailoa	56	-8.5%	307	1667	5.4	4.1	65.0%	11	5
R.Fitzpatrick*	362	7.5%	280	2026	7.2	4.7	68.8%	13	8
J.Brissett	-68	-135.2%	10	2	0.2	9.0	28.6%	0	0

Rushing

Player	DYAR	DVOA	Plays	Yds	Avg	TD	Fum	Suc
M.Gaskin	-15	-10.9%	142	584	4.1	3	2	55%
S.Ahmed	-6	-10.3%	75	319	4.3	3	0	59%
M.Breida*	-8	-11.8%	59	254	4.3	0	2	56%
D.Washington*	-28	-34.6%	28	86	3.1	0	0	46%
J.Howard	-45	-37.9%	28	33	1.2	4	0	36%
T.Tagovailoa	18	-0.9%	27	120	4.4	3	0	--
R.Fitzpatrick*	39	14.6%	24	156	6.5	2	0	--
P.Laird	-11	-33.9%	13	72	5.5	0	1	46%
L.Bowden	18	2.7%	9	32	3.6	0	0	--
M.Brown	89	11.7%	101	419	4.1	5	0	49%
J.Brissett	27	18.0%	11	23	2.1	3	0	--

Receiving

Player	DYAR	DVOA	Plays	Ctch	Yds	Y/C	YAC	TD	C%
D.Parker	70	-4.7%	103	63	793	12.6	2.7	4	61%
J.Grant	3	-11.9%	54	36	373	10.4	4.8	1	67%
I.Ford*	1	-12.3%	44	28	276	9.9	2.4	0	64%
L.Bowden	-30	-22.4%	37	28	211	7.5	4.0	0	76%
P.Williams	71	10.8%	35	18	288	16.0	2.3	4	51%
M.Hollins	-14	-19.3%	25	16	176	11.0	1.8	1	64%
M.Perry	13	-0.3%	13	9	92	10.2	3.7	1	69%
W.Fuller	326	41.2%	75	53	879	16.6	5.5	8	71%
R.Foster	-10	-33.7%	6	2	37	18.5	16.0	0	33%
M.Gesicki	108	10.4%	85	53	703	13.3	3.2	6	62%
D.Smythe	37	10.7%	29	26	208	8.0	4.7	2	90%
A.Shaheen	-9	-12.0%	22	12	150	12.5	8.8	3	55%
C.Carter	-5	-18.5%	7	5	53	10.6	2.0	0	71%
M.Gaskin	137	37.8%	47	41	388	9.5	9.5	2	87%
S.Ahmed	-10	-27.1%	14	11	61	5.5	6.5	0	79%
P.Laird	18	16.5%	12	10	68	6.8	4.0	0	83%
M.Breida*	42	49.9%	10	9	96	10.7	10.7	0	90%
D.Washington*	-10	-35.1%	9	4	28	7.0	5.5	0	44%
M.Brown	-7	-17.5%	33	23	162	7.0	7.7	0	70%

Offensive Line

Player	Pos	Age	GS	Snaps	Pen	Sk	Pass	Run	Player	Pos	Age	GS	Snaps	Pen	Sk	Pass	Run
Ted Karras*	C	28	16/16	1068	3	0.5	6	13	Robert Hunt	RT	25	16/11	721	5	1	12	2
Jesse Davis	OT/RG	30	16/15	1054	2	1	13	10	Matt Skura	C	28	15/12	661	3	0	5	8
Ereck Flowers*	LG	27	14/14	856	3	2	9	10	D.J. Fluker	RT	30	16/8	531	9	1.5	9	4
Austin Jackson	LT	22	13/12	848	4	2.5	23	8	Jermaine Eluemunor	RT	27	12/8	419	1	4	7	5
Solomon Kindley	RG/LG	24	13/13	747	6	2	9	9									

Year	Yards	ALY	Rk	Power	Rk	Stuff	Rk	2Lev	Rk	OpFld	Rk	BB Rt	Rk	Sacks	ASR	Rk	Press	Rk	BB Rt	Rk	Cont
2018	4.79	4.47	14	62%	24	18%	15	1.29	12	1.02	8	11.0%	31	52	10.5%	31	36.3%	31	12.8%	29	26
2019	2.96	3.17	32	70%	6	26%	32	0.86	32	0.25	31	15.3%	31	58	8.6%	28	36.7%	31	20.9%	32	20
2020	3.95	4.18	24	67%	13	18%	21	1.09	26	0.50	29	13.7%	30	34	6.9%	20	23.8%	11	11.6%	13	28
2020 ALY by direction:			Left End: 5.61 (3)			Left Tackle: 3.79 (24)				Mid/Guard: 4.08 (28)				Right Tackle: 5.23 (4)				Right End: 3.30 (28)			

Miami's offensive line hasn't ranked in the top 20 in adjusted line yards since 2018. They haven't been in the top 20 in adjusted sack rate since 2017. Both Ryan Fitzpatrick and Tua Tagovailoa were in the bottom 10 in time to throw, per Next Gen Stats. All five starting positions need to improve, although at least they had the third-youngest line in football last season with a snap-weighted age of 25.3. Ideally, 2020 will just be growing pains. ❧ Matt Skura suffered a torn ACL and dislocated kneecap in November 2019 and wasn't the same player in 2020, benched after missing multiple pistol snaps. His 47.2 snaps per blown block was 28th among 36 ranked centers. ❧ Austin Jackson's rookie season could have gone better—he was in the top 15 for blown blocks despite missing three games. He was a known fixer-upper when the Dolphins draft him last year, and he did improve over the course of 2020, so mark him with an "I" for incomplete through one year. ❧ Trading away Ereck Flowers will open up a spot at guard, allowing Solomon Kindley to move to the left full time; that's his more natural position and he looked significantly more comfortable there in 2020. ❧ Robert Hunt was the best of the three rookie linemen last season, and will start *somewhere*, though whether that's at tackle or guard depends more on second-round rookie Liam Eichenberg than anything else. ❧ Eichenberg allowed just one sack in the last two seasons at Notre Dame, per SIS charting, and after playing through a swollen-shut left eye against Florida State there's no doubting his toughness or tenacity. If he sticks at tackle, however, he may have issues with his speed, timing, and short arms—it's possible guard is his better long-term position.

Defensive Front

Defensive Line	Age	Pos	G	Snaps	Plays	Overall TmPct	Rk	Stop	Dfts	BTkl	Runs	vs. Run St%	Rk	RuYd	Rk	Pass Rush Sack	Hit	Hur	Dsrpt
Christian Wilkins	26	DE	14	637	52	7.4%	9	41	8	1	44	77%	39	3.3	87	1.5	1	12	4
Raekwon Davis	24	DT	16	538	40	5.0%	51	28	4	4	40	70%	60	2.8	63	0.0	1	9	0
Zach Sieler	26	DE	16	532	48	6.0%	29	36	14	2	41	76%	45	1.8	19	3.5	7	13	0
Adam Butler	27	DT	15	483	36	4.8%	54	23	10	2	26	62%	84	3.2	85	4.0	3	21	5
John Jenkins	32	DT	11	223	22	3.9%	--	18	1	1	20	80%	--	2.4	--	0.0	1	2	1

Edge Rushers	Age	Pos	G	Snaps	Plays	Overall TmPct	Rk	Stop	Dfts	BTkl	Runs	vs. Run St%	Rk	RuYd	Rk	Pass Rush Sack	Hit	Hur	Dsrpt
Kyle Van Noy*	30	OLB	14	811	75	10.7%	1	42	17	13	44	52%	94	4.5	94	6.0	4	21	2
Emmanuel Ogbah	28	DE	16	792	47	5.8%	28	41	16	7	31	81%	12	2.2	34	9.0	14	40	5
Shaq Lawson*	27	OLB	14	571	33	4.7%	49	26	13	2	22	77%	26	1.6	12	4.0	16	27	1
Andrew Van Ginkel	26	OLB	16	479	46	5.7%	29	30	12	3	30	60%	81	3.0	66	5.5	6	9	5
Duke Riley	27	OLB	13	568	47	6.8%	75	25	7	10	30	57%	39	3.4	22	0.5	0	2	0
Brennan Scarlett	28	OLB	11	286	24	4.0%	--	13	2	5	19	58%	--	3.9	--	0.0	1	4	0

Linebackers	Age	Pos	G	Snaps	Plays	Overall TmPct	Rk	Stop	Dfts	BTkl	Runs	vs. Run St%	Rk	RuYd	Rk	Pass Rush Sack	Hit	Hur	vs. Pass Tgts	Suc%	Rk	Yd/P	Rk	PD	Int
Jerome Baker	25	ILB	16	868	114	14.2%	32	55	21	12	58	45%	77	4.3	56	7.0	3	10	37	57%	19	6.3	37	3	0
Elandon Roberts	27	ILB	13	402	61	9.3%	63	30	12	10	47	57%	38	2.9	5	1.5	2	5	11	36%	--	8.3	--	0	0
Kamu Grugier-Hill*	27	ILB	15	207	23	3.1%	--	5	3	4	6	50%	--	6.2	--	1.0	1	2	9	0%	--	10.1	--	0	0
Benardrick McKinney	29	ILB	4	234	38	17.5%	9	22	5	8	29	66%	16	2.8	4	0.0	0	2	4	75%	--	1.5	--	1	0

Year	Yards	ALY	Rk	Power	Rk	Stuff	Rk	2Lev	Rk	OpFld	Rk	BB Rt	Rk	Sacks	ASR	Rk	Press	Rk	BB Rt	Rk
2018	4.53	4.36	16	65%	15	20%	15	1.29	21	1.04	23	9.3%	12	31	6.3%	28	28.5%	23	13.4%	5
2019	4.46	5.00	32	65%	18	14%	28	1.32	25	0.53	5	7.4%	32	23	4.4%	32	24.1%	31	8.3%	32
2020	4.41	4.41	16	71%	26	17%	16	1.30	19	0.66	13	14.1%	11	41	7.5%	9	29.4%	5	14.8%	10

2020 ALY by direction:	Left End: 4.14 (11)	Left Tackle: 3.41 (7)	Mid/Guard: 4.55 (19)	Right Tackle: 5.02 (25)	Right End: 4.14 (9)

Two years ago, the Dolphins ranked 31st in the league at generating pressure, succeeding only 24% of the time. In 2020, they were fifth at 29%, by far the biggest year-to-year increase in a season where overall pressure numbers were down. They hadn't been in the top 10 since 2016 in Vance Joseph's one year with the team. ◈ Emmanuel Ogbah had more pressures in 2020 than in his previous two seasons combined. A 12.5% pressure rate on 472 rushes (per SIS charting) is a fantastic combination of efficiency and volume; only Aaron Donald had a better rate on more rushes. ◈ Christian Wilkins has developed into a very solid two-gap lineman. He tied for 11th in run stops among linemen despite missing two games on the COVID list. He's no pass-rusher, but he's a hell of a spark plug and possibly the most fun personality on the team. ◈ It was never the plan for Raekwon Davis to eat up tons of snaps in 2020, but the rookie did a tremendous job filling the nose tackle role when Davon Godchaux went down in October—he made the veteran expendable. ◈ Benardrick McKinney only played four games last season due to a shoulder injury, but managed to miss eight tackles—more than he did in all of 2019. ◈ Jerome Baker's 45% run stop rate was the worst among inside linebackers with at least 50 plays against the run; he had just one tackle for a loss. ◈ An injury-free Jaelan Phillips might well have been a top-10 pick; he was SackSEER's favorite with a projection right alongside guys such as Chase Young. Instead, the Dolphins snagged him 18th overall. Multiple concussions led to his temporary retirement in college, and that's obviously a concern going forwards, but he got a clean bill of health from the NFL's doctors. ◈ The route between Miami International and Boston Logan was busy this year. The Dolphins brought in Adam Butler and Jason McCourty from New England to help run Flores' scheme while Davon Godchaux, Ted Karras, and Kyle Van Noy went in the other direction. It should make for an interesting Week 1 reunion.

Defensive Secondary

Secondary	Age	Pos	G	Snaps	Plays	TmPct	Rk	Stop	Dfts	BTkl	Runs	St%	Rk	RuYd	Rk	Tgts	Tgt%	Rk	aDOT	Suc%	Rk	Yd/P	Rk	PD	Int
Xavien Howard	28	CB	16	936	71	8.8%	37	32	17	4	8	38%	50	7.3	46	77	20.7%	35	15.9	61%	7	7.3	35	20	10
Bobby McCain*	28	FS	16	923	51	6.3%	68	5	3	7	20	0%	71	14.7	70	12	3.3%	68	17.6	58%	12	8.2	43	5	1
Eric Rowe	29	SS/CB	16	919	102	12.7%	13	39	12	10	35	46%	22	6.1	28	70	19.1%	3	9.9	54%	21	7.9	38	11	2
Byron Jones	29	CB	14	769	41	5.8%	77	12	9	10	11	27%	64	7.5	48	53	17.3%	63	13.9	43%	66	9.4	69	4	2
Nik Needham	25	CB	16	617	65	8.1%	55	20	9	8	12	8%	80	13.2	79	53	21.6%	27	10.0	45%	63	9.4	68	7	2
Brandon Jones	23	FS	16	430	60	7.5%	--	22	12	7	21	38%	--	6.2	--	14	8.2%	--	5.9	50%	--	5.3	--	1	0
Noah Igbinoghene	22	CB	16	286	12	1.5%	--	3	2	5	1	0%	--	11.0	--	25	22.0%	--	13.9	48%	--	9.2	--	2	0
Jamal Perry	27	CB	13	140	20	3.1%	--	5	2	3	8	38%	--	5.5	--	7	12.6%	--	4.6	43%	--	7.0	--	1	0
Jason McCourty	34	CB	16	666	44	5.5%	80	9	6	2	17	18%	76	10.1	72	35	14.2%	77	12.9	49%	52	10.0	78	3	0
Justin Coleman	28	CB	11	470	30	5.2%	--	11	7	9	3	33%	--	6.7	--	29	16.1%	--	9.2	45%	--	9.3	--	1	0

Year	Pass D Rank	vs. #1 WR	Rk	vs. #2 WR	Rk	vs. Other WR	Rk	WR Wide	Rk	WR Slot	Rk	vs. TE	Rk	vs. RB	Rk
2018	23	7.0%	21	5.5%	21	-2.2%	17	26.0%	32	-5.7%	10	-0.3%	14	20.2%	30
2019	32	26.0%	31	21.9%	28	-3.3%	15	17.9%	30	17.1%	26	11.3%	29	55.4%	32
2020	6	-2.2%	17	-14.3%	7	-11.3%	9	-3.2%	14	-7.9%	8	-13.1%	7	14.8%	26

Plenty of teams are better at covering the boundaries than the middle of the field and vice versa, but the 2020 Dolphins were a bit of an extreme case. Their DVOA was in the top quarter of the league against passes to the left or right but in the bottom quarter against passes down the middle, the first team to pull that off since 2016. Their DVOA was in the bottom 10 against both short and deep throws down the middle as well. ● Byron Jones only had three passes defensed in 2020, the lowest total of his career. He had a career-worst 43% success rate in coverage, too. ● Xavien Howard set career highs in interceptions and pass breakups and a career-low in broken-tackle percentage—he may well be the best cornerback in football. ● Justin Coleman is looking for a fresh start after bombing out in Detroit. In Seattle, Coleman was regularly near the top of the league in success rate. In 2020, his 9.3 yards per target was in the bottom 25 for corners with a least 25 targets. Perhaps being surrounded by more talent will help him bounce back. ● No safety was targeted more often than Eric Rowe, in part because Rowe lined up at cornerback about a quarter of the time. He handled his own there; it was when asked to make stops as a box safety that he struggled. ● Second-round pick Jevon Holland (Oregon) spent most of 2018 at free safety, most of 2019 at slot corner, and most of 2020 at home as a COVID opt-out. Cutting Bobby McCain likely tips the Dolphins' hand as to where they see Holland playing, but positional versatility never hurt anyone.

Special Teams

Year	DVOA	Rank	FG/XP	Rank	Net Kick	Rank	Kick Ret	Rank	Net Punt	Rank	Punt Ret	Rank	Hidden	Rank
2018	-1.1%	21	1.9	13	-5.8	29	2.9	6	-10.5	29	6.0	4	11.8	3
2019	-1.3%	22	-1.3	19	-1.6	22	3.4	7	-2.8	21	-4.3	26	-3.5	21
2020	3.3%	6	12.5	3	7.9	2	-2.5	19	-5.3	24	4.0	8	15.7	2

Jason Sanders hit 92.3% of his field goals, setting a new Dolphins franchise record. With 12.5 points of added value by our numbers, it comes up just short of Pete Stoyanovich in 1991, who had 12.9; kickers are more accurate today, so Sanders was less relatively valuable when compared to what average kickers can do now. ● Sanders also set a new career high in kickoff value, which tends to be more consistent from year to year than field goals. The three-pointers earned him his new contract; the kickoffs are a better sign of good performance to come. ● New punter Michael Palardy missed 2020 with a torn ACL he got playing pickup basketball. In 2019, his Panthers had the worst punt value in the league; perhaps that was due to offseason polo practice? ● Jakeem Grant was the fifth-most valuable punt returner in the league last season at 5.3 estimated points of added field position, though he had slight negative value as a kick returner. Miami only returned 12 kicks all year, though, so the punt value is much more relevant.

Minnesota Vikings

2020 Record: 7-9	**Total DVOA:** -6.4% (7)	**2021 Mean Projection:** 9.1 wins	**On the Clock (0-5):** 10%
Pythagorean Wins: 7 (21)	**Offense:** 6.3% (8)	**Postseason Odds:** 52.3%	**Mediocrity (6-8):** 31%
Snap-Weighted Age: 26.3 (20)	**Defense:** 3.4% (18)	**Super Bowl Odds:** 7.3%	**Playoff Contender (9-11):** 39%
Average Opponent: 3.7% (6)	**Special Teams:** -9.4% (31)	**Proj. Avg. Opponent:** 1.6% (7)	**Super Bowl Contender (12+):** 20%

2020: A playoff push that hid a rebuild.

2021: An NFC North contender with none of the noise.

As they entered their Week 14 matchup with the Buccaneers, the Vikings had hopes for down-the-stretch surge and postseason run. They didn't match the eventual Super Bowl champions in either playoff odds (27.3% versus 92.0%) or DVOA (-1.3%, 15th, versus 26.0%, third). But on a streak of five wins in six games, the Vikings were just one game behind in the standings. They were different enough from the usual fare of contenders—in their avoidance of 11 personnel and reliance on a running game—to give even their best opponents fits, like they did to the Packers in a Week 8 road upset. They seemed poised to do the same to the Bucs in Tampa when they traversed the bulk of the field on their first drive with six straight runs against the league's best run defense.

That drive stalled on a third-and-4 Shaq Barrett sack, but after Tampa Bay went three-and-out and punted the ball back to them, the Vikings returned to their initial rhythm. Play-action passes to Adam Thielen added a pair of 15-yard chunks, but by and large, the Vikings bullied the Bucs methodically on the ground. They took 14 plays and the rest of the first quarter to reach the end zone, and they only threatened a disruption with one third down.

Head coach Mike Zimmer must have been confident when Dalvin Cook punctuated the extended drive with a 1-yard touchdown. His top-ranked run-blocking line (5.07 adjusted line yards) had so far had its way against its defensive counterpart. But I doubt he retained that confidence when kicker Dan Bailey pulled his extra point attempt wide left.

Source 1 of likely 2021 regression: the 31st-ranked special teams (-9.4% DVOA) and 30th-ranked conversion rate on kicks inside 50 yards (83.3%).

At one time, Bailey was the most accurate kicker in NFL history. He looked like the opposite in the final month of the 2020 season. Bailey had already missed three kicks in Week 13, two of them point-after attempts. Perhaps Zimmer attributed these misses to an unexpected bad day, relieved they came in a Jaguars game that his team won despite them. But that suspicion was unlikely to survive this encore of four missed kicks in as many attempts. And neither would his team.

Zimmer would not have thrown in the towel at Minnesota's first adversity, especially once Tom Brady overthrew his second downfield receiver and produced a second straight three-and-out. The Bucs may have assembled an offensive super team, but the Vikings had drafted their way to something close to one. With the first-round pick they added in their previous offseason's Stefon Diggs trade, the team selected wide receiver Justin Jefferson, the fifth receiver taken last year but by far the best of them based on their rookie seasons. Jefferson ranked third among all receivers with 373 DYAR in 2020, and he was seventh among the 87 wideouts that saw 50 or more targets with a 25.5% DVOA. On the team's third drive, Jefferson quickly advanced the Vikings into Bucs territory with a 17-yard catch-and-run featuring a pair of broken tackles.

The Vikings made it as far as the Bucs' 11-yard line. Thielen even got a hand on an end zone target that could have put his team up by multiple scores, but he couldn't secure the fade pass with his outstretched body crashing into the turf. Backed into a third-and-7, Kirk Cousins took a Ndamukong Suh sack, and Bailey missed the resulting 36-yard field goal try, this time to the right.

Source 2 of likely 2021 regression: the fourth-ranked DVOA differential on early versus late downs (19.4%).

As you might imagine of a team with Cook and the No. 1 run-blocking offensive line, the Vikings excelled in many power situations. Most notably, they were the No. 6 offense in the red zone (27.2% DVOA). But the Vikings struggled to translate their broader success on first and second downs into success on third and fourth downs.

Cousins ended many Vikings drives prematurely with third-down sacks, in this game and all season. But his overall 7.0% sack rate fell outside the top 10 at the position and behind stars such as Russell Wilson and Lamar Jackson despite his disadvantage of a 31.4% offensive pressure rate (31st). Like so many Cousins criticisms, those of his third-down decision-making are often unfair. Discrepancies between early- and late-down DVOA rates are inconsistent from year to year. In fact, Cousins' Vikings were on the other end of the spectrum in 2019 when they were 28.1% *better* on third and fourth downs than they were on first and second downs.

If Zimmer didn't yet dread the missed opportunities from Cousins' two early sacks and Bailey's two early missed kicks, he would shortly when Brady bookended a four-play, 74-yard touchdown drive with on-target deep completions to Mike Ev-

2021 Vikings Schedule

Week	Opp.	Week	Opp.	Week	Opp.
1	at CIN	7	BYE	13	at DET
2	at ARI	8	DAL	14	PIT (Thu.)
3	SEA	9	at BAL	15	at CHI (Mon.)
4	CLE	10	at LAC	16	LAR
5	DET	11	GB	17	at GB
6	at CAR	12	at SF	18	CHI

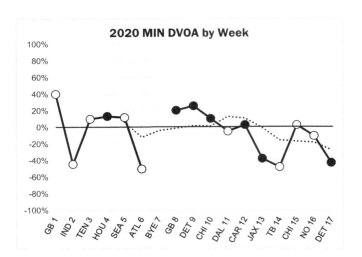

2020 MIN DVOA by Week

ans for 20 yards and Scotty Miller for 48 yards. Brady shook off his early inaccuracies and Minnesota's early ball control to put 26 points on the board in the final two and a half quarters. The 26-14 final score looked convincing. But the Vikings ran 27 more plays, converted 10 more first downs, and controlled 18:06 more clock on offense than the Bucs did. They almost certainly would have won if Cousins hadn't taken his eventual six sacks and Bailey hadn't missed his eventual four kicks—both representative of 2020 but neither likely foreshadowing of 2021—and if the team could have avoided a third issue.

Source 3 of likely 2021 regression: the third-ranked adjusted games lost on defense (64.8).

The Bucs' surplus of skill talent would force even the deepest of defenses into bad matchups. So it isn't fair to blame injuries alone for cornerback Chris Jones (undrafted in 2018 and on the Cardinals' practice squad to start 2020) failing to cover the aforementioned Scotty Miller on a 48-yard touchdown catch or linebacker Todd Davis (undrafted in 2014 and a Broncos roster cutdown victim in September) interfering with Rob Gronkowski on an end-of-half Hail Mary that earned the Bucs an untimed play at the goal line and a gifted three points. Still, the Vikings were less prepared to deal with injuries than many teams because they used the 2020 season to fix their salary cap.

The Vikings have rivaled the Saints for salary-cap savvy in the decade that general manager Rick Spielman has run the team. But after deferring payments on several contracts to extend the title window of one of the league's best defenses, their cap bill came due in 2020. Stefon Diggs was the most famous of their losses, but the Vikings also jettisoned Everson Griffen, Linval Joseph, Stephen Weatherly, Xavier Rhodes, Trae Waynes, Mackensie Alexander, and Jayron Kearse. They picked up $37 million in dead money—more than four times their last-place figure from the prior two years—to make it under the cap (Table 1).

Table 1. Vikings' Dead Cap Money

Season	Dead Cap (Millions)	Rank
2018	$7.1	32
2019	$8.4	32
2020	$37.0	6
2021	$9.9	19

2021 dead cap as of July 1.

For most teams, the dismantling of a perennial top-eight DVOA defense would kick off a complete teardown and rebuild. That line of thinking likely influenced the team's decision to trade edge rusher Yannick Ngakoue—a trade acquisition just two months prior—after a hard-luck 1-5 start that included a pair of one-point losses to the Titans and Seahawks. But after a Week 7 bye, the Vikings rallied. And as they got back to a .500 record, they seemed poised to survive more losses. The team's lone free-agent splurge, defensive tackle Michael Pierce, had opted out of the season due to COVID concerns. Two-time Pro Bowl edge rusher Danielle Hunter suffered a neck injury in early September and missed the full season. Four-time Pro Bowl linebacker Anthony Barr tore a pectoral muscle in Week 2 and missed the rest of the year. Cornerbacks Holton Hill and Mike Hughes lasted just four games with their respective foot and neck injuries. All-Pro linebacker Eric Kendricks may have been the tipping point. His Week 12 calf injury robbed the defense of its captain and signal-caller and undoubtedly made jobs harder for injury-promoted backups such as Chris Jones and Todd Davis. And the team had no chance to survive the losses of all five of Davis, edge rusher Ifeadi Odenigbo, linebacker Troy Dye, cornerback Cameron Dantzler, and defensive tackle Armon Watts in Week 15.

Without knowledge of how those injuries would spiral, the Vikings entered the week with the hope of their remaining 15.2% playoff odds. Tied in record with their opponent Chicago, the Vikings could more than make up for their Bucs loss with a win that would effectively eliminate one of their two competitors for the seventh NFC playoff seed. But then Davis and Odenigbo went down, and Bears running back David Montgomery ripped off first-half carries of 6, 8, 9, 10, and 19 yards with a touchdown. The Vikings continued their third- and fourth-down misfortune, ending consecutive drives with a third-and-4 sack at midfield and a fourth-and-1 Dalvin Cook carry for no yards and a turnover on downs deep in their own territory.

Further front-seven losses in Dye and Watts propelled Montgomery to a career-best 146 yards, but Cook nearly matched him with 132. And after Trubisky stared down his intended receiver J.P. Holtz and threw an interception in the end zone, the Vikings had close to three minutes left in the fourth quarter to tie the game with a field goal or win it with a touchdown.

That dream was short-lived. Cornerback Duke Shelley tackled Cook by the shoestrings on a second-and-7 catch-and-run, saving a new first down and likely much more. With 1 yard to go on their own 29-yard line, Cook barely made it back to the line of scrimmage on third down. On fourth down, Cousins' play-fake did not fool Khalil Mack rushing straight up the middle. Cousins got a pass off, but in a backpedal and already 20 yards behind the line of scrimmage, he had no zip. The ball fell incomplete on the right sideline in a sea of Bears defenders.

That loss didn't mathematically eliminate the Vikings from playoff contention (we still gave them 0.8% odds), but it effectively ended the season in the disposition of their players. And even if their third- and fourth-down fortunes had reversed against the Bears, the likely different outcome would have been a pyrrhic victory. Down to backups (and backups of backups) on defense, the Vikings had to travel to New Orleans on short rest for a Christmas Friday game against the Saints.

Source 4 of likely 2021 regression: the sixth-ranked schedule strength DVOA (3.7%).

Schedule strength may be the least likely to regress of the Vikings' extreme 2020 tendencies. We project the team to once again have a top-10 schedule in 2021 with divisional draws of the NFC West and AFC North, home of four teams—the Seahawks, 49ers, Rams, and Ravens—with top-10 DVOA projections, plus two teams with ceilings to join them (Cleveland and Arizona) and the No. 1 projected defense (Pittsburgh). Still, their projected schedule is a lot closer to average (1.6%) than last year's real schedule because of the wide range of possibilities for each opponent. The Vikings could be one Aaron Rodgers injury (or forced trade) away from a dramatic change in their fortunes. And better internal injury luck would likely have helped the team handle its backload of difficult opponents at the end of 2020.

Given the reality of those injuries in Week 16, it was little surprise to see the No. 1-ranked Saints (28.5% DVOA) embarrass the Vikings with six Alvin Kamara touchdowns that inform many pessimistic 2021 perceptions of the team. In total, the Saints ran 45 times for 264 yards, seven scores, and 21 first downs in a 52-33 win. And it could have been even worse. Drew Brees was in his second start back from his myriad rib and shoulder injuries, and his arm strength had not returned. He threw a soft third-and-6 pass at the edge of the red zone midway through the second quarter and gave cornerback Harrison Hand (a fifth-round rookie playing defensive snaps for just the fifth time) a chance to undercut it for an interception. He threw high on a third-quarter first-and-10 pass in his own territory, and Emmanuel Sanders deflected the ball up where linebacker Hardy Nickerson (undrafted in 2017 and also playing on defense for just the fifth time that season) could intercept it. The Vikings might even have scored their way to a shootout win if they weren't plagued by the same mistakes they had made all season—Bailey missed an extra-point attempt, the Vikings later went for two because of it and failed, and Cousins took sacks on third-and-4 and a third-and-5.

The 2020 Vikings didn't suffer from poor luck in the facets of the game most famous for their year-to-year regression. They fell in the middle of the pack in both Pythagorean-win surplus (0.0, 16th) and fumble recovery rate (49%, 18th). But their relatively inconspicuous misfortunes on special teams, on third and fourth downs, with injuries, and with their schedule strength dealt the team damage you could see in the results of its most important games. And those facets are just as likely to revert to the mean in 2021 as the famous ones (Table 2).

Table 2. Vikings' Performance in Various Unsticky Stats, 2019-2020

Stat	2019 Value (Rk)	2020 Value (Rk)	Lg Y2Y Correl
Special Teams DVOA	0.8% (14)	-9.4% (31)	0.35
Made Kick% - Inside 50	91.4% (15)	83.3% (30)	0.25
Average Starting Field Position	29.6 (5)	26.0 (32)	0.23
Average Starting Field Position Diff	1.8 (9)	-6.7 (32)	0.25
Early - Late Down DVOA	-28.1% (31)	19.4% (4)	-0.03
Adjusted Games Lost - Def	13.9 (31)	64.8 (3)	0.20
Schedule Strength DVOA	-1.3% (20)	3.7% (6)	0.16

League year-to-year correlation coefficients calculated from 2009-2020 for all stats

The timing couldn't be any better. A failed 2020 playoff push may have disappointed their fans, but the Vikings likely saw it as an overachievement for their quiet rebuild. The flip side of the team's cap resetting has been an influx of draft picks from trades and as compensation for departed free agents. The team has made 26 draft selections the last two years. And whether or not Kellen Mond becomes the franchise quarterback higher picks like Justin Fields and Mac Jones are expected to be, the Vikings have the makings of another complete roster that can compete for Super Bowls with Cousins or another mid-level quarterback as their starter.

That 2021 roster should enjoy strengths on the offensive and defensive lines to rival the team's best years from the previous decade. Riley Reiff never lived up to his $58.7-million contract; even if first-round offensive tackle Christian Darrisaw faces a learning curve as a professional left tackle, he seems likely to improve upon his predecessor's 3.5% blown pass block rate from the previous four seasons. Third-round guard Wyatt Davis should contribute in his rookie season as well, especially with his physical approach as a run-blocker. But the team has recovered their depth so they won't have to rely on him Day 1. Ezra Cleveland and Dakota Dozier were capable starters in 2020 with 2.5% and 2.4% respective blown block rates.

With improved health, Danielle Hunter should reassert himself as a star defender. But he'll have some help from an influx of defensive line talent. Free-agent additions Dalvin Tomlinson and Sheldon Richardson plus COVID opt-out returnee Michael Pierce may mean more to the team than the Pro Bowl pass-rusher since they directly address the team's bigger weakness in run defense (1.9% DVOA, 30th). The same could be true on the back end, where even modest production from veteran addition Patrick Peterson would likely improve the team's 31st-ranked performance in coverage of opposing wide receivers (9.4 yards per target).

Adam Thielen and Justin Jefferson don't leave a lot of room for other skill-player breakouts, but third-year tight end Irv Smith ranked top-10 in efficiency at his position with a 23.5% receiving DVOA last year and should enjoy expanded opportunities with Kyle Rudolph departing for New York. Even if fourth- and fifth-round rookies Kene Nwangwu and Ihmir Smith-Marsette contribute little on offense, their returning acumen plus a new kicker in either Greg Joseph or Riley Patterson could turn special teams from one of the team's major 2020 deficiencies into a 2021 strength. Altogether, their additions from the draft, from free agency, and from injury returns could plexiglass the Vikings back into the top 10 in defensive DVOA and help make the Super Bowl push the previous iteration never managed to make.

Our projections aren't quite that optimistic. They expect a defensive rebound closer to NFL average and even fewer improvements on special teams. And, as previously discussed, they predict another difficult schedule. But even those conservative projections coupled with another top-10 projected offense nets the team 9.1 predicted wins. That isn't as many as it sounds like with the expanded 17-game season, but it's still enough to rank the Vikings in the top seven when it comes to playoff odds in our season simulation. Games against the NFC West give them a chance to earn a tiebreaker over the bulk of their likely wild-card competitors, and they even have a chance to settle the NFC North in their games with Green Bay. That success could sneak up on people distracted by the Packers drama. At least it could if Vikings fans weren't liable to sound a horn to announce their return to contention.

Scott Spratt

2020 Vikings by Week

Wk	vs.	W-L	PF	PA	YDF	YDA	TO	Total	Off	Def	ST
1	GB	L	34	43	382	522	-1	40.2%	39.4%	2.3%	3.2%
2	at IND	L	11	28	175	354	-2	-44.4%	-47.5%	-7.6%	-4.6%
3	TEN	L	30	31	464	444	-2	10.1%	1.6%	-16.6%	-8.1%
4	at HOU	W	31	23	410	386	1	13.2%	21.2%	2.5%	-5.4%
5	at SEA	L	26	27	449	314	-1	11.9%	17.9%	3.9%	-2.1%
6	ATL	L	23	40	365	462	-2	-50.5%	-42.6%	10.3%	2.5%
7	BYE										
8	at GB	W	28	22	324	400	1	20.3%	32.6%	6.8%	-5.5%
9	DET	W	34	20	487	421	3	25.7%	43.1%	-13.9%	-31.2%
10	at CHI	W	19	13	385	149	0	10.4%	-3.7%	-45.3%	-31.2%
11	DAL	L	28	31	430	376	-1	-4.8%	10.4%	7.7%	-7.5%
12	CAR	W	28	27	387	374	-2	2.8%	-7.5%	-9.7%	0.6%
13	JAX	W	27	24	420	390	2	-37.8%	-30.5%	-8.5%	-15.8%
14	at TB	L	14	26	335	303	-1	-48.0%	8.2%	31.4%	-24.7%
15	CHI	L	27	33	407	397	0	2.8%	21.2%	15.9%	-2.5%
16	at NO	L	33	52	364	583	2	-10.3%	29.7%	35.5%	-4.5%
17	at DET	W	37	35	508	417	2	-42.7%	3.7%	33.7%	-12.7%

Trends and Splits

	Offense	Rank	Defense	Rank
Total DVOA	6.3%	8	3.4%	18
Unadjusted VOA	7.2%	11	6.8%	23
Weighted Trend	6.0%	11	7.8%	26
Variance	7.5%	19	4.3%	14
Average Opponent	2.0%	25	5.0%	4
Passing	18.8%	11	4.7%	14
Rushing	0.7%	6	1.9%	30
First Down	20.2%	3	6.7%	23
Second Down	-2.2%	18	10.6%	28
Third Down	-9.1%	18	-15.0%	8
First Half	-1.7%	18	0.0%	18
Second Half	13.5%	8	7.3%	20
Red Zone	27.2%	6	-22.7%	1
Late and Close	7.9%	11	-1.0%	17

Five-Year Performance

Year	W-L	Pyth W	Est W	PF	PA	TO	Total	Rk	Off	Rk	Def	Rk	ST	Rk	Off AGL	Rk	Def AGL	Rk	Off Age	Rk	Def Age	Rk	ST Age	Rk
2016	8-8	8.6	8.9	327	307	+11	1.2%	18	-9.7%	26	-9.4%	7	1.5%	10	92.4	32	28.2	10	27.1	10	27.8	3	26.3	10
2017	13-3	11.7	12.3	382	252	+5	28.7%	2	12.5%	5	-17.2%	1	-0.9%	18	41.9	20	7.1	3	26.9	17	27.9	3	25.7	23
2018	8-7-1	8.5	9.2	360	341	0	10.5%	10	-1.2%	18	-12.6%	3	-0.9%	19	35.0	15	35.2	19	26.9	13	26.7	8	25.5	25
2019	10-6	10.8	10.7	407	303	+11	17.9%	7	4.8%	10	-12.3%	4	0.8%	14	11.7	3	13.9	2	26.3	23	27.2	5	25.7	20
2020	7-9	7.0	7.1	430	475	-1	-6.4%	20	6.3%	8	3.4%	18	-9.4%	31	18.6	5	64.8	30	26.7	16	26.0	23	25.8	21

2020 Performance Based on Most Common Personnel Groups

MIN Offense					MIN Offense vs. Opponents					MIN Defense				MIN Defense vs. Opponents			
Pers	Freq	Yds	DVOA	Run%	Pers	Freq	Yds	DVOA	Run%	Pers	Freq	Yds	DVOA	Pers	Freq	Yds	DVOA
11	28%	5.8	4.0%	32%	Base	49%	6.3	6.3%	58%	Base	35%	6.4	11.0%	11	56%	6.0	-2.5%
21	26%	6.9	12.7%	59%	Nickel	33%	5.8	11.2%	34%	Nickel	63%	6.1	-3.0%	12	19%	7.1	23.9%
12	22%	5.8	5.5%	32%	Dime+	15%	7.6	20.5%	12%	Dime+	1%	10.1	-67.6%	21	9%	6.2	4.1%
22	9%	5.8	11.9%	84%	Goal Line	1%	0.8	-8.2%	71%	Goal Line	1%	4.7	104.1%	13	5%	4.7	-39.0%
02	8%	9.0	42.5%	0%	Big	1%	5.1	20.7%	100%					01	2%	8.4	29.6%
13	3%	6.2	18.1%	64%										22	2%	11.1	60.6%

Strategic Tendencies

Run/Pass		Rk	Formation		Rk	Pass Rush		Rk	Secondary		Rk	Strategy		Rk
Runs, first half	45%	5	Form: Single Back	55%	32	Rush 3	4.9%	20	4 DB	35%	6	Play Action	29%	11
Runs, first down	50%	11	Form: Empty Back	13%	5	Rush 4	70.9%	9	5 DB	63%	14	Offensive Motion	43%	16
Runs, second-long	38%	1	Form: Multi Back	32%	2	Rush 5	19.4%	19	6+ DB	1%	27	Avg Box (Off)	6.89	3
Runs, power sit.	71%	4	Pers: 3+ WR	36%	32	Rush 6+	4.9%	17	Man Coverage	31%	17	Avg Box (Def)	6.45	25
Runs, behind 2H	32%	10	Pers: 2+ TE/6+ OL	45%	3	Edge Rusher Sacks	50.0%	18	CB by Sides	73%	16	Offensive Pace	31.38	26
Pass, ahead 2H	40%	28	Pers: 6+ OL	3%	9	Interior DL Sacks	26.1%	13	S/CB Cover Ratio	15%	32	Defensive Pace	30.03	14
Run-Pass Options	4%	28	Shotgun/Pistol	38%	32	Second Level Sacks	23.9%	14	DB Blitz	11%	22	Go for it on 4th	1.79	11

Although every team in the NFL had 11 personnel as their most common grouping last season, Minnesota was the only offense that used 11 personnel less than 40% of the time. 🏈 Minnesota only ran the ball 32% of time when using 12 personnel, the lowest figure in the league. 🏈 The Vikings zoomed up from 31st to fifth in using empty backfields. They had a strong 7.2 yards per play from empty, but a few fumbles helped drop them to a very average 8.4% DVOA. 🏈 For the second straight year, Minnesota was very high with 10.3 yards after the catch on targets at or behind the line of scrimmage. (This figure was 11.2 yards in 2019.) 🏈 The Vikings finished last by throwing only 9% of passes to targets we designated as "other wide receivers," i.e., not No. 1 or No. 2. 🏈 Minnesota ran a league-low 13 wide receiver or tight end screens, although they had an excellent 39.8% DVOA in this small sample. 🏈 Vikings receivers dropped only 18 passes, tied for second in the league. 🏈 After three straight years in the top five for both stats, Minnesota's defense finished "only" 10th in both yards allowed (6.1) and DVOA (-5.8%) when blitzing. 🏈 The Vikings had no gap between where their two safeties made their average play, suggesting interchangeable safeties instead of more defined roles as free and strong safety. Minnesota has been at the bottom of the league in this stat for a few years. 🏈 Minnesota finished second with 11 coverage sacks on defense, and more than half their sacks were "non-pressure sacks" (either coverage sacks or failed scrambles).

Passing

Player	DYAR	DVOA	Plays	NtYds	Avg	YAC	C%	TD	Int
K.Cousins	837	12.0%	552	4009	7.3	5.5	68.0%	35	11

Rushing

Player	DYAR	DVOA	Plays	Yds	Avg	TD	Fum	Suc
D.Cook	335	15.6%	312	1557	5.0	16	4	56%
A.Mattison	24	-2.8%	96	434	4.5	2	0	47%
K.Cousins	57	26.3%	24	163	6.8	1	1	--
M.Boone*	14	14.5%	11	59	5.4	1	0	73%
A.Abdullah	21	50.6%	8	42	5.3	0	0	63%
C.J.Ham	3	2.8%	5	18	3.6	0	0	60%

Receiving

Player	DYAR	DVOA	Plays	Ctch	Yds	Y/C	YAC	TD	C%
J.Jefferson	373	25.5%	125	88	1400	15.9	5.1	7	70%
A.Thielen	287	19.2%	108	74	925	12.5	3.3	14	69%
C.Beebe	1	-12.3%	30	20	201	10.1	3.7	2	67%
O.Johnson	45	18.0%	19	14	189	13.5	3.5	0	74%
I.Smith	92	23.5%	43	30	365	12.2	4.2	5	70%
K.Rudolph*	33	6.7%	37	28	334	11.9	5.9	1	76%
T.Conklin	11	-1.2%	26	19	194	10.2	6.6	1	73%
D.Cook	58	5.9%	54	44	361	8.2	10.0	1	81%
A.Mattison	53	52.9%	15	13	125	9.6	8.3	1	87%
C.J.Ham	47	46.2%	13	8	97	12.1	9.4	1	62%
A.Abdullah	25	31.5%	9	8	58	7.3	7.9	2	89%

Offensive Line

Player	Pos	Age	GS	Snaps	Pen	Sk	Pass	Run	Player	Pos	Age	GS	Snaps	Pen	Sk	Pass	Run
Garrett Bradbury	C	26	16/16	1082	3	2.5	15	20	Riley Reiff*	LT	33	15/15	1002	1	2	10	10
Dakota Dozier	LG	30	16/16	1082	9	3	16	9	Ezra Cleveland	RG	23	13/9	621	1	2.5	7	8
Brian O'Neill	RT	26	16/16	1069	8	5	15	7	Dru Samia	RG	24	13/4	272	4	3	13	4

Year	Yards	ALY	Rk	Power	Rk	Stuff	Rk	2Lev	Rk	OpFld	Rk	BB Rt	Rk	Sacks	ASR	Rk	Press	Rk	BB Rt	Rk	Cont
2018	4.29	4.09	23	58%	30	21%	25	1.16	23	1.02	9	14.1%	32	40	6.1%	9	34.1%	27	14.0%	32	31
2019	4.67	4.60	7	68%	11	16%	5	1.24	13	1.04	6	10.0%	14	28	6.7%	14	29.9%	16	14.0%	19	24
2020	4.88	5.07	1	57%	27	14%	6	1.43	3	0.83	11	13.7%	31	39	7.7%	26	31.7%	30	14.4%	26	27

| 2020 ALY by direction: | Left End: 5.76 (2) | Left Tackle: 4.62 (10) | Mid/Guard: 4.77 (6) | Right Tackle: 5.53 (1) | Right End: 5.52 (7) |

There's quite a dichotomy between the Vikings' No. 1 rank in adjusted line yards and their ranks in power success (27th) and blown blocks on running plays (31st). The Vikings specialized in runs where someone got charged with a blown block but Dalvin Cook or Alexander Mattison gained positive yardage anyway. They had 37 such plays; no other offense had more than 30. ● Riley Reiff cut his blown block rate on passes in half compared to his first three years with the Vikings, but it was still an easy decision for the team to cut him and free up $11.8 million in cap space. They may not even suffer in the transition since they snagged Virginia Tech tackle Christian Darrisaw with the 23rd overall pick after a trade down. Darrisaw is smooth and strong, though he has had struggles against edge rushers with finesse and speed. ● Darrisaw continues the Vikings' recent trend of heavy draft investment in their offensive line. But despite their rushing success, those draft picks have had mixed results. 2019 first-round center Garrett Bradbury declined from a 2.5% blown block rate as a rookie to 3.8% last year. And while he has an earned reputation as a poor pass-protector, he also blew more than twice as many run blocks in his second year (22 vs. 10) despite an almost identical total of run snaps. ● 2019 fourth-round guard Dru Samia blew 10.3% of his pass blocks in his first significant playing time in 2020. That was the worst of any offensive lineman with 100 or more passing snaps. ● Fortunately, 2020 second-rounder Ezra Cleveland looks like a hit after a 2.5% rookie blown block rate. Cleveland and third-round rookie Wyatt Davis (Ohio State) should start on either side of Bradbury and can try to prop him up where previous guards such as Pat Elflein and Dakota Dozier could not. ● Brian O'Neill was the vanguard of this revamped offensive line as a second-round selection in 2018. And while his 2.2% blown block rate in 2020 was no better than his three-year career rate, it makes him a capable starter at right tackle. If he or either rookie falters, veterans Rashod Hill and Dozier offer depth at tackle and guard after returning to the team on one-year deals.

Defensive Front

Defensive Line	Age	Pos	G	Snaps	Plays	TmPct	Rk	Stop	Dfts	BTkl	Runs	St%	Rk	RuYd	Rk	Sack	Hit	Hur	Dsrpt
						Overall						vs. Run				Pass Rush			
Shamar Stephen*	30	DT	16	663	34	4.1%	65	21	4	0	30	63%	82	3.1	83	0.5	2	6	1
Jaleel Johnson*	27	DT	16	655	44	5.3%	43	24	5	4	39	54%	95	3.9	97	1.5	0	1	0
Armon Watts	25	DT	16	392	31	3.7%	--	24	3	2	29	79%	--	2.3	--	0.5	1	4	0
Hercules Mata'afa	26	DT	13	293	24	3.6%	--	17	8	2	19	63%	--	3.5	--	2.5	2	11	0
Sheldon Richardson	31	DT	16	799	66	8.0%	4	39	16	3	51	55%	94	3.3	90	4.5	5	24	3
Dalvin Tomlinson	27	DT	16	656	53	6.1%	26	42	15	1	44	75%	47	1.7	14	3.5	6	11	7

Edge Rushers	Age	Pos	G	Snaps	Plays	TmPct	Rk	Stop	Dfts	BTkl	Runs	St%	Rk	RuYd	Rk	Sack	Hit	Hur	Dsrpt
						Overall						vs. Run				Pass Rush			
Ifeadi Odenigbo*	27	DE	15	697	35	4.5%	55	22	8	1	26	50%	95	3.8	86	3.5	10	19	0
Jalyn Holmes	25	DE	14	619	37	5.1%	41	27	6	5	30	73%	40	3.0	69	0.0	4	13	3
D.J. Wonnum	24	DE	14	471	24	3.3%	78	17	8	6	20	65%	72	3.1	70	3.0	6	14	2
Stephen Weatherly	27	DE	9	358	17	3.7%	70	11	3	5	15	67%	60	1.1	4	0.0	3	10	0

Linebackers	Age	Pos	G	Snaps	Plays	TmPct	Rk	Stop	Dfts	BTkl	Runs	St%	Rk	RuYd	Rk	Sack	Hit	Hur	Tgts	Suc%	Rk	Yd/P	Rk	PD	Int
						Overall						vs. Run				Pass Rush				vs. Pass					
Eric Wilson*	27	OLB	16	1035	128	15.4%	18	45	21	14	70	36%	86	4.9	76	3.0	5	6	36	53%	30	4.6	11	8	3
Eric Kendricks	29	MLB	11	755	113	19.8%	1	61	21	4	78	51%	60	4.1	44	0.0	1	12	29	66%	6	5.3	23	6	3
Todd Davis*	29	MLB	11	281	36	6.3%	79	17	7	5	22	41%	82	5.8	86	1.0	0	1	10	50%	--	4.6	--	2	0
Troy Dye	25	OLB	11	201	29	5.1%	--	10	0	4	19	37%	--	4.1	--	0.0	1	1	8	25%	--	8.1	--	2	0
Nick Vigil	28	OLB	15	312	43	5.9%	--	22	5	3	25	44%	--	5.8	--	2.0	0	0	12	58%	--	4.6	--	1	0

Year	Yards	ALY	Rk	Power	Rk	Stuff	Rk	2Lev	Rk	OpFld	Rk	BB Rt	Rk	Sacks	ASR	Rk	Press	Rk	BB Rt	Rk
2018	4.05	4.60	24	66%	17	16%	25	1.09	6	0.48	5	10.4%	8	50	9.3%	2	32.0%	9	14.4%	2
2019	4.39	4.60	25	49%	1	16%	25	1.13	12	0.71	14	11.3%	23	48	8.2%	5	30.4%	16	12.2%	27
2020	4.70	5.16	32	76%	31	10%	31	1.30	21	0.61	10	8.4%	31	23	4.8%	28	18.9%	32	7.4%	32

2020 ALY by direction:	Left End: 4.57 (18)	Left Tackle: 5.10 (28)	Mid/Guard: 5.22 (32)	Right Tackle: 5.84 (32)	Right End: 5.14 (27)

The Vikings will have a completely new defensive line in 2021 with free-agent additions Dalvin Tomlinson and Stephen Weatherly joining COVID opt-out Michael Pierce and injury returnee Danielle Hunter. Hunter is the biggest name there and deserves to be since his 59 hurries in 2019 were the fourth-most that season. But the Vikings may gain more from the Tomlinson and Pierce additions. They had run stop rates of 75% and 71% in 2020 and 2019, respectively. Armon Watts was the team's only regular defensive tackle with a rate better than 63% last season, and the defense as a whole had the worst adjusted line yards (5.16) and third-worst run defense DVOA (1.9% DVOA) in football. ✎ Hunter is returning from a cervical spine disc herniation, which sounds terrifying but seems not to worry the Vikings if you believe their interviews. What worries them instead is probably Hunter's reported dissatisfaction with his current contract and subsequent absence from OTAs. He did return for mandatory minicamp but is a threat to hold out for a new deal. ✎ The team planned for the future with third- and fourth-round draft selections of edge rushers Patrick Jones II (Pitt) and Janarius Robinson (Florida State), but that pair will likely need time to translate their tools into NFL production. Weatherly, meanwhile, is a complementary piece. He managed just six sacks and 45 hurries in his best two seasons with the Vikings before his 2020 dalliance with the Panthers. ✎ Linebacker Anthony Barr seldom matched the reputation that landed him four Pro Bowl berths with standout run stop or coverage success rates. He finished just 18th and 46th among linebackers in those rates in 2019, and then he missed the bulk of 2020 with a torn pectoral muscle. He was inching toward cut-candidate status until he agreed to a pay cut this offseason, telling *St. Paul Pioneer Press* reporter Chris Tomasson that he "didn't want that to be [his] last memory as a Minnesota Viking." ✎ If anything, Eric Kendricks is underrated. He has had identical 66% coverage success rates the last two seasons and finished in the top six among linebackers. Even with Barr returning, Kendricks will be a defensive keystone in 2021 in part because tackle machine Eric Wilson departed in free agency for the Eagles and in part as a mentor to third-round rookie Chazz Surratt. Surratt was North Carolina's quarterback before a junior year switch to defense. He'll need to improve his feel for his new position before his exceptional speed and athleticism makes him a capable NFL starter.

Defensive Secondary

Secondary	Age	Pos	G	Snaps	Plays	TmPct	Rk	Stop	Dfts	BTkl	Runs	St%	Rk	RuYd	Rk	Tgts	Tgt%	Rk	aDOT	Suc%	Rk	Yd/P	Rk	PD	Int
						Overall						vs. Run						vs. Pass						
Anthony Harris*	30	FS	16	1075	111	13.4%	9	31	13	10	60	23%	60	7.8	50	21	5.0%	62	16.5	62%	6	8.2	44	7	0
Harrison Smith	32	SS	16	1031	99	11.9%	24	27	16	8	46	30%	48	6.4	33	22	5.5%	57	16.3	41%	59	8.9	49	10	5
Jeff Gladney	25	CB	16	959	84	10.1%	18	33	14	17	30	53%	18	4.6	16	72	19.2%	44	9.9	42%	70	8.5	57	3	0
Cameron Dantzler	23	CB	11	601	50	8.8%	41	19	8	4	15	47%	31	2.4	1	59	25.1%	7	12.1	56%	19	6.9	28	4	2
Kris Boyd	25	CB	10	344	32	6.2%	--	11	2	6	8	75%	--	4.6	--	33	24.6%	--	10.3	39%	--	8.2	--	2	0
Chris Jones	26	CB	9	273	19	4.1%	--	5	1	5	1	100%	--	3.0	--	26	24.4%	--	11.0	31%	--	9.3	--	0	0
Holton Hill*	24	CB	4	255	27	13.0%	--	8	4	2	9	11%	--	8.0	--	23	23.1%	--	12.9	48%	--	9.3	--	3	0
Patrick Peterson	31	CB	16	1098	69	8.2%	51	21	10	9	20	30%	60	10.3	73	67	15.7%	72	12.5	43%	67	8.6	61	8	3
Xavier Woods	26	FS	15	989	73	9.4%	52	26	7	10	42	43%	27	7.1	39	18	5.2%	58	6.7	61%	7	5.4	9	1	0
Bashaud Breeland	29	CB	11	688	47	8.4%	47	20	11	11	14	29%	62	4.5	13	50	19.1%	45	13.1	56%	17	6.5	18	9	2
Mackensie Alexander	28	CB	13	642	53	7.9%	59	29	8	8	12	67%	3	5.8	31	47	18.0%	56	9.2	53%	31	7.6	40	6	1

Year	Pass D Rank	vs. #1 WR	Rk	vs. #2 WR	Rk	vs. Other WR	Rk	WR Wide	Rk	WR Slot	Rk	vs. TE	Rk	vs. RB	Rk
2018	5	-23.8%	3	-20.0%	6	-11.4%	9	-33.9%	1	-4.6%	11	22.6%	30	12.5%	27
2019	7	5.4%	21	-13.9%	6	17.0%	24	15.3%	28	-7.0%	7	-46.4%	1	-9.3%	11
2020	14	18.4%	28	-10.3%	9	7.8%	22	4.6%	20	7.9%	25	-15.3%	6	-24.4%	3

Minnesota's safety strength will likely take a hit in 2021 with Anthony Harris joining the Eagles in free agency. He was dramatically more effective in coverage (62% success rate) than former All-Pro Harrison Smith (41%) in 2020, and it's asking a lot for the latter 32-year-old to bounce back to his 62% and 65% rates from 2018 and 2019 when he was still in his twenties. At least Smith continues to make game-breaking plays. He had 16 defeats and five interceptions in 2020, the latter total tied for fourth-most in football. ✏ Xavier Woods will replace Harris on a modest one-year, $2.3-million contract that reflects the disappointment of his lack of interceptions for the Cowboys in 2020. Mike Zimmer would take that if he could have a repeat of Woods' 61% coverage success rate. Woods may fit better in Zimmer's defense with standout instincts and football intelligence but underwhelming physical traits. ✏ The Vikings will aim to offset any decline they see at safety with some major investments at cornerback. Those started last year with first-, third-, and fifth-round draft selections of Jeff Gladney, Cameron Dantzler, and Harrison Hand and continued this offseason with one-year $8.0-, $4.0-, and $1.1-million contracts for Patrick Peterson, Bashaud Breeland, and Mackensie Alexander, respectively. Peterson is the big name of the bunch with three All-Pro distinctions on his resume. His recent coverage rates haven't matched that standard, but his quotes this offseason paint him as invigorated by a new team that wants him—and ready to face his old team in Week 2. ✏ Peterson led the NFL with 14 penalties last year, including seven defensive holding calls (three declined). It's rare for a defensive player to lead the NFL in penalties, and Peterson had only four the year before (in 10 games). ✏ With Dantzler showing the promise of a 56% coverage success rate to match Breeland in 2020, it may seem odd to see that latter signing, which could push Dantzler to a rotation role. But the Vikings may also be hedging their bets as Gladney faces a case of alleged assault that would carry prison time if he were convicted. ✏ Fourth-round Cal rookie Camryn Bynum is likely not a corner investment. General manager Rick Spielman has already indicated he plans to switch the undersized but intelligent Bynum to safety like he did previously with Harris to great success.

Special Teams

Year	DVOA	Rank	FG/XP	Rank	Net Kick	Rank	Kick Ret	Rank	Net Punt	Rank	Punt Ret	Rank	Hidden	Rank
2018	-0.9%	19	-15.2	32	-1.5	23	1.2	10	5.8	8	5.3	5	-11.4	29
2019	0.8%	14	4.1	10	0.0	18	-1.4	19	6.9	6	-5.7	31	-2.8	20
2020	-9.4%	31	-15.5	32	-9.6	31	0.3	12	-13.7	31	-8.3	30	1.8	13

Dan Bailey is gone after the Vikings finished dead last in placekicking for the second time in three seasons, but he leaves $2.1 million in dead money on the Vikings' cap. His replacement will likely be either journeyman Greg Joseph or undrafted rookie Riley Patterson from Memphis. Patterson made a higher percentage of his kicks in 2019 than 2020 and has just average leg strength for kickoffs, but quotes suggest he has embraced an open competition and may hint at the necessary disposition to kick for a seemingly snake-bitten special teams unit. ✏ Ameer Abdullah has seen his kick return average decline from 25.8 to 25.0 to 23.5 yards per return in three years in Minnesota. He returned to the team on a minimal one-year contract, but he'll face competition for his special teams role from fourth- and fifth-round rookies Kene Nwangwu (Iowa State) and Ihmir Smith-Marsette (Iowa). Both rookies returned at least 50 kicks in their college careers. Nwangwu had the better 2020 return average of 28.9 yards, but Smith-Marsette bested him with a 28.7-yard career rate. ✏ Veteran punter Britton Colquitt lost nearly 5.0 net yards per punt from 2019 to 2020, and he had his contract restructured and faces competition from undrafted LSU rookie and 30-year-old former minor league baseball player Zach Von Rosenberg because of it. ✏ Neither Nwangwu nor Smith-Marsette returned punts in college, and so K.J. Osborn may get another crack at the team's return job in his sophomore season. Both Osborn and Chad Beebe had negative value on punt returns in 2020.

New England Patriots

2020 Record: 7-9	**Total DVOA:** -7.1% (3)	**2021 Mean Projection:** 9.8 wins	**On the Clock (0-5):** 6%
Pythagorean Wins: 7.2 (19)	**Offense:** -7.3% (23)	**Postseason Odds:** 62.4%	**Mediocrity (6-8):** 24%
Snap-Weighted Age: 26.9 (5)	**Defense:** 7.9% (26)	**Super Bowl Odds:** 9.9%	**Playoff Contender (9-11):** 41%
Average Opponent: 1.4% (12)	**Special Teams:** 8.1% (1)	**Proj. Avg. Opponent:** -3% (32)	**Super Bowl Contender (12+):** 28%

2020: There are things you can replace (and others you cannot).

2021: I will pay, day by day / Help is on the way.

Replacing Tom Brady was never going to be an easy task. So why not throw in a global pandemic that stripped the team of half of its defensive starters, too? You know, just for a challenge.

It would be easy to chalk up the Patriots' 7-9 record in 2020, their first losing season in the 21st century, to a complete and utter lack of manpower. On offense, replacing a franchise legend didn't go as smoothly as one might have hoped. New England didn't even sign their replacement starter, Cam Newton, until June 28, prompting a frantic replacement and rewriting of preview pieces and *Almanacs* across the league. Even under normal circumstances, learning an entirely new offense and gaining chemistry with a new set of receivers in two months would have been a Herculean task; doing it with contact limitations and virtual meetings was beyond impossible. Even if Newton had been able to stay healthy—never a guarantee for a player who hasn't really been healthy since 2016—the Patriots may well still have put up their worst offensive DVOA since 1999.

And on defense? Well, of course the Patriots couldn't match their 2019 highs, and not just because defense fluctuates more year-to-year than offense does. There was some fear that 2020 would see a massive number of COVID opt-outs, disrupting the integrity of the league, but most teams dodged that bullet. Not the Patriots! With a league-high eight opt-outs, three more than any other team, including four presumed starters, the Patriots had to shuffle to refill a defense that had already lost Jamie Collins, Kyle Van Noy, and Elandon Roberts in free agency. The Patriots entered the 2020 season with the biggest net Approximate Value over replacement lost on defense we had ever recorded (since 2003), and then followed that up with a league-high 69.0 adjusted games lost due solely to the pandemic, over twice as high as any other team. With that much loss of manpower, there's no wonder the Patriots couldn't live up to their 2019 numbers.

In fact, some would say, the plan was never to be competitive in 2020. As Bill Belichick himself said during the season, 2020 was "kind of the year that we've taken to … adjust our cap from the spending that we've had in accumulation of prior years. We just haven't been able to have the kind of depth on our roster that we've had in some other years." The lack of depth on the roster last season hampered the Patriots' renowned adaptability and versatility, both on offense and defense. There was no one on the roster who could supplant Kyle Van Noy as a three-down linebacker with the flexibility to play both off the ball and on the edge; no one who could run the defense as smoothly as Dont'a Hightower; and, of course, no one who lived and breathed the offensive system as much as Tom Brady, who dragged an offense severely lacking in receiving talent to a 14.9% passing DVOA two years ago. The idea that the Patriots were tanking is overblown, but New England knew it was in a bit of an awkward spot last season, and the Pats didn't press all their resources into competing right away. Instead, they ate the ninth-most dead cap, carried over the sixth-most cap room, and bided their time.

And so we welcome the 2021 Patriots and their wild shopping spree back to the ranks of contenders. Since the Super Bowl, the Patriots have inked over $320 million in new contracts, with more than $170 million guaranteed, and just under $140 million being paid out during the 2021 season. All of those numbers lead the league, most by significant margins. It's just not the sort of thing the Patriots do—they had spent less than average on free-agent contracts in six out of seven years since 2014. They have historically been very content letting players go before they get their second contracts, picking up bargain free agents who accepted lower deals to play for a perennial Super Bowl contender, and trusting their draft picks to fill in the gaps. The Patriots could have watched players such as Joe Thuney and Jason McCourty leave and opted to continue to clear their books, following in the footsteps of the Dolphins and Browns by sacrificing short-term success for long-term gains. (How's *that* for some teams the Patriots haven't been compared to in modern times?). Instead, they simply reloaded—and they got their first-round quarterback in the bargain as well. Who needs to tank?

There's very little doubt that the 2021 Patriots will be significantly more talented than their 2020 counterparts. In this chapter last year, we ran a table of the most net AV over replacement lost on defense in a single season. The 2020 Patriots topped that table, and accordingly saw their defensive DVOA go from -25.2% to 7.9%. This year, we can run the opposite table and, as you might expect, the 2021 Patriots will add more net AV to their defense than any team in recent history (Table 1).

This table deserves a slight caveat, because AV does tend to overrate off-ball linebackers. Hightower is likely not worth

2021 Patriots Schedule

Week	Opp.	Week	Opp.	Week	Opp.
1	MIA	7	NYJ	13	at BUF (Mon.)
2	at NYJ	8	at LAC	14	BYE
3	NO	9	at CAR	15	at IND
4	TB	10	CLE	16	BUF
5	at HOU	11	at ATL (Thu.)	17	JAX
6	DAL	12	TEN	18	at MIA

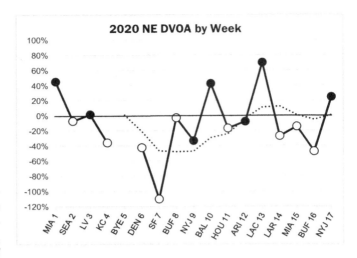

2020 NE DVOA by Week

twice as much as all these other players. However, considering all the struggles that the Patriots had finding replacements in their linebacker corps last year, it's fair to consider Hightower a crucial missing piece of the defense. And, anyway, even if you halved Hightower's value, the Patriots would *still* top the list.

And, of course, that doesn't include the complete restructuring of the passing game, with Hunter Henry, Jonnu Smith, Nelson Agholor, and Kendrick Bourne all penciled into the starting lineup. Nor does it include the return of Trent Brown to shore up the line, or a full complement of draft picks including quarterback Mac Jones. You may need a program to recognize all the players in New England this season, but the Pats have spared no expense trying to get this team back to contention, and quickly.

There's some evidence that the strategy could pay off. While spending gobs of money in free agency isn't a great way to build a long-term base, it frequently pays some immediate dividends. Since 2011, teams spending at least $50 million in cap-adjusted dollars in free agency saw an average improvement of 1.8 wins the next season and watched their DVOAs grow by an average of 11.8%. Since 2015, those numbers are even better: 2.9 wins and 14.7% DVOA (Table 2). There's obviously some selection bias here. Teams that were good the year before generally don't go out and dump millions of dollars on free agents. The average DVOA of the big-spending teams since 2011 was an uninspiring -12.9%, so we're talking a rebound back up to the vicinity of average. But for teams with a clear talent deficiency, especially at one or two key

Table 1. Biggest Net AV Over Replacement Gain on Defense, 2003-2021

Tm	Year	Net AV Change	DVOA Y-1	Rk	DVOA	Rk	Change	Players Added	Players Lost
NE	2021	+31	7.9%	26	--	--	--	D.Hightower (est. 14), M.Judon (7), K.Van Noy (5), D.Godchaux (est. 3), J.Mills (2), H.Anderson (1), H.Langi (1)	A.Butler (1), J.McCourty (1)
DET	2009	+22	20.9%	31	14.7%	30	-6.3%	L.Foote (6), P.Buchanon (5), J.Peterson (5), A.Henry (4), G.Jackson (3), K.Simpson (2), J.David (1), M.Manuel (1)	L.Bodden (2), P.Lenon (2), C.Redding (1)
NYJ	2015	+21	4.5%	22	-13.0%	6	-17.5%	D.Revis (11), A.Cromartie (6), B.Skrine (4), M.Gilchrist (3)	D.Landry (3)
KC	2005	+20	16.4%	30	-2.1%	14	-18.6%	P.Surtain (9), S.Knight (5), D.Washington (5), C.Hall (3)	S.Fujita (2)
DEN	2021	+19	-0.2%	13	--	--	--	V.Miller (est. 8), R.Darby (4), K.Fuller (4), S.Stephen (3)	NONE
HOU	2018	+18	3.4%	19	-9.7%	5	-13.1%	J.J.Watt (est. 10), W.Mercilus (est. 6), T.Mathieu (3)	M.Gilchrist (1)
DEN	2009	+17	21.5%	32	-8.6%	7	-30.1%	B.Dawkins (8), V.Holliday (5), A.Davis (4), A.Goodman (4), R.Hill (3)	D.Bly (2), E.Ekuban (1), M.Manuel (1), D.Robertson (1), N.Webster (1), J.Winborn (1)
DET	2003	+16	13.6%	29	2.6%	19	-11.0%	D.Bly (6), E.Holmes (5), A.Molden (4), W.Rainer (4), O.Smith (2), D.Wilkinson (2)	C.Claiborne (4), T.Lyght (3)
ATL	2006	+16	7.0%	26	-0.4%	13	-7.4%	J.Abraham (4), C.Crocker (4), G.Jackson (4), D.Jackson (4), L.Schulters (4), L.Milloy (2)	K.Carpenter (2), C.Lavalais (2), B.Scott (2)
TB	2014	+16	-6.3%	10	2.0%	19	+8.3%	A.Verner (9), M.Jackson (6), M.Jenkins (2), C.McDonald (2), M.Wright (2)	D.Revis (4), D.Te'o-Nesheim (1)
NYG	2009	+15	-6.6%	8	4.0%	21	+10.6%	O.Umenyiora (est. 8), R.Bernard (4), C.Canty (4), M.Boley (3)	J.Butler (4)
MIN	2005	+14	17.3%	31	0.3%	17	-17.0%	F.Smoot (7), P.Williams (6), D.Sharper (4), N.Harris (1)	B.Russell (2), C.Claiborne (1), K.Mixon (1)
KC	2019	+14	7.7%	27	-2.6%	14	-10.3%	F.Clark (7), D.Lee (4), T.Mathieu (4), E.Ogbah (4), A.Okafor (4), M.Claiborne (3), D.Wilson (1)	D.Ford (5), A.Bailey (3), J.Houston (2), S.Nelson (2), R.Parker (1)
MIA	2017	+13	3.8%	20	10.7%	28	+6.9%	L.Timmons (6), W.Hayes (4), T.J.McDonald (3)	NONE
AVG (Excluding NE/DEN)		8.6%	24	-0.2%	16	-8.8%		

positions—say, a receiving corps and off-ball linebackers?—a sudden injection of talent can provide some short-term relief.[1]

"Short-term" is the key word there, as loading up your roster with veterans can end up being a double-edged sword. The more players with large contracts you use to fill your starting lineup, the less cap flexibility you have in the future, and the fewer snaps your young prospects end up getting. The teams that turned their spending into longer-term contention, such as the Bills and Browns, generally did so by coupling that talent injection with a solid draft full of players to develop behind them, especially at quarterback. Those that didn't—see the Jaguars and Jets—saw a 10-win season that ended up unsustainable. That's more of an issue for future seasons, however. Your cash injection is your bump start, and your franchise quarterback and his draft class keep you from stalling.

And maybe we could leave the analysis there. Our projections have the Patriots rebounding to be an above-average team, led by a very good defense. They're in playoff position, thanks in part to a particularly easy schedule. They're not likely to really compete with the Bills for the division crown, but our models predict a return to respectability. And, of course, if Jones ends up as a massive hit, and the below-average offensive projection ends up underselling New England's potential, then we're talking about a team right back in contention after just one season. There's upside here.

All that is true on the surface, and no amount of criticism can refute the fact that the Patriots are, on paper, significantly more talented than they were a year ago. It would be a big surprise if they did not rebound from their worst DVOA since 1995. But there are a lot of question marks surrounding just how New England chose to spend their resources—who they paid, who they drafted, and how it's all going to fit together on the field. The hot take would be to either call this a savvy offseason from an unimpeachable mind, or a desperate attempt by a fading ex-dynasty to buy its way back into contention. We strive for slightly less spicy analysis here, so let's just say that we have a few questions.

Let's start on offense. Part of the logic behind teams improving via free agency is that if you spend so-and-so many millions of dollars, you're getting so-and-so much quality in return. That logic becomes a bit shakier when you dive into the details of the deals and see just who is making what. New England's heavily revamped receiving corps was not put together with value in mind.

The Patriots have been trying to rebuild their early 2010s two-tight end offense for a few years now, with diminishing returns. Despite using two 2020 third-round picks on Devin Asiasi and Dalton Keene, the Patriots ran only 23 snaps with more than one tight end on the field last season. Clearly set on bringing back big sets, New England went out and added both Henry and Smith, the top two tight ends available. That all makes sense and checks out. Henry's route-running ability is among the best in the league at the position, and Smith routinely features at or near the top of our YAC+ rankings. Both are versatile as well, splitting roughly half their targets lined up in tight and in the slot. That versatility is going to be a huge boost to the offense; they'll be movable chess pieces that will challenge opposing defensive coordinators throughout the league. It's not quite a return to the Gronk/Hernandez days, but Josh McDaniels will find plenty of creative ways to use his new weapons. They'll be a welcome return to form.

They're also costing the Patriots $12.5 million apiece, tied for the third-largest deals ever given to a tight end, and fifth-largest if you adjust for the rise in the salary cap over the past 20 years. The only tight ends to sign larger deals than Henry and Smith are George Kittle, Jimmy Graham, Rob Gronkowski, and Travis Kelce. Henry and Smith just aren't in that same category of player; they have the 14th- and 15th-most DYAR among tight ends over the last three seasons. Henry looked like he might be an elite talent in his first couple seasons in the league, but repeated knee and ACL injuries have knocked him down towards a top-10 player when healthy—still a solid piece, but not a spectacular one. Smith's advanced numbers have been sharper, but his jump in production in Tennessee correlated with the arrival of Ryan Tannehill. He has never topped 500 yards in a season, in part because of Tennessee's run-heavy offense. Don't get us wrong; having two top-15 tight ends is a remarkable weapon. The Buccaneers are the only other team in football to have that. But $25 million for Henry and Smith raises eyebrows.

Table 2. Most Cap-Adjusted Free Agency Spending, 2015-2020

Team	Year	APY	Wins Y-1	Wins	Dif	DVOA Y-1	DVOA	Dif
MIA	2020	67.7	5	10	5	-38.8%	4.6%	43.4%
BUF	2019	61.9	6	10	4	-18.6%	1.6%	20.2%
CHI	2017	61.7	3	5	2	-8.8%	-17.0%	-8.2%
CLE	2018	60.2	0	7	7	-28.7%	-3.3%	25.4%
CAR	2020	57.4	5	5	0	-26.5%	-6.7%	19.8%
KC	2019	57.3	12	12	0	33.2%	30.1%	-3.1%
NYJ	2018	57.0	5	4	-1	-19.2%	-17.0%	2.2%
NYJ	2015	55.3	4	10	6	-16.8%	11.7%	28.5%
OAK	2015	54.6	3	7	4	-29.5%	-0.6%	28.9%
JAX	2016	54.1	5	3	-2	-16.7%	-11.7%	5.0%
OAK	2019	54.1	4	7	3	-23.4%	-12.7%	10.7%
NYJ	2019	52.2	4	7	3	-17.0%	-17.7%	-0.7%
LV	2020	50.9	7	8	1	-12.7%	-6.2%	6.5%
JAX	2017	50.7	3	10	7	-11.7%	13.8%	25.5%
NYG	2016	50.6	6	11	5	-7.4%	9.4%	16.8%
AVERAGE			*4.8*	*7.7*	*2.9*	*-16.2%*	*-1.4%*	*14.7%*

APY (average per year) adjusted to 2021 salary cap, in millions of dollars.

[1] Note that eight different teams hit the $50-million mark in average annual compensation for new free agents this offseason, due in part to the expectation of a big TV deal pumping up future salary-cap numbers. The Patriots lead at $116.4 million, but the 49ers, Jaguars, Giants, Bengals, Washington, Jets, and Texans also hit $50 million.

But at least Henry and Smith were easily the top two tight ends available. Paying Nelson Agholor $11 million a year after one rebound season in the desert is a hard pill to swallow. Agholor's career has been as an inconsistent slot guy, with a history of critical drops and disappearing at the most crucial moments. Admittedly, the Raiders used Agholor differently than he had been used in Philly, much more as a deep threat rather than an all-around player, and you could conceivably argue that its possible Las Vegas found something that the Eagles never could uncork. Still, the Patriots are paying for the outlier here. If Agholor is as good as he was in 2020, he'll work as a deep threat, and if Henry returns to his pre-injury form, he'll be a deadly weapon over the middle, and if Smith's last two seasons aren't scheme/quarterback-induced, then he'll be great with the ball in his hands. If, if, if. These are gambles—logical gambles, defendable gambles, but gambles nonetheless.

And they're gambles that needed to be made because the Patriots have not had any real success drafting offensive weapons for years. Signing Henry and Smith signals throwing in the towel on last year's Asiasi and Keene selections; signing Agholor and Bourne in free agency became necessary because N'Keal Harry has been a non-entity. Rob Gronkowski is the last pass-catcher the Patriots drafted to top 1,000 career receiving yards; Julian Edelman was the last one the Patriots still had rostered. And the Patriots' draft struggles go beyond just skill positions. Through a combination of late draft picks (due to success on the field), stripped picks (due to DeflateGate and last year's filming snafu), and just poor picks, the Patriots rank 29th in the NFL in draft return over the past six years (based on career Approximate Value). That's what makes a $320-million spending spree necessary; when you can't get quality replacements for cheap, you have to find them in free agency. And without a Brady as a draw, you can't get quite the same bargains as you got half a decade ago.

And that brings us back around to the quarterback position. One reason the Patriots can afford to overspend around their roster is that they have the fifth-cheapest (per player) quarterback room in the league, thanks to a budget deal on Newton and a rookie contract for Jones. It seems likely at this point that Newton will begin the season as starter, but the future is obviously the first-round pick. There were rumors throughout the pre-draft process that the Patriots might make a move up the draft board to lock up one of the five first-round passers, so to sit still and get someone who was hyped up as the potential third pick in the draft at No. 15 seems like a pretty big coup.

Well, no, not really. There was a gap between Jones and the first four picks taken. Our QBASE model gives Jones a 9% chance of becoming an elite passer; the other four are all in double-digits. Jones has a predicted Total DYAR per Attempt of 0.04, so just over replacement level; it places him 44th among the 100 quarterbacks taken in the top 100 since 2004, sandwiched between Jameis Winston and Paxton Lynch. Jones does not have the arm talent of a top prospect, nor the athletic ability that strikes fear in the heart of defensive coordinators. Jones is the kind of prospect you would expect to see 40 years ago—a pocket passer who excels in accuracy and decision-making, who has to use every inch of his timing and anticipation to make up for borderline NFL-quality athletic profile. Jones has often been described as a high-floor, low-ceiling prospect—someone who will reliably play within the structure of an offense, won't put the ball at risk, and can keep a team moving as long as he stays in rhythm. That's more the profile of an Andy Dalton or Chad Pennington rather than someone who looks poised to elevate a team out of sheer talent alone.

To be clear, none of this is to say the Jones selection was bad. Jones went about where he should have, considering the positional importance of quarterbacks; this isn't a case of someone like Brandon Weeden or EJ Manuel going in the first round out of desperation. Belichick certainly doesn't take Jones if his good friend Nick Saban hadn't given him a stamp of approval. If Jones does reach Dalton/Pennington levels of performance, that's an above-average result for a pick in the middle of the first round. And, of course, no model is gospel; just check out the Buffalo chapter for more evidence of *that*. But when you see other teams shooting up the draft board for Trey Lance or Justin Fields, you have to wonder if the Pats were too passive, content to sit and take a quarterback that other passer-needy teams had let slide rather than make a bold move. Maybe in three years, we'll be sitting here talking about how Belichick outsmarted the league yet again, getting his guy without giving up anything to do it. Or maybe we'll be wondering why he couldn't beat the Chicago package to go up and get someone like Justin Fields, a move the Pats were more than capable of making. They spent all this money on a new receiving corps, they brought in Trent Brown and re-signed David Andrews to bolster their line, and they're giving the keys of their offense to the most milquetoast of the first-round prospects.

Defensively, the questions are far less prominent. It's not just the return of Hightower in the middle of the defense; the free-agent signings of Kyle Van Noy, Matthew Judon, and Jalen Mills; and a strong draft class led by Alabama's Christian Barmore. Our model also has the Patriots' defense bouncing back some due to the Plexiglass Principle, the idea that teams that significantly decline in one season tend to bounce back the next. These issues are intertwined, honestly. Part of the idea behind the Plexiglass Principle is that a significant shift in performance is based both on a change in underlying skill and a change in luck, and we would consider "a global pandemic that costs the team multiple starters" to be a significant change in luck.

In addition, the 2020 Patriots tended to be stronger in aspects of defense that correlate better year-to-year. For example, first-down run defense ends up being much more significant in projecting future success than third-down run defense, and New England's -1.4% run defense DVOA on first downs was significantly better than their 23.8% DVOA on third and fourth. That latter number helped contribute to their league-worst run defense last season, but it's the former that's more predictive going forward; New England would be unlikely to repeat their last-place finish even if they hadn't added so much talent during the offseason.

No, the Patriots biggest questions on defense affect the future more than 2021. Players such as Mills, Judon, and Davon Godchaux all fall into that serviceable-to-very-good slot, which is why they're going to be a boon to the Patriots this season. But the Patriots never used to have to pay quality free-agent prices for those kinds of players; they found draft gems or turned other teams' trash into treasures for a fraction of the cost. And if, for instance, starting Mills means less work for young players such as Kyle Dugger, getting adequate play today might hurt the team's chances of developing the next generation of starters down the road and thus do more harm than good. You want adequate veterans to put the finishing touches on a contending team, and we can no longer just assume the Patriots will be in contention year in and year out.

And that's rather the bottom line, isn't it? Our projections have the Patriots as contenders, and they should be in the mix in the AFC playoff race. But they're no longer the monsters at the end of the book; no longer the measuring stick the rest of the league holds themselves to. There's very little doubt the 2021 Patriots will be better than last year's model, and the talent influx in the receiving corps gives them a chance to have their best offensive season since 2017 or 2018. And perhaps we're being a little overly harsh with some of our criticisms, used to two decades of everything they touch turning to gold. It's difficult for any team to live up to the standards the Patriots set for themselves in the first 20 years of the 21st century. But there's a difference between making the playoffs and being a major contender for championships, and it looks like the Patriots are fitting firmly in the former category for this season. It's a positive first step after last year's disappointment, but the future remains shaky, at least by New England's standards.

Bryan Knowles

2020 Patriots by Week

Wk	vs.	W-L	PF	PA	YDF	YDA	TO	Total	Off	Def	ST
1	MIA	W	21	11	357	269	2	45.4%	34.4%	-19.3%	-8.3%
2	at SEA	L	30	35	464	429	0	-7.0%	27.3%	23.6%	-10.7%
3	LV	W	36	20	406	375	2	1.7%	15.9%	18.1%	3.9%
4	at KC	L	10	26	357	323	-3	-35.8%	-48.2%	-0.8%	11.7%
5	BYE										
6	DEN	L	12	18	288	299	-1	-42.4%	-67.5%	-13.9%	11.1%
7	SF	L	6	33	241	467	-2	-110.3%	-59.8%	52.8%	2.3%
8	at BUF	L	21	24	349	339	0	-2.9%	3.2%	11.9%	5.8%
9	at NYJ	W	30	27	433	322	1	-33.3%	20.8%	64.3%	10.2%
10	BAL	W	23	17	308	357	1	42.7%	46.4%	6.4%	2.7%
11	at HOU	L	20	27	435	399	0	-16.8%	5.9%	20.0%	-2.8%
12	ARI	W	20	17	179	298	-1	-7.9%	-50.1%	-18.2%	24.0%
13	at LAC	W	45	0	291	258	2	70.2%	-16.8%	-44.9%	42.2%
14	at LAR	L	3	24	220	318	0	-27.1%	-56.5%	-13.4%	16.0%
15	at MIA	L	12	22	303	383	0	-14.3%	-12.1%	16.8%	14.6%
16	BUF	L	9	38	201	474	0	-47.3%	-14.1%	32.3%	-0.8%
17	NYJ	W	28	14	404	350	2	24.9%	24.5%	7.5%	7.9%

Trends and Splits

	Offense	Rank	Defense	Rank
Total DVOA	-7.3%	23	7.9%	26
Unadjusted VOA	-4.0%	21	8.7%	26
Weighted Trend	-13.2%	26	6.3%	23
Variance	13.9%	32	7.7%	28
Average Opponent	-0.5%	12	0.8%	13
Passing	-10.6%	27	9.1%	18
Rushing	-1.2%	8	6.6%	32
First Down	-15.9%	26	14.6%	29
Second Down	10.9%	7	20.6%	30
Third Down	-20.1%	29	-26.6%	2
First Half	-17.1%	30	10.7%	28
Second Half	1.7%	13	5.0%	18
Red Zone	-16.5%	25	10.2%	24
Late and Close	12.2%	10	14.0%	26

Five-Year Performance

Year	W-L	Pyth W	Est W	PF	PA	TO	Total	Rk	Off	Rk	Def	Rk	ST	Rk	Off AGL	Rk	Def AGL	Rk	Off Age	Rk	Def Age	Rk	ST Age	Rk
2016	14-2	12.8	11.9	441	250	+12	25.1%	1	21.2%	2	-1.6%	16	2.3%	8	51.8	25	9.4	1	27.3	7	26.6	14	26.3	9
2017	13-3	12.0	10.8	458	296	+6	22.2%	6	27.9%	1	12.0%	31	6.3%	3	37.0	18	26.7	11	27.7	3	26.3	15	26.7	3
2018	11-5	10.8	9.9	436	325	+10	13.5%	7	14.7%	5	1.4%	19	0.1%	16	40.0	18	35.2	18	28.5	1	27.2	5	27.9	1
2019	12-4	13.1	12.3	420	225	+21	30.7%	3	4.3%	11	-25.2%	1	1.2%	11	69.7	30	11.4	1	29.3	1	28.2	1	27.9	1
2020	7-9	7.2	7.3	326	353	+3	-7.1%	22	-7.3%	23	7.9%	26	8.1%	1	83.5	31	51.3	23	26.4	23	27.3	3	27.5	1

2020 Performance Based on Most Common Personnel Groups

NE Offense					NE Offense vs. Opponents					NE Defense				NE Defense vs. Opponents			
Pers	Freq	Yds	DVOA	Run%	Pers	Freq	Yds	DVOA	Run%	Pers	Freq	Yds	DVOA	Pers	Freq	Yds	DVOA
11	54%	5.6	-7.7%	36%	Base	36%	5.3	-4.2%	68%	Base	5%	4.2	18.4%	11	60%	6.1	5.1%
21	37%	5.4	-5.1%	66%	Nickel	51%	5.5	-6.2%	38%	Nickel	47%	6.0	12.8%	12	23%	5.6	0.4%
20	4%	5.0	-3.1%	30%	Dime+	10%	6.1	-21.5%	19%	Dime+	47%	6.1	-0.2%	21	6%	7.3	46.2%
12	1%	0.8	-99.6%	46%	Goal Line	1%	1.1	55.2%	89%	Goal Line	1%	0.6	15.6%	10	3%	6.6	45.7%
10	1%	8.4	70.1%	11%	Big	3%	3.9	-7.8%	64%					22	2%	5.8	10.4%

Strategic Tendencies

Run/Pass		Rk	Formation		Rk	Pass Rush		Rk	Secondary		Rk	Strategy		Rk
Runs, first half	52%	1	Form: Single Back	65%	30	Rush 3	22.7%	1	4 DB	5%	31	Play Action	35%	4
Runs, first down	56%	4	Form: Empty Back	2%	32	Rush 4	55.9%	29	5 DB	47%	28	Offensive Motion	46%	14
Runs, second-long	32%	7	Form: Multi Back	33%	1	Rush 5	16.0%	26	6+ DB	47%	2	Avg Box (Off)	6.90	2
Runs, power sit.	82%	2	Pers: 3+ WR	59%	23	Rush 6+	5.5%	14	Man Coverage	40%	7	Avg Box (Def)	6.50	22
Runs, behind 2H	38%	3	Pers: 2+ TE/6+ OL	4%	32	Edge Rusher Sacks	56.3%	9	CB by Sides	55%	31	Offensive Pace	29.83	13
Pass, ahead 2H	37%	31	Pers: 6+ OL	2%	13	Interior DL Sacks	29.2%	10	S/CB Cover Ratio	26%	16	Defensive Pace	31.51	31
Run-Pass Options	5%	24	Shotgun/Pistol	53%	28	Second Level Sacks	14.6%	28	DB Blitz	13%	18	Go for it on 4th	1.51	17

Without Tom Brady around, the Patriots fell from the top of the league in situation-neutral pace. ✎ New England still isn't listening to the analytics people when they talk about running against light boxes. Last year, 44% of New England's runs came against boxes of eight or more, the highest figure in the league. The Patriots also ranked first in 2018 and were sixth in 2019. And yet once again, the Patriots weren't worse against these heavy boxes. In fact, in the context of the down-and-distance, they were a little better: New England had 5.0 yards per carry and -9.7% DVOA against seven in the box or fewer, compared to 4.6 yards per carry but a higher 1.3% DVOA against eight in the box or more. ✎ New England ranked eighth rushing the ball on third or fourth down but dead-last passing the ball. ✎ New England ranked first in the league with 29% of pass targets going to running backs. The Patriots called 42 running back screens, more than twice the NFL average of 20, and had 7.3 yards per play with 17.1% DVOA (compared to an NFL average of -9.9% on these plays). ✎ The Patriots rushed only three more than any other defense but they weren't particularly good when they did: 7.8 yards per play with 32.8% DVOA. New England had a strange split, with good defense rushing four (6.3 yards per play, -14.0% DVOA) but poor defense both when rushing three and when blitzing (8.0 yards per play, 23.3% DVOA). ✎ New England's defense broke down last year in many ways, but the Patriots stayed strong in a couple of important metrics. The Patriots are one of the best tackling teams every year and their charted total of 100 broken tackles was the fifth-lowest in the NFL. ✎ The Patriots also ranked fourth in DVOA against deep passes (16 or more air yards), where they were No. 1 in 2019. ✎ However, New England had the league's second-worst DVOA against play-action passes last season (40.0% DVOA with 8.6 yards per play). Only Tennessee was worse. Against non-play-action, the Patriots had above-average pass defense (-3.9% DVOA with 6.4 yards per play). ✎ The Patriots ranked No. 1 in pass defense on third downs. In every other down/play combination, the Patriots ranked 27th or worse. ✎ New England is not known as one of the top pass rushes in the league, but the Patriots were one of four teams with a league-high 31% pressure rate when bringing just the standard four pass-rushers. That's a good thing, too, because the Patriots allowed 6.3 yards per pass and -14.0% DVOA with four pass-rushers but 8.0 yards per pass and 23.3% DVOA with five or more pass-rushers. ✎ The Patriots are one of the league's least-penalized teams every year that they do not employ Brandon Browner. Last season, they had a league-low 72 penalties for only 534 yards. All other teams were above 80 penalties and 600 yards.

Passing

Player	DYAR	DVOA	Plays	NtYds	Avg	YAC	C%	TD	Int
C.Newton	-166	-17.7%	397	2462	6.2	5.2	66.1%	8	10
J.Stidham	-123	-50.5%	48	235	4.9	7.9	50.0%	2	3
B.Hoyer*	-91	-65.2%	26	112	4.3	3.7	62.5%	0	1

Rushing

Player	DYAR	DVOA	Plays	Yds	Avg	TD	Fum	Suc
D.Harris	102	9.9%	137	691	5.0	2	1	53%
C.Newton	44	-6.4%	125	572	4.6	12	5	--
S.Michel	94	19.9%	79	449	5.7	1	0	56%
R.Burkhead*	60	12.9%	67	274	4.1	3	0	55%
J.White	-27	-26.4%	35	121	3.5	2	1	37%
J.J.Taylor	13	7.0%	23	110	4.8	0	0	52%
G.Olszewski	8	-8.5%	5	23	4.6	0	0	--
J.Stidham	-7	-32.9%	5	9	1.8	0	0	--

Receiving

Player	DYAR	DVOA	Plays	Ctch	Yds	Y/C	YAC	TD	C%
J.Meyers	81	0.4%	81	59	729	12.4	3.7	0	73%
D.Byrd*	2	-12.3%	77	47	604	12.9	3.7	1	61%
N.Harry	-67	-27.8%	57	33	309	9.4	3.2	2	58%
J.Edelman*	12	-8.6%	39	21	315	15.0	3.0	0	54%
N.Agholor	277	28.0%	82	48	896	18.7	4.8	8	59%
K.Bourne	107	6.1%	74	49	667	13.6	4.5	2	66%
M.Hall	40	3.4%	32	18	302	16.8	3.2	2	56%
R.Izzo*	8	-1.8%	20	13	199	15.3	5.2	0	65%
D.Asiasi	-17	-39.4%	7	2	39	19.5	3.0	1	29%
H.Henry	27	-2.8%	93	60	613	10.2	3.8	4	65%
J.Smith	65	7.2%	65	41	448	10.9	5.8	8	63%
J.White	66	6.0%	62	49	375	7.7	8.4	1	79%
R.Burkhead*	42	8.4%	33	25	192	7.7	8.0	3	76%
S.Michel	64	101.5%	9	7	114	16.3	15.7	1	78%
J.Johnson	-6	-24.0%	9	8	35	4.4	2.5	1	89%
D.Harris	20	36.5%	7	5	52	10.4	11.0	0	71%

Offensive Line

Player	Pos	Age	GS	Snaps	Pen	Sk	Pass	Run	Player	Pos	Age	GS	Snaps	Pen	Sk	Pass	Run
Joe Thuney*	LG	29	16/16	979	3	1	6	3	Justin Herron	LT	26	12/6	351	0	3	5	2
Michael Onwenu	RT/RG	24	16/16	926	1	2	6	7	James Ferentz	C	32	7/2	161	0	0	1	1
Shaquille Mason	RG	28	13/13	782	2	0.5	9	6	Ted Karras	C	28	16/16	1068	3	0.5	6	13
David Andrews	C	29	12/12	724	1	1	6	5	Alex Redmond	RG	26	9/7	448	5	3	7	2
Isaiah Wynn	LT	26	10/10	640	2	3	9	2	Trenton Brown	RT	28	5/5	281	1	0	5	3
Jermaine Eluemunor*	RT	27	12/8	419	1	4	7	5									

Year	Yards	ALY	Rk	Power	Rk	Stuff	Rk	2Lev	Rk	OpFld	Rk	BB Rt	Rk	Sacks	ASR	Rk	Press	Rk	BB Rt	Rk	Cont
2018	4.24	5.03	3	58%	29	16%	4	1.19	21	0.63	25	2.9%	2	21	3.8%	1	22.9%	1	4.8%	1	31
2019	3.90	4.49	9	65%	17	21%	24	1.19	16	0.49	28	8.2%	5	28	5.3%	5	24.7%	2	14.9%	25	28
2020	4.82	4.94	3	78%	4	14%	3	1.38	4	0.81	13	6.7%	2	37	8.0%	28	25.2%	18	10.4%	9	27

2020 ALY by direction:	Left End: 4.58 (13)	Left Tackle: 5.09 (4)	Mid/Guard: 4.94 (2)	Right Tackle: 4.69 (9)	Right End: 5.61 (5)

Sacks are heavily influenced by quarterback. As much as we can adjust for situation and opponent, there is no formula in adjusted sack rate that can account for going from Tom Brady to Cam Newton. That's a lot of the reason the Patriots dropped to 28th after finishing in the top five the previous two years. ◥ Welcome back (again) Isaiah Wynn. Wynn has only managed to play 18 of 48 regular season games since he was drafted, but he has been very good when actually on the field; a major bully in run blocking who can hold his own in pass protection as well. He was missed. ◥ Also missed: Trent Brown, back after two seasons with the Raiders. Brown remains dominant when he's on the field, but he missed 16 out of 32 games with the Raiders with calf, pectoral, and knee injuries, plus complications with COVID and an air embolism. ◥ Our own Ben Muth argued that Michael Onwenu should have garnered Rookie of the Year consideration. While a lineman is never going to win that award, Onwenu had good-to-great level of play at right tackle and both guard positions; he gave New England tons of flexibility when rebuilding their line. He's expected to replace Joe Thuney at left guard this season. ◥ David Andrews' return after missing all of 2019 didn't always go smoothly; his 1.6% blown block rate was his worst since 2017. A thumb injury was at least partially to blame, and the Patriots are fortunate to get him back on a comparatively budget deal. ◥ Shaq Mason's run-blocking is better than his blown block total would indicate. He's a beast, moving people out of the way with ease. He's a big reason the Patriots had the second-best ALY up the gut, and you can count the better run-blocking guards in the league on one hand with fingers left over.

Defensive Front

Defensive Line	Age	Pos	G	Snaps	Plays	TmPct	Overall Rk	Stop	Dfts	BTkl	Runs	St%	vs. Run Rk	RuYd	Rk	Sack	Hit	Pass Rush Hur	Dsrpt
Lawrence Guy	31	DT	14	505	57	8.1%	2	39	5	2	51	69%	65	2.8	64	2.0	5	12	0
Adam Butler*	27	DT	15	483	36	4.8%	54	23	10	2	26	62%	84	3.2	85	4.0	3	21	5
Byron Cowart	25	DT	14	420	28	4.0%	67	20	5	1	24	71%	54	2.2	39	1.0	2	5	0
Henry Anderson	30	DE	16	549	42	4.8%	52	29	11	4	40	70%	60	1.7	16	0.5	3	13	0
Montravius Adams	26	DE	8	130	11	2.7%	--	9	2	1	11	82%	--	1.7	--	0.0	0	2	0

Edge Rushers	Age	Pos	G	Snaps	Plays	TmPct	Overall Rk	Stop	Dfts	BTkl	Runs	St%	vs. Run Rk	RuYd	Rk	Sack	Hit	Pass Rush Hur	Dsrpt
John Simon*	31	DE	16	702	56	7.0%	11	32	5	7	37	57%	87	3.1	72	2.0	2	10	3
Chase Winovich	26	DE	16	594	46	5.7%	29	28	11	6	31	58%	84	3.8	87	5.5	7	39	2
Deatrich Wise	27	DE	16	565	49	6.1%	24	25	3	0	42	52%	93	4.0	93	2.5	10	20	2
Shilique Calhoun*	29	OLB	10	257	18	3.6%	75	7	5	2	11	18%	97	4.6	95	2.0	1	6	0
Kyle Van Noy	30	OLB	14	811	75	10.7%	1	42	17	13	44	52%	94	4.5	94	6.0	4	21	2
Matt Judon	29	OLB	14	563	52	7.2%	9	35	18	2	26	81%	11	2.8	56	6.0	15	26	3

Linebackers	Age	Pos	G	Snaps	Plays	TmPct	Overall Rk	Stop	Dfts	BTkl	Runs	St%	vs. Run Rk	RuYd	Rk	Sack	Hit	Pass Rush Hur	Tgts	Suc%	vs. Pass Rk	Yd/P	Rk	PD	Int
Ja'Whaun Bentley	25	MLB	13	609	93	14.2%	31	43	11	7	61	51%	63	3.8	36	1.5	2	5	12	58%	16	3.6	4	2	0
Anfernee Jennings	24	OLB	14	292	20	2.8%	--	9	0	4	14	43%	--	4.6	--	0.0	2	6	4	25%	--	6.3	--	0	0
Terez Hall	25	MLB	8	260	52	12.9%	42	24	3	6	29	52%	59	4.4	57	0.0	0	2	11	55%	--	6.5	--	2	0
Josh Uche	23	OLB	9	178	9	2.0%	--	5	4	3	6	50%	--	3.5	--	1.0	6	11	0	0%	0	0.0	0	0	0
Harvey Langi	29	ILB	14	513	58	7.6%	71	32	7	10	28	68%	11	3.7	34	0.0	1	8	21	48%	48	6.1	32	1	0
Raekwon McMillan	26	MLB	16	169	24	2.9%	--	12	2	6	18	61%	--	7.2	--	0.0	0	0	3	67%	--	10.3	--	1	0

Year	Yards	ALY	Rk	Power	Rk	Stuff	Rk	2Lev	Rk	OpFld	Rk	BB Rt	Rk	Sacks	ASR	Rk	Press	Rk	BB Rt	Rk
2018	4.79	4.67	26	67%	18	16%	24	1.31	23	0.91	19	2.1%	32	30	5.0%	30	33.0%	6	7.0%	29
2019	4.06	3.99	6	60%	10	18%	20	1.00	5	0.68	13	8.3%	31	47	7.7%	8	37.1%	1	16.3%	6
2020	4.65	5.00	31	75%	30	10%	32	1.33	25	0.55	7	9.0%	30	24	5.2%	26	28.9%	8	12.7%	20
2020 ALY by direction:			Left End: 5.02 (24)			Left Tackle: 5.32 (30)			Mid/Guard: 4.66 (23)				Right Tackle: 5.36 (27)				Right End: 6.03 (31)			

Only Denver ran more plays with only two down linemen than New England did last year. The Patriots added a bunch of new linemen in free agency, so more three-linemen sets appear to be in the cards. ● Matt Judon has had at least six sacks in each of the past four years. The last Patriots to do that were Chandler Jones and Rob Ninkovich in 2012-2015. ● Kyle Van Noy's pressure numbers dropped in Miami, mostly because Brian Flores was using him less as a pass-rusher and more frequently in coverage. He was just as efficient on a per-play basis, so expect Bill Belichick to send him rushing more often in 2021. ● Consistency, thy name is Lawrence Guy. Guy's one of six players to have at least 35 run stops in each of the past four years, and the other five guys are all rangy linebackers, not linemen. ● Henry Anderson becomes the Patriots' top run defender; he was third in ESPN's run stop win rate among defensive tackles in 2020. ● Davon Godchaux had become expendable in Miami, but he can play; his 45 run stops in 2019, his last healthy season, led all defensive tackles. ● Dont'a Hightower opted out of 2020, and he was missed. The Patriots didn't really have another linebacker who could handle both playing off the ball and on the edge, leading to a committee approach to replace him. Ja'Whaun Bentley found himself thrust into the heart of the defense and wasn't quite up to the task; he was alright in pass coverage, but often ran himself out of plays in run defense. ● Not all of second-round pick Christian Barmore's games were as dominant as his performances for Alabama in the College Football Playoff, but when he turns it on, he's a wrecking ball. He projects as a very strong interior pass-rushing force, though only one season as a starter means we're scouting from a limited sample size. ● Ronnie Perkins, a third-round pick from Oklahoma, had the second-lowest SackSEER projection this year. His big problem is size; at just 253 pounds, he's probably going to have to stand up in the pros. He's more motor and effort than raw talent, though Belichick usually finds a way to use those kinds of guys. ● Fifth-round pick Cam McGrone (Michigan) tore his ACL in November; he'll almost assuredly sit out all of 2021.

Defensive Secondary

Secondary	Age	Pos	G	Snaps	Plays	TmPct	Rk	Stop	Dfts	BTkl	Runs	St%	Rk	RuYd	Rk	Tgts	Tgt%	Rk	aDOT	Suc%	Rk	Yd/P	Rk	PD	Int
Devin McCourty	34	FS	16	962	74	9.2%	56	14	8	7	34	15%	67	10.0	63	18	5.1%	60	12.7	28%	70	10.1	59	6	2
J.C. Jackson	26	CB	16	853	54	6.7%	73	27	12	7	8	50%	24	7.6	51	70	22.2%	19	12.9	54%	27	8.4	56	14	9
Adrian Phillips	29	SS	16	747	111	13.8%	7	45	18	8	63	46%	21	4.8	10	23	8.3%	38	6.1	48%	41	7.9	40	4	2
Jonathan Jones	28	CB	16	729	77	9.6%	22	30	14	10	21	29%	62	9.6	71	71	26.3%	4	10.7	54%	30	6.2	11	6	2
Jason McCourty*	34	CB	16	666	44	5.5%	80	9	6	2	17	18%	76	10.1	72	35	14.2%	77	12.9	49%	52	10.0	78	3	0
Stephon Gilmore	31	CB	11	633	40	7.2%	67	12	5	9	13	23%	69	5.6	29	40	17.1%	65	11.0	53%	35	7.7	42	3	1
Kyle Dugger	25	SS	14	520	59	8.4%	62	27	10	9	29	52%	12	3.9	3	24	12.5%	11	8.4	54%	23	8.0	41	0	0
Terrence Brooks*	29	SS	14	254	20	2.8%	--	5	3	3	10	30%	--	5.5	--	11	11.7%	--	15.0	27%	--	12.5	--	0	0
Myles Bryant	23	FS	9	156	11	2.4%	--	3	3	2	6	33%	--	6.0	--	5	8.7%	--	10.4	40%	--	6.0	--	1	1
Jalen Mills	27	SS	15	1012	77	9.7%	46	36	14	10	41	59%	6	6.7	35	46	12.8%	7	10.0	52%	30	7.3	27	3	1

Year	Pass D Rank	vs. #1 WR	Rk	vs. #2 WR	Rk	vs. Other WR	Rk	WR Wide	Rk	WR Slot	Rk	vs. TE	Rk	vs. RB	Rk
2018	13	0.0%	16	-6.1%	12	-17.4%	5	-14.0%	7	-2.5%	15	-12.8%	8	9.5%	22
2019	1	-34.5%	1	-49.9%	1	-40.1%	1	-46.3%	2	-38.4%	1	-10.6%	7	3.5%	21
2020	18	-13.9%	7	-2.8%	14	-3.3%	13	-10.9%	8	-3.7%	15	-11.8%	9	-6.8%	10

They may not have been up to 2019 levels, but the Patriots were one of just three teams to have negative DVOAs against all types of receivers: No. 1s, No. 2s, other wideouts, tight ends, and running backs. ✎ Stephon Gilmore had a down year in essentially all his advanced stats. That doesn't mean he wasn't important, however; the Patriots pass defense DVOA dropped from -1.4% to 34.9% in the games he missed. ✎ J.C. Jackson had a fantastic year, but he also was a bit boom-and-bust. His nine interceptions were second in the league, but he also allowed five touchdowns; he allowed the highest yards per target of any corner with at least four interceptions. ✎ Jonathan Jones' 6.2 yards allowed per pass was second-fewest among corners who lined up at least 60% of the time in the slot. ✎ Devin McCourty's 28% success rate was second-lowest among safeties. There's some sample-size bias there, though; he was only charted with 18 pass targets, fewest in his career. ✎ Adrian Phillips continues to be listed as a safety, but he was really more of a pure off-ball linebacker in 2020. With New England adding so much beef to the front seven in free agency, it wouldn't be surprising to see Phillips play more as a jack-of-all-trades defensive back in 2021. ✎ Jalen Mills routinely finished below a 50% success rate as a corner, even when he was healthy, so the Eagles tried him as a strong safety/slot corner hybrid instead. So far, so good; Mills played all over the defense last season and had much better numbers handling slot receivers and tight ends than he ever did on the boundaries.

Special Teams

Year	DVOA	Rank	FG/XP	Rank	Net Kick	Rank	Kick Ret	Rank	Net Punt	Rank	Punt Ret	Rank	Hidden	Rank
2018	0.1%	16	0.1	17	-8.7	32	5.3	5	4.5	10	-0.6	17	8.5	8
2019	1.2%	11	-9.7	30	5.0	7	-0.9	15	10.5	3	1.2	11	6.9	4
2020	8.1%	1	5.6	9	5.2	6	-2.6	20	18.9	1	13.5	1	-5.2	22

The Patriots have had a positive special teams DVOA every season since 1996, but 2020 was the first year they've ever finished first overall. ✎ The Patriots' punt unit allowed just 12 returns all year long, tied for the fewest since the 2008 Patriots allowed 11, and the fewest for a team with a losing record since the 1982 Bills allowed 10 … in a nine-game season. You don't run against Jake Bailey, Matthew Slater, and the rest of the Patriots' punt unit. (Although it was Justin Bethel, not Slater, who led the Patriots special teams with 14 tackles.) ✎ Nick Folk's 92.9% field goal rate was a new personal best, though he didn't break his personal record for value added with only 28 attempts to his name. ✎ Gunner Olszewski didn't just lead the league in punt return value; he had twice as much value as anyone else. He was only the fourth player in history to average at least 17 yards per punt return on at least 20 returns, the minimum needed to qualify for the NFL's leaderboards.

New Orleans Saints

2020 Record: 12-4	**Total DVOA:** 33.3% (2)	**2021 Mean Projection:** 9.5 wins	**On the Clock (0-5):** 8%
Pythagorean Wins: 11.4 (2)	**Offense:** 10.7% (7)	**Postseason Odds:** 57.6%	**Mediocrity (6-8):** 27%
Snap-Weighted Age: 27.3 (1)	**Defense:** -19% (2)	**Super Bowl Odds:** 9.0%	**Playoff Contender (9-11):** 41%
Average Opponent: 0.6% (15)	**Special Teams:** 3.6% (5)	**Proj. Avg. Opponent:** -0.2% (19)	**Super Bowl Contender (12+):** 24%

2020: How to Recognize Different Types of Playoff Losses from Quite a Long Way Away.

2021: ... and Now for Something Completely Different.

The careers of long-time franchise quarterbacks conclude in many different ways. Everybody dreams of a finale like John Elway, riding off into the sunset as a multiple-time champion at the peak of your profession. If not Elway, then Peyton Manning: an aging, splintered sensei, his time obviously at an end, carried home one final time by his heroic comrades-in-arms. Most would be satisfied with an outcome like Tom Brady's in New England, a champion in his penultimate season who returned for one last failed attempt at enhancing an untouchable legacy, before moving on to further success elsewhere.

The only player to top all three in career passing yards, Drew Brees, was not so fortunate. After a pair of superb drafts and some smart free-agency decisions helped them rediscover the lost art of defense in 2017, Brees and the Saints began each of the past three seasons amid the clutch of NFC favorites with arguably the most complete roster in the conference. They won at least 12 games each of those years, winning the NFC South at such a canter that it defies belief that it was their first-ever streak of division wins. Only Tampa Bay last season pushed them beyond the start of December, and the Saints swept that Buccaneers squad in the regular season by a combined score of 72-26. New Orleans finished either first or second in DVOA every year from 2017 to 2020, and its average of 31.6% DVOA was easily the highest in the league. Nobody has been better in the regular season over the last four years.

Yet for all the regular-season dominance, a series of initially incredible but increasingly predictable playoff losses left them with only a single NFC Championship Game appearance to show for four years of outstanding play. Only once in the history of the franchise have the Saints won multiple playoff games in a single season: 2009, the year they won the Super Bowl. Thanks in part to the franchise's best defense since 1992, the most recent squad was better than that one. It wasn't enough, in part because of the randomness inherent in one-and-done postseason play; in part because even in the NFC, Tom Brady trumps everything. (Brady, we should note, has one more playoff win over NFC opponents than Brees does despite only playing a single year in the actual NFC playoff bracket.)

If recent history is any indication, Brees' retirement probably brings an end to the most successful period in franchise history. Since free agency was introduced in 1993, the Saints will be the 10th different franchise to replace a quarterback who played at least 10 seasons with them and either has been or is a nailed-on certainty to be inducted into the Hall of Fame. (We are steadfastly *not* getting into Eli Manning or related debates here.) The previous nine averaged 10.8 wins in their quarterback's final season as the primary starter[1], with Troy Aikman's 5-11 2000 Cowboys the only side that did not have a winning record (Table 1). On average, these teams won 4.3 fewer games the following year, falling from 11-5 to an average of 6-9-1. Only Andrew Luck's 2012 Colts and Jay Fiedler's 2000 Dolphins had a winning record in the first season without their respective Hall of Famers. The 2020 Patriots, the first Patriots side to finish under nine wins since the Y2K bug was the major global crisis, had the third-*best* record on that list.

DVOA paints a more detailed but equally discouraging picture. The nine teams on our list averaged an overall DVOA of 13.5% in their franchise player's final season. That average dropped to -5.6% the following year. The post-Dan Marino Dolphins were the only team to improve: they were slightly better on offense, leapt to No. 3 in defense, and finished No. 1 in special teams in their first season under Dave Wannstedt. Every other team declined, both on offense and in total DVOA. The Troy Aikman Cowboys, at -14.7% overall DVOA, were by a country mile the worst of the teams in their franchise quarterback's final year, yet still declined by 6.3 percentage points the following season. Everybody else declined by at least 11 percentage points, producing an average decline of -19.1%. That effect was not only seen on offense, either: the average decline on offense was -11.5%, but it was also +6.4% on defense (remember, higher DVOA means more yards and points, so defensive DVOA increasing is bad). It turns out that not only are Hall of Fame quarterbacks extremely difficult to replace, but having one paints over a multitude of cracks that suddenly become visible when he leaves.

---

[1] This qualifier is necessary. It's no use comparing the 2011 Colts, for whom Peyton Manning missed the full year after neck surgery and Curtis Painter started most of the games, with Andrew Luck's rookie year. The same goes for 1999, when Steve Young missed 13 games. In both cases, we've compared the quarterback's final year as the primary starter with the year after they left, when the team was no longer built around them.

2021 Saints Schedule

Week	Opp.	Week	Opp.	Week	Opp.
1	GB	7	at SEA (Mon.)	13	DAL (Thu.)
2	at CAR	8	TB	14	at NYJ
3	at NE	9	ATL	15	at TB
4	NYG	10	at TEN	16	MIA (Mon.)
5	at WAS	11	at PHI	17	CAR
6	BYE	12	BUF (Thu.)	18	at ATL

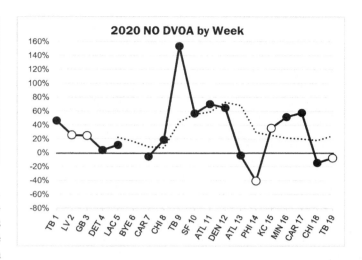

It's easy to see how the same fate could befall the Saints. The salary-cap issues created by Brees' retirement, the lowered cap due to COVID, and a practice of shoveling cap hits into future years meant the Saints began this offseason in the worst cap shape of any team, millions over the ceiling with several high-priority free agents to retain and a draft class to sign. They were able to retain their key priorities—safety Marcus Williams and quarterback Jameis Winston—and get under the cap, but at considerable cost elsewhere on the roster.

Out go last year's second- and third-leading receivers, Emmanuel Sanders and Jared Cook. Other cap casualties include defensive starters Kwon Alexander, Malcom Brown, and Janoris Jenkins. The team could not afford to bring back 13.5-sack breakout edge rusher Trey Hendrickson, who is now in Cincinnati. Sheldon Rankins (New York Jets) and Alex Anzalone (Detroit) were also valuable contributors who went elsewhere as free agents. Retired blocking tight end Josh Hill and new Chiefs fullback Michael Burton are lesser lights, but Hill played one-third of the team's offensive snaps and both players contributed extensively on special teams. Other core special-teamers also departed, including gunner Justin Hardee (New York Jets), special teams captain Craig Robertson, and beloved punter Thomas Morstead (both still unsigned). Even counting Alexander and Anzalone as a single starter lost since one replaced the other in-season, the Saints lost eight starters and a lot of veteran depth.

In their place, the Saints signed only their draft class and a handful of low-priced veteran free agents. Former Seahawks and Steelers tight end Nick Vannett arrives as a direct replacement for Hill, former Panthers fullback Alex Armah replaces Burton, and former Chiefs defensive end Tanoh Kpassagnon pads the edge rotation a little. Every other hole will be filled either by a rookie or from the existing depth chart. Payton Turner (Houston) is the team's latest developmental first-round edge rusher, while second-round rookie Pete Werner (Ohio State) and 2020 third-round pick Zack Baun will fill the roles vacated by Alexander and Anzalone. At outside cornerback, veteran Patrick Robinson is the most likely opening-day starter, but Robinson will be 34 by then and has missed time in every season since returning to New Orleans in 2018. That means third-round pick Paulson Adebo (Stanford), once touted as a potential first-rounder, may be in the lineup sooner rather than later.

At receiver, the departure of Sanders leaves Michael Thomas once again as the only established target. This is not an unfamiliar issue for Saints fans: they haven't had more than one wide receiver reach 500 receiving yards since Ted Ginn played alongside Thomas in 2017. Still, this year's crop is particularly green. Now that Sanders is in Buffalo, the presumptive second starter is Tre'Quan Smith: a perennial fantasy breakout pick with a knack for touchdown catches, who

Table 1. After Long-Time Hall of Fame Quarterbacks Leave

Tm	Player	Years	Final Season	W-L	Total DVOA	Off DVOA	Def DVOA	W-L Y+1	Total DVOA Y+1	Off DVOA Y+1	Def DVOA Y+1	Dif Wins	Dif Total DVOA	Dif Off DVOA	Dif Def DVOA
BUF	Jim Kelly	11	1996	10-6	1.8%	-12.7%	-9.1%	6-10	-16.8%	-18.3%	-7.2%	-4	-18.6%	-5.6%	1.9%
DAL	Troy Aikman	12	2000	5-11	-14.7%	-10.8%	7.1%	5-11	-21.0%	-15.6%	2.2%	0	-6.3%	-4.8%	-4.9%
DEN	John Elway	16	1998	14-2	32.2%	35.0%	5.1%	6-10	8.4%	3.6%	-6.3%	-8	-23.8%	-31.4%	-11.4%
GB	Brett Favre	16	2007	13-3	20.5%	16.0%	-1.5%	6-10	8.9%	7.5%	-2.0%	-7	-11.6%	-8.5%	-0.5%
HOIL	Warren Moon	10	1993	12-4	18.9%	-1.4%	-18.1%	2-14	-29.9%	-22.2%	5.8%	-10	-48.8%	-20.8%	23.9%
IND	Peyton Manning	13	2010*	10-6	1.0%	13.1%	5.8%	11-5	-16.2%	-2.5%	14.6%	+1	-17.2%	-15.6%	8.8%
MIA	Dan Marino	17	1999	9-7	5.9%	-6.6%	-8.4%	11-5	25.1%	-1.3%	-17.5%	+2	19.2%	5.3%	-9.1%
NE	Tom Brady	20	2019	12-4	30.7%	4.3%	-25.2%	7-9	-7.1%	-7.3%	7.9%	-5	-37.8%	-11.6%	33.1%
NO	**Drew Brees**	**15**	**2020**	**12-4**	**33.3%**	**10.7%**	**-19.0%**								
SF	Joe Montana	10	1990	14-2	18.5%	13.0%	-7.0%	10-6	26.1%	24.9%	-4.0%	-4	7.6%	11.9%	3.0%
SF	Steve Young	13	1998*	12-4	25.0%	29.3%	1.0%	4-12	-1.9%	18.8%	16.9%	-8	-26.9%	-10.5%	15.9%
	AVERAGE			11.2-4.8	13.5%	7.4%	-4.8%	6.8-9.2	-5.6%	-4.1%	1.6%	-4.3	-19.1%	-11.5%	6.4%

has nevertheless averaged just under 380 receiving yards per season during his three-year career. Behind Thomas and Smith, the rest of the receiver depth chart barely has 500 career receiving yards *combined*. Outside target Marquez Callaway impressed last season, hauling in all 21 catchable targets as charted by SIS, but that still amounted to barely over 200 yards, no touchdowns, and more games with no targets (five) than with 50 receiving yards (two). Deonte Harris was targeted in every game he played, but the speedster averaged just 9.3 yards per reception, and his career-best game amounted to just 46 yards along with his lone career receiving touchdown. Juwan Johnson and Lil'Jordan Humphrey have under 50 career yards apiece, and recent reports have Johnson splitting time between the receiver and tight end position groups. Seventh-round pick Kawaan Baker (South Alabama) is an intriguing athlete, but an inconsistent receiver. None of those players has more than three years of professional experience, and only Smith and Baker were drafted. It's likely that somebody will emerge, even if only by virtue of opportunity, but on the surface it's clearly the weakest receiver group in the division.

The Saints have always fed Thomas targets when healthy: his average season accumulates more yards on more targets than the sum of the best seasons of every other wide receiver and tight end on the roster. Last year's injury was, thankfully, an anomaly, as Thomas has played at least 15 games in every other year of his career. But if anything were to happen to him in 2020, it's unclear where any production would come from at all.

Without Cook, the tight end situation looks only marginally better. Third-round pick Adam Trautman impressed as a rookie with 171 receiving yards; if he had been targeted often enough to qualify, his DVOA of 39.7% would have ranked second in the league at a position where rookies do not typically post gaudy numbers. He is high on our list of top prospects as a young player with a clear path to a potential breakout season, but he is eligible for that list in part because he played fewer than 400 offensive snaps last year. He now needs to prove that he can flourish in an expanded role. His presumptive backup, Nick Vannett, had a career-best 269 yards for the Seahawks in 2018 but has averaged just 137 yards per season over his five-year career. Garrett Griffin scored a receiving touchdown in the 2018 NFC Championship Game, but he has one regular season target in four years mostly spent bouncing between the practice squad and the active roster. Undrafted free agent Dylan Soehner could crack the roster ahead of Griffin as a versatile depth piece that Sean Payton can move around the formation. Trautman's presence in particular gives this group potential, but that potential will need to become production quickly.

Of course, the most likely candidate to finish second behind Thomas in receiving yards doesn't play either receiver or tight end. It was halfback Alvin Kamara, not Sanders, who led the team in receiving last year. Thomas aside, every year of Kamara's career has outproduced the career best of every other

pass target the Saints employ. He has never finished lower than third on the team, and even that third-place finish came in a season he spent battling a high-ankle sprain. Last year was Kamara's most productive yet, with career highs in rushing yards, scrimmage yards, and touchdowns.

However, more than probably any other player, Kamara's contribution likely depends in significant part on the answer to the biggest offseason question in New Orleans: who will ultimately emerge as the successor to Drew Brees. If it's Taysom Hill, that spells trouble: Kamara had two or fewer receptions in three of the games with Hill at quarterback last year, including the first catchless game of his career.

Winston is a much more favorable option. Much has been made in fantasy circles of the difference in the rate at which Winston targeted running backs in Tampa Bay versus Brees in New Orleans, but a great deal of that was circumstantial. When Winston was a rookie playing alongside a healthy Charles Sims and Doug Martin, with Mike Evans and a declining Vincent Jackson as his only downfield targets, he threw 114 passes (21.3%) to his backs. When his receiving corps was Evans, DeSean Jackson, Adam Humphries, Chris Godwin, and Cameron Brate, it's not exactly surprising that he didn't check down to Peyton Barber and Jacquizz Rodgers very much. As detailed above, the receiving situation in New Orleans is much closer to the former than the latter, meaning Kamara's involvement should be secure with Winston at quarterback.

The Saints coaches have been careful not to give away their plans, presumably for more profound reasons than simply to thwart would-be fantasy prognosticators. The two options are about as different as quarterbacks get. Winston is an archetypal pocket passer and former No. 1 overall pick with five years' experience as a primary starter. He sits among the most productive passers in history at every age from 21 through 25 and is one of only eight players who have ever passed for more than 5,000 yards in a single season.[2] In Winston's least productive season for the Buccaneers, he threw for almost five times as many touchdowns (19) as Hill has in his entire career (four). Four times, he has finished No. 16 or higher in both DVOA and DYAR, marking him as a league-average starter. The only time he fell out of that bracket was in 2019, a season in which he still broke the 5,000-yard mark and threw 33 touchdown passes for a 7-9 Buccaneers squad.

Hill, on the other hand, is a former undrafted free agent who may have taken the most unconventional route to becoming a starting quarterback this side of Kendall Hinton. After being cut by the Packers and claimed by the Saints at the end of the 2017 preseason, Hill worked his way up the roster as a special teams gunner, punt protector, occasional tight end, and Wildcat quarterback before finally starting four games as the stand-in last year while Drew Brees was absent with rib fractures. In those four games, he threw for four touchdowns, rushed for four more, and compiled a 3-1 record as a starting quarterback. He also has 11 career receiving touchdowns and

---

[2] In a slightly ironic twist, Winston and Brees are the only two passers who have ever passed for 5,000 yards in a season while their team finished with a losing record.

a further five rushing (including playoffs) in his other roles as receiver, tight end, and gadget quarterback.

If analytics are any indication, this quarterback competition is no contest at all. Winston's career average DVOA, weighted by attempts per season, is around 2.5%, a figure that would have ranked 19th among qualifying passers in 2020. Hill's passing DVOA in Weeks 11 to 14 of 2020, his only action as a starting quarterback, was -23.9%, a figure that would have ranked 33rd. Winston is 27 years old with five seasons as a starter, Hill is 31 with four starts. When we run our projections with Winston as the starter, the Saints come out as a playoff contender with an offense on the fringes of the top 10. When we run them with Hill, they come out as a fringe wild-card contender with an offense nowhere close to that. (Our season simulation was split between the two.) Offseason reports suggest that Winston is more likely to win the job, but given how NFL coaches are with the media, it is entirely possible that nothing will be confirmed until the team releases its starting lineup for Week 1.

Put that all together and the Saints passing game may be the biggest unknown for any team heading into the 2020 season. We don't know who will start at quarterback. We can't be sure how that will impact Thomas and Kamara. We can only guess who will emerge as the other pass targets. We don't have the faintest clue how all of those unknowns will fit together. The staff has a history of success, not only with Brees at quarterback but also with Hill, Teddy Bridgewater, and even in a small sample with Luke McCown. With the benefit of a full offseason, they can build an offense around either player. How effective that offense will be, we simply don't know. All we can say with any confidence is it is exceedingly unlikely to be anywhere near as effective as it was under Brees.

Instead, in a remarkable turnaround from most of the Brees era, the defense is the most likely driving force if the Saints are to defy history. Last year's defense was the franchise's best since the heyday of the Dome Patrol, a top-five unit against both run and pass with dominant players at all three levels. While there are reasons to expect that mark to regress, the Saints have a sustained track record on defense and the underlying factors to back up their high rank. Their high adjusted sack rate is not especially predictive, but their third-best pressure rate is. They have three straight seasons among the top five in adjusted line yards. Their most productive edge rusher left in free agency, but they already had success with his replacement as the starter in 2019 and they don't rely on a single player to generate pressure. They enjoyed above-average health last year, but they have a clear backup plan at every position. It's true that they probably won't have another -200.9% pass defense DVOA day in 2021, as they did against Kendall Hinton's Broncos, but removing that game from their DVOA only drops them one spot, from second at -19.0% to third at -17.4%. Our projections have them remaining among the top five, which is consistent with their average ranking across the past four years.

The Saints will not begin this season as one of the favorites, as they did in each of the past three seasons. However, if the defense can sustain its level, and the offense can hold serve despite the talent drain, they can still be strong enough to make another run at the postseason. Given the history, even a wild-card berth could arguably be considered Payton's finest coaching job yet. And if, by some miracle, Winston can take over as the starter and lead the team beyond that, those Ws you see being eaten will be Words. The last head coach to successfully navigate the transition from a decade with a Hall of Fame quarterback to a winning record the following year was Bill Walsh, and he was moving from one Hall of Famer to another in an era prior to the introduction of the salary cap. Both of the successful follow-up seasons in the salary-cap era involved replacing the head coach as well.

While Brees is iconic, Payton's legacy is more complicated. He is clearly the most successful head coach in franchise history, but he is also remembered for the Bountygate scandal that cost him a season mid-tenure, as well as the historic run of appalling defense that kept Brees out of the postseason from 2014 through 2016. Payton's 143 career wins seat him among the 25 most successful head coaches in history, ranking fifth among active head coaches. The only coach above him on the list who has had only one starting quarterback for his entire tenure is Mike Tomlin, a coach who has also endured more than his fair share of criticism during his career. Success without Brees would be a significant endorsement of Payton's credentials, and perhaps prove to his doubters that the Saints were not a one-man show.

On the other hand, if the loss of veteran pieces causes a drop-off on defense, and the offense struggles thanks to inexperienced receivers or inconsistent quarterbacking, the Saints could look a lot like the 2020 Patriots. If that comparison is exasperating—we're all sick of being measured against the Patriots—it's also apt. A former No. 1 overall pick at quarterback. A depleted receiving corps. A defensive drop-off after losing key veterans. The Patriots still won seven games, the most of any incumbent coach in this situation in the salary-cap era. Seven games should be the absolute floor for the Saints with what is still one of the stronger rosters in the NFC.

The comparisons between the Patriots and Saints go deeper, of course. Both were historically moribund franchises who suddenly became consistent contenders when their future Hall of Fame quarterbacks came along. Few people expected either quarterback to be anything like the legends they became. Both have enjoyed their greatest periods of success over the past 20 years, with a quarterback-coach combination that has now been severed. And both now need to chart a way forward, boldly going where no head coach has gone before.

With this quarterback room, at the very least, it should be anything but predictable.

Andrew Potter

2020 Saints by Week

Wk	vs.	W-L	PF	PA	YDF	YDA	TO	Total	Off	Def	ST
1	TB	W	34	23	271	310	3	46.4%	8.9%	-27.3%	10.3%
2	at LV	L	24	34	424	377	0	25.6%	28.6%	3.9%	0.9%
3	GB	L	30	37	397	369	-1	24.8%	15.0%	-12.1%	-2.4%
4	at DET	W	35	29	392	281	0	4.0%	4.4%	-1.2%	-1.6%
5	LAC	W	30	27	408	350	-1	11.4%	-8.2%	-7.5%	12.2%
6	BYE										
7	CAR	W	27	24	415	283	-1	-5.3%	17.3%	23.2%	0.7%
8	at CHI	W	26	23	394	329	1	18.8%	5.8%	-7.2%	5.8%
9	at TB	W	38	3	420	194	1	153.5%	50.2%	-96.7%	6.7%
10	SF	W	27	13	237	281	2	56.8%	6.4%	-39.8%	10.6%
11	ATL	W	24	9	376	248	1	70.3%	27.5%	-49.2%	-6.4%
12	at DEN	W	31	3	292	112	2	64.8%	-20.8%	-78.8%	6.8%
13	at ATL	W	21	16	424	332	0	-3.6%	-7.6%	-15.0%	-11.0%
14	at PHI	L	21	24	358	413	-1	-40.6%	-14.6%	21.2%	-4.8%
15	KC	L	29	32	285	411	0	35.6%	-5.5%	-22.8%	18.3%
16	MIN	W	52	33	583	364	-2	51.9%	49.2%	0.5%	3.2%
17	at CAR	W	33	7	347	320	5	57.8%	7.5%	-42.7%	7.7%
18	CHI	W	21	9	385	239	-1	-14.3%	-4.3%	2.1%	-7.9%
19	TB	L	20	30	294	316	-4	-7.3%	-28.7%	-12.3%	9.1%

Trends and Splits

	Offense	Rank	Defense	Rank
Total DVOA	10.7%	7	-19.0%	2
Unadjusted VOA	12.0%	6	-16.0%	4
Weighted Trend	9.4%	7	-21.7%	2
Variance	4.3%	7	10.9%	32
Average Opponent	0.5%	19	2.9%	8
Passing	16.6%	12	-14.7%	3
Rushing	9.5%	1	-25.7%	2
First Down	23.4%	1	-19.1%	2
Second Down	1.3%	16	-21.9%	3
Third Down	1.7%	14	-15.0%	7
First Half	7.3%	11	-17.1%	3
Second Half	14.6%	6	-20.8%	4
Red Zone	42.3%	2	-17.0%	5
Late and Close	12.6%	9	-7.6%	10

Five-Year Performance

Year	W-L	Pyth W	Est W	PF	PA	TO	Total	Rk	Off	Rk	Def	Rk	ST	Rk	Off AGL	Rk	Def AGL	Rk	Off Age	Rk	Def Age	Rk	ST Age	Rk
2016	7-9	8.3	9.2	469	454	-3	2.2%	16	15.2%	6	10.4%	28	-2.6%	27	22.5	5	59.0	25	28.3	2	26.8	11	27.0	4
2017	11-5	11.1	14.1	448	326	+7	35.0%	1	22.4%	2	-11.4%	6	1.2%	15	32.6	16	66.4	29	27.5	6	24.9	31	25.7	21
2018	13-3	11.5	11.7	504	353	+9	25.2%	2	16.1%	4	-7.3%	8	1.7%	9	28.0	9	22.4	8	28.2	3	25.3	29	26.6	7
2019	13-3	10.9	13.3	458	341	+15	32.7%	2	22.0%	4	-7.1%	8	3.6%	3	23.2	8	35.1	18	27.5	5	25.8	21	26.5	6
2020	12-4	11.4	11.8	482	337	+9	33.3%	1	10.7%	7	-19.0%	2	3.6%	5	29.9	10	19.2	3	27.4	8	27.5	1	26.7	5

2020 Performance Based on Most Common Personnel Groups

NO Offense					NO Offense vs. Opponents					NO Defense					NO Defense vs. Opponents			
Pers	Freq	Yds	DVOA	Run%	Pers	Freq	Yds	DVOA	Run%	Pers	Freq	Yds	DVOA	Pers	Freq	Yds	DVOA
11	50%	6.0	8.9%	34%	Base	28%	5.4	5.9%	61%	Base	9%	3.6	-19.0%	11	54%	5.7	-21.3%
12	11%	6.9	20.7%	47%	Nickel	57%	6.0	12.4%	42%	Nickel	60%	5.4	-16.1%	12	23%	5.0	-16.4%
21	11%	6.6	25.2%	50%	Dime+	14%	7.3	17.2%	12%	Dime+	29%	5.8	-28.5%	21	7%	5.4	-13.6%
611	5%	8.5	56.8%	57%	Goal Line	1%	1.2	77.4%	93%	Goal Line	1%	0.4	-5.0%	01	3%	5.1	-30.2%
22	5%	3.4	-59.6%	54%	Big	1%	2.3	60.2%	83%					22	3%	2.9	-28.9%
612	4%	3.9	-21.0%	79%										13	2%	3.7	-13.0%
621	3%	4.5	-27.8%	96%										02	2%	5.9	7.8%

Strategic Tendencies

Run/Pass		Rk	Formation		Rk	Pass Rush		Rk	Secondary		Rk	Strategy		Rk
Runs, first half	41%	7	Form: Single Back	77%	22	Rush 3	11.4%	8	4 DB	9%	29	Play Action	22%	28
Runs, first down	50%	10	Form: Empty Back	9%	13	Rush 4	62.5%	20	5 DB	60%	17	Offensive Motion	43%	19
Runs, second-long	35%	3	Form: Multi Back	13%	9	Rush 5	21.3%	14	6+ DB	29%	5	Avg Box (Off)	6.63	11
Runs, power sit.	72%	3	Pers: 3+ WR	56%	25	Rush 6+	4.8%	18	Man Coverage	47%	1	Avg Box (Def)	6.62	14
Runs, behind 2H	25%	20	Pers: 2+ TE/6+ OL	34%	11	Edge Rusher Sacks	62.5%	5	CB by Sides	69%	24	Offensive Pace	31.54	28
Pass, ahead 2H	42%	25	Pers: 6+ OL	15%	1	Interior DL Sacks	20.5%	19	S/CB Cover Ratio	40%	1	Defensive Pace	30.48	20
Run-Pass Options	7%	17	Shotgun/Pistol	55%	26	Second Level Sacks	17.0%	27	DB Blitz	14%	11	Go for it on 4th	1.73	12

In 2019, the Saints led the league with 41.3% DVOA when running in second-and-long. Maybe the staff saw this on film, and so the Saints increased their use of running plays on second-and-long from 22% in 2019 to 35% in 2020. And instead, they were awful on these runs: 4.3 yards per carry with -38.7% DVOA last season. ❧ New Orleans was the only team in 2020 to use six offensive linemen more than 10% of the time, and the Saints had 5.8 yards per play and 31.8% DVOA with an extra lineman. ❧ New Orleans led the NFL with 16.5% DVOA when running against a heavy box of eight or more defenders. ❧ Unsurprisingly, the Saints' use of play-action went up from 20% with Drew Brees as quarterback to 29% with Taysom Hill behind center. ❧ New Orleans ranked second in DVOA rushing the ball on third or fourth down but 25th passing the ball. ❧ New Orleans had the best run defense in the league against handoffs from standard under-center formations by both DVOA (-34.1%) and yards per carry (3.0). Its run defense against handoffs from shotgun was almost exactly the league average by both DVOA (-10.4%) and yards per carry (4.8). ❧ The Saints ranked second in the league with 1,005 penalty yards, but they were also dead last with only 517 penalty yards charged to their opponents. Opposing penalty yards is not a stat that usually correlates strongly from year to year, but this was the second straight season the Saints were last in opposing penalty yards.

Passing

Player	DYAR	DVOA	Plays	NtYds	Avg	YAC	C%	TD	Int
D.Brees*	769	17.6%	401	2845	7.1	5.4	71.1%	24	6
T.Hill	-69	-19.0%	135	841	6.2	4.2	72.7%	4	2
J.Winston	-7	-20.4%	13	64	4.9	8.7	63.6%	0	0

Rushing

Player	DYAR	DVOA	Plays	Yds	Avg	TD	Fum	Suc
A.Kamara	253	23.1%	187	932	5.0	16	1	54%
L.Murray	131	12.3%	146	656	4.5	4	1	62%
T.Hill	2	-11.8%	87	449	5.2	8	7	--
T.Montgomery	-4	-13.9%	19	101	5.3	0	0	47%
D.Washington	-17	-69.3%	8	15	1.9	0	0	13%
M.Burton*	4	-1.5%	7	18	2.6	0	0	86%
D.Harris	33	59.9%	6	51	8.5	0	0	--
D.Brees	7	2.4%	6	10	1.7	2	0	--
A.Armah	2	-4.0%	6	9	1.5	0	0	83%

Receiving

Player	DYAR	DVOA	Plays	Ctch	Yds	Y/C	YAC	TD	C%
E.Sanders*	150	9.6%	82	61	726	11.9	2.8	5	74%
M.Thomas	45	-2.6%	55	40	438	11.0	2.1	0	73%
T.Smith	61	2.9%	50	34	448	13.2	4.0	4	68%
M.Callaway	27	0.1%	27	21	213	10.1	2.8	0	78%
D.Harris	29	1.3%	25	20	186	9.3	6.4	1	80%
J.Johnson	-33	-52.3%	10	4	39	9.8	5.0	0	40%
B.Fowler*	-28	-71.0%	6	2	11	5.5	0.5	0	33%
J.Cook*	88	13.9%	60	37	504	13.6	3.4	7	62%
A.Trautman	50	39.7%	16	15	171	11.4	7.8	1	94%
T.Hill	-5	-13.4%	12	8	98	12.3	4.4	1	67%
J.Hill*	-32	-51.6%	10	8	46	5.8	4.6	1	80%
N.Vannett	-35	-28.3%	21	14	95	6.8	4.6	1	67%
A.Kamara	195	19.1%	107	83	756	9.1	8.8	5	78%
L.Murray	48	21.6%	26	23	176	7.7	8.6	1	88%
T.Montgomery	-19	-67.6%	6	3	27	9.0	11.0	0	50%
A.Armah	-30	-64.3%	9	5	18	3.6	4.0	0	56%

Offensive Line

Player	Pos	Age	GS	Snaps	Pen	Sk	Pass	Run	Player	Pos	Age	GS	Snaps	Pen	Sk	Pass	Run
Erik McCoy	C	24	16/16	1073	3	1	5	5	Cesar Ruiz	RG	22	15/9	744	1	0	7	3
Ryan Ramczyk	RT	27	16/16	1038	4	2	11	3	Nick Easton*	RG	29	12/9	562	3	0	5	4
Terron Armstead	LT	30	14/14	857	4	2.5	8	8	James Hurst	LT/LG	30	12/5	377	1	1	1	1
Andrus Peat	LG	28	13/13	766	4	3.5	10	1									

Year	Yards	ALY	Rk	Power	Rk	Stuff	Rk	2Lev	Rk	OpFld	Rk	BB Rt	Rk	Sacks	ASR	Rk	Press	Rk	BB Rt	Rk	Cont
2018	4.60	5.19	2	70%	9	14%	1	1.28	14	0.77	21	6.7%	19	20	4.4%	3	23.9%	3	5.7%	4	24
2019	4.56	4.92	1	67%	13	16%	4	1.27	11	0.80	15	10.8%	21	25	4.7%	3	23.7%	1	12.7%	12	33
2020	4.69	4.89	4	78%	2	14%	2	1.28	12	0.82	12	5.9%	1	29	6.1%	13	19.4%	4	8.6%	3	26

2020 ALY by direction:	Left End: 2.92 (30)	Left Tackle: 4.97 (5)	Mid/Guard: 4.98 (1)	Right Tackle: 5.45 (2)	Right End: 5.24 (11)

New Orleans has more of its own draft capital invested in their five starting offensive linemen than any other franchise: three first-round picks, a second-rounder, and a third-rounder, all since 2013. This investment has paid off: the Saints have been in the top five by adjusted line yards for five straight seasons. No other franchise has more than three seasons in the top five over that period. New Orleans ranked in the top five in runs behind each of left tackle, mid/guard, and right tackle, the only team to be that high in all three spots. ❧ One reason for this success is a lack of blown blocks: the Saints blew a block on just 5.9% of run plays in 2020, the best rate in the league. The rate increased to 8.6% on pass plays, still good for third best, and only Pittsburgh had a lower overall rate of plays with a blown block. This was a significant improvement on the previous year. Every qualifying lineman ranked in the top 10 at his position for snaps per blown block, and the youngest three each ranked in the top six. ❧ First-round rookie Cesar Ruiz made his first start at left guard in Week 4 as an injury replacement for Andrus Peat, but otherwise worked his way into the lineup at right guard, eventually supplanting veteran Nick Easton. Ruiz was charged with just one sack all year. Easton did not allow any, but he was a salary cap casualty in the offseason and remains an unsigned free agent at the time of writing. ❧ Despite the lack of blown blocks, the Saints recorded their worst adjusted sack rate since 2005, and their first year above 5.3% in the Sean Payton/Drew Brees era. However, almost half the sacks, 14 of 29, were inflicted on Taysom Hill. Brees was sacked just 13 times in 12 games, whereas Hill was sacked 13 times in his four starts, once again demonstrating the extent to which quarterbacks influence sack rates. This is one stat where Jameis Winston has a clear edge: Winston has a career sack rate of 6.2%, considerably better than Hill's 10.7%. ❧ Sixth-round pick Landon Young (Kentucky) is a powerful but immobile potential swing tackle and sixth lineman, a former five-star recruit who helps with the depth on the offensive line. With the lone exception of backup tackle James Hurst, the Saints' depth here consists solely of young late-round picks and undrafted free agents.

Defensive Front

Defensive Line	Age	Pos	G	Snaps	Plays	TmPct	Rk	Stop	Dfts	BTkl	Runs	St%	Rk	RuYd	Rk	Sack	Hit	Hur	Dsrpt
						Overall						vs. Run				Pass Rush			
David Onyemata	29	DT	15	599	46	6.2%	24	38	19	5	32	78%	34	1.3	7	6.5	10	24	1
Sheldon Rankins*	27	DT	12	415	21	3.5%	74	13	5	1	18	56%	93	2.8	67	1.5	7	9	1
Malcom Brown*	27	DT	13	345	27	4.2%	62	23	6	1	24	88%	4	1.1	2	1.0	2	7	0
Shy Tuttle	26	DT	13	326	30	4.7%	--	23	5	3	27	78%	--	2.6	--	0.0	2	4	3
Malcolm Roach	23	DT	9	233	16	3.6%	--	9	2	0	14	64%	--	1.6	--	0.0	3	7	0

Edge Rushers	Age	Pos	G	Snaps	Plays	TmPct	Rk	Stop	Dfts	BTkl	Runs	St%	Rk	RuYd	Rk	Sack	Hit	Hur	Dsrpt
						Overall						vs. Run				Pass Rush			
Cameron Jordan	32	DE	16	816	54	6.8%	14	42	18	6	41	73%	44	1.7	15	7.5	10	31	4
Trey Hendrickson*	27	DE	15	558	26	3.5%	76	24	17	2	10	90%	2	2.0	27	13.5	13	23	3
Marcus Davenport	25	DE	11	374	23	4.2%	60	17	8	4	18	67%	60	3.4	81	1.5	8	21	3
Carl Granderson	25	DE	15	291	15	2.0%	--	12	5	6	9	67%	--	3.4	--	5.0	6	10	1
Tanoh Kpassagnon	27	DE	16	717	31	3.8%	68	25	7	9	23	74%	37	2.8	57	1.0	3	16	4

Linebackers	Age	Pos	G	Snaps	Plays	TmPct	Rk	Stop	Dfts	BTkl	Runs	St%	Rk	RuYd	Rk	Sack	Hit	Hur	Tgts	Suc%	Rk	Yd/P	Rk	PD	Int
						Overall						vs. Run				Pass Rush			vs. Pass						
Demario Davis	32	OLB	16	1032	124	15.7%	15	64	17	6	71	55%	48	3.3	17	4.0	8	19	34	68%	5	3.1	1	5	0
Kwon Alexander*	27	OLB	12	667	61	10.3%	58	41	9	11	34	74%	3	2.9	8	1.0	1	9	26	65%	7	3.8	5	4	0
Alex Anzalone*	27	MLB	16	525	40	5.1%	85	19	7	4	23	70%	8	2.5	2	0.0	0	5	14	50%	35	5.1	21	0	0

Year	Yards	ALY	Rk	Power	Rk	Stuff	Rk	2Lev	Rk	OpFld	Rk	BB Rt	Rk	Sacks	ASR	Rk	Press	Rk	BB Rt	Rk
2018	3.22	3.61	2	57%	3	24%	6	0.87	1	0.40	3	7.6%	20	49	8.7%	4	31.2%	13	11.7%	10
2019	3.65	3.94	5	58%	5	21%	8	0.95	3	0.51	4	17.5%	4	51	7.7%	9	36.2%	2	15.2%	17
2020	3.85	3.74	4	64%	12	21%	6	0.98	3	0.66	12	12.1%	19	45	8.5%	3	30.1%	3	16.1%	5

2020 ALY by direction:	Left End: 5.47 (29)	Left Tackle: 2.36 (1)	Mid/Guard: 3.72 (2)	Right Tackle: 3.88 (8)	Right End: 4.26 (11)

The Saints defense has finished in the top five in adjusted line yards for three straight seasons and the top 10 in adjusted sack rate for four straight. Their interior line was especially dominant in 2020: David Onyemata's average play came just 0.2 yards downfield, best among defensive tackles. Malcom Brown made his 0.9 yards downfield, seventh best. Sheldon Rankins also ranked among the top 20, as would Ryan Glasgow if he had enough plays to qualify. ● With Rankins and Brown gone, Shy Tuttle is expected to assume starting duties as the main run-plugger, with Glasgow and 2020 undrafted free agent Malcolm Roach filling the primary rotation. ● Cameron Jordan's streak of 145 consecutive regular-season starts is the second-longest active streak of any player, behind Ndamukong Suh (147). However, Jordan's 2020 sack, hurry, and defeat totals were all the lowest they've been since 2016. ● With Trey Hendrickson now in Cincinnati, first-round pick Marcus Davenport will get the first shot at reclaiming the vacant spot. Davenport was a starter in 2019 but lost his spot to Hendrickson last year. 2019 undrafted free agent Carl Granderson had more sacks than Davenport last year, but Davenport had more hits and way more hurries. Granderson appears best suited as a rotational piece. This year's first-round pick, Payton Turner (Houston), was considered a developmental reach near the end of the first round and will likely be brought along slowly. That leaves former Chiefs edge rusher Tanoh Kpassagnon, who had only one sack in 15 starts for Kansas City. ● Rotational depth is critical to the team's success: Jordan was the only Saints defender in the top 40 for individual hurries, but the Saints defense generated pressure on 30.1% of opposing pass plays, the third-highest rate in the league. This was down more than 5% from 2019, but the league-wide hurry rate also fell by almost 5%. ● Demario Davis pressured quarterbacks on 27.0% of his pass-rush snaps last year, the highest rate of any player with at least 100 pass rushes. ● With Alex Anzalone and Kwon Alexander gone and no veteran free-agent replacement, last year's third-round pick, Zach Baun, should compete directly with this year's second-round pick, Pete Werner, to play alongside Davis. Baun was a college edge rusher who is too small to play that role in the NFL, but his quickness and understanding in zone coverage should aid his transition to weakside linebacker. He played only 82 defensive snaps in his rookie season. Werner is a more natural off-ball linebacker, but one whose projected upside is more that of a solid role player than a top-tier starter.

Defensive Secondary

Secondary	Age	Pos	G	Snaps	Plays	TmPct	Rk	Stop	Dfts	BTkl	Runs	St%	Rk	RuYd	Rk	Tgts	Tgt%	Rk	aDOT	Suc%	Rk	Yd/P	Rk	PD	Int
						Overall					vs. Run					vs. Pass									
Malcolm Jenkins	34	SS	16	1036	101	12.8%	12	42	16	11	44	39%	32	4.9	11	48	11.5%	16	9.2	52%	31	6.9	22	10	3
Marcus Williams	25	FS	14	880	66	9.5%	48	17	9	2	33	27%	55	8.4	53	9	2.5%	71	8.7	22%	71	9.8	58	7	3
Marshon Lattimore	25	CB	14	871	73	10.6%	14	19	13	4	15	27%	66	7.1	44	76	21.6%	25	13.2	47%	57	7.8	45	11	2
Chauncey Gardner-Johnson	24	SS/CB	15	861	78	10.5%	39	47	15	15	27	70%	1	3.6	2	70	20.2%	2	9.5	60%	9	5.4	8	13	1
Janoris Jenkins*	33	CB	13	805	67	10.4%	16	26	9	5	13	46%	33	3.9	9	71	21.9%	23	14.0	52%	37	8.1	51	12	3
P.J. Williams	28	CB	15	499	39	5.3%	--	8	5	8	10	20%	--	6.5	--	22	10.9%	--	12.4	41%	--	12.1	--	2	1
Patrick Robinson	34	CB	12	248	18	3.0%	--	10	4	1	5	80%	--	1.2	--	28	28.0%	--	16.6	54%	--	8.7	--	4	2

Year	Pass D Rank	vs. #1 WR	Rk	vs. #2 WR	Rk	vs. Other WR	Rk	WR Wide	Rk	WR Slot	Rk	vs. TE	Rk	vs. RB	Rk
2018	22	17.7%	30	28.4%	31	-16.4%	6	13.5%	27	5.6%	20	-22.2%	4	19.8%	29
2019	13	-6.3%	11	-4.6%	11	10.1%	22	-9.7%	14	9.9%	20	-7.8%	8	-3.2%	16
2020	3	-10.7%	11	-8.9%	11	-1.4%	15	0.6%	16	-6.3%	12	-34.7%	2	-9.7%	9

The Saints' use of man coverage zoomed from 31% (20th) in 2019 to 47% (first) last season, yet they allowed 23.4% DVOA on passes where SIS charted them with man coverage, compared to a league-best -18.3% DVOA when SIS charted them with zone coverage. That was the largest such gap in the league. ● With that increase in man coverage came the No. 1 spot in S/CB cover ratio. That mostly comes from the use of safety Chauncey Gardner-Johnson at nickelback, as his 70 targets tied for the most among safeties, but with 48 targets Malcolm Jenkins also tied for third in that figure. ● Gardner-Johnson impressed in his busy role. He finished second among safeties in passes defensed (behind Jessie Bates of Cincinnati) and had the highest combined stop rate (run and pass) among qualifying safeties. However, he did allow more broken tackles than any other Saints defender, and only Kwon Alexander allowed them at a higher rate. ● Speaking of the impact of roles on individual stats, deep safety Marcus Williams had the worst coverage success rate of any safety, but that came on just nine targets. The Saints defense had the third-best DVOA against deep passes, so Williams was doing something right. Williams also allowed just two broken tackles with 39 solo tackles, the third-best rate among qualifying defensive backs. The Saints defense as a whole tied for second best with just 95 broken tackles, its second straight season in the top three. ● The most likely immediate replacement for outgoing starter Janoris Jenkins is veteran Patrick Robinson, who made a handful of starts before missing most of December with a hamstring injury. However, third-round pick Paulson Adebo (Stanford) is a high-upside prospect as a big, physically gifted outside cornerback who could quickly ascend into a starting role. Adebo was considered a potential first-round pick after a superb 2018 campaign as a redshirt freshman, but he had a down year in 2019 and opted out of the 2020 season.

Special Teams

Year	DVOA	Rank	FG/XP	Rank	Net Kick	Rank	Kick Ret	Rank	Net Punt	Rank	Punt Ret	Rank	Hidden	Rank
2018	1.7%	9	6.8	6	-0.9	19	-0.2	13	5.3	9	-2.4	19	23.5	1
2019	3.6%	3	8.4	4	-7.0	31	3.1	9	4.9	10	9.0	2	6.8	5
2020	3.6%	5	-1.1	16	5.0	8	1.0	11	8.3	6	4.5	6	0.7	14

The Saints' coverage teams were outstanding in 2020. Punt coverage allowed a league-low 46 return yards on 20 returns, 25 fewer than the next fewest (New England Patriots, 71). Their average of just 2.3 yards allowed per return was less than half the average of the next best Atlanta Falcons (5.5). Their longest return allowed was a league-low 12 yards, and they allowed a league-best average of just 2.9 punt return yards per game. ● On kick coverage, the Saints allowed an average return of just 17.2 yards, second best behind only the Dolphins. ● The return teams were less impressive, but the Saints still finished in the top 10 in both average punt return (10.2 yards, ninth) and kick return (25.4 yards, sixth). Seventh-round receiver Kawaan Baker may be needed most urgently on offense, but he may also feature in the return game to free up Deonte Harris for those wideout duties. ● Thomas Morstead forced more fair catches (29) than any other punter; however, he also had the third-shortest average punt among qualifying punters. Morstead was cut as a salary-cap move during the offseason. 2020 undrafted free agent Blake Gillikin (Penn State) and undrafted rookie Nolan Cooney (Syracuse) will battle to replace him, with Gillikin the early favorite. ● Wil Lutz converted just 82.1% of his field goals, the lowest rate of his career, and had his first miss from under 30 yards. However, he missed just a single extra point for the fourth time in five seasons.

New York Giants

2020 Record: 6-10	Total DVOA: -13.8% (27)	2021 Mean Projection: 7.4 wins	On the Clock (0-5): 26%
Pythagorean Wins: 5.7 (27)	Offense: -11.8% (26)	Postseason Odds: 28.3%	Mediocrity (6-8): 42%
Snap-Weighted Age: 25.7 (30)	Defense: 3.7% (19)	Super Bowl Odds: 1.8%	Playoff Contender (9-11): 26%
Average Opponent: 1% (14)	Special Teams: 1.7% (12)	Proj. Avg. Opponent: 0% (17)	Super Bowl Contender (12+): 7%

2020: The unveiling of the "Almost Won the NFC East" banner will be scheduled to coincide with Dave Gettleman's dismissal.

2021: The Decline and Fall of Danny Dimes and the Hog Mollies.

What if Dave Gettleman is right and the rest of us are wrong?

That's a question we must at least entertain in the wake of what looked on paper like a very productive New York Giants offseason. There's a slim chance that Gettleman, the NFL's least-repentant cackling Facebook uncle, has known what he was doing all along, and that the rest of us—the analytics community, the Twitter intelligentsia, the New York media, anyone with a more forward-thinking worldview than the average caveman—were the ones who were mistaken.

Rest assured that DVOA doesn't see such a scenario playing out: our average projection features just 7.4 wins in a weak division and rankings near the bottom of the league in both offense and defense. But DVOA would be the last thing to see Gettleman's vindication coming. Any Giants success, after all, would by definition fly directly into the face of all of our research and cherished assumptions.

Gettleman himself spent the offseason doubling down on his role as the analytics community's cartoon antagonist, making him hard to take seriously as a threat. During media sessions, he frequently cited the Giants' 4-2 record in the NFC East as a sign of progress ("should have been 5-1," he sometimes asserted, referencing a tight Week 5 loss to the Cowboys), insulting the intelligence of his audience by clinging to the technicality that the 6-10 Giants were a near-playoff team. When asked before the draft if the Giants were entering a Super Bowl window, he quipped that he's "not a 'window theory' guy." He then made a cringy dad joke about Microsoft Windows, stopping just short of adding a wisecrack about Millenials and avocado toast.

Yes, Gettleman still sounds like a midday WFAN caller circa 2004. Yet it's possible for a general manager who doesn't believe in windows to accidentally crash like a nearsighted pigeon into one. It's also possible that all of Gettleman's suspect-to-awful decisions—overvaluing Saquon Barkley, overrating Daniel Jones, overdrafting Andrew Thomas, trading Odell Beckham, settling upon (if not for) Joe Judge as head coach and Jason Garrett as offensive coordinator, building the Giants roster as though it were 1977, sneering at anything that smacks of data-driven reasoning—might not be enough to overcome the NFL's powerful forces of central tendency.

There are, in fact, a few faint signals that the Giants are headed in the right direction.

The Giants had the third-youngest roster in the NFL last season, with a snap-weighted age of 25.7 years. This year's free-agent haul, led by 27-year-old Kenny Golladay and 25-year-old Adoree' Jackson, won't make the Giants appreciably older. "Young" doesn't always equal "promising," but even a hardened Gettleman critic must admit that some of his acquisitions, including Jones, show flashes now and then.

The Giants lost 104.4 adjusted games to injury and COVID last year, eighth highest in the NFL. Barkley missed nearly all of the season, of course. Jones missed two starts and was hobbled for others. The receiver corps was missing a key piece or two in most weeks. The defensive line and secondary were each hit hard, losing promising young starters such as Lorenzo Carter and Xavier McKinney for long stretches. It's no stretch to assume that a healthier Giants team would be a better team.

The Giants also have a clear offensive identity and discernable plan. Judge and Garrett are going to air it the heck out, with Jones flinging deep passes to Golladay and Darius Slayton while Evan Engram, Sterling Shepard, and Kadarius Toney work underneath and Barkley powers the running and screen/flat games. It's an easy plan to poke holes in, but it's not a ridiculous plan at all.

Jones was actually one of the most effective deep passers in the NFL, ranking second to Deshaun Watson with a 46.2% completion rate on throws 25-plus yards downfield (Table 1). Sample sizes are small for such deep throws, but lower the Air Yards threshold to 15 yards (officially all "deep passes" in the league's play-by-play) and Jones still ranks fifth in the league, completing 57.7% of his 71 attempts. Completion rates are a useful metric for deep passes, of course, because there are no screens/swings/checkdowns padding the data.

Table 1: Highest Completion Rate on Passes of 25-plus Air Yards

Name	Team	Att	Comp %
Deshaun Watson	HOU	33	48.5%
Daniel Jones	**NYG**	**26**	**46.2%**
Teddy Bridgewater	CAR	35	45.7%
Aaron Rodgers	GB	51	43.1%
Derek Carr	LV	42	42.9%
Minimum 20 attempts			

185

2021 Giants Schedule

Week	Opp.	Week	Opp.	Week	Opp.
1	DEN	7	CAR	13	at MIA
2	at WAS (Thu.)	8	at KC (Mon.)	14	at LAC
3	ATL	9	LV	15	DAL
4	at NO	10	BYE	16	at PHI
5	at DAL	11	at TB (Mon.)	17	at CHI
6	LAR	12	PHI	18	WAS

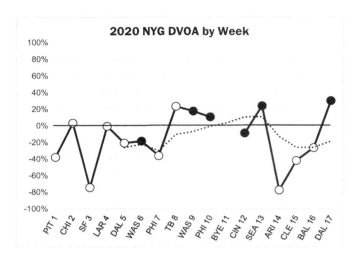

Watching Giants film, it's hard to conclude that Jones is an outstanding mad bomber just waiting to be unleashed because his placement on deep throws is all over the farm. He's clearly a willing and eager deep passer, however, one who would look much better with Golladay and Slayton screaming down the field than he did when his deep options, besides Slayton, included Dante Pettis and/or Austin Mack.

One reason the New York offense was so ineffective for long stretches, despite intermittent Jones bombs, was that the Giants were one of the worst extra-short passing teams in the NFL. As Table 2 shows, Jones finished third to the 2017 Eagles dream team of Carson Wentz and Nick Foles in yards per attempt on passes of less than 5 air yards. (Yards per attempt is the appropriate statistic for these easier-to-complete throws).

Table 2: Lowest Yards per Attempt on Passes Under 5 Air Yards

Name	Team	Att	Y/A
Carson Wentz	PHI	221	3.8
Nick Foles	CHI	177	3.8
Daniel Jones	**NYG**	**225**	**4.4**
Matt Ryan	ATL	330	4.5
Kyler Murray	ARI	319	4.5
Minimum 100 attempts			

The non-Barkley running backs were the primary culprits for the Giants' inability to get more from their micro-passing game. Wayne Gallman, Devonta Freeman, Dion Lewis, and Alfred Morris combined for just 275 yards on 66 targets (4.2 yards per target), with as many dropped passes as missed or broken tackles (six each, per Sports Info Solutions). The crispy remnants of slot receiver Golden Tate also did their part (3.2 yards per catch, 2.2 yards per target on 19 throws), and Evan Engram pitched in with three drops on short tosses. Jones certainly had a hand in the team's micro-passing misfortunes, as did Garrett, but the lack of screen-and-go type plays made the Giants offense far less consistent than it should have been. Overall, Giants ballcarriers broke just 74 tackles, the lowest total in the league, which hurt both their running game and short passing game.

Barkley was reportedly on schedule to return from his Week 2 injury as of spring, and the Giants picked up his—ugh—$7-million fifth-year option before the draft. The expectation of a fully healthy, showroom-new Barkley is more of a wish than

a plan, but the Giants took other steps to upgrade their short game. Kadarius Toney was an effective slot receiver, Wildcat quarterback, and general slash weapon at Florida; he should provide some YAC on underneath passes and be useful on the many end arounds Garrett likes to run. Devontae Booker and sixth-round pick Gary Brightwell look like replacement-level backups at running back, but they should at least keep the Giants from scouring the waiver wire for retreads like Freeman and Morris.

Protecting Jones will be a young offensive line that got better as last season wore on; the only way it could have gotten worse is if the rookie starters accidentally wandered onto the New Jersey Turnpike. Andrew Thomas turned out to be the quintessential Gettleman top pick: not nearly as good as many alternatives in a deep tackle class, but not as terrible as he could have been. By season's end, Thomas improved from "catastrophe" to "somewhat adequate," and he's talented enough to advance to "pretty good" this season.

Elsewhere on the line, veterans Kevin Zeitler and Cameron Fleming are gone, but Nate Solder returns from a COVID opt-out to provide an option at either right tackle or guard. The Giants are hoping for big strides forward from second-year linemen Shane Lemieux and Matt Peart, who were both mostly dreadful as rookies. Longtime college offensive line coach and coordinator Rob Sale arrived in February to get the youngsters on track; he replaces Dave DeGuglielmo, who won the job from Marc Colombo last year in a midseason trial by combat.

The Giants defense finished a semi-impressive 19th in the NFL in DVOA last year. Most of the improvement came from the arrivals of three veterans: lineman Leonard Williams (whom Gettleman traded for in 2019), linebacker Blake Martinez, and cornerback James Bradberry. All three are fine players, but they don't add up to the core of a championship-caliber defense.

But there's potential elsewhere on that side of the ball. Dexter Lawrence is a formidable Hog Molly. Safety McKinney and edge rusher Carter have looked solid when healthy. Rookie edge rushers Azeez Ojulari and Elerson G. Smith were considered fine values in their draft rounds. And Jabrill Peppers is bound to develop into an all-purpose defensive superweapon one of these years.

DVOA is unconvinced that this young defense is about to gel, however. One reason why is that the losses of veterans Kyler Fackrell and Dalvin Tomlinson along the front seven will offset any gains. Another concern is that the Giants defense was not truly great at anything in 2020. Their defense finished 15th against the run, 22nd against the pass, 21st in adjusted line yards, 27th in adjusted sack rate, 17th against deep passes, 29th against short passes, and so forth. Meanwhile, they finished with the third-highest variance in the NFL. That sure sounds like a mediocre defense that caught some teams starting backup quarterbacks (Andy Dalton, Kyle Allen, Brandon Allen) and others in meltdown mode (Eagles) but would be in real trouble if it faced a string of top-tier offenses that were playing well.

The 2021 Giants roster isn't really built from horrible decisions, just lots and lots of suboptimal decisions. Even if he bounces back, Barkley will never be as useful as the many players the Giants could have drafted instead. Jones may have been the best option available when Gettleman decided he was ready to draft a quarterback, but the Giants opted out of the 2018 class by picking Barkley. Jones' presence then had the additional effect of keeping them out of the deep 2021 quarterback class. Thomas should be fine but may never be Mekhi Beckton or Tristan Wirfs. Leonard Williams is excellent but cost the Giants a lot of draft picks and cap space. Beckham hasn't exactly proved his doubters wrong in Cleveland, but the return on that deal (the picks that became Lawrence and edge rusher Oshane Ximines, plus Peppers) was not exactly transformative.

Joe Judge and lieutenants Garrett and Patrick Graham fit the same paradigm of sub-optimization perfectly. Gettleman's Uncle Know-It-All routine, combined with the reduced media access to training camp, shielded the idiosyncratic Judge from criticism last year. When veterans (and coaches!) are ordered to run laps in August but the beat writers are not around to see them, it doesn't make much of a sound.

When not watching his offensive line coaches duke it out or simply following the standard Baby Belichick tutorial, Judge displayed an arch-conservative streak. The Giants' Aggressiveness Index plummeted from third to 30th on Judge's watch, perhaps fueled by the former special teams coach's desire to showcase the kicking game. Despite Barkley's absence,

the Giants' run-pass ratio went up under Garrett (from 20th to sixth in the first half of games, for example). And Graham's defense ranked 29th in the league in blitz rate despite the absence of any marquee edge rushers.

Judge, you may recall, was a consolation prize when the Giants were out-maneuvered and outspent in their quest for Matt Rhule. Like the choice of Barkley over Sam Darnold, it may turn out that neither choice was destined to work out; the best rationalization for many Gettleman decisions is "the alternative was no better." The Judge regime could also look much better in its second year, with its (ugh) culture in place, a little more talent, and some better injury luck. For now, the Giants coaching staff is most noteworthy for how little it appears to be bringing to the table.

As easy as Gettleman is to lampoon, he usually knows a good football player when he sees one. But his denial of basic concepts like positional value has resulted in a team with a maybe-kinda-hopefully franchise quarterback supported by an if-they-stay-healthy skill position arsenal and an if-they-develop offensive line, plus a won't-get-ya'-killed defense. Factor in a coaching staff that throws off some heavy Matt Patricia vibes and you get a team that's almost custom-built to max out at mediocrity.

If the Giants prove our projections wrong, it will be at least a partial validation of Gettleman the actual general manager, as opposed to Gettleman the SNL character. It will be a repudiation of the worst excesses of Gettleman's-a-shmuck, Jones-is-a-bum dogpiling many of us (including me) have engaged in over the last few years. And it will likely be an acknowledgement of what was indeed a strong offseason for the Giants, whose offense should be fun to watch this season: when Danny Dimes drops to pass, something (long gain, dropped pass, strip-sack, stumble scramble) is going to happen.

That said, the most likely scenario for the Giants is another year of flailing while Gettleman lectures us like a tipsy father-in-law at Thanksgiving. It's comforting, familiar, and entertaining in a way, especially because we know that fathers-in-law go home after dinner, and general managers who deliver more bromides than playoff appearances get fired.

Mike Tanier

2020 Giants by Week

Wk	vs.	W-L	PF	PA	YDF	YDA	TO	Total	Off	Def	ST
1	PIT	L	16	26	291	349	-1	-38.1%	-19.6%	21.0%	2.5%
2	at CHI	L	13	17	295	304	0	3.1%	-11.1%	-13.9%	0.3%
3	SF	L	9	36	231	420	-3	-74.4%	-49.7%	31.4%	6.7%
4	at LAR	L	9	17	295	240	0	-0.7%	-22.5%	-18.4%	3.4%
5	at DAL	L	34	37	300	402	1	-20.8%	-17.6%	13.4%	10.2%
6	WAS	W	20	19	240	337	1	-18.5%	-2.1%	14.5%	-2.0%
7	at PHI	L	21	22	325	442	-2	-36.2%	-21.0%	18.4%	3.1%
8	TB	L	23	25	357	344	-1	23.3%	14.6%	-3.5%	5.2%
9	at WAS	W	23	20	350	402	5	17.5%	17.0%	11.8%	12.3%
10	PHI	W	27	17	382	346	0	10.4%	18.4%	28.0%	20.0%
11	BYE										
12	at CIN	W	19	17	386	155	2	-8.9%	-26.2%	-42.9%	-25.7%
13	at SEA	W	17	12	290	327	1	23.9%	-16.3%	-45.8%	-5.7%
14	ARI	L	7	26	159	390	-3	-77.5%	-71.0%	-6.7%	-13.3%
15	CLE	L	6	20	288	392	0	-42.2%	-9.9%	37.6%	5.3%
16	at BAL	L	13	27	269	432	1	-26.5%	2.7%	26.1%	-3.0%
17	DAL	W	23	19	336	307	-1	30.3%	2.8%	-19.0%	8.6%

Trends and Splits

	Offense	Rank	Defense	Rank
Total DVOA	-11.8%	26	3.7%	19
Unadjusted VOA	-17.0%	27	1.2%	16
Weighted Trend	-11.1%	24	0.8%	17
Variance	5.6%	15	6.6%	24
Average Opponent	-5.6%	1	-5.3%	30
Passing	-11.5%	28	13.2%	22
Rushing	-3.7%	11	-9.9%	15
First Down	-1.9%	19	-1.1%	17
Second Down	-34.0%	32	2.3%	16
Third Down	3.4%	13	15.3%	26
First Half	-13.5%	27	-0.9%	16
Second Half	-10.1%	24	9.3%	24
Red Zone	-31.1%	30	3.6%	17
Late and Close	-8.4%	20	-9.9%	9

Five-Year Performance

Year	W-L	Pyth W	Est W	PF	PA	TO	Total	Rk	Off	Rk	Def	Rk	ST	Rk	Off AGL	Rk	Def AGL	Rk	Off Age	Rk	Def Age	Rk	ST Age	Rk
2016	11-5	8.8	9.8	310	284	-2	9.4%	8	-5.7%	21	-13.9%	3	1.2%	11	27.9	11	24.6	7	26.3	22	25.9	27	26.2	13
2017	3-13	4.0	4.1	246	388	-3	-24.5%	31	-9.4%	23	7.6%	25	-7.5%	32	59.0	26	36.4	17	26.5	23	26.0	20	25.6	24
2018	5-11	6.9	7.8	369	412	+2	-1.2%	16	1.1%	14	6.8%	25	4.5%	3	32.6	14	18.5	7	26.9	14	26.1	21	26.0	12
2019	4-12	5.3	3.8	341	451	-17	-18.6%	27	-7.4%	22	11.5%	28	0.3%	17	49.0	21	23.6	5	26.7	17	26.0	20	25.4	26
2020	6-10	5.7	6.5	280	357	0	-13.8%	25	-11.8%	26	3.7%	19	1.7%	12	50.9	25	53.5	24	25.8	25	25.6	28	25.9	17

2020 Performance Based on Most Common Personnel Groups

NYG Offense					NYG Offense vs. Opponents					NYG Defense				NYG Defense vs. Opponents			
Pers	Freq	Yds	DVOA	Run%	Pers	Freq	Yds	DVOA	Run%	Pers	Freq	Yds	DVOA	Pers	Freq	Yds	DVOA
11	55%	5.4	-5.5%	25%	Base	33%	4.9	-8.0%	54%	Base	18%	4.9	-5.4%	11	61%	5.4	3.0%
12	27%	5.3	-3.7%	47%	Nickel	54%	5.3	-6.7%	33%	Nickel	54%	5.5	5.4%	12	16%	4.8	-9.6%
13	10%	4.3	-28.0%	59%	Dime+	11%	5.5	-11.9%	2%	Dime+	26%	5.9	2.5%	21	7%	7.3	43.3%
22	4%	3.9	-10.9%	78%	Goal Line	1%	-0.2	11.2%	80%	Goal Line	1%	0.8	47.0%	10	4%	7.5	20.0%
21	1%	6.0	28.2%	43%	Big	1%	3.3	-108.2%	63%					13	3%	4.3	-16.5%

Strategic Tendencies

Run/Pass		Rk	Formation		Rk	Pass Rush		Rk	Secondary		Rk	Strategy		Rk
Runs, first half	42%	6	Form: Single Back	85%	8	Rush 3	16.9%	3	4 DB	18%	25	Play Action	27%	17
Runs, first down	49%	12	Form: Empty Back	7%	24	Rush 4	67.5%	13	5 DB	54%	20	Offensive Motion	30%	31
Runs, second-long	29%	16	Form: Multi Back	8%	19	Rush 5	13.9%	29	6+ DB	26%	6	Avg Box (Off)	6.64	10
Runs, power sit.	56%	23	Pers: 3+ WR	56%	26	Rush 6+	1.7%	32	Man Coverage	23%	26	Avg Box (Def)	6.22	30
Runs, behind 2H	24%	24	Pers: 2+ TE/6+ OL	43%	4	Edge Rusher Sacks	24.4%	31	CB by Sides	63%	26	Offensive Pace	30.55	19
Pass, ahead 2H	50%	13	Pers: 6+ OL	2%	16	Interior DL Sacks	53.8%	2	S/CB Cover Ratio	38%	4	Defensive Pace	29.95	11
Run-Pass Options	5%	22	Shotgun/Pistol	67%	14	Second Level Sacks	21.8%	19	DB Blitz	13%	17	Go for it on 4th	1.02	30

The Giants ranked sixth in rushing DVOA in the red zone despite the absence of Saquon Barkley, but they were dead-last passing in the red zone. ● The Giants ran two-tight end sets more than twice as often as the year before, mostly with Kaden

Smith joining Evan Engram. ● Daniel Jones struggled against defensive back blitzes, as the Giants offense had league-low numbers of both 3.7 yards per pass and -61.0% DVOA. ● Patrick Graham had the Giants sending three pass-rushers over three times as often as the year before, while only three teams blitzed less often. ● The Giants started the year with James Bradberry playing left cornerback (offensive right side) but within a couple weeks were moving him around the field covering specific receivers.

Passing

Player	DYAR	DVOA	Plays	NtYds	Avg	YAC	C%	TD	Int
D.Jones	-350	-22.4%	491	2657	5.4	4.0	62.8%	11	10
C.McCoy*	-132	-40.7%	71	351	4.9	3.2	60.6%	1	1
M.Glennon	-105	-19.8%	186	988	5.3	3.6	63.4%	7	5

Rushing

Player	DYAR	DVOA	Plays	Yds	Avg	TD	Fum	Suc
W.Gallman*	151	15.5%	147	682	4.6	6	1	54%
A.Morris*	61	19.4%	55	238	4.3	1	0	53%
D.Freeman*	4	-6.6%	54	172	3.2	1	0	43%
D.Jones	67	16.2%	51	433	8.5	1	3	--
D.Lewis*	14	1.4%	29	115	4.0	2	1	41%
S.Barkley	-32	-51.7%	19	34	1.8	0	0	26%
E.Penny	3	-1.6%	6	15	2.5	0	0	67%
S.Shepard	27	42.6%	6	49	8.2	1	0	--
E.Engram	23	9.4%	6	26	4.3	1	0	--
C.McCoy*	-14	-71.2%	5	16	3.2	0	0	--
D.Booker	26	-1.8%	93	423	4.5	3	1	46%
C.Clement	9	2.7%	21	75	3.6	1	0	43%
M.Glennon	-28	-85.3%	6	17	2.8	0	1	--

Receiving

Player	DYAR	DVOA	Plays	Ctch	Yds	Y/C	YAC	TD	C%
D.Slayton	-7	-13.6%	96	50	751	15.0	3.2	3	52%
S.Shepard	25	-9.0%	90	66	656	9.9	3.1	3	73%
G.Tate*	11	-10.0%	52	35	388	11.1	2.1	2	67%
C.J.Board	-14	-24.2%	16	11	101	9.2	3.0	0	69%
A.Mack	14	1.5%	11	7	91	13.0	5.3	0	64%
D.Ratley	-36	-59.5%	10	4	63	15.8	2.5	0	40%
K.Golladay	90	22.0%	32	20	338	16.9	1.9	2	63%
J.Ross	-29	-67.5%	7	2	17	8.5	1.5	0	29%
E.Engram	-114	-24.0%	109	63	654	10.4	4.6	1	58%
K.Smith	-14	-16.4%	21	18	112	6.2	4.9	0	86%
L.Toilolo	6	6.9%	6	5	46	9.2	5.2	0	83%
D.Lewis*	25	1.9%	30	19	127	6.7	4.2	1	63%
W.Gallman*	-11	-21.0%	27	21	114	5.4	4.8	0	78%
D.Freeman*	2	-10.4%	10	7	58	8.3	10.0	0	70%
S.Barkley	17	17.2%	9	6	60	10.0	9.2	0	67%
D.Booker	-26	-37.5%	21	17	84	4.9	4.8	0	81%
C.Clement	5	1.2%	6	5	25	5.0	6.4	0	83%

Offensive Line

Player	Pos	Age	GS	Snaps	Pen	Sk	Pass	Run	Player	Pos	Age	GS	Snaps	Pen	Sk	Pass	Run
Nick Gates	C	26	16/16	1013	6	0	7	5	Will Hernandez	LG	26	13/7	524	1	0	10	3
Kevin Zeitler*	RG	31	16/16	1001	4	2	6	4	Shane Lemieux	LG	24	12/9	504	2	3	16	7
Andrew Thomas	LT	22	16/15	976	5	9	37	5	Zach Fulton	RG	30	16/16	952	3	6.5	19	2
Cameron Fleming*	RT	29	16/16	911	7	4	22	4									

Year	Yards	ALY	Rk	Power	Rk	Stuff	Rk	2Lev	Rk	OpFld	Rk	BB Rt	Rk	Sacks	ASR	Rk	Press	Rk	BB Rt	Rk	Cont
2018	4.69	3.90	29	69%	10	21%	24	1.10	25	1.60	1	7.0%	20	47	7.4%	20	30.7%	17	9.7%	19	29
2019	4.25	3.96	25	58%	26	20%	19	1.10	24	0.99	8	10.7%	20	43	7.1%	17	33.4%	27	12.7%	11	34
2020	4.05	4.20	21	66%	20	17%	14	1.11	24	0.60	22	9.0%	13	50	7.9%	27	29.6%	25	17.4%	32	36

2020 ALY by direction:	Left End: 2.71 (31)	Left Tackle: 3.85 (23)	Mid/Guard: 4.53 (13)	Right Tackle: 3.94 (23)	Right End: 3.17 (29)

Andrew Thomas was tied for the league lead with 42 blown blocks last season, but a whopping 29 of those blocks came in his first eight games, leaving just 13 in the second half of the year. Blown blocks are not an all-encompassing stat for gauging offensive line play, but in Thomas' case they certainly illustrate his broad-based improvement in the second half of the season. ● Center Nick Gates also improved noticeably last season as he gained experience and after Dave DeGuglielmo defeated Marc Colombo in the steel cage match to become the Giants line coach. Gates blew nine blocks in the first eight games but just four in the last eight. ● Matt Peart, on the other hand, looked worse and worse the more he played at right tackle in relief of Cameron Fleming (now in Denver) late in the season. Peart will compete with returning Nate Solder at right tackle. Joe Judge spoke about the 33-year-old Solder in OTAs, stressing how hard he's working to get back into football shape after a COVID opt-out and making lots of vague statements about the value of Solder's veteran leadership. Translation: Judge really really really wants Peart to seize the job. ● Left guard Shane Lemieux blew a stunning 24 blocks in just 466 snaps. His blown-block rate of 4.8% was the highest in the NFL among players with 400 snaps; Thomas finished second. Sorry, but there is no evidence of Lemieux improving as the season wore on. Potential competitors for Lemieux include Texans castoff Zach Fulton and possibly Solder. 🏈 Will Hernandez, who was benched in favor of Lemieux after a COVID-list stint last season, is moving from left to right guard. Hernandez may also have been playing through an undisclosed injury and/or gotten caught in the middle of the DeGuglielmo/Colombo power struggle/smackdown. At any rate, he often ended up subbing into games to replace Lemieux and prevent quarterback fatalities. Hernandez could either be the Giants best linemen this year or get cut in August, which encapsulates just how much wish-casting is going on along the Giants offensive line in 2021.

Defensive Front

Defensive Line	Age	Pos	G	Snaps	Plays	TmPct	Rk	Stop	Dfts	BTkl	Runs	St%	Rk	RuYd	Rk	Sack	Hit	Hur	Dsrpt
						Overall							vs. Run				Pass Rush		
Leonard Williams	27	DE	16	800	58	6.7%	14	46	20	3	41	78%	35	1.9	23	11.5	19	30	3
Dalvin Tomlinson*	27	DT	16	656	53	6.1%	26	42	15	1	44	75%	47	1.7	14	3.5	6	11	7
Dexter Lawrence	24	DE	16	653	55	6.4%	22	44	12	2	47	77%	41	2.2	38	4.0	5	15	2
B.J. Hill	26	DE	16	372	33	3.8%	--	18	3	1	24	58%	--	4.1	--	1.0	2	14	0
Danny Shelton	28	DT	12	498	38	6.0%	28	25	5	3	33	70%	64	2.7	55	1.0	3	7	3

Edge Rushers	Age	Pos	G	Snaps	Plays	TmPct	Rk	Stop	Dfts	BTkl	Runs	St%	Rk	RuYd	Rk	Sack	Hit	Hur	Dsrpt
						Overall							vs. Run				Pass Rush		
Kyler Fackrell*	30	OLB	12	607	36	5.6%	33	24	12	9	23	65%	70	3.4	80	4.0	6	12	2
Jabaal Sheard*	32	DE	10	275	20	3.7%	71	14	8	1	14	71%	48	2.0	27	1.5	5	11	1
Ifeadi Odenigbo	27	DE	15	697	35	4.5%	55	22	8	1	26	50%	95	3.8	86	3.5	10	19	0
Ryan Anderson	27	DE	9	145	7	1.6%	--	5	1	1	7	71%	--	0.9	--	0.0	0	4	0

Linebackers	Age	Pos	G	Snaps	Plays	TmPct	Rk	Stop	Dfts	BTkl	Runs	St%	Rk	RuYd	Rk	Sack	Hit	Hur	Tgts	Suc%	Rk	Yd/P	Rk	PD	Int
						Overall							vs. Run				Pass Rush				vs. Pass				
Blake Martinez	27	ILB	16	1062	156	18.1%	6	85	27	11	88	66%	15	3.9	37	3.0	3	5	42	38%	64	6.9	50	5	1
Tae Crowder	24	ILB	11	403	57	9.6%	62	22	3	8	31	55%	49	4.1	45	1.0	2	5	15	33%	--	9.9	--	1	0
Devante Downs	26	ILB	16	232	28	3.2%	--	13	1	1	13	62%	--	3.9	--	0.0	1	1	8	50%	--	4.5	--	1	0
David Mayo	28	ILB	11	193	20	3.4%	--	10	3	3	13	77%	--	2.5	--	0.0	0	3	5	0%	--	10.0	--	0	0
Reggie Ragland	28	MLB	16	562	52	6.2%	80	28	9	2	40	58%	37	3.6	25	1.0	2	9	10	50%	--	4.8	--	1	0

Year	Yards	ALY	Rk	Power	Rk	Stuff	Rk	2Lev	Rk	OpFld	Rk	BB Rt	Rk	Sacks	ASR	Rk	Press	Rk	BB Rt	Rk
2018	4.25	4.38	18	64%	12	20%	13	1.21	16	0.85	17	8.0%	19	30	4.9%	31	30.8%	16	6.3%	31
2019	3.96	4.02	7	59%	9	21%	11	1.16	17	0.71	15	13.1%	14	36	6.3%	23	28.6%	23	12.3%	26
2020	4.23	4.27	13	74%	29	17%	17	1.18	14	0.71	17	10.1%	24	40	6.6%	17	25.1%	16	13.2%	16
2020 ALY by direction:		Left End: 4.54 (16)			Left Tackle: 4.55 (20)			Mid/Guard: 4.32 (14)				Right Tackle: 3.28 (2)				Right End: 4.88 (21)			

Opponents ran in the "middle/guard" direction against the Giants on just 41.9% of all rushes last year, the lowest rate in the entire NFL since 2017. Opponents were reluctant to run into the teeth of Dexter Lawrence, Leonard Williams, and Dalvin Tomlinson, meaning that the "stout up the middle" philosophy is working to some degree. 🏈 Blake Martinez finished third among linebackers with 151 combined tackles and fourth with 69 tackles short of the first down. 🏈 Martinez is an avid Pokemon card collector, and he participated in "box break" auctions during the offseason. Martinez described the thrill of finding a rare Charizard in an unopened pack as "like getting a sack, that adrenaline rush, those endorphins." Dave Gettleman was unavailable to comment upon Martinez's remarks, because his head exploded the moment he heard them. 🏈 Danny Shelton is likely to pick up many of the snaps vacated by Dalvin Tomlinson. That's not an upgrade. Shelton performed well as a Patriots situational run-stuffer but is now taking the traditional pre-retirement tour of Belichick assistants. 🏈 The situation on the edge is foggy. Second-round pick Azeez Ojulari (Georgia) is more of an all-around defender than a pure edge rusher. He should be effective as a hybrid DE/OLB in Patrick Graham's defense (i.e., he can drop into coverage better than the typical college edge rusher), but he won't be the sack specialist the Giants need to complement Williams. Ryan Anderson, who never really panned out as an edge rusher in Washington, won't be that player either, nor will Ifeadi Odenigbo, who flopped when elevated from situational pass-rusher to starter for the Vikings last year. That may open the door for fourth-round pick Elerson G. Smith (Northern Iowa), whose SackSEER rating of 95.5% was fueled by a 41.5-inch vertical jump; 10-foot, 7-inch broad jump; and 7.0s 3-cone drill at 262 pounds at his pro day.

Defensive Secondary

Secondary	Age	Pos	G	Snaps	Plays	Overall TmPct	Rk	Stop	Dfts	BTkl	vs. Run Runs	St%	Rk	RuYd	Rk	vs. Pass Tgts	Tgt%	Rk	aDOT	Suc%	Rk	Yd/P	Rk	PD	Int
Logan Ryan	30	FS	16	1050	100	11.6%	27	31	14	11	35	23%	62	9.2	58	33	8.7%	32	9.2	48%	40	7.2	26	9	1
James Bradberry	28	CB	15	1018	71	8.8%	40	29	15	14	15	33%	56	6.8	42	67	18.2%	55	10.7	49%	45	6.4	16	18	3
Jabrill Peppers	26	SS	15	910	100	12.3%	19	51	23	15	40	60%	5	4.6	9	40	12.1%	14	10.9	48%	43	7.8	35	11	1
Julian Love	23	FS	16	718	63	7.3%	65	15	8	5	23	35%	40	7.6	44	20	7.7%	41	10.1	40%	61	8.7	47	3	1
Isaac Yiadom	25	CB	16	633	50	5.8%	78	14	5	5	10	40%	48	6.5	37	42	18.3%	53	11.9	50%	43	7.9	49	5	0
Darnay Holmes	23	CB	12	441	35	5.4%	--	15	10	7	4	25%	--	8.0	--	28	17.5%	--	8.0	54%	--	6.7	--	5	1
Xavier McKinney	23	FS	6	209	25	7.7%	--	7	4	2	8	25%	--	7.5	--	6	7.9%	--	9.3	67%	--	7.2	--	1	1

Year	Pass D Rank	vs. #1 WR	Rk	vs. #2 WR	Rk	vs. Other WR	Rk	WR Wide	Rk	WR Slot	Rk	vs. TE	Rk	vs. RB	Rk
2018	26	15.0%	26	-18.8%	7	20.0%	28	-18.7%	4	30.3%	30	3.1%	18	-14.6%	6
2019	31	32.8%	32	-2.2%	15	37.2%	32	-6.4%	16	48.2%	32	6.1%	20	12.8%	24
2020	22	-3.8%	14	3.0%	21	29.9%	31	-4.1%	12	9.1%	26	11.4%	24	-5.7%	11

Patrick Graham's scheme was zone-heavy in 2020, using man coverage on just 23.1% of passes last year. That ranked 26th in the NFL. Lack of depth behind James Bradberry at cornerback may have made Graham reluctant to use man coverage too often. By DVOA, the difference between the Giants in man and zone was very small, less than five percentage points; it was larger by passer rating, as Giants opponents had 104.7 passer rating against man but 88.9 against zone. ➤ Bradberry is coming off a remarkable year. He averaged 0.7 yards allowed per coverage snap, third behind Jalen Ramsey and Jaire Alexander among cornerbacks with 50-plus targets. He also tied for second in the NFL in passes defensed. ➤ New arrival Adoree' Jackson, who missed most of last season with a knee injury, is an incredibly athletic defender with a flag-football-on-rollerblades tackling style. He's an odd fit for a defense that is expected to play a lot of zone. ➤ Third-round pick Aaron Robinson is a thickly built cornerback/safety hybrid who handled plays in front of him very well for Central Florida but either gave up a big play or turned into a Grabby Gus on deeper routes. Think of Robinson as the Anti-Adoree' and pencil him into a slot role. ➤ Rookie Xavier McKinney broke his foot in 2020 training camp, then returned to play very well as a multi-purpose safety down the stretch. He should push cornerback-turned-free-safety Logan Ryan into more of a nickel hybrid role. ➤ It's time to accept that Jabrill Peppers has become a pretty useful strong safety and return man but will never be the positionless three-platoon megaweapon some of us hoped he would be when he left Michigan. Peppers' production-to-expectations ratio remains low, but he's a nasty situational edge rusher, plays the run well, and doesn't get pan seared when covering slot receivers.

Special Teams

Year	DVOA	Rank	FG/XP	Rank	Net Kick	Rank	Kick Ret	Rank	Net Punt	Rank	Punt Ret	Rank	Hidden	Rank
2018	4.5%	3	11.5	2	5.3	2	2.2	7	9.6	2	-5.8	29	-16.5	31
2019	0.3%	17	-9.7	29	5.7	4	0.5	13	2.5	13	2.4	8	-2.7	19
2020	1.7%	12	14.0	1	-7.8	30	-3.4	22	2.5	13	3.4	9	-14.3	30

Graham Gano's touchback rate of 41% was the second-lowest in the league among players with more than 20 kickoffs; only Lions punter Jack Fox was lower. Joe Judge knows the value of deep kickoffs, but Gano was 31-of-32 on field goals and is also one of Dave Gettleman's Panthers imports, so Judge must learn to live with the lack of touchbacks. ➤ Riley Dixon finished fifth in the league with 27 punts inside the 20-yard line and sixth with nine inside the 10-yard line. Those numbers have a tiny bit to do with Dixon's performance (he's fine), a little to do with Judge's special teams acumen, and everything else to do with the fact that lots of Giants drives stalled and Judge was skittish about fourth-down conversions. ➤ Candidates to replace Dion Lewis on kickoff returns include rookie Kadarius Toney, former Eagles return man Corey Clement, and second-year cornerback Darnay Holmes, who returned kickoffs for UCLA. Jabrill Peppers has turned into a pretty good punt returner and will likely retain the role.

New York Jets

2020 Record: 2-14	**Total DVOA:** -30.5% (26)	**2021 Mean Projection:** 6.1 wins	**On the Clock (0-5):** 44%
Pythagorean Wins: 2.8 (32)	**Offense:** -20.5% (31)	**Postseason Odds:** 13.0%	**Mediocrity (6-8):** 39%
Snap-Weighted Age: 26.3 (19)	**Defense:** 4.7% (21)	**Super Bowl Odds:** 0.5%	**Playoff Contender (9-11):** 15%
Average Opponent: 2.6% (8)	**Special Teams:** -5.3% (29)	**Proj. Avg. Opponent:** -0.8% (20)	**Super Bowl Contender (12+):** 3%

2020: Ooh, nothing's going to bring him back (he's gone for good).

2021: The first days are the hardest days (don't you worry anymore).

>>Welcome back to Fumblr, the NFL's premier service for shopping for quick turnarounds, anti-tanking supplies, and complete franchise refurbishments. Remember: If You They Want You To Cook The Dinner, At Least They Ought To Let You Shop For The Groceries™.

>>Welcome back, The New York Jets. While we value all our customers, it's our regular returning franchises that help us make the offseason content machine run as smoothly as it does. While you're here, we'd love it if you'd rate your previous orders. How likely are you to recommend your 2019 purchase of "The Adam Gase Experience" to a friend or colleague?

>>I'm sorry; we can only accept positive numbers between 1 and 10. Your attempted inputs of "negative a zillion," a frankly impressive breadth of profanity, or a collection of rude emoji are not acceptable responses.

The failure of the Adam Gase era was more than a failure of Xs and Os, though there was plenty of that to go around. You don't go 9-23 by unleashing a high-powered, beautifully schemed offense. The Jets lacked talent, for sure, but they also lacked an identity—neither physical nor finesse, without a key sense of logic or continuity to their play calling on offense. The entire reason Gase got not one but two head coaching opportunities was based on the reputation he earned working with Peyton Manning in Denver. With only six games with a positive offensive DVOA over the last two years, the fewest in the league, Gase utterly failed at the one thing he could hang his hat on.

>> **Your request for a refund has been denied. Before making your next purchase, we advise you to read the user reviews from previous customers.**

But more than that, Gase brought with him the same disfunction and disorder that soured his time in Miami. He alienated his locker room, feuding with players in the media and alienating stars such as Jamal Adams. He practically ignored his defense, letting Gregg Williams have free reign to call all the Cover-0 blitzes he wanted. He demonstrated terrible personnel management both by placing injured players in the lineup and by continuing to run out ineffective elderly players he was comfortable with. He lied to the media about who was calling the offensive plays, out of fear it would make his assistants look more competent than he was. We called Gase a horrible result of a muddled search when he was hired, someone more concerned with protecting his power than running a team. If anything, we undersold it.

>> **You have successfully added the San Francisco Treat boxset to your shopping cart.**

Teams looking to recover from a terrible coaching regime tend to zig as hard as they can in the opposite direction with their next hire. The Jets went from a soft-spoken defensive coach in Todd Bowles to an offensive disciplinarian in Gase, and now have zagged back to the defensive side of the ball with former 49ers defensive coordinator Robert Saleh. But it's not just his on-field specialties that have made Saleh such a breath of fresh air.

>> **View our recommended reviews for Robert Saleh, from a wide variety of satisfied customers.**

It is difficult to find a coach with more universal acclaim from his former players than Saleh. When the Jets made the hiring official, it was greeted with showerings of praise from Richard Sherman, Fred Warner, DeForest Buckner, Russell Wilson, and more. Where Gase has left a trail of disgruntled players and bad vibes in his wake, Saleh has a track record of players singing his praises—Houston, Seattle, Jacksonville, San Francisco, you name it. Saleh's players would run through a wall for him, which would be convenient if playing football involved running through any walls. At the very least, bringing Saleh in should create a less toxic environment around the team. They may well be a two- or three-win team again, but getting free of the toxic atmosphere surrounding Gase should make being a Jets fan significantly more fun going forward.

In fact, the last time you could find a sense of negativity surrounding Saleh was among San Francisco fans in 2018. When Saleh took over the 49ers' defensive coordinator job, he

2021 Jets Schedule

Week	Opp.	Week	Opp.	Week	Opp.
1	at CAR	7	at NE	13	PHI
2	NE	8	CIN	14	NO
3	at DEN	9	at IND (Thu.)	15	at MIA
4	TEN	10	BUF	16	JAX
5	at ATL (U.K.)	11	MIA	17	TB
6	BYE	12	at HOU	18	at BUF

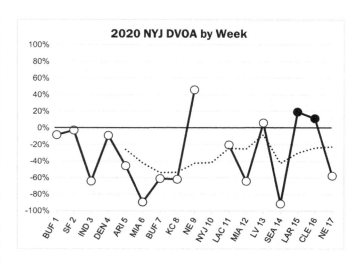

2020 NYJ DVOA by Week

inherited a woeful team lacking talent on all three levels, and he was no miracle cure. The 49ers ranked 26th and 24th in defensive DVOA in Saleh's first two years, and there were some calls from outside the organization that the team should move on and find someone else; it clearly wasn't working. Then, in 2019, Saleh adjusted his scheme, switching the defensive line to using more Wide-9 with a focus on penetration rather than reading and reacting, and switching to a Cover 2-based system in the secondary. It also helped to add Nick Bosa and Dee Ford to a line already bursting with first-round picks, but don't think the 49ers' defensive improvement was solely due to personnel. Dragging the 49ers' defense to a sixth-place ranking in 2020 despite leading the league in defensive adjusted games lost may well have been the coaching feat of the year. The 49ers had a different defensive starting lineup in all 16 games last season; they were forced to put 37 different players on the field, second-most in the league. An average performance out of that lot would have been commendable; gluing together a very good defense out of that mess deserves an award.

>> Please allow 12 to 18 months for delivery.

Saleh's no one-year wonder, but Jets fans hoping for a miracle turnaround in just one season are setting their expectations poorly. All else being equal, bad defenses with new schemes tend to improve less than bad defenses in their second or third year of a scheme. And all things are not equal in New York. You could make a strong argument that the Jets ended the 2020 season with the least talented roster in all of football. Saleh and Joe Douglas did a good job this year finding talent in free agency and the draft, and the Jets could be significantly better at pretty much every position this season. But considering the starting bar was so low, there's a lot of climbing to do before the Jets approach respectable, much less good. Considering that moderately useful players like Tarell Basham and Jordan Jenkins were let go, replaced by lesser-proven players who may be better scheme fits, it's also not a clear progression forward. This is a rebuild, no doubt about it, and it will take some time to get everything in place before .500 is a reasonable goal.

But enough talk about generalities. Let's look at the pieces Saleh has, how they'll fit into his scheme, and which parts haven't quite arrived yet.

>> You attempted to order a defensive line featuring five first-round picks, but those items are temporarily out of stock. May we suggest as a re-

placement a high-priced free agent and some oddly shaped pieces?

While the difference between a 3-4 and a 4-3 front is overblown, there's no denying that Robert Saleh's aggressive 4-3 makes for a clunky change from Gregg William's hybrid system. Going from a two-gap to a one-gap scheme will change responsibilities of linemen, alter the reads for the players behind them, and so on and so forth. Some early growing pains are to be expected.

Further complicating matters is the fact that the preexisting strengths of the Jets defense don't line up with what Saleh asks his team to do. The interior line trio of Quinnen Williams, Foley Fatukasi, and John Franklin-Myers did some great work for the Jets last season, but only Williams has an obvious place in the system. Williams fits perfectly as the DeForest Buckner-esque 3-technique. Saleh's Wide-9 front puts the edge rushers outside the tight ends, forcing the offensive line to slide outside to handle them and opening up gaps inside. Williams was already fourth in ESPN's Pass Rush Win Rate among defensive tackles; giving him more isolated "don't think, just go" snaps one-on-one with guards could see his production soar even higher.

The other interior lineman usually plays the 1-technique, and that's a problem for both Fatukasi and Franklin-Myers. Saleh asks for speed and explosion from his interior linemen, while Fatukasi is more of a power and timing guy. Sheldon Rankins, despite being comparatively undersized, is more Saleh's traditional type. Meanwhile, while moving inside helped Franklin-Myers excel last season, he's not a fit for the 1-tech role at all. Franklin-Myers did play outside with Los Angeles, but he was a bland situational pass-rusher. Despite his small frame, he performed much better inside as a 3-tech. Saleh routinely rotated seven linemen in San Francisco, so there will be plenty of snaps for both Fatukasi and Franklin-Myers, but they're not going to benefit from the scheme change nearly as much as Williams will.

On the outside, Carl Lawson comes in from Cincinnati and immediately becomes the best edge rusher the Jets have seen since 2017. His hype as a three-down breakout player last year has been a little oversold, but he had the fourth-highest pressure rate among defensive linemen last season. The slot across from him, however, is more of a mystery. Franklin-Myers will be in the mix for that other edge spot, but Vinny Curry or ex-49er Ronald Blair probably fit better.

Honestly, the best lineup the Jets might have is a NASCAR-style speed package with Williams and Franklin-Myers inside, joining Lawson and Curry on the edge. That's not something Saleh has regularly used in the past, but it fits his philosophy of putting as much speed on the field as possible, and Saleh has shown a willingness to adjust his scheme before. He'll have to be creative and flexible to squeeze the most out of the talent he has available on the line.

And he'll have to squeeze it all out, because the rest of the defense isn't ideal.

>> I'm sorry; your membership level does not qualify you for "competent NFL cornerbacks."

When Saleh switched to the Wide-9 front, he also switched to a Cover-2 behind it. Specifically, he used lots of Tampa-2, taking advantage of the excellent coverage abilities of Fred Warner to drop back and cover the deep middle. That was pretty much all the 49ers ran in 2019, blitzing just 19% of the time and trusting their front four to generate pressure on their own. The massive injuries they suffered in 2020 necessitated that blitz frequency jumping to 32%, which meant fewer linebackers dropping into coverage, but the principles were the same. It's a schematically simple defense which puts emphasis on speed and aggressive tackling.

The Jets don't really have the cornerbacks to run a Tampa-2. Or a Cover-2. Or a Cover-1, Cover-3, or frankly Cover-Anybody. New York had holes to fill everywhere on the roster, and the secondary was mostly slapped with a "wait until next year" Post-it Note. Oh, the safeties are fine—Marcus Maye isn't Jamal Adams, but he was a rare playmaking highlight in the secondary. LaMarcus Joyner was brought in to compete with Ashtyn Davis across from him. But the cornerback situation is a nightmare. Brian Poole was the only Jets corner with at least 25 targets last season to have a success rate of over 50%; he's unsigned at the moment.

There are no veterans penciled into the starting lineup. The Jets look to have the youngest cornerback group in the league, and it's not a lineup filled with young studs, either. No one in contention for a starting job was drafted earlier than the fifth round. There's a chance that the switch to a more press-/zone-based scheme from Gregg Williams' more aggressive approach could help some of these young players, however, and that's what the 2020 Jets will have to rely on. There are some places you can find optimism, if you squint—the length and physicality of Bryce Hall, the 4.2s speed of Javelin Guidry. But your guess as to who will start at cornerback is as good as anyone else's; none of last years' players (especially the overmatched Blessuan Austin) have any guarantees of a roster spot, much less a starting job. The Jets will need two or three players to take significant steps forward just to be competent in coverage. This isn't a situation like the defensive line,

where the struggle is matching scheme and talent when they don't quite perfectly align. Consider this an evaluation year to see which, if any, players will avoid getting replaced when the Jets inevitably draft a corner or three next year.

We also have no idea if the Jets are going to have that competent cover linebacker Saleh loves, because we still haven't really gotten to see C.J. Mosley in a Jets uniform. When we last saw Mosley qualify for our leaderboards, he had an acceptable 51% success rate in coverage, and he had been sharper in previous years. But that last qualified season was 2018. He played only two games in 2019 before getting injured and opted out of 2020 entirely. Scheme fit isn't the issue; he'll fit fine as the Mike. The question is just how good he'll be after such a long layoff, and whether he can play all three downs as a pass defender or will just serve as a two-down run plugger. Either is valuable compared to what the Jets rostered last season, but the questions remain very much up in the air.

>> Congratulations! Your cart full of offensive draft picks qualifies for free shipping!

The back of the Jets' defense will depend on Saleh coaching preexisting players up, because New York spent the lion's share of the offseason adding talent to their offense. Outside of Lawson, all their major free-agent acquisitions came on the offensive side of the ball, as did their first four draft picks. That means the imported San Francisco offensive coaching staff, in both coordinator Mike LaFleur and run game coordinator John Benton, get the benefit of the Jets' talent infusion right off the bat.

>> We're sorry; the last "Trevor Lawrence" just sold out. May we suggest the Famous Idaho Potato Bowl MVP instead?

That starts with second overall pick Zach Wilson, who will assuredly be the opening day starter if for no other reason than the rest of the quarterback room is bare. If you feel like the Jets have been looking for a quarterback forever, you're not entirely wrong; the last New York passer to put up multiple seasons of positive DVOA was Chad Pennington in the mid-2000s. But now there's a shiny new passer in town, who will definitely turn things around, unlike Sam Darnold. Or Christian Hackenberg. Or Geno Smith. Or Mark Sanchez.

OK, so Jets fans have reasons to be skeptical of a shiny new passer coming in to save the day. And it's fair if that skepticism is backed by the fact that we only saw one really great season from Wilson in college, in the midst of a slapped-together schedule in thanks to the pandemic; his 2019 season was derailed by injuries and he was still fairly raw as a true freshman in 2018. In addition, Jets fans may still hold a residual grudge against Adam Gase for winning *just* enough games to cost them the first overall pick and Trevor Lawrence, with Wilson feeling like something of a consolation prize.

However, Lawrence and Wilson come out with nearly identical QBASE projections, and Wilson dwarfs the five other quarterbacks the Jets have picked in the top 100 since 2004.

Lawrence's track record made him the safer pick, but Wilson's success last year wasn't just about facing inferior competition. Wilson had the best deep ball of the draft class, he's exceptionally accurate to all areas of the field, and his creativity on the move has drawn comparisons to Patrick Mahomes. Obviously, that's a massively unfair standard to hold Wilson to, and he's not a perfect prospect—his processing prowess in his progressions perhaps pale parallel to other premium players—but Jets fans should be excited with their new passer.

Shanahan-style coaches—including LaFleur's older brother in Green Bay—typically look for their quarterbacks to utilize play-action and be effective when on the move with bootlegs and rollouts and things of that nature. Wilson checks those boxes, throwing 19 touchdowns and no interceptions on play-action last season; he was good for one or two 20-plus-yard bombs per game off of play-action. When off-platform, his arm strength and improvisational skills allow him to make explosive splash plays without putting the ball in harm's way. He should be an ideal fit for what LaFleur plans to do.

All that being said, we would expect Wilson to struggle some, especially early in the year. He was rarely pressured at BYU, with quite a few games ending up with him basically playing seven-on-seven drills and picking apart defenses. He also has a bit of the Favreian gunslingerness to his game and sometimes overtrusts his arm strength in a way that might get him into trouble against NFL defenses. Watching him adjust to the speed of the pro game and handling how quick the pocket can collapse when you're not playing Western Kentucky will be key to his short-term development.

>> Your purchases qualify for speedy delivery!

At the skill positions, the Jets' offense will be based around speed mismatches and spacing. In the passing game, the 49ers love giving the ball quickly to athletic players in space. Deebo Samuel led all qualified players in YAC+ last season, with George Kittle and Jeff Wilson each finishing in the top three at their positions as well. Part of this was aided by San Francisco's heavy use of 21 personnel, trying to get opposing defenses to put that third linebacker on the field and then challenging those slower players to keep up with their receivers. The Jets won't run much 21 personnel; they do not have a fullback. Instead, they'll probably look more like Mike's brother's offense in Green Bay, substituting more two-tight end sets to try get the same effect. Chris Herndon's role should increase; he'll be asked to be a more physical player than he has in recent years, and we might see Trevon Wesco as a Kyle Juszcyzk substitute.

However the Jets manage to get their big guys onto the field, they'll be providing space for what's probably the most upgraded receiving corps in the league. They're still lacking a true No. 1, but both Corey Davis and Keelan Cole have been versatile players throughout their careers, and second-round pick Elijah Moore's exceptional athleticism (a 4.35s 40-yard dash and 6.67s 3-cone drill tell the story) has already been turning heads during OTAs and minicamp. Add in the useful Jamison Crowder returning to the fold and you have a massive improvement over the Breshad Perrimans and Braxton Berrioses of the world. And that's not including fourth-round pick Michael Carter, who had one of the top receiving indexes in our BackCAST projections, or Tevin Coleman, who has three top-10 receiving DVOA seasons in Shanahan-style offenses. Sam Darnold never got the benefit of a receiving corps of this quality.

And then there's the offensive line. While trading up for an interior player such as first-round pick Alijah Vera-Tucker is a bad use of resources, he's a great fit for the outside zone-heavy scheme that LaFleur and Benton will be bringing with them. Vera-Tucker did a lot of outside zone-blocking at USC to great effect. San Francisco's system generally asks for lighter, athletic linemen, because they're asked to move laterally more than most other systems, even other outside zone situations. Vera-Tucker fits that model, with strong results in all the various shuttle and jump drills during his pro day. He'll be fine pulling and trapping and finding moving targets in space. Put next to last year's first round pick Mekhi Becton, who also has plenty of outside zone experience from college, and the Jets look to have a very solid left side of their line. They also have to start three other linemen, but one step at a time.

>> Thank you for your continued patronage of Fumblr. We hope you enjoy your new coaching package. Please expect results in 2 to 3 business seasons.

The Jets are obviously a massive work in progress. Our projections have them once again as the worst team in the league. Everything we've talked about here is a matter of potential or projections or possibilities, and sometimes those simply do not come true. The secondary is likely to be atrocious, and too much for the defensive line to overcome even if they're used to their maximum potential. There's no evidence yet that Saleh will be an effective head coach; not all coordinators step in and succeed off the bat. Rookies flop, offensive lines crumble, regimes fall. The best-case scenario—Wilson immediately stepping in as a quality quarterback, and Saleh's scheme resulting in a Wade Phillips-esque first-year turnaround—still might not be enough to have the Jets sniffing double-digit wins. We're being charitable with some of our descriptions above because we're talking about how pieces might work or could work. Some of them won't and will need to be replaced next year.

But even if the Jets are once again battling for the top pick in the draft, they can at least feel more positive about the direction the team is going in. After a year of patiently (or impatiently) waiting for Adam Gase to get fired, New York fans can at least feel like their team has a plan towards eventually being competitive again. It won't be in 2021, but a season without such a crushing sense of despair might just do for now.

Bryan Knowles

2020 Jets by Week

Wk	vs.	W-L	PF	PA	YDF	YDA	TO	Total	Off	Def	ST
1	at BUF	L	17	27	254	404	0	-8.2%	-11.5%	-13.7%	-10.4%
2	SF	L	13	31	277	359	1	-2.7%	-12.8%	-10.4%	-0.3%
3	at IND	L	7	36	260	353	-3	-64.0%	-42.0%	14.2%	-7.7%
4	DEN	L	28	37	321	359	3	-8.9%	-9.4%	0.2%	0.7%
5	ARI	L	10	30	285	496	1	-45.4%	-3.9%	41.5%	0.0%
6	at MIA	L	0	24	263	302	1	-89.4%	-62.6%	3.6%	-23.1%
7	BUF	L	10	18	191	422	-1	-60.8%	-56.7%	-2.2%	-6.4%
8	at KC	L	9	35	221	496	-1	-61.7%	-38.8%	23.5%	0.6%
9	NE	L	27	30	322	433	-1	46.2%	55.7%	15.7%	6.2%
10	BYE										
11	at LAC	L	28	34	292	376	0	-20.1%	-10.7%	6.1%	-3.3%
12	MIA	L	3	20	260	345	0	-64.1%	-55.7%	-3.5%	-11.9%
13	LV	L	28	31	376	440	-1	6.3%	-3.1%	-9.5%	-0.1%
14	at SEA	L	3	40	185	410	0	-91.3%	-60.8%	17.7%	-12.8%
15	at LAR	W	23	20	289	303	1	19.5%	11.2%	-9.2%	-0.9%
16	CLE	W	23	16	333	299	2	11.6%	-5.1%	-29.4%	-12.7%
17	at NE	L	14	28	350	404	-2	-57.5%	-18.0%	36.4%	-3.1%

Trends and Splits

	Offense	Rank	Defense	Rank
Total DVOA	-20.5%	31	4.7%	21
Unadjusted VOA	-23.1%	32	8.9%	27
Weighted Trend	-19.7%	31	4.8%	19
Variance	9.8%	28	3.6%	8
Average Opponent	-0.4%	13	1.3%	12
Passing	-12.5%	30	22.9%	28
Rushing	-22.6%	27	-20.0%	8
First Down	-16.3%	27	4.1%	22
Second Down	-24.6%	31	4.5%	18
Third Down	-21.9%	30	6.7%	20
First Half	-11.9%	25	9.0%	27
Second Half	-30.9%	32	0.6%	13
Red Zone	-28.4%	29	5.9%	20
Late and Close	-46.0%	32	-3.8%	13

Five-Year Performance

Year	W-L	Pyth W	Est W	PF	PA	TO	Total	Rk	Off	Rk	Def	Rk	ST	Rk	Off AGL	Rk	Def AGL	Rk	Off Age	Rk	Def Age	Rk	ST Age	Rk
2016	5-11	4.4	4.4	275	409	-20	-34.5%	32	-22.3%	31	5.4%	23	-6.8%	32	67.1	29	42.6	18	27.5	6	26.4	19	26.0	19
2017	5-11	5.6	4.9	298	382	-4	-19.2%	27	-10.7%	25	5.6%	22	-3.0%	25	37.7	19	9.0	4	27.1	13	25.6	27	25.9	13
2018	4-12	5.3	5.6	333	441	-10	-17.0%	26	-20.2%	29	4.9%	22	8.1%	1	47.2	23	23.2	9	26.4	19	26.0	23	26.0	13
2019	7-9	5.6	6.2	276	359	-4	-17.7%	26	-25.4%	32	-4.2%	11	3.4%	4	76.4	31	83.7	32	27.1	9	25.7	23	26.5	5
2020	2-14	2.8	3.3	243	457	0	-30.5%	32	-20.5%	31	4.7%	21	-5.3%	29	46.6	22	77.3	31	26.7	18	26.1	21	26.3	10

2020 Performance Based on Most Common Personnel Groups

NYJ Offense					NYJ Offense vs. Opponents					NYJ Defense				NYJ Defense vs. Opponents			
Pers	Freq	Yds	DVOA	Run%	Pers	Freq	Yds	DVOA	Run%	Pers	Freq	Yds	DVOA	Pers	Freq	Yds	DVOA
11	72%	5.0	-12.9%	33%	Base	16%	5.0	-17.8%	64%	Base	16%	5.4	-1.1%	11	57%	6.0	3.2%
12	16%	4.9	-30.9%	64%	Nickel	69%	4.9	-16.1%	38%	Nickel	83%	6.1	5.8%	12	22%	6.3	15.1%
13	3%	3.4	-26.3%	78%	Dime+	15%	5.0	-20.8%	13%	Dime+	1%	6.1	-23.9%	21	11%	6.0	-7.1%
02	3%	6.3	-4.4%	0%	Goal Line	0%	0.5	-11.1%	100%	Goal Line	0%	1.0	50.7%	10	4%	7.0	24.9%
01	2%	4.6	0.7%	6%										22	1%	6.1	31.8%
10	2%	3.1	-65.6%	24%										20	1%	4.2	2.2%

Strategic Tendencies

Run/Pass		Rk	Formation		Rk	Pass Rush		Rk	Secondary		Rk	Strategy		Rk
Runs, first half	41%	8	Form: Single Back	84%	9	Rush 3	6.8%	14	4 DB	16%	27	Play Action	24%	25
Runs, first down	49%	13	Form: Empty Back	7%	25	Rush 4	58.8%	25	5 DB	83%	2	Offensive Motion	41%	22
Runs, second-long	32%	8	Form: Multi Back	9%	17	Rush 5	28.2%	5	6+ DB	1%	29	Avg Box (Off)	6.59	13
Runs, power sit.	64%	10	Pers: 3+ WR	79%	4	Rush 6+	6.2%	12	Man Coverage	30%	18	Avg Box (Def)	6.77	6
Runs, behind 2H	32%	8	Pers: 2+ TE/6+ OL	23%	24	Edge Rusher Sacks	24.2%	32	CB by Sides	89%	6	Offensive Pace	30.59	20
Pass, ahead 2H	52%	9	Pers: 6+ OL	0%	30	Interior DL Sacks	54.8%	1	S/CB Cover Ratio	23%	23	Defensive Pace	29.80	8
Run-Pass Options	4%	27	Shotgun/Pistol	62%	21	Second Level Sacks	21.0%	22	DB Blitz	15%	10	Go for it on 4th	1.25	26

The Jets ranked 31st in how often they threw to the middle of the field, just 19% of targets. ● The Jets had the league's worst numbers when running on second-and-long by both DVOA (-72.2%) and yards per carry (3.2). ● The Jets ranked 31st with just 77 broken tackles. ● Gang Green never used six offensive linemen. ● Last year, the Jets had three linemen on 46% of their defensive plays, using four linemen just 10% of the time. Robert Saleh's 49ers defense had four linemen out there 86% of the time. ● This was the second straight year the Jets were dead last in percentage of sacks coming from edge rushers. ● Showing how much they missed Jamal Adams, the Jets had the league's worst DVOA (49.3%) when blitzing a defensive back. ● The Jets led the NFL with 65 defensive penalties.

Passing

Player	DYAR	DVOA	Plays	NtYds	Avg	YAC	C%	TD	Int
S.Darnold*	-540	-32.2%	396	1974	5.0	5.3	60.1%	9	11
J.Flacco*	2	-10.9%	141	782	5.5	4.6	55.6%	6	3

Rushing

Player	DYAR	DVOA	Plays	Yds	Avg	TD	Fum	Suc
F.Gore*	-52	-15.4%	187	653	3.5	2	1	45%
L.Perine	-6	-10.7%	64	232	3.6	2	0	44%
T.Johnson	8	-5.0%	54	254	4.7	1	0	56%
S.Darnold*	72	35.3%	30	224	7.5	2	0	--
J.Adams	37	20.1%	29	157	5.4	2	0	62%
L.Bell*	-11	-21.7%	19	74	3.9	0	0	53%
J.Flacco*	-11	-44.6%	6	16	2.7	0	1	--
T.Coleman	-43	-47.0%	28	53	1.9	0	0	32%

Receiving

Player	DYAR	DVOA	Plays	Ctch	Yds	Y/C	YAC	TD	C%
J.Crowder	66	-3.2%	89	59	699	11.8	5.5	6	66%
B.Perriman*	41	-4.4%	60	30	505	16.8	5.3	3	50%
B.Berrios	39	-3.4%	55	37	394	10.6	5.8	3	67%
D.Mims	-20	-18.2%	44	23	357	15.5	4.6	0	52%
J.Smith	-72	-37.3%	37	17	167	9.8	2.9	0	46%
C.Hogan*	-55	-38.5%	26	14	118	8.4	2.9	0	54%
J.Malone	-14	-38.9%	6	4	16	4.0	2.0	0	67%
L.Cager	-15	-43.8%	6	2	35	17.5	7.0	0	33%
C.Davis	261	22.5%	92	65	984	15.1	4.5	5	71%
K.Cole	82	-1.7%	88	55	642	11.7	3.2	5	63%
C.Herndon	4	-6.1%	45	31	287	9.3	4.1	3	69%
R.Griffin	-3	-10.4%	12	9	86	9.6	5.4	0	75%
T.Kroft	42	29.2%	16	12	119	9.9	3.7	3	75%
T.Johnson	19	3.8%	20	16	99	6.2	8.1	1	80%
F.Gore*	5	-9.3%	19	16	89	5.6	4.6	0	84%
L.Perine	-8	-22.8%	15	11	63	5.7	6.1	0	73%
K.Ballage*	11	13.7%	10	9	67	7.4	9.2	0	90%
J.Adams	-3	-18.8%	8	6	29	4.8	4.0	0	75%

Offensive Line

Player	Pos	Age	GS	Snaps	Pen	Sk	Pass	Run	Player	Pos	Age	GS	Snaps	Pen	Sk	Pass	Run
Connor McGovern	C	28	16/16	969	2	1	8	8	Josh Andrews*	RG	30	15/4	311	1	0	8	3
George Fant	RT	29	14/14	829	2	2.5	14	2	Conor McDermott	RT	29	15/1	247	2	1.5	9	1
Greg Van Roten	RG	31	13/13	752	0	2	6	7	Chuma Edoga	RT	24	11/4	235	5	1	9	1
Mekhi Becton	LT	22	14/13	691	7	5	12	2	Dan Feeney	C	27	16/16	1173	2	2.5	14	16
Alex Lewis	LG	29	9/9	544	4	0.5	8	6	Morgan Moses	RT/LT	30	16/16	1066	7	1.5	24	4
Pat Elflein*	LG	27	7/7	419	2	0.5	9	7									

Year	Yards	ALY	Rk	Power	Rk	Stuff	Rk	2Lev	Rk	OpFld	Rk	BB Rt	Rk	Sacks	ASR	Rk	Press	Rk	BB Rt	Rk	Cont
2018	4.05	3.59	32	61%	26	26%	32	1.05	28	1.06	6	8.8%	29	37	6.7%	18	32.4%	21	7.0%	9	28
2019	3.29	3.80	31	69%	8	21%	25	0.91	30	0.17	32	10.6%	18	52	9.2%	30	39.8%	32	14.0%	20	21
2020	3.88	4.34	17	62%	22	15%	10	1.09	25	0.33	31	10.1%	16	43	8.1%	29	31.7%	31	14.2%	25	21

2020 ALY by direction:	Left End: 4.44 (17)	Left Tackle: 4.85 (9)	Mid/Guard: 4.15 (25)	Right Tackle: 4.59 (13)	Right End: 4.08 (22)

The Jets were the only offensive line to finish in the bottom five in pressure rate in the passing game and yards before contact in the rushing game. They were also third worst in both Pass Block Win Rate and Run Block Win Rate, per ESPN. When your high point is ranking slightly below average in adjusted line yards, you know you have problems. ● Playing Mekhi Becton injured against the Broncos should have seen Adam Gase fired right then and there. When healthy, Becton was as good as advertised and looks to be a staple at left tackle. ● Alijah Vera-Tucker impressed when kicking out to tackle in 2020 at USC, allowing just two pressures in five games before struggling in the Pac-12 title game. He's an interior prospect at the NFL level, but being able to play tackle in a pinch isn't a bad skill to have. ● Connor McGovern's 2019 season earned him his free-agent contract with New York, but so far, that seems like an outlier—he had a blown block every 111.8 snaps in the passing game in 2019, and one every 67.6 in his other three seasons. Getting 2019 McGovern would be a huge boost to the offensive line. ● Greg Van Roten was significantly better in the passing game than the rushing game. He had seven blown blocks in the rushing game, but just six on pass plays despite 75% more pass-blocking snaps. ✎ Just before we went to print, the Jets signed Morgan Moses to likely replace George Fant at right tackle. While his lack of athleticism means he's not a perfect scheme fit, he's a massive upgrade as a run blocker.

Defensive Front

Defensive Line	Age	Pos	G	Snaps	Plays	TmPct	Rk	Stop	Dfts	BTkl	Runs	St%	Rk	RuYd	Rk	Sack	Hit	Hur	Dsrpt
						Overall						vs. Run				Pass Rush			
Quinnen Williams	24	DE	13	586	57	8.0%	3	47	19	3	42	81%	23	1.3	6	7.0	8	15	4
Henry Anderson*	30	DE	16	549	42	4.8%	52	29	11	4	40	70%	60	1.7	16	0.5	3	13	0
Folorunso Fatukasi	26	DT	15	507	44	5.4%	40	35	12	3	39	79%	29	1.3	5	2.0	4	6	2
John Franklin-Myers	25	DE	15	473	21	2.6%	91	18	6	3	14	79%	32	2.1	32	3.0	11	28	2
Nathan Shepherd	28	DE	14	336	17	2.2%	--	15	4	2	14	86%	--	2.4	--	2.5	6	3	0
Bryce Huff	23	DE	14	296	16	2.1%	--	10	6	1	8	63%	--	1.6	--	2.0	2	10	0
Sheldon Rankins	27	DT	12	415	21	3.5%	74	13	5	1	18	56%	93	2.8	67	1.5	7	9	1

Edge Rushers	Age	Pos	G	Snaps	Plays	TmPct	Rk	Stop	Dfts	BTkl	Runs	St%	Rk	RuYd	Rk	Sack	Hit	Hur	Dsrpt
						Overall						vs. Run				Pass Rush			
Tarell Basham*	27	OLB	16	734	34	3.9%	67	26	13	8	23	78%	21	1.9	24	3.5	9	19	0
Jordan Jenkins*	27	OLB	12	528	33	5.0%	43	24	10	3	23	83%	10	1.7	14	2.0	5	19	2
Frankie Luvu*	25	OLB	13	257	21	3.0%	--	14	7	5	8	88%	--	0.1	--	2.0	2	8	2
Carl Lawson	26	DE	16	723	36	4.4%	56	26	8	4	28	64%	75	2.7	53	5.5	27	25	1
Vinny Curry	33	DE	11	310	16	2.7%	87	11	5	5	11	64%	77	3.5	83	3.0	6	14	0

Linebackers	Age	Pos	G	Snaps	Plays	TmPct	Rk	Stop	Dfts	BTkl	Runs	St%	Rk	RuYd	Rk	Sack	Hit	Hur	Tgts	Suc%	Rk	Yd/P	Rk	PD	Int
						Overall						vs. Run				Pass Rush				vs. Pass				
Neville Hewitt*	28	ILB	16	1130	135	15.5%	16	64	16	16	77	58%	33	4.7	68	2.0	3	8	36	44%	54	8.4	68	4	0
Harvey Langi*	29	ILB	14	513	58	7.6%	71	32	7	10	28	68%	11	3.7	34	0.0	1	8	21	48%	48	6.1	32	1	0
Jarrad Davis	27	MLB	14	329	41	5.6%	--	18	5	9	27	52%	--	4.7	--	0.5	3	9	6	33%	--	5.8	--	0	0

Year	Yards	ALY	Rk	Power	Rk	Stuff	Rk	2Lev	Rk	OpFld	Rk	BB Rt	Rk	Sacks	ASR	Rk	Press	Rk	BB Rt	Rk
2018	4.31	4.28	13	55%	2	22%	10	1.25	19	0.87	18	5.8%	27	39	6.7%	21	28.1%	24	8.3%	23
2019	3.16	3.00	1	52%	3	31%	1	1.01	6	0.56	7	17.5%	5	35	6.2%	26	30.4%	17	12.0%	29
2020	4.09	3.75	5	70%	25	20%	8	1.06	7	0.89	24	17.3%	2	31	5.9%	20	25.6%	13	14.5%	13
2020 ALY by direction:			Left End: 3.98 (10)			Left Tackle: 3.12 (3)			Mid/Guard: 3.99 (7)			Right Tackle: 3.67 (6)			Right End: 2.50 (2)					

Quinnen Williams is recovering from offseason foot surgery, which cost him OTAs and minicamp. Williams has yet to play a full season, which is about the only negative thing you can say about his game. ✎ Carl Lawson blossomed into one of the league's elite pass-rushers in 2020. While his breakout year as a three-down player is slightly oversold, he'll play the Nick Bosa role as the focal point of Saleh's pass rush. The last Jets defender to match Lawson's 14.3% pressure rate was Demario Davis in 2017, and that came rushing the passer half as often. ✎ On a better team, Vinny Curry would probably be a rotational edge rusher instead of the second guy on the outside, but he still managed a 12.7% pressure rate last year, placing him in the top 25 among edge rushers with at least 150 rushes. ✎ Sheldon Rankins hasn't played a full season since 2018, thanks to tearing his left Achilles and nearly doing the same to his right; he admitted he wasn't at 100% in 2020. While he hasn't come close to matching his eight sacks from 2018, his pressure rate last season rebounded to a respectable 8.0%, placing him in the top 20 for defensive tackles. If he can get back to 100%, he's a nice addition in the interior. ✎ It's safe to say middle linebacker C.J. Mosley's contract has been a disappointment so far—he played two games in 2019 and opted out of 2020, so we haven't had a chance to really see him in green yet. The Jets reportedly looked to shop his contract this offseason, but he's back. ✎ Going on injured reserve three times in two seasons is impressive, Blake Cashman. Cashman projects as one of the Jets' starting line-backers in nickel, but with all of three defensive snaps last year, we're doing a lot of projection off of a poor rookie season in 2019. ✎ Jarrad Davis has not lived up to his billing as a first-round pick in 2017. The Jets believe that he wasn't used properly in Detroit, and considering Detroit's defense was run by Matt Patricia, they may have a point. Davis is an outside pass-rushing linebacker who was used as a coverage/run-stopper with the Lions; expect him to be pointed more towards the quarterback in 2021. ✎ Fifth-round rookie Jamien Sherwood played his entire career at Auburn at safety, but the Jets are moving him to linebacker—he spent more time in the box last year, anyway. His 4.76s 40 killed his draft stock, but that won't be as much of a problem as a moneybacker, and his tackling is beyond reproach.

Defensive Secondary

Secondary	Age	Pos	G	Snaps	Plays	TmPct	Rk	Stop	Dfts	BTkl	Runs	St%	Rk	RuYd	Rk	Tgts	Tgt%	Rk	aDOT	Suc%	Rk	Yd/P	Rk	PD	Int
Marcus Maye	28	FS	16	1138	99	11.4%	31	48	16	10	49	51%	15	5.1	16	27	5.9%	55	12.3	70%	2	3.9	1	11	2
Blessuan Austin	25	CB	11	682	67	11.2%	11	22	10	10	19	37%	51	6.5	38	54	19.6%	42	9.1	48%	54	6.6	21	4	0
Bryce Hall	24	CB	8	547	39	8.9%	--	11	3	4	4	25%	--	6.5	--	42	19.0%	--	9.1	40%	--	8.0	--	3	1
Pierre Desir*	31	CB	12	519	54	8.3%	49	18	9	6	12	42%	45	8.7	65	44	20.9%	32	10.2	34%	79	10.2	79	8	3
Brian Poole*	29	CB	9	482	51	10.4%	--	21	8	2	13	46%	--	6.8	--	29	14.9%	--	10.5	52%	--	6.4	--	7	2
Lamar Jackson	23	CB	13	452	29	4.1%	--	9	2	2	10	50%	--	6.2	--	39	21.3%	--	12.3	41%	--	10.2	--	2	0
Bradley McDougald*	31	SS	7	433	38	10.0%	--	9	5	8	12	17%	--	9.3	--	18	10.3%	--	17.6	39%	--	11.6	--	3	0
Arthur Maulet*	28	CB	11	404	28	4.7%	--	14	6	7	8	38%	--	10.3	--	23	14.1%	--	10.7	65%	--	6.5	--	5	1
Ashtyn Davis	25	SS	10	402	36	6.6%	--	7	3	1	10	20%	--	6.6	--	18	11.1%	--	9.6	39%	--	9.1	--	1	0
Javelin Guidry	23	CB	11	171	21	3.5%	--	9	2	1	10	50%	--	5.7	--	7	10.1%	--	7.1	57%	--	7.1	--	0	0
Lamarcus Joyner	31	FS/CB	14	669	71	9.8%	45	24	9	3	28	46%	18	4.5	7	48	17.9%	4	8.5	50%	34	7.0	24	5	0
Sharrod Neasman	30	SS	16	289	20	2.5%	--	5	2	2	7	43%	--	7.9	--	4	3.3%	--	14.5	25%	--	13.3	--	0	0

Year	Pass D Rank	vs. #1 WR	Rk	vs. #2 WR	Rk	vs. Other WR	Rk	WR Wide	Rk	WR Slot	Rk	vs. TE	Rk	vs. RB	Rk
2018	19	11.5%	24	-3.5%	14	9.7%	23	-10.5%	10	21.1%	27	7.8%	20	-13.4%	7
2019	18	8.7%	24	16.9%	27	1.0%	18	18.0%	31	4.6%	13	-5.1%	12	-13.0%	5
2020	28	12.6%	22	22.5%	29	-4.9%	12	10.9%	26	10.9%	27	16.5%	27	-5.6%	12

The Jets haven't ranked in the top 20 against No. 1 wideouts since 2015, Darrelle Revis' prime. Forget being good, even a halfway-competent season would be cause for a ticker-tape parade. ✎ After flashing in limited action as a rookie, Bless Austin stumbled in 2020—his success rate dropped from 54% to 48%, and his completion percentage allowed jumped by 10 points. He fits the Saleh mold of tall and long cornerbacks, so he'll get one more shot to show the form that excited Jets fans for two months in 2019. ✎ This year's Austin is Bryce Hall, who flashed in limited action as a rookie. He was burned early, but by the end of the year, he was settling into his role. His success rate doesn't reflect that; 40% is very bad and caused by him playing too far off on receivers, letting them pick up easy catches for first downs. ✎ As of press time, the Jets still haven't come to a long-term deal with Marcus Maye. Maye's one of the best coverage safeties in the game and has more than earned a long-term extension, especially in New York's talent-starved secondary. ✎ Ashtyn Davis won't be confused for Jamal Adams anytime soon, but eight pressures on 40 rushes isn't too shabby for a defensive back. Davis' athleticism flashed in short bursts, mostly in tackling rather than coverage; his speed doesn't have a great correlation with any of Saleh's previous defensive players, so he's an interesting potential chess piece. ✎ Fifth-round pick Jason Pinnock (Pitt) is a great athlete, ranking in the upper tier in his 3-cone, short shuttle, and jumping drills. That doesn't always show up on the field, as his technique when transitioning isn't smooth—if he can work on that, he still has room to grow. ✎ Of the five Day 3 defensive backs the Jets drafted, "the other" Michael Carter (Duke) may have the biggest role as a rookie. His 4.36s 40 speed means you're not going to run by him, either as a slot corner or a deep safety. The problem is, he's stiff as a board; sharp routes leave him in the dust. He has a shot at the starting slot role, though he'll probably be more useful as a gunner as a rookie.

Special Teams

Year	DVOA	Rank	FG/XP	Rank	Net Kick	Rank	Kick Ret	Rank	Net Punt	Rank	Punt Ret	Rank	Hidden	Rank
2018	8.1%	1	10.3	4	5.1	4	13.6	2	2.7	14	8.8	1	0.8	14
2019	3.4%	4	-4.8	24	6.5	1	0.6	12	10.1	4	4.7	4	1.3	16
2020	-5.3%	29	-10.0	30	-0.1	19	-4.0	24	-12.8	30	0.3	15	-6.7	24

All five aspects of New York's special teams got worse in 2020, but the drop from Lac Edwards to Braden Mann was the worst. The Jets went from the fourth-best punting team in 2019 to the third-worst in 2020—and since the Jets were punting a lot, it was very noticeable. ✎ Kicker Sam Ficken's job is in jeopardy. He's just 35-for-48 in his career and has missed six extra points for New York. UDFA rookie Chris Naggar (SMU) will have every chance to win the role. ✎ The Jets switched from Ficken to Mann on kickoffs in Week 7. Ficken earned -1.0 net points worth of field position, while Matt was about average at 0.1 points. ✎ The midseason acquisition of Corey Ballentine helped New York's kickoff return game. Ballentine had 2.5 estimated points of field position on kick returns; Ty Johnson had -0.4 and Braxton Berrios (who also returned punts) had -1.7. Both return jobs are up in the air for 2021. Rookies Elijah Moore and Michael Carter (RB) are options, but they may be too valuable on offense to risk putting them back there. A combination of Berrios, Johnson, and Ballentine is likely to take on these roles again.

Philadelphia Eagles

2020 Record: 4-11-1	**Total DVOA:** -18.8% (11)	**2021 Mean Projection:** 7.3 wins	**On the Clock (0-5):** 27%
Pythagorean Wins: 5.8 (26)	**Offense:** -16.9% (28)	**Postseason Odds:** 27.6%	**Mediocrity (6-8):** 41%
Snap-Weighted Age: 26.5 (14)	**Defense:** 0.2% (15)	**Super Bowl Odds:** 1.7%	**Playoff Contender (9-11):** 25%
Average Opponent: 3.4% (7)	**Special Teams:** -1.6% (22)	**Proj. Avg. Opponent:** -1.3% (22)	**Super Bowl Contender (12+):** 7%

2020: Most of a Super Bowl-winning roster is still intact. What's the worst that could happen?

2021: Please be patient as we transition to our new head coach and starting quarterback.

Well, that escalated quickly.

Few, if any, could have imagined that the Philadelphia Eagles would enter the 2021 season with a new head coach and quarterback. Just a few years removed from a Super Bowl title, the round robin of deteriorating relationships between ownership, front office, coaching staff, and players ended with a disappointing 4-11-1 season, Doug Pederson fired, and Carson Wentz traded to Indianapolis.

Amazon's *All or Nothing* followed the Eagles throughout the 2019 season. A 2020 version might have been more fit for Bravo, complete with an Andy Cohen-hosted reunion special. The most successful football group in Philadelphia throughout the 2020 season might have been the beat writers, who were able to dive into how everything broke down. A January story from the *Philadelphia Inquirer* detailed the falling out between Wentz and Pederson, which included the quarterback killing plays at the line of scrimmage "for no other reason than personal distaste." An April story from The Athletic highlighted the rift between Pederson and the duo of Howie Roseman and owner Jeffery Lurie as well as growing tension between different departments within the Eagles' building.

Wentz no longer trusted Pederson's offense. Pederson's offense no longer had answers to cover up the quarterback's flaws. The coaching staff no longer had anyone willing to hold Wentz accountable for his mistakes. Lurie no longer trusted Pederson's play calling or staffing decisions. All of this combined to paint the picture of an organization that went from a Super Bowl following the 2017 season to back-to-back nine-win seasons, then a complete bottoming out and rebuild.

Since 2000 only the Tampa Bay Buccaneers, Indianapolis Colts, and Denver Broncos fell to a worse DVOA than the 2020 Eagles (-18.8%) within five years of winning the Super Bowl. Two of those teams had Peyton Manning during the Super Bowl season and then did not during the poor season in question. The 2005 Buccaneers completely collapsed on defense (25th in DVOA after eight straight years in the top 10) and offense (30th in DVOA behind 11 starts from Bruce Gradkowski) but they rebounded again the following season. The only other team that hit -15.0% within five years of a Super Bowl win was the 2013 New York Giants, and that team under Tom Coughlin and Eli Manning still scratched out seven wins to at least give the façade of success (although it could be argued that was to the long-term detriment of the franchise).

Still, no team in recent memory has dropped so far, so quickly, with so many of the same major players involved. In that context, it's not much of a surprise that fewer of those major players will be involved in 2021 and beyond.

Almost everything that could have gone wrong for the Eagles did this past season. Nowhere was that more evident than at quarterback. While Wentz (reportedly) openly rebelled against the offense, the offense also rebelled against Wentz. The 2017 version of Wentz was never going to be sustainable, a good season propped up by incredible production on third down and inside the red zone. But even as his DVOA declined in both 2018 and 2019, the worst version of Wentz appeared to be an average quarterback—a player more impacted by the situation around him rather than a player who could elevate it. The 2020 version of Wentz took a bad situation around him and made it worse.

Wentz spectacularly performed the bad quarterback combination of indecision and inaccuracy at nearly every turn. During the 2020 season, Wentz had the sixth-highest average time to throw among qualified quarterbacks according to NFL Next Gen Stats, even though a third of his dropbacks were charted as zero- or one-step drops by Sports Info Solutions. Seventeen quarterbacks had at least 100 0-/1-step drops in 2020 and Wentz's 7.7% sack rate was easily the worst of that group. The second-highest was Russell Wilson at 6.6%. Only three other quarterbacks were above 4.0%.

The Eagles' offensive line had its troubles and injuries, but those problems were not often early in the play. ESPN's Pass Block Win Rate measures the success of blocking within 2.5 seconds of the snap. Philadelphia's line ranked 11th in that metric during the 2020 season. Much of the pressure on the quarterback was brought on by the quarterback himself.

Patience in the pocket was not often a hallmark of Wentz's game, but previously the breaks from the pocket turned into positive plays. Earlier in Wentz's career, many of those plays were designed to get the quarterback out of the pocket to take advantage of his ability to throw on the move. Wentz threw as many interceptions outside the pocket in 2020 (five) as he did from 2016 to 2019 combined. His percentage of plays outside the pocket grew in each of the past three seasons from 10.9% in 2018 to 17.9% in 2019 to 19.1% in 2020. The controlled designed pocket movement turned into bailing to the outside whenever the quarterback felt pressure, which was often.

2021 Eagles Schedule

Week	Opp.	Week	Opp.	Week	Opp.
1	at ATL	7	at LV	13	at NYJ
2	SF	8	at DET	14	BYE
3	at DAL (Mon.)	9	LAC	15	WAS
4	KC	10	at DEN	16	NYG
5	at CAR	11	NO	17	at WAS
6	TB (Thu.)	12	at NYG	18	DAL

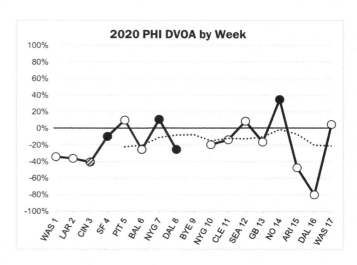

Wentz played a dysfunctional version of hero ball in 2020. It was Carson Wentz, the Snyder Cut: long, drawn out, grim, and no one looked better asking for it.

Perhaps what was more frustrating is what happened when Wentz stayed put. His -21.1% DVOA in the pocket last season was better than only the Washington duo of Dwayne Haskins and Alex Smith, quarterbacks who barely threw beyond 10 yards past the line of scrimmage.

Part of the Wentz meltdown was attributed to the way he handled the team's selection of Alabama/Oklahoma quarterback Jalen Hurts in the second round of the draft. The value of the pick was widely debated at the time, with many suggesting the Eagles had other needs that could have been a better use of resources instead of a backup quarterback. But Hurts did fill a need at a position that had seen the field often. Wentz had seen his previous three seasons ended prematurely by injuries. Roseman's reasoning for the pick stemmed from bringing in a young, cheap option with upside for both his potential as a player and as a future trade asset. The Eagles were supposed to be a "quarterback factory," a team that groomed and developed quarterbacks with the ability to profit off either their play on the field or their value across the league.

Unfortunately for the Eagles, it turned out more like an iPhone factory where, as soon as the new model gets produced, the old one stops working.

Hurts was sprinkled in early in the season with gadget plays, mostly as a runner. He was inactive in Week 1 but played at least two offensive snaps in every game except one from Weeks 2 to 12. In that time, Hurts was 3-for-3 as a passer for 33 yards and 12 carries for 53 yards. He even had a catch for 3 yards on a play where he lined up at quarterback and tossed a backward pass to Wentz split out wide; Wentz then threw it back to Hurts in a mostly failed attempt to set up a screen down the opposite sideline. The factory had some kinks to work out.

Losing 20-3 to Green Bay in Week 13, Pederson finally decided he had seen enough. Wentz was pulled and Hurts was inserted as an actual quarterback for the first time instead of playing in a Taysom Hill knockoff role. Hurts played the remainder of the game and then got the final four starts of the season.

Philadelphia's offense didn't suddenly flip a switch with a new quarterback and Hurts displayed many of the same flaws as Wentz. Hurts had the NFL's highest average time to throw (3.11 seconds) as he held on to the ball and struggled to make throws inside structure. His 52% completion rate was the low-est among qualified quarterbacks, but our model had his expected completion rate as just 59.3%, second-lowest among quarterbacks with at least 100 pass attempts. That was partially a product of his 9.7-yard average depth of target, third-highest among the same group of quarterbacks.

Hurts' -17.6% DVOA as a passer wasn't great, but it wasn't half as bad as Wentz's -35.9%. Even as Hurts faced more pressure (42.7% to 39.8%), he took a sack less often (6.5% to 9.8%) and averaged over a yard more per pass attempt (7.2 to 6.0). Two of Philadelphia's three best passing DVOA games came during Hurts starts.

No quarterback from Weeks 14 to 17 had more rushing attempts than Hurts, but nearly half of those carries (19 of 44, 43%) were scrambles. In the same time period, just 13 of Lamar Jackson's 41 rushing attempts were scrambles (32%). Hurts' legs added an extra element to the offense, but he had three fumbles in that short time, six total during the season, and his overall DVOA as a runner was -15.2%, which ranked 30th among 38 quarterbacks with at least eight rushing attempts.

In the season finale, a Sunday night game featuring a win-and-in playoff situation for the Washington Football Team, Hurts was benched after a 7-of-20 performance for 72 yards and interception. Nate Sudfeld came in, the Internet exploded, and the Eagles not-so-subtly tanked the game to improve draft position with nothing else to play for. The loss raised Philadelphia from the ninth pick in the 2021 NFL draft to the sixth. That look to the future midway through the Week 17 game foreshadowed the rebuild-on-the-fly approach the Eagles would take during the offseason.

Previous swings at roster construction had been about the Eagles getting the most out of the roster in place, acquiring pieces in attempt to put the team over the edge during a window of contention. In 2018, a third-round pick was sent to the Detroit Lions in exchange for a half-season of Golden Tate. In the 2019 NFL draft, the Eagles traded fourth- and sixth-round picks to move up in the first round to select tackle Andre Dillard. Last offseason, third- and fifth-round picks were traded to Detroit in exchange for cornerback Darius Slay. Trading draft picks for veteran players can be one of the league's biggest market inefficiencies, but in limiting the number of draft picks available, the selections made need to work out in order for the depth to replenish.

Philadelphia made just 10 total selections between the 2018 and 2019 drafts. While the 2018 class produced five contributors during the 2020 season, the 2019 class has yet to blossom. Dillard filled in for four games during what was planned to be a redshirt rookie season, then a preseason injury cost him all of 2020 when he was expected to step in as the starter. Second-round pick J.J. Arcega-Whiteside has just 30 targets, 14 receptions, and 254 receiving yards through his first two seasons. A fifth-round pick, the final in a five-player draft class, was used on Northwestern quarterback Clayton Thorson, who did not make the opening day roster and was not even signed back to Philadelphia's practice squad after he cleared waivers. He has bounced around the practice squads of the Cowboys and Giants over the past two seasons. Within the next six picks of the 2019 draft, two NFC East rivals, the Giants and Washington, drafted wide receiver Darius Slayton and linebacker Cole Holcomb, two players who broke into the starting lineup due to skill rather than necessity.

It's difficult to keep a roster moving forward when those cheap contracts don't turn into useful contributors at any level. Making that harder is the reported lack of cohesion throughout the building between the scouting and analytics staffs, each coming to the table with their own processes and lists of desired prospects rather than collaboration that blends the two sides together.

Even some of the good-process bets didn't pan out. The Eagles went heavy on trying to find deep speed at receiver prior to the season. The team brought back DeSean Jackson, traded a seventh-round pick for Marquise Goodwin, then drafted three speedsters in Jalen Reagor (first round), John Hightower (fifth), and Quez Watkins (sixth). None of those moves really panned out in 2020.

Despite some of those misses and a tightwire act to fill the back end of the roster, the Eagles were considered a deep team heading into the season. But there's a difference between having the depth required to make up for a typical year and having the ability to fill in for whatever happened to Philadelphia last season.

Losing two offensive line starters before the season would hurt any team, but it didn't just stop there. The Eagles had a league-worst 57.1 adjusted games lost along the offensive line; the next worst team was at 46.4. They were also the third-most injured team at wide receiver by AGL. Overall, Philadelphia ranked 32nd in AGL on offense (94.6), more than 10 games worse that the No. 31 Patriots (83.5). When the young players aren't developing at a rate that would be expected and that's combined with an extraordinary injury rate, that's how a team perceived as deep ends up running out Greg Ward for 70% of the offensive snaps at wide receiver and finishing dead-last in offensive line continuity score.

This is also where some evaluation questions come in. Reagor was selected one pick before the Minnesota Vikings drafted Justin Jefferson, who had one of the most impressive rookie seasons ever for a wide receiver. According to The Athletic's report, Arcega-Whiteside was a pick pushed by Jeffery Lurie while most of the scouting staff preferred Ohio State's

Parris Campbell, who was selected by the Colts two picks later. Campbell has suffered injuries through his first two seasons but both Arcega-Whiteside and Campbell were drafted just a few spots ahead of the clearly superior DK Metcalf. It's early, but Metcalf has more career AV (21) than Philly's entire 2019 draft class (19).

As the team hit the offseason, the emphasis turned from the now to the future. Wentz was traded to the Colts for picks, including a conditional pick that will be in the first round if the quarterback plays 75% of the offensive snaps, or if he plays 70% of the snaps and the Colts make the playoffs. Philadelphia also traded the sixth overall pick in a deal with the Miami Dolphins that dropped them to 12th overall and netted another 2022 first-round pick, potentially giving the Eagles three first-round picks in next year's draft. That's enough ammo to trade up for a quarterback, if necessary. Philadelphia did not take one this year, which means the 2021 season will now be about evaluating Hurts as a full-time starter.

The future at quarterback is just one piece of the puzzle. This is now a rebuild on a roster that was not supposed to be in this position. Due to the combination of veteran trades and lack of development from some of the draft picks, there isn't really a young core for this team.

Players who were expected to be part of the young core have already reached the end of their rookie contracts. Hits from the 2017 and 2018 draft classes such as Dallas Goedert, Derek Barnett, and Josh Sweat are all entering the final years of their rookie contracts in 2021. This isn't a particularly young roster in general, either. The Eagles were the 14th-oldest team by snap-weighted age in 2020 with the fifth-oldest defense. Philadelphia had the 12th-oldest offensive line and, if healthy, will get more snaps in 2021 from 31-year-old Lane Johnson and 32-year-old Brandon Brooks.

Because of that, the Eagles aren't exactly in a position to treat the 2021 season like the second half of Week 17. Philadelphia is already up against the cap for the upcoming season, thanks in part to $33 million in dead money from the Wentz deal. That forced the Eagles to push more money into future years, even on cheap contracts, using void years to prorate signing bonuses beyond the practical length of the contract. For example, Philadelphia signed safety Anthony Harris to a one-year, $4-million deal but added four void years to minimize the cap hit for the upcoming season. Because of that, Harris will cost more against the Eagles cap in 2022 after the deal expires ($2.4 million) than he will when he's actually on the team in 2021 ($1.6 million).

With those types of moves, the Eagles aren't a team looking at a ton of cap space for the 2022 season. To open some space up, more money from bigger veteran contracts would have to be restructured, continuing the cycle.

Darius Slay's post-trade extension last offseason highlights both sides of this. His three-year, $50-million extension last March included two void years in 2024 and 2025. That allowed his 2021 cap hit to be just $6.6 million, but that shoots up to $22 million in 2022. It's a contract that can be reworked to lower that number, but that will add more guaranteed money to the latter years of the deal for player who will be 31 years old for that season. It's cap flexibility, but at a cost.

The Eagles will now enter their self-branded "transition period" looking ahead to the future while still accounting for previous roster strategies. But even the new strategies aren't completely diverging from the past. In the first round of the 2021 draft, Philadelphia traded up from pick 12 to pick 10 to select *another* wide receiver. At least trading just a third-round pick (one received as part of the package in the Wentz trade) for Heisman Trophy-winner DeVonta Smith—who has Playmaker Score's highest-ever projection for a senior—might be the best bet the franchise has made at the position.

There are still a lot of questions that need to be answered about this transition in Philadelphia. Maybe there's no better example than having gotten to the end of this essay before even bringing up the new head coach responsible for overseeing it, Nick Sirianni. Sirianni spent the past three seasons as the offensive coordinator in Indianapolis under Frank Reich

and his only head coaching interview during the offseason came with the Eagles. Many details about Sirianni's coaching philosophy and scheme have been kept under wraps. The detail Sirianni has pushed the most thus far in his Eagles is his desire for competition. That has included playing rock, paper, scissors over Zoom with prospects and having three-point shooting contests with players after practice.

Philadelphia was competitive throughout the Doug Pederson era, though some of the factors that led to its success were also responsible for the downfall. Projections aren't kind for the 2021 Eagles. This transition should include some self-scouting of multiple aspects of the organization. If the Eagles want to get back to being competitive with the top teams in the NFL, they'll need to figure out what went wrong off the field just as much as what happened on it.

Dan Pizzuta

2020 Eagles by Week

Wk	vs.	W-L	PF	PA	YDF	YDA	TO	Total	Off	Def	ST
1	at WAS	L	17	27	265	239	-3	-34.2%	-46.5%	-16.9%	-4.6%
2	LAR	L	19	37	363	449	-2	-36.2%	7.1%	48.8%	5.6%
3	CIN	T	23	23	378	304	-2	-40.7%	-40.6%	5.3%	5.1%
4	at SF	W	25	20	267	417	2	-9.6%	-24.0%	-10.0%	4.4%
5	at PIT	L	29	38	336	367	-1	10.0%	37.5%	21.3%	-6.2%
6	BAL	L	28	30	364	355	-1	-25.4%	-17.0%	-6.2%	-14.6%
7	NYG	W	22	21	442	325	2	11.0%	6.3%	-10.9%	-6.2%
8	DAL	W	23	9	222	265	-2	-25.5%	-50.1%	-23.3%	1.3%
9	BYE										
10	at NYG	L	17	27	346	382	0	-19.4%	0.7%	20.5%	0.3%
11	at CLE	L	17	22	315	324	-2	-13.6%	-39.7%	-26.9%	-0.7%
12	SEA	L	17	23	250	301	-1	8.9%	-20.5%	-29.0%	0.4%
13	at GB	L	16	30	278	437	-1	-16.4%	-16.8%	20.2%	20.6%
14	NO	W	24	21	413	358	1	34.9%	28.0%	-11.4%	-4.4%
15	at ARI	L	26	33	422	526	3	-47.3%	-15.4%	7.4%	-24.6%
16	at DAL	L	17	37	477	513	-2	-80.0%	-45.5%	28.3%	-6.2%
17	WAS	L	14	20	216	248	-1	4.9%	-23.9%	-25.2%	3.7%

Trends and Splits

	Offense	Rank	Defense	Rank
Total DVOA	-16.9%	28	0.2%	15
Unadjusted VOA	-18.3%	29	-3.2%	13
Weighted Trend	-16.9%	27	-2.5%	16
Variance	6.9%	17	5.3%	20
Average Opponent	-5.0%	2	-2.8%	24
Passing	-12.1%	29	15.9%	24
Rushing	-10.2%	18	-18.2%	13
First Down	-18.9%	29	3.3%	20
Second Down	-16.2%	26	-11.8%	8
Third Down	-14.3%	23	14.3%	25
First Half	-14.8%	28	-2.6%	14
Second Half	-19.2%	29	3.1%	16
Red Zone	-15.7%	24	-3.9%	10
Late and Close	-19.9%	26	-3.2%	14

Five-Year Performance

Year	W-L	Pyth W	Est W	PF	PA	TO	Total	Rk	Off	Rk	Def	Rk	ST	Rk	Off AGL	Rk	Def AGL	Rk	Off Age	Rk	Def Age	Rk	ST Age	Rk
2016	7-9	9	9.7	367	331	+6	13.3%	6	-5.2%	20	-11.0%	4	7.5%	2	20.4	3	17.7	4	27.0	11	26.9	9	27.0	3
2017	13-3	12.0	11.3	457	295	+11	23.7%	5	10.5%	7	-12.2%	5	0.9%	16	29.0	13	24.4	9	27.1	12	26.9	9	26.4	7
2018	9-7	8.5	7.8	367	348	-9	-1.0%	15	-0.4%	16	0.9%	15	0.2%	15	46.0	22	71.0	31	27.9	5	27.6	3	25.5	26
2019	9-7	8.8	9.0	385	354	-3	5.5%	11	2.4%	14	-3.1%	12	0.0%	19	30.3	10	54.1	29	27.8	3	27.2	4	25.6	21
2020	4-11-1	5.8	4.9	334	418	-10	-18.8%	28	-16.9%	28	0.2%	15	-1.6%	22	94.6	32	33.5	12	26.5	21	27.0	5	25.4	25

2020 Performance Based on Most Common Personnel Groups

PHI Offense					PHI Offense vs. Opponents					PHI Defense					PHI Defense vs. Opponents			
Pers	Freq	Yds	DVOA	Run%	Pers	Freq	Yds	DVOA	Run%	Pers	Freq	Yds	DVOA		Pers	Freq	Yds	DVOA
11	58%	5.2	-11.7%	29%	Base	13%	5.4	2.2%	39%	Base	26%	4.8	-13.5%		11	56%	5.8	4.7%
12	34%	5.4	-13.8%	35%	Nickel	67%	4.9	-19.3%	37%	Nickel	54%	6.0	-1.5%		12	24%	6.1	8.6%
21	2%	0.6	-105.5%	56%	Dime+	19%	5.9	7.1%	11%	Dime+	15%	6.7	43.2%		21	6%	6.0	-26.3%
611	1%	3.4	-5.5%	69%	Big	1%	10.9	53.9%	46%	Goal Line	2%	0.8	-29.1%		13	3%	4.4	-38.0%
10	1%	7.8	38.7%	44%						Big	3%	5.7	12.3%		22	3%	5.2	16.5%

Strategic Tendencies

Run/Pass		Rk	Formation		Rk	Pass Rush		Rk	Secondary		Rk	Strategy		Rk
Runs, first half	38%	14	Form: Single Back	90%	3	Rush 3	0.8%	32	4 DB	26%	13	Play Action	27%	16
Runs, first down	39%	30	Form: Empty Back	8%	20	Rush 4	85.1%	1	5 DB	54%	21	Offensive Motion	35%	29
Runs, second-long	27%	19	Form: Multi Back	1%	32	Rush 5	9.4%	32	6+ DB	15%	14	Avg Box (Off)	6.30	32
Runs, power sit.	58%	16	Pers: 3+ WR	61%	21	Rush 6+	4.8%	19	Man Coverage	36%	10	Avg Box (Def)	6.83	3
Runs, behind 2H	22%	29	Pers: 2+ TE/6+ OL	38%	6	Edge Rusher Sacks	45.9%	22	CB by Sides	62%	27	Offensive Pace	30.40	17
Pass, ahead 2H	47%	19	Pers: 6+ OL	2%	11	Interior DL Sacks	32.7%	7	S/CB Cover Ratio	34%	8	Defensive Pace	30.33	17
Run-Pass Options	14%	4	Shotgun/Pistol	82%	5	Second Level Sacks	21.4%	20	DB Blitz	12%	20	Go for it on 4th	2.64	2

The Eagles dropped from 9.6 yards after the catch on passes at or behind the line of scrimmage in 2019 to just 7.7 average yards after the catch in 2020. ● Philadelphia had 45% of its handoffs against light boxes of six or fewer, third in the NFL. The Eagles had only 16% of their handoffs against heavy boxes of eight or more, the lowest rate in the league. And the Eagles were much better running against those light boxes: 5.7 yards per carry and 6.7% DVOA, compared to 4.2 yards per carry and -21.1% DVOA with seven or more men in the box. ● Part of the reason the Eagles faced so many light boxes: they had only one running play all year with two backs in the formation. It was a fake kneeldown at the end of the first half of the Week 16 loss to Dallas. ● The Eagles were losing enough that the offense finished third in total pace (one play every 25.9 seconds) despite ranking only 17th in situation-neutral pace. ● Philadelphia had the best run defense in the league against handoffs in shotgun or pistol formations: 3.1 yards per carry and -52.7% DVOA. ● In 2019, the Eagles had the largest gap in the league in favor of playing man defense: -1.8% defensive DVOA in man coverage compared to 48.9% DVOA in zone coverage. Last season, the Eagles had the league's second-largest gap in the other direction: 66.6% DVOA in man coverage compared to 27.3% DVOA in zone coverage. ● Philadelphia benefited from 125 opposing penalties for 1,036 yards. Both figures led the NFL. ● The Eagles recovered 18 of 27 fumbles on offense and 10 of 16 fumbles on defense.

Passing

Player	DYAR	DVOA	Plays	NtYds	Avg	YAC	C%	TD	Int
C.Wentz*	-780	-35.9%	486	2278	4.7	4.0	57.7%	16	15
J.Hurts	-68	-17.6%	160	992	6.2	6.1	52.7%	6	4
N.Sudfeld*	-51	-72.6%	14	16	1.1	3.6	41.7%	0	1
N.Mullens	76	-7.7%	345	2298	6.7	5.9	64.7%	12	12
J.Flacco	2	-10.9%	141	782	5.5	4.6	55.6%	6	3

Rushing

Player	DYAR	DVOA	Plays	Yds	Avg	TD	Fum	Suc
M.Sanders	110	7.0%	164	867	5.3	6	4	55%
B.Scott	32	1.4%	80	374	4.7	1	1	49%
J.Hurts	-9	-15.2%	60	350	5.8	3	6	--
C.Wentz*	62	9.2%	50	261	5.2	5	3	--
C.Clement*	9	2.7%	21	75	3.6	1	0	43%
J.Howard	-6	-29.9%	7	27	3.9	0	0	14%
J.Huntley	2	5.8%	5	19	3.8	0	0	20%
J.Flacco	-11	-44.6%	6	16	2.7	0	1	--

Receiving

Player	DYAR	DVOA	Plays	Ctch	Yds	Y/C	YAC	TD	C%
G.Ward	-47	-20.0%	79	53	419	7.9	3.1	6	67%
T.Fulgham	93	4.9%	67	38	539	14.2	2.6	4	57%
J.Reagor	-32	-20.5%	54	31	396	12.8	5.6	1	57%
J.Hightower	-55	-36.8%	29	10	167	16.7	5.7	0	34%
D.Jackson*	12	-6.9%	26	14	236	16.9	4.6	1	54%
A.Jeffery*	44	23.3%	13	6	115	19.2	4.2	1	46%
Q.Watkins	3	-9.6%	13	7	106	15.1	8.3	1	54%
JJ Arcega-Whiteside	26	24.9%	8	4	85	21.3	2.8	0	50%
Z.Ertz	-144	-37.2%	72	36	335	9.3	2.4	1	50%
D.Goedert	105	16.8%	65	46	524	11.4	4.4	3	71%
R.Rodgers	79	30.4%	31	24	345	14.4	4.0	2	77%
M.Sanders	-59	-33.5%	52	28	197	7.0	7.5	0	54%
B.Scott	40	8.1%	36	25	212	8.5	7.2	1	69%
C.Clement*	5	1.2%	6	5	25	5.0	6.4	0	83%

Offensive Line

Player	Pos	Age	GS	Snaps	Pen	Sk	Pass	Run	Player	Pos	Age	GS	Snaps	Pen	Sk	Pass	Run
Jason Kelce	C	34	16/16	1124	4	1.5	5	6	Jason Peters*	LT	39	8/8	507	0	7	15	5
Nate Herbig	RG/LG	23	15/12	891	6	0.5	10	3	Lane Johnson	RT	31	7/7	404	2	0.5	3	1
Matt Pryor	RG	27	15/10	773	7	4	22	4	Jack Driscoll	RT	24	11/4	300	2	0	8	1
Jordan Mailata	LT	24	15/10	731	4	5	19	5	Iosua Opeta	LG	25	8/2	170	2	0	3	0
Isaac Seumalo	LG	28	9/9	587	4	3	6	4									

Year	Yards	ALY	Rk	Power	Rk	Stuff	Rk	2Lev	Rk	OpFld	Rk	BB Rt	Rk	Sacks	ASR	Rk	Press	Rk	BB Rt	Rk	Cont
2018	4.12	4.14	19	62%	25	21%	26	1.28	15	0.61	27	6.0%	15	40	6.7%	17	26.0%	7	8.0%	13	30
2019	4.36	4.34	14	76%	3	18%	13	1.17	18	0.78	16	9.7%	12	37	6.4%	11	28.6%	10	14.0%	21	31
2020	4.86	4.19	23	73%	9	16%	12	1.29	11	1.18	2	8.3%	9	65	9.4%	31	32.5%	32	13.8%	21	15

2020 ALY by direction:	Left End: 3.58 (28)	Left Tackle: 4.09 (19)	Mid/Guard: 4.45 (17)	Right Tackle: 3.61 (28)	Right End: 4.47 (16)

The Eagles tied the record for the lowest offensive line continuity score and never made it through three straight games with the same five starters. They clearly blame injuries more than coaching for last year's poor performance; while the coaching staff turned over, the Eagles kept offensive line coach Jeff Stoutland for his ninth season with the team. ◥ For the second straight season, the Eagles' offensive line was a much better run-blocking unit (ninth in blown block rate) than a pass-blocking one (21st). Pass protection wasn't much different between blocking for Carson Wentz (3.0% blown block rate) and Jalen Hurts (3.3% blown block rate). The Eagles tied for the most sacks allowed on blown blocks (24). ◥ Jason Kelce turns 34 in November but is still one of the league's best centers. He finished sixth at the position in blown blocks and was one of five to not blow a block as a puller. He also played 99.6% of the offensive snaps and hasn't been below 95% since 2014. ◥ There are questions at every other position. The right side has Brandon Brooks at guard and Lane Johnson at tackle but Brooks is coming off a torn Achilles that forced him to miss all of 2020 and Johnson is returning from an ankle ligament tear that ended his 2020 in Week 11. ◥ Isaac Seumalo will return as the starting left guard. He had to miss eight weeks at midseason with a knee injury but put up a career-best 1.9% blown block rate on passes. ◥ The biggest question on the line comes at left tackle. Former first-round pick Andre Dillard was in line to start at the position in 2020 but tore his biceps last August and missed his entire sophomore campaign. 2017 seventh-round pick rugby player-turned-offensive tackle Jordan Mailata got his first NFL action with 10 starts and 65% of the offensive snaps. His 3.7% blown block rate was among the worst for tackles but there were enough flashes for the Eagles to let him compete for the starting role in 2021. ◥ Second-round rookie Landon Dickerson had a 0.6% blown block rate as a center at Alabama and could provide depth along the interior, though he is another lineman recovering from injury—a torn ACL suffered in December.

Defensive Front

Defensive Line	Age	Pos	G	Snaps	Plays	TmPct	Rk	Stop	Dfts	BTkl	Runs	St%	Rk	RuYd	Rk	Sack	Hit	Hur	Dsrpt
						Overall							vs. Run				Pass Rush		
Fletcher Cox	31	DT	15	746	42	5.3%	44	31	17	5	30	73%	51	1.7	13	6.5	4	25	2
Javon Hargrave	28	DT	15	600	38	4.8%	53	32	15	5	30	80%	26	2.0	29	4.5	2	16	1
Malik Jackson*	31	DT	15	537	30	3.8%	71	26	10	2	21	86%	7	1.5	8	2.5	10	14	2

Edge Rushers	Age	Pos	G	Snaps	Plays	TmPct	Rk	Stop	Dfts	BTkl	Runs	St%	Rk	RuYd	Rk	Sack	Hit	Hur	Dsrpt
						Overall							vs. Run				Pass Rush		
Brandon Graham	33	DE	16	757	45	5.3%	37	34	17	9	36	69%	56	1.7	16	8.0	9	29	1
Derek Barnett	25	DE	13	534	34	4.9%	45	27	12	2	23	74%	37	2.3	38	5.5	11	18	0
Josh Sweat	24	DE	14	421	38	5.1%	39	31	14	2	26	77%	29	1.8	23	6.0	8	3	2
Vinny Curry*	33	DE	11	310	16	2.7%	87	11	5	5	11	64%	77	3.5	83	3.0	6	14	0
Ryan Kerrigan	*33*	*DE*	*16*	*397*	*18*	*2.3%*	*--*	*15*	*9*	*2*	*7*	*71%*	*--*	*2.3*	*--*	*5.5*	*1*	*12*	*1*

Linebackers	Age	Pos	G	Snaps	Plays	TmPct	Rk	Stop	Dfts	BTkl	Runs	St%	Rk	RuYd	Rk	Sack	Hit	Hur	Tgts	Suc%	Rk	Yd/P	Rk	PD	Int
						Overall						vs. Run				Pass Rush				vs. Pass				
Alex Singleton	28	OLB	16	748	114	13.5%	39	63	17	15	79	63%	18	4.7	73	2.0	5	5	24	46%	51	7.0	52	1	1
Duke Riley*	27	OLB	13	568	47	6.8%	75	25	7	10	30	57%	39	3.4	22	0.5	0	2	16	50%	39	6.6	47	1	1
T.J. Edwards	25	MLB	12	490	65	10.2%	59	34	12	8	47	60%	30	3.2	14	2.0	0	2	11	27%	--	9.8	--	1	1
Nathan Gerry*	26	OLB	7	478	57	15.4%	19	33	10	4	30	73%	4	4.3	54	1.0	1	4	17	29%	73	10.0	74	2	0
Eric Wilson	*27*	*OLB*	*16*	*1035*	*128*	*15.4%*	*18*	*45*	*21*	*14*	*70*	*36%*	*86*	*4.9*	*76*	*3.0*	*5*	*6*	*36*	*53%*	*30*	*4.6*	*11*	*8*	*3*

Year	Yards	ALY	Rk	Power	Rk	Stuff	Rk	2Lev	Rk	OpFld	Rk	BB Rt	Rk	Sacks	ASR	Rk	Press	Rk	BB Rt	Rk
2018	4.56	3.93	6	62%	8	26%	2	1.22	17	1.44	32	13.7%	2	44	6.5%	26	29.7%	19	12.9%	7
2019	3.72	3.44	3	67%	22	26%	3	1.00	4	0.87	23	18.6%	3	43	7.0%	17	30.6%	14	15.4%	14
2020	3.69	3.73	3	51%	1	24%	1	0.98	4	0.71	19	14.8%	7	49	8.5%	4	29.3%	6	15.7%	7

2020 ALY by direction:	Left End: 3.15 (6)	Left Tackle: 3.10 (2)	Mid/Guard: 3.98 (6)	Right Tackle: 3.88 (9)	Right End: 4.02 (8)

Few defensive coaches believe in rushing four more than Jim Schwartz, and even as the defense moves to Jonathan Gannon, the Eagles' defensive line is set up to make the most of a four-man rush. The Eagles rushed four a league-leading 85% of the time and ranked third in pressure rate while doing so but ranked 25th in DVOA. (They also led the NFL with a 49% pressure rate when blitzing, although they didn't blitz much.) ❧ Brandon Graham, now in his 12th season, has never excelled at transforming pass pressure into sacks. He has never had a double-digit sack total, but last year was his fifth straight season with at least 25 hurries. ❧ The next two highest pressure totals came from the interior by Fletcher Cox and Javon Hargrave. No team got more pressures when lining interior linemen up at 2i (29) with Hargrave (13), Cox (seven), and Malik Jackson (seven) all excelling from inside the guard. ❧ Jackson was cut and will be replaced as part of the interior rotation by third-round pick Milton Williams (Louisiana Tech), who has the upside to develop as a pass-rusher behind the top two. Williams, who had 99th-percentile pro day numbers in the 40, broad jump, vertical jump, and 3-cone, had four solo sacks and was 12th in pressures among college interior defenders in 2020. ❧ Philadelphia hopes for another leap from either Derek Barnett or Josh Sweat, both of whom are in the final years of their rookie deals. Barnett led the Eagles with 17 quarterback knockdowns (including nullified plays) but tallied 11 fewer hurries than Graham. ❧ Veteran Ryan Kerrigan was signed as edge depth after being supplanted by the young stars in Washington. As a 32-year-old, Kerrigan played just 38% of defensive snaps but managed 5.5 sacks despite only one other quarterback hit. Regardless of playing time, Kerrigan has been a consistent hit-to-sack converter throughout his career. ❧ Linebacker hasn't been much of a priority for the franchise, but that could change under the new coaching staff influenced by Mike Zimmer. Former CFL star Alex Singleton led the team in defeats last season (17) but free-agent signing Eric Wilson topped that figure with 21 for the Vikings. Wilson gives a coverage element that was sorely missed in the middle of the Eagles defense in 2020. Wilson was 11th among linebackers in yards allowed per pass and was consistently around the ball with eight passes defensed and three interceptions. Philadelphia linebackers combined for five passes defensed and two interceptions.

Defensive Secondary

Secondary	Age	Pos	G	Snaps	Plays	TmPct	Rk	Stop	Dfts	BTkl	Runs	St%	Rk	RuYd	Rk	Tgts	Tgt%	Rk	aDOT	Suc%	Rk	Yd/P	Rk	PD	Int
Jalen Mills*	27	SS	15	1012	77	9.7%	46	36	14	10	41	59%	6	6.7	35	46	12.8%	7	10.0	52%	30	7.3	27	3	1
Darius Slay	30	CB	15	884	65	8.2%	50	24	15	5	11	27%	64	16.0	80	71	22.7%	18	12.0	39%	74	9.6	72	6	1
Rodney McLeod	31	FS	13	872	72	10.5%	40	30	11	9	37	41%	29	5.7	25	17	5.5%	56	9.9	65%	3	4.1	3	7	1
Nickell Robey-Coleman*	29	CB	15	612	45	5.7%	--	14	6	12	12	42%	--	4.6	--	35	16.1%	--	9.5	40%	--	9.7	--	1	0
Avonte Maddox	25	CB	10	508	43	8.1%	52	12	4	3	12	42%	45	4.9	21	39	21.7%	24	14.1	44%	65	9.6	74	3	0
Marcus Epps	25	SS	14	363	42	5.7%	--	17	7	6	11	64%	--	5.7	--	19	14.8%	--	7.4	53%	--	7.4	--	4	2
Cre'von LeBlanc*	27	CB	9	217	24	5.0%	--	11	7	7	5	40%	--	4.2	--	21	27.3%	--	8.5	48%	--	9.0	--	2	0
Michael Jacquet	24	CB	7	159	20	5.4%	--	7	3	0	5	40%	--	3.8	--	20	35.5%	--	15.5	35%	--	14.7	--	3	0
Anthony Harris	30	FS	16	1075	111	13.4%	9	31	13	10	60	23%	60	7.8	50	21	5.0%	62	16.5	62%	6	8.2	44	7	0

Year	Pass D Rank	vs. #1 WR	Rk	vs. #2 WR	Rk	vs. Other WR	Rk	WR Wide	Rk	WR Slot	Rk	vs. TE	Rk	vs. RB	Rk
2018	15	0.0%	15	6.5%	22	-2.7%	16	8.1%	25	-6.6%	9	-16.1%	7	11.2%	24
2019	16	2.2%	16	6.4%	21	-2.1%	17	-6.5%	15	15.4%	23	-5.2%	11	-10.2%	9
2020	24	26.3%	32	28.4%	31	7.2%	20	29.9%	32	20.9%	31	14.9%	26	-10.2%	8

Nothing involved within the Philadelphia secondary went as planned last season. The Eagles made a big trade to bring in Darius Slay to be the team's top corner. Slay had never finished with a success rate under 48% in his career, then was near the bottom of the league at 39% in 2020. Slay was put in some impossible situations, like his Week 12 matchup against DK Metcalf that saw the Seahawks star work spacing on screens and slants before a 53-yard deep shot against Slay with no safety help on a third-and-13. ❧ Avonte Maddox was the other starter on the outside, but it's yet to be determined if Maddox stays outside or will shift back to the slot this season. Maddox matched Slay's 9.6 yards allowed per pass but put up a slightly better, but still not good, success rate of 44%. ❧ There are still a lot of unknowns and not much experience in the running for the other starting corner spot, whether it be outside or in the slot. Zech McPhearson, a fourth-round pick, was the only addition in the draft and he has experience both inside and outside at Texas Tech. After the draft, Philadelphia traded for Josiah Scott, Jacksonville's

2020 fourth-round pick who played just 80 defensive snaps in his rookie season. Scott is a short (5-foot-9), athletic slot special-ist. McPhearson and Scott will join a group including the likes of Craig James, Michael Jacquet, Grayland Arnold, and Kevon Seymour, all fighting for that final starting spot. ✎ Anthony Harris was a bargain signing on a one-year, $5-million contract this offseason after playing as one of the league's best deep safeties in Minnesota. 2020 was a drop in production going from six interceptions to zero, but Harris still showed plus deep coverage in single- and two-high alignments. He was sixth among safeties in success rate and fourth in yards after the catch allowed per play. ✎ Rodney McLeod will also start at safety, but when that happens is to be determined. The 31-year-old tore his ACL in Week 14 but is shooting for a Week 1 return. ✎ Ver-satility could be a key among the options should development come from second-year slot corner/safety K'Von Wallace, who played 18% of the defensive snaps in 2020, or rookie sixth-round linebacker/safety JaCoby Stevens. In his career at LSU, the 216-pound Stevens played 29% of his snaps in the slot and 31% in the box.

Special Teams

Year	DVOA	Rank	FG/XP	Rank	Net Kick	Rank	Kick Ret	Rank	Net Punt	Rank	Punt Ret	Rank	Hidden	Rank
2018	0.2%	15	-0.5	19	3.1	7	-2.6	23	6.4	6	-5.3	28	-6.7	24
2019	0.0%	19	3.8	11	-3.6	25	-2.3	23	5.0	9	-3.1	24	-13.5	32
2020	-1.6%	22	-5.7	24	2.9	10	-4.3	26	-0.7	19	-0.4	18	-18.0	32

Jake Elliott had a strange year on field goal attempts. His 73.7% conversion rate was easily the worst of his career. Elliott was a perfect 11-for-11 from 30 to 49 yards but went 2-for-5 on attempts of 50 or more yards and just 1-for-3 on attempts within 29 yards. ✎ Elliott has remained one of the most consistent positive players on kickoffs. Over the past three seasons, Eliott has ranked third, first, and eighth in gross kickoff value. ✎ As we go to press, the only punter on the roster is Arryn Siposs, a former Australian rules player. Siposs spent the 2020 season on the Detroit practice squad. In his final season at Auburn, Siposs had the 11th-best fair catch percentage (44.3%) among 90 college punters with at least 50 punts. ✎ The Eagles need upgrades on both kick and punt returns. Boston Scott finished 58th of 61 players in kick return value (minimum five returns). Greg Ward was the main punt returner due to his reliable hands but finished 40th of 47 players in return value and averaged just 6.4 yards per return. ✎ Jalen Reagor only got four punt returns in 2020, but they included a 73-yard touchdown. His role should in-crease with better health and a new staff that could have more trust in his explosiveness. ✎ Along with Reagor, any number of receivers with return experience could take that spot from Ward including Quez Watkins, John Hightower, and 2021 first-round pick DeVonta Smith. Watkins, Hightower, and running back Jason Huntley should also be in the mix for kick returns.

Pittsburgh Steelers

2020 Record: 12-4	**Total DVOA:** 16.8% (19)	**2021 Mean Projection:** 8.8 wins	**On the Clock (0-5):** 12%
Pythagorean Wins: 10.7 (6)	**Offense:** -4.7% (22)	**Postseason Odds:** 46.0%	**Mediocrity (6-8):** 34%
Snap-Weighted Age: 26.9 (7)	**Defense:** -20.2% (1)	**Super Bowl Odds:** 6.2%	**Playoff Contender (9-11):** 37%
Average Opponent: -5.7% (31)	**Special Teams:** 1.3% (14)	**Proj. Avg. Opponent:** 3.2% (2)	**Super Bowl Contender (12+):** 17%

2020: From undefeated to unwatchable.

2021: Once more unto the breach with Big Ben.

The Steelers aren't the type of franchise that likes to admit to being in a rebuilding phase. They are a proud bunch that wears the black and gold. Deservedly so—this is a team that hasn't had a losing season since 2003 and has had two in a row just once since the 1980s. That competitive arrogance is more often than not a good thing, and surely any team that started a season 11-0 and captured a tough division title, as the Steelers did in 2020, is usually confident that the next year will be, well, super.

It is in this context that Pittsburgh decided that despite an aging roster, a lack of depth and/or experience at key positions, and a quarterback who emitted alarming signs of decay at the end of last season, they could not allow a rebuilding, or even retrenching, process to take place. Instead, they are going back into battle with 39-year-old Ben Roethlisberger and most of the same pieces they had in 2020, without much of a backup plan should Roethlisberger stumble even further into the ditch at the end of his otherwise Hall of Fame career.

Roethlisberger's return from the elbow injury that cost him virtually all of 2019 seemed a triumphant one as the team won its first 11 games. But it was among the more uneasy double-digit-unbeaten streaks in recent memory. Every win only seemed to bring more pessimism. Pittsburgh barely escaped Denver and backup quarterback Jeff Driskel in its home opener. Carson Wentz, the lowest-rated passer in the league, almost beat them with a furious late rally. Stephen Gostkowski missed a kick that would have sent the Titans game to overtime. Lamar Jackson threw an incomplete pass in the end zone that allowed a four-point escape, and the following week Pittsburgh required a fourth-quarter rally to best Dallas and third-stringer Garrett Gilbert.

Overall, the Steelers won seven of nine one-score games, recovered 14 of their 19 fumbles on offense, and got to match up with the tragicomic NFC East and punchless AFC South, making for what would be the league's second-easiest schedule. They were incapable of running the ball, and the passing game more closely resembled hot potato, with Roethlisberger unloading the ball seemingly before he gripped the laces. Their 11th straight victory was a squeaker over the COVID-depleted Ravens in a thrice-rescheduled Wednesday afternoon game. Afterward, Pittsburgh head coach Mike Tomlin was asked what the problem was with his unbeaten yet unimpressive team.

"Us sucking," was his typically tart reply.

So the last month of the season was an overdue corrective. The team faceplanted down the stretch, losing four of its last five games, including an embarrassing pratfall on Monday Night Football against their usual pigeons from Cincinnati (who were also on to a third-string quarterback). In the wild-card round, Pittsburgh was put out of its misery by an even less likely opponent, the Browns, who prior to this playoff exorcism were an astonishing 8-36-1 against their hated "rivals."

As Tomlin put it, the Steelers "died on the vine."

Predictable as the fall from the heavens may have been, it was nevertheless startling how bad the Steelers looked as autumn turned to winter. It was as though the entire team stepped into the machine that turned the Man of Steel into a mere mortal in *Superman II*. Roethlisberger was the exemplar of the collapse. When the season began it was every Steelers fan's fervent wish that they could get the full 16 games out of Big Ben. By year's end, there were plenty of Steelers fans who fervently wished he would hang up that iconic No. 7 for good. He ended up 17th in DYAR, 20th in DVOA (both the second-lowest finishes of his long career, not counting the injury-hit 2019), and genuinely looked creaky for the first time. From Week 13 through the wild-card game, Roethlisberger had a passing DVOA of -9.1%, which would have finished 27th during the regular season. A photo of Bereft Ben seated alone on the bench, hands stuck miserably in his pockets, turned into a meme favorite among rival fans.

But the greats seldom leave of their own accord, and Roethlisberger wasn't ready to hang 'em up just yet. He decided to return to the huddle for his 18th season, and the Steelers, unwilling to turn what they consider a championship contender over to a rookie or journeyman passer, agreed to bring him back—with a $5-million pay cut and severable voidable years tacked on to his contract to reduce his mammoth (roughly $41 million!) cap hit. Surely the vision of a drunken Tom Brady tossing the Lombardi Trophy around Tampa Bay after winning a ring at age 43 was a factor in the decision to return. Unfortunately, the BR7 wellness and nutrition plan has never resembled the TB12 method.

Another legend in Roethlisberger's mind is probably Peyton Manning. Last-Lap Peyton was hauled to a championship by the 2015 Broncos defense like a sherpa hauling a rich, hob-

2021 Steelers Schedule

Week	Opp.	Week	Opp.	Week	Opp.
1	at BUF	7	BYE	13	BAL
2	LV	8	at CLE	14	at MIN (Thu.)
3	CIN	9	CHI (Mon.)	15	TEN
4	at GB	10	DET	16	at KC
5	DEN	11	at LAC	17	CLE (Mon.)
6	SEA	12	at CIN	18	at BAL

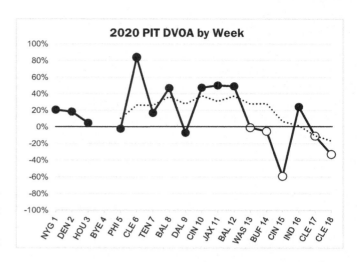

2020 PIT DVOA by Week

bled client up the slopes of Everest. Roethlisberger probably sees the Steelers defense as good enough to give him one last fighting chance at a third ring, optics be damned.

Guess what? Our projection system mostly agrees with that assessment, giving Pittsburgh the league's best forecast on defense with just enough offense to compete for a playoff berth. From there, who knows what an old magician might conjure for his final trick?

Pittsburgh was a top-eight offense by DVOA for five straight seasons spanning 2014 to 2018 before plummeting to 31st in 2019 due to the weekly ineptitude of Devlin Hodges and Mason Rudolph playing quarterback. The expected Plexiglass Principle/Roethlisberger Rebound™ wasn't exactly Superball quality, however, with the offense finishing in just 22nd place, mainly due to a horrendous (30th overall) rushing attack. The franchise of Franco and Fast Willie and The Bus was reduced to a virtual abandonment of the run. The Steelers passed on 64% of snaps, second only to the hapless Jags, who trailed pretty much the entire season while Tanking for Trevor. Even while ahead in the second half, Roethlisberger dropped back to pass 59% of the time, again second-most in the NFL, up from 46% in 2019.

Now ex-offensive coordinator Randy Fichtner's scheme operated from a defensive crouch, throwing it short and quickly, fully acknowledging both Roethlisberger's limitations (some of which can be chalked up to the elbow surgery) and those of his increasingly frail offensive line. The Steelers easily led the league with 66 wide receiver or tight end screens, sticking with the quick stuff even though other teams knew it was coming—they averaged just 4.4 yards per pass with -6.7% DVOA on those plays, poor compared to NFL averages of 5.9 yards and 12.3% DVOA.

Fortunately for Pittsburgh, an expected defensive regression didn't happen. Indeed, the Steelers were even better than in 2019, placing atop the league in DVOA and ranking No. 1 in adjusted sack rate for an unprecedented fourth straight season. The pass rush broke the NFL record for consecutive regular-season games with at least one sack, a streak that dates back to mid-2016 and is still ongoing (it currently stands at 73 in a row). While a slight falloff is perhaps inevitable, Pittsburgh is once again expected to field a shutdown defense, one that will see the return of linebacker Devin Bush from injury to offset the free-agency loss of pass-rusher Bud Dupree (who himself missed the last month of the season with an injury).

Another factor potentially working in the Steelers' favor is their continuing ability to benefit from penalties called on their foes. After topping the NFL in opponents' penalty yardage in 2018 and 2019, Pittsburgh fell all the way to … third, and only Tampa Bay was better in net penalty yardage. There isn't a great deal of year-to-year correlation when it comes to penalty yardage accrued, but you have to go back to 2014 to find a season when Pittsburgh wasn't in the top eight in beneficiary yardage. Except in 2016, they have been right at the top in net yardage as well.

One crucial reason is that Pittsburgh gets a ton of consistent love from back judges. Drawing defensive pass interference flags has been a staple of the Steelers offense in recent seasons. Despite the fact the downfield passing game was virtually non-existent in 2020 (Pittsburgh tied for 30th in yards per attempt), Steelers pass-catchers drew 19 DPI flags for 351 yards, both marks second only to the Bucs and Brady and well beyond the rest of the league. This was not a one-off (Table 1). Even in 2019, when Hodges and Rudolph were under center, the team's offense got a number of big gains thanks to the officials. Cynics who claim "the Steelers get all the calls" have a point in this particular facet of the game.

Table 1. Defensive Pass Interference Penalties Drawn by Pittsburgh, 2014-2020

Year	DPIs	Rank	Yards	Rank
2014	8	T-6	156	8
2015	14	T-2	297	2
2016	8	T-11	121	15
2017	14	T-2	299	1
2018	9	T-6	152	6
2019	15	2	299	1
2020	19	2	351	2

To be fair, Tomlin should get some credit for his team's ability to refrain from committing penalties. Indeed, "Coaching matters in the NFL" is a tried-and-true shibboleth of the pigskin commentariat. The Steelers are putting a great deal of faith in that old saw, especially with a pair of new assistants tasked with repairing the offense. First and foremost is offensive coordinator Matt Canada, who succeeds Fichtner, a man whose name is rarely uttered in Yinzerville without an accompanying sneer and angrily consumed Iron City beer.

Canada may be best known nationally for a stormy and unsuccessful run as offensive coordinator at LSU in 2017, where he openly clashed with Ed Orgeron and was bounced after a single season in Baton Rouge. (LSU shifted to Steve Ensminger and brought in a transfer named Joe Burrow to play quarterback, and the rest is history.) Around Pittsburgh, however, Canada is fondly recalled for the effect he had on the 2016 Pitt Panthers, where he transformed the offense with his creative and deceptive schemes, work that caught the eye of the SEC big boys.

Now that he is calling the shots for the local professional gridders, what should we look for in a Canadian Offense (thicker and less fatty than slices of American Offense)? His most obvious transformation of the attack figures to be in the use of play-action, a staple of Canada's offenses in his collegiate stops, as well as a stratagem about as popular lately in Pittsburgh as scab workers. In 2020 the Steelers were last in the league in using play-action; amazingly, that's the sixth-straight season the team has ranked last, making it more of a tradition than a trend. And just like every other year, Pittsburgh had a reverse split where the Steelers were worse with play-action (5.5 yards/play, -15.4% DVOA) than without it (6.4 yards/play, 15.8% DVOA).

Canada also loves to dandify his plays with motion, shifts, and receiver stacking and unstacking, other strategies the Steelers didn't do a lot with last season (they ranked just 20th in pre-snap motion percentage). There is a more basic function he needs to drum into his receivers first, however: catching the damn ball. As pretty much anyone who watched Pittsburgh in 2020 would imagine, the Steelers lapped the field in dropped passes, flubbing 47 of them, led by Diontae Johnson's remarkable 15 drops. At times it seemed there was a better chance of Roethlisberger completing a pass to the Venus de Milo than to any of his wideouts. A real offseason training schedule plus Canada's emphasis on the finer points of holding on to the oblong sphere should see those numbers regress back towards the mean.

Another aspect of the Canada system is welding all that pre-snap persiflage to simple power running schemes. Backing him up in that capacity is the new offensive line coach, Adrian Klemm, who succeeds Shaun Sarrett. Like Canada, Klemm has some collegiate baggage on his resume, in this case an NCAA suspension for paying illegal benefits while coaching at UCLA. A former Patriots lineman, he learned the art of trench warfare under the legendary Dante Scarnecchia, and he has a reputation for developing talent. The Steelers are in the midst of an overdue overhaul up front, but Klemm will have plenty of raw material to work with after the Steelers drafted a pair of linemen (Kendrick Green and Dan Moore) and a bulky tight end (Pat Freiermuth). The line has never been the same

since Mike Munchak left town—Klemm is the latest coach to attempt to recreate some of that success.

The hope is that first-round draft choice Najee Harris out of Alabama is not only the beneficiary of Klemm's blocking sled whisperings but can also make the line look better himself. He is already being counted upon as the bell-cow running back in the mold of another Harris who once carried the mail in Pittsburgh. Last seen leaping over defenders in the College Football Playoff, when not plowing through them or catching passes beyond them, there is little doubt of Harris' talent, regardless of how you feel about drafting running backs in the first round. (You know how we feel about it.) Harris has good hands, and he figures to get plenty of work out of the backfield as Canada re-enters passes to backs into the Pittsburgh playbook—last season only 12% of Roethlisberger's throws were to his running backs, fewest in the NFL. Just in case Big Ben's muscle memory fails him, Harris spent some time during rookie minicamp lining up at the X-receiver spot.

The new hires and fresh blood on offense would seem to indicate the dreaded rebuilding process is indeed underway in Pittsburgh, but the Steelers are attempting to pull off something much trickier—the rebuild on the fly, akin to a NASCAR pit stop while the car is still vying for the lead. The salary cap department, led by longtime guru Omar Khan, did well in bringing back a viable roster that at season's end seemed destined for gutting. Expiring-contract contributors such as wideout JuJu Smith-Schuster, linebacker Vince Williams, and nose tackle Tyson Alualu all returned on short-term, team-friendly deals after many assumed they would be headed elsewhere due to the money crunch. Veteran Trai Turner came in on a one-year contract after the surprising June cut of guard David DeCastro. Joe Haden is in the final year of his contract at the age of 32. It all has the feeling of a last desperate charge of the defibrillators, hoping that a jolt of electricity (and some freshly injected plasma) will rouse the mortifying corpse into one more furious spasm of life.

The FrankenSteelers will have to battle what is, by 2020 winning percentage, the hardest schedule in the NFL. (By our schedule measurement, based on average projected DVOA, Pittsburgh "only" has the hardest schedule in the AFC.) The NFC North is better than the NFC East, the AFC West is better than the AFC South, and as an added bonus the 17th game will be against Russell Wilson and the Seahawks. If Pittsburgh manages to stay competitive until December, the final three games—at Kansas City, Cleveland, at Baltimore—will be a telling crucible, especially given the 2020 collapse. If this experiment is to be successful, those three weekends at year's end figure to be the critical proving ground.

The 2022 Steelers almost certainly will look much different, starting at quarterback. In the meantime, any triumph in Roethlisberger's last stand will likely be much more dependent on a bunch of other Steelers players.

Robert Weintraub

2020 Steelers by Week

Wk	vs.	W-L	PF	PA	YDF	YDA	TO	Total	Off	Def	ST
1	at NYG	W	26	16	349	291	1	20.8%	3.5%	-27.5%	-10.2%
2	DEN	W	26	21	410	319	0	18.4%	3.2%	-9.3%	5.8%
3	HOU	W	28	21	387	260	1	5.0%	-2.8%	-4.7%	3.2%
4	BYE										
5	PHI	W	38	29	367	336	1	-2.0%	17.2%	23.5%	4.3%
6	CLE	W	38	7	277	220	2	84.1%	1.3%	-76.5%	6.2%
7	at TEN	W	27	24	362	292	-3	17.1%	-20.2%	-21.6%	15.7%
8	at BAL	W	28	24	221	457	3	47.0%	12.2%	-33.0%	1.7%
9	at DAL	W	24	19	355	364	2	-7.0%	-7.8%	-20.9%	-20.0%
10	CIN	W	36	10	377	324	2	47.5%	11.3%	-15.4%	20.7%
11	at JAX	W	27	3	373	206	3	50.2%	-7.8%	-65.4%	-7.4%
12	BAL	W	19	14	334	219	0	49.2%	2.9%	-57.5%	-11.3%
13	WAS	L	17	23	326	318	-1	-0.7%	-14.7%	-10.1%	3.9%
14	at BUF	L	15	26	224	334	0	-5.1%	-28.8%	-25.9%	-2.2%
15	at CIN	L	17	27	244	230	-3	-59.1%	-60.7%	6.1%	7.6%
16	IND	W	28	24	354	365	2	24.4%	28.4%	-0.9%	-4.8%
17	at CLE	L	22	24	394	358	-1	-10.8%	-10.4%	8.5%	8.2%
18	CLE	L	37	48	553	390	-5	-33.0%	-3.1%	31.8%	1.9%

Trends and Splits

	Offense	Rank	Defense	Rank
Total DVOA	-4.7%	22	-20.2%	1
Unadjusted VOA	1.8%	14	-21.9%	1
Weighted Trend	-7.9%	22	-20.0%	4
Variance	4.3%	8	7.4%	27
Average Opponent	2.5%	29	-4.3%	27
Passing	11.3%	21	-19.8%	1
Rushing	-26.3%	30	-20.7%	5
First Down	-8.0%	23	-22.6%	1
Second Down	-6.8%	25	-18.5%	4
Third Down	3.8%	12	-18.2%	6
First Half	-13.5%	26	-22.1%	1
Second Half	4.6%	11	-18.4%	6
Red Zone	15.3%	11	-17.2%	4
Late and Close	5.0%	14	-18.6%	4

Five-Year Performance

Year	W-L	Pyth W	Est W	PF	PA	TO	Total	Rk	Off	Rk	Def	Rk	ST	Rk	Off AGL	Rk	Def AGL	Rk	Off Age	Rk	Def Age	Rk	ST Age	Rk
2016	11-5	9.9	10.0	399	327	+5	15.6%	4	12.7%	8	-3.0%	11	-0.1%	16	34.7	15	26.4	9	27.1	9	26.5	15	25.7	23
2017	13-3	10.6	11.2	406	308	+2	25.9%	4	17.5%	3	-5.4%	9	3.1%	9	13.8	6	14.8	6	27.4	7	25.7	23	25.9	14
2018	9-6-1	9.7	9.2	428	360	-11	11.3%	9	14.3%	6	-0.5%	14	-3.5%	27	24.4	7	14.1	3	27.9	6	26.2	18	26.1	10
2019	8-8	7.6	7.3	289	303	+8	-5.8%	19	-25.1%	31	-17.8%	3	1.5%	8	30.6	11	30.0	15	27.0	11	26.1	19	25.9	16
2020	12-4	10.7	10.1	416	312	+9	16.8%	8	-4.7%	22	-20.2%	1	1.3%	14	29.1	9	26.1	7	27.4	7	26.7	9	25.8	19

2020 Performance Based on Most Common Personnel Groups

PIT Offense					PIT Offense vs. Opponents					PIT Defense					PIT Defense vs. Opponents			
Pers	Freq	Yds	DVOA	Run%	Pers	Freq	Yds	DVOA	Run%	Pers	Freq	Yds	DVOA	Pers	Freq	Yds	DVOA
11	74%	5.6	-1.0%	28%	Base	13%	5.1	-22.0%	64%	Base	36%	4.6	-17.7%	11	63%	5.6	-8.2%
12	9%	5.0	-0.1%	45%	Nickel	70%	5.4	-2.3%	32%	Nickel	40%	5.0	-29.4%	12	22%	4.5	-22.3%
01	6%	8.0	48.8%	2%	Dime+	15%	6.8	25.6%	4%	Dime+	20%	6.2	6.8%	13	6%	4.3	-55.8%
22	4%	3.9	-17.7%	76%	Goal Line	2%	2.2	-17.2%	83%	Big	4%	2.9	-53.1%	21	3%	2.7	-47.1%
612	3%	4.6	-26.4%	81%	Big	1%	1.6	-43.6%	78%					10	2%	1.3	-165.8%

Strategic Tendencies

Run/Pass		Rk	Formation		Rk	Pass Rush		Rk	Secondary		Rk	Strategy		Rk
Runs, first half	34%	26	Form: Single Back	82%	13	Rush 3	5.1%	19	4 DB	36%	4	Play Action	12%	32
Runs, first down	40%	29	Form: Empty Back	16%	2	Rush 4	56.1%	28	5 DB	40%	31	Offensive Motion	42%	20
Runs, second-long	30%	12	Form: Multi Back	2%	30	Rush 5	30.7%	2	6+ DB	20%	11	Avg Box (Off)	6.48	18
Runs, power sit.	56%	24	Pers: 3+ WR	81%	3	Rush 6+	8.1%	6	Man Coverage	32%	15	Avg Box (Def)	6.50	23
Runs, behind 2H	21%	32	Pers: 2+ TE/6+ OL	19%	29	Edge Rusher Sacks	46.4%	21	CB by Sides	93%	3	Offensive Pace	29.24	6
Pass, ahead 2H	59%	2	Pers: 6+ OL	7%	4	Interior DL Sacks	32.1%	8	S/CB Cover Ratio	21%	27	Defensive Pace	31.13	26
Run-Pass Options	8%	14	Shotgun/Pistol	83%	4	Second Level Sacks	21.4%	20	DB Blitz	17%	7	Go for it on 4th	1.21	27

The Steelers used empty backfields twice as often as they did in 2019, and these plays were successful with 28.6% DVOA, although the 6.3 yards per play wasn't much more than the league average of 6.1. ✎ Pittsburgh ranked ninth passing the ball on third and fourth down but ranked 22nd or lower for every other down/play combination. ✎ Pittsburgh's offense was sixth in situation-neutral pace but dropped to just 26th when trailing in games. ✎ The Steelers had a dismal -43.6% DVOA with just 3.1 yards per play when using six offensive linemen. ✎ Pittsburgh ranked 10th in offensive DVOA at home but 27th on the road. This is usually where we would write that these kind of home/road splits have no correlation from year to year, but in fact the Steelers have a history of a bigger gap than usual between offense at home and on the road.

Pittsburgh Offense Home vs. Road, 2015-2020

Year	Home DVOA	Rank	Road DVOA	Rank
2015	26.4%	1	9.0%	5
2016	22.7%	4	2.0%	10
2017	20.1%	2	14.5%	5
2018	23.8%	3	5.7%	11
2019	-20.2%	32	-30.0%	31
2020	5.7%	10	-15.7%	27

Leaguewide, the gap between offensive DVOA at home and on the road was always about 6% or 7%. Over the last two years that has shrunk to about 1%. ✎ You know the Steelers use play-action less than any other offense, but they also faced it less than any other defense, just 18% of pass plays. The Pittsburgh defense had a phenomenal -42.2% DVOA on passes with play-action, when no other defense was better than -10.0%. ✎ Pittsburgh allowed 7.3 yards per pass in zone compared to 5.7 yards per pass in man coverage, one of the largest gaps in the league. But the corresponding DVOA gap wasn't very big, just 6.2%.

Passing

Player	DYAR	DVOA	Plays	NtYds	Avg	YAC	C%	TD	Int
B.Roethlisberger	518	1.1%	621	3676	5.9	4.9	65.7%	33	10
M.Rudolph	1	-10.9%	44	316	7.2	4.1	58.1%	2	1
D.Haskins	-483	-40.1%	261	1298	5.0	5.8	61.4%	5	6

Rushing

Player	DYAR	DVOA	Plays	Yds	Avg	TD	Fum	Suc
J.Conner*	8	-7.5%	169	721	4.3	6	2	49%
B.Snell	-96	-26.3%	111	368	3.3	4	2	44%
A.McFarland	-30	-31.9%	33	113	3.4	0	0	36%
C.Claypool	8	-29.0%	10	16	1.6	2	0	--
J.Samuels	-14	-48.0%	9	28	3.1	0	0	33%
B.Roethlisberger	-49	-112.2%	9	14	1.6	0	3	--
K.Ballage	-56	-21.1%	88	290	3.3	3	1	57%
D.Haskins	-4	-16.2%	13	57	4.4	1	1	--

Receiving

Player	DYAR	DVOA	Plays	Ctch	Yds	Y/C	YAC	TD	C%
D.Johnson	-73	-19.1%	144	88	923	10.5	4.5	7	61%
J.Smith-Schuster	28	-10.0%	128	97	831	8.6	4.2	9	76%
C.Claypool	68	-5.4%	110	62	873	14.0	5.2	9	57%
J.Washington	18	-8.9%	56	30	392	13.1	4.6	5	54%
R.McCloud	-75	-51.6%	22	20	77	3.9	5.3	0	91%
E.Ebron	-95	-23.3%	91	56	558	10.0	3.4	5	62%
V.McDonald*	-49	-45.3%	20	15	99	6.6	5.3	0	75%
J.Conner*	-23	-23.5%	43	35	215	6.1	6.7	0	81%
B.Snell	-11	-26.5%	14	10	61	6.1	8.8	0	71%
J.Samuels	-12	-29.5%	14	9	46	5.1	6.2	0	64%
A.McFarland	7	0.9%	9	6	54	9.0	7.8	0	67%
K.Ballage	-30	-32.6%	27	20	99	5.0	6.5	0	74%

Offensive Line

Player	Pos	Age	GS	Snaps	Pen	Sk	Pass	Run	Player	Pos	Age	GS	Snaps	Pen	Sk	Pass	Run
Alejandro Villanueva*	LT	33	16/16	1098	4	1.5	21	5	David DeCastro*	RG	31	13/13	845	2	0	5	3
Chukwuma Okorafor	RT	24	16/15	1033	4	3	9	6	Kevin Dotson	RG/LG	25	13/4	358	4	0	0	3
Maurkice Pouncey*	C	32	13/13	863	1	0	4	3	J.C. Hassenauer	C	26	15/4	303	3	0	2	2
Matt Feiler	LG	29	13/13	848	2	1.5	6	4	Trai Turner	RG	28	9/9	536	2	1	6	8

Year	Yards	ALY	Rk	Power	Rk	Stuff	Rk	2Lev	Rk	OpFld	Rk	BB Rt	Rk	Sacks	ASR	Rk	Press	Rk	BB Rt	Rk	Cont
2018	4.36	4.44	15	71%	5	16%	5	1.20	20	0.80	19	4.1%	4	24	4.4%	4	23.2%	2	5.5%	2	28
2019	3.74	3.84	30	54%	27	23%	31	1.05	26	0.52	26	7.0%	2	32	6.6%	12	30.0%	17	9.9%	3	31
2020	3.82	3.78	32	56%	30	19%	28	1.02	31	0.72	17	7.8%	6	14	2.7%	1	15.2%	2	7.3%	2	24

2020 ALY by direction:	Left End: 4.44 (18)	Left Tackle: 3.19 (29)	Mid/Guard: 3.78 (31)	Right Tackle: 3.27 (30)	Right End: 4.76 (14)

The Steelers' line finished first in the NFL in adjusted sack rate while also dead last in adjusted line yards, a feat matched only by the 2003 Detroit Lions. For the second straight year, the Steelers didn't have too many easily attributable blown blocks on running plays, but they were poor in short yardage and let the backs get tackled behind the line of scrimmage too often. ◥ The declining unit loses its standard-bearer, center Maurkice Pouncey, who has retired after 11 seasons. His Hall of Fame candidacy will be interesting; he has two All-Pro selections, nine Pro Bowls, 108 career Approximate Value, and the weight of the Steelers glamour on his side. Working against Pouncey is the lack of longevity and Super Bowl rings, along with the eye test—he has always been among the league's better centers but never the clear-cut best, and his last two years were subpar by his career standards. ◥ Pittsburgh also loses tackle Alejandro Villanueva and his 21 blown blocks to the Ravens, a potential case of addition by subtraction, and versatile fellow free agent Matt Feiler to the Chargers. ◥ Right guard David DeCastro was shockingly released in late June due to ankle issues (and was reportedly contemplating joining Pouncey in retirement). Veteran Trai Turner was signed to replace him. Turner's 2020 was affected by various injuries, and the fact he was dumped by the line-desperate Chargers has to be a red flag. But he does have some strong play on his résumé, which at least separates him from the other guys on the roster. ◥ Rashaad Coward, a free agent who started 15 games over the last two seasons in Chicago, worked with the first unit when DeCastro was absent from OTAs. Fourth-year man Aviante Collins, who has played tackle in his brief time on the field (with the Vikings), has the athleticism to swap positions, if not the experience. ◥ Chukwuma "Chuks" Okorafor will flip from right to left tackle to replace Villanueva. Zach Banner, aka "The Hulk," was set to be the team's right tackle before he tore his ACL in the 2020 opener. That opened the door for Okorafor, who played decently, though he hardly popped eyeballs. The 6-foot-8, 360-pound Banner's return adds some green-tinted size and strength to the line, though he's hardly a sure thing, having played sparingly across four seasons and three teams. ◥ Fourth-rounder Dan Moore (Texas A&M) will be in the mix to contribute as a swing tackle. He's well-rounded but not particularly great in any area. ◥ Third-round pick Kendrick Green, an athletic mover from Illinois, is likely to take over at center on Day 1, much as Pouncey started as a rookie. Green is not going to match peak Pouncey right away, though he will wear the same No. 53 jersey. No pressure. ◥ At left guard is Kevin Dotson, who looked capable when forced into the lineup as a rookie but remains unseasoned. Overall, a youthful if not especially talented group for new line coach Adrian Klemm to attempt to mold.

Defensive Front

Defensive Line	Age	Pos	G	Snaps	Plays	TmPct	Rk	Stop	Dfts	BTkl	Runs	St%	Rk	RuYd	Rk	Sack	Hit	Hur	Dsrpt
Cameron Heyward	32	DE	15	807	57	7.6%	7	43	16	2	45	76%	46	2.3	43	4.0	16	33	3
Stephon Tuitt	28	DE	15	778	48	6.4%	19	42	15	5	32	84%	10	2.3	44	11.0	13	29	5
Tyson Alualu	34	DT	15	449	43	5.8%	32	34	11	3	33	79%	31	1.7	12	2.0	5	8	5

Edge Rushers	Age	Pos	G	Snaps	Plays	TmPct	Rk	Stop	Dfts	BTkl	Runs	St%	Rk	RuYd	Rk	Sack	Hit	Hur	Dsrpt
T.J. Watt	27	OLB	15	856	59	7.9%	5	57	31	4	34	97%	1	0.6	2	15.0	27	32	9
Bud Dupree*	28	OLB	11	609	33	6.0%	26	28	17	4	18	72%	47	1.7	19	8.0	7	24	6
Alex Highsmith	24	OLB	16	438	43	5.4%	35	28	10	2	32	66%	69	2.8	58	2.0	4	15	1
Cassius Marsh	29	DE	8	150	12	3.0%	--	8	2	4	10	70%	--	5.6	--	0.0	0	0	0

Linebackers	Age	Pos	G	Snaps	Plays	TmPct	Rk	Stop	Dfts	BTkl	Runs	St%	Rk	RuYd	Rk	Sack	Hit	Hur	Tgts	Suc%	Rk	Yd/P	Rk	PD	Int
Vince Williams	32	ILB	14	671	70	10.0%	60	44	16	13	46	76%	1	2.3	1	3.0	1	7	26	38%	63	8.3	66	0	0
Avery Williamson*	29	ILB	15	666	114	13.9%	35	48	7	6	66	53%	54	5.0	80	1.0	1	2	31	19%	75	8.9	71	3	1
Robert Spillane	26	ILB	12	378	47	7.9%	68	23	8	6	27	44%	78	4.9	77	2.0	1	8	23	65%	8	4.7	13	4	1
Devin Bush	23	ILB	5	278	29	11.6%	50	19	8	3	14	71%	5	4.7	71	1.0	0	2	16	69%	4	5.6	29	3	0
Marcus Allen	25	ILB	14	206	24	3.4%	--	12	7	8	18	44%	--	4.9	--	0.0	2	4	3	67%	--	3.7	--	0	0

Year	Yards	ALY	Rk	Power	Rk	Stuff	Rk	2Lev	Rk	OpFld	Rk	BB Rt	Rk	Sacks	ASR	Rk	Press	Rk	BB Rt	Rk
2018	4.04	4.24	12	69%	22	19%	17	1.17	11	0.63	8	11.2%	7	52	9.3%	1	34.5%	2	13.1%	6
2019	3.89	4.12	11	76%	31	20%	15	1.15	14	0.44	1	11.1%	25	54	9.7%	1	34.4%	5	19.8%	2
2020	4.00	3.67	2	67%	16	22%	4	1.12	10	0.78	22	14.1%	10	56	9.2%	1	30.4%	1	21.8%	1

| 2020 ALY by direction: | Left End: 6.06 (32) | Left Tackle: 4.19 (16) | Mid/Guard: 3.73 (3) | Right Tackle: 2.21 (1) | Right End: 4.90 (22) |

One position group the Steelers don't have to worry about is the defensive line. Cameron Heyward and Stephon Tuitt form an outstanding combo, and the ability to re-sign both Tyson Alualu and Chris Wormley ensures the entirety of the 2020 unit returns. ● The Steelers were far better at stopping runs between the tackles than they were at stopping runs to the outside. They were third against runs up the gut while dead last against runs around left end. ● Heyward had "only" four sacks, but actually totaled more hurries than pass-rusher deluxe and NFL sack leader T.J. Watt (34 to 32) while continuing to anchor the line against the run. ● Depth is a concern at outside linebacker. The unit loses Bud Dupree, who had at last emerged into his first-round pedigree with 19.5 sacks in his last 27 games before tearing an ACL in November. Tennessee ignored the injury and signed him to a rich free-agent deal. ● Alex Highsmith had a couple of nice moments as a rookie replacement last season, but it remains to be seen how he holds up now that he is the starter opposite Watt, who is probably the best defensive player in the league not named Aaron Donald. Watt has amassed 49.5 sacks and 17 forced fumbles while averaging around 33 hurries over his first four seasons—not bad. He was also the top-ranked edge rusher in run stop rate in 2020. ● Highsmith was drafted on the assumption that Dupree would leave, so his time has come regardless. But behind the starters are just journeyman Cassius Marsh and a sixth-round rookie, Quincy Roche (Miami). ● Inside, the situation is better, with the surprise return of Vince Williams adding depth and the crucial return of Devin Bush from his ACL tear bringing his playmaking juice back to the position. ● Robert ("I, The Jury") Spillane was a small-sample revelation in Bush's absence last year, especially in coverage, with the highlight a pick-six against the Ravens. He was mercilessly picked on by the Browns and Jarvis Landry in the playoff game, however, so playing the more run-centric position alongside Bush is probably a good thing. That position in the Steelers scheme will require Spillane to blitz more often than in 2020; he told the *Pittsburgh Post-Gazette* that he remembered being assigned just two blitzes all season.

Defensive Secondary

						Overall						vs. Run					vs. Pass						
Secondary	Age	Pos	G	Snaps	Plays	TmPct	Rk	Stop	Dfts	BTkl	Runs	St%	Rk	RuYd	Rk	Tgts	Tgt%	Rk	aDOT	Suc%	Rk	Yd/P	Rk	PD	Int
Minkah Fitzpatrick	25	FS	16	1021	90	11.3%	32	22	13	11	44	16%	66	9.4	61	19	4.7%	64	14.8	74%	1	4.5	5	11	4
Steven Nelson*	28	CB	15	907	57	7.6%	64	23	11	6	12	25%	67	11.2	77	71	19.6%	40	14.0	61%	8	6.6	20	9	2
Terrell Edmunds	24	SS	15	865	76	10.2%	43	34	14	8	33	55%	7	5.2	18	38	11.0%	18	10.3	53%	29	9.3	54	8	2
Joe Haden	32	CB	14	846	64	9.2%	28	29	13	11	18	61%	8	7.6	50	69	20.4%	36	13.7	64%	4	6.6	19	12	2
Cameron Sutton	26	CB	16	548	37	4.6%	--	23	14	9	2	50%	--	6.5	--	44	20.1%	--	10.2	68%	--	6.4	--	8	1
Mike Hilton*	27	CB	12	463	57	9.5%	--	36	22	13	23	61%	--	3.7	--	31	16.8%	--	14.7	55%	--	5.8	--	7	3
Arthur Maulet	28	CB	11	404	28	4.7%	--	14	6	7	8	38%	--	10.3	--	23	14.1%	--	10.7	65%	--	6.5	--	5	1

Year	Pass D Rank	vs. #1 WR	Rk	vs. #2 WR	Rk	vs. Other WR	Rk	WR Wide	Rk	WR Slot	Rk	vs. TE	Rk	vs. RB	Rk
2018	17	-6.0%	10	2.4%	19	10.8%	25	-6.8%	17	10.0%	22	25.5%	31	1.6%	15
2019	3	4.2%	19	-15.8%	5	20.4%	26	-30.5%	3	20.9%	29	-25.3%	3	-36.7%	3
2020	1	13.3%	24	-16.2%	4	-27.6%	2	5.7%	22	-6.5%	10	-48.4%	1	-3.8%	14

The surprise return of JuJu Smith-Schuster forced the cap-strapped Steelers to shed steady Steven Nelson (eighth in coverage success rate), a depletion that came on the heels of losing playmaking slot corner Mike Hilton and his 22 defeats to free agency. That leaves Pittsburgh with Joe Haden, who was fourth in success rate but is now 32 years old, along with Cam Sutton, a versatile player who can play on the perimeter or in the slot, and plenty of questions at the position. In a league where no team can ever have enough corners, the Steelers are banking on the great pass rush to cover some potential back-end holes. ● Third-year vet Justin Layne is the presumptive third starter; his time atop the depth chart got off to a rocky start when he was arrested on a firearms charge in April (Layne pled guilty to several misdemeanors). A converted wideout with great length but not much speed, Layne needs to improve as a run defender if he is to stick in the lineup long term. ● An intriguing contrast is Layne's fellow Michigan State alum, Shakur Brown, who surprisingly went undrafted (helping to end an 80-year streak of at least one Spartans player hearing his name called on draft day). Signed as a rookie free agent, Brown stood out against the run in East Lansing, though his athletic traits are just average. ● Minkah Fitzpatrick overcame a slow start to regain his All-Pro form, leading all safeties in success rate. His run stats reflect his position as the last line of defense, with almost half of his run tackles coming after double-digit gains. ● Running mate Terrell Edmunds surprisingly had his fifth-year option declined (on the same day Buffalo picked up the option on his brother, Tremaine—ouch). Edmunds has been more workhorse than impact player in Pittsburgh, and he hasn't lived up to his status as a first-round pick. But with little behind him on the depth chart, he has outsized importance this season. ❧ As with outside linebacker, the safeties need to stay healthy, for depth is lacking. Ex-Lion Miles Killebrew is primarily a special-teamer, so a serious injury at the position would be a hammer blow.

Special Teams

Year	DVOA	Rank	FG/XP	Rank	Net Kick	Rank	Kick Ret	Rank	Net Punt	Rank	Punt Ret	Rank	Hidden	Rank
2018	-3.5%	27	-11.0	30	3.7	6	-4.2	28	-5.5	26	-0.5	16	1.2	12
2019	1.5%	8	10.7	2	5.4	5	-5.5	31	-9.1	28	5.9	3	-3.6	22
2020	1.3%	14	6.7	7	1.7	14	0.0	13	-2.0	22	0.2	17	-4.3	21

Punter Jordan Berry was the weak link of an otherwise solid if unspectacular special teams group, and the team drafted a big leg to replace him, Pressley Harvin of Georgia Tech. Harvin was an unanimous All-American and the Ray Guy Award-winner, and is a 255-pound-weighing, 545-pound-squatting, fake-punt-bomb-throwing folk-hero-in-waiting if any of that boom translates to the pros. ❧ Kicker Chris Boswell was quietly one of the league's best on field goals, and when factoring in the treacherous Heinz Field kicking conditions, he may be right at the top. ❧ Ray-Ray McCloud is still around to be an average return man with an above-average name. Diontae Johnson had a strong year returning punts in 2019 (8.5 points of estimated field position) and still shares that role with McCloud.

San Francisco 49ers

2020 Record: 6-10	**Total DVOA:** 5.4% (5)	**2021 Mean Projection:** 9.7 wins	**On the Clock (0-5):** 7%
Pythagorean Wins: 7.6 (17)	**Offense:** -2.5% (20)	**Postseason Odds:** 58.7%	**Mediocrity (6-8):** 25%
Snap-Weighted Age: 26.4 (18)	**Defense:** -9.9% (6)	**Super Bowl Odds:** 8.7%	**Playoff Contender (9-11):** 41%
Average Opponent: 5.1% (3)	**Special Teams:** -2.1% (23)	**Proj. Avg. Opponent:** -2% (25)	**Super Bowl Contender (12+):** 26%

2020: Everyone got hurt.

2021: They should return to Super Bowl contention, but who will be the quarterback?

Each of the 32 NFL chapters in this book is designed to answer two questions: What happened in 2020? And what's going to happen in 2021? For the San Francisco 49ers, what happened in 2020 is simple: everyone got hurt. We'll expand on that and break it down in detail, but at the end of the day that's really all you need to know. What's going to happen in 2021, however, is a much more interesting question. The 49ers are going to attempt something that has never been done before: win a Super Bowl while simultaneously developing their quarterback of the future.

The 49ers suffered 161.6 adjusted games lost last year, not including COVID-related absences. That was most in the league by a wide margin, and the second-most in our database behind the 171.5 of the 2017 Chicago Bears. They had 74.7 AGL on offense, second only to Philadelphia, and a league-high 86.9 AGL on defense, 26 more than anyone else. And when we say everyone got hurt, we do really mean that *everyone* got hurt to one degree or another. Their healthiest position group was linebacker, where they ranked 15th in AGL; their healthiest position group on offense was wide receiver, where they ranked 21st. They were in the bottom five at every other position group on the field. That includes finishing third-to-last in defensive back AGL and next-to-last in quarterback AGL, and they set an all-time record with 46.3 AGL among defensive linemen. By the time the Week 2 win over the Jets was over, three of the team's top defensive ends—Nick Bosa (torn ACL), Solomon Thomas (also a torn ACL), and Dee Ford (back)—were all out for the year.

Elsewhere, Weston Richburg, the hypothetical starter at center, missed the entire season with a torn patella suffered in 2019 and thus led the team with 16.0 AGL (he retired this off-season). His backup, Ben Garland, only played in five games due to ankle and calf injuries. Cornerback Richard Sherman (11.0 AGL, calf) and strong safety Jaquiski Tartt (9.3, groin/toe) were the biggest losses in the secondary, where there were so many injuries that 11 defensive backs started at least three games. Other starters who missed at least half the season included quarterback Jimmy Garoppolo (10.0, ankle), wide receiver Deebo Samuel (9.6, foot/hamstring), and tight end George Kittle (8.0, knee/foot).

San Francisco is nearly certain to have better health in 2021, so that alone should get them deep into the playoffs, right? Well, not necessarily. The most injured teams in history typically won fewer games than they had the year before and then bounced back the next season, but the effect is less dramatic than you might think, only about one win per year (Table 1).

The 49ers were not the only team from 2020 to suffer a historic amount of injuries; the Patriots and Eagles also qualify. This is partly due to COVID ramifications, especially in the case of New England. Even before the pandemic, however, injuries have been on the rise in recent seasons ... or, perhaps, teams have been more willing to report them. Regardless, we checked the teams that saw the biggest year-to-year jumps in AGL and found a somewhat similar pattern (Table 2). The injuries caused a steeper decline, about three wins per year, but the rebound in the following season was even smaller, about half a win per year on average.

The bigger problem for San Francisco is that while 2020 was especially bad, this team always seems to suffer an abnormal amount of injuries. The 49ers have finished among the bottom 11 teams in AGL every year since general manager John Lynch and head coach Kyle Shanahan arrived in 2017 (see table on page 220). Only Washington has suffered more total AGL in the past four seasons, and while San Francisco's quarterbacks and running backs are notoriously fragile, it's their 246.9 AGL total on defense that stands out—no other team has even 200.0 AGL on that side of the ball. In plain English, that means about a dozen more games missed by a starting defender than the next most injured team, every year. The 49ers lost Malcolm Smith, Arik Armstead, and Jimmie Ward for large chunks of 2017, and Brock Coyle, Adrian Colbert, and Jaquiski Tartt in 2018. Even in the Super Bowl year of 2019, they often had to go without Jason Verrett, Kwon Alexander, Dee Ford, Ahkello Witherspoon, and others.

In defense of Lynch and Shanahan, the injuries started to pile up long before they arrived. The 49ers have fallen outside the top 20 in AGL every year since 2013, the last season they played in Candlestick Park. They had been in the top 10 six times in the seven years before that, including a first-place finish in 2012 when they reached the Super Bowl against Baltimore.

Lynch and Shanahan are well aware that injuries have been their team's biggest problem. "There's an old adage in football," Lynch has said. "I don't know if it's exclusive to football, but your best ability is availability. We haven't had a lot of guys available, and that's something we're looking into hard." Shanahan agreed, admitting that "Injuries are pretty

2021 49ers Schedule

Week	Opp.	Week	Opp.	Week	Opp.
1	at DET	7	IND	13	at SEA
2	at PHI	8	at CHI	14	at CIN
3	GB	9	ARI	15	ATL
4	SEA	10	LAR (Mon.)	16	at TEN (Thu.)
5	at ARI	11	at JAX	17	HOU
6	BYE	12	MIN	18	at LAR

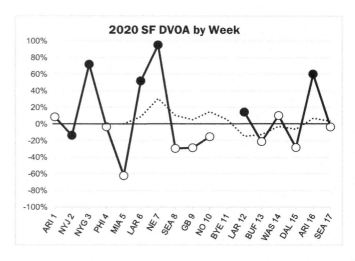

2020 SF DVOA by Week

random, but it has also affected us huge. So, that's something that we definitely have to sit back and really look at it from all angles and put a lot of time into." Unfortunately, those comments were not made this year, but back in 2019 after the team fired head athletic trainer Jeff Ferguson and strength and conditioning coach Ray Wright. The results have only gotten worse since then.

It is possible, however, that the 49ers have started to sow seeds for success down the road. An article by Nick Wagoner of ESPN.com noted that the players in San Francisco's draft class this year missed only 7% of games they were expected to play in college, a rate matched by the 49ers' draft class of 2020. Early results from that class are promising—first-round picks Javon Kinlaw and Brandon Aiyuk missed only four games due to injury. (Aiyuk missed two others due to COVID protocols.) The 2019 class, meanwhile, missed 22% of expected collegiate games, while the 2018 class missed 15%. Those are the draft classes that produced such oft-injured players as Nick Bosa, Deebo Samuel, Jalen Hurd, and Dante Pettis. Then again, the 2017 class missed only 8% of their expected college games, and that's the draft that produced Solomon Thomas, Reuben Foster, and Ahkello Witherspoon, all of whom have struggled with injuries (among other issues).

At some point, we must face the possibility that the franchise is simply cursed. In May, running back Jeff Wilson was

finishing a workout at team facilities when he tore his meniscus *while standing up out of a chair*. Safety Tarvarius Moore then tore his Achilles in a non-contact injury in June practices; three plays later, offensive lineman Justin Skule tore his ACL. Wilson underwent surgery and will miss at least the first six weeks of the season, while Moore and Skule are each out for the year. Though all three were expected to be backups this year, they offered valuable depth and experience, with a combined 44 games and 15 starts last year.

Injuries were not the only problem the 49ers had to deal with in 2020. San Francisco beat the Rams in Week 12 to move to 5-6 and keep their faint playoff hopes alive, but the next day Santa Clara County announced harsh COVID restrictions that made it impossible to run a football team. With zero notice, the 49ers packed up shop and temporarily moved to Arizona, where they proceeded to lose "home" games to Buffalo and Washington and then a road game in Dallas, effectively ending their season. The 49ers came into the year with Super Bowl aspirations but ended it stuck in a series of meaningless games, usually ending in blowouts, while living out

Table 1. Most Single-Season AGL, 2004-2020

Year	Team	AGL	Wins Y-1	DVOA Y-1	Wins	DVOA	Wins Y+1	DVOA Y+1
2016	CHI	171.5	6	-6.5%	3	-8.8%	5	-17.0%
2020	**SF**	**166.6***	**13**	**29.0%**	**6**	**5.4%**	**--**	**--**
2019	NYJ	160.1	4	-17.0%	7	-17.7%	2	-30.5%
2015	NYG	152.0	6	-7.8%	6	-7.4%	11	9.4%
2013	NYG	140.5	9	11.9%	7	-16.5%	6	-7.8%
2017	WAS	138.8	8.5	8.9%	7	-2.6%	7	-20.1%
2014	NYG	136.1	7	-16.5%	6	-7.8%	6	-7.4%
2020	NE	134.8*	12	30.7%	7	-7.1%	--	--
2019	WAS	131.0	7	-20.1%	3	-26.9%	7	-2.3%
2020	PHI	128.1*	9	5.5%	4.5	-18.8%	--	--
2016	SD	127.4	4	-16.9%	5	-1.9%	9	6.8%
2017	MIA	126.1	10	-1.4%	6	-21.7%	7	-17.7%
2015	WAS	125.5	4	-29.1%	9	-0.8%	8.5	8.9%
2016	TB	125.0	6	-9.5%	9	-3.0%	5	-12.4%
2017	CHI	124.5	3	-8.8%	5	-17.0%	12	19.1%
Average			**7.2**	**-3.2%**	**6.0**	**-10.2%**	**7.1**	**-5.9%**

* Includes COVID-related absences

of suitcases like a barnstorming team playing a century ago. They were perhaps the most depressing team in the league.

But they were not the worst—far from it, in fact, ranking 11th in both total and weighted DVOA. Their 6-10 record can somewhat be blamed on a tough schedule (third-hardest by DVOA) and a 3-5 record in one-score games. Somehow, despite the injuries, the defense actually improved throughout the year, going from a DVOA of -1.6% (11th) through Week 9 to -18.9% (fourth) from Week 10 onwards. There were a lot of areas where this defense excelled, particularly in the secondary. They were the finest team in the league when playing man coverage, allowing just 5.5 yards per pass with -6.6% DVOA. They were second best in DVOA without pressure at 13.5%. They were outstanding in preventing long runs. This is all an enormous credit to departed defensive coordinator Robert Saleh and explains why he is now head coach of the Jets. Most of the players who were executing Saleh's scheme, though, will still be in town for his replacement, DeMeco Ryans. Eight of San Francisco's defensive starters from the Super Bowl against Kansas City are still on the roster, and the three who are gone (DeForest Buckner, Sheldon Day, and Richard Sherman) have been adequately replaced (Javon Kinlaw, D.J. Jones, and Jason Verrett). Ryans, by the way, knows a thing or two about surviving on defense in the NFL—the Defensive Rookie of the Year in 2006, he started 139 games at linebacker for the Texans and Eagles.

The offense has seen more of a makeover, but it still has a perennial Pro Bowl candidate at tight end, the league's scariest YAC attack for a wide receiver corps, and about a dozen running backs alternating trips to the medical tent with trips to the end zone. Offensive line reinforcements have arrived in the form of center Alex Mack, the ideal fit for Shanahan's mobility-based offense. Mack previously worked with Shanahan in both Atlanta (where they reached the Super Bowl) and Cleveland (where they did not). With few obvious needs, the 49ers added critical backups for both the offensive line and the secondary via the draft.

It's the first of their draft picks, though, that is most compelling. A full month before draft night, the 49ers made a giant move, trading three first-round picks (including the 12th selection this year) and a 2022 third-rounder to Miami for the third pick overall. The early timing of the trade was a boon to sports talk stations around the country. Who else was trying to trade up so high? Were the 49ers really targeting Alabama's Mac Jones? Shanahan didn't help matters when he said there were five quarterbacks they would be happy with ... which opened the door to criticism, because we know the Eagles were willing to trade the sixth pick for a lower price than San Francisco paid for the third.

That's all irrelevant now, because the 49ers used that pick on North Dakota State's Trey Lance, the most intriguing quarterback prospect in the class. Lance only started one full season in Fargo, but that one season was laughably good. Lance completed 66.9% of his 287 passes, averaging 9.7 yards per throw with 28 touchdowns and no—as in zero—interceptions. He added 1,100 yards and 14 more touchdowns on the ground. The Bison went 16-0 and defeated the James Madison Dukes 28-20 in the FCS National Championship Game. Lance won the Walter Payton award as the most outstanding player in FCS and the Jerry Rice award as its best freshman. Then came the pandemic, which ruined the Bison's 2020 fall season. Lance played just one game (a thrown-together contest against Central Arkansas in which Lance ran for two touchdowns and threw for two more along with—horrors!—an interception) and then was off to the draft, where he was selected by San Francisco about a week shy of his 21st birthday.

As you might imagine, it's very rare for a team to draft a quarterback within two years of playing in a Super Bowl. The last time it happened was in 2016, when Peyton Manning retired after winning the Lombardi Trophy and the Broncos tried to replace him with Paxton Lynch. Before that you have to go way back to 1987, when the No Longer Shufflin' Bears

Table 2. Biggest Jumps in Single-Season AGL, 2004-2020

Year	Team	AGL Y-1	AGL	Change	Wins Y-1	DVOA Y-1	Wins	DVOA	Wins Y+1	DVOA Y+1
2019	NYJ	70.4	160.1	+89.6	4	-17.0%	7	-17.7%	2	-30.5%
2020	DAL	35.8	118.5*	+82.7	8	19.9%	6	-11.1%	--	--
2008	DET	28.7	103.2	+74.5	7	-24.3%	0	-45.2%	2	-48.6%
2009	BUF	47.6	121.2	+73.6	7	-8.1%	6	-11.2%	4	-22.4%
2020	**SF**	**95.8**	**166.6***	**+70.8**	**13**	**29.0%**	**6**	**5.4%**	**--**	**--**
2016	CHI	103.9	171.5	+67.7	6	-6.5%	3	-8.8%	5	-17.0%
2018	JAX	35.6	102.5	+66.9	10	13.8%	5	-8.5%	6	-19.4%
2017	SEA	40.1	104.5	+64.4	10.5	7.5%	9	2.3%	10	5.9%
2014	KC	37.4	101.3	+63.9	11	16.0%	9	9.8%	11	25.5%
2008	CIN	43.5	107.3	+63.8	7	-0.2%	4.5	-22.0%	10	-1.2%
2018	PHI	53.4	117.0	+63.6	13	23.7%	9	-1.0%	9	5.5%
2013	SF	13.9	77.3	+63.4	11.5	30.2%	12	16.8%	8	6.3%
2016	MIN	57.5	120.6	+63.1	11	5.8%	8	1.2%	13	28.7%
2004	TEN	22.9	85.5	+62.6	12	22.7%	5	-18.7%	4	-22.6%
2018	CAR	40.5	102.6	+62.1	11	12.6%	7	0.3%	5	-26.5%
Average					9.5	8.3%	6.4	-7.2%	6.8	-8.9%

Includes COVID-related absences

drafted Jim Harbaugh. Only four other quarterbacks qualify: Miami's Dan Marino in 1983, Pittsburgh's Mark Malone in 1980, Minnesota's Tommy Kramer in 1977, and Green Bay's Don Horn in 1967. None of those men, however, were drafted any higher than 25th overall, so it's hard to compare their situations to that of Lance and the 49ers.

If we extend our window to look at teams that took first-round quarterbacks three years after reaching the Super Bowl, we find more early picks, including two Colts passers nearly 40 years apart (Bert Jones and Andrew Luck) and, of all people, Mac Jones. The most similar player and team to Lance and the 49ers, however, might be Michael Vick and the 2001 Atlanta Falcons. Those Falcons were a few years removed from reaching the Super Bowl with an offense built around the running game and play-action passing, and a quarterback in Chris Chandler who was known for mixing stretches of brilliant play with frequent appearances on the injury list. Like the 49ers, they traded up for a precociously gifted quarterback who had led his college team to a National Championship Game. And like Lance, Vick was just 20 years old on draft night. If Lance can combine a fraction of Vick's athletic talent with the off-field habits and character of, oh, almost any other NFL player, he should be a perennial Pro Bowler.

The question now becomes how long it will take Lance to overtake Garoppolo. There are three basic possibilities here. The first, and least likely, is that Lance wins the starting job in training camp and finds himself under center against Detroit in Week 1. First, we must point out that Garoppolo is still on the roster—if the 49ers had truly lost all faith in him, they would not waste their time by keeping him around. Further, Lance is abnormally young for an NFL quarterback. He will be 21 years, 126 days old on opening Sunday. Only two passers younger than that have started NFL games since 1950: the Jets' Sam Darnold in 2018 and Denver's Tommy Maddox in 1992. There's further reason to question Lance's readiness for the NFL given his quality of competition in college. In that 2019 season, Lance only faced two defenders who have since played for or been drafted by NFL teams: Southern Illinois safety/linebacker Jeremy Chinn, now a member of the Carolina Panthers, and Northern Iowa defensive end Elerson Smith, a fourth-round draftee of the New York Giants. Maybe coincidence, maybe not, but those were two of Lance's lesser games of the year as he completed 56% of his passes for 7.1 yards per throw.

The second possibility—also unlikely—is that Lance serves as Garoppolo's backup all season but never actually sees the field. Even if we assume that Garoppolo will make it through 17 games (or more) unscathed, that doesn't mean Lance won't have value as a backup or goal-line weapon. And remember, Lance has barely played since that championship win over James Madison on January 11, 2020. San Francisco must optimize his odds of success by letting him gain experience whenever he can.

Which leads us to the third and most likely option: Garoppolo starts any games for which he is healthy, but often leaves the field for Lance cameos. And should he get hurt—again—Lance will get the call, but he'll be handled with kid gloves.

We turn back once again to Vick and the Falcons. Vick's first four NFL games were all relief appearances, as he had 44 combined passes, sacks, and runs before making his first start. And when Chandler was inevitably hurt and Vick opened the game in Week 9, the Falcons still refused to put the whole load on his shoulders, rotating second-year man Doug Johnson into the game periodically. (The 49ers seem very prepared for this possibility: in early April, with Garoppolo and Josh Rosen under contract, and knowing they were going to draft a quarterback, they signed Nate Sudfeld in free agency. There may not be a more important third quarterback this year than the one in San Francisco.) Only in Week 17, with the Falcons out of the playoff race at 7-8, did Vick start and finish a game, going wire to wire in a 31-13 loss to the Rams.

History suggests that if the 49ers want to make the playoffs this year, they had better make an early decision to start Lance or sit him, then stick with it. In the DVOA era, which goes back to 1983, 55 quarterbacks have been drafted in the top 10. Of the 14 that started at least 15 games in their first seasons, four (29%) made the playoffs. So did three of the 13 teams (23%) whose rookies started fewer than six times. However, only one of the 28 teams (4%) whose freshman passers started more than five games but fewer than 15 made the postseason, and that one was the Denver Broncos with John Elway way back in 1983. None of those 55 teams with top-10 quarterbacks, however, reached the Super Bowl. In fact, only one won a playoff game: the 2009 Jets, who reached the AFC Championship Game with Mark Sanchez

Whenever Lance plays, if he's going to achieve his potential, the 49ers will need to find a way to keep him upright. That has been a particular problem for Shanahan quarterbacks for years now—they put up big numbers but take a beating in the process (Table 3).

Table 3. 49ers QB Knockdowns Under Shanahan

Year	Sacks*	Rk	Hits	Rk	KD	Rk
2017	47	7	76	5	123	5
2018	48	9	87	1	135	2
2019	42	13	41	26	83	23
2020	37	14	93	1	130	2
TOTAL	174	8	297	3	471	4

Does not include strip sacks or sacks out of bounds, but does include sacks wiped out by penalty.

The 49ers don't necessarily surrender a ton of sacks, but they are practically unmatched when it comes to taking a hit after throwing the ball. Combine the two and you usually find San Francisco's starting quarterback on the turf, and it doesn't matter much which quarterback that is. C.J. Beathard had the highest knockdown rate of any qualifying quarterback in in 2017; Nick Mullens was second in both 2018 and 2020. If you include Matt Ryan in 2016, that's four times in the last five years that a Shanahan quarterback has made the top five. Garoppolo's numbers here have fluctuated pretty wildly, both a cause and effect of his inability to stay healthy, but his knockdown rate of 18.1% last season would have made the top 10 among qualifiers, and he was about average in his one healthy season in 2019.

If San Francisco can keep Lance safe, his ceiling is sky high … which makes him a perfect microcosm for their entire team. When healthy, the 49ers should be able to compete with anyone. That's why our projections have them neck-and-neck with Seattle atop the brutally tough NFC West. However, in the past, they have rarely ever managed to stay healthy for very long. And until they prove they can, it's fair to eye them with more than a little skepticism.

Vincent Verhei

2020 49ers by Week

Wk	vs.	W-L	PF	PA	YDF	YDA	TO	Total	Off	Def	ST
1	ARI	L	20	24	366	404	1	8.7%	10.0%	-7.7%	-8.9%
2	at NYJ	W	31	13	359	277	-1	-13.6%	-8.6%	10.1%	5.1%
3	at NYG	W	36	9	420	231	3	72.0%	36.7%	-37.3%	-2.1%
4	PHI	L	20	25	417	267	-2	-3.1%	-13.0%	-9.9%	-0.1%
5	MIA	L	17	43	259	436	-3	-62.0%	-29.3%	39.1%	6.4%
6	LAR	W	24	16	390	311	1	52.0%	47.6%	-3.6%	0.9%
7	at NE	W	33	6	467	241	2	95.4%	43.6%	-49.5%	2.3%
8	at SEA	L	27	37	351	350	-2	-29.2%	-14.7%	11.0%	-3.5%
9	GB	L	17	34	337	405	-2	-28.3%	-21.5%	9.6%	2.8%
10	at NO	L	13	27	281	237	-2	-15.0%	-16.9%	-11.6%	-9.7%
11	BYE										
12	at LAR	W	23	20	345	308	1	14.6%	-26.8%	-38.9%	2.5%
13	BUF	L	24	34	402	449	-1	-20.7%	-9.3%	11.1%	-0.2%
14	WAS	L	15	23	344	193	-2	10.6%	-20.0%	-33.3%	-2.7%
15	at DAL	L	33	41	458	291	-4	-28.1%	-21.5%	1.0%	-5.5%
16	at ARI	W	20	12	398	350	1	60.3%	38.1%	-44.9%	-22.7%
17	SEA	L	23	26	328	280	-1	-3.0%	-16.3%	-11.0%	2.3%

Trends and Splits

	Offense	Rank	Defense	Rank
Total DVOA	-2.5%	20	-9.9%	6
Unadjusted VOA	-7.1%	23	-7.9%	8
Weighted Trend	-6.5%	20	-13.8%	5
Variance	7.4%	18	6.1%	22
Average Opponent	-4.1%	4	-0.1%	16
Passing	8.9%	22	-3.4%	7
Rushing	-7.4%	15	-19.3%	10
First Down	4.2%	15	-10.1%	6
Second Down	-3.7%	19	-12.4%	7
Third Down	-14.1%	22	-5.9%	13
First Half	-4.2%	21	-10.7%	4
Second Half	-0.5%	16	-9.1%	8
Red Zone	7.8%	15	-14.3%	7
Late and Close	-12.5%	23	-19.4%	3

Five-Year Performance

Year	W-L	Pyth W	Est W	PF	PA	TO	Total	Rk	Off	Rk	Def	Rk	ST	Rk	Off AGL	Rk	Def AGL	Rk	Off Age	Rk	Def Age	Rk	ST Age	Rk
2016	2-14	3.9	4.4	309	247	-5	-21.5%	29	-7.3%	24	14.0%	30	-0.3%	17	38.4	20	57.8	24	27.0	13	26.2	22	26.1	17
2017	6-10	6.6	6.6	331	383	-3	-9.4%	21	-3.0%	19	9.1%	26	2.7%	11	23.8	8	69.8	32	27.3	9	25.4	29	25.8	18
2018	4-12	5.6	4.7	342	435	-25	-22.0%	30	-15.8%	27	6.5%	24	0.3%	14	54.4	26	42.8	25	26.7	17	25.1	30	25.2	30
2019	13-3	12.0	12.1	479	310	+4	29.0%	5	7.7%	7	-20.3%	2	1.0%	12	49.5	22	46.4	26	27.0	14	25.2	31	25.8	19
2020	6-10	7.6	8.6	376	390	-11	5.4%	11	-2.5%	20	-9.9%	6	-2.1%	23	78.7	30	87.9	32	26.7	17	26.2	19	26.2	12

2020 Performance Based on Most Common Personnel Groups

SF Offense					SF Offense vs. Opponents					SF Defense				SF Defense vs. Opponents			
Pers	Freq	Yds	DVOA	Run%	Pers	Freq	Yds	DVOA	Run%	Pers	Freq	Yds	DVOA	Pers	Freq	Yds	DVOA
11	45%	5.9	0.2%	19%	Base	40%	5.4	1.2%	60%	Base	31%	5.0	-15.2%	11	59%	5.3	-8.9%
21	33%	6.0	4.1%	58%	Nickel	46%	6.0	3.5%	30%	Nickel	67%	5.4	-7.2%	12	24%	5.2	-15.0%
12	12%	5.5	-2.8%	51%	Dime+	12%	6.2	-18.2%	13%	Dime+	2%	3.0	-36.2%	21	5%	4.7	-39.4%
22	9%	5.7	2.8%	61%	Goal Line	1%	0.1	-11.4%	88%	Goal Line	0%	0.8	33.6%	10	4%	6.5	0.2%
23	1%	0.1	8.6%	86%	Big	1%	9.4	105.1%	38%					13	2%	3.7	24.5%

Strategic Tendencies

Run/Pass		Rk	Formation		Rk	Pass Rush		Rk	Secondary		Rk	Strategy		Rk
Runs, first half	46%	4	Form: Single Back	64%	31	Rush 3	2.9%	29	4 DB	31%	10	Play Action	29%	12
Runs, first down	52%	6	Form: Empty Back	7%	22	Rush 4	65.0%	19	5 DB	67%	8	Offensive Motion	73%	1
Runs, second-long	25%	21	Form: Multi Back	29%	3	Rush 5	23.0%	11	6+ DB	2%	24	Avg Box (Off)	6.71	7
Runs, power sit.	63%	12	Pers: 3+ WR	45%	29	Rush 6+	9.1%	3	Man Coverage	27%	21	Avg Box (Def)	6.63	13
Runs, behind 2H	22%	28	Pers: 2+ TE/6+ OL	21%	25	Edge Rusher Sacks	58.3%	8	CB by Sides	74%	15	Offensive Pace	32.63	31
Pass, ahead 2H	45%	22	Pers: 6+ OL	0%	29	Interior DL Sacks	18.3%	24	S/CB Cover Ratio	24%	21	Defensive Pace	28.84	1
Run-Pass Options	3%	29	Shotgun/Pistol	58%	25	Second Level Sacks	23.3%	17	DB Blitz	14%	14	Go for it on 4th	1.13	29

San Francisco has led the NFL in average yards after the catch for three straight seasons, although that average has gone down each year (from 7.0 to 6.6 to 6.2). The 49ers had an average of 11.3 yards after the catch on targets at or behind the line of scrimmage, a yard more than any other offense. Their average of 4.7 yards after the catch on other targets ranked fourth. ● This was the second straight year the 49ers' offense led the NFL in using motion. ● San Francisco averaged a league-low 3.7 yards per carry with -20.2% DVOA (30th) when running the ball against a light box of six or fewer defenders. In a related stat, the 49ers ran the ball a league-low 20% of the time when they had three or more wide receivers on the field. ● The 49ers dropped from first in the league to 28th in how often they ran when behind in the second half of games. ● San Francisco dropped from first to 18th in the frequency of plays coded as max protect (seven or more blockers with at least two more blockers than pass-rushers). ● The San Francisco offense ranked 31st in situation-neutral pace but that rank shot up to ninth when the 49ers were trailing and second (behind only Dallas) when trailing by at least a touchdown. ● San Francisco receivers were tied for second with 39 drops. Meanwhile, the 49ers defense benefited from a league-low 18 drops by opponents. ● Robert Saleh's defense blitzed far more often in 2020, going from 19% of passes in 2019 (26th) to 32% of passes last season (eighth). ● The 49ers were high in how often they faced wide receiver screens for the second straight year, second only behind Washington. Some of this has to do with their schedule, as division rivals Los Angeles and Arizona were tied for second in using wide receiver screens. San Francisco's DVOA of 5.9% on these plays was a rounding error away from the NFL average. ● San Francisco was one of the worst teams in the NFL when it came to fumble recovery luck last season. The 49ers recovered six of 16 fumbles on offense and seven of 17 fumbles on defense. On special teams, they lost all four of their fumbles on returns. That includes two muffed kicks, which are usually recovered by the receiving team 79% of the time.

Passing

Player	DYAR	DVOA	Plays	NtYds	Avg	YAC	C%	TD	Int
N.Mullens*	76	-7.7%	345	2298	6.7	5.9	64.7%	12	12
J.Garoppolo	198	9.3%	151	1019	6.7	7.6	67.1%	7	4
C.J.Beathard*	75	-1.0%	112	716	6.4	5.2	64.1%	6	0
N.Sudfeld	-51	-72.6%	14	16	1.1	3.6	41.7%	0	1

Rushing

Player	DYAR	DVOA	Plays	Yds	Avg	TD	Fum	Suc
J.Wilson	86	7.3%	126	600	4.8	7	2	53%
R.Mostert	57	4.0%	104	521	5.0	2	1	49%
J.McKinnon*	53	8.3%	81	319	3.9	5	0	41%
J.Hasty	1	-8.0%	39	148	3.8	1	1	49%
T.Coleman*	-43	-47.0%	28	53	1.9	0	0	32%
K.Juszczyk	30	16.4%	17	64	3.8	2	0	82%
D.Samuel	1	-37.5%	8	26	3.3	0	0	--
J.Garoppolo	-2	-17.4%	7	28	4.0	0	1	--
B.Aiyuk	61	138.6%	6	77	12.8	2	0	--
C.J.Beathard*	3	1.3%	5	29	5.8	0	0	--
W.Gallman	151	15.5%	147	682	4.6	6	1	54%

Receiving

Player	DYAR	DVOA	Plays	Ctch	Yds	Y/C	YAC	TD	C%
B.Aiyuk	117	1.7%	96	60	748	12.5	4.8	5	63%
K.Bourne*	107	6.1%	74	49	667	13.6	4.5	2	66%
D.Samuel	64	5.5%	44	33	391	11.8	12.1	1	75%
R.James	78	16.3%	36	23	394	16.7	8.0	1	66%
T.Taylor*	-82	-58.7%	21	10	86	8.6	4.3	0	48%
R.Cracraft	-17	-37.4%	9	6	41	6.8	1.8	0	67%
M.Sanu	44	12.2%	23	16	178	11.1	2.1	1	70%
B.Fowler	-28	-71.0%	6	2	11	5.5	0.5	0	33%
G.Kittle	142	28.0%	63	48	634	13.2	6.2	2	76%
J.Reed*	-16	-12.6%	46	26	231	8.9	3.2	4	57%
R.Dwelley	56	30.8%	24	19	245	12.9	5.6	1	79%
M.Pruitt	2	-4.2%	8	5	49	9.8	2.6	2	63%
J.McKinnon*	83	22.7%	46	33	253	7.7	5.4	1	72%
K.Juszczyk	66	22.0%	29	19	202	10.6	5.3	4	66%
J.Wilson	32	8.9%	28	13	133	10.2	8.5	3	46%
R.Mostert	35	21.1%	19	16	156	9.8	8.5	1	84%
J.Hasty	-14	-54.9%	8	7	33	4.7	6.7	0	88%
W.Gallman	-11	-21.0%	27	21	114	5.4	4.8	0	78%

Offensive Line

Player	Pos	Age	GS	Snaps	Pen	Sk	Pass	Run	Player	Pos	Age	GS	Snaps	Pen	Sk	Pass	Run
Laken Tomlinson	LG	29	16/16	1092	2	4	19	9	Colton McKivitz	RG	25	14/3	299	0	0	7	2
Mike McGlinchey	RT	26	16/16	1089	6	5.5	26	8	Justin Skule	LT/RG	25	16/4	253	2	1.5	7	1
Daniel Brunskill	C/RG	27	16/16	1085	5	2.5	16	12	Hroniss Grasu*	C	30	9/3	215	0	1	2	2
Trent Williams	LT	33	14/14	957	9	3.5	12	6	Alex Mack	C	36	14/14	972	2	0.5	14	8
Ben Garland*	C	33	5/5	333	0	0	3	8	Senio Kelemete	LG	31	14/5	366	2	2	10	2

Year	Yards	ALY	Rk	Power	Rk	Stuff	Rk	2Lev	Rk	OpFld	Rk	BB Rt	Rk	Sacks	ASR	Rk	Press	Rk	BB Rt	Rk	Cont
2018	4.84	4.56	10	68%	16	19%	18	1.47	3	1.13	5	7.4%	23	48	8.0%	22	31.9%	19	11.9%	25	37
2019	4.80	4.53	8	67%	13	20%	20	1.32	7	1.16	3	8.2%	6	36	6.9%	15	26.0%	5	11.2%	5	25
2020	4.31	4.20	22	56%	29	21%	31	1.29	10	0.78	14	11.6%	23	39	5.5%	9	27.9%	22	15.3%	29	24

2020 ALY by direction:	Left End: 4.25 (22)	Left Tackle: 3.42 (27)	Mid/Guard: 4.14 (26)	Right Tackle: 4.18 (19)	Right End: 5.32 (10)

The interior of San Francisco's line was a mess last year. Daniel Brunskill started the first half of the season at right guard, then moved over to center in Week 9 after Weston Richburg and Ben Garland were both lost for the year. Of course, that just opened up a new hole at right guard, a hole that was first filled by journeyman Tom Compton, then fifth-round rookie Colton McKivitz, then Compton again, then McKivitz again, then 2019 sixth-rounder Justin Skule, and finally McKivitz a third time, all in a span of eight games. That's not even counting Hroniss Grasu, a sixth-year pro who set a career-high with nine games played, including three starts at center. ❧ Left tackle Trent Williams, left guard Laken Tomlinson, and right tackle Mike McGlinchey all return this year. Williams was outstanding in his return to the NFL after sitting out 2019 in a nasty dispute with Washington concerning a cancerous growth on his head that he claims was misdiagnosed by the team's medical staff. He was traded to San Francisco with one year left on his deal, then played so well that the 49ers made him the highest paid offensive lineman in history, signing him to a six-year, $138-million contract with $55 million guaranteed in March. ❧ Neither McGlinchey nor Tomlinson were as effective, each ranking among the worst three at their position in blown blocks. This was just two years after McGlinchey led the league in blown blocks as a rookie in 2018. That's disappointing for a former top-10 draft pick, but the 49ers did pick up his fifth-year option in May, guaranteeing his 2022 salary at $10.9 million. Tomlinson's contract effectively runs out after this season, so he'll be playing for his job. ❧ Your new center is Alex Mack, signed away from Atlanta for three years and $14.9 million ($5.0 million guaranteed) in free agency. Kyle Shanahan's offense requires mobility from all players, including his offensive linemen, the smallest in the league last year by snap-weighted size. Mack fits those physical requirements to a T, and his mental acumen and leadership skills make him even more of an asset. In his introductory press conference, he spent more time discussing his ability to survey the defense and get his teammates on the same page than his blocking. ❧ The right guard spot will be decided in a camp battle between Brunskill (re-signed for one year and $850,000 as an exclusive-rights free agent), McKivitz, and Aaron Banks, a second-round rookie out of Notre Dame who is big and strong but not very naturally athletic. It won't be Skule—the valuable swing lineman (he started two games at left tackle when Williams was out) tore his ACL in OTAs.

Defensive Front

Defensive Line	Age	Pos	G	Snaps	Plays	TmPct	Rk	Stop	Dfts	BTkl	Runs	St%	Rk	RuYd	Rk	Sack	Hit	Hur	Dsrpt
							Overall					vs. Run				Pass Rush			
Javon Kinlaw	24	DT	14	546	37	5.4%	41	31	12	3	27	85%	9	2.0	28	1.5	2	9	3
D.J. Jones	26	DT	14	419	21	3.0%	82	17	8	4	17	76%	42	1.7	15	3.0	1	10	1
Kevin Givens	24	DT	13	386	20	3.1%	81	16	7	2	18	78%	36	0.7	1	1.0	2	7	2
Zach Kerr	31	DT	13	390	34	5.1%	50	29	7	2	29	83%	15	2.1	34	2.0	6	12	1
Maurice Hurst	26	DT	11	277	28	4.9%	--	18	5	2	22	59%	--	3.0	--	0.5	5	6	1

Edge Rushers	Age	Pos	G	Snaps	Plays	TmPct	Rk	Stop	Dfts	BTkl	Runs	St%	Rk	RuYd	Rk	Sack	Hit	Hur	Dsrpt
							Overall					vs. Run				Pass Rush			
Arik Armstead	28	DE	16	749	52	6.6%	18	35	13	7	39	62%	80	2.8	54	3.5	11	26	3
Kerry Hyder*	30	DE	16	721	49	6.2%	22	38	16	10	37	78%	19	2.7	49	8.5	9	39	0
Kentavius Street	25	DE	15	381	11	1.5%	--	4	2	0	9	33%	--	3.4	--	0.0	1	2	0
Dion Jordan*	31	DE	13	373	18	2.8%	85	14	7	2	13	69%	57	2.8	59	3.0	3	8	0
Jordan Willis	26	DE	9	229	13	2.9%	--	8	4	3	8	63%	--	2.8	--	2.5	2	5	1
Arden Key	25	DE	14	433	17	2.3%	91	13	3	3	14	71%	48	2.0	27	0.0	11	16	3
Samson Ebukam	26	OLB	16	363	27	3.3%	--	22	7	5	19	74%	--	2.7	--	4.5	4	13	1

Linebackers	Age	Pos	Overall								vs. Run					Pass Rush			vs. Pass						
			G	Snaps	Plays	TmPct	Rk	Stop	Dfts	BTkl	Runs	St%	Rk	RuYd	Rk	Sack	Hit	Hur	Tgts	Suc%	Rk	Yd/P	Rk	PD	Int
Fred Warner	25	MLB	16	971	131	16.6%	11	63	15	10	75	55%	51	4.1	49	1.0	6	17	38	61%	12	4.6	10	6	2
Dre Greenlaw	24	OLB	13	699	84	13.1%	40	37	15	10	48	44%	81	4.7	70	1.0	1	2	24	50%	36	6.0	31	1	0
Azeez Al-Shaair	24	MLB	16	305	36	4.6%	--	15	4	5	18	44%	--	4.9	--	0.0	1	4	16	50%	34	4.6	12	2	1

Year	Yards	ALY	Rk	Power	Rk	Stuff	Rk	2Lev	Rk	OpFld	Rk	BB Rt	Rk	Sacks	ASR	Rk	Press	Rk	BB Rt	Rk
2018	4.08	4.39	19	61%	6	17%	21	1.19	12	0.59	6	9.0%	13	37	6.9%	18	29.9%	18	9.1%	20
2019	4.23	4.16	13	50%	2	20%	14	1.29	23	0.67	12	12.6%	17	48	9.0%	2	30.8%	13	15.8%	10
2020	3.72	4.10	8	67%	19	21%	6	1.05	5	0.48	6	11.6%	21	30	5.3%	24	26.5%	12	11.1%	24

2020 ALY by direction:	Left End: 4.49 (15)	Left Tackle: 3.79 (11)	Mid/Guard: 4.12 (10)	Right Tackle: 5.40 (29)	Right End: 1.57 (1)

There are 20-some teams that would gladly swap their perimeter defenders for Nick Bosa and company, but there is still reason for concern here. Bosa himself is returning from a torn ACL that limited him to two games in 2020, and it is a little scary that the 49ers' top edge rusher has only 9.0 career sacks (though he also has 4.0 more in the playoffs). Arik Armstead, the other starter, had 10.0 sacks in 2019, but only 12.5 in his other five NFL seasons. ● The 49ers do have depth, but it's shaky. Dee Ford has only 6.5 sacks since signing a five-year contract in 2019. He restructured his deal to stay with the team this year. San Francisco also signed Samson Ebukam away from the Rams, but he never had more than 4.5 sacks in four seasons in L.A. Only two other edge rushers on the roster have ever sacked a quarterback in the NFL: Jordan Willis and Arden Key combined for 8.5 sacks in eight NFL seasons. It doesn't help that edge rusher is one of the few positions the 49ers failed to address in the draft. ● At defensive tackle, Javon Kinlaw (a first-round draftee who made the Pro Football Writers Association All-Rookie team) and D.J. Jones will both return. San Francisco also added free-agent depth in Zach Kerr (88 NFL games with the Colts, Broncos, Cardinals, and Panthers) and Maurice Hurst Jr. (40, all with the Raiders). ● No matter who was lining up in front of him, Fred Warner kept the ship afloat and put opposing ballcarriers on the ground, earning a first-team spot on pretty much every All-Pro roster. His advanced stats were closer to good than dominant (especially in defeats, where teammate Dre Greenlaw matched him in about three-quarters the playing time), but he was versatile, ranking among the top 20 linebackers in run tackles, quarterback hurries, and targets in coverage. NFL Next Gen Stats ranked him among the top 10 defenders in pass coverage, the only linebacker to make their list. Warner, a third-round pick in 2018, is entering the final year of his rookie deal and will probably be described as the league's highest-paid linebacker in *Football Outsiders Almanac 2022*. Greenlaw has two years remaining on his rookie contract, giving the 49ers a pair of exciting young players at the position.

Defensive Secondary

Secondary	Age	Pos	Overall								vs. Run					vs. Pass									
			G	Snaps	Plays	TmPct	Rk	Stop	Dfts	BTkl	Runs	St%	Rk	RuYd	Rk	Tgts	Tgt%	Rk	aDOT	Suc%	Rk	Yd/P	Rk	PD	Int
Jimmie Ward	30	FS	14	849	75	10.9%	35	18	11	4	31	19%	65	7.3	42	32	10.5%	21	9.0	47%	44	7.6	31	4	0
Jason Verrett	30	CB	13	802	67	10.5%	15	22	8	7	14	43%	38	8.4	63	56	19.4%	43	9.4	41%	71	6.5	17	7	2
Tarvarius Moore	25	SS	16	540	50	6.3%	67	21	10	8	27	52%	11	5.5	22	9	4.6%	65	22.6	44%	51	14.6	69	1	0
Emmanuel Moseley	25	CB	12	498	56	9.5%	24	19	9	7	14	36%	53	7.7	53	51	28.4%	1	12.5	51%	40	7.5	39	9	1
Jaquiski Tartt	29	SS	7	373	31	9.0%	--	17	6	3	14	57%	--	6.6	--	11	8.2%	--	5.6	36%	--	6.3	--	4	1
Marcell Harris	27	SS	16	348	32	4.1%	--	15	4	4	16	50%	--	4.0	--	10	8.0%	--	30.0	70%	--	10.3	--	3	0
Ahkello Witherspoon*	26	CB	11	333	23	4.2%	--	12	6	1	5	20%	--	4.8	--	24	20.0%	--	12.5	58%	--	6.5	--	4	1
Richard Sherman*	33	CB	5	332	19	7.7%	--	6	2	5	8	38%	--	6.5	--	18	15.1%	--	14.8	44%	--	7.3	--	1	1
K'Waun Williams	30	CB	8	284	26	6.6%	--	19	8	1	8	88%	--	0.3	--	14	13.7%	--	4.6	64%	--	3.8	--	4	0
Dontae Johnson	30	CB	14	273	22	3.2%	--	13	5	3	7	71%	--	4.1	--	22	22.4%	--	8.1	50%	--	7.1	--	3	0
Jamar Taylor*	31	CB	8	201	25	6.3%	--	13	4	1	13	62%	--	3.2	--	11	15.2%	--	10.7	45%	--	12.2	--	3	2
Tavon Wilson	31	SS	15	219	21	2.8%	--	10	4	1	6	83%	--	3.0	--	9	9.9%	--	12.2	56%	--	7.8	--	1	0

Year	Pass D Rank	vs. #1 WR	Rk	vs. #2 WR	Rk	vs. Other WR	Rk	WR Wide	Rk	WR Slot	Rk	vs. TE	Rk	vs. RB	Rk
2018	27	4.8%	19	18.5%	26	36.9%	31	-9.9%	11	36.7%	32	9.6%	21	5.7%	19
2019	2	-9.0%	10	-2.8%	13	-15.8%	7	-22.0%	8	3.6%	11	-33.4%	2	-63.8%	1
2020	7	-25.4%	1	0.5%	17	9.3%	23	5.3%	21	-7.4%	9	-25.1%	3	1.7%	19

Injuries wreaked so much havoc here that the 49ers were starting journeymen, undrafted rookies, and practice-squad rejects at various points of the season. As the saying goes, the definition of insanity is doing the same thing over and over again and expecting different results. With that in mind, let's dig into San Francisco's secondary with a keen eye on each player's injury history. ● Jason Verrett had an excellent season and would have been a candidate for Comeback Player of the Year in non-Alex Smith circumstances. We must point out, however, that he was coming back from playing only six games in the preceding four years due to multiple torn ACLs and fallout from those injuries. ● Emmanuel Moseley opened 2020 as a starter before losing that role to Ahkello Witherspoon, but with Witherspoon now in Seattle, he likely takes it by default. He was bothered by concussion and hamstring issues all year and has just 17 starts in three NFL seasons. ● Nickelback K'Waun Williams missed eight games last year with knee, ankle, and shin problems. He has never started more than 11 games in six NFL seasons; dating back to his days in Cleveland, he has a history of concussion, shoulder, hamstring, quadriceps, ribs, and hand injuries. ● Depth is provided by Dontae Johnson, who has gone from the 49ers to the Bills to the Chargers to the Seahawks and back to the 49ers since 2017. He missed two games last year with a groin injury. The 49ers also drafted a pair of corners in Ambry Thomas (Michigan, third round) and Deommodore Lenoir (Oregon, fifth). ● At safety, Jimmie Ward has missed five starts with quadriceps and concussion issues over the past two seasons, and 21 games the three years before that with broken arms (yes, plural) and clavicle, not to mention hamstring and quadriceps woes. ● Jaquiski Tartt has started each of his 36 games in the last four years, but he has missed 28 games in that span with trauma to his arm, shoulder, ribs, groin, and toe. ● First safety off the bench is Marcell Harris, who has appeared on the injury report just once in the last two years, though he did miss eight games in 2018 with a hamstring ailment. San Francisco also signed Tony Jefferson, who has not played since tearing his ACL with Baltimore in Week 5 of 2019. Talanoa Hufanga (USC, fifth round) arrives via the draft. ● Miraculously, Tarvarius Moore had played in every game since the 49ers drafted him in the third round in 2018 (including eight starts last year), but he could not dodge the San Francisco curse forever—he tore his Achilles tendon in OTAs and will miss the season.

Special Teams

Year	DVOA	Rank	FG/XP	Rank	Net Kick	Rank	Kick Ret	Rank	Net Punt	Rank	Punt Ret	Rank	Hidden	Rank
2018	0.3%	14	6.6	7	-0.4	17	1.7	8	0.0	17	-6.4	30	3.6	10
2019	1.0%	12	-5.7	27	0.5	16	1.3	10	6.4	7	2.4	9	-5.9	24
2020	-2.1%	23	-1.5	17	-2.0	21	-5.0	31	2.0	16	-3.9	27	-9.0	26

Welcome to the inaugural edition of *Long Snapper Outsiders Almanac*. Kyle Nelson had done most of the long snapping for San Francisco since 2014, but after a series of botches against the Giants in Week 3, he was benched midgame and replaced by Swiss Army lineman Justin Skule. Nelson was released and the 49ers signed a man called Taybor Pepper, who is a real person and not a glitch in a Madden create-a-player algorithm. Pepper lasted until Week 17, which he missed due to COVID protocols; the 49ers then turned to Colin Holba, an emergency backup snapper they have kept in a glass case since 2018. Pepper re-signed with San Francisco this spring for two years and almost $2 million, so he should have plenty of cash to spend on his hobbies, which include playing Apex Legends on Twitch and assembling Highend Master Model Zoids kits. This concludes the inaugural edition of *Long Snapper Outsiders Almanac*. ● There is little else of interest to discuss here. For two years now, Mitch Wishnowsky has been slightly below average on both punts and kickoffs, another reminder to never, ever draft special-teamers. Only three 49ers made more tackles in kick coverage, which tells you all you need to know about the 49ers' performance in kick coverage. ● Robbie Gould may or may not be the active leader in points scored, pending Stephen Gostkowski's ongoing job hunt. He was having a fine year before missing two field goals and an extra point in Week 16 against Arizona and missing all of Week 17 due to COVID protocols. Tristan Vizcaino made all five of his kicks in the finale against Seattle, but Gould should return this fall. ● Richie James did a fine job on both punt and kickoff returns in both 2018 and 2019, but he gave up most of those responsibilities last year as he took on a bigger role in the offense. His primary replacements, Jerick McKinnon and Trent Taylor, weren't nearly as successful. Now they're both gone, so James figures to take back the special teams spotlight in 2021.

Seattle Seahawks

2020 Record: 12-4	**Total DVOA:** 20.1% (8)	**2021 Mean Projection:** 9.7 wins	**On the Clock (0-5):** 7%
Pythagorean Wins: 10.1 (10)	**Offense:** 13.7% (6)	**Postseason Odds:** 59.9%	**Mediocrity (6-8):** 25%
Snap-Weighted Age: 26.8 (9)	**Defense:** 0.4% (16)	**Super Bowl Odds:** 10.3%	**Playoff Contender (9-11):** 41%
Average Opponent: -1% (19)	**Special Teams:** 6.8% (3)	**Proj. Avg. Opponent:** 0.2% (14)	**Super Bowl Contender (12+):** 27%

2020: Russ cooks, but the season result makes Pete Carroll an unhappy customer.

2021: The heat is on, and a lack of playoff success may have the chef wanting out.

Entering the 2020 season, the Seattle Seahawks were coming off of back-to-back early playoff exits in which it seemed that Pete Carroll refused to acknowledge his team's relative strengths. While reality suggested a team that should lean on its quarterback to win shootout-oriented games, Carroll was managing games as if he still had a good defense. Sure, there were some defensive pieces around—Bobby Wagner, K.J. Wright, Quandre Diggs, and the newly acquired Jamal Adams—but it seemed more likely that if Seattle was going to make a serious run at Super Bowl LV, it was going to be driven by the offense.

Observers were in awe when Carroll and offensive coordinator Brian Schottenheimer appeared to completely change their philosophy through the first half of the season. Russell Wilson and the offense led an all-out aerial assault, and while the team was by no means balanced, they were still winning games. Wilson was dropping back to pass on over 68% of plays through their first eight games—only Kansas City passed more often when the score was within a touchdown—and the Seahawks were averaging over 34 points per game in the process. Up to that point in the year, Wilson was playing like an MVP favorite, and the fans who had been begging the team to lean more on the star quarterback were seemingly vindicated.

Wilson's MVP-level start was absolutely needed for Seattle to succeed early in the year because as overwhelming as the offense was, the defense was similarly impressive for the wrong reasons. Through that same eight-game span, the run defense was playing well, but the pass defense was a major liability, ranking 29th in the league in DVOA. Seattle's struggles were best encapsulated by a Week 9 contest where Buffalo handed the ball off only four times in the first three quarters while the Seahawks offered Josh Allen little resistance. The pass defense's struggles allowed opposing offenses to gobble up yards and put up points in bunches without having to deal with running the ball.

Then some cracks started to show, and the formerly fearsome offense began to sputter. Wilson coughed up 10 turnovers in a four-game span from Weeks 7 through 10, and Seattle only managed to break the 30-point barrier once in the second half of 2020, against the lowly Jets. If the defense had continued to play as poorly for the remainder of the season, the decline in offensive production may have been a death knell for the season, but Seattle continued tweaking things and made some key changes that turned an abominable defense into an average one by year's end.

Adams had sustained a groin injury in Week 3; once he returned in Week 9, the Seahawks blitzed him frequently to add some juice to their pass rush. In addition, Seattle brought in Bengals edge rusher Carlos Dunlap at minimal cost in a midseason trade. While 5.0 sacks in eight games may not seem like superstar-level production, just having Dunlap in the lineup forced offensive lines to account for a legitimate threat off the edge and opened up opportunities for the Seahawks' other defensive linemen. The pass-rush improvements took pressure off Seattle's defensive backs because the team no longer had to blitz whenever they wanted to rush the quarterback effectively. These personnel improvements combined with a weaker slate of opposing offenses late in the year resulted in a substantial uptick in their defensive performance, allowing the Seahawks to finish 12-4.

Seattle had a strong team entering the postseason, finishing fifth in overall DVOA on the year. Well, no one told the Rams, who came into Seattle and pulled the upset. Wilson again was not at his sharpest, and a pick-six in the first half forced the Seahawks to chase the game from then on. After halftime, Seattle never cut the lead to less than seven, and the Seahawks were left with another sour taste in their mouths as they lost in the wild-card round for the second time in three seasons.

The team parted ways with Schottenheimer shortly after that loss, and that was only the start of the team's offseason upheaval. Rumors began circulating like wildfire that Wilson was unhappy and wanted out of Seattle. Wilson attended the Super Bowl in person as he was set to receive the Walter Payton Man of the Year award, and after watching the juxtaposition of Patrick Mahomes running for his life while Tom Brady calmly picked apart Kansas City's defense with nary a scratch, Wilson began expressing frustration with Seattle's offensive line through the media. Wilson also reportedly started voicing more concerns regarding lingering issues with Carroll's offensive philosophy and coaching practices.

As is often the case, neither side in this kerfuffle was completely correct. On one hand, Wilson tends to hold the ball searching for a big play when he drops back to pass, which lends itself to taking more sacks. On the other hand, Wilson has played behind some absolutely atrocious offensive lines

2021 Seahawks Schedule

Week	Opp.	Week	Opp.	Week	Opp.
1	at IND	7	NO (Mon.)	13	SF
2	TEN	8	JAX	14	at HOU
3	at MIN	9	BYE	15	at LAR
4	at SF	10	at GB	16	CHI
5	LAR (Thu.)	11	ARI	17	DET
6	at PIT	12	at WAS (Mon.)	18	at ARI

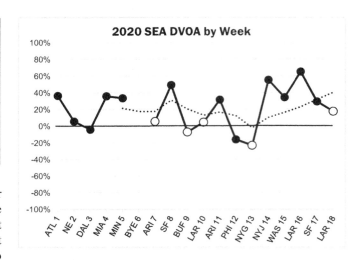

2020 SEA DVOA by Week

over the years, with 2016 and 2017 representing the nadir for that group. It is easy to see why he might be frustrated with the overall level of play he has had in front of him. It's true that throwing the ball more often tends to lead to more efficient results, but Seattle still has a head coach who led the team to a Super Bowl with a defensive-first approach that he would surely love to replicate—and he may have a bad taste in his mouth from the way the passing game faded in the second half of last year.

Whatever direction Seattle ends up choosing moving forward, that tension is not going to go away overnight. However, there does appear to be some common ground in the building, and everything that has come out from both Wilson and the team lately has signified a more unified approach and a shared vision for how to move forward. Some degree of discontent likely still exists beneath the surface, regardless of what is said publicly, but there have been some positive signs for their relationship over the course of the offseason. Reportedly, Wilson was on board with the hire of offensive coordinator Shane Waldron and the trade for veteran guard Gabe Jackson, which suggests that Seattle has been at least trying to appease some of Wilson's concerns.

With that rough patch in the relationship addressed to the extent that it can be in the offseason, Seattle is pushing forward with the hope that it can make the deep playoff run that has been so elusive in recent years. Frankly, the 2020 team had component parts that would have made that possible had everything synced up come playoff time. The offensive performance from the first half of the season was absolutely good enough to power a playoff run. The defense in the second half of the season was better than the one Kansas City fielded on its way back to the Super Bowl. And the special teams group was a consistent strength for Seattle over the course of the season, finishing third in the league in DVOA. Now, the question is how everything comes together moving forward.

Based on the level of public concern about the offense heading into the offseason, one would think that Waldron is facing a nightmare situation. However, things are not quite as doom-and-gloom as Seattle's late-season performance might make it seem. Six of Seattle's final nine games (including the playoffs) came against defenses that finished in the top 10 in defensive DVOA, which can at least partially explain the decline in performance. Additionally, Waldron will be able to leverage what he learned in his time with the Rams to combine certain play-calling concepts to make different plays look the same at the snap.

While Waldron was not the primary offensive mind in Los Angeles, he can bring some high-level strategic tendencies up the coast with him that might benefit the Seahawks' offensive outlook in 2021. Los Angeles finished sixth in the league in play-action frequency whereas Seattle was merely in the middle of the pack. In conjunction with those play-action fakes, the Rams tend to put their quarterback under center much more than the Seahawks. Over the past three years, Seattle has averaged 70% of plays from shotgun, while Los Angeles has averaged 42% of plays from shotgun. While shotgun formations are more efficient in general, putting Wilson under center should work for an offense that has been one of the best from those formations over the last three seasons (Table 1). The Rams also played at an above-average pace despite not fully trusting their quarterback; Seattle operated at a more lethargic pace despite Wilson's past success when playing at a higher tempo. Based on reports from OTAs, it sounds like Waldron is already implementing a faster-paced approach, and if the Rams' history is any guide, we could see a larger share of the passing offense come via play-action as well.

There is also some real talent here. Having Wilson at quarterback gives Seattle a high floor regardless of who is currently the offensive coordinator. The receiving duo of DK Metcalf and veteran Tyler Lockett is an excellent one-two punch, with Metcalf in particular enjoying a major second-year breakout

Table 1. Seattle in Shotgun vs. Under Center, 2018-2020

Year	DVOA Shotgun	Rk	Yd/Play Shotgun	Rk	DVOA Not Shotgun	Rk	Yd/Play Not Shotgun	Rk	Shotgun Use	Rk
2018	9.3%	12	5.7	21	8.6%	8	6.3	3	69%	10
2019	22.6%	5	5.9	13	7.4%	5	5.9	3	71%	10
2020	13.8%	6	5.9	17	13.5%	4	6.0	4	70%	12

last season. Seattle then augmented their pass-catching corps by signing tight end Gerald Everett away from the Rams in free agency and drafting Western Michigan receiver D'Wayne Eskridge in the second round. Everett fits in as an athletic receiving tight end to give Wilson an outlet that the aging Greg Olsen was unable to consistently provide, and Eskridge's speed adds yet another threat to take the top off of defenses that already have to worry about a physical freak like Metcalf, who competed in the USA Track and Field Golden Games during the spring.

All of that speed on the outside should help open up more rushing lanes for Chris Carson at running back, which could help Seattle build on its ninth-place finish in rushing offense DVOA from 2020. If you are going to run the ball at higher volume, as Carroll surely would love to do, it helps if you can do so efficiently. The dominant Rams offense of 2018 had a better rushing offense DVOA than most teams' passing offense DVOA that year (no easy feat), and while that is not a reasonable expectation, a quality running game will help prevent teams from sitting on deep passing concepts designed for Lockett and Metcalf. This is a team that still finished sixth in offensive DVOA a year ago, and it may not take much schematically to elevate this group even further.

There is also reason to believe that a good chunk of the defensive improvements will stick heading into this season. Rather than rest on their laurels and be content with the mid-season improvements, the Seahawks made a concerted effort during the offseason to avoid the pass-rush issues that contributed to the horrendous early-season defense, re-signing Dunlap to a multi-year contract after initially cutting him to clear cap space (a move necessitated by the pandemic's impact on the salary cap) and adding Kerry Hyder to play a hybrid role along the defensive line in the mold of Michael Bennett.

After years of sticking to Carroll's preferred single-high alignment with four defensive linemen, Seattle adjusted to use more bear fronts with three defensive tackles in 2020, which likely played a large role in the improved run defense because of the better personnel fit it provided. The Seahawks used a heavy dose of base defense with three linebackers in 2019 because they felt they did not have good answers at nickel corner, but their base-defense snap rate dropped from 69% to 38% in 2020 due to increased faith in the team's defensive backs. Carroll may be a stubborn game manager, but he has at least shown some schematic flexibility on defense recently. In 2021, it seems likely that Seattle will continue to use two linebackers on the field most of the time rather than revert to the base-heavy tendencies of 2019 because as of press time Wright has not re-signed with the team.

An added benefit of playing with one less linebacker is that it allows more freedom for Adams to play around the line of scrimmage, where Seattle can leverage his blitzing ability to cause headaches for opposing offensive lines. Adams led the Seahawks in both sacks and tackles for loss despite missing four games, and that was partly a result of Seattle's willingness to send him (and other defensive backs) after the quarterback, as they ranked first in the league in defensive back blitz frequency at 21%. If Seattle continues to utilize Adams in a way that will maximize his talents, he can be a major impact player for the Seahawks defense.

With the additions made over the past year, Seattle should not be the defensive disaster it was at the start of 2020, which will alleviate some of the pressure on the offense to carry the team by itself from Week 1. And for all the ink spilled about a potential Wilson trade during the offseason, the fact of the matter remains that he is still Seattle's quarterback, which gives the Seahawks a high baseline for offensive success. Competition in the NFC West will again be strong, as both the Rams and 49ers look playoff-caliber, but the pieces are there for Seattle to be a playoff team yet again.

But just being a playoff team is not the goal in the Pacific Northwest. Years of sustained winning have justifiably raised expectations, and Seattle has not broken past the divisional round of the playoffs since its most recent Super Bowl appearance in 2014. The trades for veterans such as Adams, Jackson, and Dunlap over the past year were made with pursuing a championship in mind. Those moves may not be enough to put them over the top. And if they cannot at least make the conference championship game, let alone win a Super Bowl, we might be hearing more about Wilson being unhappy in February 2022.

Carl Yedor

2020 Seahawks by Week

Wk	vs.	W-L	PF	PA	YDF	YDA	TO	Total	Off	Def	ST
1	at ATL	W	38	25	383	506	2	36.7%	41.5%	12.5%	7.6%
2	NE	W	35	30	429	464	0	5.8%	22.4%	27.4%	10.8%
3	DAL	W	38	31	412	522	2	-3.9%	3.7%	6.9%	-0.7%
4	at MIA	W	31	23	441	415	1	36.1%	32.2%	-4.5%	-0.6%
5	MIN	W	27	26	314	449	1	33.9%	25.6%	2.0%	10.3%
6	BYE										
7	at ARI	L	34	37	572	519	-1	5.8%	11.0%	7.2%	2.0%
8	SF	W	37	27	350	351	2	49.5%	36.8%	-3.8%	8.9%
9	at BUF	L	34	44	419	420	-4	-7.0%	7.0%	13.2%	-0.8%
10	at LAR	L	16	23	333	389	-2	4.7%	1.0%	15.8%	19.5%
11	ARI	W	28	21	347	314	0	31.9%	29.6%	5.3%	7.6%
12	at PHI	W	23	17	301	250	1	-16.0%	-18.5%	1.6%	4.1%
13	NYG	L	12	17	327	290	-1	-23.1%	-43.4%	-11.8%	8.5%
14	NYJ	W	40	3	410	185	0	55.5%	30.6%	-27.3%	-2.5%
15	at WAS	W	20	15	302	353	1	34.7%	23.7%	1.6%	12.6%
16	LAR	W	20	9	292	334	1	65.3%	11.5%	-33.8%	20.1%
17	at SF	W	26	23	280	328	1	29.6%	10.2%	-17.4%	2.0%
18	LAR	L	20	30	278	333	-2	17.9%	-21.6%	-13.9%	25.6%

Trends and Splits

	Offense	Rank	Defense	Rank
Total DVOA	13.7%	6	0.4%	16
Unadjusted VOA	10.7%	7	-2.1%	14
Weighted Trend	9.5%	6	-5.2%	11
Variance	4.7%	11	2.5%	1
Average Opponent	-4.1%	5	-4.4%	28
Passing	30.4%	6	12.3%	20
Rushing	-1.4%	9	-20.1%	7
First Down	10.7%	7	-2.8%	15
Second Down	20.2%	5	-2.1%	13
Third Down	8.2%	11	10.0%	22
First Half	13.3%	7	-8.5%	6
Second Half	14.1%	7	8.5%	22
Red Zone	32.7%	4	4.2%	18
Late and Close	15.8%	7	-1.5%	16

Five-Year Performance

Year	W-L	Pyth W	Est W	PF	PA	TO	Total	Rk	Off	Rk	Def	Rk	ST	Rk	Off AGL	Rk	Def AGL	Rk	Off Age	Rk	Def Age	Rk	ST Age	Rk
2016	10-5-1	9.8	9.0	354	292	+1	7.5%	11	-2.5%	16	-10.1%	5	-0.1%	15	23.2	6	17.0	3	25.7	29	27.2	7	26.4	8
2017	9-7	9.0	8.2	366	332	+8	2.3%	15	2.2%	14	-2.1%	13	-2.0%	20	55.1	24	49.5	26	26.1	29	27.0	8	25.8	20
2018	10-6	10.1	8.7	428	347	+16	5.9%	12	9.1%	8	1.0%	17	-2.2%	24	31.5	12	31.3	14	27.2	11	25.5	27	25.8	16
2019	11-5	8.2	10.7	405	398	+12	12.7%	8	17.7%	5	4.1%	21	-0.9%	20	31.5	12	25.0	8	27.2	8	26.6	12	25.3	28
2020	12-4	10.1	11.4	459	371	+4	20.1%	5	13.7%	6	0.4%	16	6.8%	3	33.6	13	54.7	25	27.4	6	26.6	11	25.7	23

2020 Performance Based on Most Common Personnel Groups

SEA Offense					SEA Offense vs. Opponents					SEA Defense					SEA Defense vs. Opponents			
Pers	Freq	Yds	DVOA	Run%	Pers	Freq	Yds	DVOA	Run%	Pers	Freq	Yds	DVOA		Pers	Freq	Yds	DVOA
11	65%	5.8	14.1%	31%	Base	22%	6.2	27.6%	42%	Base	38%	4.5	-20.9%		11	54%	5.9	5.8%
12	30%	6.7	30.8%	39%	Nickel	66%	5.9	14.9%	34%	Nickel	54%	6.2	12.2%		12	18%	5.3	-12.9%
10	2%	7.2	13.3%	18%	Dime+	11%	6.1	17.7%	14%	Dime+	7%	6.4	21.9%		21	7%	3.6	-43.2%
13	1%	1.9	-41.4%	50%	Goal Line	0%	1.5	71.7%	0%	Goal Line	1%	0.8	57.6%		10	7%	8.4	46.6%
21	1%	2.6	7.7%	70%											13	5%	3.6	-5.0%
															22	4%	6.1	6.4%

Strategic Tendencies

Run/Pass		Rk	Formation		Rk	Pass Rush		Rk	Secondary		Rk	Strategy		Rk
Runs, first half	32%	29	Form: Single Back	91%	1	Rush 3	8.4%	11	4 DB	38%	2	Play Action	27%	15
Runs, first down	42%	27	Form: Empty Back	5%	27	Rush 4	60.5%	24	5 DB	54%	22	Offensive Motion	50%	10
Runs, second-long	20%	27	Form: Multi Back	3%	25	Rush 5	24.8%	8	6+ DB	7%	20	Avg Box (Off)	6.46	21
Runs, power sit.	51%	29	Pers: 3+ WR	67%	14	Rush 6+	6.3%	11	Man Coverage	20%	31	Avg Box (Def)	6.67	11
Runs, behind 2H	23%	27	Pers: 2+ TE/6+ OL	32%	13	Edge Rusher Sacks	45.7%	23	CB by Sides	95%	2	Offensive Pace	30.68	22
Pass, ahead 2H	56%	4	Pers: 6+ OL	0%	27	Interior DL Sacks	20.7%	18	S/CB Cover Ratio	28%	12	Defensive Pace	29.80	9
Run-Pass Options	8%	16	Shotgun/Pistol	70%	12	Second Level Sacks	33.7%	5	DB Blitz	21%	1	Go for it on 4th	1.26	25

Seattle preferred to hand the ball off when facing lighter boxes. They ranked fifth with 40% of their handoffs coming against a light box of six or fewer. They ranked 29th with 22% of their handoffs coming against a heavy box of eight or more. Seattle only gained 2.3 yards per carry against those heavy boxes, lowest in the league, with -18.4% DVOA. ◆ After two straight years where they led the NFL in usage of six offensive linemen, the Seahawks used a sixth lineman on a grand total of one play in 2020. ◆ The Seahawks were an excellent tackling defense in 2020, the best in the league with in both total broken tackles (89) and rate of plays with at least one broken tackle (7.6%). ◆ One play where Seattle's defense excelled: the wide receiver screen. The Seahawks faced an above-average 48 of these screens and allowed just 4.1 yards per pass with -16.9% DVOA.

Passing

Player	DYAR	DVOA	Plays	NtYds	Avg	YAC	C%	TD	Int
R.Wilson	773	8.1%	604	3879	6.4	4.8	69.3%	40	13
G.Smith	3	-2.7%	6	30	5.0	3.5	80.0%	0	0

Rushing

Player	DYAR	DVOA	Plays	Yds	Avg	TD	Fum	Suc
C.Carson	153	15.1%	141	681	4.8	5	1	65%
C.Hyde*	46	4.7%	81	356	4.4	4	0	49%
R.Wilson	99	21.3%	66	515	7.8	2	4	--
D.Dallas	11	-1.8%	34	108	3.2	2	0	53%
T.Homer	-41	-50.5%	25	88	3.5	0	0	40%
A.Collins	49	56.5%	18	77	4.3	2	0	61%
R.Penny	5	2.5%	11	34	3.1	0	0	55%
D.Moore*	47	57.6%	8	61	7.6	0	0	--
B.Scarbrough*	-1	-11.5%	6	31	5.2	0	0	67%

Receiving

Player	DYAR	DVOA	Plays	Ctch	Yds	Y/C	YAC	TD	C%
T.Lockett	238	9.8%	132	100	1054	10.5	3.3	10	76%
DK Metcalf	334	19.5%	129	83	1303	15.7	4.4	10	64%
D.Moore*	76	7.0%	47	35	417	11.9	4.8	6	74%
F.Swain	4	-10.1%	21	13	159	12.2	7.8	2	62%
J.Hollister*	-11	-11.5%	40	25	209	8.4	3.2	3	63%
G.Olsen*	14	-2.0%	37	24	239	10.0	2.0	1	65%
W.Dissly	42	13.3%	29	24	251	10.5	7.0	2	83%
G.Everett	0	-7.3%	62	41	417	10.2	5.9	1	66%
C.Carson	108	23.5%	46	37	287	7.8	6.9	4	80%
D.Dallas	31	13.7%	20	17	111	6.5	6.5	1	85%
C.Hyde*	-19	-33.6%	20	16	93	5.8	6.8	0	80%
T.Homer	37	48.5%	10	9	90	10.0	10.2	1	90%

Offensive Line

Player	Pos	Age	GS	Snaps	Pen	Sk	Pass	Run	Player	Pos	Age	GS	Snaps	Pen	Sk	Pass	Run
Duane Brown	LT	36	16/16	1048	2	1	8	4	Mike Iupati*	LG	34	10/10	498	4	0	3	5
Damien Lewis	RG	24	16/16	967	11	3	17	12	Cedric Ogbuehi	RT	29	8/4	277	1	1	4	4
Ethan Pocic	C	26	14/14	932	1	0	5	7	Jamarco Jones	RT/RG	25	11/2	192	3	1.5	7	2
Brandon Shell	RT	29	11/11	673	4	1	6	4	Gabe Jackson	RG	30	16/16	1061	3	1	13	10
Jordan Simmons	LG	27	14/6	593	2	2	6	0									

Year	Yards	ALY	Rk	Power	Rk	Stuff	Rk	2Lev	Rk	OpFld	Rk	BB Rt	Rk	Sacks	ASR	Rk	Press	Rk	BB Rt	Rk	Cont
2018	4.64	4.50	12	71%	5	17%	8	1.30	10	0.85	15	6.6%	18	51	10.4%	30	35.7%	30	10.2%	21	26
2019	4.61	4.32	16	68%	10	18%	9	1.33	6	0.93	13	11.2%	24	48	7.9%	24	36.6%	30	13.4%	17	28
2020	4.35	4.53	10	62%	22	17%	17	1.33	6	0.58	23	11.2%	21	48	8.2%	30	30.5%	28	9.3%	4	24

2020 ALY by direction: Left End: 4.38 (19) Left Tackle: 4.57 (11) Mid/Guard: 4.87 (4) Right Tackle: 4.41 (16) Right End: 3.01 (30)

Veteran Duane Brown locked down the left tackle spot for the Seahawks again in 2020, allowing only one sack on the year and ranking fourth in snaps per blown block among NFL left tackles. On the right side, Brandon Shell joined Seattle from the Jets on a modest two-year contract and provided a steadying presence when he was on the field. Shell matched Brown's positional ranking by finishing fourth among right tackles in snaps per blown block. ◆ In his first year as a starter, center Ethan Pocic won the job over free-agent acquisition B.J. Finney in training camp and never let it go. Finney was traded to Cincinnati in the Carlos Dunlap deal at midseason. The team did not seem happy with Pocic's play, as he only earned a small one-year deal to return to Seattle in free agency, but Pocic likely has the edge over Kyle Fuller in the competition for this year's starting job. ◆ Longtime veteran Mike Iupati played his final season in 2020 and was effective when healthy, but he was limited to 10 games because of knee and neck injuries. Iupati's replacement Jordan Simmons did not blow a run block but struggled a bit in pass protection. ◆ When it comes to guards, Seattle seems to have a type. Third-round rookie Damien Lewis stepped in at right guard immediately and was in the starting lineup for every game (though he did play center in an emergency against Arizona). While the coaching staff loved his run-blocking, he struggled mightily as a pass-blocker. ◆ Russell Wilson voiced concerns about the offensive line during the offseason, which may have pushed the Seahawks to trade a fifth-round pick for Raiders guard Gabe Jackson. The former Raiders starter will slide in at right guard, pushing Lewis to the opposite side.   ❧   Seattle also drafted Florida tackle Stone Forsythe in the sixth round. Forsythe profiles as a developmental left tackle with strong pass-blocking ability, though his height works as a disadvantage for him in the run game. He may be Brown's eventual successor.

Defensive Front

Defensive Line	Age	Pos	G	Snaps	Plays	TmPct	Overall Rk	Stop	Dfts	BTkl	Runs	St%	vs. Run Rk	RuYd	Rk	Sack	Pass Rush Hit	Hur	Dsrpt
Jarran Reed*	29	DT	16	847	38	4.3%	60	28	11	2	27	70%	58	2.9	70	6.5	8	17	1
Poona Ford	26	DT	16	670	40	4.5%	58	32	10	4	29	79%	30	2.1	31	2.0	7	15	2
Bryan Mone	26	DT	10	228	9	1.6%	--	7	3	1	8	75%	--	1.9	--	0.5	1	3	0

Edge Rushers	Age	Pos	G	Snaps	Plays	TmPct	Overall Rk	Stop	Dfts	BTkl	Runs	St%	vs. Run Rk	RuYd	Rk	Sack	Pass Rush Hit	Hur	Dsrpt
Carlos Dunlap	32	DE	15	593	36	4.3%	57	26	13	2	21	62%	79	4.0	91	6.0	11	19	5
Benson Mayowa	30	DE	13	571	27	3.7%	69	23	13	3	15	73%	40	2.8	55	6.0	5	17	2
L.J. Collier	26	DE	16	559	24	2.7%	89	20	5	0	16	88%	4	1.9	25	3.0	4	15	3
Rasheem Green	24	DE	10	365	10	1.8%	94	8	5	1	6	67%	60	5.0	96	2.0	4	13	0
Alton Robinson	23	DE	14	336	22	2.8%	--	15	7	1	15	73%	--	1.6	--	4.0	2	10	0
Aldon Smith	32	DE	16	808	50	6.0%	25	40	10	8	42	76%	31	2.9	63	5.0	9	37	5
Kerry Hyder	30	DE	16	721	49	6.2%	22	38	16	10	37	78%	19	2.7	49	8.5	9	39	0

Linebackers	Age	Pos	G	Snaps	Plays	TmPct	Overall Rk	Stop	Dfts	BTkl	Runs	St%	vs. Run Rk	RuYd	Rk	Sack	Pass Rush Hit	Hur	Tgts	vs. Pass Suc%	Rk	Yd/P	Rk	PD	Int
Bobby Wagner	31	MLB	16	1141	146	16.5%	12	73	18	8	79	61%	25	3.4	23	3.0	7	14	64	56%	21	5.5	27	8	0
K.J. Wright*	32	OLB	16	990	95	10.7%	56	57	20	10	34	68%	12	2.9	6	2.0	1	6	41	59%	15	6.2	33	10	1
Jordyn Brooks	24	OLB	14	367	59	7.6%	70	35	8	2	42	71%	5	4.4	59	0.0	0	2	20	45%	52	5.9	30	2	0

Year	Yards	ALY	Rk	Power	Rk	Stuff	Rk	2Lev	Rk	OpFld	Rk	BB Rt	Rk	Sacks	ASR	Rk	Press	Rk	BB Rt	Rk
2018	4.55	4.55	22	58%	5	19%	19	1.28	20	0.91	20	6.8%	22	43	7.3%	14	28.9%	21	10.6%	17
2019	4.28	4.36	21	67%	22	20%	12	1.21	20	0.82	21	11.7%	22	28	5.1%	30	24.0%	32	10.5%	31
2020	3.91	4.20	12	63%	9	19%	10	1.06	6	0.59	9	14.3%	9	46	6.6%	16	23.9%	22	11.1%	26
2020 ALY by direction:			Left End: 3.05 (5)			Left Tackle: 3.49 (8)			Mid/Guard: 4.20 (12)				Right Tackle: 5.38 (28)				Right End: 5.18 (28)			

The longtime linebacker duo of Bobby Wagner and K.J. Wright had another strong year together. Wagner was named to the All-Pro team for the fifth year in a row, and Wright had a productive all-around season, knocking down 10 passes while posting 20 defeats. Wagner will be back to anchor the Seattle defense in 2021, but at press time, Wright was still unsigned as he enters his age-32 season.   ❧   Seattle originally planned to have Bruce Irvin flanking Wright and Wagner at strongside linebacker and sub-package edge rusher, but a torn ACL opened the door for first-rounder Jordyn Brooks to get on the field. The Seahawks saw enough from Brooks to feel comfortable moving forward with him as Wagner's running mate up the middle.   ❧   Nose tackle Poona Ford flashed some disruptive ability as a secondary pass-rusher, but he primarily earns his keep against the run. Seattle rewarded Ford with a two-year contract in the offseason, representing a big raise for the former undrafted free agent.   ❧   Jarran Reed struggled to get much going as a pass-rusher early in the season, but he thrived after Seattle added Carlos Dunlap. Seattle released Reed after he declined a restructure; Reed has since signed with the Chiefs to rejoin old teammate Frank Clark. The Seahawks will be relying on the combination of Bryan Mone and Al Woods to replace Reed in the interior defensive line rotation.   ❧   Carlos Dunlap started the year unhappy in Cincinnati, effectively forcing a trade to a contender, and with Seattle's pass-rush problems, the Seahawks happily obliged. In addition to Dunlap's own production, his presence led to a knock-on effect where supporting edge rushers such as Benson Mayowa, L.J. Collier, Rasheem Green, and rookie Alton Robinson received less defensive attention. Even before the Dunlap trade, Robinson had been a bright spot in a rotational role as a pass-rush specialist.   ❧   In addition to bringing back Dunlap on a new contract, Seattle signed experienced defensive ends Kerry Hyder and Aldon Smith as free agents. Hyder profiles as a bigger defensive end who can kick inside on passing downs, and Smith will be more of a strict edge rusher depending on his legal status, as he was arrested on a battery charge during the offseason.   ❧   The Seahawks traded up in the second round last year for Tennessee's Darrell Taylor, but he missed his entire rookie season following surgery to insert a metal rod into his leg. He participated in rookie minicamp this spring and left Pete Carroll raving about his athletic ability. He could fill the Bruce Irvin role as a strongside linebacker who moves to edge rusher on passing downs.

Defensive Secondary

Secondary	Age	Pos	G	Snaps	Plays	TmPct	Rk	Stop	Dfts	BTkl	Runs	St%	Rk	RuYd	Rk	Tgts	Tgt%	Rk	aDOT	Suc%	Rk	Yd/P	Rk	PD	Int
Quandre Diggs	28	FS	16	1075	74	8.3%	63	19	9	9	27	22%	63	11.3	66	15	3.2%	70	15.5	47%	46	13.3	68	10	5
Shaquill Griffin*	26	CB	12	812	75	11.3%	9	30	11	5	15	47%	31	5.2	26	75	21.0%	31	12.8	47%	59	7.9	48	12	3
Jamal Adams	26	SS	12	784	86	12.9%	11	44	27	13	33	61%	4	3.0	1	33	9.6%	25	10.7	42%	56	10.4	61	3	0
Tre Flowers	26	CB	12	577	48	7.2%	68	11	2	5	7	43%	38	6.6	39	51	20.1%	38	11.3	35%	77	8.9	64	2	0
D.J. Reed	25	CB	10	560	69	12.4%	2	28	12	5	21	52%	21	5.1	25	43	17.5%	62	10.6	49%	47	6.7	22	7	2
Ugo Amadi	24	FS	14	551	56	7.2%	66	23	13	5	9	44%	24	5.0	13	36	14.9%	5	9.1	56%	17	6.4	16	7	0
Quinton Dunbar*	29	CB	6	397	35	10.5%	--	12	4	3	8	50%	--	4.5	--	39	22.3%	--	12.1	46%	--	8.7	--	5	1
Ryan Neal	26	CB/SS	13	393	41	5.7%	--	17	9	5	15	47%	--	5.3	--	23	13.3%	--	10.5	48%	--	8.5	--	5	2
Pierre Desir	31	CB	12	519	54	8.3%	49	18	9	6	12	42%	45	8.7	65	44	20.9%	32	10.2	34%	79	10.2	79	8	3
Ahkello Witherspoon	26	CB	11	333	23	4.2%	--	12	6	1	5	20%	--	4.8	--	24	20.0%	--	12.5	58%	--	6.5	--	4	1

Year	Pass D Rank	vs. #1 WR	Rk	vs. #2 WR	Rk	vs. Other WR	Rk	WR Wide	Rk	WR Slot	Rk	vs. TE	Rk	vs. RB	Rk
2018	14	13.1%	25	4.6%	20	-10.3%	10	18.8%	30	-3.7%	14	-12.3%	10	-3.7%	13
2019	15	-2.9%	12	-5.6%	10	-9.6%	11	-27.8%	5	5.9%	16	3.3%	17	-9.4%	10
2020	20	9.5%	21	-8.9%	12	14.3%	25	4.2%	19	6.9%	23	-7.6%	11	15.8%	28

Jamal Adams, the former All-Pro acquired via trade from the Jets, battled injuries in his first season in Seattle and was underwhelming in coverage, but the Seahawks seriously needed his pass-rushing ability, blitzing him frequently enough to rack up 9.5 sacks. ◥ At free safety, Quandre Diggs led the team with five interceptions and nearly matched No. 1 cornerback Shaquill Griffin in passes defensed. ◥ Griffin was clearly Seattle's most talented corner from 2018 through 2020. Bouts of inconsistency and occasional injuries made Seattle hesitant to pony up what it would take to keep him, so he signed a three-year deal for a large payday with Jacksonville. ◥ Seattle traded for Quinton Dunbar heading into 2020, but the fallout from a May incident in which Dunbar was arrested for alleged armed robbery (charges were later dropped) combined with nagging knee injuries prevented him from solidifying a spot. Former starter Tre Flowers struggled when pressed into action, showing why Seattle traded for Dunbar in the first place. ◥ Their struggles opened the door for D.J. Reed to win the right cornerback job late in the year. Reed had signed with Seattle as a depth piece at nickel after being waived by the 49ers due to injury; he enters 2021 as a likely starter on the outside. The other spot is up for grabs between Flowers, free-agent signee Ahkello Witherspoon, and fourth-round rookie Tre Brown (Oklahoma). ◥ Former second-round pick Marquise Blair entered 2020 as the starting nickel after the addition of Adams, but he tore his ACL in Week 2, opening up time at nickel for Ugo Amadi. Blair will be back in 2021, though it may be hard for him to get on the field initially after Amadi claimed the role with his play down the stretch.

Special Teams

Year	DVOA	Rank	FG/XP	Rank	Net Kick	Rank	Kick Ret	Rank	Net Punt	Rank	Punt Ret	Rank	Hidden	Rank
2018	-2.2%	24	-0.8	20	-6.6	30	1.4	9	-2.2	20	-2.7	22	-1.7	18
2019	-1.0%	20	-0.1	18	-0.9	20	-2.1	22	-1.2	20	-0.5	15	4.9	10
2020	6.8%	3	14.0	2	6.3	5	1.2	10	13.9	3	-1.3	19	-1.6	17

Seattle's special teams unit vaulted into the top five in DVOA in 2020 after spending the previous four years languishing below average. Longtime special teams coordinator Brian Schneider stepped away from the team for personal reasons just before the start of the season and the unit made a dramatic improvement under Larry Izzo. ◥ The big free-agent contract signed by kicker Jason Myers in 2019 looked very bad a year ago. It looked a bit better after he ranked second in placekicking value and fifth in net kickoff value in 2020. ◥ Punter Michael Dickson bounced back from an underwhelming 2019 to finish third in net points of field position from punts, which played a major role in the four-year contract extension he earned over the offseason that makes him one of the highest paid punters in the league. ◥ Seattle was the only team where two players had at least a dozen special teams tackles. Fullback Nick Bellore made the Pro Bowl as a special-teamer and tied for third in the league with 14; despite the lack of accolades, linebacker Cody Barton exceeded Bellore's tackle total with 16. ◥ Seattle cycled through a few different players on punt and kickoff returns, but the best in both areas was cornerback D.J. Reed. After being waived by the 49ers due to an injury in August, Reed quickly earned a role once he was able to get on the field in Seattle. Given that he has the inside track to start at corner entering 2021, do not be surprised if some combination of running back Travis Homer and wide receivers Freddie Swain and D'Wayne Eskridge handle return duties in 2021. Eskridge in particular earned MAC Special Teams Player of the Year honors in 2020 for his play as a kick returner.

Tampa Bay Buccaneers

2020 Record: 11-5	**Total DVOA:** 31.5% (14)	**2021 Mean Projection:** 11.1 wins	**On the Clock (0-5):** 2%
Pythagorean Wins: 11.2 (3)	**Offense:** 19.8% (3)	**Postseason Odds:** 79.8%	**Mediocrity (6-8):** 13%
Snap-Weighted Age: 26.9 (8)	**Defense:** -14.6% (5)	**Super Bowl Odds:** 22.6%	**Playoff Contender (9-11):** 38%
Average Opponent: 1.7% (11)	**Special Teams:** -2.9% (26)	**Proj. Avg. Opponent:** -2.6% (30)	**Super Bowl Contender (12+):** 47%

2020: Winning a Super Bowl is easy, just sign the best quarterback in NFL history and don't suffer many injuries.

2021: Repeating as champion is easy, just bring back your entire team and hope you don't suffer many injuries.

Tom Brady sat in his living room and waited. And waited. And waited some more.

He began to think about life after football.

Then, finally, the Patriots called. They decided to take him with the 199th pick in the 2000 NFL draft.

Over the next two decades in New England, Brady went on to win six Super Bowls and four Super Bowl MVPs. A lot of teams came to regret overlooking him. Surely, if given the chance, they wouldn't do it again.

And yet when Brady became a free agent in March 2020, only one team openly pursued him: the Tampa Bay Buccaneers.

At the time, it seemed like an odd union—a quarterback known for winning and a franchise known for losing. The Buccaneers hadn't been relevant for years … or put another way, as long as you had been reading Football Outsiders. From 2003 to 2019, they posted a .393 win percentage, fourth worst in the NFL. They finished last in their division 10 times and missed the playoffs 15 times, including 12 straight seasons. The organization was a disaster, bungling coaching hires, draft picks, MRSA outbreaks, and uniform redesigns.

So when the Buccaneers signed Brady, they wanted him to do more than win football games. They wanted him to set a new standard. "He's going to bring the best out of everybody," general manager Jason Licht said during an appearance on Sirius XM NFL Radio.

And ultimately, he did. Tampa Bay showed flashes of dominance early and shot up the DVOA leaderboard. Four weeks into the season, the Buccaneers were No. 1 (No. 7 on offense and No. 2 on defense). Despite sometimes streaky play, they never dropped out of the top three for the rest of the year.

That inconsistency, however, raised questions about their viability as a Super Bowl contender. One week, they played their sloppiest game of the season, committing 11 penalties and surrendering three sacks in a narrow loss to the Bears; the next, they played their cleanest, committing zero penalties and surrendering zero sacks in a blowout win over the Packers. One week, they jumped out to a double-digit lead against the Raiders; the next, they had to rally from a double-digit deficit against the Giants. One week, Brady threw three interceptions and no touchdowns in a 38-3 loss to the Saints (the biggest loss, by point margin, of his career); the next, he threw three touchdowns and no interceptions in a 46-23 win over the Pan-

thers. No team experienced more game-to-game variance in total DVOA.

Even the Buccaneers seemed skeptical of the Buccaneers. "Everybody tried to hand us the Lombardi Trophy in August," coach Bruce Arians said after a Week 12 loss to the Chiefs dropped his team to 7-5. "You don't just throw guys out there with names. You've got to practice. You've got to learn to get in sync with each other. That takes time."

As it turns out, the high variance wasn't predictive. Tampa Bay never lost again. After a Week 13 bye, the Buccaneers won eight straight games, including three straight on the road in the playoffs to become the first team to play a Super Bowl in its home stadium.

What happened? It indeed took time for Brady to gel with his new teammates and learn the intricacies of the offense. He wasn't bad by any stretch, but through 12 games, he was on track to post his highest interception rate (2.3%) since 2006. "It's like anything—the longer you're together, the less you'll have to say certain things because you will already have experienced them, you will have talked about them, you'll work through them," Brady said early in the season. "There's a lot of black and white in football, and there's a lot of gray. The problem is when there is too much gray—*I thought one thing, you thought another.*"

But improved chemistry doesn't explain the suddenness of the Buccaneers' transformation. Brady spent the first three-quarters of the season adapting to his coaches, but after the loss to the Chiefs, it was time for them to adapt to him, a point Tony Romo hammered during CBS' broadcast. "Just talking to him, I sit here and watch the tape, and I'm watching an offense that's very different" from the offense he led in New England, he said, adding later that "they need to do more easy things."

One of the "easy things" Romo wanted to see more of was play-action. Arians' offenses never have been heavy on play-action, but the Buccaneers' 18.5% rate through Week 13 was exceptionally low. Only one team (Steelers) had used play-action less often, and four teams had used it twice as often (Patriots, Rams, Bills, and Titans).

Romo also called for the Buccaneers to make a change before Brady even touched the ball. Pre-snap motion, he argued, would help Brady detect coverage disguises and allow him to more accurately identify whether the defense was playing

2021 Buccaneers Schedule

Week	Opp.	Week	Opp.	Week	Opp.
1	DAL (Thu.)	7	CHI	13	at ATL
2	ATL	8	at NO	14	BUF
3	at LAR	9	BYE	15	NO
4	at NE	10	at WAS	16	at CAR
5	MIA	11	NYG (Mon.)	17	at NYJ
6	at PHI (Thu.)	12	at IND	18	CAR

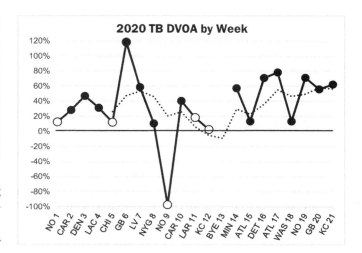

man-to-man or zone. Arians brushed off the criticism, saying "I'm not a big fan of it if it's going to disrupt what you're doing versus just blocking people."

Whatever the reason—rigidity or indifference—Tampa Bay's relatively minimal use of these concepts was confounding, so much so that ESPN's Dan Orlovsky accused the Buccaneers of "coaching malpractice" and "wasting Tom Brady." He wasn't wrong. When they used play-action or motion, their efficiency improved dramatically. On non-play-action passes, they averaged 6.3 yards (17th); on play-action passes, they averaged 9.3 yards (second). On non-motion plays, they averaged 4.9 yards (30th); on motion plays, they averaged 6.5 yards (third).

The Buccaneers got Brady's message via Romo, and after the bye week, the offense's play-action and motion rates spiked (Tables 1 and 2). Over the final four weeks of the season, the play-action rate rose 7 percentage points—the fourth-largest increase in that span—and the motion rate rose 10 percentage points. Tampa Bay's efficiency didn't suffer, either. In fact, no team averaged more yards on play-action passes or motion plays. And in the Super Bowl, the Buccaneers relied on play-action and motion even more, using play-action on nearly half of Brady's dropbacks and motion on about three-quarters of all plays.

The Buccaneers didn't go from inconsistent to invincible because "things just clicked." They went from inconsistent to invincible because they leaned into their strengths. So, rest of the NFL, there's your winning formula: Sign Tom Brady and do more of the things you do well.

Brady's influence wasn't limited to the offense. He was a factor on the other side of the ball, too. Yes, Tampa Bay already had a good defense, finishing sixth in DVOA in 2019, but barely anyone outside the analytics community noticed. They saw that the Buccaneers allowed 28.1 points per game, more than all but three teams. The defense wasn't to blame,

however. The quarterback was. Jameis Winston threw an NFL record seven pick-sixes, plus a bunch more pick-soon-to-be-sixes (interceptions that gave opponents short fields). With Winston, the Buccaneers had an offense that set the defense up to fail. With Brady, the Buccaneers had an offense that set the defense up to succeed. The upgrade helped Tampa Bay jump from 32nd in average opponent starting field position to 13th.

While Brady proved to be the missing piece of a complementary offense, the Buccaneers' defensive revival was set in motion well before his arrival thanks to these transactions:

• A pair of draft-day trades in 2018. In the first, Tampa Bay sent the seventh pick to Buffalo for the 12th, 53rd, and 56th picks. In the second, it flipped that 56th to New England for the 63rd and 117th picks. In the end, the Buccaneers came away with three of their Super Bowl starters—defensive tackle Vita Vea, cornerback Carlton Davis, and safety Jordan Whitehead. (Fans will appreciate this coincidence: The last time Tampa Bay traded down from No. 7 to No. 12, it landed Warren Sapp, part of the dominant defensive core that carried the Buccaneers to their first Super Bowl championship.)

• The hiring of Todd Bowles as defensive coordinator. From 2014 through 2017, the Buccaneers drafted just eight players on defense, fewest in the NFL. The lack of investment showed on the field. When Tampa Bay hired Arians in 2019, his first move was to bring Bowles aboard to fix a unit that had finished last in DVOA in consecutive seasons. The squad Bowles inherited was young and inexperienced, but

Table 1. Tampa Bay's Use of Play-Action

Weeks	Rate	Rank	PA Yd/Play	Rank	Non-PA Yd/Play	Rank
Weeks 1-12	18.5%	31	9.3	2	6.3	17
Weeks 14-17	25.5%	21	11.4	1	8.9	2
Playoffs	28.5%	5*	9.7	2*	6.1	7*

Represents position among the 14 postseason teams, not all 32 teams.

Table 2. Tampa Bay's Use of Motion

Weeks	Rate	Rank	Motion Yd/Play	Rank	Non-Motion Yd/Play	Rank
Weeks 1-12	46.4%	13	6.5	3	4.9	30
Weeks 14-17	56.6%	6	8	1	6.1	10
Playoffs	60.8%	4*	5.7	7*	5.7	5*

that worked in his favor. He didn't have to break bad habits. He could be a teacher. The players bought in immediately, and though they suffered some lapses early, they steadily improved throughout 2019.

You would expect a defense to experience some regression after a dramatic turnaround, but that never happened for the Buccaneers. Tampa Bay rose up the leaderboards in yards allowed per drive, three-and-outs per drive, punts per drive, turnovers forced per drive, and drive success rate. The Buccaneers repeated as the No. 1 rush defense (the first team to do so since the 2015-2016 Jets, also coached by Bowles) and jumped from No. 13 to No. 5 in DVOA against the pass. Under Bowles' tutelage, the Buccaneers have shed their reputation as a soft defense. They attack quarterbacks (finishing among the top seven in pressure rate in back-to-back seasons) and are no longer prone to explosive plays (allowing the fourth-fewest plays of 20 or more yards last season).

• The signing of Shaquil Barrett. In his first five seasons, Barrett was mostly a backup, stuck behind Von Miller and De-Marcus Ware and later Miller and Bradley Chubb on the Broncos' depth chart. All he needed was a chance. Seeking an edge rusher to play opposite Jason Pierre-Paul, the Buccaneers gave him that chance in 2019, and he became a star. In his first season in Tampa, he led the NFL in sacks (19.5) and finished fifth in hurries (55). That breakout season wasn't enough to secure a long-term contract, however. Playing under the franchise tag last season, he again proved his worth. While his sack total dropped (8.0), he remained disruptive, recording a league-high 48 hurries, three of which resulted in interceptions. He added another four sacks and 12 hurries in the playoffs. This offseason, he finally received the big money he had been seeking, signing a four-year deal worth up to $72 million.

How much longer can the defense sustain this level of play? Though it's difficult to post a -10.0% DVOA for three straight seasons, it's not uncommon. Since 1983, 74 teams have been in position to do it, and 32 have, most recently the 2017-2019 Ravens and 2017-2019 Vikings. Even the Buccaneers have done it before—and in five straight seasons (1999-2003). Given that this defense, like the offense, is returning all 11 starters from the Super Bowl, Tampa Bay very well could be next.

The bigger question, of course, is whether the Buccaneers can become the first team to repeat since the 2003-2004 Patriots. Two things could derail their hopes. One is obvious: the sudden decline of Tom Brady. If he is, in fact, human and isn't regularly replacing his mechanical parts at his Armenia Avenue "recovery" center, we can't completely rule out the possibility. The other: a lack of depth. Though Tampa Bay has options at wide receiver, tight end, and running back, the

drop-off from starter to reserve is severe at offensive tackle, edge rusher, linebacker, and cornerback. During the draft, the Buccaneers missed an opportunity to add insurance, instead burning a second-round pick on quarterback Kyle Trask, who won't throw a pass until Brady says he can.

Depth also was a concern last season, but Tampa Bay was remarkably healthy. That could be a testament to the team's conditioning and medical staffs. Youth also could have been a factor, as well as just plain luck. The Buccaneers didn't go unscathed—they lost Vea for three months and right guard Alex Cappa for most of the playoffs—but they didn't experience injuries to the degree that other teams did. In a season in which we saw a record average of 83.2 adjusted games lost per team, Tampa Bay actually saw a decline. In 2019, the Bucs suffered 39.5 adjusted games lost, second-fewest; in 2020, they suffered a league-low 30.6.

Otherwise, the Buccaneers are set up for another deep run. With a projected top-five offense and defense and a relatively light schedule, they're clear-cut favorites not only in their division but also in the NFC. Ironically, the road to the Super Bowl in Inglewood, California, this season looks easier than the road to the Super Bowl in Tampa last season.

Staying relevant in the seasons ahead? That's another matter. The Buccaneers' focus has been on keeping their Super Bowl roster intact, and to do so they've had to deviate from their preference for frontloaded contracts. The new deals they gave Brady, Barrett, Donovan Smith, Lavonte David, Ndamukong Suh, and Rob Gronkowski include signing bonuses and/or void years that create short-term salary-cap relief but cause long-term pain.

The pain starts in 2022. The cap hits for Barrett, Smith, David, and Vea spike. The dead-cap void-year charges for Suh and Gronkowski kick in. And several starters can become free agents, including Chris Godwin (playing under the franchise tag this season), O.J. Howard, Ryan Jensen, Jason Pierre-Paul, Carlton Davis, and Jordan Whitehead. The year to watch, though, is 2023. Tampa Bay could incur $30 million in dead-cap charges because of the void years in Brady and David's contracts. Plus, Devin White's cap hit spikes and Vea can become a free agent. The Buccaneers are counting on the cap rising by tens of millions of dollars by then, and while that might give them some breathing room, it won't be a cure. Every Super Bowl contender that retains its veteran core by postponing cap hits eventually faces a reckoning.

But that's eventually. The Buccaneers know, perhaps better than any NFL franchise, that opportunity is not a lengthy visitor. For them, a chance like this comes around only once every couple of decades.

Thomas Bassinger

2020 Buccaneers by Week

Wk	vs.	W-L	PF	PA	YDF	YDA	TO	Total	Off	Def	ST
1	at NO	L	23	34	310	271	-3	12.5%	10.1%	-20.0%	-17.6%
2	CAR	W	31	17	339	427	2	28.3%	12.0%	-12.4%	3.9%
3	at DEN	W	28	10	353	226	2	47.0%	19.6%	-33.7%	-6.3%
4	LAC	W	38	31	484	324	1	31.4%	29.0%	-0.2%	2.2%
5	at CHI	L	19	20	339	243	0	12.1%	-4.5%	-10.1%	6.5%
6	GB	W	38	10	324	201	2	118.5%	21.4%	-94.9%	2.2%
7	at LV	W	45	20	454	347	1	58.8%	29.2%	-26.2%	3.4%
8	at NYG	W	25	23	344	357	1	10.6%	12.6%	3.3%	1.3%
9	NO	L	3	38	194	420	-1	-97.1%	-68.2%	21.1%	-7.8%
10	at CAR	W	46	23	544	187	0	40.6%	31.1%	-24.1%	-14.6%
11	LAR	L	24	27	251	413	0	18.5%	7.6%	-8.6%	2.3%
12	KC	L	24	27	417	543	-1	2.7%	14.4%	14.1%	2.4%
13	BYE										
14	MIN	W	26	14	303	335	1	57.6%	46.3%	-11.5%	-0.1%
15	at ATL	W	31	27	416	369	0	13.7%	18.7%	6.7%	1.7%
16	at DET	W	47	7	588	186	2	71.2%	38.7%	-63.3%	-30.8%
17	ATL	W	44	27	485	385	1	78.5%	75.8%	1.7%	4.4%
18	at WAS	W	31	23	507	375	0	13.6%	35.1%	24.7%	3.2%
19	at NO	W	30	20	316	294	4	71.6%	28.5%	-49.8%	-6.7%
20	at GB	W	31	26	351	381	-1	56.2%	13.3%	-35.4%	7.5%
21	KC	W	31	9	340	350	2	62.6%	5.6%	-53.8%	3.2%

Trends and Splits

	Offense	Rank	Defense	Rank
Total DVOA	19.8%	3	-14.6%	5
Unadjusted VOA	19.9%	4	-14.2%	5
Weighted Trend	24.6%	2	-12.0%	6
Variance	8.8%	23	8.5%	31
Average Opponent	-0.3%	15	2.5%	10
Passing	37.1%	5	-5.4%	5
Rushing	-2.0%	10	-31.4%	1
First Down	9.4%	9	-16.7%	3
Second Down	21.2%	4	-18.1%	5
Third Down	40.3%	3	-5.6%	14
First Half	17.7%	5	4.3%	23
Second Half	22.2%	2	-35.6%	2
Red Zone	31.8%	5	5.6%	19
Late and Close	31.3%	2	-36.3%	2

Five-Year Performance

Year	W-L	Pyth W	Est W	PF	PA	TO	Total	Rk	Off	Rk	Def	Rk	ST	Rk	Off AGL	Rk	Def AGL	Rk	Off Age	Rk	Def Age	Rk	ST Age	Rk
2016	9-7	7.6	7.2	354	369	+2	-3.0%	22	-3.9%	19	-2.8%	12	-1.8%	20	75.9	30	49.1	20	25.7	28	26.2	21	25.8	22
2017	5-11	6.7	6.0	335	382	-1	-12.4%	23	5.2%	11	12.0%	32	-5.5%	29	25.4	9	55.3	27	26.2	27	27.0	7	25.9	12
2018	5-11	6.4	5.4	396	464	-18	-14.4%	25	5.9%	12	16.2%	32	-4.1%	28	14.3	3	91.4	32	26.3	22	26.5	12	25.6	22
2019	7-9	8.2	6.9	458	449	-13	0.3%	14	-7.4%	23	-10.5%	6	-2.8%	27	17.0	6	22.5	4	26.2	25	25.6	24	25.5	22
2020	11-5	11.2	12.8	492	355	+8	31.5%	2	19.8%	3	-14.6%	5	-2.9%	26	12.4	1	18.2	2	27.7	3	26.3	17	26.1	14

2020 Performance Based on Most Common Personnel Groups

TB Offense					TB Offense vs. Opponents					TB Defense					TB Defense vs. Opponents			
Pers	Freq	Yds	DVOA	Run%	Pers	Freq	Yds	DVOA	Run%	Pers	Freq	Yds	DVOA	Pers	Freq	Yds	DVOA
1.1	58%	6.2	13.1%	27%	Base	17%	5.8	20.0%	56%	Base	34%	5.7	-4.4%	1.1	56%	5.1	-21.9%
1.2	21%	6.6	28.7%	50%	Nickel	59%	6.7	25.1%	35%	Nickel	63%	5.1	-22.3%	1.2	15%	6.1	-8.3%
1.0	6%	6.7	25.6%	7%	Dime+	23%	6.7	15.5%	12%	Dime+	1%	7.5	-90.0%	2.1	10%	5.0	-33.3%
61.1	5%	7.7	36.8%	66%	Goal Line	1%	0.9	71.8%	29%	Goal Line	1%	2.2	49.2%	1.3	5%	6.2	35.0%
1.3	5%	8.8	62.8%	53%										2.2	5%	5.1	-13.8%

Strategic Tendencies

Run/Pass		Rk	Formation		Rk	Pass Rush		Rk	Secondary		Rk	Strategy		Rk
Runs, first half	32%	28	Form: Single Back	86%	7	Rush 3	6.3%	16	4 DB	34%	7	Play Action	20%	30
Runs, first down	48%	16	Form: Empty Back	11%	9	Rush 4	56.3%	27	5 DB	63%	12	Offensive Motion	49%	11
Runs, second-long	19%	28	Form: Multi Back	3%	27	Rush 5	29.3%	3	6+ DB	1%	30	Avg Box (Off)	6.44	24
Runs, power sit.	47%	30	Pers: 3+ WR	67%	15	Rush 6+	8.2%	4	Man Coverage	24%	24	Avg Box (Def)	6.61	17
Runs, behind 2H	21%	30	Pers: 2+ TE/6+ OL	35%	8	Edge Rusher Sacks	39.4%	28	CB by Sides	76%	12	Offensive Pace	28.82	4
Pass, ahead 2H	54%	7	Pers: 6+ OL	7%	3	Interior DL Sacks	27.7%	11	S/CB Cover Ratio	20%	30	Defensive Pace	31.22	28
Run-Pass Options	11%	7	Shotgun/Pistol	59%	23	Second Level Sacks	33.0%	6	DB Blitz	18%	6	Go for it on 4th	1.56	16

With Tom Brady at quarterback, the Buccaneers moved up to fourth in situation-neutral pace. Bruce Arians' offenses had usually been around the league average. ✎. Tampa Bay had 28.2% DVOA with six offensive linemen and was the team most likely to pass the ball from a six-lineman set (36% of plays). ✎. Tampa Bay's offense was fourth with 38 drops. The Buccaneers led the league with 16 dropped passes from running backs. ✎. Another issue for the offense: It ranked 29th in the league with only 83 broken tackles. ✎. Tampa Bay's defense dropped from 37% (seventh) to 24% (24th) in frequency of using man coverage. ✎. The Buccaneers were fourth in defensive DVOA on passes at or behind the line of scrimmage after ranking first the year before. A big part of that was allowing just 7.3 average yards after the catch (fifth) on these passes, compared to the NFL average of 8.4 yards after the catch. ✎. The Bucs were one of four teams with a league-high 31% pressure rate when bringing just the standard four pass-rushers. ✎. The Tampa Bay run defense was remarkably well-rounded. The Bucs had the best run defense by DVOA and yards per carry with three or more wide receivers on the field, and the best run defense by DVOA and second-best by yards per carry with less than three wide receivers. The Bucs ranked No. 2 in both stats against handoffs from shotgun, and No. 2 in both stats against handoffs from under center. Tampa Bay was second in run defense on first down and first on second down, although only 13th on third and fourth downs. ✎. The Buccaneers ranked 26th in defensive DVOA in the first quarter of games, then improved to 16th in the second quarter, sixth in the third quarter, and first in the fourth quarter or overtime. ✎. Tampa Bay won the Super Bowl despite finishing 24th in average time of possession (28:54) during the regular season.

Passing

Player	DYAR	DVOA	Plays	NtYds	Avg	YAC	C%	TD	Int
T.Brady	1518	25.0%	627	4466	7.1	4.5	66.4%	40	12
B.Gabbert	13	-0.1%	17	136	8.0	8.9	56.3%	2	0

Rushing

Player	DYAR	DVOA	Plays	Yds	Avg	TD	Fum	Suc
R.Jones	195	15.5%	192	978	5.1	7	0	57%
L.Fournette	46	2.1%	97	367	3.8	6	0	49%
K.Vaughn	-17	-25.6%	26	109	4.2	0	0	46%
T.Brady	-22	-37.5%	13	12	0.9	3	3	--
L.McCoy*	-14	-41.7%	10	31	3.1	0	0	40%
G.Bernard	-29	-13.9%	124	416	3.4	3	1	48%

Receiving

Player	DYAR	DVOA	Plays	Ctch	Yds	Y/C	YAC	TD	C%
M.Evans	354	25.6%	109	70	1006	14.4	3.8	13	64%
C.Godwin	267	28.0%	84	65	840	12.9	4.3	7	77%
A.Brown	110	8.9%	62	45	483	10.7	5.6	4	73%
S.Miller	113	13.2%	53	33	501	15.2	3.3	3	62%
T.Johnson	50	24.4%	17	12	169	14.1	6.0	2	71%
J.Watson	19	11.7%	11	7	94	13.4	2.7	0	64%
J.Mickens	15	4.6%	10	7	58	8.3	4.4	0	70%
R.Gronkowski	77	6.4%	77	45	623	13.8	5.5	7	58%
C.Brate	65	22.8%	34	28	282	10.1	2.5	2	82%
O.J.Howard	25	11.8%	19	11	146	13.3	1.5	2	58%
T.Hudson	-5	-17.3%	7	3	41	13.7	4.0	0	43%
L.Fournette	-9	-17.4%	47	36	233	6.5	6.5	0	77%
R.Jones	-89	-53.4%	42	28	165	5.9	5.6	1	67%
L.McCoy*	-16	-30.3%	19	15	101	6.7	6.8	0	79%
K.Vaughn	-25	-61.9%	10	5	34	6.8	4.6	1	50%
G.Bernard	40	-1.7%	59	47	355	7.6	7.4	3	80%

Offensive Line

Player	Pos	Age	GS	Snaps	Pen	Sk	Pass	Run	Player	Pos	Age	GS	Snaps	Pen	Sk	Pass	Run
Tristan Wirfs	RT	22	16/16	1074	3	1	12	4	Donovan Smith	LT	28	15/15	963	11	4	22	5
Alex Cappa	RG	26	16/16	1071	2	0	13	7	Ali Marpet	LG	28	13/13	850	3	0	6	3
Ryan Jensen	C	30	16/16	1062	4	2.5	9	8									

Year	Yards	ALY	Rk	Power	Rk	Stuff	Rk	2Lev	Rk	OpFld	Rk	BB Rt	Rk	Sacks	ASR	Rk	Press	Rk	BB Rt	Rk	Cont
2018	3.55	3.78	31	64%	22	25%	30	1.06	27	0.49	29	8.5%	28	41	6.6%	15	31.4%	18	7.8%	11	40
2019	3.59	4.00	23	53%	30	23%	30	0.94	28	0.55	24	9.9%	13	47	7.6%	22	29.2%	11	10.0%	4	29
2020	4.57	4.55	9	88%	1	14%	4	1.15	21	0.97	6	8.8%	12	22	4.3%	3	15.0%	1	11.1%	12	32

2020 ALY by direction:	Left End: 4.46 (16)	Left Tackle: 3.44 (26)	Mid/Guard: 4.64 (7)	Right Tackle: 4.61 (10)	Right End: 5.37 (9)

Left tackle Donovan Smith tied for the league lead with 11 penalties (10 accepted), but he didn't commit any in the play-offs. ✏ Smith regressed in pass protection, averaging 35.7 snaps per blown block, which ranked 24th among left tackles. In 2019, he averaged 56.6, which ranked fifth. Though he has been inconsistent in that regard, the Buccaneers have been able to count on him suiting up almost every game day since they drafted him in 2015. He has played at least 1,000 snaps in each of his six seasons and missed only two games (one last season because of COVID protocols). Tampa Bay signed him to a two-year, $31-million extension that should keep him in pewter through 2023. It also dropped his 2021 cap hit from $14.3 million to $3.7 million. ✏ On the right side, rookie Tristan Wirfs lived up to his first-round billing and then some. He was on the field for every dropback and allowed only one sack. Wirfs ranked 11th among all tackles in snaps per blown block, well ahead of the tackles drafted before him—Andrew Thomas (70th), Jedrick Wills (42nd), and Mekhi Becton (33rd). ✏ Early in the season, Rob Gronkowski playfully declared, "I came here to block, baby!" With Gronk and Wirfs anchoring the right side, the Buccaneers improved significantly in short-yardage situations as well as runs to the right side in general. Compared to 2019, the Buccaneers improved by 1.5 adjusted line yards per carry on runs behind right tackle and nearly 2.0 ALY on runs around right end. ✏ How good is left guard Ali Marpet? When he missed the Buccaneers' Week 9 game against the Saints because of a concussion, the offense cratered and Tom Brady, constantly under pressure, had his worst game of the season. The next week, Tampa Bay shook up its line, moving Ryan Jensen to left guard and inserting A.Q. Shipley at center. ✏ A couple of weeks after coming off the bench, Shipley suffered a career-ending neck injury. In May, he joined Arians' staff as an offensive assistant. ✏ Right guard Alex Cappa ranked 57th among interior linemen in snaps per blown block. With Cappa as well as Jensen entering a contract year, the Buccaneers used a third-round pick on Robert Hainsey, who started at right tackle at Notre Dame but is projected to play on the interior in the NFL. During rookie minicamp, he took some reps at center.

Defensive Front

Defensive Line	Age	Pos	G	Snaps	Plays	Overall TmPct	Rk	Stop	Dfts	BTkl	vs. Run Runs	St%	Rk	RuYd	Rk	Pass Rush Sack	Hit	Hur	Dsrpt
Ndamukong Suh	34	DE	16	786	47	5.6%	35	35	18	4	32	75%	47	1.9	26	6.0	15	27	3
William Gholston	30	DE	16	606	46	5.5%	38	29	11	2	38	63%	83	2.4	46	3.0	19	20	2
Rakeem Nunez-Roches	28	DT	16	482	20	2.4%	95	13	0	2	19	68%	66	2.7	56	0.0	3	5	0
Steve McLendon	35	DT	15	443	31	4.0%	68	24	3	3	31	77%	38	2.3	42	0.0	3	4	0

Edge Rushers	Age	Pos	G	Snaps	Plays	Overall TmPct	Rk	Stop	Dfts	BTkl	vs. Run Runs	St%	Rk	RuYd	Rk	Pass Rush Sack	Hit	Hur	Dsrpt
Jason Pierre-Paul	32	OLB	16	943	61	7.3%	8	50	22	6	36	83%	7	2.5	43	9.5	5	27	3
Shaquil Barrett	29	OLB	15	822	60	7.7%	7	41	19	4	30	73%	40	2.3	35	8.0	9	48	5
Anthony Nelson	24	OLB	16	322	17	2.0%	--	12	3	3	15	67%	--	2.7	--	1.0	6	9	3

Linebackers	Age	Pos	G	Snaps	Plays	Overall TmPct	Rk	Stop	Dfts	BTkl	vs. Run Runs	St%	Rk	RuYd	Rk	Pass Rush Sack	Hit	Hur	vs. Pass Tgts	Suc%	Rk	Yd/P	Rk	PD	Int
Lavonte David	31	ILB	16	1056	123	14.8%	24	76	29	16	55	75%	2	3.1	12	1.5	1	3	60	58%	17	4.4	8	6	1
Devin White	23	ILB	15	991	144	18.4%	5	76	33	17	61	61%	26	3.3	16	9.0	7	13	51	41%	58	7.0	54	4	0

Year	Yards	ALY	Rk	Power	Rk	Stuff	Rk	2Lev	Rk	OpFld	Rk	BB Rt	Rk	Sacks	ASR	Rk	Press	Rk	BB Rt	Rk
2018	4.59	4.36	15	71%	24	23%	8	1.45	29	1.04	24	4.7%	31	38	8.0%	8	25.0%	31	7.0%	28
2019	3.02	3.14	2	62%	11	29%	2	0.81	1	0.45	2	18.8%	2	47	6.7%	20	32.9%	7	17.6%	3
2020	3.35	3.60	1	70%	21	22%	2	0.85	1	0.40	5	18.6%	1	48	7.9%	6	29.0%	7	16.7%	3

2020 ALY by direction:	Left End: 2.62 (2)	Left Tackle: 3.36 (6)	Mid/Guard: 3.65 (1)	Right Tackle: 3.54 (3)	Right End: 4.51 (15)

The Buccaneers had the oldest defensive line (29.2 years old) and sixth-oldest linebacker corps (27.0) by snap-weighted age. ✏ Devin White, the fifth overall pick in 2019, tied for the league lead in defeats (33). Lavonte David finished fourth (29). ✏ White and David were also among the seven linebackers to be charted with at least 16 broken tackles. That's more of a quibble than cause for concern. They're relentless defenders who cover a lot of ground. When you reach the ballcarrier more often than other players, you're likely to whiff a little more often than other players. ✎ White has been a menace when rushing the passer (he was first among inside linebackers in sacks, hits, and hurries) but a liability when dropping back (he was 58th among 75 qualifying linebackers in success rate on passes into his coverage). ✎ Tampa Bay recorded about the same number of sacks in 2020 as it did in 2019. The distribution, however, was completely different, due in large part to White's success as a pass-rusher. The Buccaneers went from second in edge-rusher sacks to 28th and from 26th in second-level sacks to sixth. The Tampa Bay defense also led the league with 12 sacks attributed to "rusher untouched." ✎ Only one tandem of edge rushers (T.J. Watt and Bud Dupree of the Steelers) has generated more sacks over the past two seasons than the 45.5 combined sacks for Shaquil Barrett and Jason Pierre-Paul. No other edge rusher on the roster has more than one. Joe Tryon, whom the Buccaneers drafted at the end of the first round in May, and Anthony Nelson, whom they drafted in the fourth round in 2019, are projected to be the primary backups. ✎ When Vita Vea broke his leg in Week 5 against the Bears, the Buccaneers turned to Rakeem "Nacho" Nunez-Roches, a good player to have on your roster in queso an emergency.

Defensive Secondary

Secondary	Age	Pos	G	Snaps	Plays	TmPct	Overall Rk	Stop	Dfts	BTkl	Runs	St%	vs. Run Rk	RuYd	Rk	Tgts	Tgt%	Rk	aDOT	vs. Pass Suc%	Rk	Yd/P	Rk	PD	Int
Antoine Winfield	23	FS	16	1034	97	11.6%	25	24	8	11	34	29%	50	9.9	62	26	6.0%	53	11.7	42%	57	8.5	46	6	1
Jordan Whitehead	24	SS	16	918	78	9.4%	54	30	16	11	39	51%	13	4.3	5	23	6.0%	54	12.2	43%	52	10.5	62	4	2
Carlton Davis	25	CB	14	904	86	11.8%	5	36	15	16	15	40%	48	6.4	35	87	23.0%	16	12.9	51%	41	7.6	41	18	4
Sean Murphy-Bunting	24	CB	16	882	69	8.3%	48	28	13	11	13	77%	1	2.8	2	59	16.0%	70	10.7	37%	75	9.8	76	3	1
Jamel Dean	25	CB	14	708	66	9.1%	30	31	10	7	12	58%	9	7.7	52	58	19.6%	41	11.2	57%	15	5.7	5	7	1
Ross Cockrell	30	CB	12	237	12	1.9%	--	8	3	3	0	0%	--	0.0	--	12	12.1%	--	8.5	75%	--	5.1	--	1	0
Raven Greene*	26	FS	10	326	46	9.1%	58	21	13	6	10	70%	2	4.5	7	29	23.1%	1	7.1	31%	69	7.4	29	5	1

Year	Pass D Rank	vs. #1 WR	Rk	vs. #2 WR	Rk	vs. Other WR	Rk	WR Wide	Rk	WR Slot	Rk	vs. TE	Rk	vs. RB	Rk
2018	30	16.0%	29	25.1%	29	-1.4%	18	-11.2%	9	28.7%	29	21.1%	28	2.2%	16
2019	12	3.7%	17	2.2%	18	-20.0%	6	-4.2%	18	-2.8%	8	10.7%	27	-49.0%	2
2020	5	-15.5%	6	5.9%	22	-28.6%	1	-23.2%	4	-12.0%	3	11.5%	25	-16.1%	5

In contrast to its defensive front, Tampa Bay's secondary was the league's youngest (24.0 years old) by snap-weighted age. From 2017 to 2020, the Buccaneers drafted seven defensive backs in the first four rounds, a total matched by only the Raiders. Six of the seven played significant snaps last season and remain with the team. (Tampa Bay waived former second-round pick M.J. Stewart before the 2020 season started.) ✎ When the Buccaneers drafted Antoine Winfield Jr. in the second round last year, they were looking for a physical playmaker, and that's exactly what they got. They might not have reached the Super Bowl without him. In their divisional-round game against the Saints, they were trailing 20-13 late in the third quarter when Drew Brees, on third-and-2, hit Jared Cook across the middle. Winfield closed in and punched the ball loose, wiping out a first down in Tampa Bay territory and changing the course of the game. ✎ Another Winfield highlight: in the Buccaneers' Week 12 game against the Chiefs, Tyreek Hill threw up a peace sign after burning the defense for a 75-yard touchdown. Winfield remembered and got revenge in the Super Bowl. After breaking up a fourth-down pass intended for Hill, Winfield celebrated with … a peace sign. The NFL fined him $7,815. He responded by donating the same amount to a Tampa-area middle school. ✎ Aside from that first game against the Chiefs, the Buccaneers clamped down on the deep ball. Tampa Bay posted a 58.3% DVOA (29th) against such passes in 2019 but a 24.5% DVOA (12th) in 2020. Most of that improvement came against deep passes down the right, which is usually Carlton Davis' side of the field. ✎ Davis, who had one interception in his first two seasons, became the first Buccaneers cornerback since Brent Grimes in 2016 to pick off four passes. ✎ Jamel Dean already has established himself as one of the league's top cover corners. Only four cornerbacks allowed fewer yards per pass into their coverage last season—Bryce Callahan (4.0), Jaire Alexander (4.5), Jalen Ramsey (4.8), and Bradley Roby (5.5). Dean intercepted only one pass, but it was a special one. With the Buccaneers trailing the Packers 10-0 in Week 8, he jumped on an Aaron Rodgers pass to Davante Adams and returned it for a touchdown, the first of 38 straight points for Tampa Bay. Rodgers had thrown only two other pick-sixes in his career. ✎ Tampa Bay's overall pass defense improved despite Sean Murphy-Bunting's extended struggles in coverage. Usually the slot corner when the Buccaneers use five defensive backs, Murphy-Bunting ranked 75th in success rate in 2019 and again in 2020. Then he got hot in January with three postseason interceptions. Playing in the slot didn't necessarily keep Murphy-Bunting away from the opposition's top receivers, which explains the discrepancy between his charting numbers and Tampa Bay ranking No. 1 against "other wide receivers." ✎ Safety Mike Edwards saw a diminished role after the Buccaneers drafted Winfield but delivered one of the most satisfying moments in team history: he intercepted the final pass of Brees' career.

Special Teams

Year	DVOA	Rank	FG/XP	Rank	Net Kick	Rank	Kick Ret	Rank	Net Punt	Rank	Punt Ret	Rank	Hidden	Rank
2018	-4.1%	28	-12.9	31	1.7	12	-2.2	20	-2.9	23	-4.0	26	-8.3	25
2019	-2.8%	27	-3.7	22	4.7	9	-4.4	29	-3.6	22	-6.9	32	-11.3	30
2020	-2.9%	26	-0.9	15	-5.5	26	-0.6	16	-5.4	26	-2.3	21	6.5	9

The Buccaneers finally figured out how to solve their eternal special teams problems: Score more touchdowns! Tampa Bay scored a team-record 59 last season, making it easier to overlook that they were below average in all five aspects of special teams that we track. The Buccaneers have posted a negative special teams DVOA for nine straight seasons. Our projections say they will make it 10 straight. New placekicker Ryan Succop was above average on field goals, converting 28 of 31 attempts. The problem came on extra points, where he had three misses and two blocks. Tampa Bay retained him on a deal that will pay him $8.3 million over the next two seasons. Bradley Pinion was close to average in both gross kickoff value and gross punt value, but the coverage teams were an issue. Tampa Bay allowed the fourth-highest value for opponent kick returns and the sixth-highest value for opponent punt returns. Jaydon Mickens and Kenjon Barner were the primary returners. Neither impressed, though Mickens did produce a positive value on kickoffs. Fourth-round pick Jaelon Darden returned kickoffs and punts at North Texas and will get a chance this summer to win both jobs. Compared to the year before, the Buccaneers saw a nearly 18-point swing in their favor in "hidden points." They can thank Dan Bailey for most of that. In the Vikings' Week 14 visit to Tampa, Bailey missed four kicks (three field goals and one extra point) in the first half. All other enemy kickers made 21 of their 23 field goals and all 37 of their extra points.

Tennessee Titans

2020 Record: 11-5	**Total DVOA:** 2.5% (10)	**2021 Mean Projection:** 8.2 wins	**On the Clock (0-5):** 17%
Pythagorean Wins: 9.2 (12)	**Offense:** 18.4% (4)	**Postseason Odds:** 42.1%	**Mediocrity (6-8):** 38%
Snap-Weighted Age: 27 (3)	**Defense:** 11.5% (29)	**Super Bowl Odds:** 3.6%	**Playoff Contender (9-11):** 33%
Average Opponent: -2.7% (26)	**Special Teams:** -4.4% (28)	**Proj. Avg. Opponent:** -1.2% (21)	**Super Bowl Contender (12+):** 12%

2020: Derrick Henry stuffs regression into a locker.

2021: Derrick Henry's posse has dwindled and regression has hit the gym this summer.

The 2020 Tennessee Titans defied basic mathematical expectations in many ways. It wasn't likely for an offense that came from out of nowhere like the Titans did in 2019 to continue to ascend. But they did. It wasn't likely for the Titans to return to the playoffs with a defense that fell to the bottom five in DVOA. But they did. It wasn't likely that they would avoid injuries two years in a row, or shred opponents with play-action passes two years in a row, but they did, once again finishing near the top of the leaderboards in both categories.

Quarterbacks that played as great as Ryan Tannehill did in 2019, with no history of elite play, are not supposed to stick around and remain great. Not only did Tannehill remain great but he improved on his 2019 season, posting a 19.6% DVOA in a bigger sample of games, remaining a deadly play-action passer despite offensive line injuries, and leading the Titans to an NFL-high six game-winning drives. Those are the situations that Derrick Henry isn't supposed to help out with, because you can't run the ball as often with time dwindling. Somebody forgot to let Tannehill know about that. He got Corey Davis more involved in this offense than ever before, and even garnered some fringe MVP buzz from People Who Just Want To Recognize Great Seasons (as opposed to serious analysis).

To find a quarterback who improved as much as Tannehill did with a similar sample size—and then kept most of the gains—you have to go back to Matt Schaub and Eli Manning's ascension from adequate to good in the late-aughts. There's some sort of Tannehill hybrid lurking between those two players: the arm and the draft status of Manning, and the play-action-focused dominance of Schaub's years in the Gary Kubiak offense. There have been plenty of out-of-nowhere success stories and plenty of wild improvements—including some we can't fully explain yet such as Josh Allen—but Tannehill will now become the standard example for a quarterback improving in new surroundings, mentioned whenever any team makes a hopeful trade for a Jared Goff or Sam Darnold. Our projection systems are now pretty set on Tannehill being a good quarterback. His KUBIAK projection for 2021 doesn't quite match Patrick Mahomes or Aaron Rodgers, but it resembles the top-10 quarterback that we've seen for the past two seasons.

Henry received an NFL-high 378 carries. Those of you who are long-time readers may remember The Curse of 370. Nearly every NFL running back who has received that level of wear and tear has seen a real decline in their output next season, usually via injury, sometimes via effectiveness (Table 1). Because NFL running backs have been platooned more and more often in recent seasons, this is a concept that lives on mostly in theory now. Only two NFL running backs have received more than 370 carries in a season since 2008: Henry and DeMarco Murray with 392 carries for the 2014 Cowboys. Moving on to Philadelphia the next season, Murray put together a paltry 702 yards in 15 games as part of Chip Kelly's last hurrah.

Table 1. The Curse of 370 since 2000

Player	Team	Year	Carries	DYAR	Carries Y+1	DYAR Y+1
Eddie George	TEN	2000	403	124	315	-199
Edgerrin James	IND	2000	387	351	151	27
Ricky Williams	MIA	2002	383	211	392	-75
LaDainian Tomlinson	SD	2002	372	186	313	365
Ricky Williams	MIA	2003	392	-75	Retired	Retired
Jamal Lewis	BAL	2003	387	292	235	135
Curtis Martin	NYJ	2004	371	398	220	-17
Shaun Alexander	SEA	2005	370	453	252	-57
Larry Johnson	KC	2006	416	236	158	-38
Michael Turner	ATL	2008	376	155	178	132
DeMarco Murray	PHI	2014	392	382	193	-29
Derrick Henry	TEN	2020	378	386	--	--
AVERAGE			385.5	258.3	218	24.4

Now, does that mean you should be predicting doom and gloom for Henry? Should we let regression guide everything we feel about this team? I don't think so. Henry is sculpted in such a way that he's pushing barbells off of exercise balls and doing air push-ups with a giant chain around his neck. He's 247 pounds and the game has gotten lighter at linebacker. Maybe he's just an exception to the rule, and we should be prepared for that.

This is where I remind you that the Curse of 370 is not a hard and fast line where running backs suddenly become injury risks. It is more of a concept where the number 370 roughly represents the point at which additional carries start to become more and more of a problem. But look at Henry's

2021 Titans Schedule

Week	Opp.	Week	Opp.	Week	Opp.
1	ARI	7	KC	13	BYE
2	at SEA	8	at IND	14	JAX
3	IND	9	at LAR	15	at PIT
4	at NYJ	10	NO	16	SF (Thu.)
5	at JAX	11	HOU	17	MIA
6	BUF (Mon.)	12	at NE	18	at HOU

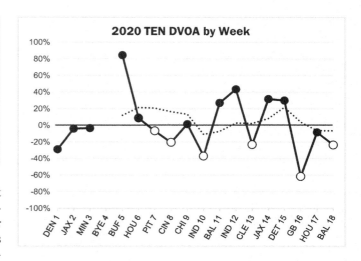

2020 TEN DVOA by Week

additional playoff rushing loads, and he has clearly gone past that point, toting the ball 782 times over the last two calendar years. Only three running backs on Table 1 had a higher two-year workload. Edgerrin James carried the ball 797 times between 1999 and 2000, Shaun Alexander had 798 total carries between 2003 and 2004, and Eddie George had 858 (!!) total carries including playoff games between 1999 and 2000. Rounding out the closest comps to Henry's workload, Ricky Williams had 775 carries and Larry Johnson had 765.

Neither Alexander, George, nor Johnson ever had another positive DVOA season in their collective careers. Williams temporarily retired and missed two of the next three seasons while trying to cope with his pain. James—who got this massive workload before he even turned 23—missed eight games between 2001 and 2002 and didn't rediscover his franchise back form until 2003. Henry is an impressive runner who is pretty much unparalleled in his era, but the history of backs with the kind of workload he has had in the modern era is also pretty much undefeated.

Head coach Mike Vrabel showed no signs of pulling the brakes on Henry, noting at OTAs that "as far as Derrick's workload, I think we all understand—and Derrick's fully aware of—what that may be and how he prepares to go through that."

The possibility of a Henry breakdown is just one of the things the Titans needed to consider as they built their 2021 roster. Tennessee had a 7-2 record in close games last year that led to an 11-5 record despite just a 2.5% DVOA. They were extremely healthy, ranking sixth in adjusted games lost. They had a defense that was among the league's worst despite ranking seventh in takeaways per drive. And they needed to respond to coaching and personnel losses over the offseason.

Arthur Smith, the architect of their play-action-heavy offensive scheme, is off to Atlanta to work his black magic on Matt Ryan. Enter Todd Downing, an offensive coordinator with exactly one year of experience with the job—he coordinated the Raiders to a 3.6% offensive DVOA in 2017 as they dropped from seventh to 13th in the NFL. Derek Carr had thrived under Bill Musgrave in 2016 but regressed so heavily in the next two years that the Raiders broke open the pocketbook and reeled in Jon Gruden to try to save him. Downing didn't speak to the media until June, where he noted that "There'd be pressure if I looked at it as my job to fill Arthur's shoes. ... Each year is its own year and its own components. ... It's my job to be the best version of me and best coordinator for this offense I can be," and "It's certainly an easier job

having Derrick Henry back there." It wasn't exactly a press availability that betrayed a lot of actionable insights, but that doesn't necessarily mean the offense is heading off a cliff either. As great as Smith was for this offense, it's not like he was elevated to offensive coordinator as some hotshot whiz kid—he took over as a complete unknown and did a great job. The Titans are largely hoping the same thing will happen here, albeit with an offensive coordinator that is wearing one bad season around his neck. Sometimes that past season is a bellwether for the future, but sometimes Brian Daboll turns Josh Allen into a superstar.

The Titans responded to personnel losses by coming out spending, particularly on defense. They gave Bud Dupree a five-year, $82.5-million deal with $35 million of guarantees—but a ridiculously small cap hit in 2021 of just $5.1 million. They patched cornerback with Janoris Jenkins in a deal built largely the same way—a $4.6-million cap hit in 2021 becomes $10.2 million in 2022. Denico Autry signed up for $21.5 million over three years ($3.5-million cap number in 2021, $8.6 million in 2022). Then, in the coup de grace, they landed star wideout Julio Jones from the Falcons in early June as an over-the-top move to take the lead in the AFC South arms race for all media intents and purposes. To do that, they had to restructure Tannehill's contract to the point that Tannehill's cap hit in 2022 is now (not a typo) $38.6 million. The 2022 Titans already have almost $200 million in committed cap space right now, before they even get into the question of how long Jones is going to be there. There are a lot of long-term ramifications to the way that the Titans have crafted this offseason, but it's absolutely what they needed to do to stay in the AFC South discussion.

General manager Jon Robinson wouldn't really take the bait on "win-now" mode or "all-in" questions, but he told *Sports Illustrated*'s Albert Breer that "It's my responsibility to try to get as many good football players on the team as possible. You understand that part about winning and wanting to compete for championships. You've got to have the players in place to go do that, and that's part of my job—to make decisions to try to put our team in position to compete for that."

Both Robinson and Vrabel credited the blessing of Nick Saban with chasing Jones. "When we've got a chance to shoot, we shoot," Robinson told reporters at a post-trade press availability, "Like all these basketball players do, they don't quit shooting three-pointers if they miss one, they keep shooting." From a scouting standpoint, the only thing that went wrong with Jones last season was when he tried to play through injury—he finished second in receiving DVOA and hasn't finished below 21st in receiving DVOA since 2015. Jones turned 32 in May, but as with Henry, he's built to take punishment and hasn't shown any signs of speed slippage yet.

Robinson has by no means been a bad general manager, but declining Davis' fifth-year option and losing Jonnu Smith in free agency means the team employs just four offensive non-rookies he drafted since starting in 2016: Henry, A.J. Brown, Nate Davis, and Darrynton Evans. (It sure would help if Isaiah Wilson hadn't rapped his way out of the NFL.) The Titans have largely focused on drafting defensive players over that timespan, notably trading up at a heavy cost for edge rusher Harold Landry. But that defense stunk out loud last season and there is almost no cause for optimism on that front.

Vrabel has been a sneaky-smart situational head coach who has stolen some big seconds for his team with strategic maneuvers during games, but he had no success actually coordinating a defense in Houston (without J.J. Watt in 2017) and his right-hand man, Shane Bowen, was destroyed last season by both local media and raw numbers. (Bowen called the plays as linebackers coach last season and was officially promoted to defensive coordinator for 2021.)

Only two teams had a worse pass defense DVOA than Tennessee last season, and no team has a worse defensive projection for 2021 even after all of that money was spent on Dupree, Jenkins, and Autry. The Titans also took two high-round swings at defensive backs on draft day, Caleb Farley and Elijah Molden. At least the Titans decided to turn over much of the defense instead of just standing pat, and they get credit for the additions in our projection system. But the Titans also lost useful veteran starters such as DaQuan Jones and Malcolm Butler. Of the Titans' top 11 players by defensive snaps, only six return: Landry, Kevin Byard, Rashaan Evans, Jeffery Simmons, Jayon Brown, and Amani Hooker. Simmons flashed star power last year and was a major bright spot for the unit, but the only other returning player in that group who feels like a core building block as we sit here in summer 2021 is Byard. The guys that were tasked with fixing the pass rush last year, Jadeveon Clowney and Vic Beasley, were such busts that they are already gone.

Vrabel led off his post-free agency press conference by saying that he doesn't know how much better anybody is—that wasn't surprising because Vrabel often comes off a little irritated and at times can feel downright angsty in pressers—and refused to answer a question about why he was confident in elevating Bowen to defensive coordinator beyond saying he was confident and excited. That was part of a frequent questioning process about Bowen from the local media that seemed to tick off Vrabel. It's easy to understand why the media wants to understand more given how poor the results on the field were last year.

"Finding ways to be more aggressive in coverage, to challenge receivers more, I think that's all part of it as we progress on," Bowen said at OTAs, as he promoted getting players into a position to succeed and getting better at communication without promising widespread scheme changes. Vrabel noted the next day that communication failures were on the players, which seems to point more towards the cause for the 30th-ranked pass defense DVOA not being coaching. We're not saying that the players didn't blow coverages at times last season, but Bowen and Vrabel have a combined zero seasons of coordinating a top-20 DVOA defense between them and neither has much experience in the role. We think it's OK to be skeptical of the grander plan.

Dupree and Autry are an honest stab at fixing the pressure problem; the Titans have three straight seasons in the bottom 10 of pressure rate and finished just 31st in adjusted sack rate. They went sackless for almost the entire month of December. But those are only two solid pass-rushers. Dupree and Autry aren't going to command double-teams or handily win one-on-one on a down-by-down basis. Only four players on the team had more than a single sack last year, and two of them—DaQuan Jones and Jack Crawford—weren't brought back. None of these guys is a flat-out monster in a vacuum, so the unit will be reliant on winning mismatches. Dupree's sack rate is high, but his pressure rates have been consistently mediocre, i.e., lower than Landry's. Dupree also played on a high-sack, high-pressure defense and is coming off a torn ACL. The Titans should probably be thrilled if he finds eight more sacks this year. So unless this extremely young cornerback corps is going to be up to covering for four seconds every other passing down, the Titans are going to need to be more creative in both getting pressure and finishing it.

From a non-analytical standpoint, it's easy to see how people are coming to the conclusion that the Titans should be AFC South favorites. No unit in this division has a higher established ceiling than the Titans' offense, and their division rivals are either struggling with quarterback uncertainty or coming off a 1-15 season. It makes a lot of sense to just believe that the Titans will continue to roll behind Tannehill and Henry, particularly now that they have yet another superstar receiver to line up across from Brown.

But there are absolutely a few warning beacons on the horizon, from Henry's workload over the past two years, to the loss of Arthur Smith and some of the key offensive core in 2020, to the plan on defense and the continued employment of Bowen. The defense is the biggest reason for our underwhelming prediction, but we also have the Titans with a surprisingly low offensive projection for a team that has finished fourth and sixth in offensive DVOA over the last two years. That is why our forecast for this division settles more on the Colts and Titans battling for the division title rather than giving the Titans a major step ahead on the field.

We can absolutely understand someone who would take these underlying metrics, weigh them against the Titans' recent history, and scoff at the numbers (or, as is more common, tell us that Dorks Value Only Analytics, maybe with an added Titan Up! or two). But even if you do believe this offense is going to avoid a stumble, the defense is going to need to take a major step forward for Tennessee to become an upper-crust

AFC contender rather than the team that makes the playoffs because someone in this division has to.

Robinson has pushed a lot of the costs to the future to keep this team competitive, and I think that's something that we should applaud a little. For every team that should be trying to maximize their chances in the now, there are probably two or three teams that marry themselves to their process. We have seen what happened to Aaron Rodgers this offseason when the Packers drafted Jordan Love instead of receiver help and failed to go after free agents aggressively. The Broncos have a stellar roster attached to quarterbacks that nobody wants. The reason the Falcons had to deal Jones in the first place is because they got very attached to their roster and paid to keep it together even though it wasn't good enough, all the while telling Jones they'd get him another restructure eventually until he ran out of interest in waiting. It's refreshing to see a process that can be as simple as "we would like to collect as many good players as we can."

Certainly, the Titans will have some business decisions to make in 2022 because of this. From an analytical standpoint, this team is pushing its chips in with a pair of fours and hoping nobody catches a high card. But at least they're pushing.

Rivers McCown

2020 Titans by Week

Wk	vs.	W-L	PF	PA	YDF	YDA	TO	Total	Off	Def	ST
1	at DEN	W	16	14	377	323	1	-28.9%	6.9%	5.1%	-30.7%
2	JAX	W	33	30	354	480	2	-3.8%	20.4%	32.6%	8.4%
3	at MIN	W	31	30	444	464	2	-3.3%	-8.2%	2.9%	7.8%
4	BYE										
5	BUF	W	42	16	334	370	3	84.6%	44.3%	-27.4%	12.9%
6	HOU	W	42	36	607	412	-2	8.9%	50.9%	23.8%	-18.2%
7	PIT	L	24	27	292	362	3	-6.5%	15.7%	-6.7%	-28.9%
8	at CIN	L	20	31	441	367	-1	-20.4%	31.9%	38.4%	-14.0%
9	CHI	W	24	17	228	375	2	1.6%	0.9%	-2.5%	-1.8%
10	IND	L	17	34	294	430	0	-36.9%	12.0%	20.7%	-28.2%
11	at BAL	W	30	24	423	306	0	27.1%	17.4%	-7.5%	2.1%
12	at IND	W	45	26	449	336	1	43.6%	44.2%	10.6%	10.0%
13	CLE	L	35	41	431	458	-2	-23.1%	-10.6%	15.1%	2.7%
14	at JAX	W	31	10	454	354	0	31.8%	34.7%	8.1%	5.2%
15	DET	W	46	25	463	430	3	30.2%	46.0%	17.0%	1.2%
16	at GB	L	14	40	260	448	-1	-61.4%	-30.8%	32.8%	2.3%
17	at HOU	W	41	38	492	457	0	-8.1%	8.7%	16.0%	-0.8%
18	BAL	L	13	20	209	401	0	-23.4%	-26.7%	4.7%	8.0%

Trends and Splits

	Offense	Rank	Defense	Rank
Total DVOA	18.4%	4	11.5%	29
Unadjusted VOA	21.9%	3	9.5%	28
Weighted Trend	19.1%	4	12.2%	29
Variance	5.4%	14	3.0%	4
Average Opponent	2.6%	30	-0.5%	18
Passing	39.5%	4	25.3%	30
Rushing	6.1%	2	-8.8%	16
First Down	10.3%	8	11.0%	26
Second Down	22.3%	3	2.6%	17
Third Down	29.8%	4	24.8%	29
First Half	20.2%	4	6.6%	25
Second Half	16.8%	4	16.9%	30
Red Zone	33.1%	3	11.0%	25
Late and Close	16.1%	6	5.9%	22

Five-Year Performance

Year	W-L	Pyth W	Est W	PF	PA	TO	Total	Rk	Off	Rk	Def	Rk	ST	Rk	Off AGL	Rk	Def AGL	Rk	Off Age	Rk	Def Age	Rk	ST Age	Rk
2016	9-7	8.1	8.5	381	378	0	2.0%	17	10.8%	9	7.6%	26	-1.1%	19	20.7	4	13.1	2	26.2	24	27.0	8	26.2	14
2017	9-7	7.4	7.5	334	356	-4	-6.2%	18	-2.1%	18	5.7%	23	1.6%	13	10.8	5	16.6	7	26.5	22	26.9	10	26.8	2
2018	9-7	8.2	7.5	310	303	-1	-6.0%	21	-5.6%	23	1.3%	18	0.8%	13	29.4	10	35.3	20	26.2	23	26.4	14	26.6	6
2019	9-7	9.9	9.1	402	331	+6	7.6%	10	13.0%	6	1.9%	18	-3.5%	29	19.7	7	23.9	6	26.7	18	26.3	17	26.0	13
2020	11-5	9.2	8.4	491	439	+11	2.5%	14	18.4%	4	11.5%	29	-4.4%	28	27.8	7	29.7	10	27.5	5	26.5	13	27.3	2

2020 Performance Based on Most Common Personnel Groups

TEN Offense					TEN Offense vs. Opponents					TEN Defense				TEN Defense vs. Opponents			
Pers	Freq	Yds	DVOA	Run%	Pers	Freq	Yds	DVOA	Run%	Pers	Freq	Yds	DVOA	Pers	Freq	Yds	DVOA
11	40%	6.2	26.2%	36%	Base	45%	6.6	12.5%	62%	Base	21%	5.8	-2.9%	11	66%	6.0	12.5%
12	33%	6.9	16.9%	53%	Nickel	45%	6.2	27.2%	39%	Nickel	52%	5.9	13.3%	12	15%	6.4	26.0%
21	10%	6.7	5.6%	69%	Dime+	8%	5.9	30.3%	11%	Dime+	26%	6.4	21.3%	13	4%	6.3	9.8%
13	8%	5.7	33.8%	53%	Goal Line	0%	1.0	122.9%	75%	Goal Line	1%	0.8	15.0%	21	4%	7.0	-15.1%
22	4%	6.8	20.6%	64%						Big	1%	7.8	-23.1%	22	3%	4.5	-12.8%

Strategic Tendencies

Run/Pass		Rk	Formation		Rk	Pass Rush		Rk	Secondary		Rk	Strategy		Rk
Runs, first half	46%	3	Form: Single Back	77%	24	Rush 3	11.1%	9	4 DB	21%	21	Play Action	36%	3
Runs, first down	62%	1	Form: Empty Back	3%	30	Rush 4	67.4%	14	5 DB	52%	26	Offensive Motion	57%	4
Runs, second-long	34%	4	Form: Multi Back	20%	6	Rush 5	18.0%	22	6+ DB	26%	7	Avg Box (Off)	6.85	4
Runs, power sit.	67%	8	Pers: 3+ WR	43%	30	Rush 6+	3.5%	23	Man Coverage	36%	12	Avg Box (Def)	6.61	16
Runs, behind 2H	40%	2	Pers: 2+ TE/6+ OL	49%	2	Edge Rusher Sacks	39.5%	27	CB by Sides	74%	14	Offensive Pace	28.56	3
Pass, ahead 2H	39%	30	Pers: 6+ OL	2%	14	Interior DL Sacks	36.8%	6	S/CB Cover Ratio	23%	24	Defensive Pace	30.38	19
Run-Pass Options	2%	30	Shotgun/Pistol	42%	31	Second Level Sacks	23.7%	16	DB Blitz	14%	15	Go for it on 4th	1.95	7

One trend that continued from 2019 is that the Titans offense was best when it could stay on schedule. Tennessee ranked in the top eight for every down-and-distance split except third-and-long, where they were 19th. ● The Titans were one of just two teams, along with Miami, to allow a lower pressure rate on third downs (17.0%) than on first and second down (20.4%). ● Tennessee ranked second behind Cleveland using max protect blocking on 12.5% of pass plays (defined as seven or more blockers with at least two more blockers than pass-rushers). ● Tennessee was next to last, narrowly ahead of Pittsburgh, throwing just 12% of passes to running backs. ● The Titans dropped significantly in broken tackles, going from second with 166 broken tackles in 2019 to 20th with 109 broken tackles in 2020. Derrick Henry still ranked third with 61 broken tackles and A.J. Brown was tied for fifth among receivers with 21, but the rest of the team had far fewer than the year before. ● The tackling numbers were better on defense, where Tennessee was tied for seventh with only 102 broken tackles. Since the Titans faced so many plays, they were second best in the rate of plays with at least one broken tackle (8.4%). ● Tennessee's top three safeties all made their average plays in at about the same yardage downfield, suggesting that their roles were fairly interchangeable.

Passing

Player	DYAR	DVOA	Plays	NtYds	Avg	YAC	C%	TD	Int
R.Tannehill	1046	19.6%	505	3636	7.2	4.9	65.6%	33	7

Rushing

Player	DYAR	DVOA	Plays	Yds	Avg	TD	Fum	Suc
D.Henry	386	15.5%	377	2027	5.4	17	3	57%
J.McNichols	-4	-10.9%	47	204	4.3	1	0	45%
R.Tannehill	127	49.3%	35	254	7.3	7	1	--
D.Foreman*	26	20.4%	22	95	4.3	0	0	41%
D.Evans	-8	-19.7%	14	54	3.9	0	0	64%
B.Hill	0	-8.6%	100	465	4.7	1	1	48%

Receiving

Player	DYAR	DVOA	Plays	Ctch	Yds	Y/C	YAC	TD	C%
A.J.Brown	332	25.0%	106	70	1075	15.4	6.2	11	66%
C.Davis*	261	22.5%	92	65	984	15.1	4.5	5	71%
A.Humphries*	18	-5.8%	35	23	228	9.9	2.0	2	66%
K.Raymond*	34	16.2%	15	9	187	20.8	4.2	0	60%
C.Batson	38	23.2%	13	12	100	8.3	3.6	1	92%
N.Westbrook-Ikhine	-19	-42.6%	8	3	33	11.0	1.7	0	38%
J.Reynolds	13	-10.6%	81	52	618	11.9	4.3	2	64%
J.Jones	231	29.8%	68	51	771	15.1	4.5	3	75%
J.Smith*	65	7.2%	65	41	448	10.9	5.8	8	63%
A.Firkser	36	2.8%	53	39	387	9.9	3.7	1	74%
G.Swaim	18	13.6%	11	9	83	9.2	3.9	1	82%
M.Pruitt*	2	-4.2%	8	5	49	9.8	2.6	2	63%
D.Henry	-75	-53.3%	31	19	114	6.0	6.7	0	61%
J.McNichols	-32	-50.0%	17	12	55	4.6	4.3	0	71%
B.Hill	29	3.7%	30	25	199	8.0	6.5	0	83%

Offensive Line

Player	Pos	Age	GS	Snaps	Pen	Sk	Pass	Run	Player	Pos	Age	GS	Snaps	Pen	Sk	Pass	Run
Nate Davis	RG	25	16/16	1072	6	1	11	13	David Quessenberry	LT	31	12/6	436	2	3.5	11	4
Dennis Kelly*	RT	31	16/16	1047	2	1	15	10	Ty Sambrailo	LT	29	10/5	413	2	3.5	11	3
Ben Jones	C	32	16/16	1041	4	0.5	3	14	Taylor Lewan	LT	30	5/5	239	0	0	5	2
Rodger Saffold	LG	33	15/15	870	3	4	13	8									

Year	Yards	ALY	Rk	Power	Rk	Stuff	Rk	2Lev	Rk	OpFld	Rk	BB Rt	Rk	Sacks	ASR	Rk	Press	Rk	BB Rt	Rk	Cont
2018	4.25	4.33	17	67%	17	19%	17	1.15	24	0.83	18	7.1%	21	47	10.2%	29	25.7%	5	7.8%	12	24
2019	4.83	4.65	4	73%	5	18%	15	1.36	3	1.05	5	10.9%	23	56	11.2%	32	28.6%	9	15.0%	28	34
2020	5.17	4.97	2	71%	10	15%	9	1.44	2	1.14	3	11.9%	26	25	5.5%	11	21.4%	7	13.6%	20	32

| 2020 ALY by direction: | Left End: 4.58 (11) | Left Tackle: 4.20 (16) | Mid/Guard: 4.94 (3) | Right Tackle: 5.43 (3) | Right End: 5.73 (4) |

The plan to replace Jack Conklin hit a roadblock last year when first-round pick Isaiah Wilson went AWOL and the Titans had to release him, leaving swing tackle Dennis Kelly starting for the entire season. The Titans didn't invite Kelly back, so the competition at right tackle appears to be between Kendall Lamm, David Quessenberry, Ty Sambrailo, and rookie second-round pick Dillon Radunz (North Dakota State). Radunz noted that he was a big follower of Taylor Lewan's podcast in his post-draft availability and profiles as a toolsy (5.16s 40-yard dash at 301 pounds, 7.26s 3-cone drill) tackle who will look to continue the recent tradition of high-round picks on non-FBS linemen paying off. Jon Robinson mentioned meeting Radunz at the Senior Bowl as a big factor in being comfortable with the pick. The bar to clear isn't high, with Lamm and Sambrailo being more journeymen than obvious starters. ● Sambrailo and Quessenberry got playing time last year because of Lewan's torn ACL in Week 6. The stalwart tackle has now missed 15 games in the last two years while carrying an $18.6-million cap figure. He has been very good, but another year dinged up might make it awfully hard to consider keeping him at that contract level. ● Rodger Saffold had yet another slow start—in 2019 he allowed nine blown blocks and six sacks in his first five weeks, and in 2020 nine of his blown blocks came in the first six weeks. The good news is that Saffold was better in 2020 than in 2019 and shut down pass-rushers during the stretch run. ● Saffold and center Ben Jones are both pushing the bounds of "grizzled veteran," but Jones continues to be excellent. He has started every game of the last five seasons but one—almost 4,766 snaps— and has been charted with just 61 total blown blocks over that timespan. ● At right guard, Nate Davis continues to show a lot of push and get a lot of movement as a run-blocker, and he took a step forward in cutting his overall blown block rate from 4.2% as a rookie to 2.4% last season. He still could stand to take another step forward in pass-protection, but last year was very encouraging for his growth.

Defensive Front

Defensive Line	Age	Pos	G	Snaps	Plays	TmPct	Rk	Stop	Dfts	BTkl	Runs	St%	Rk	RuYd	Rk	Sack	Hit	Hur	Dsrpt
						Overall							vs. Run				Pass Rush		
Jeffery Simmons	24	DE	15	838	54	6.6%	16	37	11	4	41	66%	74	2.8	59	3.0	12	21	7
DaQuan Jones*	30	DT	16	704	49	5.7%	34	32	9	3	43	65%	75	2.2	40	2.0	3	11	0
Jack Crawford*	33	DE	16	473	28	3.2%	79	19	6	2	24	71%	54	2.8	58	2.0	9	13	0
Matt Dickerson*	26	DT	10	196	10	1.8%	--	6	1	0	8	63%	--	2.4	--	0.0	1	0	0

Edge Rushers	Age	Pos	G	Snaps	Plays	TmPct	Rk	Stop	Dfts	BTkl	Runs	St%	Rk	RuYd	Rk	Sack	Hit	Hur	Dsrpt
						Overall							vs. Run				Pass Rush		
Harold Landry	25	OLB	16	1048	74	8.5%	3	47	16	8	48	67%	60	3.0	68	5.5	10	37	5
Jadeveon Clowney*	28	OLB	8	425	22	5.1%	42	14	5	2	16	56%	88	2.3	40	0.0	6	17	4
Derick Roberson	26	OLB	8	246	7	1.6%	97	5	2	0	5	60%	81	4.0	92	0.0	2	10	1
Denico Autry	31	DE	14	631	33	4.6%	51	26	12	5	23	74%	37	2.3	38	7.5	2	22	1
Bud Dupree	28	OLB	11	609	33	6.0%	26	28	17	4	18	72%	47	1.7	19	8.0	7	24	6

Linebackers	Age	Pos	G	Snaps	Plays	TmPct	Rk	Stop	Dfts	BTkl	Runs	St%	Rk	RuYd	Rk	Sack	Hit	Hur	Tgts	Suc%	Rk	Yd/P	Rk	PD	Int
						Overall						vs. Run				Pass Rush				vs. Pass					
Rashaan Evans	26	ILB	16	893	101	11.6%	49	47	13	4	64	56%	41	4.7	69	0.5	4	10	17	41%	57	6.5	41	5	0
Jayon Brown	26	ILB	10	653	83	15.3%	20	42	13	3	42	52%	57	4.7	74	1.0	1	3	30	53%	28	5.5	26	8	1
David Long	25	ILB	14	378	52	6.9%	74	27	8	11	28	64%	17	2.8	3	0.0	0	3	20	40%	61	7.9	64	2	0

Year	Yards	ALY	Rk	Power	Rk	Stuff	Rk	2Lev	Rk	OpFld	Rk	BB Rt	Rk	Sacks	ASR	Rk	Press	Rk	BB Rt	Rk
2018	4.29	4.82	28	64%	13	16%	23	1.19	13	0.64	9	5.7%	29	39	6.7%	22	27.6%	26	10.5%	18
2019	4.01	4.09	9	63%	13	18%	18	1.03	7	0.76	17	11.7%	21	43	7.1%	14	25.1%	30	12.1%	28
2020	4.60	4.31	14	63%	8	16%	20	1.23	18	1.01	27	13.6%	14	19	3.9%	31	23.0%	24	11.1%	25
2020 ALY by direction:		Left End: 4.99 (23)			Left Tackle: 3.76 (10)			Mid/Guard: 4.12 (9)				Right Tackle: 4.38 (18)					Right End: 5.14 (26)			

As pointed out earlier, Bud Dupree's sack-to-hurry ratio tends to be a bit out of alignment. On the other hand, the biggest reason he didn't have yet another 10-sack season was that he tore his ACL in Week 12. "I'll be full speed in camp," Dupree told reporters at a post-signing availability. "I'll be healthy way before camp, I'll be full-speed training in May." Dupree is working out on his own so we won't know the truth behind those words until training camp. ● What Jeffery Simmons did last year while only having three sacks was incredible. He was credited with 21 hurries, which is a huge step up from just four in 2019 and puts him solidly in the upper tier of interior pass-rushers. If he puts it all together this year and converts some of those hurries to sacks, he could be an easy one-for-one replacement for an in-his-prime Jurrell Casey. ● Harold Landry finished in the top 10 in quarterback hurries after finishing in the top 25 last year, but between the two seasons he has only 14.5 sacks to show for it. To Landry's credit, he did cut his broken tackle numbers a little bit, but eight of his hurries came in a Week 17 game that was meaningless for Houston without Laremy Tunsil. Titans fans are still waiting for him to put it all together, which isn't a sentence you want to write about someone entering the last year of their rookie contract. ◥ With DaQuan Jones gone, the Titans have a real hole at nose tackle—they signed Abry Jones (ex-Jaguars) in May and otherwise have Trevon Coley and a bunch of UDFA's and inexperienced depth at the position. ◥ The Titans were very fortunate that Jayon Brown found the market wanting and took a one-year prove-it deal to come back after missing the last six games of the year with an elbow injury, as Brown was the only linebacker the team rostered last year who could provide any semblance of pass coverage. Brown backed defensive coordinator Shane Bowen at OTAs: "Shane's a really good coach and we trust him and he makes great play-call decisions and we've just gotta go out there and execute it." ◥ David Long was bullied as often as that missed tackle number up there says he was, and Rashaan Evans has become more notable for his ejections and playing the run solidly than he has for being a three-down linebacker. Evans became the second first-round pick in two years to have his fifth-year option declined by the club. ◥ With Evans on his way out, it was an easy decision for the Titans to spend a high pick on Georgia linebacker Monty Rice. Rice popped a 4.58s 40-yard dash at his pro day and showed a lot of production at a major program as a run-stuffer. As a pass defender? Well, there are tools, but his shiftiness was questioned by draftniks and he had just five passes defensed his entire college career. As a rookie, Rice will likely be a special teams contributor behind Long unless he wows the team in training camp.

Defensive Secondary

Secondary	Age	Pos	G	Snaps	Plays	Overall TmPct	Rk	Stop	Dfts	BTkl	vs. Run Runs	St%	Rk	RuYd	Rk	vs. Pass Tgts	Tgt%	Rk	aDOT	Suc%	Rk	Yd/P	Rk	PD	Int
Kevin Byard	28	FS	16	1101	118	13.6%	8	33	11	5	56	32%	43	6.3	31	35	7.7%	42	9.4	43%	54	6.4	17	7	1
Malcolm Butler*	31	CB	16	1085	114	13.1%	1	40	10	10	34	32%	59	8.8	67	111	24.7%	8	11.1	49%	51	7.5	37	14	4
Kenny Vaccaro*	30	SS	13	871	87	12.4%	18	37	12	11	36	64%	3	5.5	23	31	8.6%	33	9.4	45%	49	7.7	34	5	0
Desmond King*	27	CB	15	708	56	6.9%	72	26	7	4	17	53%	19	4.8	20	38	12.6%	78	7.7	53%	33	6.8	24	2	0
Amani Hooker	23	FS	16	466	52	6.0%	--	18	7	9	14	64%	--	4.4	--	14	7.3%	--	15.6	29%	--	10.9	--	8	4
Johnathan Joseph*	37	CB	11	423	37	6.2%	--	13	6	4	10	60%	--	3.0	--	36	20.6%	--	12.1	39%	--	8.8	--	6	1
Breon Borders	26	CB	6	359	31	9.5%	--	15	4	4	5	40%	--	5.4	--	41	27.6%	--	12.5	59%	--	7.0	--	5	1
Chris Jackson	23	CB	11	239	22	3.7%	--	6	4	5	7	43%	--	3.7	--	20	20.2%	--	11.0	35%	--	7.9	--	1	0
Janoris Jenkins	33	CB	13	805	67	10.4%	16	26	9	5	13	46%	33	3.9	9	71	21.9%	23	14.0	52%	37	8.1	51	12	3
Chris Jones	26	CB	9	273	19	4.1%	--	5	1	5	1	100%	--	3.0	--	26	24.4%	--	11.0	31%	--	9.3	--	0	0

Year	Pass D Rank	vs. #1 WR	Rk	vs. #2 WR	Rk	vs. Other WR	Rk	WR Wide	Rk	WR Slot	Rk	vs. TE	Rk	vs. RB	Rk
2018	21	5.8%	20	26.1%	30	5.3%	21	8.5%	26	19.2%	26	-10.6%	11	-31.6%	2
2019	21	19.5%	29	-39.4%	2	25.3%	30	9.5%	24	-0.9%	9	4.4%	19	12.1%	23
2020	30	-2.7%	15	1.0%	19	-14.8%	8	-27.2%	3	-6.5%	11	36.6%	32	5.9%	22

Here's where it sinks or swims. Last year's top three corners in snap count are gone. So is Adoree' Jackson, who was cut after a year lost to injury. ◥ 2020 second-rounder Kristian Fulton only saw 12 coverage targets last year, mostly out of the slot, and his sample from the Week 6 game against the Texans (four catches on four targets, 34 yards, one touchdown, one 28-yard DPI) was not great. After Week 7, the Titans placed him on injured reserve, and after he was activated again the Titans made him a healthy scratch until Week 17. Fulton had plenty of buzz coming into the draft and most rookie corners struggle, but his improvement or lack thereof will have a major impact for the Titans at the position. ◥ Spending on Janoris Jenkins to be the veteran stopgap should be fine as long as the Titans aren't expecting an ace corner. Jackrabbit has been one of the better outside corners in the league over his tenure, but he's turning 33 in October, was frequently targeted as the Saints' non-Marshon Lattimore corner, and gave up some plays deep while getting called for DPI six times last year. At his inaugural presser Jenkins summed up his mindset as "I'm not concerned about nothin'. Wherever I go I'm going to be a baller, I'm gonna ball, I'm gonna continue to ball and just lead." ◥ The Titans spent two top-100 picks on corners, and it sure seems that first-rounder Caleb Farley (Virginia Tech) has the inside track to an outside corner job early. You may remember Farley watching the draft alone because of COVID concerns. Medical questions pushed him further down in the pecking order than the tape might have otherwise merited. (Farley has had multiple back surgeries, but only missed two 2019 games because of it. He was a COVID opt-out in 2020.) Describing his best fit in a defense as "Caleb, you've got that guy," Farley profiles as an outside corner with a 6-foot-1 frame and 4.3s 40 speed. ◥ Elijah Molden (Washington), son of former NFLer Alex, is only 5-foot-9 but diagnoses well as a slot/safety hybrid and plays beyond his physical traits. That led to some around the scouting circuit slapping a Tyrann Mathieu comp on him. Jon Robinson raved about Molden in a post-draft show on Titans All-Access where he noted Molden had watched some of Tennessee's games last season and enjoyed the way they used their nickel corners. ◥ Breon Borders has played for four different teams in four NFL years—on the active roster for all of them—and was targeted eight times per game in his five starts. ❧ Last year was the first season that Kevin Byard didn't record at least four picks since his debut in 2016, and his passes defensed were also low while his tackle numbers were way up as he played a lot more in the box than he had in the years prior. ❧ The one bright spot in last year's secondary was young safety Amani Hooker, who broke in behind Kenny Vaccaro and had a successful sophomore season. Hooker should step into Vaccaro's role ably this season and came to OTAs notably slimmer than he was in 2020.

Special Teams

Year	DVOA	Rank	FG/XP	Rank	Net Kick	Rank	Kick Ret	Rank	Net Punt	Rank	Punt Ret	Rank	Hidden	Rank
2018	0.8%	13	-1.8	21	-7.2	31	13.6	1	2.3	15	-2.8	23	-5.6	23
2019	-3.5%	29	-14.9	32	-2.9	23	-2.9	27	5.1	8	-1.7	19	6.3	6
2020	-4.4%	28	-8.2	28	-1.4	20	-4.7	29	-8.5	28	0.8	14	4.3	12

The Titans have moved on from veteran kicker Stephen Gostkowski, who hit only 69% of his field goals last season. They're going with a camp battle between 2020 UDFA Tucker McCann and 2021 UDFA Blake Haubeil. Jon Robinson more or less dismissed a reunion with Gostkowski at his post-draft presser. ❧ Primary punt returner Kalif Raymond signed with the Lions in free agency, making Cameron Batson, the primary kick returner, the likely replacement. This may also open up some return reps for Darrynton Evans, who returned kicks in all three of his seasons at Appalachian State and had three return touchdowns. ❧ While the Titans punt unit struggled last year, Brett Kern still finished in the top 10 in gross punt value. The team has brought in UDFA James Smith to work in camp in an ominous move. Kern has been a franchise stalwart since 2009, but he's now 35, missed three games last season, and has a top-five cap hit among all punters at $3.8 million. The non-Kern punters the Titans used last year, Trevor Daniel and Ryan Allen, combined for -8.8 gross points of field position.

Washington Football Team

2020 Record: 7-9	**Total DVOA:** -2.3% (30)	**2021 Mean Projection:** 8.1 wins	**On the Clock (0-5):** 18%
Pythagorean Wins: 8.2 (14)	**Offense:** -21.8% (32)	**Postseason Odds:** 39.4%	**Mediocrity (6-8):** 38%
Snap-Weighted Age: 26 (25)	**Defense:** -18.3% (3)	**Super Bowl Odds:** 3.6%	**Playoff Contender (9-11):** 32%
Average Opponent: -3.8% (28)	**Special Teams:** 1.1% (15)	**Proj. Avg. Opponent:** 1% (11)	**Super Bowl Contender (12+):** 11%

2020: Nothing we did at quarterback worked.

2021: Bah Gawd, that's Ryan Fitzpatrick's music.

Any number of things could have derailed the 2020 season for the Washington Football Team, a franchise that has been no stranger to cultivating a circus environment. The organization was finally in the midst of changing the team's racist nickname, settling for the simple and temporary (or potentially permanent) "Washington Football Team," and that might not have made the top five of wild stories from the season.

Owner Dan Snyder and the franchise were hit with sexual misconduct claims in July from current and former cheerleaders, as well as other women around the organization. In August, new head coach Ron Rivera announced he had cancer, which caused him to receive chemo treatments until his final session at the end of October. In December, benched-then-reinstated starter Dwayne Haskins was photographed maskless in a strip club during a pandemic season. He started the following week against Rivera's old team, the Carolina Panthers, but was benched mid-game and released the following day. Yet this team won the NFC East, albeit with only seven wins thanks to an awful division, and hung close with the eventual Super Bowl champions in the wild-card round.

Expectations couldn't have been much lower going into the 2020 season for Washington. In last year's *Almanac*, Washington had the lowest projected DVOA, second-lowest projected win total, and second-lowest odds to make the playoffs. Much of that stemmed from a projected league-worst offense that lived down to those expectations. Instead, the catalyst for the playoff appearance was a massive defensive turnaround in the first year under head coach Ron Rivera and defensive coordinator Jack Del Rio.

Defensive improvement was always a possibility. Last year's *Almanac* even hinted at it: "The defense is rich with talent so that Rivera and defensive coordinator Jack Del Rio have a chance to find immediate success." So a potential Year 1 leap was in the cards under a new coaching staff, but immediately turning into one of the league's best defenses wasn't the expectation. That's what happened as a defense that ranked 27th in DVOA during 2019 jumped to third in 2020.

Washington's improvement on defense was the culmination of high draft picks and breakout seasons coming together, especially along the defensive line. With the second overall pick last year, Washington selected Ohio State edge rusher Chase Young. Young played in 15 games during his rookie season and was on the field for 74% of the defensive snaps. He totaled 7.5 sacks with four passes defensed and four forced fumbles. He was seventh among edge rushers in ESPN's Pass Rush Win Rate metric. All of that resulted in Young being named Defensive Rookie of the Year.

Young was added to a defensive line that already had 2019 first-round pick Montez Sweat on the other edge plus 2017 first-round pick Jonathan Allen and 2018 first-round pick Daron Payne inside. With that star-studded line, Washington relied heavily on rushing just four on pass plays, which they did 68% of the time (11th in the NFL). Washington ranked sixth in yards per play and ninth in defensive DVOA with a four-man rush.

Washington had a league-average blitz rate, but the defense was among the best when rushing five or more. The defense had the lowest yards per play allowed and the lowest DVOA by 10% with a pass rush of five or more. A lot of that came from effective defensive back blitzes, where Washington also ranked first in DVOA (-65.4%).

The ability to rely consistently on the four-man defensive line allowed the defense to use those blitzes as well-timed weapons rather than a necessity to create pressure. It also allowed the defense to keep seven defenders back in coverage and flood the shallow areas of the field, where Washington ranked second in DVOA against short passes.

Can this type of defensive production continue for the 2021 season? The Plexiglass Principle is certainly in play here, where teams that significantly improve on one side of the ball tend to see that unit decline the following season. Washington's defensive improvement was the eighth-biggest year-to-year jump in the DVOA database, which now goes back to 1983. Of the seven defenses with bigger year-to-year jumps, only two stayed in the top 10 the following season and three dropped to 26th or worse (Table 1).

On a more positive note, the seven teams immediately behind Washington on Table 1 all finished in the top six the following season. The Washington defense could be more aligned with that group of teams than the ones above them.

The bottom of Table 1 presents three case studies over the past two seasons, two of which offer optimism for Washington's 2021 defense. Each of the 49ers, Buccaneers, and Patriots made big leaps from the 2018 to 2019 seasons. In their leap years, the 49ers (second-youngest) and Buccaneers

2021 Football Team Schedule

Week	Opp.	Week	Opp.	Week	Opp.
1	LAC	7	at GB	13	at LV
2	NYG (Thu.)	8	at DEN	14	DAL
3	at BUF	9	BYE	15	at PHI
4	at ATL	10	TB	16	at DAL
5	NO	11	at CAR	17	PHI
6	KC	12	SEA (Mon.)	18	at NYG

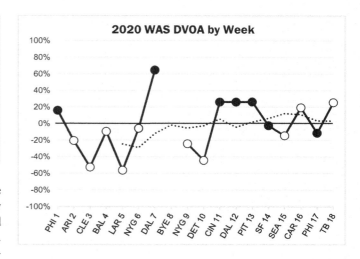

2020 WAS DVOA by Week

(ninth-youngest) were two of the youngest defenses in the league by snap-weighted age. Both were top-six defenses by DVOA in 2020 as they added some experience and fell toward league average in snap-weighted age on that side of the ball. The Patriots, on the other hand, had the league's oldest defense in their leap year and stayed among the oldest while they dropped back to 26th in DVOA this past season.

Washington profiles more like the San Francisco and Tampa Bay defenses. Washington had the fifth-youngest defense in the league last season, and the youth comes at the unit's best positions. The defensive line was the youngest in the league (24.3) and the defensive backs were the fourth-youngest (24.9). We currently have Washington projected to have a top-10 defense again in 2021.

Even if the Washington defense doesn't remain one of the best in the league, it's difficult to see it dropping all the way back down to the bottom-third unit that it was previously. The depth and youth of the front four should be a solid enough base, and it's a position group that will get back Matt Ioannidis, who suffered a torn biceps in Week 3. In the secondary, Landon Collins is also scheduled to return from a torn Achilles suffered in Week 7.

Additions made could also help the defense in areas where they were more likely to regress. Washington signed William Jackson III in free agency, which gives the defense a top corner it didn't have last season. Washington had the second-best

DVOA against the pass in 2020, but only ranked 27th against opposing No. 1 receivers.

In the first round of the 2021 NFL Draft, Washington selected Jamin Davis, an uber athletic linebacker out of Kentucky. Davis was more athlete than instinct in college, but he was often able to find his way to the ball and he'll have an easier job doing that behind this defensive line. He has some developing to do in coverage, but that's another area where the Washington defense got by with some struggles in 2020, ranked 17th in DVOA against tight ends.

With the late offseason signing of safety Bobby McCain, the Washington secondary is now deeper than it was last season. The return of Collins and the breakout of 2020 seventh-round safety Kamren Curl could allow more defensive backs on the field. Washington used dime or lighter personnel on just 2% of plays last season. Since Collins and Curl can excel as downhill players, some three-safety looks in dime could put Washington's best players on the field at the same time without losing much against the run.

Washington's 2021 season won't necessarily have to be determined by how close the defense can come to the 2020 ver-

Table 1. Biggest Year-to-Year Improvement in Defensive DVOA, 1983-2020

Years	Team	Y1	Rk	Y2	Rk	Dif	Y3	Rk
1997-1999	MIA	13.4%	28	-22.0%	1	-35.4%	-8.4%	8
1999-2001	TEN	5.8%	22	-25.0%	1	-30.8%	10.5%	26
2008-2010	DEN	21.5%	32	-8.6%	7	-30.1%	18.8%	31
1997-1999	OAK	15.7%	29	-14.2%	3	-30.0%	-5.1%	11
1988-1990	DEN	14.1%	27	-15.8%	4	-29.9%	8.4%	19
2010-2012	JAX	18.8%	32	-9.9%	8	-28.7%	13.0%	29
1990-1992	PHI	-13.6%	5	-42.0%	1	-28.5%	-18.3%	2
2019-2021	WAS	8.9%	27	-18.3%	3	-27.3%	--	--
2000-2002	STL	11.0%	26	-16.2%	1	-27.3%	-7.8%	6
1983-1985	SEA	5.3%	19	-21.8%	2	-27.1%	-16.8%	2
1990-1992	NO	-0.4%	16	-27.4%	2	-27.0%	-21.1%	1
2010-2012	HOU	16.3%	30	-10.6%	7	-26.9%	-17.1%	2
2008-2010	NYJ	1.2%	16	-25.6%	1	-26.8%	-9.7%	6
2018-2020	SF	6.5%	24	-20.3%	2	-26.7%	-9.9%	6
2018-2020	TB	16.2%	32	-10.5%	6	-26.7%	-14.6%	5
2018-2020	NE	1.4%	19	-25.2%	1	-26.6%	7.9%	26

sion. It could be more about how good the defense will have to be to complement the offense.

To be a competitive team, last year's defense *needed* to be great while the offense struggled to do much of anything productive. Washington's 2020 offense was centered around the hope Haskins would develop in his second season and that just didn't happen. Haskins' initial run to start the season lasted just four games before he was benched for Kyle Allen. Haskins eventually returned late in the season out of injury necessity, a stretch that lasted three games and two starts before his release. In that limited time, Haskins put up a passing DVOA that was nearly identical to his historically poor rookie season (-40.1% compared to -42.0% in 2019).

In between Haskins' two disastrous turns as the starting quarterback came a four-game Kyle Allen interlude and then the inspirational return of Alex Smith. Smith replaced an injured Allen during a Week 5 game against the Los Angeles Rams, but was not given the starting job until he again came in for Allen in Week 9 against the New York Giants. Smith's well-documented recovery from not just a broken leg but multiple infections made him the league's best feel-good story and a deserving Comeback Player of the Year as soon as he stepped on the field.

Unfortunately, after that point, the football just wasn't very good. Smith dumpoffed (dumped off?) his way to a -39.7% DVOA that was barely better than Haskins'. Among 44 quarterbacks with at least 100 pass attempts on the season, Smith's average depth of target (5.1 yards) ranked 44th and a full yard below the 43rd-ranked quarterback.

Smith was always known as a checkdown artist, but that was taken to the extreme in his 2020 return to play. 81% of Smith's passes traveled fewer than 10 yards past the line of scrimmage, easily the lowest rate in the league. The next-lowest passer was Jared Goff at 74%. Fittingly, Smith ranked dead last in ALEX with his average throw on third down coming 2.6 yards short of the first down marker.

The Smith era in Washington, and eventually his career, ended with a calf strain on his injured leg prior to the wildcard game against the Buccaneers that left the quarterback inactive. In his place, Taylor Heinicke got the start and put up what might have been Washington's best quarterback performance of the season. His 85 DYAR was the highest in a single game for Washington during the 2020 season, topping Smith's 58 from Week 13 against San Francisco—a figure that only ranked ninth among quarterbacks *that week*.

In previous seasons, a Washington team with a potentially dominant defense and a clear need at quarterback could have gone wild in the offseason. Maybe that was the plan had the highest tier of quarterbacks actually been available. Washington reportedly offered a first- and third-round pick for Matthew Stafford before he was traded to the Rams. Deshaun Watson and Russell Wilson never became realistic options for multiple reasons. The Carson Wentz Reclamation Project wasn't going to happen in the NFC East. Statistically, Sam Darnold offered less than the quarterbacks already on the roster, though Washington reportedly inquired on the former third overall pick before the start of free agency.

That eliminated almost every major avenue for quarterback improvement and led to Washington having a normal, fairly well-received offseason. The new Washington regime—including Rivera, team president Jason Wright, and general manager Martin Mayhew—has provided a calm and sensible approach that hasn't really been seen around this organization in some time.

The more laidback strategy landed Washington quarterback Ryan Fitzpatrick on a reasonable one-year, $10-million deal. Fitzpatrick's presence brings a baseline of competency to the position, but betting on consistency from Fitzpatrick is always a gamble. Historically, the worst time to invest in Fitzpatrick is right after he has played well enough to get paid.

Washington will also become the first team since the 2016 New York Jets to fully buy in to Fitzpatrick as the unquestioned starter. (They also had Geno Smith and Bryce Petty on that roster, both of whom eventually started games. You could make the case the 2012 Buffalo Bills were actually the last.) In that 2016 season, he finished 32nd in both DYAR and DVOA just one year after ranking 13th in DYAR and 14th DVOA.

Fitzpatrick's "good" in 2020 also comes with a few asterisks. We remember the spectacular plays like the deep heave with his facemask turned sideways against the Las Vegas Raiders, but that's part of the issue. Much of Fitzpatrick's success with the Dolphins in 2020 came under pressure. Fitzpatrick had an insane 8.3% DVOA under pressure, which was easily the best in the league among qualified quarterbacks (minimum 200 passes). Patrick Mahomes was the only other quarterback to have positive DVOA under pressure at 0.6%.

The concern comes from what happened when there was no pressure. Mahomes, for instance, was still third in DVOA without pressure (71.6%) while Fitzpatrick was just 27th (30.1%), ranked between Mitchell Trubisky and Carson Wentz. His yards per play under pressure (7.6) was also higher than his yards per play without pressure (7.5). The next highest difference in yards per play was -2.2. The last qualified quarterback to put up more yards per play under pressure than without pressure was Seneca Wallace with Cleveland in 2011.

Play under pressure is not something that is sustainable and projectable from year-to-year. On top of that, Fitzpatrick hasn't been an outlier in terms of consistently performing well under pressure. His previous two seasons featured DVOA under pressure of -42.8% and -76.0%.

Fitzpatrick was also one of the luckier quarterbacks in the league in terms of dropped interceptions in 2020. He threw eight interceptions, which already gave him one of the highest interception rates at 3.0%, but he had another five dropped interceptions. That would have put his total up at 13 with an adjusted interception rate of 4.3%, which would have been better than only Darnold and Nick Foles.

There is a certain amount of YOLO ball that needs to be accepted when Fitzpatrick is at quarterback, but last year's performance wasn't based on a high volume of low-percentage deep throws. Just 7.2% of Fitzpatrick's passes traveled at least 20 air yards, which was the fifth-lowest rate in the league among quarterbacks with at least 100 total attempts. Fitzpatrick did luck out in the sense that 60% of those passes were completed, the highest rate in the league, though he ranked just 12th in "catchable" rate per Sports Info Solutions charting.

Despite the lack of deep throws, only Mike Glennon threw into tight windows (considered a yard or fewer of separation) more often than Fitzpatrick (21.7%) in 2020, according to NFL Next Gen Stats. Separation and target depth have a negative correlation (shorter passes typically have more separation), so it would have made sense if many of Fitzpatrick's throws were into tight windows deep down the field. Instead, Fitzpatrick was throwing short and intermediate routes into tight coverage. The hope will be that the type of tight throws Fitzpatrick attempted in 2020 was a product of a Miami offense that was mostly void of separators (just look at the assets the Dolphins put into finding those types of players this offseason).

With Washington, Fitzpatrick will be paired with Terry McLaurin, who remains one of the league's most underrated receivers. Stuck with some poor quarterback play, McLaurin is still just one of 30 players since the merger to eclipse 2,000 receiving yards over his first two seasons. He's one of just three, along with Mike Wallace and Marques Colston, to do so as a third-round pick or later. McLaurin has the ability to win and separate at all areas of the field but hasn't often been able to showcase that ability on a consistent basis. McLaurin didn't have much help from the other receivers, which led to some inefficient targets and left him 72nd in DYAR and 74th in DVOA. Among 41 players with at least 100 targets last season, McLaurin's catchable target rate ranked just 33rd per SIS.

Both McLaurin and Fitzpatrick will get some help with the addition of Curtis Samuel, Washington's other big offensive free-agent signing, brought over from the Carolina Panthers on a three-year, $34.5-million deal. A receiver reuniting with a former coaching staff usually signals a familiarity and seamless fit into an old role, but that might not be the case here. In the Norv/Scott Turner offense in Carolina, Samuel was used as an outside deep threat. There was clearly talent and potential, but things never clicked and Samuel had negative DVOA in both 2018 and 2019.

Then last season, Samuel was moved inside more often under new Panthers offensive coordinator Joe Brady and his average depth of target dropped from 14.9 yards in 2019 to 7.1 in 2020. Samuel had fewer targets in 2020 than 2019 but more than doubled his yards after the catch (158 to 343) while his completed air yards also increased (473 to 508). A lack of

scoring (a problem across the entire 2020 Carolina offense) stopped Samuel's metrics from truly popping, but the catch-and-run role with some deep shots sprinkled in appeared to suit him better.

Getting the most out of Samuel might rely less on familiarity and more on how much Washington wants to steal from a different coaching staff that got a little more production out of the player. The selection of North Carolina receiver Dyami Brown in the third round might signal some more slot time for Samuel, since Brown was strictly an outside deep threat (and a good one) for the Tar Heels with the highest aDOT in the 2021 draft class. (The signing of veteran slot receiver Adam Humphries could also indicate the opposite.)

Either way, there's hope a bit more stability could spark more positive results out of the offense with an increase in talent across the board. There was an effort last season—Washington used motion at the sixth-highest rate in the league—but there is only so much that can be done when even the most creative play designs turn into swing passes targeting J.D. McKissic.

Given all that, it's hard to place exactly what this team is. There is a solid foundation in place, something that hasn't been said about this franchise in a while, but it's unclear exactly what that foundation is building toward. If everything breaks right, Washington rides a dominant defense and an above-average offense back to the postseason for its first back-to-back playoff appearances since 1991-1992. It's probably still not enough to be a Super Bowl contender. It would also leave them with a draft slot at the end of the first round, not quite striking distance for a quarterback of the future.

If Washington then trades up for a quarterback, they'll be banking on a rookie and a third-straight year of a top-tier defense to keep the success going. That's a tough ask. Or maybe the rest of the roster proves to be good enough—and the franchise has become stable enough outside of the owner—to be a desirable trade destination for the next disgruntled star quarterback.

Washington didn't do much to mortgage its future for a quick fix this offseason, but there are still questions about what that future looks like. It's a strange place for the Washington Football Team to be, but the organization has certainly seen stranger.

Dan Pizzuta

2020 Football Team Stats by Week

Wk	vs.	W-L	PF	PA	YDF	YDA	TO	Total	Off	Def	ST
1	PHI	W	27	17	239	265	3	16.0%	-34.2%	-53.1%	-2.8%
2	at ARI	L	15	30	316	438	-1	-20.5%	-21.4%	-5.3%	-4.5%
3	at CLE	L	20	34	309	300	-5	-52.5%	-50.8%	-0.8%	-2.5%
4	BAL	L	17	31	343	350	1	-9.2%	2.0%	3.7%	-7.5%
5	LAR	L	10	30	108	429	1	-56.2%	-50.7%	9.8%	4.3%
6	at NYG	L	19	20	337	240	-1	-5.6%	-12.2%	-11.0%	-4.3%
7	DAL	W	25	3	397	142	1	64.8%	5.9%	-71.1%	-12.3%
8	BYE										
9	NYG	L	20	23	402	350	-5	-24.1%	-25.7%	1.6%	3.2%
10	at DET	L	27	30	464	372	-1	-44.3%	-14.5%	28.0%	-1.8%
11	CIN	W	20	9	325	272	1	26.2%	-4.0%	-25.6%	4.7%
12	at DAL	W	41	16	338	247	1	26.3%	-14.4%	-37.1%	3.6%
13	at PIT	W	23	17	318	326	1	26.4%	-12.4%	-22.4%	16.4%
14	at SF	W	23	15	193	344	2	-2.2%	-46.5%	-34.3%	10.0%
15	SEA	L	15	20	353	302	-1	-14.2%	-23.8%	-9.4%	0.1%
16	CAR	L	13	20	386	280	-2	19.5%	-15.5%	-34.0%	1.0%
17	at PHI	W	20	14	248	216	1	-11.2%	-48.1%	-26.8%	10.1%
18	TB	L	23	31	375	507	0	25.8%	25.9%	4.5%	4.4%

Trends and Splits

	Offense	Rank	Defense	Rank
Total DVOA	-21.8%	32	-18.3%	3
Unadjusted VOA	-18.2%	28	-19.4%	2
Weighted Trend	-20.7%	32	-21.0%	3
Variance	3.4%	5	6.3%	23
Average Opponent	0.1%	17	-4.7%	29
Passing	-26.7%	32	-18.0%	2
Rushing	-6.0%	14	-18.8%	11
First Down	-26.6%	31	-15.4%	4
Second Down	-17.9%	28	-25.8%	2
Third Down	-18.6%	27	-12.9%	10
First Half	-25.9%	32	-2.2%	15
Second Half	-17.8%	28	-38.8%	1
Red Zone	-15.0%	23	-20.4%	3
Late and Close	-39.2%	31	-37.2%	1

Five-Year Performance

Year	W-L	Pyth W	Est W	PF	PA	TO	Total	Rk	Off	Rk	Def	Rk	ST	Rk	Off AGL	Rk	Def AGL	Rk	Off Age	Rk	Def Age	Rk	ST Age	Rk
2016	8-7-1	8.3	9.6	396	383	0	8.9%	9	15.5%	5	7.0%	25	0.4%	13	27.8	10	70.2	31	27.1	8	27.4	4	26.1	15
2017	7-9	6.8	6.9	342	388	-4	-2.6%	16	-3.8%	20	-3.5%	12	-2.4%	22	69.4	31	69.3	31	27.1	15	26.3	16	25.3	26
2018	7-9	5.7	5.8	281	359	+7	-20.1%	29	-19.8%	28	2.8%	20	2.5%	8	86.6	31	9.1	1	28.4	2	26.2	19	25.1	32
2019	3-13	3.7	4.4	266	435	+1	-26.9%	30	-20.7%	30	8.9%	27	2.7%	7	81.9	32	49.1	28	27.1	10	25.5	28	25.1	30
2020	7-9	8.2	7.6	335	329	-4	-2.3%	16	-21.8%	32	-18.3%	3	1.1%	15	62.5	28	34.6	14	26.8	15	25.2	29	25.6	24

2020 Performance Based on Most Common Personnel Groups

WAS Offense					WAS Offense vs. Opponents					WAS Defense				WAS Defense vs. Opponents			
Pers	Freq	Yds	DVOA	Run%	Pers	Freq	Yds	DVOA	Run%	Pers	Freq	Yds	DVOA	Pers	Freq	Yds	DVOA
11	67%	5.1	-17.1%	24%	Base	15%	3.7	-27.8%	56%	Base	31%	5.1	-15.3%	11	56%	4.8	-19.7%
12	15%	4.5	-28.9%	48%	Nickel	63%	5.0	-14.1%	37%	Nickel	65%	5.0	-20.2%	12	25%	5.7	-10.4%
21	12%	5.6	0.6%	55%	Dime+	19%	6.1	-19.9%	9%	Dime+	2%	6.8	91.2%	21	7%	4.8	-30.1%
13	3%	4.6	-24.4%	71%	Goal Line	1%	2.9	-50.6%	91%	Goal Line	1%	-0.2	-69.6%	22	4%	4.8	-17.8%
612	1%	2.8	-23.7%	93%	Big	1%	2.8	-81.1%	67%					13	2%	1.7	-71.7%
613	1%	0.3	-107.9%	89%										10	2%	4.5	-51.0%

Strategic Tendencies

Run/Pass		Rk	Formation		Rk	Pass Rush		Rk	Secondary		Rk	Strategy		Rk
Runs, first half	35%	24	Form: Single Back	81%	18	Rush 3	6.0%	17	4 DB	31%	9	Play Action	28%	13
Runs, first down	42%	26	Form: Empty Back	13%	6	Rush 4	67.7%	11	5 DB	65%	11	Offensive Motion	53%	8
Runs, second-long	30%	13	Form: Multi Back	6%	23	Rush 5	21.2%	15	6+ DB	2%	25	Avg Box (Off)	6.45	23
Runs, power sit.	60%	14	Pers: 3+ WR	67%	13	Rush 6+	5.1%	16	Man Coverage	24%	25	Avg Box (Def)	6.25	29
Runs, behind 2H	24%	22	Pers: 2+ TE/6+ OL	20%	26	Edge Rusher Sacks	48.9%	19	CB by Sides	90%	5	Offensive Pace	29.92	14
Pass, ahead 2H	39%	29	Pers: 6+ OL	2%	12	Interior DL Sacks	25.0%	15	S/CB Cover Ratio	24%	19	Defensive Pace	29.73	7
Run-Pass Options	12%	5	Shotgun/Pistol	77%	9	Second Level Sacks	26.1%	12	DB Blitz	11%	23	Go for it on 4th	1.49	19

Washington's run/pass ratios fell with new offensive coordinator Scott Turner, going from sixth both in the first half and on first downs to 24th for the former and 26th for the latter. However, Washington went from dead-last in rate of runs in short-yardage "power situations" to a rank close to the NFL average. Washington was second in the league throwing 28% of passes to running backs, trailing only New England. Washington ranked sixth in DVOA rushing the ball on third or fourth down but 31st passing the ball. Washington ranked seventh in pace when trailing in games (one play every 24.7 seconds) but 27th in pace when leading (30.0 seconds). Washington faced a league-high 51 wide receiver screens and had a very good -20.3% DVOA with just 4.3 yards allowed per pass on these plays. Washington's defense went from 15th in DVOA in the first half of games to first in the second half of games. Washington benefited from a league-leading 42 dropped passes by opponents.

Passing

Player	DYAR	DVOA	Plays	NtYds	Avg	YAC	C%	TD	Int
A.Smith*	-506	-39.7%	274	1443	5.3	5.6	66.7%	6	8
D.Haskins*	-483	-40.1%	261	1298	5.0	5.8	61.4%	5	6
K.Allen	20	-8.0%	94	566	6.0	5.4	69.0%	4	1
T.Heinicke	33	12.7%	20	130	6.5	4.1	63.2%	1	0
R.Fitzpatrick	362	7.5%	280	2026	7.2	4.7	68.8%	13	8

Rushing

Player	DYAR	DVOA	Plays	Yds	Avg	TD	Fum	Suc
A.Gibson	193	18.8%	170	795	4.7	11	0	52%
P.Barber	-3	-9.2%	94	258	2.7	4	0	44%
J.D.McKissic	57	7.7%	85	365	4.3	1	1	52%
D.Haskins*	-4	-16.2%	13	57	4.4	1	1	--
K.Allen	7	9.7%	5	28	5.6	1	0	--
C.Samuel	99	3.1%	41	200	4.9	2	0	--
R.Fitzpatrick	39	14.6%	24	156	6.5	2	0	--

Receiving

Player	DYAR	DVOA	Plays	Ctch	Yds	Y/C	YAC	TD	C%
T.McLaurin	18	-11.0%	134	87	1118	12.9	5.5	4	65%
C.Sims	48	0.3%	48	32	477	14.9	7.8	1	67%
S.Sims	-15	-17.9%	37	27	265	9.8	4.7	1	73%
I.Wright	-22	-20.3%	35	27	197	7.3	5.3	0	77%
D.Inman*	-25	-24.5%	28	18	163	9.1	2.4	2	64%
A.Gandy-Golden	-46	-102.1%	7	1	3	3.0	1.0	0	14%
R.Foster*	-10	-33.7%	6	2	37	18.5	16.0	0	33%
C.Samuel	95	0.1%	97	77	851	11.1	4.2	3	79%
A.Humphries	18	-5.8%	35	23	228	9.9	2.0	2	66%
L.Thomas	-4	-7.8%	110	72	670	9.3	4.0	6	65%
J.D.McKissic	30	-9.0%	110	80	589	7.4	6.3	2	73%
A.Gibson	-34	-27.2%	44	36	247	6.9	8.4	0	82%
P.Barber	-20	-62.3%	7	4	12	3.0	2.8	0	57%

Offensive Line

Player	Pos	Age	GS	Snaps	Pen	Sk	Pass	Run	Player	Pos	Age	GS	Snaps	Pen	Sk	Pass	Run
Chase Roullier	C	28	16/16	1090	4	1.5	7	7	Geron Christian*	LT	25	6/6	399	1	4.5	9	1
Morgan Moses*	RT/LT	30	16/16	1066	7	1.5	24	4	Wes Martin	LG	25	16/5	340	1	5	9	2
Wes Schweitzer	LG	28	16/13	991	2	4	10	6	David Sharpe	RT	26	10/2	184	2	2	5	4
Brandon Scherff	RG	30	13/13	857	2	2	9	6	Charles Leno	LT	30	16/16	1066	7	3.5	19	4
Cornelius Lucas	LT	30	14/8	536	1	1.5	7	1	Ereck Flowers	LG	27	14/14	856	3	2	9	10

Year	Yards	ALY	Rk	Power	Rk	Stuff	Rk	2Lev	Rk	OpFld	Rk	BB Rt	Rk	Sacks	ASR	Rk	Press	Rk	BB Rt	Rk	Cont
2018	4.16	3.96	26	76%	2	23%	28	1.24	19	0.93	13	6.1%	16	44	8.5%	24	32.7%	23	11.1%	23	19
2019	4.36	4.28	18	61%	22	19%	17	1.14	20	0.89	14	7.5%	3	50	9.8%	31	30.7%	21	14.3%	22	29
2020	4.06	4.35	16	73%	7	15%	11	1.20	16	0.51	28	8.4%	11	50	7.3%	22	22.9%	10	12.0%	15	28

2020 ALY by direction:	Left End: 3.87 (25)	Left Tackle: 3.90 (21)	Mid/Guard: 4.48 (15)	Right Tackle: 4.45 (15)	Right End: 4.52 (15)

As a team, Washington ranked 15th in blown block rate on passes, but only the Bengals, Eagles, and Cowboys had more blown blocks turn into sacks. Just four teams used five-man protection more than Washington last season. Center Chase Roullier signed a four-year extension following the 2020 season. The 2017 sixth-round pick was one of four centers to finish in the top 10 of both Pass Block Win Rate and Run Block Win Rate in 2020, according to ESPN. Brandon Scherff will return on his second straight franchise tag. He made his first All-Pro team in 2020. Scherff put up an identical blown block rate as in 2019 (1.8%) but significantly cut down on his rate of blown pass blocks (from 2.7% down to 1.7%). Wes Sch-weitzer started 13 games at left guard for Washington and put up a lower blown block rate than Scherff. He'll be in competi-tion with the reacquired Ereck Flowers, who was traded back to Washington with a reworked contract this offseason. Flowers struggled in 2020 with Miami, especially run-blocking with a 3.3% blown block rate. The tackle spots raise questions, but there are answers. Washington released tackles Morgan Moses and Geron Christian in May. Christian, a 2018 third-round pick, started six games at left tackle in 2020. Moses started 96 consecutive regular season games at right tackle. While his release came as a surprise, there were some low points to his play while he battled through some injuries. His 2.8% blown block rate ranked 21st among 34 right tackles with at least 400 snaps in 2020. Moses particularly struggled in those five-man protection schemes that Washington liked to use, with the worst blown block rate of the 17 tackles who had at least 100 snaps with only five blockers. ❧ Charles Leno will be the starter at left tackle on a one-year deal. Leno cut down on his penalties and blown blocks in 2020 and has been an average to above-average tackle throughout his career outside of a down year in 2019 where he had 25 blown blocks and 13 penalties. ❧ Second-round pick Sam Cosmi is the likely starter at right tackle. Cosmi had a standout season as a redshirt freshman at Texas playing right tackle before he made the switch to the left side. He'll likely follow a similar career path in the NFL. Cosmi has plus-plus athleticism and good hand usage that help make up for 13th-percentile arm length. His 1.2% blown block rate was eighth-best among tackles in the 2021 draft class. ❧

Defensive Front

Defensive Line	Age	Pos	G	Snaps	Plays	TmPct	Rk	Stop	Dfts	BTkl	Runs	St%	Rk	RuYd	Rk	Sack	Hit	Hur	Dsrpt
						Overall						**vs. Run**				**Pass Rush**			
Daron Payne	24	DT	16	881	58	7.3%	11	51	16	3	49	88%	3	2.0	30	3.0	4	16	5
Jonathan Allen	26	DT	16	809	61	7.6%	8	43	10	2	54	70%	58	2.8	67	2.0	11	15	2
Tim Settle	24	DT	16	348	19	2.4%	--	17	6	0	14	86%	--	2.1	--	5.0	2	8	0

Edge Rushers	Age	Pos	G	Snaps	Plays	TmPct	Rk	Stop	Dfts	BTkl	Runs	St%	Rk	RuYd	Rk	Sack	Hit	Hur	Dsrpt
						Overall						**vs. Run**				**Pass Rush**			
Chase Young	22	DE	15	770	47	6.3%	21	34	21	0	28	64%	75	1.6	13	7.5	10	26	5
Montez Sweat	25	DE	16	693	51	6.4%	20	41	21	1	32	75%	33	3.1	71	9.0	12	32	6
Ryan Kerrigan*	33	DE	16	397	18	2.3%	--	15	9	2	7	71%	--	2.3	--	5.5	1	12	1
Ryan Anderson*	27	DE	9	145	7	1.6%	--	5	1	1	7	71%	--	0.9	--	0.0	0	4	0

Linebackers	Age	Pos	G	Snaps	Plays	TmPct	Rk	Stop	Dfts	BTkl	Runs	St%	Rk	RuYd	Rk	Sack	Hit	Hur	Tgts	Suc%	Rk	Yd/P	Rk	PD	Int
						Overall						**vs. Run**				**Pass Rush**				**vs. Pass**					
Jon Bostic	30	MLB	16	966	121	15.1%	21	58	23	11	60	55%	47	3.6	27	3.0	3	7	39	49%	45	5.1	20	3	1
Cole Holcomb	25	MLB	11	555	71	12.9%	43	31	13	4	38	47%	72	3.4	19	2.5	1	4	22	55%	23	3.1	2	1	1
Kevin Pierre-Louis*	30	OLB	13	505	58	8.9%	67	29	6	7	26	58%	36	4.7	72	1.0	1	6	21	52%	31	7.1	55	2	0
Shaun Dion Hamilton*	26	OLB	14	109	20	2.9%	--	10	3	2	14	57%	--	3.1	--	0.0	1	0	5	60%	--	6.4	--	0	0
David Mayo	28	ILB	11	193	20	3.4%	--	10	3	3	13	77%	--	2.5	--	0.0	0	3	5	0%	--	10.0	--	0	0

Year	Yards	ALY	Rk	Power	Rk	Stuff	Rk	2Lev	Rk	OpFld	Rk	BB Rt	Rk	Sacks	ASR	Rk	Press	Rk	BB Rt	Rk
2018	4.57	4.97	29	76%	28	16%	26	1.37	26	0.71	11	5.7%	28	46	7.6%	11	31.3%	12	12.3%	8
2019	4.71	4.85	29	64%	16	16%	26	1.22	21	0.95	27	10.0%	28	46	8.3%	4	26.1%	29	14.1%	21
2020	3.93	4.06	7	72%	27	21%	5	1.15	13	0.56	8	14.0%	12	47	7.9%	7	27.7%	9	16.0%	6

2020 ALY by direction:	Left End: 4.28 (13)	Left Tackle: 5.03 (27)	Mid/Guard: 4.12 (11)	Right Tackle: 3.64 (5)	Right End: 3.51 (4)

Few teams if any can sport as dominant of an edge rush duo as Chase Young and Montez Sweat. Young got the much of the hype, but Sweat had an impressive second season. He finished 13th in hurries and 16th in quarterback hits. Sweat was also able to impact the play when he didn't quite get to the quarterback with six passes batted at the line, which tied for seventh. Young was right behind him with five. ❧ As good as Young's rookie season was, his 7.5 sacks came with just 10 other quarterback hits. Young will get to the quarterback more often, but it remains to be seen if he'll be able to keep such a high hit-to-sack conversion rate. Ryan Kerrigan had been a consistently high converter throughout his career in Washington. ❧ Washington can match the star power of the edges with incredible depth on the inside. Daron Payne was a dominant force who led the interior in run stop rate and hurries. Jonathan Allen finished his third straight season with 10 or more quarterback hits. The interior should be even deeper with the return of Matt Ioannidis. ❧ No team had more defensive snaps with five defensive linemen on the field (58), mostly early downs outside of the red zone, and Washington averaged 3.9 yards per play allowed on those snaps. ❧ First-round pick Jamin Davis is a raw, athletic linebacker out of Kentucky. He put up high tackle numbers, but only 50 of his 107 tackles (46.7%) were solo in 2020. His average tackle also came 22% further down the field than would be expected, according to Sports Info Solutions. ❧ After a promising rookie season, Cole Holcomb turned into one of the league's best-tackling linebackers with a 9% broken-tackle rate. He also had a significant jump in coverage. Holcomb allowed just 3.1 yards per target after he allowed 8.2 in 2019. ❧ After two years playing 91% and 92% of the defensive snaps, Jon Bostic is likely to see that play time decrease with a deeper linebacker rotation, even if he remains the main Mike.

Defensive Secondary

Secondary	Age	Pos	G	Snaps	Plays	Overall TmPct	Rk	Stop	Dfts	BTkl	Runs	vs. Run St%	Rk	RuYd	Rk	Tgts	vs. Pass Tgt%	Rk	aDOT	Suc%	Rk	Yd/P	Rk	PD	Int
Ronald Darby*	27	CB	16	1001	71	8.9%	34	34	10	4	17	53%	19	6.2	33	85	23.3%	14	14.0	58%	12	7.0	29	16	0
Kendall Fuller	26	CB	14	892	61	8.7%	42	23	12	6	16	19%	73	7.8	55	70	21.5%	28	10.9	56%	22	6.3	12	11	4
Kamren Curl	22	SS	16	764	92	11.5%	29	45	14	13	41	54%	9	4.1	4	26	9.3%	28	7.7	54%	24	8.1	42	4	3
Jimmy Moreland	26	CB	16	599	45	5.6%	--	21	10	11	10	50%	--	8.4	--	40	18.3%	--	8.1	60%	--	5.1	--	1	1
Troy Apke	26	FS	16	441	33	4.1%	--	9	5	6	15	20%	--	8.9	--	13	8.1%	--	26.6	62%	--	10.9	--	2	0
Landon Collins	27	SS	7	397	42	12.0%	--	24	10	9	27	59%	--	3.6	--	14	9.7%	--	11.9	50%	--	10.2	--	1	1
Deshazor Everett	29	SS	11	355	32	5.8%	--	6	1	7	15	7%	--	8.1	--	7	5.4%	--	15.6	43%	--	13.3	--	4	0
Jeremy Reaves	25	FS	9	263	26	5.8%	--	7	3	2	11	27%	--	11.0	--	6	6.3%	--	15.7	67%	--	10.5	--	2	1
Bobby McCain	28	FS	16	923	51	6.3%	68	5	3	7	20	0%	71	14.7	70	12	3.3%	68	17.6	58%	12	8.2	43	5	1
William Jackson	29	CB	14	886	56	7.8%	61	27	13	3	9	56%	14	4.7	17	67	18.6%	51	14.4	63%	5	7.1	33	11	1
Darryl Roberts	31	CB	11	469	45	7.8%	--	16	6	5	7	29%	--	7.9	--	40	22.3%	--	10.4	45%	--	6.8	--	6	1

Year	Pass D Rank	vs. #1 WR	Rk	vs. #2 WR	Rk	vs. Other WR	Rk	WR Wide	Rk	WR Slot	Rk	vs. TE	Rk	vs. RB	Rk
2018	11	3.9%	18	-7.2%	10	13.8%	26	17.8%	29	-9.3%	4	-17.4%	6	-6.1%	12
2019	24	-10.5%	9	43.4%	32	12.2%	23	-13.6%	11	34.9%	31	23.6%	31	-3.9%	15
2020	2	14.1%	27	-30.0%	2	-24.3%	3	-21.1%	5	-9.4%	5	4.0%	17	-46.9%	1

Washington bought low on a bounce-back year for Ronald Darby, and then traded that in for a three-year upgrade with free agent William Jackson III. Jackson was fifth in success rate in 2020 and provides the ability to cover opposing No. 1 receivers, which was a struggle for Washington last season. The only receiver to really get the best of Jackson in 2020 was now-teammate Terry McLaurin. Jackson was tied for the league lead with nine targets on go routes but allowed just one reception for 46 yards with two passes defensed. ◥ Kendall Fuller impressed in a transition to full-time outside corner from the slot/box player he had been previously. His yards per pass allowed decreased from 8.8 in 2019 to 6.4 in 2020 as his success rate improved from 46% to 58%. ◥ Jimmy Moreland, a 2019 seventh-round pick from James Madison, played solid but unspectacular coverage in the slot. He didn't make many impact plays (only one pass defensed) but allowed just 5.1 yards per pass with a 60% success rate. ◥ With Landon Collins out for much of the season, 2020 seventh-round pick Kamren Curl stepped into his role quite well. Curl led the team in run stops and ranked top-10 league-wide in run stop rate and average yards per run tackle. ◥ The question becomes what the playing time split will look like with Collins heathy. After some rumors that Collins could shift toward a more traditional linebacker role, it was confirmed by both Collins and Jack Del Rio that there would be no position switch. But neither Collins nor Curl really has the coverage ability to transition more into the slot or a free safety role. ◥ Jeremy Reaves and Troy Apke teamed up to play deep safety, but most of those snaps are likely to go to post-draft signing Bobby McCain. McCain can cover ground along the back end and was an excellent tackler for a defensive back in 2020 with only seven broken tackles and 0.8 yards after the catch allowed per reception, which was the best rate among safeties.

Special Teams

Year	DVOA	Rank	FG/XP	Rank	Net Kick	Rank	Kick Ret	Rank	Net Punt	Rank	Punt Ret	Rank	Hidden	Rank
2018	2.5%	8	9.2	5	2.8	9	-3.0	24	6.1	7	-2.5	20	-1.1	17
2019	2.7%	7	1.2	15	2.5	11	6.8	3	4.8	11	-1.8	20	1.0	17
2020	1.1%	15	-2.0	18	1.7	15	-1.3	18	17.9	2	-10.8	32	-14.8	31

Tress Way has finished in the top two of gross punting value in each of the past three seasons. As an added benefit, the coverage unit finally stepped up. Washington finished with negative return value allowed for the first time in those three seasons. ◥ Similarly, Dustin Hopkins has gone from fifth to fourth to second in gross kickoff value over the past three seasons. However, conversion rates on both extra points (93.8%) and field goals (79.4%) hit career lows. Hopkins had a rocky go from 40 to 49 yards out, with just 13-of-17 field goals made. He was asked to kick the most field goals of any kicker from that range. A little more riverboating from Ron Rivera could help in that area. ◥ Steven Sims was one of the most dynamic kick returners in 2019, but that role went to Danny Johnson in 2020. Johnson averaged just 22 yards per return, which ranked 11th among 13 players with at least 20 returns. Johnson did have positive value on those returns, but barely. ◥ Sims did take over as the lead punt returner, but he finished with just 6.7 yards per return with a long gain of 22 yards. He rated as the least valuable punt returner in the league. His hands were an issue, with three muffs and a lost fumble. ◥ New slot receiver Adam Humphries has experience as a punt returner but had negative value in both 2018 and 2019.

Quarterbacks

On the following pages, we provide the last three years of statistics for the top two quarterbacks on each team's depth chart, as well as a number of other quarterbacks who played significant time in 2020. Each quarterback who is currently on a roster also gets a 2021 projection from our KUBIAK fantasy football projection system, explained further in the Statistical Toolbox at the front of the book.

It is difficult to accurately project statistics for a 162-game baseball season, but it is exponentially more difficult to accurately project statistics for a 17-game football season because of the small size of the data samples involved. With that in mind, we ask that you consider the listed projections not as a prediction of exact numbers, but the mean of a range of possible performances. What's important is not so much the exact number of yards and touchdowns we project, but whether or not we're projecting a given player to improve or decline. Along those same lines, rookie projections will not be as accurate as veteran projections due to lack of data.

Our quarterback projections look a bit different from our projections for the other skill positions. At running back and wide receiver, second-stringers see plenty of action, but, at quarterback, either a player starts or he does not start. We recognize that, when a starting quarterback gets injured in Week 8, you don't want to grab your *Football Outsiders Almanac* to find out if his backup is any good only to find that we've projected that the guy will throw 12 passes this year. Therefore, each year we project all quarterbacks to start all 17 games. If Tom Brady goes down in November, you can look up Blaine Gabbert, divide the stats by 17, and get an idea of what we think he will do in an average week (and then, if you are a Tampa Bay fan, pass out). There are full-season projections for the top two quarterbacks on all 32 depth charts. You'll find projections which incorporate the possibility of injury in the fantasy appendix on page 457.

The first line of each quarterback table contains biographical data—the player's name, height, weight, college, draft position, birth date, and age. Height and weight are the best data we could find; weight, of course, can fluctuate during the offseason. **Age** is very simple: the number of years between the player's birth year and 2021, but birthdate is provided if you want to figure out exact age.

Draft position gives draft year and round, with the overall pick number with which the player was taken in parentheses. In the sample table, it says that Tom Brady was chosen in the sixth round of the 2000 NFL draft, with the 199th overall pick. Undrafted free agents are listed as "FA" with the year they came into the league, even if they were only in training camp or on a practice squad.

To the far right of the first line is the player's Risk variable for fantasy football in 2021, which measures the likelihood of the player hitting his projection. The default rating for each player is Green. As the risk of a player failing to hit his projection rises, he's given a rating of Yellow or, in the worst cases, Red. The Risk variable is not only based on age and injury probability, but how a player's projection compares to his recent performance as well as our confidence (or lack thereof) in his offensive teammates.

Next, we give the last three years of player stats. The majority of these statistics are passing numbers, although the shaded five columns on the right are the quarterback's rushing statistics.

The first few columns after the year and team the player played for are standard numbers: games and games started (**G/GS**), offensive **Snaps**, pass attempts (**Att**), pass completions (**Cmp**), completion percentage (**C%**), passing yards (**Yds**), passing touchdowns (**TD**). These numbers are official NFL totals and therefore include plays we leave out of our own metrics, such as clock-stopping spikes, and omit plays we include in our metrics, such as sacks and aborted snaps. (Other differences between official stats and Football Outsiders stats are described in the "Statistical Toolbox" introduction at the front of the book.)

The exception among these standard stats is **CPOE**, or Completion Percentage Over Expectation. The probability of a pass completion is calculated on each play based on numerous factors such as down and distance and location of the pass. There are multiple models of CPOE around the Internet and the numbers in our book come from our model, which removes passes that are marked "Thrown Away," "Batted Down," "Quarterback Hit in Motion," or "Miscommunication." In 2020, Deshaun Watson's actual completion percentage was 5.5% higher than his expected completion percentage, the best difference in the league. Dwayne Haskins was last at -6.8%.

The column for interceptions contains two numbers, representing the official NFL total for interceptions (**Int**) as well as our own metric for adjusted interceptions (**Adj**). For example, if you look at our sample table, Tom Brady had 12 intercep-

Tom Brady				Height: 6-4		Weight: 225		College: Michigan				Draft: 2000/6 (199)		Born: 3-Aug-1977			Age: 44			Risk: Green
Year	Tm	G/GS	Snaps	Att	Cmp	C%	CPOE	Yds	TD	INT/Adj	FUM	ASR	NY/P	Rk	DVOA	Rk	DYAR	Rk	Runs	Yds	TD	DVOA	DYAR	QBR
2018	NE	16/16	1092	570	375	65.8%	0.0%	4355	29	11/12	4	3.8%	7.1	8	15.4%	7	1034	8	23	35	2	18.1%	30	70.6
2019	NE	16/16	1142	613	373	60.8%	-3.8%	4057	24	8/14	4	5.2%	6.1	21	2.4%	17	550	16	26	34	3	22.0%	32	53.7
2020	TB	16/16	1025	610	401	65.7%	1.2%	4633	40	12/14	4	4.2%	7.1	11	25.0%	4	1518	3	30	6	3	-37.5%	-22	72.4
2021	TB			611	391	64.0%		4561	35	11	5		6.7		12.2%				33	27	3	-4.1%		

2019: 14% Behind 54% Short 20% Mid 12% Deep aDOT: 7.9 (27) YAC: 5 (24) ALEX: 1.0 2020: 12% Behind 50% Short 21% Mid 17% Deep aDOT: 9.7 (1) YAC: 4.5 (29) ALEX: 2.6

tions and 14 adjusted interceptions in 2020. Adjusted interceptions use game charting data to add dropped interceptions, plays where a defender most likely would have had an interception but couldn't hold onto the ball. Then we remove Hail Mary passes and interceptions thrown on fourth down when losing in the final two minutes of the game. We also remove "tipped interceptions," when a perfectly catchable ball deflected off the receiver's hands or chest and into the arms of a defender.

Overall, adjusted interception rate is higher than standard interception rate, so most quarterbacks will have more adjusted interceptions than standard interceptions. On average, a quarterback will have one additional adjusted interception for every 100 pass attempts. Once this difference is accounted for, adjusted interceptions are a better predictor of next year's interception total than standard interceptions.

The next column is fumbles (**FUM**), which adds together all fumbles by this player, whether turned over to the defense or recovered by the offense (explained in the essay "Pregame Show"). Even though this fumble total is listed among the passing numbers, it includes all fumbles, including those on sacks, aborted snaps, and rushing attempts. By listing fumbles and interceptions next to one another, we're giving readers a general idea of how many total turnovers the player was responsible for.

Next comes Adjusted Sack Rate (**ASR**). This is the same statistic you'll find in the team chapters, only here it is specific to the individual quarterback. It represents sacks plus intentional grounding calls per pass play (total pass plays = pass attempts + sacks) adjusted based on down, distance, and strength of schedule. For reference, the NFL average was 7.1% in 2018, 7.0% in 2019, and 6.4% in 2020.

The next two columns are Net Yards per Pass (**NY/P**), a standard stat but a particularly good one, and the player's rank (**Rk**) in Net Yards per Pass for that season. Net Yards per Pass consists of passing yards minus yards lost on sacks, divided by total pass plays.

The four columns remaining in passing stats give our advanced metrics: **DVOA** (Defense-adjusted Value Over Average) and **DYAR** (Defense-adjusted Yards Above Replacement), along with the player's rank in both. These metrics compare each quarterback's passing performance to league-average or replacement-level baselines based on the game situations that quarterback faced. DVOA and DYAR are also adjusted based on the opposing defense. The methods used to compute these numbers are described in detail in the "Statistical Toolbox" introduction at the front of the book. The important distinctions between them is that DVOA is a rate statistic, while DYAR is a cumulative statistic. Thus, a higher DVOA means more value per pass play, while a higher DYAR means more aggregate value over the entire season.

To qualify for a ranking in Net Yards per Pass, passing DVOA, and passing DYAR in a given season, a quarterback must have had 200 pass plays in that season. 35 quarterbacks are ranked for 2018, 34 for 2019, and 36 for 2020.

The shaded five columns on the right contain rushing statistics, starting with **Runs**, rushing yards (**Yds**), and rushing touchdowns (**TD**). Once again, these are official NFL totals and include kneeldowns, which means you get to enjoy statistics such as Jameis Winston rushing eight times for -6 yards. The final two columns give **DVOA** and **DYAR** for quarterback rushing, which are calculated separately from passing. Rankings for these statistics, as well as numbers that are not adjusted for defense (YAR and VOA) can be found on our website, FootballOutsiders.com.

The last number listed is the Total **QBR** metric from ESPN Stats & Information. Total QBR is based on the expected points added by the quarterback on each play, then adjusts the numbers to a scale of 0-100. There are four main differences between Total QBR and DVOA:

- Total QBR incorporates information from game charting, such as passes dropped or thrown away on purpose.
- Total QBR splits responsibility on plays between the quarterback, his receivers, and his blockers. Drops, for example, are more on the receiver, as are yards after the catch, and some sacks are more on the offensive line than others.
- Total QBR has a clutch factor which adds (or subtracts) value for quarterbacks who perform best (or worst) in high-leverage situations.
- Total QBR combines passing and rushing value into one number and differentiates between scrambles and planned runs.

The italicized row of statistics for the 2021 season is our 2021 KUBIAK projection, as detailed above. Again, in the interest of producing meaningful statistics, all quarterbacks are projected to start a full 17-game season, regardless of the likelihood of them actually doing so.

The final line below the KUBIAK projection represents data on how far the quarterback throws his passes. First, we break down charted passes based on distance: **Behind** (anything behind the line of scrimmage), **Short** (0 to 9 yards), **Mid** (10 to 19 yards), and **Deep** (20 or more yards). These numbers are based on distance in the air only and include both complete and incomplete passes. Passes thrown away or tipped at the line are not included, nor are passes on which the quarterback's arm was hit by a defender while in motion. We also give average depth of target (**aDOT**) and average yards after catch (**YAC**) with the rank in parentheses for the 34 quarterbacks who qualify. The final number listed here is **ALEX**, which stands for Air Less EXpected, and measures the distance of each quarterback's average third-down throw compared to how many yards were needed for a first down. Aaron Rodgers' ALEX of 4.8 means his average third-down pass was thrown 4.8 yards deeper than the sticks, the highest in the league; Alex Smith (whom the stat is named for) had the lowest ALEX at -2.6.

A number of third- and fourth-string quarterbacks are briefly discussed at the end of the chapter in a section we call "Going Deep."

Top 20 QB by Passing DYAR (Total Value), 2020

Rank	Player	Team	DYAR
1	Patrick Mahomes	KC	1720
2	Aaron Rodgers	GB	1649
3	Tom Brady	TB	1518
4	Josh Allen	BUF	1460
5	Deshaun Watson	HOU	1234
6	Ryan Tannehill	TEN	1046
7	Derek Carr	LV	925
8	Justin Herbert	LAC	861
9	Kirk Cousins	MIN	837
10	Matt Ryan	ATL	817
11	Russell Wilson	SEA	773
12	Drew Brees	NO	769
13	Philip Rivers	IND	765
14	Matthew Stafford	DET	684
15	Kyler Murray	ARI	590
16	Baker Mayfield	CLE	545
17	Ben Roethlisberger	PIT	518
18	Teddy Bridgewater	CAR	446
19	Dak Prescott	DAL	399
20	Jared Goff	LAR	385

Minimum 200 passes

Top 20 QB by Passing DVOA (Value per Pass), 2020

Rank	Player	Team	DVOA
1	Aaron Rodgers	GB	33.7%
2	Patrick Mahomes	KC	31.7%
3	Josh Allen	BUF	25.9%
4	Tom Brady	TB	25.0%
5	Deshaun Watson	HOU	20.2%
6	Ryan Tannehill	TEN	19.6%
7	Drew Brees	NO	17.6%
8	Dak Prescott	DAL	14.0%
9	Derek Carr	LV	14.0%
10	Kirk Cousins	MIN	12.0%
11	Justin Herbert	LAC	10.2%
12	Philip Rivers	IND	9.9%
13	Russell Wilson	SEA	8.1%
14	Matthew Stafford	DET	7.7%
15	Matt Ryan	ATL	7.6%
16	Ryan Fitzpatrick	MIA	7.5%
17	Baker Mayfield	CLE	5.1%
18	Kyler Murray	ARI	4.6%
19	Teddy Bridgewater	CAR	2.0%
20	Ben Roethlisberger	PIT	1.1%

Minimum 200 passes

Brandon Allen

Height: 6-2   Weight: 209   College: Arkansas   Draft: 2016/6 (201)   Born: 5-Sep-1992   Age: 29   Risk: Green

Year	Tm	G/GS	Snaps	Att	Cmp	C%	CPOE	Yds	TD	INT/Adj	FUM	ASR	NY/P	Rk	DVOA	Rk	DYAR	Rk	Runs	Yds	TD	DVOA	DYAR	QBR
2019	DEN	3/3	180	84	39	46.4%	-12.9%	515	3	2/4	0	9.1%	4.9	--	-30.5%	--	-115	--	10	39	0	41.2%	21	38.1
2020	CIN	5/5	277	142	90	63.4%	-4.3%	925	5	4/6	1	5.2%	5.8	--	-23.8%	--	-125	--	13	27	0	-31.8%	-14	44.8
2021	CIN			561	342	60.9%		3669	22	14	6		5.8		-16.5%				58	164	2	-27.0%		

2019	20% Behind	46% Short	18% Mid	16% Deep	aDOT: 8.1 (--)	YAC: 6.0 (--)	ALEX: 0.7	2020	17% Behind	53% Short	18% Mid	12% Deep	aDOT: 7.1 (--)	YAC: 6.2 (--)	ALEX: 1.3

Allen is immobile and scatter-armed. There's no evidence that he can execute an offense any more sophisticated than the easy-reader game plan coaches might whip up for a late-round rookie or street free agent. His career highlights are two decent performances in victories against opponents in self-destruct mode: last year's post-Bill O'Brien Texans and the 2019 Browns during one of their swoons. His qualification for remaining on an NFL depth chart is that he is someone who always ends up on an NFL depth chart. Allen's competition behind Joe Burrow is Kyle Shurmur, whose qualification for being on an NFL depth chart is that his dad was a coach. This is how mediocrity perpetuates itself.

Josh Allen

Height: 6-5   Weight: 237   College: Wyoming   Draft: 2018/1 (7)   Born: 21-May-1996   Age: 25   Risk: Green

Year	Tm	G/GS	Snaps	Att	Cmp	C%	CPOE	Yds	TD	INT/Adj	FUM	ASR	NY/P	Rk	DVOA	Rk	DYAR	Rk	Runs	Yds	TD	DVOA	DYAR	QBR
2018	BUF	12/11	719	320	169	52.8%	-8.3%	2074	10	12/16	8	8.4%	5.3	33	-35.9%	33	-534	33	89	631	8	33.3%	192	52.0
2019	BUF	16/16	1010	461	271	58.8%	-2.4%	3089	20	9/12	14	8.2%	5.8	28	-11.8%	28	-21	28	109	510	9	6.5%	100	47.3
2020	BUF	16/16	1035	572	396	69.2%	4.6%	4544	37	10/15	9	4.8%	7.3	5	25.9%	3	1460	4	102	421	8	3.0%	74	81.7
2021	BUF			619	413	66.7%		4812	32	11	11		7.0		7.1%				117	552	8	10.2%		

2019	11% Behind	50% Short	22% Mid	16% Deep	aDOT: 9.7 (4)	YAC: 5.0 (25)	ALEX: 3.4	2020	14% Behind	51% Short	22% Mid	13% Deep	aDOT: 9.0 (7)	YAC: 4.7 (25)	ALEX: 2.0

It's very easy to find superlatives for Allen's 2020 season, but here's one we didn't use in the Buffalo team chapter: Allen led the league with 293 attempts, 874 DYAR, and a 33.1% DVOA when throwing on first down. That's the most first-down DYAR since Matt Ryan's MVP year in 2016. Defenses generally are keyed against the run more on first down than on others, making it a prime passing down. But because the Bills passed so much, they faced an average of 5.02 defensive backs on first down, most in the league, with just 6.48 average players in the box—no easy pitches and catches against undermanned secondaries here. Allen was going to throw on first down, every defense knew he was going to throw on first down, and yet he still led the league. It's one thing to have accuracy schemed up for you; it's another entirely to put up those kind of efficiency numbers when you're the engine that runs the offense.

Kyle Allen Height: 6-3 Weight: 211 College: Houston Draft: 2018/FA Born: 8-Mar-1996 Age: 25 Risk: Green

Year	Tm	G/GS	Snaps	Att	Cmp	C%	CPOE	Yds	TD	INT/Adj	FUM	ASR	NY/P	Rk	DVOA	Rk	DYAR	Rk	Runs	Yds	TD	DVOA	DYAR	QBR
2018	CAR	2/1	68	31	20	64.5%	3.0%	266	2	0/0	0	-0.7%	8.6	--	67.4%	--	158	--	5	19	1	52.8%	19	95.7
2019	CAR	13/12	897	489	303	62.0%	-1.1%	3322	17	16/26	13	9.0%	5.5	32	-22.4%	32	-395	33	32	106	2	-9.0%	4	36.4
2020	WAS	4/4	177	87	60	69.0%	5.3%	610	4	1/1	1	6.9%	6.0	--	-8.0%	--	20	--	7	26	1	9.7%	7	74.4
2021	WAS			577	376	65.1%		4057	24	14	10		6.2		-10.7%				50	193	4	-5.1%		

2019	14% Behind	50% Short	23% Mid	13% Deep	aDOT: 8.5 (19)	YAC: 5.4 (12)	ALEX: 2.2	2020	21% Behind	51% Short	21% Mid	8% Deep	aDOT: 6.3 (--)	YAC: 5.4 (--)	ALEX: -0.4

Allen got a brief stint as the starter in Washington after the team traded a fifth-round pick to get a backup familiar with the Scott Turner offense. Allen's -8.0% DVOA looked fantastic compared to some of the other Washington performances, but much of that was due to a 26.2% DVOA on third downs; he was -20.0% or worse on both first and second downs. Allen completed 69% of his passes by following the Washington formula of short passes. Among 45 quarterbacks with at least 85 pass attempts in 2020, only Alex Smith had a lower aDOT than Allen.

C.J. Beathard Height: 6-2 Weight: 215 College: Iowa Draft: 2017/3 (104) Born: 16-Nov-1993 Age: 28 Risk: Green

Year	Tm	G/GS	Snaps	Att	Cmp	C%	CPOE	Yds	TD	INT/Adj	FUM	ASR	NY/P	Rk	DVOA	Rk	DYAR	Rk	Runs	Yds	TD	DVOA	DYAR	QBR
2018	SF	6/5	340	169	102	60.4%	-6.7%	1252	8	7/8	5	8.7%	5.9	--	-24.3%	--	-156	--	19	69	1	-25.2%	-13	43.3
2020	SF	6/2	186	104	66	63.5%	-1.3%	787	6	0/2	3	7.2%	6.4	--	-1.0%	--	75	--	6	28	0	1.3%	3	53.4
2021	JAX			548	349	63.7%		3816	25	16	11		6.2		-13.5%				65	316	4	0.5%		

2019										2020	8% Behind	62% Short	18% Mid	12% Deep	aDOT: 8.1 (--)	YAC: 5.2 (--)	ALEX: 1.0

One of the wild mid-round picks from the early Kyle Shanahan days (remember Joe Williams?), Beathard lost his job as primary mistake-prone backup to Nick Mullens in 2019, but 2020 brought enough Mullens to everyone's life that he was benched in some games and injured for the Week 17 finale, where Beathard led the 49ers to an upset and playoff-denying win over the Cardinals. The Jaguars came calling in the offseason and Beathard probably slots in as a below-average backup who is stretched if the run game is bad.

Tim Boyle Height: 6-4 Weight: 233 College: Eastern Kentucky Draft: 2018/FA Born: 3-Oct-1994 Age: 27 Risk: Green

Year	Tm	G/GS	Snaps	Att	Cmp	C%	CPOE	Yds	TD	INT/Adj	FUM	ASR	NY/P	Rk	DVOA	Rk	DYAR	Rk	Runs	Yds	TD	DVOA	DYAR	QBR
2019	GB	3/0	21	4	3	75.0%	-3.7%	15	0	0/0	0	-1.9%	3.8	--	37.2%	--	17	--	5	-7	0	--	--	96.4
2020	GB	8/0	22	0	0	0.0%	0.0%	0	0	0/0	1	97.3%	-11.0	--	-666.1%	--	-40	--	13	-9	0	--	--	0.0
2021	DET			605	362	59.8%		4414	28	14	8		6.5		-6.8%				43	64	2	-38.2%		

2019	20% Behind	60% Short	20% Mid	0% Deep	aDOT: 4.4 (--)	YAC: 4.7 (--)	ALEX: -4.0	2020	0% Behind	0% Short	0% Mid	0% Deep	aDOT: 0.0 (--)	YAC: 0.0 (--)	ALEX: 0.0

Boyle has one of the more unusual stat lines in football with just four pass attempts in two seasons but 18 carries for -16 yards. He got a workout from his many kneeldowns in Aaron Rodgers victories. Now that the Packers have Jordan Love to take a knee, Boyle has left for Detroit. Despite his lack of pedigree as an undrafted free agent, Boyle has told reporters he believes he can win the Lions' starting job. That may sound crazy after the team traded for Jared Goff, but that trade included multiple draft picks as well as Goff because the quarterback isn't worth his contract. He's a sunk cost for his new team, and so Boyle has a better chance to earn his way onto the field there than he would almost anywhere else. Meanwhile, Boyle led all quarterbacks with a 112.9 passer rating in the 2019 preseason, the only one he has played in his career since COVID cancelled those games in 2020. It isn't much of a reason for optimism, but it's better than if he had played poorly in those opportunities.

Tom Brady Height: 6-4 Weight: 225 College: Michigan Draft: 2000/6 (199) Born: 3-Aug-1977 Age: 44 Risk: Yellow

Year	Tm	G/GS	Snaps	Att	Cmp	C%	CPOE	Yds	TD	INT/Adj	FUM	ASR	NY/P	Rk	DVOA	Rk	DYAR	Rk	Runs	Yds	TD	DVOA	DYAR	QBR
2018	NE	16/16	1092	570	375	65.8%	0.0%	4355	29	11/12	4	3.8%	7.1	8	15.4%	7	1034	8	23	35	2	18.1%	30	70.6
2019	NE	16/16	1142	613	373	60.8%	-3.8%	4057	24	8/14	4	5.2%	6.1	21	2.4%	17	550	16	26	34	3	22.0%	32	53.7
2020	TB	16/16	1025	610	401	65.7%	1.2%	4633	40	12/14	4	4.2%	7.1	11	25.0%	4	1518	3	30	6	3	-37.5%	-22	72.4
2021	TB			660	422	64.0%		4989	37	12	6		6.8		14.1%				35	29	3	-24.6%		

| 2019 | 14% Behind | 54% Short | 20% Mid | 12% Deep | aDOT: 7.9 (27) | YAC: 5.0 (24) | ALEX: 1.0 | 2020 | 12% Behind | 50% Short | 21% Mid | 17% Deep | aDOT: 9.7 (1) | YAC: 4.5 (29) | ALEX: 2.6 |

He did it. Tom Brady proved he no longer needed Bill Belichick to win. All he needed was the best group of pass-catchers on the face of the Earth.

In many ways, Brady's 2020 was on par with his 2017 (4,577 yards, 32 touchdowns, seven interceptions, 27.8% DVOA). Other than that time he lost track of downs against the Bears, he showed no obvious signs of decline. One vulnerability has emerged, however. Brady used to burn defenses when they blitzed him. That's not so anymore. Last season, the Buccaneers had a 41.4% DVOA (8.1 yards per pass) against four pass-rushers but a -0.5% DVOA (5.8 yards per pass) against five or more, and the Patriots had a similar drop-off in 2019. You have to go back to 2016 to find the last season Brady was better against a blitz than against a four-man rush. In fact, Brady had trouble with pressure in general in 2020. He had the league's third-largest gap in DVOA between plays without pressure (61.8%, sixth) and plays with pressure (-108.3%, 28th). It's no coincidence Brady threw a fit over the NFL's relaxed jersey number rule. "Good luck trying to block the right people now !! !!" he said in an Instagram post. "Going to make for a lot of bad football."

Tom Brady vs. the Blitz, 2016-2020

Season	Team	Four Rushers		Five or More Rushers		Diff	
		DVOA	Yd/Pass	DVOA	Yd/Pass	DVOA	Yd/Pass
2016	NE	53.8%	7.7	71.8%	8.8	+18.0%	+1.1
2017	NE	58.7%	7.9	26.1%	6.6	-32.6%	-1.3
2018	NE	41.2%	7.9	17.9%	7.3	-23.3%	-0.6
2019	NE	21.8%	6.5	-16.1%	5.0	-37.9%	-1.5
2020	TB	41.4%	8.1	-0.5%	5.8	-41.9%	-2.3

Stats listed are team totals and include a handful of passes by backup QBs and other players.

Drew Brees Height: 6-0 Weight: 209 College: Purdue Draft: 2001/2 (32) Born: 15-Jan-1979 Age: 42 Risk: N/A

Year	Tm	G/GS	Snaps	Att	Cmp	C%	CPOE	Yds	TD	INT/Adj	FUM	ASR	NY/P	Rk	DVOA	Rk	DYAR	Rk	Runs	Yds	TD	DVOA	DYAR	QBR
2018	NO	15/15	978	489	364	74.4%	8.5%	3992	32	5/7	5	4.0%	7.6	3	36.7%	2	1631	2	31	22	4	29.0%	43	80.8
2019	NO	11/11	646	378	281	74.3%	8.5%	2979	27	4/10	0	3.6%	7.5	5	39.8%	1	1316	3	9	-4	1	70.9%	14	71.7
2020	NO	12/12	717	390	275	70.5%	1.2%	2942	24	6/13	6	4.4%	7.1	12	17.6%	7	769	12	18	-2	2	2.4%	7	74.5

| 2019 | 18% Behind | 52% Short | 22% Mid | 8% Deep | aDOT: 6.7 (33) | YAC: 5.3 (15) | ALEX: 0.8 | 2020 | 17% Behind | 53% Short | 24% Mid | 5% Deep | aDOT: 6.4 (35) | YAC: 5.4 (13) | ALEX: 0.1 |

It's difficult to quantify the legacy of Drew Brees, as it transcends the Saints to impact not only New Orleans sports but even the city itself. He arrived alongside Sean Payton in 2006, the summer after Hurricane Katrina. The Saints were coming off a 3-13 season, spent playing games anywhere but home while the city began to rebuild. By the end of that year, the Saints were not only back in the Superdome but back in the playoffs as division champions, Payton was Coach of the Year, and Brees was the MVP runner-up and first-team All-Pro quarterback. More significantly for the city, he was also the joint-holder of the Walter Payton Man of the Year award for his contribution to the city's rebuilding effort. It's no exaggeration to assert that Brees, the Saints, and the Superdome became iconic, a living symbol of the city's recovery from the previous devastation.

The years with Brees at quarterback were by far the best in Saints franchise history. In the 34 seasons before his arrival, the franchise had three division titles; with him, they won twice as many in less than half the time. Prior to Brees, the Saints had one playoff win; with Brees, they won nine playoff games in 15 seasons. The pinnacle was a victory in Super Bowl XLIV against the Colts, with Brees himself as game MVP. Though he famously never won league MVP, arguably the greatest quarterback never to do so, he was selected to the Pro Bowl in 12 of 15 seasons, won Offensive Player of the Year twice, and led the league in passing yards seven times. At the time of his retirement, there have only been a dozen 5,000-yard passing seasons in league history. Brees has five of them and is the only player in history to have done it more than once.

Brees retires as the career leader in completions and passing yards, and as the holder of the records for completion rate in a season and most consecutive games with a touchdown pass. He finished in DVOA's top 10 quarterbacks an unprecedented 17 straight times (including his final two seasons in San Diego) and only injury last year capped him at 16 straight seasons in the top eight by DYAR. He was one of the most prolific, productive, efficient passers in league annals, one of the very few players who could justifiably be mentioned in the same breath as Peyton Manning and Tom Brady over the past decade and a half. By any measure, he is the greatest player in Saints history, probably the greatest sportsman ever in the city of New Orleans, one of the greatest NFL quarterbacks of all time, and a certainty for the Hall of Fame. Somehow, his legacy for the city itself might be greater still.

Teddy Bridgewater Height: 6-2 Weight: 215 College: Louisville Draft: 2014/1 (32) Born: 10-Nov-1992 Age: 29 Risk: Green

Year	Tm	G/GS	Snaps	Att	Cmp	C%	CPOE	Yds	TD	INT/Adj	FUM	ASR	NY/P	Rk	DVOA	Rk	DYAR	Rk	Runs	Yds	TD	DVOA	DYAR	QBR
2018	NO	5/1	71	23	14	60.9%	-3.3%	118	1	1/1	0	8.6%	4.4	--	-39.7%	--	-46	--	11	5	0	-58.4%	-13	33.6
2019	NO	9/5	408	196	133	67.9%	2.2%	1384	9	2/1	1	6.4%	6.2	16	15.3%	9	340	20	28	31	0	-32.7%	-19	48.9
2020	CAR	15/15	929	492	340	69.1%	3.4%	3733	15	11/18	6	6.4%	6.7	14	2.0%	19	446	18	53	279	5	6.6%	43	64.1
2021	DEN			563	372	66.2%		4285	25	12	7		6.9		1.1%				58	271	4	6.2%		

| 2019 | 17% Behind | 59% Short | 16% Mid | 8% Deep | aDOT: 6.2 (34) | YAC: 5.6 (9) | ALEX: -1.4 | 2020 | 17% Behind | 52% Short | 19% Mid | 12% Deep | aDOT: 7.6 (28) | YAC: 5.5 (11) | ALEX: -0.3 |

Just as everyone could have predicted, Bridgewater was the league's most average quarterback last season. Bridgewater finished 18th in DYAR, 18th in QBR, and 18th in difference between DVOA under pressure vs. without pressure among the league's 36 qualifying quarterbacks. The degree to which Bridgewater was perfectly fine is almost painful. What's interesting about Bridgewater's overall production, though, is that he fared better against man coverage (56.5% DVOA) than zone coverage (24.8% DVOA), which is counterintuitive for a player who wins with decision-making and patience rather than playmaking. While relatively productive on the whole, Bridgewater was frustrating to watch in large part because of how many cheap, somewhat useless yards he took in favor of gambling on tougher, more efficient plays. Bridgewater threw failed completions on a league-high 20% of his pass attempts, essentially meaning he took a ton of guaranteed short yet inefficient gains. Perhaps that will be a welcomed change in Denver, but there is no clear starter for the Broncos at the time of writing this, so it's hard to gauge how the Broncos feel about leaning into Drew Lock's polar opposite.

Jacoby Brissett Height: 6-4 Weight: 235 College: North Carolina State Draft: 2016/3 (91) Born: 11-Dec-1992 Age: 29 Risk: Green

Year	Tm	G/GS	Snaps	Att	Cmp	C%	CPOE	Yds	TD	INT/Adj	FUM	ASR	NY/P	Rk	DVOA	Rk	DYAR	Rk	Runs	Yds	TD	DVOA	DYAR	QBR
2018	IND	4/0	18	4	2	50.0%	1.6%	2	0	0/0	0	1.2%	0.5	--	-70.3%	--	-16	--	7	-7	0	--	--	100.0
2019	IND	15/15	961	447	272	60.9%	-2.6%	2942	18	6/8	7	5.8%	5.9	24	2.6%	16	414	19	56	228	4	10.1%	57	50.1
2020	IND	11/0	48	8	2	25.0%	-42.1%	17	0	0/0	0	30.6%	0.2	--	-135.2%	--	-68	--	17	19	3	18.0%	27	66.2
2021	MIA			579	357	61.7%		4006	26	10	8		6.2		-5.2%				65	202	6	1.7%		

| 2019 | 14% Behind | 51% Short | 24% Mid | 11% Deep | aDOT: 8.4 (21) | YAC: 5.6 (10) | ALEX: -0.3 | 2020 | 14% Behind | 57% Short | 14% Mid | 14% Deep | aDOT: 9.4 (--) | YAC: 9.0 (--) | ALEX: 4.0 |

With the aging, statuesque Philip Rivers under center, the Colts used Brissett as a situational specialist. Brissett had 47 offensive snaps in 2020; 21 were in garbage time or kneeling, one was an end-of-half Hail Mary, and the other 25 were all in high-leverage, short-yardage situations. His mobility gave them a dimension the statuesque Rivers couldn't and allowed them to play 11-on-11. As a strategic concept, we're 100% on board with that—Brissett may have peaked as an average quarterback, but coupled with the threat of a run, that makes him a more effective short-yardage player than Rivers was. And unlike the random nature of New Orleans' Taysom Hill experiments, the Colts' usage of Brissett was in specific situations for obvious purposes. As for the results? Brissett had 34 rushing DYAR with 3 or fewer yards to go, sixth among quarterbacks, and his 32.1% rushing DVOA was fifth among players with at least five short-yardage rushes. Those distinct services won't be necessary in Miami; Tua Tagoviloa had 29 rushing DYAR and a 23.8% DVOA on his short-yardage rushes.

Joe Burrow Height: 6-3 Weight: 221 College: Louisiana State Draft: 2020/1 (1) Born: 10-Dec-1996 Age: 25 Risk: Yellow

Year	Tm	G/GS	Snaps	Att	Cmp	C%	CPOE	Yds	TD	INT/Adj	FUM	ASR	NY/P	Rk	DVOA	Rk	DYAR	Rk	Runs	Yds	TD	DVOA	DYAR	QBR
2020	CIN	10/10	709	404	264	65.3%	0.2%	2688	13	5/10	9	7.3%	5.7	28	-7.3%	23	108	23	37	142	3	-31.8%	-43	56.5
2021	CIN			644	435	67.5%		4659	28	10	14		6.4		-3.3%				68	292	5	-1.6%		

| 2019 | | | | | | | | 2020 | 10% Behind | 54% Short | 25% Mid | 11% Deep | aDOT: 8.4 (15) | YAC: 4.3 (31) | ALEX: 1.6 |

When the Bengals unveiled their new uniforms across social media platforms in early spring, Burrow appeared seated and cross-legged, wearing shorts that revealed a 4-inch surgical scar on his knee. The scar looked as though the procedure was performed at the Gotham Henchmen Free Clinic by a supervillain with a tree saw; it was the sort of thing most folks would conceal beneath, say, team-appropriate tiger-striped sweatpants. Nothing quite illustrates the Bengals' inability to think things through like a promotional photo that screams "Our most important player was severely injured last year, to the point where it's unclear whether he could stand up for this photo. Season ticket plans are on sale now!"

Burrow's pressure rate of 33.6% (per Sports Info Solutions) was the 18th highest (and 19th lowest) among quarterbacks with 200 or more attempts. His average time to throw (per Next Gen Stats) was also a middle-of-the-pack 2.65 seconds. In other words, the numbers don't suggest that Burrow was constantly under siege or that Zac Taylor was forced to build his whole passing game out of tunnel screens to protect his quarterback.

Closer scrutiny of the numbers and the film indicates that Burrow's protection waxed and waned with the personnel on the offensive line, the opponent, and the game plan. At its best (healthy Jonah Williams, opponent with a weak pass rush like the Titans), it was kinda OK. At its worst (Hakeem Adenji and Fred Johnson at tackle against the Steelers, the Ravens blitzing from all angles against empty backfields) it was a devastating injury waiting to happen. Burrow's protection will be marginally better at best this year. His mobility may be limited. On the plus side, his weapons got an upgrade. If that sounds like the sort of fantasy risk that you like to take, go nuts.

Derek Carr

Height: 6-3   Weight: 210   College: Fresno State   Draft: 2014/2 (36)   Born: 3/28/1991   Age: 30   Risk: Green

Year	Tm	G/GS	Snaps	Att	Cmp	C%	CPOE	Yds	TD	INT/Adj	FUM	ASR	NY/P	Rk	DVOA	Rk	DYAR	Rk	Runs	Yds	TD	DVOA	DYAR	QBR
2018	OAK	16/16	1034	553	381	68.9%	3.4%	4049	19	10/20	12	8.6%	6.3	21	-1.0%	22	392	21	24	47	1	-0.3%	8	48.9
2019	OAK	16/16	1014	513	361	70.4%	6.1%	4054	21	8/9	7	6.0%	7.2	9	18.7%	8	1064	6	27	82	2	-60.6%	-49	62.2
2020	LV	16/16	1006	517	348	67.3%	2.1%	4103	27	9/10	11	5.4%	7.3	6	14.0%	9	925	7	39	140	3	-10.8%	3	71.2
2021	LV			580	398	68.6%		4612	28	11	11		7.2		7.7%				47	169	3	-6.7%		

| 2019 | 13% Behind | 61% Short | 18% Mid | 9% Deep | aDOT: 6.8 (32) | YAC: 5.9 (4) | ALEX: 1.3 | 2020 | 13% Behind | 54% Short | 19% Mid | 14% Deep | aDOT: 8.8 (8) | YAC: 5.6 (8) | ALEX: 4.4 |

There's something to appreciate about Derek Carr's consistency. His low-volatility play style often leaves one wanting more, but it's easier to gauge what Carr should provide at a base level than most any other quarterback in the league. Save for his rookie season, Carr has been just above-average in passing DVOA without pressure. He has never been higher than 12.0% DVOA or lower than -12.0% DVOA outside the pocket in each of the last three seasons, even settling right in on a neutral 0.0% in 2020. It's easy to chastise Carr for not taking his chances outside the pocket, but he also seldom puts the ball at risk and is often more of a non-factor than someone actively hindering the Raiders offense. That said, Carr did make an aggressive evolution from within the pocket last season, jumping his average depth of target from 6.8 yards to 8.8 yards. It took some time, but it seems Carr finally fully bought into Gruden's run-heavy, touchdown-to-checkdown approach, which is a lot easier to do with deep threats such as Henry Ruggs and Nelson Agholor in the offense. Hopefully the losses along the offensive line do not force Carr back to his conservative ways.

Kirk Cousins

Height: 6-3   Weight: 202   College: Michigan State   Draft: 2012/4 (102)   Born: 19-Aug-1988   Age: 33   Risk: Green

Year	Tm	G/GS	Snaps	Att	Cmp	C%	CPOE	Yds	TD	INT/Adj	FUM	ASR	NY/P	Rk	DVOA	Rk	DYAR	Rk	Runs	Yds	TD	DVOA	DYAR	QBR
2018	MIN	16/16	1051	606	425	70.1%	5.4%	4298	30	10/13	9	6.1%	6.2	23	2.7%	20	595	13	44	123	1	-13.2%	-2	62.0
2019	MIN	15/15	982	444	307	69.1%	6.2%	3603	26	6/8	10	7.0%	7.2	8	14.3%	10	795	7	31	63	1	-19.8%	-9	58.4
2020	MIN	16/16	1082	516	349	67.6%	4.6%	4265	35	13/12	9	7.7%	7.3	7	12.0%	10	837	9	32	156	1	26.3%	57	63.3
2021	MIN			538	373	69.4%		4373	31	12	10		7.3		9.7%				44	178	2	-6.3%		

| 2019 | 18% Behind | 51% Short | 16% Mid | 15% Deep | aDOT: 8.0 (24) | YAC: 5.8 (5) | ALEX: 2.3 | 2020 | 14% Behind | 53% Short | 21% Mid | 12% Deep | aDOT: 8.3 (20) | YAC: 5.5 (10) | ALEX: 1.4 |

You won't find a traditional passing metric that reflects poorly on Cousins. He has finished in the top 10 in completion percentage, yards per attempt, passing DVOA, and passing DYAR in each of the last two seasons. If the Vikings' decision to draft Kellen Mond in the third round is an indication they are dissatisfied with Cousins' performance, it's likely because of the confidence they have in their offensive scheme. The Vikings were a top-12 user of play-action in 2020 and a top-eight beneficiary with 1.8 more yards per attempt than on traditional dropbacks. Cousins showed splits that suggest he benefits from that scheme, such as his 23.7% passing DVOA on first downs versus 2.4% second and third downs, and 15.8% under center versus 7.9% on shotgun snaps. Still, the Vikings shouldn't hurry to move on from Cousins. He has shepherded top-10 offenses for the team and has not missed a game with an injury in six years as a starter. Other quarterbacks might not be so productive and so durable while taking hits on 15.5% of their dropbacks, second-most in football in 2020.

Andy Dalton

Height: 6-2 Weight: 220 College: TCU Draft: 2011/2 (35) Born: 29-Oct-1987 Age: 34 Risk: Red

Year	Tm	G/GS	Snaps	Att	Cmp	C%	CPOE	Yds	TD	INT/Adj	FUM	ASR	NY/P	Rk	DVOA	Rk	DYAR	Rk	Runs	Yds	TD	DVOA	DYAR	QBR
2018	CIN	11/11	627	365	226	61.9%	-3.1%	2566	21	11/13	1	5.8%	6.3	20	5.2%	17	404	19	16	99	0	11.9%	14	61.9
2019	CIN	13/13	927	528	314	59.5%	-3.7%	3494	16	14/21	8	6.7%	5.8	27	-10.6%	26	19	26	32	73	4	-7.7%	7	40.1
2020	DAL	11/9	619	333	216	64.9%	-1.5%	2170	14	8/12	2	6.8%	5.5	29	-16.7%	30	-136	29	28	114	0	5.2%	24	54.0
2021	CHI			588	377	64.1%		3931	25	14	7		6.0		-11.2%				56	207	3	-17.2%		

2019 13% Behind 49% Short 29% Mid 10% Deep aDOT: 8.6 (18) YAC: 4.9 (27) ALEX: 1.2 2020 15% Behind 57% Short 19% Mid 9% Deep aDOT: 7.1 (31) YAC: 4.8 (22) ALEX: 2.2

Dalton's reputation as a capable shepherd of his surrounding talent took a hit in 2020 when Dak Prescott's ankle injury forced him into a Cowboys lineup more gifted than any he ever had in Cincinnati and he underwhelmed. Dalton may become the next Ryan Fitzpatrick, a competent veteran to start for teams in transition and mentor rookie quarterbacks that will soon replace him, although he's four teams behind where Fitzpatrick was at age 33. Dalton should fill that role nicely for the Bears and Justin Fields in 2021, assuming Chicago general manager Ryan Pace is true to his word that Dalton will start in Week 1 over the team's quarterback of the future.

Chase Daniel

Height: 6-0 Weight: 229 College: Missouri Draft: 2009/FA Born: 7-Oct-1986 Age: 35 Risk: Green

Year	Tm	G/GS	Snaps	Att	Cmp	C%	CPOE	Yds	TD	INT/Adj	FUM	ASR	NY/P	Rk	DVOA	Rk	DYAR	Rk	Runs	Yds	TD	DVOA	DYAR	QBR
2018	CHI	5/2	148	76	53	69.7%	0.8%	515	3	2/3	4	10.7%	5.6	--	-37.9%	--	-152	--	13	3	0	-107.0%	-26	29.6
2019	CHI	3/1	131	64	45	70.3%	0.7%	435	3	2/2	0	9.8%	5.5	--	-13.2%	--	-9	--	6	6	0	-38.3%	-10	57.6
2020	DET	4/0	65	43	29	67.4%	-0.3%	264	1	2/3	0	7.1%	5.2	--	-23.5%	--	-36	--	2	16	0	57.0%	5	20.6
2021	LAC			559	385	68.9%		4124	26	15	5		6.6		-5.5%				31	140	1	-1.1%		

2019 16% Behind 63% Short 11% Mid 11% Deep aDOT: 6.9 (--) YAC: 3.0 (--) ALEX: -1.3 2020 10% Behind 65% Short 18% Mid 8% Deep aDOT: 6.6 (--) YAC: 4.1 (--) ALEX: 2.8

Chase Daniel is the definition of a backup who offers the bare minimum for non-disastrous quarterback play. Nothing more, nothing less. With the Bears, Daniels got progressively worse the later in a series he was working, seeing his DVOA fall from first down to second down to third/fourth down in both 2018 and 2019. Daniels' completion rate through those two years was also a flat 70%, only further solidifying that he is someone who will give an offense the easy throws and nothing more. Though creeping up on 35 years old in 2021, Daniels can still move around fairly well, but his indecisiveness outside the pocket and lack of arm strength often negate the possible upside of his mobility.

Sam Darnold

Height: 6-3 Weight: 225 College: USC Draft: 2018/1 (3) Born: 5-Jun-1997 Age: 24 Risk: Yellow

Year	Tm	G/GS	Snaps	Att	Cmp	C%	CPOE	Yds	TD	INT/Adj	FUM	ASR	NY/P	Rk	DVOA	Rk	DYAR	Rk	Runs	Yds	TD	DVOA	DYAR	QBR
2018	NYJ	13/13	810	414	239	57.7%	-4.7%	2865	17	15/21	5	6.7%	6.0	27	-15.2%	30	-110	30	44	138	1	0.2%	23	48.4
2019	NYJ	13/13	853	441	273	61.9%	0.5%	3024	19	13/15	11	7.2%	6.0	23	-20.4%	31	-290	32	33	62	2	-20.1%	-7	43.6
2020	NYJ	12/12	739	364	217	59.6%	-3.5%	2208	9	11/19	4	8.8%	5.0	34	-32.2%	33	-540	35	37	217	2	35.3%	72	40.7
2021	CAR			588	368	62.5%		4144	22	13	9		6.2		-11.3%				53	260	3	-3.2%		

2019 11% Behind 50% Short 26% Mid 13% Deep aDOT: 8.9 (13) YAC: 5.4 (13) ALEX: 2.5 2020 15% Behind 48% Short 25% Mid 12% Deep aDOT: 8.4 (16) YAC: 5.3 (15) ALEX: 1.5

By almost any measure, Sam Darnold's third year was a disappointment. A third successive decline in DVOA and the second-worst DYAR of any quarterback barely scratches the surface of his struggles:

- Darnold was pressured more often than any other quarterback, on 33.0% of his dropbacks versus a league average of 25.2%. Only Carson Wentz and Daniel Jones were sacked at a higher rate.
- When not under pressure, his 7.2% DVOA ranked third worst behind only the Washington duo of Alex Smith and Dwayne Haskins.
- He threw the fourth-most adjusted interceptions (19), and his 5.3% adjusted interception rate was second behind only Nick Foles. His raw interception rate, without adjustment, was still fifth worst.
- He had the fifth-worst rate of failed completions, ahead of only Foles, the Washington pair, and the man he is replacing in Carolina, Teddy Bridgewater.

In summary, however you slice it, Darnold sits quite comfortably among the very worst passers of the 2020 season. It is likely that his struggles were heightened by a talent-starved and poorly coached offense, and that better coaching and a stronger supporting cast in Carolina will help Darnold look significantly better than he did in New York. His predecessor, Teddy Bridgewater, set career highs in completion rate, yards, touchdowns, net yards per attempt, and DVOA with the Panthers last year (min. 200 attempts), and we project Darnold to do the same. That might go some way toward justifying Carolina's investment, because based on Darnold's history alone, the trade looks very iffy indeed.

Ben DiNucci — Height: 6-3 — Weight: 210 — College: James Madison — Draft: 2020/7 (231) — Born: 24-Nov-1996 — Age: 25 — Risk: Green

Year	Tm	G/GS	Snaps	Att	Cmp	C%	CPOE	Yds	TD	INT/Adj	FUM	ASR	NY/P	Rk	DVOA	Rk	DYAR	Rk	Runs	Yds	TD	DVOA	DYAR	QBR
2020	DAL	3/1	94	43	23	53.5%	-12.5%	219	0	0/2	4	11.7%	3.0	--	-78.0%	--	-199	--	6	22	0	-32.9%	-7	13.5
2021	DAL			573	337	58.8%		3949	23	12	13		6.1		-10.9%				57	233	3	-3.9%		
2019														2020	22% Behind		44% Short		22% Mid	12% Deep	aDOT: 8.4 (--)		YAC: 5.8 (--)	ALEX: 0.4

DiNucci was a typical seventh-round, small-program rookie emergency starter when he faced the Eagles in Week 8. Mike McCarthy called a double reverse on the second play from scrimmage and an Ezekiel Elliott direct snap on the fourth, signaling to the defense that "yep, this is gonna be mostly bullsh*t." DiNucci completed enough simple passes and ran well enough to not embarrass himself, but the Cowboys replaced him with Garrett Gilbert (who had been on the team's Zoom meeting list for about two weeks) in Week 9. DiNucci is probably no worse than Gilbert and Cooper Rush, the two other competitors for the clipboard job behind Dak Prescott.

Jeff Driskel — Height: 6-4 — Weight: 235 — College: Louisiana Tech — Draft: 2016/6 (207) — Born: 23-Apr-1993 — Age: 28 — Risk: Green

Year	Tm	G/GS	Snaps	Att	Cmp	C%	CPOE	Yds	TD	INT/Adj	FUM	ASR	NY/P	Rk	DVOA	Rk	DYAR	Rk	Runs	Yds	TD	DVOA	DYAR	QBR
2018	CIN	9/5	372	176	105	59.7%	-6.0%	1003	6	2/8	4	9.4%	4.5	--	-16.4%	--	-61	--	25	130	2	-2.8%	10	31.6
2019	DET	3/3	223	105	62	59.0%	-4.4%	685	4	4/5	1	9.8%	5.6	--	-24.2%	--	-91	--	22	151	1	37.0%	52	47.9
2020	DEN	3/1	115	64	35	54.7%	-10.1%	432	3	2/2	0	12.1%	4.5	--	-18.9%	--	-36	--	6	28	0	24.8%	14	42.8
2021	HOU			546	330	60.4%		3763	24	13	7		6.1		-14.0%				80	441	4	3.4%		
2019	17% Behind	47% Short		23% Mid	13% Deep		aDOT: 8.7 (--)		YAC: 4.7 (--)		ALEX: -1.6			2020	13% Behind		38% Short		37% Mid	13% Deep	aDOT: 10.6 (--)		YAC: 3.7 (--)	ALEX: -0.8

Jeff Driskel may be trying to institute his own Ryan Fitzpatrick-esque curse. Driskel was on three different teams the last three years, totaling nine starts over that span with at least one per team. Last year's action was a good example of Driskel's limitations as a backup, though. As far as non-pressured plays and plays within the pocket, Driskel was at or around average for an NFL quarterback, but his -90.2% DVOA under pressure was subpar and his -80.6% DVOA outside the pocket was abysmal. Of course, these are volatile statistics on a small sample, but Driskel is the kind of quarterback who constantly tries to push the envelope and test tight windows without the timing or arm talent to do so at a consistent level. Driskel's non-disastrous performance on "standard" plays as well as his mobility still make him a decent backup option, though.

Jacob Eason — Height: 6-6 — Weight: 231 — College: Washington — Draft: 2020/4 (122) — Born: 17-Nov-1997 — Age: 24 — Risk: Green

Year	Tm	G/GS	Snaps	Att	Cmp	C%	CPOE	Yds	TD	INT/Adj	FUM	ASR	NY/P	Rk	DVOA	Rk	DYAR	Rk	Runs	Yds	TD	DVOA	DYAR	QBR
2021	IND			573	349	60.8%		3946	25	14	9		6.2		-9.7%				45	162	3	-10.4%		

A telling start of a question asked to Eason in OTAs was: "Any time we talk to Frank or Chris about you, they sort of agree that the next step is … playing." Well, yeah. Eason was inactive for the entire season behind Philip Rivers and Jacoby Brissett. With them gone and Carson Wentz in, Eason stands to be the top choice to be the backup. When Football Outsiders draft analyst Derrik Klassen charted Eason he saw weaknesses in accuracy under pressure—Eason was the worst of the quarterbacks Klassen scouted in that class by over 4%—and deep accuracy. Those are two pretty important things for an NFL quarterback to have. We'll see if he developed any further on those two things while learning how to play football by osmosis last year.

Justin Fields — Height: 6-3 — Weight: 228 — College: Ohio State — Draft: 2021/1 (11) — Born: 5-Mar-1999 — Age: 22 — Risk: Green

Year	Tm	G/GS	Snaps	Att	Cmp	C%	CPOE	Yds	TD	INT/Adj	FUM	ASR	NY/P	Rk	DVOA	Rk	DYAR	Rk	Runs	Yds	TD	DVOA	DYAR	QBR
2021	CHI			525	341	64.8%		3609	24	15	12		6.1		-12.6%				125	821	7	2.8%		

Fields seems to have the widest range of scouting opinions in his class, and that may be due to outside uncertainty in how he played versus how Ohio State asked him to play. He routinely held the ball in the pocket for more time than other rookie passers this year, but that allowed him to work down the field. He has the arm strength to avoid the anticipatory throws other passers must make and the athleticism to tuck and run for first downs when plays fail to develop. In fact, he has all the tools. With 83.2% adjusted accuracy, Fields is the most accurate passer that Football Outsiders draft analyst Derrik Klassen has charted since 2016. Fields' traditional statistics, however, are hurt by a class-leading 5.3% drop rate, and his perception seems to suffer from an association with recent Ohio State quarterback bust Dwayne Haskins that has no bearing on his own NFL potential. The Bears paid a lot to move up to draft him, but Fields looks more like a No. 1 pick than a No. 11 pick in his metrics.

Ryan Finley

Height: 6-4 Weight: 207 College: North Carolina State Draft: 2019/4 (104) Born: 26-Dec-1994 Age: 27 Risk: N/A

Year	Tm	G/GS	Snaps	Att	Cmp	C%	CPOE	Yds	TD	INT/Adj	FUM	ASR	NY/P	Rk	DVOA	Rk	DYAR	Rk	Runs	Yds	TD	DVOA	DYAR	QBR
2019	CIN	3/3	196	87	41	47.1%	-18.5%	474	2	2/5	4	10.5%	4.0	--	-59.8%	--	-290	--	10	77	0	35.4%	22	23.5
2020	CIN	5/1	90	32	17	53.1%	-9.1%	164	1	2/3	0	19.4%	2.5	--	-82.9%	--	-167	--	11	66	1	23.0%	20	49.3

| 2019 | 6% Behind | 56% Short | 24% Mid | 14% Deep | aDOT: 8.7 (--) | YAC: 5.0 (--) | ALEX: 1.0 | 2020 | 17% Behind | 47% Short | 17% Mid | 20% Deep | aDOT: 10.2 (--) | YAC: 4.2 (--) | ALEX: 5.8 |

Finley spurred a Monday Night Football upset of the Steelers in his lone 2020 start, but through 119 career passing attempts he has been sacked 20 times and has averaged 3.5 net yards per pass attempt. He is averaging 6.8 yards per rush attempt, though! Maybe he could do more of that. Anyway, it was weird that the Texans traded for him, weird that they traded for him to release him, and weird that he was valued enough to be traded for in the first place.

Ryan Fitzpatrick

Height: 6-2 Weight: 228 College: Harvard Draft: 2005/7 (250) Born: 24-Nov-1982 Age: 39 Risk: Green

Year	Tm	G/GS	Snaps	Att	Cmp	C%	CPOE	Yds	TD	INT/Adj	FUM	ASR	NY/P	Rk	DVOA	Rk	DYAR	Rk	Runs	Yds	TD	DVOA	DYAR	QBR
2018	TB	8/7	428	246	164	66.7%	3.4%	2366	17	12/14	4	5.5%	8.8	1	16.8%	6	473	15	36	152	2	15.9%	40	63.7
2019	MIA	15/13	885	502	311	62.0%	-0.6%	3529	20	13/15	9	7.4%	6.2	19	1.3%	19	432	18	54	243	4	2.2%	33	66.5
2020	MIA	9/7	496	267	183	68.5%	1.7%	2091	13	8/13	2	6.2%	7.2	9	7.5%	16	362	21	30	151	2	14.6%	39	77.3
2021	WAS			615	405	65.8%		4408	26	15	7		6.3		-8.0%				57	282	4	2.9%		

| 2019 | 10% Behind | 47% Short | 30% Mid | 13% Deep | aDOT: 9.4 (7) | YAC: 4.0 (34) | ALEX: 4.0 | 2020 | 10% Behind | 51% Short | 30% Mid | 9% Deep | aDOT: 8.3 (21) | YAC: 4.7 (27) | ALEX: 2.2 |

Assessing the outlook for Fitzpatrick's 2021 comes with untangling all the indicators for regression from 2020. No quarterback was better under pressure than Fitzpatrick with 11.2% DVOA and more yards per play with pressure than without. Fitzpatrick was below average in DVOA without pressure. At the same time, Fitzpatrick was good on early downs (12.7% on each of first and second downs) but posted negative DVOA on third downs (-10.8%). Fitzpatrick is always going to be a quarterback willing to test tight windows, but he might not need to as often with a plus route runner in Terry McLaurin and a yards-after-the-catch threat in Curtis Samuel. That type of supporting cast could work to push back some of the regression bound to hit the 39-year-old quarterback.

Joe Flacco

Height: 6-6 Weight: 245 College: Delaware Draft: 2008/1 (18) Born: 16-Jan-1985 Age: 36 Risk: Green

Year	Tm	G/GS	Snaps	Att	Cmp	C%	CPOE	Yds	TD	INT/Adj	FUM	ASR	NY/P	Rk	DVOA	Rk	DYAR	Rk	Runs	Yds	TD	DVOA	DYAR	QBR
2018	BAL	9/9	641	379	232	61.2%	-1.8%	2465	12	6/11	3	4.3%	6.1	25	5.4%	16	429	18	19	45	0	2.9%	13	57.4
2019	DEN	8/8	537	262	171	65.3%	2.3%	1822	6	5/6	8	9.7%	5.8	29	-18.8%	29	-144	29	12	20	0	-9.3%	1	48.7
2020	NYJ	5/4	250	134	74	55.2%	-3.3%	864	6	3/5	1	5.4%	5.5	--	-10.9%	--	2	--	6	22	0	-44.6%	-11	57.9
2021	PHI			579	372	64.2%		4043	25	12	8		6.1		-10.7%				30	96	1	-15.2%		

| 2019 | 18% Behind | 52% Short | 21% Mid | 10% Deep | aDOT: 7.3 (29) | YAC: 5.3 (17) | ALEX: -0.3 | 2020 | 4% Behind | 59% Short | 17% Mid | 20% Deep | aDOT: 11.4 (--) | YAC: 4.6 (--) | ALEX: 4.0 |

Flacco has somehow made seamless transition from frustrating starting quarterback to perfect YOLO backup. In his time with the Denver Broncos in 2019, Flacco was a checkdown obsessive and had one of the lowest average depth of targets in the league at 7.3 yards past the line of scrimmage. That increased to an 11.4-yard aDOT with the Jets in 2020. He also went from a -0.3 ALEX in 2019 to 4.0 in 2020. It still didn't turn into good football, but it was significantly more interesting to watch, clearing a very low bar.

Nick Foles

Height: 6-6 | Weight: 243 | College: Arizona | Draft: 2012/3 (88) | Born: 20-Jan-1989 | Age: 32 | Risk: Green

Year	Tm	G/GS	Snaps	Att	Cmp	C%	CPOE	Yds	TD	INT/Adj	FUM	ASR	NY/P	Rk	DVOA	Rk	DYAR	Rk	Runs	Yds	TD	DVOA	DYAR	QBR
2018	PHI	5/5	357	195	141	72.3%	2.6%	1413	7	4/5	4	4.4%	6.8	13	-5.4%	25	74	26	9	17	0	-2.7%	5	67.4
2019	JAX	4/4	188	117	77	65.8%	2.4%	736	3	2/3	2	7.1%	5.5	--	-21.3%	--	-77	--	4	23	0	26.7%	7	33.6
2020	CHI	9/7	496	312	202	64.7%	-0.5%	1852	10	8/17	2	6.0%	5.1	33	-16.3%	29	-112	28	16	1	1	-31.8%	-7	43.6
2021	CHI			638	409	64.2%		4225	25	16	7		5.9		-12.9%				52	99	3	-31.0%		

2019   20% Behind   47% Short   17% Mid   16% Deep   aDOT: 8.6 (--)   YAC: 4.6 (--)   ALEX: 1.8   2020   14% Behind   55% Short   15% Mid   15% Deep   aDOT: 8.5 (14)   YAC: 3.5 (36)   ALEX: 0.2

The Bears were desperate for a quarterback when they traded a fourth-round pick for Foles last offseason and agreed (even after a contract restructure) to pay him $21 million guaranteed. That decision looks terrible in hindsight since incumbent Mitchell Trubisky had the better 2020 season and even worse since the Bears drafted Justin Fields this offseason. They would prefer to trade Foles away after the first year of a three-year deal, but Foles wasn't as bad as his 5.9 yards per attempt or 10:8 touchdown-to-interception ratio would on their own suggest. Because of the timing of Trubisky's benching and his own hip injury, Foles played against opponents with an average of a -5.5% defensive DVOA, the second-hardest schedule in football, while Trubisky enjoyed opponents with an average defensive DVOA of 8.1%, the easiest schedule. Foles would likely produce better statistics with better fortune in 2021, but he seems unlikely to get a chance to start even if the Bears find a willing trade partner.

Blaine Gabbert

Height: 6-4 | Weight: 235 | College: Missouri | Draft: 2011/1 (10) | Born: 15-Oct-1989 | Age: 32 | Risk: Green

Year	Tm	G/GS	Snaps	Att	Cmp	C%	CPOE	Yds	TD	INT/Adj	FUM	ASR	NY/P	Rk	DVOA	Rk	DYAR	Rk	Runs	Yds	TD	DVOA	DYAR	QBR
2018	TEN	8/3	211	101	61	60.4%	-6.8%	626	4	4/7	0	5.7%	5.4	--	-35.5%	--	-154	--	6	0	0	39.6%	8	28.4
2020	TB	4/0	49	16	9	56.3%	3.1%	143	2	0/0	1	7.4%	8.0	--	-0.1%	--	13	--	9	16	0	-20.5%	-1	60.9
2021	TB			573	343	59.9%		4087	28	13	10		6.4		-2.6%				62	220	3	-9.8%		

2019   2020   25% Behind   31% Short   25% Mid   19% Deep   aDOT: 9.0 (--)   YAC: 8.9 (--)   ALEX: -4.8

In just about every photograph of Tom Brady working out, you'll see a man standing beside him. Usually, that's his trainer and business partner, Alex Guerrero. But when it's not Guerrero, it's Blaine Gabbert. When the Buccaneers re-signed Ryan Griffin and drafted Kyle Trask, it seemed as if Gabbert's days in Tampa were over, but they ultimately decided it was worth paying him $2 million to keep standing in the background.

Jimmy Garoppolo

Height: 6-2 | Weight: 225 | College: Eastern Illinois | Draft: 2014/2 (62) | Born: 11-Feb-1991 | Age: 30 | Risk: Red

Year	Tm	G/GS	Snaps	Att	Cmp	C%	CPOE	Yds	TD	INT/Adj	FUM	ASR	NY/P	Rk	DVOA	Rk	DYAR	Rk	Runs	Yds	TD	DVOA	DYAR	QBR
2018	SF	3/3	197	89	53	59.6%	-5.4%	718	5	3/3	4	11.3%	6.1	--	-12.5%	--	-9	--	8	33	0	-48.2%	-14	29.9
2019	SF	16/16	1079	476	329	69.1%	1.2%	3978	27	13/17	10	7.0%	7.3	6	10.8%	11	724	12	46	62	1	-18.0%	-9	58.8
2020	SF	6/6	305	140	94	67.1%	-3.7%	1096	7	5/5	2	6.4%	6.7	--	9.3%	--	198	--	10	25	0	-17.4%	-2	61.4
2021	SF			522	350	67.0%		4013	26	14	8		6.9		-0.3%				41	83	1	-30.6%		

2019   19% Behind   49% Short   25% Mid   7% Deep   aDOT: 6.8 (31)   YAC: 6.6 (1)   ALEX: -0.1   2020   20% Behind   49% Short   23% Mid   9% Deep   aDOT: 6.6 (--)   YAC: 7.6 (--)   ALEX: 1.4

If you listen to the 49ers, you would believe that Garoppolo's job is secure for 2021 and beyond. Kyle Shanahan called Trey Lance "a very good backup" after the draft. Both John Lynch and CEO Jed York have gone so far as to hint that Garoppolo could still be their starter for two years or more. It sounds nice, and in their position it's the kind of thing they have to say, but their words inspire skepticism. It's difficult to envision a scenario in which Garoppolo plays so well that the 49ers haven't turned to Lance and the three first-round picks they invested in him by this point next year. Even reaching the Super Bowl might not be enough—Garoppolo already did that and they have still picked out his replacement. Even York has said that when Lance is ready to play, he'll play, and it didn't sound like there was anything Garoppolo could do to prevent that.

This makes Garoppolo's upcoming season one long audition. His contract runs through 2022 with reasonable terms that would make a trade simple for both teams involved. He doesn't turn 30 till November, and his production is nearly unmatched—of the 47 quarterbacks with at least 500 passes since 2017, the year Garoppolo arrived in San Francisco, only Patrick Mahomes has averaged more yards per pass. The weaknesses are, obviously, the injuries, but also the interceptions—he has thrown two more than Mahomes in barely half as many passes. If he can cut those down, stay healthy, and get the 49ers back to the playoffs? They'll have no shortage of teams looking to grab him for draft picks—draft picks they could use, since they spent so many of theirs to get Lance.

Gilbert Garrett

Height: 6-4   Weight: 230   College: Southern Methodist   Draft: 2014/6 (214)   Born: 19-Jul-1991   Age: 30   Risk: Green

Year	Tm	G/GS	Snaps	Att	Cmp	C%	CPOE	Yds	TD	INT/Adj	FUM	ASR	NY/P	Rk	DVOA	Rk	DYAR	Rk	Runs	Yds	TD	DVOA	DYAR	QBR
2018	CAR	1/0	13	3	2	66.7%	-4.8%	40	0	0/0	0	23.9%	8.8	--	-0.2%	--	3	--	0	0	0	--	--	42.8
2019	CLE	5/0	8	3	0	0.0%	-65.8%	0	0	0/0	0	-5.1%	0.0	--	-103.1%	--	-13	--	3	-3	0	--	--	21.4
2020	DAL	1/1	72	38	21	55.3%	1.5%	243	1	1/2	0	1.6%	5.6	--	-0.5%	--	25	--	3	28	0	88.1%	12	63.9
2021	DAL			559	330	59.0%		3888	24	12	6		6.2		-7.0%				49	245	2	9.2%		

2019   0% Behind   50% Short   50% Mid   0% Deep   aDOT: 15.7 (--)   YAC: 0.0 (--)   ALEX: 1.0   2020   3% Behind   50% Short   28% Mid   19% Deep   aDOT: 10.4 (--)   YAC: 2.5 (--)   ALEX: 3.5

Gilbert survived his spot start against the Steelers. He threw a touchdown pass to CeeDee Lamb on a wheel route with T.J. Watt in coverage, threw an interception in the end zone at a point when the Cowboys could have cut the Steelers' heart out, and looked exactly like a 29-year-old with six previous career attempts as soon as the Steelers defense figured out the few things he could do well. According to NFL logic, however, Gilbert nearly beat a playoff team, and will therefore get a half-dozen more opportunities as a backup based on three or four decent passes and a few stumbling scrambles.

Mike Glennon

Height: 6-7   Weight: 225   College: North Carolina State   Draft: 2013/3 (73)   Born: 12-Dec-1989   Age: 32   Risk: Green

Year	Tm	G/GS	Snaps	Att	Cmp	C%	CPOE	Yds	TD	INT/Adj	FUM	ASR	NY/P	Rk	DVOA	Rk	DYAR	Rk	Runs	Yds	TD	DVOA	DYAR	QBR
2018	ARI	2/0	26	21	15	71.4%	7.8%	174	1	0/0	0	5.0%	7.5	--	45.4%	--	73	--	0	0	0	--	--	76.4
2019	OAK	2/0	23	10	6	60.0%	5.0%	56	1	0/0	3	0.6%	5.6	--	-20.2%	--	-6	--	2	0	0	-262.0%	-9	23.7
2020	JAX	5/5	288	179	111	62.0%	-2.6%	1072	7	5/8	2	6.7%	5.3	--	-19.8%	--	-105	--	6	17	0	-85.3%	-28	37.0
2021	NYG			577	356	61.7%		4007	26	14	8		6.1		-14.3%				39	127	1	-19.9%		

2019   11% Behind   44% Short   22% Mid   22% Deep   aDOT: 12.1 (--)   YAC: 3.0 (--)   ALEX: -2.7   2020   14% Behind   50% Short   23% Mid   13% Deep   aDOT: 8.6 (--)   YAC: 3.6 (--)   ALEX: 1.0

What's left to write about Mike Freakin' Glennon the year 2021 of the Common Era? He led the Jaguars to five increasingly uncompetitive losses at the end of 2020. His passing DVOA was lower than Taysom Hill's. The theory that he does anything a mid-round rookie couldn't do has been thoroughly debunked once again. Yet he keeps getting "proven veteran" opportunities because the Bears gave him a big contract in 2017, when the NFL personnel establishment was professing its love for immobile quarterbacks as part of their cover for blackballing Colin Kaepernick. Glennon replaces Colt McCoy as the perfect backup for Daniel Jones: someone who has been around long enough to qualify as a "mentor" while being so clearly awful that no one will clamor for him to take over if Jones struggles.

Jared Goff

Height: 6-4   Weight: 223   College: California   Draft: 2016/1 (1)   Born: 14-Oct-1994   Age: 27   Risk: Green

Year	Tm	G/GS	Snaps	Att	Cmp	C%	CPOE	Yds	TD	INT/Adj	FUM	ASR	NY/P	Rk	DVOA	Rk	DYAR	Rk	Runs	Yds	TD	DVOA	DYAR	QBR
2018	LAR	16/16	1064	561	364	64.9%	2.9%	4688	32	12/18	12	5.5%	7.5	5	17.0%	5	1114	6	43	108	2	-11.8%	0	66.4
2019	LAR	16/16	1120	626	394	62.9%	-0.3%	4638	22	16/20	10	3.7%	6.9	12	2.0%	18	552	15	33	40	2	-36.7%	-32	48.5
2020	LAR	15/15	1047	552	370	67.0%	1.2%	3952	20	13/18	7	4.3%	6.6	17	-1.1%	22	385	20	51	99	4	-14.8%	-6	58.5
2021	DET			597	381	63.8%		4584	25	12	8		6.8		-0.8%				54	111	4	-22.2%		

2019   15% Behind   48% Short   28% Mid   10% Deep   aDOT: 7.9 (26)   YAC: 5.7 (8)   ALEX: 1.8   2020   15% Behind   58% Short   17% Mid   10% Deep   aDOT: 6.9 (33)   YAC: 5.8 (5)   ALEX: 1.6

Football Outsiders writer Ben Muth once compared Goff to a JUGS machine. When he's pointed in the right direction pre-snap and left undisturbed, Goff delivers some of the most beautiful, on-target spirals at the position. When conditions are imperfect, however, he often fails to rise above the circumstances. You can see that disparity in Goff's performance with and without pressure. He suffered a league-high decline in 2020 from a 55.8% passing DVOA in clean pockets to a -126.8% passing DVOA with pressure. You can also see it in the strategy of his opponents: defenses tried to confuse Goff by playing zone coverage on 75% of his dropbacks, a rate so high that it is otherwise reserved for dual-threat quarterbacks such as Lamar Jackson and Kyler Murray. Sean McVay seemed particularly annoyed with Goff's inability to complete passes downfield. Goff and his replacement Matthew Stafford were on opposite ends of that leaderboard with -5.9% and 113.9% respective DVOAs on passes thrown to targets 20 or more yards downfield in 2020. It's probably good news that Goff's new Lions team has one of the best pass-protecting lines in football and more talent at running back and tight end than at wide receiver. Big picture, it likely means that Goff is a temporary solution until the Lions can draft a new franchise quarterback with fewer limitations.

Dwayne Haskins Height: 6-4 Weight: 230 College: Ohio State Draft: 2019/1 (15) Born: 3-May-1997 Age: 24 Risk: Green

Year	Tm	G/GS	Snaps	Att	Cmp	C%	CPOE	Yds	TD	INT/Adj	FUM	ASR	NY/P	Rk	DVOA	Rk	DYAR	Rk	Runs	Yds	TD	DVOA	DYAR	QBR
2019	WAS	9/7	442	203	119	58.6%	-6.7%	1365	7	7/6	6	12.7%	5.0	34	-42.0%	34	-443	34	20	101	0	-20.9%	-8	26.4
2020	WAS	7/6	429	241	148	61.4%	-6.8%	1439	5	7/8	6	7.2%	5.0	35	-40.1%	36	-483	33	20	46	1	-16.2%	-4	30.8
2021	PIT			573	354	61.8%		3764	23	15	11		6.0		-17.0%				57	200	3	-17.9%		

2019	13% Behind	48% Short	28% Mid	12% Deep	aDOT: 8.9 (15)	YAC: 5.2 (19)	ALEX: 0.2	2020	16% Behind	55% Short	20% Mid	10% Deep	aDOT: 6.9 (34)	YAC: 5.8 (4)	ALEX: -0.3

Haskins and Alex Smith had virtually identical numbers in 2020—identically terrible, that is. Smith had the incredible comeback story working for him, not to mention the pelts on the wall. Haskins, by contrast, is a guy with zero accomplishments who, by all accounts, refused to put in the work required to be a professional quarterback. Therefore, he was unceremoniously dumped by Washington after just two seasons. Nevertheless, he does retain the athletic traits that made him a first-round pick, and with Pittsburgh's quarterback situation composed of Praying for Ben Roethlisberger, the Steelers have brought him in for a look-see. Haskins' size brought Roethlisberger comparisons as a prospect; now he can learn from the man himself, if he cares to.

Taylor Heinicke Height: 6-1 Weight: 210 College: Old Dominion Draft: 2015/FA Born: 15-Mar-1993 Age: 28 Risk: Green

Year	Tm	G/GS	Snaps	Att	Cmp	C%	CPOE	Yds	TD	INT/Adj	FUM	ASR	NY/P	Rk	DVOA	Rk	DYAR	Rk	Runs	Yds	TD	DVOA	DYAR	QBR
2018	CAR	6/1	91	57	35	61.4%	-1.1%	320	1	3/3	1	4.4%	5.2	--	-49.1%	--	-140	--	5	31	0	-49.7%	-5	19.9
2020	WAS	1/0	25	19	12	63.2%	-1.1%	137	1	0/3	0	6.8%	6.5	--	12.7%	--	33	--	3	22	0	42.5%	8	48.3
2021	WAS			555	342	61.7%		3758	23	13	7		6.0		-13.6%				48	282	3	11.4%		

2019						2020	5% Behind	42% Short	26% Mid	26% Deep	aDOT: 13.4 (--)	YAC: 4.1 (--)	ALEX: -1.5

Heinicke's playoff start against the Buccaneers was easily Washington's best performance from a quarterback during the 2020 season. In that game, Heinicke showed the ability to push the ball down the field, which just wasn't a consistent element in the Washington offense during the regular season. 20 of Heinicke's passes traveled at least 10 yards past the line of scrimmage. Neither Alex Smith nor Dwayne Haskins ever hit 15 during a game in 2020. Still, even after Heinicke's performance, Washington brought in Ryan Fitzpatrick to be the starter in 2021. Heinicke showed the ability to play at a productive level as a spot starter, and given Fitzpatrick's history, he should be prepared to do that at some point this season.

Chad Henne Height: 6-3 Weight: 222 College: Michigan Draft: 2008/2 (57) Born: 2-Jul-1985 Age: 36 Risk: Green

Year	Tm	G/GS	Snaps	Att	Cmp	C%	CPOE	Yds	TD	INT/Adj	FUM	ASR	NY/P	Rk	DVOA	Rk	DYAR	Rk	Runs	Yds	TD	DVOA	DYAR	QBR
2018	KC	1/0	13	3	2	66.7%	-9.6%	29	0	0/0	0	3.9%	9.7	--	38.8%	--	11	--	1	3	0	-51.8%	-2	71.8
2020	KC	3/1	75	38	28	73.7%	1.4%	248	2	0/0	2	6.2%	6.1	--	22.3%	--	89	--	7	-2	1	-113.9%	-33	32.7
2021	KC			590	384	65.2%		4442	29	13	7		6.8		6.3%				31	82	2	-7.3%		

2019						2020	32% Behind	49% Short	14% Mid	5% Deep	aDOT: 4.0 (--)	YAC: 7.1 (--)	ALEX: -5.1

Last season, Henne started his first game since being benched for rookie Blake Bortles with the Jaguars in 2014. Since then, Henne had only been briefly seen time as an emergency backup, with a grand total of five attempts until Week 17 of last year. While the game was a completely meaningless final-week contest against a mediocre Chargers defense, Henne showed enough to retain his job as the Chiefs backup. What's funny about Henne's lone start is that he became more productive when the stakes were higher. He posted a poor -6.1% DVOA on 13 first-down plays, yet his DVOA climbed to 84.8% on 10 third- or fourth-down passes, half of which he converted for a fresh set of downs. It's worth noting that head coach Andy Reid did not ask a whole lot of Henne until those downs, but it was still nice to see the old vet make some daring plays when it mattered most. He did it again in the playoffs, filling in for a shaken-up Patrick Mahomes and icing the win over Cleveland with a 13-yard scramble on third-and-14 and a completion for a first down on the ensuing fourth-and-1.

Justin Herbert Height: 6-6 Weight: 237 College: Oregon Draft: 2020/1 (6) Born: 10-Mar-1998 Age: 23 Risk: Green

Year	Tm	G/GS	Snaps	Att	Cmp	C%	CPOE	Yds	TD	INT/Adj	FUM	ASR	NY/P	Rk	DVOA	Rk	DYAR	Rk	Runs	Yds	TD	DVOA	DYAR	QBR
2020	LAC	15/15	1096	595	396	66.6%	0.0%	4336	31	10/14	8	6.0%	6.6	16	10.2%	11	861	8	55	234	5	-23.2%	-29	69.7
2021	LAC			679	455	67.0%		5070	37	10	8		6.7		6.3%				68	286	3	-7.9%		

2019						2020	19% Behind	50% Short	19% Mid	12% Deep	aDOT: 7.7 (26)	YAC: 5.6 (9)	ALEX: 1.2

Herbert bursting onto the scene with one of the best rookie seasons ever was a pleasant surprise after he was drafted as the third quarterback in his own class. Herbert broke the rookie records for passing touchdowns and total touchdowns, topping Cam Newton's 35 from 2011 in the latter category. A good portion of Herbert's production can be credited to his work in volatile splits such as play under pressure and on third down, but those were not the only interesting splits he posted. Despite coming from a full spread offense at Oregon, Herbert actually posted a higher DVOA from under center (18.9%) than from shotgun (7.5%). Herbert was also one of the league's best throwers versus man coverage right out of the gate. The rookie finished eighth in the league in DVOA versus man coverage, showcasing his blend of arm talent to test tight windows and mobility to scramble around while looking for plays. Herbert may not take the MVP leap in Year 2 the way Patrick Mahomes and Lamar Jackson did, but Chargers fans should feel good about what they have at the position.

Taysom Hill Height: 6-2 Weight: 221 College: Brigham Young Draft: 2017/FA Born: 23-Aug-1990 Age: 31 Risk: Blue

Year	Tm	G/GS	Snaps	Att	Cmp	C%	CPOE	Yds	TD	INT/Adj	FUM	ASR	NY/P	Rk	DVOA	Rk	DYAR	Rk	Runs	Yds	TD	DVOA	DYAR	QBR
2018	NO	16/4	181	7	3	42.9%	-11.0%	64	0	1/1	1	14.4%	7.6	--	-40.8%	--	-19	--	37	196	2	-7.1%	12	43.5
2019	NO	16/5	242	6	3	50.0%	4.1%	55	0	0/0	0	14.4%	6.6	--	4.2%	--	6	--	27	156	1	-7.5%	7	83.9
2020	NO	16/8	472	121	88	72.7%	3.5%	928	4	2/3	10	10.4%	6.2	--	-19.0%	--	-69	--	87	457	8	-11.8%	2	58.7
2021	NO			540	354	65.6%		3869	22	11		19		6.4		-10.8%				145	761	11	10.4%		

2019 0% Behind 0% Short 100% Mid 0% Deep aDOT: 12.3 (--) YAC: 4.0 (--) ALEX: 0.0   2020 19% Behind 48% Short 25% Mid 8% Deep aDOT: 7.3 (--) YAC: 4.2 (--) ALEX: -1.6

Hill finally started games as an actual quarterback in 2020, rather than being restricted to his usual gadgetry-and-goal-line role. The surface results were pleasant enough: a 3-1 record, four passing touchdowns versus two interceptions, and a further four scores on the ground. However, during those four starts, Hill also piled up 14 sacks in just 140 dropbacks—one more than Drew Brees had in over 400—and fumbled an alarming six times, losing three. Among quarterbacks with at least 100 dropbacks, only Carson Wentz was sacked at a higher rate. Over the whole season, Hill's 10 fumbles would have ranked tied for eighth among *offenses*, not just individual players; only Daniel Jones and Derek Carr fumbled more often, and both of them started all season long. In large part because of his ball-security issues, Hill finished with negative DVOA both running and passing, and a cumulative -67 passing and rushing DYAR. (He also had -5 receiving DYAR on 13 targets.)

Hill's inexperience makes it easy to forget that these aren't the struggles of a young player: he will be 31 by opening day. He remains a positive contributor to the Saints offense as a role player: his passing DVOA outside Weeks 11 to 14 leapt to 48.6%, albeit on only eight attempts, and his overall contribution outside his starts amounted to 15 DYAR. When Hill comes in at quarterback and plays like he did during the 2019 playoff loss, it is easy to see the allure for Sean Payton. On last season's evidence, he would be very much a longshot to replicate that as the primary starter.

Jalen Hurts Height: 6-1 Weight: 222 College: Oklahoma Draft: 2020/2 (53) Born: 7-Aug-1998 Age: 23 Risk: Yellow

Year	Tm	G/GS	Snaps	Att	Cmp	C%	CPOE	Yds	TD	INT/Adj	FUM	ASR	NY/P	Rk	DVOA	Rk	DYAR	Rk	Runs	Yds	TD	DVOA	DYAR	QBR
2020	PHI	15/4	334	148	77	52.0%	-6.6%	1061	6	4/7	9	7.7%	6.2	--	-17.6%	--	-68	--	63	357	3	-15.2%	-9	41.2
2021	PHI			575	335	58.4%		3885	26	13		16		5.9		-19.5%				113	637	6	-4.7%		

2019   2020 13% Behind 47% Short 25% Mid 16% Deep aDOT: 9.7 (--) YAC: 6.1 (--) ALEX: 2.3

Hurts got thrown into the deep end of an offense that had already crumbled late in the season, but for a rookie second-round pick, he had some flashes through his four games as a starter. Hurts struggled as a passer against man coverage with just -17.7% DVOA, though by the time Hurts took over at quarterback, the Eagles weren't running out many receivers who could easily win against man. Hurts was much better against zone (40.4% DVOA) and saw that coverage more often. He was also just slightly below average on plays without pressure—38.2% DVOA compared to a 40.7% league average. As a passer, Hurts had positive DVOA on first and third downs when he was able to push the ball down the field. But when his average depth of target dropped to 6.6 yards on second downs, his DVOA dropped to an awful -56.5%. Hurts' ability as a runner should also improve. Nine fumbles—some off poor snaps—tanked his DVOA, but when Hurts did get into the open field, he was successful.

Lamar Jackson

Height: 6-2 | Weight: 212 | College: Louisville | Draft: 2018/1 (32) | Born: 7-Jan-1997 | Age: 24 | Risk: Green

Year	Tm	G/GS	Snaps	Att	Cmp	C%	CPOE	Yds	TD	INT/Adj	FUM	ASR	NY/P	Rk	DVOA	Rk	DYAR	Rk	Runs	Yds	TD	DVOA	DYAR	QBR
2018	BAL	16/7	585	170	99	58.2%	-5.5%	1201	6	3/6	12	10.2%	6.0	--	-9.2%	--	24	--	147	695	5	-27.2%	-112	45.2
2019	BAL	15/15	987	401	265	66.1%	2.4%	3127	36	6/6	9	5.6%	7.2	10	34.9%	2	1261	5	176	1206	7	20.5%	273	81.8
2020	BAL	15/15	917	376	242	64.4%	-0.2%	2757	26	9/16	10	7.5%	6.5	21	-0.7%	21	265	22	159	1005	7	-3.6%	69	73.9
2021	BAL			461	292	63.4%		3454	27	11	12		6.6		2.6%				173	1119	8	0.5%		

| 2019 | 12% Behind | 54% Short | 20% Mid | 14% Deep | aDOT: 9.2 (8) | YAC: 5.1 (20) | ALEX: 1.8 | 2020 | 13% Behind | 50% Short | 24% Mid | 13% Deep | aDOT: 9.1 (6) | YAC: 4.8 (23) | ALEX: 1.4 |

Jackson currently ranks 13th on the all-time quarterback rushing list with 2,906 yards. If he meets the projection above, he will leap all the way to sixth place, passing Tobin Rote, Aaron Rodgers, John Elway, Donovan McNabb, Charley Trippi, Steve McNair, and Fran Tarkenton. Rodgers could theoretically stay ahead of Jackson, of course, and perhaps will if Brian Gutekunst gives him a direct mandate to never leave the pocket and sets his oppositional-defiant impulse to "ludicrous." Anyway, only Steve Young, Russell Wilson, Randall Cunningham, Cam Newton, and Michael Vick will be ahead of Jackson once he rushes for another 1,000 yards.

Five of the players ahead of Jackson on the quarterback rushing list (Vick, Newton, Young, Trippi, and Elway) were first overall picks, McNabb was a second overall pick, and McNair a third. Apparently, the NFL really does like mobile quarterbacks, given certain parameters, and such quarterbacks can indeed have successful careers. That said, the most similar player to Jackson might be Trippi, the quarterback/tailback/safety/return man/punter who led the Cardinals to their last NFL title in 1947. Trippi evolved into more of a traditional quarterback by his sixth season, but he was 31 years old by then. When Trippi was Jackson's age, he was playing for the Third Air Force Gremlins, a morale-boosting unit that faced off against other military bases duing World War II.

In other words, there's no real precedent for a quarterback doing what Jackson is doing as successfully as Jackson is doing it. At some point, Jackson will slow down or get hurt, or the Ravens will yoke him to a more traditional offense, and his 1,000-yard rushing seasons will turn into Newton-like 500- to 600-yard seasons. Either that, or Jackson leads the Ravens to back-to-back Super Bowls and every quarterback more mobile than Nick Foles starts running 10 times per game.

For now, there is no evidence that Jackson will slow down or run less in 2021, so let's let history rest and the long-range future take care of itself.

Daniel Jones

Height: 6-5 | Weight: 220 | College: Duke | Draft: 2019/1 (6) | Born: 27-May-1997 | Age: 24 | Risk: Green

Year	Tm	G/GS	Snaps	Att	Cmp	C%	CPOE	Yds	TD	INT/Adj	FUM	ASR	NY/P	Rk	DVOA	Rk	DYAR	Rk	Runs	Yds	TD	DVOA	DYAR	QBR
2019	NYG	13/12	826	459	284	61.9%	-2.4%	3027	24	12/18	18	7.8%	5.5	31	-19.2%	30	-256	31	45	279	2	7.9%	45	53.6
2020	NYG	14/14	868	448	280	62.5%	-4.2%	2943	11	10/12	11	8.2%	5.4	31	-22.4%	32	-350	32	65	423	1	16.2%	67	61.5
2021	NYG			583	371	63.6%		4318	25	12	14		6.5		-9.3%				80	497	2	-6.9%		

| 2019 | 13% Behind | 56% Short | 19% Mid | 13% Deep | aDOT: 8.2 (22) | YAC: 4.9 (28) | ALEX: 0.7 | 2020 | 9% Behind | 61% Short | 21% Mid | 9% Deep | aDOT: 7.8 (25) | YAC: 4.0 (34) | ALEX: 0.1 |

Jones threw just five touchdown passes from inside the 10-yard line last season. That's a low total for even an inexperienced/ineffective starter—Drew Lock threw 11 touchdown passes inside the 10-yard line, for example—and it rendered Jones nearly useless in fantasy after he looked like someone who would at least rack up the raw stats as a rookie.

Jones should bounce back this season as a QB3, QB2 in deeper leagues, or DFS starter against weak opponents. He will have a thousand weapons when healthy, runs well when not tripping over his own destiny on the way to the end zone, and is likely to have slightly better luck as a goal-line passer this season, plus the job security you want from an emergency fantasy starter. Mild statistical success may not be what the Giants have in mind for Jones, but maybe it is. At any rate, that's not your fantasy team's problem.

Mac Jones

Height: 6-3 | Weight: 214 | College: Alabama | Draft: 2021/1 (15) | Born: 5-Sep-1998 | Age: 23 | Risk: Green

Year	Tm	G/GS	Snaps	Att	Cmp	C%	CPOE	Yds	TD	INT/Adj	FUM	ASR	NY/P	Rk	DVOA	Rk	DYAR	Rk	Runs	Yds	TD	DVOA	DYAR	QBR
2021	NE			563	374	66.4%		4054	26	10	9		6.4		-4.0%				49	215	3	-1.2%		

QBASE had Jones as the fifth-best passer in this year's rookie class, and he was taken as the fifth quarterback in the draft. A logical outcome, if we ignore the month-long frenzy that attempted to push him all the way up to the third slot. Jones doesn't have eye-popping arm talent, nor is he an athletic marvel. To succeed in New England, Jones will have to translate his accuracy, touch, finesse, and decision-making to the NFL level. Per Football Outsiders draft analyst Derrik Klassen's charting, Jones was the second-most accurate passer in this year's class, and his 68.1% accuracy under pressure was tops. He also threw the fewest passes contested or defended; his timing, anticipation, and ball placement when he's in rhythm are fantastic. Of course, it's quite possible he was playing with better receivers at Alabama than he will have in New England.

Case Keenum

Height: 6-1 Weight: 215 College: Houston Draft: 2012/FA Born: 17-Feb-1988 Age: 33 Risk: Green

Year	Tm	G/GS	Snaps	Att	Cmp	C%	CPOE	Yds	TD	INT/Adj	FUM	ASR	NY/P	Rk	DVOA	Rk	DYAR	Rk	Runs	Yds	TD	DVOA	DYAR	QBR
2018	DEN	16/16	1073	586	365	62.3%	-2.7%	3890	18	15/17	11	6.3%	5.9	29	-12.7%	28	-63	29	26	93	2	31.2%	40	46.9
2019	WAS	10/8	460	247	160	64.8%	-1.5%	1707	11	5/8	6	6.3%	6.0	22	-8.1%	23	51	24	9	12	1	-36.8%	-12	43.5
2020	CLE	2/0	15	10	5	50.0%	-20.3%	46	0	0/0	0	0.0%	4.6	--	-32.9%	--	-16	--	0	0	0	--	--	41.7
2021	CLE			571	362	63.3%		4009	27	18	9		6.3		-8.9%				44	165	3	-5.0%		

2019 15% Behind 59% Short 17% Mid 9% Deep aDOT: 7.1 (30) YAC: 5.0 (23) ALEX: -1.3   2020 22% Behind 56% Short 22% Mid 0% Deep aDOT: 3.0 (--) YAC: 5.6 (--) ALEX: 0.5

Few teams can boast a backup quarterback who once led the NFL in passing DVOA, which Keenum did in 2017 with the Vikings (under the tutelage of then-quarterbacks coach, now-head coach Kevin Stefanski). Keenum, if nothing else, won't embarrass anyone if called into duty. Surprisingly enough, 2021 will be the first time since 2015 Keenum hasn't changed teams in the offseason, and it feels like he could remain Cleveland's backup for as long as his rabbi, Stefanski, remains on the sidelines. One of Mayfield's primary comparisons as a prospect was Keenum, which may not be what you want from a top overall draft choice, but plenty of higher touted players have had worse careers.

Trey Lance

Height: 6-4 Weight: 226 College: North Dakota State Draft: 2021/1 (3) Born: 9-May-2000 Age: 21 Risk: Green

Year	Tm	G/GS	Snaps	Att	Cmp	C%	CPOE	Yds	TD	INT/Adj	FUM	ASR	NY/P	Rk	DVOA	Rk	DYAR	Rk	Runs	Yds	TD	DVOA	DYAR	QBR
2021	SF			545	345	63.3%		3933	24	14	13		6.4		-8.4%				134	764	9	12.6%		

It's impossible to watch Lance's highlights at North Dakota State and imagine what this tall, skinny, hyper-athlete would look like in a 49ers uniform without getting Colin Kaepernick flashbacks. According to Pro Football Reference, the two players are the exact same height, while Lance is heavier by a single pound. Lance ended up at North Dakota State because he didn't get any Power 5 scholarship offers to play quarterback; it was a similar story for Kaepernick, who played college football for Nevada simply because they were the only team to offer him a football scholarship (though other schools wanted him to play baseball). Our old colleague Doug Farrar has noted there also similarities between Lance and the late Steve McNair, the former MVP who played for Alcorn State because bigger schools wanted him to switch positions. Both McNair and Kaepernick spent the better part of their first two seasons on the bench behind, respectively, Chris Chandler and Alex Smith, two veterans who had trouble staying healthy.

There are a lot of parallels here that tell us Lance won't be the top guy in San Francisco anytime soon. On the other hand, unlike McNair and Kaepernick, Lance plays in an era when everyone realizes the financial benefits of a quarterback on a rookie contract, and the 49ers may not afford him the same patience that his predecessors received.

Due to the unique nature of his career and the COVID-ravaged state of college football, we must take Lance's QBASE numbers with multiple helpings of salt. But for what it's worth, he is among the top 15 highest-graded quarterback prospects since 2004, with a projection similar to those of Ben Roethlisberger, Vince Young, and—yes—Colin Kaepernick.

Trevor Lawrence

Height: 6-6 Weight: 220 College: Clemson Draft: 2021/1 (1) Born: 6-Oct-1999 Age: 22 Risk: Green

Year	Tm	G/GS	Snaps	Att	Cmp	C%	CPOE	Yds	TD	INT/Adj	FUM	ASR	NY/P	Rk	DVOA	Rk	DYAR	Rk	Runs	Yds	TD	DVOA	DYAR	QBR
2021	JAX			554	368	66.5%		3906	25	12	10		6.3		-6.9%				66	364	4	7.7%		

We live in an age in sports information where there is a hot take for just about everything. If you wanted to believe that Mitchell Trubisky was going to be good, there were content farms designed around that fact, even after the Bears started becoming bad. The truth is that there are enough of you out there willing to read something that will confirm your priors that it is just an inescapable fact of the way content is created today. If you are a die-hard Georgia fan who wants to believe that Jake Fromm can still become an NFL starter, there are people who will cater to you. In light of that fact, it speaks a real truth about how good Lawrence was in college, how fast he was good, and how many boxes he checked that nobody could really muster up much of a hot take about how Justin Fields or Trey Lance was better. We found some position-only people arguing about Kyle Pitts' potential greatness, and OK, but the intersection of value and talent was very obvious here and in a way that probably helped influence Jacksonville's decision to "evaluate" some Mike Glennon tape down the stretch. Brian Schottenheimer, Jaguars passing game coordinator, tried to claim that it was too early to name a starting quarterback in a June presser and he was roundly roasted. This has been pre-ordained since at least December, and probably November. The only question left is if Lawrence is taking the world by storm in Year 1 or if NFL teams will find some flaws that college teams couldn't.

Drew Lock

Height: 6-4		Weight: 228			College: Missouri				Draft: 2019/2 (42)			Born: 10-Nov-1996			Age: 25							Risk: Red		

Year	Tm	G/GS	Snaps	Att	Cmp	C%	CPOE	Yds	TD	INT/Adj	FUM	ASR	NY/P	Rk	DVOA	Rk	DYAR	Rk	Runs	Yds	TD	DVOA	DYAR	QBR
2019	DEN	5/5	307	156	100	64.1%	-1.3%	1020	7	3/4	3	4.2%	6.2	--	2.2%	--	138	--	18	72	0	-10.9%	1	48.2
2020	DEN	13/13	834	443	254	57.3%	-6.3%	2933	16	15/16	8	6.1%	6.0	25	-16.2%	28	-151	30	44	160	3	-16.0%	-8	49.2
2021	DEN			611	359	58.7%		4216	26	19	10		6.2		-15.9%				63	246	4	-7.8%		

2019	19% Behind	52% Short	19% Mid	11% Deep	aDOT: 7.1 (--)	YAC: 5.5 (--)	ALEX: 1.3	2020	11% Behind	51% Short

23% Mid	16% Deep	aDOT: 9.3 (3)	YAC: 5.4 (12)	ALEX: 1.7

The second-year leap did not happen for Drew Lock. The former Missouri quarterback instead took a step back, which is not too surprising in hindsight. Lock finished his five-game rookie year with a 138 passing DYAR, but that includes 149 DYAR in a fluky match against Houston. Lock, while certainly not bad in that performance, got away with a number of tightly contested throws and questionable decisions, most of which appeared unstable to the degree he made it work in that game. In his second season, Lock showed little to no improvement in any area. Lock's footwork, in particular, remains a mess and he still is not confident executing any dropback concept beyond your standard Day 1 install stuff. Funny enough, Lock was nearly the same quarterback regardless of what kind of coverage defenses tossed at him in 2020, posting a 2.7% DVOA vs man coverage and a 3.8% DVOA vs zone coverage; only Dak Prescott (about 35.0% in both categories) had a smaller gap. Lock needs to show more than the occasional flash if he wants to earn a second contract in Denver.

Jordan Love

Height: 6-4		Weight: 224			College: Utah State				Draft: 2020/1 (26)			Born: 2-Nov-1998			Age: 23			Risk: Green

Year	Tm	G/GS	Snaps	Att	Cmp	C%	CPOE	Yds	TD	INT/Adj	FUM	ASR	NY/P	Rk	DVOA	Rk	DYAR	Rk	Runs	Yds	TD	DVOA	DYAR	QBR
2021	GB			565	330	58.4%		3873	27	14	10		6.1		-7.5%				70	290	5	3.6%		

The Packers made a mistake by not communicating their intentions to trade up and draft a quarterback to their star incumbent Aaron Rodgers. It remains to be seen whether they made a mistake in the selection itself. Advanced metrics were never optimistic. Love had the second-worst adjusted accuracy (69.7%) of the nine quarterbacks in his 2020 draft class, and he was below average under pressure and on play-action, the latter of which has become a staple under head coach Matt LaFleur's Packers offense. But like so many prospects with traits, Love will now point to Josh Allen's development as a precedent. The comparison is especially apt for Love since he played in college at Utah State in the same Mountain West Conference as Allen's Wyoming Cowboys.

Jake Luton

Height: 6-6		Weight: 229			College: Oregon State				Draft: 2020/6 (189)			Born: 11-Apr-1996			Age: 25			Risk: Green

Year	Tm	G/GS	Snaps	Att	Cmp	C%	CPOE	Yds	TD	INT/Adj	FUM	ASR	NY/P	Rk	DVOA	Rk	DYAR	Rk	Runs	Yds	TD	DVOA	DYAR	QBR
2020	JAX	3/3	191	110	60	54.5%	-7.9%	624	2	6/10	2	4.5%	4.9	--	-48.6%	--	-287	--	1	13	1	183.5%	12	40.6
2021	JAX			595	359	60.3%		3922	25	17	9		5.8		-18.0%				41	181	4	10.0%		

2019					2020	15% Behind	53% Short	18% Mid	14% Deep aDOT: 8.5 (--) YAC: 4.6 (--) ALEX: 2.6

On the second dropback of his career, Luton hit DJ Chark for a 73-yard touchdown pass over Vernon Hargreaves. Over his next 33 pass attempts against one of the worst passing defenses in the league, he created six first downs. It's a pretty nice success story for a sixth-round pick to come on the field and do anything at quarterback, and it's cool as hell for Luton that he almost came up with a game-tying drive at the end of that contest before missing a 2-point attempt. With Trevor Lawrence now in town, Luton can be a nice little story for Duval bar patrons and sports radio callers, which is about the extent of what he showed he could be on the field in three starts last year.

Patrick Mahomes

Height: 6-3 Weight: 230 College: Texas Tech Draft: 2017/1 (10) Born: 17-Sep-1995 Age: 26 Risk: Green

Year	Tm	G/GS	Snaps	Att	Cmp	C%	CPOE	Yds	TD	INT/Adj	FUM	ASR	NY/P	Rk	DVOA	Rk	DYAR	Rk	Runs	Yds	TD	DVOA	DYAR	QBR
2018	KC	16/16	1032	580	383	66.0%	1.9%	5097	50	12/21	9	5.4%	8.1	2	39.9%	1	2031	1	60	272	2	3.0%	39	81.6
2019	KC	14/14	889	484	319	65.9%	2.7%	4031	26	5/10	3	4.3%	7.8	2	30.0%	3	1320	2	43	218	2	28.1%	66	76.3
2020	KC	15/15	1027	588	390	66.3%	0.7%	4740	38	6/13	5	4.4%	7.5	4	31.7%	2	1720	1	62	308	2	6.0%	44	82.9
2021	KC			667	440	65.9%		5350	37	9	6		7.3		17.8%				64	304	3	6.3%		

| 2019 | 18% Behind | 45% Short | 23% Mid | 14% Deep | aDOT: 9.0 (12) | YAC: 6.1 (2) | ALEX: 1.5 | 2020 | 15% Behind | 50% Short | 22% Mid | 13% Deep | aDOT: 8.6 (13) | YAC: 5.7 (6) | ALEX: 3.0 |

Mahomes' magic bears itself out in the data as it does on film. Play under pressure is generally a volatile split for any quarterback, regardless of whether or not they are perceived as playmakers, but Mahomes is a legitimately special and consistent producer under pressure. Mahomes has been top-two in the league in DVOA under pressure in all three seasons as a starter. No other quarterback over that span has even had multiple top-five finishes. Mahomes is also every bit as dominant on third down as he feels, thanks to his mobility and unmatched arm talent. For the third year in a row, Mahomes posted a DVOA higher than 60.0% on third-/fourth-down passes, giving him the highest mark in the league by the wide margin. We all saw that magic run out in the Super Bowl when he was tasked with overcoming an offensive line almost entirely made of backups, but Mahomes is very much still the best playmaker in the league despite our most recent memory of him. With a much-improved offensive line in 2021, expect Mahomes to only feel more emboldened to hold onto the ball and try to create plays late in the down.

Marcus Mariota

Height: 6-4 Weight: 222 College: Oregon Draft: 2015/1 (2) Born: 30-Oct-1993 Age: 28 Risk: Green

Year	Tm	G/GS	Snaps	Att	Cmp	C%	CPOE	Yds	TD	INT/Adj	FUM	ASR	NY/P	Rk	DVOA	Rk	DYAR	Rk	Runs	Yds	TD	DVOA	DYAR	QBR
2018	TEN	14/13	775	331	228	68.9%	2.5%	2528	11	8/10	9	11.6%	6.1	24	-8.5%	27	65	27	64	357	2	15.1%	86	55.5
2019	TEN	7/6	367	160	95	59.4%	-4.9%	1203	7	2/3	3	13.6%	5.7	--	-17.0%	--	-62	--	24	129	0	-13.7%	-2	33.7
2020	LV	1/0	65	28	17	60.7%	2.2%	226	1	1/2	0	1.6%	8.4	--	13.0%	--	45	--	9	88	1	76.2%	48	98.1
2021	LV			529	347	65.6%		4047	23	11	8		6.9		2.0%				83	587	5	20.4%		

| 2019 | 18% Behind | 44% Short | 29% Mid | 10% Deep | aDOT: 7.4 (--) | YAC: 6.4 (--) | ALEX: 0.2 | 2020 | 8% Behind | 42% Short | 27% Mid | 23% Deep | aDOT: 10.8 (--) | YAC: 4.5 (--) | ALEX: -5.3 |

In a rare turn of events, Raiders starting quarterback Derek Carr missed some time last season. Carr left the Week 15 match against the Chargers with a groin injury, leaving Mariota to play most of the game. The brief showing was Mariota's first (and only) appearance since being benched halfway through the 2019 season in Tennessee. Mariota ripped a sideline throw to tight end Foster Moreau from outside the pocket on his first attempt, then finished off that drive with a one-on-one deep ball to Darren Waller down the sideline to give the Raiders a brief early lead. The rest of his performance in the narrow loss was not quite as dazzling, but Mariota did at least prove himself capable of quality play again, as a passer and runner alike. Mariota restructured his contract to take much less money this season and will not push Carr for the starting job, but he's one of the best backups in the NFL right now and may well be a late-offseason or midseason trade piece.

Baker Mayfield

Height: 6-1 Weight: 215 College: Oklahoma Draft: 2018/1 (1) Born: 14-Apr-1995 Age: 26 Risk: Green

Year	Tm	G/GS	Snaps	Att	Cmp	C%	CPOE	Yds	TD	INT/Adj	FUM	ASR	NY/P	Rk	DVOA	Rk	DYAR	Rk	Runs	Yds	TD	DVOA	DYAR	QBR
2018	CLE	14/13	906	486	310	63.8%	0.4%	3725	27	14/14	7	5.5%	7.0	11	8.1%	14	628	12	39	131	0	-28.6%	-20	53.9
2019	CLE	16/16	1058	534	317	59.4%	-2.8%	3827	22	21/23	6	7.1%	6.2	17	-9.8%	25	48	25	28	141	3	21.9%	48	52.4
2020	CLE	16/16	1046	486	305	62.8%	1.4%	3563	26	8/12	8	6.7%	6.6	18	5.1%	17	545	16	54	165	1	-6.8%	13	72.4
2021	CLE			549	347	63.3%		4004	27	12	8		6.6		-0.7%				55	182	2	-19.3%		

| 2019 | 17% Behind | 45% Short | 23% Mid | 15% Deep | aDOT: 8.9 (14) | YAC: 5.7 (6) | ALEX: 1.6 | 2020 | 11% Behind | 51% Short | 25% Mid | 12% Deep | aDOT: 8.8 (11) | YAC: 4.5 (30) | ALEX: 1.8 |

Incredibly, barring some tragic preseason injury, 2021 will mark the first time since 1950 that the Browns will start the same quarterback on opening Sunday three straight seasons—namely, Mayfield, who made some fans wonder whether he would join Automatic Otto Graham in that stat after his mediocre 2019. A key to Mayfield's improvement last season was less usage. His 486 pass attempts (identical to 2018, when he played two fewer games) were down nearly 50 from the year before, and he cut his interceptions from 21 to eight. His growing maturity in that department can also be seen in his willingness to live to play another down—only four passers threw it away more than Mayfield (24). Mayfield was most effective in 2020 throwing short. Only Nick Mullens had a better DVOA on passes thrown behind the line of scrimmage, though it wasn't a huge part of Mayfield's game (50 attempts; Justin Herbert led the league with 107).

AJ McCarron

Height: 6-3   Weight: 220   College: Alabama   Draft: 2014/5 (164)   Born: 13-Sep-1990   Age: 31   Risk: Green

Year	Tm	G/GS	Snaps	Att	Cmp	C%	CPOE	Yds	TD	INT/Adj	FUM	ASR	NY/P	Rk	DVOA	Rk	DYAR	Rk	Runs	Yds	TD	DVOA	DYAR	QBR
2018	OAK	2/0	12	3	1	33.3%	24.2%	8	0	0/0	1	24.6%	0.3	--	-157.0%	--	-30	--	3	-2	0	-118.4%	-12	0.4
2019	HOU	2/1	69	37	21	56.8%	0.1%	225	0	1/1	0	12.1%	4.3	--	-43.6%	--	-96	--	5	39	1	48.3%	19	25.5
2020	HOU	2/0	1	1	1	100.0%	54.9%	20	0	0/0	0	52.6%	4.0	--	-78.8%	--	-13	--	0	0	0	--	--	0.0
2021	ATL			569	349	61.3%		3786	25	12	7		5.9		-11.7%				40	163	2	-5.3%		

2019 13% Behind 58% Short 16% Mid 13% Deep aDOT: 8.7 (--) YAC: 6.2 (--) ALEX: 3.0   2020 0% Behind 0% Short 0% Mid 0% Deep aDOT: 0.0 (--) YAC: 2.0 (--) ALEX: 0.0

McCarron played one offensive snap for the Texans last season. In Week 14, he entered the game when Deshaun Watson's elbow collided with a linebacker's helmet. On the fourth-and-goal play from the 1, McCarron dropped back … and just held onto the ball. After the sack, he returned to the bench and picked up a tablet to review what went wrong. The game film confirmed that the ball never left his hand. Mystery solved.

Turns out, that was an excellent audition for one of the cushiest jobs in football: backup to Matt Ryan, who has missed only three starts in 13 seasons. If all goes well, McCarron will continue not throwing passes.

Colt McCoy

Height: 6-1   Weight: 212   College: Texas   Draft: 2010/3 (85)   Born: 5-Sep-1986   Age: 35   Risk: Green

Year	Tm	G/GS	Snaps	Att	Cmp	C%	CPOE	Yds	TD	INT/Adj	FUM	ASR	NY/P	Rk	DVOA	Rk	DYAR	Rk	Runs	Yds	TD	DVOA	DYAR	QBR
2018	WAS	3/2	100	54	34	63.0%	1.4%	372	3	3/4	1	10.9%	5.8	--	-40.8%	--	-119	--	10	63	0	48.3%	30	41.5
2019	WAS	1/1	59	27	18	66.7%	0.1%	122	0	1/2	2	16.9%	2.4	--	-73.8%	--	-114	--	2	14	0	90.1%	9	13.9
2020	NYG	4/2	145	66	40	60.6%	-7.8%	375	1	1/2	1	6.9%	4.9	--	-40.7%	--	-132	--	9	12	0	-71.2%	-14	36.0
2021	ARI			580	368	63.4%		3841	23	11	9		5.9		-9.8%				62	196	2	-23.8%		

2019 12% Behind 64% Short 16% Mid 8% Deep aDOT: 6.9 (--) YAC: 1.9 (--) ALEX: -3.7   2020 11% Behind 48% Short 29% Mid 12% Deep aDOT: 8.9 (--) YAC: 3.2 (--) ALEX: 4.5

Only four quarterbacks started games against the Seahawks in the regular season last year and came away with a win. The first three were Kyler Murray, Josh Allen, and Jared Goff. The fourth, as you have likely guessed, was Colt McCoy, who filled in for a gimpy Daniel Jones and led the Giants to a win in Seattle. "Led," of course, is a relative term—McCoy threw for barely 100 yards while giving up an interception and a pair of sacks, and two of the Giants' three scoring drives in the 17-12 upset started in Seattle territory—but McCoy at least showed enough flashes of competence that a brilliant day by the New York defense did not go to waste.

McCoy lost his next start to the Browns two weeks later; the Seahawks game, which broke McCoy's six-start losing streak, remains his only win as a starter since 2014. He'll remain a low-end backup for as long as his 35-year-old body will allow, but should serve the Cardinals better in that role than Chris Streveler did last year.

Trace McSorley

Height: 6-0   Weight: 202   College: Penn State   Draft: 2019/6 (197)   Born: 23-Aug-1995   Age: 26   Risk: Green

Year	Tm	G/GS	Snaps	Att	Cmp	C%	CPOE	Yds	TD	INT/Adj	FUM	ASR	NY/P	Rk	DVOA	Rk	DYAR	Rk	Runs	Yds	TD	DVOA	DYAR	QBR
2019	BAL	1/0	1	0	0	0.0%	--	0	0	0/0	0	--	--	--	--	--	--	--	1	1	0	6.9%	2	--
2020	BAL	2/0	20	10	3	30.0%	-29.7%	90	1	0/1	0	0.0%	9.0	--	14.0%	--	15	--	5	17	0	-14.2%	-1	35.0
2021	BAL			449	257	57.2%		3023	21	11	9		5.9		-15.7%				123	538	6	-11.6%		

2019   2020 0% Behind 63% Short 38% Mid 0% Deep aDOT: 9.3 (--) YAC: 17.7 (--) ALEX: -1.8

McSorley replaced an injured Robert Griffin against the Steelers and fluttered a sideline pass to Marquise Brown which turned into a 70-yard touchdown; rewatching the tape of that play, it looked as though everyone from the Steelers defenders to Brown himself was surprised to see a pass attempt along the intermediate sideline. McSorley then filled in against the Browns when Lamar Jackson had a case of the scoots (figure it out, big shoots) but suffered a knee injury that forced Jackson to return to the game, McSorley was then lost for the year, which is why Tyler Huntley replaced Jackson in the playoff loss to the Bills.

A pint-sized, cost-effective scrambler, McSorley has the skill set to back up Jackson and just about only Jackson. There's a chance that Huntley wins the backup job in camp. In the event Jackson misses significant time, either backup could end up with about 50 rushing yards per game, helping your fantasy team while the Ravens rapidly sink into oblivion.

Davis Mills   Height: 6-4   Weight: 212   College: Stanford   Draft: 2021/3 (67)   Born: 21-Oct-1998   Age: 23   Risk: Green

Year	Tm	G/GS	Snaps	Att	Cmp	C%	CPOE	Yds	TD	INT/Adj	FUM	ASR	NY/P	Rk	DVOA	Rk	DYAR	Rk	Runs	Yds	TD	DVOA	DYAR	QBR
2021	HOU		556	327	58.7%			3704	21	16	9		5.9		-21.6%				46	206	3	-3.8%		

Well, the Texans had to have somebody with some youth, right? Mills doesn't exactly have the deep arm that gets scouts drooling, but he showed a little bit of everything else at Stanford. The problem was that he only played in 14 college games and his accuracy was puzzlingly bad on some throws. He showed some good play up the seam, he showed some solid poise under pressure, and he's not afraid to throw a receiver open. He also had the highest passes defensed rate of anyone in the class that Football Outsiders draft analyst Derrik Klassen charted. This was a high-risk, low-floor swing in the third round, but the good news is that the Texans don't seem likely to be married to Mills if they happen to find themselves with a high first-round pick next year.

Gardner Minshew   Height: 6-1   Weight: 225   College: Washington State   Draft: 2019/6 (178)   Born: 16-May-1996   Age: 25   Risk: Green

Year	Tm	G/GS	Snaps	Att	Cmp	C%	CPOE	Yds	TD	INT/Adj	FUM	ASR	NY/P	Rk	DVOA	Rk	DYAR	Rk	Runs	Yds	TD	DVOA	DYAR	QBR
2019	JAX	14/12	920	470	285	60.6%	-4.0%	3271	21	6/10	13	7.0%	6.1	20	-5.0%	22	193	22	67	344	0	8.1%	48	42.6
2020	JAX	9/8	558	327	216	66.1%	0.8%	2259	16	5/7	5	8.9%	6.0	26	-11.0%	27	4	27	29	153	1	-4.2%	11	52.2
2021	JAX			546	363	66.6%			3742	27	9	10		6.1		-9.8%				64	312	2	-10.0%		

| 2019 | 16% Behind | 54% Short | 19% Mid | 12% Deep | aDOT: 7.7 (28) | YAC: 5.4 (14) | ALEX: 2.0 | 2020 | 14% Behind | 52% Short | 22% Mid | 12% Deep | aDOT: 8.3 (19) | YAC: 4.7 (26) | ALEX: 0.1 |

Minshew's Jaguars career has certainly not been dull. He has not exactly been bad, yet he has irked the Jaguars enough to have Nick Foles and Mike Glennon start over him. He has advanced pocket feel and does a great job avoiding sacks, scrambling, and not turning the ball over, but his accuracy leaves something to be desired. He's kind of the perfect backup quarterback in a way, it's just that he doesn't realize it yet and clearly wants a chance to make things work as a starter. There was not a more Florida Man Quarterback than Minshew, and for that we weep for the inevitable breakup, but the spirit of Ryan Fitzpatrick flows through Minshew's veins and we're probably going to get plenty of him over the next 10 years. Minshew's starts were not, altogether, good. But there was enough there to sell someone else on his worth, and the Doug Marrone Jags were hardly an offensive paragon.

Kellen Mond   Height: 6-3   Weight: 217   College: Texas A&M   Draft: 2021/3 (66)   Born: 22-Jun-1999   Age: 22   Risk: Green

Year	Tm	G/GS	Snaps	Att	Cmp	C%	CPOE	Yds	TD	INT/Adj	FUM	ASR	NY/P	Rk	DVOA	Rk	DYAR	Rk	Runs	Yds	TD	DVOA	DYAR	QBR
2021	MIN		543	325	59.8%			3810	25	13	11		6.2		-9.4%				103	580	6	5.0%		

Mond has the athleticism and rushing ability to rival even the Round 1 dual-threat quarterbacks such as Trey Lance and Justin Fields, but he never matched those prospects in accuracy or frequency of explosive passing plays, and so he slipped to the third round. Mond has some fans beyond the Vikings team that drafted him—NBC Sports analyst Chris Simms ranked him fourth in the class ahead of both Lance and Fields, and reports have suggested that the Texans would have taken Mond over Davis Mills if he had slipped one spot further in the draft. It's probably for the best he landed where he did. With an increased reliance on play-action on a run-oriented Texas A&M team, Mond dramatically cut his interception rate in 2020. He could excel in a Gary Kubiak-inspired offensive scheme that does not demand its passers to do everything themselves.

James Morgan   Height: 6-4   Weight: 213   College: Florida International   Draft: 2020/4 (125)   Born: 28-Feb-1997   Age: 24   Risk: Green

Year	Tm	G/GS	Snaps	Att	Cmp	C%	CPOE	Yds	TD	INT/Adj	FUM	ASR	NY/P	Rk	DVOA	Rk	DYAR	Rk	Runs	Yds	TD	DVOA	DYAR	QBR
2021	NYJ		571	332	58.2%			3801	24	15	9		5.9		-20.6%				46	172	3	-8.6%		

RIP the James Morgan, QB1 era; April 5, 2021—April 29, 2021. Between the Sam Darnold trade and the Zach Wilson pick, Morgan, who has never been active for an NFL game, was the dean in New York's quarterback room. Should something happen to Wilson, Morgan does have a cannon for an arm and a willingness to go deep, but does not have touch, accuracy, mobility, or solid footwork. A 58% completion rate in Conference USA does not bode well for one's success on the professional level, and being drafted by a since-fired coaching staff does not bode well for one's continued employment.

Nick Mullens

Height: 6-1 | Weight: 210 | College: Southern Mississippi | Draft: 2017/FA | Born: 21-Mar-1995 | Age: 26 | Risk: Green

Year	Tm	G/GS	Snaps	Att	Cmp	C%	CPOE	Yds	TD	INT/Adj	FUM	ASR	NY/P	Rk	DVOA	Rk	DYAR	Rk	Runs	Yds	TD	DVOA	DYAR	QBR
2018	SF	8/8	519	274	176	64.2%	1.4%	2277	13	10/12	2	6.3%	7.5	6	4.2%	18	286	24	18	-16	0	-118.6%	-43	54.9
2019	SF	1/0	7	0	0	0.0%	--	0	0	0/0	0	--	--	--	--	--	--	--	3	-3	0	--	--	--
2020	SF	10/8	603	326	211	64.7%	-1.9%	2437	12	12/14	6	4.5%	6.7	15	-7.7%	25	76	25	9	8	0	-24.8%	-3	44.4
2021	PHI			587	377	64.3%		4212	25	19	8		6.3		-14.9%				26	68	1	-20.7%		

2019 | | 2020 15% Behind | 54% Short | 23% Mid | 8% Deep | aDOT 7.0 (32) | YAC: 5.9 (3) | ALEX: 0.1

Last year was a season of great extremes for Mullens. Among quarterbacks with at least 200 passes, he had the highest DVOA on throws to receivers behind the line of scrimmage because he got to play with Brandon Aiyuk, Deebo Samuel, and the other Human YAC Machines in San Francisco. He also had the highest DVOA on throws to receivers 20-plus yards downfield because he rarely threw that deep unless his targets were wide open—only Drew Brees threw deep less frequently. However, he was next to last in DVOA on short throws (0 to 9 yards downfield) and well below average on medium throws (10 to 19 yards) because his inaccuracy and failure to spot defenders dropping into coverage led to turnovers—all 12 of his interceptions were thrown in this range, most in the NFL. That includes a pair of pick-sixes when targeting receivers within 5 yards of the line of scrimmage. Further complicating all this, a massive share of Mullens' production came in garbage time. He was only 26th in total passing yardage, but he led the NFL with 663 passing yards when trailing by 10 points or more in the fourth quarter, and 473 yards when down by 17 or more.

In three years since joining San Francisco as an undrafted free agent, Mullens has completed 64.5% of his passes and averaged 7.9 yards per throw, 12.2 yards per completion. He has a low sack rate of just 5.6% and has produced at a high volume, averaging 248.1 passing yards per game. Those numbers are all superior to those of any quarterback drafted in the first round in Mullens' rookie class of 2018, including Baker Mayfield, Josh Allen, and Lamar Jackson. Unfortunately, his 1.2 interceptions per game are also higher than any of those first-rounders, higher even than Sam Darnold's or Josh Rosen's. That, and the elbow injury he suffered in Week 15 against Dallas that ended his season and led to December surgery, is why he was available to sign with the Eagles in mid-June as a backup to Jalen Hurts and Joe Flacco.

Kyler Murray

Height: 5-10 | Weight: 207 | College: Oklahoma | Draft: 2019/1 (1) | Born: 7-Aug-1997 | Age: 24 | Risk: Green

Year	Tm	G/GS	Snaps	Att	Cmp	C%	CPOE	Yds	TD	INT/Adj	FUM	ASR	NY/P	Rk	DVOA	Rk	DYAR	Rk	Runs	Yds	TD	DVOA	DYAR	QBR
2019	ARI	16/16	1025	542	349	64.4%	0.5%	3722	20	12/15	5	8.2%	5.9	26	-3.1%	21	305	21	93	544	4	8.5%	87	55.7
2020	ARI	16/16	1103	558	375	67.2%	3.9%	3971	26	12/20	9	5.3%	6.5	19	4.6%	18	590	15	133	819	11	15.8%	186	69.1
2021	ARI			613	404	65.9%		4501	29	12	8		6.6		0.8%				107	642	8	18.4%		

2019 | 19% Behind | 50% Short | 17% Mid | 14% Deep | aDOT 7.9 (25) | YAC: 5.3 (18) | ALEX: 1.5 | 2020 17% Behind | 52% Short | 17% Mid | 13% Deep | aDOT 8.3 (18) | YAC: 4.7 (28) | ALEX: 2.8

Sixteen of Murray's passes were batted down at the line of scrimmage, the second-highest total in the league. The natural conclusion to jump to is that this is due to Murray's short stature … until you realize that every other quarterback in the top five (Ben Roethlisberger, Cam Newton, Philip Rivers, and Justin Herbert) was 6-foot-5 or taller. Turns out that batted passes are an issue for many quarterbacks, regardless of height.

It's difficult to discuss Murray without mentioning his diminutive size. It's his most obvious and defining trait. The last NFL quarterback of note shorter than Murray was the Little General, Eddie LeBaron, of the 1960s. (Go look up some LeBaron highlights—the similarities to Murray and the Cardinals' offense are uncanny.) Seth Wickersham wrote an excellent article for ESPN+ in May breaking down how Murray uses his small frame to his advantage, playing less like a short quarterback and more like a short point guard, breaking defenders down "off the dribble" like 5-foot-3 former NBA star Muggsy Bogues to open passing and running lanes. That's how he's able to stay in the pocket more often than you might guess. Even counting his 50 scrambles (third most in the league), he only left the pocket on 21.7% of his dropbacks. That's more than average, but less often than some of his more lead-footed peers, including Baker Mayfield, Drew Lock, and Mitchell Trubisky.

There's an undeniably comic element to this. Murray looks like a little kid playing dress-up in his big brother's helmet, with this gargantuan head perched atop his itty-bitty body scampering all over the field. He looks as if he has just ordered Spaceball One to hit Ludicrous Speed. He's a Funko Pop! come to life. He's the NFL's answer to M.O.D.O.K. The real comedy, of course, comes when Murray breaks defenders' ankles, leaving world-class athletes falling all over themselves, Keystone Kops-style, as he skitters for a first down. After all, rabbits are also small, but have you ever tried to tackle one?

Cam Newton

Height: 6-5   Weight: 245   College: Auburn   Draft: 2011/1 (1)   Born: 11-May-1989   Age: 32   Risk: Red

Year	Tm	G/GS	Snaps	Att	Cmp	C%	CPOE	Yds	TD	INT/Adj	FUM	ASR	NY/P	Rk	DVOA	Rk	DYAR	Rk	Runs	Yds	TD	DVOA	DYAR	QBR
2018	CAR	14/14	885	471	320	67.9%	1.9%	3395	24	13/17	6	6.6%	6.4	18	-1.4%	23	321	23	101	488	4	2.7%	71	55.9
2019	CAR	2/2	146	89	50	56.2%	-5.4%	572	0	1/1	2	6.1%	5.6	--	-8.0%	--	19	--	5	-2	0	-230.2%	-48	21.1
2020	NE	15/15	876	368	242	65.8%	-1.0%	2657	8	10/11	6	8.0%	6.2	23	-17.7%	31	-166	31	137	592	12	-6.4%	44	47.4
2021	NE			464	295	63.6%		3236	17	11	10		6.2		-12.9%				158	687	13	19.3%		

2019	10% Behind	45% Short	30% Mid	15% Deep	aDOT: 9.3 (--)	YAC: 4.1 (--)	ALEX: -0.5	2020	20% Behind	47% Short	25% Mid	8% Deep	aDOT: 7.3 (30)	YAC: 5.2 (16)	ALEX: -2.1

Piecing together how much of Newton's 2020 struggles were due to his bout of COVID, how much were due to his deteriorated shoulder, how much were due to the neck and abdomen injuries he picked up throughout the year, and how much were due to the lack of talent around him makes evaluating him very difficult. He had four games above a 20.0% passing DVOA and seven games below -20.0% as he fluctuated from week to week. One thing that did stay consistent was his struggles against pressure. Patriots quarterbacks were blitzed on 42% of pass plays, more than any other in the league by leaps and bounds. And New England's DVOA fell from 18.0% with four pass-rushers to a league-worst -51.0% with five or more. There was a time when Newton would make you pay for sending extra men, either bulldozing his way up the middle or rifling a pass into single coverage. That was half a decade and roughly 10 zillion injuries ago, however, and that Newton may never be coming back.

Dak Prescott

Height: 6-2   Weight: 238   College: Mississippi State   Draft: 2016/4 (135)   Born: 29-Jul-1993   Age: 28   Risk: Yellow

Year	Tm	G/GS	Snaps	Att	Cmp	C%	CPOE	Yds	TD	INT/Adj	FUM	ASR	NY/P	Rk	DVOA	Rk	DYAR	Rk	Runs	Yds	TD	DVOA	DYAR	QBR
2018	DAL	16/16	1071	526	356	67.7%	0.9%	3885	22	8/12	12	9.7%	6.1	26	-8.1%	26	112	25	75	305	6	2.0%	45	57.8
2019	DAL	16/16	1124	596	388	65.1%	1.2%	4902	30	11/17	6	4.3%	7.7	3	27.1%	6	1541	1	52	277	3	15.6%	71	70.2
2020	DAL	5/5	360	222	151	68.0%	1.0%	1856	9	4/9	3	4.4%	7.7	1	14.0%	8	399	19	18	93	3	33.3%	46	78.4
2021	DAL			646	429	66.3%		5135	30	12	9		7.1		12.5%				73	380	7	29.5%		

2019	10% Behind	51% Short	26% Mid	13% Deep	aDOT: 9.7 (6)	YAC: 4.8 (29)	ALEX: 2.3	2020	15% Behind	52% Short	20% Mid	13% Deep	aDOT: 8.2 (22)	YAC: 5.4 (14)	ALEX: 2.5

The Cowboys' passing DVOA was over 15.0% in all four games that Prescott played to completion. Prescott threw for over 450 yards in three of those games, in part because he was playing catch-up after opponents took significant early leads thanks to turnovers (a few by Prescott himself) and putrid defense. And Prescott finished 19th in DYAR for the year despite playing one-fourth of a season, a testament to both the quality and quantity of his passing.

So there's plenty of evidence that Prescott will produce gobs of yardage and scoring opportunities in Mike McCarthy's system, given his current weapons. But can he cut down on the strip-sacks and interceptions? Better protection will help. Not being forced to drop back 60 times while playing from behind would also help. Prescott himself could make a better decision now and then, but nearly all of his 2020 problems appeared to be Cowboys problems that he was forced to cope with. Whatever else happens in Dallas this year, he should hold up his end of the bargain.

Philip Rivers

Height: 6-5   Weight: 228   College: North Carolina State   Draft: 2004/1 (4)   Born: 8-Dec-1981   Age: 40   Risk: N/A

Year	Tm	G/GS	Snaps	Att	Cmp	C%	CPOE	Yds	TD	INT/Adj	FUM	ASR	NY/P	Rk	DVOA	Rk	DYAR	Rk	Runs	Yds	TD	DVOA	DYAR	QBR
2018	LAC	16/16	964	508	347	68.3%	2.0%	4308	32	12/16	2	6.1%	7.6	4	27.2%	3	1316	3	18	7	0	-96.5%	-55	70.2
2019	LAC	16/16	1044	591	390	66.0%	2.9%	4615	23	20/26	8	6.3%	7.1	11	6.6%	14	714	14	12	29	0	-41.9%	-10	48.6
2020	IND	16/16	1044	543	369	68.0%	1.2%	4169	24	11/16	2	4.8%	7.2	8	9.9%	12	765	13	18	-8	0	-62.1%	-4	62.7

2019	15% Behind	45% Short	25% Mid	15% Deep	aDOT: 9.0 (10)	YAC: 5.5 (11)	ALEX: 2.0	2020	18% Behind	48% Short	24% Mid	10% Deep	aDOT: 7.6 (27)	YAC: 6.0 (2)	ALEX: 0.5

As weird as it was to let literally Drew Brees walk out the door because of a first-round pick, the Chargers made a lot of hay with Philip Rivers. He passed the 15,000-career-DYAR mark in his lone season with the Colts, really only had one bad season (2012, behind a Mike Harris-Tyronne Green-Nick Hardwick-Louis Vasquez-Jeromey Clary offensive line), and checked pretty much every franchise quarterback box besides appearing in and winning a Super Bowl. He finished in the top 10 in passing DVOA nine times, and the top five six times, and he did it all with a funky side-arm delivery. Rivers teared up after the season-ending loss to the Bills in the AFC wild-card game, saying "After your 17th year and you're about to be 40, and you're not sure if you walked up your last tunnel, heck yeah, heck yeah, it's more (emotional)." He's destined to become a coach somewhere in South Alabama as he deals with his kids playing high school football, and destined in our little section of the football world to become the subject of a bunch of Hall of Fame debates, ones where our statistically brightest try to tell someone to not count the rings. Nick Drake isn't in the Rock & Roll Hall of Fame, and that's fine, *Pink Moon* still ruled.

Aaron Rodgers

Height: 6-2			Weight: 225		College: California				Draft: 2005/1 (24)			Born: 2-Dec-1983			Age: 38			Risk: Yellow			

Year	Tm	G/GS	Snaps	Att	Cmp	C%	CPOE	Yds	TD	INT/Adj	FUM	ASR	NY/P	Rk	DVOA	Rk	DYAR	Rk	Runs	Yds	TD	DVOA	DYAR	QBR
2018	GB	16/16	1013	597	372	62.3%	-0.1%	4442	25	2/8	6	8.0%	6.3	22	8.1%	12	817	9	43	269	2	18.4%	66	60.6
2019	GB	16/16	1082	569	353	62.0%	0.1%	4002	26	4/6	4	6.5%	6.2	18	9.0%	13	794	8	46	183	1	35.9%	61	50.4
2020	GB	16/16	1018	526	372	70.7%	5.3%	4299	48	5/11	4	4.8%	7.6	3	33.7%	1	1649	2	38	149	3	2.9%	24	84.4
2021	GB			584	397	67.9%		4616	39	7	5		7.1		19.6%				49	188	3	2.0%		

2019	18% Behind	46% Short	18% Mid	19% Deep	aDOT: 9.1 (9)	YAC: 5.7 (7)	ALEX: 4.1	2020	20% Behind	49% Short	16% Mid	16% Deep	aDOT: 8.3 (17)	YAC: 6.0 (1)	ALEX: 4.8

Under head coach Matt LaFleur, the Packers have made some analytically savvy offensive adjustments to make life easier for their quarterback. They've increased their play-action rate from 18% in 2018 (29th) to 36% last year (second), and they've increased their rate of offensive motion from 28% (26th) to 54% (sixth) over the same period. That would all be great for the team's sophomore quarterback Jordan Love if the changes hadn't also made life easier for star incumbent Aaron Rodgers. And since Rodgers remains tremendous at aspects of the position you can't improve with scheme — he was top five in 2020 in yards per play without play-action and in DVOA with pressure and on deep attempts — he has returned to MVP form and put the team in a bind. It's unclear now whether Rodgers will return to the Packers this season or force a trade to another team. But based on his recent productivity, it is clear that he could turn just about any team he joined into a Super Bowl contender.

Ben Roethlisberger

Height: 6-5			Weight: 240		College: Miami (Ohio)			Draft: 2004/1 (11)			Born: 2-Mar-1982			Age: 39			Risk: Yellow

Year	Tm	G/GS	Snaps	Att	Cmp	C%	CPOE	Yds	TD	INT/Adj	FUM	ASR	NY/P	Rk	DVOA	Rk	DYAR	Rk	Runs	Yds	TD	DVOA	DYAR	QBR
2018	PIT	16/16	1086	675	452	67.0%	0.4%	5129	34	16/20	7	4.4%	7.1	9	14.5%	8	1204	5	31	98	3	37.8%	62	71.8
2019	PIT	2/2	96	62	35	56.5%	-11.1%	351	0	1/2	1	3.1%	5.3	--	5.4%	--	69	--	1	7	0	26.2%	2	27.1
2020	PIT	15/15	1010	608	399	65.6%	-2.3%	3803	33	10/20	5	2.8%	5.9	27	1.1%	20	518	17	25	11	0	-112.2%	-49	60.8
2021	PIT			690	443	64.3%		4603	33	14	7		6.1		-2.6%				32	46	1	-38.0%		

2019	10% Behind	60% Short	16% Mid	15% Deep	aDOT: 9.5 (--)	YAC: 5.5 (--)	ALEX: 3.3	2020	16% Behind	53% Short	18% Mid	13% Deep	aDOT: 7.5 (29)	YAC: 4.9 (20)	ALEX: 0.7

As Roethlisberger enters his age-39 season, he will be looking to his contemporaries in the pantheon of great passers of this era as to what he can expect at such a wizened age. If he gazes at Drew Brees, who posted 1,631 DYAR and a 36.7% DVOA in his age-39 season in 2018, he will be encouraged. Likewise Tom Brady in 2016: 1,286 and 33.4%. He should avert his eyes from Peyton Manning's 2015, however—the legend finished his career with -326 DYAR and a -25.8% DVOA, both next-to-last among qualifying quarterbacks that year.

We mentioned that the Steelers benefited from outsized defensive pass interference flags in the Pittsburgh chapter. Roethlisberger was fortunate in another respect: he had 20 adjusted interceptions in 2020, just one behind the league leader, the abominable Carson Wentz. No quarterback had more dropped or defensed interceptions (10), which would have doubled Roethlisberger's 10 actual interceptions. Roethlisberger had some good deep-dive numbers, however, including a 16.5% DVOA on third/fourth downs and 22.8% DVOA in the red zone, good for 10th among qualifying quarterbacks. If this is the end for Roethlisberger, our projection expects him to go out throwing.

Mason Rudolph

Height: 6-5			Weight: 235		College: Oklahoma State			Draft: 2018/3 (76)			Born: 17-Jul-1995			Age: 26			Risk: Green

Year	Tm	G/GS	Snaps	Att	Cmp	C%	CPOE	Yds	TD	INT/Adj	FUM	ASR	NY/P	Rk	DVOA	Rk	DYAR	Rk	Runs	Yds	TD	DVOA	DYAR	QBR
2019	PIT	10/8	534	283	176	62.2%	-1.1%	1765	13	9/9	4	5.7%	5.5	30	-23.0%	33	-225	30	21	42	0	-12.5%	0	34.4
2020	PIT	5/1	79	43	25	58.1%	-6.0%	324	2	1/1	0	1.6%	7.2	--	-10.9%	--	1	--	7	-6	0	-113.9%	-5	77.8
2021	PIT			619	385	62.1%		4006	29	15	7		5.9		-8.5%				42	77	2	-34.6%		

2019	21% Behind	43% Short	19% Mid	16% Deep	aDOT: 8.7 (16)	YAC: 5.3 (16)	ALEX: -0.2	2020	10% Behind	57% Short	14% Mid	19% Deep	aDOT: 10.3 (--)	YAC: 4.1 (--)	ALEX: 1.0

Rudolph appears to have bought another season in Pittsburgh with his strong performance in a Week 17 glorified scrimmage in Cleveland, one week before the teams squared off for real in the wild-card round. Re-signed to an extra year on top of his rookie deal, Rudolph is at the moment the lone quarterback under contract in Pittsburgh for 2022, which means the team wants at least one guy around who knows which toilet beneath Heinz Field requires jimmying the handle. Bathroom metaphors have been Rudolph's milieu over three seasons of largely crappy appearances when Ben Roethlisberger didn't play. Yet for the time being, his roster spot appears safe.

Matt Ryan

Height: 6-4 Weight: 217 College: Boston College Draft: 2008/1 (3) Born: 17-May-1985 Age: 36 Risk: Green

Year	Tm	G/GS	Snaps	Att	Cmp	C%	CPOE	Yds	TD	INT/Adj	FUM	ASR	NY/P	Rk	DVOA	Rk	DYAR	Rk	Runs	Yds	TD	DVOA	DYAR	QBR
2018	ATL	16/16	1048	608	422	69.4%	3.5%	4924	35	7/11	10	6.7%	7.1	7	18.2%	4	1232	4	33	125	3	33.9%	68	68.2
2019	ATL	15/15	1087	616	408	66.2%	3.2%	4466	26	14/18	9	6.8%	6.3	15	6.5%	15	732	11	34	147	1	18.1%	38	57.6
2020	ATL	16/16	1113	626	407	65.0%	1.4%	4581	26	11/18	6	6.8%	6.5	20	7.6%	15	817	10	29	92	2	-30.3%	-21	66.8
2021	ATL			641	429	66.9%		4758	29	14	7		6.6		4.2%				40	146	2	-6.1%		

| 2019 | 9% Behind | 55% Short | 26% Mid | 11% Deep | aDOT: 8.6 (17) | YAC: 4.0 (33) | ALEX: 2.5 | 2020 | 9% Behind | 54% Short | 24% Mid | 13% Deep | aDOT: 8.8 (9) | YAC: 4.0 (33) | ALEX: 1.7 |

In the Atlanta chapter, we explored some of the reasons why Arthur Smith could rejuvenate Matt Ryan's career like he did Ryan Tannehill's. In this space, let's drill down to a specific situation: second down.

On first, third, and fourth downs last season, Ryan was solid, posting a combined 22.7% DVOA, which ranked fourth. But on second down, his DVOA plummeted to -22.3%, which ranked 30th, barely better than Nick Foles, Gardner Minshew, and Sam Darnold (minimum 50 passes). That wasn't an aberration. Ryan's splits in 2019 were similar, though not as severe. As for Tannehill, his 24.2% DVOA on second down last season put him among the league leaders.

Why the difference? One of the hallmarks of Smith's offense is putting his quarterback in favorable down-and-distance situations. On second down last season, the Titans needed, on average, 7.2 yards to reach a first down, third lowest. And with a 53-47 pass-run ratio (excluding the fourth quarter), they kept defenses guessing. That, of course, fueled a high first-down percentage—43.7% on passes (second behind the Chiefs) and 42.9% on runs (second behind the Seahawks).

Brett Rypien

Height: 6-2 Weight: 200 College: Boise State Draft: 2019/FA Born: 9-Jul-1996 Age: 25 Risk: Green

Year	Tm	G/GS	Snaps	Att	Cmp	C%	CPOE	Yds	TD	INT/Adj	FUM	ASR	NY/P	Rk	DVOA	Rk	DYAR	Rk	Runs	Yds	TD	DVOA	DYAR	QBR
2020	DEN	3/1	83	40	27	67.5%	4.2%	295	2	4/6	1	5.4%	7.0	--	-63.0%	--	-143	--	5	-5	0	--	--	57.8
2021	DEN			596	358	60.1%		4172	28	18	9		6.3		-13.2%				55	99	3	-33.3%		

| 2019 | | | | | | 2020 | 8% Behind | 65% Short | 14% Mid | 14% Deep | aDOT: 8.8 (--) | YAC: 3.0 (--) | ALEX: 2.5 |

Rypien is as good a case as any that understanding how to play quarterback is not the same as having the talent to do it. A four-year starter at Boise State, Rypien is a generally fluid processor and decision-maker in the pocket, but his arm strength is such that he has to be exactly right and exactly on time in order for his game to work. For seasoned vets such as Drew Brees and Philip Rivers, that's fine, but not so much for a mid-tier backup. Blend that together with some of Rypien's stubbornness with regards to hanging in the pocket, and you get a quarterback who is smart in theory but only partially in practice, which is how his lone start ended with a volatile ratio of two touchdowns with three interceptions. Rypien was pressured on one-third of his dropbacks last season and his stubbornness, lack of mobility, and middling arm strength left him floundering to the tune of 3.0 yards per attempt on those plays, compared to his fairly impressive 9.0 yards per attempt while unpressured. Rypien will not likely see the field in 2021, but if he does, perhaps a sound pass-protection plan could squeeze competent play from him in a pinch.

Alex Smith

Height: 6-4 Weight: 217 College: Utah Draft: 2005/1 (1) Born: 7-May-1984 Age: 37 Risk: N/A

Year	Tm	G/GS	Snaps	Att	Cmp	C%	CPOE	Yds	TD	INT/Adj	FUM	ASR	NY/P	Rk	DVOA	Rk	DYAR	Rk	Runs	Yds	TD	DVOA	DYAR	QBR
2018	WAS	10/10	651	328	205	62.5%	-1.4%	2180	10	5/7	6	6.9%	5.9	31	-13.5%	29	-53	28	41	168	1	13.8%	42	49.3
2020	WAS	8/6	459	252	168	66.7%	-3.0%	1582	6	8/9	2	7.7%	5.3	32	-39.7%	35	-506	34	10	3	0	-133.8%	-22	34.7

| 2019 | | | | | | 2020 | 25% Behind | 55% Short | 9% Mid | 11% Deep | aDOT: 5.3 (36) | YAC: 5.6 (7) | ALEX: -2.6 |

Smith had quite the career arc as No. 1 overall pick. He didn't hit positive passing DVOA until Year 7, then did so in six of the next seven seasons. He ranked inside the top 10 just twice, but even when the upside wasn't there, Smith rarely made back-breaking mistakes. He had the lowest interception rate in the league in 2011 and 2017, with seven total seasons under 2.0%. Of course, his hesitancy to throw the ball down the field inspired our ALEX metric, measuring the distance of a pass compared to the first-down marker on third down. Smith's entire career touches on some of the major shifts in offensive innovation. Under Urban Meyer at Utah, Smith was part of some of the earliest modern spread option offenses. He held down the San Francisco offense before Colin Kaepernick and the read-option took over the 49ers. He was also the placeholder for the Chiefs before Patrick Mahomes was unleashed on the NFL. Of course, Smith's most noteworthy accomplishment could be his recovery from a nasty broken leg suffered during the 2018 season to come back and end his career on his own terms in 2020.

Geno Smith

Height: 6-3　Weight: 221　College: West Virginia　Draft: 2013/2 (39)　Born: 10-Oct-1990　Age: 31　Risk: Green

Year	Tm	G/GS	Snaps	Att	Cmp	C%	CPOE	Yds	TD	INT/Adj	FUM	ASR	NY/P	Rk	DVOA	Rk	DYAR	Rk	Runs	Yds	TD	DVOA	DYAR	QBR
2018	LAC	5/0	32	4	1	25.0%	-27.4%	8	0	0/0	1	16.8%	-1.0	--	-282.0%	--	-49	--	8	2	0	45.4%	3	0.8
2020	SEA	1/0	18	5	4	80.0%	2.1%	33	0	0/0	1	17.3%	5.0	--	-2.7%	--	3	--	2	-2	0	-231.2%	-27	5.2
2021	SEA			566	339	59.9%		3847	27	14	11		5.9		-13.1%				57	229	3	-2.9%		

| 2019 | | | | | | | | | | | | 2020 | 20% Behind | 80% Short | 0% Mid | 0% Deep | aDOT: 5.0 (--) | | YAC: 3.5 (--) | ALEX: -4.5 |

Smith is entering his third season as Russell Wilson's backup, and while he did not get a chance to play at all in 2019, he did see some action on the field this past year against the Jets, the team that originally drafted him in 2013. Smith was only on the field for two drives in that game, but if we subtract all points on drives led by Wilson, the Seahawks still tie the Jets 3-3 that day. This says more about Adam Gase's group than anything about Smith, but it must have been nice to get a small measure of revenge on the team that gave up on him all those years ago.

Matthew Stafford

Height: 6-3　Weight: 220　College: Georgia　Draft: 2009/1 (1)　Born: 7-Feb-1988　Age: 33　Risk: Green

Year	Tm	G/GS	Snaps	Att	Cmp	C%	CPOE	Yds	TD	INT/Adj	FUM	ASR	NY/P	Rk	DVOA	Rk	DYAR	Rk	Runs	Yds	TD	DVOA	DYAR	QBR
2018	DET	16/16	1053	555	367	66.1%	-1.5%	3777	21	11/16	6	6.4%	5.9	28	-0.8%	21	396	20	25	71	0	1.9%	12	54.0
2019	DET	8/8	558	291	187	64.3%	2.2%	2499	19	5/7	5	6.0%	7.7	4	28.8%	4	776	9	20	66	0	-40.1%	-19	69.6
2020	DET	16/16	969	528	339	64.2%	-1.0%	4084	26	10/14	2	7.2%	6.8	13	7.7%	14	684	14	29	112	0	23.0%	42	68.8
2021	LAR			619	418	67.5%		4898	31	11	5		7.1		10.3%				37	141	1	-10.0%		

| 2019 | 7% Behind | 53% Short | 19% Mid | 21% Deep | aDOT: 11.3 (1) | YAC: 4.8 (30) | ALEX: 3.0 | 2020 | 15% Behind | 46% Short | 26% Mid | 13% Deep | aDOT: 9.2 (4) | YAC: 5.1 (18) | ALEX: 2.2 |

Over the past three seasons, Stafford has exhibited some wild swings in how he has performed without pressure in his face; he finished in the bottom five in 2018, the top three in 2019, then below the middle of the pack in 2020. The Los Angeles offensive line likely represents an upgrade over what was in front of Stafford in Detroit and head coach Sean McVay is excellent at scheming open receivers down the field, so it would not be a complete surprise if Stafford's performance under pressure yo-yos back up to the top of the league again.

Jarrett Stidham

Height: 6-3　Weight: 214　College: Auburn　Draft: 2019/4 (133)　Born: 8-Aug-1996　Age: 25　Risk: Green

Year	Tm	G/GS	Snaps	Att	Cmp	C%	CPOE	Yds	TD	INT/Adj	FUM	ASR	NY/P	Rk	DVOA	Rk	DYAR	Rk	Runs	Yds	TD	DVOA	DYAR	QBR
2019	NE	3/0	15	4	2	50.0%	-11.2%	14	0	1/1	0	19.7%	1.4	--	-306.6%	--	-68	--	2	-2	0	--	--	0.1
2020	NE	5/0	85	44	22	50.0%	-11.7%	256	2	3/2	0	8.3%	4.9	--	-50.5%	--	-123	--	7	7	0	-32.9%	-7	16.4
2021	NE			574	358	62.4%		4011	28	17	6		6.2		-11.8%				45	109	2	-22.3%		

| 2019 | 0% Behind | 100% Short | 0% Mid | 0% Deep | aDOT: 5.3 (--) | YAC: 2.5 (--) | ALEX: -4.5 | 2020 | 16% Behind | 59% Short | 14% Mid | 11% Deep | aDOT: 7.0 (--) | YAC: 7.9 (--) | ALEX: -3.2 |

While you hate to pass final judgment on a player with fewer than 50 career pass attempts, Stidham's brief appearances in relief of Cam Newton last season would have dispelled any idea of him being the secret quarterback of the future even before Mac Jones was added on draft day. While he has never had the benefit of a full week of practice before a start, Stidham's 2020 performance can best be described as deer-in-headlights-esque: jumpy in the pocket, poor coverage reading skills, a lack of accuracy. In other words, the problems that plagued Stidham at Auburn did not suddenly go away after sitting on the bench for two years. Tom Brady apparently took whatever magic juice that turns underwhelming third-day quarterbacks into superstars with him to Tampa Bay.

Tua Tagovailoa

Height: 6-0　Weight: 217　College: Alabama　Draft: 2020/1 (5)　Born: 2-Mar-1998　Age: 23　Risk: Yellow

Year	Tm	G/GS	Snaps	Att	Cmp	C%	CPOE	Yds	TD	INT/Adj	FUM	ASR	NY/P	Rk	DVOA	Rk	DYAR	Rk	Runs	Yds	TD	DVOA	DYAR	QBR
2020	MIA	10/9	572	290	186	64.1%	-3.5%	1814	11	5/13	1	7.6%	5.4	30	-8.5%	26	56	26	36	109	3	-0.9%	18	52.9
2021	MIA			607	386	63.5%		4438	30	14	6		6.6		-1.4%				69	247	3	-11.6%		

| 2019 | | | | | | | | | | | | 2020 | 11% Behind | 58% Short | 19% Mid | 12% Deep | aDOT: 8.0 (24) | | YAC: 4.1 (32) | ALEX: 2.5 |

Tagovailoa had a 4.9% passing DVOA before missing the Week 12 Jets game with a jammed thumb and a -15.0% DVOA afterwards, with his four final games all ending up in the negatives. That makes for a compelling offseason narrative as he throws a bunch of camp interceptions in a rainstorm, but it may not foreshadow anything; rookies with declining second-half splits fare no worse in their sophomore seasons than those with similar overall efficiencies and increasing splits. Still, the broader pessimism may make for a fantasy opportunity since the Dolphins' improved offensive talent — in particular at receiver with Will Fuller and top draft pick Jaylen Waddle — should magnify the improvements second-year starters tend to enjoy from the added experience. Of course, the team's improvements also accelerate their need for better quarterback play, and the Dolphins have a war chest of assets to make an upgrade if Tagovailoa can't better his play in Year 2.

Ryan Tannehill   Height: 6-4   Weight: 207   College: Texas A&M   Draft: 2012/1 (8)   Born: 27-Jul-1988   Age: 33   Risk: Green

Year	Tm	G/GS	Snaps	Att	Cmp	C%	CPOE	Yds	TD	INT/Adj	FUM	ASR	NY/P	Rk	DVOA	Rk	DYAR	Rk	Runs	Yds	TD	DVOA	DYAR	QBR
2018	MIA	11/11	580	274	176	64.2%	-0.7%	1979	17	9/16	5	12.0%	5.5	32	-20.8%	32	-186	31	32	145	0	34.9%	39	35.0
2019	TEN	12/10	651	286	201	70.3%	7.7%	2742	22	6/5	6	9.8%	8.1	1	28.0%	5	773	10	43	185	4	48.9%	82	62.2
2020	TEN	16/16	1051	481	315	65.5%	1.1%	3819	33	7/12	6	5.4%	7.2	10	19.6%	6	1046	6	43	266	7	49.3%	127	78.7
2021	TEN			533	344	64.5%		4313	30	10	7		7.3		8.9%				60	326	6	24.6%		

2019	11% Behind	47% Short	27% Mid	15% Deep	aDOT: 10.1 (3)	YAC: 6.1 (3)	ALEX: 2.9	2020	9% Behind	54% Short	28% Mid	9% Deep	aDOT: 8.8 (12)	YAC: 4.9 (21)	ALEX: 1.2

Last year's Tennessee chapter posited that Ryan Tannehill would decline on play-action passes because that tends to be the case for most teams and quarterbacks who perform as well as Tannehill and the Titans did in 2019. It sort of happened. In 2019, the Titans had averaged a mind-boggling 11.2 yards per play with play-action. In 2020, the Titans averaged 9.7 yards per play, still tied for second in the league. It was the highest average gain of any team that ran play-action more than 22% of the time, and the Titans used it as often as any team in the NFL. The funny thing is that the Titans actually had a better DVOA when *not* using play-action.

Tannehill's only real weakness at this point is that he's extremely poor under pressure. His DVOA difference of -167.1% between pressure and no pressure ranked 31st out of 36 quarterbacks. This is normally something that is less consistent from year to year, but in 2019 Tannehill had a gap of -139.2% which was 30th out of 34 quarterbacks. In his final year in Miami, Tannehill's gap between pressure and no pressure ranked 29th of 34 quarterbacks. Though he cut his sack rate drastically last year despite a very combustible offensive tackle situation, he's still obviously not comfortable when hurried. But hey, you know, keep on doubting that he'll retain his gains. He'll use that fuel to get us to talk about his MVP season in *Football Outsiders Almanac 2022*.

Tyrod Taylor   Height: 6-1   Weight: 215   College: Virginia Tech   Draft: 2011/6 (180)   Born: 3-Aug-1989   Age: 32   Risk: Red

Year	Tm	G/GS	Snaps	Att	Cmp	C%	CPOE	Yds	TD	INT/Adj	FUM	ASR	NY/P	Rk	DVOA	Rk	DYAR	Rk	Runs	Yds	TD	DVOA	DYAR	QBR
2018	CLE	4/3	185	85	42	49.4%	-12.5%	473	2	2/2	3	13.3%	3.9	--	-53.5%	--	-264	--	16	125	1	-6.8%	4	29.1
2019	LAC	8/0	32	6	4	66.7%	-5.0%	33	1	0/0	0	-1.6%	5.5	--	59.3%	--	23	--	10	7	0	-48.0%	-8	3.1
2020	LAC	2/1	75	30	16	53.3%	-7.8%	208	0	0/0	0	8.8%	6.5	--	-0.7%	--	20	--	6	7	0	-61.4%	-14	21.3
2021	HOU			558	334	59.8%		3832	19	9	9		6.1		-12.8%				88	482	4	-3.9%		

2019	50% Behind	17% Short	17% Mid	17% Deep	aDOT: 5.3 (--)	YAC: 4.8 (--)	ALEX: 1.7	2020	7% Behind	41% Short	31% Mid	21% Deep	aDOT: 11.3 (--)	YAC: 5.0 (--)	ALEX: 7.0

A list of players from the last 10 years that have had between 60 and 121 pass attempts between their age-29 and -31 seasons: Matt Barkley, Blaine Gabbert, T.J. Yates, Mark Sanchez, Chad Henne, Derek Anderson, Luke McCown. None of those guys were good, and the odds are that Tyrod Taylor won't be either. The last quarterback to bounce back from that kind of stretch and become as much as a part-time starter somewhere? Billy Joe Tolliver started 11 games for the Saints between 1998 and 1999, with 349 passing DYAR in that first year but only -119 passing DYAR in the second, and then he never played again. To get to an actual 16-game starter, you have to go back to the legend of Rich Gannon. Usually when you are down to a backup around age 30, you don't get to become a starter again. Taylor offers upside with his legs and he lost his job in Los Angeles to a punctured lung that a team doctor administered, but it would be pretty surprising if he were a 17-game—or even 10-game—starter for this year's Texans.

Kyle Trask   Height: 6-5   Weight: 240   College: Florida   Draft: 2021/2 (64)   Born: 6-Mar-1998   Age: 23   Risk: Green

Year	Tm	G/GS	Snaps	Att	Cmp	C%	CPOE	Yds	TD	INT/Adj	FUM	ASR	NY/P	Rk	DVOA	Rk	DYAR	Rk	Runs	Yds	TD	DVOA	DYAR	QBR
2021	TB			571	338	59.2%		4022	27	14	9		6.3		-5.1%				47	172	3	0.6%		

At first glance, Trask-to-the-Buccaneers makes sense. Tom Brady is 44 and under contract through the 2022 season. Let's draft his successor—he won't have to play right away and he can learn from the best to ever play the game.

Think about it more, though, and the flaws in the plan become more apparent. First, let's review the list of quarterbacks Brady has taken under his wing and groomed to take his job:

That's it. That's the list.

Yes, Brady is in the twilight of his career. But this is the same guy who reportedly forced the Patriots to trade Jimmy Garoppolo. (Brady denies this.) Also, the Trask pick doesn't mesh with Tampa Bay's all-in approach to this season and smacks of overconfidence in the current roster. The Buccaneers don't have any glaring holes, but things go wrong every season. At some point, they're going to wish they had something they don't have. Maybe an edge rusher. Or an offensive tackle. Or a cornerback. But it probably won't be a quarterback. If Brady suffers an injury, Bruce Arians is turning to Blaine Gabbert, not a rookie.

Plus, there's the fact that Trask might not be very good. Our QBASE projection system gives him a greater than 80% chance of becoming a bust. His senior season at Florida was phenomenal, but how much did he benefit from throwing to two first-round pass-catchers (tight end Kyle Pitts and wide receiver Kadarius Toney)? If his performance against Oklahoma in the Cotton Bowl is any indication, the answer is "a lot." Pitts and Toney didn't play in the game, and Trask struggled badly, completing 16 of 28 passes for 158 yards, no touchdowns, and three interceptions.

Mitchell Trubisky

Height: 6-2 **Weight:** 215 **College:** North Carolina **Draft:** 2017/1 (2) **Born:** 20-Aug-1994 **Age:** 27 **Risk:** Green

Year	Tm	G/GS	Snaps	Att	Cmp	C%	CPOE	Yds	TD	INT/Adj	FUM	ASR	NY/P	Rk	DVOA	Rk	DYAR	Rk	Runs	Yds	TD	DVOA	DYAR	QBR
2018	CHI	14/14	929	434	289	66.6%	0.7%	3223	24	12/16	6	5.1%	6.7	15	3.6%	19	448	17	68	421	3	22.9%	114	72.8
2019	CHI	15/15	960	516	326	63.2%	-3.7%	3138	17	10/15	5	7.0%	5.3	33	-11.0%	27	5	27	48	193	2	-17.6%	-12	39.5
2020	CHI	10/9	570	297	199	67.0%	-1.5%	2055	16	8/14	6	6.6%	6.1	24	-7.5%	24	79	24	33	195	1	-7.0%	9	61.8
2021	BUF			549	347	63.2%		3891	23	13	9		6.4		-6.1%				68	359	3	0.6%		

2019 19% Behind 47% Short 22% Mid 13% Deep aDOT: 8.2 (23) YAC: 4.3 (32) ALEX: 1.5   2020 14% Behind 51% Short 24% Mid 11% Deep aDOT: 8.0 (23) YAC: 5.0 (19) ALEX: 1.7

Trubisky goes from overmatched starter to quality backup in one simple career move! From Week 12 onwards, Trubisky had a passing DVOA of 2.9%, the first time he had been above average since his Pro Bowl year in 2018. Trubisky was particularly solid when he had the benefit of pre-snap motion, throwing seven touchdowns and just one interception. The Bills were in the upper quartile in pre-snap motion in 2020, and few coordinators did a better job giving his quarterback favorable looks than Brian Daboll. In other words, if Trubisky has to start a game or three, it's not the end of the world.

P.J. Walker

Height: 5-11 **Weight:** 212 **College:** Temple **Draft:** 2017/FA **Born:** 26-Feb-1995 **Age:** 26 **Risk:** Green

Year	Tm	G/GS	Snaps	Att	Cmp	C%	CPOE	Yds	TD	INT/Adj	FUM	ASR	NY/P	Rk	DVOA	Rk	DYAR	Rk	Runs	Yds	TD	DVOA	DYAR	QBR
2020	CAR	4/1	107	56	32	57.1%	-5.6%	368	1	5/5	1	7.3%	5.6	--	-71.1%	--	-217	--	5	-2	0	-121.6%	-17	12.6
2021	CAR			583	370	63.5%		4318	24	19	10		6.6		-12.1%				76	220	4	-26.2%		

2019   2020 19% Behind 43% Short 19% Mid 20% Deep aDOT: 10.8 (--) YAC: 4.4 (--) ALEX: 2.7

A former student-athlete under Matt Rhule during their time at Temple, Walker holds the school records in most major passing categories, including wins by a starting quarterback, passing yards, and passing touchdowns. Despite some expectation that he would be a Day 3 pick, he passed undrafted in 2017 before spending the next couple of years bouncing off and on the Colts practice squad. He briefly shot to niche stardom in 2020 as the starter for the Houston Roughnecks in the rebooted XFL, where he led the league with 1,338 passing yards and 15 touchdowns before the COVID pandemic stopped play. He then joined the Panthers on a two-year contract shortly after Rhule was appointed head coach. An athletic but relatively diminutive quarterback, Walker played his first NFL games, including his first start, in 2020, but a low completion rate and just one touchdown versus five interceptions suggests he is no threat to new arrival Sam Darnold regardless of his history with Rhule or the Roughnecks.

Deshaun Watson

Height: 6-2   Weight: 221   College: Clemson   Draft: 2017/1 (12)   Born: 14-Sep-1995   Age: 26   Risk: Red

Year	Tm	G/GS	Snaps	Att	Cmp	C%	CPOE	Yds	TD	INT/Adj	FUM	ASR	NY/P	Rk	DVOA	Rk	DYAR	Rk	Runs	Yds	TD	DVOA	DYAR	QBR
2018	HOU	16/16	1093	505	345	68.3%	3.7%	4165	26	9/14	9	11.6%	6.8	14	9.5%	11	737	10	99	551	5	7.8%	95	63.8
2019	HOU	15/15	1026	495	333	67.3%	2.6%	3852	26	12/17	10	8.1%	6.7	14	9.5%	12	722	13	82	413	7	9.9%	77	68.7
2020	HOU	16/16	978	544	382	70.2%	5.5%	4823	33	7/12	8	9.3%	7.7	2	20.2%	5	1234	5	90	444	3	-14.9%	-12	71.0
2021	HOU			588	416	70.7%		4805	30	10	10		7.3		10.2%				99	495	5	-5.0%		

2019   13% Behind   55% Short   17% Mid   15% Deep   aDOT: 9.0 (11)   YAC: 5.0 (22)   ALEX: 1.2   2020   12% Behind   49% Short   28% Mid   12% Deep   aDOT: 9.1 (5)   YAC: 5.2 (17)   ALEX: 2.1

First, let's talk about Watson's breakout season on the field. In Weeks 6-16, Watson was picked off exactly one time, and that interception was essentially a ball that was right on the money but Kenny Moore stripped away from Brandin Cooks. Watson managed to fuse his prowess under pressure with a better overall process, creating a reel of highlight plays as good as any career montage and an understanding of the field that had him throwing guys open without having an A-plus rocket arm. The next step forward will be to cut his sack rate, which has hovered in the 8.5% range for the last two seasons, where he's so explosive and good in creating under pressure that he sometimes just decides to see what happens when an obvious pass-rusher comes through instead of throwing the ball away. Keep in mind he did what he did last season with almost no help, throwing to Chad Hansen and Keke Coutee for the last five weeks of the season, and had his personal stats affected by a wind bowl game in Cleveland in Week 10. If you don't think he's a top-tier, A-plus quarterback already, it might surprise you how good he could be with actual infrastructure around him.

However, we obviously don't want to give short shrift to the allegations placed against Watson. They are real, and they will be heard. Nobody—neither the Texans nor Watson's camp—knew what they were in for when this started with one accuser and bloomed further and further. What he's accused of doing is shameful behavior that is worthy of the kind of rebuke he has received. It's been a tough fall from grace to watch through a football lens. Between Watson's legal situation and his request to be traded, we are not projecting him to start games for the Texans this season. But there is a KUBIAK projection for him in case he does.

Carson Wentz

Height: 6-5   Weight: 237   College: North Dakota State   Draft: 2016/1 (2)   Born: 30-Dec-1992   Age: 29   Risk: Yellow

Year	Tm	G/GS	Snaps	Att	Cmp	C%	CPOE	Yds	TD	INT/Adj	FUM	ASR	NY/P	Rk	DVOA	Rk	DYAR	Rk	Runs	Yds	TD	DVOA	DYAR	QBR
2018	PHI	11/11	724	401	279	69.6%	2.7%	3074	21	7/11	9	7.8%	6.6	16	8.1%	13	545	14	34	93	0	-6.8%	7	64.2
2019	PHI	16/16	1169	607	388	63.9%	-0.5%	4039	27	7/16	16	6.5%	5.9	25	0.1%	20	476	17	62	243	1	6.1%	56	60.8
2020	PHI	12/12	808	437	251	57.4%	-6.5%	2620	16	15/21	10	10.0%	4.7	36	-35.9%	34	-780	36	52	276	5	9.2%	62	49.7
2021	IND			597	381	63.7%		4149	26	12	13		6.3		-7.1%				56	271	4	3.4%		

2019   15% Behind   50% Short   21% Mid   14% Deep   aDOT: 8.4 (20)   YAC: 4.7 (31)   ALEX: 2.7   2020   13% Behind   49% Short   24% Mid   14% Deep   aDOT: 9.6 (2)   YAC: 4.0 (35)   ALEX: 2.9

Not only did Wentz perform poorly, he saved his worst for when the stakes were the highest last year. He had a -48.5% DVOA on third- and fourth-down passes, creating more negative DYAR on those throws than any passer in the NFL. When Wentz was pressured, he averaged 1.5 yards per play, which was worse than anyone not named Joe Burrow who didn't play for the Washington Football Team. Wentz had the highest number of knockdowns in the NFL, taking a hit on 23% of his dropbacks. He was one of the three quarterbacks—again grouped with those WFT passers—to have a negative DVOA on throws in the pocket.

Last year's Wentz comment noted that Howie Roseman wanted the Eagles to have more of a downfield passing attack in 2020 and pointed out that his average depth of target was slipping drastically. Well, Wentz boosted his aDOT significantly! It did nothing to help anybody. If you look at the raw underlying hopes of what the Colts are doing here, they want to turn Wentz back into his 2019 version with essentially the same game plan they used for Philip Rivers last year, but with a plus-arm in the spot instead of what was left for Rivers. At a raw statistical level, that's the easy step to try to salvage Wentz. Is he capable of that? Possibly! Is he a guy we need to spend time focusing on MVPs for anymore? Probably not.

Russell Wilson

Height: 5-11   Weight: 215   College: Wisconsin   Draft: 2012/3 (75)   Born: 29-Nov-1988   Age: 33   Risk: Green

Year	Tm	G/GS	Snaps	Att	Cmp	C%	CPOE	Yds	TD	INT/Adj	FUM	ASR	NY/P	Rk	DVOA	Rk	DYAR	Rk	Runs	Yds	TD	DVOA	DYAR	QBR
2018	SEA	16/16	1069	427	280	65.6%	5.1%	3448	35	7/11	10	10.4%	6.6	17	11.3%	10	673	11	67	376	0	23.3%	83	65.6
2019	SEA	16/16	1124	516	341	66.1%	4.9%	4110	31	5/7	8	7.9%	6.8	13	24.3%	7	1265	4	75	342	3	-0.3%	33	69.8
2020	SEA	16/16	1047	558	384	68.8%	3.9%	4212	40	13/14	7	8.1%	6.4	22	8.1%	13	773	11	83	513	2	21.3%	99	73.7
2021	SEA			577	387	67.1%		4414	35	12	7		6.7		5.4%				90	544	3	-0.7%		

2019   15% Behind   46% Short   24% Mid   16% Deep   aDOT: 9.7 (5)   YAC: 5.1 (21)   ALEX: 3.7   2020   14% Behind   55% Short   18% Mid   13% Deep   aDOT: 8.8 (10)   YAC: 4.8 (24)   ALEX: 2.9

When Wilson's play tailed off in the latter part of the 2020 season, a lot of the coverage centered around the fact that opponents had figured out that they only needed to play two deep safeties and sit in zone coverage to neuter the Seattle passing attack. A quick look at Wilson's passing splits over the past three years shows that he performed only slightly better against man defenses than zone defenses in 2020, but his DVOA against zone was significantly lower than it had been in 2018 and 2019. Wilson finished with 89.2% DVOA against zone in 2018 and 85.1% in 2019, but that number dropped to 48.6% in 2020 (these numbers are quite high in part because they exclude runs, penalties, and sacks). This could have been a function of teams using more "third-down" defenses earlier in series because they knew Seattle was throwing. New offensive coordinator Shane Waldron's task is then pretty simple: get Wilson back to something resembling his performance from 2018 and 2019, and good things should follow.

Zach Wilson

Height: 6-3		Weight: 210		College: Brigham Young			Draft: 2021/1 (2)		Born: 3-Aug-1999		Age: 22			Risk: Green						

Year	Tm	G/GS	Snaps	Att	Cmp	C%	CPOE	Yds	TD	INT/Adj	FUM	ASR	NY/P	Rk	DVOA	Rk	DYAR	Rk	Runs	Yds	TD	DVOA	DYAR	QBR
2021	NYJ			554	339	61.2%		3829	23	15	9		6.1		-17.4%				61	287	4	0.7%		

If anything, Wilson's 2020 stats at BYU could have been even bigger. Wilson had the highest adjusted accuracy in the class on play-action—81.4%, per Football Outsiders draft analyst Derrik Klassen. And yet he actually had the lowest percentage of play-action and designed rollouts among the five first-round passers. Expect to see all those numbers jump up in the Shanahan-style offense the Jets are importing. On the move, Wilson's accuracy does drop a tad: a below-average 62.5%, with 7.2% of his completions coming only after his receivers adjusted their routes, worst among the top five passers. But at least Wilson somewhat makes up for that with exceptional off-platform arm strength. No one minds if your receiver has to slightly alter his route if the end result is a 50-yard bomb.

Jameis Winston

Height: 6-4		Weight: 231		College: Florida State			Draft: 2015/1 (1)		Born: 6-Jan-1994		Age: 28			Risk: Red						

Year	Tm	G/GS	Snaps	Att	Cmp	C%	CPOE	Yds	TD	INT/Adj	FUM	ASR	NY/P	Rk	DVOA	Rk	DYAR	Rk	Runs	Yds	TD	DVOA	DYAR	QBR
2018	TB	11/9	688	378	244	64.6%	0.7%	2992	19	14/19	7	7.4%	7.0	10	6.9%	15	470	16	49	281	1	4.7%	37	68.6
2019	TB	16/16	1149	626	380	60.7%	0.7%	5109	33	30/40	12	7.6%	7.2	7	-9.8%	24	57	23	59	250	1	12.6%	53	53.7
2020	NO	4/0	54	11	7	63.6%	-12.3%	75	0	0/1	0	15.4%	4.9	--	-20.4%	--	-7	--	8	-6	0	18.3%	2	13.5
2021	NO			623	396	63.6%		4441	27	20	9		6.4		-9.5%				54	178	2	-17.0%		

2019	9% Behind	44% Short	27% Mid	19% Deep	aDOT: 10.9 (2)	YAC: 4.9 (26)	ALEX: 2.2	2020	18% Behind	55% Short	27% Mid	0% Deep	aDOT: 4.6 (--)	YAC: 8.7 (--)	ALEX: -4.8

A dozen dropbacks against the 49ers in relief of an injured Drew Brees don't tell us a great deal about the quarterback Jameis Winston will be in New Orleans. Neither does his touchdown bomb against the Buccaneers in the postseason, coming as it did off a trick play stolen from the Bears' playbook the week before. Winston didn't throw a single deep pass during the regular season, and fully a third of his snaps were kneeldowns. It may say something about his prospects for 2020 that Taysom Hill started while Drew Brees was out injured, or it may tell us nothing at all.

Statistically, DVOA pegged Winston in Tampa Bay as a slightly above-average starter: a 61% passer who usually lingered among the top 16 quarterbacks in efficiency. Certainly, he benefited from a stellar supporting cast in 2018 and 2019, but Winston was also above average in 2015, when his second-leading receiver was Charles Sims, and 2016, when his second outside target was Russell Shepard. It wasn't until 2019, when he was paired with the aggressive deep passing game of Bruce Arians, that Winston's interception rate finally became unmanageable.

Now 27 years old, Winston may never be a franchise quarterback. But if he can earn the Saints starting job and return his interception rate (and especially his pick-six rate—he threw seven in 2019) to the levels of his early career, he could again be above average in one of the league's most quarterback-friendly offenses. Paired with one of its best defenses, that should be enough for the Saints to stay competitive as the post-Brees era begins.

John Wolford

Height: 6-1		Weight: 199		College: Wake Forest			Draft: 2018/FA		Born: 16-Oct-1995		Age: 26			Risk: Green						

Year	Tm	G/GS	Snaps	Att	Cmp	C%	CPOE	Yds	TD	INT/Adj	FUM	ASR	NY/P	Rk	DVOA	Rk	DYAR	Rk	Runs	Yds	TD	DVOA	DYAR	QBR
2020	LAR	1/1	73	38	22	57.9%	1.2%	231	0	1/1	0	3.1%	5.6	--	-35.9%	--	-63	--	6	56	0	25.6%	14	74.7
2021	LAR			546	335	61.3%		3805	21	12	9		6.2		-7.6%				102	598	5	2.4%		

2019						2020	19% Behind	39% Short	19% Mid	22% Deep	aDOT: 9.9 (--)	YAC: 4.2 (--)	ALEX: 1.2

The all-time Alliance of American Football passing touchdown leader entered 2020 as the backup to Jared Goff, but by season's end he was starting crucial games in the wake of Goff's thumb injury to help the Rams secure their spot in the play-offs. There was some consideration that Wolford would have been the better option regardless of Goff's health because of the additional element his running ability brought to the offense, but Wolford sustained a neck injury early in the wild-card game against the Seahawks, knocking him out for the rest of the playoffs. Wolford will again be the backup in Los Angeles, this time to Matthew Stafford, but hopefully he can keep his job holding the clipboard so that he does not have to keep updating his LinkedIn profile.

Logan Woodside

Height: 6-1   Weight: 213   College: Toledo   Draft: 2018/7 (249)   Born: 27-Jan-1995   Age: 26   Risk: Green

Year	Tm	G/GS	Snaps	Att	Cmp	C%	CPOE	Yds	TD	INT/Adj	FUM	ASR	NY/P	Rk	DVOA	Rk	DYAR	Rk	Runs	Yds	TD	DVOA	DYAR	QBR
2020	TEN	6/0	21	3	1	33.3%	-38.3%	7	0	0/0	0	0.0%	2.3	--	-24.3%	--	-3	--	7	10	0	73.9%	7	71.7
2021	TEN			579	336	58.1%		4025	24	15		9		6.2		-11.8%				45	145	2	-17.0%		
2019													2020	0% Behind	100% Short	0% Mid	0% Deep	aDOT: 5.0 (--)		YAC: 0.0 (--)		ALEX: -3.0		

What a wild stat line last year held for Woodside, who came into a December game against the Jaguars with Tennessee up 31-10 with 5:03 left and proceeded to hand off to Jeremy McNichols five times and, on third-and-1, gain 18 yards on a naked bootleg against a nine-man box. Woodside also knelt out two other games and completed one pass against the Ravens in Week 10. Woodside continues to have no relevant passing experience besides carrying a 99.3 passer rating in the 2019 preseason, and the Titans will be screwed if Ryan Tannehill gets seriously injured.

Going Deep

Matt Barkley, FA: Barkley played the second half of Week 17 against a Dolphins team that needed to win to make the playoffs. He went out on a high note, going 6-for-13 for 164 yards and a score to clinch the victory and eliminate Buffalo's division rivals—48 DYAR isn't too shabby for a half of work. For the second time in his career, however, Barkley lost his job to Mitchell Trubisky, and was unsigned as of press time. Not a bad way to go out if it's over.

David Blough, DET: Blough threw just 10 passes in 2020 behind a healthy Matthew Stafford, but he lost all five of his starts in 2019 after Stafford injured his back, finishing that year with -101 DYAR and -19.5% DVOA. And while one might be tempted to offer him the benefit of the doubt in his rookie season playing behind below-average pass protection (he saw a 30.8% pressure rate), Blough managed a meager 17.4% passing DVOA without pressure. Among quarterbacks with at least 150 snaps, only Dwayne Haskins (-0.1%) was worse. And so while Blough is the only Lions quarterback with team tenure, he seems likely to play third string behind former Packers backup Tim Boyle.

Ian Book, NO: Despite having more wins as a starting quarterback than anybody else in the illustrious history of Notre Dame football, Book was considered a reach when the Saints took him in the fourth round of April's draft. An undersized passer with subpar arm strength and middling athleticism, Book struggles with pressure and relies too heavily on making plays outside the structure of the offense. He may stick on the roster as a third quarterback, but he will need to make serious progress even to become a viable backup.

Blake Bortles, GB: Bortles is one of the most efficient rushing quarterbacks in NFL history. He exceeded a 20.0% rushing DVOA in all five of his seasons as the Jaguars starter, and his 6.2 career yards per carry average bests those of modern dual threats Lamar Jackson (6.0), Kyler Murray (6.0), and Josh Allen (5.2). But Bortles never took 60 carries in a season. It makes one wonder if he was the No. 3 draft pick seven years too soon ... or it would, if Bortles hadn't consistently produced passing DVOA rates of -10.0% or worse over more than 2,500 career attempts.

Jake Browning, MIN: Browning is the most productive quarterback in University of Washington history and is the all-time Pac-12 wins leader (39), but he lacked NFL arm strength even before he suffered shoulder injuries in 2015 and 2016. With third-round rookie Kellen Mond jumping both Browning and teammate Nate Stanley on the Vikings depth chart, he seems unlikely to take his first NFL snap in 2021.

Sam Ehlinger, IND: There are worse spots for an unlikely story to start than behind Carson Wentz and Jacob Eason. Ehlinger mixes fairly stellar scrambling and running ability with a command of a middle-of-the-field offense, and he started games in each of his four seasons at Texas. There's probably a good NFL backup or journeyman starter in his tools. Texas' deep passing was brutal the last few years with Ehlinger and he will need to be more consistent with accuracy to stick.

Feleipe Franks, ATL: How polarizing is Franks? He once shushed fans—at home. After transferring from Florida to Arkansas for his senior season, Franks hit his stride in offensive coordinator Kendal Briles' RPO-heavy system, completing about 70% of his passes, averaging 8.9 yards per attempt, and throwing 17 touchdowns to four interceptions. Scouts like his arm but question his accuracy. Contextual metrics suggest they're underrating him. Signed in Atlanta as an undrafted free agent.

Jake Fromm, BUF: We have yet to see Fromm in action, thanks to the cancelled 2020 preseason, but from all reports he has yet to impress. There were rumors last year that the fifth-round rookie would be cut, first due to racist text messages and then due to being outperformed by Matt Barkley. The Bills will need to keep three quarterbacks for Fromm to make the roster; they only kept three last season due to COVID. Otherwise, Fromm will have to beat out Davis Webb to even earn a practice squad slot.

Will Grier, CAR: As uncertainty about the health of Cam Newton's shoulder lingered after the 2019 season, the Panthers drafted West Virginia senior Will Grier in the third round as a contingency plan. Grier started the final two games of his rookie season after injuries to Newton, Taylor Heinicke, and Kyle Allen. He completed less than 55% of his passes with no touchdowns and four interceptions, including a spectacular 1-for-8 with a pick-six performance before leaving injured against the Saints in Week 17. He finished that season with -60.6% DVOA and hasn't seen the field since.

Robert Griffin, FA: Griffin threw two interceptions against the Steelers before suffering a hamstring injury in his lone start in Week 12. He has done nothing that really justifies a role as even a premium backup since 2013. He could be a useful mentor in the cautionary tale/*how to navigate the hype* sense, which is not insignificant, but it's hard to imagine him contributing much else at this point in his career. Griffin spent all of 2017 as a free agent and may do so again unless one of the NFL's combustible quarterback situations (Texans, Packers) goes thermonuclear. Multiple networks are also rumored to be interested in signing him as a commentator.

Ryan Griffin, TB: Griffin took his job as Tom Brady's backup seriously. Last we saw him, he was keeping a drunk Brady upright after the Buccaneers' Super Bowl boat parade. Though Tampa Bay re-signed Griffin, he might not be on the roster for much longer. One backup spot will go to second-round pick Kyle Trask; the other will likely go to Blaine Gabbert, who received more guaranteed money than Griffin.

Brian Hoyer, NE: The NFL requires 1,500 career pass attempts to qualify for their rate leaderboards, and Hoyer just squeaked over that mark in 2020. Hoyer now proudly takes over the mantle of quarterback with the fewest career starts to be qualified—just 39, as Hoyer has been the definition of career backup. The Patriots have re-signed him as a clipboard holder/backup in case Mac Jones beats out Cam Newton for the starting job. Considering Hoyer hasn't been above replacement level since 2016, they should probably keep looking.

Tyler Huntley, BAL: Huntley was a Florida high school rival of Lamar Jackson who became a capable starter for three years in a Utah offense that mixed spread-option and single-setback rollout concepts. He signed with the Ravens as an undrafted rookie last year, climbed the depth chart by default due to the Robert Griffin and Trace McSorley injuries, and ended up replacing Jackson after a concussion in the playoff loss to the Bills. One advantage of running an option-heavy NFL offense is that the Ravens can use pesky 6-foot-1 college scramblers that don't fit any other team's schemes as system-fitting backups. Huntley enters camp as the Ravens' No. 3 quarterback behind McSorley, but there's not much really separating the pair.

DeShone Kizer, TEN: Kizer had one of the worst seasons in Football Outsiders history with -756 passing DYAR as a rookie in 2017. He spent 2020 on the practice squad as Tennessee's emergency COVID quarterback and when he looked good at this summer's OTAs, reports had the Titans seriously considering Kizer as this season's backup ahead of Logan Woodside. This would be bad for your Titans fantasy receivers.

Jamie Newman, PHI: By the time you're done reading this, Jamie Newman might still be holding the mesh point on an RPO. Newman was supposed to get experience outside of the unorthodox Wake Forest offense when he transferred to Georgia, but he opted out of the 2020 season. In his final season at Wake Forest, Newman threw 87% of his passes beyond the line of scrimmage; nearly 55% came between 1 and 10 yards past the line, and 19% came over 20 air yards. Newman wasn't particularly accurate to any area of the field, though, ranking 60th in adjusted net yards per attempt among quarterbacks in 2019. Signed by Philadelphia as an undrafted free agent.

Nathan Peterman, LV: Peterman is the worst quarterback of the modern era, at least relative to how much he has played. Of the 132 quarterbacks to have thrown at least 100 passes since 2011, Peterman ranks dead last with 0.26 adjusted net yards per attempt. He is the only player below 1.00 ANY/A and is the worst of those 132 quarterbacks by almost a full yard. Granted, Peterman has only thrown five total passes over the past two seasons, so there is a slim chance he has improved. Probably not, though.

Josh Rosen, SF: In his first 32 months in the NFL, Rosen was drafted in the first round by the Cardinals, traded to the Dolphins, waived by the Dolphins, signed to the Buccaneers' practice squad, and finally signed to the 49ers' active roster. That's a new team every eight months, putting him on pace to sign with each of the NFL's 32 franchises by sometime in 2039. He re-signed with San Francisco last February and will battle Nate Sudfeld for the third quarterback spot behind Jimmy Garoppolo and Trey Lance. Should he come up short, well, at least he's used to moving.

Cooper Rush, DAL: Rush, an eerie clone of Jason Garrett, followed Garrett to New York last year, spent a few weeks on the Giants practice squad, then resurfaced in Dallas during the Ben DiNucci/Garrett Gilbert circus. Had he stayed in Dallas, Rush would have earned a few starts, increasing his career regular-season passing attempts well beyond his current total of three. But part of the secret of rising from third-string quarterback to offensive coordinator is playing as little as possible, and Rush is learning the craft from a master.

Trevor Siemian, NO: A late-round pick turned former Broncos starter who is now firmly in the "veteran backup" phase of his career, Siemian's only action since 2017 came in one game with the Jets and resulted in a gruesome ankle injury that ended his 2019 season. The kind of quarterback teams sign specifically as a backup who won't threaten the starter, Siemian probably won't make the initial 53-man roster in New Orleans, but he likely will end up rostered somewhere at some point during the season.

Nate Stanley, MIN: Unlike Jake Browning, his competition for the No. 3 quarterback job in Minnesota, Stanley has NFL traits. He has ideal size at 6-foot-4 and 235 pounds and throws an effortless deep ball even off-platform. But Stanley lacks Browning's feel for the game, which manifested in too-frequent fastballs in touch-pass situations and a 58.3% career completion rate at Iowa. You can't make it in the NFL with poor accuracy and poor mobility.

Tommy Stevens, FA: One of a recent slew of college quarterbacks attempting to take the Logan Thomas route to a professional career, Stevens failed to make the transition to tight end in New Orleans. Former coach Joe Brady and the Panthers picked him up, gave him a handful of carries against the Saints in the season finale, then waived him in June. He is unsigned at the time of writing.

Easton Stick, LAC: A fifth-round pick in 2019, some speculated that Stick would move to wide receiver out of college. He ran a 4.62s 40-yard dash and an outrageous 6.65s 3-cone drill, which suggested he had the movement skills required to survive as a pass-catcher. Alas, Stick has primarily stuck around as the Chargers' third quarterback. The team signed Chase Daniel this offseason to play the actual backup role, so it's unlikely Stick is seen as anything but a potential gadget piece with desirable athletic tools.

Chris Streveler, ARI: Streveler played college ball for Minnesota and South Dakota before starting his pro career with the Winnipeg Blue Bombers. He spent two years in Manitoba as a part-time starter and full-time running threat, scoring more touchdowns rushing (22) than passing (19) and once running 13 times in a playoff game without throwing a single pass. His first significant NFL action came in Week 17 against the Rams. He was so ineffective (95 net yards in 18 dropbacks, -45.9% DVOA) that Arizona put a gimpy Kyler Murray back into the game, then signed Colt McCoy after the season to battle for the backup spot.

Nate Sudfeld, SF: Four years into his NFL career, Sudfeld is best known as the "I can't believe Doug Pederson pulled Jalen Hurts for this guy" guy. Sudfeld threw 37 passes in four games with the Eagles, none of them starts, and failed to amass 200 yards even before accounting for the 40 yards he lost on sacks. The 49ers signed him knowing full well they had Jimmy Garoppolo and Josh Rosen under contract and having already traded for the third pick they would eventually use on Trey Lance. It's not clear why they bothered.

Running Backs

In the following section we provide the last three years of statistics, as well as a 2021 KUBIAK projection, for every running back who either played a significant role in 2020 or is expected to do so in 2021.

The first line contains biographical data—each player's name, height, weight, college, draft position, birth date, and age. Height and weight are the best data we could find; weight, of course, can fluctuate during the offseason. **Age** is very simple, the number of years between the player's birth year and 2021, but birthdate is provided if you want to figure out exact age.

Draft position gives draft year and round, with the overall pick number with which the player was taken in parentheses. In the sample table, it says that Dalvin Cook was chosen in the 2017 NFL draft in the second round with the 41st overall pick. Undrafted free agents are listed as "FA" with the year they came into the league, even if they were only in training camp or on a practice squad.

To the far right of the first line is the player's Risk for fantasy football in 2021. As explained in the quarterback section, the standard is for players to be marked Green. Players with higher than normal risk are marked Yellow, and players with the highest risk are marked Red. Players who are most likely to match or surpass our forecast—primarily second-stringers with low projections but also some particularly strong breakout candidates—are marked Blue. Risk is not only based on age and injury probability, but how a player's projection compares to his recent performance as well as our confidence (or lack thereof) in his offensive teammates.

Next we give the last three years of player stats. First come games played and games started (**G/GS**). Games played is the official NFL total and may include games in which a player appeared on special teams but did not carry the ball or catch a pass. We also have a total of offensive **Snaps** for each season. The next four columns are familiar: **Runs**, rushing yards (**Yds**), yards per rush (**Yd/R**) and rushing touchdowns (**TD**).

The entry for fumbles (**FUM**) includes all fumbles by this running back, no matter whether they were recovered by the offense or defense. Holding onto the ball is an identifiable skill; fumbling it so that your own offense can recover it is not. (For more on this issue, see the essay "Pregame Show" in the front of the book.) This entry combines fumbles on both carries and receptions. Fumbles on special teams are not included.

The next four columns give our advanced metrics for rushing: **DVOA** (Defense-adjusted Value Over Average) and

DYAR (Defense-adjusted Yards Above Replacement), along with the player's rank (**Rk**) in both. These metrics compare every carry by the running back to a league-average baseline based on the game situations in which that running back carried the ball. DVOA and DYAR are also adjusted based on the opposing defense. The methods used to compute these numbers are described in detail in the "Statistical Toolbox" introduction in the front of the book. The important distinctions between them is that DVOA is a rate statistic, while DYAR is a cumulative statistic. Thus, a higher DVOA means more value per play, while a higher DYAR means more aggregate value over the entire season.

To qualify for ranking in rushing DVOA and DYAR, a running back must have had 100 carries in that season. Last year, 47 running backs qualified to be ranked in these stats, compared to 45 backs in 2019 and 47 in 2018.

Numbers without opponent adjustment (YAR and VOA) can be found on our website, FootballOutsiders.com.

Success Rate (**Suc%**), listed along with rank, represents running back consistency as measured by successful running plays divided by total running plays. (The definition for success is explained in the "Statistical Toolbox" introduction in the front of the book.) A player with high DVOA and a low Success Rate mixes long runs with plays on which he was stuffed at or behind the line of scrimmage. A player with low DVOA and a high Success Rate generally gets the yards needed, but rarely gets more. The league-average Success Rate in 2020 was 51%. Success Rate is not adjusted for the defenses a player faced.

We also give a total of broken tackles (**BTkl**) according to charting from Sports Info Solutions. This total includes broken tackles on both runs and receptions. Please note that SIS marked broken tackles roughly 10% more often in 2019 than in either 2018 or 2020.

New this year is yards after contact (**YafC**), which measures how many yards a runner gained after making contact with any defensive player.

The shaded columns to the right of yards after contact give data for each running back as a pass receiver. Receptions (**Rec**) counts passes caught, while Passes (**Pass**) counts total passes thrown to this player, complete or incomplete. The next four columns list receiving yards (**Yds**), receiving touchdowns (**TD**), catch rate (**C%**), yards per catch (**Yd/C**), and average yards after the catch (**YAC**).

Our research has shown that receivers bear some responsi-

Dalvin Cook				Height: 5-10				Weight: 210		College: Florida State				Draft: 2017/2 (41)			Born: 10-Aug-1995			Age: 26			Risk: Green
Year	Tm	G/GS	Snaps	Runs	Yds	TD	Yd/R	FUM	DVOA	Rk	DYAR	Rk	Suc%	Rk	BTkl	YafC	Pass	Rec	Yds	TD	C%	Yd/C	YAC	DVOA	Rk	DYAR	Rk
2018	MIN	11/10	490	133	615	2	4.6	2	-13.7%	41	-27	38	41%	41	42	2.8	49	40	305	2	82%	7.6	9.3	2.1%	26	45	24
2019	MIN	14/14	615	250	1135	13	4.5	4	9.3%	10	183	8	49%	23	68	2.7	63	53	519	0	84%	9.8	11.2	29.2%	5	144	4
2020	MIN	14/14	669	312	1557	16	5.0	5	15.6%	8	335	2	56%	10	71	2.8	54	44	361	1	81%	8.2	10.0	5.9%	21	58	16
2021	MIN			313	1443	14	4.6	4	9.1%								66	53	434	2	80%	8.2		7.5%			

bility for incomplete passes, even though only their catches are tracked in official statistics. Catch rate represents receptions divided by all intended passes for this running back. The average NFL running back caught 77% of passes in 2020. Unfortunately, we don't have room to post the best and worst running backs in receiving plus-minus, but you'll find the top 10 and bottom 10 running backs in this metric listed in the statistical appendix.

Finally we have receiving DVOA and DYAR, which are entirely separate from rushing DVOA and DYAR. To qualify for ranking in receiving DVOA and DYAR, a running back must have 25 passes thrown to him in that season. There are 50 players ranked for 2020, 49 for 2019, and 53 players ranked for 2018.

The italicized row of statistics for the 2021 season is our 2021 KUBIAK projection as explained further in the Statistical Toolbox at the front of the book. Be aware that projections account for the possibility of injury so workload projections may seem low for the top players.

It is difficult to accurately project statistics for a 162-game baseball season, but it is exponentially more difficult to accurately project statistics for a 17-game football season. Consider the listed projections not as a prediction of exact numbers, but the mean of a range of possible performances. What's important

Top 20 RB by Rushing DYAR (Total Value), 2020

Rank	Player	Team	DYAR
1	Derrick Henry	TEN	386
2	Dalvin Cook	MIN	335
3	Nick Chubb	CLE	276
4	Aaron Jones	GB	254
5	Alvin Kamara	NO	253
6	J.K. Dobbins	BAL	196
7	Ronald Jones	TB	195
8	Antonio Gibson	WAS	193
9	Darrell Henderson	LAR	185
10	Gus Edwards	BAL	177
11	Chris Carson	SEA	153
12	Wayne Gallman	NYG	151
13	Latavius Murray	NO	131
14	Jonathan Taylor	IND	127
15	Miles Sanders	PHI	110
16	D'Andre Swift	DET	106
17	Damien Harris	NE	102
18	Tony Pollard	DAL	91
19	Malcolm Brown	LAR	89
20	Ezekiel Elliott	DAL	87

Minimum 100 carries.

Top 20 RB by Rushing DVOA (Value per Rush), 2020

Rank	Player	Team	DVOA
1	J.K. Dobbins	BAL	26.1%
2	Nick Chubb	CLE	25.5%
3	Alvin Kamara	NO	23.1%
4	Darrell Henderson	LAR	21.4%
5	Aaron Jones	GB	20.3%
6	Antonio Gibson	WAS	18.8%
7	Gus Edwards	BAL	17.4%
8	Dalvin Cook	MIN	15.6%
9	Wayne Gallman	NYG	15.5%
10	Derrick Henry	TEN	15.5%
11	Ronald Jones	TB	15.5%
12	Chris Carson	SEA	15.1%
13	Tony Pollard	DAL	13.0%
14	D'Andre Swift	DET	13.0%
15	Latavius Muray	NO	12.3%
16	Malcolm Brown	LAR	11.7%
17	Damien Harris	NE	9.9%
18	Jeff Wilson	SF	7.3%
19	Miles Sanders	PHI	7.0%
20	Raheem Mostert	SF	4.0%

Minimum 100 carries.

Top 10 RB by Receiving DYAR (Total Value), 2020

Rank	Player	Team	DYAR
1	Alvin Kamara	NO	195
2	Nyheim Hines	IND	158
3	Kareem Hunt	CLE	148
4	Myles Gaskin	MIA	137
5	Chase Edmonds	ARI	135
6	David Montgomery	CHI	113
7	Austin Ekeler	LAC	111
8	Chris Carson	SEA	108
9	D'Andre Swift	DET	94
10	Jerick McKinnon	SF	83

Minimum 25 passes.

Top 10 RB by Receiving DVOA (Value per Pass), 2020

Rank	Player	Team	DVOA
1	Myles Gaskin	MIA	37.8%
2	Kerryon Johnson	DET	37.1%
3	Kareem Hunt	CLE	35.1%
4	Chase Edmonds	ARI	24.0%
5	Nyheim Hines	IND	23.7%
6	Chris Carson	SEA	23.5%
7	Jerick McKinnon	SF	22.7%
8	Jonathan Taylor	IND	22.2%
9	Kyle Juszcyk	SF	22.0%
10	Latavius Murray	NO	21.6%

Minimum 25 passes.

is less the exact number of yards we project, and more which players are projected to improve or decline. Actual performance will vary from our projection less for veteran starters and more for rookies and third-stringers, for whom we must base our projections on much smaller career statistical samples. Touchdown numbers will vary more than yardage numbers.

Finally, in a section we call "Going Deep," we briefly discuss lower-round rookies, free-agent veterans, and practice-squad players who may play a role during the 2021 season or beyond.

Salvon Ahmed

			Height: 5-11		Weight: 196			College: Washington					Draft: 2020/FA			Born: 29-Dec-1998			Age: 23		Risk: Green

Year	Tm	G/GS	Snaps	Runs	Yds	TD	Yd/R	FUM	DVOA	Rk	DYAR	Rk	Suc%	Rk	BTkl	YafC	Pass	Rec	Yds	TD	C%	Yd/C	YAC	DVOA	Rk	DYAR	Rk
2020	MIA	6/4	205	75	319	3	4.3	0	-10.3%	--	-6	--	59%	--	9	1.7	14	11	61	0	79%	5.5	6.5	-27.1%	--	-10	--
2021	MIA			44	183	2	4.2	0	-2.6%								5	4	30	0	80%	7.5		-3.8%			

When you only have 75 carries, one bad day at the office can ruin your numbers. Excluding Week 16, Ahmed was the Dolphins' leading running back in our stats, with 26 DYAR and an even 0.0% DVOA, the only Miami back to hit that mark. Against the Raiders on Boxing Day, however, Ahmed was boxed in to the tune of 2 yards on six attempts, knocking him back into the negatives for the season. That was still enough to lead all Miami running backs, which is more indicative of Miami's running game troubles than it is Ahmed's success. Frankly, Ahmed may still be the best pure runner on the Dolphins roster, though his lack of skill in pass protection or the receiving game limits how much he can actually see the field.

Cam Akers

			Height: 5-11		Weight: 212			College: Florida State					Draft: 2020/2 (52)			Born: 22-Jun-1999			Age: 22		Risk: Green

Year	Tm	G/GS	Snaps	Runs	Yds	TD	Yd/R	FUM	DVOA	Rk	DYAR	Rk	Suc%	Rk	BTkl	YafC	Pass	Rec	Yds	TD	C%	Yd/C	YAC	DVOA	Rk	DYAR	Rk
2020	LAR	13/5	297	145	625	2	4.3	1	-13.7%	41	-33	41	48%	34	23	2.4	14	11	123	1	79%	11.2	8.3	37.0%	--	46	--
2021	LAR			267	1150	9	4.3	2	1.5%								50	40	335	2	80%	8.4		12.4%			

As a rookie in 2020, Akers took a little while to get rolling in Los Angeles. The second-round pick from Florida State won the starting job in training camp, but an early injury forced him down the depth chart until late in the year. It took him a while to regain his spot, with fellow running back Darrell Henderson performing well enough in his absence to merit the work, but when the calendar turned to December, Akers took over the backfield. Akers averaged nearly 24 touches per game from Week 12 onward and enters camp as the Rams' lead back. Sean McVay has said a lot this offseason about Akers as a "special player" and a "complete back" and we expect passes to Akers to be a larger part of the Rams offense in 2021.

Kalen Ballage

			Height: 6-2		Weight: 230			College: Arizona State					Draft: 2018/4 (131)			Born: 22-Dec-1995			Age: 26		Risk: Green

Year	Tm	G/GS	Snaps	Runs	Yds	TD	Yd/R	FUM	DVOA	Rk	DYAR	Rk	Suc%	Rk	BTkl	YafC	Pass	Rec	Yds	TD	C%	Yd/C	YAC	DVOA	Rk	DYAR	Rk
2018	MIA	12/0	92	36	191	1	5.3	1	1.0%	--	16	--	42%	--	2	4.4	11	9	56	0	82%	6.2	8.4	-39.6%	--	-17	--
2019	MIA	12/6	256	74	135	3	1.8	0	-33.9%	--	-75	--	32%	--	5	1.3	24	14	63	0	58%	4.5	6.2	-66.6%	--	-65	--
2020	2TM	11/2	301	91	303	3	3.3	1	-19.2%	--	-49	--	57%	--	18	2.1	37	29	166	0	78%	5.7	7.3	-23.3%	42	-19	42
2021	PIT			30	102	1	3.4	0	-13.7%								15	13	76	0	87%	6.0		-12.1%			

Now on his fourth team in four seasons, Ballage started 2020 with the Jets, who released him after three weeks. The Chargers grabbed him to step into their injury-decimated backfield and gave him 49 carries (for 181 yards, a 3.7-yard average) in three games. But he only had 39 carries the rest of the season, and the Chargers moved on. Ballage possesses a bruising body and can fill the James Conner role in the Steelers running back room, or be cut loose in the preseason just as easily. Don't bet a fortune on either turnout, but if you must wager, do it at the Ballage-io (rim shot).

Peyton Barber

			Height: 5-11		Weight: 225			College: Auburn					Draft: 2016/FA			Born: 27-Jun-1994			Age: 27		Risk: Green

Year	Tm	G/GS	Snaps	Runs	Yds	TD	Yd/R	FUM	DVOA	Rk	DYAR	Rk	Suc%	Rk	BTkl	YafC	Pass	Rec	Yds	TD	C%	Yd/C	YAC	DVOA	Rk	DYAR	Rk
2018	TB	16/16	616	234	871	5	3.7	1	-12.4%	38	-37	41	44%	36	44	2.3	29	20	92	1	69%	4.6	3.2	-35.1%	53	-34	53
2019	TB	16/7	347	154	470	6	3.1	1	-29.8%	45	-140	45	40%	43	17	2.0	24	16	115	1	67%	7.2	7.4	0.3%	--	17	--
2020	WAS	16/2	194	94	258	4	2.7	0	-9.2%	--	-3	--	44%	--	5	1.4	7	4	12	0	57%	3.0	2.8	-62.3%	--	-20	--
2021	WAS			43	135	2	3.1	0	-18.2%								4	3	23	0	75%	6.8		-3.2%			

Few things were more surprising in Week 1 than Peyton Barber's 17 carries. Those only went for 27 yards, but seven of them came inside the 5-yard line and resulted in two touchdowns. Barber wouldn't have double-digit carries in a game again until Week 7. Barber worked in as a short-yardage back, which somewhat explains his low yards per carry, but doesn't completely justify it. Barber had a 12.1% rushing DVOA inside the red zone, though that role also decreased as Antonio Gibson's grew.

Saquon Barkley

Height: 5-11   Weight: 233   College: Penn State   Draft: 2018/1 (2)   Born: 9-Feb-1997   Age: 24   Risk: Yellow

Year	Tm	G/GS	Snaps	Runs	Yds	TD	Yd/R	FUM	DVOA	Rk	DYAR	Rk	Suc%	Rk	BTkl	YafC	Pass	Rec	Yds	TD	C%	Yd/C	YAC	DVOA	Rk	DYAR	Rk
2018	NYG	16/16	853	261	1307	11	5.0	0	3.3%	18	127	14	41%	40	94	3.2	121	91	721	4	75%	7.9	8.4	-0.7%	28	86	13
2019	NYG	13/13	737	217	1003	6	4.6	1	0.4%	19	84	18	44%	38	55	3.1	73	52	438	2	71%	8.4	8.4	-22.8%	45	-37	46
2020	NYG	2/2	67	19	34	0	1.8	0	-51.7%	--	-32	--	26%	--	5	1.5	9	6	60	0	67%	10.0	9.2	17.2%	--	17	--
2021	NYG			247	1029	10	4.2	1	-0.5%								63	47	346	1	75%	7.4		-5.6%			

By all accounts, Barkley was on his way to a full recovery from his September ACL/MCL/meniscus injury as of April, when the Giants picked up the fifth-year option on his rookie contract. What "full recovery" means is unclear for such a devastating injury to an athlete who already coped with an ankle injury for much of the 2019 season. There's a strong chance that the Giants will be paying a premium cap price over the next two seasons for something slightly better than Todd Gurley's 2019/2020 seasons. The good news for fantasy gamers is A) the Giants have enough deep-threat receivers to keep defenders out of the box, so Barkley will at least have room to grind; and B) the Giants should continue to feature him in their backfield. They added some depth at the position in Devontae Booker (2-year, $5.5-million free-agent contract) and Gary Brightwell (sixth-round draft pick) so they have a viable backup plan if he suffers another injury. But as long as he's healthy, Barkley should have a major workload if not the same extreme one he had in his rookie year.

Le'Veon Bell

Height: 6-1   Weight: 225   College: Michigan State   Draft: 2013/2 (48)   Born: 18-Feb-1992   Age: 29   Risk: N/A

Year	Tm	G/GS	Snaps	Runs	Yds	TD	Yd/R	FUM	DVOA	Rk	DYAR	Rk	Suc%	Rk	BTkl	YafC	Pass	Rec	Yds	TD	C%	Yd/C	YAC	DVOA	Rk	DYAR	Rk
2019	NYJ	15/15	798	245	789	3	3.2	1	-16.6%	44	-76	44	42%	40	55	2.3	78	66	461	1	85%	7.0	6.7	-13.2%	39	3	39
2020	2TM	11/4	270	82	328	2	4.0	1	0.6%	--	34	--	54%	--	21	2.5	20	16	138	0	80%	8.6	8.5	-2.1%	--	14	--

Bell was seen as a menace to all Clyde Edwards-Helaire managers in fantasy football last season. The real-life reception to Bell's work with the Chiefs was not a whole lot friendlier, despite him being largely what he has always been as a runner. Bell held a 57% success rate through his 60 carries on first and second downs, making him every bit as productive on a base level as Edwards-Helaire. Like the rookie, however, Bell struggled to generate explosive plays, which is not necessarily a foreign concept for Bell. Bell's best days in Pittsburgh were about minimizing losses and squeezing an extra yard or two out of seemingly mundane runs, rather than being a home-run hitter. That just served less value when K.C.'s other running back was a first-round pick who provides the same thing. If anything, Bell's value as a receiver was missing—he earned a career-low 16 receptions. Bell offered close to nothing on third down getting four carries and zero targets. Bell still pass protects effectively, but that's about it.

Giovani Bernard

Height: 5-9   Weight: 205   College: North Carolina   Draft: 2013/2 (37)   Born: 22-Nov-1991   Age: 30   Risk: Green

Year	Tm	G/GS	Snaps	Runs	Yds	TD	Yd/R	FUM	DVOA	Rk	DYAR	Rk	Suc%	Rk	BTkl	YafC	Pass	Rec	Yds	TD	C%	Yd/C	YAC	DVOA	Rk	DYAR	Rk
2018	CIN	12/4	329	56	211	3	3.8	0	-1.6%	--	16	--	41%	--	10	2.1	48	35	218	0	73%	6.2	6.5	-11.8%	37	5	37
2019	CIN	16/2	457	53	170	0	3.2	2	-33.5%	--	-52	--	32%	--	11	2.0	43	30	234	0	70%	7.8	7.3	-38.5%	48	-55	49
2020	CIN	16/10	517	124	416	3	3.4	1	-13.9%	42	-29	40	48%	35	19	2.0	59	47	355	3	80%	7.6	7.4	-1.7%	28	40	22
2021	TB			31	128	1	4.1	1	-4.6%								56	44	317	2	79%	7.2		-0.3%			

Per reports, Bernard was added to a crowded Tampa Bay backfield due to the Buccaneers' struggles with drops in 2020; their running backs collectively had 16 drops and a drop rate of 13.4%. Bernard is comparatively sure-handed, with positive receiving DYAR in every year of his career but 2019, and he's a very solid pass-blocker as well. There's always room for a James White type in a Tom Brady offense.

Devontae Booker

Height: 5-11   Weight: 219   College: Utah   Draft: 2016/4 (136)   Born: 27-May-1992   Age: 29   Risk: Green

Year	Tm	G/GS	Snaps	Runs	Yds	TD	Yd/R	FUM	DVOA	Rk	DYAR	Rk	Suc%	Rk	BTkl	YafC	Pass	Rec	Yds	TD	C%	Yd/C	YAC	DVOA	Rk	DYAR	Rk
2018	DEN	16/0	316	34	183	1	5.4	1	9.6%	--	27	--	50%	--	21	3.2	51	38	275	0	75%	7.2	6.3	-13.5%	39	1	39
2019	DEN	16/0	26	2	9	0	4.5	0	-13.8%	--	0	--	0%	--	3	6.0	9	6	57	0	67%	9.5	7.3	-33.6%	--	-9	--
2020	LV	16/1	238	93	423	3	4.5	1	-1.8%	--	26	--	46%	--	14	2.4	21	17	84	0	81%	4.9	4.8	-37.5%	--	-26	--
2021	NYG			37	158	1	4.2	0	-4.5%								16	12	82	0	75%	6.6		-11.2%			

A classic expensive, overcomplicated Dave Gettleman solution to a simple problem. The Giants plowed through multiple veteran committee backs last season after Saquon Barkley was injured. The takeaway for most forward-thinking general managers would be, "hmm, adequate committee backs are plentiful." Gettleman's takeaway was: "I better rush out and get an adequate committee back in free agency!" Booker doesn't really cost that much (two years, $5.5 million) but doesn't offer much, either, particularly as a receiver. If Barkley is limited, Booker should be about as effective in relief as Wayne Gallman was.

Mike Boone

Height: 5-10   Weight: 206   College: Cincinnati   Draft: 2018/FA   Born: 30-Jun-1995   Age: 26   Risk: Green

Year	Tm	G/GS	Snaps	Runs	Yds	TD	Yd/R	FUM	DVOA	Rk	DYAR	Rk	Suc%	Rk	BTkl	YafC	Pass	Rec	Yds	TD	C%	Yd/C	YAC	DVOA	Rk	DYAR	Rk
2018	MIN	8/0	36	11	47	0	4.3	0	-4.2%	--	2	--	36%	--	0	3.7	3	2	1	0	67%	0.5	2.5	-105.0%	--	-15	--
2019	MIN	16/2	82	49	273	3	5.6	0	9.0%	--	35	--	51%	--	10	3.1	4	3	17	0	75%	5.7	8.7	-10.6%	--	1	--
2020	MIN	16/0	31	11	59	1	5.4	0	14.5%	--	14	--	73%	--	5	3.5	2	2	10	0	100%	5.0	8.5	0.5%	--	2	--
2021	DEN			41	194	2	4.7	0	6.0%								6	4	27	0	67%	6.8		-26.2%			

Boone was almost entirely phased out of the Vikings lineup last season—his 11 total carries matched his previous career low from 2018. Minnesota fully indexed into Dalvin Cook handling the bulk of the workload, so all of the carries that trickled down to Boone in 2019 just returned back to Cook. While some running backs can still find their way into the lineup via pass-catching, that is not really Boone's strength. Boone has never seen more than four targets in a season and there is no reason to believe that will change in 2021. In Denver, Boone will likely be buried behind Javonte Williams, Melvin Gordon, and perhaps Royce Freeman.

Matt Breida

Height: 5-10   Weight: 190   College: Georgia Southern   Draft: 2017/FA   Born: 28-Feb-1995   Age: 26   Risk: Green

Year	Tm	G/GS	Snaps	Runs	Yds	TD	Yd/R	FUM	DVOA	Rk	DYAR	Rk	Suc%	Rk	BTkl	YafC	Pass	Rec	Yds	TD	C%	Yd/C	YAC	DVOA	Rk	DYAR	Rk
2018	SF	14/13	364	153	814	3	5.3	1	1.3%	23	58	23	46%	30	28	2.4	31	27	261	2	87%	9.7	8.7	44.8%	2	105	10
2019	SF	13/5	259	123	623	1	5.1	2	-1.8%	22	33	25	46%	31	16	2.3	22	19	120	1	86%	6.3	6.7	19.5%	--	39	--
2020	MIA	12/1	152	59	254	0	4.3	2	-11.8%	--	-8	--	56%	--	4	1.9	10	9	96	0	90%	10.7	10.7	49.9%	--	42	--
2021	BUF			11	48	0	4.4	0	-2.1%								3	3	19	0	100%	7.6		-2.5%			

Breida's stats dropping after going from the San Francisco offensive line to Miami's isn't a stunning turn of events, but getting only 68 touches in the Dolphins' talent-strapped backfield is. Injuries didn't help, and Breida has certainly spent more than his fair share of time on the injury report, but he also failed to impress Miami's coaching staff. It appears he's another in the long line of backs who have looked better than their talent level in a Shanahan offense, as that family has been plugging-and-playing backs since the mid-1990s. Breida will fit comfortably behind Devin Singletary and Zack Moss, but Buffalo's offense is a better fit for him than Miami's, and he could easily find more room to run behind a better offensive line.

Malcolm Brown

Height: 5-11   Weight: 222   College: Texas   Draft: 2015/FA   Born: 15-May-1993   Age: 28   Risk: Green

Year	Tm	G/GS	Snaps	Runs	Yds	TD	Yd/R	FUM	DVOA	Rk	DYAR	Rk	Suc%	Rk	BTkl	YafC	Pass	Rec	Yds	TD	C%	Yd/C	YAC	DVOA	Rk	DYAR	Rk
2018	LAR	12/0	123	43	212	0	4.9	0	9.7%	--	36	--	67%	--	7	3.0	7	5	52	1	71%	10.4	7.8	43.5%	--	23	--
2019	LAR	14/1	226	69	255	5	3.7	0	-0.1%	--	25	--	46%	--	16	2.2	6	2	16	0	33%	8.0	3.5	-71.9%	--	-19	--
2020	LAR	16/0	472	101	419	5	4.1	1	11.7%	16	89	19	49%	32	16	1.5	33	23	162	0	70%	7.0	7.7	-17.5%	40	-7	39
2021	MIA			77	306	3	4.0	1	-4.7%								19	14	110	0	74%	7.9		-3.4%			

Brown's 89 rushing DYAR would have led Miami last season, though that says more about the state of the Dolphins' offense than anything about Brown as a player. For the second offseason in a row, Brown begins the year as the most accomplished rusher in an inexperienced backfield, and if things go as hoped, he'll end the year buried on the depth chart once again. Brown is fine as a rusher and has use as a short-yardage hammer, but he's a liability in the passing game both as a receiver and a blocker. A situational-use player only.

Rex Burkhead Height: 5-10 Weight: 215 College: Nebraska Draft: 2013/6 (190) Born: 2-Jul-1990 Age: 31 Risk: Yellow

Year	Tm	G/GS	Snaps	Runs	Yds	TD	Yd/R	FUM	DVOA	Rk	DYAR	Rk	Suc%	Rk	BTkl	YafC	Pass	Rec	Yds	TD	C%	Yd/C	YAC	DVOA	Rk	DYAR	Rk
2018	NE	8/4	151	57	186	0	3.3	2	-8.2%	--	1	--	40%	--	14	2.4	20	14	131	1	70%	9.4	8.6	-9.1%	--	5	--
2019	NE	13/1	264	65	302	3	4.6	1	22.2%	--	85	--	52%	--	14	3.1	38	27	279	0	71%	10.3	8.5	4.0%	21	37	23
2020	NE	10/0	269	67	274	3	4.1	0	12.9%	--	60	--	55%	--	10	1.9	33	25	192	3	76%	7.7	8.0	8.4%	18	42	21
2021	HOU			9	35	0	4.0	0	-6.5%								3	2	18	0	67%	8.6		-0.9%			

Ezekiel Elliott. Derrick Henry. Mark Ingram. Aaron Jones. Alvin Kamara … Rex Burkhead? It's an odd stat that puts Burkhead in with that group, but it's true—these are the six running backs who have put up positive rushing DVOAs in four of the past five seasons, with a minimum of 50 carries each year. Obviously, that last caveat is carrying serious weight here, but Burkhead's consistently solid play as part of rotations in Cincinnati and New England is worth celebrating in its own right. He'll attempt to carve out the same role in the Houston backfield as the Texans continue to sign every veteran willing to take a cheap deal in the name of competition.

Chris Carson Height: 5-11 Weight: 222 College: Oklahoma State Draft: 2017/7 (249) Born: 16-Sep-1994 Age: 27 Risk: Green

Year	Tm	G/GS	Snaps	Runs	Yds	TD	Yd/R	FUM	DVOA	Rk	DYAR	Rk	Suc%	Rk	BTkl	YafC	Pass	Rec	Yds	TD	C%	Yd/C	YAC	DVOA	Rk	DYAR	Rk
2018	SEA	14/14	454	247	1151	9	4.7	3	3.9%	17	133	12	51%	15	61	3.0	24	20	163	0	83%	8.2	8.2	21.2%	--	43	--
2019	SEA	15/15	736	278	1230	7	4.4	7	1.9%	16	130	10	57%	3	78	3.3	47	37	266	2	79%	7.2	8.6	8.9%	18	57	18
2020	SEA	12/12	403	141	681	5	4.8	1	15.1%	12	153	11	65%	1	25	2.8	46	37	287	4	80%	7.8	6.9	23.5%	6	108	8
2021	SEA			194	869	6	4.5	2	1.9%								50	39	298	2	78%	7.6		7.3%			

Carson has earned a well-deserved reputation as a bulldozing tackle-breaker through his first four seasons in the NFL, but with Russell Wilson looking to him out of the backfield more often in 2019 and 2020, he has recently provided some value as a receiver as well. While he does not have the flashy breakaway speed of someone such as Saquon Barkley, Carson has quietly and consistently produced for Seattle, and the Seahawks rewarded him with a two-year contract to remain the starting running back for the immediate future. Even though he has not been named to the Pro Bowl at any point in his career, he has still more than exceeded expectations after entering the league as a seventh-round pick.

Michael Carter Height: 5-10 Weight: 199 College: North Carolina Draft: 2021/4 (107) Born: 7-May-1999 Age: 22 Risk: Green

Year	Tm	G/GS	Snaps	Runs	Yds	TD	Yd/R	FUM	DVOA	Rk	DYAR	Rk	Suc%	Rk	BTkl	YafC	Pass	Rec	Yds	TD	C%	Yd/C	YAC	DVOA	Rk	DYAR	Rk
2021	NYJ			131	563	4	4.3	1	-3.8%								33	26	197	1	79%	7.7		-1.2%			

We're fairly certain that the Jets drafted two Michael Carters just to make our database a little bit more difficult to parse. Carter gets dinged some in our BackCAST projections for never carrying a heavy load at North Carolina, splitting time with Javonte Williams. We do have Carter as the superior Tar Heels back, though—6.6 yards per carry is very good, and he projects as one of the better receiving backs in the draft. Size is a worry, and Carter didn't break out until his senior year, but he has the skill set to at least contribute as a third-down back right away.

Nick Chubb Height: 5-11 Weight: 225 College: Georgia Draft: 2018/2 (35) Born: 27-Dec-1995 Age: 26 Risk: Green

Year	Tm	G/GS	Snaps	Runs	Yds	TD	Yd/R	FUM	DVOA	Rk	DYAR	Rk	Suc%	Rk	BTkl	YafC	Pass	Rec	Yds	TD	C%	Yd/C	YAC	DVOA	Rk	DYAR	Rk
2018	CLE	16/9	395	192	996	8	5.2	0	1.1%	24	80	18	50%	19	47	4.3	29	20	149	2	69%	7.5	9.1	-4.6%	30	14	32
2019	CLE	16/16	728	298	1494	8	5.0	3	4.5%	12	162	9	45%	37	74	3.5	49	36	278	0	73%	7.7	8.8	-15.3%	41	-4	41
2020	CLE	12/12	410	190	1067	12	5.6	1	25.5%	2	276	3	52%	20	56	3.7	18	16	150	0	89%	9.4	8.3	52.7%	--	63	--
2021	CLE			248	1265	9	5.1	1	14.6%								31	24	199	1	77%	8.3		9.2%			

Chubb shrugged off the knee injury that cost him a month of action without missing a beat. His combination of efficiency and volume was apparent on his first-down carries. Of the 17 backs who had 100 or more first-down carries, only Alvin Kamara had a better DVOA than Chubb (35.4% to 34.5%). It's not like he fell off on later downs, as his 82% success rate on third/fourth down will attest. Chubb was also sensational in the red zone, with a 44.7% DVOA on 41 carries inside the 20. Weirdly, however, he wasn't great inside the 5-yard line, where Chubb scored on just five of 12 chances, below league average. Chubb also struggled in shotgun runs—just a -20.8% DVOA on those totes.

Chubb isn't necessarily thought of as an all-purpose back, but he also did damage in the passing game when given the chance. In other words, you'd be hard-pressed to find many better all-around backs in the league, and he's a no-brainer early pick in your fantasy draft, even with the injury worries.

Tarik Cohen Height: 5-6   Weight: 191   College: North Carolina A&T   Draft: 2017/4 (119)   Born: 26-Jul-1995   Age: 26   Risk: Yellow

Year	Tm	G/GS	Snaps	Runs	Yds	TD	Yd/R	FUM	DVOA	Rk	DYAR	Rk	Suc%	Rk	BTkl	YafC	Pass	Rec	Yds	TD	C%	Yd/C	YAC	DVOA	Rk	DYAR	Rk
2018	CHI	16/7	495	99	444	3	4.5	3	-12.9%	--	-17	--	44%	--	37	1.7	91	71	725	5	78%	10.2	7.3	21.3%	6	184	4
2019	CHI	16/11	543	64	213	0	3.3	1	-17.2%	--	-23	--	42%	--	22	1.6	104	79	456	3	76%	5.8	5.4	-20.1%	43	-36	45
2020	CHI	3/0	77	14	74	0	5.3	0	16.4%	--	13	--	50%	--	2	1.9	9	6	41	0	67%	6.8	10.2	-38.8%	--	-12	--
2021	CHI			32	137	1	4.3	0	-3.6%								35	26	191	1	74%	7.4		-4.0%			

Cohen has the shiftiness and top-end speed to excel as a punt returner, so it's strange to see him carry -10.4% career rushing and -9.7% career receiving DVOAs after four years in the league. It's tempting to blame quarterback Mitchell Trubisky for putting Cohen in bad spots. He threw 42 of Cohen's 104 total targets behind the line of scrimmage in 2019, where Cohen compiled a league-worst -87 DYAR with -51.4% DVOA (compared to a league average of -13.2% for running backs on passes behind the line of scrimmage). Cohen has had few chances to try his luck with another quarterback under center—he tore his ACL in Week 3 before Nick Foles made his first Bears start in 2020. Cohen also deserves some blame for his own inefficiency. His 15.4% broken tackle rate in 2019 was just 34th of the 51 running backs with 100 or more touches.

Tevin Coleman Height: 6-1   Weight: 210   College: Indiana   Draft: 2015/3 (73)   Born: 16-Apr-1993   Age: 28   Risk: Red

Year	Tm	G/GS	Snaps	Runs	Yds	TD	Yd/R	FUM	DVOA	Rk	DYAR	Rk	Suc%	Rk	BTkl	YafC	Pass	Rec	Yds	TD	C%	Yd/C	YAC	DVOA	Rk	DYAR	Rk
2018	ATL	16/14	580	167	800	4	4.8	2	-6.4%	30	14	30	43%	37	26	2.4	44	32	276	5	73%	8.6	8.6	17.2%	10	77	16
2019	SF	14/11	392	137	544	6	4.0	0	-15.3%	43	-38	41	39%	44	19	2.1	30	21	180	1	70%	8.6	9.7	0.0%	24	23	30
2020	SF	8/1	63	28	53	0	1.9	0	-47.0%	--	-43	--	32%	--	5	1.9	5	4	34	0	80%	8.5	5.3	13.2%	--	8	--
2021	NYJ			134	552	5	4.1	1	-3.5%								37	28	235	1	76%	8.4		2.6%			

What do you do when you're bringing a new offense to a new team? Why, bring in as many veterans who know the scheme as you can, of course! Coleman was drafted to be in a Shanahan offense, has spent the last two years in a Shanahan offense, and now comes with Mike LaFleur and John Belton to kick-start the Shanahan offense in New York. Coleman has never been a great runner, and his -43 rushing DYAR last season was the worst of his career. He is still a high-quality *receiving* back, however, and would be ideal as a third-down back for the Jets. He may have to be an every-down back due to lack of overall talent, but hey, a role is a role.

James Conner Height: 6-1   Weight: 233   College: Pittsburgh   Draft: 2017/3 (105)   Born: 5-May-1995   Age: 26   Risk: Green

Year	Tm	G/GS	Snaps	Runs	Yds	TD	Yd/R	FUM	DVOA	Rk	DYAR	Rk	Suc%	Rk	BTkl	YafC	Pass	Rec	Yds	TD	C%	Yd/C	YAC	DVOA	Rk	DYAR	Rk
2018	PIT	13/12	718	215	973	12	4.5	4	2.3%	21	99	16	49%	24	56	2.8	71	55	497	1	77%	9.0	10.0	15.2%	11	112	9
2019	PIT	10/10	334	116	464	4	4.0	1	-11.3%	38	-13	37	45%	35	33	2.3	38	34	251	3	89%	7.4	8.8	21.2%	10	75	14
2020	PIT	13/11	561	169	721	6	4.3	2	-7.5%	34	8	34	49%	29	39	2.4	43	35	215	0	81%	6.1	6.7	-23.5%	43	-23	43
2021	ARI			182	739	7	4.1	2	-4.5%								33	26	183	1	79%	7.1		-2.6%			

The most important number in that table is 39—as in, the 39 attempted tackles Conner broke last year. Dividing that by 169 carries gives us a broken tackle rate of 23%, well above the league average of about 20%. Kenyan Drake, the man Conner is replacing in Arizona, only broke 24 attempted tackles in 239 runs, a rate of 10% that was second worst among qualifying backs, ahead of only Frank Gore the Undying. Conner's season was no fluke, either; he ranked in the top 10 in broken tackle rate in both 2018 and 2019. The Cardinals got Conner to sign a one-year, $1.8-million contract—a steal given his past production—in part because he is recovering from toe surgery following an ATV accident. Between Kliff Kingsbury's Air Raid formations and

Kyler Murray's threat as a ballcarrier, Cardinals running backs are going to get plenty of opportunities to beat tacklers one-on-one. Arizona is counting on Conner to win there when Drake so often lost.

Dalvin Cook

Height: 5-10 **Weight:** 210 **College:** Florida State **Draft:** 2017/2 (41) **Born:** 10-Aug-1995 **Age:** 26 **Risk:** Green

Year	Tm	G/GS	Snaps	Runs	Yds	TD	Yd/R	FUM	DVOA	Rk	DYAR	Rk	Suc%	Rk	BTkl	YafC	Pass	Rec	Yds	TD	C%	Yd/C	YAC	DVOA	Rk	DYAR	Rk
2018	MIN	11/10	490	133	615	2	4.6	2	-13.7%	41	-27	38	41%	41	42	2.8	49	40	305	2	82%	7.6	9.3	2.1%	26	45	24
2019	MIN	14/14	615	250	1135	13	4.5	4	9.3%	10	183	8	49%	23	68	2.7	63	53	519	0	84%	9.8	11.2	29.2%	5	144	4
2020	MIN	14/14	669	312	1557	16	5.0	5	15.6%	8	335	2	56%	10	71	2.8	54	44	361	1	81%	8.2	10.0	5.9%	21	58	16
2021	MIN			313	1443	14	4.6	4	4.6%								66	53	434	2	80%	8.2		7.5%			

Cook may not be worth the five-year, $63-million contract extension he coaxed out of the Vikings with a preseason holdout in 2020, but that says more about the position than it does Cook as a player. Cook was exceptional in 2020, finishing in the top 13 at his position in broken tackle rate, yards after contact per attempt, rushing success rate, and rushing DVOA all while pacing the position with 25.4 touches per game. He was particularly effective with a 63% rushing success rate on third and fourth down, a rate that rose to 69% in the red zone. And while the Vikings led the league with 5.07 adjusted line yards, they blew more run blocks than all but one other team. Cook would be a Pro Bowl back no matter his circumstances.

DeeJay Dallas

Height: 5-10 **Weight:** 215 **College:** Miami **Draft:** 2020/4 (144) **Born:** 16-Sep-1998 **Age:** 23 **Risk:** Green

Year	Tm	G/GS	Snaps	Runs	Yds	TD	Yd/R	FUM	DVOA	Rk	DYAR	Rk	Suc%	Rk	BTkl	YafC	Pass	Rec	Yds	TD	C%	Yd/C	YAC	DVOA	Rk	DYAR	Rk
2020	SEA	12/2	146	34	108	2	3.2	0	-1.8%	--	11	--	53%	--	11	2.5	20	17	111	1	85%	6.5	6.5	13.7%	--	31	--
2021	SEA			13	49	1	3.8	0	-6.4%								4	3	21	0	75%	7.3		-0.6%			

Seattle's fourth-round rookie entered the season buried on the depth chart, but a rash of injuries at midseason forced Dallas to enter the lineup and start earlier than anyone would have anticipated. Dallas did not make much of an impact with his chance to play, but that should not be considered a huge disappointment given that he was a Day 3 selection. With Rashaad Penny fully recovered from his 2019 ACL injury and Travis Homer back as well, Dallas will be fighting to get on the field unless the injury bug bites again. If he can improve his pass protection, he may get the nod over Homer on passing downs, but until that happens, we should not expect to see a whole lot of Dallas in the immediate future.

Mike Davis

Height: 5-9 **Weight:** 221 **College:** South Carolina **Draft:** 2015/4 (126) **Born:** 19-Feb-1993 **Age:** 28 **Risk:** Yellow

Year	Tm	G/GS	Snaps	Runs	Yds	TD	Yd/R	FUM	DVOA	Rk	DYAR	Rk	Suc%	Rk	BTkl	YafC	Pass	Rec	Yds	TD	C%	Yd/C	YAC	DVOA	Rk	DYAR	Rk
2018	SEA	15/2	393	112	514	4	4.6	0	9.0%	12	80	19	52%	14	24	2.8	42	34	214	1	81%	6.3	6.9	-0.1%	27	31	28
2019	2TM	12/1	80	13	27	0	2.1	0	-67.8%	--	-34	--	15%	--	0	1.2	8	7	22	0	88%	3.1	3.9	-33.4%	--	-9	--
2020	CAR	15/12	581	165	642	6	3.9	1	-3.5%	31	37	31	50%	27	56	2.7	70	59	373	2	84%	6.3	7.2	0.2%	26	55	17
2021	ATL			224	857	9	3.8	1	-5.6%								55	43	278	1	78%	6.4		-9.7%			

While Davis performed solidly as an injury replacement for Christian McCaffrey last season, he was still squarely in negative DVOA as a rusher; his fantasy impact was far greater than his actual football impact. Considering the state of Carolina's offense last season, perhaps we should cut Davis a bit more slack. He had a top-15 broken tackle rate and averaged a healthy 2.7 yards after contact. Davis is a solid player who won't hurt you when you give him the ball, but he's not someone who's going to break a lot of highlight-worthy carries. It's a surprise Atlanta didn't draft a runner this year, leaving Davis as the favorite in the clubhouse to lead Arthur Smith's offense in carries. Derrick Henry he isn't.

AJ Dillon

Height: 6-0 **Weight:** 250 **College:** Boston College **Draft:** 2020/2 (62) **Born:** 2-May-1998 **Age:** 23 **Risk:** Blue

Year	Tm	G/GS	Snaps	Runs	Yds	TD	Yd/R	FUM	DVOA	Rk	DYAR	Rk	Suc%	Rk	BTkl	YafC	Pass	Rec	Yds	TD	C%	Yd/C	YAC	DVOA	Rk	DYAR	Rk
2020	GB	11/0	97	46	242	2	5.3	0	21.6%	--	56	--	54%	--	13	3.5	2	2	21	0	100%	10.5	8.0	153.7%	--	15	--
2021	GB			140	635	4	4.5	2	2.1%								31	24	183	1	77%	7.7		3.8%			

With his size, speed (4.53s 40), and agility (7.17s 3-cone), Dillon is a 97th-percentile SPARQ athlete that Packers head coach Matt LaFleur likely drafted to fill the role that Derrick Henry fills for his previous Titans team. Dillon didn't take many attempts as a rookie and will likely never make major receiving contributions, but he teased that potential with 3.5 yards after contact per attempt in 2020. That would have ranked third behind Derrick Henry and Nick Chubb if Dillon had reached 100 carries to qualify for our rankings.

J.K. Dobbins

Height: 5-9   Weight: 209   College: Ohio State   Draft: 2020/2 (55)   Born: 17-Dec-1998   Age: 23   Risk: Green

Year	Tm	G/GS	Snaps	Runs	Yds	TD	Yd/R	FUM	DVOA	Rk	DYAR	Rk	Suc%	Rk	BTkl	YafC	Pass	Rec	Yds	TD	C%	Yd/C	YAC	DVOA	Rk	DYAR	Rk
2020	BAL	15/1	456	134	805	9	6.0	2	26.1%	1	196	6	59%	4	32	2.9	24	18	120	0	75%	6.7	7.2	-20.0%	--	-9	--
2021	BAL			224	1190	8	5.3	2	15.2%								36	25	211	1	69%	8.4		-2.5%			

Dobbins rushed for 265 yards on 32 carries (8.3 yards per carry) on runs to the outside, per Sports Info Solutions. He finished third in the NFL in rushing yards to the outside, behind Derrick Henry (283) and teammate Lamar Jackson (265). Dobbins led the league with 167 rushing yards to the outside left, 17 more yards than Jackson and 55 more yards than Nick Chubb, who ranked second among running backs. The data includes a 72-yard touchdown but a number of other runs of 15-plus yards, as Dobbins was particularly effective on outside zone-read concepts in which Jackson threatened the offense with a possible keeper between the tackles. Dobbins will take on an increased workload with Mark Ingram gone. He's more than up for the challenge, though his fantasy value may be nerfed a bit by sharing carries with Gus Edwards at the goal line and with his quarterback everywhere else.

Kenyan Drake

Height: 6-1   Weight: 211   College: Alabama   Draft: 2016/3 (73)   Born: 26-Jan-1994   Age: 27   Risk: Green

Year	Tm	G/GS	Snaps	Runs	Yds	TD	Yd/R	FUM	DVOA	Rk	DYAR	Rk	Suc%	Rk	BTkl	YafC	Pass	Rec	Yds	TD	C%	Yd/C	YAC	DVOA	Rk	DYAR	Rk
2018	MIA	16/7	545	120	535	4	4.5	2	4.7%	16	58	22	45%	33	41	2.4	74	53	477	5	73%	9.0	7.8	14.0%	12	123	8
2019	2TM	14/10	622	170	817	8	4.8	2	19.7%	3	202	5	51%	16	34	2.3	68	50	345	0	74%	6.9	8.5	-7.9%	33	23	29
2020	ARI	15/13	615	239	955	10	4.0	3	-3.4%	29	57	28	50%	26	24	2.0	31	25	137	0	81%	5.5	6.6	-8.1%	34	10	36
2021	LV			138	566	6	4.1	2	-2.6%								53	41	286	1	77%	7.0		-11.3%			

The Kenyan Drake revival tour in Arizona was short-lived. Drake flourished with the Cardinals after being traded from Miami in the middle of the 2019 season and looked like the perfect fit for Kliff Kingsbury's spread-to-run ground game. Kingsbury's offense as a whole became stale in 2020, however, and the Cardinals offensive line took a step back in adjusted line yards. Drake suffered for that, seeing his success rate crash back to league average while his production on both first and second down sat below 4.0 yards per carry. Last year was Drake's only season with more than 200 carries, yet also happened to be his only season with fewer than 4.5 yards per carry. One year does not entirely disqualify Drake from ever being a lead back, but there's a reason the Dolphins were always hesitant to make him one, and it's not too surprising he was lackluster in his one season in that role. That said, Drake is being moved back to a change-of-pace role behind Josh Jacobs in Las Vegas, which is probably a better fit for his explosive style and pass-catching chops anyway. We expect Drake to eat all the carries Devontae Booker took last year, and then some.

Chase Edmonds

Height: 5-9   Weight: 210   College: Fordham   Draft: 2018/4 (134)   Born: 13-Apr-1996   Age: 25   Risk: Yellow

Year	Tm	G/GS	Snaps	Runs	Yds	TD	Yd/R	FUM	DVOA	Rk	DYAR	Rk	Suc%	Rk	BTkl	YafC	Pass	Rec	Yds	TD	C%	Yd/C	YAC	DVOA	Rk	DYAR	Rk
2018	ARI	16/0	198	60	208	2	3.5	1	-18.9%	--	-27	--	45%	--	14	2.1	23	20	103	0	87%	5.2	6.1	-27.7%	--	-19	--
2019	ARI	13/2	209	60	303	4	5.1	0	31.7%	--	84	--	40%	--	10	2.6	21	12	105	1	57%	8.8	8.8	-15.3%	--	-2	--
2020	ARI	16/2	526	97	448	1	4.6	2	1.8%	--	42	--	49%	--	19	2.1	67	53	402	4	79%	7.6	6.2	24.0%	4	135	5
2021	ARI			147	659	4	4.5	2	-0.7%								55	44	320	3	80%	7.3		8.5%			

Edmonds brought unusual versatility to Arizona's offense, one of eight players league-wide to log at least 90 carries and 60 targets in 2020. He didn't produce much value on targets out of the backfield, but the Cardinals liked to line him up in the slot or split wide—26 of his targets came from those positions, second most among running backs behind Washington's J.D. McKissic. And he was dominant out there, with a 92% catch rate (not a typo) and an average gain of 8.7 yards per target. Edmonds has made it very clear that he would like to be Arizona's starting running back in this, the final year of his rookie deal, though James Conner is going to have a lot to say about that. It doesn't help Edmonds' case that he was at his worst in his one game with 20 carries last season, averaging 2.8 yards on 25 runs in a 34-31 loss to Miami.

Gus Edwards   Height: 6-1   Weight: 235   College: Rutgers   Draft: 2018/FA   Born: 13-Apr-1995   Age: 26   Risk: Green

Year	Tm	G/GS	Snaps	Runs	Yds	TD	Yd/R	FUM	DVOA	Rk	DYAR	Rk	Suc%	Rk	BTkl	YafC	Pass	Rec	Yds	TD	C%	Yd/C	YAC	DVOA	Rk	DYAR	Rk
2018	BAL	11/6	286	137	718	2	5.2	0	13.9%	9	130	13	63%	1	19	2.6	2	2	20	0	100%	10.0	8.5	69.1%	--	10	--
2019	BAL	16/1	402	133	711	2	5.3	2	11.8%	8	126	11	56%	6	23	3.1	7	7	45	0	100%	6.4	6.4	24.7%	--	15	--
2020	BAL	16/6	347	144	723	6	5.0	1	17.4%	7	177	10	63%	2	26	3.0	13	9	129	0	69%	14.3	10.3	46.3%	--	35	--
2021	BAL			162	807	6	5.0	2	10.0%								14	10	90	0	71%	8.8		6.3%			

Edwards led the Ravens with nine rushes inside the 5-yard line, producing three touchdowns. J.K. Dobbins rushed eight times inside the 5-yard line last year, producing seven touchdowns. (Lamar Jackson rushed just once inside the 5-yard line but 16 times inside the 10-yard line; his game works best when he has a little more space to operate.) We have lots and lots of data that proves that there's no such thing as an effective "goal-line back," but what matters is what John Harbaugh and Greg Roman believe, not what we believe. Edwards has carved out a productive niche as the big back in the Ravens rotation, and with 5.2 career yards per carry, he has earned the chance to split the carries left behind by Mark Ingram 50-50 or so with Dobbins. They may end up splitting the touchdown opportunities as well. If all goes according to plan in Baltimore, there will be a lot of them.

Clyde Edwards-Helaire   Height: 5-7   Weight: 207   College: Louisiana State   Draft: 2020/1 (32)   Born: 11-Apr-1999   Age: 22   Risk: Green

Year	Tm	G/GS	Snaps	Runs	Yds	TD	Yd/R	FUM	DVOA	Rk	DYAR	Rk	Suc%	Rk	BTkl	YafC	Pass	Rec	Yds	TD	C%	Yd/C	YAC	DVOA	Rk	DYAR	Rk
2020	KC	13/13	542	181	803	4	4.4	0	-6.9%	33	13	33	56%	9	41	2.2	54	36	297	1	67%	8.3	8.2	-13.2%	38	2	38
2021	KC			199	862	7	4.3	1	2.6%								57	38	294	1	67%	7.7		-12.5%			

First-round picks are supposed to be flashy, even more so if they play a position that is generally believed to be devalued such as running back. Clyde Edwards-Helaire was anything but flashy as a rookie, which makes it easy to chastise the Chiefs for the pick. The rookie running back showed plenty of encouraging signs, though. If any piece of Edwards-Helaire's production profile highlights where he shines, it's his success rate. Edwards-Helaire came out of LSU as someone known for minimizing losses and getting the most out of each run, similar to prime Le'Veon Bell, and he proved that to be true with his 56% success rate despite a middling and increasingly injured Chiefs offensive line. All of the Chiefs' moves on this line this offseason suggest that they want to move to more duo and pulling schemes, both of which Edwards-Helaire excelled in at the college level. Edwards-Helaire may never be an explosive-play threat (only three 20-plus-yard rushes last season), but he may well blossom into one of the league's best down-to-down runners with improved offensive line play and a fuller workload with Bell out of the picture.

Austin Ekeler   Height: 5-10   Weight: 200   College: Western State   Draft: 2017/FA   Born: 17-May-1995   Age: 26   Risk: Yellow

Year	Tm	G/GS	Snaps	Runs	Yds	TD	Yd/R	FUM	DVOA	Rk	DYAR	Rk	Suc%	Rk	BTkl	YafC	Pass	Rec	Yds	TD	C%	Yd/C	YAC	DVOA	Rk	DYAR	Rk
2018	LAC	14/3	348	106	554	3	5.2	1	4.9%	15	59	21	52%	13	39	3.8	53	39	404	3	74%	10.4	10.5	30.3%	4	131	7
2019	LAC	16/8	609	132	557	3	4.2	3	-10.0%	35	-8	35	45%	32	62	2.8	108	92	993	8	85%	10.8	10.2	38.8%	3	320	2
2020	LAC	10/10	411	116	530	1	4.6	1	-13.4%	40	-23	39	43%	45	39	2.7	65	54	403	2	83%	7.5	8.8	16.6%	14	111	7
2021	LAC			171	735	5	4.3	2	-2.2%								98	83	632	3	85%	7.7		16.3%			

Ekeler cannot be a team's lead back, but the Chargers may not have another option. Since entering the league in 2017, Ekeler has only gotten worse each year in direct correlation with his rushing volume going up. It's an oversimplification, but the more he carries the ball, the less efficient he becomes on those carries. Ekeler set a career high with 11.6 carries per game last year, while his success rate plummeted to 43% to net him a career low and the third-worst mark in the league. He is still good for some explosive runs, but the floor for the Chargers run game bottoms out when Ekeler is the lead man. Granted, the Chargers offensive line has done him zero favors, but it's still concerning that Ekeler has yet to prove capable of handling a heavy rushing workload well. That said, Ekeler's real strength is and always was his ability as a pass-catcher, even from wide receiver alignments. Ekeler has seen at least 20% of his targets from a wide receiver spot in each of the past two seasons, making him one of the league's truly versatile pass-catching backs.

Ezekiel Elliott

Height: 6-0 Weight: 228 College: Ohio State Draft: 2016/1 (4) Born: 22-Jul-1995 Age: 26 Risk: Green

Year	Tm	G/GS	Snaps	Runs	Yds	TD	Yd/R	FUM	DVOA	Rk	DYAR	Rk	Suc%	Rk	BTkl	YafC	Pass	Rec	Yds	TD	C%	Yd/C	YAC	DVOA	Rk	DYAR	Rk
2018	DAL	15/15	890	304	1434	6	4.7	6	2.9%	20	149	9	50%	18	46	3.0	95	77	567	3	81%	7.4	7.5	-3.2%	29	52	20
2019	DAL	16/16	941	301	1357	12	4.5	3	16.5%	4	324	1	56%	4	54	2.6	71	54	420	2	76%	7.8	7.3	12.6%	16	99	10
2020	DAL	15/15	787	244	979	6	4.0	6	-0.9%	27	87	20	50%	25	42	2.4	71	52	338	2	73%	6.5	6.9	-5.2%	32	35	25
2021	DAL			262	1159	11	4.4	4	2.2%								63	46	328	1	73%	7.1		-11.4%			

Elliott fumbled just once in his final nine games after fumbling five times (losing four) in the Cowboys' first six games. On the downside, Elliott scored just one rushing and one receiving touchdown after Week 5, when Dak Prescott was injured. For the year, Elliott rushed 22 times inside the 5-yard line (tied with Dalvin Cook for the league lead) but scored just five touchdowns; let that be yet another reminder that "great goal-line runner" isn't really a thing.

It sure looks like Elliott executed a brief swan dive into "terrible, fumble-prone running back" early in the season before bouncing back to being an "overpaid, incrementally above replacement level running back," which will likely be his status for the next year or two. The goal-line opportunities and about 20 touches per game will still come, and Elliott will putter along at 4 yards per carry, with the occasional highlight and "feed me" gesture after the whistle. Assuming he holds onto the ball, he won't actively hurt the Cowboys, unless you consider that his salary would have been better spent on Byron Jones, Chidobe Awuzie, a veteran pass-rusher, etc.

Travis Etienne

Height: 5-10 Weight: 210 College: Clemson Draft: 2021/1 (25) Born: 26-Jan-1999 Age: 22 Risk: Green

Year	Tm	G/GS	Snaps	Runs	Yds	TD	Yd/R	FUM	DVOA	Rk	DYAR	Rk	Suc%	Rk	BTkl	YafC	Pass	Rec	Yds	TD	C%	Yd/C	YAC	DVOA	Rk	DYAR	Rk
2021	JAX			114	505	4	4.4	1	-1.0%								42	35	237	1	83%	6.8		1.2%			

Can Etienne succeed in the role that he was drafted for? Absolutely, and he can do more than that. Etienne showcased speed and big-play ability as a receiver out of the backfield at Clemson. As a runner, he's got some polishing to do, and how the Jaguars develop him is probably going to have a lot to do with where he ends up. If he starts mainlining James Robinson tape, gets better on keys, and evolves with footwork minimalism, he's got a chance to be a franchise back. If he doesn't, well, there are plenty of speedy satellite backs who have long careers as third-down or third-down-and-a-series options. Etienne absolutely has the talent to stay out of that spectrum, but he will need some improvement. Dabo Swinney, known for high praise of his own players, compared Etienne to Walter Payton. Urban Meyer's own praise for Etienne? "Travis has got the gift of ... if that guy touches the ball, there's a chance it's going."

Leonard Fournette

Height: 6-0 Weight: 228 College: Louisiana State Draft: 2017/1 (4) Born: 18-Jan-1995 Age: 26 Risk: Green

Year	Tm	G/GS	Snaps	Runs	Yds	TD	Yd/R	FUM	DVOA	Rk	DYAR	Rk	Suc%	Rk	BTkl	YafC	Pass	Rec	Yds	TD	C%	Yd/C	YAC	DVOA	Rk	DYAR	Rk
2018	JAX	8/8	280	133	439	5	3.3	0	-9.3%	32	-4	33	47%	26	17	2.1	26	22	185	1	85%	8.4	9.7	9.6%	17	37	26
2019	JAX	15/15	918	265	1152	3	4.3	1	-8.6%	34	0	34	42%	39	56	2.9	101	76	522	0	76%	6.9	7.2	-17.0%	42	-17	42
2020	TB	13/3	383	97	367	6	3.8	0	2.1%	--	46	--	49%	--	17	2.1	47	36	233	0	77%	6.5	6.5	-17.4%	39	-9	40
2021	TB			159	643	6	4.0	1	-1.8%								26	20	140	1	77%	7.0		-7.0%			

Fournette didn't do all that much in the regular season. He didn't have enough volume for our rushing rankings and his stone hands made him a liability in the passing game. He was nearly cut in December. And then the postseason rolled around, and Playoff Lenny emerged. Fournette racked up 154 DYAR in the postseason, most of it in the wild-card and divisional rounds. He became the third player ever to score a touchdown in four playoff games in the same year, after 1997 Terrell Davis and 2008 Larry Fitzgerald. That has earned him an eternal place in Tampa Bay lore, whether or not he performs in 2021.

Devonta Freeman

Height: 5-8 Weight: 206 College: Florida State Draft: 2014/4 (103) Born: 15-Mar-1992 Age: 29 Risk: N/A

Year	Tm	G/GS	Snaps	Runs	Yds	TD	Yd/R	FUM	DVOA	Rk	DYAR	Rk	Suc%	Rk	BTkl	YafC	Pass	Rec	Yds	TD	C%	Yd/C	YAC	DVOA	Rk	DYAR	Rk
2018	ATL	2/2	67	14	68	0	4.9	0	-6.9%	--	1	--	50%	--	2	1.9	7	5	23	0	71%	4.6	4.0	-109.8%	--	-30	--
2019	ATL	14/14	675	184	656	2	3.6	3	-11.1%	37	-19	39	41%	41	38	2.0	70	59	410	4	84%	6.9	5.8	-0.9%	25	51	19
2020	NYG	5/4	136	54	172	1	3.2	0	-6.6%	--	4	--	43%	--	7	1.4	10	7	58	0	70%	8.3	10.0	-10.4%	--	2	--

Freeman was active for five early-season games in between shoulder and ankle injuries, with a trip to the COVID list sprinkled in for good measure. He wasn't effective as a rusher or receiver when he was available and is now three full seasons removed from being anything more than a high-volume guy. The Giants released Freeman in December and he spent January on the Buffalo practice squad. This is the way that former 1,000-yard rushers who started in Super Bowls slowly fade from the NFL.

Royce Freeman Height: 6-0 Weight: 238 College: Oregon Draft: 2018/3 (71) Born: 24-Feb-1996 Age: 25 Risk: Green

Year	Tm	G/GS	Snaps	Runs	Yds	TD	Yd/R	FUM	DVOA	Rk	DYAR	Rk	Suc%	Rk	BTkl	YafC	Pass	Rec	Yds	TD	C%	Yd/C	YAC	DVOA	Rk	DYAR	Rk
2018	DEN	14/8	308	130	521	5	4.0	1	-6.8%	31	10	31	46%	29	31	2.8	20	14	72	0	70%	5.1	4.2	-32.2%	--	-20	--
2019	DEN	16/0	513	132	496	3	3.8	0	-11.0%	36	-12	36	41%	42	22	2.1	50	43	256	1	86%	6.0	6.0	-10.1%	36	10	36
2020	DEN	16/0	192	35	170	0	4.9	0	12.4%	--	30	--	43%	--	5	2.5	13	12	81	0	92%	6.8	5.3	2.1%	--	11	--
2021	DEN			10	44	0	4.3	0	-2.7%								3	2	13	0	67%	6.1		-5.6%			

Freeman got buried on last year's roster after the signing of Melvin Gordon. This year will be no different given the arrival of second-round pick Javonte Williams. What's perhaps even more worrisome for Freeman is that there is so much overlap with his skill set ahead of him on the depth chart, compared to when the smaller, speedier Philip Lindsay was on the team. Freeman is a strong but plodding runner who mostly thrives when he can immediately cut downhill on inside zone. Gordon and Williams can provide that and a whole lot more. It's not like Freeman was particularly efficient and only lacking in explosive plays, either. Freeman's success rate has been below 50% for three straight years. Freeman does not offer reliable hands out of the backfield and he's not a special route-runner or someone who can flex outside, so the value there is not enough to warrant keeping him on the field over more complete players.

Kenneth Gainwell Height: 5-11 Weight: 201 College: Memphis Draft: 2021/5 (150) Born: 14-Mar-1999 Age: 22 Risk: Green

Year	Tm	G/GS	Snaps	Runs	Yds	TD	Yd/R	FUM	DVOA	Rk	DYAR	Rk	Suc%	Rk	BTkl	YafC	Pass	Rec	Yds	TD	C%	Yd/C	YAC	DVOA	Rk	DYAR	Rk
2021	PHI			23	97	1	4.2	0	-5.5%								19	13	104	0	68%	7.7		-10.4%			

Gainwell is the next in line of Memphis all-purpose backs, a stable that has produced Darrell Henderson, Tony Pollard, and Antonio Gibson over the previous two drafts. Gainwell isn't as explosive as Henderson and wasn't used as creatively as Gibson in the passing game, but he still showed plus traits in those areas. Gainwell opted out of the 2020 season, but he was the main runner in 2019 (230 carries) with Gibson on the team. His 6.3 yards per carry in 2019 were part excellent blocking and part great vision. Gainwell is a one-cut runner with the ability to make the most of holes created, but he lacks open field speed. Gainwell measured at 201 pounds at his pro day, and a 4.47s 40 at that size would have produced just an average 100.7 speed score at the combine. With a smaller frame, Gainwell's size could also be an issue if he's asked to pass protect on third downs.

Wayne Gallman Height: 6-0 Weight: 210 College: Clemson Draft: 2017/4 (140) Born: 1-Oct-1994 Age: 27 Risk: Green

Year	Tm	G/GS	Snaps	Runs	Yds	TD	Yd/R	FUM	DVOA	Rk	DYAR	Rk	Suc%	Rk	BTkl	YafC	Pass	Rec	Yds	TD	C%	Yd/C	YAC	DVOA	Rk	DYAR	Rk
2018	NYG	15/1	155	51	176	1	3.5	2	7.3%	--	30	--	39%	--	12	2.1	22	14	89	0	64%	6.4	5.8	-63.8%	--	-47	--
2019	NYG	10/2	167	29	110	2	3.8	1	-15.5%	--	-9	--	41%	--	5	1.7	15	11	102	1	73%	9.3	9.5	6.0%	--	14	--
2020	NYG	15/10	391	147	682	6	4.6	1	15.5%	9	151	12	54%	14	19	2.6	27	21	114	0	78%	5.4	4.8	-21.0%	41	-11	41
2021	SF			73	322	3	4.4	1	0.8%								22	16	139	1	73%	8.5		1.7%			

Very quietly, Gallman was a quality fill-in for Saquon Barkley last season. He started every game from Week 8 onwards, finishing 12th in the league with 572 rushing yards over that span, putting up good efficiency numbers as the Giants went 5-4 down the stretch. His reward for a job well done: a one-year contract for the veteran's minimum with zero dollars guaranteed on the league's most crowded running back depth chart. Jeff Wilson's meniscus tear opens the door for some snaps behind Raheem Mostert, but Gallman must still beat out Trey Sermon, Elijah Mitchell, and JaMycal Hasty for playing time.

Welcome to Choose Your Own Adventure: 49ers Running Back Fantasy Draft! *If you would like to draft Wayne Gallman, turn to Elijah Mitchell's comment on page 322. If you would prefer a more boom-and-bust player, turn to Raheem Mostert's comment on page 312. If you would rather draft a rookie, turn to Trey Sermon's comment on page 315.*

Myles Gaskin

Height: 5-10   Weight: 205   College: Washington   Draft: 2019/7 (234)   Born: 15-Feb-1997   Age: 24   Risk: Red

Year	Tm	G/GS	Snaps	Runs	Yds	TD	Yd/R	FUM	DVOA	Rk	DYAR	Rk	Suc%	Rk	BTkl	YafC	Pass	Rec	Yds	TD	C%	Yd/C	YAC	DVOA	Rk	DYAR	Rk
2019	MIA	7/0	125	36	133	1	3.7	0	-10.3%	--	-3	--	42%	--	8	3.0	12	7	51	0	58%	7.3	6.6	-32.9%	--	-14	--
2020	MIA	10/7	453	142	584	3	4.1	2	-10.9%	36	-15	36	55%	12	31	2.4	47	41	388	2	87%	9.5	9.5	37.8%	1	137	4
2021	MIA			183	733	7	4.0	2	-5.6%								44	34	279	1	77%	8.2		0.2%			

No one was happier with Miami's draft than Gaskin. The Dolphins passed on running backs until the seventh round, leaving Gaskin as the presumed starter in the clubhouse. Adding Will Fuller and Jaylen Waddle should give him more room to work, too—the cards could not have come out any better for him. The Dolphins clearly aren't 100% set on Gaskin being their top guy, considering they put in a waiver claim on Kerryon Johnson, but Gaskin is a perfectly acceptable back. He led all running backs in receiving DVOA, and we would blame most of his struggles on the ground to the line in front of him rather than a lack of skill on his part. If Gaskin's performance clawing his way up the depth chart last season convinced Miami to not spend a draft pick on a running back, he has done the Dolphins an immeasurable service.

Antonio Gibson

Height: 6-0   Weight: 228   College: Memphis   Draft: 2020/3 (66)   Born: 23-Jun-1998   Age: 23   Risk: Green

Year	Tm	G/GS	Snaps	Runs	Yds	TD	Yd/R	FUM	DVOA	Rk	DYAR	Rk	Suc%	Rk	BTkl	YafC	Pass	Rec	Yds	TD	C%	Yd/C	YAC	DVOA	Rk	DYAR	Rk
2020	WAS	14/10	406	170	795	11	4.7	2	18.8%	6	193	8	52%	21	40	2.0	44	36	247	0	82%	6.9	8.4	-27.2%	44	-34	45
2021	WAS			206	947	8	4.6	1	6.0%								32	26	185	1	81%	7.2		-3.1%			

With so much more experience as a receiver than a runner in college, there were questions about whether Gibson would be anything other than a third-down back at the NFL level. The question entering 2021 is whether Gibson will be used more in the passing game after taking such a heavy workload on the ground as a rookie. After just 33 college carries, Gibson had 170 carries with just 44 targets in 2020. Just eight of Gibson's carries and three targets came on third down. We're not expecting Gibson to catch a ton of balls this season, because dumping down to the running back just isn't Ryan Fitzpatrick's game.

Gibson didn't rip off as many big plays as he did in college (eight of his carries went for 15 or more yards), but he had a few, some taking advantage of misdirection used from jet motion. He still ranked seventh among backs with at least 100 carries in broken tackle rate. Gibson was also the leading rusher inside the red zone, where he put up a 51.4% DVOA and had nine rushing touchdowns.

Melvin Gordon

Height: 6-1   Weight: 215   College: Wisconsin   Draft: 2015/1 (15)   Born: 13-Apr-1993   Age: 28   Risk: Red

Year	Tm	G/GS	Snaps	Runs	Yds	TD	Yd/R	FUM	DVOA	Rk	DYAR	Rk	Suc%	Rk	BTkl	YafC	Pass	Rec	Yds	TD	C%	Yd/C	YAC	DVOA	Rk	DYAR	Rk
2018	LAC	12/12	524	175	885	10	5.1	1	20.8%	3	210	5	53%	9	55	3.2	66	50	490	4	76%	9.8	10.7	5.5%	22	72	19
2019	LAC	12/11	433	162	612	8	3.8	4	-7.5%	33	8	32	51%	15	37	2.1	55	42	296	1	76%	7.0	7.6	-7.3%	32	19	31
2020	DEN	15/10	627	215	986	9	4.6	4	-1.8%	28	59	27	44%	44	51	2.5	44	32	158	1	73%	4.9	5.1	-51.9%	47	-93	50
2021	DEN			191	815	6	4.3	3	-3.3%								36	27	159	1	75%	5.9		-22.0%			

Gordon's two-year, $16-million contract signed last offseason did not stop the Broncos from investing a second-round pick at running back in the draft. On the surface, Gordon's 4.6 yards per carry seems rather nice, but Gordon returned to posting a horrid success rate, which was an issue early in his career with the Chargers; it was the fourth time in Gordon's six-year career that he's been at or below the 45% mark. That said, the Broncos may still feel comfortable with Gordon as a red zone back. Both in his final two years with the Chargers and last year with the Broncos, Gordon has been a menace inside the 20. He produced a success rate of 59% or better in all three seasons, and was easily Denver's most trusted back in that area last year, when he earned 29 red zone carries compared to a total of 10 between Denver's two other backs. Gordon has been horrendous in pass protection recently, so it's not like he is a situational monster, but perhaps the drafting of Williams re-inspires Gordon in that department.

Frank Gore | Height: 5-9 | Weight: 212 | College: Miami | Draft: 2005/3 (65) | Born: 14-May-1983 | Age: 38 | Risk: N/A

Year	Tm	G/GS	Snaps	Runs	Yds	TD	Yd/R	FUM	DVOA	Rk	DYAR	Rk	Suc%	Rk	BTkl	YafC	Pass	Rec	Yds	TD	C%	Yd/C	YAC	DVOA	Rk	DYAR	Rk
2018	MIA	14/14	330	156	722	0	4.6	1	5.7%	14	86	17	50%	19	28	2.6	16	12	124	1	75%	10.3	9.6	35.4%	--	49	--
2019	BUF	16/8	381	166	599	2	3.6	0	-15.2%	42	-50	43	45%	36	16	2.3	16	13	100	0	81%	7.7	6.8	-9.6%	--	4	--
2020	NYJ	15/14	380	187	653	2	3.5	1	-15.4%	44	-52	42	45%	42	17	2.1	19	16	89	0	84%	5.6	4.6	-9.3%	--	5	--

If this is it for Gore—and we'll believe it when we see it, he may well still be playing when his son enters the league in a couple seasons—he leaves behind an impressive record. Three men have had at least 50 rushing DYAR in 10 or more seasons: Marcus Allen, Emmitt Smith, and Gore. He's one of 23 backs to have five seasons of at least 100 DYAR, and one of only six to have positive DYAR in at least a dozen seasons. And Gore did most of that work on a team with the worst stretch of passing offenses in DVOA history; there were plenty of years in San Francisco where Gore *was* the offense. It has been clear for a couple of years that Gore is a sub-replacement level player now, getting by on veteran savvy and name recognition, and that has knocked him down a few spots on our leaderboards. He still ranks 20th in career rushing DYAR since 1983.

Todd Gurley | Height: 6-1 | Weight: 224 | College: Georgia | Draft: 2015/1 (10) | Born: 3-Aug-1994 | Age: 27 | Risk: N/A

Year	Tm	G/GS	Snaps	Runs	Yds	TD	Yd/R	FUM	DVOA	Rk	DYAR	Rk	Suc%	Rk	BTkl	YafC	Pass	Rec	Yds	TD	C%	Yd/C	YAC	DVOA	Rk	DYAR	Rk
2018	LAR	14/14	825	256	1251	17	4.9	1	23.6%	1	366	1	57%	4	42	3.0	81	59	580	4	73%	9.8	9.9	6.9%	20	98	12
2019	LAR	15/15	805	223	857	12	3.8	3	-2.4%	25	58	21	48%	26	40	2.5	49	31	207	2	63%	6.7	6.3	-13.8%	40	0	40
2020	ATL	15/15	507	195	678	9	3.5	2	-14.9%	43	-54	44	46%	38	35	2.3	35	25	164	0	71%	6.6	4.9	-28.6%	45	-29	44

As of press time, Gurley remains unsigned. He hasn't drawn a ton of interest, either; the man who had three top-five finishes in rushing DYAR in his first four seasons is persona non grata around the league. He finished in the bottom seven in both rushing and receiving value last season and simply doesn't seem to have much more left in his knees. Rumors at the moment have Baltimore being the team most likely to bring him into the fold, but it's hard to imagine him as more than third on a depth chart at this point.

Damien Harris | Height: 5-11 | Weight: 216 | College: Alabama | Draft: 2019/3 (87) | Born: 11-Feb-1997 | Age: 24 | Risk: Green

Year	Tm	G/GS	Snaps	Runs	Yds	TD	Yd/R	FUM	DVOA	Rk	DYAR	Rk	Suc%	Rk	BTkl	YafC	Pass	Rec	Yds	TD	C%	Yd/C	YAC	DVOA	Rk	DYAR	Rk
2019	NE	2/0	5	4	12	0	3.0	0	-74.0%	--	-5	--	0%	--	0	0.8	--	0	0	0	--	0.0	--	--	--	--	--
2020	NE	10/10	251	137	691	2	5.0	1	9.9%	17	102	17	53%	19	17	2.6	7	5	52	0	71%	10.4	11.0	36.5%	--	20	--
2021	NE			170	802	5	4.7	1	4.5%								17	13	103	1	76%	8.1		-1.3%			

Harris became the first Patriots running back to top 100 rushing DYAR since Dion Lewis in 2017, and he did it on fewer than 150 carries. That gets even more impressive when you realize just how often Harris was running into a wall. 82 of Harris' 137 carries came with eight or more men in the box. That's the fifth-highest raw total in the league, and his average of 7.7 men in the box per carry was most in the league among qualified rushers. Given that context, placing in the top 20 in success rate is a minor miracle.

Najee Harris | Height: 6-2 | Weight: 230 | College: Alabama | Draft: 2021/1 (24) | Born: 9-Mar-1998 | Age: 23 | Risk: Green

Year	Tm	G/GS	Snaps	Runs	Yds	TD	Yd/R	FUM	DVOA	Rk	DYAR	Rk	Suc%	Rk	BTkl	YafC	Pass	Rec	Yds	TD	C%	Yd/C	YAC	DVOA	Rk	DYAR	Rk
2021	PIT			237	955	8	4.0	2	-5.4%								40	31	211	1	78%	6.8		-9.9%			

Harris drove all night so he could put in an appearance at the Alabama pro day—one he wasn't participating in, mind you. He merely wanted to be there to support his fellow Crimson Tide prospects. If Pittsburgh wasn't already convinced about taking Harris with the 24th overall pick, that little tidbit sealed the deal. Fortunately, Harris had a fairly light load by Alabama superback standards, even though he surprised many when he returned for his senior season. Harris amassed 530 touches over the last two seasons, helped in part by the shorter COVID campaign as well as Nick Saban's reinvention as the Mouse Davis of Tuscaloosa. His immediate predecessors in the Alabama backfield, Josh Jacobs and Damien Harris, seem to have fit into the NFL without much difficulty. Najee was a much better receiver in college than either, and we expect him to surpass 1,000 yards from scrimmage quite comfortably despite the issues with an inexperienced Pittsburgh offensive line.

Jamycal Hasty

Jamycal Hasty — Height: 5-9 — Weight: 205 — College: Baylor — Draft: 2020/FA — Born: 12-Sep-1996 — Age: 25 — Risk: Green

Year	Tm	G/GS	Snaps	Runs	Yds	TD	Yd/R	FUM	DVOA	Rk	DYAR	Rk	Suc%	Rk	BTkl	YafC	Pass	Rec	Yds	TD	C%	Yd/C	YAC	DVOA	Rk	DYAR	Rk
2020	SF	8/0	97	39	148	1	3.8	1	-8.0%	--	1	--	49%	--	5	1.6	8	7	33	0	88%	4.7	6.7	-54.9%	--	-14	--
2021	SF			11	45	0	4.2	0	-3.3%								2	1	8	0	50%	6.7		-2.9%			

The bulk of Hasty's carries came in Weeks 6-10 when Jeff Wilson, Raheem Mostert, and Tevin Coleman were mostly inactive due to the usual assortment of injuries suffered by 49ers running backs. Hasty joined them in the trainer's room after breaking his collarbone against the Saints, ending his season. He wasn't very good in 2020, and the acquisitions of Wayne Gallman, Trey Sermon, and Elijah Mitchell make it unlikely that he'll get much playing time in 2021.

Welcome to Choose Your Own Adventure: 49ers Running Back Fantasy Draft! If you would like to draft JaMycal Hasty, you are doomed. Fantasy football is not for you. Time to find a new hobby.

THE END

Darrell Henderson

Darrell Henderson — Height: 5-8 — Weight: 208 — College: Memphis — Draft: 2019/3 (70) — Born: 19-Aug-1997 — Age: 24 — Risk: Blue

Year	Tm	G/GS	Snaps	Runs	Yds	TD	Yd/R	FUM	DVOA	Rk	DYAR	Rk	Suc%	Rk	BTkl	YafC	Pass	Rec	Yds	TD	C%	Yd/C	YAC	DVOA	Rk	DYAR	Rk
2019	LAR	13/0	95	39	147	0	3.8	0	-11.6%	--	-5	--	46%	--	15	3.1	6	4	37	0	67%	9.3	9.3	-8.1%	--	2	--
2020	LAR	15/11	348	138	624	5	4.5	0	21.4%	4	185	9	55%	11	19	2.2	25	16	159	1	67%	9.9	9.4	17.2%	12	43	20
2021	LAR			80	350	3	4.4	0	1.7%								27	22	174	1	81%	8.0		7.9%			

Henderson entered the league in 2019 as a well-regarded prospect for a third-round pick, but he failed to impress in his rookie year in a crowded backfield. Henderson began 2020 third on the depth chart behind second-round draft pick Cam Akers and Malcolm Brown, but an injury to Akers opened the door for Henderson to earn more time. Henderson was pretty efficient when he had the opportunity, but Akers regained the starting job late in the year and appears entrenched as the starter heading into 2021.

Derrick Henry

Derrick Henry — Height: 6-3 — Weight: 247 — College: Alabama — Draft: 2016/2 (45) — Born: 4-Jan-1994 — Age: 28 — Risk: Yellow

Year	Tm	G/GS	Snaps	Runs	Yds	TD	Yd/R	FUM	DVOA	Rk	DYAR	Rk	Suc%	Rk	BTkl	YafC	Pass	Rec	Yds	TD	C%	Yd/C	YAC	DVOA	Rk	DYAR	Rk
2018	TEN	16/12	401	215	1059	12	4.9	1	23.1%	2	281	2	51%	16	55	3.6	18	15	99	0	83%	6.6	7.7	-18.0%	--	-4	--
2019	TEN	15/15	602	303	1540	16	5.1	5	6.7%	11	192	6	50%	17	69	3.2	24	18	206	2	75%	11.4	13.1	21.8%	--	46	--
2020	TEN	16/16	704	378	2027	17	5.4	3	15.5%	10	386	1	57%	7	61	3.6	31	19	114	0	61%	6.0	6.7	-53.3%	48	-75	47
2021	TEN			348	1697	12	4.9	3	9.7%								28	20	143	1	71%	7.2		-13.4%			

In six games against his division rivals last year, Henry rushed for 1,042 yards. That number would have ranked him ninth on the season-long rushing yards list, ahead of backs such as Ezekiel Elliott and Alvin Kamara. Yes, two of those teams have bad defenses. But in the game of guts and stomps—our earliest research on how predictive wins were—the stomps mean a lot about how good you are. Hard to imagine the Titans coming away 5-1 in the division without his contributions of running all over everybody. The best way to explain Henry's season is to note that Google autocomplete thinks you want to search for "Derrick Henry (stiff arm)," and several of his opponents were asked about not getting stiff-armed and, well, still couldn't help but get stiff-armed. Henry only had 22 carries on third or fourth down. As you would imagine, the average yards to a first-down conversion on those carries was fairly low: 2.2. Only one of them was over 5 yards; boxes were obviously stacked. Henry converted all but five of them for first downs or touchdowns, piling up a DVOA of 53.3% on those runs.

Brian Hill

Brian Hill — Height: 6-1 — Weight: 219 — College: Wyoming — Draft: 2017/5 (156) — Born: 9-Nov-1995 — Age: 26 — Risk: Green

Year	Tm	G/GS	Snaps	Runs	Yds	TD	Yd/R	FUM	DVOA	Rk	DYAR	Rk	Suc%	Rk	BTkl	YafC	Pass	Rec	Yds	TD	C%	Yd/C	YAC	DVOA	Rk	DYAR	Rk
2018	ATL	10/0	66	20	157	0	7.9	1	-10.8%	--	-2	--	50%	--	7	5.6	2	1	9	0	50%	9.0	5.0	-82.6%	--	-5	--
2019	ATL	12/2	238	78	323	2	4.1	0	-4.1%	--	14	--	44%	--	9	2.9	14	10	69	1	71%	6.9	5.4	16.5%	--	23	--
2020	ATL	16/1	327	100	465	1	4.7	2	-8.6%	35	0	35	48%	33	19	2.1	30	25	199	0	83%	8.0	6.5	3.7%	22	29	31
2021	TEN			21	94	1	4.4	0	-2.1%								19	14	99	1	74%	7.1		-11.6%			

If you've spent any amount of time over the last three years playing fantasy football, you'll know that at about Week 13, the waiver wire for running backs is barren, and Brian Hill will be there with a supposed chance at real carries. Behind Todd Gurley last year, Hill lost a lot of playing time to Ito Smith. 62 of Hill's 465 yards came on one carry against Tampa in Week 17, superficially boosting his yards per carry average away from what generally was about six to 10 carries for about 20 to 40 yards when Hill was more involved. He's not a tackle-breaker, but Hill is a willing special-teamer. It's not like Darrynton Evans proved he was a real backup last year, so Hill should have a real shot at playing time in the event the Curse of 370 takes Derrick Henry.

Nyheim Hines Height: 5-9 Weight: 198 College: North Carolina State Draft: 2018/4 (104) Born: 12-Nov-1996 Age: 25 Risk: Green

Year	Tm	G/GS	Snaps	Runs	Yds	TD	Yd/R	FUM	DVOA	Rk	DYAR	Rk	Suc%	Rk	BTkl	YafC	Pass	Rec	Yds	TD	C%	Yd/C	YAC	DVOA	Rk	DYAR	Rk
2018	IND	16/4	499	85	314	2	3.7	1	-11.8%	--	-12	--	46%	--	21	2.4	81	63	425	2	78%	6.7	5.5	3.5%	23	79	15
2019	IND	16/2	341	52	199	2	3.8	1	8.4%	--	38	--	52%	--	14	2.0	58	44	320	0	76%	7.3	7.2	-21.5%	44	-24	43
2020	IND	16/2	391	89	380	3	4.3	0	-2.5%	--	22	--	44%	--	20	2.4	76	63	482	4	83%	7.7	7.5	23.7%	5	158	2
2021	IND			72	321	3	4.5	1	2.5%								65	46	349	2	71%	7.6		-9.1%			

Hines combines great returns and stellar third-down receiver work in a way that some of the greats of his genre have: your Darren Sproleses, Brian Mitchells, and so on. Hines isn't quite the gnat that Sproles was, but he does have superb durability, generates yards after the catch, and can make a tackler miss in space. Entering the final year of his rookie contract, Hines has been an absolute hit for the draft price. The Colts haven't really found or drafted another running back like him for the depth chart, either, so it stands to reason that the team plans to re-sign him after the season. As is, he was the third-most targeted back in the NFL last year despite only playing 36% of Indianapolis' offensive snaps.

Kareem Hunt Height: 5-11 Weight: 216 College: Toledo Draft: 2017/3 (86) Born: 6-Aug-1995 Age: 26 Risk: Blue

Year	Tm	G/GS	Snaps	Runs	Yds	TD	Yd/R	FUM	DVOA	Rk	DYAR	Rk	Suc%	Rk	BTkl	YafC	Pass	Rec	Yds	TD	C%	Yd/C	YAC	DVOA	Rk	DYAR	Rk
2018	KC	11/11	503	181	824	7	4.6	0	9.1%	11	134	11	55%	7	54	3.2	35	26	378	7	74%	14.5	13.0	79.4%	1	198	1
2019	CLE	8/3	313	43	179	2	4.2	1	7.9%	--	26	--	53%	--	34	2.7	44	37	285	1	84%	7.7	7.5	14.2%	15	71	16
2020	CLE	16/5	548	198	841	6	4.2	2	-0.6%	25	64	24	51%	24	50	2.5	51	38	304	5	75%	8.0	7.4	35.1%	3	148	3
2021	CLE			116	493	4	4.3	1	-0.6%								46	36	290	2	78%	8.1		10.2%			

Like his backfield mate Nick Chubb, Hunt struggled to run from the shotgun formation, though Hunt at least offset his -11.6% DVOA on those 25 carries with a 4.6-yard average. His main running contribution came on first down, where he took the bulk of his carries (121 of 188) and admirably filled in while Chubb was sidelined, to the tune of a solid 10.4% DVOA. Hunt fell off notably on later downs, and was brutal on third downs (-27.8% DVOA). But as a receiver Hunt had no weak downs, and caught an otherworldly 92% of his first-down targets. He was also incredible as a receiving weapon in the red zone, with the second-most targets down deep on the Browns and a 124.5% DVOA on those passes.

Hunt is not close to the back he was during the two lofty seasons in Kansas City before off-field issues took him to Cleveland, but he has reinvented himself as a wicked curveball to Chubb's 100-mph heater, and is as effective a second pitch as there is in pro football, if you'll pardon the blending of national pastimes for a moment. A recent contract extension will keep him a with the Browns through 2022 at least, and presuming the team ponies up to keep Chubb, the duo figures to remain dynamic for the foreseeable future.

Carlos Hyde Height: 6-0 Weight: 229 College: Ohio State Draft: 2014/2 (57) Born: 20-Sep-1990 Age: 31 Risk: Green

Year	Tm	G/GS	Snaps	Runs	Yds	TD	Yd/R	FUM	DVOA	Rk	DYAR	Rk	Suc%	Rk	BTkl	YafC	Pass	Rec	Yds	TD	C%	Yd/C	YAC	DVOA	Rk	DYAR	Rk
2018	2TM	14/7	385	172	571	5	3.3	2	-11.0%	35	-18	36	39%	42	28	2.4	16	10	33	0	63%	3.3	5.9	-73.3%	--	-51	--
2019	HOU	16/14	538	245	1070	6	4.4	4	-3.3%	26	54	22	52%	13	34	2.3	16	10	42	0	63%	4.2	5.1	-50.3%	--	-36	--
2020	SEA	10/1	260	81	356	4	4.4	1	4.7%	--	46	--	49%	--	11	2.5	20	16	93	0	80%	5.8	6.8	-33.6%	--	-19	--
2021	JAX			55	229	2	4.1	1	-4.4%								18	15	96	0	83%	6.6		-6.5%			

A solid zone runner between the tackles without much in the way of tackle-breaking ability, Hyde surprisingly lingered in free agency last season before signing with the Seahawks in late May—he had a labrum tear that wasn't really made public. When Hyde wasn't dealing with his own injuries, he popped up for four games of 15-plus carries as Chris Carson's primary relief and did fairly well in three of them. Signed to a two-year, $6-million contract by college coach Urban Meyer, Hyde said in his post-signing availability that he had been "waiting for Coach Meyer to become a head coach in the NFL," and that it was a "no-brainer" to join him in Jacksonville. If Travis Etienne gets chained into the hybrid role Meyer was talking about in OTAs and rookie minicamp, Hyde could wind up as James Robinson's primary backup in much the same role he played with Seattle last year.

Mark Ingram

Height: 5-9		Weight: 215			College: Alabama					Draft: 2011/1 (28)			Born: 21-Dec-1989				Age: 32				Risk: Green					

Year	Tm	G/GS	Snaps	Runs	Yds	TD	Yd/R	FUM	DVOA	Rk	DYAR	Rk	Suc%	Rk	BTkl	YafC	Pass	Rec	Yds	TD	C%	Yd/C	YAC	DVOA	Rk	DYAR	Rk
2018	NO	12/6	350	138	645	6	4.7	3	2.9%	19	71	20	57%	3	24	2.9	27	21	170	1	78%	8.1	7.4	-18.8%	46	-7	43
2019	BAL	15/15	511	202	1018	10	5.0	2	19.8%	2	257	3	60%	1	46	2.7	29	26	247	5	90%	9.5	8.5	74.6%	1	145	3
2020	BAL	11/9	160	72	299	2	4.2	0	-6.8%	--	5	--	51%	--	5	1.9	8	6	50	0	75%	8.3	8.2	-10.9%	--	1	--
2021	HOU			60	247	2	4.2	1	-2.9%								15	12	92	0	80%	7.7		0.1%			

Ingram was a healthy inactive for much of last season, getting over 20% of the offensive snaps just twice in the last 11 weeks of the season, then being inactive for both playoff games. Nearly 10% of his total yardage came on one carry against the Texans in Week 2 where he was untouched on a fourth-down touchdown against a stacked box. That must have impressed Jack Easterby enough to get him in the building early, as Ingram was signed before free agency officially opened. There's probably not a lot of tread left on the tires at this point for Ingram, but he was signed to be a veteran leader more than anything.

Justin Jackson

Height: 6-0		Weight: 200			College: Northwestern					Draft: 2018/7 (251)			Born: 22-Apr-1996				Age: 25				Risk: Yellow					

Year	Tm	G/GS	Snaps	Runs	Yds	TD	Yd/R	FUM	DVOA	Rk	DYAR	Rk	Suc%	Rk	BTkl	YafC	Pass	Rec	Yds	TD	C%	Yd/C	YAC	DVOA	Rk	DYAR	Rk
2018	LAC	13/1	149	50	206	2	4.1	0	-6.0%	--	6	--	56%	--	20	2.4	19	15	135	0	79%	9.0	10.1	29.9%	--	37	--
2019	LAC	7/0	95	29	200	0	6.9	0	34.9%	--	50	--	62%	--	9	4.9	11	9	22	0	82%	2.4	4.2	-74.9%	--	-33	--
2020	LAC	9/4	190	59	270	0	4.6	0	9.2%	--	40	--	46%	--	16	2.2	24	19	173	0	79%	9.1	11.6	23.1%	--	50	--
2021	LAC			79	371	2	4.7	1	3.3%								30	25	181	1	83%	7.4		0.9%			

Justin Jackson looked to be a promising role player early in his career before injuries began chipping away at him. There is always something bothering Jackson, including an ankle injury in 2019 as well as quad and patella strains on separate occasions in 2020. It's worth noting that Jackson was the running back the Chargers trusted the least in the red zone; he only had five carries inside the 20, while Austin Ekeler, Joshua Kelley, and Kalen Ballage each had 18 or more. Jackson also earned just two third-down carries, further suggesting that he is not really someone the Chargers want on the field in critical situations. Jackson will still be a first- and second-down rotational piece, but do not expect to see him during situational football.

Josh Jacobs

Height: 5-10		Weight: 220			College: Alabama					Draft: 2019/1 (24)			Born: 11-Feb-1998				Age: 23				Risk: Green					

Year	Tm	G/GS	Snaps	Runs	Yds	TD	Yd/R	FUM	DVOA	Rk	DYAR	Rk	Suc%	Rk	BTkl	YafC	Pass	Rec	Yds	TD	C%	Yd/C	YAC	DVOA	Rk	DYAR	Rk
2019	OAK	13/13	469	242	1150	7	4.8	1	3.5%	14	126	12	51%	14	68	3.0	27	20	166	0	74%	8.3	9.2	4.6%	20	28	27
2020	LV	15/15	616	273	1065	12	3.9	2	-12.9%	39	-54	43	51%	23	50	2.4	45	33	238	0	73%	7.2	7.2	-5.2%	31	20	33
2021	LV			233	929	9	4.0	2	-3.4%								43	34	253	1	79%	7.5		-2.3%			

After a phenomenal rookie campaign in 2019, Jacobs stumbled through his sophomore season, thanks in large part to an injured Raiders offensive line that took a major step back. The Raiders fell from sixth to 18th in ALY, thus opening up fewer opportunities for Jacobs to shine. Jacobs still did his part to keep the offense moving at the most basic level, though—his 51% success rate, the same figure he posted as a rookie in 2019, was league average, showcasing both Jacob's year-over-year consistency and ability to scrape something valuable out of seemingly doomed runs. Where Jacobs himself failed in his second season was breaking tackles. A menace to tackle as a rookie, Jacobs was merely slightly above average as a tackle-breaker in 2020, finishing 25th out of 57 running backs in broken tackle rate last year (minimum 100 touches), which explains his drop in yards after contact. Jacobs still proved he could provide the Raiders with a stable floor for their run game, but he's going to need to return to making plays at the second level if he's ever going to get back to what he was as a rookie.

As for Jacobs' fantasy value, we were as shocked as anyone else that the Raiders signed Kenyan Drake and made him a top-15 running back in average annual contract value. It suggests that Las Vegas wants a backfield share similar to Cleveland's, which is why we're projecting a drop in usage for Jacobs in 2021.

David Johnson

| | Height: 6-1 | Weight: 224 | College: Northern Iowa | | Draft: 2015/3 (86) | | Born: 16-Dec-1991 | Age: 30 | Risk: Yellow |

Year	Tm	G/GS	Snaps	Runs	Yds	TD	Yd/R	FUM	DVOA	Rk	DYAR	Rk	Suc%	Rk	BTkl	YafC	Pass	Rec	Yds	TD	C%	Yd/C	YAC	DVOA	Rk	DYAR	Rk
2018	ARI	16/16	749	258	940	7	3.6	3	-12.6%	40	-42	42	38%	43	45	2.2	76	50	446	3	66%	8.9	7.7	-17.1%	43	-13	50
2019	ARI	13/9	445	94	345	2	3.7	1	-10.8%	--	-9	--	43%	--	14	2.0	47	36	370	4	77%	10.3	6.3	29.2%	6	114	8
2020	HOU	12/12	550	147	691	6	4.7	2	2.2%	23	71	23	46%	41	24	2.3	46	33	314	2	72%	9.5	7.1	0.1%	27	39	24
2021	HOU			148	629	6	4.3	1	-1.2%								43	30	269	1	70%	9.1		-0.9%			

Johnson has spoken about meeting with a therapist as the season was winding down, and it's hard to blame him. He was the target of a lot of undeserved derision as the main on-field return in an absolute bamboozle of a trade, and he played poorly for most of the season. He has never been a good zone running back, but the Texans continue to believe he is. He pressed holes often rather than waiting for things to develop—something he called himself out on in his own pressers—and the only reason his raw stats look as good as they do is because of a combined 212 yards in the last two weeks of the season against a couple of abysmal run defenses in Cincinnati and Tennessee. (Until those last two games, Johnson had -8.8% rushing DVOA and just 4.0 yards per carry.) Any tackles Johnson breaks are incidental, and he needs pitch-perfect blocking to use his speed. His only 100-yard receiving game came as a result of two long catches generated by Deshaun Watson buying time outside of the scope of the play. But, hey, great news! He got $4.3 million guaranteed in a restructure and is going to be Houston's 1A back again this year.

Duke Johnson

| | Height: 5-9 | Weight: 210 | College: Miami | | Draft: 2015/3 (77) | | Born: 23-Sep-1993 | Age: 28 | Risk: N/A |

Year	Tm	G/GS	Snaps	Runs	Yds	TD	Yd/R	FUM	DVOA	Rk	DYAR	Rk	Suc%	Rk	BTkl	YafC	Pass	Rec	Yds	TD	C%	Yd/C	YAC	DVOA	Rk	DYAR	Rk
2018	CLE	16/2	459	40	201	0	5.0	1	7.2%	--	24	--	50%	--	20	3.6	62	47	429	3	76%	9.1	8.0	12.9%	14	103	11
2019	HOU	16/2	531	83	410	2	4.9	1	-2.0%	--	21	--	48%	--	35	3.1	62	44	410	3	71%	9.3	8.2	24.6%	9	125	6
2020	HOU	11/5	354	77	235	1	3.1	3	-45.1%	--	-117	--	43%	--	18	2.0	35	28	249	1	80%	8.9	7.9	1.4%	24	30	29

Despite how bad the idea to trade for him was, the schematic idea of uniting Duke Johnson with Deshaun Watson in empty formations should have produced booms at a much higher rate than it did. The Texans simply refused to use Johnson's best trait: he's a great receiver. The Texans showcased this on Thanksgiving, and only on Thanksgiving, by having Johnson catch three balls for 43 yards and a touchdown where he beat man coverage outside. They seemed incapable of making Johnson's skill set a part of their offensive game plan under Bill O'Brien and the O'Brienettes, and while last year was disappointing for Johnson, a lot of that is because of a spiked fumble rate and an interior line that just couldn't block for anybody. Unsigned at age 27, Johnson must still be hurt, because on paper he's a solid third-down back.

Kerryon Johnson

| | Height: 5-11 | Weight: 212 | College: Auburn | | Draft: 2018/2 (43) | | Born: 30-Jun-1997 | Age: 24 | Risk: Green |

Year	Tm	G/GS	Snaps	Runs	Yds	TD	Yd/R	FUM	DVOA	Rk	DYAR	Rk	Suc%	Rk	BTkl	YafC	Pass	Rec	Yds	TD	C%	Yd/C	YAC	DVOA	Rk	DYAR	Rk
2018	DET	10/7	346	118	641	3	5.4	1	17.5%	5	124	15	53%	12	35	2.6	39	32	213	1	82%	6.7	8.3	-4.8%	31	20	30
2019	DET	8/7	281	113	403	3	3.6	1	-13.7%	41	-26	40	52%	11	18	2.3	15	10	127	1	67%	12.7	11.6	29.3%	--	39	--
2020	DET	16/2	296	52	181	2	3.5	1	-11.7%	--	-7	--	56%	--	7	2.0	26	19	187	1	73%	9.8	9.6	37.1%	2	72	12
2021	PHI			38	151	1	3.9	0	-7.3%								7	4	37	0	57%	8.3		-6.4%			

For the first time in Johnson's career, he was heathy for 16 games. But after the Lions drafted D'Andre Swift in the second round in 2020, Johnson saw just 52 carries. The Lions cut Johnson this offseason and he was claimed by the Eagles. Johnson was a broken tackle machine in his rookie season with a 14.8% broken tackle rate. That dropped to 9.7% in 2019 and just 3.8% in 2020. Johnson joins a crowded Philadelphia backfield. The 2018 version would be a useful piece behind Miles Sanders; the 2019/2020 version might not make the roster.

Ty Johnson

| | Height: 5-10 | Weight: 208 | College: Maryland | | Draft: 2019/6 (186) | | Born: 17-Sep-1997 | Age: 24 | Risk: Green |

Year	Tm	G/GS	Snaps	Runs	Yds	TD	Yd/R	FUM	DVOA	Rk	DYAR	Rk	Suc%	Rk	BTkl	YafC	Pass	Rec	Yds	TD	C%	Yd/C	YAC	DVOA	Rk	DYAR	Rk
2019	DET	16/1	318	63	273	0	4.3	1	3.5%	--	28	--	44%	--	8	2.5	31	24	109	0	77%	4.5	3.9	-40.2%	50	-45	47
2020	2TM	13/1	174	54	254	1	4.7	0	-5.0%	--	8	--	56%	--	7	1.9	21	16	99	1	76%	6.2	8.1	0.7%	--	16	--
2021	NYJ			15	64	0	4.4	0	-1.8%								3	2	16	0	67%	7.5		-1.4%			

Johnson played two games for Detroit last year, getting no carries and only five offensive snaps, then was waived and picked up by the Jets early in October. He carried the ball 22 times in Week 13 against the Raiders, rushing for 104 yards. Adam Gase gave him just 32 more carries the rest of the season, leading some to say this was another example of Gase's terrible personnel management—why keep handing the ball to Frank Gore when you have a young prospect who could be getting work? Admittedly, the Raiders' run defense was third worst in the league last year, leading to a huge 15.5% gap between Johnson's VOA and DVOA; his standard numbers are among the most inflated in the league. Still, it probably would have been better giving him a run than some of the other backs New York trotted out there.

Aaron Jones

Height: 5-9   Weight: 208   College: Texas-El Paso   Draft: 2017/5 (182)   Born: 2-Dec-1994   Age: 27   Risk: Green

Year	Tm	G/GS	Snaps	Runs	Yds	TD	Yd/R	FUM	DVOA	Rk	DYAR	Rk	Suc%	Rk	BTkl	YafC	Pass	Rec	Yds	TD	C%	Yd/C	YAC	DVOA	Rk	DYAR	Rk
2018	GB	12/8	376	133	728	8	5.5	1	17.1%	7	146	10	55%	6	34	2.7	35	26	206	1	74%	7.9	8.5	2.2%	25	33	27
2019	GB	16/16	676	236	1084	16	4.6	3	12.0%	7	207	4	56%	5	54	2.6	68	49	474	3	72%	9.7	8.9	-5.1%	29	35	24
2020	GB	14/14	539	201	1104	9	5.5	2	20.3%	5	254	4	59%	5	49	3.3	63	47	355	2	75%	7.6	7.8	-5.6%	33	30	30
2021	GB			206	1027	8	5.0	3	10.6%								69	52	398	2	75%	7.7		1.8%			

Fantasy players may have lamented Jones' decline from a league-leading 19 total touchdowns in 2019 to just 11 last season, but that decline says more about Jones' opportunities than his efficiency. With Aaron Rodgers running up his touchdown total with 30 pass attempts within 5 yards of the end zone, Jones saw his own total of goal-line carries cut from 17 to 10 last season. Broadly speaking, Jones was more effective in 2020 than he has ever been. He set new career highs with a 59% success rate and 3.3 yards after contact per attempt. That latter rate is particularly impressive for a back whose 208-pound frame makes him 19 and 39 pounds lighter than qualifying leaders Nick Chubb and Derrick Henry. Jones is also 39 pounds lighter than his second-year backfield mate AJ Dillon, so it will be interesting to see whether Jones' success in short yardage earns him as many of those opportunities in 2021 as he had last year.

Ronald Jones

Height: 5-11   Weight: 208   College: USC   Draft: 2018/2 (38)   Born: 3-Aug-1997   Age: 24   Risk: Green

Year	Tm	G/GS	Snaps	Runs	Yds	TD	Yd/R	FUM	DVOA	Rk	DYAR	Rk	Suc%	Rk	BTkl	YafC	Pass	Rec	Yds	TD	C%	Yd/C	YAC	DVOA	Rk	DYAR	Rk
2018	TB	9/0	90	23	44	1	1.9	0	-24.3%	--	-15	--	30%	--	3	2.0	9	7	33	0	78%	4.7	6.0	-42.4%	--	-15	--
2019	TB	16/9	422	172	724	6	4.2	3	-2.3%	24	43	23	45%	33	43	3.1	40	31	309	0	78%	10.0	9.5	9.2%	17	47	20
2020	TB	14/13	451	192	978	7	5.1	2	15.5%	11	195	7	57%	8	29	3.3	42	28	165	1	67%	5.9	5.6	-53.4%	49	-89	49
2021	TB			148	662	5	4.5	1	3.6%								19	13	98	0	68%	7.3		-13.5%			

Jones played through a broken pinky during Tampa's Super Bowl run, leaving the door open for Leonard Fournette to excel. The two running backs saw their usage flip back and forth throughout the season, with Jones seeing about four more snaps a game than Fournette. Neither really gained a foothold on the starting job, and that status quo looks to continue in 2021. For the record, our numbers had Jones as the significantly superior rusher, but he may well have been the worst pass-catching back in the game last year, with a 14.3% drop rate and just two first downs on 42 targets. Jones had an above-average receiving DVOA in 2019; if he can find that form again, he could and should get the lion's share of the work for Tampa Bay this year.

Kyle Juszczyk

Height: 6-1   Weight: 240   College: Harvard   Draft: 2013/4 (130)   Born: 23-Apr-1991   Age: 30   Risk: Green

Year	Tm	G/GS	Snaps	Runs	Yds	TD	Yd/R	FUM	DVOA	Rk	DYAR	Rk	Suc%	Rk	BTkl	YafC	Pass	Rec	Yds	TD	C%	Yd/C	YAC	DVOA	Rk	DYAR	Rk
2018	SF	16/14	662	8	30	0	3.8	2	-86.7%	--	-29	--	38%	--	6	1.5	41	30	324	1	73%	10.8	5.8	18.7%	8	76	18
2019	SF	12/12	396	3	7	0	2.3	0	-49.0%	--	-7	--	33%	--	1	3.0	24	20	239	1	83%	12.0	7.9	47.6%	2	98	11
2020	SF	16/15	472	17	64	2	3.8	1	16.4%	--	30	--	82%	--	3	1.7	29	19	202	4	66%	10.6	5.3	22.0%	9	66	13
2021	SF			12	47	1	3.8	0	-1.2%								25	18	164	1	72%	9.0		8.9%			

In his 1986 book *One Knee Equals Two Feet*, Hall of Fame coach John Madden explained that fullbacks have three jobs: blocking, receiving, and short-yardage running. Let's check how Juszczyk fared in those three categories:

- The 49ers had 191 runs with two backs in the formation (only Minnesota had more) and they averaged 4.7 yards per carry on those plays. That's nearly a yard better than their 3.9-yard average out of single-back sets; only Houston and Philadelphia saw bigger boosts, and they didn't use fullbacks nearly as often as San Francisco. (The Eagles had exactly one two-back run all year.)

- Juszczyk also perennially ranks highly in receiving DVOA, in part because he runs such deep routes—he led all qualifying running backs with a 6.5-yard average depth of target, and only Houston's David Johnson saw more targets 10 yards or more downfield. (This is definitely a Kyle Shanahan thing—Juszczyk's teammate Jerick McKinnon was second with a 4.0-yard aDOT, and Jeff Wilson also made the top 10.)
- Finally, Juszczyk was nearly automatic in short yardage. Thirteen of his 17 runs came with exactly 1 yard to go; he picked up a first down 11 times.

The few fullbacks left in the NFL these days usually play like undersized guards, but Juszczyk is definitely a multi-purpose throwback. The 49ers realize how hard he would be to replace, re-signing him to a five-year, $27-million contract ($9.6 million guaranteed) in March.

Welcome to Choose Your Own Adventure: 49ers Running Back Fantasy Draft! *You should never draft fullbacks, but Juszczyk is such a good real-life player that we can't blame you for considering it. Start over by turning back to Wayne Gallman's comment on page 299.*

Alvin Kamara

Height: 5-10   Weight: 215   College: Tennessee   Draft: 2017/3 (67)   Born: 25-Jul-1995   Age: 26   Risk: Yellow

Year	Tm	G/GS	Snaps	Runs	Yds	TD	Yd/R	FUM	DVOA	Rk	DYAR	Rk	Suc%	Rk	BTkl	YafC	Pass	Rec	Yds	TD	C%	Yd/C	YAC	DVOA	Rk	DYAR	Rk
2018	NO	15/13	657	194	883	14	4.6	0	18.5%	4	238	3	58%	2	43	2.4	105	81	709	4	77%	8.8	7.9	19.4%	7	197	2
2019	NO	14/9	636	171	797	5	4.7	4	3.1%	15	81	19	52%	12	56	2.6	97	81	533	1	84%	6.6	6.9	1.6%	23	83	13
2020	NO	15/10	658	187	932	16	5.0	1	23.1%	3	253	5	54%	15	59	2.5	107	83	756	5	78%	9.1	8.8	19.1%	11	195	1
2021	NO			181	836	8	4.6	2	6.8%								102	74	626	2	73%	8.5		1.6%			

Kamara enjoyed a return to form in 2020 after battling through a high-ankle sprain in 2019. He led all running backs in both receiving and total DYAR, with the highest target share and most catches and yards at the position. He was also tied for the lead in touchdown catches, and third in yards per catch. He was even more productive on the ground, setting career highs in both rushing yards and touchdowns, and converting first downs at a higher rate than any other primary back.

Although still just 26 years old, Kamara is very unlikely to be quite so productive in 2021. For one thing, he will not get a six-touchdown day against the Vikings again. Thanks in no small part to that game, he converted a near-impossible 11 of his 15 goal-line carries (73%), almost twice as many as we would expect given average conversion rates in that situation. Eleven rushing touchdowns to go with his five receiving would be much more in line with his career average, random one-off matchups be damned.

Still, a healthy Kamara producing at a career-average rate is a very valuable player. That injury-blighted 2019 season is the only time he has fallen outside the top five in rushing DYAR, and his only season outside the top *two* in receiving DYAR. It was also his only season below 1,500 yards from scrimmage, a figure that is almost always among the top 10 league-wide. The loss of Drew Brees will almost certainly impact his efficiency, and Taysom Hill being named the starter would definitely be reason for caution based on Hill's starts in 2020, but Kamara should remain a fantasy stud and one of the most productive pass-catching backs of his generation.

Joshua Kelley

Height: 5-11   Weight: 219   College: UCLA   Draft: 2020/4 (112)   Born: 20-Nov-1997   Age: 24   Risk: Green

Year	Tm	G/GS	Snaps	Runs	Yds	TD	Yd/R	FUM	DVOA	Rk	DYAR	Rk	Suc%	Rk	BTkl	YafC	Pass	Rec	Yds	TD	C%	Yd/C	YAC	DVOA	Rk	DYAR	Rk
2020	LAC	14/0	297	111	354	2	3.2	2	-36.4%	47	-141	47	42%	46	13	1.6	23	23	148	0	100%	6.4	7.5	7.3%	--	27	--
2021	LAC			88	346	3	3.9	1	-7.9%								18	15	104	0	83%	7.1		-1.4%			

In a Chargers running back room filled with middling runners, Joshua Kelley may be the least inspiring. Kelley was a disaster on first down—his success rate, DVOA, and yards per carry were all the worst among Los Angeles' top four running backs last season. And he saw 62 first-down carries, second on the team, so it's not as though his failures were the result of a poor sample size. The Chargers also tried to make use of Kelley's low, barreling style in the red zone, but to little avail. On 22 red zone carries, he produced -41.4% DVOA and a 36% success rate, both far worse than the stats of their other red zone back, Kalen Ballage. That said, Kelley did accomplish a wild feat in the receiving game: he caught every one of his 23 targets, making him the only player in the league with at least 20 targets to do so. Of course, all of those targets were cheap checkdowns, but it's still a credit to his consistency given that plenty of running backs around the league drop these passes on the regular.

Dion Lewis

Height: 5-8 Weight: 195 College: Pittsburgh Draft: 2011/5 (149) Born: 27-Sep-1990 Age: 31 Risk: N/A

Year	Tm	G/GS	Snaps	Runs	Yds	TD	Yd/R	FUM	DVOA	Rk	DYAR	Rk	Suc%	Rk	BTkl	YafC	Pass	Rec	Yds	TD	C%	Yd/C	YAC	DVOA	Rk	DYAR	Rk
2018	TEN	16/7	600	155	517	1	3.3	1	-20.1%	43	-69	43	34%	47	53	2.2	67	59	400	1	88%	6.8	8.1	-9.8%	35	15	31
2019	TEN	16/1	379	54	209	0	3.9	1	-20.7%	--	-26	--	46%	--	25	2.5	32	25	164	1	78%	6.6	7.7	-11.9%	38	3	38
2020	NYG	16/0	304	29	115	2	4.0	1	1.4%	--	14	--	41%	--	5	2.1	30	19	127	1	63%	6.7	4.2	1.9%	23	25	32

Lewis spent three seasons touring the Patriots cosplay circuit after three solid years as a product of the Bill Belichick/Josh McDaniels/Tom Brady system. He bottomed out last season as an utterly replaceable change-up back and kick returner who could barely wrest touches away from Alfred Morris or Elijhaa Penny for the Giants. A free agent at press time, Lewis is exactly the type of player the Texans spent all of the 2020 offseason signing, so don't be surprised if he ends up trying to win a job as the backup to Duke Johnson, Mark Ingram, and Phillip Lindsay in Houston.

Phillip Lindsay

Height: 5-8 Weight: 190 College: Colorado Draft: 2018/FA Born: 24-Jul-1994 Age: 27 Risk: Green

Year	Tm	G/GS	Snaps	Runs	Yds	TD	Yd/R	FUM	DVOA	Rk	DYAR	Rk	Suc%	Rk	BTkl	YafC	Pass	Rec	Yds	TD	C%	Yd/C	YAC	DVOA	Rk	DYAR	Rk
2018	DEN	15/8	453	192	1037	9	5.4	0	17.3%	6	203	6	49%	22	36	2.2	47	35	241	1	74%	6.9	8.5	-10.4%	36	9	36
2019	DEN	16/16	516	224	1011	7	4.5	0	1.9%	17	94	16	50%	19	45	2.4	48	35	196	0	73%	5.6	6.9	-39.7%	49	-69	50
2020	DEN	11/8	270	118	502	1	4.3	0	-24.2%	45	-70	45	40%	47	15	2.2	14	7	28	0	50%	4.0	5.6	-62.3%	--	-38	--
2021	HOU			96	414	3	4.3	0	-2.6%								22	15	130	0	68%	8.7		-4.2%			

Despite the fact that he had two 1,000-yard rushing seasons for Denver, it's hard to imagine a team believing in a player less than the Broncos believed in Lindsay. After he made the Pro Bowl in Year 1 with Case Keenum as his quarterback and outplayed highly drafted Royce Freeman twice in two years, Lindsay was sentenced to a lesser backfield role behind Melvin Gordon and succumbed to a toe sprain early in the season, then a hip injury that put him on IR. The Broncos rescinded his qualifying offer and Lindsay signed a one-year deal with the Texans. He certainly has the most recent success of anyone in the backfield, but he's a small player without small skills (not a dominant pass-catcher), and so he'll be underestimated the whole way as he tries to get the Texans to open their eyes about the David Johnson trade.

Marlon Mack

Height: 6-0 Weight: 210 College: South Florida Draft: 2017/4 (143) Born: 7-Mar-1996 Age: 25 Risk: Yellow

Year	Tm	G/GS	Snaps	Runs	Yds	TD	Yd/R	FUM	DVOA	Rk	DYAR	Rk	Suc%	Rk	BTkl	YafC	Pass	Rec	Yds	TD	C%	Yd/C	YAC	DVOA	Rk	DYAR	Rk
2018	IND	12/10	445	195	908	9	4.7	2	16.8%	8	216	4	54%	8	27	2.6	26	17	103	1	65%	6.1	7.2	-21.3%	49	-10	48
2019	IND	14/12	517	247	1091	8	4.4	0	1.0%	18	102	15	52%	10	39	2.3	17	14	82	0	82%	5.9	5.7	-18.5%	--	-4	--
2020	IND	1/1	11	4	26	0	6.5	0	23.5%	--	6	--	75%	--	0	2.0	3	3	30	0	100%	10.0	10.3	51.9%	--	11	--
2021	IND			46	203	2	4.4	0	0.7%								12	9	66	0	75%	7.6		-9.9%			

A torn Achilles on the fourth carry of the season destroyed Mack's contract year, and the resulting cold market of the COVID offseason led him to re-sign a one-year contract with the Colts for $2 million. Jonathan Taylor pretty much took over down the stretch for the Colts, but Frank Reich has tended to prefer a more balanced backfield usage in the past and it shouldn't surprise anyone if a healthy Mack is annoying fantasy football owners in 2021. If the Achilles takes some of his juice away, that's a brutal break for someone who might have been in line for a huge payday with a good 2020. Asked to ponder on the future of the running back position at his post-signing presser, Mack said: "It's tough, man ... right now it's tough being a running back as everybody can see by these contracts." Mack's a runner-only, head-of-committee capable guy who will be used in more of a change-up role because of Taylor's obvious talents.

Alexander Mattison

Height: 5-11 Weight: 221 College: Boise State Draft: 2019/3 (102) Born: 19-Jun-1998 Age: 23 Risk: Blue

Year	Tm	G/GS	Snaps	Runs	Yds	TD	Yd/R	FUM	DVOA	Rk	DYAR	Rk	Suc%	Rk	BTkl	YafC	Pass	Rec	Yds	TD	C%	Yd/C	YAC	DVOA	Rk	DYAR	Rk
2019	MIN	13/0	200	100	462	1	4.6	1	-2.2%	23	24	27	38%	45	16	2.7	12	10	82	0	83%	8.2	7.4	21.2%	--	18	--
2020	MIN	13/2	229	96	434	2	4.5	0	-2.8%	--	24	--	47%	--	25	2.8	15	13	125	1	87%	9.6	8.3	52.9%	--	53	--
2021	MIN			77	331	3	4.3	1	-0.5%								22	18	148	1	82%	8.1		8.5%			

Mattison has nearly matched his two-time Pro Bowl teammate Dalvin Cook with 4.6 versus 4.8 yards per carry the last two seasons, but their disparate 42.3% and 52.8% success rates add some important context. Mattison has taken fewer than half as many carries in power situations (third or fourth down, 1-2 yards to go), but he has nearly doubled his teammate in percentage of breakaway runs of 15 or more yards. Mattison would likely be good enough to earn 150 carries per season as part of a committee if he weren't stuck behind one of the game's handful of standout workhorse backs.

Christian McCaffrey Height: 5-11   Weight: 205   College: Stanford   Draft: 2017/1 (8)   Born: 7-Jun-1996   Age: 25   Risk: Yellow

Year	Tm	G/GS	Snaps	Runs	Yds	TD	Yd/R	FUM	DVOA	Rk	DYAR	Rk	Suc%	Rk	BTkl	YafC	Pass	Rec	Yds	TD	C%	Yd/C	YAC	DVOA	Rk	DYAR	Rk
2018	CAR	16/16	965	219	1098	7	5.0	4	9.6%	10	167	7	55%	5	63	2.7	124	107	867	6	86%	8.1	8.0	11.5%	15	183	5
2019	CAR	16/16	1056	287	1387	15	4.8	1	14.9%	5	278	2	47%	28	73	2.0	142	116	1005	4	82%	8.7	8.5	34.8%	4	386	1
2020	CAR	3/3	171	59	225	5	3.8	0	5.0%	--	37	--	56%	--	11	2.2	20	17	149	1	89%	8.8	6.8	42.5%	--	60	--
2021	CAR			262	1120	10	4.3	2	0.9%								95	76	564	3	80%	7.4		9.7%			

Perhaps the most productive dual-threat running back since Marshall Faulk across 2018 and 2019, McCaffrey's 2020 season was defined by a lingering high-ankle sprain that first landed him on injured reserve from Week 3 to Week 8, then kept him inactive from Week 10 through the end of the season. Fortunately, though high-ankle sprains are severely debilitating in-season, the long NFL offseason should ensure that McCaffrey is fully healed ahead of the new campaign. Though his loss was definitely painful, the news from 2020 was not *entirely* doom and gloom for fantasy owners. If Week 1 is any indication, we learned that Carolina's new coaching staff will use McCaffrey just as much as the old one did: he played 65 of 67 possible snaps on offense, piling up 135 yards from scrimmage and two touchdowns. However, KUBIAK expects a little less receiving usage given the way the Panthers have upgraded their receiving corps over the last two years.

Anthony McFarland Height: 5-9   Weight: 198   College: Maryland   Draft: 2020/4 (124)   Born: 4-Mar-1999   Age: 22   Risk: Green

Year	Tm	G/GS	Snaps	Runs	Yds	TD	Yd/R	FUM	DVOA	Rk	DYAR	Rk	Suc%	Rk	BTkl	YafC	Pass	Rec	Yds	TD	C%	Yd/C	YAC	DVOA	Rk	DYAR	Rk
2020	PIT	11/0	89	33	113	0	3.4	0	-31.9%	--	-30	--	36%	--	5	1.5	9	6	54	0	67%	9.0	7.8	0.9%	--	7	--
2021	PIT			10	40	0	4.0	0	-8.8%								3	2	14	0	67%	7.6		-2.0%			

McFarland didn't get much work as a rookie, but his elite speed (4.44s 40, which made him fifth in speed score among 2020 prospects) should keep him on the roster. Unfortunately, that speed hasn't shown up on the field much since an ankle injury fouled up his 2019 season at Maryland. After redshirting due to a broken leg in 2017, he bolted for three separate 50-plus-yard runs against Ohio State en route to freshman All-American status in 2018. Even with the Steelers dying for an injection of burst out of the backfield last year, McFarland didn't do much to seize the opportunity. His best path forward to playing time might be with his hands instead of his legs, as McFarland has shown good adjustment and tracking skills as a receiver in the past.

Jerick McKinnon Height: 5-9   Weight: 209   College: Georgia Southern   Draft: 2014/3 (96)   Born: 3-May-1992   Age: 29   Risk: Yellow

Year	Tm	G/GS	Snaps	Runs	Yds	TD	Yd/R	FUM	DVOA	Rk	DYAR	Rk	Suc%	Rk	BTkl	YafC	Pass	Rec	Yds	TD	C%	Yd/C	YAC	DVOA	Rk	DYAR	Rk
2020	SF	16/4	372	81	319	5	3.9	0	8.3%	--	53	--	41%	--	18	2.2	46	33	253	1	72%	7.7	5.4	22.7%	7	83	10
2021	KC			34	153	1	4.5	0	3.4%								15	11	75	0	73%	7.1		-13.8%			

It's a shame Jerick McKinnon's career unfolded the way it has due to injury. A four-year contributor in Minnesota, McKinnon was signed before the 2018 season to play for the 49ers in Kyle Shanahan's offense, which would have been a wonderful fit for his speed and skills. Alas, McKinnon missed all of 2018 and 2019 due to knee injuries suffered one year apart almost to the day. When McKinnon finally saw the field in 2020, he did not look like the player he once was. While McKinnon had always posted poor success rates (sub-45% in all qualifying seasons), he lost his big-play spark a bit in 2020. McKinnon had just one 20-plus-yard carry in 2020, though it was an impressive 55-yard pickup. McKinnon still serves value as a pass-catcher, 10th among running backs in receiving DYAR last year, which is presumably his role in Kansas City. He's still got just enough wiggle and reliable hands to be a factor in the pass game, even if his inconsistencies in the ground game are not worth the gamble the way they used to be. McKinnon could supplant Darrel Williams for the Chiefs' No. 2 role, health permitting.

J.D. McKissic   Height: 5-10   Weight: 195   College: Arkansas State   Draft: 2016/FA   Born: 15-Aug-1993   Age: 28   Risk: Green

Year	Tm	G/GS	Snaps	Runs	Yds	TD	Yd/R	FUM	DVOA	Rk	DYAR	Rk	Suc%	Rk	BTkl	YafC	Pass	Rec	Yds	TD	C%	Yd/C	YAC	DVOA	Rk	DYAR	Rk
2018	SEA	5/0	9	3	8	0	2.7	0	-38.3%	--	-3	--	33%	--	0	0.3	1	0	0	0	0%	0.0	0.0	-171.3%	--	-1	--
2019	DET	16/3	262	38	205	0	5.4	0	6.5%	--	23	--	47%	--	14	3.1	42	34	233	1	81%	6.9	7.0	-8.2%	34	12	35
2020	WAS	16/7	641	85	365	1	4.3	3	7.7%	--	57	--	52%	--	21	2.2	110	80	589	2	73%	7.4	6.3	-9.0%	37	30	28
2021	WAS			43	183	1	4.3	1	-4.1%								56	46	337	1	82%	7.3		1.1%			

There might not have been a more surprising 100-target season in 2020 than McKissic's. Over his first four seasons and two teams, McKissic had 70 receptions on 91 targets. Those figures were 80 catches on 110 targets in 2020 alone. McKissic became the favored outlet for Dwayne Haskins and Alex Smith, two quarterbacks who preferred to not push the ball down the field. McKissic was able to put up positive DVOA on first- and second-down passes, but that dropped to -40.7% on third downs. It didn't help that a third of those third-down targets (11 of 33) came behind the line of scrimmage. Even as Antonio Gibson took over as the top rushing option, McKissic continued to be the top pass-catching back. That role could diminish for McKissic should Gibson be worked in more of the passing game, though Washington used 21 personnel on 11% of plays last year and many of those included Gibson and McKissic on the field together.

Jeremy McNichols   Height: 5-9   Weight: 205   College: Boise State   Draft: 2017/5 (162)   Born: 26-Dec-1995   Age: 26   Risk: Green

Year	Tm	G/GS	Snaps	Runs	Yds	TD	Yd/R	FUM	DVOA	Rk	DYAR	Rk	Suc%	Rk	BTkl	YafC	Pass	Rec	Yds	TD	C%	Yd/C	YAC	DVOA	Rk	DYAR	Rk
2018	2TM	1/0	2	2	4	0	2.0	0	-4.2%	--	1	--	50%	--	0	3.5	0	0	0	0	--	0.0	--	--	--	--	--
2019	JAX	1/0	3	0	0	0	0.0	0	--	--	--	--	--	--	--	--	0	0	0	0	--	0.0	--	--	--	--	--
2020	TEN	16/0	271	47	204	1	4.3	0	-10.9%	--	-4	--	45%	--	5	2.1	17	12	55	0	71%	4.6	4.3	-50.0%	--	-32	--
2021	TEN			14	59	0	4.2	0	-2.9%								1	1	8	0	100%	7.5		-3.1%			

McNichols was so lowly regarded that he didn't even get a Going Deep mention in last year's book. He has been on the offseason roster or practice squad of seven different teams since being drafted in 2017. But he came out of nowhere to be the Titans third-down back after Darrynton Evans wasn't quite ready to seize the job. The Titans sprinkled in some Khari Blasingame as an H-back, but McNichols was the one constantly on the field. Mike Vrabel praised his pass protection. McNichols actually showed some pretty decent burst and good cuts out of the backfield at times, but wasn't much of an open-field creator as a receiving back. His job status probably relies more on what the Titans see from Evans than what they see from McNichols in camp.

Sony Michel   Height: 5-11   Weight: 215   College: Georgia   Draft: 2018/1 (31)   Born: 17-Feb-1995   Age: 26   Risk: Blue

Year	Tm	G/GS	Snaps	Runs	Yds	TD	Yd/R	FUM	DVOA	Rk	DYAR	Rk	Suc%	Rk	BTkl	YafC	Pass	Rec	Yds	TD	C%	Yd/C	YAC	DVOA	Rk	DYAR	Rk
2018	NE	13/8	320	209	931	6	4.5	1	-2.7%	26	58	24	53%	11	23	2.4	11	7	50	0	64%	7.1	7.1	-18.4%	--	-3	--
2019	NE	16/14	422	247	912	7	3.7	2	-6.4%	29	23	28	49%	22	30	2.4	20	12	94	0	60%	7.8	10.1	-21.3%	--	-9	--
2020	NE	9/6	181	79	449	1	5.7	0	19.9%	--	94	--	56%	--	17	3.2	9	7	114	1	78%	16.3	15.7	101.5%	--	64	--
2021	NE			109	485	3	4.5	1	0.9%								15	11	95	0	73%	8.9		-0.6%			

The Patriots opting to decline Michel's fifth-year option and draft Rhamondre Stevenson doesn't exactly give confidence for Michel's long-term future in New England. That doesn't mean he can't be a useful player in 2021, mind you. Michel had the best rushing DVOA on the Patriots and averaged 3.2 yards after contact in 2020, fifth among backs with at least 50 carries. The Pats do like to redshirt rookie running backs, so Michel may end up spelling Damien Harris on rushing downs for one more year before moving on.

Joe Mixon   Height: 6-1   Weight: 220   College: Oklahoma   Draft: 2017/2 (48)   Born: 24-Jul-1996   Age: 25   Risk: Yellow

Year	Tm	G/GS	Snaps	Runs	Yds	TD	Yd/R	FUM	DVOA	Rk	DYAR	Rk	Suc%	Rk	BTkl	YafC	Pass	Rec	Yds	TD	C%	Yd/C	YAC	DVOA	Rk	DYAR	Rk
2018	CIN	14/13	596	237	1168	8	4.9	0	6.4%	13	154	8	49%	23	46	2.7	55	43	296	1	78%	6.9	7.7	-15.3%	41	-5	42
2019	CIN	16/15	661	278	1137	5	4.1	0	-0.9%	20	90	17	46%	30	71	2.8	45	35	287	3	78%	8.2	9.5	19.3%	13	86	12
2020	CIN	6/6	290	119	428	3	3.6	1	-11.6%	38	-16	37	46%	39	18	2.1	26	21	138	1	81%	6.6	8.1	-4.8%	30	13	34
2021	CIN			263	997	8	3.8	2	-7.8%								67	54	384	3	81%	7.1		6.3%			

Mixon ripped off 34- and 23-yard touchdown runs against the Jaguars in Week 4. Take those runs away and he averaged 3.2 yards per carry for six games before getting shelved with a foot injury. With Gio Bernard liberated to chase a Super Bowl ring in Tampa, Mixon is expected to be an every-down back in 2021. Because the Bengals only made token upgrades to their offensive line, that likely means a whole season of 24-carry, 59-yard (Ravens, Week 5) and 19-carry, 69-yard (Chargers, Week 1) stat lines, with one or two 25-151-2 (Jaguars, Week 4) Sundays sprinkled in against weakling opponents.

David Montgomery Height: 5-10   Weight: 222   College: Iowa State   Draft: 2019/3 (73)   Born: 7-Jun-1997   Age: 24   Risk: Green

Year	Tm	G/GS	Snaps	Runs	Yds	TD	Yd/R	FUM	DVOA	Rk	DYAR	Rk	Suc%	Rk	BTkl	YafC	Pass	Rec	Yds	TD	C%	Yd/C	YAC	DVOA	Rk	DYAR	Rk
2019	CHI	16/8	625	242	889	6	3.7	2	-13.0%	40	-46	42	46%	29	53	1.9	35	25	185	1	71%	7.4	6.2	-5.5%	30	15	34
2020	CHI	15/14	759	247	1070	8	4.3	1	-3.4%	30	57	30	47%	36	70	2.8	68	54	438	2	79%	8.1	7.3	14.1%	15	113	6
2021	CHI			221	879	8	4.0	1	-4.5%								33	26	196	1	79%	7.7		0.7%			

Montgomery has not been satisfied by his two NFL seasons with subpar rates of 4.0 yards per carry and a -8.1% rushing DVOA, and so he has worked this offseason with sports science trainer Chris Korfist to rebuild his running mechanics. That work could lead to more breakaway runs if Korfist is correct that his client has added about 1.5 mph of foot speed. Either way, Montgomery shouldn't be so hard on himself. The Bears have finished 29th and 25th in adjusted line yards in his two professional seasons. He has overachieved to accumulate his modest production. Referencing a metric he can better control himself, Montgomery ranks sixth among the 30 running backs with 300 or more touches the last two seasons with a 22.0% broken tackle rate. That has him just between Pro Bowlers Alvin Kamara (22.2%) and Dalvin Cook (21.2%).

Alfred Morris Height: 5-10   Weight: 224   College: Florida Atlantic   Draft: 2012/6 (173)   Born: 12-Dec-1988   Age: 33   Risk: N/A

Year	Tm	G/GS	Snaps	Runs	Yds	TD	Yd/R	FUM	DVOA	Rk	DYAR	Rk	Suc%	Rk	BTkl	YafC	Pass	Rec	Yds	TD	C%	Yd/C	YAC	DVOA	Rk	DYAR	Rk
2018	SF	12/1	250	111	428	2	3.9	2	-30.5%	47	-103	45	41%	38	18	2.8	13	8	73	0	62%	9.1	8.4	-6.7%	--	6	--
2019	ARI	1/0	3	1	4	0	4.0	0	69.1%	--	5	--	100%	--	0	2.0	0	0	0	0	--	0.0	--	--	--	--	--
2020	NYG	9/0	111	55	238	1	4.3	0	19.4%	--	61	--	53%	--	4	2.5	4	3	19	1	75%	6.3	5.7	81.7%	--	21	--

If we ever get around to creating a "replacement value Hall of Fame," Morris will be a charter member. The former sixth-round pick and three-time 1,000-yard rusher for Washington was a free agent at press time, having played for four teams in the last four years. The Giants pulled him off the scrap heap during an injury crunch last season, and Morris provided several seven- to eight-carry, 28- to 39-yard stat lines as a passable committee back, plus two touchdowns in the upset over the Seahawks. Morris' nine-year career is a testament to the fact that a team can find a decent running back nearly anywhere, and that a decent running back can look like a sensation given the right opportunities at the start of his career.

Zack Moss Height: 5-9   Weight: 222   College: Utah   Draft: 2020/3 (86)   Born: 15-Dec-1997   Age: 24   Risk: Green

Year	Tm	G/GS	Snaps	Runs	Yds	TD	Yd/R	FUM	DVOA	Rk	DYAR	Rk	Suc%	Rk	BTkl	YafC	Pass	Rec	Yds	TD	C%	Yd/C	YAC	DVOA	Rk	DYAR	Rk
2020	BUF	13/0	403	112	481	4	4.3	0	-4.1%	32	23	32	53%	18	23	2.8	18	14	95	1	78%	6.8	6.2	13.4%	--	29	--
2021	BUF			134	548	5	4.1	1	-2.9%								27	20	144	1	74%	7.1		-7.6%			

Moss was the best Bills running back at actually rushing in 2020, which is a bit like being the best theremin player in The Strokes—a cool attribute to have, but not exactly one that comes up all the time considering how pass-heavy the Bills were last season. Fantasy players take note: while Devin Singletary had more touches last season, Moss had 29 carries to Singletary's 22 in the red zone. A -7.9% DVOA and a 38% success rate inside the 20 isn't great, but it's better than Singletary could manage. The Bills just hope their running game does a little bit better than that in tough situations this season.

Raheem Mostert

Height: 5-10   **Weight:** 197   **College:** Purdue   **Draft:** 2015/FA   **Born:** 9-Apr-1992   **Age:** 29   **Risk:** Red

Year	Tm	G/GS	Snaps	Runs	Yds	TD	Yd/R	FUM	DVOA	Rk	DYAR	Rk	Suc%	Rk	BTkl	YafC	Pass	Rec	Yds	TD	C%	Yd/C	YAC	DVOA	Rk	DYAR	Rk
2018	SF	9/0	89	34	261	1	7.7	1	19.4%	--	40	--	65%	--	5	3.9	7	6	25	0	86%	4.2	7.3	-32.1%	--	-6	--
2019	SF	16/0	370	137	772	8	5.6	1	26.8%	1	191	7	53%	9	30	2.9	22	14	180	2	64%	12.9	11.1	39.3%	--	62	--
2020	SF	8/8	237	104	521	2	5.0	1	4.0%	20	57	29	49%	30	13	2.5	19	16	156	1	84%	9.8	8.5	21.1%	--	35	--
2021	SF			159	794	5	5.0	1	10.1%								30	23	198	1	77%	8.5		7.7%			

Per NFL Next Gen Stats, Mostert reached speeds of 23.1 mph on his 80-yard touchdown run against the Jets in Week 2 and 22.7 mph on his 76-yard touchdown catch against Arizona in Week 1. That gave him both the gold and silver medals in the NFL's fastest ballcarrier 2020 Olympics. The bad news is that those two plays made up more than 20% of his yards from scrimmage all year as he was otherwise unreliable or injured, or both. By December, he was splitting carries nearly 50-50 with Jeff Wilson even before the ankle injury that ended his season in Week 15. It's not clear whether this was a re-aggravation of the ankle injury that caused him to miss most of November, but it was definitely not the MCL sprain that caused him to miss Weeks 3 and 4. Mostert goes into training camp atop San Francisco's running back depth chart, but he will need to stay healthy to keep an army of competitors at bay.

Welcome to Choose Your Own Adventure: 49ers Running Back Fantasy Draft! Mostert has been productive, but can't seem to stay healthy. Let's try someone else—turn to Jeff Wilson's comment on page 319.

Latavius Murray

Height: 6-3   **Weight:** 230   **College:** Central Florida   **Draft:** 2013/6 (181)   **Born:** 21-Feb-1991   **Age:** 30   **Risk:** Blue

Year	Tm	G/GS	Snaps	Runs	Yds	TD	Yd/R	FUM	DVOA	Rk	DYAR	Rk	Suc%	Rk	BTkl	YafC	Pass	Rec	Yds	TD	C%	Yd/C	YAC	DVOA	Rk	DYAR	Rk
2018	MIN	16/6	461	140	578	6	4.1	0	-4.2%	27	25	29	46%	31	18	2.7	26	22	141	0	85%	6.4	5.2	-7.5%	33	9	35
2019	NO	16/8	442	146	637	5	4.4	0	10.7%	9	125	13	60%	2	34	2.5	43	34	235	1	79%	6.9	8.4	-5.6%	31	19	32
2020	NO	15/7	364	146	656	4	4.5	1	12.3%	15	131	13	62%	3	17	2.3	26	23	176	1	88%	7.7	8.6	21.6%	10	48	19
2021	NO			80	338	2	4.2	1	-2.5%								23	16	138	1	70%	8.4		-5.4%			

The bruising complement to Alvin Kamara, Murray handled his usual 40% of rushing attempts with typical effectiveness, almost perfectly duplicating his 2019 figures on the ground while ceding pass targets to a healthier Kamara. Murray won't shock anybody with what he can do, but three straight seasons of 140 or so attempts, four-and-a-bit yards a pop, and a handful of touchdowns is exactly the sort of reliability that turns sixth-round picks into eight-year veterans. If the New Orleans offense isn't as good this year -- and it probably won't be -- fewer lasting drives will mean fewer carries for Murray.

Qadree Ollison

Height: 6-1   **Weight:** 228   **College:** Pittsburgh   **Draft:** 2019/5 (152)   **Born:** 8-Sep-1996   **Age:** 25   **Risk:** Green

Year	Tm	G/GS	Snaps	Runs	Yds	TD	Yd/R	FUM	DVOA	Rk	DYAR	Rk	Suc%	Rk	BTkl	YafC	Pass	Rec	Yds	TD	C%	Yd/C	YAC	DVOA	Rk	DYAR	Rk
2019	ATL	8/0	57	22	50	4	2.3	1	-11.1%	--	-3	--	55%	--	0	1.2	2	1	7	0	50%	7.0	3.0	35.3%	--	5	--
2020	ATL	3/0	13	1	3	0	3.0	0	11.6%	--	1	--	100%	--	0	2.0	0	0	0	0	--	0.0	--	--	--	--	--
2021	ATL			91	356	4	3.9	1	-6.7%								15	12	84	0	80%	7.0		-9.1%			

The Falcons didn't draft a running back this year, so Qadree Ollison gets a full player comment and the tag of "potential breakout player" almost by default. The 2019 fifth-round pick lacks short-area quickness or acceleration, has subpar field vision, and is awkward when shaking second-level tacklers. One thing Ollison *has* done well, at least in camp, is pass protect. That's a plus, as neither Mike Davis nor Cordarrelle Patterson particularly stand out there. He also would look to be in line for goal-line carries, making him a touchdown vulture candidate. His presence in these writeups says more about the Falcons' running backs than it does about Ollison.

Rashaad Penny

Height: 5-11 | Weight: 220 | College: San Diego State | Draft: 2018/1 (27) | Born: 2-Feb-1996 | Age: 25 | Risk: Yellow

Year	Tm	G/GS	Snaps	Runs	Yds	TD	Yd/R	FUM	DVOA	Rk	DYAR	Rk	Suc%	Rk	BTkl	YafC	Pass	Rec	Yds	TD	C%	Yd/C	YAC	DVOA	Rk	DYAR	Rk
2018	SEA	14/0	180	85	419	2	4.9	0	8.9%	--	56	--	40%	--	12	2.6	12	9	75	0	75%	8.3	8.1	8.3%	--	12	--
2019	SEA	10/0	152	65	370	3	5.7	1	32.4%	--	115	--	57%	--	8	2.6	11	8	83	1	73%	10.4	11.4	45.4%	--	37	--
2020	SEA	3/0	38	11	34	0	3.1	0	2.5%	--	5	--	55%	--	1	2.1	0	0	0	0	--	0.0	--	--	--	--	--
2021	SEA			126	578	4	4.6	1	4.3%								27	21	157	1	78%	7.5		2.8%			

The disappointing former first-round pick missed the majority of the 2020 season while recovering from a torn ACL sustained late in 2019, and the timing of that injury ensured that 2020 was going to be a dud for Penny as well. Chris Carson has been the clear starter here, and Seattle intends to keep it that way, as they re-signed the bruising Carson to a two-year deal in free agency. Penny has one last shot on his rookie contract to make an impact in 2021, but to this point in his career, he has only shown flashes of explosiveness in fits and starts.

La'Mical Perine

Height: 5-11 | Weight: 218 | College: Florida | Draft: 2020/4 (120) | Born: 30-Jan-1998 | Age: 23 | Risk: Red

Year	Tm	G/GS	Snaps	Runs	Yds	TD	Yd/R	FUM	DVOA	Rk	DYAR	Rk	Suc%	Rk	BTkl	YafC	Pass	Rec	Yds	TD	C%	Yd/C	YAC	DVOA	Rk	DYAR	Rk
2020	NYJ	10/0	200	64	232	2	3.6	0	-10.7%	--	-6	--	44%	--	6	2.0	15	11	63	0	73%	5.7	6.1	-22.8%	--	-8	--
2021	NYJ			64	251	2	3.9	0	-10.6%								15	11	87	0	73%	7.7		-2.1%			

Switching coaching staffs is often tough for players in a rotation, who might find the skill set they were drafted for no longer in vogue with the new administration. Shanahan-style running backs typically have high-level speed and cutting ability; Perine's more of a grinder, plowing forward without tons of burst. Had Perine performed well as a rookie, that might not have mattered, but 3.6 yards per carry isn't exactly a "rejigger your offensive plans to fit this guy" statistic. With the Jets bringing in Tevin Coleman and drafting Michael Carter, it's entirely possible Perine finds himself the odd man out.

Samaje Perine

Height: 5-11 | Weight: 240 | College: Oklahoma | Draft: 2017/4 (114) | Born: 16-Sep-1995 | Age: 26 | Risk: Green

Year	Tm	G/GS	Snaps	Runs	Yds	TD	Yd/R	FUM	DVOA	Rk	DYAR	Rk	Suc%	Rk	BTkl	YafC	Pass	Rec	Yds	TD	C%	Yd/C	YAC	DVOA	Rk	DYAR	Rk
2018	WAS	5/0	30	8	32	0	4.0	0	19.3%	--	9	--	63%	--	1	2.4	4	3	5	0	75%	1.7	3.0	-105.1%	--	-21	--
2019	2TM	7/0	11	5	16	0	3.2	0	-9.2%	--	0	--	40%	--	0	2.2	0	0	0	0	--	0.0	--	--	--	--	--
2020	CIN	16/1	207	63	301	3	4.8	0	4.4%	--	35	--	43%	--	12	2.9	12	11	66	0	92%	6.0	8.1	11.8%	--	17	--
2021	CIN			37	154	1	4.2	0	-3.9%								24	20	138	1	83%	6.8		5.4%			

Perine is a burly halfback/fullback tweener and special-teamer who saw his first regular playing time in three years last season when Joe Mixon got injured. He went 13-95-2 (with four catches for 41 yards) in Week 16 against a Texans defense that had little interest in being in the stadium that day. With Gio Bernard gone, Perine is Joe Mixon's top backup, even though he's not exactly the "change-up back" type. The Bengals don't make the same commitment to self-scouting and quality control that better run organizations do, and may have reached some false conclusions from that Texans win. That would explain why Perine and Brandon Allen were invited back in important backup roles.

Adrian Peterson

Height: 6-1 | Weight: 220 | College: Oklahoma | Draft: 2007/1 (7) | Born: 21-Mar-1985 | Age: 36 | Risk: N/A

Year	Tm	G/GS	Snaps	Runs	Yds	TD	Yd/R	FUM	DVOA	Rk	DYAR	Rk	Suc%	Rk	BTkl	YafC	Pass	Rec	Yds	TD	C%	Yd/C	YAC	DVOA	Rk	DYAR	Rk
2018	WAS	16/16	481	251	1042	7	4.2	3	-6.0%	29	26	28	47%	28	56	3.0	26	20	208	1	77%	10.4	10.1	22.3%	5	50	21
2019	WAS	15/15	407	211	898	5	4.3	3	-4.1%	27	39	24	47%	27	45	2.5	23	17	142	0	74%	8.4	9.5	-14.9%	--	-1	--
2020	DET	16/10	316	156	604	7	3.9	0	0.9%	24	64	25	46%	40	18	2.4	18	12	101	0	67%	8.4	8.6	9.0%	--	22	--

With even another modest season of production like he had for the Lions in 2020, Peterson would pass Barry Sanders for the fourth-most rushing yards in NFL history, and he's already fourth all-time in rushing touchdowns. That kind of resume paired with an above-average rushing DVOA in 2020 would have landed the veteran at least another committee job -- if it were still 2007, back when Peterson was drafted. To the 36-year-old's credit, Peterson has played his way into a new era of football that prefers versatility at the position and often leans on inexpensive Day 3 prospects over established veterans with even modest contract demands of $1 million or $2 million.

Tony Pollard Height: 6-0 Weight: 210 College: Memphis Draft: 2019/4 (128) Born: 30-Apr-1997 Age: 24 Risk: Blue

Year	Tm	G/GS	Snaps	Runs	Yds	TD	Yd/R	FUM	DVOA	Rk	DYAR	Rk	Suc%	Rk	BTkl	YafC	Pass	Rec	Yds	TD	C%	Yd/C	YAC	DVOA	Rk	DYAR	Rk
2019	DAL	15/0	204	86	455	2	5.3	1	11.6%	--	71	--	52%	--	26	4.0	20	15	107	1	75%	7.1	9.0	-2.7%	--	12	--
2020	DAL	16/2	363	101	435	4	4.3	0	13.0%	13	91	18	47%	37	27	3.0	40	28	193	1	70%	6.9	8.3	-8.3%	35	12	35
2021	DAL			98	424	3	4.3	1	4.1%								30	23	162	1	77%	7.1		-9.8%			

"Backup running back is almost indistinguishable from the overpaid starter" is practically a literary subgenre here at Football Outsiders. So you know what's coming. Pollard went 12-69-2 rushing and 6-63 receiving as a starter in place of Ezekiel Elliott in Week 15 against the 49ers. He did not fumble at all on offense last season, though he dropped a few catchable passes, and nothing in his splits or on film suggests any deficiencies as a short-yardage runner or third-down back. To be diplomatic, the Cowboys are set with a solid committee backfield, and they should experience little drop-off if Pollard takes over as the featured back for any reason.

Jalen Richard Height: 5-8 Weight: 207 College: Southern Mississippi Draft: 2016/FA Born: 15-Oct-1993 Age: 28 Risk: Green

Year	Tm	G/GS	Snaps	Runs	Yds	TD	Yd/R	FUM	DVOA	Rk	DYAR	Rk	Suc%	Rk	BTkl	YafC	Pass	Rec	Yds	TD	C%	Yd/C	YAC	DVOA	Rk	DYAR	Rk
2018	OAK	16/1	413	55	259	1	4.7	2	-20.3%	--	-28	--	45%	--	27	3.2	81	68	607	0	84%	8.9	7.3	17.4%	9	138	6
2019	OAK	16/0	305	39	145	0	3.7	1	-3.6%	--	8	--	46%	--	7	1.1	43	36	323	0	84%	9.0	6.6	2.7%	22	39	21
2020	LV	13/0	190	22	123	1	5.6	1	46.8%	--	46	--	50%	--	6	3.4	23	19	138	0	83%	7.3	5.1	1.5%	--	19	--
2021	LV			12	54	0	4.5	0	0.7%								6	4	32	0	67%	7.5		-0.7%			

Richard once appeared to be a blooming pass-catching specialist after hitting career-highs in his first year with Jon Gruden as the head coach. In 2018, Richard saw 81 targets, third on the team behind Jared Cook and Jordy Nelson (what an odd collection that 2018 squad was). Alas, the team drafted Josh Jacobs in the first-round in 2019, and Richard's carries and targets have fallen in each of the past two seasons as a result. Moreover, the Raiders signed Kenyan Drake this offseason, who has a lot of overlap with Richard's explosive yet inefficient rushing style. Richard's eye-popping 5.6 yards per carry last season is heavily influenced by a handful of explosive runs he ripped off in third-and-long situations, but he averaged fewer than 3.5 yards with a sub-45% success rate on both first and second down. Richard may still slot in as a backup receiving back, but do not expect his role to expand in any way in 2021.

James Robinson Height: 5-10 Weight: 220 College: Illinois State Draft: 2020/FA Born: 9-Aug-1998 Age: 23 Risk: Yellow

Year	Tm	G/GS	Snaps	Runs	Yds	TD	Yd/R	FUM	DVOA	Rk	DYAR	Rk	Suc%	Rk	BTkl	YafC	Pass	Rec	Yds	TD	C%	Yd/C	YAC	DVOA	Rk	DYAR	Rk
2020	JAX	14/14	641	240	1070	7	4.5	2	-0.8%	26	76	22	49%	28	55	2.8	60	49	344	3	82%	7.0	7.8	1.2%	25	50	18
2021	JAX			168	714	4	4.3	1	-3.6%								33	26	185	1	79%	7.0		0.6%			

Being an undrafted free-agent success story is a land of contrasts. The Jaguars celebrated what Robinson meant to the team, then drafted Travis Etienne in the first round and brought in Carlos Hyde to spell him. "When they brought those guys in … I've got to go out there and control what I can control, and once I get the opportunity, make the most of it." Robinson said at OTAs. He certainly did that last year, showing a full skill set of tools as a runner and a receiver. He's not quite an A-plus tackle-breaker; Robinson just manipulates you in very subtle ways with his foot movement to create space and uses that to work with. Urban Meyer called Robinson an "integral" player in a March presser, noting that the Jaguars wanted to build the running back room around him. There's probably plenty of space for him to get 160 carries this year if everything breaks right, but with Etienne hanging on his heels, well, undrafted backs have no choice but to keep proving it. As Phillip Lindsay taught us, they aren't afforded a lot of leeway for a bad season.

Miles Sanders Height: 5-11 Weight: 211 College: Penn State Draft: 2019/2 (53) Born: 1-May-1997 Age: 24 Risk: Green

Year	Tm	G/GS	Snaps	Runs	Yds	TD	Yd/R	FUM	DVOA	Rk	DYAR	Rk	Suc%	Rk	BTkl	YafC	Pass	Rec	Yds	TD	C%	Yd/C	YAC	DVOA	Rk	DYAR	Rk
2019	PHI	16/11	626	179	818	3	4.6	2	-6.6%	30	14	30	45%	34	36	2.8	63	50	509	3	79%	10.2	8.3	20.0%	12	121	7
2020	PHI	12/11	602	164	867	6	5.3	4	7.0%	19	110	15	55%	13	32	2.8	52	28	197	0	54%	7.0	7.5	-33.5%	46	-59	46
2021	PHI			208	994	8	4.8	3	4.6%								39	26	207	1	67%	7.9		-15.2%			

Given the rest of the Philadelphia offense last season, Sanders pulling out positive DVOA is something of a miracle. Sanders consistently got what was given to him, and his 55% success rate was impressive considering the state of the Eagles' offensive line. Only six of his carries gained over 10 yards, but his explosive gains were really explosive. Sanders had runs of 82, 74, and 74 yards, three of the 10 longest runs in the NFL during 2020. None of those explosive plays came on first down, when Sanders put up a -14.4% DVOA and just 3.8 yards per carry. Sanders could see a bigger workload in 2021 as the lead back, should the Eagles have more favorable game scripts. He received 20 and 18 carries in each of his first two games in 2020, then hit 15 carries just four more times during the season.

Boston Scott   Height: 5-6   Weight: 203   College: Louisiana Tech   Draft: 2018/6 (201)   Born: 27-Apr-1995   Age: 26   Risk: Green

Year	Tm	G/GS	Snaps	Runs	Yds	TD	Yd/R	FUM	DVOA	Rk	DYAR	Rk	Suc%	Rk	BTkl	YafC	Pass	Rec	Yds	TD	C%	Yd/C	YAC	DVOA	Rk	DYAR	Rk
2019	PHI	11/2	187	61	245	5	4.0	2	22.2%	--	85	--	52%	--	17	1.9	26	24	204	0	92%	8.5	11.4	29.0%	7	67	17
2020	PHI	16/4	383	80	374	1	4.7	1	1.4%	--	32	--	49%	--	14	2.7	36	25	212	1	69%	8.5	7.2	8.1%	19	40	23
2021	PHI			52	228	2	4.4	1	-1.8%								12	9	70	0	75%	8.0		-1.5%			

Scott took over as the Eagles' No. 2 back in 2020. Given the Eagles' overall lack of running back carries and Miles Sanders' ability to hang on to an every-down role, Scott's four starts were his only games with more than five carries. Scott had nearly identical yards after contact and first-down rates to Sanders, but a lack of scoring and negative DVOA in the red zone kept him from similar overall efficiency. Scott now faces more competition in the backfield, mainly from fifth-round rookie Kenneth Gainwell. He does have the advantage of being useful on kick returns, though that role could also be up for grabs—Scott had one of the lowest values on returns in the league last season.

Trey Sermon   Height: 6-1   Weight: 215   College: Ohio State   Draft: 2021/3 (88)   Born: 30-Jan-1999   Age: 22   Risk: Green

Year	Tm	G/GS	Snaps	Runs	Yds	TD	Yd/R	FUM	DVOA	Rk	DYAR	Rk	Suc%	Rk	BTkl	YafC	Pass	Rec	Yds	TD	C%	Yd/C	YAC	DVOA	Rk	DYAR	Rk
2021	SF			116	500	4	4.3	1	-1.9%								16	12	96	1	75%	7.8		-0.7%			

The 49ers took one look at Sermon's postseason run with the Buckeyes—331 rushing yards against Northwestern in the Big Ten Championship Game, 193 more against Clemson in the Sugar Bowl, one carry and a broken collarbone against Alabama in the National Championship Game—and knew he had the right mix of talent and brittleness to fit in with the rest of their roster. Our BackCAST projections looked at Sermon's track record as a committee player at both Oklahoma and Ohio State and came away unimpressed. Sermon lost his starting job with the Sooners to Kennedy Brooks and transferred to Ohio State, where he got fewer carries per game than Master Teague. Add in a slower-than-average 4.61s 40 and Sermon ended up 16th in BackCAST out of 23 running back prospects invited to the combine this year. Sermon has the size to be an effective blocker and scouts liked what they saw in the rare occasions when he was used as a receiver, so he should at the very least bring three-down versatility to the NFL, even if he never approaches the kind of numbers he posted against the Wildcats and Tigers.

Welcome to Choose Your Own Adventure: 49ers Running Back Fantasy Draft! *If you would like to draft Sermon, turn to Elijah Mitchell's comment on page 322. If your league awards six points per reception, turn to Kyle Juszczyk's comment on page 306. If you would like to draft JaMycal Hasty for some reason, turn to his comment on page 302.*

Devin Singletary   Height: 5-7   Weight: 203   College: Florida Atlantic   Draft: 2019/3 (74)   Born: 3-Sep-1997   Age: 24   Risk: Green

Year	Tm	G/GS	Snaps	Runs	Yds	TD	Yd/R	FUM	DVOA	Rk	DYAR	Rk	Suc%	Rk	BTkl	YafC	Pass	Rec	Yds	TD	C%	Yd/C	YAC	DVOA	Rk	DYAR	Rk
2019	BUF	12/8	540	151	775	2	5.1	4	3.7%	13	75	20	50%	21	42	2.4	41	29	194	2	71%	6.7	6.7	-35.2%	47	-47	48
2020	BUF	16/16	621	156	687	2	4.4	1	-11.5%	37	-20	38	49%	31	45	2.9	50	38	269	0	76%	7.1	7.1	-2.2%	29	32	27
2021	BUF			138	596	4	4.3	1	-2.1%								43	32	233	1	74%	7.3		-7.8%			

Brandon Beane said neither of his running backs were "home-run hitters" in a pre-draft Zoom meeting, and that's not entirely without merit; only three of Singletary's 156 rushes gained 20 or more yards in 2020. But it wasn't like Singletary never had any solid gains—in fact, 48.2% of his rushing yards came 5 or more yards downfield, once he had gotten past what the blockers had blocked for him. That was 14th among qualified rushers. Singletary's issue has been finding holes, or creating his own when his line can't get a push, not what he can do when he gets into some open space.

Ito Smith Height: 5-9 Weight: 195 College: Southern Mississippi Draft: 2018/4 (126) Born: 11-Sep-1995 Age: 26 Risk: N/A

Year	Tm	G/GS	Snaps	Runs	Yds	TD	Yd/R	FUM	DVOA	Rk	DYAR	Rk	Suc%	Rk	BTkl	YafC	Pass	Rec	Yds	TD	C%	Yd/C	YAC	DVOA	Rk	DYAR	Rk
2018	ATL	14/0	311	90	315	4	3.5	1	-13.4%	--	-19	--	48%	--	20	2.4	32	27	152	0	84%	5.6	5.9	-17.7%	45	-8	44
2019	ATL	7/0	153	22	106	1	4.8	0	13.7%	--	27	--	55%	--	9	2.3	14	11	87	0	79%	7.9	6.5	-14.7%	--	-1	--
2020	ATL	14/0	225	63	268	1	4.3	1	0.0%	--	21	--	60%	--	10	1.6	26	17	75	0	65%	4.4	4.8	-62.1%	50	-77	48

As of press time, Smith remains unsigned—and when you're cut from the Falcons backfield, while still on your rookie contract, that's not a great sign for your continued future in the league. Smith wasn't terrible as a runner; perfectly average by our numbers, in fact. The problem was that he finished dead last in receiving DVOA and has never been above replacement level there; a 65% catch rate when your average target comes behind the line of scrimmage is woeful beyond belief. Smith may pick up a spot as a third back somewhere during camp as injuries pile up, but likely will not be a factor in 2021.

Rodney Smith Height: 5-11 Weight: 210 College: Minnesota Draft: 2020/FA Born: 28-Feb-1996 Age: 25 Risk: Green

Year	Tm	G/GS	Snaps	Runs	Yds	TD	Yd/R	FUM	DVOA	Rk	DYAR	Rk	Suc%	Rk	BTkl	YafC	Pass	Rec	Yds	TD	C%	Yd/C	YAC	DVOA	Rk	DYAR	Rk
2020	CAR	7/1	133	41	156	1	3.8	1	-0.8%	--	16	--	61%	--	8	1.9	11	9	59	0	82%	6.6	5.1	-8.0%	--	3	--
2021	CAR			12	50	0	4.0	0	-7.2%								3	2	15	0	67%	7.0		-3.7%			

Undrafted former Minnesota Golden Gophers halfback Rodney Smith played an unexpectedly large role for the Panthers as a rookie, earning 40 carries and a Week 17 start in relief of Mike Davis following the injury to Christian McCaffrey. With Davis now in Atlanta, Smith begins the summer as the hypothetical top backup. However, he faces a challenge to hold onto that role ahead of talented fourth-round rookie Chuba Hubbard. Even if he does cling on, his value appears entirely dependent on garbage time or a McCaffrey injury, as Matt Rhule has shown no sign of changing the policy that the Panthers basically never take a healthy McCaffrey off the field.

Benny Snell Height: 5-10 Weight: 224 College: Kentucky Draft: 2019/4 (122) Born: 27-Feb-1998 Age: 23 Risk: Green

Year	Tm	G/GS	Snaps	Runs	Yds	TD	Yd/R	FUM	DVOA	Rk	DYAR	Rk	Suc%	Rk	BTkl	YafC	Pass	Rec	Yds	TD	C%	Yd/C	YAC	DVOA	Rk	DYAR	Rk
2019	PIT	13/2	171	108	426	2	3.9	1	-11.7%	39	-14	38	49%	24	17	2.9	4	3	23	0	75%	7.7	7.3	-13.2%	--	0	--
2020	PIT	16/3	281	111	368	4	3.3	2	-26.3%	46	-96	46	44%	43	18	2.1	14	10	61	0	71%	6.1	8.8	-26.5%	--	-11	--
2021	PIT			51	200	3	3.9	1	-5.6%								13	11	66	0	85%	5.9		-9.8%			

The great-nephew of former Jets back and Super Bowl III hero Matt Snell hasn't done much in his first two seasons to make anyone compare him to his kin. The Steelers gave him plenty of chances—Snell had 15 carries inside the 5-yard line, and he repaid the team by scoring on just four of them, the third-worst percentage among qualifying runners (after Zeke Elliott and Clyde Edwards-Helaire). His first-down success rate was a horrific 30%. Matt Snell's career ended with knee injuries and bitterness towards the Jets. Benny's trajectory seems headed for similar disappointment, especially after the drafting of Najee Harris.

D'Andre Swift Height: 5-9 Weight: 215 College: Georgia Draft: 2020/2 (35) Born: 14-Jan-1999 Age: 22 Risk: Green

Year	Tm	G/GS	Snaps	Runs	Yds	TD	Yd/R	FUM	DVOA	Rk	DYAR	Rk	Suc%	Rk	BTkl	YafC	Pass	Rec	Yds	TD	C%	Yd/C	YAC	DVOA	Rk	DYAR	Rk
2020	DET	13/4	398	114	521	8	4.6	3	13.0%	14	106	16	54%	16	26	2.1	57	46	357	2	81%	7.8	7.6	17.1%	13	94	9
2021	DET			220	959	9	4.4	3	3.1%								66	48	363	2	73%	7.6		-8.4%			

Swift spent his three-year Georgia career in time-shares with Elijah Holyfield and Brian Herrien, and so despite the exceptional athletic traits that made him a second-round draft selection, he may have sparked some apprehension of an NFL learning curve. Those concerns lasted all of seven games. In that first half of the Lions season, Swift contributed excellent 16.2% and 16.3% rushing and receiving DVOAs. He subsequently saw an increase in his workload from 9.1 touches per game to 16.0 per game from Week 9 on, and he maintained comparable rushing and receiving efficiencies. Swift is relatively small at 5-foot-9 and 215 pounds, and so he will likely never rival Derrick Henry's workload. The Lions added Jamaal Williams in free agency and will lean on him in pass protection, but Swift could follow in Alvin Kamara's footsteps, especially as part of a Lions roster that lacks a traditional No. 1 wide receiver.

Jonathan Taylor

Height: 5-10　　Weight: 226　　College: Wisconsin　　Draft: 2020/2 (41)　　Born: 19-Jan-1999　　Age: 22　　Risk: Green

Year	Tm	G/GS	Snaps	Runs	Yds	TD	Yd/R	FUM	DVOA	Rk	DYAR	Rk	Suc%	Rk	BTkl	YafC	Pass	Rec	Yds	TD	C%	Yd/C	YAC	DVOA	Rk	DYAR	Rk
2020	IND	15/13	511	232	1169	11	5.0	1	3.8%	21	127	14	52%	22	38	2.6	39	36	299	1	92%	8.3	10.1	22.2%	8	76	11
2021	IND			270	1257	11	4.7	2	7.5%								46	34	259	1	74%	7.6		-6.0%			

How was that first year for the best player in the history of our BackCAST projection system? The criticisms of Taylor coming out were his fumble rate and his lack of demonstrated pass-catching prowess. He fumbled one time in 2020 and caught 36 of 39 balls with a high DVOA. Oh, and he did this despite having to learn at an accelerated pace, on the fly, after Marlon Mack's injury. "Now it's from a perspective of I kind of know the basics … now it's just how can I make the job a little bit easier … anticipate that pre-snap read, understanding it ... it's fun seeing the growth," Taylor said at OTAs.

The year is going to be very simple for Taylor: Is he going to be so good that Frank Reich can't leave him off the field, or is Marlon Mack going to be a true threat to his touches? One makes him a fantasy football league-winner and starts to set him up as the next great back in the NFL, and the other puts him about where he was last season. Either way, he is obviously one of the most promising young backs in the NFL and someone who runs in a way that manages to be angry and introspective at the same time.

James White

Height: 5-10　　Weight: 205　　College: Wisconsin　　Draft: 2014/4 (130)　　Born: 3-Feb-1992　　Age: 29　　Risk: Green

Year	Tm	G/GS	Snaps	Runs	Yds	TD	Yd/R	FUM	DVOA	Rk	DYAR	Rk	Suc%	Rk	BTkl	YafC	Pass	Rec	Yds	TD	C%	Yd/C	YAC	DVOA	Rk	DYAR	Rk
2018	NE	16/3	600	94	425	5	4.5	0	1.6%	--	42	--	47%	--	14	1.5	123	87	751	7	71%	8.6	7.6	13.5%	13	194	3
2019	NE	15/1	493	67	263	1	3.9	0	-9.0%	--	-1	--	42%	--	20	2.1	95	72	645	5	76%	9.0	7.4	14.8%	14	142	5
2020	NE	14/0	330	35	121	2	3.5	1	-26.4%	--	-27	--	37%	--	10	2.1	62	49	375	1	79%	7.7	8.4	6.0%	20	66	14
2021	NE			50	198	2	4.0	1	-6.7%								64	47	373	2	73%	7.9		-0.3%			

Calling James White a "running" back continues to be one of the NFL's best ongoing jokes. For the sixth season in a row, White failed to qualify for our rushing leaderboard (he has never hit the 100 carries needed to be ranked) but *did* qualify for our running back receiving tables. He's the only running back in the DVOA era to have over 1,000 rushing yards while still having more receptions than carries. Since the post-Brady era saw New England throw far fewer checkdowns and handoff far more often, White's usage plummeted in 2020. Perhaps Mac Jones will be more interested in checking down than Cam Newton was.

Jordan Wilkins

Height: 6-1　　Weight: 217　　College: Mississippi　　Draft: 2018/5 (169)　　Born: 18-Jul-1994　　Age: 27　　Risk: Green

Year	Tm	G/GS	Snaps	Runs	Yds	TD	Yd/R	FUM	DVOA	Rk	DYAR	Rk	Suc%	Rk	BTkl	YafC	Pass	Rec	Yds	TD	C%	Yd/C	YAC	DVOA	Rk	DYAR	Rk
2018	IND	16/3	198	60	336	1	5.6	2	15.0%	--	61	--	58%	--	9	2.4	17	16	85	0	94%	5.3	6.6	-47.8%	--	-34	--
2019	IND	14/1	178	51	307	2	6.0	0	20.9%	--	64	--	57%	--	13	3.2	11	7	43	0	64%	6.1	4.6	-31.5%	--	-9	--
2020	IND	15/0	183	84	308	1	3.7	0	-18.0%	--	-34	--	45%	--	13	2.9	16	12	105	0	75%	8.8	11.9	-21.1%	--	-6	--
2021	IND			9	38	0	4.1	0	-5.5%								4	3	23	0	75%	7.5		-3.1%			

Slippery and with good size, Wilkins was supposed to get a year as the change-up back behind Jonathan Taylor this year, but Marlon Mack's re-signing has thrown that into a state of flux. Through three seasons, outside of staying healthy, there's not a whole lot more that Wilkins can do empirically to get playing time. The raw numbers tell the story well here. He's a solid back who could handle more of a workload as the run-first part of the committee, but he was born into the wrong NFL for that to matter. The Colts have enough backfield talent that he'll have a hard time making a case for himself. He'll make an interesting free agent if he gets through this year with another healthy, clean season.

Damien Williams

Height: 5-11　　Weight: 224　　College: Oklahoma　　Draft: 2014/FA　　Born: 3-Apr-1992　　Age: 29　　Risk: Blue

Year	Tm	G/GS	Snaps	Runs	Yds	TD	Yd/R	FUM	DVOA	Rk	DYAR	Rk	Suc%	Rk	BTkl	YafC	Pass	Rec	Yds	TD	C%	Yd/C	YAC	DVOA	Rk	DYAR	Rk
2018	KC	16/3	207	50	256	4	5.1	1	26.4%	--	79	--	62%	--	9	2.2	24	23	160	2	96%	7.0	9.3	33.9%	--	74	--
2019	KC	11/6	368	111	498	5	4.5	1	-6.8%	31	8	31	50%	18	40	3.2	37	30	213	2	81%	7.1	7.7	-3.7%	28	24	28
2021	CHI			45	192	2	4.3	0	-0.9%								13	10	76	1	77%	7.4		2.0%			

Williams is the player whose NFL career was hurt most by a decision to opt out of the 2020 season over COVID concerns. After five years as a backup, he won the 2019 Chiefs starting job at 27 over prominent veteran LeSean McCoy, leading all backs with a 28.4% broken tackle rate (minimum 100 touches). He starred with 133 yards, 11 first downs, and two touchdowns in the team's Super Bowl win. Now a year removed from that performance and entering 2021 at 29 years old at a position that rarely ages gracefully, Williams settled for a one-year, $1.3-million contract with the Bears to compete with Tarik Cohen and rookie Khalil Herbert to back up starter David Montgomery.

Darrel Williams Height: 5-11 Weight: 229 College: Louisiana State Draft: 2018/FA Born: 15-Apr-1995 Age: 26 Risk: Green

Year	Tm	G/GS	Snaps	Runs	Yds	TD	Yd/R	FUM	DVOA	Rk	DYAR	Rk	Suc%	Rk	BTkl	YafC	Pass	Rec	Yds	TD	C%	Yd/C	YAC	DVOA	Rk	DYAR	Rk
2019	KC	12/0	199	41	141	3	3.4	1	-15.7%	--	-15	--	56%	--	7	1.3	19	15	167	1	79%	11.1	11.9	38.9%	--	57	--
2020	KC	16/0	280	39	169	1	4.3	0	2.7%	--	22	--	59%	--	3	1.7	26	18	116	0	69%	6.4	8.7	-8.4%	36	8	37
2021	KC			85	370	3	4.3	1	0.7%								25	17	121	0	67%	7.3		-18.6%			

After being ahead of Clyde Edwards-Helaire on the LSU depth chart a few years ago, Williams is now behind him on the Chiefs depth chart. It does not feel like the Chiefs are particularly sold on him though. Williams handled the No. 2 spot to start last season, but the team then signed Le'Veon Bell in October, pushing Williams down the depth chart until Edwards-Helaire suffered a late-season injury. Williams' value is as a competent pass-catcher, but his average depth of target was in the negatives last year, so it's not as though he is anything but a screen-and-checkdown guy. Pass-blocking is not Williams' strength, either, which negates any talk of him being a true third-down back. Regardless of Williams' incomplete skill set and the Chiefs balking on him before, it looks like 2021 will be his chance to prove he's a legitimate No. 2.

Jamaal Williams Height: 6-0 Weight: 213 College: BYU Draft: 2017/4 (134) Born: 3-Apr-1995 Age: 26 Risk: Blue

Year	Tm	G/GS	Snaps	Runs	Yds	TD	Yd/R	FUM	DVOA	Rk	DYAR	Rk	Suc%	Rk	BTkl	YafC	Pass	Rec	Yds	TD	C%	Yd/C	YAC	DVOA	Rk	DYAR	Rk
2018	GB	16/8	523	121	464	3	3.8	0	1.7%	22	52	25	45%	32	21	2.2	41	27	210	0	66%	7.8	8.5	-9.3%	34	11	33
2019	GB	14/2	385	107	460	1	4.3	0	-1.5%	21	31	26	53%	7	25	2.5	45	39	253	5	87%	6.5	7.2	27.4%	8	103	9
2020	GB	14/3	419	119	505	2	4.2	0	2.8%	22	60	26	58%	6	18	2.6	35	31	236	1	89%	7.6	7.1	14.0%	16	58	15
2021	DET			98	403	4	4.1	0	-2.0%								25	18	137	1	72%	7.6		-10.4%			

It likely frustrated some Packers fans and fantasy football players that Williams saw as much work as he did despite trailing his teammate and 2017 draft class member Aaron Jones by at least 10.0% rushing DVOA in each of their four seasons. Williams, though, routinely bested his more elusive teammate in one critical aspect of the position: pass protection. Keep that in mind before you spend a first-round fantasy pick on his new Lions teammate D'Andre Swift. Williams will likely spell his more heralded teammate more than you would expect for a player on a two-year, $6-million contract. Perhaps a bit too concerned with toughness, Lions head coach Dan Campbell will undoubtedly love him.

Javonte Williams Height: 5-10 Weight: 220 College: North Carolina Draft: 2021/2 (35) Born: 25-Apr-2000 Age: 21 Risk: Green

Year	Tm	G/GS	Snaps	Runs	Yds	TD	Yd/R	FUM	DVOA	Rk	DYAR	Rk	Suc%	Rk	BTkl	YafC	Pass	Rec	Yds	TD	C%	Yd/C	YAC	DVOA	Rk	DYAR	Rk
2021	DEN			120	521	4	4.3	1	-2.3%								24	18	118	1	75%	6.5		-11.7%			

Williams is another attempt by the Broncos to find a true lead back, which is funny given that Williams split time in the North Carolina backfield with Michael Carter (since drafted by the Jets). Williams rocks a sturdy 5-foot-10 and 220-pound build and runs with all the power one might expect from that kind of body. He may not bully people the same way Derrick Henry does, but Williams' low, balanced rushing style with that much weight behind him makes it easy to bounce off of tacklers, especially since his adequate burst and change of direction make it trickier to get a clean tackle attempt on him than it would appear. Williams's 4.57s 40-yard dash was nothing special, but he did show enough speed on film to break away from time to time, even if that will never be his true calling card.

What may really bring Williams to the forefront of Denver's rotation is his three-down ability. Not only is Williams a sturdy and willing pass-protector, but he's got the chops to be an above-average pass-catcher. He falls well short of the Alvin Kamara and Christian McCaffrey tier, but Williams snagged 42 passes over his final two years at North Carolina. The Broncos will likely split their backfield to some degree with Melvin Gordon, but Gordon will be gone after this season, giving way to Williams eventually becoming the full-time guy.

Jeffery Wilson Height: 6-0 Weight: 194 College: North Texas Draft: 2018/FA Born: 16-Nov-1995 Age: 26 Risk: Red

Year	Tm	G/GS	Snaps	Runs	Yds	TD	Yd/R	FUM	DVOA	Rk	DYAR	Rk	Suc%	Rk	BTkl	YafC	Pass	Rec	Yds	TD	C%	Yd/C	YAC	DVOA	Rk	DYAR	Rk
2018	SF	6/2	197	66	266	0	4.0	3	-9.4%	--	-2	--	52%	--	9	2.2	15	12	98	0	80%	8.2	8.1	4.9%	--	17	--
2019	SF	10/0	60	27	105	4	3.9	0	20.3%	--	39	--	52%	--	2	2.8	5	3	34	1	60%	11.3	7.0	8.9%	--	7	--
2020	SF	12/3	311	126	600	7	4.8	2	7.3%	18	86	21	53%	17	18	3.0	28	13	133	3	46%	10.2	8.5	8.9%	17	32	26
2021	SF			12	56	1	4.5	0	2.6%								2	2	15	0	100%	8.3		0.1%			

A slippery runner, Wilson has a knack for approaching a crowded line of scrimmage and suddenly popping out the other side with no obvious explanation of how he got from Point A to Point B. His total numbers in three starts last year: 59 carries for 371 yards (a 6.3-yard average) and four touchdowns, plus six catches for 41 yards and two more scores. That looks like RB1 potential, but Wilson may never get a full season to prove what he can do. He missed time last year with calf and knee issues, then tore his meniscus in the 49ers' locker room in May. He will begin the season on the reserve/PUP list, which means he will miss at least the first six games of the year. Given San Francisco's crowded backfield, he may not play much after that either.

Welcome to Choose Your Own Adventure: 49ers Running Back Fantasy Draft! Wilson has been productive, but can't seem to stay healthy. Let's try someone else—turn to Raheem Mostert's comment on page 312.

Going Deep

Ameer Abdullah, MIN: The former Detroit second-round pick never worked out as a starter, but he has extended his NFL career to seven seasons now thanks to his contributions on special teams. He has returned kickoffs for the Vikings for the past three seasons, but that role is in jeopardy after the team drafted top college returners Kene Nwangwu and Ihmir Smith-Marsette in the fourth and fifth rounds. And since his average yards per return has declined from 26.1 yards in 2018 to 25.0 yards in 2019 to 23.5 yards in 2020, Abdullah's days in the NFL may be numbered.

Josh Adams, NYJ: Adams led all Jets running backs with 37 rushing DYAR, which says less about Adams and more about the woeful Jets offense. It did earn him his first day with double-digit carries since his rookie year—11 rushes for 47 yards and -3 DYAR against the Patriots in Week 17. New York's top running back spot is wide open for the taking, but it's hard to see Adams being more than a special teams and depth player at this point.

Reggie Bonnafon, CAR: The last man standing from the clutch of young backs the Panthers picked up in 2019, Bonnafon played just two games last year despite Christian McCaffrey's extended injury absence. He did score his first career receiving touchdown, but that was one of only two targets to go with his 12 carries. Bonnafon remains efficient when called on—he has positive rushing and receiving DVOA in both seasons—but his usage dropped sharply in his second year.

Gary Brightwell, NYG: A sixth-round pick by the Giants, Brightwell produced 100-yard games against USC and Colorado last season in Arizona's wide-open offense during a truncated Pac-12 schedule. He's a burly rusher with nifty open-field jump cuts. He caught 19 passes in five games, but his role as a receiver mostly involved flair and bench routes. Brightwell has NFL traits but is likely to max out as the No. 3 back in a committee, or (if Saquon Barkley stays healthy) as a special-teamer.

Trenton Cannon, CAR: One 98-yard return that somehow did not result in a touchdown was enough for Cannon to lead the Panthers in kickoff return average last year, but his 10 returns were barely a third of the team's total. He had the exact same number of carries on offense in a season that saw lead back Christian McCaffrey miss 13 games. As a second-choice kick returner and possible fourth-string running back, in an offense that seldom takes its main back off the field, Cannon's path to playing time is a long one.

Corey Clement, NYG: Clement was a Philly local hero who caught the second-most famous and important Super Bowl touchdown in franchise history, then spent most of the next three seasons battling injuries. He went 21-75-1 with 2.7% DVOA last season and could stick as the Giants' third-down back if rookie Gary Brightwell cannot claim a roster spot.

Alex Collins, SEA: Originally drafted by the Seahawks in 2016, Collins had been out of the league for all of 2019 before re-signing with Seattle amidst a midseason slew of running back injuries. He got his first start for the Seahawks against the Rams in Week 9, but he was only used sparingly (18-77-2, 56.5% DVOA) and spent a lot of time on the expanded practice squad. Collins will be competing for a roster spot this offseason, but that's a better position than where he was entering 2020.

Gerrid Doaks, MIA: A seventh-round pick out of Cincinnati, Doaks is a strong finisher with good forward lean and the ability to bounce off defenders. His issue is that he's not a particularly good starter—poor vision, slow cuts, little elusiveness with fumbling issues, and no real history of production. He did manage a 4.5s 40 at his pro day, impressive for a 230-pounder.

Tyler Ervin, FA: Ostensibly a running back, Ervin had 13 carries and 15 targets in 2020, doubling the totals of his first four NFL seasons. The bulk of that workload came in Week 9 in San Francisco, when Jamaal Williams was out and Aaron Jones' was gimpy with an injured calf. Ervin did well with a 32.6% rushing and 17.0% receiving DVOA, but he remains a free agent because he has declined in his primary role as a returner, suffering a three-year decline on both kickoff returns (from 25.3 to 24.3 to 19.6 yards per return) and on punt returns (from 8.3 to 7.2 to 4.0).

Chris Evans, CIN: Evans rushed for over 600 yards in his freshman and sophomore seasons at Michigan. His junior year was less impressive, and he was suspended by the university for an undisclosed academic infraction in 2019. He returned as a fifth-year player in 2020 but rushed for just 73 yards as a little-used backup. The Bengals, who are so wildly successful and deep across their roster that they can futz around with square peg prospects who have not played well in three years, drafted Evans in the sixth round, because of course they did.

Darrynton Evans, TEN: On IR for a majority of his rookie season with a hamstring strain, Evans is headed to training camp to compete with Brian Hill for the No. 2 spot on the depth chart. Eight of Evans' 14 carries last year came in a Week 15 blowout of the Lions, and he played in just 31 snaps while the Titans turned to Jeremy McNichols on passing downs. Evans needs to stay healthy and refine his passing-down skills, both routes and blocking.

Demetric Felton, CLE: In an offseason when every draft prospect's pro day seemed to feature 40-yard dashes run downhill and trampolines boosting vertical jumps, Felton's athletic testing was poor, running a 4.55s 40 (at 189 pounds). For a hybrid player caught between running back and wideout, that was a red flag. On the other hand, Felton looked good catching the ball at the Senior Bowl. Fortunately for Cleveland, Felton won't be required to run the ball too often, so this sixth-round rookie can spend his time learning the presumed gadget package that will be his calling card until he finds a niche at the pro level.

D'Onta Foreman, FA: The former Texans back finally bubbled up again at the fringe of Tennessee's roster after being suddenly released by Houston in 2019's training camp. There was not much workload behind Derrick Henry, and the Titans moved on quickly this offseason. Foreman had a tryout with the Seahawks in April but remains unsigned as we go to press; he's a bruiser with almost no special-teams value, which makes him a tough roster spot fit unless he's a major part of the backfield.

Jake Funk, LAR: A rookie seventh-round pick from Maryland, Funk is expected to make his biggest contributions on special teams (as most late-round picks do). With the Rams having used Day 2 picks on running backs in both 2019 and 2020, Funk is near the bottom of the depth chart entering camp. Funk dealt with injury issues in college and never exceeded 60 carries in a season, but he topped 500 yards during the Terrapins five-game season in 2020.

Khalil Herbert, CHI: Herbert carries a massive red flag since he lost his job at Kansas to the undrafted Pooka Williams. That said, the sixth-round rookie enjoyed his best season by far in 2020 as a graduate transfer to Virginia Tech. And while he won't translate his 7.6 yards per carry to the next level with his lack of elusiveness, Herbert has a compact power and one-cut style that makes sense for Matt Nagy's increasing reliance on an outside zone scheme. He could also replace the departed Cordarrelle Patterson as the team's kick returner.

Dontrell Hilliard, HOU: A return specialist with some passing-down chops, Hilliard was claimed off waivers by the Texans towards the end of last season and has since been drowned in a tidal wave of additions such as Phillip Lindsay and Mark Ingram. As someone who can't be directly linked to Nick Caserio and who didn't have strong in-roads to playing time last season, Hilliard will probably need a rash of injuries or other extenuating circumstances to make Houston's 53-man roster this fall.

Justice Hill, BAL: Hill was relegated to special teams duty with the arrival of J.K. Dobbins last season, carrying the ball just 12 times for 60 yards (28.4% DVOA). Mark Ingram's departure should elevate him back to the No. 3 running back role, which over the past two years came with extensive mop-up duties. Hill is a compact bruiser who would probably be about as effective as Gus Edwards, given similar opportunities.

Kylin Hill, GB: Packers head coach Matt LaFleur came from Tennessee, and his running back selections the past two drafts echo an appreciation for Derrick Henry. Hill isn't massive like Henry or AJ Dillon, and that and disproportionate success against Mississippi State's lesser opponents such as Southern Mississippi, Louisiana, and Abilene Christian caused his drop to the seventh round. But Hill plays bigger than his 214 pounds since he's just 5-foot-11, and he smashes into would-be tacklers with low pads.

Travis Homer, SEA: After a late-season tryout in a more expansive role in 2019 due to a rash of running back injuries, Homer slid back into a third-down role in 2020 when he was healthy. His pass protection is solid and Seattle trusts him to be on the field in those situations, but that is about where the trust ends. He has limited ability to run between the tackles, which caps his upside, but his pass-blocking and special teams chops should keep him on the roster.

Jordan Howard, PHI: Howard's rushing yardage totals have dropped every season of his career. In 2020, he received under 10 carries per game for the first time. He got five carries per game in his short stint with the Dolphins but just 3.5 per game when he re-signed with the Eagles. Still, Howard totaled nine carries inside the 5-yard line, which tied for 27th among running backs, and included all four of his rushing touchdowns. He finished with -51 rushing DYAR and -36.7% DVOA despite the touchdowns.

Buddy Howell, HOU: Howell has generated some decent preseason buzz over the years and has been a core Texans special-teamer. Playing against the Bears in what would become a 36-7 blowout, Howell managed 11 carries for 42 yards. That may not seem amazing, but for a team that finished dead last in rushing DVOA, it was cause for a little optimism. The Texans immediately buried that by making sure the 25-year-old Howell was stapled to the bench in service of the delusion that the DeAndre Hopkins trade can return some value for them. Howell remains in that exact spot headed into 2021.

Chuba Hubbard, CAR: 18 months ago, Hubbard was a longshot Heisman candidate and likely Day 2 pick coming off a 2,000-yard, 21-touchdown season at Oklahoma State. After an injury-blighted 2020 season, he fell to the Panthers in the fourth round this April. A powerful, bruising back with near-elite speed, a healthy Hubbard looks an ideal complement to Christian McCaffrey. If he can recapture his 2019 form and fitness, he could even become the rare back the Panthers allow to eat into McCaffrey's workload. At the very least, he looks the strongest bet to emerge from the clutch of backup options.

Jermar Jefferson, DET: The Lions snagged Jefferson, BackCAST's No. 4 running back prospect, as the 18th selection at the position at the end of the seventh round. Jefferson presumably fell because of a poor 4.6s 40 time and because his vision and rhythmic style pigeonhole him into a zone rushing scheme. Well, NFL backs rarely can reach their top-end speeds, and new Lions offensive coordinator Anthony Lynn uses a zone scheme. It may not happen Year 1, but Jefferson could outplay his draft position if the Lions offer him the consistent workload he enjoyed at Oregon State.

D'Ernest Johnson, CLE: The former member of the Orlando Apollos of the AAF may not have received his final paychecks from the destitute spring league, but Johnson used what he put on tape to earn a much better contract in Cleveland in 2019. It may have been more impressive that he stuck around in 2020, making his second Browns roster, and even expanded his role. His Week 4 eruption for 95 yards on just 13 carries in Dallas may have been the greatest moment for an alternative leaguer since Rod Smart's "He Hate Me" jersey. Johnson returns kicks and punts as well, if not with much aplomb, and it is his willingness to play special teams that makes it likely Johnson sees a third season in the varsity fall league.

John Kelly, CLE: After spending 2020 on the practice squad, Kelly is clearly on the roster bubble. If the Browns decide to keep five running backs, the former Rams backup has a shot to stick on the roster. If Cleveland goes with four, Kelly will rue the fact the luck of the Irish eluded him.

Patrick Laird, MIA: Laird caught Tua Tagovailoa's first NFL pass, which possibly will make him the answer to a trivia question someday. Laird saw significant action against Kansas City, splitting snaps 50/50 with DeAndre Washington due to COVID issues, and yet he only touched the ball five times. Laird will not be the answer to the "who was Miami's lead running back in 2021?" trivia question.

LeSean McCoy, FA: During the first 10 years of McCoy's career, his teams didn't win any playoff games. During the past two, they've won seven, including two Super Bowls, though he didn't play in either. Could his next stop be Canton? Pro Football Reference's Hall of Fame Monitor gives him a score of 83.2, ahead of several running backs already enshrined, including Curtis Martin, Leroy Kelly, Tony Dorsett, Jerome Bettis, John Riggins, and Paul Hornung. His 11,102 rushing yards rank 22nd all-time, his 15,000 yards from scrimmage rank 18th among running backs, and his 4.5 yards per carry average ranks seventh (minimum 2,000 carries).

Elijah Mitchell, SF: Despite splitting carries with Trey Ragas (who signed with Las Vegas as an undrafted free agent), Mitchell ran for 3,000-plus yards and 37 touchdowns in his last three years at Louisiana-Lafayette. He fell to the 49ers in the sixth round of this year's draft, but thanks to a 6.2-yard average and a sub-4.4s 40-yard dash, he had a better BackCAST score than six of the running backs drafted before him—including new teammate Trey Sermon. Mitchell could be a potential sleeper, but given the absurd running back depth in San Francisco, we may not find out this year.

Welcome to Choose Your Own Adventure: 49ers Running Back Fantasy Draft! If you have made it this far, you have probably figured out that whichever 49ers running back you pick, he'll score three times in one week and then immediately suffer some terrible injury, like tearing five muscles at once or something. Just do the safe, boring thing and take Gus Edwards or somebody instead.

THE END

Ty Montgomery, NO: Drafted into the league as a wide receiver with the Packers, Montgomery switched back to his college role of halfback during a 2016 season that saw a plethora of backfield injuries in Green Bay. He led the Packers with 457 rushing yards that season but hasn't exceeded 200 yards on the ground since 2017. Usually a competent kickoff returner, Montgomery is most remembered for playing his way out of Green Bay by defying coaches' orders to return a kick that he then fumbled, leading to a loss against the Rams. He went 19-101-0 with -13.9% DVOA on the ground last season and caught only three passes.

Kene Nwangwu, MIN: Nwangwu has exceptional athletic traits, but he struggled to translate that to the field with his hesitance to hit holes and his poor footwork in and out of cuts. The Vikings were likely comfortable to reach for Nwangwu in the fourth round because of his success as a kickoff returner. He averaged 26.8 yards over 92 returns in four years at Iowa State, and he and fifth-round receiver Ihmir Smith-Marsette could revitalize a special teams unit that finished 31st in DVOA last year.

Dare Ogunbowale, JAX: A credible third-down back/kick returner type, Ogunbowale briefly generated a ton of hype last summer as fantasy football players looked for a passing game target that could be Tom Brady's James White in Tampa Bay. He failed to make the Bucs roster, however, and was snapped up by the Jaguars. Jacksonville has since added Carlos Hyde and Travis Etienne to the depth chart, and Ogunbowale is in for another training camp fight to keep his roster spot with Devine Ozigbo and Nathan Cottrell trying to hone in on it.

Troymaine Pope, TB: Since joining the Seahawks as an undrafted free agent in 2016, Pope has bounced around from practice squad to practice squad. In stints with the Chargers last season, he gained 118 yards on 23 touches (-12.2% rushing DVOA). The Buccaneers signed Pope after he impressed during a May tryout. The running back room is crowded in Tampa, so if Pope sticks around, it will be primarily as a special-teamer.

C.J. Prosise, TB: Oft-injured Prosise found 10 carries behind David Johnson's concussions and missed COVID games, returning eight kicks, and fumbling once. He even caught a touchdown against the Lions on Thanksgiving. Prosise was on the Tampa Bay practice squad in the playoffs but never played; he re-signed in February but is unlikely to make the team.

Theo Riddick, LV: Riddick has slowly faded from the spotlight over each of his last three seasons, thanks in part to a clavicle injury in 2019. Riddick earned just over 100 touches in both 2017 and 2018, but just 11 with the Raiders in 2020 after having missed the 2019 season. Riddick was a pass-catching specialist in Detroit, but that's not something that is necessary in Las Vegas, where three other running backs caught more than 15 passes. Do not expect Riddick to overtake Jalen Richard as the team's pass-catching back, which is a limited role in the offense as is.

Larry Rountree, LAC: A sixth-round draft pick, Rountree is the quintessential boring running back who provides little more than baseline inside zone rushing ability and competent pass-protection qualities, like a lesser Jamaal Williams. Rountree sports passable vision and downhill decisiveness, though his explosiveness and balance through contact are ordinary. Rountree never caught more than 15 passes in a season at Missouri, and his targets were limited to basic routes in the flat or underneath area. Rountree may work his way into a legit rotational role thanks in part to his pass-blocking.

Jaylen Samuels, PIT: As a rookie in 2018, Samuels cranked out a 142-yard performance on the ground against the Patriots; in his 42 other games over three NFL seasons, he has amassed 317 rushing yards—about 7.5 yards per game. More of a receiving threat in his first two years, the coaches' lack of trust in him and the overall disinterest in throwing to backs in Pittsburgh sapped that part of his skill set in 2020. With Matt Canada's scheme more amenable to passes to backs, Samuels might earn a larger role, but the Steelers didn't spend a first-round pick on Najee Harris to have him come out on third down too often.

Rhamondre Stevenson, NE: Stevenson received a thoroughly mediocre BackCAST score of +14.2%, in large part because he never dominated the backfield at Oklahoma. While averaging 7.2 yards per carry is great, it's worrisome that he was splitting carries with T.J. Pledger and Kennedy Brooks. A 4.64s 40 isn't any great shakes either at 230 pounds. He'll fight with Sony Michel for a role on the offense and may end up using 2021 as more of a redshirt year.

J.J. Taylor, NE: Taylor was repeatedly praised by the coaching staff during 2020's training camp, called a mini version of Dion Lewis. He then spent most of last season firmly planted on the bench, a healthy scratch as he basically took a redshirt developmental year. Lewis was pretty mini on his own, but Taylor takes it to another level at 5-foot-6, 185 pounds. Only one back smaller than that has ever qualified for our leaderboards: Lionel "Little Train" James in 1985.

Chris Thompson, FA: There are a lot of guys who wind up in Going Deep as Not My Guy—the guys that the previous administration loved. Thompson was very much Jay Gruden's guy, and very much not Urban Meyer's. Thompson lost a lot of playing time when James Robinson turned out to be better than anyone could have imagined before training camp started. Thompson still showed his chops by catching 20-of-23 targets out of the backfield with a 16.7% DVOA but hit IR with a back injury after Week 8. Released, Thompson could be a solid third-down back somewhere if healthy.

Darwin Thompson, KC: Thompson was getting regular playing time by the end of his rookie season in 2019, but was an afterthought for most of last season, getting most of his action in a meaningless Week 17 rest-the-starters game against the Chargers (27-97-1, -17.8% DVOA). All the additions to the running back room in 2020 pushed him out of the picture, and it's hard to imagine how he claws back into the lineup for 2021. At 5-foot-8 and 200 pounds, it has been difficult for Thompson to find a role as anything more than a depth player or very situational pass-catcher.

Ke'Shawn Vaughn, TB: Vaughn's chance of a breakout last season crashed when the Buccaneers added Leonard Fournette, and they haven't improved with the addition of Gio Bernard to the backfield. That means Vaughn will most likely see the bulk of his work on special teams, when he's not a healthy scratch, as he was five times in 2020. He saw significant action in Week 16, carrying the ball 15 times for 62 yards and -7 DYAR. He also remains in Bruce Arians' good graces, which is at least a good sign for his future, if not for his 2021.

DeAndre Washington, FA: Washington has suffered a steep decline since his rookie year of 2016, failing to clear 3.8 yards per carry in any season since. A small, determined back, Washington split time last year between Kansas City and Miami. He had seven carries in the red zone, totaling just 12 yards for a 43% success rate. He did not score on any of those touches, or any other touch for that matter. Washington's avenue back onto a roster is through the air, as evidenced by his 14th-place 74 receiving DYAR in 2019 with the Raiders.

Antonio Williams, BUF: Antonio Williams putting up 20 rushing DYAR against the Dolphins in Week 17, second-highest total for a Bills running back last season, might be the most random thing that has ever happened, especially considering the undrafted free agent actually retired and went back to North Carolina as a graduate assistant after being cut in training camp. Despite helping squash Miami's playoff hopes, Williams will probably go back to bouncing between the practice squad and the main roster in 2021.

Pooka Williams, CIN: Williams rushed for over 1,000 yards for Kansas in 2018 and 2019 before rushing for just 196 yards in 2020 due to a shortened schedule, numerous injuries, and a terrible team. Williams is an explosive jump-cutter but weighs just 170 pounds after a firehouse breakfast. His 2019 tape was a blast to watch, but it's hard to tell if he's another Antonio Gibson or another Donnel Pumphrey whose entire game will fall apart if he tries to gain six pounds. As an undrafted rookie on a thin Bengals depth chart, Williams will get a long look as a potential third-down back and/or return man.

Trayveon Williams, CIN: A sixth-round pick in 2019, Williams is a low-center-of-gravity runner who earned some snaps at the ends of blowouts last year and ripped off a 55-yarder in silly time near the end of the Ravens beatdown in the season finale. (Season totals: 26-157-0, -4.1% DVOA.) He's now in line for the No. 3 role for the Bengals and could inherit some of Gio Bernard's touches by virtue of being the guy on the roster who looks the most like a third-down back.

T.J. Yeldon, FA: Shockingly, the market for a 28-year-old running back with 11 touches in 2020 hasn't been super strong. Yeldon was a healthy scratch most of the season, as long as both Zack Moss and Devin Singletary were both active. He had some success in garbage time early in the year, but he's mostly just a league-minimum body at this point in time—still worth a roster spot somewhere, but not as a contributor.

Wide Receivers

In the following two sections we provide the last three years of statistics, as well as a 2021 KUBIAK projection, for every wide receiver and tight end who either played a significant role in 2020 or is expected to do so in 2021.

The first line contains biographical data—each player's name, height, weight, college, draft position, birth date, and age. Height and weight are the best data we could find; weight, of course, can fluctuate during the off-season. **Age** is very simple, the number of years between the player's birth year and 2021, but birth date is provided if you want to figure out exact age.

Draft position gives draft year and round, with the overall pick number with which the player was taken in parentheses. In the sample table, it says that Julio Jones was chosen in the 2011 NFL draft with the sixth overall pick in the first round. Undrafted free agents are listed as "FA" with the year they came into the league, even if they were only in training camp or on a practice squad.

To the far right of the first line is the player's Risk for fantasy football in 2021. As explained in the quarterback section, the standard is for players to be marked Green. Players with higher than normal risk are marked Yellow, and players with the highest risk are marked Red. Players who are most likely to match or surpass our forecast—primarily second-stringers with low projections but also some particularly strong breakout candidates—are marked Blue. Risk is not only based on age and injury probability, but how a player's projection compares to his recent performance as well as our confidence (or lack thereof) in his offensive teammates.

Next we give the last three years of player stats. Note that rushing stats are not included for receivers, but that any receiver with at least five carries last year will have his 2020 rushing stats appear in his team's chapter.

Next we give the last three years of player stats. First come games played and games started (**G/GS**). Games played represents the official NFL total and may include games in which a player appeared on special teams but did not play wide receiver or tight end. We also have a total of offensive **Snaps** for each season. Receptions (**Rec**) counts passes caught, while Passes (**Pass**) counts passes thrown to this player, complete or incomplete. Receiving yards (**Yds**) and touchdowns (**TD**) are the official NFL totals for each player. End Zone Targets (**EZ**) count how often a player was targeted while in the end zone.

Catch rate (**C%**) includes all passes listed in the official play-by-play with the given player as the intended receiver, even if those passes were listed as "Thrown Away," "Batted Down," or "Quarterback Hit in Motion." The average NFL wide receiver has caught between 58% and 63% of passes over the last five seasons; tight ends caught between 64% and 68% of passes over the last five seasons.

Plus/minus (**+/-**) is a metric that we introduced in *Football Outsiders Almanac 2010*. It estimates how many passes a receiver caught compared to what an average receiver would have caught, given the location of those passes. Unlike simple catch rate, plus/minus does not consider passes listed as "Thrown Away," "Batted Down," "Quarterback Hit in Motion," or "Miscommunication." Player performance is compared to a historical baseline of how often a pass is caught based on the pass distance, the distance required for a first down, and whether it is on the left, middle, or right side of the field. Note that plus/minus is not scaled to a player's target total.

Drops (**Drop**) list the number of dropped passes according to charting from Sports Info Solutions. Our totals may differ from the drop totals kept by other organizations. Yards per catch (**Yd/C**) is a standard statistic.

Next you'll find each player's average depth of target (**aDOT**). This is the average distance beyond the line of scrimmage on all throws to this player, not counting passes listed as "Thrown Away," "Batted Down," or "Quarterback Hit in Motion." Long-ball specialists will rank high in this category (Marquez Valdes-Scantling of the Packers had an 18.5 aDOT, most of any qualifying wide receiver) while players who see a lot of passes on slots and screens will rank low (Pittsburgh's JuJu Smith-Schuster was lowest at 5.7 aDOT).

Next we list yards after catch (**YAC**), rank (**Rk**) in yards after catch, and **YAC+.** YAC+ is similar to plus-minus; it estimates how much YAC a receiver gained compared to what we would have expected from an average receiver catching passes of similar length in similar down-and-distance situations. This is imperfect—we don't base YAC+ on what route a player runs, and obviously a go route will have more YAC than a comeback—but it does a fairly good job of telling you if this receiver gets more or less YAC than other receivers with similar usage patterns. We also give a total of broken tackles (**BTkl**) according to Sports Info Solutions charting.

The next four columns include our main advanced metrics for receiving: **DVOA** (Defense-adjusted Value Over Average) and **DYAR** (Defense-adjusted Yards Above Replacement), along with the player's rank in both. These metrics compare

Julio Jones				Height: 6-3		Weight: 220	College: Alabama				Draft: 2011/1 (6)		Born: 8-Feb-1989		Age: 32		Risk: Green	

Year	Tm	G/GS	Snaps	Pass	Rec	Yds	TD	EZ	C%	+/-	Drop	Yd/C	aDOT	Rk	YAC	Rk	YAC+	BTkl	DVOA	Rk	DYAR	Rk	Use	Rk	Slot
2018	ATL	16/16	818	170	113	1677	8	10	66%	+10.1	6	14.8	14.5	14	4.0	51	-0.4	13	15.9%	17	382	6	28.2%	5	43%
2019	ATL	15/15	834	157	99	1394	6	11	63%	+4.5	5	14.1	12.6	34	3.5	61	-0.7	10	11.6%	21	299	7	25.6%	11	49%
2020	ATL	9/9	468	68	51	771	3	8	75%	+8.0	2	15.1	11.7	35	4.5	35	+0.4	7	29.8%	2	231	16	20.3%	34	57%
2021	TEN			124	80	1146	7		65%	--		14.3							4.2%						

every pass intended for a receiver and the results of that pass to a league-average baseline based on the game situations in which passes were thrown to that receiver. DVOA and DYAR are also adjusted based on the opposing defense and include Defensive Pass Interference yards on passes intended for that receiver. The methods used to compute these numbers are described in detail in the "Statistical Toolbox" introduction in the front of the book. The important distinction between them is that DVOA is a rate statistic, while DYAR is a cumulative statistic. Thus, a higher DVOA means more value per pass play, while a higher DYAR means more aggregate value over the entire season. Numbers without opponent adjustment (YAR and VOA) can be found on our website, FootballOutsiders.com.

To qualify for ranking in YAC, receiving DVOA, or receiving DYAR, a wide receiver must have had 50 passes thrown to him in that season. We ranked 87 wide receivers in 2020, 81 in 2019, and 84 in 2018. Tight ends qualify with 25 targets in a given season; we ranked 50 tight ends in 2020, 48 in 2019, and 49 in 2018.

The final columns measure each player's role in his offense. Usage rate (**Use**) measures each player's share of his team's targets, adjusted for games played. Green Bay's Davante Adams was targeted on 29.6% of his team's targets, but he also missed two games. Adjusting for those missing games gives Adams a usage rate of 33.8%, the highest in the league and a more accurate assessment of his workload. The final column shows the percentage of each player's targets that came when he lined up in the **Slot** (or at tight end). Larry Fitzgerald of the Arizona Cardinals saw 96% of his targets from the slot, the

highest rate in the league; the Cowboys' Michael Gallup had the lowest rate of slot targets at 23%. Tight ends have an additional column listing how frequently they were split **Wide**, from a high of 21% (the Rams' Gerald Everett) to a low of 0% (lots of guys).

"Slot" and "Wide" here are defined based on where the players are lined up in relation to the field, not based on where they are lined up in relation to other receivers. For example, if three wide receivers are in a trips bunch that is tight to the formation, all three receivers are marked as "slot" even if no other receiver is further out wide on that same side of the formation.

The italicized row of statistics for the 2021 season is our 2021 KUBIAK projection as explained further in the Statistical Toolbox at the front of the book. Be aware that projections account for the possibility of injury so workload projections may seem low for the top players.

It is difficult to accurately project statistics for a 162-game baseball season, but it is exponentially more difficult to accurately project statistics for a 17-game football season. Consider the listed projections not as a prediction of exact numbers, but as the mean of a range of possible performances. What's important is less the exact number of yards we project, and more which players are projected to improve or decline. Actual performance will vary from our projection less for veteran starters and more for rookies and third-stringers, for whom we must base our projections on much smaller career statistical samples. Touchdown numbers will vary more than yardage numbers. Players facing suspension or recovering from injury have those missed games taken into account.

Top 20 WR by DYAR (Total Value), 2020

Rank	Player	Team	DYAR
1	Davante Adams	GB	395
2	Stefon Diggs	BUF	377
3	Justin Jefferson	MIN	373
4	Mike Evans	TB	354
5	DK Metcalf	SEA	334
6	A.J. Brown	TEN	332
7	Will Fuller	HOU	326
8	Tyreek Hill	KC	322
9	Adam Thielen	MIN	287
10	Nelson Agholor	LV	277
11	Chris Godwin	TB	267
12	Cole Beasley	BUF	267
13	Corey Davis	TEN	261
14	Tyler Lockett	SEA	238
15	Marvin Jones	DET	235
16	Julio Jones	ATL	231
17	Calvin Ridley	ATL	230
18	Brandin Cooks	HOU	207
19	DeAndre Hopkins	ARI	207
20	D.J. Moore	CAR	191

Minimum 50 passes.

Top 20 WR by DVOA (Value per Pass), 2020

Rank	Player	Team	DVOA
1	Will Fuller	HOU	41.2%
2	Julio Jones	ATL	29.8%
3	Rashard Higgins	CLE	29.4%
4	Nelson Agholor	LV	28.0%
5	Chris Godwin	TB	28.0%
6	Mike Evans	TB	25.6%
7	Justin Jefferson	MIN	25.5%
8	A.J. Brown	TEN	25.0%
9	Corey Davis	TEN	22.5%
10	Cole Beasley	BUF	19.9%
11	Davante Adams	GB	19.7%
12	DK Metcalf	SEA	19.5%
13	Adam Thielen	MIN	19.2%
14	Tyreek Hill	KC	17.3%
15	Tim Patrick	DEN	16.1%
16	Stefon Diggs	BUF	15.8%
17	Scott Miller	TB	13.2%
18	Marvin Jones	DET	12.3%
19	John Brown	BUF	11.4%
20	Gabriel Davis	BUF	10.7%

Minimum 50 passes.

A few low-round rookies, guys listed at seventh on the depth chart, and players who are listed as wide receivers but really only play special teams are briefly discussed at the end of the chapter in a section we call "Going Deep."

Two notes regarding our advanced metrics: We cannot yet fully separate the performance of a receiver from the performance of his quarterback. Be aware that one will affect the other. In addition, these statistics measure only passes thrown to a receiver, not performance on plays when he is not thrown the ball, such as blocking and drawing double teams.

Davante Adams　Height: 6-1　Weight: 215　College: Fresno State　Draft: 2014/2 (53)　Born: 12/24/1992　Age: 29　Risk: Yellow

Year	Tm	G/GS	Snaps	Pass	Rec	Yds	TD	EZ	C%	+/-	Drop	Yd/C	aDOT	Rk	YAC	Rk	YAC+	BTkl	DVOA	Rk	DYAR	Rk	Use	Rk	Slot
2018	GB	15/15	954	169	111	1386	13	18	66%	+5.0	5	12.5	11.2	44	4.3	43	-0.5	10	6.1%	30	246	16	29.3%	4	32%
2019	GB	12/12	695	127	83	997	5	13	65%	+0.3	8	12.0	10.5	51	4.7	31	-0.1	5	0.6%	43	139	31	31.7%	2	48%
2020	GB	14/14	775	149	115	1374	18	18	77%	+13.6	2	11.9	9.0	63	5.2	21	+0.8	12	19.7%	11	395	1	33.8%	1	59%
2021	GB			152	104	1254	12		68%	--		12.1							10.1%						

Adams quickly developed the savvy and route-running skills to outplay the physical tools that dropped him to the second round of the 2014 draft. Already a Pro Bowler in the previous three seasons, Adams raised his play level even higher in 2020. He dropped just two of his 117 catchable targets for a 1.7% drop rate that was fifth lowest of the 87 wide receivers with 50 or more targets, and he led the position with 18 touchdowns and was second with a 55.5% DVOA in the red zone. His production ceiling may be tied to Aaron Rodgers, but Adams earned his All-Pro distinction on his own merits and deserves consideration as maybe the best wide receiver in football.

Nelson Agholor　Height: 6-0　Weight: 198　College: USC　Draft: 2015/1 (20)　Born: 24-May-1993　Age: 28　Risk: Green

Year	Tm	G/GS	Snaps	Pass	Rec	Yds	TD	EZ	C%	+/-	Drop	Yd/C	aDOT	Rk	YAC	Rk	YAC+	BTkl	DVOA	Rk	DYAR	Rk	Use	Rk	Slot
2018	PHI	16/16	985	97	64	736	4	4	66%	+2.0	4	11.5	10.5	48	5.5	17	-0.2	11	-21.8%	77	-69	78	16.2%	56	78%
2019	PHI	11/10	706	69	39	363	3	6	57%	-1.4	4	9.3	11.8	41	3.4	62	-2.0	8	-35.0%	79	-123	80	16.7%	59	83%
2020	LV	16/13	731	82	48	896	8	15	59%	-1.4	8	18.7	16.4	3	4.8	29	+0.6	9	28.0%	4	277	10	16.3%	56	57%
2021	NE			59	37	516	3		63%	--		13.9							-0.8%						

Agholor's ALEX skyrocketed to 7.1 last season, up from 2.0 in his entire time in Philadelphia. Las Vegas basically removed the short passing game from Agholor's responsibilities, and Agholor responded with career highs in DVOA, DYAR, and YAC+. The Patriots are definitely paying for a career outlier, but the vastly changed role Agholor had last season at least makes an argument other than random chance for why Agholor suddenly became a top-five receiver in 2020. Suffice it to say, we don't expect top-five production again from Agholor … but then, neither do the Patriots. A competent deep option, opening up room underneath, is something New England has lacked since Josh Gordon and Chris Hogan left.

Brandon Aiyuk　Height: 6-0　Weight: 206　College: Arizona State　Draft: 2020/1 (25)　Born: 17-Mar-1998　Age: 23　Risk: Green

Year	Tm	G/GS	Snaps	Pass	Rec	Yds	TD	EZ	C%	+/-	Drop	Yd/C	aDOT	Rk	YAC	Rk	YAC+	BTkl	DVOA	Rk	DYAR	Rk	Use	Rk	Slot
2020	SF	12/11	728	96	60	748	5	7	63%	-1.8	5	12.5	10.3	48	4.8	28	-0.0	14	1.7%	40	117	31	23.7%	18	59%
2021	SF			93	59	753	4		63%	--		12.7							-2.5%						

Despite concerns that he would be just another slants-and-screens guy in the 49ers offense, Aiyuk may have been the most complete wide receiver in San Francisco in his rookie year. He led the team not only in total targets, but also in targets in the short, middle, and deep ranges, and in targets down the middle of the field (which is saying something for a team that had as many good tight ends as the 49ers did). Mind you, he ran a lot of slants too (18, twice as many as any of his teammates) and even took the occasional screen away from Deebo Samuel. That's not even including his rushing numbers—six carries for 77 yards and two touchdowns. He really caught fire late in the year, gaining 70-plus yards in six of his last seven games. With the obvious exception of George Kittle, Aiyuk is likely the 49ers' safest pick in a fantasy draft.

Keenan Allen

Height: 6-2 Weight: 211 College: California Draft: 2013/3 (76) Born: 27-Apr-1992 Age: 29 Risk: Green

Year	Tm	G/GS	Snaps	Pass	Rec	Yds	TD	EZ	C%	+/-	Drop	Yd/C	aDOT	Rk	YAC	Rk	YAC+	BTkl	DVOA	Rk	DYAR	Rk	Use	Rk	Slot
2018	LAC	16/14	794	136	97	1196	6	8	71%	+7.2	4	12.3	8.9	68	4.2	45	-0.3	9	18.1%	15	320	9	27.0%	7	64%
2019	LAC	16/16	944	149	104	1199	6	12	70%	+8.5	5	11.5	10.2	55	3.5	59	-0.7	11	7.3%	28	232	16	25.7%	10	63%
2020	LAC	14/13	874	147	100	992	8	11	68%	+0.9	3	9.9	7.8	78	4.4	44	-0.4	16	-8.1%	64	53	57	27.7%	4	67%
2021	LAC			144	96	1088	9		67%	--		11.3							1.5%						

Allen saw a dip in efficiency last season, but there's a good case to be made that it had more to do with his situation than any sort of real regression. With the Chargers switching from Philip Rivers to Justin Herbert, the offense saw a shift in passing focus because Herbert is someone who wants to target down the field as much as possible. Herbert is also nowhere near as sharp as Rivers was in the quick game. Additionally, the emergence of Jalen Guyton and Tyron Johnson as pure vertical threats made it so that Allen did not need to be a deep threat, leaving him to be the offense's best option in the short-to-intermediate range with a young quarterback who was not yet fully comfortable throwing at that distance. Allen's target share to the short area of the field jumped 12% last season, while his deep target share dropped by 10%. That said, Allen did find explosive plays on horizontal stretches, producing a league-best 107 DYAR on nine deep crossing route targets. Expect Allen to continue being the team's best short-to-intermediate option while others roam deeper downfield.

Danny Amendola

Height: 5-11 Weight: 185 College: Texas Tech Draft: 2008/FA Born: 2-Nov-1985 Age: 36 Risk: N/A

Year	Tm	G/GS	Snaps	Pass	Rec	Yds	TD	EZ	C%	+/-	Drop	Yd/C	aDOT	Rk	YAC	Rk	YAC+	BTkl	DVOA	Rk	DYAR	Rk	Use	Rk	Slot
2018	MIA	15/15	682	79	59	575	1	1	75%	+5.1	1	9.7	7.4	78	3.9	53	-1.3	2	-6.2%	55	38	55	19.1%	36	91%
2019	DET	15/10	656	97	62	678	1	4	64%	-2.2	6	10.9	8.9	66	3.3	64	-0.9	6	-10.2%	64	18	64	18.6%	47	88%
2020	DET	14/5	462	69	46	602	0	2	67%	-1.8	3	13.1	8.1	75	6.4	5	+1.0	6	-1.0%	46	62	50	13.8%	73	90%

Amendola has played 155 games in his 12-year career, but if 2020 proves to be his final season, then injuries will lead his legacy. He dealt with numerous concussions and sprains over the years and more recently missed time with chest and hip injuries. He did have several seasons with a DVOA of 12.0% or better, a major accomplishment for an undrafted free agent, but he never lived up to his comparisons to similarly built Wes Welker, even when Amendola found his way to the Patriots for five seasons.

Robby Anderson

Height: 6-3 Weight: 190 College: Temple Draft: 2016/FA Born: 9-May-1993 Age: 28 Risk: Green

Year	Tm	G/GS	Snaps	Pass	Rec	Yds	TD	EZ	C%	+/-	Drop	Yd/C	aDOT	Rk	YAC	Rk	YAC+	BTkl	DVOA	Rk	DYAR	Rk	Use	Rk	Slot
2018	NYJ	14/9	682	94	50	752	6	14	53%	+0.3	1	15.0	16.4	4	3.6	61	-0.6	3	-11.8%	65	6	66	21.2%	28	32%
2019	NYJ	16/15	944	96	52	779	5	10	54%	-2.3	2	15.0	15.6	10	3.7	53	-0.8	4	-4.2%	53	66	52	20.0%	39	21%
2020	CAR	16/16	804	137	95	1096	3	8	70%	+3.8	6	11.5	9.6	58	5.2	22	-0.0	14	-10.9%	73	19	68	26.3%	6	64%
2021	CAR			106	64	783	4		60%	--		12.3							-11.1%						

Anderson's first year in Carolina saw him set a career high in receiving yards, which accompanied a dramatic change in how he was deployed compared to his time in New York. His average depth of target in 2020 was cut by more than one-third from his days in New York. Consequently, he gained just 11.5 yards per reception after averaging 15.0 yards per catch in each of the previous two seasons. However, his catch rate increased by 15% over his Jets average, meaning he ended up with the exact same 8.1 yards per target as 2019 despite the divergent route he took to get there.

Despite being the newcomer to an offense that also featured D.J. Moore and Curtis Samuel, Anderson ranked sixth among wide receivers in Usage (target share, adjusted for games played). However, that translated to just three touchdowns, his lowest total since his rookie year. Still, fantasy owners will take a 50% increase in reception volume over his previous career high, even if he did have the worst advanced statistics of the three main Panthers pass-catchers.

Tutu Atwell

Height: 5-9 Weight: 165 College: Louisville Draft: 2021/2 (57) Born: 7-Oct-1999 Age: 22 Risk: Green

Year	Tm	G/GS	Snaps	Pass	Rec	Yds	TD	EZ	C%	+/-	Drop	Yd/C	aDOT	Rk	YAC	Rk	YAC+	BTkl	DVOA	Rk	DYAR	Rk	Use	Rk	Slot
2021	LAR			36	25	317	2		69%	--		12.7							6.5%						

The diminutive Atwell was an explosive play waiting to happen at Louisville, and he showed enough promise for the Rams to select him in the second round of the draft. Atwell should fit in as a long-term answer for the Rams' field-stretching needs—while DeSean Jackson has been a premium deep threat for much of his career, he likely does not have a ton left in the tank. One of the Rams' biggest issues in their passing attack was the inability to push the ball down the field, and Atwell should help provide a spark in that regard, even if it is not to a huge degree in his first season. The main question with Atwell is how his size impacts his ability to get open, as he could potentially get outmuscled by larger defenders. He may be shifty enough for that not to matter, especially if the Rams keep him in favorable alignments to avoid heavy press coverage, but only time will tell.

Rashod Bateman

Height: 6-2 **Weight:** 210 **College:** Minnesota **Draft:** 2021/1 (27) **Born:** 29-Nov-1999 **Age:** 22 **Risk:** Green

Year	Tm	G/GS	Snaps	Pass	Rec	Yds	TD	EZ	C%	+/-	Drop	Yd/C	aDOT	Rk	YAC	Rk	YAC+	BTkl	DVOA	Rk	DYAR	Rk	Use	Rk	Slot
2021	BAL		52	34	458	3		65%	--		13.3								4.6%						

Bateman spent much of his truncated 2020 season operating out of the slot and catching short timing passes in an RPO-heavy Golden Gophers scheme. That could make him the missing piece of the Ravens offense: someone Lamar Jackson feels comfortable flipping quick passes to when the defense is worried about the handoff and the option-keeper threat. Bateman should provide more YAC than Willie Snead did in a similar role, but of course his success depends on Jackson and the design of the offense.

The Ravens now have a thrilling deep threat in Marquise Brown, well-built possession receivers and blockers in Sammy Watkins and Myles Boykin, a screen-and-reverse specialist in Devin Duvernay, and a slot specialist in Bateman, all of whom except Watkins (a former fourth overall pick) were drafted in the top three rounds over the last three years, plus Mark Andrews and Nick Boyle at tight end. The "Jackson needs more weapons" argument no longer carries any water.

Cole Beasley

Height: 5-8 **Weight:** 174 **College:** Southern Methodist **Draft:** 2012/FA **Born:** 26-Apr-1989 **Age:** 32 **Risk:** Green

Year	Tm	G/GS	Snaps	Pass	Rec	Yds	TD	EZ	C%	+/-	Drop	Yd/C	aDOT	Rk	YAC	Rk	YAC+	BTkl	DVOA	Rk	DYAR	Rk	Use	Rk	Slot
2018	DAL	16/4	713	87	65	672	3	5	75%	+5.1	2	10.3	7.5	77	3.3	71	-1.1	5	2.1%	38	100	41	16.9%	50	89%
2019	BUF	15/10	747	106	67	778	6	2	63%	-2.9	6	11.6	8.4	68	5.0	21	+0.8	4	1.3%	41	112	37	23.3%	19	89%
2020	BUF	15/10	680	107	82	967	4	5	77%	+9.7	2	11.8	8.0	76	4.3	45	-0.4	7	19.9%	10	267	12	19.7%	36	94%
2021	BUF			93	65	771	5		70%	--		11.8							5.3%						

Had Beasley not fractured his fibula in Week 16, he likely would have had the first 1,000-yard season of his career; it remains remarkable that he was able to gut things out in the playoffs. That doesn't explain his one All-Pro vote, but the logic isn't too hard to figure out there: Peter King seemed determined to include one pure slot receiver in his three All-Pro wideouts, and Beasley was the right choice there. His 308 DYAR out of the slot led all wide receivers last season, and his 28.0% DVOA out of the slot was the highest among the 15 qualified players who had at least 85% of their targets come there.

Odell Beckham

Height: 5-11 **Weight:** 198 **College:** Louisiana State **Draft:** 2014/1 (12) **Born:** 5-Nov-1992 **Age:** 29 **Risk:** Red

Year	Tm	G/GS	Snaps	Pass	Rec	Yds	TD	EZ	C%	+/-	Drop	Yd/C	aDOT	Rk	YAC	Rk	YAC+	BTkl	DVOA	Rk	DYAR	Rk	Use	Rk	Slot
2018	NYG	12/12	716	124	77	1052	6	21	62%	+1.7	3	13.7	12.2	30	4.1	50	-0.8	18	2.5%	37	151	27	29.5%	3	44%
2019	CLE	16/15	1017	133	74	1035	4	13	56%	-5.5	9	14.0	13.2	27	4.4	38	-0.3	8	-5.4%	56	79	46	26.6%	6	30%
2020	CLE	7/7	316	43	23	319	3	5	53%	-2.9	1	13.9	13.7	--	2.0	--	-2.1	8	-8.8%	--	13	--	21.3%	--	33%
2021	CLE			101	62	841	5		61%	--		13.6							-2.2%						

Cleveland's strong rushing attack allowed Beckham to flourish on first down to the tune of a 45.5% DVOA before his injury in Week 7. Conversely, the attention he drew on third and fourth down resulted in a scandalous -58.8% DVOA and just 3.2 yards per reception. It has been a frustrating stint in Cleveland for OBJ, culminating in the torn ACL he suffered while chasing down a defensive back who had made an interception on a pass thrown his way. Given the outsized expectations Beckham brought to town, the fact the Browns made the playoffs while he was in rehab led to plenty of "Is Cleveland better off without Odell?" chatter in the media. Obviously no team is "better" without a player of Beckham's caliber, though he is hardly irreplaceable. Beckham has now missed 30 games in his seven years, and is entering his age-29 season, so it's fair to wonder what the Browns would get in return for the flighty star, who hasn't hit double digits in touchdowns since 2016. It wouldn't be a shock if Beckham was dealt; it wouldn't be a surprise if he turned in a "Y'all forgot about me, huh?" season in Cleveland, either. And perhaps least surprising would be a season plagued, once again, by injury.

Braxton Berrios

Height: 5-9 Weight: 190 College: Miami Draft: 2018/6 (210) Born: 6-Oct-1995 Age: 26 Risk: Green

Year	Tm	G/GS	Snaps	Pass	Rec	Yds	TD	EZ	C%	+/-	Drop	Yd/C	aDOT	Rk	YAC	Rk	YAC+	BTkl	DVOA	Rk	DYAR	Rk	Use	Rk	Slot
2019	NYJ	16/0	85	13	6	115	0	0	46%	-0.7	1	19.2	9.3	--	14.5	--	+9.7	1	-15.2%	--	-2	--	2.6%	--	67%
2020	NYJ	16/2	290	55	37	394	3	3	67%	-0.3	3	10.6	7.8	77	5.8	8	+0.5	8	-3.4%	52	39	63	11.8%	78	81%
2021	NYJ			14	8	94	1		57%	--		11.9							-16.3%						

Berrios ranked third in targets on the Jets in 2020, in large part because the Jets ranked sixth in adjusted games lost at the wide receiver position. That being said, although the Jets didn't particularly want to turn to Berrios, he did step up when asked. In the four games Jamison Crowder missed, Berrios had 22 DYAR and a -3.0% DVOA—not bad for a receiver fourth or fifth on the depth chart when the season began. The Jets are hoping to see much less of Berrios in 2021, but OTAs saw him once again taking a major role with Crowder and Corey Davis not around. Don't be shocked if Berrios fights his way into a role on offense yet again.

Kendrick Bourne

Height: 6-1 Weight: 203 College: Eastern Washington Draft: 2017/FA Born: 4-Aug-1995 Age: 26 Risk: Green

Year	Tm	G/GS	Snaps	Pass	Rec	Yds	TD	EZ	C%	+/-	Drop	Yd/C	aDOT	Rk	YAC	Rk	YAC+	BTkl	DVOA	Rk	DYAR	Rk	Use	Rk	Slot
2018	SF	16/8	606	67	42	487	4	3	63%	+0.5	4	11.6	9.0	67	3.5	65	-0.4	4	-4.5%	51	42	52	12.8%	74	52%
2019	SF	16/0	475	44	30	358	5	5	68%	+0.1	3	11.9	9.3	--	4.1	--	+0.3	6	25.7%	--	130	--	9.4%	--	78%
2020	SF	15/5	688	74	49	667	2	5	66%	+0.8	5	13.6	9.7	56	4.5	41	+0.7	8	6.1%	29	107	36	14.2%	67	61%
2021	NE			49	31	390	2		63%	--		12.6							-5.2%						

While Bourne is no superstar, he developed into something of a jack of all trades in San Francisco. He may be the closest thing the Patriots have to a replacement for Julian Edelman. Like Edelman, Bourne's main bailiwick is the short, sharp game, where his quickness and route-running precision can help him get open quickly. Bourne had a 6.37-second 3-cone drill, and that top change-of-direction ability has been his calling card to this point in his career. It's a useful skill set to have with a pair of quarterbacks who don't necessarily have the best deep balls; while Nelson Agholor drags defenders deep, Bourne might just feast underneath.

Lynn Bowden

Height: 5-11 Weight: 204 College: Kentucky Draft: 2020/3 (80) Born: 14-Oct-1997 Age: 24 Risk: Green

Year	Tm	G/GS	Snaps	Pass	Rec	Yds	TD	EZ	C%	+/-	Drop	Yd/C	aDOT	Rk	YAC	Rk	YAC+	BTkl	DVOA	Rk	DYAR	Rk	Use	Rk	Slot
2020	MIA	10/4	337	37	28	211	0	1	76%	+0.2	0	7.5	5.1	--	4.0	--	-1.4	12	-22.4%	--	-30	--	10.5%	--	86%
2021	MIA			7	5	50	0		71%	--		10.5							-2.3%						

It's rare to see players traded the same year they were drafted, but Bowden went from Las Vegas to Miami in September. The college quarterback/running back/receiver had a bit of a steep learning curve, but did develop some quick chemistry with Tua Tagovailoa. Unfortunately for his DVOA, that resulted in a lot of quick checkdowns and short routes, leading to things like eight catches for 44 yards in the season-ending loss to the Bills. Bowden has Swiss Army Knife potential—I believe we're supposed to call those "Taysom Hill" players now—but he was a master of no trades last season. Expect him to go back to gadget plays in 2021 now that the Dolphins have upgraded their receiving corps.

Tyler Boyd

Height: 6-2 Weight: 203 College: Pittsburgh Draft: 2016/2 (55) Born: 15-Nov-1994 Age: 27 Risk: Green

Year	Tm	G/GS	Snaps	Pass	Rec	Yds	TD	EZ	C%	+/-	Drop	Yd/C	aDOT	Rk	YAC	Rk	YAC+	BTkl	DVOA	Rk	DYAR	Rk	Use	Rk	Slot
2018	CIN	14/14	773	108	76	1028	7	4	70%	+7.4	6	13.5	9.8	55	5.5	17	+0.6	5	24.1%	4	305	12	22.9%	21	82%
2019	CIN	16/15	1001	148	90	1046	5	3	61%	-3.4	5	11.6	9.8	62	3.9	48	-0.9	16	-12.4%	68	3	67	25.2%	12	77%
2020	CIN	15/8	746	110	79	841	4	9	72%	+4.1	2	10.6	8.6	69	4.4	42	-0.0	7	-6.2%	62	56	56	20.8%	33	91%
2021	CIN			118	81	901	5		69%	--		11.2							-1.4%						

Boyd caught just 10 passes for 131 yards on 23 targets in five games started by Brandon Allen or Ryan Finley; 72 of those yards came on one touchdown run after a short flat pass against the Dolphins. Boyd also missed the Texans game with a concussion after getting sandwiched between two Steelers while retrieving a Finley floater. Boyd's metrics have slipped over the last two seasons because the situation surrounding him keeps deteriorating, but he's still a quality receiver when paired with an adequate quarterback. Joe Burrow may have a new No. 1 target in rookie and former LSU teammate Ja'Marr Chase, but Boyd should still plenty of work in the slot with Chase and Tee Higgins out wide. The Bengals will be playing catch-up a lot, so there should be plenty of footballs to go around.

Miles Boykin   Height: 6-4   Weight: 220   College: Notre Dame   Draft: 2019/3 (93)   Born: 12-Oct-1996   Age: 25   Risk: Green

Year	Tm	G/GS	Snaps	Pass	Rec	Yds	TD	EZ	C%	+/-	Drop	Yd/C	aDOT	Rk	YAC	Rk	YAC+	BTkl	DVOA	Rk	DYAR	Rk	Use	Rk	Slot
2019	BAL	16/11	433	22	13	198	3	5	59%	+2.0	1	15.2	17.2	--	0.9	--	-2.3	0	16.2%	--	50	--	5.2%	--	23%
2020	BAL	16/13	546	33	19	266	4	6	58%	-0.6	1	14.0	12.1	--	4.2	--	+0.4	1	5.7%	--	45	--	8.4%	--	39%
2021	BAL			12	7	91	1		58%	--		13.4							-7.7%						

Since the passing-friendly rule changes of 1978, just eight wide receivers have started 10 or more games and caught 15 or fewer passes. Just two have done so since 1984: Darrius Heyward-Bey in 2009 (9-124-1 on a shocking 40 targets in 11 starts for the Raiders) and Boykin as a rookie in 2019. Increase the catch threshold to 20 and you get several other deep threats like Heyward-Bey, including Torrey Smith for the 2016 49ers (20-267-3 in 12 starts for an offense with a read-option flavor) and James Jett for the 2000 Raiders (20-356-2 in 13 starts), as well as Boykin last year. In other words, to start for most of a season at wide receiver but catch 20 passes or fewer, you must either be a track star whose primary job is to run the safeties out to the stadium parking lot or Myles Boykin.

Boykin is a fine blocker, which would keep him in the lineup for a run-heavy offense if he averaged 2.8 catches per game instead of 0.8. Sammy Watkins, Rashod Bateman, and others will be clamoring for Boykin's playing time this year. Boykin was a draftnik binky and has the athletic profile of a go-to receiver, but he's likely to get relegated to a package role this season.

A.J. Brown   Height: 6-0   Weight: 226   College: Mississippi   Draft: 2019/2 (51)   Born: 30-Jun-1997   Age: 24   Risk: Green

Year	Tm	G/GS	Snaps	Pass	Rec	Yds	TD	EZ	C%	+/-	Drop	Yd/C	aDOT	Rk	YAC	Rk	YAC+	BTkl	DVOA	Rk	DYAR	Rk	Use	Rk	Slot
2019	TEN	16/11	695	84	52	1051	8	5	62%	+0.8	2	20.2	13.2	26	8.9	1	+4.4	20	26.2%	4	251	11	19.4%	43	40%
2020	TEN	14/12	759	106	70	1075	11	6	66%	+3.6	6	15.4	11.5	36	6.2	6	+2.2	21	25.0%	8	332	6	26.6%	5	44%
2021	TEN			122	81	1177	8		66%	--		14.5							8.5%						

Slowed by a knee injury that kept him out for two of the team's first three games, Brown revealed after the season that he had undergone surgery on both of his knees and that both he and the team feared his season was over after Week 2. Instead, Brown outpaced his 2019 production in 12 games. He didn't quite match his yards after catch production from 2019, but that number was obviously unsustainable and what he produced instead was still wildly good. Brown is tough to press against, beats man coverage easily, and breaks tackles in the open field. He now gets to play next to Julio Jones after his successful social media recruiting pitch, which left Titans general manager Jon Robinson suggesting he "would go on Amazon and get him a $40 arts and crafts kit" to make sure he can properly craft the Julio Jones jersey. Brown noted that the pitch came about because "he was bored" at OTAs. This could be the prelude to his best year yet, and given the competition, that's saying a lot.

Antonio Brown   Height: 5-10   Weight: 185   College: Central Michigan   Draft: 2010/6 (195)   Born: 10-Jul-1988   Age: 33   Risk: Red

Year	Tm	G/GS	Snaps	Pass	Rec	Yds	TD	EZ	C%	+/-	Drop	Yd/C	aDOT	Rk	YAC	Rk	YAC+	BTkl	DVOA	Rk	DYAR	Rk	Use	Rk	Slot
2018	PIT	15/15	998	168	104	1297	15	24	62%	-4.2	2	12.5	11.1	46	4.7	34	-0.3	17	1.7%	41	191	19	26.4%	10	38%
2019	NE	1/0	24	8	4	56	1	4	50%	-1.0	0	14.0	11.5	--	1.8	--	-0.9	0	-14.0%	--	-1	--	21.3%	--	50%
2020	TB	8/4	323	62	45	483	4	4	73%	+3.0	1	10.7	8.9	65	5.6	12	+0.6	6	8.9%	24	110	35	20.0%	35	42%
2021	TB			86	60	686	5		70%	--		11.5							6.0%						

Brown kept a lid on any unprofessional/antisocial/abhorrent tendencies last season. His probation for a battery case was terminated, and his myriad other issues have receded to the background. So why not sign him to a one-year, incentive-laden deal to remain in Tom Brady's entourage? As a No. 3 receiver, Brown is both terrifying to opponents and a low risk for the Bucs if he flakes out. Brown might have enough good behavior in him for one more year of image rehabilitation and possible championship glory, with the carrot of one more big contract at the end of the stick. If not, well, we'll all have something to tweet about this autumn.

John Brown

Height: 5-11 Weight: 179 College: Pittsburg State (KS) Draft: 2014/3 (91) Born: 4-Mar-1990 Age: 31 Risk: Yellow

Year	Tm	G/GS	Snaps	Pass	Rec	Yds	TD	EZ	C%	+/-	Drop	Yd/C	aDOT	Rk	YAC	Rk	YAC+	BTkl	DVOA	Rk	DYAR	Rk	Use	Rk	Slot
2018	BAL	16/15	757	97	42	715	5	15	43%	-11.2	6	17.0	16.9	2	3.8	56	-0.5	1	-12.2%	67	4	67	18.1%	42	51%
2019	BUF	15/15	934	115	72	1060	6	5	63%	+4.6	5	14.7	14.6	12	3.0	73	-1.2	13	11.0%	23	205	19	25.0%	14	34%
2020	BUF	9/8	453	52	33	458	3	5	63%	+1.6	2	13.9	13.2	20	5.4	17	+0.9	2	11.4%	19	99	38	16.6%	54	41%
2021	LV			72	48	665	4		67%	--		14.0							5.5%						

Small sample size theatre: On just six screen passes, Brown earned 48 DYAR, best in the league by 25 DYAR. However, a decent portion of that production stems from a 33-yard play against the Seahawks on a third-and-goal from the 35-yard line (yes, you read that correctly). Brown was tracked down just before reaching the end zone, which makes it even funnier seeing as Brown's production in this small split could have been even more absurd with a touchdown.

Brown is best known for what he offers to the intermediate-to-deep area as a field-stretcher. His role was somewhat toned down in that regard last season thanks to the addition of speedster Gabriel Davis, but Brown's average depth of target was above 14 yards in both 2018 and 2019, and should be expected to return to that range as he steps in to replace Nelson Agholor in Las Vegas. Expect Brown and Henry Ruggs to threaten down the field in order to open up space for Darren Waller, Hunter Renfrow, and others in the underneath area.

Marquise Brown

Height: 5-9 Weight: 170 College: Oklahoma Draft: 2019/1 (25) Born: 4-Jun-1997 Age: 24 Risk: Green

Year	Tm	G/GS	Snaps	Pass	Rec	Yds	TD	EZ	C%	+/-	Drop	Yd/C	aDOT	Rk	YAC	Rk	YAC+	BTkl	DVOA	Rk	DYAR	Rk	Use	Rk	Slot
2019	BAL	14/11	571	71	46	584	7	10	65%	+1.3	3	12.7	12.1	37	4.9	22	-0.4	6	4.2%	35	98	42	19.6%	41	63%
2020	BAL	16/14	802	100	58	769	8	13	58%	-2.9	9	13.3	13.4	18	4.7	31	+0.2	8	-6.5%	63	48	58	25.6%	8	56%
2021	BAL			85	52	704	6		61%	--		13.5							-0.9%						

Brown's average depth of target of 13.4 yards ranked 11th overall among receivers with more than 75 targets. Unfortunately, his average depth of catch of 8.5 ranked 32nd and wedged him between New England's Jakobi Meyers and Jacksonville's Keelan Cole, neither of whom can be described as dangerous big-play threats. In other words, Brown and Lamar Jackson weren't connecting downfield as often as they should have. That was due in part to Jackson's hesitancy/ineffectiveness as a sideline passer: Brown was targeted along the sidelines past the line of scrimmage just 41 times, tied with Marquez Valdes-Scantling and Christian Kirk for 39th in the NFL. Nine drops by Brown, several of them on catchable short passes, also played a role.

Brown may max out at about 100 targets and 50 or 60 receptions in the Ravens' run-heavy offense, but the Ravens need him to average over 15 yards per catch in his role as a 1970s-style vertical receiver. There's nothing wrong with being an occasional home run threat; Brown, Jackson, and the Ravens just need to create a lot more occasions.

Damiere Byrd

Height: 5-9 Weight: 180 College: South Carolina Draft: 2015/FA Born: 27-Jan-1993 Age: 28 Risk: Green

Year	Tm	G/GS	Snaps	Pass	Rec	Yds	TD	EZ	C%	+/-	Drop	Yd/C	aDOT	Rk	YAC	Rk	YAC+	BTkl	DVOA	Rk	DYAR	Rk	Use	Rk	Slot
2018	CAR	8/0	44	2	1	8	0	0	50%	-0.1	0	8.0	12.5	--	1.0	--	-2.9	0	-25.3%	--	-2	--	0.7%	--	50%
2019	ARI	11/3	461	46	32	359	1	1	70%	+2.3	0	11.2	10.0	--	4.7	--	-0.4	7	-4.6%	--	30	--	12.7%	--	11%
2020	NE	16/14	901	77	47	604	1	1	61%	-4.3	5	12.9	11.4	37	3.7	62	-1.0	5	-12.3%	76	2	76	18.5%	46	28%
2021	CHI			29	18	220	1		62%	--		12.6							-7.1%						

Byrd was the No. 2 Patriots receiver by both targets and DVOA, but his latter rate of -12.3% does not spark much optimism for a late-twenties breakout with his new team in Chicago. That said, the Bears have clearly made a point to get faster in recent seasons. They are poised to start sophomore receiver Darnell Mooney opposite Allen Robinson, and he ran a 4.38s 40. Byrd was even faster at his pro day with a 4.28s time, and with rookie Dazz Newsome out for much of the preseason with a broken collarbone, Byrd has a chance to start in the slot as the Bears try to trade incumbent Anthony Miller. At the very least, Byrd can contribute as a returner for a team that lost the best to ever return kicks this offseason when Cordarrelle Patterson joined the Falcons.

Marquez Callaway

Marquez Callaway   Height: 6-2   Weight: 204   College: Tennessee   Draft: 2020/FA   Born: 27-Mar-1998   Age: 23   Risk: Green

Year	Tm	G/GS	Snaps	Pass	Rec	Yds	TD	EZ	C%	+/-	Drop	Yd/C	aDOT	Rk	YAC	Rk	YAC+	BTkl	DVOA	Rk	DYAR	Rk	Use	Rk	Slot
2020	NO	11/3	266	27	21	213	0	0	78%	+2.3	0	10.1	8.1	--	2.8	--	-1.0	2	0.1%	--	27	--	7.6%	--	48%
2021	NO			51	31	400	3		61%	--		13.0							-5.3%						

Earning a significant role in the Saints offense partly thanks to injuries ahead of him, undrafted rookie Marquez Callaway hauled in every one of his 21 targets that SIS marked as catchable in 2020. That includes Drew Brees' 7000th career completion, guaranteeing Callaway immortality as a trivia answer if nothing else. Callaway had the most catchable passes without an incompletion of any receiver, which fits his college scouting reports as a big target with elite ball skills, but his average target came just 8.1 yards downfield. He did show flashes of his speed on both punt and kick returns, and his ball skills should be enough to earn him increased opportunities amid a very inexperienced receiver group, but he'll need to convert opportunities deeper downfield to make a lasting impact.

Parris Campbell   Height: 6-0   Weight: 205   College: Ohio State   Draft: 2019/2 (59)   Born: 16-Jul-1997   Age: 24   Risk: Red

Year	Tm	G/GS	Snaps	Pass	Rec	Yds	TD	EZ	C%	+/-	Drop	Yd/C	aDOT	Rk	YAC	Rk	YAC+	BTkl	DVOA	Rk	DYAR	Rk	Use	Rk	Slot
2019	IND	7/3	200	24	18	127	1	1	75%	+1.3	1	7.1	8.1	--	5.9	--	-0.5	5	-73.4%	--	-104	--	11.0%	--	63%
2020	IND	2/2	63	9	6	71	0	0	67%	+0.5	0	11.8	11.9	--	3.0	--	-1.8	0	-21.3%	--	-7	--	13.1%	--	100%
2021	IND			87	56	584	4		64%	--		10.4							-9.7%						

A popular preseason sleeper, Campbell immediately lived up to that notion with a nine-target, 71-yard Week 1. And then ... he tore his MCL and PCL as he took an end around on the first snap of Week 2. "Sundays were hard for me, man, I can't lie," Campbell told The Athletic's Zak Keefer, "I was in a rough place for a long time." Two years into his career, there has not been a lot of Campbell. This is a make-it-or-break-it year, and Carson Wentz has not historically been the best screen-tosser in the yard, but Campbell's waterbug game should draw plenty of targets if he can stay healthy.

Quintez Cephus   Height: 6-1   Weight: 207   College: Wisconsin   Draft: 2020/5 (166)   Born: 1-Apr-1998   Age: 23   Risk: Green

Year	Tm	G/GS	Snaps	Pass	Rec	Yds	TD	EZ	C%	+/-	Drop	Yd/C	aDOT	Rk	YAC	Rk	YAC+	BTkl	DVOA	Rk	DYAR	Rk	Use	Rk	Slot
2020	DET	13/2	365	35	20	349	2	2	57%	-0.3	2	17.5	14.9	--	4.3	--	-0.1	2	10.6%	--	66	--	7.5%	--	44%
2021	DET			37	24	323	2		65%	--		13.4							0.4%						

A fifth-round sophomore receiver who had just 20 catches in his rookie season would not normally merit a full *Almanac* table, but Cephus' 20 catches are 20 more than any current Lions wide receiver had for the team in 2020. That's not to say that Cephus will be the team's new No. 1 receiver; that role will likely belong to either free-agent addition Breshad Perriman or Tyrell Williams. But Cephus was efficient in his limited opportunities, and he has something that new head coach Dan Campbell is sure to love: a 6-foot-1 and 201-pound frame to help him body up smaller defensive backs as a run-blocker.

DJ Chark   Height: 6-4   Weight: 198   College: Louisiana State   Draft: 2018/2 (61)   Born: 23-Sep-1996   Age: 25   Risk: Yellow

Year	Tm	G/GS	Snaps	Pass	Rec	Yds	TD	EZ	C%	+/-	Drop	Yd/C	aDOT	Rk	YAC	Rk	YAC+	BTkl	DVOA	Rk	DYAR	Rk	Use	Rk	Slot
2018	JAX	11/0	291	32	14	174	0	3	44%	-4.7	2	12.4	10.3	--	3.2	--	-1.5	1	-47.4%	--	-90	--	8.8%	--	34%
2019	JAX	15/14	864	118	73	1008	8	12	62%	+1.8	4	13.8	11.9	39	4.3	39	-0.3	14	1.9%	38	134	32	22.8%	21	50%
2020	JAX	13/12	702	93	53	706	5	9	57%	-2.9	3	13.3	14.3	11	3.1	75	-1.2	3	-9.1%	68	26	66	19.4%	39	34%
2021	JAX			99	65	842	5		66%	--		12.9							1.4%						

The challenge Urban Meyer threw Chark as they went through OTAs and minicamp was that Chark was a big receiver who played small last year. Chark agreed with that, saying "I love the challenge. I love talking to Coach Meyer. He's a competitor. He's going to push me." However, at the end of Week 4 last year, Chark was second in the NFL in DYAR on only 17 targets. The talent was absolutely put on display, but Chark admitted at OTAs that as the Jaguars fell to 1-3 and it became pretty clear that they wouldn't be competitive, there were times where he let "the circumstances control the output." Chark was particularly bad with Mike Glennon, finishing with a -31.0% DVOA in his three games when Glennon started. Hooked up with Trevor Lawrence, there are a lot of good reasons to believe that Chark can be put on the rejuvenation machine.

Ja'Marr Chase

Height: 6-0   Weight: 208   College: Louisiana State   Draft: 2021/1 (5)   Born: 1-Mar-2000   Age: 21   Risk: Green

Year	Tm	G/GS	Snaps	Pass	Rec	Yds	TD	EZ	C%	+/-	Drop	Yd/C	aDOT	Rk	YAC	Rk	YAC+	BTkl	DVOA	Rk	DYAR	Rk	Use	Rk	Slot
2021	CIN			125	83	1079	6		66%	--		12.9							1.5%						

The Bengals targeted A.J. Green 7.9 times per game over the last three seasons despite a revolving cast of quarterbacks and Green's vacillating health and enthusiasm for remaining with the organization. Chase should earn a similar target load and do more with it than the fading, disinterested Green did last season. Chase is a "safe" prospect whose game contains shades of Allen Robinson and JuJu Smith-Schuster, and of course he arrives with pre-established chemistry with Joe Burrow. The 83-catch, 1,000-yard season projected for Chase would vindicate the Bengals for selecting him to a degree -- not because such a season is unlikely, but because it will only happen if the Bengals offensive line plays well enough to keep Burrow alive.

Chase Claypool

Height: 6-4   Weight: 229   College: Notre Dame   Draft: 2020/2 (49)   Born: 7-Jul-1998   Age: 23   Risk: Green

Year	Tm	G/GS	Snaps	Pass	Rec	Yds	TD	EZ	C%	+/-	Drop	Yd/C	aDOT	Rk	YAC	Rk	YAC+	BTkl	DVOA	Rk	DYAR	Rk	Use	Rk	Slot
2020	PIT	16/6	692	110	62	873	9	9	57%	+1.1	7	14.1	14.6	7	5.2	20	+0.6	12	-5.4%	58	68	48	17.6%	52	42%
2021	PIT			116	74	965	7		64%	--		13.0							1.0%						

Claypool exploded on the national scene in Week 4 with a four-touchdown game (including one on an end around) against the Eagles, producing a lot of "the Steelers just know how to draft wide receivers" takes. He caught only five more touchdowns all season (and added another on the ground) and was caught up in the general malaise that affected the Pittsburgh passing attack. Over the 10 games from Halloween to Christmas, he averaged four receptions for 44 yards. Still, the size/speed combo that made him a top-50 draft pick were displayed often enough to expect a more consistent and productive sophomore season. One positive was that Claypool saved his best work—by far—for third and fourth downs. His first- and second-down DVOAs were poor, -32.5% and -18.1% respectively. But when the money downs came, Claypool delivered to the tune of a 44.3% DVOA and averaged 13.6 yards on 36 targets.

Randall Cobb

Height: 5-10   Weight: 192   College: Kentucky   Draft: 2011/2 (64)   Born: 22-Aug-1990   Age: 31   Risk: Green

Year	Tm	G/GS	Snaps	Pass	Rec	Yds	TD	EZ	C%	+/-	Drop	Yd/C	aDOT	Rk	YAC	Rk	YAC+	BTkl	DVOA	Rk	DYAR	Rk	Use	Rk	Slot
2018	GB	9/6	466	61	38	383	2	4	62%	-3.3	4	10.1	8.4	71	6.2	6	+0.1	5	-22.1%	78	-45	76	17.7%	46	90%
2019	DAL	15/6	727	83	55	828	3	4	66%	+0.9	10	15.1	9.9	61	6.0	7	+1.5	16	5.4%	33	119	35	15.2%	63	98%
2020	HOU	10/2	369	48	38	441	3	5	79%	+3.0	2	11.6	6.7	--	4.5	--	-0.3	1	15.8%	--	107	--	14.5%	--	90%
2021	HOU			72	45	497	3		63%	--		11.1							-11.8%						

After his signing was panned as a wild overpay, Cobb hurt his toe in Week 11 and missed the last six weeks of the season. When he was on the field, he showed his trademark competent route-running and cut down on his Dallas drop issue by a large amount, but just wasn't a frequent target for Deshaun Watson. Cobb had just one game with more than six targets—against the Packers in Week 7—and was never seriously involved in the offense. Keke Coutee showed more separation than Cobb in his late-season trial. However, Cobb still has a guaranteed contract for this season, he is the veteran, and the Texans definitely don't have many other receivers of note to throw to. Could seniority make him a volume-based fantasy football sleeper? The low average depth of target will certainly help.

Keelan Cole

Height: 6-1   Weight: 194   College: Kentucky Wesleyan   Draft: 2017/FA   Born: 20-Apr-1993   Age: 28   Risk: Green

Year	Tm	G/GS	Snaps	Pass	Rec	Yds	TD	EZ	C%	+/-	Drop	Yd/C	aDOT	Rk	YAC	Rk	YAC+	BTkl	DVOA	Rk	DYAR	Rk	Use	Rk	Slot
2018	JAX	16/11	687	70	38	491	1	4	54%	-4.8	8	12.9	10.2	51	3.6	60	-0.7	1	-21.3%	76	-48	77	13.5%	67	51%
2019	JAX	16/1	380	35	24	361	3	2	69%	+2.4	1	15.0	11.0	--	4.1	--	-0.7	1	24.8%	--	105	--	6.3%	--	67%
2020	JAX	16/5	785	88	55	642	5	8	63%	-1.1	3	11.7	11.3	39	3.2	73	-1.1	5	-1.7%	47	82	43	15.6%	60	90%
2021	NYJ			47	27	336	2		57%	--		12.3							-12.6%						

After spending his first two seasons bouncing between slot and wide roles, the Jaguars stuck Cole in the slot the last two years and kept him there. That will likely be Cole's role in New York, which brings up questions as to the future of Jamison Crowder. It also might bring up questions about the future of Denzel Mims, as Cole leapfrogged him on the depth chart at OTAs, drawing rave reviews for his chemistry with Zach Wilson. Even if he doesn't earn a starting job in the offense, Cole could contribute on special teams; he was third in the league with 6.9 estimated points of punt return value last season in his first year in that role in the NFL.

Nico Collins   Height: 6-4   Weight: 222   College: Michigan   Draft: 2021/3 (89)   Born: 19-Mar-1999   Age: 22   Risk: Green

Year	Tm	G/GS	Snaps	Pass	Rec	Yds	TD	EZ	C%	+/-	Drop	Yd/C	aDOT	Rk	YAC	Rk	YAC+	BTkl	DVOA	Rk	DYAR	Rk	Use	Rk	Slot
2021	HOU			30	17	224	1		57%	--		13.3							-13.4%						

A humongous receiver, Collins ran fast at his pro day, but that upper-echelon speed is hit-or-miss on his tape and will essentially dictate his ultimate upside. He can be a fairly productive wideout in the sort of peak Hakeem Nicks way if his speed on the field matches that on the track. If not, he might be something more like a latter day Michael Westbrook—a big possession receiver who could box out and win outside. The Texans don't really have an established receiver of this kind on the roster as a result of ... various idiotic moves ... so Collins is worth keeping an eye on. If this administration had any history of actually trusting rookies, there might be some alarm bells sounding about him.

Chris Conley   Height: 6-3   Weight: 205   College: Georgia   Draft: 2015/3 (76)   Born: 25-Oct-1992   Age: 29   Risk: Green

Year	Tm	G/GS	Snaps	Pass	Rec	Yds	TD	EZ	C%	+/-	Drop	Yd/C	aDOT	Rk	YAC	Rk	YAC+	BTkl	DVOA	Rk	DYAR	Rk	Use	Rk	Slot
2018	KC	16/13	802	52	32	334	5	10	62%	-3.1	5	10.4	9.0	64	4.4	39	+0.1	4	-1.0%	47	48	50	9.5%	83	66%
2019	JAX	16/14	880	90	47	775	5	4	52%	-4.4	5	16.5	14.3	18	5.1	17	+1.1	9	-2.7%	50	68	50	15.9%	61	22%
2020	JAX	15/4	439	63	40	471	2	6	63%	-0.6	4	11.8	10.3	46	4.5	37	+0.5	4	-9.0%	66	18	70	11.3%	79	48%
2021	HOU			50	28	359	2		56%	--		12.8							-14.2%						

At some point, the Jaguars clearly had the idea that Conley could be a red zone target because of his size. After his first five red zone targets went for -1 yard, they kind of moved on from that one. As an outside receiver, Conley was startlingly limited last season. He was only targeted deep on 14 balls, and only caught four of them. The Jaguars seemed to use a random number generator to determine how much they were into Conley. They'd go months at a time with him never passing 32% of the snaps, then suddenly he'd go back up to 86%, then he'd be inactive two weeks later. Houston is a great port in a storm as an outside receiver trying to find consistent NFL snaps, but Conley hasn't really shown a lot to indicate that he is going to seize on the opportunity.

Brandin Cooks   Height: 5-10   Weight: 183   College: Oregon State   Draft: 2014/1 (20)   Born: 25-Sep-1993   Age: 28   Risk: Green

Year	Tm	G/GS	Snaps	Pass	Rec	Yds	TD	EZ	C%	+/-	Drop	Yd/C	aDOT	Rk	YAC	Rk	YAC+	BTkl	DVOA	Rk	DYAR	Rk	Use	Rk	Slot
2018	LAR	16/16	989	117	80	1204	5	6	68%	+9.1	1	15.1	14.0	19	4.3	41	-1.0	9	21.5%	12	318	10	21.7%	26	70%
2019	LAR	14/14	716	72	42	583	2	3	58%	+2.5	4	13.9	14.3	17	4.0	44	-1.0	3	0.0%	46	71	49	13.5%	67	63%
2020	HOU	15/15	801	119	81	1150	6	10	68%	+6.2	4	14.2	11.9	33	4.2	52	-0.1	4	8.9%	23	207	18	24.1%	17	64%
2021	HOU			106	60	807	4		57%	--		13.4							-12.6%						

Nobody benefited from Bill O'Brien's firing quite as much as Cooks, who produced just 128 yards in the first four games, in which he was used mostly as an outside, stagnant receiver, including a three-target shutout against Minnesota. The Texans introduced more motion under Tim Kelly's play calling and Cooks immediately put up four straight games with at least 60 yards, catching touchdowns in three of them. The play-action game never really came around for the Texans in a meaningful way, which kept Cooks from being targeted on bombs for most of the year, but like David Johnson he finished the year in a fury. An Easterby ally from his Patriots days, Cooks threatened a public holdout when asked if he would welcome a trade after the season. The good news is that he's absolutely this team's No. 1 target. The bad news is that No. 1 deep threats playing with Tyrod Taylor, as Sammy Watkins can tell you, don't have it made.

Amari Cooper

| | | Height: 6-1 | | Weight: 211 | | College: Alabama | | | | Draft: 2015/1 (4) | | | Born: 17-Jun-1994 | | | Age: 27 | | Risk: Green |

Year	Tm	G/GS	Snaps	Pass	Rec	Yds	TD	EZ	C%	+/-	Drop	Yd/C	aDOT	Rk	YAC	Rk	YAC+	BTkl	DVOA	Rk	DYAR	Rk	Use	Rk	Slot
2018	2TM	15/15	838	107	75	1005	7	9	70%	+6.4	5	13.4	9.9	53	5.5	15	+1.2	13	8.7%	27	187	20	21.9%	25	31%
2019	DAL	16/16	850	119	79	1189	8	9	66%	+6.2	6	15.1	13.1	28	3.0	72	-1.0	6	22.3%	10	324	3	20.6%	34	29%
2020	DAL	16/15	943	130	92	1114	5	12	71%	+7.1	5	12.1	8.9	64	4.5	38	+0.3	11	4.7%	34	184	21	21.1%	31	48%
2021	DAL			122	84	1088	6		69%	--		12.9							7.6%						

Cooper was targeted on routes marked as "curl" by Sports Info Solutions 30 times last season, the third-highest total in the NFL. (Stefon Diggs was targeted a remarkable 50 times, DeAndre Hopkins 34.) Cooper went 25-224-0 on those routes. The appeal of the curl route for the Cowboys is obvious: defenders often played off Cooper, and it's a short timing-based throw that Andy Dalton could complete without incident. Also, Mike McCarthy's game plans are about as creative as an elementary accounting textbook.

Cooper went 37-401-1 on 51 targets in Dak Prescott's four full starts. Despite a crowded receiving corps, he should be at least a high-end WR2 in fantasy and a potential league leader in receptions and yards if the Cowboys season works out the way they hope it will.

Keke Coutee

| | | Height: 5-11 | | Weight: 180 | | College: Texas Tech | | | | Draft: 2018/4 (103) | | | Born: 14-Jan-1997 | | | Age: 24 | | Risk: Green |

Year	Tm	G/GS	Snaps	Pass	Rec	Yds	TD	EZ	C%	+/-	Drop	Yd/C	aDOT	Rk	YAC	Rk	YAC+	BTkl	DVOA	Rk	DYAR	Rk	Use	Rk	Slot
2018	HOU	6/2	267	41	28	287	1	0	68%	-2.5	3	10.3	5.1	--	7.5	--	+1.1	2	-10.5%	--	7	--	21.9%	--	73%
2019	HOU	9/4	350	36	22	254	0	1	61%	-2.7	3	11.5	7.7	--	6.4	--	+1.6	3	-25.5%	--	-37	--	12.3%	--	67%
2020	HOU	8/4	292	40	33	400	3	6	83%	+5.3	2	12.1	9.4	--	4.5	--	-0.1	6	14.6%	--	85	--	15.1%	--	90%
2021	HOU			67	40	480	2		60%	--		11.9							-12.8%						

Entering the final year of his rookie contract, Coutee spent his third season making just enough miscues to get everybody upset at him—fumbling on the goal line in Indianapolis as the Texans were driving to tie the game in Week 15, fumbling against the Ravens on a short catch in Week 2 to set them up in the red zone. Yet he still flashed the kind of talent that this team needs from its slot receiver after Randall Cobb gave way, closing the year out with three-straight 50-yard games where he was targeted 19 total times. It sure would be great if the Texans simply acted in the interests of their future and gave Coutee a 1,000-snap season at slot receiver just to see what happens. But if they did that, they wouldn't be the Texans.

Jamison Crowder

| | | Height: 5-9 | | Weight: 177 | | College: Duke | | | | Draft: 2015/4 (105) | | | Born: 17-Jun-1993 | | | Age: 28 | | Risk: Red |

Year	Tm	G/GS	Snaps	Pass	Rec	Yds	TD	EZ	C%	+/-	Drop	Yd/C	aDOT	Rk	YAC	Rk	YAC+	BTkl	DVOA	Rk	DYAR	Rk	Use	Rk	Slot
2018	WAS	9/7	428	49	29	388	2	1	59%	-1.1	2	13.4	10.2	52	7.0	4	+1.6	4	-6.2%	54	23	56	18.0%	43	84%
2019	NYJ	16/12	815	122	78	833	6	5	64%	-3.4	7	10.7	8.0	73	4.5	34	-0.4	17	-11.8%	66	9	65	24.4%	15	85%
2020	NYJ	12/7	593	89	59	699	6	4	66%	+1.8	3	11.8	7.7	80	5.5	13	+1.0	8	-3.2%	50	66	49	25.0%	12	84%
2021	NYJ			102	64	736	4		63%	--		11.6							-10.0%						

The Jets spent most of the offseason trying to get Crowder to take a significant pay cut, resulting in him skipping OTAs. Using a second-round pick on Elijah Moore and bringing in Keelan Cole doesn't help Crowder's long-term outlook. But Crowder was the Jets' most valuable receiver last season, at least partially because someone had to be; Crowder hasn't had a positive DVOA since 2016. Crowder did have some soft hands last season; his +1.8 receiving plus/minus was the highest for any Jets receiver in the last three years. Then again, he's just one year removed from having seven drops, so it's far from a sure thing that he'll provide Zach Wilson with a reliable receiver in 2021.

Corey Davis

| | | Height: 6-3 | | Weight: 209 | | College: Western Michigan | | | | Draft: 2017/1 (5) | | | Born: 11-Jan-1995 | | | Age: 26 | | Risk: Green |

Year	Tm	G/GS	Snaps	Pass	Rec	Yds	TD	EZ	C%	+/-	Drop	Yd/C	aDOT	Rk	YAC	Rk	YAC+	BTkl	DVOA	Rk	DYAR	Rk	Use	Rk	Slot
2018	TEN	16/16	872	112	65	891	4	9	58%	-2.7	5	13.7	11.2	43	4.1	49	-0.8	10	-1.2%	48	104	40	27.1%	6	62%
2019	TEN	15/11	733	69	43	601	2	3	62%	+1.9	3	14.0	12.5	35	5.0	19	+0.8	17	5.4%	34	99	41	17.5%	57	63%
2020	TEN	14/12	718	92	65	984	5	8	71%	+6.7	4	15.1	12.1	29	4.5	40	+0.7	4	22.5%	9	261	13	22.3%	26	61%
2021	NYJ			89	52	718	4		58%	--		13.7							-9.1%						

Davis broke out in 2020, putting career highs in DVOA and DYAR to go along with all his traditional stats. Some of that is actual improvement from the former top-five pick; he has seen both his DYAR and DVOA increase in every season in the league. It's perhaps not surprising that Davis performed better when catching passes from Ryan Tannehill instead of Marcus Mariota; his 71% catch rate was a career high, but it was sparked in part by seeing more catchable balls. More concerning is Davis going from a solid No. 2 receiver next to A.J. Brown to being the top guy on paper in New York; his DVOA dropped from 27.3% to -3.1% in the games Brown did not start.

Gabriel Davis   Height: 6-2   Weight: 216   College: Central Florida   Draft: 2020/4 (128)   Born: 1-Apr-1999   Age: 22   Risk: Blue

Year	Tm	G/GS	Snaps	Pass	Rec	Yds	TD	EZ	C%	+/-	Drop	Yd/C	aDOT	Rk	YAC	Rk	YAC+	BTkl	DVOA	Rk	DYAR	Rk	Use	Rk	Slot
2020	BUF	16/11	797	62	35	599	7	10	56%	-1.3	1	17.1	15.7	6	3.7	60	-0.2	4	10.7%	20	115	32	10.9%	82	52%
2021	BUF			56	35	578	3		63%	--		16.7							1.7%						

Davis' breakout year in 2020 was enough for the Bills to part with John Brown, though the subsequent pickup of Emmanuel Sanders will eat up some of those vacated snaps. Davis had some odd splits in 2020. His 15.7-yard aDOT was sixth among all qualified receivers, profiling him as a deep threat. But 20.6% of his targets came in the red zone, leading all qualified receivers and helping him put up a touchdown every 8.9 targets, fourth in the league. We'll go out on a limb and predict he won't keep that level of scoring rate up, but when you can produce as both a deep threat and a close-range scoring threat, you're doing something right.

Stefon Diggs   Height: 6-0   Weight: 191   College: Maryland   Draft: 2015/5 (146)   Born: 29-Nov-1993   Age: 28   Risk: Green

Year	Tm	G/GS	Snaps	Pass	Rec	Yds	TD	EZ	C%	+/-	Drop	Yd/C	aDOT	Rk	YAC	Rk	YAC+	BTkl	DVOA	Rk	DYAR	Rk	Use	Rk	Slot
2018	MIN	15/14	874	149	102	1021	9	13	68%	+9.7	3	10.0	9.1	61	4.3	42	-0.7	24	-12.0%	66	8	64	26.7%	8	42%
2019	MIN	15/15	783	95	63	1130	6	8	67%	+9.0	4	17.9	15.6	9	4.7	28	+0.1	12	24.0%	7	272	10	22.9%	20	38%
2020	BUF	16/15	965	166	127	1535	8	10	77%	+17.4	5	12.1	10.6	45	3.7	63	-0.5	23	15.8%	16	377	2	29.3%	3	51%
2021	BUF			158	109	1393	8		69%	--		12.7							6.9%						

Diggs did not quite set the Buffalo franchise record for receiving DYAR, which still belongs to Eric Moulds' 459 in 1998. That's about the only bad thing you can say about Diggs' 2020 season as he immediately developed fantastic chemistry with Josh Allen. He's the first receiver not named Michael Thomas to lead the league in receiving plus-minus since 2016. Diggs had the most DYAR in the league on curls (88) and slants (116), two of the three most common routes in football. (Diggs ran 51 curl routes, with no other receiver in the league over 35.) He led the league with 188 DYAR in the "mid" zone, between the 40s. And he did all this while retaining a DVOA of over 15.0% on over 150 targets, one of 48 players in DVOA history to pull that feat off. So, yeah, it's safe to say trading for him was a decent idea.

Devin Duvernay   Height: 5-11   Weight: 210   College: Texas   Draft: 2020/3 (92)   Born: 12-Sep-1997   Age: 24   Risk: Green

Year	Tm	G/GS	Snaps	Pass	Rec	Yds	TD	EZ	C%	+/-	Drop	Yd/C	aDOT	Rk	YAC	Rk	YAC+	BTkl	DVOA	Rk	DYAR	Rk	Use	Rk	Slot
2020	BAL	16/3	347	26	20	201	0	0	77%	+2.0	1	10.1	6.2	--	5.9	--	-0.6	3	-14.0%	--	-2	--	6.6%	--	69%
2021	BAL			23	15	174	1		65%	--		11.3							0.2%						

Thirteen of Duvernay's 26 targets came on screens or jet sweep shovel passes. He averaged a respectable 7.6 yards per reception on these glorified handoffs, plus 17.5 yards per carry on actual handoffs and he ranked second in the league in kickoff return value. But even the most dedicated screen-and-reverse specialist needs to provide a little more than just screens and reverses, especially when playing about 20 offensive snaps per game. Rookie Rashod Bateman should leapfrog Duvernay on the depth chart, as will Sammy Watkins in the eight to 10 games when he is healthy, but Myles Boykin could sink below him. Duvernay is gifted enough to earn an expanded role in the Ravens offense; the Ravens offense just might not have one for him.

Julian Edelman   Height: 5-10   Weight: 200   College: Kent State   Draft: 2009/7 (232)   Born: 22-May-1986   Age: 35   Risk: N/A

Year	Tm	G/GS	Snaps	Pass	Rec	Yds	TD	EZ	C%	+/-	Drop	Yd/C	aDOT	Rk	YAC	Rk	YAC+	BTkl	DVOA	Rk	DYAR	Rk	Use	Rk	Slot
2018	NE	12/12	747	108	74	850	6	5	69%	+1.3	8	11.5	7.9	75	4.7	30	+0.1	10	1.7%	42	122	35	25.5%	13	82%
2019	NE	16/13	1009	153	100	1117	6	6	65%	-1.7	11	11.2	9.7	64	3.2	68	-1.1	9	-8.6%	62	48	55	26.3%	8	84%
2020	NE	6/1	265	39	21	315	0	2	54%	-3.2	3	15.0	10.9	--	3.0	--	-1.4	1	-8.6%	--	12	--	24.6%	--	90%

After two years of nursing a knee injury, Edelman finally called it a career in April. A lock for the Patriots Hall of Fame, and second only to Wes Welker in receptions in franchise history, Edelman leaves behind one of the most prolific playoff resumes we have ever seen, a key player on a dynasty for a decade. All that being said, no, Edelman should not be going to Canton. Edelman's 776 DYAR ranks 153rd among receivers in the DVOA era. He never made a Pro Bowl team or finished in the top 20 of DYAR or top 30 of DVOA. He'll have to console himself with his Super Bowl MVP, and with never having to buy a beer in Boston again.

Bryan Edwards   Height: 6-3   Weight: 215   College: South Carolina   Draft: 2020/3 (81)   Born: 13-Nov-1998   Age: 23   Risk: Green

Year	Tm	G/GS	Snaps	Pass	Rec	Yds	TD	EZ	C%	+/-	Drop	Yd/C	aDOT	Rk	YAC	Rk	YAC+	BTkl	DVOA	Rk	DYAR	Rk	Use	Rk	Slot
2020	LV	12/3	259	15	11	193	1	2	73%	+0.7	0	17.5	9.3	--	7.3	--	+2.3	3	36.6%	--	64	--	4.0%	--	47%
2021	LV			26	18	242	1		69%	--		13.6							9.4%						

Edwards is a familiar case of a player peaking early in college, then never quite blossoming beyond that. A former four-star recruit, Edwards started right away for the Gamecocks and turned heads with his contested catch ability. Not only does Edwards have proper strength to jostle with defensive backs, but he has an uncanny feel for finding the ball in the air while contorting his body around. As much as Edwards shines in that regard, though, his route-running never developed beyond average while at South Carolina and he is not someone who adds value as a burner down the field. Edwards' rookie year was stunted more by injury than anything, though. He was earning about half the team's offensive snaps before suffering an ankle injury that kept him out for four weeks. Edwards is not a burner anyway, and that extra tick in lost speed put a damper on his rookie season. Hopefully a full offseason of recovery may allow Edwards to find his way back onto the field as a YAC and contested-catch bully, which is something the Raiders lack at wide receiver right now.

D'Wayne Eskridge   Height: 5-9   Weight: 190   College: Western Michigan   Draft: 2021/2 (56)   Born: 23-Mar-1997   Age: 24   Risk: Green

Year	Tm	G/GS	Snaps	Pass	Rec	Yds	TD	EZ	C%	+/-	Drop	Yd/C	aDOT	Rk	YAC	Rk	YAC+	BTkl	DVOA	Rk	DYAR	Rk	Use	Rk	Slot
2021	SEA			18	13	163	1		72%	--		12.5							9.2%						

Seattle's second-round pick did not truly break out at receiver until his final season at Western Michigan, and he primarily succeeded using his deep speed to run past players. Western Michigan's passing attack did not use the most sophisticated passing concepts, and as a result, a large share of Eskridge's best plays came from taking a post or a slant to the house on a run-pass option. Eskridge also excelled as a kick returner, and he displayed some versatility in college by playing cornerback during his injury-shortened 2019 season. Eskridge slots in as the third option in Seattle's receiver room, so he should have plenty of opportunities to take advantage of opposing secondaries that are focused on Tyler Lockett and DK Metcalf.

Mike Evans   Height: 6-5   Weight: 231   College: Texas A&M   Draft: 2014/1 (7)   Born: 21-Aug-1993   Age: 28   Risk: Green

Year	Tm	G/GS	Snaps	Pass	Rec	Yds	TD	EZ	C%	+/-	Drop	Yd/C	aDOT	Rk	YAC	Rk	YAC+	BTkl	DVOA	Rk	DYAR	Rk	Use	Rk	Slot
2018	TB	16/16	940	138	86	1524	8	16	62%	+10.3	6	17.7	15.8	6	3.3	70	-1.0	6	26.3%	3	420	4	22.3%	24	29%
2019	TB	13/13	810	118	67	1157	8	18	57%	+1.1	7	17.3	15.8	6	3.8	49	-0.5	3	18.0%	14	301	6	25.1%	13	25%
2020	TB	16/16	857	109	70	1006	13	14	64%	+3.7	7	14.4	13.1	24	3.8	59	+0.1	7	25.6%	6	354	4	18.7%	45	39%
2021	TB			100	62	909	7		62%	--		14.6							10.3%						

Evans finished second in the NFL to Davante Adams of the Packers with 14 targets when the offense was inside the 10-yard line, resulting in nine of his touchdowns. Evans also finished tied with Chase Claypool for the league lead by drawing seven pass interference penalties. Evans' status as Tom Brady's favorite among many targets appears secure, despite a few high-profile drops and an injury scare before last year's playoffs. Evans will get plenty of red zone opportunities and either flag down

Brady's sideline launches or make sure his defender gets flagged. He's generally a safe fantasy pick, but be aware that there are only so many balls to go around in Tampa Bay this season.

Larry Fitzgerald   Height: 6-3   Weight: 225   College: Pittsburgh   Draft: 2004/1 (3)   Born: 31-Aug-1983   Age: 38   Risk: N/A

Year	Tm	G/GS	Snaps	Pass	Rec	Yds	TD	EZ	C%	+/-	Drop	Yd/C	aDOT	Rk	YAC	Rk	YAC+	BTkl	DVOA	Rk	DYAR	Rk	Use	Rk	Slot
2018	ARI	16/16	872	112	69	734	6	11	62%	-1.4	2	10.6	9.5	58	3.0	76	-1.7	12	-15.3%	71	-23	72	23.6%	18	89%
2019	ARI	16/16	903	109	75	804	4	7	69%	+3.7	2	10.7	8.4	69	4.6	32	-0.9	12	-2.0%	48	90	44	20.6%	32	86%
2020	ARI	13/13	745	72	54	409	1	3	75%	+1.9	1	7.6	6.1	85	3.4	66	-1.7	2	-18.1%	78	-30	78	16.2%	57	96%

Fitzgerald's raw career totals through his age-37 season: 1,432 catches (over 100 more than anyone else except Jerry Rice), 17,492 yards (second only to Rice), 121 touchdowns (sixth, because he was stuck with horrible quarterbacks for large chunks of his career). He's the active leader in all three categories and needs 117 receptions to catch Rice's all-time record in that department. He could get there with two more decent years, but there has been zero indication whether or not that interests him. He hit free agency after the season but hasn't met with any teams aside from brief conversations with Cardinals brass. At the same time, he has not made any move to retire, leaving us all to throw out wild guesses about where he might be playing this fall. Arizona, Minnesota, and Tampa Bay are among his rumored destinations, but nothing is off the table.

If Fitzgerald does play again, it's important that teams know what they're getting. He is practically a tight end at this point; he led all wide receivers in slot rate last season and also finished in the top 10 in 2018 and 2019. His deep speed is gone—he was third-to-last in average depth of target and dead last in average depth of reception (4.1 yards) and yards per catch. He could be your guy, however, if you need some blocking on the perimeter and an effective short-yardage receiver; he picked up a first down on 61% of his targets with 6 yards or less to go for a first down, right at league average for wideouts.

Travis Fulgham   Height: 6-2   Weight: 215   College: Old Dominion   Draft: 2019/6 (184)   Born: 13-Sep-1995   Age: 26   Risk: Green

Year	Tm	G/GS	Snaps	Pass	Rec	Yds	TD	EZ	C%	+/-	Drop	Yd/C	aDOT	Rk	YAC	Rk	YAC+	BTkl	DVOA	Rk	DYAR	Rk	Use	Rk	Slot
2019	DET	3/0	63	3	0	0	0	0	0%	-1.5	0	0.0	22.0	--	0.0	--	+0.0	0	-103.6%	--	-21	--	2.9%	--	33%
2020	PHI	13/8	552	67	38	539	4	10	57%	-1.2	5	14.2	13.3	19	2.6	82	-1.3	3	4.9%	33	93	40	15.1%	62	40%
2021	PHI			45	27	377	3		60%	--		14.0							-4.2%						

There were few faster surprise rises and falls than Fulgham's during the 2020 season. The receiver was cut by the Packers in training camp, claimed by the Eagles, and sat on the practice squad for the first three weeks of the season. In his first game, Fulgham caught a 42-yard touchdown pass late in the fourth quarter to give the Eagles the lead over the 49ers. His next four games had yardage totals of 152, 75, 73, and 78 with three touchdowns. Then, after the Eagles' Week 9 bye, Fulgham didn't eclipse 30 yards receiving in any game. More defensive attention and a returning Alshon Jeffery played a part in that second-half disappearance. He won't be the center of attention in 2021 either, not with DeVonta Smith and Jalen Reagor as the top two targets. In 2020, Fulgham had positive DVOA both from the slot and outside, versatility that should help if he grabs the No. 3 receiver role.

Will Fuller   Height: 6-0   Weight: 184   College: Notre Dame   Draft: 2016/1 (21)   Born: 16-Apr-1994   Age: 27   Risk: Yellow

Year	Tm	G/GS	Snaps	Pass	Rec	Yds	TD	EZ	C%	+/-	Drop	Yd/C	aDOT	Rk	YAC	Rk	YAC+	BTkl	DVOA	Rk	DYAR	Rk	Use	Rk	Slot
2018	HOU	7/7	375	45	32	503	4	5	71%	+6.0	0	15.7	16.3	--	5.2	--	+0.6	4	34.6%	--	180	--	21.5%	--	40%
2019	HOU	11/11	580	71	49	670	3	9	69%	+7.8	4	13.7	14.6	14	4.5	37	-0.5	2	1.8%	39	82	45	20.1%	36	63%
2020	HOU	11/11	577	75	53	879	8	6	71%	+6.7	3	16.6	13.1	25	5.5	15	+1.2	3	41.2%	1	326	7	21.4%	29	60%
2021	MIA			109	67	910	6		61%	--		13.6							-1.3%						

Fuller finally managed a healthy season, parlayed that into a league-leading DVOA—and then still failed to appear in all 16 games as a PED suspension cost him the last five games of the season. Watching him in Miami will be interesting, as 45% of Fuller's DYAR came on go/fly routes. The deep go route was not in Tua Tagovailoa's wheelhouse last season; he only attempted 10 such passes and completed just three. Fuller could have gone anywhere in free agency; we'll see if his speed can unlock Tua's deep ball.

Devin Funchess Height: 6-4 Weight: 225 College: Michigan Draft: 2015/2 (41) Born: 21-May-1994 Age: 27 Risk: Green

Year	Tm	G/GS	Snaps	Pass	Rec	Yds	TD	EZ	C%	+/-	Drop	Yd/C	aDOT	Rk	YAC	Rk	YAC+	BTkl	DVOA	Rk	DYAR	Rk	Use	Rk	Slot
2018	CAR	14/12	622	79	44	549	4	8	56%	-2.0	7	12.5	13.0	22	1.7	84	-1.9	1	-10.5%	62	13	61	16.4%	54	39%
2019	IND	1/1	36	5	3	32	0	1	60%	-0.3	0	10.7	9.8	--	2.0	--	-2.1	0	-7.6%	--	2	--	16.0%	--	0%
2021	GB			7	5	56	0		71%	--		12.2							1.1%						

Funchess missed nearly all of 2019 with a broken collarbone and then missed all of 2020 after a COVID opt-out. It's a long shot that he'll live up to the Packers' initial hope that he could become the team's No. 2 receiver opposite Davante Adams, but it was a long shot when he initially signed his rolled over $2.5-million contract last offseason. Funchess has just one career season with an above-average DVOA, and even that year he averaged an underwhelming 2.5 yards of separation according to Next Gen Stats. Aaron Rodgers (or whomever quarterbacks the Packers this year) would have to trust Funchess to win jump balls to bolster his target total. That just doesn't seem necessary for a team with Davante Adams and secondary receivers in Allen Lazard and Robert Tonyan among the top 10 at their positions in average separation.

Russell Gage Height: 6-0 Weight: 184 College: Louisiana State Draft: 2018/6 (194) Born: 22-Jan-1996 Age: 25 Risk: Green

Year	Tm	G/GS	Snaps	Pass	Rec	Yds	TD	EZ	C%	+/-	Drop	Yd/C	aDOT	Rk	YAC	Rk	YAC+	BTkl	DVOA	Rk	DYAR	Rk	Use	Rk	Slot
2018	ATL	15/0	60	10	6	63	0	0	60%	-1.1	2	10.5	10.5	--	3.2	--	-1.8	0	-24.2%	--	-9	--	1.7%	--	10%
2019	ATL	16/4	527	74	49	446	1	3	66%	-1.5	4	9.1	7.1	80	3.1	71	-1.5	13	-14.1%	70	-8	70	11.2%	73	76%
2020	ATL	16/8	762	109	72	786	4	10	66%	-1.3	9	10.9	8.6	67	3.9	57	-0.4	13	-1.7%	48	93	41	17.9%	49	77%
2021	ATL			99	64	747	4		65%	--		11.7							-4.7%						

Gage caught just 16 passes for 126 yards (7.9 yards per catch) when split wide, as opposed to 53-641-4 from the slot, even though he frequently lined up wide when Julio Jones was injured for the final six games of the season. In other words, Gage is a pure slot receiver, which is all fine and dandy, except that *someone* must be split wide besides Calvin Ridley. Gage went 23-264-2 in the final four Falcons games and should be able to extend similar production over a full year if not asked to do too much. Look for Gage to be the starter but move inside when the Falcons go three-wide, possibly with a department store mannequin flanking him.

Michael Gallup Height: 6-1 Weight: 200 College: Colorado State Draft: 2018/3 (81) Born: 4-Mar-1996 Age: 25 Risk: Green

Year	Tm	G/GS	Snaps	Pass	Rec	Yds	TD	EZ	C%	+/-	Drop	Yd/C	aDOT	Rk	YAC	Rk	YAC+	BTkl	DVOA	Rk	DYAR	Rk	Use	Rk	Slot
2018	DAL	16/8	739	68	33	507	2	6	49%	-5.7	1	15.4	14.3	16	5.2	23	-0.1	2	-14.3%	68	-9	68	13.4%	69	16%
2019	DAL	14/12	853	113	66	1107	6	5	58%	-1.8	10	16.8	12.9	32	5.0	20	+1.1	10	13.5%	19	233	15	22.6%	24	19%
2020	DAL	16/15	1003	105	59	843	5	14	56%	-5.1	6	14.3	12.1	30	4.3	48	-0.1	5	-5.7%	60	58	53	17.6%	51	23%
2021	DAL			83	52	840	4		63%	--		16.3							1.7%						

Gallup served as the designated boundary deep threat in Mike McCarthy's system. It was a thankless job because A) Andy Dalton could not throw deep, and B) the injury-plagued Cowboys line couldn't protect Dalton long enough to throw deep if he could. Gallup had some big games against teams with thin secondaries (6-121-2 against the Eagles in Week 16) and should catch a few more bombs with Dak Prescott back in the saddle. At the same time, Gallup is likely to be the odd man out in the battle for touches now that CeeDee Lamb has established himself.

Chris Godwin Height: 6-1 Weight: 209 College: Penn State Draft: 2017/3 (84) Born: 27-Feb-1996 Age: 25 Risk: Green

Year	Tm	G/GS	Snaps	Pass	Rec	Yds	TD	EZ	C%	+/-	Drop	Yd/C	aDOT	Rk	YAC	Rk	YAC+	BTkl	DVOA	Rk	DYAR	Rk	Use	Rk	Slot
2018	TB	16/5	717	95	59	842	7	15	62%	+1.2	1	14.3	11.9	33	4.2	46	+0.1	10	1.3%	43	105	39	15.5%	60	49%
2019	TB	14/14	957	121	86	1333	9	9	71%	+11.6	1	15.5	10.6	49	6.7	4	+2.0	19	32.8%	1	415	2	22.5%	25	82%
2020	TB	12/12	675	84	65	840	7	6	77%	+9.7	4	12.9	10.1	51	4.3	47	-0.4	6	28.0%	5	267	11	18.0%	48	82%
2021	TB			110	70	933	7		64%	--		13.3							8.4%						

Godwin battled hamstring and hand injures for the first half of last season. By the time he returned, Antonio Brown had joined the Tom Brady Orchestra as a featured soloist. Godwin's numbers dipped sharply from 2019 as a result, but he was still productive when healthy and went 14-253-4 in the final three Bucs regular season games. The Bucs franchise-tagged Godwin in the offseason and are reportedly seeking a long-term deal. Godwin sounds content to play under the tag and share targets with Brown, Mike Evans, and many others this season, even if it hurts his raw totals and potential market value. Such is the magic of riding shotgun with Tom Brady for a defending Super Bowl champion.

Kenny Golladay   Height: 6-4   Weight: 213   College: Northern Illinois   Draft: 2017/3 (96)   Born: 3-Nov-1993   Age: 28   Risk: Yellow

Year	Tm	G/GS	Snaps	Pass	Rec	Yds	TD	EZ	C%	+/-	Drop	Yd/C	aDOT	Rk	YAC	Rk	YAC+	BTkl	DVOA	Rk	DYAR	Rk	Use	Rk	Slot
2018	DET	15/13	904	119	70	1063	5	13	59%	-0.5	5	15.2	12.9	23	5.0	25	+0.7	10	13.3%	21	250	15	23.2%	19	46%
2019	DET	16/16	957	116	65	1190	11	15	56%	+1.0	6	18.3	15.7	7	4.7	30	+0.6	7	18.0%	13	279	9	21.1%	30	45%
2020	DET	5/5	226	32	20	338	2	4	63%	+0.4	3	16.9	14.9	--	1.9	--	-2.3	0	22.0%	--	90	--	19.1%	--	35%
2021	NYG			105	64	1030	7		61%	--		16.2							-0.8%						

Golladay missed a chunk of 2020 training camp due to a COVID quarantine, then missed the first two games of the season with a tweaked hamstring, then suffered a hip injury in Week 8 that kept him on the week-to-week list until he finally ended up on IR in December. In the four full games he played for the Lions, Golladay went over 100 yards twice and scored touchdowns in the other two. Golladay was relatively productive when third-stringer David Blough quarterbacked the Lions in 2019 (18-240-1 in four December games), which is an encouraging sign that his skills as a deep threat will travel with him. His price tag was high, but Dave Gettleman always splurges for the platinum soft-cloth car wash. Golladay and Darius Slayton will either turn Daniel Jones into the NFL's most dangerous mad bomber or become the primary witnesses when the Giants offense blows itself up.

Jakeem Grant   Height: 5-7   Weight: 169   College: Texas Tech   Draft: 2016/6 (186)   Born: 30-Oct-1992   Age: 29   Risk: Green

Year	Tm	G/GS	Snaps	Pass	Rec	Yds	TD	EZ	C%	+/-	Drop	Yd/C	aDOT	Rk	YAC	Rk	YAC+	BTkl	DVOA	Rk	DYAR	Rk	Use	Rk	Slot
2018	MIA	10/2	282	34	21	268	2	0	62%	-0.4	2	12.8	8.5	--	6.7	--	+1.3	3	-4.6%	--	21	--	12.7%	--	31%
2019	MIA	10/2	219	33	19	164	0	0	58%	-0.2	2	8.6	12.4	--	4.6	--	-1.5	2	-33.1%	--	-52	--	8.6%	--	61%
2020	MIA	14/4	370	54	36	373	1	1	67%	+0.8	4	10.4	10.9	42	4.8	30	-0.1	16	-11.9%	75	3	75	11.1%	80	53%
2021	MIA			17	11	123	1		65%	--		11.2							-6.0%						

Grant's receiving numbers are nearly the textbook definition of replacement-level player, but he justifies his spot on the roster with his special teams play. His 5.3 estimated points added as a punt returner was fifth in the league, and he was tied for second with 16 positive-value punt returns. Grant has now finished in the top five in punt return value in two of the past three years, only missing out in 2019 because Adam Gase for some reason opted not to take advantage of Grant's speed in the return game. Grant may never be more than a gadget player as a receiver, but as long as he can provide value on punts, he won't have to worry about having a roster slot.

A.J. Green   Height: 6-4   Weight: 210   College: Georgia   Draft: 2011/1 (4)   Born: 31-Jul-1988   Age: 33   Risk: Red

Year	Tm	G/GS	Snaps	Pass	Rec	Yds	TD	EZ	C%	+/-	Drop	Yd/C	aDOT	Rk	YAC	Rk	YAC+	BTkl	DVOA	Rk	DYAR	Rk	Use	Rk	Slot
2018	CIN	9/9	457	77	46	694	6	13	60%	-1.2	4	15.1	12.7	24	3.5	64	-0.4	4	12.4%	23	155	24	26.1%	11	47%
2020	CIN	16/14	820	104	47	523	2	13	45%	-11.1	3	11.1	13.5	17	1.8	87	-2.2	5	-33.0%	87	-172	87	18.8%	44	24%
2021	ARI			82	49	643	4		60%	--		13.3							-6.5%						

Could there be anything left in the tank? Green is the 20th wide receiver since the merger to average 40 yards per game or less with at least 10 starts in their age-32 seasons. Of the 19 others, eight never played again; three others remained useful for 40-plus games. (The best was James Lofton, who moved to the Bills and became a key player for several Super Bowl teams.) The rest put up a few hundred yards and were gone a year later. None of them, however, had advanced statistics as bad as Green's last year—Green's total of -172 DYAR is among the bottom 10 on record and the worst since Tavon Austin had -219 with the Rams in 2016.

Worst Wide Receiver Seasons by Receiving DYAR, 1983-2020

Year	Player	Team	DYAR	DVOA	Pass	Rec	Yards	TD	C%	Yd/C
2006	Chris Chambers	MIA	-294	-36.8%	153	59	677	4	39%	11.5
2016	Tavon Austin	LAR	-219	-39.1%	106	58	509	3	55%	8.8
2004	Bobby Wade	CHI	-210	-44.3%	89	42	481	0	47%	11.5
1994	Kelvin Martin	SEA	-188	-31.1%	135	56	681	1	41%	12.2
2003	Az Hakim	DET	-185	-34.1%	108	49	449	4	45%	9.2
2014	Cecil Shorts	JAX	-183	-33.7%	110	53	557	1	48%	10.5
2001	Peter Warrick	CIN	-180	-30.0%	137	70	667	1	51%	9.5
2020	**A.J. Green**	**CIN**	**-172**	**-33.0%**	**104**	**47**	**523**	**2**	**45%**	**11.1**
2013	Greg Little	CLE	-171	-34.7%	99	41	465	2	41%	11.3
2011	Devin Aromashodu	MIN	-171	-38.9%	84	26	468	1	31%	18.0

No, the offensive environment in Cincinnati was not ideal, but neither Tee Higgins nor Tyler Boyd struggled anywhere near as badly as Green did in 2020. Sports Info Solutions charts balls as "catchable" or "uncatchable" and Green had just 60% catchable passes, the lowest rate of any qualifying wide receiver. But he also caught just 76% of those catchable passes, the sixth-lowest rate of any qualifying wide receiver. And when he caught them, he didn't get much YAC with them.

It's not obvious where Green fits in Arizona's wideout corps either. Only 24% of his targets came from the slot last year, the second-lowest rate in the league. His new teammate Christian Kirk was third lowest, and DeAndre Hopkins was also in the bottom 10. Second-round draftee Rondale Moore figures to get the bulk of the team's slot targets this year, but one of these veterans will probably also be spending more time inside.

Jalen Guyton

Height: 6-1   Weight: 212   College: North Texas   Draft: 2019/FA   Born: 7-Jun-1997   Age: 24   Risk: Green

Year	Tm	G/GS	Snaps	Pass	Rec	Yds	TD	EZ	C%	+/-	Drop	Yd/C	aDOT	Rk	YAC	Rk	YAC+	BTkl	DVOA	Rk	DYAR	Rk	Use	Rk	Slot
2019	LAC	3/0	18	2	0	0	0	0	0%	-0.6	0	0.0	37.5	--	0.0	--	+0.0	0	-110.1%	--	-12	--	1.8%	--	50%
2020	LAC	16/9	919	55	28	511	3	8	51%	-4.0	6	18.3	16.1	4	6.4	4	+1.3	2	-3.7%	53	39	62	9.2%	85	53%
2021	LAC			33	21	302	2		64%	--		14.6							0.7%						

As is the case for most of the Chargers' tertiary receivers, Guyton is a speed threat with the tools to punish defenses down the field. Guyton toiled away at the bottom of the roster in 2019 before emerging into a contributing role last season. Unsurprising for a former UDFA, Guyton does have issues with holding onto the ball (six drops on 55 targets). That boom-or-bust factor is an accepted trade-off for Guyton's 4.39s speed, which netted him seven 20-plus-yard gains last season. Oddly enough, Guyton struggles more when playing out wide than from the slot despite his solid 6-foot-1 and 212-pound build. Guyton caught just 38% of his targets from wide alignments, though a healthy portion of those were strictly go balls down the sideline. Guyton was much better from the slot, snagging 62% of his passes while posting a DVOA that was 55.7% higher than his work from wide alignments. Guyton probably will not see his role expanded in 2021, but he can continue to be a deep threat that helps open up the short-to-intermediate area for his teammates.

DaeSean Hamilton

Height: 6-1   Weight: 206   College: Penn State   Draft: 2018/4 (113)   Born: 10-Mar-1995   Age: 26   Risk: N/A

Year	Tm	G/GS	Snaps	Pass	Rec	Yds	TD	EZ	C%	+/-	Drop	Yd/C	aDOT	Rk	YAC	Rk	YAC+	BTkl	DVOA	Rk	DYAR	Rk	Use	Rk	Slot
2018	DEN	14/5	471	46	30	243	2	2	65%	-0.9	1	8.1	8.5	--	2.3	--	-2.3	0	-18.1%	--	-20	--	9.4%	--	77%
2019	DEN	16/2	660	52	28	297	1	2	54%	-4.6	4	10.6	8.3	70	4.6	33	-0.2	2	-18.0%	74	-21	72	10.6%	75	85%
2020	DEN	16/2	533	44	23	293	2	5	52%	-2.5	3	12.7	14.0	--	4.1	--	+0.2	0	-20.3%	--	-27	--	8.4%	--	59%

Early this offseason, Hamilton was looking like the odd man out in Denver's wide receiver room and was being shopped as a potential trade piece. Hamilton then tore his ACL in mid-May, giving the Broncos an easy decision to simply cut the injured player they were trying to trade anyway. Hamilton looked somewhat promising early on but never developed beyond his rookie year and the team saw fit to draft KJ Hamler last year to replace him in the slot. Hamilton earned negative DVOA on first, second, and third/fourth downs while sharing snaps last season, which all but sealed his fate given some of the flashes Hamler showed. Assuming he can return to good health after 2021, Hamilton may still be a decent No. 4 for a team, but it's not hard to see how he got pushed out of Denver given their investment in more explosive options at the position.

KJ Hamler

Height: 5-9 | Weight: 176 | College: Penn State | Draft: 2020/2 (46) | Born: 8-Jul-1999 | Age: 22 | Risk: Green

Year	Tm	G/GS	Snaps	Pass	Rec	Yds	TD	EZ	C%	+/-	Drop	Yd/C	aDOT	Rk	YAC	Rk	YAC+	BTkl	DVOA	Rk	DYAR	Rk	Use	Rk	Slot
2020	DEN	13/4	521	56	30	381	3	2	54%	-6.5	6	12.7	10.9	43	4.1	55	-0.6	6	-20.3%	82	-33	80	12.8%	76	88%
2021	DEN			85	46	570	4		54%	--		12.3							-18.2%						

Seeing as Hamler is a tiny third-round rookie whose defining trait was YAC ability when he entered the league, it's not terribly surprising that he proved to be something of a rollercoaster in his first pro season. The floor for Hamler's game is lowered given his size and questionable hands—he dropped six passes, an alarming number considering he saw only 56 targets. Hamler's effective route tree was also lacking in 2020. He was a trusted underneath YAC weapon and a useful deep threat both down the seam and the sideline, but his work over the middle of the field left something to be desired. That issue showed up very clearly in the red zone, where Hamler earned just four targets for 0.5 yards per pass as he was reduced to being nothing more than a quick screen option. Hamler either needs to take the next step as a route-runner or hope that the rest of Denver's pass-catchers are so good in the intermediate area that Hamler does not need to provide much there (which may well be the case).

Mecole Hardman

Height: 5-10 | Weight: 187 | College: Georgia | Draft: 2019/2 (56) | Born: 12-Mar-1998 | Age: 23 | Risk: Green

Year	Tm	G/GS	Snaps	Pass	Rec	Yds	TD	EZ	C%	+/-	Drop	Yd/C	aDOT	Rk	YAC	Rk	YAC+	BTkl	DVOA	Rk	DYAR	Rk	Use	Rk	Slot
2019	KC	16/5	479	41	26	538	6	0	63%	+1.5	1	20.7	11.3	--	11.2	--	+5.3	12	44.1%	--	181	--	7.6%	--	60%
2020	KC	16/8	499	62	41	560	4	3	66%	-0.4	7	13.7	10.6	44	7.0	3	+1.5	6	6.4%	28	90	42	10.1%	83	65%
2021	KC			69	43	606	4		62%	--		14.0							1.8%						

Hardman's real value to Kansas City is to serve as an emergency plan in the case that Tyreek Hill ever suffers an injury, but he has become a decent weapon in his own right. A 4.33s speed guy coming out of Georgia, Hardman was primarily used as a pure vertical weapon during his rookie season before stepping into a slightly fuller role in 2020. Granted, Hardman is still mostly a gadget weapon and deep threat, but his target share to the middle portion of the field did jump from 26% to 34%. The next evolution for Hardman has to be finding work in the red zone. Last season, Hardman earned just four targets inside the 20, the same amount as Byron Pringle, who is otherwise an afterthought in the Chiefs offense. With Sammy Watkins now out of the picture, some of those targets should fall to Hardman, and it's on him to learn to find space in those tight areas rather than relying only on his speed like he can between the 20s. That said, with Kansas City's improved offensive line, Hardman should still be plenty productive down the field on the Chiefs' many vertical passing concepts.

Kelvin Harmon

Height: 6-2 | Weight: 213 | College: North Carolina State | Draft: 2019/6 (206) | Born: 15-Dec-1996 | Age: 25 | Risk: Yellow

Year	Tm	G/GS	Snaps	Pass	Rec	Yds	TD	EZ	C%	+/-	Drop	Yd/C	aDOT	Rk	YAC	Rk	YAC+	BTkl	DVOA	Rk	DYAR	Rk	Use	Rk	Slot
2019	WAS	16/8	493	44	30	365	0	4	68%	+2.0	2	12.2	11.6	--	3.1	--	-1.1	3	-2.8%	--	33	--	9.3%	--	45%
2021	WAS			25	17	210	1		68%	--		12.3							2.3%						

At this time last year, Harmon was in the running to be Washington's No. 2 receiver opposite Terry McLaurin. Unfortunately, a torn ACL in training camp forced him to miss the entire 2020 season. Now he comes back to a significantly more crowded wide receiver room that includes the additions of Curtis Samuel, Adam Humphries, and Dyami Brown. When he was on the field in 2019, Harmon's best role was on first-down shot plays. He had 31.6% DVOA on 12 first-down passes with a 13.5-yard average depth of target, but negative DVOA on all other downs.

Deonte Harris

Height: 5-6 | Weight: 170 | College: Assumption | Draft: 2019/FA | Born: 4-Dec-1997 | Age: 24 | Risk: Green

Year	Tm	G/GS	Snaps	Pass	Rec	Yds	TD	EZ	C%	+/-	Drop	Yd/C	aDOT	Rk	YAC	Rk	YAC+	BTkl	DVOA	Rk	DYAR	Rk	Use	Rk	Slot
2019	NO	14/1	68	6	6	24	0	0	100%	+0.8	0	4.0	-2.2	--	6.2	--	-3.1	5	-47.1%	--	-14	--	1.2%	--	83%
2020	NO	1/0	169	25	20	186	1	2	80%	+2.4	2	9.3	4.9	--	6.4	--	+0.2	13	1.3%	--	29	--	9.0%	--	54%
2021	NO			57	36	437	3		63%	--		12.3							-4.5%						

Harris was named first-team All-Pro as a return specialist in his rookie year, making him the first undrafted Saints rookie ever to make the Pro Bowl. Although he didn't return to the Pro Bowl last season, his average kick and punt return distance both increased, and he scored his first career receiving touchdown against the Panthers in Week 7. Harris is one of a group of young

Saints receivers whose kicking game contributions should help secure their roster spots. It's tougher to figure out which, if any, will also emerge as a contributor on offense.

N'Keal Harry

Height: 6-4 Weight: 225 College: Arizona State Draft: 2019/1 (32) Born: 17-Dec-1997 Age: 24 Risk: Green

Year	Tm	G/GS	Snaps	Pass	Rec	Yds	TD	EZ	C%	+/-	Drop	Yd/C	aDOT	Rk	YAC	Rk	YAC+	BTkl	DVOA	Rk	DYAR	Rk	Use	Rk	Slot
2019	NE	7/5	220	24	12	105	2	4	50%	-3.2	1	8.8	9.6	--	3.5	--	-0.6	8	-26.1%	--	-25	--	9.5%	--	25%
2020	NE	14/9	584	57	33	309	2	5	58%	-4.0	2	9.4	8.6	68	3.2	71	-1.4	2	-27.8%	86	-67	83	15.7%	59	62%
2021	NE			12	8	88	0		67%	--		11.2							-8.4%						

We've reached the "anonymous scouts claim they preferred tons of other receivers in the draft" stage of Harry's career, which is rarely a good sign. Harry's sophomore season went just about as bad as it possibly could have; he ended up with the second-worst DYAR for a wide receiver in franchise history, just losing out to Greg McMurtry's -110 DYAR in 1993. Harry joined A.J. Green as one of only two qualified receivers to finish in the bottom 10 in both receiving plus-minus and YAC+, meaning he had trouble catching the ball and had trouble doing anything afterwards. There's a reason the same two players finished in the bottom two slots in DVOA. Harry is on his last chance in New England, if he even gets a chance at all; rumors during OTAs had him fighting for a roster spot along with the likes of Isaiah Zuber and Kristian Wilkerson, who we assure you are actual players and not names made up for a gag.

Rashard Higgins

Height: 6-1 Weight: 198 College: Colorado State Draft: 2016/5 (172) Born: 7-Oct-1994 Age: 27 Risk: Green

Year	Tm	G/GS	Snaps	Pass	Rec	Yds	TD	EZ	C%	+/-	Drop	Yd/C	aDOT	Rk	YAC	Rk	YAC+	BTkl	DVOA	Rk	DYAR	Rk	Use	Rk	Slot
2018	CLE	13/1	483	53	39	572	4	4	74%	+7.6	3	14.7	11.6	38	3.7	57	-1.0	3	22.3%	11	143	28	11.6%	76	57%
2019	CLE	10/1	177	11	4	55	1	2	36%	-2.6	0	13.8	11.1	--	2.3	--	-0.6	0	-27.0%	--	-11	--	3.3%	--	64%
2020	CLE	13/6	502	52	37	599	4	6	71%	+7.1	0	16.2	14.5	9	2.1	85	-1.4	1	29.4%	3	176	23	14.1%	68	33%
2021	CLE			23	14	206	1		61%	--		14.3							0.5%						

Much like his teammate Jarvis Landry, Higgins was a second-down machine, with a 69.5% DVOA and 89% catch percentage. Unlike Landry, Higgins also made plays on the money downs—on third and fourth down his DVOA was 30.3%, and on deep passes as well (15.4-yard average depth of target).

Higgins was a free agent who would have made a smart under-the-radar buy for some team; he told the media he turned down more money elsewhere to come back to Cleveland. "It's just like, going to another team, how does that really benefit me?" Higgins stated. "To go somewhere for another $1 million or another $2 million, then you start over with a whole other quarterback and then you start over with a whole new playbook." Higgins and his current quarterback, Baker Mayfield, have vibed from the beginning, and reportedly the Progressive pitchman lobbied heavily for his favorite binky to return to the Lake. The Browns getting Higgins for just over $2 million on a one-year deal is smart business. At some point, however, should Higgins continue to play well, he will earn a long-term deal and may have to relocate after all.

Tee Higgins

Height: 6-4 Weight: 215 College: Clemson Draft: 2020/2 (33) Born: 18-Jan-1999 Age: 22 Risk: Green

Year	Tm	G/GS	Snaps	Pass	Rec	Yds	TD	EZ	C%	+/-	Drop	Yd/C	aDOT	Rk	YAC	Rk	YAC+	BTkl	DVOA	Rk	DYAR	Rk	Use	Rk	Slot
2020	CIN	16/14	805	108	67	908	6	10	62%	+1.8	7	13.6	11.9	32	4.6	34	+0.4	7	3.9%	37	142	26	19.0%	41	56%
2021	CIN			112	69	872	5		62%	--		12.7							-6.9%						

Higgins' average depth of target of 11.9 yards ranked 13th among receivers with 100-plus targets in 2020. A.J. Green's aDOT was higher (13.5 yards), but Green was the target of many more hopeless moon launches. Higgins was effective both working the deep sidelines and the short middle of the field, with lots of traits that could translate to stardom: excellent concentration and tracking on long passes, the ability to rumble through some tackles on shorter ones. Higgins must share targets with Ja'Marr Chase and Tyler Boyd, but the Bengals lack a truly dangerous receiving weapon at tight end or running back, so there should be just enough footballs to go around.

Tyreek Hill Height: 5-10 Weight: 185 College: West Alabama Draft: 2016/5 (165) Born: 1-Mar-1994 Age: 27 Risk: Green

Year	Tm	G/GS	Snaps	Pass	Rec	Yds	TD	EZ	C%	+/-	Drop	Yd/C	aDOT	Rk	YAC	Rk	YAC+	BTkl	DVOA	Rk	DYAR	Rk	Use	Rk	Slot
2018	KC	16/16	905	137	87	1479	12	11	64%	+8.3	8	17.0	15.3	10	6.1	8	+0.5	19	23.8%	6	387	5	24.0%	17	59%
2019	KC	12/12	567	89	58	860	7	4	65%	+4.6	3	14.8	12.9	33	4.8	24	-0.2	13	22.4%	9	237	12	20.9%	31	58%
2020	KC	15/15	901	135	87	1276	15	15	64%	+3.3	10	14.7	13.1	22	5.0	26	+0.4	21	17.3%	14	322	8	23.4%	22	74%
2021	KC			133	89	1305	9		67%	--		14.7							11.3%						

The NFL is littered with track stars, but none seem to move at quite the same speed as Tyreek Hill. Since Patrick Mahomes took over at quarterback in 2018, Hill leads the league with 19 receptions of 40-plus yards. That includes 13 touchdowns, also the most in the league of that span. (The next-closest players are tied with just seven such scores.) Not all of those plays are vertical shots, either. Hill is as electric with the ball in his hands as anyone in the league and regularly generates these explosive plays on his own. Just last season, Hill broke 21 tackles on 100 touches, giving him the ninth-highest broken tackle rate among wide receivers with at least 50 touches. And that does not account for all the times Hill simply outruns someone and breaks their pursuit angle entirely without being touched. For that reason, it's no wonder Hill is one of the league's best screen weapons, even at the volume he sees those plays. Hill handled 12 screens last season for 22 DYAR, putting him fourth in the league. Assuming he remains on this trajectory, Hill is the league's most explosive receiver and one of the best pass-catchers period.

T.Y. Hilton Height: 5-10 Weight: 183 College: Florida International Draft: 2012/3 (92) Born: 14-Nov-1989 Age: 32 Risk: Yellow

Year	Tm	G/GS	Snaps	Pass	Rec	Yds	TD	EZ	C%	+/-	Drop	Yd/C	aDOT	Rk	YAC	Rk	YAC+	BTkl	DVOA	Rk	DYAR	Rk	Use	Rk	Slot
2018	IND	14/14	763	120	76	1270	6	8	63%	-0.4	3	16.7	11.8	34	6.0	9	+1.0	8	23.4%	8	359	7	22.4%	23	50%
2019	IND	10/10	485	68	45	501	5	4	66%	+0.5	2	11.1	10.1	56	4.7	26	-0.2	4	1.6%	40	76	47	22.7%	22	52%
2020	IND	15/15	688	93	56	762	5	13	60%	-1.1	3	13.6	13.0	26	3.5	65	-0.7	3	5.7%	30	138	27	19.5%	38	40%
2021	IND			81	49	653	4		60%	--		13.3							-5.1%						

Was it the injury, or was it the age? Hilton took a one-year prove-it deal after the COVID-driven scarcity of the market proved cool for him—he admitted in a presser that he turned down more cash from the Browns. Last year he labored a bit with a long-term groin injury and also had problems winning in a way that Philip Rivers could connect with. Hilton noted at OTAs that he was "excited" for the return of deep balls, so nobody show him any of Carson Wentz's 2020 deep-ball film, OK? That would be mean. The biggest difference between the unhealthy Hilton and the healthy Hilton is he just found it harder to get off the line of scrimmage. If he's past the injury, his speed will help set a tone for the Colts offense. If he's not, well, Michael Pittman might just take over as the No. 1.

DeAndre Hopkins Height: 6-1 Weight: 212 College: Clemson Draft: 2013/1 (27) Born: 6-Jun-1992 Age: 29 Risk: Green

Year	Tm	G/GS	Snaps	Pass	Rec	Yds	TD	EZ	C%	+/-	Drop	Yd/C	aDOT	Rk	YAC	Rk	YAC+	BTkl	DVOA	Rk	DYAR	Rk	Use	Rk	Slot
2018	HOU	16/16	1084	163	115	1572	11	20	71%	+14.2	1	13.7	11.6	40	3.4	69	-0.9	10	22.6%	10	455	2	33.0%	1	33%
2019	HOU	15/15	1000	150	104	1165	7	11	69%	+7.5	5	11.2	10.2	54	3.7	54	-1.0	17	6.2%	31	224	17	30.8%	3	52%
2020	ARI	16/16	1044	160	115	1407	6	11	72%	+9.1	1	12.2	9.3	61	4.5	36	-0.2	26	3.4%	38	207	19	29.9%	2	29%
2021	ARI			152	104	1221	7		68%	--		11.8							0.7%						

As you read these words, know that somewhere, somehow, DeAndre Hopkins is probably open … and if he's not, just throw him the ball anyway, he'll probably still come down with it. Just ask the Buffalo Bills—they had three defenders engulfing him in the end zone and he still reeled in a 43-yard touchdown that became known as the "Hail Murray" to beat them in one of the great plays of the 2020 NFL season.

Hopkins' raw totals mostly reflect his dominance—he was third or better in targets, receptions, and yards—but his advanced stats aren't quite as kind. He was among the victims of Arizona's late-season slump, ranking 15th among wide receivers in DYAR through Week 11 but 40th in DYAR from Week 12 on. He was also somewhat misused as a possession receiver, which is not what he's best at. He had a league-high 109 targets within 9 yards of the line of scrimmage, but a -21.2% DVOA on those throws, below the wide receiver average of -16.2%. Meanwhile, he was only 15th in deeper targets of 10 yards or more, where his DVOA (51.1%) was much better than average (22.6%).

Mostly, though, Hopkins' efficiency suffered because of the predictable nature of Arizona's offense. He had more than twice as many targets as any of his teammates, which meant double the attention from opposing defenses. Hopkins was very hard to bring down—he led all wide receivers in broken tackles—but every time he got by one defender, he found two more waiting for him, which explains his middling YAC numbers. If the Cardinals can diversify Hopkins' route tree and find a reliable No. 2 receiver, Hopkins' efficiency will improve. Arizona will probably win more games, too, if you're interested in that sort of thing.

Adam Humphries

Height: 5-11 Weight: 195 College: Clemson Draft: 2015/FA Born: 24-Jun-1993 Age: 28 Risk: Red

Year	Tm	G/GS	Snaps	Pass	Rec	Yds	TD	EZ	C%	+/-	Drop	Yd/C	aDOT	Rk	YAC	Rk	YAC+	BTkl	DVOA	Rk	DYAR	Rk	Use	Rk	Slot
2018	TB	16/10	781	105	76	816	5	5	72%	+0.6	3	10.7	6.4	84	5.5	20	+0.5	6	6.7%	28	152	26	16.7%	52	84%
2019	TEN	12/3	390	47	37	374	2	2	79%	+4.3	1	10.1	7.5	--	3.2	--	-1.5	4	11.7%	--	84	--	14.4%	--	98%
2020	TEN	7/1	227	35	23	228	2	2	66%	+0.7	2	9.9	9.9	--	2.0	--	-1.9	0	-5.8%	--	18	--	16.8%	--	89%
2021	WAS			29	19	221	1		66%	--		11.5							-4.1%						

After a career year in 2018, Humphries signed a four-year deal with the Titans. Two seasons in Tennessee included just 19 games and four starts due to injuries, including a concussion in 2020 that forced Humphries to miss four midseason games, attempt to return, then finish the season on injured reserve. His combined 2019-2020 stat line falls short of his 2018 season. That 2018 season becomes slightly more relevant now since it was mostly with Ryan Fitzpatrick at quarterback with the Buccaneers. Humphries won't be the top target in Washington's lineup, but he wasn't during that 2018 season in Tampa Bay either. He was third in both DYAR and DVOA on that 2018 Buccaneers team behind Mike Evans and DeSean Jackson, with a not-yet-emerged Chis Godwin behind them.

Andy Isabella

Height: 5-9 Weight: 190 College: Massachusetts Draft: 2019/2 (62) Born: 18-Nov-1996 Age: 25 Risk: Green

Year	Tm	G/GS	Snaps	Pass	Rec	Yds	TD	EZ	C%	+/-	Drop	Yd/C	aDOT	Rk	YAC	Rk	YAC+	BTkl	DVOA	Rk	DYAR	Rk	Use	Rk	Slot
2019	ARI	15/1	160	13	9	189	1	1	69%	+0.3	0	21.0	6.3	--	15.6	--	+9.3	4	33.4%	--	44	--	2.6%	--	46%
2020	ARI	13/2	306	35	21	224	2	3	60%	-1.6	3	10.7	12.1	--	3.9	--	-1.9	5	-24.4%	--	-31	--	7.7%	--	97%
2021	ARI			10	6	80	0		60%	--		13.6							-3.0%						

Isabella's first catch of the 2020 season was a 54-yard gain against Washington; his next 20 catches gained only 170 yards between them. He had similar results in 2019, when nearly half of his total yardage came on one 88-yard touchdown against San Francisco. Isabella's only two starts in 2020 came in Weeks 12 and 13 against New England and the Rams. He came out of those two starts with six catches for all of 40 yards, and that sealed his fate for the year. He was a healthy inactive for each of the next three weeks, then played only three offensive snaps in the do-or-die Week 17 loss to the Rams. The Cardinals then signed A.J. Green and drafted Rondale Moore, putting Isabella's job on very, very thin ice.

DeSean Jackson

Height: 5-10 Weight: 175 College: California Draft: 2008/2 (49) Born: 1-Dec-1986 Age: 35 Risk: Red

Year	Tm	G/GS	Snaps	Pass	Rec	Yds	TD	EZ	C%	+/-	Drop	Yd/C	aDOT	Rk	YAC	Rk	YAC+	BTkl	DVOA	Rk	DYAR	Rk	Use	Rk	Slot
2018	TB	12/10	453	74	41	774	4	6	55%	+1.3	2	18.9	19.5	1	4.4	38	-0.2	3	12.2%	25	153	25	16.4%	53	32%
2019	PHI	3/3	67	10	9	159	2	1	90%	+2.7	1	17.7	14.1	--	1.7	--	-2.6	1	41.6%	--	47	--	9.6%	--	64%
2020	PHI	5/5	179	26	14	236	1	1	54%	-0.7	2	16.9	16.7	--	4.6	--	+0.1	0	-6.9%	--	12	--	14.4%	--	35%
2021	LAR			42	28	494	2		67%	--		17.6							9.9%						

Jackson has long been one of the NFL's premier field-stretching deep threats, and his mere presence opens up opportunities for the rest of the receivers on the field. The question for Jackson has always been about his health. Entering his age-35 season, Jackson is coming off back-to-back years that were cut significantly short due to injury, and he has not played a full 16-game slate since 2013. Los Angeles struggled to create explosive passing plays down the field in 2020, so the addition of both new quarterback Matthew Stafford and Jackson should give defenses something to worry about if the latter can remain available. Maybe returning to play in his hometown will be what he needs to stay on the field.

Richie James Height: 5-9 Weight: 185 College: Middle Tennessee State Draft: 2018/7 (240) Born: 5-Sep-1995 Age: 26 Risk: Green

Year	Tm	G/GS	Snaps	Pass	Rec	Yds	TD	EZ	C%	+/-	Drop	Yd/C	aDOT	Rk	YAC	Rk	YAC+	BTkl	DVOA	Rk	DYAR	Rk	Use	Rk	Slot
2018	SF	13/2	192	14	9	130	1	1	64%	-0.8	0	14.4	4.3	--	11.2	--	+5.6	0	-2.8%	--	11	--	3.3%	--	69%
2019	SF	16/1	207	10	6	165	1	0	60%	-0.4	0	27.5	11.9	--	17.2	--	+11.3	2	64.5%	--	54	--	2.1%	--	90%
2020	SF	11/7	405	36	23	394	1	0	66%	-0.1	3	17.1	10.9	--	8.0	--	+2.1	7	16.3%	--	78	--	9.6%	--	72%
2021	SF			32	22	289	1		69%	--		13.3							6.7%						

Relegated mostly to return duty in his first two seasons, James was the 49ers' fourth wideout by default last season. He was the closest thing they had to a deep-ball specialist—his 10.9-yard average depth of target seems pretty mundane for a wideout, but it was most of any San Francisco player. Fifteen of his 36 targets came at least 10 yards beyond the line of scrimmage; he had a 90.1% DVOA on those throws (average for a wide receiver: 22.6%), picking up 10 first downs and averaging 17.9 yards per target. With Mohamed Sanu returning to San Francisco this fall, James will probably return to return duty.

Justin Jefferson Height: 6-1 Weight: 202 College: Louisiana State Draft: 2020/1 (22) Born: 16-Jun-1999 Age: 22 Risk: Green

Year	Tm	G/GS	Snaps	Pass	Rec	Yds	TD	EZ	C%	+/-	Drop	Yd/C	aDOT	Rk	YAC	Rk	YAC+	BTkl	DVOA	Rk	DYAR	Rk	Use	Rk	Slot
2020	MIN	16/14	886	125	88	1400	7	10	70%	+9.1	4	15.9	12.0	31	5.1	23	+0.6	15	25.5%	7	373	3	26.2%	7	59%
2021	MIN			124	85	1208	8		69%	--		14.2							10.4%						

It could have been a disaster for the Vikings when Stefon Diggs put up 377 DYAR in the season after they traded him to the Bills. But Jefferson, drafted with the pick Minnesota got back in the deal, nearly matched Diggs with 373 DYAR, the third-highest wide receiver total in 2020 and fifth highest by a rookie wide receiver in our database going back to 1983.

Top Rookie Wide Receivers by Receiving DYAR, 1983-2020

Year	Player	Team	DYAR	Rk	DVOA	Pass	Rec	Yards	TD	C%	Y/C
2016	Michael Thomas	NO	431	2	31.6%	121	92	1,137	9	76%	12.4
1998	Randy Moss	MIN	428	2	30.1%	124	69	1,317	17	56%	19.1
2014	Odell Beckham	NYG	396	6	25.8%	130	91	1,305	12	70%	14.3
2004	Michael Clayton	TB	389	3	26.1%	122	80	1,196	7	66%	15.0
2020	**Justin Jefferson**	**MIN**	**373**	**3**	**25.5%**	**125**	**88**	**1,400**	**7**	**70%**	**15.9**
2013	Keenan Allen	SD	343	8	28.2%	104	71	1,053	8	68%	14.8
2017	JuJu Smith-Schuster	PIT	317	6	37.3%	79	58	917	7	73%	15.8
2011	A.J. Green	CIN	288	9	17.4%	115	65	1,057	7	57%	16.3
2004	Lee Evans	BUF	284	14	36.0%	75	48	843	9	64%	17.6
2017	Cooper Kupp	LAR	272	10	24.8%	92	60	869	5	65%	14.5

He may have been the fifth receiver taken in the 2020 draft, but Jefferson clearly looks like the best of that class after one year. And with a lower than anticipated 59% slot target rate, he showed the versatility to excel on the outside, where he will need to win consistently to settle in as one of the best receivers in football.

Van Jefferson Height: 6-2 Weight: 197 College: Florida Draft: 2020/2 (57) Born: 26-Jul-1996 Age: 25 Risk: Green

Year	Tm	G/GS	Snaps	Pass	Rec	Yds	TD	EZ	C%	+/-	Drop	Yd/C	aDOT	Rk	YAC	Rk	YAC+	BTkl	DVOA	Rk	DYAR	Rk	Use	Rk	Slot
2020	LAR	16/0	256	31	19	220	1	1	61%	-0.5	1	11.6	11.3	--	2.4	--	-1.6	2	-12.9%	--	-1	--	5.4%	--	58%
2021	LAR			51	34	403	3		67%	--		12.0							-0.2%						

In his rookie year, Jefferson played a very limited role in the Rams passing offense, appearing in all 16 games but only getting on the field for 23% of the team's offensive snaps. Matthew Stafford may be likely to help the offense as a whole produce at a higher level, but the offseason additions of DeSean Jackson in free agency and Tutu Atwell in the draft will add further competition to the Los Angeles receiver room and may make it difficult for Jefferson to get on the field yet again. Jefferson entered the league drawing praise for his route-running ability, which could still give him an opportunity to produce out the slot, but with Cooper Kupp still around, that opportunity seems unlikely to be significant in 2021.

Jerry Jeudy

Height: 6-1 **Weight:** 192 **College:** Alabama **Draft:** 2020/1 (15) **Born:** 24-Apr-1999 **Age:** 22 **Risk:** Green

Year	Tm	G/GS	Snaps	Pass	Rec	Yds	TD	EZ	C%	+/-	Drop	Yd/C	aDOT	Rk	YAC	Rk	YAC+	BTkl	DVOA	Rk	DYAR	Rk	Use	Rk	Slot
2020	DEN	16/14	805	113	52	856	3	8	46%	-13.3	13	16.5	14.1	13	5.0	25	+0.4	13	-22.9%	84	-92	86	21.4%	30	47%
2021	DEN			105	57	821	5		54%	--		14.5							-13.4%						

Jeudy's rookie season was as frustrating as it could be. An infuriating blend of poor quarterback play and Jeudy's own drop issues lead to a rookie year that left a ton of meat on the bone. While Denver's passers are partly responsible for Jeudy's putrid 46% catch rate on targets, Jeudy did have the highest drop rate in the league at a stunning 17.6% (minimum 50 targets). He caught only 70% of passes charted as "catchable," the lowest rate among qualifying wide receivers. Truthfully, Jeudy is likely to continue having drop issues, just as he did in college. That said, Jeudy's obscene explosiveness and calculated route-running skills allowed him to consistently get himself wide open as a rookie, and he should grow in those areas with time in the league. Denver's offensive staff also clearly trusted Jeudy to get open to the intermediate area, be that on crossers, digs, comebacks, etc., and Jeudy proved himself to be efficient when he did hang onto the ball. Three-quarters of Jeudy's receptions went for first downs, making him just one of 13 players to hit or cross the 75% mark (minimum 50 targets). While Jeudy's drop issues will continue to be bothersome, he is a clearly talented wide receiver who can separate to all three levels. Jeudy should become a more effective pro with another offseason under his belt and (hopefully) some more stable quarterback play.

Diontae Johnson

Height: 5-10 **Weight:** 181 **College:** Toledo **Draft:** 2019/3 (66) **Born:** 5-Jul-1996 **Age:** 25 **Risk:** Green

Year	Tm	G/GS	Snaps	Pass	Rec	Yds	TD	EZ	C%	+/-	Drop	Yd/C	aDOT	Rk	YAC	Rk	YAC+	BTkl	DVOA	Rk	DYAR	Rk	Use	Rk	Slot
2019	PIT	16/12	666	91	59	680	5	2	64%	+2.6	5	11.5	10.0	59	5.2	16	+0.2	22	-8.9%	63	26	61	18.6%	48	33%
2020	PIT	15/13	733	144	88	923	7	10	61%	-7.9	15	10.5	8.2	73	4.5	39	-0.6	17	-19.1%	79	-73	84	23.3%	23	27%
2021	PIT			139	87	958	7		63%	--		11.1							-9.1%						

Johnson was a dropped-pass machine, and his worst errors often came at critical moments—his catch rate on third/fourth downs was just 55%, his DVOA -28.8%. The good news going forward is that he can't possibly drop as many again—right? Even with all those miscues Johnson's overall catch rate was decent, and his production a grade above decent. With a dozen touchdowns in his first two seasons, Johnson has proven to be a playmaker, if he can just sort out the basics.

Julio Jones

Height: 6-3 **Weight:** 220 **College:** Alabama **Draft:** 2011/1 (6) **Born:** 8-Feb-1989 **Age:** 32 **Risk:** Green

Year	Tm	G/GS	Snaps	Pass	Rec	Yds	TD	EZ	C%	+/-	Drop	Yd/C	aDOT	Rk	YAC	Rk	YAC+	BTkl	DVOA	Rk	DYAR	Rk	Use	Rk	Slot
2018	ATL	16/16	818	170	113	1677	8	10	66%	+10.1	6	14.8	14.5	14	4.0	51	-0.4	13	15.9%	17	382	6	28.2%	5	43%
2019	ATL	15/15	834	157	99	1394	6	11	63%	+4.5	5	14.1	12.6	34	3.5	61	-0.7	10	11.6%	21	299	7	25.6%	11	49%
2020	ATL	9/9	468	68	51	771	3	8	75%	+8.0	2	15.1	11.7	35	4.5	35	+0.4	7	29.8%	2	231	16	20.3%	34	57%
2021	TEN			124	80	1146	7		65%	--		14.3							4.2%						

Jones now ranks 20th on the all-time receiving yardage list; a 1,000-yard season would move him up to 14th (three yards behind Cris Carter), while back-to-back 1,000-yard seasons would launch him all the way up to eighth. Those numbers should be achievable in 17-game seasons, even if Jones declines a bit due to age, injuries, and landing in a run-oriented offense after getting a zillion targets because his team was always playing from behind over the last three years. Jones enjoyed a four-game stretch of 28-425-4 between injuries from Weeks 6 through 9 last year. That's the Jones the Titans assume they are getting. We're skeptical about whether Jones is the missing piece of a Super Bowl puzzle, but that doesn't mean we think he's washed up by any means.

Marvin Jones

Height: 6-2 **Weight:** 198 **College:** California **Draft:** 2012/5 (166) **Born:** 12-Mar-1990 **Age:** 31 **Risk:** Green

Year	Tm	G/GS	Snaps	Pass	Rec	Yds	TD	EZ	C%	+/-	Drop	Yd/C	aDOT	Rk	YAC	Rk	YAC+	BTkl	DVOA	Rk	DYAR	Rk	Use	Rk	Slot
2018	DET	9/9	538	62	35	508	5	13	56%	-0.6	1	14.5	15.5	9	3.1	74	-0.6	3	15.7%	18	142	29	20.5%	30	23%
2019	DET	13/11	837	91	62	779	9	9	68%	+6.0	5	12.6	13.4	24	1.7	80	-2.1	6	11.8%	20	180	24	20.6%	33	66%
2020	DET	16/16	942	115	76	978	9	13	66%	+4.4	6	12.9	13.2	21	2.6	83	-1.3	8	12.3%	18	235	15	21.0%	32	67%
2021	JAX			67	43	531	4		64%	--		12.5							-2.9%						

Jones has the my-ball mentality that coaches crave. According to Matt Harmon's work at ReceptionPerception.com, Jones registered an 81.8% contested catch rate last year and has never been below average in the stat. Of course you see the downfield highlights because he's a speed receiver, but he's also pretty good contesting over the middle and on curls. Jaguars offensive coordinator Darrell Bevell had the job in Detroit the last few years, and the emphasis on speed that Urban Meyer placed this offseason made Jones an easy fit in Jacksonville. Jones is getting up there in age and isn't quite the coverage-buster he once was, but he's still plenty capable of going viral with Trevor Lawrence on any given go route.

Christian Kirk Height: 5-11 Weight: 200 College: Texas A&M Draft: 2018/2 (47) Born: 18-Nov-1996 Age: 25 Risk: Green

Year	Tm	G/GS	Snaps	Pass	Rec	Yds	TD	EZ	C%	+/-	Drop	Yd/C	aDOT	Rk	YAC	Rk	YAC+	BTkl	DVOA	Rk	DYAR	Rk	Use	Rk	Slot
2018	ARI	12/7	542	68	43	590	3	4	63%	-0.5	3	13.7	9.8	54	5.3	22	-0.1	3	-1.8%	49	57	49	19.2%	35	48%
2019	ARI	13/13	804	108	68	709	3	6	63%	+1.6	2	10.4	10.9	45	4.2	40	-0.9	8	-5.1%	55	67	51	25.9%	9	52%
2020	ARI	14/10	781	79	48	621	6	10	61%	+3.5	3	12.9	13.1	23	3.6	64	-0.9	2	-5.5%	59	46	59	16.9%	53	26%
2021	ARI			100	67	806	5		67%	--		12.1							0.5%						

While the Arizona offense as a whole began to collapse in Week 12 against New England, Kirk's decline began a few weeks earlier than that. His last touchdown of the year was a 56-yard catch in Week 9 against Miami. In seven games after that, he had 25 catches for only 221 yards, an average of just 8.8 yards per grab. Through the Dolphins game, he was 31st at the position with 97 receiving DYAR; from Week 10 on, he was in the bottom 10 with -52 DYAR. Kirk was the dedicated deep-ball specialist in the Arizona offense, leading the club with 20 targets that came 20-plus yards downfield. (Yes, that was one more than DeAndre Hopkins had, and no, we have no idea why.) Once he proved unable to stretch the field, that was effectively the end of Arizona's season. His performance this fall will go a long way in determining whether or not the Cardinals can return to the playoffs.

Cooper Kupp Height: 6-2 Weight: 208 College: Eastern Washington Draft: 2017/3 (69) Born: 15-Jun-1993 Age: 28 Risk: Green

Year	Tm	G/GS	Snaps	Pass	Rec	Yds	TD	EZ	C%	+/-	Drop	Yd/C	aDOT	Rk	YAC	Rk	YAC+	BTkl	DVOA	Rk	DYAR	Rk	Use	Rk	Slot
2018	LAR	8/8	439	55	40	566	6	4	73%	+3.9	1	14.2	7.4	79	7.6	2	+2.2	8	23.8%	7	158	23	19.9%	31	100%
2019	LAR	16/14	905	134	94	1161	10	7	70%	+4.4	5	12.4	7.4	76	5.7	11	+1.0	12	7.1%	30	205	18	22.0%	27	92%
2020	LAR	15/12	842	124	92	974	3	5	74%	+6.4	2	10.6	6.7	83	5.7	10	+0.8	24	-0.8%	45	118	29	23.6%	21	90%
2021	LAR			127	90	1058	7		71%	--		11.8							5.8%						

Kupp, who signed a three-year extension with the Rams early in the 2020 season, did most of his work in the short and intermediate areas of the field. In an odd quirk, Kupp's target distribution was perfectly even across first downs, second downs, and third/fourth downs for the Rams at 42 in each split. When it got to those later downs, Kupp's average target depth increased substantially to 9.3, which was more than double the average depth of his first-down targets. It seems pretty clear that Kupp was a trusted outlet for former quarterback Jared Goff when he was under pressure; we will see if that remains the case with new signal-caller Matthew Stafford.

CeeDee Lamb Height: 6-2 Weight: 198 College: Oklahoma Draft: 2020/1 (17) Born: 8-Apr-1999 Age: 22 Risk: Green

Year	Tm	G/GS	Snaps	Pass	Rec	Yds	TD	EZ	C%	+/-	Drop	Yd/C	aDOT	Rk	YAC	Rk	YAC+	BTkl	DVOA	Rk	DYAR	Rk	Use	Rk	Slot
2020	DAL	16/14	730	111	74	935	5	10	67%	+0.3	9	12.6	9.7	57	4.2	51	-0.7	6	-3.8%	54	78	46	17.9%	50	94%
2021	DAL			119	76	1025	6		64%	--		13.5							0.4%						

Lamb was the Cowboys' top third-down target by a wide margin (38 targets; Michael Gallup was second with 27) and led the team with a 77% conversion rate on those throws. Lamb was targeted 25 times on third down with 4-9 yards to go, catching 17 passes for 15 first downs, all fine numbers for a guy who caught more passes from Ben DiNucci and Garrett Gilbert than anyone should be asked to do. It's unusual for a rookie receiver on a team with two solid veteran starters to end up as the top third-down target, but such are the mysteries of a Mike McCarthy-coached team. At any rate, effectiveness in high-leverage situations bodes well for Lamb's development and future. He may face a "not enough footballs" crunch in 2021, but that's about the only thing that should hold Lamb back.

Jarvis Landry

Height: 5-11 Weight: 196 College: Louisiana State Draft: 2014/2 (63) Born: 11/28/1992 Age: 29 Risk: Green

Year	Tm	G/GS	Snaps	Pass	Rec	Yds	TD	EZ	C%	+/-	Drop	Yd/C	aDOT	Rk	YAC	Rk	YAC+	BTkl	DVOA	Rk	DYAR	Rk	Use	Rk	Slot
2018	CLE	16/14	957	149	81	976	4	11	54%	-7.9	6	12.0	11.7	36	3.4	67	-1.6	9	-22.2%	79	-111	83	26.6%	9	75%
2019	CLE	16/16	998	138	83	1174	6	8	60%	-0.3	3	14.1	10.3	52	5.3	15	+0.5	23	4.1%	36	182	23	26.6%	7	77%
2020	CLE	15/14	699	101	72	840	3	9	71%	+4.8	6	11.7	8.2	72	4.8	27	+0.3	14	4.0%	36	130	28	22.8%	25	81%
2021	CLE			106	68	830	5		64%	--		12.2							-3.0%						

Landry was particularly inefficient in his first season in Cleveland, 2018, but has bounced back to have a couple of pretty good campaigns. Landry was awful on first downs (-31.5%, 66% catch rate) and poor on third downs (-9.8%, 63% catch rate), but the Browns used Landry as their Canadian football option—on second down, Landry put up a 39.2% DVOA and 81% catch rate on 42 targets. Landry was forced in 2018 to run much deeper routes than he prefers, and that average depth of target has come down into his comfort zone, from 32% of his targets charted as 16 yards or more past the line of scrimmage in 2018 to just 18% in 2020.

Landry has never been the receiver his media mentions have made him out to be, and hasn't exactly earned his contract (which has two years remaining). He and teammate Odell Beckham are also no longer the cool LSU wideouts in the NFL, having been supplanted by Justin Jefferson and incoming rookie Ja'Marr Chase. But Landry has been an emotional leader in the Browns locker room, and unlike Beckham can be counted on to play—the game he missed due to COVID protocols last year was the first he missed in his entire career. His fantasy value is low, and he isn't particularly fun to watch, but the suspicion is the Browns will happily take what they get from Landry.

Allen Lazard

Height: 6-5 Weight: 227 College: Iowa State Draft: 2018/FA Born: 11-Dec-1995 Age: 26 Risk: Green

Year	Tm	G/GS	Snaps	Pass	Rec	Yds	TD	EZ	C%	+/-	Drop	Yd/C	aDOT	Rk	YAC	Rk	YAC+	BTkl	DVOA	Rk	DYAR	Rk	Use	Rk	Slot
2018	GB	1/0	1	1	1	7	0	0	100%	+0.3	0	7.0	7.0	--	0.0	--	-3.6	0	-2.6%	--	1	--	2.6%	--	100%
2019	GB	16/3	484	52	35	477	3	8	67%	+4.0	5	13.6	13.9	22	3.7	51	-0.4	2	14.6%	18	118	36	9.7%	81	72%
2020	GB	10/9	470	46	33	451	3	5	72%	+2.7	5	13.7	10.3	--	5.9	--	+1.2	2	28.3%	--	153	--	14.7%	--	87%
2021	GB			68	44	615	4		65%	--		14.0							5.7%						

Lazard's 28.3% DVOA paints him as top-five receiver in football, but there is a lot to unpack in that rate. Aaron Rodgers deserves much of the credit. Fellow Packers receivers Davante Adams and Marquez Valdes-Scantling joined Lazard in the top 25 in DVOA at the position. Meanwhile, Lazard was dramatically more effective with a 76.0% DVOA and position-leading 124 DYAR in the first three weeks before a core muscle injury landed him on injured reserve. From his return in Week 10 on, Lazard was pedestrian with a -0.5% DVOA and 28 DYAR. The Packers will have to hope that a healthier Lazard can play to his pre-injury standard in 2021. They can take solace in Lazard's 3.7 yards of average separation, a top-five rate at the position according to Next Gen Stats.

Tyler Lockett

Height: 5-10 Weight: 182 College: Kansas State Draft: 2015/3 (69) Born: 28-Sep-1992 Age: 29 Risk: Green

Year	Tm	G/GS	Snaps	Pass	Rec	Yds	TD	EZ	C%	+/-	Drop	Yd/C	aDOT	Rk	YAC	Rk	YAC+	BTkl	DVOA	Rk	DYAR	Rk	Use	Rk	Slot
2018	SEA	16/14	908	70	57	965	10	9	81%	+17.7	0	16.9	15.9	5	3.7	58	-1.5	7	66.3%	1	464	1	18.5%	39	58%
2019	SEA	16/16	1010	110	82	1057	8	14	75%	+13.6	4	12.9	13.0	29	3.7	55	-1.1	4	24.6%	6	317	4	22.4%	26	83%
2020	SEA	16/16	944	132	100	1054	10	16	76%	+9.8	7	10.5	10.1	50	3.3	70	-0.9	8	9.8%	21	238	14	24.8%	14	73%
2021	SEA			124	86	1040	8		69%	--		12.1							8.1%						

Early in his career, Lockett primarily served as a deep threat for the Seahawks, which made sense when Doug Baldwin was the main slot option underneath. In recent years, though, he has filled a role closer to the line of scrimmage now that DK Metcalf is around to take the top off of defenses. 2020 represented a bit of an up-and-down year for Lockett. This may sound strange given that he set the franchise record for receptions in a season, but Lockett's production exhibited a considerable amount of variance. He recorded 36% of his catches, 37% of his receiving yards, and 80% of his touchdowns in just three regular-season games, an incredibly boom-or-bust profile for a player who is supposed to be more than a deep-ball threat. A nagging knee injury may have had something to do with that, so a healthy season from Lockett would go a long way toward more consistent production.

Terrace Marshall

Height: 6-3   Weight: 200   College: Louisiana State   Draft: 2021/2 (59)   Born: 9-Jun-2000   Age: 21   Risk: Green

Year	Tm	G/GS	Snaps	Pass	Rec	Yds	TD	EZ	C%	+/-	Drop	Yd/C	aDOT	Rk	YAC	Rk	YAC+	BTkl	DVOA	Rk	DYAR	Rk	Use	Rk	Slot
2021	CAR			71	41	563	3		58%	--		13.6							-9.6%						

A college teammate of last year's rookie stud Justin Jefferson and this year's fifth overall pick Ja'Marr Chase, Marshall scored 10 touchdowns and averaged over 100 yards in seven games last year as LSU's No. 1 receiver before opting out of the rest of the season in November. Even with both Jefferson and Chase on the team in 2019, Marshall pitched in 13 touchdowns and over 650 yards as a true sophomore. Standing 6-foot-3 with a broad frame, Marshall also ran the 40-yard dash in 4.38 seconds, marking him as an outstanding athlete who can beat defenders with both his size and speed. Given his attributes and production, it is possible that only being overshadowed by Chase and Jefferson kept Marshall out of the first round himself. He already has experience with Joe Brady from their time at LSU, and though the Panthers have said they plan to bring him along slowly, he certainly has the natural ability to step straight into the void created by Curtis Samuel's departure to Washington in free agency.

Isaiah McKenzie

Height: 5-8   Weight: 173   College: Georgia   Draft: 2017/5 (172)   Born: 9-Apr-1995   Age: 26   Risk: Green

Year	Tm	G/GS	Snaps	Pass	Rec	Yds	TD	EZ	C%	+/-	Drop	Yd/C	aDOT	Rk	YAC	Rk	YAC+	BTkl	DVOA	Rk	DYAR	Rk	Use	Rk	Slot
2018	2TM	8/1	225	30	18	179	0	2	60%	-2.6	1	9.9	7.7	--	4.2	--	-1.5	3	-23.8%	--	-25	--	12.3%	--	90%
2019	BUF	15/8	454	39	27	254	1	3	69%	-1.7	2	9.4	4.3	--	7.6	--	+0.4	5	-21.0%	--	-24	--	8.5%	--	67%
2020	BUF	16/7	270	34	30	282	5	1	88%	+4.5	1	9.4	4.0	--	6.3	--	-0.0	8	25.1%	--	99	--	5.9%	--	70%
2021	BUF			22	15	169	1		68%	--		11.2							0.2%						

Do you know who had the most receiving touchdowns out of the slot for Buffalo in 2020? It wasn't Cole Beasley; McKenzie had five to Beasley's three. McKenzie's Week 17 performance against the Dolphins was obviously the highlight of his season—six receptions for 65 yards and a pair of touchdowns, and a punt return for another score, with all three touchdowns coming within seven minutes of game time. Often times, a player with a small sample size and one huge game will have their numbers distorted, but not McKenzie; he would have an 18.8% DVOA even if Week 17 had never occurred. McKenzie will have to fight off rookie Marquez Stevenson for the gadget/returner role for 2021, but he has been effective enough to be favored pretty heavily in that battle.

Terry McLaurin

Height: 6-0   Weight: 210   College: Ohio State   Draft: 2019/3 (76)   Born: 15-Apr-1996   Age: 25   Risk: Green

Year	Tm	G/GS	Snaps	Pass	Rec	Yds	TD	EZ	C%	+/-	Drop	Yd/C	aDOT	Rk	YAC	Rk	YAC+	BTkl	DVOA	Rk	DYAR	Rk	Use	Rk	Slot
2019	WAS	14/14	784	93	58	919	7	12	62%	+3.3	5	15.8	14.3	19	3.7	52	-0.3	6	18.9%	12	237	13	23.3%	18	34%
2020	WAS	15/15	950	134	87	1118	4	7	65%	+0.5	3	12.9	9.8	55	5.5	14	+0.6	14	-11.0%	74	18	72	25.1%	11	46%
2021	WAS			122	82	1063	5		67%	--		13.0							1.2%						

McLaurin broke out in his rookie season as a plus route-runner able to take advantage of intermediate and deep targets. In an offense helmed by quarterbacks who either wouldn't or couldn't push the ball down the field, passes that went McLaurin's way became significantly less efficient. On first down, McLaurin's average depth of target dropped from 14.2 yards in 2019 to 10.8 in 2020. On second down, aDOT dropped from 16.3 to 8.9; on third down, 10.3 down to 8.5. Among 33 players with at least 40 targets of more than 10 air yards, McLaurin ranked 26th in catchable target rate. With more short passes, McLaurin upped his YAC and broken tackles to get the most out of what he was given. With better quarterback play, McLaurin could look like a combination of 2019 efficiency with 2020 volume.

DK Metcalf

Height: 6-4   Weight: 230   College: Mississippi   Draft: 2019/2 (64)   Born: 14-Dec-1997   Age: 24   Risk: Green

Year	Tm	G/GS	Snaps	Pass	Rec	Yds	TD	EZ	C%	+/-	Drop	Yd/C	aDOT	Rk	YAC	Rk	YAC+	BTkl	DVOA	Rk	DYAR	Rk	Use	Rk	Slot
2019	SEA	16/15	940	100	58	900	7	21	58%	-1.1	7	15.5	13.0	31	4.8	25	+0.3	13	0.6%	44	105	39	20.2%	35	17%
2020	SEA	16/16	980	129	83	1303	10	18	64%	+6.8	9	15.7	14.2	12	4.4	43	+0.2	16	19.5%	12	334	5	24.2%	16	30%
2021	SEA			118	78	1164	9		66%	--		14.9							10.7%						

After impressing as the No. 2 receiver as a rookie in 2019, the musclebound Metcalf took a major step forward in his second year, breaking Steve Largent's franchise record for single-season receiving yards. Metcalf's combination of size and speed made him a near-impossible cover for most cornerbacks, and Russell Wilson's proficiency throwing the deep ball allowed Metcalf to flex the traits that make him special. Metcalf will only be 24 in December, and if he puts up another explosive campaign this year, he will be in an excellent position to sign a market-setting extension next offseason.

Jakobi Meyers   Height: 6-2   Weight: 200   College: North Carolina State   Draft: 2019/FA   Born: 9-Nov-1996   Age: 25   Risk: Green

Year	Tm	G/GS	Snaps	Pass	Rec	Yds	TD	EZ	C%	+/-	Drop	Yd/C	aDOT	Rk	YAC	Rk	YAC+	BTkl	DVOA	Rk	DYAR	Rk	Use	Rk	Slot
2019	NE	15/1	420	41	26	359	0	3	63%	+2.9	3	13.8	11.2	--	4.4	--	-0.4	5	5.9%	--	61	--	7.8%	--	67%
2020	NE	14/9	665	81	59	729	0	3	73%	+5.1	2	12.4	10.3	47	3.7	61	-0.8	9	0.4%	42	81	45	21.9%	28	85%
2021	NE			65	42	507	2		65%	--		12.1							-4.9%						

The offseason acquisitions of Nelson Agholor and Kendrick Bourne have eaten up all the headlines about the Patriots receiver corps, but don't be surprised if Meyers remains the Patriots' top wideout in 2021, especially if Cam Newton gets a long stretch in the starting lineup. Meyers was the only qualified Patriots wideout to have an above-average DVOA, and his +5.1 receiving plus-minus was the most for a New England receiver since Danny Amendola in 2017. He developed a real rapport with Newton over the last half of the season and could serve as a vital cog while all the rest of the new pass-catchers are still learning the system.

Anthony Miller   Height: 5-11   Weight: 199   College: Memphis   Draft: 2018/2 (51)   Born: 9-Oct-1994   Age: 27   Risk: Red

Year	Tm	G/GS	Snaps	Pass	Rec	Yds	TD	EZ	C%	+/-	Drop	Yd/C	aDOT	Rk	YAC	Rk	YAC+	BTkl	DVOA	Rk	DYAR	Rk	Use	Rk	Slot
2018	CHI	15/4	576	54	33	423	7	8	61%	-2.0	4	12.8	11.8	35	5.2	24	+0.4	4	3.9%	36	71	46	11.4%	77	82%
2019	CHI	16/7	704	85	52	656	2	7	61%	-2.5	4	12.6	10.3	53	4.2	42	-0.9	4	-7.6%	59	34	58	14.8%	66	88%
2020	CHI	16/6	584	76	49	485	2	8	64%	-1.0	5	9.9	9.8	54	3.0	79	-1.7	5	-26.4%	85	-80	85	12.6%	77	91%
2021	CHI			36	23	254	1		64%	--		11.0							-9.6%						

Sixth-round rookie slot receiver Dazz Newsome broke his collarbone in OTAs. While that won't likely keep him sidelined into the regular season, it could disrupt the Bears' Ian Rapoport-reported plan to trade Miller this offseason. On one hand, a delay makes sense. Miller has one more year on an inexpensive second-round rookie contract, and new quarterback Justin Fields could potentially unlock the once-heralded receiver who hasn't been any less efficient than Mitchell Trubisky's other wideouts apart from No. 1 Allen Robinson. On the other hand, Miller seems more responsible for his poor performance than his teammates. Playing out of the slot, Miller saw a relatively low average depth of target last season, but still finished in the bottom five in YAC+.

Scotty Miller   Height: 5-11   Weight: 174   College: Bowling Green   Draft: 2019/6 (208)   Born: 31-Jul-1997   Age: 24   Risk: Blue

Year	Tm	G/GS	Snaps	Pass	Rec	Yds	TD	EZ	C%	+/-	Drop	Yd/C	aDOT	Rk	YAC	Rk	YAC+	BTkl	DVOA	Rk	DYAR	Rk	Use	Rk	Slot
2019	TB	10/2	180	26	13	200	1	4	50%	-0.3	0	15.4	17.9	--	2.8	--	-1.9	0	-15.5%	--	-5	--	6.7%	--	40%
2020	TB	16/5	440	53	33	501	3	6	62%	+2.4	3	15.2	16.9	2	3.3	68	-1.3	4	13.2%	17	113	33	9.0%	86	38%
2021	TB			30	19	268	2		63%	--		14.2							1.5%						

Miller has the ideal name for a Tom Brady fan-favorite slot sidekick. "Scotty Miller" is both generic and diminutive. It chimes with Scottie Pippen and Reggie Miller, providing a callback from Brady to the Michael Jordan era. It screams "spunky interchangeability." If we told you that Scotty Miller was the Robin between Jason Todd and Tim Drake, you might believe us. Anyway, Miller did a little more than catch quick slants and shallow crosses last year: he was one of Brady's favorite targets on sneaky deep shots, with six receptions for 244 yards on passes of 20-plus air yards in the regular season, plus a 39-yard bomb in the NFC Championship Game. Miller may be stuck in a numbers game as part of Brady's deep supporting cast, but he'll find the field in four-receiver packages, when Mike Evans and/or Chris Godwin are banged up, and during any Antonio Brownouts.

Denzel Mims

| | Height: 6-3 | | Weight: 207 | | College: Baylor | | | | | Draft: 2020/2 (59) | | Born: 10-Oct-1997 | | Age: 24 | | Risk: Green | |

Year	Tm	G/GS	Snaps	Pass	Rec	Yds	TD	EZ	C%	+/-	Drop	Yd/C	aDOT	Rk	YAC	Rk	YAC+	BTkl	DVOA	Rk	DYAR	Rk	Use	Rk	Slot
2020	NYJ	9/8	439	44	23	357	0	4	52%	-2.0	1	15.5	15.7	--	4.6	--	-0.3	5	-18.2%	--	-20	--	16.8%	--	38%
2021	NYJ			50	30	407	2		60%	--		13.8							-8.0%						

Intriguingly, last year's second-round pick found himself banished to the second team during OTAs, as newcomers Keelan Cole and Elijah Moore elbowed him out of snaps. The problem with Mims in Mike LaFleur's offense is that he's a fairly linear player and not a great route-runner or YAC guy; Mims had the lowest YAC+ of any Jets receiver with 40 or more targets last season. Mims is often hyped as a potential breakout candidate for 2021, and a healthy year with a regular offseason would certainly seem to help his potential, which flashed on occasion last year. At the moment, however, he's still the fifth receiver on his own team; he's got a lot of ground to make up.

Darnell Mooney

| | Height: 5-11 | | Weight: 175 | | College: Tulane | | | | | Draft: 2020/5 (173) | | Born: 29-Oct-1997 | | Age: 24 | | Risk: Yellow | |

Year	Tm	G/GS	Snaps	Pass	Rec	Yds	TD	EZ	C%	+/-	Drop	Yd/C	aDOT	Rk	YAC	Rk	YAC+	BTkl	DVOA	Rk	DYAR	Rk	Use	Rk	Slot
2020	CHI	16/9	781	98	61	631	4	9	62%	-1.2	3	10.3	11.8	34	4.2	53	-1.2	14	-20.3%	81	-60	82	16.4%	55	58%
2021	CHI			80	52	582	3		65%	--		11.1							-6.4%						

Mooney endured an inefficient rookie season with a -20.3% DVOA, but the Bears clearly blamed those underwhelming results on poor quarterback play. They were optimistic enough for Mooney's second season to forgo a major free agent to challenge him for the team's No. 2 role, and they didn't draft a receiver until the sixth round. If Justin Fields can fulfil his potential as a deep passer, that hope makes sense. Mooney had the third-lowest receiving DYAR (-58) on deep passes thrown 20 or more yards downfield, but his 4.38s speed offers him a chance to excel on those targets if they can make it to him with better accuracy.

D.J. Moore

| | Height: 5-11 | | Weight: 215 | | College: Maryland | | | | | Draft: 2018/1 (24) | | Born: 14-Apr-1997 | | Age: 24 | | Risk: Green | |

Year	Tm	G/GS	Snaps	Pass	Rec	Yds	TD	EZ	C%	+/-	Drop	Yd/C	aDOT	Rk	YAC	Rk	YAC+	BTkl	DVOA	Rk	DYAR	Rk	Use	Rk	Slot
2018	CAR	16/10	732	82	55	788	2	6	67%	+1.2	1	14.3	8.6	70	7.7	1	+2.2	27	4.1%	35	109	38	15.4%	61	35%
2019	CAR	15/15	925	135	87	1175	4	7	64%	+3.6	3	13.5	11.6	42	4.5	36	+0.3	17	3.2%	37	167	25	24.0%	17	26%
2020	CAR	15/14	835	118	66	1193	4	11	56%	-4.5	7	18.1	13.6	15	5.8	9	+0.9	12	7.9%	26	191	20	23.6%	20	53%
2021	CAR			107	63	932	4		59%	--		14.7							-7.0%						

Under new offensive coordinator Joe Brady, Moore's usage changed exactly inverse to that of teammate Robby Anderson's—while Anderson found himself running shorter routes than he had with the Jets, Moore was used more as a downfield weapon than he had in prior seasons. Moore's catch rate plummeted to a career low 56%, but his 18.1 yards per reception was the third-highest figure of any receiver to qualify for our official leaderboard. His average target depth increased for the second successive season and he averaged a further 5.8 yards after catch, second most among receivers with at least 100 targets. Over 80% of his receptions resulted in a first down or touchdown, third among qualifying receivers. That, added to his opponent adjustments, meant his DVOA increased to a career high despite the lower catch rate. Although Anderson took more of the target share, Moore still comfortably led all Panthers receivers in yards per game.

If there is one lingering criticism of Moore, it is a lack of touchdowns, but that appears at least partly a function of his quarterbacks; Curtis Samuel and Washington receiver Terry McLaurin are the other players whose low touchdown totals stand out among the 1,000-yard receiving crowd. Otherwise, his success in a new role in 2020 demonstrated that Moore can be productive as a No. 1 receiver pretty much however he is deployed. The Panthers evidently agree, picking up his $11.1-million fifth-year option this summer as a prelude to an intended long-term deal. Sam Darnold may have an existing rapport with Robby Anderson, but in his three seasons as a professional Moore has exceeded 850 yards receiving from each of Teddy Bridgewater, Kyle Allen, and the shattered remains of Cam Newton. There's little reason to doubt that he'll be just as productive with Darnold.

David Moore

| | | Height: 6-0 | | Weight: 215 | | College: East Central (OK) | | | | Draft: 2017/7 (226) | | | Born: 15-Jan-1995 | | Age: 26 | | Risk: Green | |

Year	Tm	G/GS	Snaps	Pass	Rec	Yds	TD	EZ	C%	+/-	Drop	Yd/C	aDOT	Rk	YAC	Rk	YAC+	BTkl	DVOA	Rk	DYAR	Rk	Use	Rk	Slot
2018	SEA	16/7	620	53	26	445	5	14	49%	-3.5	1	17.1	15.6	7	3.6	62	-1.2	5	-7.4%	57	20	58	12.9%	72	4%
2019	SEA	14/1	318	34	17	301	2	9	50%	-1.7	2	17.7	14.6	--	7.5	--	+2.3	8	-5.5%	--	19	--	7.8%	--	24%
2020	SEA	16/6	482	47	35	417	6	8	74%	+3.5	3	11.9	9.0	--	4.8	--	-0.3	7	7.0%	--	76	--	8.6%	--	34%
2021	CAR			35	21	266	2		60%	--		12.9							-10.0%						

When Curtis Samuel left Carolina to join his old coach in Washington in free agency, new Panthers general manager Scott Fitterer returned to his old club in Seattle to pluck David Moore as his replacement. While nowhere near as productive as Samuel, Moore has similar height, a knack for making plays downfield, and the agility to run the sweeps and end arounds that were a part of Samuel's repertoire in Carolina. He also has experience as a punt returner, which could be significant for the Panthers with last season's primary returner, Pharoh Cooper, now in Jacksonville.

Elijah Moore

| | | Height: 5-9 | | Weight: 184 | | College: Mississippi | | | | Draft: 2021/2 (34) | | | Born: 27-Mar-2000 | | Age: 21 | | Risk: Blue | |

Year	Tm	G/GS	Snaps	Pass	Rec	Yds	TD	EZ	C%	+/-	Drop	Yd/C	aDOT	Rk	YAC	Rk	YAC+	BTkl	DVOA	Rk	DYAR	Rk	Use	Rk	Slot
2021	NYJ			37	23	274	2		62%	--		12.1							-10.2%						

Playmaker Score loved Moore, marking him as the third-best receiver in the class. Moore was second in the nation in receptions and yards despite playing just eight games last year, racking up double-digit catches in every game but one. He was also heavily used in the running game, as Ole Miss did everything they could to get the ball into his hands. While his size implies that Moore will be stuck in the slot in New York, expect the Jets to turn him into their version of Deebo Samuel—a guy who lines up all over the field and uses his exceptional route-running to get open, with lots of little crosses, jet sweeps and shovel passes to get him the ball and let him use his 4.35 speed to run around defenders.

Rondale Moore

| | | Height: 5-9 | | Weight: 180 | | College: Purdue | | | | Draft: 2021/2 (49) | | | Born: 9-Jun-2000 | | Age: 21 | | Risk: Green | |

Year	Tm	G/GS	Snaps	Pass	Rec	Yds	TD	EZ	C%	+/-	Drop	Yd/C	aDOT	Rk	YAC	Rk	YAC+	BTkl	DVOA	Rk	DYAR	Rk	Use	Rk	Slot
2021	ARI			60	40	464	3		67%	--		11.6							-1.4%						

Due to hamstring injuries, Moore appeared in only three of the six games in Purdue's COVID-shortened 2020 campaign. He caught 35 passes, nearly a dozen per week, but averaged only 7.7 yards per catch and failed to score a single touchdown as the Boilermakers lost all three contests. The Cardinals saw all those failed completions leading to eventual defeat and knew that yes, this man would fit into Kliff Kingsbury's offense just fine.

In all seriousness, Moore brings a lot of potential to the table. He caught a nation-high 114 passes as a freshman in 2018, leading the Big Ten with 1,258 yards and a dozen touchdowns, before hamstring injuries ruined his next two years. He was also a dangerous runner in West Lafayette, finishing with 30 carries for 248 yards (that's 8.3 yards per pop, which, wow) and three scores. As a bonus, he has experience on both kickoff and punt returns. He won the Paul Hornung Award as a true freshman as the nation's most versatile college football player. Then he ran a 4.3s 40 at Purdue's pro day, second fastest of any player in this year's draft class.

The best-case scenario for Moore is that he becomes Arizona's version of Curtis Samuel, starting in the slot from Day 1. He could add yet another dimension to Kingsbury's running game—the coach has specifically mentioned jet sweeps, a play that he called just once last year (for zero yards) but which Moore ran 19 times (for 195 yards) at Purdue. Moore should also show that tackle-dodging ability by taking screen targets away from DeAndre Hopkins and will get the occasional shot target to scare the bejeezus out of opposing coordinators.

Josh Palmer

| | | Height: 6-2 | | Weight: 210 | | College: Tennessee | | | | Draft: 2021/3 (77) | | | Born: 22-Sep-1999 | | Age: 22 | | Risk: Green | |

Year	Tm	G/GS	Snaps	Pass	Rec	Yds	TD	EZ	C%	+/-	Drop	Yd/C	aDOT	Rk	YAC	Rk	YAC+	BTkl	DVOA	Rk	DYAR	Rk	Use	Rk	Slot
2021	LAC			26	18	239	2		69%	--		13.1							8.8%						

Palmer is a bet on film over production and measurables. Palmer's athletic profile is unspectacular, sporting figures that placed below the 50th percentile in every drill but the broad jump. More worrisome, however, is that Palmer never eclipsed

500 yards in any season at Tennessee. He also maxed out at just four touchdowns. In fairness to Palmer, some of that has to do with poor quarterback play and having teammates at wide receiver who were also fringe NFL talents, but it's concerning that he never really emerged from the pack there. Palmer's selling points on film are his ability to see the ball cleanly, both in stride and in the air, as well as bring the ball in with strong hands. Palmer's route-running still needs work, though, which may be the biggest reason he won't see too much playing time this season. The Chargers already have two studs in Keenan Allen and Mike Williams, in addition to some speedster role players, so rushing Palmer onto the field is not a necessity.

DeVante Parker   Height: 6-3   Weight: 216   College: Louisville   Draft: 2015/1 (14)   Born: 20-Jan-1993   Age: 28   Risk: Green

Year	Tm	G/GS	Snaps	Pass	Rec	Yds	TD	EZ	C%	+/-	Drop	Yd/C	aDOT	Rk	YAC	Rk	YAC+	BTkl	DVOA	Rk	DYAR	Rk	Use	Rk	Slot
2018	MIA	11/7	411	48	24	309	1	3	52%	-3.1	1	12.9	13.6	--	3.9	--	-1.1	2	-26.6%	--	-52	--	15.8%	--	15%
2019	MIA	16/14	914	128	72	1202	9	11	56%	+0.1	4	16.7	14.4	15	3.7	56	-0.4	9	14.9%	17	283	8	21.4%	28	40%
2020	MIA	14/11	726	103	63	793	4	15	61%	-3.0	7	12.6	10.2	49	2.7	81	-1.0	10	-4.7%	57	70	47	22.2%	27	34%
2021	MIA			102	64	827	5		63%	--		12.9							-2.5%						

Parker averaged just 1.7 yards of separation on his targets in 2020, worst in the league; he does not excel at running himself open, nor did his quarterbacks do him many favors with their choices of targets. This helps explain why he had a -3.0 receiving plus-minus; he had a cornerback draped over him more often than not, which makes hauling in balls that much more difficult. With that in mind, hauling in 63 passes feels a little more impressive; about a third of them were tough, contested grabs. Those seven drops didn't exactly help his cause, however.

Zach Pascal   Height: 6-2   Weight: 214   College: Old Dominion   Draft: 2017/FA   Born: 18-Dec-1994   Age: 27   Risk: Green

Year	Tm	G/GS	Snaps	Pass	Rec	Yds	TD	EZ	C%	+/-	Drop	Yd/C	aDOT	Rk	YAC	Rk	YAC+	BTkl	DVOA	Rk	DYAR	Rk	Use	Rk	Slot
2018	IND	16/4	527	46	27	268	2	4	59%	-2.8	2	9.9	8.9	--	3.0	--	-1.4	2	-20.5%	--	-28	--	7.1%	--	48%
2019	IND	16/13	809	72	41	607	5	8	57%	-3.6	3	14.8	11.8	40	5.8	8	+1.6	6	8.4%	26	121	33	15.0%	64	60%
2020	IND	16/14	834	71	44	629	5	8	62%	-1.3	5	14.3	11.0	41	5.3	19	+0.2	6	5.5%	31	99	37	13.0%	75	84%
2021	IND			46	28	373	2		61%	--		13.3							-3.9%						

Parris Campbell's loss was Pascal's gain, as he put in another year of yeoman's work as Indy's big slot receiver. Pascal's best game for the Colts last year was Week 15 versus the Texans, when he finished with 50 receiving DYAR, second most in the NFL that week, after catching five of six targets for 79 yards and two touchdowns. A UDFA in 2017, Pascal is on the final year of his team control with the Colts after signing a one-year, $3.4-million tender. He's a valuable backup and has been there when the Colts needed him over the past couple of seasons—Carson Wentz will be his fourth starting quarterback in four years. He's probably not a priority re-sign guy, but plenty of teams have done worse at fourth wideout.

Tim Patrick   Height: 6-4   Weight: 212   College: Utah   Draft: 2017/FA   Born: 23-Nov-1993   Age: 28   Risk: Blue

Year	Tm	G/GS	Snaps	Pass	Rec	Yds	TD	EZ	C%	+/-	Drop	Yd/C	aDOT	Rk	YAC	Rk	YAC+	BTkl	DVOA	Rk	DYAR	Rk	Use	Rk	Slot
2018	DEN	16/4	393	41	23	315	1	2	56%	-1.9	2	13.7	10.7	--	4.9	--	+0.1	0	-17.6%	--	-16	--	7.2%	--	44%
2019	DEN	8/2	290	31	16	218	0	2	52%	-2.2	2	13.6	10.7	--	2.4	--	-1.7	3	-7.8%	--	11	--	12.6%	--	52%
2020	DEN	15/15	750	79	51	742	6	5	65%	+3.6	2	14.5	12.9	27	4.7	32	+0.1	6	16.1%	15	183	22	16.2%	58	46%
2021	DEN			55	33	443	3		60%	--		13.3							-6.0%						

The Broncos wide receiver room is crowded, but Patrick will vie for the No. 3 spot after a bit of a breakout last season. A UDFA in 2017, Patrick bounced around some practice squads before finally making the Broncos roster in 2018, then ascended to become a legitimate No. 3 option in 2020. Part of Patrick's value, and what may keep him ahead of slot receiver KJ Hamler, is that he has inside-outside flexibility like his teammates Jerry Jeudy and Courtland Sutton. Patrick and Jeudy saw 46% and 47% of their targets from the slot last season, respectively, while Sutton earned 43% of his targets from the slot in 2019 when he was healthy. Patrick allows Denver's three-receiver looks to be shuffled all around into different formations. Though not the scariest player with the ball in his hands, Patrick's tall, thick frame enables him to be a tough and reliable target over the intermediate area of the field when paired with how comfortably he sees the ball into his hands. Jeudy and Sutton should be the bread-winners, but Patrick is the kind of glue guy that holds together a high-end wide receiver unit.

Cordarrelle Patterson

Height: 6-2   Weight: 238   College: Tennessee   Draft: 2013/1 (29)   Born: 17-Mar-1991   Age: 30   Risk: Green

Year	Tm	G/GS	Snaps	Pass	Rec	Yds	TD	EZ	C%	+/-	Drop	Yd/C	aDOT	Rk	YAC	Rk	YAC+	BTkl	DVOA	Rk	DYAR	Rk	Use	Rk	Slot
2018	NE	15/5	230	28	21	247	3	2	75%	+0.7	1	11.8	6.2	--	7.7	--	+0.9	11	0.6%	--	29	--	5.3%	--	46%
2019	CHI	16/4	203	17	11	83	0	1	65%	-1.8	0	7.5	5.2	--	6.5	--	+0.2	8	-35.1%	--	-32	--	3.1%	--	78%
2020	CHI	16/3	201	25	21	132	0	0	84%	+1.6	1	6.3	3.6	--	5.4	--	-1.3	13	-33.2%	--	-39	--	4.1%	--	26%
2021	ATL			20	14	148	1		70%	--		10.4							-0.6%						

There's no question that Patterson is a game-changing kick returner, but after eight seasons he has yet to develop into a home-run threat as a receiver or a rusher. Though he saw an increase in touches last season in Chicago (from 28 to 85), he wasn't any more effective. In 2019, he broke off six gains of at least 10 yards; in 2020, with three times as many opportunities, he had nine such gains. Patterson may not see very many targets for new coach Arthur Smith. Only the Broncos attempted fewer screen passes (including jet sweep passes) last season than Smith's Titans. (Patterson's rushing numbers, not listed above, included 64 carries for 232 yards and a touchdown last year, with 67 DYAR and -20.6% DVOA.)

Breshad Perriman

Height: 6-2   Weight: 215   College: Central Florida   Draft: 2015/1 (26)   Born: 10-Sep-1993   Age: 28   Risk: Yellow

Year	Tm	G/GS	Snaps	Pass	Rec	Yds	TD	EZ	C%	+/-	Drop	Yd/C	aDOT	Rk	YAC	Rk	YAC+	BTkl	DVOA	Rk	DYAR	Rk	Use	Rk	Slot
2018	CLE	10/2	218	25	16	340	2	4	64%	+2.2	0	21.3	18.4	--	4.7	--	-0.4	1	36.6%	--	97	--	7.1%	--	28%
2019	TB	14/4	652	69	36	645	6	11	52%	+1.3	0	17.9	17.4	2	3.5	60	-1.1	3	16.5%	15	155	29	13.1%	68	34%
2020	NYJ	12/12	651	60	30	505	3	9	50%	-3.7	4	16.8	15.9	5	5.3	18	+0.6	3	-4.4%	56	41	61	18.2%	47	59%
2021	DET			92	55	928	4		60%	--		17.0							-4.6%						

The one-time first-round Ravens pick and apparent bust Perriman seemed to revive his career with tremendously efficient low-volume seasons with the Browns and Bucs in 2018 and 2019. But Perriman did not have much of a chance to parlay that efficiency into a major offensive role in 2020 since he suffered ankle and head injuries that cost him four games and limited him in his other starts for the Jets. That sort of career trajectory has exhausted the chances of other 28-year-olds, but Perriman found an exciting opportunity as a temporary No. 1 option for a rebuilding Lions team desperate for receivers. Perriman broke out after a shift to a more niche role as a deep threat. He finished second at his position with a 17.4-yard average depth of target in his season in Tampa Bay that meshes well with his 4.25s speed. But at 6-foot-2 and 215 pounds, Perriman is bulkier than the team's other lankier deep threat Tyrell Williams. And that size could allow Perriman to work a bigger route tree and even see some time in the slot in 2021.

Michael Pittman

Height: 6-4   Weight: 220   College: USC   Draft: 2020/2 (34)   Born: 5-Oct-1997   Age: 24   Risk: Yellow

Year	Tm	G/GS	Snaps	Pass	Rec	Yds	TD	EZ	C%	+/-	Drop	Yd/C	aDOT	Rk	YAC	Rk	YAC+	BTkl	DVOA	Rk	DYAR	Rk	Use	Rk	Slot
2020	IND	13/8	699	61	40	503	1	0	66%	-1.0	3	12.6	8.5	70	7.3	1	+2.7	3	-5.8%	61	32	64	13.9%	70	50%
2021	IND			88	56	716	4		64%	--		12.7							-3.5%						

Losing a lot of the first half of the season to his rookieness and a short IR stint, Pittman came on hard starting in Week 8 against the Ravens. There were some definite growing pains with his skill set vis a vis Philip Rivers' arm strength to the outside last year, but Pittman thrived on the slants that the Colts ran for him and comes into Year 2 with a quarterback who will expand the risk-taking portfolio quite a bit in Carson Wentz. Pittman will box out and win against man coverage on the outside—he did that at USC and he's going to do it in the NFL—and with a non-COVID offseason in the books he should be a good bet to take a step forward. He maintains a fairly popular YouTube channel (372K subscribers as of this typing) with his wife Kianna, so if you want to see them buying a new car or cooking a lobster dinner, the content is out there, man. There's some football stuff and awkward ad reads, too! Did you know Pittman always takes the hotel key card with him? He sure does. Yup. #Content

Jalen Reagor

Height: 5-11   Weight: 195   College: Texas Christian   Draft: 2020/1 (21)   Born: 2-Jan-1999   Age: 23   Risk: Green

Year	Tm	G/GS	Snaps	Pass	Rec	Yds	TD	EZ	C%	+/-	Drop	Yd/C	aDOT	Rk	YAC	Rk	YAC+	BTkl	DVOA	Rk	DYAR	Rk	Use	Rk	Slot
2020	PHI	11/11	510	54	31	396	1	6	57%	-3.4	1	12.8	13.6	16	5.6	11	+0.1	4	-20.5%	83	-32	79	13.9%	71	38%
2021	PHI			73	44	586	4		60%	--		13.3							-5.7%						

Reagor was drafted in the first round for his speed and ability to create in space. Neither of those skills really flourished during his rookie season, when Reagor battled poor quarterback play, inconsistency, and some injuries (a torn thumb ligament put him on IR from Weeks 3-7). Neither Philadelphia quarterback was able to get on the same page with Reagor, who caught 19 of 33 passes for 222 yards from Carson Wentz and 12 of 21 for 174 yards from Jalen Hurts. There were some flashes that showed what Reagor could do. Of the 27 wide receivers who had at least 10 screen targets, Reagor ranked third with 7.8 yards per reception. Despite terrible production on early downs, Reagor had positive DVOA (2.4%) on third downs riding out a high-variance deep attack. He had just a 47% catch rate on third downs but with an 18.7-yard average depth of target.

Hunter Renfrow Height: 5-10 Weight: 185 College: Clemson Draft: 2019/5 (149) Born: 21-Dec-1995 Age: 26 Risk: Green

Year	Tm	G/GS	Snaps	Pass	Rec	Yds	TD	EZ	C%	+/-	Drop	Yd/C	aDOT	Rk	YAC	Rk	YAC+	BTkl	DVOA	Rk	DYAR	Rk	Use	Rk	Slot
2019	OAK	13/4	445	71	49	605	4	5	69%	+3.4	6	12.3	7.2	78	6.1	6	+1.8	14	7.9%	27	112	38	17.6%	56	97%
2020	LV	16/6	550	77	56	656	2	2	73%	+1.8	4	11.7	7.3	81	6.0	7	+0.7	14	-3.2%	51	59	52	14.8%	64	94%
2021	LV			75	53	663	4		71%	--		12.6							7.5%						

It's hard not to stereotype Hunter Renfrow as your standard quick-game slot receiver. Renfrow, all 5-foot-10 and 185 pounds of him, held the fifth-highest ratio of his targets being from the slot versus outside, with 94% of his targets coming from slot alignments. Renfrow's 7.7-yard average depth of target from the slot also ranked just 70th out of 87 qualifying wide receivers, while his five targets from outside alignments combined for a negative depth of target, suggesting Renfrow was only a screen or gadget player when lined up there. Moreover, Renfrow had a catch rate of 70% or higher on all three downs, making him the only non-running back on the team to do so last season. Slants, shallows, etc., are all Renfrow specials, even if he adds very little down the field. Renfrow's overall DYAR has sat close to average in each of the past two seasons, but that's a plenty useful player to have around when others such as Darren Waller and Henry Ruggs can be the explosive play threats.

Josh Reynolds Height: 6-3 Weight: 196 College: Texas A&M Draft: 2017/4 (117) Born: 16-Feb-1995 Age: 26 Risk: Green

Year	Tm	G/GS	Snaps	Pass	Rec	Yds	TD	EZ	C%	+/-	Drop	Yd/C	aDOT	Rk	YAC	Rk	YAC+	BTkl	DVOA	Rk	DYAR	Rk	Use	Rk	Slot
2018	LAR	16/8	611	53	29	402	5	12	55%	-1.6	2	13.9	11.7	37	4.4	37	+0.4	4	1.9%	40	62	48	9.6%	82	79%
2019	LAR	16/2	490	43	21	326	1	4	49%	-5.5	1	15.5	10.8	--	6.6	--	+1.6	6	-16.1%	--	-11	--	7.0%	--	65%
2020	LAR	16/13	803	81	52	618	2	6	64%	+1.4	2	11.9	11.3	38	4.3	46	+0.1	8	-10.6%	71	13	73	14.4%	66	49%
2021	TEN			56	36	478	3		64%	--		13.2							0.8%						

L.A.'s main outside wideout in three-wide sets, with Cooper Kupp shifting inside, Reynolds struggled through some relentless up-and-downs stapled to Jared Goff's pocket presence and didn't gain much in the way of targets despite Brandin Cooks moving on because the Rams simply couldn't operate their run game without two tight ends on the field. Reynolds is an intriguing buy-low for Titans general manager Jon Robinson as a size-speed guy with experience in play-action who, all in all, had his best year yet in 2020. But with Julio Jones now in Tennessee, the path to targets didn't clear up all that much for Reynolds unless there's a shift away from Arthur Smith's preferred two-tight end sets by new offensive coordinator Todd Downing.

Calvin Ridley Height: 6-1 Weight: 190 College: Alabama Draft: 2018/1 (26) Born: 20-Dec-1994 Age: 27 Risk: Green

Year	Tm	G/GS	Snaps	Pass	Rec	Yds	TD	EZ	C%	+/-	Drop	Yd/C	aDOT	Rk	YAC	Rk	YAC+	BTkl	DVOA	Rk	DYAR	Rk	Use	Rk	Slot
2018	ATL	16/5	644	92	64	821	10	5	70%	+3.9	9	12.8	10.6	47	5.7	13	+0.7	5	10.2%	26	167	21	15.3%	63	49%
2019	ATL	13/10	732	93	63	866	7	8	68%	+8.3	3	13.7	14.1	21	2.2	78	-1.9	6	30.6%	2	310	5	17.8%	53	32%
2020	ATL	15/15	822	143	90	1374	9	21	63%	+8.0	6	15.3	14.4	10	3.1	78	-1.1	15	6.7%	27	230	17	25.5%	9	37%
2021	ATL			145	98	1314	7		68%	--		13.4							5.2%						

Calvin Ridley emerged from Julio Jones' shadow last season and has all the tools to be one of the best wide receivers in the league. That said, the roster around him is full of question marks. After yet another contract restructuring, Matt Ryan is still here and capable of playing at a reasonably high level, but Jones has been replaced by some cardboard cutouts. Good news is that Ridley should be used to shouldering the load. Jones either missed or was severely limited in nine of Ridley's 15 starts last season. In those games, Ridley saw an uptick in targets (10.3 vs. 8.3), catches (6.1 vs. 5.8) and receiving yards (95.0 vs. 86.5). However, without Jones to pull away coverage, he wasn't able to score touchdowns as often (0.3 vs. 1.0). Put another way, in the six games Ridley and Jones played together, they were near equals in efficiency. Jones' DVOA was 27.9%; Ridley's was

26.3%. Without Jones, Ridley was closer to average. Throw in his offseason foot surgery, and it's easy to be a little ambivalent about Ridley. He might have a mammoth season, but only because he leads the league in targets, garbage-time production, and empty calories.

Allen Robinson   Height: 6-2   Weight: 220   College: Penn State   Draft: 2014/2 (61)   Born: 8/24/1993   Age: 28   Risk: Green

Year	Tm	G/GS	Snaps	Pass	Rec	Yds	TD	EZ	C%	+/-	Drop	Yd/C	aDOT	Rk	YAC	Rk	YAC+	BTkl	DVOA	Rk	DYAR	Rk	Use	Rk	Slot
2018	CHI	13/12	765	94	55	754	4	11	59%	-2.0	2	13.7	12.0	31	3.9	52	-0.4	9	-4.8%	52	62	47	24.3%	15	52%
2019	CHI	16/15	1025	154	98	1147	7	14	64%	+0.4	4	11.7	11.3	44	2.6	77	-1.9	9	0.4%	45	165	26	27.9%	4	65%
2020	CHI	16/16	911	151	102	1250	6	15	68%	+2.5	0	12.3	10.0	52	3.1	74	-1.2	13	1.4%	41	175	24	25.5%	10	56%
2021	CHI			132	83	1001	6		63%	--		12.0							-6.3%						

Robinson's 1.4% DVOA in 2020 may not be impressive without extra context. It was just 41st of the 87 wide receivers with 50 or more targets, but relative to the other Bears wide receivers, it popped. None of Darnell Mooney, Anthony Miller, and Cordarrelle Patterson—the other three Bears receivers with 25 or more targets—beat -20.0%. Robinson was also the only wideout with 60 or more targets in 2020 that did not drop a pass. The Bears retained Robinson on a franchise tag in 2021. It would be odd if the team didn't work out a long-term deal before Robinson hit the market next winter.

Demarcus Robinson   Height: 6-1   Weight: 203   College: Florida   Draft: 2016/4 (126)   Born: 21-Sep-1994   Age: 27   Risk: Blue

Year	Tm	G/GS	Snaps	Pass	Rec	Yds	TD	EZ	C%	+/-	Drop	Yd/C	aDOT	Rk	YAC	Rk	YAC+	BTkl	DVOA	Rk	DYAR	Rk	Use	Rk	Slot
2018	KC	16/5	419	33	22	288	4	4	67%	+0.6	1	13.1	12.1	--	5.3	--	+0.0	4	13.5%	--	68	--	5.8%	--	45%
2019	KC	16/10	743	55	32	449	4	6	58%	-1.4	1	14.0	13.3	25	3.2	67	-1.1	9	1.0%	42	61	53	10.1%	79	45%
2020	KC	16/9	711	59	45	466	3	6	76%	+5.4	2	10.4	8.7	66	3.8	58	-0.5	7	5.2%	32	81	44	9.6%	84	41%
2021	KC			60	40	487	4		67%	--		12.0							3.1%						

Robinson saw another shift in his role last season and was better for it. Previously, Robinson had seen an overwhelming target share on shot plays. In 2018 and 2019, Robinson's target share on "bomb" passes (26 or more air yards) was 14% and 16%, respectively. That number fell to just 7% in 2020, while his share of short passes skyrocketed to 44% after a career-low 30% in 2019. Coincidentally, Robinson produced the best DYAR of his career, perhaps proving that his short-area explosiveness is best used as a quick-game separator and YAC threat rather than someone who ought to be sprinting up and down the field. With Sammy Watkins now out of the fold, that may become even more true as Robinson is likely the best suited player on the roster to eat up some of Watkins' targets. That said, Robinson has never cleared 500 yards in five seasons with the Chiefs and it's hard to imagine he would suddenly do much better than that.

Amari Rodgers   Height: 5-10   Weight: 210   College: Clemson   Draft: 2021/3 (85)   Born: 23-Sep-1999   Age: 22   Risk: Green

Year	Tm	G/GS	Snaps	Pass	Rec	Yds	TD	EZ	C%	+/-	Drop	Yd/C	aDOT	Rk	YAC	Rk	YAC+	BTkl	DVOA	Rk	DYAR	Rk	Use	Rk	Slot
2021	GB			37	27	325	2		73%	--		11.9							10.8%						

With a compact build and quick acceleration playing out of the slot, Rodgers fits the mold of recent productive Packers receiver Randall Cobb. And although he did not cost a first- or second-round draft pick, Rodgers is exactly the sort of receiver his new offense has been missing—Equanimeous St. Brown and Allen Lazard led the Packers in slot target percentage in 2020 despite both being 6-foot-5. Rodgers' addition might well have placated disgruntled star quarterback Aaron Rodgers if the damage had not already been done with the team's draft decisions and lack of communication last year. And that could be a shame for the receiver Rodgers, who undoubtedly would be less productive catching passes from unproven sophomore quarterback Jordan Love.

Henry Ruggs

Height: 5-11 Weight: 188 College: Alabama Draft: 2020/1 (12) Born: 24-Jan-1999 Age: 22 Risk: Green

Year	Tm	G/GS	Snaps	Pass	Rec	Yds	TD	EZ	C%	+/-	Drop	Yd/C	aDOT	Rk	YAC	Rk	YAC+	BTkl	DVOA	Rk	DYAR	Rk	Use	Rk	Slot
2020	LV	13/12	581	43	26	452	2	2	60%	+0.3	1	17.4	17.8	--	5.6	--	+0.6	3	-2.4%	--	38	--	10.1%	--	82%
2021	LV			67	42	663	4		63%	--		15.7							2.2%						

Ruggs was the best version of Ted Ginn Jr., for better or worse. He was as electric down the field as advertised. Whether Ruggs worked open himself or helped generate space for others, his track speed forced defenses to respect the Raiders' deep game as much as any team in the league, especially when paired with Nelson Agholor's sudden breakout season. Ruggs' presence even got Derek Carr to attack down the field above the league average rate. Like Ginn, however, Ruggs needed to be wide open to make himself a useful pass-catcher, which was not always something he proved capable of. Some of the league's better cornerbacks did a decent job pinning him to the sideline on vertical routes, and he was seldom able to muscle his way back. Ruggs was useless in the red zone for the same reasons, only earning two targets with zero catches over the course of the year. It's fine for Ruggs to be primarily a vertical stretcher, but he is going to need to add some muscle and ability to fight at the catch point in order to ascend beyond being a high-end role player.

Curtis Samuel

Height: 5-11 Weight: 195 College: Ohio State Draft: 2017/2 (40) Born: 11-Aug-1996 Age: 25 Risk: Green

Year	Tm	G/GS	Snaps	Pass	Rec	Yds	TD	EZ	C%	+/-	Drop	Yd/C	aDOT	Rk	YAC	Rk	YAC+	BTkl	DVOA	Rk	DYAR	Rk	Use	Rk	Slot
2018	CAR	13/8	466	65	39	494	5	9	60%	-2.2	3	12.7	12.3	29	2.8	77	-1.7	14	-5.4%	53	39	54	14.9%	65	24%
2019	CAR	16/15	970	105	54	627	6	10	51%	-6.0	7	11.6	15.3	11	2.8	74	-1.5	7	-15.1%	71	-21	73	17.9%	52	34%
2020	CAR	15/5	658	97	77	851	3	2	79%	+11.4	5	11.1	7.7	79	4.2	54	-1.4	15	0.1%	43	95	39	19.5%	37	89%
2021	WAS			98	65	761	4		66%	--		11.8							-2.9%						

After years of trying to find the right role as a gadget guy and outside deep threat, Samuel became a low-aDOT slot receiver who was able to take advantage of open space in the middle of the field in Joe Brady's offense. There were still gadget plays—Samuel led all wide receivers with 11 targets from the backfield, which resulted in a -33.7% DVOA—but more importantly Samuel 's slot numbers went from 35% of his passes with a 13.7-yard average depth of target and -15.3% DVOA in 2019 to 89% of his passes with an 8.0-yard aDOT and 9.2% DVOA in 2020. It remains to be seen how much of Samuel's 2020 role will come over to Washington, especially since he's again under the coaching staff responsible for his 2019 usage.

Deebo Samuel

Height: 5-11 Weight: 214 College: South Carolina Draft: 2019/2 (36) Born: 15-Jan-1996 Age: 25 Risk: Yellow

Year	Tm	G/GS	Snaps	Pass	Rec	Yds	TD	EZ	C%	+/-	Drop	Yd/C	aDOT	Rk	YAC	Rk	YAC+	BTkl	DVOA	Rk	DYAR	Rk	Use	Rk	Slot
2019	SF	15/11	728	81	57	802	3	5	70%	+1.6	8	14.1	7.6	75	8.3	2	+2.4	28	7.3%	29	121	34	18.1%	51	66%
2020	SF	7/5	305	44	33	391	1	0	75%	-0.7	3	11.8	2.4	--	12.1	--	+4.7	12	5.5%	--	64	--	17.9%	--	70%
2021	SF			87	57	697	4		66%	--		12.2							-1.8%						

Samuel was almost exclusively a gadget player in 2020—398 of his 391 receiving yards (not a typo) came after the catch. Per Sports Info Solutions, his most common targets were labeled as some variety of screen, followed closely by "jet sweep pass." He didn't even qualify for our main wide receiver tables, but he was still in the top five at the position with 21 targets behind the line of scrimmage. Fortunately, he was a really *good* gadget player, leading all wideouts with 229 yards on behind-the-line targets, nearly 100 more than the next-most productive player (Mecole Hardman, 131). He also had eight rushes for 26 yards (and a -37.5% DVOA). Meanwhile, he had only three catches 10 or more yards downfield. The foot and hamstring injuries that knocked him out for nine games likely still affected him when he did play, forcing him into that extreme role—note his year-to-year drop in average depth of target—but he'll probably always be a possession receiver more than a downfield threat.

Emmanuel Sanders

Height: 5-11 Weight: 180 College: Southern Methodist Draft: 2010/3 (82) Born: 17-Mar-1987 Age: 34 Risk: Green

Year	Tm	G/GS	Snaps	Pass	Rec	Yds	TD	EZ	C%	+/-	Drop	Yd/C	aDOT	Rk	YAC	Rk	YAC+	BTkl	DVOA	Rk	DYAR	Rk	Use	Rk	Slot
2018	DEN	12/12	658	99	71	868	4	4	73%	+6.8	5	12.2	9.7	56	4.3	44	-1.3	10	2.0%	39	113	36	23.1%	20	68%
2019	2TM	17/16	859	97	66	869	5	8	68%	+3.7	2	13.2	10.8	46	3.6	58	-0.6	6	10.5%	24	188	22	20.1%	38	67%
2020	NO	14/5	559	82	61	726	5	8	74%	+5.5	4	11.9	9.3	59	2.8	80	-1.4	3	9.6%	22	150	25	18.9%	43	61%
2021	BUF			65	44	523	3		68%	--		11.8							3.6%						

Here's a tidbit to win you points at future trivia nights: Sanders became the first receiver to pick a single-digit number under the NFL's new relaxed uniform rules. With Josh Allen, Mitchell Trubisky and Dawson Knox all holding Sanders' previous numbers, he'll now be No. 1. He'll be more like No. 4 in the Bills' receiving hierarchy, but that's less of a problem in Buffalo than it would be elsewhere. The Bills ran 158 snaps with at least four receivers on the field in 2020, second-most in the league, and that number's only going to go up with Tyler Kroft out of town. Sanders is one of only 16 receivers to put up triple-digit DYARs in each of the last three years; he probably won't hit that again in the crowded Buffalo receiver room, but he'll be a plus addition to the passing attack.

Anthony Schwartz

Height: 6-0 Weight: 179 College: Auburn Draft: 2021/3 (91) Born: 5-Sep-2000 Age: 21 Risk: Green

Year	Tm	G/GS	Snaps	Pass	Rec	Yds	TD	EZ	C%	+/-	Drop	Yd/C	aDOT	Rk	YAC	Rk	YAC+	BTkl	DVOA	Rk	DYAR	Rk	Use	Rk	Slot
2021	CLE			28	18	228	1		64%	--		12.6							-1.9%						

The Browns needed to add a pure burner to their wideout group, and that is what Schwartz is—the 2018 Gatorade National Track and Field Athlete of the Year as a prep sprinter in Florida, in fact. Schwartz remains more track star than polished wideout, however, and his years at Auburn didn't exactly shine that diamond—Schwartz averaged fewer than 40 yards per game and just 12 yards per reception in his three seasons on the Plains. His speed can wreck defenses, and Schwartz could be a weapon in jet sweeps and other spacial plays, but he will have to prove he can catch the ball regularly for defenses to respect that great speed to the point it changes games.

Laviska Shenault

Height: 6-1 Weight: 227 College: Colorado Draft: 2020/2 (42) Born: 5-Oct-1998 Age: 23 Risk: Green

Year	Tm	G/GS	Snaps	Pass	Rec	Yds	TD	EZ	C%	+/-	Drop	Yd/C	aDOT	Rk	YAC	Rk	YAC+	BTkl	DVOA	Rk	DYAR	Rk	Use	Rk	Slot
2020	JAX	14/12	585	79	58	600	5	6	73%	+2.9	4	10.3	6.5	84	5.1	24	+0.1	24	-4.0%	55	56	55	15.3%	61	60%
2021	JAX			86	56	619	4		65%	--		11.1							-6.3%						

Remember when the Jaguars wanted to list Denard Robinson as "OW" for "offensive weapon?" That was Laviska Shenault last year, except Shenault could catch the ball. The Jaguars tried to manufacture touches for him, created packages for him to join the backfield, and used him to send defenses scrambling. Offensive coordinator Darrell Bevell said in OTAs that Shenault "needs the ball in his hands," but also added "there's routes ... where I want to progress, too, and see what he was able to do as a wide receiver and I really like what I see." Shenault profiles as the main slot player on the team with DJ Chark and Marvin Jones outside, which is just as well because 45 of Shenault's targets came lined up in the slot or at tight end. Safe to say that whatever the Jaguars are brewing with Travis Etienne could jeopardize some targets for Shenault, but his first-year tape points to a player who could succeed as a big slot and create after the catch. If Shenault gets the opportunities, he could be quite the fantasy football find. Percy Harvin was an Urban Meyer creation, you know.

Sterling Shepard

Height: 5-10 Weight: 201 College: Oklahoma Draft: 2016/2 (40) Born: 10-Feb-1993 Age: 28 Risk: Yellow

Year	Tm	G/GS	Snaps	Pass	Rec	Yds	TD	EZ	C%	+/-	Drop	Yd/C	aDOT	Rk	YAC	Rk	YAC+	BTkl	DVOA	Rk	DYAR	Rk	Use	Rk	Slot
2018	NYG	16/16	936	107	66	872	4	12	62%	-2.6	7	13.2	10.2	50	4.7	33	-0.1	9	-0.9%	46	97	42	18.5%	40	69%
2019	NYG	10/10	608	83	57	576	3	7	69%	+1.6	3	10.1	9.9	60	3.1	70	-1.2	8	-8.1%	61	30	60	22.6%	23	65%
2020	NYG	12/12	561	90	66	656	3	3	73%	+4.1	1	9.9	8.3	71	3.1	77	-1.4	8	-9.0%	67	25	67	23.7%	19	53%
2021	NYG			94	64	700	4		68%	--		11.0							-2.7%						

Over the last three years, Shepard's average depth of target has dropped from 10.2 yards to 9.9 to 8.3. His average depth of catch has dropped from 8.4 yards to 7.0 to 6.7. His YAC per reception has fallen from 4.7 yards to 3.1. Shepard has also spent the last three seasons drifting from a role as slot weapon to that of a more traditional outside receiver, largely due to the unavailability/ineffectiveness of various teammates. In other words, Shepard is becoming an outside receiver who catches micro-passes and doesn't do much with them, which is not a very useful battery of skills. A September toe injury likely slowed Shepard a bit last season, and he has little control over his role in the Giants offense, but something's gotta give now that Shepard's yards per reception have dropped below the Mendoza line.

Kenny Golladay's arrival should allow Shepard to return to his more natural slot role and give him more room underneath to work. It could also relegate him to role-player status. Though really, that's what Shepard has always been.

Cam Sims   Height: 6-5   Weight: 214   College: Alabama   Draft: 2018/FA   Born: 6-Jan-1996   Age: 26   Risk: Green

Year	Tm	G/GS	Snaps	Pass	Rec	Yds	TD	EZ	C%	+/-	Drop	Yd/C	aDOT	Rk	YAC	Rk	YAC+	BTkl	DVOA	Rk	DYAR	Rk	Use	Rk	Slot
2019	WAS	7/1	57	3	2	27	0	0	67%	-0.0	0	13.5	11.7	--	4.0	--	-0.1	0	7.2%	--	4	--	1.5%	--	33%
2020	WAS	16/10	639	48	32	477	1	2	67%	+0.7	3	14.9	10.9	--	7.8	--	+2.7	9	0.3%	--	48	--	8.3%	--	44%
2021	WAS			28	19	247	1		68%	--		13.0							3.2%						

Sims got himself on the field for 59% of the offensive snaps and 10 starts in 2020. At 6-foot-5, Sims quite literally stands out among the Washington receivers, given the main targets are a 6-foot-0 Terry McLaurin and 5-foot-11 Curtis Samuel. Despite that size, Sims wasn't a big red zone threat last season (just three passes, one touchdown, and a -53.8% DVOA), but he did find a niche as a productive third-down receiver with a 51.1% DVOA on 15 passes. Sims has the ability to get down the field, but that third-down production came with an 8.1-yard average depth of target and 11.7 yards after the catch per reception. His big plays caught on in the second half of the season. A 4-yard mesh crosser on third-and-4 turned into a 33-yard gain against the Giants in Week 9. In Week 13, Sims took a screen 31 yards on a third-and-14 and had a 29-yard one-handed reception on a slot fade for a conversion on a third-and-4. Sims could be the favorite to start outside in three-receiver sets should Washington favor using Samuel more in the slot.

Steven Sims   Height: 5-10   Weight: 176   College: Kansas   Draft: 2019/FA   Born: 31-Mar-1997   Age: 24   Risk: Green

Year	Tm	G/GS	Snaps	Pass	Rec	Yds	TD	EZ	C%	+/-	Drop	Yd/C	aDOT	Rk	YAC	Rk	YAC+	BTkl	DVOA	Rk	DYAR	Rk	Use	Rk	Slot
2019	WAS	16/2	314	56	34	310	4	8	61%	-1.8	5	9.1	7.2	77	5.1	18	-0.5	8	-24.6%	78	-53	75	12.5%	71	78%
2020	WAS	12/2	379	37	27	265	1	2	73%	+0.1	4	9.8	7.2	--	4.7	--	-0.3	2	-17.9%	--	-15	--	8.8%	--	87%
2021	WAS			4	3	27	0		75%	--		11.0							-1.1%						

In last year's Top 25 Prospects section, we likened Sims to Tavon Austin if the latter knew how to play receiver. We might have been half right. Sims couldn't translate his late-2019 production into 2020. Even though he turned in more yards per game and more yards per reception, the impact of those plays wasn't the same. Sims scored just once and wasn't nearly the red zone threat that he had been in 2019 when he scored five touchdowns inside the 20. He only ran the ball once after nine carries for 85 yards and a touchdown in 2019. Sims also struggled shifting from kick returns to punt returns and developed a ball security issue with five fumbles. There may not be room for him on the depth chart in 2021.

Darius Slayton   Height: 6-1   Weight: 190   College: Auburn   Draft: 2019/5 (171)   Born: 12-Jan-1997   Age: 24   Risk: Green

Year	Tm	G/GS	Snaps	Pass	Rec	Yds	TD	EZ	C%	+/-	Drop	Yd/C	aDOT	Rk	YAC	Rk	YAC+	BTkl	DVOA	Rk	DYAR	Rk	Use	Rk	Slot
2019	NYG	14/9	709	84	48	740	8	6	57%	+2.0	3	15.4	14.1	20	4.0	45	-0.2	5	9.6%	25	148	30	16.5%	60	21%
2020	NYG	16/15	877	96	50	751	3	9	52%	-6.6	5	15.0	13.8	14	3.2	72	-0.7	6	-13.6%	77	-7	77	18.9%	42	27%
2021	NYG			43	26	405	2		60%	--		15.3							-0.3%						

Slayton's average depth of target of 13.8 yards ranked eighth in the NFL among receivers with at least 75 targets, while his average depth of catch of 11.7 yards ranked sixth. Slayton picked up a first down on 82.0% of his receptions, the highest rate in the league among receivers with at least 75 targets. So what we have here is an underrated deep threat who has been trapped on a bad offense with iffy quarterback play and an awful offensive line for two seasons. SIS only charted 61.5% of passes to Slayton as "catchable," the second-lowest rate among qualifying wide receivers.

Slayton must now share deep targets with the similar (and better, when healthy) Kenny Golladay for an organization that may want them both to simply lift the lid off the defense for the running game. Either Slayton and Golladay turn into Henry Ellard and Flipper Anderson, or lots of people are gonna be really disappointed.

DeVonta Smith   Height: 6-1   Weight: 175   College: Alabama   Draft: 2021/1 (10)   Born: 14-Nov-1998   Age: 23   Risk: Green

Year	Tm	G/GS	Snaps	Pass	Rec	Yds	TD	EZ	C%	+/-	Drop	Yd/C	aDOT	Rk	YAC	Rk	YAC+	BTkl	DVOA	Rk	DYAR	Rk	Use	Rk	Slot
2021	PHI			109	64	867	7		59%	--		13.6							-5.9%						

Pick a receiving stat and Smith led college football in it during the 2020 season. Perhaps no stat shows how Smith can win all over the field more than the fact he led all college receivers in both completed air yards and yards after the catch. Smith had over 300 more yards after the catch than the next player, Clemson running back Travis Etienne (952 to 650). Or maybe it's that Smith led all of college football in yards on short targets (447), intermediate targets (464), and deep targets (6,576). Or maybe how Smith had the best Playmaker Score given out to a senior in the model's history. Smith's 175-pound frame is a concern, but the receiver has shown the ability to get off of press and beat some of the best defensive backs in college football.

JuJu Smith-Schuster
Height: 6-1   Weight: 215   College: USC   Draft: 2017/2 (62)   Born: 22-Nov-1996   Age: 25   Risk: Green

Year	Tm	G/GS	Snaps	Pass	Rec	Yds	TD	EZ	C%	+/-	Drop	Yd/C	aDOT	Rk	YAC	Rk	YAC+	BTkl	DVOA	Rk	DYAR	Rk	Use	Rk	Slot
2018	PIT	16/13	960	167	111	1426	7	14	67%	+3.1	5	12.8	9.0	63	5.8	11	+0.7	12	4.4%	34	235	17	24.8%	14	65%
2019	PIT	12/12	580	71	42	552	3	6	59%	-2.8	6	13.1	10.0	58	5.3	13	+0.2	4	-11.3%	65	8	66	19.7%	40	74%
2020	PIT	16/14	923	128	97	831	9	10	76%	+4.7	3	8.6	5.7	87	4.2	50	-0.6	6	-10.0%	69	28	65	19.3%	40	88%
2021	PIT			127	88	881	7		69%	--		10.1							-1.9%						

Much has changed for JJSS since his remarkable 2018 season. Antonio Brown and his Stanislavski Method moved on, allowing defenses to focus on JuJu and apparently encouraging the young receiver to fill the drama vacuum left behind. Meanwhile, Ben Roethlisberger missed almost all of 2019 and the passing attack went locavore in 2020. It's enough to make a kid want to go on TikTok and dance away the blues. Smith-Schuster made up for plummeting yards per catch and YAC numbers by grabbing every ball thrown his way, contrasting with his career to date and the general sloppiness in the Steelers receiving corps. He is a full-time slot receiver now, which, along with the perception that he's more concerned with his social media standing than his gridiron one, depressed his free agency market. His return to Pittsburgh reflected the surprisingly soft interest in a player who certainly remains effective, if not the equal of Brown, which many in the Steel City expected him to become. JuJu, unsurprisingly, was at his best nearest the big painted logos—of the 32 players with 15 or more red zone targets in 2020, only Davante Adams and Adam Thielen had a better receiving DVOA than Smith-Schuster's 50.1%.

Tre'Quan Smith
Height: 6-2   Weight: 210   College: Central Florida   Draft: 2018/3 (91)   Born: 7-Jan-1996   Age: 26   Risk: Green

Year	Tm	G/GS	Snaps	Pass	Rec	Yds	TD	EZ	C%	+/-	Drop	Yd/C	aDOT	Rk	YAC	Rk	YAC+	BTkl	DVOA	Rk	DYAR	Rk	Use	Rk	Slot
2018	NO	15/7	567	44	28	427	5	7	64%	+2.8	2	15.3	11.7	--	4.1	--	+0.1	2	22.7%	--	126	--	9.0%	--	55%
2019	NO	11/6	464	25	18	234	5	3	72%	+0.9	2	13.0	7.8	--	6.4	--	+2.8	8	53.6%	--	135	--	6.7%	--	69%
2020	NO	14/10	672	50	34	448	4	4	68%	+0.6	4	13.2	9.2	62	4.0	56	-0.3	8	2.9%	39	61	51	11.1%	81	66%
2021	NO			68	40	564	4		59%	--		14.1							-4.2%						

Smith has been a popular fantasy breakout pick for every year of his professional career as the Saints have struggled to find a consistent No. 2 receiver. However, he has never quite lived up to that billing, and even with Michael Thomas missing most of the 2020 season Smith's career-high 448 yards ranked just fourth on the team. With Emmanuel Sanders and Jared Cook now gone, and only a smattering of undrafted receivers and low picks to challenge him for second spot behind Thomas, a contract year would be the ideal time for Smith to finally turn promise into production.

Willie Snead
Height: 5-11   Weight: 205   College: Ball State   Draft: 2014/FA   Born: 17-Oct-1992   Age: 29   Risk: Green

Year	Tm	G/GS	Snaps	Pass	Rec	Yds	TD	EZ	C%	+/-	Drop	Yd/C	aDOT	Rk	YAC	Rk	YAC+	BTkl	DVOA	Rk	DYAR	Rk	Use	Rk	Slot
2018	BAL	16/10	821	95	62	651	1	1	65%	+0.1	5	10.5	9.0	66	4.5	36	-0.3	9	-9.8%	60	21	57	17.6%	47	91%
2019	BAL	16/11	688	46	31	339	5	4	67%	+1.3	3	10.9	9.0	--	4.1	--	-0.0	6	12.4%	--	88	--	10.8%	--	93%
2020	BAL	4/2	535	48	33	432	3	3	69%	+0.1	3	13.1	8.8	--	5.7	--	+1.2	7	10.1%	--	81	--	15.0%	--	94%
2021	LV			16	11	140	1		69%	--		12.8							5.7%						

It's unlikely that Snead's production will ever return to what he put up in New Orleans, where he threatened to top 1,000 yards as a rookie, but his final year in Baltimore showed some encouraging signs that he can still be a useful player. Snead's 69% catch rate and 5.7 average yards after the catch were both career highs, topping the numbers he had posted in 2016. That said, Snead is best off remaining as a role player, which should be the case for him with the Raiders. There is some overlap between his skill set and John Brown's, and Brown should handily beat out Snead for reps. Snead can still come off the bench as a speed threat on shallows, crossers, posts, and go balls, but do not expect him to be stealing anyone's reps for any reason other than injury or giving someone a rest.

Amon-Ra St. Brown

Height: 6-1   Weight: 195   College: USC   Draft: 2021/4 (112)   Born: 24-Oct-1999   Age: 22   Risk: Green

Year	Tm	G/GS	Snaps	Pass	Rec	Yds	TD	EZ	C%	+/-	Drop	Yd/C	aDOT	Rk	YAC	Rk	YAC+	BTkl	DVOA	Rk	DYAR	Rk	Use	Rk	Slot
2021	DET			44	31	361	2		70%	--		11.7							3.3%						

A fourth-round rookie receiver wouldn't normally spark the excitement St. Brown has this offseason, but the Lions lost six of the seven wide receivers that received targets for them in 2020 and retained just fifth-round sophomore wideout Quintez Cephus. Placeholder signings Breshad Perriman and Tyrell Williams will likely start the season atop the team's receiver depth chart, but St. Brown has the versatility to work in the slot and out wide and has a path to an immediate impact in the former role. He also has great bloodlines—his brother Equanimeous plays for the Packers and his father was a two-time Mr. Universe bodybuilder.

Courtland Sutton

Height: 6-4   Weight: 216   College: Southern Methodist   Draft: 2018/2 (40)   Born: 10-Oct-1995   Age: 26   Risk: Yellow

Year	Tm	G/GS	Snaps	Pass	Rec	Yds	TD	EZ	C%	+/-	Drop	Yd/C	aDOT	Rk	YAC	Rk	YAC+	BTkl	DVOA	Rk	DYAR	Rk	Use	Rk	Slot
2018	DEN	16/9	819	84	42	704	4	17	50%	-5.9	9	16.8	14.3	17	3.9	54	-0.5	5	1.3%	44	95	44	15.4%	62	25%
2019	DEN	16/14	942	124	72	1112	6	12	58%	+1.1	6	15.4	12.4	36	4.9	23	+0.6	18	5.7%	32	189	21	26.9%	5	43%
2020	DEN	1/1	31	6	3	66	0	0	50%	-0.4	1	22.0	17.7	--	2.3	--	-5.7	0	1.3%	--	6	--	17.5%	--	17%
2021	DEN			97	55	791	5		57%	--		14.4							-9.5%						

As promising as Jerry Jeudy looked at times last season, Sutton will still run the show in Denver. Sutton missed almost all of last season with an ACL injury, but had blossomed into a bona fide star wide receiver the year before. Sutton is the definition of a modern day No. 1 receiver as someone who can reliably win on the outside while still bumping inside on occasion. With KJ Hamler and Jeudy now in the picture, in addition to Tim Patrick's emergence, Sutton may not kick inside as frequently as he used to, but it's certainly something he is capable of. Moreover, Sutton's 14.8% drop rate as a rookie was concerning, but that figure fell to just 7.2% over a much larger target workload in 2019. Sutton is also a red zone machine. Back in 2019, Sutton's 21 red zone targets were more than Denver's next two players combined. No Broncos player earned more than 12 red zone targets in 2020, making it quite clear that Sutton was missed in that area of the field. With their No. 1 receiver back in the fold, the rest of Denver's pass-catchers—particularly Jeudy and tight end Noah Fant—should be able to thrive.

Golden Tate

Height: 5-10   Weight: 197   College: Notre Dame   Draft: 2010/2 (60)   Born: 2-Aug-1988   Age: 33   Risk: N/A

Year	Tm	G/GS	Snaps	Pass	Rec	Yds	TD	EZ	C%	+/-	Drop	Yd/C	aDOT	Rk	YAC	Rk	YAC+	BTkl	DVOA	Rk	DYAR	Rk	Use	Rk	Slot
2018	2TM	15/7	606	114	74	795	4	3	66%	-3.6	9	10.7	6.7	80	5.7	12	+0.6	29	-27.8%	81	-134	84	20.8%	29	86%
2019	NYG	11/10	629	86	49	676	6	4	58%	-5.1	4	13.8	10.0	57	5.8	9	+1.1	12	-2.0%	47	71	48	21.3%	29	91%
2020	NYG	12/4	424	52	35	388	2	3	67%	-0.2	2	11.1	9.3	60	2.1	84	-2.5	2	-10.0%	70	11	74	13.9%	69	89%

Tate out-muscled slot defenders for deep receptions up the seam of 39, 39, and 38 yards last season. Take those three catches out of his data and Tate's yards per reception dipped to 8.5 as he spent much of the season catching micro-passes from the slot. Tate remained useful on third downs (12 conversions on 21 targets, 8-of-11 with 4-9 yards to go) and could help a team as a hard-nosed veteran slot guy. Unfortunately, there's a lot of those guys floating around and only so many teams who need one.

Adam Thielen

Height: 6-2   Weight: 200   College: Minnesota State   Draft: 2013/FA   Born: 22-Aug-1990   Age: 31   Risk: Yellow

Year	Tm	G/GS	Snaps	Pass	Rec	Yds	TD	EZ	C%	+/-	Drop	Yd/C	aDOT	Rk	YAC	Rk	YAC+	BTkl	DVOA	Rk	DYAR	Rk	Use	Rk	Slot
2018	MIN	16/16	1011	153	113	1373	9	11	74%	+16.6	2	12.2	9.7	57	3.7	59	-0.7	5	15.2%	19	341	8	25.7%	12	70%
2019	MIN	10/10	443	48	30	418	6	7	63%	+2.0	3	13.9	13.0	30	3.9	46	-0.0	4	15.4%	16	103	40	17.7%	55	58%
2020	MIN	15/15	926	108	74	925	14	22	69%	+5.1	4	12.5	11.2	40	3.3	69	-0.3	6	19.2%	13	287	9	24.2%	15	59%
2021	MIN			102	67	881	8		66%	--		13.2							7.0%						

Thielen doesn't check the size and athleticism boxes that many of the game's other best wide receivers like Julio Jones and DK Metcalf do. But a 6-foot-2, 200-pound frame and lack of draft pedigree didn't prevent Thielen from becoming the best touchdown scorer at the position in 2020. He didn't quite take the crown with a third-place total of 14 receiving scores, but Thielen had a 70.0% DVOA in the red zone that was the highest among the 34 wide receivers with 15 or more targets inside the

20, and he paced his position with more than a fifth of his total targets (20.4%) coming in the end zone. His ability to maintain his current impact will be key for a Vikings team that has lost Stefon Diggs and Kyle Rudolph the last two offseasons.

Michael Thomas

Height: 6-3   Weight: 212   College: Ohio State   Draft: 2016/2 (47)   Born: 3-Mar-1993   Age: 28   Risk: Green

Year	Tm	G/GS	Snaps	Pass	Rec	Yds	TD	EZ	C%	+/-	Drop	Yd/C	aDOT	Rk	YAC	Rk	YAC+	BTkl	DVOA	Rk	DYAR	Rk	Use	Rk	Slot
2018	NO	16/16	927	147	125	1405	9	8	85%	+24.2	3	11.2	8.0	74	4.1	48	-0.0	18	23.1%	9	442	3	29.6%	2	59%
2019	NO	16/15	959	185	149	1725	9	7	81%	+24.9	3	11.6	8.1	71	3.9	47	-0.2	12	23.9%	8	538	1	33.2%	1	48%
2020	NO	7/5	345	55	40	438	0	2	73%	+3.4	1	11.0	9.9	53	2.1	86	-1.8	3	-2.6%	49	45	60	24.9%	13	41%
2021	NO			152	100	1222	7		66%	--		12.3							-0.7%						

Thomas suffered an opening-day high-ankle sprain that cost him most of the 2020 season. Although he returned for six games in the middle of the campaign, he was clearly still impaired by the injury and the team shut him down in early December to rest for the postseason. That didn't exactly work out: though he scored the lone touchdown of his season in the wild-card win over the Bears, he then had the first catchless game (0-for-4) of his career in the divisional round against the Buccaneers. He recorded career lows in basically everything: yards, targets, yards per target, yards per catch, yards per game, touchdowns, DVOA, and DYAR.

Yet even an impaired Michael Thomas is a very productive player by normal human standards. Thomas still had 62.6 yards per game, which prorates to just barely a 1,000-yard season. He still caught 73% of passes thrown his way. He also had two nine-catch, 100-yard days with Taysom Hill at quarterback, both against the Falcons. Hill's four starts were the most productive stretch of the season for Thomas, when he caught 30 of 37 targets (81%) for 343 yards. That suggests that no matter who wins the quarterback battle this offseason, a healthy Thomas will be back to his usual dominant self.

Kadarius Toney

Height: 6-0   Weight: 193   College: Florida   Draft: 2021/1 (20)   Born: 27-Jan-1999   Age: 22   Risk: Green

Year	Tm	G/GS	Snaps	Pass	Rec	Yds	TD	EZ	C%	+/-	Drop	Yd/C	aDOT	Rk	YAC	Rk	YAC+	BTkl	DVOA	Rk	DYAR	Rk	Use	Rk	Slot
2021	NYG			45	30	376	2		67%	--		12.4							0.6%						

Toney was used as an all-purpose weapon and sometime Wildcat quarterback for Florida last year. He looked like he could do even more in Senior Bowl practices, where he displayed impressive route-running talent and looked sturdier than his 193-pound pro day weight suggests. Toney should eat up most of Golden Tate's old targets, could swipe some opportunities from Sterling Shepard and Evan Engram, and may even run the one direct snap play that Jason Garrett put in his playbook for Tashard Choice back in 2009. It should all add up to a rather substantial role.

Marquez Valdes-Scantling

Height: 6-4   Weight: 207   College: South Florida   Draft: 2018/5 (174)   Born: 10-Oct-1994   Age: 27   Risk: Green

Year	Tm	G/GS	Snaps	Pass	Rec	Yds	TD	EZ	C%	+/-	Drop	Yd/C	aDOT	Rk	YAC	Rk	YAC+	BTkl	DVOA	Rk	DYAR	Rk	Use	Rk	Slot
2018	GB	16/10	692	73	38	581	2	6	52%	-5.6	3	15.3	12.5	26	5.6	14	+0.2	4	-11.3%	63	8	63	12.4%	75	56%
2019	GB	16/10	556	56	26	452	2	8	46%	-3.4	2	17.4	17.2	3	5.8	10	+0.0	3	-15.5%	72	-13	71	10.5%	76	45%
2020	GB	16/12	794	63	33	690	6	5	52%	-2.3	7	20.9	18.5	1	7.3	2	+2.3	4	8.5%	25	112	34	13.1%	74	55%
2021	GB			55	34	598	4		62%	--		17.8							0.7%						

Three seasons into his NFL career, Valdes-Scantling has settled into a Ted Ginn Jr. type of receiver role. He led all qualifying wideouts in average depth of target, and when Valdes-Scantling could squeeze the ball, good things happened. He scored six touchdowns and finished second in YAC+, ahead of even YAC monster A.J. Brown. Valdes-Scantling's issue was a 17.5% drop rate that trailed just Jerry Jeudy (20.0%) and Jalen Guyton (17.6%) at the position. But if that flaw makes him an imperfect role player, Valdes-Scantling is still an excellent draft value as a former fifth-round selection. It remains to be seen if the Packers will be willing to pay for that when Valdes-Scanting becomes a free agent in 2022.

Jaylen Waddle

Height: 5-10   Weight: 182   College: Alabama   Draft: 2021/1 (6)   Born: 25-Nov-1998   Age: 23   Risk: Green

Year	Tm	G/GS	Snaps	Pass	Rec	Yds	TD	EZ	C%	+/-	Drop	Yd/C	aDOT	Rk	YAC	Rk	YAC+	BTkl	DVOA	Rk	DYAR	Rk	Use	Rk	Slot
2021	MIA			84	56	642	4		67%	--		11.6							-2.0%						

Waddle's Playmaker Rating of 75.5% was 12th in the class, not exactly what you hope to see out of the sixth overall pick. His Playmaker Score (accounting for his draft position) bounces back into the top five, but the model is nervous about his relatively small sample size. He played just six games last season and had his best season as a freshman with just 848 yards; it considers Waddle to be more DeVante Parker than superstar in the making. On the other hand, his 18.9 yards per reception is second-all time for Alabama among receivers with at least 100 catches. He is a big play machine waiting to happen. The question is what happens when he's no longer playing third fiddle to DeVonta Smith and Ja'Marr Chase and has to manufacture space for himself.

Greg Ward Height: 5-11 Weight: 190 College: Houston Draft: 2017/FA Born: 12-Jul-1995 Age: 26 Risk: Green

Year	Tm	G/GS	Snaps	Pass	Rec	Yds	TD	EZ	C%	+/-	Drop	Yd/C	aDOT	Rk	YAC	Rk	YAC+	BTkl	DVOA	Rk	DYAR	Rk	Use	Rk	Slot
2019	PHI	7/3	310	40	28	254	1	3	70%	+1.6	0	9.1	7.0	--	3.5	--	-0.9	3	-19.0%	--	-20	--	15.0%	--	75%
2020	PHI	16/10	791	79	53	419	6	5	67%	-3.0	4	7.9	5.8	86	3.1	76	-1.7	6	-20.0%	80	-47	81	13.9%	72	94%
2021	PHI			18	11	122	1		61%	--		11.4							-14.9%						

In two seasons, Ward has turned himself from college quarterback to necessary savior of the Eagles' receiving rotation. OK, so "savior" is strong given the actual production, but over the past two seasons Ward has found himself in a place to be the go-to player when the rest of the receiver group crumbles around him. After a stint on Philadelphia's practice squad and time with the AAF, Ward came on late in the 2019 season, then found himself in the lineup for 70% of Philadelphia's 2020 snaps. Among qualifying receivers with at least 50 targets, Ward's -28.8% DVOA from the slot was better than only the Denver duo of KJ Hamler (-29.9%) and Jerry Jeudy (-31.5%).

James Washington Height: 5-11 Weight: 213 College: Oklahoma State Draft: 2018/2 (60) Born: 2-Apr-1996 Age: 25 Risk: Blue

Year	Tm	G/GS	Snaps	Pass	Rec	Yds	TD	EZ	C%	+/-	Drop	Yd/C	aDOT	Rk	YAC	Rk	YAC+	BTkl	DVOA	Rk	DYAR	Rk	Use	Rk	Slot
2018	PIT	14/6	526	38	16	217	1	2	42%	-4.7	2	13.6	17.0	--	3.3	--	-1.2	1	-25.1%	--	-37	--	6.3%	--	45%
2019	PIT	15/10	649	80	44	735	3	6	55%	+0.2	6	16.7	16.4	4	4.2	41	-0.5	2	11.2%	22	156	28	18.3%	50	48%
2020	PIT	16/7	486	56	30	392	5	11	54%	-2.6	5	13.1	12.8	28	4.6	33	+0.5	6	-8.9%	65	18	71	8.9%	87	35%
2021	PIT			30	19	248	2		63%	--		13.0							-2.6%						

Washington was similar to his teammate Diontae Johnson in that they were both terrible on third and fourth down. In Washington's case, his catch rate plummeted from 58% to 44% in money situations, and his DVOA—quite good on first down (23.1%)—fell to -33.6% on almost the same number of targets. Washington seemed poised for a breakout after a solid 2019 with Larry, Moe, and Curly playing quarterback in Pittsburgh, but the Steelers apparently felt otherwise, drafting Chase Claypool with a premium pick and subsequently welcoming JuJu Smith-Schuster and his iPhone back to town. Even Johnson and his innumerable drops seem more in the team's plans. Washington has shown flashes, but for now he is on the fringe of the rotation.

Sammy Watkins Height: 6-1 Weight: 211 College: Clemson Draft: 2014/1 (4) Born: 14-Jun-1993 Age: 28 Risk: Yellow

Year	Tm	G/GS	Snaps	Pass	Rec	Yds	TD	EZ	C%	+/-	Drop	Yd/C	aDOT	Rk	YAC	Rk	YAC+	BTkl	DVOA	Rk	DYAR	Rk	Use	Rk	Slot
2018	KC	10/9	459	55	40	519	3	1	73%	+3.8	1	13.0	9.0	65	6.0	10	+1.2	14	24.1%	5	161	22	16.3%	55	57%
2019	KC	14/13	744	90	52	673	3	5	58%	-4.8	4	12.9	9.7	63	5.7	12	+0.9	14	-12.3%	67	3	68	18.3%	49	65%
2020	KC	10/9	527	55	37	421	2	4	67%	-1.0	4	11.4	8.2	74	4.2	49	+0.5	2	-0.4%	44	57	54	14.6%	65	54%
2021	BAL			61	38	492	4		62%	--		13.1							-2.3%						

Watkins hasn't gone over 100 receiving yards in a regular-season game since he went 9-198-3 in the 2019 season opener. He has only gone over 75 yards one other time in the last two regular seasons: 7-82-1 in the 2020 season opener. The Sammy Watkins experience, for both his employers and fantasy gamers, consists of a productive season opener, followed by long weeks as a big-name third option in the passing game, with several appearances on the injury report ladled in. Watkins is a willing blocker and (despite a rather offbeat worldview) a well-regarded locker room presence, so he may replace Myles Boykin as the Ravens starting receiver who mostly stalk-blocks on options. He could also disappear onto injured reserve for most of the season.

Mike Williams

Height: 6-4 Weight: 218 College: Clemson Draft: 2017/1 (7) Born: 4-Oct-1994 Age: 27 Risk: Yellow

Year	Tm	G/GS	Snaps	Pass	Rec	Yds	TD	EZ	C%	+/-	Drop	Yd/C	aDOT	Rk	YAC	Rk	YAC+	BTkl	DVOA	Rk	DYAR	Rk	Use	Rk	Slot
2018	LAC	16/5	622	66	43	664	10	13	65%	+4.9	2	15.4	14.7	13	2.7	79	-1.1	8	39.2%	2	262	13	13.2%	70	51%
2019	LAC	15/15	850	90	49	1001	2	13	54%	+1.1	2	20.4	17.7	1	3.8	50	-0.8	3	20.6%	11	235	14	17.1%	58	43%
2020	LAC	15/11	799	85	48	756	5	14	56%	-0.0	4	15.8	14.5	8	3.4	67	-0.7	2	4.5%	35	117	30	15.0%	63	28%
2021	LAC			90	57	843	6		63%	--		14.7							4.4%						

Contested-catch superstars do not work out as often in the league as they do in college. When they work out the wrong way, you get N'Keal Harry. When they work out the right way, though, the result is Mike Williams, who must have more leaping catches with devastating crashes to the ground than any other receiver in the league. Williams hangs onto the ball despite the perilous landings, though. Williams is a premier downfield option as a contested-catch and back-shoulder ball receiver, making him a wonderful fit with new quarterback Justin Herbert. Oddly enough, Williams' skills in that regard do not show up very well in the red zone. Williams earned 29 combined targets in the red zone over that past two years, but failed to finish above a 20% catch rate in either season. His DVOA was also firmly in the negatives for both years. While that does not track with his skill set at all, it would make sense that Williams is such a trusted contested-catch player that the Chargers have used a majority of his red zone targets on goal line fades, which are a low-percentage play regardless of the talent of the receiver. With tight end Hunter Henry now out of the picture, Williams may be required to step up in the red zone in a more legitimate way next season.

Preston Williams

Height: 6-5 Weight: 218 College: Colorado State Draft: 2019/FA Born: 27-Mar-1997 Age: 24 Risk: Yellow

Year	Tm	G/GS	Snaps	Pass	Rec	Yds	TD	EZ	C%	+/-	Drop	Yd/C	aDOT	Rk	YAC	Rk	YAC+	BTkl	DVOA	Rk	DYAR	Rk	Use	Rk	Slot
2019	MIA	8/7	412	60	32	428	3	8	53%	-2.3	4	13.4	14.4	16	1.9	79	-1.8	3	-5.9%	57	32	59	20.1%	37	19%
2020	MIA	8/7	336	35	18	288	4	5	51%	-1.5	2	16.0	15.5	--	2.3	--	-1.5	0	10.8%	--	71	--	13.4%	--	22%
2021	MIA			22	13	171	1		59%	--		13.7							-9.9%						

Williams' Week 9 foot injury not only cost him his season but may well have cost him his career in Miami. When he went down, Williams was 44th in DYAR and 50th in DVOA among qualified receivers, both steps up from his rookie season and totally acceptable numbers for a second wideout working with a rookie passer. He has now missed the second half of both of his first two seasons with injuries, however, and this time, the Dolphins went shopping for Will Fuller and Jaylen Waddle. In 2021, the snaps might just not be there for the former UDFA.

Tyrell Williams

Height: 6-4 Weight: 205 College: Western Oregon Draft: 2015/FA Born: 12-Feb-1992 Age: 29 Risk: Green

Year	Tm	G/GS	Snaps	Pass	Rec	Yds	TD	EZ	C%	+/-	Drop	Yd/C	aDOT	Rk	YAC	Rk	YAC+	BTkl	DVOA	Rk	DYAR	Rk	Use	Rk	Slot
2018	LAC	16/10	761	65	41	653	5	7	63%	+1.2	2	15.9	12.6	25	4.8	29	-0.0	3	12.3%	24	128	32	12.8%	73	62%
2019	OAK	14/12	743	64	42	651	6	8	66%	+3.5	5	15.5	13.5	23	4.5	35	+0.1	4	27.2%	3	204	20	14.9%	65	49%
2021	DET			82	52	718	4		63%	--		13.8							0.0%						

Williams could only enjoy the first year of the four-year, $44.3-million contract he signed with the Raiders in 2019. A torn labrum ended his 2020 season before it began, and the team released him early this offseason. With better luck, he would have filled the role Nelson Agholor did for the team last year. In fact, his targets skewed deeper than Agholor's. His 13.5-yard average depth of target landed in the top 25 at the position in 2019. As it stands, Williams joins the Lions on a modest one-year, $4-million deal and will try to revive new quarterback Jared Goff's deep passing game. It's not as far-fetched as it sounds. Williams has routinely beaten a 10.0% receiving DVOA in his career, and Goff should have plenty of time to hit his placeholder No. 2 receiver with one of the better offensive lines in football.

Robert Woods — Height: 6-0 — Weight: 193 — College: USC — Draft: 2013/2 (41) — Born: 10-Apr-1992 — Age: 29 — Risk: Green

Year	Tm	G/GS	Snaps	Pass	Rec	Yds	TD	EZ	C%	+/-	Drop	Yd/C	aDOT	Rk	YAC	Rk	YAC+	BTkl	DVOA	Rk	DYAR	Rk	Use	Rk	Slot
2018	LAR	16/16	1041	130	86	1219	6	9	66%	+4.1	3	14.2	11.3	42	4.9	27	+0.1	11	17.5%	16	316	11	24.3%	16	85%
2019	LAR	15/15	1009	139	90	1134	2	4	65%	+2.4	4	12.6	8.6	67	6.4	5	+0.7	12	-4.0%	51	94	43	24.2%	16	67%
2020	LAR	16/16	1000	129	90	936	6	6	70%	+2.5	5	10.4	7.2	82	5.5	16	+0.2	15	-10.9%	72	18	69	22.8%	24	82%
2021	LAR			119	80	955	6		67%	--		12.0							1.9%						

After a 2019 season when he only scored two touchdowns in nearly 140 total targets, Woods was the Rams' most consistent red zone producer in 2020. He essentially flip-flopped with Cooper Kupp in terms of red zone efficiency—while Kupp was significantly more efficient than Woods in the red zone in 2019 and drew twice as many targets, they received a much more equitable distribution in 2020, with Woods performing at a high level while Kupp struggled. A lot of this is likely small sample noise, as Woods' red zone target totals for 2019 and 2020 were only 10 and 12, respectively. Either way, Woods and Kupp will be duking it out for red zone looks for years to come as they both signed contract extensions to stay in Los Angeles early in the 2020 season.

Isaiah Wright — Height: 6-2 — Weight: 220 — College: Temple — Draft: 2020/FA — Born: 13-Jan-1997 — Age: 24 — Risk: Green

Year	Tm	G/GS	Snaps	Pass	Rec	Yds	TD	EZ	C%	+/-	Drop	Yd/C	aDOT	Rk	YAC	Rk	YAC+	BTkl	DVOA	Rk	DYAR	Rk	Use	Rk	Slot
2020	WAS	14/6	347	35	27	197	0	1	77%	+0.9	0	7.3	4.4	--	5.3	--	-0.8	8	-20.3%	--	-22	--	7.1%	--	81%
2021	WAS			4	3	27	0		75%	--		10.6							-1.5%						

As an undrafted free agent out of Temple, Wright made his way onto the field for 32% of Washington's offensive snaps. Now Wright is likely to find himself deeper in the wide receiver rotation after numerous additions in the offseason. Wright could still secure his spot on the roster as a special teams contributor as he has been in the early battle to be the team's punt returner throughout the offseason.

Olamide Zaccheaus — Height: 5-8 — Weight: 193 — College: Virginia — Draft: 2019/FA — Born: 23-Jul-1997 — Age: 24 — Risk: Green

Year	Tm	G/GS	Snaps	Pass	Rec	Yds	TD	EZ	C%	+/-	Drop	Yd/C	aDOT	Rk	YAC	Rk	YAC+	BTkl	DVOA	Rk	DYAR	Rk	Use	Rk	Slot
2019	ATL	10/0	88	5	3	115	1	0	60%	-0.1	0	38.3	13.8	--	21.0	--	+14.9	1	82.2%	--	33	--	1.2%	--	60%
2020	ATL	11/2	308	32	20	274	1	3	63%	+1.4	1	13.7	14.1	--	3.2	--	-1.2	2	8.5%	--	51	--	7.6%	--	31%
2021	ATL			56	37	497	3		66%	--		13.3							3.4%						

You're probably here because it's the 15th round of your fantasy football draft and you're trying to decide between Emmanuel Sanders and Olamide Zaccheaus. Zaccheaus doesn't have the track record, but he is 10 years younger. A UDFA signing in 2019, he has flashed big-play potential in limited snaps. In Week 9 last season against the Broncos, the second start of his career, he caught passes of 51 and 42 yards en route to his first 100-yard receiving game. Two weeks later, he suffered a toe injury that ultimately ended his season. With Julio Jones gone, Zaccheaus is in line for a more prominent role. But temper your expectations. When Arthur Smith was the offensive coordinator in Tennessee, Adam Humphries was the No. 3 wide receiver. He topped out at 47 targets.

Going Deep

Jamal Agnew, JAX: More All-Pro punt returner than wideout, Agnew has returned four punts and a kickoff for touchdowns over four seasons. The converted cornerback went 13-89-0 with -36.2% DVOA last season but added six carries for 33 yards. He follows his former Detroit offensive coordinator Darrell Bevell to Jacksonville and cited "picking up where he left off" with Bevell as a main reason for signing with the Jaguars in his introductory presser. With Collin Johnson and Phillip Dorsett ahead of him in the pecking order, there will probably not be quite as many catches by Agnew in 2021, but he should still be a contributor on returns.

Geronimo Allison, DET: Allison opted out of the 2020 season with a touching statement about his newborn baby daughter. He's impossible not to root for, but his meager career statistics and subsequent absence net him a tenuous hold on one of the last Lions receiver spots even with their lack of depth at the position and the rollover of his one-year deal. Allison underwhelmed with a -11.8% receiving DVOA in four years in Green Bay, and it's difficult to imagine that will improve dramatically as he switches from Aaron Rodgers to Jared Goff under center.

JJ Arcega-Whiteside, PHI: It would be hard to have a more disappointing start to a career than Arcega-Whiteside's. The former second-round pick had only 10 catches in his rookie season for -12.3% DVOA, but he was at least active for all 16 games. In 2020, Arcega-Whiteside was a healthy scratch for most of the season and saw just eight targets in eight games. Since 2000, Arcega-Whiteside is one of 12 wide receivers drafted in the first or second round to have fewer than 15 career receptions through two years. He has played in the most games (24) with the most starts (five) among that group.

Kawaan Baker, NO: Chosen in the seventh round, Baker is the first wide receiver the Saints have drafted since Tre'Quan Smith in 2018, and one of only three drafted receivers on the Saints roster. He has an outstanding athletic profile and was very productive against limited competition at South Alabama. Baker has the size and speed to excel as an outside receiver and also the elusiveness with the ball in his hands to play inside. He also has experience as a returner, which could help him stick on what is a crowded but very inexperienced depth chart.

Cameron Batson, TEN: After missing the 2019 season with a shoulder injury suffered in July, Batson returned with a vengeance as someone who benefitted from those wide-open play-action throwing lanes to the tune of a 92% catch rate (12-100-1, 23.2% DVOA). Batson is a 5-foot-8 flyer who does some returns on the side, but Kalif Raymond had the main role last season. Raymond fled the Titans to sign with the Lions in free agency, so the Titans will likely have a camp battle between Darrynton Evans and Batson for the primary return spot.

Chad Beebe, MIN: Beebe is one of the most likely candidates for the Vikings' No. 3 receiver job, but he has a less secure position on the team's depth chart than one might imagine because Minnesota uses so many two-tight end sets, and because he never plays special teams. At 5-foot-10 and 183 pounds and with football intelligence (his dad Don was a receiver on the Bills Super Bowl teams), Beebe is a reasonable slot option, but Adam Thielen and Justin Jefferson can play in the slot too. (20-201-2, -12.3% DVOA in 2020.)

Christian Blake, ATL: Blake played 50 snaps in the Falcons' Week 11 win over the Raiders, but Matt Ryan targeted him only once. He barely saw the field after that, even after Julio Jones and Olamide Zaccheaus landed on injured reserve in December. Over the final four weeks of the season, he barely outsnapped (60 to 59) Laquon Treadwell, whom Atlanta promoted from the practice squad. Heading into his third season, he'll compete with sixth-round pick Frank Darby for one of the Falcons' reserve spots. (13-141-0, -7.8% DVOA in 2020.)

C.J. Board, NYG: Board should stick on the Giants roster as an all-purpose special-teamer and fifth wideout. He earned a few targets on underneath and flat routes last year during various Giants injury crunches. If he catches more than two passes per month in 2021, it's a sign that the Giants master plan has gone straight to heck. (11-101-0, -24.2% DVOA in 2020.)

Dyami Brown, WAS: At North Carolina, Brown was thrown into the DK Metcalf plan under offensive coordinator Phil Longo, who had been Metcalf's offensive coordinator at Ole Miss. Most of Brown's routes were vertical on the left side of the field, but similar to Metcalf, Brown excelled at doing exactly what he was asked. Brown was tied for fourth in college football last season in receptions over 20 air yards, and his 543 yards on those receptions trailed only DeVonta Smith. Washington drafted Brown in the third round but he starts out fifth or sixth on the depth chart so don't expect too much rookie production.

Noah Brown, DAL: Noah Brown and Cedrick Wilson are essentially the same person: a tall, speedy, hustling former late-round draft pick turned special-teamer. They also play about the same role in the Cowboys offense: fourth receiver who sometimes replaces one of the starters (usually CeeDee Lamb last year) in certain packages. Therefore, Wilson and Brown also share a Going Deep comment this year.

Dez Bryant, FA: Bryant caught just six passes in late-season games for Baltimore and was targeted just twice in two playoff games. The Ravens decided in the offseason that Sammy Watkins was a better fit in the big-name role player role. Bryant is currently a free agent who will make headlines when he expresses interest in a team on social media or is rumored to be on a tryout list. He's toast, but as we say in the media biz, he still clicks.

Jalen Camp, JAX: A very "yes sir" man, to the point where he actually had to correct himself and say "yes ma'am" to a question from a woman at his post-draft media availability. Selected in the sixth round, Camp joins a long list of Georgia Tech size/ speed wideout combos that have tempted NFL teams over the years. Demaryius Thomas was one of them. Stephen Hill was another. Camp had just 27 catches in his senior year, but he brings 6-foot-2, 226 pounds with 4.4s speed outside and is an excellent ball-tracker. If Collin Johnson doesn't take a step forward this year, Camp might be nipping on his heels sooner rather than later.

Frank Darby, ATL: At 19.7 yards per catch, this Atlanta sixth-round pick led all of this year's drafted wide receivers, though he's behind Rams tight end Jacob Harris (20.1). The former Arizona State Sun Devil's downfield ability gives him a shot at cracking the final roster, but to develop into more than the Falcons' No. 5 receiver, he'll need to expand his route tree and cut the drops (12 on 136 targets).

Jaelon Darden, TB: The Buccaneers ranked 25th in average yards after the catch, and that's where the diminutive Darden excels. His 7.8-yard average YAC ranked sixth among drafted wide receivers. Quick and elusive, the fourth-round pick out of North Texas can stretch the field, but given Tampa Bay's depth at the position, he could make a more immediate impact as a returner.

Phillip Dorsett, JAX: A speed merchant who has spent a career shedding a first-round bust label as a Pagano/Grigson-era Colts pick, Dorsett missed all of last season in Seattle with a foot injury that sent him to IR after Week 2. Joining the Jaguars, in a speed-emphasized offense, should give Dorsett yet another chance to showcase his wares out of the slot and away from press coverage if he can stay healthy. (29-397-5, -2.1% DVOA in 2019.)

Alex Erickson, HOU: A quality return man, adequate slot receiver, and typical Bengals journeyman who went five years without a challenge for his roster spot, Erickson caught 43 passes in 2019 but got lost in a crowd of No. 4 receivers with the emergence of Tee Higgins last season. The Texans signed Erickson in the offseason, because of course a team destined to go 2-15 simply MUST have a 28-year-old return man eating up a roster spot.

Simi Fehoko, DAL: Fehoko is the cousin of Alfred Pupunu, the former Chargers tight end best known for pretending to crack the football open like a coconut and drink from it as his end zone celebration. Fehoko is a 6-foot-4 run-up-the-seam receiver who averaged 18.5 yards per catch on 62 receptions in his Stanford career. He's about as nifty and agile as a school bus when changing direction. Place JJ Arcega-Whiteside and DK Metcalf in a blender, and what do you get? Someone to challenge Cedrick Wilson and Noah Brown for a role as the Cowboys' fourth wideout, special-teamer, and oversized track guy!

Dez Fitzpatrick, TEN: While many people will benefit from a year of Julio Jones, nobody needed that pressure off them quite like Fitzpatrick, who comes out of Louisville extremely raw in his route-running and will have to be a lot better against smarter NFL corners. Without the pressure to play right away, Tennessee's fourth-round pick can work on his craft a little more and not be hurried on to the field. He's a nice size-speed prospect (6-foot-2, 210 pounds) who isn't afraid to take contact, and he could profile as a big slot to ease him into a less press-intensive NFL role, which is part of what he did at the Senior Bowl.

Isaiah Ford, FA: Ford was traded midseason from the Dolphins to the Patriots for a late-round pick in 2022. Ford then played zero snaps for New England, was cut when Donte Moncrief returned, and ended up back in Miami about a month after he left. That's a deal the Dolphins will take any time. Ford is again not on the Dolphins roster in 2021, but because he was cut, not because Miami found someone else to pay them for not playing him.

Antonio Gandy-Golden, WAS: A fourth-round pick out of Liberty in 2020, Gandy-Golden's rookie season was cut short due to a hamstring injury that forced him onto injured reserve for nine games. He only had one reception for three yards on seven targets when he was on the field. At 6-foot-5, Gandy-Golden is bigger than the primary Washington receiver targets. In 2019, he had 19 end zone targets, seventh-most in college football, though only three were charted as catchable, per SIS—all three were caught for touchdowns.

Marvin Hall, NE: The Patriots are the seventh team on Hall's resume; the question is whether he gets more snaps in New England than he did in Week 16 for Cleveland. That was the game against the Jets that saw the entirety of the Browns wideout corps sidelined due to COVID restrictions, forcing the recently signed Hall to be called up to the show and play 74 snaps, catching one pass for 12 yards. Hall ran a 4.28s 40-yard dash once upon a time when coming out of Washington, and that blurry speed has given him multiple opportunities, if not actual production. (18-302-2, 3.4% DVOA in 2020, mostly for Detroit.)

Chad Hansen, DET: Life's not fair. Hansen came out of nowhere to get 24 targets for the Texans towards the end of their lost season, connecting with Deshaun Watson after spending a ton of time with the quarterback in previous training camps and offseason activities. Watson's future with the Texans is tenuous, and Nick Caserio took over as general manager and released Hansen. Hansen has slot receiver chops and while he's not going to be a main producer, wouldn't be out of place in that role for Detroit, which signed him in mid-June. (17-236-1, 12.5% DVOA in 2020.)

DeMichael Harris, IND: Southern Miss' lead running back during the 2019 season, Harris became De'Michael on the spot after injuries to Michael Pittman, T.Y. Hilton, and Parris Campbell blew open the Colts depth chart at wideout midseason. Seven of his 10 targets came in Weeks 6 and 9, and he showcased his versatility with a couple of 10-yard carries against the Ravens. Harris returned kicks in college as well, though the Colts haven't needed that because of Nyheim Hines. Harris has enough versatility to cling to the end of the roster if nobody Indy drafted blows him off of it. (10-79-0, 3.0% DVOA in 2020.)

John Hightower, PHI: Hightower was a fifth-round pick out of Boise State in 2020. His 16.7-yard average depth of target was the second highest in the 2020 draft class, and he followed that up with a team-leading 21.6-yard aDOT on 29 targets during his rookie season. However, those deep shots didn't lead to a ton of completions as his catch rate was just 34%. Hightower ranked 77th in DYAR (-55) and 72nd in DVOA (-36.8%) among the 80 wideouts who saw between 10 and 49 targets. He had consecutive games with a 50-plus-yard reception in Weeks 6 and 7, both of which could have gone for longer gains but he was forced to wait on the ball in the air.

Kendall Hinton, DEN: Thanks to COVID, Hinton has thrown more NFL passes than he has caught. Hinton was Denver's emergency quarterback for one game last year, completing one of his nine pass attempts with two interceptions. He has not caught an NFL pass, not even in the preseason, since there was no 2020 preseason for Hinton's rookie campaign. Hinton is explosive and sports surprisingly natural hands, but he is entering just his third year as a wide receiver after converting from quarterback late in his college career.

KhaDarel Hodge, CLE: After a strong 2019 in special teams, when he led the Browns with 19 tackles, a hamstring injury limited Hodge to nine games a year ago. With the re-signing of Rashard Higgins and the drafting of Anthony Schwartz, the numbers are against Hodge in Cleveland, though his usefulness in the third phase should get him a gig somewhere. (11-180-0, 22.9% DVOA in 2020.)

Chris Hogan, FA: Hogan has opted to retire from the NFL rather than stick around for the Jets rebuild. Instead, he has joined the Premier Lacrosse League, signing with the Cannons Lacrosse Club in Boston before being traded to Whipsnakes LC. Stay tuned to *Lacrosse Outsiders Almanac 2021* for full Hogan projections, in bookstores the 12th of Never.

Mack Hollins, MIA: Hollins had the fifth-most pass routes on the 2020 Dolphins out of sheer necessity. With the revamped Miami receiving corps, Hollins still has a chance to make the 53-man roster as a special teams contributor; in weeks where he wasn't forced into the lineup as a starting receiver, he played 61% of Miami's special teams snaps. (16-176-1, -19.3% DVOA in 2020.)

Jalen Hurd, SF: A third-round draft pick in 2019, Hurd missed all of his rookie season with a back injury and all of 2020 with a torn ACL. He was working on the sidelines in May minicamp, though, and expected to be 100% for training camp. The 49ers go into the season with plenty of wide receivers, but since none of them played in more than 12 games in 2020, odds are good that Hurd will finally get a chance to see the field sooner or later.

Dontrelle Inman, FA: Inman had his peak with 97 targets in 2016 with the Chargers, but he has bounced around over the past four seasons. Inman spent all of 2020 with Washington and got on the field for 10 games and 30% of the offensive snaps, but he put up just 18-163-2 with -24.5% DVOA. He was released in December and remains unsigned.

Alshon Jeffery, FA: Jeffery suffered a Lisfranc injury in December of 2019. He didn't return to the field until Week 10 of 2020 and played sparingly after. Jeffery's return to the field wasn't impressive, though he nearly topped his 2019 DYAR (50 on 73 passes) with 44 DYAR on 13 passes. He caught six of those for 115 yards and a touchdown but also drew three DPI flags for 83 yards. Jeffery turned 31 years old in February and was released in March. He has missed games in all but two of his nine seasons. He could potentially serve as a depth piece/red zone threat for a team desperate for receiving help in training camp.

Collin Johnson, JAX: Johnson started 2020 out as a guy who had a primary role inside the opponent's 40, with four red zone targets in the first five weeks of the season. He played primarily out of the slot. Then, over the last five weeks of the year, almost all of his targets came out wide. Johnson has NFL-caliber size and blocking ability, with some inconsistency in playing the ball as well as he could, but now finds himself as an inherited lower-roster player from a man who has emphasized speed in Urban Meyer. We'd take the under on another 31 targets. (18-272-2, -5.0% DVOA in 2020.)

KeeSean Johnson, ARI: Through two NFL seasons, Johnson has been targeted 65 times with a catch rate of 55% and an average of exactly 10 yards per catch, making him both inefficient and inexplosive. Between those stats, the signing of A.J. Green, and the drafting of Rondale Moore, Johnson is a longshot to make Arizona's roster, though Kliff Kingsbury's Air Raid and its reliance on a deep crew of wideouts at least gives him a fighting shot. (15-173-0, -20.8% DVOA in 2020.)

Marcus Johnson, TEN: Johnson spent most of 2020 on Indianapolis' active roster but ended it on Tennessee's practice squad. His 108-yard game against a pitiful Bengals defense, bouyed by a 55-yarder where he dusted safety Vonn Bell, was the high-water mark of yet another season where he reliably stepped up when injuries forced him to in good situations against bad teams. Should he win a job with the Titans, he will remain the steady outside guy that plays special teams and threatens to catch 20 or 30 balls a season because he does his job right. A Justin Gage for Generation Z. (14-255-0, -10.9% DVOA in 2020.)

Olabisi Johnson, MIN: Johnson has a bit more size (he's 6-foot-0 and 204 pounds versus 5-foot-10 and 183 pounds) and a slightly better pedigree (he was a seventh-rounder versus undrafted) than Chad Beebe, his major competition for the Vikings' No. 3 receiver job. But his target total declined from 45 in his rookie year to 19 last year in the same number of games. He does have a 6.0% receiving DVOA in his two seasons, but is a modest special teams contributor, something that could threaten his roster spot with returners such as K.J. Osborn and rookie Ihmir Smith-Marsette close behind him.

Tyler Johnson, TB: Widely considered one of the steals of the 2020 draft with an outstanding Playmaker Score, Johnson, a fifth-round pick, had a quiet regular season (12-169-2 with 24.4% DVOA). He did, however, play a large role in postseason, making a pivotal catch on third-and-long late in the divisional-round game against the Saints and drawing the pass interference penalty that sealed the Buccaneers' NFC championship win over the Packers. Unfortunately for Johnson, he remains buried on the depth chart. Mike Evans, Chris Godwin, Antonio Brown, and Scotty Miller are back, plus Tampa Bay drafted Jaelon Darden, a potential downfield threat.

Tyron Johnson, LAC: Johnson averaged 19.9 yards on his 20 catches; his 20.5-yard average depth of target last year was the second highest among players with at least 10 catches. He had the highest DVOA for part-time receivers with 10 to 49 targets, beating out quality role players such as Donovan Peoples-Jones (Browns) and Bryan Edwards (Raiders). The Chargers drafted Josh Palmer (Tennessee) this spring, but he is not a burner and is no threat to Johnson's role as the designated field stretcher. (20-398-3, 61.5% DVOA in 2020.)

Zay Jones, LV: Jones swallowed up just over 100 targets in a desolate Buffalo Bills wide receiver room in 2018. He was traded halfway through the following season to the Raiders, and he then returned to being nothing more than a short-area possession receiver with limited YAC skills. That said, Jones saw 27 targets in just seven games with the Raiders in 2019 before falling to just 20 over a full season in 2020. Jones does have some inside/outside flexibility, but it's hard to imagine why he would come onto the field in favor of either Bryan Edwards or Hunter Renfrow. (14-154-1, -9.9% DVOA in 2020.)

Ray-Ray McCloud, PIT: Ray-Ray was better than so-so as a returner in 2020; once his special teams value drops, Ray-Ray will go bye-bye.

Racey McMath, TEN: What is a football pass if not a creation of a math race? Racey (named that way because he never stayed still during his mom's pregnancy, per the LSU media guide) McMath is a size/speed prospect with limited playing time for the Tigers and not much feel for playing the position at an advanced level. McMath's 4.39s 40-yard dash at the LSU pro day was the main eye-catcher, and Tennessee selected him in the sixth round. If this whole football thing doesn't pan out, McMath can always license his name to those Amazon Web Services commercials for Next Gen Stats.

Dax Milne, WAS: A seventh-round pick out of BYU, Milne was Zach Wilson's go-to target and experienced a similar breakout to Wilson during the 2020 season. Milne doesn't have outstanding size or speed, but has the proverbial walk-on work ethic that shows in route-running, effort, and footwork. His breakout came with more routes on the outside (77% in 2020), but if he's going to succeed in the NFL, it's likely going to have to be back in the slot where he spent more time in 2018 and 2019.

Dazz Newsome, CHI: At 5-foot-10 and 190 pounds and quicker than fast, Newsome is a no-doubt slot prospect. That explains his fall to the sixth round while similarly productive North Carolina teammate Dyami Brown went to Washington in the third. But Newsome could make an immediate impact as a punt returner, and that should secure his roster spot with the Bears while he aims to develop his route technique and receiving mechanics.

Tre Nixon, NE: Nixon has the honor of having the lowest Playmaker Projection of 2021, albeit because he was projected as an undrafted free agent rather than as a seventh-round pick. Nixon has speed for days, running a 4.44s at his pro day, but his ball skills, route-running, and hands all need work, and he's coming off of a broken collarbone. He's very much a work in progress.

Dezmon Patmon, IND: Active only for the finale against Jacksonville in Week 17, and not given any preseason action, it's hard to really understand as an outsider how Patmon's development went in 2020. What we do know is that the former Washington State receiver came out of college seeming pretty raw to draftniks and that even the Great Colts Wideout Injury Scare of 2020 couldn't push him on to the field. We'll probably know a lot more about Patmon by the end of this preseason, but so far this has the look of a tools pick that hasn't panned out.

Donovan Peoples-Jones, CLE: There was a feeling DPJ, a sixth-round rookie last year, had more to offer as a pro than he had a chance to show at Michigan. He had a couple of big moments in 2020, namely the game-winning touchdown catch in the dying seconds in Cincinnati and a 75-yard score against the Titans. It's difficult to know just who will be catching passes in Cleveland come 2022; the fervent hope is that DPJ will take a leap and be a player to be counted on for the future. (14-304-2, 51.9% DVOA in 2020.)

Malcolm Perry, MIA: The former Navy quarterback/slotback never really found a home in Chan Gailey's offense, garnering just 12 touches despite starting multiple games for the skill position-challenged Dolphins. Perry's skill set could be interesting in the hands of a creative offensive coordinator, but Miami has added enough playmakers this offseason that Perry is likely going to have to win the returner job to stay on the 53-man roster.

Brandon Powell, BUF: Powell saw a career-high 181 snaps last season as injuries to Julio Jones required the Falcons to call all hands on deck. He caught 12 balls for 69 yards and 2 touchdowns, but a -41.2% DVOA shows why he typically doesn't get much call for offensive work. Powell was more successful as Atlanta's primary returner in 2020, and he'll be part of the competition to replace Andre Roberts.

Cornell Powell, KC: A fifth-round rookie, Powell was as late of a bloomer as it gets. He failed to produce until his redshirt senior season at Clemson and didn't even really produce until the second half of that year, going 39-730-5 in Clemson's final six games. Powell is a lackluster route-runner with little nuance, but he is explosive in his stride, both when working vertically and with the ball in his hands. Powell also shows natural hands and the ability to track the ball from anywhere.

Byron Pringle, KC: Pringle is a burner who serves as insurance to Tyreek Hill and Mecole Hardman more than anything. A 4.46s-40 guy coming out of Kansas State, Pringle wants to go one direction very fast rather than being a legitimate route-runner and wide receiver. Pringle showed signs of life as a playmaker last season, averaging 13.9 yards and a 75% success rate on nine third- or fourth-down targets. Pringle also stepped up to lead the team in kickoff returns (10) and produced the team's only kickoff return touchdown on the year. (13-160-1, 18.3% DVOA in 2020.)

James Proche, BAL: Proche was used primarily as a punt returner last season, catching just one pass on three targets for the Ravens. With the rookie arrivals of Rashod Bateman and Tylan Wallace, and with Devin Duvernay capable of handling return chores very well, Proche is likely to be squeezed out of a roster spot.

Kalif Raymond, DET: The 5-foot-8, 182-pound Raymond is too small to shoulder much of the burden of the Lions' receiving corps, but with 4.34s speed, he can get deep if new Detroit quarterback Jared Goff has any inclination to throw the ball downfield this season. More important for his roster security, Raymond is a capable punt and kickoff returner, something the Lions desperately needed since the departed Jamal Agnew and Danny Amendola handled the bulk of those responsibilities in 2020. (9-187-0, 16.2% DVOA in 2020.)

John Ross, NYG: Welcome to Year 5 of waiting for Ross to be more than a combine legend whose only skill is running very fast in a straight line. Where has the time gone? Year 4 was a greatest hits compilation: minor injuries, deactivations for non-injury reasons, mumblings about a move to cornerback, trade speculation, and a midseason disappearance onto injured reserve. The Giants signed Ross so they won't have to alter their "everyone go deep" offensive plans if they lose Kenny Golladay and/or Darius Slayton. Ross was quasi-useful at times in 2018 and 2019, so he's worth a tire kick.

Mohamed Sanu, SF: Since the start of the 2019 season, Sanu has gone from the Falcons to the Patriots to the 49ers to the Lions and now back to the 49ers. His first stint in San Francisco was forgettable—one catch for 9 yards in three games—but he averaged better than 25 yards per game with a 12.2% DVOA in Detroit, so there are still some signs of life here. The 49ers are very young at wide receiver, and Sanu is the best bet to bring some veteran savvy to the position.

Tajae Sharpe, ATL: Sharpe has bounced around quite a bit since last fall. He started the season in Minnesota (played in four games but didn't catch any passes) and finished it in Kansas City (didn't play in any games). The Chiefs re-signed him in March and then cut him in May. Soon after, he landed in Atlanta, where his familiarity with Arthur Smith's offense might help him land a backup role. With Smith as his coordinator for the 2019 Titans, he caught 34 passes for 329 yards and 4 touchdowns — good enough for a 45.1% DVOA.

Ben Skowronek, LAR: A seventh-round pick from Notre Dame, Skowronek brings a bit of a different dynamic to the Rams' receiver room. Skowronek spent the first four years of his college career at Northwestern before joining the Fighting Irish as a graduate transfer. He projects as a capable run-blocker with the ability to win on contested catches, though his lack of ideal speed may prevent him from becoming a consistent starter in the league absent a possible move to tight end.

Ihmir Smith-Marsette, MIN: No one will confuse fifth-round draftee Ihmir Smith-Marsette for Justin Jefferson, who shares the former player's 6-foot-1 height but is 20 pounds heavier. But Smith-Marsette has a clear place in the NFL with tremendous speed that should at least play on jet sweeps and kick returns. Smith-Marsette averaged 28.7 yards per kickoff return at Iowa, almost 2 yards better than the team's fourth-round selection Kene Nwangwu managed at Iowa State.

Jeff Smith, NYJ: Smith made a number of appearances thanks to the Jets' significant injury concerns. That included catching three passes on 11 targets against the Cardinals, including a touchdown dropped when he was standing all alone in the end zone. That earned him -59 receiving DYAR, the second-lowest single-game total of 2020. Apart from that one game, Smith played at replacement level, and he'll serve as replacement-level depth once again in 2021. (17-167-0, -37.3% DVOA in 2020.)

Shi Smith, CAR: Undersized but tough, explosive but lacking long speed, with a knack for gadget plays and a larger than expected catch radius, Smith's draft profile appears ideally suited to a role as a developmental slot receiver. In Carolina, that could mean assuming a portion of Curtis Samuel's role on jet sweeps and end arounds, but the sixth-round pick has some climbing to do first on a crowded receiver depth chart.

Equanimeous St. Brown, GB: St. Brown's 14.5% receiving DVOA last season would have landed him in the top 20 at the position if he had enough targets to qualify … but then, he only had 13 targets. St. Brown will have a chance to progress if Rodgers stays in town, but the smart money is on his brother, fourth-round Detroit rookie Amon-Ra, to carry the NFL torch for the St. Brown family.

Marquez Stevenson, BUF: A sixth-round rookie out of Houston, Stevenson is not a receiver who is going to get open on his own, but if you can figure out ways to get the ball in his hands, look out. Stevenson has been clocked in the 4.3-second 40 range on the track; he doesn't always play at that speed and doesn't blow past defenders running routes, but he can absolutely turn on the jets when needs be. That means his best shot at a roster spot is as a returner, where he doesn't have to worry about fighting off cornerbacks to get the ball in his hands.

Kenny Stills, FA: A pretty solid deep receiver who lost his real shot at a job last year when the Texans traded for Brandin Cooks and signed Randall Cobb; then they released Stills before the rash of injuries that had practice squad players like Steven Mitchell get December run. Stills signed on to the Buffalo practice squad in the postseason and was on the active roster for the AFC Championship Game but has not had a real suitor so far this offseason. Stills hasn't had a negative DVOA since 2015 and isn't yet 30. Someone should be interested. (11-144-1, 10.8% DVOA in 2020.)

Mike Strachan, IND: Not to be confused with the Mike Strachan who played six seasons for the 1970s Saints and had teammates testify that he was a drug dealer. This Strachan is 6-foot-5, won conference championships in the 200- and 400-meter dashes, and opted out of the 2020 season after putting up 78 catches for 1,319 yards and 19 touchdowns for Charleston in 2019. It wasn't great competition, and he's less fast on the field than on the racetrack, but this is another talented late-round project the Colts are taking on.

Freddie Swain, SEA: Seattle's 2020 sixth-round pick from Florida got limited run as a rookie, but he seems to have the inside track to being the No. 4 receiver for the Seahawks. Swain has to hope that a somewhat more normal offseason allows him to build more of a rapport with Russell Wilson so that the veteran quarterback looks Swain's way more frequently than the 21 times he did in 2020. (13-159-2, -10.1% DVOA in 2020.)

Auden Tate, CIN: Tate earned a few starts last year when A.J. Green and Tyler Boyd were unavailable or limited, catching seven passes for 65 yards in the Bengals' big Week 8 win over the Titans. He then went from the COVID list to a shoulder injury, missing the final five games of the season. The tall, rugged Tate can do many of the things Boyd and Tee Higgins do, making him the Bengals' likely fourth wideout. If only they were this deep at literally any other position…

Trent Taylor, CIN: Taylor's playing time and targets decreased in each of his three seasons with the 49ers, despite annual injury rashes at wide receiver that should have resulted in extra opportunities when he was healthy. He left Louisiana Tech as a fun-sized nifty-shifty mid-major draftnik darling, but if you can't make it as a YAC guy in Kyle Shanahan's offense, you ain't gonna make it anywhere. Taylor is now looking for a slot/punt returner role for the Bengals, a team that's dangerously thin at every position on the field except the one Taylor plays.

Mike Thomas, CIN: The Other One, of course: the longtime Rams special-teamer and fourth/fifth wideout who caught six passes for 85 yards and one touchdown in the two high-scoring losses to the Browns last season. The departures of Alex Erickson and John Ross move Thomas closer to the top of the receiver depth chart, a place where he does not really belong.

Tylan Wallace, BAL: Wallace led the Big 12 in receiving yards in both 2018 (1,491 yards) and 2020 (922). He's a classic boundary threat who ran the fly and a variety of comeback routes against soft coverage well in the wide-open playground conference. Such receivers are easy to overrate, but Wallace looked like a good one, and the price was right in the fourth round. Wallace joins Devin Duvernay, James Proche, and others on a speedy, crowded Ravens bench. Someone very fast will be streaking up the sideline for the Ravens this year, whether Lamar Jackson chooses to throw to him or not.

Quez Watkins, PHI: Watkins, a sixth-round pick in 2020, was another dart throw for speed by the Eagles last offseason. He had above average yards per route run, percentage of deep routes, and average depth of target during his final year at Southern Miss to go along with a 4.35s 40. He started his rookie season on IR, got 20 snaps and no targets in Weeks 5 and 6, then didn't appear again until Week 14. His big highlight was a 32-yard touchdown catch on a third-and-20 screen against Arizona in Week 16. (7-106-1, -9.6% DVOA in 2020.)

Nick Westbrook-Ikhine, TEN: An undrafted free agent from Indiana, Westbrook-Ikhine stayed active almost the entirety of last season. The only game he saw massive playing time in was the Week 4 "Tuesday Night Football" game that Tennessee's COVID situation created, but Westbrook-Ikhine carved out a role for himself on special teams and in creating exactly one target per game on six different occasions. The crowd at UDFA wideout grows larger this year as the Titans cast a wide net to try to replace Corey Davis and Adam Humphries. Westbrook-Ikhine has incumbency in his favor, but this won't be an easy roster spot to win again.

Seth Williams, DEN: Williams, a sixth-round pick out of Auburn, is your standard sure-handed bully who needs to prove he can separate at an NFL level. At 6-foot-3 and 211 pounds, Williams sees the ball well, uses his body to shield the catch point, and extends his arms away from his body to consistently snatch passes from the air. There is not much quickness or agility to Williams' game before the catch point, though, which is why his contested-catch ability is a necessity. Expect Williams to need a year or two of development before potentially blooming.

Albert Wilson, MIA: Wilson returns after opting out of 2020 to find the Dolphins' receiver room substantially more crowded than he remembered. Wilson's -23.7% DVOA was 77th out of 80 qualified receivers in 2019, with the second-highest failed reception rate; Wilson specialized in catching short passes in front of the sticks and then not doing anything with them. He'll have to regain his Kansas City form if he's going to get significant playing time in 2021.

Cedrick Wilson, DAL: Noah Brown and Cedrick Wilson are essentially the same person: a tall, speedy, hustling former late-round draft pick turned special-teamer. They also play about the same role in the Cowboys offense: fourth receiver who sometimes replaces one of the starters (usually CeeDee Lamb last year) in certain packages. Therefore, Wilson and Brown also share a Going Deep comment this year.

Tight Ends

Top 20 TE by DYAR (Total Value), 2020

Rank	Player	Team	DYAR
1	Travis Kelce	KC	415
2	Robert Tonyan	GB	242
3	Darren Waller	LV	190
4	George Kittle	SF	142
5	Tyler Higbee	LAR	112
6	Mike Gesicki	MIA	108
7	Dallas Goedert	PHI	105
8	Dan Arnold	ARI	101
9	Irv Smith	MIN	92
10	Darren Fells	HOU	90
11	Jared Cook	NO	88
12	Richard Rodgers	PHI	79
13	Rob Gronkowski	TB	77
14	Cameron Brate	TB	65
15	Jonnu Smith	TEN	65
16	Jordan Akins	HOU	65
17	Mo Alie-Cox	IND	57
18	Ross Dwelley	SF	56
19	Mark Andrews	BAL	52
20	Will Dissly	SEA	42

Minimum 25 passes.

Top 20 TE by DVOA (Value per Pass), 2020

Rank	Player	Team	DVOA
1	Robert Tonyan	GB	51.7%
2	Darren Fells	HOU	38.6%
3	Travis Kelce	KC	35.7%
4	Ross Dwelley	SF	30.8%
5	Richard Rodgers	PHI	30.4%
6	George Kittle	SF	28.0%
7	Dan Arnold	ARI	26.7%
8	Irv Smith	MIN	23.5%
9	Cameron Brate	TB	22.8%
10	Tyler Higbee	LAR	19.6%
11	Dallas Goedert	PHI	16.8%
12	Mo Alie-Cox	IND	14.7%
13	Jared Cook	NO	13.9%
14	Will Dissly	SEA	13.3%
15	Jordan Akins	HOU	12.4%
16	Darren Waller	LV	11.4%
17	Durham Smythe	MIA	10.7%
18	Mike Gesicki	MIA	10.4%
19	Jonnu Smith	TEN	7.2%
20	Kyle Rudolph	MIN	6.7%

Minimum 25 passes.

Jordan Akins

Height: 6-4   Weight: 243   College: Central Florida   Draft: 2018/3 (98)   Born: 19-Apr-1992   Age: 29   Risk: Green

Year	Tm	G/GS	Snaps	Pass	Rec	Yds	TD	EZ	C%	+/-	Drop	Yd/C	aDOT	Rk	YAC	Rk	YAC+	BTkl	DVOA	Rk	DYAR	Rk	Use	Rk	Slot	Wide
2018	HOU	16/6	388	25	17	225	0	1	68%	-0.2	0	13.2	6.9	30	7.2	5	+1.8	4	8.3%	16	24	24	5.0%	47	44%	4%
2019	HOU	16/9	672	55	36	418	2	3	65%	-1.8	3	11.6	7.1	26	6.8	4	+1.9	10	-5.6%	27	6	27	10.6%	30	40%	0%
2020	HOU	13/5	405	49	37	403	1	6	76%	+3.4	3	10.9	7.4	23	4.6	22	+0.2	6	12.4%	15	65	16	11.4%	24	20%	4%
2021	HOU			49	33	359	2		67%	--		10.8							-8.2%							

Heading into the final year of his rookie deal, Akins has a very typical Texans development problem where nobody really knows what he can be yet. He has shown some phenomenal separation, catching ability, and evasion in small bursts. He also missed some of last season with a concussion and is already 29 because he was a former baseball prospect, and the Texans seem unable to actually get him even 70 targets in a season. With Darren Fells gone, Akins and Pharoah Brown should be the main two tight ends, and that should lead to plenty of snaps for Akins. Should, not will.

Mo Alie-Cox

Height: 6-5   Weight: 267   College: Virginia Commonwealth   Draft: 2017/FA   Born: 19-Sep-1993   Age: 28   Risk: Green

Year	Tm	G/GS	Snaps	Pass	Rec	Yds	TD	EZ	C%	+/-	Drop	Yd/C	aDOT	Rk	YAC	Rk	YAC+	BTkl	DVOA	Rk	DYAR	Rk	Use	Rk	Slot	Wide
2018	IND	9/1	241	13	7	133	2	2	54%	-0.7	1	19.0	11.7	--	7.1	--	+3.1	2	9.5%	--	16	--	3.6%	--	31%	0%
2019	IND	16/2	357	11	8	93	0	1	73%	+0.3	1	11.6	4.4	--	7.5	--	+2.9	2	13.6%	--	14	--	2.2%	--	0%	0%
2020	IND	15/6	503	39	31	394	2	3	79%	+5.0	1	12.7	7.1	34	5.9	8	+1.2	2	14.7%	12	57	17	7.8%	37	32%	3%
2021	IND			32	23	261	2		72%	--		11.5							5.2%							

A mountain of a tight end. Alie-Cox has the ability to block solid defensive ends and help anchor some combo blocks. He's got the frame and arms to go win balls over smaller middle-of-the-field players, and as you see in the above stat line, he did that with some wild efficiency last season in his first real taste of playing time. That positioned Alie-Cox as someone worth a second-round RFA tender, and he enters his walk year trying to prove that he is worth a Cameron Brate-esque contract somewhere. Alie-Cox certainly brings the physical upside most NFL teams are looking for at tight end, just don't expect that to translate into broken tackles or move roles. He's an in-line mauler with good enough hands and ball instincts to rise into a 60- or 70-target role in the right spot.

Mark Andrews

Height: 6-5 Weight: 255 College: Oklahoma Draft: 2018/3 (86) Born: 6-Sep-1996 Age: 25 Risk: Green

Year	Tm	G/GS	Snaps	Pass	Rec	Yds	TD	EZ	C%	+/-	Drop	Yd/C	aDOT	Rk	YAC	Rk	YAC+	BTkl	DVOA	Rk	DYAR	Rk	Use	Rk	Slot	Wide
2018	BAL	16/3	414	50	34	552	3	6	68%	+4.3	3	16.2	11.4	4	5.7	17	+1.5	1	36.2%	2	159	4	9.6%	25	51%	8%
2019	BAL	15/4	467	98	64	852	10	13	65%	+1.2	4	13.3	10.8	2	4.5	29	+0.6	9	12.1%	15	123	7	24.5%	2	72%	2%
2020	BAL	14/2	597	88	58	701	7	13	66%	+0.6	5	12.1	10.7	6	3.1	45	-0.8	4	1.6%	25	52	19	25.8%	2	67%	1%
2021	BAL			82	55	648	6		67%	--		11.9							6.6%							

Andrews tied Tyler Boyd for second in the NFL with 22 targets listed as "middle" (between the hashmarks, essentially) by Sports Info Solutions; 49ers rookie Brandon Aiyuk led the NFL with 23 targets. Andrews caught 16 of these targets for just 141 yards; his average depth of target of 6.2 yards ranked 57th in the category among those with 10 targets, three slots behind teammate Willie Sneed, who averaged 6.8 yards per target on 13 throws over the middle of the field. Andrews is a fine receiving weapon, but opponents start to notice when a quarterback keeps floating low-post entry passes to teammates 20 feet directly in front of him. Andrews caught lots of passes in very heavy traffic last year, and Lamar Jackson spent a little too much time locked onto his tight end. The whole Ravens offense would benefit if about half of those tosses to Andrews over the middle turned into accurate throws to wide receivers along the sidelines.

Dan Arnold

Height: 6-6 Weight: 220 College: Wisconsin–Platteville Draft: 2017/FA Born: 15-Mar-1995 Age: 26 Risk: Green

Year	Tm	G/GS	Snaps	Pass	Rec	Yds	TD	EZ	C%	+/-	Drop	Yd/C	aDOT	Rk	YAC	Rk	YAC+	BTkl	DVOA	Rk	DYAR	Rk	Use	Rk	Slot	Wide
2018	NO	10/1	141	19	12	150	1	1	63%	+0.2	1	12.5	10.8	--	2.5	--	-2.0	0	-21.0%	--	-18	--	5.8%	--	53%	11%
2019	2TM	5/1	105	14	8	127	2	3	57%	+0.4	0	15.9	13.6	--	3.6	--	-0.1	0	16.6%	--	21	--	8.1%	--	57%	0%
2020	ARI	16/5	470	45	31	438	4	5	69%	+3.9	2	14.1	12.5	1	5.6	13	+1.1	0	26.7%	7	101	8	8.3%	36	40%	4%
2021	CAR			45	28	338	2		62%	--		11.9							-2.0%							

By our numbers, the two-year, $6-million contract to which the Panthers signed Dan Arnold was the best-value contract at the position this offseason, barely beating out Jared Cook's deal in Los Angeles. Arnold, a converted receiver out of Division III Wisconsin-Platteville, finished third in receiving yards for the Cardinals last year despite playing barely 40% of snaps, somehow beating both DeAndre Hopkins and Christian Kirk in yards per catch. He has already played under Panthers offensive coordinator Joe Brady during their time in New Orleans, which should help ease his transition to a new team. Given the absolute dearth of receiving production from Panthers tight ends last year, Arnold has a clear path to take over as the primary receiving option while Ian Thomas and Tommy Tremble handle the majority of the blocking. Arnold has the size and wingspan to be a useful red zone option, and he can line up just as happily on the outside as in-line. He's unlikely to make Panthers fans forget Greg Olsen, but a similar arrangement to his time in Arizona has a good chance to produce similar results.

Nick Boyle

Height: 6-4 Weight: 270 College: Delaware Draft: 2015/5 (171) Born: 17-Feb-1993 Age: 28 Risk: Green

Year	Tm	G/GS	Snaps	Pass	Rec	Yds	TD	EZ	C%	+/-	Drop	Yd/C	aDOT	Rk	YAC	Rk	YAC+	BTkl	DVOA	Rk	DYAR	Rk	Use	Rk	Slot	Wide
2018	BAL	16/13	651	37	23	213	0	2	62%	-1.9	1	9.3	3.5	48	6.1	13	+0.8	2	-26.6%	44	-50	43	6.7%	40	19%	0%
2019	BAL	16/15	783	43	31	321	2	3	72%	+0.1	2	10.4	6.4	33	5.2	14	+0.5	2	-0.8%	21	18	26	10.1%	32	14%	0%
2020	BAL	9/9	380	17	14	113	2	1	82%	+2.0	0	8.1	5.7	--	2.4	--	-1.3	0	14.5%	--	25	--	7.7%	--	18%	0%
2021	BAL			22	15	150	2		68%	--		10.4							-11.0%							

Boyle suffered a severe leg injury against the Patriots last season but is expected back this season. Mark Andrews gets the majority of targets, but Boyle is among the best run-blocking tight ends in the NFL, which of course is a big deal in the Ravens offense. When everything else is clicking, Boyle gets about one target per game, which sounds about right.

Cameron Brate

Height: 6-5   Weight: 245   College: Harvard   Draft: 2014/FA   Born: 3-Jul-1991   Age: 30   Risk: Blue

Year	Tm	G/GS	Snaps	Pass	Rec	Yds	TD	EZ	C%	+/-	Drop	Yd/C	aDOT	Rk	YAC	Rk	YAC+	BTkl	DVOA	Rk	DYAR	Rk	Use	Rk	Slot	Wide
2018	TB	16/2	534	49	30	289	6	7	61%	-2.9	5	9.6	8.4	15	1.7	49	-1.9	1	-6.8%	31	2	31	7.8%	34	53%	12%
2019	TB	16/6	437	55	36	311	4	3	65%	-1.2	3	8.6	7.3	23	2.5	48	-1.6	3	-8.0%	32	-3	32	8.9%	37	49%	4%
2020	TB	16/1	318	34	28	282	2	3	82%	+3.8	1	10.1	8.6	11	2.5	48	-1.3	0	22.8%	9	65	14	5.4%	46	53%	6%
2021	TB			25	17	179	2		68%	--		10.7							-5.0%							

If you had Brate leading the Buccaneers' tight end room in targets and receptions over the last six weeks of the season, including the playoffs, then go out and buy some lotto tickets. Brate began the year buried on the depth chart, worked his way into a couple of catches a game when O.J. Howard blew out his Achilles, and then became the primary target with Rob Gronkowski mostly blocking down the stretch. It wasn't just a couple of hot playoff games, either; Brate's 46 receiving DYAR in Weeks 10-17 ranked 12th in the NFL. More reliable than explosive, Brate returns to the bench with Howard healthy, but the Bucs also made sure to renegotiate his contract to keep him around.

Harrison Bryant

Height: 6-5   Weight: 240   College: Florida Atlantic   Draft: 2020/4 (115)   Born: 23-Apr-1998   Age: 23   Risk: Green

Year	Tm	G/GS	Snaps	Pass	Rec	Yds	TD	EZ	C%	+/-	Drop	Yd/C	aDOT	Rk	YAC	Rk	YAC+	BTkl	DVOA	Rk	DYAR	Rk	Use	Rk	Slot	Wide
2020	CLE	15/9	590	38	24	238	3	5	63%	-1.7	3	9.9	8.2	15	4.9	19	+0.9	4	-18.8%	43	-33	43	9.0%	35	45%	10%
2021	CLE			13	9	86	1		69%	--		10.1							-14.5%							

Bryant was a "he fell into our laps, let's find a place for him" draftee when Cleveland took him in the fourth round in 2020. Unsurprisingly, given the presence of David Njoku and Austin Hooper ahead of him on the depth chart, Bryant didn't get as many opportunities as he might have if another team had selected him, but he developed nicely anyway. Bryant was a steady blocker, which was a question mark coming out of Florida Atlantic, but suffered through plenty of newbie moments—he struggled with fumbles and seemingly with Baker Mayfield's trust. Rookie tight ends seldom have a bravura immediate impact, and Bryant certainly showed he belonged in the league. Now he just needs to develop some chemistry with his quarterback and cut down on the mistakes.

Trey Burton

Height: 6-2   Weight: 238   College: Florida   Draft: 2014/FA   Born: 29-Oct-1991   Age: 30   Risk: N/A

Year	Tm	G/GS	Snaps	Pass	Rec	Yds	TD	EZ	C%	+/-	Drop	Yd/C	aDOT	Rk	YAC	Rk	YAC+	BTkl	DVOA	Rk	DYAR	Rk	Use	Rk	Slot	Wide
2018	CHI	16/16	860	76	54	569	6	4	71%	+3.1	3	10.5	8.4	16	3.5	42	-1.0	1	-2.7%	27	24	25	14.7%	11	58%	5%
2019	CHI	8/5	291	24	14	84	0	1	58%	-3.7	2	6.0	5.0	--	2.6	--	-2.9	0	-49.1%	--	-65	--	8.4%	--	58%	0%
2020	IND	13/4	375	47	28	250	3	4	60%	-2.5	3	8.9	7.3	25	3.1	46	-0.8	1	-22.2%	45	-47	44	10.8%	28	56%	8%

Pushed off the Colts roster by the acquisition of Kylen Granson, and thus shunned by the offensive coordinator who made him Philly Special, Burton's career has been marred by injury ever since signing with the Bears in 2018. Calf and hip labrum injuries requiring surgery held him out of most of 2019 and he was an IR-return guy for the Colts in 2020. As a free agent in June, the biggest noise out of the Burton camp is spillover stories about how his fellow former Florida teammate, Tim Tebow, deserves a chance. When we can Google you and Clay Travis and get the same content, that's not a good sign for your football career.

Tyler Conklin

Height: 6-3   Weight: 254   College: Central Michigan   Draft: 2018/5 (157)   Born: 30-Jul-1995   Age: 26   Risk: Green

Year	Tm	G/GS	Snaps	Pass	Rec	Yds	TD	EZ	C%	+/-	Drop	Yd/C	aDOT	Rk	YAC	Rk	YAC+	BTkl	DVOA	Rk	DYAR	Rk	Use	Rk	Slot	Wide
2018	MIN	16/3	146	7	5	77	0	0	71%	+0.1	1	15.4	8.4	--	6.2	--	+1.3	0	37.6%	--	20	--	1.2%	--	14%	14%
2019	MIN	15/1	276	10	8	58	0	1	80%	+1.6	0	7.3	6.8	--	2.3	--	-3.2	0	-27.9%	--	-14	--	2.4%	--	10%	0%
2020	MIN	16/2	448	26	19	194	1	1	73%	+0.7	1	10.2	4.5	48	6.6	4	+1.5	4	-1.2%	27	11	30	5.3%	48	8%	0%
2021	MIN			26	19	193	2		73%	--		10.3							-2.2%							

The Vikings were offered a preview of their 2021 tight end room when departed free agent Kyle Rudolph missed the final four weeks of 2020 with a foot injury. While 2019 second-rounder Irv Smith was dramatically more efficient with 42.3% DVOA (compared to 6.2% with Rudolph in the lineup), Conklin saw more targets (21 versus 20). That is unlikely to hold true over the course of a full season, but Conklin is the better skills replacement for Rudolph. He matched his predecessor with an

8% slot and 0% wide target rate in 2020 while Smith saw 21% of his targets from the slot and 9% out wide. Meanwhile, Conklin is scouted as the better blocker, even if his seven blown blocks in 2020 were excessive over just 205 blocking snaps.

Jared Cook

Height: 6-5   Weight: 254   College: South Carolina   Draft: 2009/3 (89)   Born: 7-Apr-1987   Age: 34   Risk: Green

Year	Tm	G/GS	Snaps	Pass	Rec	Yds	TD	EZ	C%	+/-	Drop	Yd/C	aDOT	Rk	YAC	Rk	YAC+	BTkl	DVOA	Rk	DYAR	Rk	Use	Rk	Slot	Wide
2018	OAK	16/14	770	101	68	896	6	9	67%	+1.8	8	13.2	8.4	17	5.0	24	+0.6	8	13.8%	11	146	5	19.3%	5	36%	18%
2019	NO	14/7	513	65	43	705	9	11	66%	+3.3	4	16.4	10.6	3	5.8	9	+2.4	5	37.7%	1	205	2	13.3%	21	68%	12%
2020	NO	15/5	466	60	37	504	7	9	62%	-0.6	4	13.6	11.7	3	3.4	41	-0.1	5	13.9%	13	88	11	12.6%	21	67%	15%
2021	LAC			58	36	454	5		62%	--		12.6							6.8%							

Cook could not be any more different from Hunter Henry, the player he is replacing. The 34-year-old veteran may still be the league's best vertical presence from the tight end spot, even in his old age. Cook's 11.7-yard average depth of target was essentially tied for second highest in the league, trailing only Dan Arnold in Arizona's vertical passing offense. Los Angeles' former tight end, Henry, finished with just an 8.3-yard average depth per target. Cook also finished in the DYAR top 12 for the third time in a row last season and could have been higher if not for Drew Brees seeing such a dramatic decline. To no surprise, Cook earned most of his production from wide receiver alignments, not as an in-line player. Cook's 82% target share from wide alignments was the highest in the NFL among tight ends last season, nearly 30% higher than Henry's. The Chargers may need to figure something out at the in-line position, hopefully with third-round pick Tre' McKitty, but it's clear that the addition of Cook further bolsters an already impressive pass-catching group in Los Angeles.

Will Dissly

Height: 6-4   Weight: 267   College: Washington   Draft: 2018/4 (120)   Born: 8-Jul-1996   Age: 25   Risk: Green

Year	Tm	G/GS	Snaps	Pass	Rec	Yds	TD	EZ	C%	+/-	Drop	Yd/C	aDOT	Rk	YAC	Rk	YAC+	BTkl	DVOA	Rk	DYAR	Rk	Use	Rk	Slot	Wide
2018	SEA	4/4	127	14	8	156	2	2	57%	-0.3	1	19.5	10.8	--	11.6	--	+7.4	2	30.6%	--	36	--	13.7%	--	21%	0%
2019	SEA	6/6	256	27	23	262	4	5	85%	+5.5	0	11.4	9.1	12	3.0	42	-1.5	1	36.0%	2	74	13	14.4%	18	30%	7%
2020	SEA	16/12	557	29	24	251	2	4	83%	+1.8	2	10.5	4.8	47	7.0	2	+2.1	5	13.3%	14	42	20	5.3%	47	10%	3%
2021	SEA			59	40	417	4		68%	--		10.5							-5.6%							

Dissly returned from a 2019 Achilles injury with some additional competition in the tight end room courtesy of the veteran Greg Olsen, and between injury recovery and Olsen's presence, he was mostly relegated to a blocking role in his third season. With Gerald Everett joining Seattle from the division-rival Rams, Dissly's primary responsibility will again be more focused on blocking, but an increase in play-action concepts could offer Dissly a greater chance to shine. He showed flashes of receiving ability in the seam during his first two seasons, and it would certainly help his pocketbook if he can do that on a more consistent basis as he enters the final year of his rookie contract.

Jack Doyle

Height: 6-6   Weight: 262   College: Western Kentucky   Draft: 2013/FA   Born: 5-May-1990   Age: 31   Risk: Yellow

Year	Tm	G/GS	Snaps	Pass	Rec	Yds	TD	EZ	C%	+/-	Drop	Yd/C	aDOT	Rk	YAC	Rk	YAC+	BTkl	DVOA	Rk	DYAR	Rk	Use	Rk	Slot	Wide
2018	IND	6/6	332	33	26	245	2	1	79%	+2.3	0	9.4	5.4	43	4.2	36	-0.1	2	-7.4%	33	0	33	13.7%	15	48%	6%
2019	IND	16/16	811	72	43	448	4	7	60%	-4.4	5	10.4	7.2	25	5.0	18	+0.6	1	-6.7%	30	3	30	14.6%	16	46%	3%
2020	IND	14/12	540	33	23	251	3	4	70%	-0.9	0	10.9	6.9	37	4.0	34	-0.1	1	4.9%	22	27	25	6.9%	41	27%	0%
2021	IND			38	27	299	3		71%	--		11.0							4.3%							

Did you know that Jack Doyle has been to two Pro Bowls? If you aren't a Colts fan, probably not. He has never had more than 690 receiving yards in a season. Doyle missed major portions of 2018 with a hip strain and, later, a lacerated kidney. In 2020, a knee strain and ankle sprain hit at about the same time, holding him out for a few games. Doyle remains a do-it-all tight end—good blocker, solid receiver without any open-field juice—signed to a reasonable contract with an average cap hit of about $6 million for the next two years. As long as he remains healthy and spry as he gets into his thirties, he should provide enough value to be worth the contract.

Eric Ebron

Height: 6-4   Weight: 253   College: North Carolina   Draft: 2014/1 (10)   Born: 10-Apr-1993   Age: 28   Risk: Green

Year	Tm	G/GS	Snaps	Pass	Rec	Yds	TD	EZ	C%	+/-	Drop	Yd/C	aDOT	Rk	YAC	Rk	YAC+	BTkl	DVOA	Rk	DYAR	Rk	Use	Rk	Slot	Wide
2018	IND	16/8	634	110	66	750	13	17	60%	-4.9	8	11.4	9.6	8	3.8	41	-0.4	6	2.0%	22	68	11	17.1%	6	76%	4%
2019	IND	11/2	328	52	31	375	3	5	60%	-1.4	5	12.1	9.8	8	5.0	19	+1.0	3	-1.1%	23	21	25	15.4%	12	73%	4%
2020	PIT	15/9	766	91	56	558	5	6	62%	-6.5	6	10.0	7.2	27	3.4	39	-0.9	3	-23.3%	46	-95	48	14.4%	16	38%	12%
2021	PIT			83	52	527	4		63%	--		10.1							-13.6%							

Pittsburgh didn't get anything close to a hoped-for change-of-scenery rebirth when they acquired the former first-rounder before the season. Ebron's efficiency, never great, plummeted in the Steel City. The Steelers drafted a tight end in the second round, Pat Freiermuth, but he is unlikely to replace Ebron as a down-the-seam threat in 2021.

Tyler Eifert

Height: 6-6   Weight: 255   College: Notre Dame   Draft: 2013/1 (21)   Born: 8-Sep-1990   Age: 31   Risk: N/A

Year	Tm	G/GS	Snaps	Pass	Rec	Yds	TD	EZ	C%	+/-	Drop	Yd/C	aDOT	Rk	YAC	Rk	YAC+	BTkl	DVOA	Rk	DYAR	Rk	Use	Rk	Slot	Wide
2018	CIN	4/2	133	19	15	179	1	3	79%	+3.1	0	11.9	8.2	--	3.6	--	-0.9	1	21.1%	--	36	--	15.6%	--	70%	0%
2019	CIN	16/4	507	63	43	436	3	7	68%	+1.0	4	10.1	8.4	15	2.6	46	-1.4	1	-1.8%	24	22	24	10.6%	29	59%	16%
2020	JAX	15/4	548	60	36	349	2	6	60%	-1.6	0	9.7	9.0	8	2.8	47	-1.2	1	-20.7%	44	-56	46	11.1%	26	56%	5%

Eifert has—stunningly—played 31 of the last 32 possible games. Unfortunately, it doesn't look like the prospect who caught 13 touchdowns in 2015 survived the back and ankle injuries. He's now just a serviceable bottom-of-the-roster move tight end. Unsigned as we go to deadline and on the wrong side of 30, the end could be coming soon.

Evan Engram

Height: 6-3   Weight: 240   College: Mississippi   Draft: 2017/2 (23)   Born: 2-Sep-1994   Age: 27   Risk: Green

Year	Tm	G/GS	Snaps	Pass	Rec	Yds	TD	EZ	C%	+/-	Drop	Yd/C	aDOT	Rk	YAC	Rk	YAC+	BTkl	DVOA	Rk	DYAR	Rk	Use	Rk	Slot	Wide
2018	NYG	11/8	475	64	45	577	3	3	70%	-1.8	2	12.8	5.4	42	8.6	3	+2.8	10	4.8%	19	50	19	16.2%	7	54%	2%
2019	NYG	8/6	454	68	44	467	3	3	65%	-4.0	3	10.6	6.0	36	5.7	11	+0.8	2	-15.7%	36	-37	41	22.9%	6	46%	7%
2020	NYG	16/14	837	109	63	654	1	5	58%	-11.4	8	10.4	7.4	24	4.6	24	-0.9	6	-24.0%	47	-114	49	22.3%	5	64%	4%
2021	NYG			79	49	514	3		62%	--		10.5							-18.4%							

Sports Info Solutions charged Engram with eight dropped passes last year, Pro Football Reference with 11, and the consensus of WFAN callers charged him with eleventeen gazillion. Engram just isn't very good at hauling in slightly off-target passes or snatching contested balls, which contributes to both his high/varying drop rate and to his low catch rate in general.

Engram earned Pro Bowl status last year, in part because of his raw numbers and in part because he just looks like he should be a Pro Bowler from the moment the huddle breaks to the split second before the ball reaches his hands. The Giants tried to feature him as a slot superweapon last year, and he did have some impressive moments between the catastrophic drops. Engram probably won't lead the Giants in targets this year, but players rarely appear near the top of the dropped pass leaderboard in back-to-back seasons, for one reason or another. Engram could prove to be much more effective on a per-target basis when given a reduced role.

Zach Ertz

Height: 6-5   Weight: 250   College: Stanford   Draft: 2013/2 (35)   Born: 10-Nov-1990   Age: 31   Risk: Red

Year	Tm	G/GS	Snaps	Pass	Rec	Yds	TD	EZ	C%	+/-	Drop	Yd/C	aDOT	Rk	YAC	Rk	YAC+	BTkl	DVOA	Rk	DYAR	Rk	Use	Rk	Slot	Wide
2018	PHI	16/16	1000	155	116	1163	8	10	74%	+7.7	5	10.0	7.4	27	3.1	46	-1.4	7	1.6%	23	93	8	26.2%	3	65%	4%
2019	PHI	15/15	953	135	88	916	6	9	65%	-2.1	7	10.4	8.8	13	2.9	44	-1.1	8	-4.3%	26	27	22	23.8%	5	59%	4%
2020	PHI	11/11	634	72	36	335	1	2	50%	-10.1	5	9.3	7.6	20	2.4	49	-2.2	1	-37.2%	50	-144	50	18.4%	7	73%	1%
2021	PHI			69	40	419	2		58%	--		10.5							-23.1%							

Ertz had been on a bit of a decline over the previous two seasons, but the wheels completely came off in 2020 with career lows in catch rate, yards per reception, touchdowns, DYAR, and DVOA. Ertz was never a broken tackle threat, but last year his broken tackle rate dropped to just 2.8%. In 2019, Ertz found more success when he was lined up in-line as a traditional tight end (0.1% DVOA) but he didn't line up there as often in 2020—a -65.8% DVOA on those passes didn't help much either. One thing that should help Ertz in 2021 is a better catch rate. Ertz's 11.8% drop rate was well above his previous two seasons of 4.5% and 6.7%. Even if his athleticism has started to decrease, his hands shouldn't drop off as quickly.

Gerald Everett

Height: 6-3 Weight: 240 College: South Alabama Draft: 2017/2 (44) Born: 25-Jun-1994 Age: 27 Risk: Green

Year	Tm	G/GS	Snaps	Pass	Rec	Yds	TD	EZ	C%	+/-	Drop	Yd/C	aDOT	Rk	YAC	Rk	YAC+	BTkl	DVOA	Rk	DYAR	Rk	Use	Rk	Slot	Wide
2018	LAR	16/0	380	50	33	320	3	5	66%	-0.4	0	9.7	6.4	37	4.4	33	+0.0	7	-6.6%	29	2	29	9.1%	27	26%	20%
2019	LAR	13/2	453	60	37	408	2	3	62%	-1.0	1	11.0	8.1	16	4.8	26	+0.3	14	-10.4%	34	-13	34	12.1%	24	51%	18%
2020	LAR	16/7	636	62	41	417	1	3	66%	-1.5	7	10.2	6.3	44	5.9	7	+0.9	12	-7.3%	34	0	34	11.1%	27	37%	21%
2021	SEA			58	37	367	3		64%	--		9.9							-14.3%							

In 2020, Everett played more than 50% of the overall offensive snaps for the first time in his career, but he was not able to turn that into any sort of consistent receiving production in the final year of his rookie contract. Part of that lack of production can likely be attributed to some of the quarterback issues present with the 2020 Rams, but for a player whose athletic ability should make him a strong field-stretcher at tight end, the actual output was a bit underwhelming. Everett departed for Seattle in free agency, following new offensive coordinator Shane Waldron to the Pacific Northwest, and should have a chance to carve out a larger role in a tight end room without a clear top-end option. Will Dissly profiles better as a blocking tight end who can beat you off play-action, so the opportunity is there for Everett to break out in his fifth season.

Noah Fant

Height: 6-4 Weight: 249 College: Iowa Draft: 2019/1 (20) Born: 20-Nov-1997 Age: 24 Risk: Green

Year	Tm	G/GS	Snaps	Pass	Rec	Yds	TD	EZ	C%	+/-	Drop	Yd/C	aDOT	Rk	YAC	Rk	YAC+	BTkl	DVOA	Rk	DYAR	Rk	Use	Rk	Slot	Wide
2019	DEN	16/11	703	66	40	562	3	8	61%	+0.2	4	14.1	7.9	19	8.3	1	+2.4	8	-5.9%	28	6	28	13.4%	20	23%	6%
2020	DEN	15/14	732	93	62	673	3	4	67%	-3.9	3	10.9	6.7	39	6.1	6	+1.0	9	-1.0%	26	37	22	18.1%	9	16%	3%
2021	DEN			93	62	697	5		67%	--		11.2							-1.6%							

If anyone in the league has the tools and early production profile to be the next great tight end, it is Noah Fant. Known by many as the "other" Iowa tight end coming out in the 2019 NFL draft, Fant's otherworldly athleticism was often seen as an afterthought to his severe case of the dropsies. Fant's inconsistent hands seemed to work themselves out last year, though, as his rookie drop rate of 8.5% fell to just 4.2% last season. Those drop issues seemingly going away helped Fant become one of the most productive tight ends of the modern era. Since the passing rules changed in 2004, only six tight ends—George Kittle, Rob Gronkowski, Jimmy Graham, Aaron Hernandez, Mark Andrews, and Evan Engram—have earned more yards through their first two seasons than Fant's total of 1,235. That is a pretty studly group of players to be barely trailing in early-career production. Fant did this in two different schemes while catching passes from Joe Flacco, Drew Lock, occasionally Jeff Driskel and Brett Rypien. Though Fant has not been asked to do much splitting out as a wide receiver, he does function well as a traditional in-line Y, showing off the necessary blocking chops to be a legitimate full-time player at the position. Fant's future production will likely have more to do with quarterback stability than taking any sort of developmental step forward.

Darren Fells

Height: 6-7 Weight: 270 College: California-Irvine Draft: 2013/FA Born: 22-Apr-1986 Age: 35 Risk: Green

Year	Tm	G/GS	Snaps	Pass	Rec	Yds	TD	EZ	C%	+/-	Drop	Yd/C	aDOT	Rk	YAC	Rk	YAC+	BTkl	DVOA	Rk	DYAR	Rk	Use	Rk	Slot	Wide
2018	CLE	16/11	420	12	11	117	3	2	92%	+1.8	0	10.6	4.8	--	6.0	--	+1.1	2	53.9%	--	52	--	2.1%	--	17%	0%
2019	HOU	16/14	759	48	34	341	7	6	71%	+0.3	3	10.0	5.4	42	4.9	21	+1.2	3	15.6%	10	75	12	9.2%	35	20%	0%
2020	HOU	16/14	537	28	21	312	4	3	75%	+0.7	1	14.9	7.1	33	8.4	1	+4.3	7	38.6%	2	90	10	5.3%	49	39%	0%
2021	DET			37	25	287	2		68%	--		11.3							1.2%							

Known primarily for his blocking, Fells suffered an unusually terrible 2019 season with 22 blown blocks on just 396 blocking snaps (5.6%). He snapped back to his typical standard with just three blown blocks on 293 blocking snaps (1.0%) last season, and apparently that was all the Lions needed to see to bring him back for his second stint with the team. This run in Detroit, the 35-year-old Fells may make his greatest impact as a mentor for third-year tight end T.J. Hockenson. Don't sleep on Fells' ability to contribute as a part-time receiver, however. He led tight ends with a 33.3% broken tackle rate (minimum 20 receptions) in 2020, and he been a consistent red zone threat with 11 touchdowns on just 76 targets the last two years.

Anthony Firkser

Height: 6-2   Weight: 246   College: Harvard   Draft: 2017/FA   Born: 19-Feb-1995   Age: 26   Risk: Green

Year	Tm	G/GS	Snaps	Pass	Rec	Yds	TD	EZ	C%	+/-	Drop	Yd/C	aDOT	Rk	YAC	Rk	YAC+	BTkl	DVOA	Rk	DYAR	Rk	Use	Rk	Slot	Wide
2018	TEN	12/0	181	20	19	225	1	0	95%	+4.7	0	11.8	6.7	--	5.1	--	+0.8	1	59.3%	--	85	--	6.2%	--	55%	5%
2019	TEN	15/1	202	24	14	204	1	1	58%	-0.9	1	14.6	10.1	6	5.1	16	+1.1	1	13.0%	12	31	20	6.1%	44	84%	4%
2020	TEN	16/1	348	53	39	387	1	4	74%	+2.1	1	9.9	6.9	38	3.7	38	-0.5	4	2.8%	24	36	23	11.5%	23	74%	2%
2021	TEN			55	38	414	4		69%	--		10.9							1.7%							

On a one-year, $3-million deal, Firkser enters the year with a wildly successful history as a receiver in smaller samples, and on a depth chart where the next-best player heading into training camp is probably Geoff Swaim. Before Julio Jones joined the Titans, we might have been looking at an extremely interesting fantasy football player. Post-Jones, Firkser will slot into a target role he's more qualified for. It'll be interesting to see if Firkser becomes less of a tell than he was in 2020—when he was on the field, it was a bit of a red flag that a pass was incoming.

Pat Freiermuth

Height: 6-5   Weight: 260   College: Penn State   Draft: 2021/2 (55)   Born: 25-Oct-1998   Age: 23   Risk: Blue

Year	Tm	G/GS	Snaps	Pass	Rec	Yds	TD	EZ	C%	+/-	Drop	Yd/C	aDOT	Rk	YAC	Rk	YAC+	BTkl	DVOA	Rk	DYAR	Rk	Use	Rk	Slot	Wide
2021	PIT			27	18	186	1		67%	--		10.1							0.0%							

Freiermuth was hung with the unfortunate nickname "Baby Gronk," which seems more a matter of his Massachusetts upbringing then any actual similarity to the noble savage and Hall of Famer in waiting. To his credit, Freiermuth has said he "hates" the moniker. Pittsburgh will be happy enough if Freiermuth, who has good size and blocking tenacity but is raw and wasn't the best pass-catching tight end on the Notre Dame roster last season, bears even a slight resemblance to Heath Miller, much less Gronkowski. Regardless, it is even money on a "Muuuuuuuuthhhhh" chant becoming a thing at Heinz Field this fall.

Mike Gesicki

Height: 6-6   Weight: 252   College: Penn State   Draft: 2018/2 (42)   Born: 3-Oct-1995   Age: 26   Risk: Green

Year	Tm	G/GS	Snaps	Pass	Rec	Yds	TD	EZ	C%	+/-	Drop	Yd/C	aDOT	Rk	YAC	Rk	YAC+	BTkl	DVOA	Rk	DYAR	Rk	Use	Rk	Slot	Wide
2018	MIA	16/7	400	32	22	202	0	2	69%	+1.1	1	9.2	9.2	10	4.4	33	-0.7	3	-37.3%	47	-70	45	7.5%	37	21%	21%
2019	MIA	16/5	705	89	51	570	5	11	57%	-1.7	0	11.2	10.5	4	3.4	40	-1.1	0	-16.3%	39	-51	45	14.7%	15	39%	4%
2020	MIA	15/9	621	85	53	703	6	14	62%	-1.2	3	13.3	11.1	4	3.2	44	-0.7	3	10.4%	18	108	6	16.8%	13	79%	2%
2021	MIA			73	49	577	5		67%	--		11.8							5.0%							

Gesicki broke out in 2020. It's not just that he ranked sixth in DYAR among tight ends—it was the first year he ever had positive DYAR, and he set career high in receptions, yards and touchdowns. It should be noted that that didn't translate into the red zone, however. Gesicki only caught eight of his 18 targets inside the 20, with a -12.8% DVOA. The Dolphins' offense inside the 20 last season boiled down to "force the ball to Gesicki or Devante Parker." Hopefully, adding more talent at the receiver position will open Gesicki up for easier looks in 2021.

Dallas Goedert

Height: 6-5   Weight: 256   College: South Dakota State   Draft: 2018/2 (49)   Born: 3-Jan-1995   Age: 27   Risk: Yellow

Year	Tm	G/GS	Snaps	Pass	Rec	Yds	TD	EZ	C%	+/-	Drop	Yd/C	aDOT	Rk	YAC	Rk	YAC+	BTkl	DVOA	Rk	DYAR	Rk	Use	Rk	Slot	Wide
2018	PHI	16/8	524	44	33	334	4	6	75%	+2.4	1	10.1	7.8	20	5.2	22	+0.3	5	5.1%	18	38	21	7.5%	36	29%	7%
2019	PHI	15/9	781	87	58	607	5	7	67%	+2.0	3	10.5	6.2	35	5.8	10	+0.7	9	-2.1%	25	30	21	15.2%	14	43%	3%
2020	PHI	11/9	602	65	46	524	3	5	71%	+2.1	1	11.4	9.4	7	4.4	26	+0.0	10	16.8%	11	105	7	16.9%	12	52%	3%
2021	PHI			95	58	640	4		61%	--		11.0							-16.5%							

Goedert was one of the few pieces to emerge positively from the 2020 Eagles offense. His 8-101-1 line from Week 1 wasn't exactly a sign of things to come, but he made the most of his opportunity, especially considering he missed four midseason games with a fractured ankle. He split his passes nearly evenly between the slot and in-line and had impressive production from both. The raw stats look slightly better from the slot (11.1-yard average depth of target and 5.2 yards after the catch per reception) compared to in-line (7.4, 4.0), but he had better DVOA in-line (19.3%) than in the slot (12.0%). It helped that two of his three touchdowns came lined up on the line.

Jimmy Graham

Height: 6-7   Weight: 265   College: Miami   Draft: 2010/3 (95)   Born: 24-Nov-1986   Age: 35   Risk: Green

Year	Tm	G/GS	Snaps	Pass	Rec	Yds	TD	EZ	C%	+/-	Drop	Yd/C	aDOT	Rk	YAC	Rk	YAC+	BTkl	DVOA	Rk	DYAR	Rk	Use	Rk	Slot	Wide
2018	GB	16/12	795	89	55	636	2	8	62%	+0.7	3	11.6	9.4	9	4.7	28	-0.0	5	-6.6%	30	4	28	14.4%	13	57%	8%
2019	GB	16/10	638	60	38	447	3	9	63%	+0.6	3	11.8	9.9	7	6.5	5	+1.5	7	2.1%	19	38	18	11.4%	25	55%	2%
2020	CHI	16/15	636	76	50	456	8	14	66%	-3.1	2	9.1	7.0	35	4.0	32	-0.1	4	-5.8%	31	8	31	12.7%	20	55%	14%
2021	CHI			42	29	302	3		69%	--		10.4							-1.1%							

The Athletic's Adam Jahns reported that Graham considered retirement this offseason, but Bears general manager Ryan Pace and head coach Matt Nagy convinced him to return. That team stance may sound strange since Graham has a -4.6% receiving DVOA since his last standout efficiency season in 2016, and since a $7-million potential cap savings made Graham a cut candidate in some outsiders' eyes. But while Graham has lost some athleticism in the back nine of his career, he hasn't stopped being really big. The Bears leaned on Graham in the end zone, where he saw 18.4% of his targets, the fourth-highest rate among the 131 receivers with 50 or more total targets. Meanwhile, Graham continued his typical red zone success with an 11.7% DVOA in that compressed area of the field.

Rob Gronkowski

Height: 6-6   Weight: 264   College: Arizona   Draft: 2010/2 (42)   Born: 14-May-1989   Age: 32   Risk: Green

Year	Tm	G/GS	Snaps	Pass	Rec	Yds	TD	EZ	C%	+/-	Drop	Yd/C	aDOT	Rk	YAC	Rk	YAC+	BTkl	DVOA	Rk	DYAR	Rk	Use	Rk	Slot	Wide
2018	NE	13/11	838	72	47	682	3	8	65%	+1.8	2	14.5	12.4	1	3.9	40	-0.3	5	13.3%	12	98	6	16.1%	8	38%	11%
2020	TB	16/16	809	77	45	623	7	17	58%	-3.0	2	13.8	11.7	2	5.5	14	+0.7	2	6.4%	21	77	13	13.2%	18	12%	2%
2021	TB			52	34	435	4		65%	--		12.9							13.1%							

Gronkowski's 77 DYAR were the most ever by a former WWE 24/7 champion. Gronk was obviously a step slower on his return to the league, but considering his starting point, that still made him an above-average player for most of the year. Gronkowski started the year sluggish, as you might expect following a year off; he was fifth among tight ends with 85 receiving DYAR in the last eight weeks of the season as he got himself back into game shape, both physically and mentally. At this point in his career, Gronkowski wins on his experience and chemistry with Tom Brady more than the athleticism that marked his time in New England, but it works for now.

Hunter Henry

Height: 6-5   Weight: 250   College: Arkansas   Draft: 2016/2 (35)   Born: 7-Dec-1994   Age: 27   Risk: Green

Year	Tm	G/GS	Snaps	Pass	Rec	Yds	TD	EZ	C%	+/-	Drop	Yd/C	aDOT	Rk	YAC	Rk	YAC+	BTkl	DVOA	Rk	DYAR	Rk	Use	Rk	Slot	Wide
2019	LAC	12/12	621	76	55	652	5	6	72%	+4.9	3	11.9	10.2	5	2.9	45	-1.1	0	19.0%	8	136	5	17.6%	8	59%	3%
2020	LAC	14/14	913	93	60	613	4	10	65%	-1.2	2	10.2	7.9	19	3.8	36	-0.7	7	-2.8%	29	27	26	17.2%	11	55%	0%
2021	NE			70	48	516	4		69%	--		10.9							-2.9%							

Henry is coming off his worst season as a pro, setting new lows in DVOA, DYAR, yards per reception, and catch rate. Part of that is the effect of going from Philip Rivers to Justin Herbert; Henry's average depth of target dropped as he served as a safety valve for his rookie passer. But he also just hasn't been the same player he was before his knee injuries cost him a year and a half. When healthy, he's still a top-10 player at the position and gives New England a receiving threat at tight end, which they haven't had since Rob Gronkowski retired (the first time). But the Patriots are paying him like the receiver who looked set to be the best tight end in the league in 2016 and 2017, not the receiver he has been over the past two years.

Christopher Herndon

Height: 6-4   Weight: 252   College: Miami   Draft: 2018/4 (107)   Born: 23-Feb-1996   Age: 25   Risk: Green

Year	Tm	G/GS	Snaps	Pass	Rec	Yds	TD	EZ	C%	+/-	Drop	Yd/C	aDOT	Rk	YAC	Rk	YAC+	BTkl	DVOA	Rk	DYAR	Rk	Use	Rk	Slot	Wide
2018	NYJ	16/12	625	56	39	502	4	3	70%	+3.4	1	12.9	10.5	6	4.7	29	-0.1	4	6.3%	17	50	18	11.1%	22	53%	2%
2019	NYJ	1/0	18	2	1	7	0	0	50%	-0.4	0	7.0	6.0	--	5.0	--	-0.4	0	-57.8%	--	-6	--	6.4%	--	100%	0%
2020	NYJ	16/13	675	45	31	287	3	4	69%	-1.9	4	9.3	7.1	32	4.1	30	-1.2	1	-6.1%	32	4	33	9.7%	33	17%	4%
2021	NYJ			33	21	211	2		64%	--		10.2							-16.1%							

2020 was supposed to be a breakout year for Herndon and he garnered massive training camp buzz with his rapport with Sam Darnold. Instead, a bad case of the drops and the general Gase-itis of the Jets offense dropped him out of the top 30 in DYAR and DVOA. That mostly describes the first half of Herndon's season, however; both fumbles and all but one drop came before New York's bye week. Herndon's DVOA rose from -46.3% before the bye to 41.6% afterwards as he became the Jets' most reliable receiver. So here we go again, with Herndon expected to play the discount George Kittle/Jonnu Smith role in the Jets' new Shanahan offense. The talent is there, but he has never put it together for a full season before.

Tyler Higbee   Height: 6-6   Weight: 257   College: Western Kentucky   Draft: 2016/4 (110)   Born: 1-Jan-1993   Age: 29   Risk: Green

Year	Tm	G/GS	Snaps	Pass	Rec	Yds	TD	EZ	C%	+/-	Drop	Yd/C	aDOT	Rk	YAC	Rk	YAC+	BTkl	DVOA	Rk	DYAR	Rk	Use	Rk	Slot	Wide
2018	LAR	16/16	788	34	24	292	2	3	71%	+1.3	1	12.2	7.0	28	5.7	16	+1.4	4	15.0%	8	54	16	6.2%	42	30%	6%
2019	LAR	15/15	710	89	69	734	3	8	78%	+7.0	2	10.6	6.7	29	5.6	12	+1.1	9	5.5%	17	79	11	15.4%	13	26%	4%
2020	LAR	15/15	815	60	44	521	5	3	73%	+3.4	4	11.8	8.1	16	5.4	15	+1.1	7	19.6%	10	112	5	11.2%	25	45%	10%
2021	LAR			64	44	482	4		69%	--		11.0							-1.0%							

Higbee took a major step forward in productivity late in 2019, and the hope for 2020 was that he would be able to build off that even more to add a consistent third receiving threat to the Rams offense. From a volume standpoint, Higbee regressed to a point in between his 2019 high and his prior career norms, but he was quite efficient with his 60 targets as he finished fifth in DYAR among tight ends. Higbee remains the starter in Los Angeles moving forward, and with Gerald Everett moving on in free agency, he should have a good chance to increase the share of the Los Angeles target volume headed his way. Rookie tight end Jacob Harris of Central Florida has drawn rave reviews during OTAs, but he is still a fourth-round rookie who may take some time to adjust to the NFL.

T.J. Hockenson   Height: 6-5   Weight: 248   College: Iowa   Draft: 2019/1 (8)   Born: 3-Jul-1997   Age: 24   Risk: Green

Year	Tm	G/GS	Snaps	Pass	Rec	Yds	TD	EZ	C%	+/-	Drop	Yd/C	aDOT	Rk	YAC	Rk	YAC+	BTkl	DVOA	Rk	DYAR	Rk	Use	Rk	Slot	Wide
2019	DET	12/7	539	59	32	367	2	5	54%	-8.7	2	11.5	7.7	20	6.3	8	+1.8	6	-18.1%	40	-41	44	14.2%	19	62%	5%
2020	DET	16/16	768	101	67	723	6	9	66%	-1.6	6	10.8	7.2	29	4.9	18	+0.3	4	-6.2%	33	7	32	17.9%	10	42%	6%
2021	DET			102	69	749	5		68%	--		10.9							-3.3%							

Hockenson was more efficient in 2020 when both he and Matthew Stafford were fully healthy than he was as a rookie in 2019, but his Pro Bowl berth owes more to a heavy volume of 101 targets—fifth most at his position—than it does to underwhelming efficiencies of an 8.2% drop rate and -6.2% receiving DVOA. The good news is that new Lions tight end coach Ben Johnson recognizes "there's plenty of meat still on the bone" for the third-year tight end. Hockenson won't need to match his former Iowa teammate and fellow NFL third-year Noah Fant in broken tackle rate to make a major impact on Dan Campbell's Lions; he can continue his progression from a 4.0% blown block rate in 2019 to a 2.6% rate in 2020 and succeed as an all-around contributor.

Jacob Hollister   Height: 6-4   Weight: 245   College: Wyoming   Draft: 2017/FA   Born: 18-Nov-1993   Age: 28   Risk: Green

Year	Tm	G/GS	Snaps	Pass	Rec	Yds	TD	EZ	C%	+/-	Drop	Yd/C	aDOT	Rk	YAC	Rk	YAC+	BTkl	DVOA	Rk	DYAR	Rk	Use	Rk	Slot	Wide
2018	NE	8/1	59	5	4	52	0	0	80%	+0.5	0	13.0	8.2	--	4.0	--	+0.4	0	21.2%	--	10	--	1.8%	--	40%	20%
2019	SEA	11/3	521	59	41	349	3	6	69%	-0.1	1	8.5	6.6	31	4.1	35	-0.5	2	-0.8%	22	25	23	17.5%	9	47%	3%
2020	SEA	16/5	374	40	25	209	3	6	63%	-3.0	4	8.4	6.1	45	3.2	43	-1.1	1	-11.5%	40	-11	39	7.3%	40	53%	5%
2021	BUF			16	11	104	1		69%	--		9.9							-12.0%							

Josh Allen-to-Jacob Hollister played a huge role in Wyoming's 2016 upset of Boise State. Hollister's 144 yards and two touchdowns that day dwarf anything he has done in the pros, despite Seattle trying to insist repeatedly that he would be a thing in their offense. Hollister has only averaged 8.5 yards per reception over the last two years; that ranks 42nd of the 48 tight ends with at least 50 targets. Even with that frankly terrible production, Hollister is still technically an upgrade over Dawson Knox, with better DVOA and DYAR in each of the last two seasons. And it's not too hard to imagine that either the Bills' pass-happy offense or residual Wyoming vibes helping Hollister realize that potential Pete Carroll was always on about; there's upside here.

Austin Hooper

Height: 6-4 Weight: 254 College: Stanford Draft: 2016/3 (81) Born: 29-Oct-1994 Age: 27 Risk: Yellow

Year	Tm	G/GS	Snaps	Pass	Rec	Yds	TD	EZ	C%	+/-	Drop	Yd/C	aDOT	Rk	YAC	Rk	YAC+	BTkl	DVOA	Rk	DYAR	Rk	Use	Rk	Slot	Wide
2018	ATL	16/7	809	88	71	660	4	6	81%	+8.1	1	9.3	6.8	32	3.3	44	-1.3	9	2.2%	21	56	15	14.5%	12	47%	7%
2019	ATL	13/10	743	97	75	787	6	8	77%	+8.9	3	10.5	6.6	30	4.4	33	-0.4	13	12.5%	13	130	6	18.2%	7	47%	1%
2020	CLE	13/13	684	70	46	435	4	7	66%	-1.6	4	9.5	6.6	41	3.7	37	-1.1	1	-9.4%	37	-10	38	18.2%	8	29%	4%
2021	CLE			58	39	384	4		67%	--		9.7							-8.0%							

Hooper's first season in Cleveland wasn't exactly what the team envisioned when they signed him to a $44-million free-agent contract with $23 million guaranteed. Hooper ranked 38th among tight ends in DYAR, which ranks somewhere between Matt Hooper's cage dive in *Jaws* and Tom Hooper's directorial effort with *Cats* in the "Hooper Disaster" rankings. Hooper has struggled in the red zone the past two years, with below-average DVOAs on a combined 27 targets. The Browns apparently realized this weakness in Hooper's game and shifted the close-in passing game elsewhere. Hooper usually had much better numbers than that in Atlanta, and scored touchdowns in three of his last four games (including the playoffs) with the Falcons, so a rebound is possible, though Baker Mayfield isn't Matt Ryan, especially when it comes to throwing to tight ends.

O.J. Howard

Height: 6-6 Weight: 250 College: Alabama Draft: 2017/1 (19) Born: 18-Nov-1994 Age: 27 Risk: Yellow

Year	Tm	G/GS	Snaps	Pass	Rec	Yds	TD	EZ	C%	+/-	Drop	Yd/C	aDOT	Rk	YAC	Rk	YAC+	BTkl	DVOA	Rk	DYAR	Rk	Use	Rk	Slot	Wide
2018	TB	10/8	436	48	34	565	5	2	71%	+3.3	2	16.6	11.7	3	6.1	12	+1.8	4	44.0%	1	169	3	12.2%	17	57%	6%
2019	TB	14/14	793	53	34	459	1	4	64%	+0.1	4	13.5	10.9	1	4.4	32	-0.7	3	3.2%	18	37	19	10.0%	34	26%	2%
2020	TB	4/1	132	19	11	146	2	2	58%	-0.4	1	13.3	12.1	--	1.5	--	-2.6	1	11.8%	--	25	--	12.7%	--	40%	0%
2021	TB			45	28	381	3		62%	--		13.8							6.7%							

Howard tore his Achilles in Week 4 but is on pace to return during training camp with no major setbacks. Before his injury, Howard was developing quite the chemistry with Tom Brady, catching 11 of 19 targets for a pair of touchdowns and 25 DYAR; he was 10th among qualified tight ends in DYAR before he went down. The sheer number of weapons Tampa Bay has might stop Howard from recording his third top-10 DYAR season; there's only so many balls to go around. But a full season of Howard and Gronkowski in this offense is an exciting prospect.

Hayden Hurst

Height: 6-4 Weight: 245 College: South Carolina Draft: 2018/1 (25) Born: 24-Aug-1993 Age: 28 Risk: Green

Year	Tm	G/GS	Snaps	Pass	Rec	Yds	TD	EZ	C%	+/-	Drop	Yd/C	aDOT	Rk	YAC	Rk	YAC+	BTkl	DVOA	Rk	DYAR	Rk	Use	Rk	Slot	Wide
2018	BAL	12/0	275	23	13	163	1	0	57%	-2.6	0	12.5	7.5	--	5.7	--	+1.0	2	-17.5%	--	-16	--	5.6%	--	30%	13%
2019	BAL	16/4	466	39	30	349	2	4	77%	+3.6	1	11.6	8.7	14	4.9	22	+1.0	3	28.1%	4	89	10	9.2%	36	46%	5%
2020	ATL	16/9	785	88	56	571	6	5	64%	-4.2	2	10.2	6.9	36	4.4	27	-0.3	5	-5.2%	30	13	29	14.5%	15	38%	4%
2021	ATL			55	37	386	3		67%	--		10.5							-5.0%							

The addition of Kyle Pitts obviously hurts Hurst's stock, as does Atlanta declining to pick up his fifth-year option, but don't write Hurst off just yet. The Titans had the fourth-most dropbacks with two tight ends under new Falcons head coach Arthur Smith, and Atlanta doesn't have a Derrick Henry to eat up carries. Hurst will be mostly the in-line tight end when Pitts splits out wide. There should be enough volume for Hurst to get his, though his chances of repeating as a fantasy TE1 are essentially dead.

Blake Jarwin

Height: 6-5 Weight: 260 College: Oklahoma State Draft: 2017/FA Born: 16-Jul-1994 Age: 27 Risk: Yellow

Year	Tm	G/GS	Snaps	Pass	Rec	Yds	TD	EZ	C%	+/-	Drop	Yd/C	aDOT	Rk	YAC	Rk	YAC+	BTkl	DVOA	Rk	DYAR	Rk	Use	Rk	Slot	Wide
2018	DAL	16/4	387	36	27	307	3	2	75%	+2.1	2	11.4	8.3	18	4.1	37	-0.6	5	24.0%	4	68	12	6.9%	38	58%	0%
2019	DAL	16/7	436	41	31	365	3	2	76%	+2.5	1	11.8	8.0	17	5.1	17	+1.0	3	12.1%	14	52	15	7.0%	40	51%	2%
2020	DAL	1/1	25	1	1	12	0	0	100%	+0.5	0	12.0	12.0	--	0.0	--	-3.7	0	67.9%	--	7	--	2.6%	--	100%	0%
2021	DAL			61	45	489	4		74%	--		11.0							6.5%							

The Cowboys always keep an oft-injured, athletically gifted tight end on the payroll as a sort of mascot. Eric Bjornson, a converted Pac-10 quarterback, held the job for a few years in the late 1990s. Jerry Jones then personally scouted 6-foot-7 David LaFleur and drafted him with the 22nd overall pick to be Troy Aikman's late-career bodyguard. Much later, former Baylor basketball star Rico Gathers was given several training camps to prove that he was the next Antonio Gates (he was not), while second-round pick Gavin Escobar spent a few years proving without a doubt that he was the NFL's greatest abstract artist/tight end.

Jarwin tore his ACL in the season opener last year. Before that, he spent three seasons sharing playing time with Geoff Swaim, Dalton Schultz, and the desiccated husk of Jason Witten. His claim to an uncontested starting job after Schultz's 63-catch season rests on a 7-119-3 performance in the 2018 season finale. Look for Jarwin to win the starting job by Jerry fiat and then split time with Schultz, each leeching just enough production from the other to make them useless in fantasy and probably less effective than the sturdy Schultz would be on his own.

Travis Kelce				Height: 6-5		Weight: 260			College: Cincinnati				Draft: 2013/3 (63)			Born: 5-Oct-1989		Age: 32		Risk: Green	
Year	Tm	G/GS	Snaps	Pass	Rec	Yds	TD	EZ	C%	+/-	Drop	Yd/C	aDOT	Rk	YAC	Rk	YAC+	BTkl	DVOA	Rk	DYAR	Rk	Use	Rk	Slot	Wide
2018	KC	16/16	993	150	103	1336	10	14	69%	+5.0	6	13.0	9.0	11	5.5	18	+1.1	16	11.5%	14	196	2	26.6%	1	66%	8%
2019	KC	16/16	981	136	97	1229	5	10	71%	+11.5	6	12.7	9.3	10	4.2	34	-0.0	19	14.8%	11	203	3	24.3%	3	63%	10%
2020	KC	15/15	899	145	105	1416	11	12	72%	+8.9	4	13.5	8.9	9	5.6	12	+1.5	26	35.7%	3	415	1	25.5%	3	63%	7%
2021	KC			148	109	1372	10		74%	--		12.6							29.4%							

That Travis Kelce has been one of the league's few elite tight ends for years is no secret. He ranked in the top five in DYAR in every season between 2016 and 2019, the first of those two years being with Alex Smith rather than Patrick Mahomes. Kelce then took his reputation to the next level last year and posted one of the best tight end seasons of the modern era. Since 1983, Kelce's 415 DYAR in 2020 ranks second only to Rob Gronkowski's unholy 2011 mark of 461 DYAR.

Best Tight End Seasons by Receiving DYAR, 1983-2020

Year	PBP ID	Team	DYAR	DVOA	Passes	Catches	Yards	TD	Catch %	Yd/C
2011	Rob Gronkowski	NE	461	46.2%	125	91	1329	18	73%	14.6
2020	**Travis Kelce**	**KC**	**415**	**35.7%**	**145**	**105**	**1416**	**11**	**72%**	**13.5**
2000	Tony Gonzalez	KC	362	28.1%	150	93	1203	9	62%	12.9
2010	Antonio Gates	SD	361	77.1%	65	50	782	10	77%	15.6
1993	Shannon Sharpe	DEN	360	40.5%	110	81	995	9	74%	12.3
1987	Mark Bavaro	NYG	343	65.9%	73	55	865	8	75%	15.7
2017	Rob Gronkowski	NE	339	40.4%	105	69	1084	8	66%	15.7
2009	Antonio Gates	SD	339	35.9%	114	79	1157	8	69%	14.6
1983	Todd Christensen	LARD	334	32.4%	126	92	1255	12	73%	13.6
2004	Tony Gonzalez	KC	330	25.6%	148	102	1258	7	69%	12.3

As is the case with many of the league's best pass-catchers at the position now, Kelce did most of his work from receiver alignments, not as an in-line tight end. 70% of Kelce's targets were from wide receiver alignments, good for seventh in the league. Kelce was still plenty effective in-line, though, which is what makes him so special. Kelce posted a solid 12.5% DVOA and a 77% catch rate through 44 targets as a tight end. He can block as well as anyone from those spots, too; Kelce has blown just five blocks in 622 run snaps over the last three seasons, with only one last year. Kelce's dominance from any alignment and assignment goes a long way in allowing the Chiefs' offensive to be as creative as it is.

George Kittle				Height: 6-4		Weight: 250			College: Iowa				Draft: 2017/5 (146)			Born: 9-Oct-1993		Age: 28		Risk: Yellow	
Year	Tm	G/GS	Snaps	Pass	Rec	Yds	TD	EZ	C%	+/-	Drop	Yd/C	aDOT	Rk	YAC	Rk	YAC+	BTkl	DVOA	Rk	DYAR	Rk	Use	Rk	Slot	Wide
2018	SF	16/16	928	136	88	1377	5	9	65%	-3.9	4	15.6	7.5	25	9.9	1	+4.7	19	15.1%	7	207	1	26.5%	2	40%	4%
2019	SF	14/14	815	107	85	1053	5	7	79%	+9.0	2	12.4	5.9	37	7.1	3	+1.6	27	18.9%	9	187	4	26.1%	1	40%	6%
2020	SF	8/8	443	63	48	634	2	1	76%	+3.1	8	13.2	7.5	21	6.2	5	+1.2	7	28.0%	6	142	4	22.4%	4	56%	5%
2021	SF			107	75	918	7		70%	--		12.2							13.6%							

George Kittle rocks. As his table shows, he gets open, he makes tough catches, and he gains yards with the ball in his hands—his usage rate, +/-, and YAC+ numbers are all exceptional year-in and year-out. He's also a dominant blocker; Sports Info Solutions charged him with zero blown run blocks last year and only seven in his career. In his eight starts, the 49ers had a rush offense DVOA of 10.9%, which would have led the league over the full season; in the eight games he missed, it fell to -23.8%, which would have ranked 28th.

And yet there is room for improvement, particularly in health—it was knee and foot injuries that sidelined him for those eight games. (He was back in the lineup by season's end, stampeding the Cardinals and Seahawks for 160 total yards in Weeks 16 and 17.) Also, he had a career-high eight drops.

Just last year, Kittle signed a massive extension that will keep him in San Francisco for a long time, but it's fun to think about what he could do in Jacksonville. Kittle stole his signature *zero miedo* first-down signal from renowned luchador Penta El Zero Miedo. Penta El Zero Miedo is best known in the United States for performing on All-Elite Wrestling on TNT. All-Elite Wrestling is owned by Shahid Khan, who also owns the Jaguars. Forget about what Kittle can do on the field—the cross-promotional opportunities alone would have Jaguars fans going crazy. Far be it from us, though, to accuse Jacksonville of acquiring a tight end based on name value alone.

Cole Kmet

Height: 6-6   Weight: 262   College: Notre Dame   Draft: 2020/2 (43)   Born: 10-Mar-1999   Age: 22   Risk: Green

Year	Tm	G/GS	Snaps	Pass	Rec	Yds	TD	EZ	C%	+/-	Drop	Yd/C	aDOT	Rk	YAC	Rk	YAC+	BTkl	DVOA	Rk	DYAR	Rk	Use	Rk	Slot	Wide
2020	CHI	16/9	603	44	28	243	2	2	64%	-3.2	0	8.7	6.4	43	4.9	20	-0.4	4	-29.0%	48	-63	47	7.5%	39	38%	2%
2021	CHI			59	41	405	3		69%	--		10.0							-9.8%							

Kmet struggled to break out of the Bears' logjam of tight ends in 2020, but after playing between 30% and 50% of the team's offensive snaps the first nine weeks, Kmet jumped to 70% or more in the team's final seven games. He was eighth at the position with 30 targets from Weeks 13 to 17. Kmet has a pathway to a 2021 breakout, especially if the Bears see better quarterback play from Andy Dalton or Justin Fields, but it would help his receiving fortunes to see more than his rookie rates of 38% of targets from the slot and only 2% from out wide. Even with a top-20 rate of 4.9 yards after the catch, Kmet had the third-worst DVOA of the 50 tight ends with 25 or more targets.

Dawson Knox

Height: 6-4   Weight: 254   College: Mississippi   Draft: 2019/3 (96)   Born: 14-Nov-1996   Age: 25   Risk: Yellow

Year	Tm	G/GS	Snaps	Pass	Rec	Yds	TD	EZ	C%	+/-	Drop	Yd/C	aDOT	Rk	YAC	Rk	YAC+	BTkl	DVOA	Rk	DYAR	Rk	Use	Rk	Slot	Wide
2019	BUF	15/11	655	50	28	388	2	5	56%	-4.9	7	13.9	9.3	9	5.1	15	+0.3	6	-14.0%	35	-23	38	11.1%	26	22%	12%
2020	BUF	12/7	487	44	24	288	3	6	55%	-6.7	3	12.0	8.7	10	6.7	3	+1.8	2	-11.6%	41	-13	41	10.3%	30	29%	2%
2021	BUF			37	24	272	3		65%	--		11.4							-2.0%							

Knox was just about the only Bills player who didn't benefit from the all-passing, all-the-time Buffalo offense. The second-year tight end saw his target share dry up as the Bills just had too many mouths to feed; he ended up as your fantasy TE33 and had only two games with more than eight PPR points. It is worth noting that the Bills did start working Knox in more towards the end of the season, with five touchdowns over his final nine games (including the postseason). His DVOA rose from -45.1% over the first 10 weeks to 6.3% the rest of the way. There's no reason to believe that's anything other than random noise, however, and the fact that Buffalo spent the offseason kicking the tires on every moderately priced tight end in the league should tell you their confidence level in Knox.

David Njoku

Height: 6-4   Weight: 246   College: Miami   Draft: 2017/1 (29)   Born: 10-Jul-1996   Age: 25   Risk: Green

Year	Tm	G/GS	Snaps	Pass	Rec	Yds	TD	EZ	C%	+/-	Drop	Yd/C	aDOT	Rk	YAC	Rk	YAC+	BTkl	DVOA	Rk	DYAR	Rk	Use	Rk	Slot	Wide
2018	CLE	16/14	871	88	56	639	4	8	64%	-2.9	5	11.4	8.7	13	5.5	19	+0.3	9	-18.1%	41	-63	44	15.8%	9	25%	10%
2019	CLE	4/1	101	10	5	41	1	2	50%	-2.3	3	8.2	6.4	--	3.2	--	-0.7	1	-23.7%	--	-10	--	7.5%	--	40%	20%
2020	CLE	13/5	410	29	19	213	2	6	66%	-1.2	2	11.2	7.4	22	4.6	23	+0.2	1	3.0%	23	21	27	7.5%	38	38%	0%
2021	CLE			33	21	228	2		64%	--		10.9							-10.8%							

After loud requests to be dealt in the wake of the Austin Hooper signing/Harrison Bryant drafting a year ago, Njoku appears to have come to terms with his situation as a depth piece in a crowded tight end room, saying he wants to stay in Cleveland this spring. With free agency looming and a potential playoff run in the offing with the Browns, give Njoku credit for reading the tea leaves, at least. Njoku has little trade value, though he managed his first positive DVOA of his career in a small sample, including several tough catches in traffic. He also has improved his blocking since his early turnstile days. Njoku came into the league raw and has been injury-prone. For some time the thinking has been a change of scenery might well benefit him, but it probably won't happen until 2022.

Greg Olsen

Height: 6-5   Weight: 255   College: Miami   Draft: 2007/1 (31)   Born: 11-Mar-1985   Age: 36   Risk: N/A

Year	Tm	G/GS	Snaps	Pass	Rec	Yds	TD	EZ	C%	+/-	Drop	Yd/C	aDOT	Rk	YAC	Rk	YAC+	BTkl	DVOA	Rk	DYAR	Rk	Use	Rk	Slot	Wide
2018	CAR	9/9	429	38	27	291	4	5	71%	+2.3	2	10.8	8.8	12	3.1	45	-1.0	0	14.6%	9	57	14	12.6%	16	54%	0%
2019	CAR	14/14	805	82	52	597	2	6	63%	-1.7	3	11.5	9.1	11	3.9	37	-0.4	2	-6.5%	29	4	29	15.5%	11	54%	1%
2020	SEA	11/8	429	37	24	239	1	7	65%	-0.6	1	10.0	8.0	18	2.0	50	-1.7	0	-2.0%	28	14	28	10.1%	31	76%	3%

Olsen signed a one-year deal with Seattle to serve as an underneath option for the Seahawks passing attack, but the veteran's swan song did not go as planned. Olsen ruptured his plantar fascia at midseason, and while he was able to return for the stretch run, he could only get on the field in a limited capacity. After a lengthy career, he will be heading into the FOX broadcast booth this upcoming season, so we can expect him to still be relevant in football circles for years to come. While he was not quite as dominant as some of his contemporary tight end peers, he had an excellent three-year stretch in Carolina and was one of the main offensive weapons in their run to the 2015 Super Bowl.

James O'Shaughnessy

Height: 6-4   Weight: 245   College: Illinois State   Draft: 2015/5 (173)   Born: 14-Jan-1992   Age: 29   Risk: Green

Year	Tm	G/GS	Snaps	Pass	Rec	Yds	TD	EZ	C%	+/-	Drop	Yd/C	aDOT	Rk	YAC	Rk	YAC+	BTkl	DVOA	Rk	DYAR	Rk	Use	Rk	Slot	Wide
2018	JAX	14/9	533	38	24	214	0	0	63%	-2.2	1	8.9	6.9	31	5.1	23	-0.4	7	-28.9%	45	-49	42	8.2%	33	32%	3%
2019	JAX	5/5	212	20	14	153	2	2	70%	-0.4	1	10.9	6.1	--	5.8	--	+1.0	2	19.3%	--	34	--	11.2%	--	30%	0%
2020	JAX	15/13	466	38	28	262	0	0	74%	+0.3	0	9.4	7.2	30	3.4	40	-1.1	2	-11.0%	39	-10	37	6.8%	42	37%	0%
2021	JAX			25	18	180	1		72%	--		10.0							-7.4%							

The pure consistency here is to be lauded. O'Shaughnessy has four Jaguars seasons with fewer than 40 targets, has never received over 51% of the snaps, has an average target depth of target of less than 7.2 yards in every season, and almost never breaks a tackle. He is Joe Second-String Move Tight End, never a good enough blocker to want to play on run downs, but always a fine checkdown after the real routes are covered. Except the Jaguars don't have a No. 1 tight end, so guess what, it's James O'Shaughnessy.

Kyle Pitts

Height: 6-6   Weight: 240   College: Florida   Draft: 2021/1 (4)   Born: 6-Oct-2000   Age: 21   Risk: Green

Year	Tm	G/GS	Snaps	Pass	Rec	Yds	TD	EZ	C%	+/-	Drop	Yd/C	aDOT	Rk	YAC	Rk	YAC+	BTkl	DVOA	Rk	DYAR	Rk	Use	Rk	Slot	Wide
2021	ATL			79	55	618	5		70%	--		11.3							0.0%							

Will Pitts break the first-year tight end curse? The only rookie tight end to ever break 1,000 yards was Mike Ditka in 1961. The only rookie tight ends to break 200 DYAR are Rob Gronkowski (2010) and Ken Dilger (1995); only 16 players have even had 100 DYAR as a rookie. When you take someone with the fourth overall pick, and ignore trade offers to do it, you're expecting a massive return right off the bat, but tight ends rarely live up to that billing. Pitts should be an exception; he's got speed for days, he can separate from coverage like a receiver, and he has a catch radius like you wouldn't believe. He's not much of a blocker, but then, you don't draft a tight end fourth overall because he can block.

Jordan Reed

Height: 6-2   Weight: 242   College: Florida   Draft: 2013/3 (85)   Born: 3-Jul-1990   Age: 31   Risk: N/A

Year	Tm	G/GS	Snaps	Pass	Rec	Yds	TD	EZ	C%	+/-	Drop	Yd/C	aDOT	Rk	YAC	Rk	YAC+	BTkl	DVOA	Rk	DYAR	Rk	Use	Rk	Slot	Wide
2018	WAS	13/8	511	84	54	558	2	3	64%	-4.7	2	10.3	6.9	29	4.2	35	-0.7	5	-22.2%	43	-80	48	20.9%	4	63%	13%
2020	SF	10/1	247	46	26	231	4	4	57%	-3.6	3	8.9	8.4	13	3.2	42	-0.9	4	-12.6%	42	-16	42	13.1%	19	67%	7%

Here's your wacky stat of this chapter: the 49ers got 10 games out of Jordan Reed and eight games out of George Kittle, and they had one or the other every single week, but they only had both for two games, and both were against Arizona. Reed had a disappointing, injury-marred season, then announced his retirement. His career peaked in 2015, when he was fantasy's TE3 with 952 yards and 11 touchdowns for Washington. He was also fourth at the position in receiving DYAR that season, eighth in DVOA.

It was a torn MCL that cost Reed six games last season, but it was his 10 concussions (that we know of) and their aftermath that ended his career. Reed spoke to Dan Pompei of The Athletic about the tinnitus, headaches, insomnia, and mood swings from which he is still suffering. He also explained how he has successfully used cannabis instead of opiates to treat those symptoms since 2013, how he has been investing in the cannabis industry since 2017, and how he hopes it can help others he way it has helped him.

Richard Rodgers

Height: 6-4 Weight: 257 College: California Draft: 2014/3 (98) Born: 1/22/1992 Age: 29 Risk: Green

Year	Tm	G/GS	Snaps	Pass	Rec	Yds	TD	EZ	C%	+/-	Drop	Yd/C	aDOT	Rk	YAC	Rk	YAC+	BTkl	DVOA	Rk	DYAR	Rk	Use	Rk	Slot	Wide
2018	PHI	7/0	42	1	1	7	0	0	100%	+0.2	0	7.0	-2.0	--	9.0	--	+2.3	0	20.9%	--	3	--	0.4%	--	0%	100%
2019	PHI	1/0	5	0	0	0	0	--	--	--	--	--	--	--	--	--	--	--	--	--	--	--	--	--	--	--
2020	PHI	14/4	273	31	24	345	2	2	77%	+5.9	0	14.4	10.9	5	4.0	33	-0.3	1	30.4%	5	79	12	6.1%	43	19%	0%
2021	PHI			8	5	55	0		63%	--		11.8							-5.5%							

Rodgers might have been the most impressive Philadelphia tight end when he made his way into the lineup. His opportunity mostly came when either Dallas Goedert or Zach Ertz was out. He finished with more receiving yards than Ertz (345 to 335) on 40 fewer targets and 12 fewer receptions. Unlike the top two tight ends, Rodgers did most of his work lined up as a traditional tight end, where his 26.2% DVOA was seventh at the position. Rodgers sat available as a free agent until the Eagles re-signed him in mid-June for what will somehow be his fourth season in Philadelphia.

Kyle Rudolph

Height: 6-6 Weight: 265 College: Notre Dame Draft: 2011/2 (43) Born: 9-Nov-1989 Age: 32 Risk: Green

Year	Tm	G/GS	Snaps	Pass	Rec	Yds	TD	EZ	C%	+/-	Drop	Yd/C	aDOT	Rk	YAC	Rk	YAC+	BTkl	DVOA	Rk	DYAR	Rk	Use	Rk	Slot	Wide
2018	MIN	16/16	925	82	64	634	4	10	78%	+6.7	1	9.9	6.5	35	3.9	39	-0.7	6	8.6%	15	91	9	13.9%	14	46%	7%
2019	MIN	16/16	807	48	39	367	6	8	81%	+7.3	0	9.4	7.3	24	4.9	23	+0.1	1	26.9%	5	118	8	11.1%	27	6%	0%
2020	MIN	12/12	572	37	28	334	1	3	76%	+1.3	0	11.9	7.2	31	5.9	9	+1.1	3	6.7%	20	33	24	10.0%	32	8%	0%
2021	NYG			38	27	273	2		71%	--		10.2							-4.6%							

Seventeen of Rudolph's 28 receptions came on first down last year, and an awful lot of them came on bootleg/rollout concepts. That's the receiving profile of a No. 2 tight end, and that's the role Rudolph should assume beside/behind Evan Engram. Rudolph is an effective enough in-line blocker to make him useful in two-tight end sets, and he still has the receiving chops to be the fifth or sixth option in a passing game. Rudolph's March foot surgery clouds his future a bit, but what would a Giants offensive weapon be without a significant injury concern?

Drew Sample

Height: 6-4 Weight: 259 College: Washington Draft: 2019/2 (52) Born: 16-Apr-1996 Age: 25 Risk: Green

Year	Tm	G/GS	Snaps	Pass	Rec	Yds	TD	EZ	C%	+/-	Drop	Yd/C	aDOT	Rk	YAC	Rk	YAC+	BTkl	DVOA	Rk	DYAR	Rk	Use	Rk	Slot	Wide
2019	CIN	9/2	111	6	5	30	0	1	83%	+0.5	0	6.0	8.1	--	2.6	--	-3.2	0	-0.8%	--	2	--	2.1%	--	14%	0%
2020	CIN	16/13	868	53	40	349	1	4	75%	-1.4	3	8.7	4.2	49	5.0	17	-0.4	7	-10.8%	38	-12	40	9.2%	34	19%	9%
2021	CIN			28	21	198	1		75%	--		9.4							-5.3%							

Sample caught 12 flat passes (per Sports Info Solutions) for 86 yards (7.2 yards per catch) last season. He also caught seven screens for 58 yards, 8.3 yards per catch. Throw in lots of use as a pass-protector in empty backfield formations and Sample had a rather predictable, non-nourishing offensive role.

With Joe Burrow more experienced, Ja'Marr Chase in the fold, and the offensive line (fingers crossed) less pathetic, Zac Taylor should be able to open up his offense more and use Sample as a destitute man's Zach Ertz a little less. As at most other positions on the roster, there's no real depth at tight end, so Sample at least has job security.

Dalton Schultz

Height: 6-5 Weight: 242 College: Stanford Draft: 2018/4 (137) Born: 11-Jul-1996 Age: 25 Risk: Blue

Year	Tm	G/GS	Snaps	Pass	Rec	Yds	TD	EZ	C%	+/-	Drop	Yd/C	aDOT	Rk	YAC	Rk	YAC+	BTkl	DVOA	Rk	DYAR	Rk	Use	Rk	Slot	Wide
2018	DAL	11/7	300	17	12	116	0	1	71%	-0.4	1	9.7	4.3	--	5.5	--	+0.9	2	-4.0%	--	4	--	4.7%	--	24%	0%
2019	DAL	16/0	118	2	1	6	0	0	50%	-0.3	0	6.0	10.0	--	1.0	--	-3.1	0	-52.3%	--	-6	--	0.3%	--	0%	0%
2020	DAL	16/14	971	89	63	615	4	4	71%	-0.0	3	9.8	6.6	40	4.4	25	+0.4	11	-8.5%	36	-8	36	14.2%	17	56%	3%
2021	DAL			42	31	317	2		74%	--		10.4							0.8%							

Schultz lined up as a flex tight end and caught the shallow curl over the middle of the field over and over again. For variety, he sometimes ran to the flat as an H-back or from a trips bunch, or split wide to the left and caught a slant. Really, there's not much to the Mike McCarthy playbook, folks.

Schultz's mediocre DVOA/DYAR results were partially the result of lots of empty-calorie short receptions and partly due to Garrett Gilbert and Ben DiNucci bouncing passes in his general direction. Schultz is athletic enough to exploit mismatches and break some tackles, making him useful enough in the old Jermichael Finley role. The Cowboys appear committed to Blake Jarwin as their top tight end in 2021, because Jerry Jones loves his pet perma-projects. Either player should perform adequately given such simple, well-defined responsibilities. From a fantasy standpoint, Schultz and Jarwin could cancel one another out.

Irv Smith Height: 6-2 Weight: 240 College: Alabama Draft: 2019/2 (50) Born: 9-Aug-1998 Age: 23 Risk: Green

Year	Tm	G/GS	Snaps	Pass	Rec	Yds	TD	EZ	C%	+/-	Drop	Yd/C	aDOT	Rk	YAC	Rk	YAC+	BTkl	DVOA	Rk	DYAR	Rk	Use	Rk	Slot	Wide
2019	MIN	16/7	620	47	36	311	2	4	77%	+3.5	2	8.6	5.9	38	3.8	38	-1.5	2	-18.5%	41	-39	42	10.6%	28	40%	4%
2020	MIN	13/7	545	43	30	365	5	7	70%	+1.6	1	12.2	8.5	12	4.2	29	+0.4	2	23.5%	8	92	9	10.7%	29	21%	9%
2021	MIN			64	46	506	5		72%	--		10.9							8.8%							

Smith may not see the field more in 2021 than he did in 2020. Head coach Mike Zimmer intimated this offseason that Tyler Conklin would be the bigger workload beneficiary of Kyle Rudolph's departure in free agency, and the Vikings don't have much room to expand on a perennial top-three reliance on two-tight end formations. Still, Smith remains a strong bet to enjoy a production breakout in his third season. Limited by relatively poor hands and slower transitions from the catch to run—as demonstrated by equal 6.1% drop and broken tackle rates in his two-year career—Smith flipped from inefficient to efficient when Kirk Cousins increased his average depth of target from 5.9 yards as a rookie to 8.5 yards as a sophomore to take advantage of Smith's build-up speed.

Jonnu Smith Height: 6-3 Weight: 248 College: Florida International Draft: 2017/3 (100) Born: 22-Aug-1995 Age: 26 Risk: Green

Year	Tm	G/GS	Snaps	Pass	Rec	Yds	TD	EZ	C%	+/-	Drop	Yd/C	aDOT	Rk	YAC	Rk	YAC+	BTkl	DVOA	Rk	DYAR	Rk	Use	Rk	Slot	Wide
2018	TEN	13/12	610	30	20	258	3	2	67%	-2.0	3	12.9	5.4	44	9.0	2	+3.7	4	-1.8%	26	11	27	8.5%	31	23%	13%
2019	TEN	16/14	718	44	35	439	3	2	80%	+2.7	1	12.5	5.7	40	7.8	2	+2.4	17	25.6%	6	91	9	10.4%	31	36%	7%
2020	TEN	15/14	745	65	41	448	8	9	63%	-5.3	2	10.9	5.9	46	5.8	10	+1.4	4	7.2%	19	65	15	14.8%	14	41%	3%
2021	NE			53	35	393	4		66%	--		11.1							-2.0%							

While Smith has never wowed with volume, never topping 500 receiving yards in his career, there are few players in the league more dangerous with the ball in their hands. Over the last three seasons, Smith has +2.2 YAC+, or yards after catch over expected. That trails only George Kittle among qualified tight ends and is sixth among all players with at least 75 targets since 2018. Some of that comes from a very friendly offense in Tennessee, but Smith has top-tier athleticism, and it shows up on the field. New England hasn't had a player like this in quite some time.

Durham Smythe Height: 6-6 Weight: 260 College: Notre Dame Draft: 2018/4 (123) Born: 9-Aug-1995 Age: 26 Risk: Green

Year	Tm	G/GS	Snaps	Pass	Rec	Yds	TD	EZ	C%	+/-	Drop	Yd/C	aDOT	Rk	YAC	Rk	YAC+	BTkl	DVOA	Rk	DYAR	Rk	Use	Rk	Slot	Wide
2018	MIA	15/2	176	11	6	50	0	0	55%	-1.6	0	8.3	4.5	--	1.2	--	-3.4	0	-31.2%	--	-17	--	2.7%	--	10%	10%
2019	MIA	16/14	485	14	7	65	0	1	50%	-2.6	1	9.3	9.9	--	1.4	--	-3.1	0	-31.0%	--	-20	--	2.3%	--	36%	14%
2020	MIA	15/13	449	29	26	208	2	2	90%	+4.0	0	8.0	3.5	50	4.7	21	+0.1	0	10.7%	17	37	21	5.5%	45	21%	7%
2021	MIA			28	19	189	2		68%	--		9.9							-7.6%							

Durham Smythe, sure-handed safety blanket? Not only did Smythe lead all tight ends with a 90% reception rate, but his +4.0 receiving plus/minus was sixth among tight ends. You'd expect numbers like that to come out higher in DVOA and DYAR, but Smythe has essentially zero big-play ability. There's value to a guy who will get positive yards every time you look his way, though with an average depth of target of just 3.0 with Tua Tagovailoa under center, that value is somewhat limited.

Logan Thomas   Height: 6-6   Weight: 250   College: Virginia Tech   Draft: 2014/4 (120)   Born: 1-Jul-1991   Age: 30   Risk: Green

Year	Tm	G/GS	Snaps	Pass	Rec	Yds	TD	EZ	C%	+/-	Drop	Yd/C	aDOT	Rk	YAC	Rk	YAC+	BTkl	DVOA	Rk	DYAR	Rk	Use	Rk	Slot	Wide
2018	BUF	12/3	284	17	12	77	0	1	71%	+0.7	0	6.4	5.3	--	2.8	--	-3.6	0	-43.5%	--	-37	--	4.7%	--	69%	0%
2019	DET	16/3	342	28	16	173	1	3	57%	-2.5	1	10.8	7.6	22	4.8	24	+0.4	0	-18.9%	42	-21	37	5.0%	46	50%	11%
2020	WAS	16/15	1009	110	72	670	6	8	65%	-2.8	4	9.3	7.2	28	4.0	31	-0.6	7	-7.8%	35	-4	35	19.2%	6	68%	2%
2021	WAS			103	63	671	7		61%	--		10.7							-6.1%							

Thomas got his first true run as a full-time tight end with Washington in 2020. The converted quarterback had never played more than 31% of his team's offensive snaps during stops with the Cardinals, Bills, and Lions before he played 93% last season in his seventh year in the league. Thomas was better from the slot (-3.6% DVOA) than in-line (-14.1%), both major improvements from his previous small samples at the position. He spent the offseason studying the releases of Travis Kelce, Darren Waller, and George Kittle to improve off the line. Thomas was at his best using his 6-foot-6 frame in the red zone, where he put up a 36.4% DVOA, though only six of his 17 red zone targets came in the end zone. Despite entering Year 8, this will be the first time Thomas has been in the same offense in back-to-back seasons.

Robert Tonyan   Height: 6-5   Weight: 237   College: Indiana State   Draft: 2017/FA   Born: 30-Apr-1994   Age: 27   Risk: Green

Year	Tm	G/GS	Snaps	Pass	Rec	Yds	TD	EZ	C%	+/-	Drop	Yd/C	aDOT	Rk	YAC	Rk	YAC+	BTkl	DVOA	Rk	DYAR	Rk	Use	Rk	Slot	Wide
2018	GB	16/1	67	6	4	77	1	0	67%	+0.1	1	19.3	13.8	--	2.5	--	-1.0	0	38.7%	--	19	--	1.0%	--	67%	0%
2019	GB	11/1	199	15	10	100	1	2	67%	-0.1	0	10.0	10.5	--	2.6	--	-2.0	0	4.5%	--	10	--	3.9%	--	20%	13%
2020	GB	16/8	638	59	52	586	11	7	88%	+12.6	0	11.3	8.3	14	4.3	28	+0.2	1	51.7%	1	242	2	11.8%	22	27%	12%
2021	GB			57	45	497	6		79%	--		11.1							28.0%							

Tonyan did not receive an FBS scholarship offer, and he and his family had to write dozens of letters to colleges for him to find a chance to play for Indiana State. It would have been incredible had he simply made an NFL roster, but two seasons after going undrafted, Tonyan flew past the more heralded and athletic tight end prospect Jace Sternberger on the Packers depth chart, then became one of the most productive players at his position. Tonyan comes from the Greg Olsen mold. He broke just one tackle on 52 catches, a 1.9% broken tackle rate that was the worst of 73 tight ends with 20 or more catches. But he did not drop a ball and hasn't since his rookie year in 2018.

Adam Trautman   Height: 6-6   Weight: 253   College: Dayton   Draft: 2020/3 (105)   Born: 5-Feb-1997   Age: 24   Risk: Green

Year	Tm	G/GS	Snaps	Pass	Rec	Yds	TD	EZ	C%	+/-	Drop	Yd/C	aDOT	Rk	YAC	Rk	YAC+	BTkl	DVOA	Rk	DYAR	Rk	Use	Rk	Slot	Wide
2020	NO	15/6	393	16	15	171	1	1	94%	+2.8	0	11.4	4.0	--	7.8	--	+2.8	2	39.7%	--	50	--	3.3%	--	19%	0%
2021	NO			58	39	428	3		67%	--		10.9							-3.5%							

Trautman played in all but one game during his rookie year and played at least 40% of offensive snaps in eight of his 15 appearances. The biggest surprise is that he did so mainly as a blocker: Trautman was considered more of a receiving tight end prospect, but he saw only 16 targets in almost 400 snaps and his biggest catches both came in the fourth quarter of blowout victories. Instead, he was very effective in the ground game and on special teams. That's not to say that he didn't contribute as a receiver: his 39.7% DVOA would have ranked second at the position if he had enough targets to qualify, and no tight end had a higher catch rate on at least 10 targets. With Jared Cook now in San Diego and Josh Hill having retired, a lot more of that receiving work will land on Trautman's shoulders this year.

Darren Waller   Height: 6-6   Weight: 255   College: Georgia Tech   Draft: 2015/6 (204)   Born: 13-Sep-1992   Age: 29   Risk: Green

Year	Tm	G/GS	Snaps	Pass	Rec	Yds	TD	EZ	C%	+/-	Drop	Yd/C	aDOT	Rk	YAC	Rk	YAC+	BTkl	DVOA	Rk	DYAR	Rk	Use	Rk	Slot	Wide
2018	OAK	4/0	42	6	6	75	0	0	100%	+1.5	0	12.5	3.2	--	9.3	--	+4.8	1	26.7%	--	15	--	4.5%	--	0%	33%
2019	OAK	16/16	940	117	90	1145	3	7	77%	+9.5	5	12.7	7.6	21	6.4	6	+1.5	15	22.0%	7	234	1	23.9%	4	53%	13%
2020	LV	16/15	992	145	107	1196	9	9	74%	+8.5	4	11.2	8.1	17	5.3	16	+0.8	11	11.4%	16	190	3	27.5%	1	36%	13%
2021	LV			120	89	1005	8		74%	--		11.3							17.0%							

Waller's breakout 2019 season was impressive enough, but his 2020 campaign cemented him among the league's small group of elite tight ends. The burden of responsibility the Raiders offense puts on Waller's shoulders is telling. Waller saw 145 passes last season, tying Travis Kelce for the most in the league among tight ends. They were the only tight ends with over 110 targets. Waller was also instrumental in Derek Carr's success on third downs: on 39 passes, Waller caught 77% of his targets, produced a 27.1% DVOA, and converted 22 first downs. Waller was as reliable as anyone could ask for in the red zone, too. He caught 18 of his 22 targets inside the 20, punching in six touchdowns. Stack all of Waller's situational savvy on top of his ability to stretch the field vertically and horizontally on base downs and you get a pass-catching tight end who is as complete as any. Waller may not be the toughest blocker, but with pass-catching chops as rare as his, that's a sacrifice the Raiders are willing to live with.

Maxx Williams — Height: 6-4　Weight: 252　College: Minnesota　Draft: 2015/2 (55)　Born: 12-Apr-1994　Age: 27　Risk: Yellow

Year	Tm	G/GS	Snaps	Pass	Rec	Yds	TD	EZ	C%	+/-	Drop	Yd/C	aDOT	Rk	YAC	Rk	YAC+	BTkl	DVOA	Rk	DYAR	Rk	Use	Rk	Slot	Wide
2018	BAL	13/6	374	17	16	143	1	0	94%	+3.6	0	8.9	2.9	--	6.1	--	+0.2	2	8.2%	--	18	--	3.8%	--	6%	6%
2019	ARI	16/10	493	19	15	202	1	1	79%	+2.4	1	13.5	7.2	--	6.9	--	+2.6	4	30.0%	--	51	--	3.5%	--	33%	0%
2020	ARI	9/8	326	10	8	102	1	0	80%	+1.8	0	12.8	4.5	--	8.3	--	+4.2	1	29.5%	--	27	--	3.2%	--	10%	0%
2021	ARI			32	21	250	2		66%	--		11.9							1.4%							

In a tiny sample size, Williams has been a dynamo in two years working with Kliff Kingsbury. To put his numbers in Arizona into perspective, only four qualifying tight ends had DVOAs of 30.0% or higher last season, though Williams hasn't hit the 25 targets needed to qualify since his rookie year in Baltimore in 2015. His 2020 numbers are also skewed by two big catches (a 25-yarder in Seattle in Week 11, a 42-yarder against Philadelphia in Week 15) that produced nearly two-thirds of his yardage on the season. Williams spent five games on IR last season due to an ankle injury and was inactive on two other occasions. Somebody has to start at tight end for the Cardinals, however, and Williams' experience should give him the edge over Darrell Daniels.

Jason Witten — Height: 6-6　Weight: 265　College: Tennessee　Draft: 2003/3 (69)　Born: 6-May-1982　Age: 39　Risk: N/A

Year	Tm	G/GS	Snaps	Pass	Rec	Yds	TD	EZ	C%	+/-	Drop	Yd/C	aDOT	Rk	YAC	Rk	YAC+	BTkl	DVOA	Rk	DYAR	Rk	Use	Rk	Slot	Wide
2019	DAL	16/16	851	83	63	529	4	5	76%	+3.7	6	8.4	6.7	28	2.6	47	-1.5	0	-0.5%	20	38	17	14.4%	17	61%	4%
2020	LV	16/7	404	17	13	69	2	4	76%	+0.8	0	5.3	5.4	--	1.5	--	-2.6	0	-16.5%	--	-13	--	3.2%	--	12%	0%

When Witten first retired three years ago, his comment in *Football Outsiders Almanac 2018* ran down all his numbers as the all-time leader for the Dallas Cowboys in various categories. But Witten was not a member of the Cowboys in his final season, spending his last NFL year as a blocking specialist for the Raiders. The 38-year-old vet played 37% of the team's offensive snaps but finished with just 17 targets. Witten had negative DVOA in his final five seasons and had negative DYAR for the first time in 2020. Witten still got it done as the blocking counterpart to Darren Waller, but with the decline in his receiving skills, it was time to hang 'em up.

Going Deep

Stephen Anderson, LAC: Anderson left the spotlight as quickly as he arrived. He snagged 25 passes for 342 yards with the Texans in 2017 but finished 42nd out of 50 qualifying tight ends with -22 DYAR. The Texans promptly cut him, then he spent the 2018 season inactive on the Patriots roster before joining the Chargers for the last two years. Anderson caught eight passes in 2020, but with players such as Jared Cook and rookie Tre' McKitty around, it's hard to see how someone with Anderson's athletic, non-blocking skill set finds reps.

Devin Asiasi, NE: Tight ends nearly always struggle as rookies, but two receptions in 2020, both in Week 17, is less than ideal. With New England doling out an unprecedented amount of money to Jonnu Smith and Hunter Henry this offseason, the outlook doesn't look great for Asiasi's 2021, either.

John Bates, WAS: Bates was a fourth-round pick out of Boise State. At 6-foot-6, Bates is a huge target, but that size hasn't completely translated to the field. He has struggled against man coverage and had a 4.2% passing blown block rate in 2020. He also only had two career receiving touchdowns. But Bates has the athleticism to find holes and take advantage of zone coverage. He could be most successful as an H-back who is able to move around the formation.

Blake Bell, KC: After a year away, Bell is making his return to the Chiefs. The former Oklahoma Sooners quarterback spent last season with the Cowboys, where he had one of the best seasons of his career as part of the committee replacing Jason Witten. Bell's 110-yard season in 2020 marked just the second time he as cleared the century mark since entering the league in 2015. Perhaps more important to his potential role in Kansas City, Bell saw 189 snaps as a run-blocker (roughly 44% of the team's running plays) and only blew two blocks.

Pharaoh Brown, HOU: The Browns released Brown at last cuts and the Texans plugged him in and got a much better blocker than Darren Fells at a league-minimum cost. Brown even contributed a few catches where he carried defenders on his back for multiple yards at a time. He's a fine blocking tight end and a great story given how gruesome his college knee injury was. He should have an inside track to a roster spot despite Houston's tight end-heavy offseason acquisition list. (14-163-2, 37.4% DVOA in 2020.)

Darrell Daniels, ARI: Daniels is a blocker by trade—he started eight of his 12 games last year and played nearly a third of Arizona's offensive snaps but was only targeted 11 times. Dan Arnold's departure to Carolina, however, leaves a hole in Arizona's starting lineup, and there's at least a glimmer of hope Daniels could beat out Maxx Williams for the job. He had a 27.1% DVOA on those 11 throws and produced the first three 20-yard games of his four-year career. And if it doesn't work out, he'll still get plenty of time at the goal line and on special teams.

Zach Davidson, MIN: This fifth-round pick may be the most mysterious prospect in the 2021 draft. He had 894 yards and 15 touchdowns for Central Missouri State in 2019 before the Division II MIAA conference shut down in 2020 due to COVID. His 245 pounds look lanky on his 6-foot-7 frame and call into question his long-term ceiling as a blocker. But he dominated lesser competition as a receiver, and he distracted scouts with an unusual second-position commitment as the Mules' punter. Clearly he's a project, but his position flexibility suggests an athleticism that body improvements could help blossom in time.

Josiah Deguara, GB: Deguara was among the early-round 2019 draft picks that seemed like poor fits for an Aaron Rodgers-led Packers team and may have spurred the contentious relationship between the quarterback and his front office. But Deguara makes a lot of sense for the power-rushing, play-action-heavy future Packers that Jordan Love and AJ Dillon foreshadow. Listed as a tight end, Deguara is more of a versatile H-back who does his best work as a run blocker. An early-2020 ACL tear effectively delayed his rookie season a year, and he may have to wait for Love to become a starter to enjoy a healthy percentage of the team's offensive snaps.

Ross Dwelley, SF: Dwelley had a 30.8% DVOA on 24 targets—exactly one target shy of qualifying for our leaderboards. Had he qualified, that DVOA would have finished in the top five at his position, ahead of his more celebrated teammate George Kittle. The 49ers are reportedly high on Charlie Woerner, a sixth-round draft pick in 2020, and added journeyman MyCole Pruitt late in free agency, but Dwelley and his 79% catch rate won't give up the No. 2 job without a fight.

Luke Farrell, JAX: Recruited in college by Urban Meyer, and selected by Meyer—literally, Shad Khan told Farrell right before the pick that "it was all Coach Meyer here" on a recorded Jaguars.com video of the call—Farrell comes to town as a fifth-round pick with a chance at real playing time on a barren depth chart. Chris Manhertz is definitely the veteran Farrell will be trying to shadow as Farrell is a run-block-first tight end. Whenever Farrell catches a pass he will almost instantly fall down, so any receiving production he creates will mostly be incidental or late-read based.

Troy Fumagalli, NE: Fumagalli, perhaps best known for having just four fingers on his left hand, was the odd man out in Denver's loaded tight end room. Fumagalli has enough athletic tools and a quality catch radius to be a mismatch versus lesser linebackers and safeties, but he does not boast the strength to be any sort of impact player as a blocker. Fumagalli would be better served in a role that moved him around between the slot and H-back roles, which was not something he got the luxury of in Denver.

Kylen Granson, IND: Here's how Frank Reich felt about Granson per Indy's With The Next Pick series: "I like Granson a lot, he's gonna play." And from the same video, a Colts scout related: "Frank came into the draft room one day and was like 'Hey, I watched this Granson kid, he can run, he's athletic, I really like this guy.'" There's a bit of an uphill battle to instant playing time on a depth chart with Jack Doyle and Mo Alie-Cox, but Granson projects as a zone-buster who can contribute in a limited role à la Trey Burton.

Noah Gray, KC: Gray, a fifth-round pick, is Andy Reid's cheap attempt at finding another move tight end. Undersized at 6-foot-3 and 240 pounds, Gray regularly lined up as an H-back, wing, or slot receiver for Duke. He has legitimate pass-catching talent, as evidenced by his 100 receptions over his final three seasons. Gray's 6.90s 3-cone drill is in the 90th percentile among tight end prospects since 1999, which is why he works as a slot player. Gray does not have the toughness at the catch point expected of a tight end, though, so he really needs space to operate.

Ryan Griffin, NYJ: Griffin is still a solid, if unspectacular, run-blocker—just three blown blocks on 188 rushing snaps last season. He's the best in-line tight end the Jets have, and assuming he stays on the team, he should play the Marcedes Lewis role in Mike LaFleur's offense: lots of blocking, maybe one target a game.

Jacob Harris, LAR: Harris was drafted in the fourth round this year from Central Florida, and he should have a chance to win the second tight end spot behind incumbent Tyler Higbee. Central Florida primarily used Harris as a downfield threat at receiver, leveraging his impressive athletic ability to stretch defenses. In two years with the Knights, Harris averaged over 20 yards per reception, so he should fit into a role as a receiving tight end as a pro.

Ryan Izzo, HOU: Izzo was given every opportunity to show something for a New England team that had nothing going on at tight end last year, accumulating 626 offensive snaps, and turned it into just 20 targets and pedestrian blocking. Houston traded a seventh-round pick for him this offseason and he may have a leg up on a roster spot because, despite assurances to the contrary, Houston is very much Patriots South. But it says a lot that the O.G.'s watched those 600 snaps and immediately dropped more than $50 million in guarantees on Jonnu Smith and Hunter Henry.

Jesse James, FA: Unsigned at press time, James will forever be remembered for a dropped touchdown catch against New England in 2017 that cost the Steelers the top overall seed. What may not be remembered is that James followed that season with a 27.3% receiving DVOA in 2018. That netted him a four-year, $23-million free agent contract with the Lions, but he only lasted two years in Detroit as his receiving efficiency regressed to his typical standard of -10.0% DVOA per year or worse.

Brevin Jordan, HOU: A highly-productive receiver last year after D'Eriq King transferred to Miami, Jordan was at or near the top of most draftnik "best available" lists as he slid to the Texans in the fifth round, and head coach David Culley accentuated after initial rookie minicamps that "We felt like that guy would probably be gone before the fifth round ... it was a no-brainer with the ability that he has as far as being a prototype tight end in this business." Jordan is a bit of a tweener in that he's undersized for an in-line tight end but, paradoxically, blocked really well in college. Jordan produced but without an elite trait as far as speed/size in his toolkit as a receiver.

Dalton Keene, NE: The Patriots may not be able to roster both of last year's third-round tight ends. If Keene gets the nod, it will because of his potential to be used as an H-Back and fullback as well as an in-line tight end. Keene was a slightly sharper blocker than Devin Asiasi as a rookie, but Asiasi was the better receiver. Neither has really earned any sort of long-term role yet.

Tyler Kroft, NYJ: Kroft had a weird COVID-related season. He got dinged once for being a close contact and once for a false positive but was the only active tight end in Week 7 because he missed a team meeting (a meeting in which his teammates at the position were exposed) for the birth of his daughter, so, swings and roundabouts. When on the field, Kroft blew four blocks in just 88 run-blocking snaps, by far the worst performance of his career.

Matt LaCosse, NE: LaCosse was slowed in 2019 by knee and ankle injuries and opted out of 2020. While he is coming back, it's safe to say the Patriots have moved on at the position, drafting a pair of tight ends in the third round in 2020 and bringing in another pair of high-priced free agents this last offseason. That makes LaCosse's path back to the field tricky, to say the least. (13-131-1, -10.8% DVOA in 2019.)

Marcedes Lewis, GB: Lewis never lived up to his first-round draft selection, but you don't reach the 16th year of your career without doing something right. In Lewis' case, that right thing is blocking. He has seen just 40 targets in three seasons with the Packers, but he has blown just 12 blocks on 1,099 offensive snaps and allowed Aaron Rodgers to be sacked just 1.5 times. Second-year H-back Josiah Deguara will likely eat into Lewis' playing time if he makes a healthy return from his torn ACL, but Lewis has outlasted too much competition to rule out as a relevant 2021 player. (10-107-3, 3.0% DVOA in 2020.)

Hunter Long, MIA: A third-round rookie out of Boston College, Long is a jack-of-all-trades, master-of-none sort of player. He has solid speed, but nothing spectacular. Nice hands, but not a polished route-runner. A sound blocker, but not one that is going to blow up a linebacker. He produced well in college, but doesn't have that A-plus trait that leads you to project him blowing up in the pros. The lack of serious holes in his game should give him a good chance to have a successful career, albeit one that probably tops out at fourth receiving option.

Chris Manhertz, JAX: At the conclusion of Manhertz's senior year at Canisius, "someone from the Bills" (in Manhertz's words) brought the basketball player in for a pro day-type workout. Manhertz didn't attempt a single three-pointer for the Golden Griffins in four seasons, and has similarly been sort of a one-dimensional, block-first tight end in the NFL, mostly for Carolina. It has been a great story and the two-year contract with $4.3 million in guarantees should get Manhertz plenty of playing time while the Jaguars see if they can develop anything else internally at the position.

Tre' McKitty, LAC: Unlike Hunter Henry, McKitty is more of a modern move tight end who should align at H-back or in a wing position as often as possible. A third-round pick, McKitty is not particularly strong or violent, which puts a ceiling on his contributions as a blocker as well as his ability to separate from more physical coverage defenders. The 6-foot-4, 246-pounder is surprisingly agile for his size, though, and proved himself a YAC threat at Florida State in 2018 and 2019 before transferring to Georgia in 2020, where he missed about half the season with knee issues.

Foster Moreau, LV: An early Day 3 pick in 2019, Moreau had a fairly successful rookie season, catching 21 passes for 174 yards and 29.6% DVOA. He was targeted seven times in the red zone that season, catching all seven passes and scoring touchdowns on five of them. However, the team brought in Jason Witten in 2020 with the idea that he would be a better blocker and short-area security blanket than Moreau, which left Moreau in the tough position of not being as good a blocker as Witten but not as good a pass-catcher as Darren Waller. That cut his snap share for 36% to 24%. With Witten gone, it may go back up this season.

Albert Okwuegbunam, DEN: An ACL injury nixed what was shaping up to be a decent rookie season for Okwuegbunam. In just four games, Okwuegbunam snagged 11 passes and was fairly efficient with those chances (17.9% DVOA). Granted, five of those receptions were in the second half of a blowout loss to the Chiefs, but it's still meaningful that Okwuegbunam saw 20% to 40% of the team's snaps in each of his four games. It's unlikely Okwuegbunam ascends beyond a decent No. 2, but that would still be a nice get for someone the Broncos drafted in the fourth round.

Donald Parham, LAC: An undrafted free agent in 2019, Parham spent time with Detroit and Washington (not to mention the XFL's Dallas Renegades) before making his NFL debut with the Chargers in 2020, mostly finding work in and near the red zone. Parham's highlight of the season was a 22-yard touchdown down the seam in Week 7 versus the Jags, showing off both his decent long speed and ability to climb the ladder and find the ball in the air. Parham offers nothing as a blocker, but his size (6-foot-8, 237 pounds) is valuable as a rotational pass catcher. (10-159-3, 5.3% DVOA in 2020.)

Colby Parkinson, SEA: Parkinson was a fourth-round pick in 2020 for Seattle, but a foot injury sustained over the summer prevented him from getting on the field until November. Parkinson will be third on the depth chart to start 2021 behind free agent acquisition Gerald Everett and the returning Will Dissly. He was a massive red zone threat in college, so if Seattle decides to go heavy at the goal line more in 2021, that could be his time to shine.

Adam Shaheen, MIA: Shaheen had three receptions for 51 yards and a touchdown against the Jets in Week 6, the only game in his career where he has topped 50 yards. Shaheen received a two-year extension last year which should mean his roster slot is safe, but the drafting of Hunter Long in the third round will probably cut into his playing time sooner rather than later. (12-150-3, -12.0% DVOA in 2020.)

Kaden Smith, NYG: If you feel the need to enter training camp with veterans Kaden Smith, Kyle Rudolph, and Levine Toilolo battling for the No. 2 tight end job on your six-win team, chances are that you are turning into Dave Gettleman. Take two Hog Mollies and call us before you start telling Marv Levy stories. (18-112-0, -16.4% DVOA in 2020.)

Lee Smith, ATL: After a trade from Buffalo, Smith takes over as the Falcons' blocking tight end (and surprise red zone target). "I'd much rather be wrestling in a phone booth with somebody my size than having little 200-pound submarine missiles diving at my kneecaps all damn day long," the 10-year veteran told the Atlanta media in March. "I'm all about what I've done forever. I just want to grab my lunch pail and come to work."

Jeremy Sprinkle, DAL: The very definition of a useful blocking third tight end and core special-teamer. Bill Callahan tried to make Sprinkle a passing-game weapon when he was Washington's interim coach in 2019. Callahan would also hand off a dozen times per game to a left guard, given the opportunity.

Jace Sternberger, GB: The third-round 2019 draftee was a trendy pick to break out in his sophomore season in 2020. Instead, he had only 12 catches and one touchdown as undrafted third-year player Robert Tonyan emerged as one of Aaron Rodgers' preferred pass-catchers. Despite a reputation as a smooth route-runner and an improved second-year 0.5% receiving DVOA, Sternberger may be in a roster crunch between Tonyan on one hand and superior blockers such as Marcedes Lewis, Josiah Deguera, and Dominique Dafney on the other.

Geoff Swaim, TEN: Swaim has a knack for picking great depth charts for himself. He was with the Cowboys when Jason Witten retired, and that got him a fleeting shot of glory with Dak Prescott in 2018 before he broke his wrist. The Jaguars tight end room was cursed by Julius Thomas and Swaim saw solid snap counts there as well, and finally Swaim benefits from the injury to and defection of Jonnu Smith in Tennessee. Sliding into Anthony Firkser's No. 2 role on the depth chart this year, the opportunities might come for Swaim to randomly wind up with 30 more targets. (9-83-1, 13.6% DVOA in 2020.)

Tim Tebow, JAX: No.

Ian Thomas, CAR: Handed the chance to establish himself as the long-term answer in Carolina following Greg Olsen's departure, Thomas recorded just 20 receptions, as many fumbles as touchdowns, and the second-worst DVOA at the position (-30.1%) in 2020. Thomas started only one of the last five games, and his role as the primary receiving tight end has now been supplanted by incoming free agent Dan Arnold. He may even face a fight to hold onto the backup job ahead of Tommy Tremble as his productive rookie year fades further out of view.

Tommy Tremble, CAR: Widely considered one of the best blockers at his position in this rookie class, this third-round pick from Notre Dame should earn immediate playing time in Carolina as a move tight end who has experience playing I-formation fullback. His receiving game needs work, but Tremble has earned comparisons to Kyle Juszczyk for his versatility and athleticism. That may not mean impressive fantasy production, but it would be a very valuable piece for one of the league's more creative offensive coordinators.

C.J. Uzomah, CIN: Uzomah replaced Tyler Eifert and started for the Bengals for two years before suffering an Achilles injury in Week 2 last year and losing his starting job to Drew Sample. He was medically cleared and ready to compete with Sample for playing time as of April. If "replacement-level guy who hangs around forever and gets too much playing time" were a position on the Bengals depth chart, it would be about 12 deep most years.

Nick Vannett, NO: You might expect a player with the nickname of "Baby Gronk" to be a productive player in his own right, but alas Nick Vannett earned the nickname for his athletic profile, not his production on the field. Although a willing and capable blocker, the sixth-year professional still has fewer than 700 career receiving yards to his name and has only eclipsed 200 receiving yards in a season once. Vannett will probably see the field plenty as a blocker, but 2020 third-round pick Adam Trautman will limit Vannett's opportunities to enhance his receiving numbers. (14-95-1, -28.3% DVOA in 2020.)

2021 Kicker Projections

Listed below are the 2021 KUBIAK projections for kickers. Kicker effectiveness is inconsistent from one year to the next, so the major differentiator between kickers in our fantasy projections is their projected field goal and extra point opportunities that vary based on their offenses, schedules, and other contextual factors. That said, the projections do aim to estimate kicker ranges, which in turn influence the volume of their projected deep field goal attempts.

Kickers are listed with their total fantasy points based on two different scoring systems. For **Pts1**, all field goals are worth three points. For **Pts2**, all field goals up to 39 yards are worth three points, field goals of 40-49 yards are worth four points, and field goals over 50 yards are worth five points. Kickers are also listed with a Risk of Green, Yellow, or Red, as explained in the introduction to the section on quarterbacks.

Note that field goal totals below are rounded, but "fantasy points" are based on the actual projections, so the total may not exactly equal (FG * 3 + XP).

Fantasy Kicker Projections, 2021

Kicker	Team	FG	Pct	XP	Pts1	Pts2	Risk	Kicker	Team	FG	Pct	XP	Pts1	Pts2	Risk
Younghoe Koo	ATL	30-34	87.4%	41	132	150	Green	Randy Bullock	DET	27-32	83.1%	39	120	135	Green
Ryan Succop	TB	28-32	86.9%	48	131	145	Yellow	Nick Folk	NE	27-31	87.3%	37	119	135	Yellow
Harrison Butker	KC	28-32	87.4%	46	130	146	Green	Cairo Santos	CHI	27-32	85.7%	38	119	134	Red
Greg Zuerlein	DAL	27-33	83.1%	46	129	143	Green	Robbie Gould	SF	27-32	82.7%	40	119	134	Green
Jason Sanders	MIA	29-33	86.7%	43	128	146	Green	Cody Parkey	CLE	26-30	85.8%	39	118	133	Red
Daniel Carlson	LV	28-33	84.7%	44	127	141	Green	Evan McPherson	CIN	26-33	80.0%	39	118	132	Red
Justin Tucker	BAL	27-32	84.5%	45	126	141	Green	Dustin Hopkins	WAS	26-32	81.7%	39	117	131	Green
Mason Crosby	GB	26-29	88.8%	49	126	141	Green	Tucker McCann	TEN	24-30	79.3%	44	116	131	Red
Jason Myers	SEA	27-31	89.1%	43	125	142	Green	Jake Elliott	PHI	25-31	81.2%	39	114	127	Green
Tyler Bass	BUF	27-33	80.9%	45	125	141	Green	Ka'imi Fairbairn	HOU	27-32	83.5%	32	112	127	Green
Matt Gay	LAR	27-32	84.4%	42	124	140	Green	Joey Slye	CAR	26-32	81.9%	34	112	125	Yellow
Michael Badgley	LAC	26-33	79.4%	45	123	136	Red	Sam Ficken	NYJ	26-32	81.7%	34	111	125	Red
Brandon McManus	DEN	28-33	86.0%	37	123	141	Green								
Matt Prater	ARI	27-33	81.8%	42	123	137	Green								
Graham Gano	NYG	28-32	89.7%	36	121	138	Green								
Greg Joseph	MIN	25-30	84.1%	44	121	135	Red								
Chris Boswell	PIT	26-30	86.4%	42	121	135	Green								
Wil Lutz	NO	26-32	81.0%	42	121	134	Green								
Josh Lambo	JAX	28-32	88.0%	36	120	137	Green								
Rodrigo Blankenship	IND	26-32	81.6%	41	120	134	Yellow								

Other kickers who may win jobs:							
Kicker	Team	FG	Pct	XP	Pts1	Pts2	Risk
Austin Seibert	CIN	26-33	80.4%	39	118	131	Red
Chase McLaughlin	CLE	25-30	83.7%	40	116	129	Red
Matthew Wright	DET	28-32	85.4%	38	121	137	Red
Eddy Pineiro	IND	27-32	82.4%	40	120	135	Red
Aldrick Rosas	JAX	26-32	80.4%	37	113	127	Red
Sam Sloman	PIT	25-30	82.4%	42	117	130	Red

2021 Fantasy Defense Projections

listed below are the 2021 KUBIAK projections for fantasy team defense. The main elements of team defense projections are:

- Schedule strength is very important for projecting fantasy defense.
- Categories used for scoring in fantasy defense have no consistency from year-to-year whatsoever, with the exception of sacks and interceptions.

Fumble recoveries and defensive touchdowns are forecast based on league averages, rather than the team's totals in these categories from a year ago. This is why the 2021 projections may look very different from the fantasy defense values from the 2020 season. Safeties and shutouts are not common enough to have a significant effect on the projections. Team defenses are also projected with Risk factor of Green, Yellow, or Blue.

In addition to projection of separate categories, we also give an overall total based on our generic fantasy scoring formula: one point for a sack, two points for a fumble recovery or interception, and six points for a touchdown. Remember that certain teams (for example, New England) will score better if your league also gives points for limiting opponents' scoring or yardage. Special teams touchdowns are listed separately and are not included in the fantasy scoring total listed.

Fantasy Team Defense Projections, 2021

Team	Fant Pts	Sack	Int	FR	Def TD	Risk	ST TD	Team	Fant Pts	Sack	Int	FR	Def TD	Risk	ST TD
TB	100	41.2	15.3	8.7	1.8	Green	0.5	CLE	87	31.0	12.1	10.9	1.7	Green	0.6
WAS	100	41.7	14.1	9.6	1.8	Green	0.4	KC	87	34.2	13.4	7.9	1.6	Green	0.7
PIT	97	43.3	13.1	8.9	1.6	Green	0.7	NYJ	86	32.2	12.3	9.8	1.6	Green	0.5
PHI	95	42.6	12.9	8.4	1.6	Green	0.4	ARI	86	38.3	10.9	8.5	1.5	Green	0.5
MIA	94	37.6	14.0	8.9	1.7	Green	0.6	CAR	85	33.3	12.1	9.1	1.6	Green	0.5
LAR	94	42.3	11.3	9.7	1.5	Green	0.6	SF	84	33.7	12.7	7.8	1.6	Blue	0.5
NYG	94	38.1	13.6	9.1	1.7	Green	0.5	CHI	84	33.3	11.4	9.2	1.5	Green	0.6
NO	92	41.7	12.7	7.6	1.6	Yellow	0.9	LAC	83	31.8	11.5	9.4	1.5	Blue	0.6
GB	90	38.2	13.6	7.4	1.6	Green	0.5	TEN	82	27.4	13.6	8.7	1.7	Green	0.6
DEN	89	40.2	11.5	8.6	1.5	Green	0.7	IND	82	35.1	11.1	8.0	1.4	Green	0.8
DAL	88	34.7	12.1	9.9	1.6	Green	0.4	HOU	80	35.2	9.0	9.2	1.3	Green	0.5
BUF	88	34.0	13.4	8.6	1.7	Green	0.7	JAX	78	27.0	12.5	8.2	1.6	Green	0.9
SEA	88	35.1	13.0	8.4	1.6	Green	0.5	DET	78	30.4	10.3	9.1	1.4	Green	0.5
BAL	87	32.7	11.9	10.5	1.6	Green	0.6	MIN	77	26.9	12.0	8.3	1.5	Green	0.5
ATL	87	31.6	12.4	10.3	1.7	Green	0.8	CIN	75	25.1	12.4	7.8	1.5	Green	0.8
NE	87	30.4	15.2	7.7	1.8	Green	1.0	LV	74	29.0	11.0	7.3	1.4	Green	0.8

Projected Defensive Leaders, 2021

Solo Tackles			Total Tackles			Sacks			Interceptions		
Player	Team	Tkl	Player	Team	Tkl	Player	Team	Sacks	Player	Team	Int
R.Smith	CHI	101	B.Wagner	SEA	150	A.Donald	LAR	13.6	T.Mathieu	KC	3.6
D.White	TB	99	Z.Cunningham	HOU	147	T.J.Watt	PIT	13.0	J.Simmons	DEN	3.5
Z.Cunningham	HOU	94	D.Leonard	IND	147	C.Young	WAS	12.8	C.Davis	TB	3.4
B.Wagner	SEA	90	B.Martinez	NYG	145	C.Jones	ARI	12.2	CJ Henderson	JAX	3.3
D.Leonard	IND	90	R.Smith	CHI	145	D.Hunter	MIN	12.2	X.Howard	MIA	3.3
B.Baker	ARI	86	D.White	TB	142	M.Garrett	CLE	11.8	D.J.Reed	SEA	3.3
F.Oluokun	ATL	84	J.Schobert	JAX	130	N.Bosa	SF	11.6	J.Bates	CIN	3.3
J.Baker	MIA	83	J.Smith	DAL	129	Z.Smith	GB	11.1	Q.Diggs	SEA	3.2
J.Smith	DAL	82	J.Baker	MIA	126	B.Burns	CAR	10.8	C.Awuzie	CIN	3.2
E.Kendricks	MIN	82	T.Edmunds	BUF	125	K.Mack	CHI	10.6	H.Smith	MIN	3.1
B.Martinez	NYG	82	E.Kendricks	MIN	125	M.Sweat	WAS	10.6	L.Ryan	NYG	3.1
F.Warner	SF	81	F.Oluokun	ATL	121	J.Bosa	LAC	10.5	S.Griffin	JAX	3.0

College Football Introduction and Statistical Toolbox

There are many ways to construct a college football season projection model, and volumes of data points to consider and test as inputs. Our annual projections have primarily been rooted in recent success measures of offensive and defensive drive and play efficiency. Despite fielding rosters that turn over significantly year after year, college football programs are remarkably consistent and predictable in the aggregate. Some teams unexpectedly leap forward or fall back each season, but the bulk of the 130-team Football Bowl Subdivision (FBS) universe performs within the meat of its projection curve and deviates from the norm only marginally each season.

Our F/+ ratings are strongly correlated year-to-year, and our F/+ preseason ratings are even more strongly correlated with season-ending F/+ ratings. When we scrutinize our projection forecasts of games at the very beginning of seasons in particular, when the only priors available to be applied are data from previous seasons, F/+ preseason ratings project more game winners than Vegas betting lines themselves. Since 2016, teams with an F/+ preseason ratings projection advantage won 78.2% of games in the first two weeks of the season, whereas the closing line favorite according to covers.com won only 76.9% of the same matchups.

The reliability of year-over-year performance measures to predict results was stress-tested in 2020. As of the publication of the *Football Outsiders Almanac* last summer, it was unknown (and in some areas of the country, doubtful) whether a college football season would happen at all due to the global pandemic. We put the finishing touches on our preseason projection model and individual team win distributions just before conferences elected to blow up and rebuild the regular-season schedule. Testing protocols sidelined teams and canceled games abruptly throughout the year. Stretches of the season felt more like an experiment than a traditional competitive endeavor.

Still, there were remarkable team and individual performances that grabbed our attention as with any college football season, punctuated with extraordinary games and exhilarating moments. It was unusual and familiar all at once. And it raised questions throughout the year and into the offseason. How should we best handle data from such a strange season? Can we sort out the good data from the junk data?

Consider that only 534 games were played between FBS opponents in the 2020 season, 240 fewer total games than were played one year prior. The vast majority of those lost games were non-conference matchups. There were only 12 non-conference games played between Power 5 (P5) conference opponents, none in the regular season. There were only 19 non-conference games played between P5 and Group of 5 (G5) opponents, 96 fewer than a year before.

Those "missing" results had a significant impact on established standards of success. Some G5 teams surged in our overall team rating indexes in part because they played with ruthless efficiency in a truncated season, and in part because they never faced a P5 opponent. Would G5 teams have been humbled had the non-conference schedules been more traditional, or did some P5 teams dodge a few embarrassing losses to G5 juggernauts by cancelling those games? We don't really know because they didn't play.

Some of the data we have come to trust as fundamental to our preseason projection model was simply unavailable in 2020, and other projection data inputs are unusually skewed in 2021. Overall, teams are returning much higher percentages of offensive and defensive roster talent than in a typical season because of extended eligibility granted by the NCAA due to the pandemic. Might that mean that last year's data will be an even more important factor for the particularly experienced teams this year? The 2021 season may prove to present even more challenges in projection modeling than 2020. There aren't any applicable reference points for coming out of a "COVID Year" just as there weren't any heading into it.

In spite of all that uncertainty, we're still very confident that the College Football Playoff field will be populated by the same crop of super programs as it has been since its inception. Alabama, Clemson, Ohio State, Oklahoma, and Georgia are all proven contenders, and each projects to have at least a 33% chance to grab a playoff bid. Only six other teams—Wisconsin, Iowa State, Washington, Oregon, Utah, and USC—project to have at least a 10% chance to be selected to the four-team field, and none of that group projects to have better than a 5% chance of running the table undefeated through the regular season. We are higher on more G5 teams than ever—10 of our top-50 team profiles come from outside the power conferences—but we're not high on any of them being true playoff challengers.

We're still at least a few years away from the installation of an expanded 12-team playoff field that college football leaders floated this summer and all of the enhanced season-ending excitement that will come with it. This fall, the hundreds of non-conference regular season games that disappeared from the calendar a year ago are back, and we can't wait. From marquee matchups such as Clemson vs. Georgia in Week 1 to stat-padding blowouts and jaw-dropping upsets that shock the system, every game still means something and we're gearing up to enjoy them and analyze them along with you at FootballOutsiders.com all season long.

No. 1: Alabama Crimson Tide (11.0 mean wins)

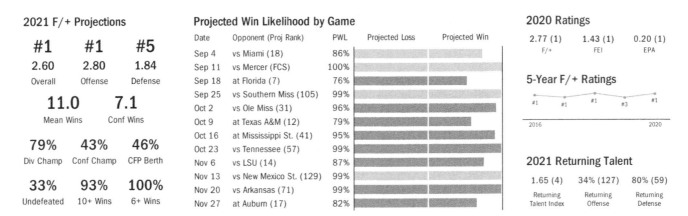

2021 F/+ Projections

#1	#1	#5
2.60	2.80	1.84
Overall	Offense	Defense

11.0	7.1
Mean Wins	Conf Wins

79%	43%	46%
Div Champ	Conf Champ	CFP Berth

33%	93%	100%
Undefeated	10+ Wins	6+ Wins

Projected Win Likelihood by Game

Date	Opponent (Proj Rank)	PWL
Sep 4	vs Miami (18)	86%
Sep 11	vs Mercer (FCS)	100%
Sep 18	at Florida (7)	76%
Sep 25	vs Southern Miss (105)	99%
Oct 2	vs Ole Miss (31)	96%
Oct 9	at Texas A&M (12)	79%
Oct 16	at Mississippi St. (41)	95%
Oct 23	vs Tennessee (57)	99%
Nov 6	vs LSU (14)	87%
Nov 13	vs New Mexico St. (129)	99%
Nov 20	vs Arkansas (71)	99%
Nov 27	at Auburn (17)	82%

2020 Ratings

2.77 (1)	1.43 (1)	0.20 (1)
F/+	FEI	EPA

5-Year F/+ Ratings

#1 (2016), #1, #1, #3, #1 (2020)

2021 Returning Talent

1.65 (4)	34% (127)	80% (59)
Returning Talent Index	Returning Offense	Returning Defense

College Statistics Toolbox

Regular readers of FootballOutsiders.com may be familiar with our college football stats published throughout the year. Others may be learning about our advanced approach to college football stats analysis for the first time by reading this book. In either case, this College Statistics Toolbox section is highly recommended reading before getting into our top-50 team capsules.

Each capsule begins with a statistical snapshot, highlighting the team's 2021 mean wins projection along with projected likelihoods of reaching key performance benchmarks—the chance to claim a division or conference championship, appear in the College Football Playoff, and to meet or exceed total win thresholds. Game-by-game win likelihoods, recent performance data, and other projection factors are also included in the snapshot.

Fremeau Efficiency Index (FEI)

Approximately 20,000 possessions are contested annually in FBS vs. FBS games, an average of 26.5 total game possessions per game. First-half clock-kills and end-of-game garbage drives are filtered out, and the resulting possessions (23.6 per game) are evaluated to determine the success rates of each team's offensive, defensive, and special teams units. Raw possession efficiency rates are adjusted for opponent team unit strength. FEI ratings represent the opponent-adjusted per-possession scoring advantage a team would be expected to have on a neutral field against an average opponent.

Offensive and Defensive FEI

Maximizing success on offensive possessions and minimizing success on opponent possessions begins with an understanding of the value of field position. An average offense facing an average defense may expect to score 2.1 points on average at the conclusion of each drive. If a given drive begins at the offense's own 15-yard line, the average scoring value is only 1.6 points. If it begins at the opponent's 15-yard line, the average scoring value is 4.8 points. Offensive and defensive efficiency is in part a function of the intrinsic value of starting field position.

Drive-ending field position is an important component as well. Touchdowns represent the ultimate goal of an offensive possession but drives that fall short of the end zone can also add scoring value attributed to the offense. National field goal success rates correlate strongly with proximity of the attempt to the end zone and an offense that drives deep into opponent territory to set up a chip-shot field goal generates more scoring value than one that ends a drive at the edge of or outside field goal range.

The value generated by an offense on a given possession is the difference between the drive-ending value and the value of field position at the start of the drive. Offensive efficiency is the average per-possession value generated or lost by the offense. Defensive efficiency is the average per-possession value generated or lost by the defense. Offensive FEI and Defensive FEI are the opponent-adjusted per-possession values generated or lost by these units, adjusted according to the strength of the opponent defense and offenses faced.

F/+ Projected Ratings

Introduced in *Football Outsiders Almanac 2009*, our F/+ ratings combine Brian Fremeau's drive-based FEI ratings and Bill Connelly's play-by-play-based SP+ ratings. Though team efficiency performance leaders at the drive and play level are often similar, there is a clear distinction between the two individual approaches. Merging the two rating systems produces a reliable rating that counterbalances outliers produced by each individual rating system. The resulting metric is both powerfully predictive and sensibly evaluative (Table 1). F/+ overall team ratings, offensive unit ratings, and defensive unit ratings represent each team and unit's projected standard deviation above or below average.

Five years of recent performance history data are the foundation of the annual projection model, weighted for the most recent results. Weighted recruiting ratings from several sources and returning production data are additional projection model inputs.

Table 1. F/+ Projected Ratings Accuracy

	2016	2017	2018	2019	2020
Correlation of Projected F/+ Ratings to End of Year F/+ Ratings	0.850	0.848	0.847	0.822	0.737
Win Percentage of Teams with Projected F/+ Ratings Advantage	0.674	0.669	0.680	0.672	0.650
Win Percentage of Teams in Weeks 0-2 with Projected F/+ Ratings Advantage	0.828	0.822	0.734	0.769	0.684

Mean Wins and Win Distributions

Our win likelihood formula calculates the likelihood of victory for a given team in its individual games based on F/+ projections and the site (home, road, or neutral) of the games. The sum of individual game win likelihoods represents the average number of wins each team projects to tally over the course of its regular season schedule. Potential conference championship games and bowl games are not included in the mean wins calculation.

Individual game win likelihoods are also used to calculate the likelihood of winning a division or conference championship, and to produce win probability distributions. Our formula for calculating the likelihood of a College Football Playoff berth includes factors such as the likelihood of an undefeated regular season record, the likelihood of winning at least 10 games, and the strength of a team's conference and overall schedule.

Strength of Schedule

Our strength of schedule (SOS) calculations are not a simple average of the Projected F/+ ratings of each team's opponents. Instead, SOS represents the average number of losses that an elite team (two standard deviations better than average) would have against the schedule. The distinction is important. An elite team that plays No. 1 Alabama and No. 130 Massachusetts in a two-game stretch would be more likely to lose a game than if it played No. 65 Liberty and No. 66 Wake Forest instead. A simple average of opponent ratings might judge these two schedules to be equivalent.

FBS teams dominate FCS opponents, winning 94.6% of these matchups over the last five seasons. Though not all FCS opponents are created equal, our win likelihood formula only takes the projected strength of the FBS team into account, and all teams with a positive F/+ projected rating are projected to have a 100% win likelihood against any FCS opponents they face.

Returning Talent Index and Returning Production

Developed by Parker Fleming and introduced at Football-Outsiders.com in March, returning talent index is a given team's talent composite weighted by returning production, net transfer ratings, and incoming recruiting ratings, normalized to a mean of 0 and a standard deviation of 1. A returning talent index of 1.5 means a team's talent improved by 1.5 standard deviations relative to average, and a returning talent index of -0.25 means a team's talent got worse by a quarter of a standard deviation relative to average.

Returning offensive and defensive production represent the percentage of key statistical performance measures recorded last season by unit personnel that return to the roster again this season.

Expected Points Added (EPA)

Though not an explicit factor in our F/+ projected ratings, expected points added (EPA) is a versatile, descriptive efficiency metric referenced throughout the top-50 team capsules. EPA measures success and explosion on any given play, considering the context of down, distance, yards to the end zone, and game situation to translate the result of every play into a point value; specifically, the change in point value between the beginning and the end of the play. It is designed to precisely answer the question "How well did a team or unit perform compared to expectations?" on a single play or even across drives, games, and seasons. There are a number of EPA models across the Internet; the college football EPA model in this book was calculated by Parker Fleming based on publicly available play-by-play data.

Brian Fremeau

NCAA Top 50

No. 1: Alabama Crimson Tide (11.0 mean wins)

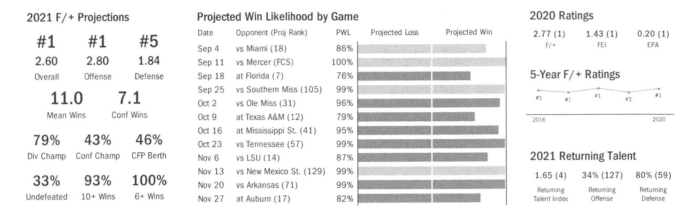

2021 F/+ Projections

#1	#1	#5
2.60	2.80	1.84
Overall	Offense	Defense

11.0	7.1
Mean Wins	Conf Wins

79%	43%	46%
Div Champ	Conf Champ	CFP Berth

33%	93%	100%
Undefeated	10+ Wins	6+ Wins

Projected Win Likelihood by Game

Date	Opponent (Proj Rank)	PWL	Projected Loss	Projected Win
Sep 4	vs Miami (18)	86%		
Sep 11	vs Mercer (FCS)	100%		
Sep 18	at Florida (7)	76%		
Sep 25	vs Southern Miss (105)	99%		
Oct 2	vs Ole Miss (31)	96%		
Oct 9	at Texas A&M (12)	79%		
Oct 16	at Mississippi St. (41)	95%		
Oct 23	vs Tennessee (57)	99%		
Nov 6	vs LSU (14)	87%		
Nov 13	vs New Mexico St. (129)	99%		
Nov 20	vs Arkansas (71)	99%		
Nov 27	at Auburn (17)	82%		

2020 Ratings

2.77 (1)	1.43 (1)	0.20 (1)
F/+	FEI	EPA

5-Year F/+ Ratings

#1   #1   #1   #3   #1
2016 — 2020

2021 Returning Talent

1.65 (4)	34% (127)	80% (59)
Returning Talent Index	Returning Offense	Returning Defense

Nick Saban's Crimson Tide had a lot of pieces in place to put together a big year in 2020 with DeVonta Smith and Jaylen Waddle back at receiver, the offensive line returning multiple starters, and Najee Harris at running back. The main question was whether Mac Jones would continue to grow and be able to manage it all effectively or whether 5-star freshman Bryce Young would supplant him.

As it turned out, Mac was more than ready to take over for Tua Tagovailoa. One year after Tagovailoa threw for 11.3 yards per attempt with 33 touchdowns to three interceptions over nine games, Mac Jones threw for 11.2 yards per attempt with 41 touchdowns to four interceptions over 13 games, which included an SEC Championship Game and two playoff games, all victories for the Tide. The talent Alabama brought to bear on offense was completely overwhelming, finishing second nationally with 0.39 EPA/play, and then seeing five offensive players taken in the first round of the NFL draft and two more in later rounds. On top of those losses, offensive coordinator Steve Sarkisian left to become the head coach at the University of Texas and took offensive line coach Kyle Flood and tight ends coach Jeff Banks with him.

Such sweeping departures suggest "reload vs rebuild?" narratives for the offense. The case for this simply being a reload includes the sheer talent accumulated by Nick Saban along with his track record for putting it all together. Young is now a sophomore quarterback working behind an offensive line with three returning starters, including massive offensive tackle Evan Neal (6-foot-7, 360 pounds) who slides from right tackle to left tackle. Wide receiver John Metchie stepped up in 2020 after Waddle went down with injury and had 55 catches for 916 yards and six touchdowns. Young slot receiver Slade Bolden is also back after snagging 24 catches for 270 yards and young power back Brian Robinson Jr.

steps in for Harris.

Nick Saban hired Bill O'Brien, fresh off being fired as the head coach of the Houston Texans, to guide it all. Whereas last year's team was all about landing shots on RPOs and a particularly nasty brand of play-action devised by Sarkisian to mimic RPOs, this squad may evolve some. Young is a particularly mobile passer who may shine brightest when allowed to move around and find the shifty Bolden, perhaps in some of the spread passing sets Bill O'Brien utilized in the NFL. The Tide will continue to have an imposing run game and accompanying passing attack, of course.

Defense is where this squad may find a National Championship ceiling. This is the best-looking Alabama defensive unit since the 2017 title team which was powered by Minkah Fitzpatrick and Daron Payne. Last year's unit finished just 57th nationally with 0.167 EPA/play but took fewer losses from the draft or graduation and now returns multiple starters.

This is their strongest looking unit up the middle of the field in some time. They finally have an upperclassman nose tackle in D.J. Dale, a third-year starter who's only now a junior, and behind him return inside linebacker Christian Harris, safeties Jordan Battle and DeMarcco Hellams, and nickel Malachi Moore. They'll need to find another lockdown corner after losing Patrick Surtain in the first round of the draft, but they have options with senior Josh Jobe joined by 5-star freshman Kool-Aid McKinstry. (Yes, that's his name.)

If the Tide are going to bounce back with another championship defense in the Saban era, this might be the year it happens. It's possible they'll need it, but the overall talent level on offense is such that a strong offseason and strong plan by Bill O'Brien could allow them to maintain their more recent formula of simply blowing away the competition by dropping 50 points a game on opponents.

No. 2: Clemson Tigers (11.3 mean wins)

2021 F/+ Projections

#2	#4	#1
2.25	1.79	2.32
Overall	Offense	Defense

11.3	7.7
Mean Wins	Conf Wins

98%	73%	63%
Div Champ	Conf Champ	CFP Berth

46%	99%	100%
Undefeated	10+ Wins	6+ Wins

Projected Win Likelihood by Game

Date	Opponent (Proj Rank)	PWL	Projected Loss	Projected Win
Sep 4	vs Georgia (5)	64%		
Sep 11	vs S. Carolina St. (FCS)	100%		
Sep 18	vs Georgia Tech (85)	99%		
Sep 25	at NC State (64)	94%		
Oct 2	vs Boston College (77)	99%		
Oct 15	at Syracuse (100)	99%		
Oct 23	at Pittsburgh (44)	90%		
Oct 30	vs Florida St. (75)	99%		
Nov 6	at Louisville (45)	91%		
Nov 13	vs Connecticut (127)	99%		
Nov 20	vs Wake Forest (66)	99%		
Nov 27	at South Carolina (92)	99%		

2020 Ratings

1.99 (3)	0.95 (3)	0.13 (8)
F/+	FEI	EPA

5-Year F/+ Ratings

#2   #5   #3   #4   #3
2016   2020

2021 Returning Talent

1.55 (6)	43% (123)	88% (34)
Returning Talent Index	Returning Offense	Returning Defense

The world got a glimpse of the post-Trevor Lawrence era last season in Clemson's highly anticipated battle on the road against Notre Dame. True freshman quarterback D.J. Uiagalelei stepped in for Lawrence (out for COVID protocol) and threw for 449 yards and two touchdowns while rushing for one more and taking the Irish into overtime before succumbing to defeat.

Uiagalelei is a different sort of player than Lawrence. He's 6-foot-4, 250 pounds and can bring some power running skills to the position while also possessing a strong and accurate arm to execute Clemson's spread passing game. The Tigers should be able to spread opponents out extra thin in 2021 by flexing their running backs out wide while leaning on Uiagalelei to allow them to maintain a power run dimension between the tackles. Last season's team was a touch limited trying to run inside against better opponents. Their rebuilt offensive line struggled to move the defensive tackles from Notre Dame or Ohio State in the team's two losses. Clemson also lacked the same level of skill talent they had boasted at receiver in 2018 or 2019. They finished 16th in offensive EPA with 0.28 EPA/play.

Star receiver Justyn Ross is looking to make a comeback after missing 2020 with back surgery. When healthy, Ross was dominant in both 2018 and 2019 with a combined 1,865 receiving yards and 17 touchdowns. If he is back on form, the Tigers are a clear favorite to make the playoffs again. Otherwise, they'll need the next generation of wideouts to make a leap. Slot receiver Amari Rodgers and outside receiver Cornell Powell are both gone now. Tight end Braden Galloway was just the fifth option in the passing game a year ago but had the most catches of any returning target. Juniors Joseph Ngata and Frank Ladson will take the baton at outside receiver with Ross likely moving inside to replace Rodgers.

The offensive line is retooling a bit as well, moving on from the Jackson Carman era at left tackle and promoting sopho-more Walker Parks to cover Uiagalelei's blind side. The rest of the offensive line returns three starters from a year ago and will hope to generate more movement against top opponents. Clemson also needs a new feature running back after losing superstar Travis Etienne and may opt for speed and receiving skill in choosing the replacement given Uiagalelei's aptitude for the power run game. Watch for freshman Will Shipley to emerge here as the season progresses.

Much like Alabama, Clemson's hope for finding wins while breaking in a new generation of offensive players is to play great defense. Defensive coordinator Brent Venables brings back a treasure trove of experienced talent for a unit which finished 41st in EPA margin in 2020 with 0.151 EPA/play. Clemson also gains an extra year of eligibility for safety Nolan Turner and linebacker James Skalski.

Up front, the Tigers hope for a return to their 2018 standard of fielding future pros at every position. Tackle Tyler Davis is back and joined by rising sophomore and former 5-star recruit Bryan Bresee. Myles Murphy, K.J. Henry, Justin Foster, and Xavier Thomas will create a rotation at defensive end. Behind them, two starting linebackers come back along with strong safety Lannden Zanders. At strongside linebacker, where the Tigers have started big-time playmakers in the past such as Dorian O'Daniel and Isaiah Simmons, the Tigers lost Mike Jones who transferred to LSU. This should lead to the promotion of Trenton Simpson, another 5-star recruit with a Simmons-esque profile as a 6-foot-3, 225-pound athlete who can cover and blitz (four sacks in 2020).

The corners need to improve after a spotty 2020 and a big year from one senior Mario Goodrich would give the Tigers one of their most imposing and athletic defenses yet. The ceiling for the team will ultimately hinge on exactly how dominant the defensive line can be and then whether Justyn Ross is healthy or another star receiver can emerge and consistently get open for Uiagalelei.

No. 3: Ohio State Buckeyes (10.7 mean wins)

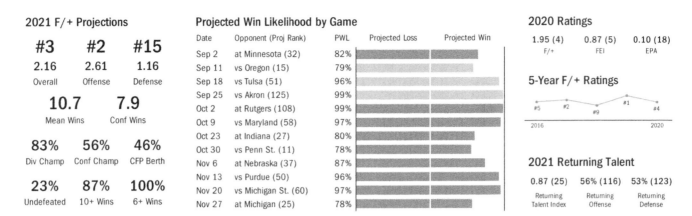

2021 F/+ Projections

#3	#2	#15
2.16	2.61	1.16
Overall	Offense	Defense

10.7	7.9
Mean Wins	Conf Wins

83%	56%	46%
Div Champ	Conf Champ	CFP Berth

23%	87%	100%
Undefeated	10+ Wins	6+ Wins

Projected Win Likelihood by Game

Date	Opponent (Proj Rank)	PWL	Projected Loss	Projected Win
Sep 2	at Minnesota (32)	82%		
Sep 11	vs Oregon (15)	79%		
Sep 18	vs Tulsa (51)	96%		
Sep 25	vs Akron (125)	99%		
Oct 2	at Rutgers (108)	99%		
Oct 9	vs Maryland (58)	97%		
Oct 23	at Indiana (27)	80%		
Oct 30	vs Penn St. (11)	78%		
Nov 6	at Nebraska (37)	87%		
Nov 13	vs Purdue (50)	96%		
Nov 20	vs Michigan St. (60)	97%		
Nov 27	at Michigan (25)	78%		

2020 Ratings

1.95 (4)	0.87 (5)	0.10 (18)
F/+	FEI	EPA

5-Year F/+ Ratings

#5 #2 #9 #1 #4

2016   2020

2021 Returning Talent

0.87 (25)	56% (116)	53% (123)
Returning Talent Index	Returning Offense	Returning Defense

The Buckeyes have a quiet advantage over many of the other top-rated teams in the country: the return of key offensive players. While Ohio State is losing first-round quarterback Justin Fields, they will return leading receivers Chris Olave (50 catches, 729 yards, and seven touchdowns) and Garrett Wilson (43 catches, 723 yards, and six touchdowns) along with starting offensive tackles Thayer Munford and Nicholas Petit-Frere.

Last year's team put together an imposing formula of running the football, often with the NFL's favored wide zone-blocking scheme and taking deep shots on play-action to Olave and Wilson running adjustable vertical patterns. Justin Fields has a very strong arm for reaching the vertical routes and threw for 2,100 yards in eight games at 9.3 yards per attempt with 22 touchdowns and six interceptions. For all those traits, the Buckeyes finished 17th in EPA margin on offense with 0.277 EPA/play.

The run game will need to be retooled with a new cast of blockers and the backfield will see newer faces, most likely redshirt freshman quarterback C.J. Stroud and redshirt junior running back Master Teague. The spring game was promising and reports from Columbus have been optimistic about Stroud, who has a knack for progression passing and delivering accurate throws. An X-factor could be freshman running back TreVeyon Henderson, a 5-star recruit who was an early enrollee for the Buckeyes. At tight end, the Buckeyes will feature Jeremy Ruckert, mostly a red zone target with five touchdowns out of 13 overall catches in 2020. Next to him at inside receiver figures to be Jaxon Smith-Njigba as Wilson moves outside opposite Olave.

Ohio State was grievously limited last season by injuries and off-field issues for their defense, which finished 98th at 0.241 EPA/play, and got caught in a drubbing from Alabama in which Heisman winner DeVonta Smith had 12 catches for 215 yards and three touchdowns. The Buckeyes were able to get away with playing their base 4-3 defense against Clemson by spreading the linebackers wide and daring the Tigers to run inside on a talented tackle tandem lead by Tommy Togiai. Against Alabama, their 4-3 and occasional 4-4 formations on defense were successful in stopping Najee Harris and the run game but at the expense of allowing Alabama to destroy their secondary.

The secondary lost three starting defensive backs to the NFL after 2019 and another one (Shaun Wade) in this year's NFL draft. Ohio State's strategy under defensive coordinator Kerry Coombs has been heavy on playing man coverage when possible. Upperclassman cornerbacks Sevyn Banks and Cameron Brown have yet to play at the level of Damon Arnette and Jeff Okudah in 2019 but Ohio State will have another offseason to try and recreate the magic of their previous playoff secondary.

The defensive line should be in better shape with Zach Harrison and Tyreke Smith as bookends and returning tackle Haskell Garrett paired with big Jerron Cage inside. Inside linebacker is also retooling but could gain a boost from rumored USC transfer Palaie Gaoteote, a thick and powerful player who missed most of 2020 with injury. There's a lot of talent across the defense overall and they seem poised to generate real problems for opponents with their big men along the defensive line, but can they duplicate their ability to match up and lock down opponents' top receiving threats as they did in 2019 or will they be vulnerable against higher-level passing teams?

No. 4: Oklahoma Sooners (10.3 mean wins)

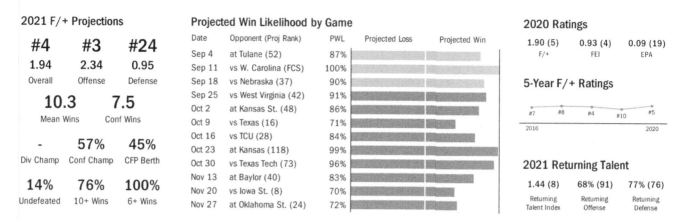

2021 F/+ Projections

#4	#3	#24
1.94	2.34	0.95
Overall	Offense	Defense

10.3	7.5
Mean Wins	Conf Wins

-	57%	45%
Div Champ	Conf Champ	CFP Berth

14%	76%	100%
Undefeated	10+ Wins	6+ Wins

Projected Win Likelihood by Game

Date	Opponent (Proj Rank)	PWL	Projected Loss	Projected Win
Sep 4	at Tulane (52)	87%		
Sep 11	vs W. Carolina (FCS)	100%		
Sep 18	vs Nebraska (37)	90%		
Sep 25	vs West Virginia (42)	91%		
Oct 2	at Kansas St. (48)	86%		
Oct 9	vs Texas (16)	71%		
Oct 16	vs TCU (28)	84%		
Oct 23	at Kansas (118)	99%		
Oct 30	vs Texas Tech (73)	96%		
Nov 13	at Baylor (40)	83%		
Nov 20	vs Iowa St. (8)	70%		
Nov 27	at Oklahoma St. (24)	72%		

2020 Ratings

1.90 (5)	0.93 (4)	0.09 (19)
F/+	FEI	EPA

5-Year F/+ Ratings

#7   #8   #4   #10   #5
2016   2020

2021 Returning Talent

1.44 (8)	68% (91)	77% (76)
Returning Talent Index	Returning Offense	Returning Defense

The Oklahoma Sooners are in less of a "reload" stage and more of a "reloaded and aimed" position. Oklahoma had to replace CeeDee Lamb and Jalen Hurts in 2020 and did so with redshirt freshman quarterback Spencer Rattler, often throwing to true freshman receiver Marvin Mims.

After a solid 2020 in which they finished 39th in offensive EPA with 0.21 EPA/play, Rattler and Mims return for 2021. The Sooners will also bring back three starting offensive linemen, star running back Kennedy Brooks (who opted out in 2020), and receivers Jadon Haselwood and Theo Wease, who are aiming to finally break out after quiet seasons as underclassmen. Oklahoma also returns Nik Bonitto and Isaiah Thomas after the pair had 16.5 sacks in 2020. The Sooners leaned on defense more in 2020, finishing 35th nationally with 0.133 EPA/play.

Overall, the Sooners have a lot of knowns and their biggest questions center around how much improvement to expect from quarterback Spencer Rattler in his second season. In Year 1, Rattler threw for 3,031 yards at 9.6 yards per attempt with 28 touchdowns to seven interceptions and had multiple highs and lows over the course of the year. Oklahoma opened the Big 12 slate with consecutive losses against Kansas State and Iowa State, both of which featured Rattler throwing interceptions on the Sooners' final possessions in single-possession games. During the Red River Shootout against Texas, Rattler had an interception and fumble early which set up a pair of Texas scores before he was benched until after the half to adjust and relax. Then Rattler bounced back to lead the Sooners to a victory in triple overtime and OU didn't lose again in 2020.

Head coach Lincoln Riley is hoping Rattler's growing pains in 2020 will lead to a major leap in 2021 and a playoff run. In pursuit of this aim, the Sooners added Tennessee transfers Wanya Morris (left tackle), Eric Gray (running back), and Key Lawrence (defensive back). Oklahoma lost promising receiver Trejan Bridges and running back Seth McGowan after off-field issues in the spring but brought in Arkansas transfer wide receiver Mike Woods and LSU running back Tre Bradford. After the infusion of talent through the transfer portal, there aren't any glaring holes on the roster.

It's a reasonable bet Riley fashions another lethal offense with Rattler. The more interesting dimension to the Sooners over the last two seasons has been their defense since Riley hired defensive coordinator Alex Grinch.

Grinch immediately downsized the Oklahoma defensive front into a 3-down/4-down hybrid front which features lighter personnel such as 290-pounder Perrion Winfrey at the nose flanked by 284-pound Jalen Redmond and 262-pound Isaiah Thomas as end/tackles and the 234-pound Bonitto at outside linebacker. The Sooners are constantly moving and shuffling along the front to confuse blocking assignments and help both linemen and linebackers shoot gaps and disrupt schemes. This dynamic has been more pronounced each year under Grinch and in 2020 the Sooners were dominating contests with the ability of their speedy defensive line to create negative plays.

The middle of the defense is loaded with experience and depth. Linebackers Brian Asamoah, Dashaun White, and David Ugwoegbu will battle for two spots while Patrick Fields, Delarrin Turner-Yell, and Justin Harrington battle for two safety positions.

At nickelback, the Sooners lost two-year starter Brendan Radley-Hiles to Washington via the transfer portal. Radley-Hiles was a smaller defender at 5-foot-9, 180 pounds who struggled with bigger players but offered the Sooners a lot of flexibility with his coverage skill. In addition to replacing Radley-Hiles, the Sooners will start young cornerbacks D.J. Graham and Woodi Washington. Their growth and play in 2021 will set the ceiling for the defense.

To get back to the playoffs OU needs only to beat Nebraska at home and navigate a Big 12 schedule which brings Iowa State and TCU to Norman.

No. 5: Georgia Bulldogs (10.0 mean wins)

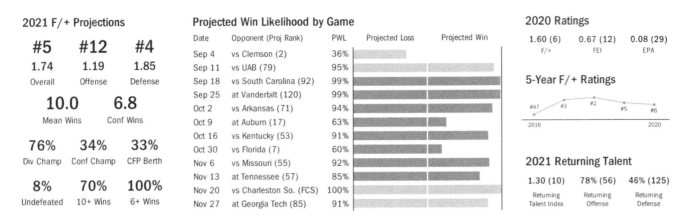

2021 F/+ Projections

#5	#12	#4
1.74	1.19	1.85
Overall	Offense	Defense

10.0	6.8
Mean Wins	Conf Wins

76%	34%	33%
Div Champ	Conf Champ	CFP Berth

8%	70%	100%
Undefeated	10+ Wins	6+ Wins

Projected Win Likelihood by Game

Date	Opponent (Proj Rank)	PWL
Sep 4	vs Clemson (2)	36%
Sep 11	vs UAB (79)	95%
Sep 18	vs South Carolina (92)	99%
Sep 25	at Vanderbilt (120)	99%
Oct 2	vs Arkansas (71)	94%
Oct 9	at Auburn (17)	63%
Oct 16	vs Kentucky (53)	91%
Oct 30	vs Florida (7)	60%
Nov 6	vs Missouri (55)	92%
Nov 13	at Tennessee (57)	85%
Nov 20	vs Charleston So. (FCS)	100%
Nov 27	at Georgia Tech (85)	91%

2020 Ratings

1.60 (6)	0.67 (12)	0.08 (29)
F/+	FEI	EPA

5-Year F/+ Ratings

#47 (2016) · #3 · #2 · #5 · #6 (2020)

2021 Returning Talent

1.30 (10)	78% (56)	46% (125)
Returning Talent Index	Returning Offense	Returning Defense

Kirby Smart's Bulldogs have been stockpiling talent for several years now. The results have been positive, including a 52-14 record, three SEC Eastern division titles, and a National Championship appearance, but everyone is still waiting for the championship breakthrough. Many have 2021 pegged as the year when it needs to happen and Georgia has certainly behaved as though it sees a title window opportunity.

The Bulldogs made good use of the relaxed rules on transfers to add defensive backs Derion Kendrick from Clemson and Tykee Smith from West Virginia along with former 5-star tight end Arik Gilbert from LSU. They join a team returning four starters on the offensive line and another former 5-star transfer, quarterback J.T. Daniels.

Daniels stepped in for the Dawgs at the end of 2020 and threw for 1,231 yards at 10.3 yards per attempt with 10 touchdowns to two interceptions in just four games. He had a mixed outing overall against Cincinnati, mostly because of the pressure the Bearcats put on him (three sacks), but also throwing for 392 yards at 10.3 yards per attempt against Cincinnati's pressure and helping to set up a game-winning field goal. Georgia finished 57th with 0.177 EPA/play on offense but Daniels' ability to hit vertical shots down the field or to the sidelines paired very effectively with the Bulldogs' power run game late in the year. Improvement is expected.

The complication is at receiver, where George Pickens could be a potential breakout star in college football after a 513-yard season in 2020 but now owns a future clouded by a torn ACL suffered during spring practice. The Bulldogs do still have Kearis Jackson, who had 514 yards a year ago, and then big promising tight end Darnell Washington and potential flex tight

end transfer Arik Gilbert (ex-LSU). The running game is not a concern with running backs Zamir White and Kenny McIntosh both returning. Starting 2020 linemen Jamaree Salyer (6-foot-4, 325 pounds) and Justin Shaffer (6-foot-4, 330 pounds) could end up giving the Dawgs All-SEC caliber players at both guard positions should Salyer slide inside from tackle.

Defense isn't expected to be an issue at Georgia while Kirby Smart is around but the Dawgs do need to replace a lot of starters. The biggest losses are on the perimeter, as cornerbacks Eric Stokes and Tyson Campbell were drafted within a few picks of each other late in the first round and early in the second. Edge rusher Azeez Ojulari went in the second round, longtime linebacker Monty Rice went in the third, and safety Richard LeCounte and nickelback Mark Webb went later in the draft.

The Bulldogs have three different former 5-star recruits vying to replace Ojulari on the edge and former 5-star recruit Nakobe Dean is back at inside linebacker after leading the team in tackles in 2020. Adding West Virginia's star nickel Tykee Smith was a big win for the defense and returning safety Lewis Cine was second in tackles last season.

If they can find a lockdown corner from among Jalen Kimber, Kelee Ringo, or incoming Clemson transfer Derion Kendrick, then the depth of freakishly big and athletic defenders up front should allow the formation of another top defense. They finished 27th in 2020 with 0.11 EPA/play.

The schedule includes an opener against Clemson in Charlotte, a home game against Arkansas, and a road trip against Auburn from the West. The path to their goals will ultimately run through the Florida Gators in their rivalry game in Jacksonville.

No. 6: Wisconsin Badgers (9.6 mean wins)

2021 F/+ Projections

#6	#32	#2
1.56	0.70	1.96
Overall	Offense	Defense

9.6	7.1
Mean Wins	Conf Wins

60%	20%	14%
Div Champ	Conf Champ	CFP Berth

5%	53%	100%
Undefeated	10+ Wins	6+ Wins

Projected Win Likelihood by Game

Date	Opponent (Proj Rank)	PWL	Projected Loss	Projected Win
Sep 4	vs Penn St. (11)	64%		
Sep 11	vs Eastern Michigan (91)	97%		
Sep 25	vs Notre Dame (10)	58%		
Oct 2	vs Michigan (25)	74%		
Oct 9	at Illinois (95)	93%		
Oct 16	vs Army (82)	93%		
Oct 23	at Purdue (50)	80%		
Oct 30	vs Iowa (9)	63%		
Nov 6	at Rutgers (108)	98%		
Nov 13	vs Northwestern (61)	89%		
Nov 20	vs Nebraska (37)	83%		
Nov 27	at Minnesota (32)	69%		

2020 Ratings

0.99 (18)	0.37 (26)	0.04 (64)
F/+	FEI	EPA

5-Year F/+ Ratings

#12 #6 #25 #6 #18
2016   2020

2021 Returning Talent

0.56 (40)	73% (71)	78% (70)
Returning Talent Index	Returning Offense	Returning Defense

For a moment early in 2020, the Badgers appeared to be a potential Big Ten contender as redshirt freshman quarterback Graham Mertz was throwing five touchdown passes in a 45-7 rout of Illinois in the season opener. As it turned out, the Badgers did not have their normally overpowering rushing attack rolling to add up the normal "run game plus defense equals Big Ten West crown" equation. The passing game also proved to be less capable of propelling the offense than the opening-game success suggested.

The Badgers struggled through their schedule after initial success against Illinois and hapless Michigan, dropping three consecutive contests with Northwestern, Indiana, and Iowa. Over those three losses Mertz completed 56% of his passes for 601 yards at 5.3 yards per attempt with one touchdown pass and five interceptions. The Badgers finished 99th in the nation at 0.092 EPA/play on offense.

In 2021 the goal for Wisconsin will be clear: to rebuild the run game and offer Mertz more play-action opportunities. The line will return four starters, all redshirt seniors. Running back Jalen Berger was established as the main guy during the 2020 season but he'll have fresh competition from Clemson transfer Chez Mellusi, who could bring more speed to offer a change up to Berger's power running. The passing game will include weapons such as slot receiver Danny Davis, outside receiver (and strong breakout candidate) Kendric Pryor, and tight end Jake Ferguson.

Defensively, the Badgers were stout in 2020 and ranked eighth with 0.053 EPA/play allowed. They return nearly a full lineup's worth of players with starting experience in defensive coordinator Jim Leonhard's schemes. Leonhard utilizes a few different varieties of base 3-4 defense but switches to a 2-4-5 for nickel sub packages. In either event, the beating heart of this defense is the linebacker play. At inside linebacker the Badgers are in great shape with Jack Sanborn and Leo Chenal back after leading the team in tackles in 2020. On the outside, they'll be looking for growth from Nick Herbig and Noah Burks, who combined for only two sacks last season.

The Badger secondary brings back veteran safeties Collin Wilder and Scott Nelson but more importantly will have all three of Faion Hicks, Donte Burton, and Caesar Williams to man the top three cornerback positions in the nickel package. The Badgers are at their best when they can play some match/man coverage outside and introduce uncertainty in the middle of the field regarding where the linebackers and safeties will end up after the snap.

Overall, this looks like a pretty typical Wisconsin team with a potential boost if they can add a more dangerous play-action passing component to the normal formula. Their schedule is not typical though and considerably more difficult than in seasons when they've coasted to the Big Ten title playing mostly West division teams.

The Big Ten draw is challenging but the toughest games are mostly at home. Penn State, Michigan, Iowa, and Northwestern all travel up to Camp Randall. However, Wisconsin also has a home game against Army and a trip to Chicago to play Notre Dame. It's one of the tougher schedules we've seen for the Badgers in recent seasons and it could be tricky for them to aim higher than winning the West and making a return trip to the Big Ten Championship Game. A playoff resume would require minimal slip-ups on a schedule with several top 25-caliber opponents.

No. 7: Florida Gators (9.2 mean wins)

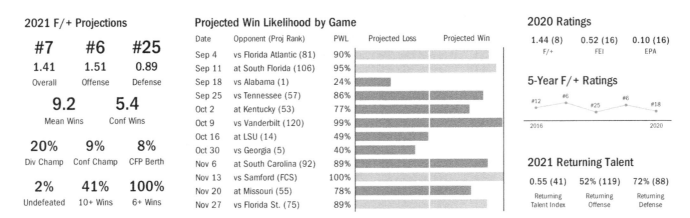

2021 F/+ Projections

#7	#6	#25
1.41	1.51	0.89
Overall	Offense	Defense

9.2	5.4
Mean Wins	Conf Wins

20%	9%	8%
Div Champ	Conf Champ	CFP Berth

2%	41%	100%
Undefeated	10+ Wins	6+ Wins

Projected Win Likelihood by Game

Date	Opponent (Proj Rank)	PWL
Sep 4	vs Florida Atlantic (81)	90%
Sep 11	at South Florida (106)	95%
Sep 18	vs Alabama (1)	24%
Sep 25	vs Tennessee (57)	86%
Oct 2	at Kentucky (53)	77%
Oct 9	vs Vanderbilt (120)	99%
Oct 16	at LSU (14)	49%
Oct 30	vs Georgia (5)	40%
Nov 6	at South Carolina (92)	89%
Nov 13	vs Samford (FCS)	100%
Nov 20	at Missouri (55)	78%
Nov 27	vs Florida St. (75)	89%

2020 Ratings

1.44 (8)	0.52 (16)	0.10 (16)
F/+	FEI	EPA

5-Year F/+ Ratings

#12 · #6 · #25 · #6 · #18
2016 — 2020

2021 Returning Talent

0.55 (41)	52% (119)	72% (88)
Returning Talent Index	Returning Offense	Returning Defense

Although the Gators lost several big games in 2020—Texas A&M, Alabama in the SEC title game, and then Oklahoma in the Cotton Bowl (albeit with multiple starters opting out)—it was a pretty strong "proof of concept" season for head coach Dan Mullen. The Gators built a lethal spread offense and did so with a former 3-star quarterback (Kyle Trask) who backed up cross-state rival D'Eriq King (Miami) in high school. Trask had a sensational season throwing to a dominant pair of receivers in slot Kadarius Toney and tight end Kyle Pitts.

Trask finished with 4,283 yards at 9.8 yards per attempt with 43 touchdowns to eight interceptions, Pitts had 770 yards and 12 touchdowns, and Toney had 984 yards and 10 more. It was a master class session by Mullen of scheming to the strengths of the roster and using the spread offense as a way to create space and matchups for top players. Florida finished 10th with 0.305 EPA/play on offense.

This forced a recalibration of the reputation Mullen built at Utah, Florida, and Mississippi State with dual-threat quarterbacks Alex Smith, Tim Tebow, and Dak Prescott. As it happens though, the 2021 Gators will probably look like one of those teams.

Emory Jones is next in line to replace Trask and he's a redshirt junior who spent the last two seasons as a change-of-pace quarterback who would come in to run the ball. At 6-foot-2 and 210 pounds, he's a faster and more explosive runner than we've seen in the past from Mullen. If he doesn't get the job, it will probably go to redshirt freshman Anthony Richardson, who at 6-foot-4 and 232 pounds is closer to Tebow or Prescott in terms of his skill set. The offensive line the Gators will put in front of their dual-threat quarterback will feature an interior of Ethan White (6-foot-5, 346 pounds), Stewart Reese (6-foot-6, 354 pounds), and Josh Braun (6-foot-6, 352 pounds), who have an obvious profile

as straight-ahead mashers. It looks like Tebow-style power-option football is back in Gainesville.

Florida has a number of talented running backs, including returning starter Dameon Pierce and Clemson transfer Demarkcus Bowman. The upshot of having a dual-threat quarterback who can run power schemes between the tackles, as both Jones and Richardson can, is that it will be very easy for Mullen to scheme open speed on the perimeter for screens and 1-on-1 option routes. Redshirt junior wideout Jacob Copeland had 435 yards a year ago and likely owns the slot with Toney gone while big Justin Shorter (6-foot-5, 227 pounds) could potentially step into the Pitts role getting isolated 1-on-1 outside against undersized defensive backs.

Defensively, the Gators have a lot to clean up after finishing 111th with 0.281 EPA/play. They're using the transfer portal to help shore up the major weak spots. They've struggled with run defense for years and added Auburn defensive tackle Daquan Newkirk and Penn State nose tackle Antonio Shelton to give them some needed size and obstructive capacity inside. Defensive end Brenton Cox already transferred from rival Georgia a year ago and will be a weapon in the pass rush after collecting 3.5 sacks for the Gators in 2020.

Inside linebackers Ventrell Miller and Mohamoud Diabate return after leading the team in tackles and star cornerback Kaiir Elam will be in a junior "contract" year. There are a lot of pieces on defense for the Gators and they typically don't struggle to find skill athletes for the secondary given their recruiting access to South Florida. If they can build a stronger run defense, the Gators will be situated to win games in the SEC with a power-spread offensive approach which helps them control games in the trenches. But their schedule will make this a challenge as their West division draw includes Alabama and a road trip to LSU.

No. 8: Iowa State Cyclones (8.9 mean wins)

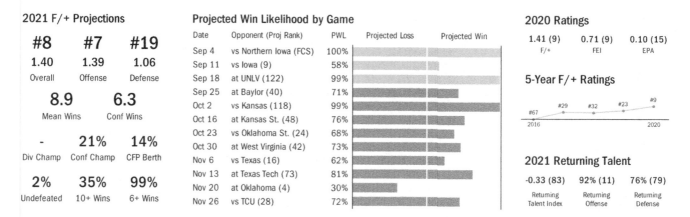

2021 F/+ Projections

#8	#7	#19
1.40	1.39	1.06
Overall	Offense	Defense

8.9	6.3
Mean Wins	Conf Wins

-	21%	14%
Div Champ	Conf Champ	CFP Berth

2%	35%	99%
Undefeated	10+ Wins	6+ Wins

Projected Win Likelihood by Game

Date	Opponent (Proj Rank)	PWL	Projected Loss	Projected Win
Sep 4	vs Northern Iowa (FCS)	100%		
Sep 11	vs Iowa (9)	58%		
Sep 18	at UNLV (122)	99%		
Sep 25	at Baylor (40)	71%		
Oct 2	vs Kansas (118)	99%		
Oct 16	at Kansas St. (48)	76%		
Oct 23	vs Oklahoma St. (24)	68%		
Oct 30	at West Virginia (42)	73%		
Nov 6	vs Texas (16)	62%		
Nov 13	at Texas Tech (73)	81%		
Nov 20	at Oklahoma (4)	30%		
Nov 26	vs TCU (28)	72%		

2020 Ratings

1.41 (9)	0.71 (9)	0.10 (15)
F/+	FEI	EPA

5-Year F/+ Ratings

#67 (2016)   #29   #32   #23   #9 (2020)

2021 Returning Talent

-0.33 (83)	92% (11)	76% (79)
Returning Talent Index	Returning Offense	Returning Defense

Iowa State are media darlings for the 2021 season because they have the highest number of obvious "knowns" of most any team you've ever read about in a preseason college football publication. They return 11 starters on offense, including dangerous slot receiver Tarique Milton who was injured for most of 2020, and nine starters on defense. Among the returnees are quarterback Brock "Pump Fake" Purdy, star running back Breece Hall, the entire back eight on defense, and top pass-rusher Will McDonald.

Their losses are meaningful but relatively light given college football's regular annual turnover. They're losing one of their three main tight ends, Dylan Soehner, who was an essential component last season because of his superior blocking. Soehner could vacillate between giving them a sixth offensive lineman to help a spotty line hold up or release into the flats or down the seams as a huge and sure-handed target. The offense was 25th following this formula with 0.239 EPA/play.

On defense the main loss is starting end and other top pass-rusher JaQuan Bailey. Another major part of Iowa State's formula in 2020 was pairing McDonald and Bailey at either end on passing downs to create an excellent three-man pass rush while dropping eight into coverage. They were 43rd on defense with 0.152 EPA/play.

The identity for the Cyclones will need to evolve, but head coach Matt Campbell has excelled in shaping the team's strategies from year to year in order to maximize the talent on the roster. Last year was a breakthrough season for Campbell's Cyclones; they posted a 9-3 record and beat Oklahoma in the regular season before giving them a good challenge in the Big 12 title game. With so many players back, the assumption is Iowa State will keep chugging along with the same tactics and success we saw in 2020, perhaps improved due to having a more experienced collection of receivers.

Offensively, senior quarterback Purdy paired with Milton, 2020's lead receiver Xavier Hutchinson, and star receiving tight end Charlie Kolar might give the Cyclones more of a drop-back passing emphasis akin to what we saw in 2019. They won't stop utilizing Breece Hall and the run game but with five starters back along the line and a better cast of targets for Purdy they'll likely look to evolve in the direction of the passing game.

Defensively the Cyclones are losing a lot because of how Bailey allowed them to rush the passer so effectively with only three. On the bright side, McDonald remains to step into Bailey's starting role and Iowa State has all three starting linebackers returning including the Big 12's Defensive Player of the Year Mike Rose. Iowa State likely needs to rush at least one linebacker, forgoing their strategy of rushing just three, but it's an exchange they may be able to afford given the experience back in the secondary and continued growth of senior cornerback Anthony Johnson.

The Cyclones' overall resume would be well served by getting off to a better start; they've been flat the last few years in their openers (losing to Louisiana in 2020) and have dropped the mid-September Iowa "Cy-Hawk" rivalry game five straight times. The Hawkeyes were not on the schedule last year; other than winning a Big 12 title, that win is the biggest remaining obstacle for Campbell's Cyclones.

No. 9: Iowa Hawkeyes (8.7 mean wins)

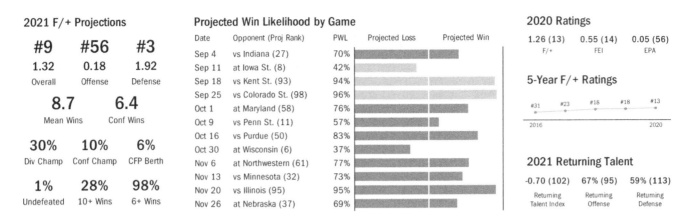

2021 F/+ Projections

#9	#56	#3
1.32	0.18	1.92
Overall	Offense	Defense

8.7	6.4
Mean Wins	Conf Wins

30%	10%	6%
Div Champ	Conf Champ	CFP Berth

1%	28%	98%
Undefeated	10+ Wins	6+ Wins

Projected Win Likelihood by Game

Date	Opponent (Proj Rank)	PWL
Sep 4	vs Indiana (27)	70%
Sep 11	at Iowa St. (8)	42%
Sep 18	vs Kent St. (93)	94%
Sep 25	vs Colorado St. (98)	96%
Oct 1	at Maryland (58)	76%
Oct 9	vs Penn St. (11)	57%
Oct 16	vs Purdue (50)	83%
Oct 30	at Wisconsin (6)	37%
Nov 6	at Northwestern (61)	77%
Nov 13	vs Minnesota (32)	73%
Nov 20	vs Illinois (95)	95%
Nov 26	at Nebraska (37)	69%

2020 Ratings

1.26 (13)	0.55 (14)	0.05 (56)
F/+	FEI	EPA

5-Year F/+ Ratings

#31   #23   #18   #18   #13
2016   2020

2021 Returning Talent

-0.70 (102)	67% (95)	59% (113)
Returning Talent Index	Returning Offense	Returning Defense

The Hawkeyes ended strong in 2020, finishing 6-2 after a pair of opening losses (by four to Purdue and by one to Northwestern) which eliminated them from the Big Ten title hunt. They were able to get their run game rolling in subsequent games and better set up first-year quarterback Spencer Petras to avoid interceptions and make plays.

Petras is back along with Sam LaPorta, the latest in a long line of strong Iowa tight ends, as well as wide receiver Nico Ragaini. Running back Tyler Goodson also returns to give the Hawkeyes a solid cast of skill talents after running for 762 yards at 5.3 yards per carry with seven touchdowns in 2020. Some of the most crucial features to the Iowa offense are the outside zone run game, which has been a staple under head coach Kirk Ferentz, and dual-threat tight ends such as LaPorta. What makes their outside zone run game work so well is their commitment to developing players for the scheme and having a parade of NFL centers to execute the lateral blocks inside.

They had Austin Blythe (drafted in 2016) and James Daniels (drafted in 2018), and this offseason starting center Tyler Linderbaum decided to come back for one more year before joining his fellow Iowa centers in the NFL. Elsewhere the Hawkeyes need to find a pair of starting tackles from converted redshirt junior guard Cody Ince, redshirt junior Jack Plumb, and sophomore Nick DeJong. Last year's offense finished 93rd with 0.106 EPA/play but Iowa could see that number climb with better passing from Petras.

Another consistent feature of the Hawkeye machine under Ferentz has been a fundamentally strong defense which tends to have real length and size on the defensive line and one or two NFL linebackers. Last year's unit just had all those features in defensive end Chauncey Golston, tackle Daviyon Nixon, and linebacker and leading tackler Nick Niemann, who were all drafted. The defense carried the team, ranking ninth nationally with 0.059 EPA/play.

The next generation may not be quite as far along. Zach VanValkenburg will look to carry the pass rush after picking up 3.5 sacks last year playing opposite Golston, while redshirt freshman Yahya Black will be counted on at defensive tackle. Linebacker is in better shape, as redshirt junior Seth Benson got off to a strong start at middle linebacker in 2020 and junior Jack Campbell played regularly.

On the back end, Iowa is much better off due to the return of all five starters in the nickel package. Safety Jack Koerner finished third on the team in tackles and picked off three passes while roving in the middle of the field. Cornerback has long been a program strength for Iowa and they return starters Matt Hankins and Riley Moss. The Hawkeyes don't play a particularly aggressive scheme but they always keep the ball in front and tackle well.

The schedule sets up well for Iowa to make a run at the Big Ten West and a 10-win season. The Hawkeyes dodged Michigan and Ohio State from the East and draw Penn State at home. Their challenges are facing Iowa State on the road in Week 2 and drawing Wisconsin and Northwestern on the road in back-to-back weeks. They'll need Petras to be ready as a redshirt junior to protect the ball and make plays on the road behind a retooling offensive line. Iowa could also use a go-to receiver for Petras to find on passing downs in the big games, a role either LaPorta or Ragaini might be able to fill.

No. 10: Notre Dame Fighting Irish (8.7 mean wins)

2021 F/+ Projections

#10	#23	#11
1.29	0.94	1.30
Overall	Offense	Defense

8.7	-
Mean Wins	Conf Wins

-	-	1%
Div Champ	Conf Champ	CFP Berth

2%	32%	98%
Undefeated	10+ Wins	6+ Wins

Projected Win Likelihood by Game

Date	Opponent (Proj Rank)	PWL	Projected Loss	Projected Win
Sep 5	at Florida St. (75)	79%		
Sep 11	vs Toledo (54)	83%		
Sep 18	vs Purdue (50)	82%		
Sep 25	vs Wisconsin (6)	42%		
Oct 2	vs Cincinnati (20)	62%		
Oct 9	at Virginia Tech (36)	65%		
Oct 23	vs USC (21)	62%		
Oct 30	vs North Carolina (22)	62%		
Nov 6	vs Navy (96)	92%		
Nov 13	at Virginia (47)	73%		
Nov 20	vs Georgia Tech (85)	90%		
Nov 27	at Stanford (76)	79%		

2020 Ratings

1.26 (12)	0.68 (10)	0.05 (48)
F/+	FEI	EPA

5-Year F/+ Ratings

#25 (2016) → #10 → #13 → #14 → #12 (2020)

2021 Returning Talent

-0.28 (79)	39% (126)	61% (108)
Returning Talent Index	Returning Offense	Returning Defense

The Irish were arguably the most well-situated football team in the country to handle a diminished 2020 offseason and consequently put together a playoff season. Ian Book and his entire offensive line were multi-year starters while the receiving corps got a boost from adding grad transfer Ben Skowronek from Northwestern. The defense similarly had a lot of experience up the middle of the unit and was able to add grad transfer cornerback Nick McCloud from North Carolina State, who served as the island corner on the boundary.

The offense was steady, not great, with 0.202 EPA/play (48th nationally) while the veteran defense was 42nd with 0.169 EPA/play. Notre Dame leaned on experience to bring winning, situational play on both sides of the ball.

All of this experience is gone now, at least on offense where Book and the offensive line have all graduated. To patch the quarterback position while developing some younger talents, they've added Wisconsin grad transfer Jack Coan, who started every game for the 10-4 Badgers in 2019. Coan made 339 passing attempts in 2019 for 2,727 yards at 8.0 yards per attempt and threw 18 touchdowns to five interceptions. Coan missed the 2020 season with injury and was replaced by young blue-chip quarterback Graham Mertz. Now he's in South Bend to hold down the fort for Brian Kelly's Irish. A major benefit of adding Coan is his familiarity working in a run-centric, pro-style offense and throwing to a receiving tight end like the Irish do.

The Irish will emphasize returning running back Kyren Williams after his 1,125 rushing yards and 13 total touchdowns and sophomore tight end Michael "Baby Gronk" Mayer who caught 42 balls for 450 yards for the Irish last season. The rest of the Notre Dame offensive infrastructure will hinge on plugging in the next generation of ultra-talented but very young offensive linemen. The 2021 unit may start true freshmen at both left tackle (Blake Fisher) and left guard (Rocco Spindler) and could be quite young overall.

Defensively Notre Dame is in better shape, although the Irish will likely have an evolved approach after coordinator Clark Lea left to take the Vanderbilt head coaching job and was replaced by Cincinnati's star coordinator Marcus Freeman. Whereas Lea emphasized zone coverages and careful, sound defense, Freeman will bring more aggressive coverage and pressure while possibly simplifying coverages in pursuit of maintaining sound, steady play.

The Irish will have to rebuild the secondary to achieve these results but return surefire NFL draft pick Kyle Hamilton at safety. The defensive line is in phenomenal shape with the return of starting tackles Myron Tagovailoa-Amosa (moving to strongside end) and Kurt Hinish plus the rise of former blue chips Jayson Ademilola and Isaiah Foskey, the latter of whom had 4.5 sacks in spot duty last season.

Overall, Notre Dame has a tremendous amount of talent, but they're in a bridge year with younger talent on the offense which will need to be managed effectively by Coan. Their schedule is challenging early on with a road trip in the season opener to Florida State and a neutral(ish)-site game in Chicago against Wisconsin in Week 4 before facing Cincinnati in Week 5. If they have the offense pieced together coming out of fall camp, the schedule lacks many nationally elite threats until home games against USC and North Carolina on the back half of the schedule. An early start could put the Irish on a roll; otherwise they may be aiming for a solid season while buying time for the next wave of NFL talents up front on offense to get their feet wet.

No. 11: Penn State Nittany Lions (8.3 mean wins)

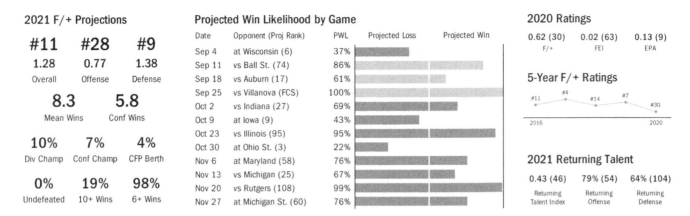

2021 F/+ Projections

#11	#28	#9
1.28	0.77	1.38
Overall	Offense	Defense

8.3	5.8
Mean Wins	Conf Wins

10%	7%	4%
Div Champ	Conf Champ	CFP Berth

0%	19%	98%
Undefeated	10+ Wins	6+ Wins

Projected Win Likelihood by Game

Date	Opponent (Proj Rank)	PWL
Sep 4	at Wisconsin (6)	37%
Sep 11	vs Ball St. (74)	86%
Sep 18	vs Auburn (17)	61%
Sep 25	vs Villanova (FCS)	100%
Oct 2	vs Indiana (27)	69%
Oct 9	at Iowa (9)	43%
Oct 23	vs Illinois (95)	95%
Oct 30	at Ohio St. (3)	22%
Nov 6	at Maryland (58)	76%
Nov 13	vs Michigan (25)	67%
Nov 20	vs Rutgers (108)	99%
Nov 27	at Michigan St. (60)	76%

Projected Loss   Projected Win

2020 Ratings

0.62 (30)	0.02 (63)	0.13 (9)
F/+	FEI	EPA

5-Year F/+ Ratings

#11   #4   #14   #7   #30
2016   2020

2021 Returning Talent

0.43 (46)	79% (54)	64% (104)
Returning Talent Index	Returning Offense	Returning Defense

The Nittany Lions would like to move on from 2020 and just count it as lost. Heading into the season, head coach James Franklin hired offensive coordinator Kirk Ciarrocca from Minnesota to install an RPO spread offense but this went awry without an offseason while the defense lost star linebacker Micah Parsons to an opt-out. They started 0-5, the worst start in school history— for a program which began to play the game in 1887—before rallying to win the final four games on the schedule. This boost occurred in part because the Lions started bringing in quarterback Will Levis to handle the running game instead of starting quarterback Sean Clifford. Levis then transferred to Kentucky in the offseason.

In the offseason Franklin was able to keep his job despite the rough year but made several big moves including hiring Mike Yurich from Texas to coordinate the offense and bringing in several transfers on the defensive line. Duke transfer tackle Derrick Tangelo joined the front along with Temple defensive end Arnold Ebiketie who's replacing Baltimore first-round selection Odafe Oweh.

At linebacker, defensive coordinator Brent Pry has taken the opportunity to shuffle the lineup to get their next generation of star athletes together. Ellis Brooks returns in the middle after leading the team in tackles but former strongside linebacker Brandon Smith flips to the weakside position and sophomore Curtis Jacobs steps in as the new strongside linebacker. Ja-

cobs brings some speed in coverage to help the Lions maintain a 4-3 base defense without subbing in a nickel and ideally frees up Smith to play around the box. The secondary returns both starting cornerbacks and safety Jaquan Brisker, then adds Johnny Dixon from South Carolina. The overall defense looked disengaged early last year but then finished 17th with 0.079 EPA/play and will be looking to put together a complete season in 2021.

The Lions' defense should be solid but the offense will need to protect the ball better to seize the Big Ten East away from Ohio State. They finished 28th nationally with 0.234 EPA/play but Clifford threw nine picks.

Yurich's new offense will emphasize tempo and downfield shot taking, which will require Clifford to start finding targets down the field. The Lions have several quick receivers such as Parker Washington and Jahan Dotson and then tight end Brenton Strange to play inside. They'll need Dotson, their big play threat in 2020, to come alive in this scheme as a play-action weapon. Yurich's offensive line is well suited to help him with Rasheed Walker and Caedan Wallace returning at tackle while guard Mike Miranda slides inside to center.

Penn State's schedule opens on the road against Wisconsin, a stiff test for the new offense, and hosts Auburn in Week 3 before sending them on the road against Iowa, Ohio State, and Michigan State. A bounce back year from 4-5 should be manageable.

No. 12: Texas A&M Aggies (8.9 mean wins)

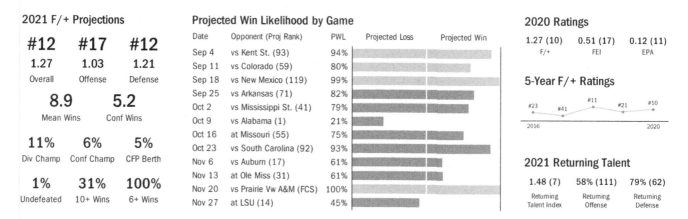

2021 F/+ Projections

#12	#17	#12
1.27	1.03	1.21
Overall	Offense	Defense

8.9	5.2
Mean Wins	Conf Wins

11%	6%	5%
Div Champ	Conf Champ	CFP Berth

1%	31%	100%
Undefeated	10+ Wins	6+ Wins

Projected Win Likelihood by Game

Date	Opponent (Proj Rank)	PWL	Projected Loss	Projected Win
Sep 4	vs Kent St. (93)	94%		
Sep 11	vs Colorado (59)	80%		
Sep 18	vs New Mexico (119)	99%		
Sep 25	vs Arkansas (71)	82%		
Oct 2	vs Mississippi St. (41)	79%		
Oct 9	vs Alabama (1)	21%		
Oct 16	at Missouri (55)	75%		
Oct 23	vs South Carolina (92)	93%		
Nov 6	vs Auburn (17)	61%		
Nov 13	at Ole Miss (31)	61%		
Nov 20	vs Prairie Vw A&M (FCS)	100%		
Nov 27	at LSU (14)	45%		

2020 Ratings

1.27 (10)	0.51 (17)	0.12 (11)
F/+	FEI	EPA

5-Year F/+ Ratings

#23　#41　#11　#21　#10
2016　　　　　　　　　2020

2021 Returning Talent

1.48 (7)	58% (111)	79% (62)
Returning Talent Index	Returning Offense	Returning Defense

The Aggies had some breakthrough success in 2020, Year 3 for head coach Jimbo Fisher, finishing 9-1 with big wins over Florida and North Carolina in the Orange Bowl. After the season, A&M saw quarterback Kellen Mond drafted in the third round along with left tackle Dan Moore (fourth round). On defense they lost nose tackle Bobby Brown and linebacker Buddy Johnson (both drafted in the fourth round). Despite those losses, the 2021 Aggies have one of their strongest collections of potential NFL talent since the 2012 team and Johnny Manziel. They just need their next star quarterback.

Since Fisher came to College Station, Texas A&M's offense has been centered around winning games in the box with line play and effective tight ends. Junior tight end Jalen Wydermyer lead the team last season with 46 catches for 506 yards and six touchdowns while running back/wide receiver hybrid Ainias Smith was second with 43 catches for 564 yards and six more scores. Both return along with lead runner Isaiah Spiller (1,036 rushing yards at 5.5 yards per carry with nine touchdowns) and his blazing fast back-up Devon Achane (364 rushing yards at 8.5 yards per carry with four touchdowns). They finished 22nd nationally with 0.253 EPA/play.

Highly athletic Haynes King will compete with strong-armed Zach Calzada for the quarterback position. With a new starter at quarterback, the Aggies figure to again emphasize their play in the box but they must do so with four new offensive linemen. Their sole returnee is Kenyon Green, a junior who started at left guard as a true freshman and sophomore and now slides out to left tackle. A pair of 300-plus-pounders named Aki Ogunbiyi and Layden Robinson are stepping in at guard, legacy Luke Matthews is at center, and Tennessee transfer Jahmir Johnson is expected to be the right tackle.

On defense everything starts with DeMarvin Leal, a 6-foot-4, 290-pounder who played strongside end last season. His numbers weren't particularly gaudy, 37 tackles with seven for loss and 2.5 sacks, but he was often two-gapping the wide edge and freeing up their linebackers. The Aggies also have defensive ends Tyree Johnson and Micheal Clemons back (eight combined sacks) who could allow Leal to slide inside to defensive tackle. Off the ball, the Aggies have linebacker Aaron Hansford back with safeties Leon O'Neal and Demani Richardson, and cornerbacks Jaylon Jones and Myles Jones. Richardson is the star, a rangy field safety who helped the Aggies protect the deep field. The Aggies were 33rd last year allowing .128 EPA/play.

The schedule includes normal challenges such as Alabama and a road trip against LSU, but their SEC East draw is lighter with a road trip to Missouri and South Carolina at home. Their road trip to Ole Miss is probably the dividing line between another acclaimed season and a disappointing finish.

No. 13: Washington Huskies (9.4 mean wins)

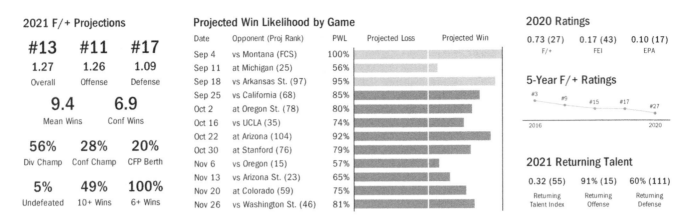

2021 F/+ Projections

#13	#11	#17
1.27	1.26	1.09
Overall	Offense	Defense

9.4	6.9
Mean Wins	Conf Wins

56%	28%	20%
Div Champ	Conf Champ	CFP Berth

5%	49%	100%
Undefeated	10+ Wins	6+ Wins

Projected Win Likelihood by Game

Date	Opponent (Proj Rank)	PWL	Projected Loss	Projected Win
Sep 4	vs Montana (FCS)	100%		
Sep 11	at Michigan (25)	56%		
Sep 18	vs Arkansas St. (97)	95%		
Sep 25	vs California (68)	85%		
Oct 2	at Oregon St. (78)	80%		
Oct 16	vs UCLA (35)	74%		
Oct 22	at Arizona (104)	92%		
Oct 30	at Stanford (76)	79%		
Nov 6	vs Oregon (15)	57%		
Nov 13	vs Arizona St. (23)	65%		
Nov 20	at Colorado (59)	75%		
Nov 26	vs Washington St. (46)	81%		

2020 Ratings

0.73 (27)	0.17 (43)	0.10 (17)
F/+	FEI	EPA

5-Year F/+ Ratings

#3 · #9 · #15 · #17 · #27
2016 — 2020

2021 Returning Talent

0.32 (55)	91% (15)	60% (111)
Returning Talent Index	Returning Offense	Returning Defense

The Huskies are still largely in a transition phase from the Chris Petersen era, which concluded after the 2019 season. The Huskies promoted defensive coordinator and secondary coach Jimmy Lake to head coach, but then they only played four games (going 3-1) in 2020. After the season they took some losses with defensive coordinator Pete Kwiatkowski hired away by Texas for the same job and defensive players Joe Tryon (first-round defensive end), Levi Onwuzurike (second-round defensive tackle), Elijah Molden (third-round corner), and Keith Taylor (fifth-round corner) all drafted.

It was a substantial talent drain, but there's quite a bit left for the Huskies. The most promising dimension to their team is along either side around the box. On offense they return the entire starting line with tight ends Cade Otton (leading receiver in 2020) and Jack Westover (blocking specialist). The interior trio is particularly imposing with skilled center Luke Wattenberg bookended by 365-pound Ulumoo Ale and 340-pound Henry Bainivalu.

The Huskies need to find some explosive skill players to feed the ball off play-action and to this point added Michigan transfer Giles Jackson, who can bring real speed in the slot. Who distributes the ball is another question. Dylan Morris returns after throwing for 897 yards at 8.2 yards per attempt with four touchdowns to three interceptions, but the Huskies also add 5-star freshman Sam Huard at the position. To add to the intrigue, Colorado State quarterback Patrick O'Brien,

originally a blue chip who went to Nebraska, transferred in for a shot at the job. This unit finished 14th in 2020 with 0.287 EPA/play.

On defense, the Husky line is formidable despite the losses of Joe Tryon and Levi Onwuzurike. Zion Tupuola-Fetui was a revelation at outside linebacker last season with seven sacks in just four games and long-time contributor Ryan Bowman returns opposite him. The interior linemen include Tuli Letuligasenoa and Sam Taimani while inside linebacker returns the tandem of Jackson Sirmon and Edefuan Ulofoshio, who paced the team in tackles last season. Last year's unit finished an uncharacteristic 104th with 0.252 EPA/play

Back in the secondary, Lake plugged in Oklahoma nickel Brendan Radley-Hiles through the transfer portal, who can combine with Kyler Gordon and Trent McDuffie to give the Huskies experienced defensive backs at the outside and slot corner positions. The Huskies have specialized in great defensive back play since Lake arrived with Petersen in 2014.

Lake has proposed the Huskies maintain a "defense and run game wins the day" formula for competing in the Pac-12 North and they certainly have the personnel to continue this trend. The schedule avoids USC and allows the Huskies to host rival Oregon in Seattle. An early road trip to Michigan will set up the rest of the season and its expectations but however it goes, this team should be in the thick of it for the North crown and a chance at another Pac-12 Championship.

No. 14: LSU Tigers (8.2 mean wins)

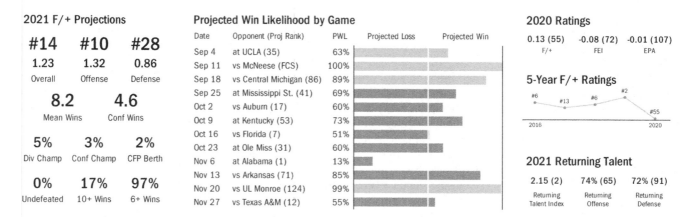

2021 F/+ Projections

#14	#10	#28
1.23	1.32	0.86
Overall	Offense	Defense

8.2	4.6
Mean Wins	Conf Wins

5%	3%	2%
Div Champ	Conf Champ	CFP Berth

0%	17%	97%
Undefeated	10+ Wins	6+ Wins

Projected Win Likelihood by Game

Date	Opponent (Proj Rank)	PWL
Sep 4	at UCLA (35)	63%
Sep 11	vs McNeese (FCS)	100%
Sep 18	vs Central Michigan (86)	89%
Sep 25	at Mississippi St. (41)	69%
Oct 2	vs Auburn (17)	60%
Oct 9	at Kentucky (53)	73%
Oct 16	vs Florida (7)	51%
Oct 23	at Ole Miss (31)	60%
Nov 6	at Alabama (1)	13%
Nov 13	vs Arkansas (71)	85%
Nov 20	vs UL Monroe (124)	99%
Nov 27	vs Texas A&M (12)	55%

2020 Ratings

0.13 (55)	-0.08 (72)	-0.01 (107)
F/+	FEI	EPA

5-Year F/+ Ratings

#6, #13, #6, #2, #55 (2016 – 2020)

2021 Returning Talent

2.15 (2)	74% (65)	72% (91)
Returning Talent Index	Returning Offense	Returning Defense

This could be a make-or-break year for LSU head coach Ed Orgeron, despite the historic success in 2019 when they won the National Championship and quarterback Joe Burrow won the Heisman trophy. The Tigers lost both coordinators and most of that 2019 team and went 5-5 in 2020. Then after their 2020 season, they hired two more new coordinators and had to part ways with offensive line coach James Cregg.

Orgeron's staff remake included hiring Minnesota Vikings' secondary coach Daronte Jones to coordinate the defense and Carolina Panthers quarterback coach Jake Peetz as the offensive coordinator. Peetz worked with LSU's 2019 offensive coordinator Joe Brady at Carolina and the goal is to recover the magic of 2019 with a similar offensive scheme and hope it elevates Myles Brennan, who started in 2020, or sophomore Max Johnson who replaced him after injury.

Out at receiver the Tigers are expecting sophomore Kayshon Boutte to lead the way in providing another wide receiver corps rich with NFL talent. The former 5-star recruit caught 45 balls for 735 yards and five touchdowns last season and will be the tip of the spear for their offense. Running back Tyrion Davis-Price is back with all five offensive linemen starters and tight end Kole Taylor to try and restart the power run game which was so dangerous with Clyde Edwards-Helaire in 2019. The offense was just 92nd in 2020 with 0.11 EPA/play.

On defense the Tigers should be improved simply from having a full season of cornerback Derek Stingley at the helm of an experienced secondary. At linebacker they added Clemson transfer strongside linebacker Mike Jones to play the role filled by North Dakota State transfer Jabril Cox in 2020. Defensive ends Andre Anthony (5.5 sacks in 2020), Ali Gaye (9.5 tackles for loss, 2.0 sacks), and B.J. Ojulari (four sacks) are back after a promising 2020 in the new four-lineman defense. Defensive tackle is also loaded with talent, highlighted by sophomore Jaquelin Roy who showed game changing pass-rushing talent in 2020. LSU was 94th on defense at 0.225 EPA/play.

The Tigers have loads of great players and more time now to recoup and reload from the post-title talent drain. They'll have to face Florida and travel to Kentucky for their SEC East draw and play Alabama and Ole Miss on the road, so the schedule won't be easy. However, if the talent comes back together this squad could be a contender in the SEC West.

No. 15: Oregon Ducks (8.7 mean wins)

2021 F/+ Projections

#15	#20	#16
1.22	0.99	1.12
Overall	Offense	Defense

8.7	6.6
Mean Wins	Conf Wins

40%	20%	13%
Div Champ	Conf Champ	CFP Berth

1%	28%	99%
Undefeated	10+ Wins	6+ Wins

Projected Win Likelihood by Game

Date	Opponent (Proj Rank)	PWL
Sep 4	vs Fresno St. (89)	90%
Sep 11	at Ohio St. (3)	21%
Sep 18	vs Stony Brook (FCS)	100%
Sep 25	vs Arizona (104)	97%
Oct 2	at Stanford (76)	77%
Oct 15	vs California (68)	84%
Oct 23	at UCLA (35)	63%
Oct 30	vs Colorado (59)	83%
Nov 6	at Washington (13)	43%
Nov 13	vs Washington St. (46)	80%
Nov 20	at Utah (19)	48%
Nov 27	vs Oregon St. (78)	86%

2020 Ratings

0.76 (26)	0.15 (47)	0.14 (5)
F/+	FEI	EPA

5-Year F/+ Ratings

#60, #43, #44, #11, #26 (2016 – 2020)

2021 Returning Talent

2.17 (1)	74% (64)	85% (41)
Returning Talent Index	Returning Offense	Returning Defense

Oregon has been a program back on the national scene since hiring Mario Cristobal as head coach in late 2017. They went 9-4 in Year 1, jumped to 12-2 in Year 2 and won the Pac-12 Championship, then slogged through the bizarre 2020 year and defended their Pac-12 title before falling flat in the Fiesta Bowl against Iowa State.

Much of 2020 was quarterbacked by Tyler Shough, who transferred after the season to Texas Tech. Now Boston College transfer Anthony Brown and freshman Ty Thompson are battling for the starting job. Offensive coordinator Joe Moorhead only had some of his offense installed for 2020 and will now have a full offseason with these two dual-threat quarterbacks to get his RPO and option-heavy system rolling. The Ducks had to rebuild the entire offensive line last season, even losing standout Penei Sewell who opted out and was drafted in the first round.

The retooled offensive line had a strong year and both running backs Travis Dye and C.J. Verdell are back after combining for 728 rushing yards and four touchdowns in 2020. The run game paced an offense which ranked seventh with 0.324 EPA/play.

Tight end D.J. Johnson, who was a regular target in Oregon's RPO schemes and caught three touchdowns while splitting time with since departed Hunter Kampmoyer, is back. Receivers Jaylon Redd and Johnny Johnson also return. It will be fun to observe how Moorhead fits all the skill talent around whichever quarterback he chooses as the starter.

On defense Oregon put together a scheme reminiscent of their old days under Chip Kelly, playing good man coverage on the back end. They finished just 75th though with 0.198 EPA/play. Then the NFL came and took safeties Jevon Holland (second round) and Brady Breeze (sixth round) and cornerbacks Deommodore Lenoir (fifth round) and 2020 opt-out Thomas Graham Jr. (sixth round). Mykael Wright had a strong sophomore year at cornerback in place of Graham but the Ducks will need to rebuild around him.

Up front, Oregon is in better shape. Inside linebacker Noah Sewell led the team in solo tackles and sophomore defensive end Kayvon Thibodeaux flashed with 9.5 tackles for loss and three sacks. Thibodeaux crushed USC in the Pac-12 Championship Game and will play opposite Mase Funa in 2020. The Ducks attacked offenses with five-man fronts in 2020 backed by match coverage. When it worked, opponents struggled to handle all of their athletes set up with 1-on-1 matchups. This Oregon front should be more consistent with Thibodeaux and Funa both one year better.

Oregon's schedule takes them on the road against Ohio State as well as conference opponents Utah, Stanford and Washington, but they avoid USC from the South entirely. The Ohio State game should be a terrific test of whether their defensive pressure will work against high-level offenses.

No. 16: Texas Longhorns (8.2 mean wins)

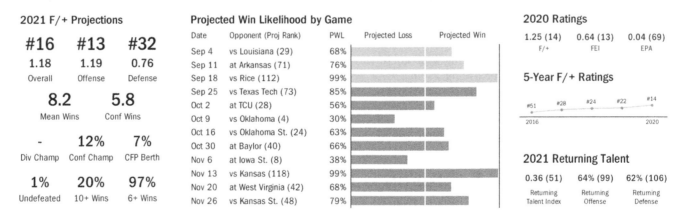

The 2020 season had been circled for a few years by the Longhorns as a "now or never" year for head coach Tom Herman. Texas had senior quarterback Sam Ehlinger (sixth-round pick) leading the way for a team with left tackle Sam Cosmi (second-round pick), edge rusher Joseph Ossai (third-round pick), defensive tackle Ta'Quon Graham (fifth-round pick), and safety Caden Sterns (fifth-round pick). But the Longhorns stumbled early against TCU and Oklahoma before ultimately losing their chance at a Big 12 Championship on fourth-and-1 at home against Iowa State when Ehlinger was tackled an inch shy of the chains.

Tom Herman was fired and Texas brought in Alabama offensive coordinator Steve Sarkisian. Sarkisian's style is more familiar to the Big 12, as he'll dial up RPOs and play-action from spread sets and look to overpower opponents with sheer firepower.

To this end, he inherited a decent situation. Wideout was a big hole for the Longhorns in 2020 but Sarkisian will have former blue-chip wideouts Josh Moore, Troy Omeire, and Jordan Whittington. To cement the chances of having playmaking here, Sarkisian also recruited transfer Xavier Worthy, a 10.5s 100-meter runner from the 2021 class who'd committed to Michigan but changed his mind when Texas hired Sarkisian. Worthy is a Jaylen Waddle/DeVonta Smith type, slight (150 pounds) but with elite speed as a deep threat.

At quarterback the Longhorns return Casey Thompson, a

dual threat who played well in the Alamo Bowl, and blue-chip redshirt freshman Hudson Card. Thompson was the back-up in 2020 but Card is a highly skilled passer who may end up fitting the Sarkisian offense better. The Longhorns were 77th last year with 0.142 EPA/play on offense and need more explosiveness in the passing game.

The more surefire talents left behind by Herman are clear fits for a "run game plus defense" formula. At the end of 2020 the Longhorns started freshman center Jacob Majors, who proved highly adept in the outside zone run scheme, and freshman running back Bijan Robinson. In Texas' final two games when Majors took over at center, Bijan had 19 carries for 355 yards at 18.7 yards per carry with four rushing touchdowns and another two receiving touchdowns.

Texas' defense will now be coordinated by Pete Kwiatkowski (formerly of Washington) and is on solid footing. The Longhorns return cornerbacks D'Shawn Jamison and Josh Thompson, nickel Chris Adimora, potential star linebacker DeMarvion Overshown, and then nose tackle Keondre Coburn and fellow tackles Moro Ojomo and Alfred Collins. Texas used the transfer portal to add three edge rushers to help replace Ossai and allow the roster to execute Kwiatkowski's preferred 2-4-5 nickel package. Last year's unit finished 51st with 0.157 EPA/play.

The schedule includes the Oklahoma game in Dallas and then road trips against Iowa State and TCU. Texas also faces Louisiana fresh off a second consecutive 10-win season in the season opener before taking the road against Arkansas.

No. 17: Auburn Tigers (7.6 mean wins)

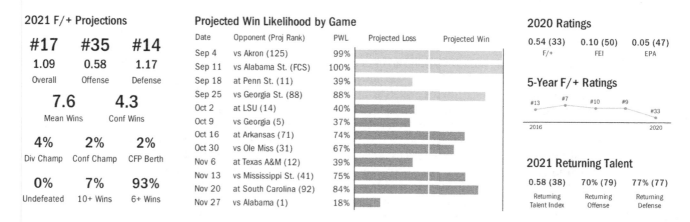

After a 68-35 record with two SEC West division titles and a National Championship appearance way back in Year 1, the Tigers fired Gus Malzahn. After a dramatic hiring process, they landed on Bryan Harsin of Boise State as his replacement.

The first challenge for Harsin will be trying to make the most of 5-star quarterback Bo Nix and an Auburn offense which fell in 2020 to 63rd with 0.166 EPA/play. He'll have to do so without any of the Tigers' top three receivers from 2020 although they do return star running back Tank Bigsby.

Harsin's offenses at Boise State always featured a running back in an inside zone/power run game and then play-action and some pro-style passing concepts. Bo Nix was supposed to bring a stronger pro-style passing element to Malzahn's Auburn formula but did some of his best work in the run game (14 touchdowns in his career). This is particularly ironic in light of Auburn transfer quarterback Malik Willis' stunning success at Liberty in 2020. Harsin's tutelage of Nix will be instrumental in setting the early course for his tenure as the Tiger head man. The run game should be in good shape with all five offensive linemen returning to block for Bigsby and Nix.

Harsin hired Derek Mason, who'd recently been fired as the head coach of Vanderbilt, to try to carry on the Tigers' recent stretch of dominant defensive play as coordinator. Auburn was solid in 2020, finishing 45th with 0.153 EPA/play. Mason recruited Vanderbilt free safety Donovan Kaufman, an early breakout star of 2020, to transfer in and join Smoke Monday and Roger McCreary to give the Tigers a strong secondary.

Auburn was normally defined under previous coordinator Kevin Steele by fielding teams rich with future NFL defensive linemen and press-man cornerbacks. The new scheme will ostensibly move them to a 3-4 base but Mason tended to play four-lineman alignments at Vanderbilt. The main adjustment may be for defensive tackle turned defensive end Colby Wooden, who was a breakout star in 2020 with nine tackles for loss and 3.5 sacks. At 6-foot-5 and 278 pounds he has the athleticism to play on the edge but the reach and size to slide inside as well. Auburn may use him in both roles. On the edge, they return Derick Hall after his four-sack 2020 season and add Northwestern outside linebacker Andrew Leota (four sacks in 2020 as well). They could leverage those talents in 2-4-5 looks.

Having flexibility in the defensive front will be key with linebackers Zakoby McClain and Owen Pappoe returning after combining for 11.5 tackles for loss and seven sacks. At nose tackle, big Tyrone Truesdell (6-foot-2, 335 pounds) is back to guarantee size and obstruction when other teams look to bully the Tigers.

The schedule includes a trip to Penn State early in the year and then their traditional gauntlet of Georgia, Alabama, at LSU, and at Texas A&M. There's a reason Malzahn struggled to win more than nine games a year.

No. 18: Miami Hurricanes (8.5 mean wins)

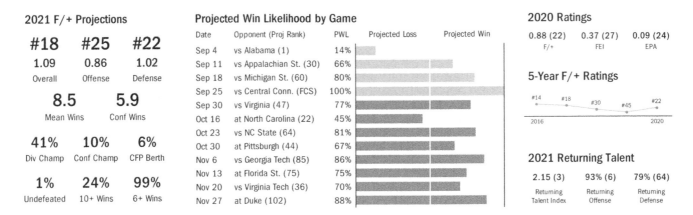

2021 F/+ Projections

#18	#25	#22
1.09	0.86	1.02
Overall	Offense	Defense

8.5	5.9
Mean Wins	Conf Wins

41%	10%	6%
Div Champ	Conf Champ	CFP Berth

1%	24%	99%
Undefeated	10+ Wins	6+ Wins

Projected Win Likelihood by Game

Date	Opponent (Proj Rank)	PWL
Sep 4	vs Alabama (1)	14%
Sep 11	vs Appalachian St. (30)	66%
Sep 18	vs Michigan St. (60)	80%
Sep 25	vs Central Conn. (FCS)	100%
Sep 30	vs Virginia (47)	77%
Oct 16	at North Carolina (22)	45%
Oct 23	vs NC State (64)	81%
Oct 30	at Pittsburgh (44)	67%
Nov 6	vs Georgia Tech (85)	86%
Nov 13	at Florida St. (75)	75%
Nov 20	vs Virginia Tech (36)	70%
Nov 27	at Duke (102)	88%

2020 Ratings

0.88 (22)	0.37 (27)	0.09 (24)
F/+	FEI	EPA

5-Year F/+ Ratings

#14 (2016) #18 #30 #45 #22 (2020)

2021 Returning Talent

2.15 (3)	93% (6)	79% (64)
Returning Talent Index	Returning Offense	Returning Defense

Miami's head coach Manny Diaz made two huge additions for the 2020 season after finishing 6-7 in Year 1. He hired former Gus Malzahn offensive assistant Rhett Lashlee as offensive coordinator, fresh off a great season with SMU, and asked him to build an offense with Houston transfer quarterback D'Eriq King.

King is a very different quarterback from SMU's Shane Buechele, more akin to someone like Nick Marshall whom Lashlee coached to the BCS Championship Game at Auburn. Lashlee's specialty has been designing formations that put top players into good matchups while setting up his quarterbacks to distribute the ball in accordance with their own skill sets. For King in 2020 this meant swing passes, flat routes, and verticals up the seams to tight ends Will Mallory and Brevin Jordan or slot Mike Harley. All of those weapons return except Jordan (a fifth-round draft pick), as do all five starting offensive linemen, King, and lead running back Cam'Ron Harris.

Adding more of a vertical passing threat would push this team further along but this may be a dimension they wait to develop until the next quarterback after King. As it was, this unit finished 31st in offense last year with 0.228 EPA/play.

On defense the Hurricanes pulled off the interesting feat of sending three different defensive ends to the NFL draft. They started Jaelan Phillips (first-round pick) and Quincy Roche (sixth-round pick) while Greg Rousseau (first-round pick) opted out of the season. To replace all of that pass-rushing they added Tennessee transfer Deandre Johnson, fresh off a nice season with six tackles for loss and 4.5 sacks and spun down linebacker Zach McCloud to play defensive end opposite him.

The Hurricanes return the entire secondary, which includes their safeties and leading tacklers Bubba Bolden, Amari Carter, and Gilbert Frierson. Al Blades and D.J. Ivey return at corner but they also added Georgia transfer Tyrique Stevenson who will likely turn one of those two into a backup with his size and talent. They were 65th in 2020 with 0.179 EPA/play.

Miami's schedule doesn't include ACC powerhouse Clemson but they open the season against Alabama in Atlanta, take on Appalachian State and Michigan State at home, and will need to go through North Carolina on the road to win their division.

No. 19: Utah Utes (8.5 mean wins)

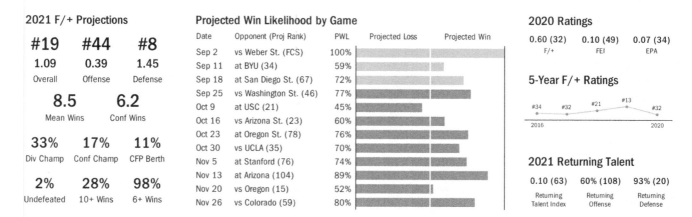

2021 F/+ Projections

#19	#44	#8
1.09	0.39	1.45
Overall	Offense	Defense

8.5	6.2
Mean Wins	Conf Wins

33%	17%	11%
Div Champ	Conf Champ	CFP Berth

2%	28%	98%
Undefeated	10+ Wins	6+ Wins

Projected Win Likelihood by Game

Date	Opponent (Proj Rank)	PWL	Projected Loss	Projected Win
Sep 2	vs Weber St. (FCS)	100%		
Sep 11	at BYU (34)	59%		
Sep 18	at San Diego St. (67)	72%		
Sep 25	vs Washington St. (46)	77%		
Oct 9	at USC (21)	45%		
Oct 16	vs Arizona St. (23)	60%		
Oct 23	at Oregon St. (78)	76%		
Oct 30	vs UCLA (35)	70%		
Nov 5	at Stanford (76)	74%		
Nov 13	at Arizona (104)	89%		
Nov 20	vs Oregon (15)	52%		
Nov 26	vs Colorado (59)	80%		

2020 Ratings

0.60 (32)	0.10 (49)	0.07 (34)
F/+	FEI	EPA

5-Year F/+ Ratings

#34   #32   #21   #13   #32
2016   2020

2021 Returning Talent

0.10 (63)	60% (108)	93% (20)
Returning Talent Index	Returning Offense	Returning Defense

Like many teams with delayed starts to 2020, the Utes started slow with a pair of losses but rebounded with wins in their final three contests. It was a good year to break in a lot of new starters for Utah and the COVID exemption year has allowed for all their top senior contributors to come back for another year.

More than that, the COVID exemption year offered a sixth year of eligibility for Baylor quarterback Charlie Brewer, who joined Oklahoma running back T.J. Pledger in transferring out to help rebuild the Utah offensive backfield. The Utes are generally a run-centric team and put much of their emphasis on star running back Ty Jordan, who tragically died in the offseason at only 19 years of age.

T.J. Pledger was a main back for Oklahoma last season and ran for 451 yards at 4.7 yards per carry with five touchdowns. Brewer was a big part of the Baylor run game each of the last three seasons and ran for 22 touchdowns for the Bears, some of it typical fare such as draws and scrambles and some of it short-yardage power running off tackle. Injuries were a routine issue for Brewer, often limiting his accurate but already borderline arm strength and generating problems for Baylor's passing game.

He should carry a lesser load in Utah where the offensive line and multi-tight ends sets will allow Pledger or redshirt freshman running back Micah Bernard to handle the short-yardage running. Instead, Utah will try to maximize Brewer's accuracy, as they did in the spring game where he was a perfect 15-for-15. Slot receiver Britain Covey and outside receiver Solomon Enis return for the Utes along with flex tight end Brant Kuithe, who led the team in receptions last season. Last year's team was 48th in EPA/play at 0.194.

The Utes under head coach Kyle Whittingham have always hung their hats on running the ball, punting exceedingly well, and playing great defense. The defense slipped some in 2020 and finished 52nd at 0.159 EPA/play. However middle linebacker Devin Lloyd was still on form with 10 tackles for loss and two sacks while new linebacker Nephi Sewell had five tackles for loss and two interceptions. Defensive end Mika Tafua was also having a potential breakout season with three sacks.

Their approach on defense hinges on being able to scheme pressure up front with the ends and linebackers moving around while holding up in match coverage on the back end. 2020's five game season gave the Utes a chance to break in freshman blue-chip cornerback Clark Phillips and sophomore Malone Mataele at nickel. They'll return with cornerback JaTravis Broughton and safety Vonte Davis in the secondary.

All the pieces are in place for the Utes and Brewer's veteran leadership at quarterback could give them a big edge. They'll need his experience to navigate a schedule including Oregon at home and Stanford, rival BYU, and USC on the road.

No. 20: Cincinnati Bearcats (9.3 mean wins)

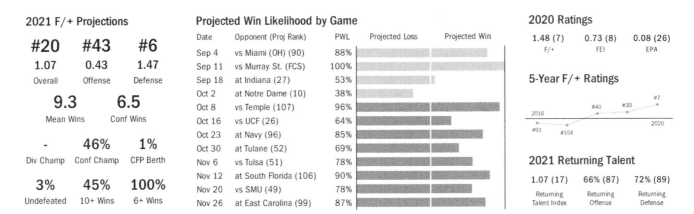

2021 F/+ Projections

#20	#43	#6
1.07	0.43	1.47
Overall	Offense	Defense

9.3	6.5
Mean Wins	Conf Wins

-	46%	1%
Div Champ	Conf Champ	CFP Berth

3%	45%	100%
Undefeated	10+ Wins	6+ Wins

Projected Win Likelihood by Game

Date	Opponent (Proj Rank)	PWL
Sep 4	vs Miami (OH) (90)	88%
Sep 11	vs Murray St. (FCS)	100%
Sep 18	at Indiana (27)	53%
Oct 2	at Notre Dame (10)	38%
Oct 8	vs Temple (107)	96%
Oct 16	vs UCF (26)	64%
Oct 23	at Navy (96)	85%
Oct 30	at Tulane (52)	69%
Nov 6	vs Tulsa (51)	78%
Nov 12	at South Florida (106)	90%
Nov 20	vs SMU (49)	78%
Nov 26	at East Carolina (99)	87%

2020 Ratings

1.48 (7)	0.73 (8)	0.08 (26)
F/+	FEI	EPA

5-Year F/+ Ratings

2021 Returning Talent

1.07 (17)	66% (87)	72% (89)
Returning Talent Index	Returning Offense	Returning Defense

The Bearcats came very close to putting together a historic 2020 season comparable to Central Florida's famous 2017 run. Staring at the chance of going undefeated with a Peach Bowl win over an SEC power (Georgia), two major events occurred before the half. The Bearcats scored a touchdown to take a 14-10 lead and their left tackle James Hudson was ejected for unnecessary roughness.

Cincinnati made it 21-10 with a big run after the half, but the loss of Hudson took its toll as Georgia had six sacks in the second half. The Bulldogs ended up ruining Cincinnati's undefeated season with a last-minute field goal.

On the surface the Bearcats still look imposing heading into 2021 with star quarterback Desmond Ridder returning along with tight end Josh Whyle and several starters from a strong defense. Ridder is a terrific start to an offense; the 6-foot-4, 215-pound quarterback shocked the Bulldogs with his speed and arm strength. He threw for 2,296 yards on the year at 8.2 yards per attempt with 19 touchdowns to six interceptions while adding 592 more yards and another 12 touchdowns on the ground. Cincinnati was 41st in offense with 0.205 EPA/play.

The offense is designed to maximize Ridder's abilities with zone-read keepers, RPOs to tight ends like Whyle, and throws outside when defenses load up on the inside zone plays. Their offensive line will return all of the interior starters who paved a way on those inside runs and Alabama transfer running back Jerome Ford is in line to replace big Gerrid Doaks as the main inside runner. Finding another left tackle of Hudson's caliber could be a real challenge.

Defense was the strongest engine for Cincinnati's success in 2020, finishing 18th nationally with 0.079 EPA/play. Their success led to defensive coordinator Marcus Freeman getting hired away by Notre Dame. Head coach Luke Fickell replaced him with Mike Tressell, longtime Michigan State assistant and nephew of former Ohio State head coach Jim Tressell. Tressell will inherit star cornerbacks Coby Bryant (four interceptions and seven break-ups in 2020) and Ahmad Gardner (three interceptions and six pass break-ups) as well as defensive end Myjai Sanders (seven sacks, five pass break-ups) but will have to rebuild elsewhere.

He'll also face an interesting question in whether to continue Freeman's man coverage defense which included a "dollar package" last year that functioned like a 3-4 defense but with dime personnel. Tressell was part of Michigan State's "no fly zone" defense in the 2010s and has been developing linebackers in the 4-3 press quarters defense for most of his time as a coach.

Tresell's ability to feature Cincinnati's existing strengths on defense while adding his own touches will play a major role in whether Cincinnati can continue their brilliant run under Fickell and defend their AAC Championship. An October 2 road trip against Notre Dame will set the ceiling for the season and determine whether they have a playoff resume if undefeated.

21. USC Trojans (8.3 mean wins)

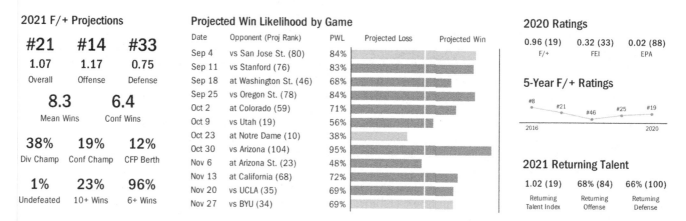

2021 F/+ Projections

#21	#14	#33
1.07	1.17	0.75
Overall	Offense	Defense

8.3	6.4
Mean Wins	Conf Wins

38%	19%	12%
Div Champ	Conf Champ	CFP Berth

1%	23%	96%
Undefeated	10+ Wins	6+ Wins

Projected Win Likelihood by Game

Date	Opponent (Proj Rank)	PWL
Sep 4	vs San Jose St. (80)	84%
Sep 11	vs Stanford (76)	83%
Sep 18	at Washington St. (46)	68%
Sep 25	vs Oregon St. (78)	84%
Oct 2	at Colorado (59)	71%
Oct 9	vs Utah (19)	56%
Oct 23	at Notre Dame (10)	38%
Oct 30	vs Arizona (104)	95%
Nov 6	at Arizona St. (23)	48%
Nov 13	at California (68)	72%
Nov 20	vs UCLA (35)	69%
Nov 27	vs BYU (34)	69%

2020 Ratings

0.96 (19)	0.32 (33)	0.02 (88)
F/+	FEI	EPA

5-Year F/+ Ratings

#8 (2016), #21, #46, #25, #19 (2020)

2021 Returning Talent

1.02 (19)	68% (84)	66% (100)
Returning Talent Index	Returning Offense	Returning Defense

USC went undefeated in the 2020 regular season, with four of five wins coming by one score. The Trojans' lone loss came in the Pac-12 Championship Game, where they played Oregon instead of Washington due to conference health protocols. The Trojans' record, though, belies struggles on both sides of the ball. The offense never really found an identity, finishing a meager 55th in EPA/play (0.180). Quarterback Kedon Slovis had a solid season, completing 67% of his passes, averaging 7.2 yards per attempt, and throwing for 17 touchdowns, and enters his junior year as one of the more respected quarterbacks in the nation. In the rushing game, the additions of transfers Keaontay Ingram (4.6 yards per carry in 2020) from Texas and Darwin Barlow (5.8 yards per carry, four touchdowns) from TCU bolster a ground attack that largely stalled, averaging 4.3 yards per carry and scoring eight touchdowns. Of course, with Graham Harrell as offensive coordinator, the run game is nothing more than a second option to the pass. While leading target Amon-Ra St. Brown left for the NFL (11.7 yards per reception, seven touchdowns), the duo of Drake London (33 receptions, 15.2 yards per reception) and Bru McCoy (21 receptions, 11.2 yards per reception) will more than fill his shoes, with interesting pieces like four-star freshman Gary Bryant Jr. and Texas transfer Malcolm Epps rounding out the attack.

On defense, end Nick Figueroa (four sacks, 13 tackles) shined in limited time in 2020, but the defensive line depth took a hit with the departures of Caleb Tremblay and Jay Toia. The linebacker corps is thin, but a healthy Drake Jackson should be one of the better edge rushers in the conference (two sacks, 15 tackles), and free safety Isaiah Pola-Mao will again anchor the secondary. The Trojans allowed 0.292 EPA/play on defense, 116th overall. They brought in Todd Orlando from Texas to shake up the scheme, specifically to play to the strengths of USC's edge rushers; Orlando likes to show multiple aggressive blitzes. It's hard to make too much of a short and volatile 2020 for the Trojans, and they're turning over almost 35% of the defense this fall. The offense will be able to score enough to keep USC competitive in most games, but the defense has a few questions to answer before USC can make a push from good to great.

22. North Carolina Tar Heels (8.9 mean wins)

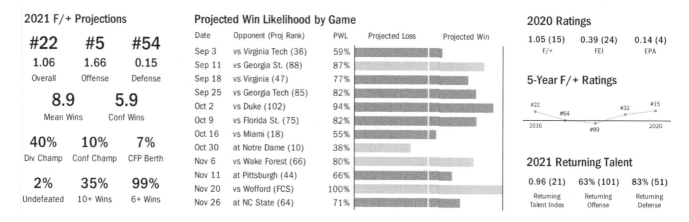

2021 F/+ Projections

#22	#5	#54
1.06	1.66	0.15
Overall	Offense	Defense

8.9	5.9
Mean Wins	Conf Wins

40%	10%	7%
Div Champ	Conf Champ	CFP Berth

2%	35%	99%
Undefeated	10+ Wins	6+ Wins

Projected Win Likelihood by Game

Date	Opponent (Proj Rank)	PWL
Sep 3	vs Virginia Tech (36)	59%
Sep 11	vs Georgia St. (88)	87%
Sep 18	vs Virginia (47)	77%
Sep 25	vs Georgia Tech (85)	82%
Oct 2	vs Duke (102)	94%
Oct 9	vs Florida St. (75)	82%
Oct 16	vs Miami (18)	55%
Oct 30	at Notre Dame (10)	38%
Nov 6	vs Wake Forest (66)	80%
Nov 11	at Pittsburgh (44)	66%
Nov 20	vs Wofford (FCS)	100%
Nov 26	at NC State (64)	71%

2020 Ratings

1.05 (15)	0.39 (24)	0.14 (4)
F/+	FEI	EPA

5-Year F/+ Ratings

#22 (2016), #64, #89, #32, #15 (2020)

2021 Returning Talent

0.96 (21)	63% (101)	83% (51)
Returning Talent Index	Returning Offense	Returning Defense

Sam Howell entered 2020 with a lot of hype and lived up to it. Howell threw for 30 touchdowns and 3,500 yards, completing 68% of his passes and leading the Tar Heels to an 8-3 regular season record. Carolina had a fierce rushing attack, and an offense capable of scoring with the best in the nation, but 2020 felt like a tragedy of missed timing for the Tar Heels. North Carolina largely feasted on lesser competition, punctuating their regular season with a 62-26 rout of Miami, but struggled to move the ball consistently at times (17 points against Notre Dame, 28 against Florida State) and the defense gave up points in big moments that induced presumably avoidable losses and tight situations (44 points to Virginia, 53 to Wake Forest, and 31 to Florida State). The Tar Heels return 82% of their defense, but the unit finished 103rd in EPA/play in 2020 (0.252). The most notable hole to fill will be the departure of linebacker Chazz Suratt, who led the team in tackles in 2020. Eugene Asante, a junior, will most likely fill that role, building on a 2020 where he had 19 tackles in limited time behind Suratt. Given the Tar Heels tendency to get into shootouts, pass coverage will be a primary concern,

and the trio of cornerbacks Kyler McMichael, Tony Grimes, and Storm Duck will be more than suited to the task. With a full offseason of work, those three should be among the best in the ACC.

Standout running backs Javonte Williams and Michael Carter have both left for the NFL after combining for over 2,000 rushing yards and 28 touchdowns last season. Tennessee transfer Ty Chandler will have to bear much of the rushing load. In the passing game, Howell will have to find new favorite targets, as Dyami Brown and Dazz Newsome (combined 1,773 yards, 109 receptions, and 14 touchdowns) left for the NFL. Who replaces those two is an open question, but two names to watch are Khafre Brown and Emery Simmons, who both had limited but productive targets in 2020. The Tar Heels made a New Year's Six Bowl, the first time in the Playoff era, and eight wins matches their second-best total since 2012. What does improvement look like for the Tar Heels after such a season? The wide receiver question must get settled, but a dynamic running attack coupled with a veteran Heisman contender at quarterback makes the ceiling high.

23. Arizona State Sun Devils (8.3 mean wins)

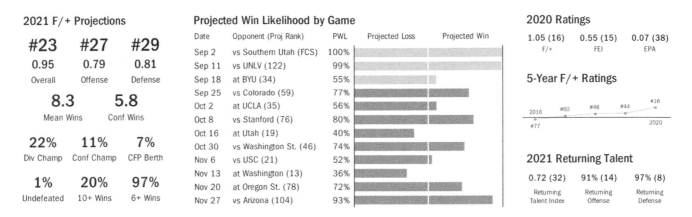

Like the rest of the Pac-12, Arizona State had a short season that's hard to take any conclusions from. They lost one-score games to USC and UCLA, then finished the season by blowing out Arizona 70-7 and beating Oregon State by double digits. Despite a 2-2 record, the Sun Devils were a top-40 team, averaging a 0.066 EPA margin on the season. Arizona State's play was highlighted by 0.290 EPA/play on offense (13th overall), built primarily on big plays. Quarterback Jayden Daniels completed 58.3% of his passes last year for 8.3 yards per attempt, but the offense was mostly driven by the rushing game: Freshman Chip Trayanum rushed for four touchdowns and averaged 5.9 yards per carry in 2020, and junior Rachaad White had five touchdowns and 10.0 yards per carry on 42 carries. That combination of consistency and explosiveness in the run game should continue, as the Sun Devils return four of five starters across the offensive line. The weapons on the edge are a question, as top target LV Bunkley-Shelton (11 receptions, 96 yards) showed some

flashes of greatness but has a thin supporting cast around him. Offensive coordinator Zak Hill has historically gotten tight ends more involved, and so it will be interesting to see how the three transfer tight ends joining the Sun Devils will factor into the offense. Overall, Daniels gives a very high potential to this offense, coupled with the solid run game and returning offensive line, and Arizona State will look to keep that explosive ceiling high while raising the floor with more consistent success.

The defense lagged for Arizona State, allowing an almost absurd 0.349 EPA/play, 123rd nationally. Almost 97% of that unit returns, including leading tackler Evan Fields (28 tackles) at safety and top edge rusher Tyler Johnson (five sacks, 11 tackles). Including those two, the Sun Devils return their 11 top tacklers from 2020, and the unit will have a full offseason in which to work and improve. Again, with such a short 2020 season, not too much should be taken away from defensive struggles, but it will be a unit to watch as Arizona State's defensive efficiency will be the limiting factor in their Pac-12 success. Arizona State hosts USC, but has road games at UCLA, Washington, and Utah on the schedule that all present as daunting threats. Daniels is a highly entertaining player, and Herm Edwards' team has made progress every year he's been in Tempe. 2021 lines up to be a year where Edwards has

a roster full of his guys and his vision for the program will get tested on the field.

Of course, none of this considers pending NCAA action on allegations of recruiting violations at Arizona State, and so 2021 could have plenty of opportunities for off-field distractions for the Sun Devils.

24. Oklahoma State Cowboys (7.6 mean wins)

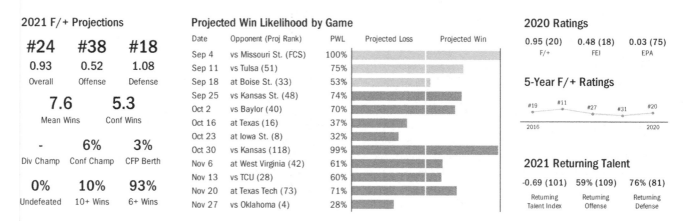

2021 F/+ Projections

#24	#38	#18
0.93	0.52	1.08
Overall	Offense	Defense

7.6	5.3
Mean Wins	Conf Wins

-	6%	3%
Div Champ	Conf Champ	CFP Berth

0%	10%	93%
Undefeated	10+ Wins	6+ Wins

Projected Win Likelihood by Game

Date	Opponent (Proj Rank)	PWL	Projected Loss	Projected Win
Sep 4	vs Missouri St. (FCS)	100%		
Sep 11	vs Tulsa (51)	75%		
Sep 18	at Boise St. (33)	53%		
Sep 25	vs Kansas St. (48)	74%		
Oct 2	vs Baylor (40)	70%		
Oct 16	at Texas (16)	37%		
Oct 23	at Iowa St. (8)	32%		
Oct 30	vs Kansas (118)	99%		
Nov 6	at West Virginia (42)	61%		
Nov 13	vs TCU (28)	60%		
Nov 20	at Texas Tech (73)	71%		
Nov 27	vs Oklahoma (4)	28%		

2020 Ratings

0.95 (20)	0.48 (18)	0.03 (75)
F/+	FEI	EPA

5-Year F/+ Ratings

#19   #11   #27   #31   #20
2016   2020

2021 Returning Talent

-0.69 (101)	59% (109)	76% (81)
Returning Talent Index	Returning Offense	Returning Defense

Quarterback Spencer Sanders threw two passes against Tulsa in the 2020 opener before going out with a leg injury, but thanks to a bye week, a cancellation, and games against then-struggling West Virginia and the all-but-inept Kansas Jayhawks, Oklahoma State was able to tread water until Sanders rejoined the team against Iowa State. The Cowboys went 5-3 over the next eight games, largely beating teams they should have and losing to those they should have. A one-score loss at TCU and another beatdown at the hands of rival Oklahoma were certainly letdowns, but Sanders completed 61.8% of his passes with 14 touchdowns.

The Cowboys offense, usually potent under Mike Gundy, was primarily built around Tylan Wallace and Chubba Hubbard. The two were involved on 31% of all of Oklahoma State's offensive snaps, leading the team in receptions and rushing attempts, respectively. Unfortunately, Wallace missed time with a knee injury and Hubbard battled an ankle injury all season, opting out after the Oklahoma game. With all the injuries, the Cowboys offense had its worst statistical season in years, averaging just 0.089 EPA/play, 101st in the nation. Sanders returns and running backs LD Brown (5.3 yards per carry and two touchdowns on 82 carries) and Dezmon Jackson (5.4 yards per carry and four touchdowns on 100 carries)

will have their chance to take over in the rushing game. At receiver, top targets Wallace (15.6 yards per reception, six touchdowns) and Dillon Stoner (42 receptions, 13.6 yards per reception) moved up to the next level, and redshirt freshman Braydon Johnson returns as the most experienced receiver (12.4 yards per reception, 20 receptions), but Washington State transfer Tay Martin should play a substantial role. The offensive line brings in JUCO transfer Caleb Ettienne and experienced Miami-Ohio center Danny Godlevske to round out the unit.

On defense, Oklahoma State allowed just 0.082 EPA/play, 19th nationally, which perhaps makes the offensive struggles sting that much more. They'll return 76% of their production, with the most notable loss being sixth-round corner Rodarius Williams. Linebacker Malcolm Rodriguez (66 tackles, two sacks) and Safety Kolby Harvell-Peel (35 tackles, two interceptions) look to repeat the stellar 2020 defensive effort as the offense grows up a bit and stays healthier for Oklahoma State. The Big 12's middle class is crowded, and the Cowboys have daunting road games in Austin, Morgantown, and Lubbock this fall, but with defensive consistency and the usual Gundy-quality offense, Oklahoma State should be in the conversation for the Big 12 Championship Game again.

25. Michigan Wolverines (7.1 mean wins)

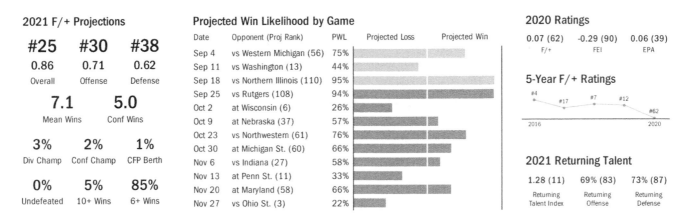

2021 F/+ Projections

#25	#30	#38
0.86	0.71	0.62
Overall	Offense	Defense

7.1	5.0
Mean Wins	Conf Wins

3%	2%	1%
Div Champ	Conf Champ	CFP Berth

0%	5%	85%
Undefeated	10+ Wins	6+ Wins

Projected Win Likelihood by Game

Date	Opponent (Proj Rank)	PWL
Sep 4	vs Western Michigan (56)	75%
Sep 11	vs Washington (13)	44%
Sep 18	vs Northern Illinois (110)	95%
Sep 25	vs Rutgers (108)	94%
Oct 2	at Wisconsin (6)	26%
Oct 9	at Nebraska (37)	57%
Oct 23	vs Northwestern (61)	76%
Oct 30	at Michigan St. (60)	66%
Nov 6	vs Indiana (27)	58%
Nov 13	at Penn St. (11)	33%
Nov 20	at Maryland (58)	66%
Nov 27	vs Ohio St. (3)	22%

2020 Ratings

0.07 (62)	-0.29 (90)	0.06 (39)
F/+	FEI	EPA

5-Year F/+ Ratings

#4 #17 #7 #12 #62
2016 — 2020

2021 Returning Talent

1.28 (11)	69% (83)	73% (87)
Returning Talent Index	Returning Offense	Returning Defense

Jim Harbaugh has won 49 games during his tenure in Ann Arbor, averaging 8.2 wins a season (9.4 if one ignores a shortened 2020 season). His predecessors averaged 7.8 and 5.0 wins per season, respectively. In fact, Harbaugh has won more games in six seasons with the Wolverines than the program had won between Lloyd Carr's 2007 departure and the start of Harbaugh's tenure. And yet, the hope at Michigan is to compete for a national championship. On that account, despite consistently having one of the better teams in college football, Harbaugh has failed. 2020 saw a 2-4 record, with the only wins coming over a Minnesota team in disarray and lowly Rutgers in a one-score affair. If the Wolverines could forget about 2020 altogether, they'd like to. Neither the offense nor the defense was abysmal in 2020, averaging 0.186 EPA/play (49th) and allowing 0.162 (54th), but both were well below the expectation and talent level of Michigan. Quarterback Joe Milton transferred after losing his starting job to Cade McNamara, who will take over the role full time in 2021. In four games last season, McNamara threw for five touchdowns and completed 60.6% of his passes, but the offense was far from mature with McNamara at the helm, focusing more on short, quick passes than the deeper throws Milton had been asked to make. McNamara will have a full offseason to work through the offense, and he'll have some nice playmaking options around him. Receiver Ronnie Bell returns, leading the team in receptions (26) and yards per reception (15.4) in 2020, and Cornelius Johnson (three touchdowns, 15.3 yards per reception) will complement him. The offensive line allowed just two sacks last season and returns four experienced starters, while running back Hassaan Haskins will drive the ground game (6.1 yards per carry and six touchdowns in 2020).

The defense returns just shy of 73% of its production, and they'll miss especially end Kwity Paye. Linebacker Josh Ross (36 tackles and an interception), safety Daxton Hill (43 tackles and an interception), and edge Aidan Hutchinson (13 tackles) are the foundations on which new defensive coordinator Mike Macdonald will build. Macdonald takes over for longtime coordinator Don Brown, and with shakeups at both coordinator positions over the last two years, Harbaugh is hoping he finally has the right recipe for Michigan to play up to their own expectations, and that of their fans. The Wolverines face a tough November, hosting Indiana and traveling to Penn State and Maryland before their annual rivalry game against Ohio State. Michigan can have a good season without a great November, but for Harbaugh to get the program where he wants it, they'll have to be ready for that tricky four-game stretch.

26. UCF Knights (9.0 mean wins)

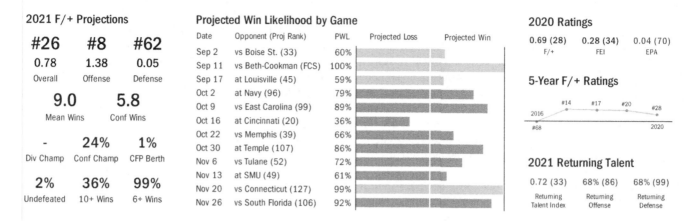

2021 F/+ Projections

#26	#8	#62
0.78	1.38	0.05
Overall	Offense	Defense

9.0	5.8
Mean Wins	Conf Wins

-	24%	1%
Div Champ	Conf Champ	CFP Berth

2%	36%	99%
Undefeated	10+ Wins	6+ Wins

Projected Win Likelihood by Game

Date	Opponent (Proj Rank)	PWL	Projected Loss	Projected Win
Sep 2	vs Boise St. (33)	60%		
Sep 11	vs Beth-Cookman (FCS)	100%		
Sep 17	at Louisville (45)	59%		
Oct 2	at Navy (96)	79%		
Oct 9	vs East Carolina (99)	89%		
Oct 16	at Cincinnati (20)	36%		
Oct 22	vs Memphis (39)	66%		
Oct 30	at Temple (107)	86%		
Nov 6	vs Tulane (52)	72%		
Nov 13	at SMU (49)	61%		
Nov 20	vs Connecticut (127)	99%		
Nov 26	vs South Florida (106)	92%		

2020 Ratings

0.69 (28)	0.28 (34)	0.04 (70)
F/+	FEI	EPA

5-Year F/+ Ratings

2016: #68 · #14 · #17 · #20 · #28 · 2020

2021 Returning Talent

0.72 (33)	68% (86)	68% (99)
Returning Talent Index	Returning Offense	Returning Defense

Since going winless in 2015, UCF has averaged 9.4 wins per year across two coaches, including two undefeated regular seasons and two New Year's Six bowl appearances. After another solid season in 2020, coach Josh Heupel took the Tennessee job, leaving UCF with a coaching search and some questions about its future. When faced with a problem, one can either go big or go home, and UCF certainly went big. Recently freed from the malaise on the plains, former Auburn coach Gus Malzahn takes over in Orlando after nine straight winning seasons in the SEC West, including a BCS championship appearance and two New Year's Six bowls. UCF, after hiring and succeeding with two up and comers, has hedged its bets in advance of structural changes in college football like playoff expansion by hiring an establishment coach. Malzahn, lauded for his offensive mind, will get to work with veteran Dillon Gabriel at quarterback. Gabriel has started for two seasons in Orlando, throwing for more than 3,500 yards in both. In 2020, Gabriel averaged 8.6 yards per attempt and completed 60% of his passes, throwing for 32 touchdowns in 10 games. Gabriel also averaged 5.4 yards per rushing attempt, adding two touchdowns on the ground. Leading target Marlon Williams left for the NFL draft last season, so look for juniors Jaylen Robinson (17.8 yards per reception, six touchdowns) and Ryan O'Keefe to play prominent roles in the pass game, although the Knights also bring in transfer Jordan Johnson from Notre Dame, a former four-star recruit.

On defense, UCF takes substantial losses. The Knights struggled last season, allowing 0.299 EPA/play on defense (119th) and giving up 30 or more points to six opponents. Senior linebacker Eriq Gilyard (second in tackles with 44) returns for another season, adding some stability, as does safety Derek Gainous (41 tackles). Travis Williams, a long-time Malzahn assistant, takes over as defensive coordinator for UCF, and he'll have to get creative to improve the Knights on that side of the ball. UCF's biggest hurdle in reclaiming their AAC championship is a regular-season road game at Cincinnati. The Knights and Bearcats have split the series three and three, with Cincinnati taking the last two games by one score each. With Gabriel as one of the conference's more experienced and talented quarterbacks, the offensive pieces are there for UCF to have another excellent season and a shot at a third New Year's Six appearance in just five years, if Malzahn and Williams can revitalize the defense.

27. Indiana Hoosiers (7.0 mean wins)

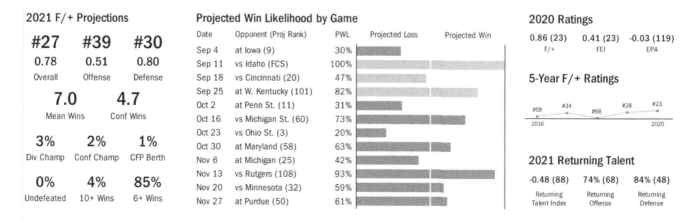

2021 F/+ Projections

#27	#39	#30
0.78	0.51	0.80
Overall	Offense	Defense

7.0	4.7
Mean Wins	Conf Wins

3%	2%	1%
Div Champ	Conf Champ	CFP Berth

0%	4%	85%
Undefeated	10+ Wins	6+ Wins

Projected Win Likelihood by Game

Date	Opponent (Proj Rank)	PWL	Projected Loss	Projected Win
Sep 4	at Iowa (9)	30%		
Sep 11	vs Idaho (FCS)	100%		
Sep 18	vs Cincinnati (20)	47%		
Sep 25	at W. Kentucky (101)	82%		
Oct 2	at Penn St. (11)	31%		
Oct 16	vs Michigan St. (60)	73%		
Oct 23	vs Ohio St. (3)	20%		
Oct 30	at Maryland (58)	63%		
Nov 6	at Michigan (25)	42%		
Nov 13	vs Rutgers (108)	93%		
Nov 20	vs Minnesota (32)	59%		
Nov 27	at Purdue (50)	61%		

2020 Ratings

0.86 (23)	0.41 (23)	-0.03 (119)
F/+	FEI	EPA

5-Year F/+ Ratings

2016: #59 · #34 · #66 · #28 · #23 · 2020

2021 Returning Talent

-0.48 (88)	74% (68)	84% (48)
Returning Talent Index	Returning Offense	Returning Defense

Indiana has improved their winning percentage every year since 2018, as head coach Tom Allen has molded the roster to meet his needs. In 2019, they finished a respectable 8-5, ranked during the season in the AP poll for the first time since 1994. In 2020, they finished 12th in the polls, and in 2021, Allen and the Hoosiers want to compete for the Big Ten championship. The Hoosiers might have a chip on their shoulder in 2021 after the conference blatantly reconfigured the rules regarding selection into the Big Ten Championship Game, preferring to protect Ohio State's playoff resume rather than consistently applying agreed-upon procedures. That energy, plus returning 80% of total production, lends itself to 2021 being a big year for Indiana.

Quarterback Michael Penix Jr. was less accurate than he had been in his career, with a 56.4% completion rate, but was also more productive, throwing for 1,645 yards and 14 touchdowns in just six games. Due to injury, Penix was out against Wisconsin (a 14-6 loss for the Hoosiers) and the bowl game against Mississippi (a 26-20 loss), and it's hard to imagine what the expectations for the Indiana Hoosiers would be in 2021 if either or both of those games had involved Penix. As is, Penix returns in 2021, along with dynamic deep threat Ty Fryfogle at receiver (seven touchdowns, 19.3 yards per reception), but there are holes to fill with the departure of Whop Phylor (54 receptions, 9.1 yards per reception) and running back Stevie Scott III (3.6 yards per carry, 10 touchdowns). USC transfer Stephen Carr, a former five-star recruit, should slot into the running back role, and two transfer wide receivers (D.J. Matthews from Florida State and Camron Buckley from Texas A&M) could contribute immediately.

On defense, Indiana's 2020 could be described as stingy enough; they held opponents to 21 or fewer points in five of their games and did enough to give the offense a shot to win in the other three. The highlight of the Indiana defense will be the return of Marcelino McCrary-Ball, the team captain who suffered an ACL injury in fall camp last year. McCrary-Ball will be a nice shot in the arm for Indiana, and the secondary led by corner Tiawan Mullen (13 tackles, three interceptions) should continue to be a strength. A team like Indiana, with such an explosive offensive threat, needs less from their defense. To take the step from being a fun top-20 team with a good story to a competitor for the conference championship and the playoff, the Hoosiers will need a defensive improvement. Watch for Cincinnati coming to Bloomington in the third game of the year, which may end up being one of the Hoosiers' tougher opponents on the season.

28. TCU Horned Frogs (7.3 mean wins)

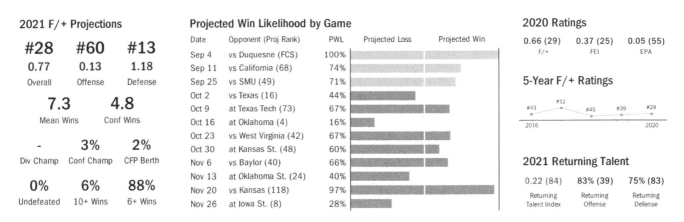

The TCU Horned Frogs have been in the desert for a couple of years. Quarterback issues have plagued the Frogs since 2018, and a revolving door of injury and opportunity at offensive line have only made things worse. The Frogs missed a bowl in 2019, only the second time TCU had won single-digit games in back-to-back seasons in Gary Patterson's 20-year career. TCU eked out wins against Texas and Oklahoma State, but looked troubled on offense for much of the 2020 campaign. Inside receivers coach Doug Meachem, back at TCU, takes over as the coordinator after Sonnie Cumbie left for the Texas Tech job. The Frogs finished 91st in EPA/play in 2021 (0.112), and instability along the offensive line was largely responsible -- the TCU offensive line allowed 12 sacks, and 11 players started games in 2020. In addition to offensive line woes, TCU's offensive design struggled to play to the strengths of its roster.

Max Duggan completed 59.9% of his passes for 7.4 yards per attempt and rushed for 6.5 yards per carry and ten touchdowns, but almost one third of his carries were scrambles. TCU brings in Memphis transfer Obina Eze, a two-year starter, to alleviate some issues on the offensive line, and the health of guard Wes Harris should stabilize the unit some. The two names to know on the TCU offense are wide receiver Quentin Johnston and running back Zach Evans. Johnston (22 receptions, 22.1 yards per reception) is TCU's deep threat receiver, and his athleticism and 6-foot-4 frame make him one of the more dangerous players in the conference. Evans has positioned himself as the feature back in TCU's offense; he averaged 7.7 yards per carry on the season and had two 100-yard performances down the stretch for TCU.

Patterson defenses are predictably consistent, and although

the Frogs lose three starters from the 2020 unit that finished 13th in EPA/play allowed (0.067), 2021 should be no different. At the corner position, TCU has a fearsome duo in Tre-Vius Hodges-Tomlinson and Noah Daniels, and Memphis transfer TJ Carter will slot into one of the safety roles. Second-team All-Conference defensive end Ochaun Mathis made huge strides in 2020 (nine sacks, 33 tackles), and improved defensive line play should only decrease the pressure on the secondary to replace three NFL draft picks. With improved line play on both sides of the ball and the first full offseason of work for quarterback Duggan, TCU has an opportunity to play itself into the Big 12 Championship in Arlington. Look for a late-November matchup against Iowa State in Ames to be a de facto play-in game.

29. Louisiana Ragin' Cajuns (9.1 mean wins)

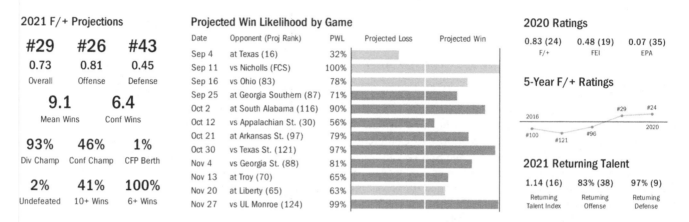

2021 F/+ Projections

#29	#26	#43
0.73	0.81	0.45
Overall	Offense	Defense

9.1	6.4
Mean Wins	Conf Wins

93%	46%	1%
Div Champ	Conf Champ	CFP Berth

2%	41%	100%
Undefeated	10+ Wins	6+ Wins

Projected Win Likelihood by Game

Date	Opponent (Proj Rank)	PWL
Sep 4	at Texas (16)	32%
Sep 11	vs Nicholls (FCS)	100%
Sep 16	vs Ohio (83)	78%
Sep 25	at Georgia Southern (87)	71%
Oct 2	at South Alabama (116)	90%
Oct 12	vs Appalachian St. (30)	56%
Oct 21	at Arkansas St. (97)	79%
Oct 30	vs Texas St. (121)	97%
Nov 4	vs Georgia St. (88)	81%
Nov 13	at Troy (70)	65%
Nov 20	at Liberty (65)	63%
Nov 27	vs UL Monroe (124)	99%

2020 Ratings

0.83 (24)	0.48 (19)	0.07 (35)
F/+	FEI	EPA

5-Year F/+ Ratings

2021 Returning Talent

1.14 (16)	83% (38)	97% (9)
Returning Talent Index	Returning Offense	Returning Defense

The Louisiana Ragin' Cajuns never got their shot at a rematch with Coastal Carolina. The Chanticleers won in Lafayette 30-27, and the Ragin' Cajuns' chance at vengeance was cancelled due to health protocols. Billy Napier and his team feel they were the best of the Sun Belt, and Louisiana has their eyes on proving themselves this season. They'll have the opportunity, for sure; Louisiana kicks off the season in Austin, facing the Texas Longhorns and new coach Steve Sarkesian. They'll have to make it to the Sun Belt championship to get another shot at Coastal, but they have the opportunity for a stellar resume with games against Appalachian State and Liberty on the schedule, not to mention expected improvements from division rivals South Alabama, Arkansas State, and Texas State this season. Louisiana returns the 15th-most production in the FBS this fall, led by quarterback Levi Lewis (59.1% completion rate, 19 touchdowns in 2020) and running back Trey Ragas (5.8 yards per carry, 10 touchdowns). In fact, on offense, Louisiana brings back all but two starters from the nation's 30th-most efficient team (0.229 EPA/play). The receiving corps of Kyren Lacy, Peter Leblanc, and Jalen Williams will be the best in the conference (71 combined completions, 13 touchdowns, 1,060 yards in 2020) and an experienced and deep offensive line will allow the Ragin' Cajuns to impose their will on offense.

On defense, redshirt junior Zi'Yon Hill (four sacks, 33 tackles) will cause disruption up front, while the back seven will be anchored by safeties Bralen Trahan and Percy Butler (73 combined tackles, six interceptions). The linebacking duo of Ferrod Gardner and Lorenzo McCaskill led the team in tackles with 55 and 47 respectively, and you can see the imposing depth of this experienced defense start to take shape. Especially in a conference like the Sun Belt, where Louisiana should be substantially more talented than many of its opponents, this returning experience will go a long way. Louisiana sacked opponents 23 times in 2020 and intercepted 16 passes. While Lewis and the offense get a lot of the praise, the Ragin' Cajun defense was solid last year and should mature this fall. Look for Louisiana to be in the Sun Belt Championship Game, but more importantly, look for them to be posturing for a New Year's Six bid with their resume.

30. Appalachian State Mountaineers (8.9 mean wins)

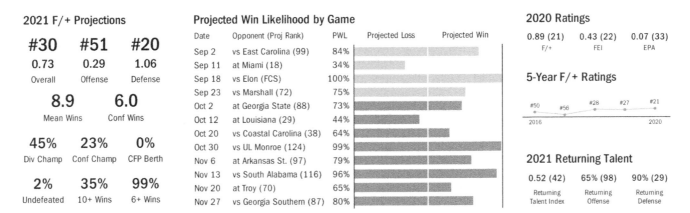

2021 F/+ Projections

#30	#51	#20
0.73	0.29	1.06
Overall	Offense	Defense

8.9	6.0
Mean Wins	Conf Wins

45%	23%	0%
Div Champ	Conf Champ	CFP Berth

2%	35%	99%
Undefeated	10+ Wins	6+ Wins

Projected Win Likelihood by Game

Date	Opponent (Proj Rank)	PWL	Projected Loss	Projected Win
Sep 2	vs East Carolina (99)	84%		
Sep 11	at Miami (18)	34%		
Sep 18	vs Elon (FCS)	100%		
Sep 23	vs Marshall (72)	75%		
Oct 2	at Georgia State (88)	73%		
Oct 12	at Louisiana (29)	44%		
Oct 20	vs Coastal Carolina (38)	64%		
Oct 30	vs UL Monroe (124)	99%		
Nov 6	at Arkansas St. (97)	79%		
Nov 13	vs South Alabama (116)	96%		
Nov 20	at Troy (70)	65%		
Nov 27	vs Georgia Southern (87)	80%		

2020 Ratings

0.89 (21)	0.43 (22)	0.07 (33)
F/+	FEI	EPA

5-Year F/+ Ratings

#50   #56   #28   #27   #21
2016   2020

2021 Returning Talent

0.52 (42)	65% (98)	90% (29)
Returning Talent Index	Returning Offense	Returning Defense

What a privilege for App State to say that 2020 was a down year. The Mountaineers finished 6-3, losing to two ranked teams by a total of 14 points plus a road loss to Conference USA runner-up Marshall. Since joining the Sun Belt in 2014, App State has lost more than four games once, and won 10 or more four times. This program expects to be at the top of the conference year in and year out, and the 2021 Sun Belt race between the Mountaineers, Coastal Carolina, and Louisiana could be the most exciting storyline of the Group of 5. App State unfortunately draws both Coastal Carolina and Louisiana, making their road to the conference championship game much tougher than the other two, who don't play each other. The Mountaineers return 78% of total production, though, and are poised in head coach Shawn Clark's second year to play up to their historical level of consistency.

The big storyline is how new offensive coordinator Frank Ponce will replace three-year starter Zac Thomas at quarterback. In 2020, Thomas threw for 2,184 yards and 20 touchdowns, averaging 7.4 yards per attempt. The Mountaineers will bring in former Clemson and Duke quarterback Chase Brice as a grad transfer, and he should start immediately. Brice had a rough year as the starter at Duke (2,169 yards, 6.2 yards per attempt, 15 interceptions to 10 touchdowns), and only limited experience at Clemson, but a change of scenery and competition level might suit his experience well. Brice can connect with a deep stable of receivers, including yards leader Thomas Hennigan (47 receptions, 13.1 yards per reception) and Malik Williams (41 receptions, 13.1 yards per reception). The Mountaineers had five receivers with at least three touchdowns in 2020, and all five return for 2021. On defense, the Mountaineers return 90% of the nation's 24th-best defense. Replacing Shemar Jean-Charles' coverage at cornerback is the only real uncertainty this season, but senior Shaun Jolly played well opposite him in 2020 (34 tackles, four pass breakups) and should continue to progress. There are sure to be growing pains in replacing a coordinator and an experienced quarterback, but Appalachian State has the defensive continuity and offensive depth to continue this program's tradition of high-level competition.

31. Ole Miss Rebels (7.0 mean wins)

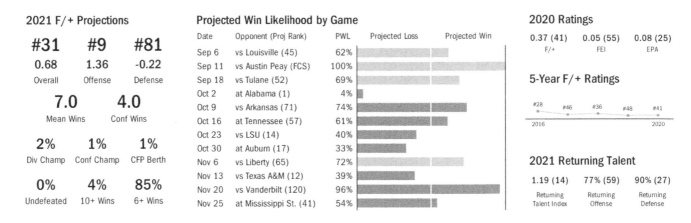

2021 F/+ Projections

#31	#9	#81
0.68	1.36	-0.22
Overall	Offense	Defense

7.0	4.0
Mean Wins	Conf Wins

2%	1%	1%
Div Champ	Conf Champ	CFP Berth

0%	4%	85%
Undefeated	10+ Wins	6+ Wins

Projected Win Likelihood by Game

Date	Opponent (Proj Rank)	PWL	Projected Loss	Projected Win
Sep 6	vs Louisville (45)	62%		
Sep 11	vs Austin Peay (FCS)	100%		
Sep 18	vs Tulane (52)	69%		
Oct 2	at Alabama (1)	4%		
Oct 9	vs Arkansas (71)	74%		
Oct 16	at Tennessee (57)	61%		
Oct 23	vs LSU (14)	40%		
Oct 30	at Auburn (17)	33%		
Nov 6	vs Liberty (65)	72%		
Nov 13	vs Texas A&M (12)	39%		
Nov 20	vs Vanderbilt (120)	96%		
Nov 25	at Mississippi St. (41)	54%		

2020 Ratings

0.37 (41)	0.05 (55)	0.08 (25)
F/+	FEI	EPA

5-Year F/+ Ratings

#28   #46   #36   #48   #41
2016   2020

2021 Returning Talent

1.19 (14)	77% (59)	90% (27)
Returning Talent Index	Returning Offense	Returning Defense

Lane Kiffin has turned Ole Miss into the team they've always wanted to be. Quarterback Matt Corral threw for 29 touchdowns, and almost 25% of his attempts were 20 yards downfield or longer. Kiffin came to Oxford to chew bubble-gum and score touchdowns, and he's all out of bubble gum. The Rebels averaged 0.299 EPA/play on offense, 12th in the nation. They scored 30 points in seven games, 40 points in five games, and three of their five losses were one-score games. The particular brand of chaos and deep throws that Kiffin and offensive coordinator Jeff Lebby brought to Ole Miss should frustrate the SEC West for years to come. In 2020, they'll return with Corrall at quarterback and four starters along the offensive line but have to replace the uber-productive Elijah Moore at receiver (1,193 yards, 13.9 yards per reception, eight touchdowns). Look for Jonathan Mingo, a four-star recruit, to be a high-volume contributor for the pass-happy offense. He had 27 receptions for three touchdowns in 2020 and averaged 14 yards per reception. On defense, the Rebels are blessed with continuity, except in the interior defensive line. Ole Miss

returns 90% of its 2020 production with a couple of junior college transfers expected to fill in for transfer Ryder Anderson (three sacks, 22 tackles), who left for Indiana.

The Rebels open with Louisville on Monday of Labor Day weekend, which should be a chance to show off their offensive prowess. They kick off conference play a month later with a visit to Tuscaloosa. It does help that their draw from the Eastern division this season is Tennessee and Vanderbilt. Ole Miss is a team to watch in the SEC West; whereas they have neither the depth nor talent of Alabama, Texas A&M, or LSU, they have offensive firepower perhaps unmatched in the entire conference. With Auburn taking a new coach, and Arkansas and Mississippi State taking on new quarterbacks, the Rebels could position themselves firmly in the top half of the division and pull off one or two upsets.

32. Minnesota Golden Gophers (7.0 mean wins)

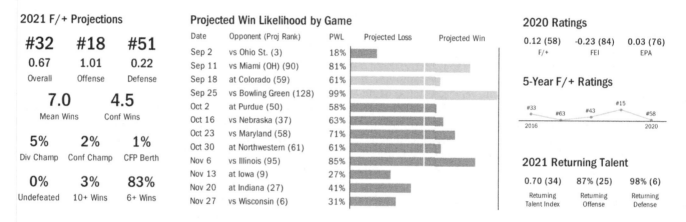

2021 F/+ Projections

#32	#18	#51
0.67	1.01	0.22
Overall	Offense	Defense

7.0	4.5
Mean Wins	Conf Wins

5%	2%	1%
Div Champ	Conf Champ	CFP Berth

0%	3%	83%
Undefeated	10+ Wins	6+ Wins

Projected Win Likelihood by Game

Date	Opponent (Proj Rank)	PWL
Sep 2	vs Ohio St. (3)	18%
Sep 11	vs Miami (OH) (90)	81%
Sep 18	at Colorado (59)	61%
Sep 25	vs Bowling Green (128)	99%
Oct 2	at Purdue (50)	58%
Oct 16	vs Nebraska (37)	63%
Oct 23	vs Maryland (58)	71%
Oct 30	at Northwestern (61)	61%
Nov 6	vs Illinois (95)	85%
Nov 13	at Iowa (9)	27%
Nov 20	at Indiana (27)	41%
Nov 27	vs Wisconsin (6)	31%

2020 Ratings

0.12 (58)	-0.23 (84)	0.03 (76)
F/+	FEI	EPA

5-Year F/+ Ratings

#33, #63, #43, #15, #58 (2016–2020)

2021 Returning Talent

0.70 (34)	87% (25)	98% (6)
Returning Talent Index	Returning Offense	Returning Defense

Minnesota's 2020 began as a letdown, starting out 1-3 and giving up 49, 45, and 35 points in losses to Michigan, Maryland, and Iowa. Quarterback Tanner Morgan struggled to find the same magic as he had in 2019, completing more than 60% of his passes in just three games as the Gophers stumbled to a 3-4 record and an EPA margin of 0.199, 76th in the nation. The good news? The Gophers are seventh in returning production, bringing back almost 95% of their 2020 team. Tanner Morgan returns for his third full season as the starter, and supporting receivers Chris Autman-Bell (22 receptions, 19.5 yards per reception) and Daniel Jackson (12 reception, 13.9 yards per reception) will have expanded roles as Rashod Bateman (472 yards, 36 receptions, 13.1 yards per reception) heads to the NFL. On the offensive line, Minnesota returns 2020 opt-out Daniel Faalele, one of the largest human beings in college football at

6-foot 9-inches and over 400 pounds, to shore up the unit, and running back Mohamed Ibrahim should improve after a standout 2020 (5.3 yards per carry, 15 touchdowns, 1,079 yards).

The defense needs to improve, having allowed 0.286 EPA/play in 2020, 116th nationally, but they'll have the experience and depth to do so. End Boye Mafe will return as the spear of the defensive line (six sacks, 17 tackles in 2020), and middle linebacker Mariona Sori-Marin made some strides last season, leading the team in tackles (41). The Gophers draw Ohio State, Indiana, and Maryland from the East this year, which makes their task in climbing atop the Big Ten West that much more difficult, but they'll have time to get right before finishing the season with a three week stretch against Iowa, Indiana, and Wisconsin, hopefully with a place in the championship game on the line.

33. Boise State Broncos (8.4 mean wins)

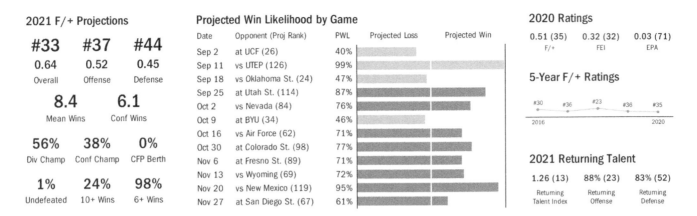

2021 F/+ Projections

#33	#37	#44
0.64	0.52	0.45
Overall	Offense	Defense

8.4	6.1
Mean Wins	Conf Wins

56%	38%	0%
Div Champ	Conf Champ	CFP Berth

1%	24%	98%
Undefeated	10+ Wins	6+ Wins

Projected Win Likelihood by Game

Date	Opponent (Proj Rank)	PWL	Projected Loss	Projected Win
Sep 2	at UCF (26)	40%		
Sep 11	vs UTEP (126)	99%		
Sep 18	vs Oklahoma St. (24)	47%		
Sep 25	at Utah St. (114)	87%		
Oct 2	vs Nevada (84)	76%		
Oct 9	at BYU (34)	46%		
Oct 16	vs Air Force (62)	71%		
Oct 30	at Colorado St. (98)	77%		
Nov 6	at Fresno St. (89)	71%		
Nov 13	vs Wyoming (69)	72%		
Nov 20	vs New Mexico (119)	95%		
Nov 27	at San Diego St. (67)	61%		

2020 Ratings

0.51 (35)	0.32 (32)	0.03 (71)
F/+	FEI	EPA

5-Year F/+ Ratings

#30 (2016), #36, #23, #36, #35 (2020)

2021 Returning Talent

1.26 (13)	88% (23)	83% (52)
Returning Talent Index	Returning Offense	Returning Defense

The question for Boise State the last few years was not whether head coach Bryan Harsin would take another job, but when he would take another job. Under Harsin, the Broncos have won 10 games five times, finishing ranked in the AP poll four times. Harsin left for the Auburn job after a 5-2 season where quarterback injury really limited opportunities for the Broncos. They bring in Andy Avalos from Oregon, and this fall, he will have plenty of continuity on the roster to begin to take Boise to the next level. The Broncos return 88% of their offense and 83% of their defense for 2020, and with some health at quarterback, the Broncos should be able to improve on both sides of the ball. The defense wasn't bad, finishing 31st in EPA/play allowed (0.121), but the offense struggled, at 0.135 EPA/play (82nd).

At quarterback, the Broncos have an open competition between junior Hank Bachmeier and redshirt senior Jack Sears. Bachmeier was the starter in 2019 and for most of last season when not hurt, and he should have the edge. He averaged 7.1 yards per attempt and completed 60% of his passes in 2020. Senior running back Andrew Van Buren averaged 3.4 yards per carry and scored eight touchdowns, heading up an effective, if limited, rushing attack. Expect his usage and output to improve as the Broncos, healthy at quarterback, will be able to pose a more credible passing threat. On defense, linebacker Riley Whimpey elected to use his fifth year of eligibility. He led the team in tackles last season. Redshirt freshman Kaonohi Kaniho (32 tackles, six pass breakups) will anchor a secondary looking to improve after allowing 250 passing yards in four games last season. The experience of San Jose State and the defensive excellence at San Diego State pose credible threats to Boise's 2021 run at a conference championship, but Andy Avalos's first season in Boise shouldn't look too different from what the Broncos have come to expect.

34. BYU Cougars (7.6 mean wins)

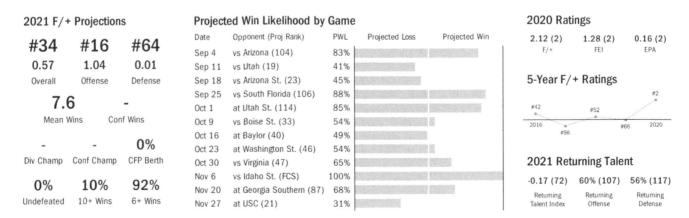

2021 F/+ Projections

#34	#16	#64
0.57	1.04	0.01
Overall	Offense	Defense

7.6	-
Mean Wins	Conf Wins

-	-	0%
Div Champ	Conf Champ	CFP Berth

0%	10%	92%
Undefeated	10+ Wins	6+ Wins

Projected Win Likelihood by Game

Date	Opponent (Proj Rank)	PWL	Projected Loss	Projected Win
Sep 4	vs Arizona (104)	83%		
Sep 11	vs Utah (19)	41%		
Sep 18	vs Arizona St. (23)	45%		
Sep 25	vs South Florida (106)	88%		
Oct 1	at Utah St. (114)	85%		
Oct 9	vs Boise St. (33)	54%		
Oct 16	at Baylor (40)	49%		
Oct 23	at Washington St. (46)	54%		
Oct 30	vs Virginia (47)	65%		
Nov 6	vs Idaho St. (FCS)	100%		
Nov 20	at Georgia Southern (87)	68%		
Nov 27	at USC (21)	31%		

2020 Ratings

2.12 (2)	1.28 (2)	0.16 (2)
F/+	FEI	EPA

5-Year F/+ Ratings

#42 (2016), #98, #52, #66, #2 (2020)

2021 Returning Talent

-0.17 (72)	60% (107)	56% (117)
Returning Talent Index	Returning Offense	Returning Defense

How do you replicate a lightning strike like Zach Wilson? The Cougars' offense finished fourth in EPA/play on offense, averaging 0.377 EPA/play and scoring 40 points in nine of their games. Strength of schedule was certainly a concern, but Zach Wilson made the slate look feeble for the most part, throwing for 32 touchdowns and 3,694 yards, and averaging 11.0 yards per attempt. The BYU Cougars' offense in 2020 was unequivocally and inarguably great.

So, what now? How can Kalani Sitake follow up 2020? Wilson left for the NFL, and offensive coordinator Jeff Grimes took the same position at Baylor. The good news on the coaching front is that newly promoted offensive coordinator Aaron Roderick and passing game coordinator Fesi Sitake have largely been the architects of BYU's offense during the last two seasons, and there is potential. Redshirt sophomore Jaren Hall should take over at quarterback as a first-time starter. Running back Tyler Allgeier returns after leading the team with 1,113 rushing yards, 13 touchdowns, and 7.6 yards per carry. They lose star tackle Brady Christensen but return three starters and have viable options to replace him in Blake Freeland and Harris LaChance. At wide receiver, Dax Milne's 70 receptions, 1,188 yards, and eight touchdowns will be missed, but Gunner Romney and Neil Pau'u combined for 83 receptions, over 1,300 yards, and five touchdowns last season. Tight end Issac Rex will surely be a force to be reckoned with;

he had 12 touchdowns on 37 receptions in 2020 and averaged 11.6 yards per reception.

The BYU defense is hard to project because they largely played well enough against a bad slate of teams. Holding UCF to just 23 points in the bowl game may be a good sign, but BYU returns only 56% of defensive production from last season, seven of their top 10 tacklers. Linebacker should be a strength for the Cougars, though, as Keenan Pili (56 tackles) and Payton Wilgar return (47 tackles), but the defense will have plenty of holes to fill. This season might be a rude awakening for BYU. Not only will they have to replace Wilson and most of the defense, they will also play seven Power 5 opponents and four Group of 5 opponents, a schedule almost infinitely more taxing than the year before. To the extent that scheduling realities drove BYU's success last season, they'll have to figure out their new quarterback quickly or face a slate of tough games that could get away from them.

35. UCLA Bruins (6.4 mean wins)

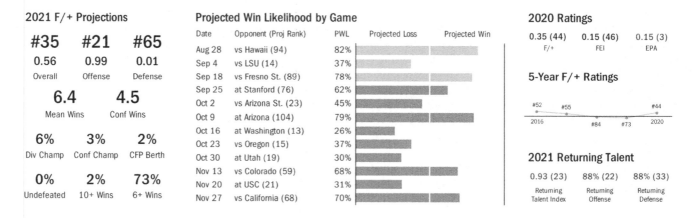

2021 F/+ Projections

#35	#21	#65
0.56	0.99	0.01
Overall	Offense	Defense

6.4	4.5
Mean Wins	Conf Wins

6%	3%	2%
Div Champ	Conf Champ	CFP Berth

0%	2%	73%
Undefeated	10+ Wins	6+ Wins

Projected Win Likelihood by Game

Date	Opponent (Proj Rank)	PWL
Aug 28	vs Hawaii (94)	82%
Sep 4	vs LSU (14)	37%
Sep 18	vs Fresno St. (89)	78%
Sep 25	at Stanford (76)	62%
Oct 2	vs Arizona St. (23)	45%
Oct 9	at Arizona (104)	79%
Oct 16	at Washington (13)	26%
Oct 23	vs Oregon (15)	37%
Oct 30	at Utah (19)	30%
Nov 13	vs Colorado (59)	68%
Nov 20	at USC (21)	31%
Nov 27	vs California (68)	70%

2020 Ratings

0.35 (44)	0.15 (46)	0.15 (3)
F/+	FEI	EPA

5-Year F/+ Ratings

2021 Returning Talent

0.93 (23)	88% (22)	88% (33)
Returning Talent Index	Returning Offense	Returning Defense

It has to work for Chip Kelly this year. If his brand of college football Moneyball doesn't show teeth this fall, will it ever? Kelly's Bruins have gone 3-9, 4-8, and 3-4 in his three seasons, and while his offensive innovation has been entertaining and commendable, it hasn't translated to an improvement in win-loss record. There are reasons for optimism, though: UCLA finished ninth on offense in 2020 (0.311 EPA/play) and 42nd on defense (0.151) and their four losses came by a total of 15 points. They return 88% of their offensive production and 88% of their defense, good enough for 22nd and 33rd in the country. At quarterback, Dorian Thompson-Robinson had a career year (65% completion rate, 8.1 yards per attempt, 12 touchdowns to four interceptions). He should be the starter, but don't be surprised to see transfer Ethan Garbers (pending eligibility issues) or backup Chase Griffin (64.5% completion rate and six touchdowns in two starts last year) eat into his time or compete in fall

camp. Receiver Kyle Phillips is poised for a big year. He led the team in receptions (38) last season as a dependable, short-range option. As Kelly has committed to involving multiple tight ends in his offense, watch for Greg Dulcich (26 receptions, five touchdowns, 19.9 yards per reception) to play a prominent role.

On defense, UCLA returns its top three tacklers: safeties Qwuantrezz Knight (35), and Stephan Blaylock (33), and cornerback Mo Osling III (33). Progress on defense might look like the Bruins having a linebacker step up and lead in tackles, but some of that depends on how opponents attack. The schedule this season will be tough, as they face LSU and Fresno State in the non-conference portion and their Pac-12 slate features trips to Washington and Utah, but if Kelly is right, and what he's been doing all along is actually working, the Bruins should be able to overcome some adversity on the schedule and compete for a Pac-12 championship.

36. Virginia Tech Hokies (7.6 mean wins)

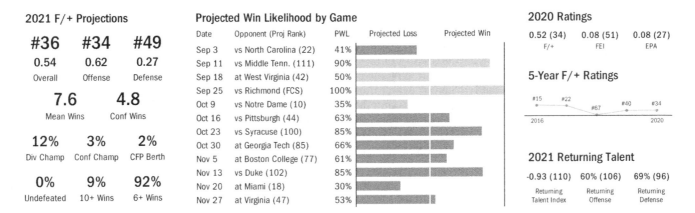

2021 F/+ Projections

#36	#34	#49
0.54	0.62	0.27
Overall	Offense	Defense

7.6	4.8
Mean Wins	Conf Wins

12%	3%	2%
Div Champ	Conf Champ	CFP Berth

0%	9%	92%
Undefeated	10+ Wins	6+ Wins

Projected Win Likelihood by Game

Date	Opponent (Proj Rank)	PWL	Projected Loss	Projected Win
Sep 3	vs North Carolina (22)	41%		
Sep 11	vs Middle Tenn. (111)	90%		
Sep 18	at West Virginia (42)	50%		
Sep 25	vs Richmond (FCS)	100%		
Oct 9	vs Notre Dame (10)	35%		
Oct 16	vs Pittsburgh (44)	63%		
Oct 23	vs Syracuse (100)	85%		
Oct 30	at Georgia Tech (85)	66%		
Nov 5	at Boston College (77)	61%		
Nov 13	vs Duke (102)	85%		
Nov 20	at Miami (18)	30%		
Nov 27	at Virginia (47)	53%		

2020 Ratings

0.52 (34)	0.08 (51)	0.08 (27)
F/+	FEI	EPA

5-Year F/+ Ratings

#15 #22 #67 #40 #34
2016 — 2020

2021 Returning Talent

-0.93 (110)	60% (106)	69% (96)
Returning Talent Index	Returning Offense	Returning Defense

Virginia Tech began 2020 3-1 and proceeded to lose five of their next seven games, including three one-score losses. Blowout losses to Pitt and Clemson certainly left a bad taste in the Hokies' mouth, although a convincing win against rival Virginia was a good way to finish things up. What to make of Justin Fuente's time in Blacksburg? The former TCU offensive coordinator and Memphis head coach won 10 and nine games his first two seasons, making four straight bowl appearances, but his tenure feels flatter than it looks on paper. Fuente will try to galvanize Virginia Tech in 2021 to break through the ceiling of mediocrity and become a real contender, but the turnover for the Hokies will make that a tall task. Virginia Tech returns just 65% of 2020 production (60% offense, 69% defense), 104th in the nation.

On defense, defensive back Divine Deablo leaves substantial shoes to fill in coverage (44 tackles, four interceptions), but the return of leading tackler Chamarri Conner makes that a little easier. The defensive line gets a boost with Clemson transfer Jordan Williams, and linebackers Alan Tisdale and Dax Hollifield combined for 74 tackles last season. On offense, the Hokies' line gets a makeover, with Christian Darrishaw leaving for the NFL and Doug Nester transferring. Leading rusher Khalil Herbert left for the NFL draft, and Rasheem Blackshear (3.8 yards per carry, two touchdowns) will look to take the brunt the workload. Quarterback will look different, too, as two-year starter Hendon Hooker transferred to Tennessee. Braxton Burmeister, a redshirt junior, will direct the offense; he completed 57.1% of attempts last season, averaging 8.2 yards per attempt.

Virginia Tech's schedule breaks oddly, with tough non-conference games against Notre Dame and West Virginia. With North Carolina, Miami, and Pitt on the schedule, all at home, the Hokies get a favorable draw. There's so much uncertainty with so much turnover, but Burmeister showed some flashes of competency last year. The questions are clear for Virginia Tech, and the opportunities to surpass projections present themselves; their fate in the ACC will depend on how quickly Virginia Tech can integrate key additions and replace departing production.

37. Nebraska Cornhuskers (5.6 mean wins)

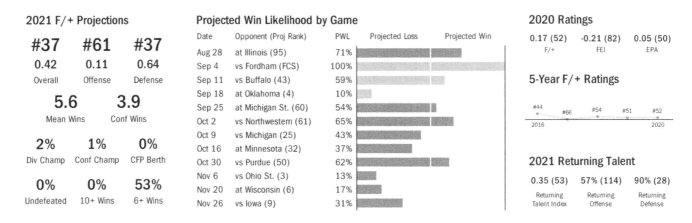

2021 F/+ Projections

#37	#61	#37
0.42	0.11	0.64
Overall	Offense	Defense

5.6	3.9
Mean Wins	Conf Wins

2%	1%	0%
Div Champ	Conf Champ	CFP Berth

0%	0%	53%
Undefeated	10+ Wins	6+ Wins

Projected Win Likelihood by Game

Date	Opponent (Proj Rank)	PWL	Projected Loss	Projected Win
Aug 28	at Illinois (95)	71%		
Sep 4	vs Fordham (FCS)	100%		
Sep 11	vs Buffalo (43)	59%		
Sep 18	at Oklahoma (4)	10%		
Sep 25	at Michigan St. (60)	54%		
Oct 2	vs Northwestern (61)	65%		
Oct 9	vs Michigan (25)	43%		
Oct 16	at Minnesota (32)	37%		
Oct 30	vs Purdue (50)	62%		
Nov 6	vs Ohio St. (3)	13%		
Nov 20	at Wisconsin (6)	17%		
Nov 26	vs Iowa (9)	31%		

2020 Ratings

0.17 (52)	-0.21 (82)	0.05 (50)
F/+	FEI	EPA

5-Year F/+ Ratings

#44 #66 #54 #51 #52
2016 — 2020

2021 Returning Talent

0.35 (53)	57% (114)	90% (28)
Returning Talent Index	Returning Offense	Returning Defense

Nebraska is yet to have a winning season under Scott Frost. Frost left Orlando for Lincoln after an undefeated 2017 at UCF, a much-heralded homecoming for the former Nebraska star, and the process of rebuilding the Cornhuskers has been slow. In 2020, Nebraska suffered a 52-17 blowout to Ohio State, but they also went 1-4 in one-score games. The Huskers finished just average on offense and defense in 2020 (58th in EPA/play on offense and 63rd on defense), and they averaged more than two turnovers a game, indicating that while Frost may be implementing his vision, the going is slow and messy.

Quarterback Adrian Martinez, a highly touted player who has struggled to live up to his reputation, returns at the helm, having successfully won a contest for the role against Luke McCaffery (transferring to Rice). Martinez completed 70% of his passes in 2020, but threw for only four touchdowns to three interceptions, and his options at wide receiver will look a little different; Wan'Dale Robinson leaves for Kentucky, although the Huskers bring in intriguing options at the wide receiver position in Samori Toure (Montana) and Oliver Martin (Iowa). Nebraska's defense will have an opportunity to build, as they return 90% of 2020's production. Look for Garrett Nelson (23 tackles, two sacks) to cause some havoc on the edge, and cornerback Quinton Newsome (40 tackles, four pass breakups) to make strides as a coverage defender. The Huskers will need to build a head of steam, as they end their season with Ohio State, Wisconsin, and Iowa, three games which will largely determine the narrative of Nebraska's season.

38. Coastal Carolina Chanticleers (9.3 mean wins)

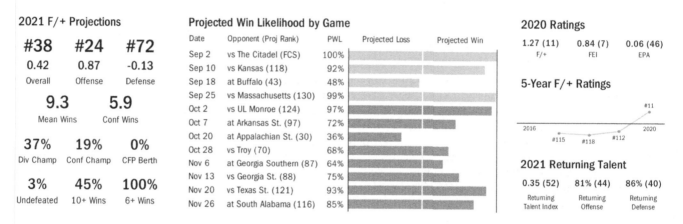

2021 F/+ Projections

#38	#24	#72
0.42	0.87	-0.13
Overall	Offense	Defense

9.3	5.9
Mean Wins	Conf Wins

37%	19%	0%
Div Champ	Conf Champ	CFP Berth

3%	45%	100%
Undefeated	10+ Wins	6+ Wins

Projected Win Likelihood by Game

Date	Opponent (Proj Rank)	PWL	Projected Loss	Projected Win
Sep 2	vs The Citadel (FCS)	100%		
Sep 10	vs Kansas (118)	92%		
Sep 18	at Buffalo (43)	48%		
Sep 25	vs Massachusetts (130)	99%		
Oct 2	vs UL Monroe (124)	97%		
Oct 7	at Arkansas St. (97)	72%		
Oct 20	at Appalachian St. (30)	36%		
Oct 28	vs Troy (70)	68%		
Nov 6	at Georgia Southern (87)	64%		
Nov 13	vs Georgia St. (88)	75%		
Nov 20	vs Texas St. (121)	93%		
Nov 26	at South Alabama (116)	85%		

2020 Ratings

1.27 (11)	0.84 (7)	0.06 (46)
F/+	FEI	EPA

5-Year F/+ Ratings

2021 Returning Talent

0.35 (52)	81% (44)	86% (40)
Returning Talent Index	Returning Offense	Returning Defense

The Chanticleers made waves in the world of college football last season, completing an undefeated regular season while playing a peculiar brand of pass-heavy option football. Coastal Carolina's offense wrapped triple-option concepts inside multiple formations to put defenders in conflict, pressuring defenses with snap decisions and employing a mobile-if-undersized offensive line to drive their rushing attack. The team also made waves with an ambitious scheduling maneuver, working amidst some logistical oddities of the 2020 season to schedule and play a game with then-undefeated BYU in an effort to enhance both teams' resumes. Coastal won that game, and they were rewarded with a trip to the Cure Bowl, for whatever that's worth. The Chanticleers lost that bowl game, but Jamey Chadwell's work is far from done in Conway.

Quarterback Grayson McCall will lead an offense looking to build on a top-25 performance in 2020; Coastal averaged 0.257 EPA/play and scored 30 points in nine of their 12 games. McCall was quietly brilliant, completing 66.7% of his passes for 26 touchdowns, averaging 9.7 yards per attempt. He comes into 2021 with a claim to the mantle of "Best Group of 5 quarterback" and is joined by almost the entire 2020 offense. Targets Javion Heiligh (15.4 yards per reception, 10 touchdowns) and Isaiah Likely (20.0 yards per reception, five touchdowns) will draw attention from opponents, and the offensive line returns all five starters. On the defensive side of the ball, the Chanticleers return 10 of 11 starters, lead by linebacker Teddy Gallagher (63 tackles) and cornerback D'Jordan Strong (five interceptions, 32 tackles). The defense allowed 0.257 EPA/play in 2020, which lagged far behind their offense, but the depth is there for this unit to make substantial progress. The question lingering over Coastal Carolina's 2021 season is whether Chadwell's charming option offense simply caught opponents off guard or if he and the Chanticleers can still execute now that there's an entire body of film out there. They play at Appalachian State but avoid Louisiana in the regular season, setting themselves up for another run at the Sun Belt Championship.

39. Memphis Tigers (8.2 mean wins)

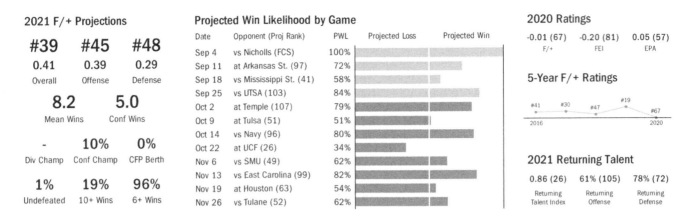

2021 F/+ Projections

#39	#45	#48
0.41	0.39	0.29
Overall	Offense	Defense

8.2	5.0
Mean Wins	Conf Wins

-	10%	0%
Div Champ	Conf Champ	CFP Berth

1%	19%	96%
Undefeated	10+ Wins	6+ Wins

Projected Win Likelihood by Game

Date	Opponent (Proj Rank)	PWL
Sep 4	vs Nicholls (FCS)	100%
Sep 11	at Arkansas St. (97)	72%
Sep 18	vs Mississippi St. (41)	58%
Sep 25	vs UTSA (103)	84%
Oct 2	at Temple (107)	79%
Oct 9	at Tulsa (51)	51%
Oct 14	vs Navy (96)	80%
Oct 22	at UCF (26)	34%
Nov 6	vs SMU (49)	62%
Nov 13	vs East Carolina (99)	82%
Nov 19	at Houston (63)	54%
Nov 26	vs Tulane (52)	62%

2020 Ratings

-0.01 (67)	-0.20 (81)	0.05 (57)
F/+	FEI	EPA

5-Year F/+ Ratings

#41 (2016), #30, #47, #19, #67 (2020)

2021 Returning Talent

0.86 (26)	61% (105)	78% (72)
Returning Talent Index	Returning Offense	Returning Defense

Coming off the school's first BCS/New Year's Six bowl in history, the Memphis Tigers knew 2020 would be somewhat of a letdown. Head coach Mike Norvell left to take the Florida State job, and the Tigers made an internal hire, hoping to keep some semblance of continuity. With Ryan Silverfield, it largely worked. Quarterback Brady White threw for 3,300 yards and led the team to an 8-3 record and a double-digit bowl win. The Tiger offense was ferocious, averaging 0.200 EPA/play and scoring at least 30 points in six of their 11 games. They lose White and 40% of their total production but replace him with either Arizona transfer Grant Gunnell (67.7% completion rate, 6.7 yards per attempt in four games last season) or the unknown but promising four-star LSU transfer Peter Parrish. Thousand-yard receiver Calvin Austin III and running back

Rodrigues Clark (546 yards, 4.0 yards per carry) both return, providing the Tigers with upside and experience on offense. Safety Quindell Johnson (69 tackles, three interceptions) will star in a secondary that returns five starters. That experience should provide a nice cushion for turnover on the defensive line, although the defensive interior will be a problem for opposing offensive lines. Morris Joseph recorded eight sacks and 34 tackles last season. Memphis misses AAC-favorite Cincinnati in conference play this year, but has tricky road games against Tulsa, UCF, and Houston. With an SEC school on the non-conference schedule, the Tigers will have a chance to build a competitive resume, but they'll have to break in a new quarterback quickly to compete with the rest of a tough American Athletic Conference.

40. Baylor Bears (6.4 mean wins)

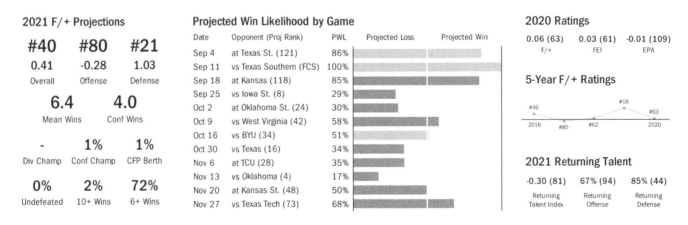

2021 F/+ Projections

#40	#80	#21
0.41	-0.28	1.03
Overall	Offense	Defense

6.4	4.0
Mean Wins	Conf Wins

-	1%	1%
Div Champ	Conf Champ	CFP Berth

0%	2%	72%
Undefeated	10+ Wins	6+ Wins

Projected Win Likelihood by Game

Date	Opponent (Proj Rank)	PWL
Sep 4	at Texas St. (121)	86%
Sep 11	vs Texas Southern (FCS)	100%
Sep 18	at Kansas (118)	85%
Sep 25	vs Iowa St. (8)	29%
Oct 2	at Oklahoma St. (24)	30%
Oct 9	vs West Virginia (42)	58%
Oct 16	vs BYU (34)	51%
Oct 30	vs Texas (16)	34%
Nov 6	at TCU (28)	35%
Nov 13	vs Oklahoma (4)	17%
Nov 20	at Kansas St. (48)	50%
Nov 27	vs Texas Tech (73)	68%

2020 Ratings

0.06 (63)	0.03 (61)	-0.01 (109)
F/+	FEI	EPA

5-Year F/+ Ratings

#46 (2016), #80, #62, #16, #63 (2020)

2021 Returning Talent

-0.30 (81)	67% (94)	85% (44)
Returning Talent Index	Returning Offense	Returning Defense

When Dave Aranda took over Baylor, the job came with a blueprint for success. Matt Rhule had taken the Bears from a 1-11 laughingstock to a team just a touchdown short of a conference championship. On the back of an experienced group he played as freshmen, Rhule built the roster his way and his vision came together in 2019. Aranda will try to take a similar path, hoping that a 2-7 2020 season was just a step along

the way. The Bears struggled on offense, limited by a not-entirely-healthy Charlie Brewer at quarterback (0.021 EPA/play ranked 118th nationally), but their defense was feisty, as one would expect from an Aranda team, holding opponents to just 0.065 EPA/play. Leading tacklers Jalen Pitre (49 tackles, two sacks) and Dillon Doyle (52 tackles, two sacks) bolster the linebacker unit and the defense overall returns 85% of production, not to mention the addition of LSU defensive tackle Siaki Ika.

The Bears will be a defense-heavy team, and their ceiling on offense will largely depend on quarterback play. Brewer transferred to Utah, and Baylor will let Gerry Bohanon and Jacob Zeno compete for the job; neither had much experience in 2020, and so the Baylor offense will be a completely blank slate. Coordinator Jeff Grimes from BYU takes over for Larry Fedora, and he'll have plenty of talent to work with. Versatile back Trestan Ebner returns, and he poses a strong threat in the passing game (11.5 yards per reception and three touchdowns in 2020), and R.J. Sneed, who led the team with 504 receiving yards in 2020 (12.6 yards per reception), joins him. Along the offensive line, Baylor gets reinforcements in transfers Jacob Gall and Grant Miller, who fill holes along a line that allowed 14 sacks last season. The Bears are probably a season away from competing for the Big 12 title again, but a stout Aranda defense and a fresh start on offense should see the football team in Waco make strides towards the returning to the top half of the conference.

41. Mississippi State Bulldogs (6.2 mean wins)

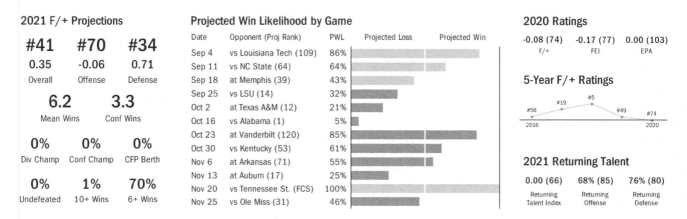

2021 F/+ Projections

#41	#70	#34
0.35	-0.06	0.71
Overall	Offense	Defense

6.2	3.3
Mean Wins	Conf Wins

0%	0%	0%
Div Champ	Conf Champ	CFP Berth

0%	1%	70%
Undefeated	10+ Wins	6+ Wins

Projected Win Likelihood by Game

Date	Opponent (Proj Rank)	PWL
Sep 4	vs Louisiana Tech (109)	86%
Sep 11	vs NC State (64)	64%
Sep 18	at Memphis (39)	43%
Sep 25	vs LSU (14)	32%
Oct 2	at Texas A&M (12)	21%
Oct 16	vs Alabama (1)	5%
Oct 23	at Vanderbilt (120)	85%
Oct 30	vs Kentucky (53)	61%
Nov 6	at Arkansas (71)	55%
Nov 13	at Auburn (17)	25%
Nov 20	vs Tennessee St. (FCS)	100%
Nov 25	vs Ole Miss (31)	46%

2020 Ratings

-0.08 (74)	-0.17 (77)	0.00 (103)
F/+	FEI	EPA

5-Year F/+ Ratings

#56 #19 #5 #49 #74
2016 ... 2020

2021 Returning Talent

0.00 (66)	68% (85)	76% (80)
Returning Talent Index	Returning Offense	Returning Defense

In 2020, Mississippi State beat LSU 44-34, throwing for five touchdowns and 623 yards. The Air Raid had evidently come to take over the SEC. The Bulldogs, though, went on to throw just four passing touchdowns in their next six games, losing five of six and only narrowly sneaking by Vanderbilt. Mike Leach's Mississippi State offense struggled with quarterback play, as Will Rogers and K.J. Costello combined to complete 66.8% of their passes, but for only 5.8 yards per attempt, and the Bulldogs largely ran out of steam against an SEC schedule evidently already familiar with the Air Raid. The Bulldogs averaged just 0.061 EPA/play on offense, 113th nationally, even as the defense found its rhythm down the stretch: 0.111 EPA/play allowed (32nd). The question for a Mike Leach team is rarely one of offensive production, and ex-Southern Miss transfer quarterback Jack Abraham (65.3% completion rate, 8.2 yards per attempt) has a skill set that should translate nicely into the hyper-aggressive Leach offense.

The question with a Leach team is often one of defense, and the Bulldogs return 76% of a unit that grew and improved throughout the season. They lose four starters to the NFL draft and will look to Nathaniel Watson (40 tackles) and Jack Harris to fill big holes at linebacker and edge rusher. The Bulldogs' SEC West conference schedule speaks for itself in terms of difficulty but keep an eye on their non-conference games; hosting Louisiana Tech and North Carolina State then traveling to Memphis to start the season is a stouter slate than it looks at first blush. With LSU, Alabama, Texas A&M, and Kentucky on the schedule, Mississippi State will need those wins to find a bowl in 2021.

42. West Virginia Mountaineers (5.8 mean wins)

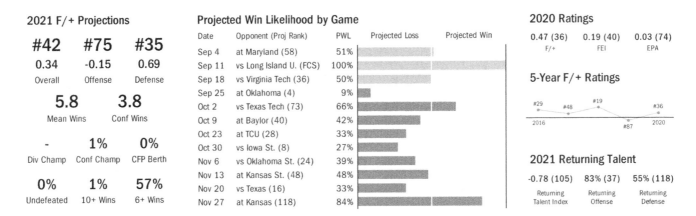

2021 F/+ Projections

#42	#75	#35
0.34	-0.15	0.69
Overall	Offense	Defense

5.8	3.8
Mean Wins	Conf Wins

-	1%	0%
Div Champ	Conf Champ	CFP Berth

0%	1%	57%
Undefeated	10+ Wins	6+ Wins

Projected Win Likelihood by Game

Date	Opponent (Proj Rank)	PWL	Projected Loss	Projected Win
Sep 4	at Maryland (58)	51%		
Sep 11	vs Long Island U. (FCS)	100%		
Sep 18	vs Virginia Tech (36)	50%		
Sep 25	at Oklahoma (4)	9%		
Oct 2	vs Texas Tech (73)	66%		
Oct 9	at Baylor (40)	42%		
Oct 23	at TCU (28)	33%		
Oct 30	vs Iowa St. (8)	27%		
Nov 6	vs Oklahoma St. (24)	39%		
Nov 13	at Kansas St. (48)	48%		
Nov 20	vs Texas (16)	33%		
Nov 27	at Kansas (118)	84%		

2020 Ratings

0.47 (36)	0.19 (40)	0.03 (74)
F/+	FEI	EPA

5-Year F/+ Ratings

#29 (2016), #48, #19, #87, #36 (2020)

2021 Returning Talent

-0.78 (105)	83% (37)	55% (118)
Returning Talent Index	Returning Offense	Returning Defense

When Neal Brown came to Morgantown, West Virginia sat in a precarious position: their best season as members of the Big 12 was a 10-win Russell Athletic Bowl appearance in 2016, and the program had not been able to break into the upper echelon of Big 12 competition. Brown has strung together two above-average seasons with the Mountaineers, and Year 3 will be the one where he either cements his identity for the future of West Virginia or he kicks the can for another year.

The Mountaineers played stout defense in 2020, allowing 0.043 EPA/play, sixth in the nation, but face substantial turnover, returning only 55% of production. The defense loses All-Conference defensive back Tykee Smith to transfer and leading tackler Tony Fields II. to the NFL. Linebacker Josh Chandler-Semedo, the teams' second-leading tackler, will be one of the more experienced pieces of this defense, joined by Penn State transfer Lance Dixon.

On offense, the Mountaineers return 83% of production, 37th in the nation, as quarterback Jarrett Doege looks to take a step forward (63.5% completion percentage, 6.9 yards per attempt). He'll be helped by standout running back Leddie Brown, who averaged 5.1 yards per carry and scored nine rushing touchdowns in 2020, and top receiver Winston Wright (11.8 yards per reception, two touchdowns). Along the offensive line, the Mountaineers get some much-needed help in transfer guard Doug Nester. Brown's West Virginia has proved that in the right circumstances, its defense can be elite, and the returning production on offense is encouraging -- whether the Mountaineers can repeat their defensive performance from 2020 and improve on offense will decide their place in a crowded Big 12 middle class.

43. Buffalo Bulls (8.7 mean wins)

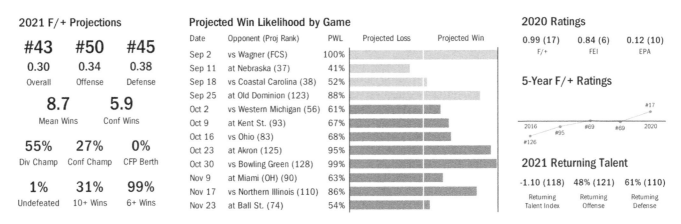

2021 F/+ Projections

#43	#50	#45
0.30	0.34	0.38
Overall	Offense	Defense

8.7	5.9
Mean Wins	Conf Wins

55%	27%	0%
Div Champ	Conf Champ	CFP Berth

1%	31%	99%
Undefeated	10+ Wins	6+ Wins

Projected Win Likelihood by Game

Date	Opponent (Proj Rank)	PWL	Projected Loss	Projected Win
Sep 2	vs Wagner (FCS)	100%		
Sep 11	at Nebraska (37)	41%		
Sep 18	vs Coastal Carolina (38)	52%		
Sep 25	at Old Dominion (123)	88%		
Oct 2	vs Western Michigan (56)	61%		
Oct 9	at Kent St. (93)	67%		
Oct 16	vs Ohio (83)	68%		
Oct 23	at Akron (125)	95%		
Oct 30	vs Bowling Green (128)	99%		
Nov 9	at Miami (OH) (90)	63%		
Nov 17	vs Northern Illinois (110)	86%		
Nov 23	at Ball St. (74)	54%		

2020 Ratings

0.99 (17)	0.84 (6)	0.12 (10)
F/+	FEI	EPA

5-Year F/+ Ratings

#126 (2016), #95, #69, #69, #17 (2020)

2021 Returning Talent

-1.10 (118)	48% (121)	61% (110)
Returning Talent Index	Returning Offense	Returning Defense

Lance Leipold came to Buffalo and won 37 games in six seasons, including the first two bowl wins in Bulls history. Prior to Leipold, Buffalo had just two winning seasons since their 1999 resurrection, and only two bowl appearances. The Bulls' offense finished eighth overall in EPA/play in 2020 behind a fierce rushing attack from Jarrett Patterson. Leipold left for Kansas, Patterson left for the draft, and 12 other players left via the transfer portal. New head coach Maurice Linguist has a task in front of him: Buffalo ranks 121st in returning production overall, 121st on offense, and 110th on defense. Quarterback Kyle Vantrease returns in 2021 to anchor the offense (62.3% completion rate, 8.6 yards per completion), but three starters on the offensive line have transferred in addition to the graduation of Patterson. Buffalo in 2020 is as blank a slate as a college football team can be, but Leipold's tenure demonstrated proof of concept for success in Buffalo. 2021 may not be that year, though, with non-conference games against Nebraska, Coastal Carolina, and Old Dominion, and trips to Kent State and Ball State in conference. Linguist has a recipe for success, inherited from Leipold: tenacious offensive line play, a fierce commitment to the run game, and a low-variance defense, but it might take him another year of recruiting to get the Bulls back to where they have been.

44. Pittsburgh Panthers (6.8 mean wins)

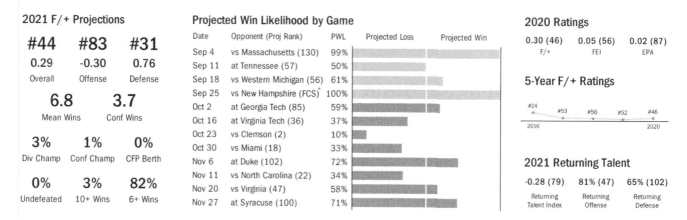

2021 F/+ Projections

#44	#83	#31
0.29	-0.30	0.76
Overall	Offense	Defense

6.8	3.7
Mean Wins	Conf Wins

3%	1%	0%
Div Champ	Conf Champ	CFP Berth

0%	3%	82%
Undefeated	10+ Wins	6+ Wins

Projected Win Likelihood by Game

Date	Opponent (Proj Rank)	PWL
Sep 4	vs Massachusetts (130)	99%
Sep 11	at Tennessee (57)	50%
Sep 18	vs Western Michigan (56)	61%
Sep 25	vs New Hampshire (FCS)*	100%
Oct 2	at Georgia Tech (85)	59%
Oct 16	at Virginia Tech (36)	37%
Oct 23	vs Clemson (2)	10%
Oct 30	vs Miami (18)	33%
Nov 6	at Duke (102)	72%
Nov 11	vs North Carolina (22)	34%
Nov 20	vs Virginia (47)	58%
Nov 27	at Syracuse (100)	71%

2020 Ratings

0.30 (46)	0.05 (56)	0.02 (87)
F/+	FEI	EPA

5-Year F/+ Ratings

#24   #53   #56   #52   #46
2016   2020

2021 Returning Talent

-0.28 (79)	81% (47)	65% (102)
Returning Talent Index	Returning Offense	Returning Defense

Were there a dictionary of college football words, Pittsburgh coach Pat Narduzzi's name would be the entry for "quiet consistency." Narduzzi's Pitt teams have finished with winning records in five of his six seasons, and the defense has given conference opponents fits for years. Pitt allowed just 0.120 EPA/play on defense in 2020, 25th in the nation, and held six opponents to 20 or fewer points. Five Panthers were selected in the 2021 NFL draft, both defensive ends, a defensive tackle, and two defensive backs. Filling those shoes will be a tall order. Deslin Alexandre, who started 13 games in 2019, will slot in as the top edge rusher.. Linebacker Sirvocea Dennis will anchor the defense this season; he finished second on the team in tackles last season.

On the offensive side of things, veteran quarterback Kenny Pickett returns for his fourth season of full-time work for the Panthers. In 2020, Pickett averaged 7.3 yards per completion and completed 61.1% of his passes. The offense as a whole had its moments, but mostly sputtered, averaged 0.079 EPA/play, 108th in the nation. But Pitt returns 81% of offensive production from 2020, raising their floor immensely. Jordan Addison averaged 11 yards per reception last season and looks to be Pickett's primary target, and former Florida tight end Lucas Krull returns to Pitt for 2021 as another weapon for a well-balanced attack. Pitt has a manageable non-conference schedule, and gets Miami, North Carolina, and Clemson at home; the Panthers will need some measured improvement from Pickett but have a clear path to being a top-25 team in 2021.

45. Louisville Cardinals (6.7 mean wins)

2021 F/+ Projections

#45	#19	#96
0.27	1.00	-0.57
Overall	Offense	Defense

6.7	4.3
Mean Wins	Conf Wins

2%	1%	1%
Div Champ	Conf Champ	CFP Berth

0%	3%	80%
Undefeated	10+ Wins	6+ Wins

Projected Win Likelihood by Game

Date	Opponent (Proj Rank)	PWL
Sep 6	vs Ole Miss (31)	38%
Sep 11	vs E. Kentucky (FCS)	100%
Sep 17	vs UCF (26)	41%
Sep 25	at Florida St. (75)	53%
Oct 2	at Wake Forest (66)	51%
Oct 9	vs Virginia (47)	57%
Oct 23	vs Boston College (77)	64%
Oct 30	at NC State (64)	50%
Nov 6	vs Clemson (2)	9%
Nov 13	vs Syracuse (100)	79%
Nov 18	at Duke (102)	71%
Nov 27	vs Kentucky (53)	59%

2020 Ratings

0.37 (42)	0.04 (59)	0.14 (6)
F/+	FEI	EPA

5-Year F/+ Ratings

#10   #16   #58   #42
2016   #108   2020

2021 Returning Talent

-0.99 (114)	70% (78)	58% (115)
Returning Talent Index	Returning Offense	Returning Defense

Louisville averaged 0.301 EPA/play on offense in 2020, an exciting if unstable mix of explosive potential and inconsistency. Quarterback Malik Cunningham threw 12 interceptions to 20 touchdowns on the season, and the Cardinals were able to put up big numbers against the lesser defenses on their schedule. Cunningham completed 63.3% of his passes last season, but averaged just 8.6 yards per attempt, as Lousiville sought to find playmakers in space. Cunningham returns, but both sides of the ball will look different for Scott Satterfield's third year; the Cardinals are 107th in returning production, 78th on offense and 115th on defense. The loss of leading receivers Tutu Atwell and Dez Fitzpatrick to the NFL leaves huge holes in the receiver room, but transfer Shai Werts, who demonstrated athletic versatility as quarterback at Georgia Southern, will slot in as a playmaker. On defense, Louisville lost five starters to the NFL, but leading tackler C.J. Avery returns to bolster the linebacking corps and edge rusher Tabarius Peterson will pose more than a passing threat to opposing offensive tackles. The non-conference slate for Louisville is daunting, with games against an explosive Ole Miss team and an experienced UCF to start the season and a rivalry game with Kentucky to end, and they face tough games in Tallahassee and Raleigh in the regular season. Given the turnover, the defensive struggles, and the offensive upside, Louisville will probably be scrapping for a bowl in 2021 in a highly entertaining manner.

46. Washington State Cougars (6.1 mean wins)

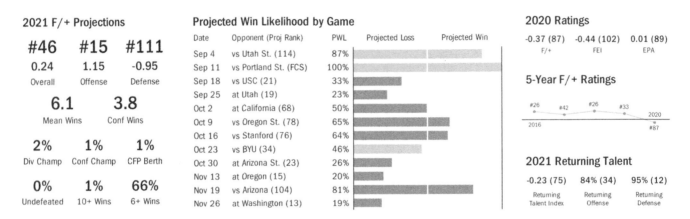

2021 F/+ Projections

#46	#15	#111
0.24	1.15	-0.95
Overall	Offense	Defense

6.1	3.8
Mean Wins	Conf Wins

2%	1%	1%
Div Champ	Conf Champ	CFP Berth

0%	1%	66%
Undefeated	10+ Wins	6+ Wins

Projected Win Likelihood by Game

Date	Opponent (Proj Rank)	PWL		
			Projected Loss	Projected Win
Sep 4	vs Utah St. (114)	87%		
Sep 11	vs Portland St. (FCS)	100%		
Sep 18	vs USC (21)	33%		
Sep 25	at Utah (19)	23%		
Oct 2	at California (68)	50%		
Oct 9	vs Oregon St. (78)	65%		
Oct 16	vs Stanford (76)	64%		
Oct 23	vs BYU (34)	46%		
Oct 30	at Arizona St. (23)	26%		
Nov 13	at Oregon (15)	20%		
Nov 19	vs Arizona (104)	81%		
Nov 26	at Washington (13)	19%		

2020 Ratings

-0.37 (87)	-0.44 (102)	0.01 (89)
F/+	FEI	EPA

5-Year F/+ Ratings

#26 (2016)   #42   #26   #33   2020   #87

2021 Returning Talent

-0.23 (75)	84% (34)	95% (12)
Returning Talent Index	Returning Offense	Returning Defense

The Cougars had less than a full season in 2020, relative to everyone else in the nation, playing only four games. Surely, Nick Rolovich had bigger plans for his first season in Pullman. The biggest news for Washington State is the addition of Tennessee transfer Jarrett Guarantano, who solves the quarterback problem nicely. Guarantano struggled on a team desperate to run the ball in 2020, and his skill set should match well with Rolovich's brand of the run-and-shoot. There are more answers than questions with Washington State in 2021, with a new quarterback and such a short 2020 season, but Rolovich has proven his ability to build solid offenses; despite some chaos last season, the Cougars averaged 0.212 EPA/play on offense, 37th in the nation, and will be offense-heavy headed into 2021. They bring in some help on defense, with three transfer defensive backs who should start immediately, but that unit may need some more time than the offense to develop (0.334 EPA/play allowed, 124th nationally). In the Cougars' favor is their schedule, which features only five road games and three home non-conference games. With a full offseason to break Guarantano into the run-and-shoot and some help on the defensive side of things, Washington State will look to right the ship and establish an identity in the Pac-12.

47. Virginia Cavaliers (6.2 mean wins)

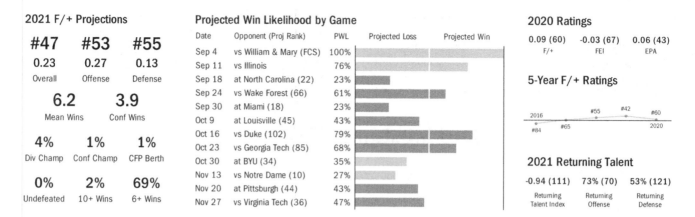

2021 F/+ Projections

#47	#53	#55
0.23	0.27	0.13
Overall	Offense	Defense

6.2	3.9
Mean Wins	Conf Wins

4%	1%	1%
Div Champ	Conf Champ	CFP Berth

0%	2%	69%
Undefeated	10+ Wins	6+ Wins

Projected Win Likelihood by Game

Date	Opponent (Proj Rank)	PWL
Sep 4	vs William & Mary (FCS)	100%
Sep 11	vs Illinois	76%
Sep 18	at North Carolina (22)	23%
Sep 24	vs Wake Forest (66)	61%
Sep 30	at Miami (18)	23%
Oct 9	at Louisville (45)	43%
Oct 16	vs Duke (102)	79%
Oct 23	vs Georgia Tech (85)	68%
Oct 30	at BYU (34)	35%
Nov 13	vs Notre Dame (10)	27%
Nov 20	at Pittsburgh (44)	43%
Nov 27	vs Virginia Tech (36)	47%

2020 Ratings

0.09 (60)	-0.03 (67)	0.06 (43)
F/+	FEI	EPA

5-Year F/+ Ratings

2021 Returning Talent

-0.94 (111)	73% (70)	53% (121)
Returning Talent Index	Returning Offense	Returning Defense

Virginia's defense lagged behind a better-than-average offense in 2020, as the Cavaliers allowed 30 points to six opponents. The offense, averaging 0.197 EPA/play (47th in the nation), was led by quarterback Brennan Armstrong, who struggled at the beginning of the season but matured quickly, completing more than 65% of his passes in three of four final games. He'll be joined by leading receiver Billy Kemp IV (9.6 yards per reception) and Oklahoma State transfer Jelani Woods, who looks to feature prominently in an offense unafraid to bend conventions. The Cavaliers employed multiple quarterbacks, trick plays, and fakes aplenty last season, and that brand of chaotic offense will be Virginia at their best in 2021.

On the defensive side of the ball, the Cavaliers return 53% of the team who allowed 0.222 EPA/play (77th in the nation). That defense will get some help in the return of a healthy Joey Blount, a safety who led the team in tackles in 2019. The loss of defensive lineman Jowon Briggs to Cincinnati and the graduation of leading tackler Zane Zandier raise some questions about the run-stopping ability of the defense, but with so much turnover, the defense is a blank slate. For Virginia to take a step forward this fall, they'll have to continue their offensive surge from the end of 2020 and have the defense coalesce into a coherent unit. The Cavaliers showed they could compete with the top of the conference in beating UNC last season; they'll miss Clemson in the regular season, so their ACC ceiling is high, but a non-conference trip to Provo and hosting Notre Dame will determine whether Virginia is simply an ACC upper middle-class team or a fringe national contender.

48. Kansas State Wildcats (5.9 mean wins)

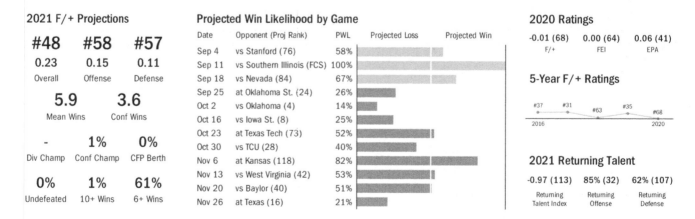

2021 F/+ Projections

#48	#58	#57
0.23	0.15	0.11
Overall	Offense	Defense

5.9	3.6
Mean Wins	Conf Wins

-	1%	0%
Div Champ	Conf Champ	CFP Berth

0%	1%	61%
Undefeated	10+ Wins	6+ Wins

Projected Win Likelihood by Game

Date	Opponent (Proj Rank)	PWL
Sep 4	vs Stanford (76)	58%
Sep 11	vs Southern Illinois (FCS)	100%
Sep 18	vs Nevada (84)	67%
Sep 25	at Oklahoma St. (24)	26%
Oct 2	vs Oklahoma (4)	14%
Oct 16	vs Iowa St. (8)	25%
Oct 23	at Texas Tech (73)	52%
Oct 30	vs TCU (28)	40%
Nov 6	at Kansas (118)	82%
Nov 13	vs West Virginia (42)	53%
Nov 20	vs Baylor (40)	51%
Nov 26	at Texas (16)	21%

2020 Ratings

-0.01 (68)	0.00 (64)	0.06 (41)
F/+	FEI	EPA

5-Year F/+ Ratings

2021 Returning Talent

-0.97 (113)	85% (32)	62% (107)
Returning Talent Index	Returning Offense	Returning Defense

Kansas State opened 2020 with a humiliating loss to Arkansas State, but that loss obscures much of the progress the Wildcats made last season. An injury to starting quarterback Skylar Thompson effectively eliminated the Wildcats from Big 12 contention down the stretch, but in beating Oklahoma to start Big 12 play, Chris Klieman demonstrated proof of concept. Running back Deuce Vaughn is a legitimate two-dimensional offensive threat (seven touchdowns on the ground and two through the air) and an offensive line with little experience coalesced into a solid unit (12 sacks) despite struggles with quarterback play. Thompson returns this season as one of the most experienced quarterbacks in the conference, and in addition to Vaughn and an experienced offensive line, will be joined by Illinois transfer Daniel Imatorbhebhe, a tight end who will round out the Wildcats' offense. Too often last season Kansas State relied on missed tackles and big plays, but with Thompson back and Vaughn more experienced, they should have a more consistent, robust offensive attack. The defense faces some substantial turnover, losing almost 40% of snaps from 2020. Defensive back Jahron McPherson will lead the team, but the loss of stalwart defensive end Wyatt Hubert and cornerback A.J. Parker will be tough to fill. Many teams in the Big 12 are circling 2021 as their year, and Kansas State is no different. Klieman will be looking to establish his brand of winning football at the Power 5 level this season, and Kansas State has the pieces to pose a lethal explosive offensive threat, even as the defense will need some room to grow.

49. SMU Mustangs (7.0 mean wins)

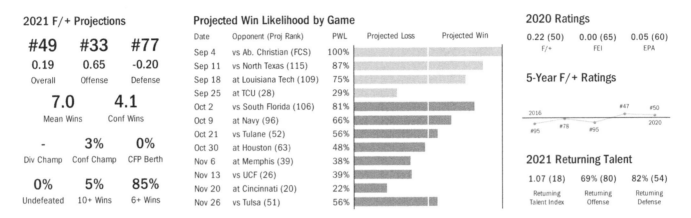

2021 F/+ Projections

#49	#33	#77
0.19	0.65	-0.20
Overall	Offense	Defense

7.0	4.1
Mean Wins	Conf Wins

-	3%	0%
Div Champ	Conf Champ	CFP Berth

0%	5%	85%
Undefeated	10+ Wins	6+ Wins

Projected Win Likelihood by Game

Date	Opponent (Proj Rank)	PWL	Projected Loss	Projected Win
Sep 4	vs Ab. Christian (FCS)	100%		
Sep 11	vs North Texas (115)	87%		
Sep 18	at Louisiana Tech (109)	75%		
Sep 25	at TCU (28)	29%		
Oct 2	vs South Florida (106)	81%		
Oct 9	at Navy (96)	66%		
Oct 21	vs Tulane (52)	56%		
Oct 30	at Houston (63)	48%		
Nov 6	at Memphis (39)	38%		
Nov 13	vs UCF (26)	39%		
Nov 20	at Cincinnati (20)	22%		
Nov 26	vs Tulsa (51)	56%		

2020 Ratings

0.22 (50)	0.00 (65)	0.05 (60)
F/+	FEI	EPA

5-Year F/+ Ratings

2016 #47 #50
#95 #78 #95 2020

2021 Returning Talent

1.07 (18)	69% (80)	82% (54)
Returning Talent Index	Returning Offense	Returning Defense

A knee injury sidelined SMU wide receiver Reggie Roberson Jr. after a near unbelievable 243-yard performance against Memphis, and the passing game took a bit of a dive. In games against Tulsa, Cincinnati, and East Carolina, the Mustangs struggled to find consistency downfield. Roberson returns for 2021, but the Mustangs still have problems with consistency. Quarterback Shane Buchele (13.0 yards per completion, 65.1% completion rate) departs for the NFL along with productive tight end Kylen Granson (15.3 yards per reception, five touchdowns), and the passing game gets a makeover. Oklahoma transfer Tanner Mordecai will take the starting job for Sonny Dykes' Mustangs, alongside Oklahoma transfer and recently unretired tight end Grant Calcaterra. These two will try to mesh with Roberson and running back Ulysses S. Bentley IV to keep the SMU offense a potent threat, and the pieces are there -- especially as Dykes has added two tackles through the transfer portal. The Mustangs finished 36th in EPA/play (0.223) on offense, and part of their success in 2021 will rest on whether the defense can improve from 100th in EPA/play (0.242). The Mustangs return 82% of their defense from 2020, and Florida transfer Jahari Rogers should shore up a weak secondary. The Mustangs face a gauntlet in a much-improved AAC West, and the offensive production is there on paper; whether the defense can keep up will be the question that determines SMU's fate.

50. Purdue Boilermakers (5.2 mean wins)

2021 F/+ Projections

#50	#36	#82
0.18	0.53	-0.23
Overall	Offense	Defense

5.2	3.5
Mean Wins	Conf Wins

1%	0%	0%
Div Champ	Conf Champ	CFP Berth

0%	0%	43%
Undefeated	10+ Wins	6+ Wins

Projected Win Likelihood by Game

Date	Opponent (Proj Rank)	PWL	Projected Loss — Projected Win
Sep 4	vs Oregon St. (78)	63%	
Sep 11	at Connecticut (127)	95%	
Sep 18	at Notre Dame (10)	18%	
Sep 25	vs Illinois (95)	75%	
Oct 2	vs Minnesota (32)	42%	
Oct 16	at Iowa (9)	17%	
Oct 23	vs Wisconsin (6)	20%	
Oct 30	at Nebraska (37)	38%	
Nov 6	vs Michigan St. (60)	58%	
Nov 13	at Ohio St. (3)	4%	
Nov 20	vs Northwestern (61)	53%	
Nov 27	vs Indiana (27)	39%	

2020 Ratings

0.08 (61)	-0.16 (76)	0.06 (42)
F/+	FEI	EPA

5-Year F/+ Ratings

2016	#39	#39		#61
#106			#65	2020

2021 Returning Talent

-0.64 (96)	88% (21)	73% (86)
Returning Talent Index	Returning Offense	Returning Defense

Jeff Brohm's Purdue has yet to arrive. The Boilermakers finished 2020 an underwhelming 2-4 but have hopes for 2021 to be a rebound year. They return 88.2% of offensive production from a unit that averaged 0.185 EPA/play on offense, 52nd in the nation, and 73% of a defense that ranked 58th in EPA/play (0.168). Purdue made bowl appearances in their first two seasons under Brohm, but since then have been plagued by injuries at the quarterback position. This season, Brohm will have an honest-to-God quarterback battle on his hands, with Aidan O'Connell and Jack Plummer again battling it out in fall camp. The two split time last season, each starting three games, but neither flashed, as Purdue's passing offense averaged a decent but limited 0.254 EPA/play. Star receiver Rondale Moore departed for the NFL, but the explosive upside on offense is still there, with David Bell returning as the No. 1 receiver (11.2 yards per reception), and a healthy Jackson Anthrop looking to have an expanded role. Purdue looked to the transfer market on defense, bringing in four starting-caliber players who add immediate and needed depth. The Boilermakers will look to do more than just recreate the magic of upsetting Ohio State in 2018, hoping that an experienced offense, a reinforced defense, and some Jeff Brohm creativity can launch them into contention for the Big Ten West.

NCAA Win Projections

Projected Win Probabilities For ACC Teams

ACC Atlantic	Overall Wins													Conference Wins								
	12-0	11-1	10-2	9-3	8-4	7-5	6-6	5-7	4-8	3-9	2-10	1-11	0-12	8-0	7-1	6-2	5-3	4-4	3-5	2-6	1-7	0-8
Boston College	-	-	3	8	18	26	24	14	5	2	-	-	-	-	1	4	18	30	26	15	5	1
Clemson	46	42	11	1	-	-	-	-	-	-	-	-	-	71	26	3	-	-	-	-	-	-
Florida State	-	-	-	1	4	14	25	28	19	7	2	-	-	-	-	2	9	23	31	26	8	1
Louisville	-	-	3	9	20	25	23	13	6	1	-	-	-	-	3	17	27	28	17	6	2	-
NC State	-	-	1	4	12	22	28	20	10	3	-	-	-	-	-	3	12	24	29	21	9	2
Syracuse	-	-	-	-	1	4	12	20	26	23	12	2	-	-	-	-	2	7	22	31	28	10
Wake Forest	-	-	2	7	16	25	26	16	7	1	-	-	-	-	2	9	22	30	22	11	4	-

ACC Coastal	12-0	11-1	10-2	9-3	8-4	7-5	6-6	5-7	4-8	3-9	2-10	1-11	0-12	8-0	7-1	6-2	5-3	4-4	3-5	2-6	1-7	0-8
Duke	-	-	-	-	2	5	12	23	27	20	9	2	-	-	-	-	1	5	19	32	32	11
Georgia Tech	-	-	-	-	1	5	14	26	28	19	6	1	-	-	-	-	5	14	28	30	18	5
Miami	1	6	17	27	26	16	6	1	-	-	-	-	-	7	26	35	21	9	2	-	-	-
North Carolina	2	9	24	27	22	11	4	1	-	-	-	-	-	7	27	31	23	9	3	-	-	-
Pittsburgh	-	-	3	10	19	27	23	13	4	1	-	-	-	-	2	6	19	31	27	12	3	-
Virginia	-	-	2	5	14	23	25	19	9	3	-	-	-	-	2	8	20	31	24	13	2	-
Virginia Tech	-	2	7	18	26	24	15	6	2	-	-	-	-	1	7	21	31	26	11	2	1	-

Projected Win Probabilities For American Teams

American	Overall Wins													Conference Wins								
	12-0	11-1	10-2	9-3	8-4	7-5	6-6	5-7	4-8	3-9	2-10	1-11	0-12	8-0	7-1	6-2	5-3	4-4	3-5	2-6	1-7	0-8
Cincinnati	3	14	28	29	18	7	1	-	-	-	-	-	-	15	36	32	14	3	-	-	-	-
East Carolina	-	-	-	-	1	7	15	24	26	18	7	2	-	-	-	2	5	16	34	27	14	2
Houston	-	2	10	21	26	23	12	5	1	-	-	-	-	1	7	18	29	26	14	5	-	-
Memphis	1	4	14	24	26	18	9	3	1	-	-	-	-	1	11	24	29	22	10	2	1	-
Navy	-	-	-	-	1	4	8	17	24	24	16	5	1	-	-	2	6	16	27	28	17	4
SMU	-	1	4	11	21	26	22	11	3	1	-	-	-	-	3	10	23	33	19	10	2	-
South Florida	-	-	-	-	-	1	5	13	24	29	20	7	1	-	-	-	3	10	24	34	22	7
Temple	-	-	-	-	2	7	15	24	25	17	8	2	-	-	-	1	2	10	25	30	23	9
Tulane	-	-	1	5	12	22	25	20	10	5	-	-	-	-	2	10	24	30	21	11	2	-
Tulsa	-	-	1	6	17	25	25	17	7	2	-	-	-	-	5	15	28	29	17	4	2	-
UCF	2	11	23	29	21	10	3	1	-	-	-	-	-	6	22	34	26	10	2	-	-	-

Projected Win Probabilities For Big 12 Teams

Big 12	Overall Wins													Conference Wins									
	12-0	11-1	10-2	9-3	8-4	7-5	6-6	5-7	4-8	3-9	2-10	1-11	0-12	9-0	8-1	7-2	6-3	5-4	4-5	3-6	2-7	1-8	0-9
Baylor	-	-	2	6	15	24	25	18	7	3	-	-	-	-	1	4	10	22	27	24	10	2	-
Iowa State	2	10	23	28	22	11	3	1	-	-	-	-	-	4	17	28	26	18	6	1	-	-	-
Kansas	-	-	-	-	-	-	-	1	7	20	36	30	6	-	-	-	-	-	1	4	16	40	39
Kansas State	-	-	1	4	10	20	26	22	12	4	1	-	-	-	-	2	7	15	28	28	15	5	-
Oklahoma	14	31	31	17	6	1	-	-	-	-	-	-	-	19	33	31	14	3	-	-	-	-	-
Oklahoma State	-	2	8	19	25	24	15	6	1	-	-	-	-	-	4	13	26	29	18	8	2	-	-
TCU	-	1	5	14	24	26	18	8	3	1	-	-	-	-	1	9	19	29	24	13	4	1	-
Texas	1	5	14	24	26	19	8	2	1	-	-	-	-	1	9	22	30	22	12	3	1	-	-
Texas Tech	-	-	-	1	4	12	23	28	21	10	1	-	-	-	-	2	7	21	30	27	11	2	
West Virginia	-	-	1	3	9	19	25	23	14	5	1	-	-	-	2	8	20	27	27	13	3	-	

Projected Win Probabilities For Big Ten Teams

Big Ten East	Overall Wins													Conference Wins									
	12-0	11-1	10-2	9-3	8-4	7-5	6-6	5-7	4-8	3-9	2-10	1-11	0-12	9-0	8-1	7-2	6-3	5-4	4-5	3-6	2-7	1-8	0-9
Indiana	-	1	3	12	22	26	21	11	3	1	-	-	-	-	1	9	21	27	25	13	4	-	-
Maryland	-	-	-	2	7	17	25	25	16	7	1	-	-	-	-	1	3	12	25	31	20	7	1
Michigan	-	1	4	12	22	26	20	10	3	2	-	-	-	1	2	9	24	29	20	12	3	-	-
Michigan State	-	-	-	2	6	15	25	26	17	8	1	-	-	-	-	1	5	15	27	29	18	4	1
Ohio State	23	38	26	10	3	-	-	-	-	-	-	-	-	31	39	23	6	1	-	-	-	-	-
Penn State	-	4	15	27	27	18	7	2	-	-	-	-	-	1	7	22	30	26	11	3	-	-	-
Rutgers	-	-	-	-	-	2	8	20	30	27	11	2		-	-	-	-	-	1	10	26	40	23
Big Ten West	12-0	11-1	10-2	9-3	8-4	7-5	6-6	5-7	4-8	3-9	2-10	1-11	0-12	9-0	8-1	7-2	6-3	5-4	4-5	3-6	2-7	1-8	0-9
Illinois	-	-	-	-	1	3	9	20	27	24	12	4	-	-	-	-	-	2	13	25	32	23	5
Iowa	1	8	19	28	24	13	5	2	-	-	-	-	-	4	15	29	29	17	5	1	-	-	-
Minnesota	-	-	3	11	21	26	22	11	4	2	-	-	-	-	1	7	17	24	29	16	5	1	-
Nebraska	-	-	-	2	8	17	26	25	15	6	1	-	-	-	-	2	10	22	28	25	11	2	-
Northwestern	-	-	1	4	12	22	26	21	10	3	1	-	-	-	-	2	8	20	29	25	14	2	-
Purdue	-	-	-	1	6	13	23	26	20	9	2	-	-	-	-	1	6	15	28	28	16	6	-
Wisconsin	5	19	29	26	14	5	2	-	-	-	-	-	-	13	28	32	18	7	2	-	-	-	-

Projected Win Probabilities For Conference USA Teams

Conf USA East	Overall Wins													Conference Wins								
	12-0	11-1	10-2	9-3	8-4	7-5	6-6	5-7	4-8	3-9	2-10	1-11	0-12	8-0	7-1	6-2	5-3	4-4	3-5	2-6	1-7	0-8
Charlotte	-	-	-	1	4	9	17	23	23	15	6	2	-	-	1	2	11	24	30	20	11	1
Florida Atlantic	-	2	8	20	27	23	14	5	1	-	-	-	-	4	19	32	28	13	4	-	-	-
Florida International	-	-	-	1	6	15	23	25	17	9	3	1	-	-	2	5	18	30	23	16	6	-
Marshall	1	4	15	24	26	18	8	3	1	-	-	-	-	5	23	28	26	14	3	1	-	-
Middle Tennessee	-	-	-	1	6	14	23	25	18	9	3	1	-	-	1	7	16	24	29	16	6	1
Old Dominion	-	-	-	-	-	2	8	17	26	25	15	5	2	-	-	2	7	20	27	28	13	3
Western Kentucky	-	-	1	4	11	19	25	21	12	5	2	-	-	-	6	15	25	26	20	6	2	-
Conf USA West	12-0	11-1	10-2	9-3	8-4	7-5	6-6	5-7	4-8	3-9	2-10	1-11	0-12	8-0	7-1	6-2	5-3	4-4	3-5	2-6	1-7	0-8
Louisiana Tech	-	-	-	2	8	17	25	23	16	7	2	-	-	-	4	13	28	27	19	7	2	-
North Texas	-	-	-	1	2	7	17	23	24	17	7	2	-	-	1	3	13	27	29	20	6	1
Rice	-	-	-	1	5	13	22	25	20	9	4	1	-	1	2	9	22	29	25	9	2	1
Southern Mississippi	-	-	1	4	12	21	25	21	11	4	1	-	-	1	4	16	26	27	20	5	1	-
UAB	-	1	5	15	26	25	17	8	3	-	-	-	-	4	19	32	26	14	4	1	-	-
UTEP	-	-	-	-	-	1	3	10	20	29	23	12	2	-	-	-	1	3	17	30	34	15
UTSA	-	-	2	8	17	24	23	15	7	4	-	-	-	1	5	16	25	27	16	9	1	-

Projected Win Probabilities For Independent Teams

Independents	Overall Wins												
	12-0	11-1	10-2	9-3	8-4	7-5	6-6	5-7	4-8	3-9	2-10	1-11	0-12
Army	-	1	5	13	23	28	20	8	2	-	-	-	-
BYU	-	2	8	18	25	24	15	6	2	-	-	-	-
Connecticut	-	-	-	-	-	-	1	3	13	29	32	18	4
Liberty	1	4	13	23	29	20	8	2	-	-	-	-	-
Massachusetts	-	-	-	-	-	-	-	-	3	12	31	37	17
Notre Dame	2	10	20	26	23	12	5	2	-	-	-	-	-
New Mexico State	-	-	-	-	-	-	-	1	9	25	35	24	6

Projected Win Probabilities For MAC Teams

MAC East	Overall Wins													Conference Wins								
	12-0	11-1	10-2	9-3	8-4	7-5	6-6	5-7	4-8	3-9	2-10	1-11	0-12	8-0	7-1	6-2	5-3	4-4	3-5	2-6	1-7	0-8
Akron	-	-	-	-	-	-	-	2	6	20	34	29	9	-	-	-	-	1	6	23	45	25
Bowling Green	-	-	-	-	-	-	-	1	6	18	32	32	11	-	-	-	-	1	4	21	44	30
Buffalo	1	9	21	28	24	12	4	1	-	-	-	-	-	5	26	32	25	9	2	1	-	-
Kent State	-	-	-	1	6	16	26	27	16	6	2	-	-	-	2	11	29	31	20	6	1	-
Miami (OH)	-	-	1	4	12	22	27	22	10	2	-	-	-	1	3	15	29	30	16	5	1	-
Ohio	-	1	4	13	23	26	20	9	3	1	-	-	-	2	10	24	28	24	10	2	-	-
MAC West	12-0	11-1	10-2	9-3	8-4	7-5	6-6	5-7	4-8	3-9	2-10	1-11	0-12	8-0	7-1	6-2	5-3	4-4	3-5	2-6	1-7	0-8
Ball State	-	1	4	12	20	24	22	12	4	1	-	-	-	1	7	19	32	22	15	3	1	-
Central Michigan	-	-	1	6	13	23	25	18	10	3	1	-	-	1	3	12	23	28	22	9	2	-
Eastern Michigan	-	-	2	7	17	25	25	16	6	2	-	-	-	-	2	10	22	30	24	9	3	-
Northern Illinois	-	-	-	-	1	4	11	20	28	23	11	2	-	-	-	1	6	17	31	31	13	1
Toledo	1	5	17	29	27	15	5	1	-	-	-	-	-	4	19	33	28	13	3	-	-	-
Western Michigan	-	2	6	15	24	26	17	8	2	-	-	-	-	2	12	24	32	21	6	3	-	-

Projected Win Probabilities For MWC Teams

MWC Mountain	Overall Wins													Conference Wins								
	12-0	11-1	10-2	9-3	8-4	7-5	6-6	5-7	4-8	3-9	2-10	1-11	0-12	8-0	7-1	6-2	5-3	4-4	3-5	2-6	1-7	0-8
Air Force	-	3	11	21	26	21	12	4	2	-	-	-	-	2	11	25	31	21	8	2	-	-
Boise State	1	6	17	25	25	17	7	2	-	-	-	-	-	10	29	32	19	9	1	-	-	-
Colorado State	-	-	-	1	5	13	23	25	19	10	3	1	-	-	1	4	13	22	29	23	7	1
New Mexico	-	-	-	-	2	6	15	26	27	16	6	2	-	-	-	-	3	12	29	32	19	5
Utah State	-	-	-	-	2	6	15	23	27	18	7	2	-	-	-	2	4	17	31	30	14	2
Wyoming	-	4	12	23	27	20	10	3	1	-	-	-	-	1	8	24	29	24	10	3	1	-
MWC West	12-0	11-1	10-2	9-3	8-4	7-5	6-6	5-7	4-8	3-9	2-10	1-11	0-12	8-0	7-1	6-2	5-3	4-4	3-5	2-6	1-7	0-8
Fresno State	-	-	2	4	12	23	27	21	9	2	-	-	-	-	2	10	23	29	24	10	2	-
Hawaii*	-	1	5	12	21	25	20	11	3	2	-	-	-	-	1	10	20	30	24	11	3	1
Nevada	-	-	3	10	20	26	22	12	5	2	-	-	-	-	2	14	28	29	18	7	2	-
San Diego State	-	2	9	21	27	22	12	5	2	-	-	-	-	2	9	22	29	25	9	4	-	-
San Jose State	-	1	6	15	24	26	18	8	2	-	-	-	-	1	8	21	30	25	12	3	-	-
UNLV	-	-	-	-	-	-	2	7	19	28	27	14	3	-	-	-	2	7	18	32	32	9

*Hawaii will play 13 regular season games; for projected overall records, 12-0 means 12-1, 11-1 means 11-2, etc.

Projected Win Probabilities For Pac-12 Teams

Pac 12 North	Overall Wins													Conference Wins								
	12-0	11-1	10-2	9-3	8-4	7-5	6-6	5-7	4-8	3-9	2-10	1-11	0-12	9-0	8-1	7-2	6-3	5-4	4-5	3-6	2-7	1-8	0-9
California	-	-	-	2	7	17	25	24	16	7	2	-	-	-	-	2	7	17	27	27	15	4	1
Oregon	1	7	20	30	24	13	4	1	-	-	-	-	-	4	17	31	29	14	4	1	-	-	-
Oregon State	-	-	-	-	2	8	18	26	24	15	5	2	-	-	-	-	2	7	18	29	25	15	4
Stanford	-	-	-	-	2	5	13	22	25	20	10	3	-	-	-	-	2	9	17	28	27	13	4
Washington	5	16	28	26	17	7	1	-	-	-	-	-	-	8	28	29	22	10	3	-	-	-	-
Washington State	-	-	1	4	12	22	27	21	10	3	-	-	-	-	-	1	9	19	27	26	15	3	-
Pac 12 South	12-0	11-1	10-2	9-3	8-4	7-5	6-6	5-7	4-8	3-9	2-10	1-11	0-12	9-0	8-1	7-2	6-3	5-4	4-5	3-6	2-7	1-8	0-9
Arizona	-	-	-	-	-	-	1	6	15	28	30	17	3	-	-	-	-	-	2	10	26	40	22
Arizona State	1	5	14	25	27	17	8	3	-	-	-	-	-	1	10	23	29	23	11	3	-	-	-
Colorado	-	-	-	1	3	10	20	26	23	12	4	1	-	-	-	1	5	14	24	29	19	7	1
UCLA	-	-	2	7	16	23	25	16	7	3	1	-	-	-	2	6	15	26	28	16	6	1	-
USC	1	6	16	24	25	17	7	3	1	-	-	-	-	4	15	28	30	15	6	2	-	-	-
Utah	2	7	19	26	23	15	6	2	-	-	-	-	-	2	15	26	29	18	7	3	-	-	-

Projected Win Probabilities For SEC Teams

SEC East	Overall Wins													Conference Wins								
	12-0	11-1	10-2	9-3	8-4	7-5	6-6	5-7	4-8	3-9	2-10	1-11	0-12	8-0	7-1	6-2	5-3	4-4	3-5	2-6	1-7	0-8
Florida	2	11	28	31	19	7	2	-	-	-	-	-	-	2	14	34	31	16	3	-	-	-
Georgia	8	27	35	21	7	2	-	-	-	-	-	-	-	24	41	27	7	1	-	-	-	-
Kentucky	-	-	3	9	20	29	24	12	3	-	-	-	-	-	1	6	16	26	30	17	4	-
Missouri	-	-	2	7	17	26	26	15	6	1	-	-	-	-	1	6	16	29	29	15	4	-
South Carolina	-	-	-	-	-	2	8	21	29	26	12	2	-	-	-	-	1	8	21	38	27	5
Tennessee	-	-	1	5	15	28	29	16	5	1	-	-	-	-	-	1	10	25	36	21	6	1
Vanderbilt	-	-	-	-	-	-	2	9	21	31	26	10	1	-	-	-	-	1	6	20	40	33
SEC West	12-0	11-1	10-2	9-3	8-4	7-5	6-6	5-7	4-8	3-9	2-10	1-11	0-12	8-0	7-1	6-2	5-3	4-4	3-5	2-6	1-7	0-8
Alabama	33	40	20	6	1	-	-	-	-	-	-	-	-	36	42	19	3	-	-	-	-	-
Arkansas	-	-	-	-	1	6	16	27	28	16	5	1	-	-	-	-	1	7	20	34	29	9
Auburn	-	1	6	18	28	25	15	5	2	-	-	-	-	-	2	16	28	29	18	6	1	-
LSU	-	4	13	25	27	19	9	3	-	-	-	-	-	1	5	20	29	27	14	4	-	-
Mississippi State	-	-	1	5	13	24	27	19	9	2	-	-	-	-	-	2	14	26	32	21	5	-
Ole Miss	-	1	3	12	22	26	21	11	3	1	-	-	-	-	1	9	23	31	27	8	1	-
Texas A&M	1	8	22	31	23	11	4	-	-	-	-	-	-	1	12	28	30	21	7	1	-	-

Projected Win Probabilities For Sun Belt Teams

Sun Belt East	Overall Wins													Conference Wins								
	12-0	11-1	10-2	9-3	8-4	7-5	6-6	5-7	4-8	3-9	2-10	1-11	0-12	8-0	7-1	6-2	5-3	4-4	3-5	2-6	1-7	0-8
Appalachian State	2	10	23	28	22	11	3	1	-	-	-	-	-	9	28	32	22	8	1	-	-	-
Coastal Carolina	3	14	28	28	18	7	2	-	-	-	-	-	-	8	24	31	25	10	2	-	-	-
Georgia Southern	-	-	1	4	11	20	25	22	12	4	1	-	-	-	2	7	22	33	24	10	2	-
Georgia State	-	-	-	2	6	14	24	25	19	8	2	-	-	-	1	7	21	30	29	10	2	-
Troy	-	1	7	15	25	25	17	8	2	-	-	-	-	1	6	17	32	26	14	4	-	-
Sun Belt West	12-0	11-1	10-2	9-3	8-4	7-5	6-6	5-7	4-8	3-9	2-10	1-11	0-12	8-0	7-1	6-2	5-3	4-4	3-5	2-6	1-7	0-8
Arkansas State	-	-	-	1	3	10	19	27	23	12	4	1	-	-	1	4	16	28	31	15	4	1
Louisiana	2	13	26	28	20	8	3	-	-	-	-	-	-	13	33	34	16	4	-	-	-	-
South Alabama	-	-	-	-	1	4	12	23	27	20	10	3	-	-	-	-	2	10	24	34	25	5
Texas State	-	-	-	-	-	1	7	17	25	27	16	6	1	-	-	1	2	11	26	33	22	5
UL Monroe	-	-	-	-	-	-	1	4	14	27	32	19	3	-	-	-	-	3	14	33	34	16

NCAA F+ Projections

F+: Projected overall F/+

OF+: Projected offensive F/+ with rank

DF+: Projected defensive F/+ with rank

MW: Mean wins

CW: Mean conference wins

Div: Odds of winning division

Conf: Odds of winning conference

CFP: Odds of making College Football Playoff

U: Odds of going undefeated

10+: Odds of winning 10 or more games

6+: Odds of winning 6 or more games

SOS: Strength of Schedule (number of losses an elite team would have against this schedule) and rank

CSOS: Conference strength of schedule with rank

NCAA Teams, No. 1 to No. 130

Rk	Team	F+	OF+	Rk	DF+	Rk	MW	CW	Div	Conf	CFP	U	10+	6+	SOS	Rk	CSOS	Rk
1	Alabama	2.60	2.80	1	1.84	5	11.0	7.1	79%	43%	46%	33%	93%	100%	1.94	23	1.66	26
2	Clemson	2.25	1.79	4	2.32	1	11.3	7.7	98%	73%	63%	46%	99%	100%	0.95	81	0.49	81
3	Ohio State	2.16	2.61	2	1.16	15	10.7	7.9	83%	56%	46%	23%	87%	100%	1.59	43	1.28	47
4	Oklahoma	1.94	2.34	3	0.95	24	10.3	7.5	-	57%	45%	14%	76%	100%	1.61	42	1.40	40
5	Georgia	1.74	1.19	12	1.85	4	10.0	6.8	76%	34%	33%	8%	70%	100%	1.55	46	0.91	60
6	Wisconsin	1.56	0.70	32	1.96	2	9.6	7.1	60%	20%	14%	5%	53%	100%	1.52	48	1.19	49
7	Florida	1.41	1.51	6	0.89	25	9.2	5.4	20%	9%	8%	2%	41%	100%	1.75	36	1.69	25
8	Iowa State	1.40	1.39	7	1.06	19	8.9	6.3	-	21%	14%	2%	35%	99%	1.92	26	1.64	30
9	Iowa	1.32	0.18	56	1.92	3	8.7	6.4	30%	10%	6%	1%	28%	98%	1.82	32	1.41	38
10	Notre Dame	1.29	0.94	23	1.30	11	8.7	-	-	-	1%	2%	32%	98%	1.62	40	0.00	
11	Penn State	1.28	0.77	28	1.38	9	8.3	5.8	10%	7%	4%	0%	19%	98%	2.20	7	1.95	4
12	Texas A&M	1.27	1.03	17	1.21	12	8.9	5.2	11%	6%	5%	1%	31%	100%	1.74	37	1.65	29
13	Washington	1.27	1.26	11	1.09	17	9.4	6.9	56%	28%	20%	5%	49%	100%	1.19	68	0.93	58
14	LSU	1.23	1.32	10	0.86	28	8.2	4.6	5%	3%	2%	0%	17%	97%	2.20	6	1.99	3
15	Oregon	1.22	0.99	20	1.12	16	8.7	6.6	40%	20%	13%	1%	28%	99%	1.73	38	1.11	52
16	Texas	1.18	1.19	13	0.76	32	8.2	5.8	-	12%	7%	1%	20%	97%	1.94	24	1.70	22
17	Auburn	1.09	0.58	35	1.17	14	7.6	4.3	4%	2%	2%	0%	7%	93%	2.39	3	2.01	2
18	Miami	1.09	0.86	25	1.02	22	8.5	5.9	41%	10%	6%	1%	24%	99%	1.62	41	0.76	68
19	Utah	1.09	0.39	44	1.45	8	8.5	6.2	33%	17%	11%	2%	28%	98%	1.42	56	1.13	51
20	Cincinnati	1.07	0.43	43	1.47	6	9.3	6.5	-	46%	1%	3%	45%	100%	1.03	79	0.43	85
21	USC	1.07	1.17	14	0.75	33	8.3	6.4	38%	19%	12%	1%	23%	96%	1.49	51	1.00	57
22	North Carolina	1.06	1.66	5	0.15	54	8.9	5.9	40%	10%	7%	2%	35%	99%	1.18	70	0.77	67
23	Arizona State	0.95	0.79	27	0.81	29	8.3	5.8	22%	11%	7%	1%	20%	97%	1.49	52	1.29	46
24	Oklahoma State	0.93	0.52	38	1.08	18	7.6	5.3	-	6%	3%	0%	10%	93%	1.95	20	1.69	24
25	Michigan	0.86	0.71	30	0.62	38	7.1	5.0	3%	2%	1%	0%	5%	85%	2.17	9	1.85	11
26	UCF	0.78	1.38	8	0.05	62	9.0	5.8	-	24%	1%	2%	36%	99%	0.89	82	0.62	73
27	Indiana	0.78	0.51	39	0.80	30	7.0	4.7	3%	2%	1%	0%	4%	85%	2.10	12	1.87	7
28	TCU	0.77	0.13	60	1.18	13	7.3	4.8	-	3%	2%	0%	6%	88%	1.93	25	1.83	12
29	Louisiana	0.73	0.81	26	0.45	43	9.1	6.4	93%	46%	1%	2%	41%	100%	0.78	95	0.33	98
30	Appalachian State	0.73	0.29	51	1.06	20	8.9	6.0	45%	23%	0%	2%	35%	99%	0.84	89	0.49	82
31	Ole Miss	0.68	1.36	9	-0.22	81	7.0	4.0	2%	1%	1%	0%	4%	85%	2.02	16	1.82	13
32	Minnesota	0.67	1.01	18	0.22	51	7.0	4.5	5%	2%	1%	0%	3%	83%	1.91	27	1.78	18
33	Boise State	0.64	0.52	37	0.45	44	8.4	6.1	56%	38%	0%	1%	24%	98%	0.88	84	0.26	106
34	BYU	0.57	1.04	16	0.01	64	7.6	-	-	-	0%	0%	10%	92%	1.27	67	0.00	
35	UCLA	0.56	0.99	21	0.01	65	6.4	4.5	6%	3%	2%	0%	2%	73%	1.84	30	1.57	34

444

Rk	Team	F+	OF+	Rk	DF+	Rk	MW	CW	Div	Conf	CFP	U	10+	6+	SOS	Rk	CSOS	Rk
36	Virginia Tech	0.54	0.62	34	0.27	49	7.6	4.8	12%	3%	2%	0%	9%	92%	1.29	62	0.88	61
37	Nebraska	0.42	0.11	61	0.64	37	5.6	3.9	2%	1%	0%	0%	0%	53%	2.40	2	1.79	17
38	Coastal Carolina	0.42	0.87	24	-0.13	72	9.3	5.9	37%	19%	0%	3%	45%	100%	0.52	116	0.36	94
39	Memphis	0.41	0.39	45	0.29	48	8.2	5.0	-	10%	0%	1%	19%	96%	0.70	101	0.60	74
40	Baylor	0.41	-0.28	80	1.03	21	6.4	4.0	-	1%	1%	0%	2%	72%	1.83	31	1.70	23
41	Mississippi State	0.35	-0.06	70	0.71	34	6.2	3.3	0%	0%	0%	0%	1%	70%	2.02	15	1.81	14
42	West Virginia	0.34	-0.15	75	0.69	35	5.8	3.8	-	1%	0%	0%	1%	57%	2.03	14	1.81	15
43	Buffalo	0.30	0.34	50	0.38	45	8.7	5.9	55%	27%	0%	1%	31%	99%	0.50	118	0.23	108
44	Pittsburgh	0.29	-0.30	83	0.76	31	6.8	3.7	3%	1%	0%	0%	3%	82%	1.43	54	1.27	48
45	Louisville	0.27	1.00	19	-0.57	96	6.7	4.3	2%	1%	1%	0%	3%	80%	1.29	63	0.91	59
46	Washington State	0.24	1.15	15	-0.95	111	6.1	3.8	2%	1%	1%	0%	1%	66%	1.77	35	1.64	31
47	Virginia	0.23	0.27	53	0.13	55	6.2	3.9	4%	1%	1%	0%	2%	69%	1.51	49	1.05	54
48	Kansas State	0.23	0.15	58	0.11	57	5.9	3.6	-	1%	0%	0%	1%	61%	1.80	33	1.73	20
49	SMU	0.19	0.65	33	-0.20	77	7.0	4.1	-	3%	0%	0%	5%	85%	1.11	76	0.86	62
50	Purdue	0.18	0.53	36	-0.23	82	5.2	3.5	1%	0%	0%	0%	0%	43%	2.26	5	1.87	8
51	Tulsa	0.18	-0.43	89	0.87	27	6.5	4.5	-	5%	0%	0%	1%	74%	1.59	44	0.71	70
52	Tulane	0.18	0.37	47	-0.16	74	6.1	4.0	-	3%	0%	0%	1%	65%	1.51	50	0.85	63
53	Kentucky	0.17	-0.20	77	0.47	41	6.9	3.6	2%	1%	1%	0%	3%	85%	1.45	53	1.30	43
54	Toledo	0.14	0.48	41	-0.22	79	8.5	5.6	40%	20%	0%	1%	23%	99%	0.67	103	0.29	103
55	Missouri	0.12	0.08	62	0.12	56	6.5	3.5	2%	1%	1%	0%	2%	78%	1.40	57	1.30	44
56	Western Michigan	0.10	0.97	22	-0.69	101	7.4	5.1	24%	12%	0%	0%	8%	90%	0.75	98	0.35	95
57	Tennessee	0.10	-0.25	79	0.55	39	6.5	3.1	1%	0%	0%	0%	1%	78%	1.95	22	1.86	10
58	Maryland	0.10	-0.13	73	0.15	53	5.5	3.3	0%	0%	0%	0%	0%	51%	1.88	29	1.79	16
59	Colorado	0.10	0.16	57	0.08	59	4.9	3.3	1%	0%	0%	0%	0%	34%	2.14	10	1.71	21
60	Michigan State	0.10	-0.73	99	0.98	23	5.5	3.5	0%	0%	0%	0%	0%	48%	1.95	21	1.64	32
61	Northwestern	0.08	-1.22	117	1.46	7	6.1	3.8	2%	0%	0%	0%	1%	65%	1.43	55	1.41	39
62	Air Force	0.07	-0.02	68	0.08	60	7.9	5.1	22%	15%	0%	0%	14%	94%	0.46	121	0.38	90
63	Houston	0.07	0.03	64	0.05	63	7.9	4.7	-	7%	0%	0%	12%	94%	0.50	117	0.43	86
64	NC State	0.07	-0.20	76	0.33	47	6.1	3.2	0%	0%	0%	0%	1%	67%	1.54	47	1.37	41
65	Liberty	0.06	0.50	40	-0.34	90	8.2	-	-	-	0%	1%	18%	98%	0.60	113	0.00	
66	Wake Forest	0.05	0.24	55	-0.07	69	6.5	3.9	0%	0%	0%	0%	2%	76%	1.37	59	1.00	56
67	San Diego State	0.05	-1.25	118	1.34	10	7.8	4.9	31%	10%	0%	0%	11%	93%	0.60	114	0.36	93
68	California	0.05	-0.30	82	0.45	42	5.6	3.7	2%	1%	1%	0%	0%	51%	1.57	45	1.32	42
69	Wyoming	0.02	-0.85	103	0.88	26	8.1	4.9	18%	12%	0%	0%	16%	96%	0.48	120	0.43	87
70	Troy	-0.02	-0.01	66	-0.01	67	7.4	4.6	10%	5%	0%	0%	8%	90%	0.61	110	0.54	77
71	Arkansas	-0.02	-0.11	72	0.05	61	4.5	1.9	0%	0%	0%	0%	0%	23%	2.66	1	2.41	1
72	Marshall	-0.03	-0.45	90	0.38	46	8.2	5.7	40%	20%	0%	1%	20%	96%	0.40	126	0.15	117
73	Texas Tech	-0.04	0.14	59	-0.19	76	5.2	2.9	-	0%	2%	0%	0%	40%	1.96	19	1.88	6
74	Ball State	-0.04	0.25	54	-0.25	84	6.9	4.8	18%	9%	0%	0%	5%	83%	0.76	97	0.30	100
75	Florida State	-0.04	0.07	63	-0.19	75	5.3	3.0	0%	0%	0%	0%	0%	44%	2.10	11	1.44	37
76	Stanford	-0.04	0.47	42	-0.63	97	4.2	2.8	0%	0%	0%	0%	0%	20%	2.02	17	1.65	28
77	Boston College	-0.05	0.38	46	-0.53	94	6.7	3.5	0%	0%	0%	0%	3%	79%	1.12	75	1.05	55
78	Oregon State	-0.09	0.75	29	-1.08	115	4.7	2.7	0%	0%	0%	0%	0%	28%	1.79	34	1.66	27
79	UAB	-0.11	-0.79	102	0.64	36	7.4	5.5	45%	22%	0%	0%	6%	89%	0.81	93	0.16	113
80	San Jose State	-0.12	-0.07	71	-0.14	73	7.3	4.8	29%	9%	0%	0%	7%	90%	0.62	109	0.20	111
81	Florida Atlantic	-0.12	-0.61	95	0.48	40	7.7	5.6	38%	19%	0%	0%	10%	94%	0.66	104	0.16	115
82	Army	-0.14	-0.47	92	0.23	50	7.2	-	-	-	0%	0%	6%	90%	0.82	92	0.00	
83	Ohio	-0.17	0.36	48	-0.73	103	7.2	4.9	23%	11%	0%	0%	5%	87%	0.60	111	0.27	105
84	Nevada	-0.18	-0.14	74	-0.22	80	6.9	4.2	17%	6%	0%	0%	3%	81%	0.67	102	0.44	84
85	Georgia Tech	-0.22	-0.22	78	-0.11	70	4.4	2.5	0%	0%	0%	0%	0%	20%	2.28	4	1.54	36
86	Central Michigan	-0.24	-0.33	85	-0.01	68	6.2	4.1	9%	4%	0%	0%	1%	68%	0.83	90	0.37	92
87	Georgia Southern	-0.26	-0.67	97	0.21	52	5.9	3.9	4%	2%	0%	0%	1%	61%	0.86	87	0.59	75
88	Georgia State	-0.32	0.29	52	-0.76	105	5.3	3.8	4%	2%	0%	0%	0%	46%	1.28	64	0.65	72
89	Fresno State	-0.33	-0.01	65	-0.55	95	6.2	4.0	11%	4%	0%	0%	2%	68%	0.98	80	0.44	83
90	Miami (OH)	-0.36	-0.45	91	-0.21	78	6.1	4.5	13%	7%	0%	0%	1%	66%	0.88	85	0.30	99

Rk	Team	F+	OF+	Rk	DF+	Rk	MW	CW	Div	Conf	CFP	U	10+	6+	SOS	Rk	CSOS	Rk
91	Eastern Michigan	-0.47	0.36	49	-1.21	117	6.6	3.9	7%	4%	0%	0%	2%	76%	0.74	99	0.28	104
92	South Carolina	-0.47	-0.42	87	-0.30	85	3.9	2.1	0%	0%	0%	0%	0%	10%	2.18	8	1.62	33
93	Kent State	-0.51	0.70	31	-1.65	124	5.5	4.3	9%	5%	0%	0%	0%	49%	1.16	71	0.34	96
94	Hawaii	-0.52	-0.03	69	-0.83	107	7.1	3.9	12%	4%	0%	0%	6%	84%	0.54	115	0.25	107
95	Illinois	-0.55	-0.42	88	-0.64	98	3.9	2.3	0%	0%	0%	0%	0%	13%	1.72	39	1.57	35
96	Navy	-0.57	-0.61	94	-0.31	87	3.7	2.6	-	0%	0%	0%	0%	13%	1.27	65	0.83	64
97	Arkansas State	-0.61	-0.01	67	-0.99	112	4.9	3.5	6%	3%	0%	0%	0%	33%	1.07	78	0.51	79
98	Colorado State	-0.61	-0.75	100	-0.31	86	5.2	3.3	3%	2%	0%	0%	0%	42%	0.82	91	0.33	97
99	East Carolina	-0.67	-0.30	81	-0.84	109	4.4	2.7	-	0%	0%	0%	0%	23%	1.08	77	0.80	66
100	Syracuse	-0.69	-1.07	112	-0.23	83	4.0	1.9	0%	0%	0%	0%	0%	17%	1.27	66	1.16	50
101	Western Kentucky	-0.69	-1.26	119	0.10	58	5.9	4.3	12%	6%	0%	0%	1%	60%	0.49	119	0.16	112
102	Duke	-0.71	-1.21	114	-0.12	71	4.2	1.8	0%	0%	0%	0%	0%	19%	1.14	72	1.08	53
103	UTSA	-0.76	-0.69	98	-0.74	104	6.6	4.5	16%	8%	0%	0%	2%	74%	0.28	129	0.09	123
104	Arizona	-0.78	-0.37	86	-0.93	110	2.6	1.3	0%	0%	0%	0%	0%	1%	1.97	18	1.78	19
105	Southern Mississippi	-0.84	-0.95	107	-0.49	93	6.0	4.3	15%	7%	0%	0%	1%	63%	0.85	88	0.09	122
106	South Florida	-0.85	-1.05	111	-0.34	89	3.3	2.1	-	0%	0%	0%	0%	6%	1.39	58	0.81	65
107	Temple	-0.90	-1.17	113	-0.32	88	4.4	2.1	-	0%	0%	0%	0%	24%	0.79	94	0.74	69
108	Rutgers	-0.96	-1.32	122	-0.47	92	2.9	1.2	0%	0%	0%	0%	0%	2%	1.88	28	1.86	9
109	Louisiana Tech	-0.97	-1.00	109	-0.72	102	5.6	4.3	12%	6%	0%	0%	0%	52%	0.45	123	0.14	118
110	Northern Illinois	-0.98	-1.21	116	-0.42	91	4.1	2.7	1%	1%	0%	0%	0%	16%	0.77	96	0.42	88
111	Middle Tennessee	-0.99	-0.65	96	-1.03	113	5.3	3.5	4%	2%	0%	0%	0%	44%	0.46	122	0.16	116
112	Rice	-1.00	-1.72	125	0.00	66	5.2	4.0	8%	4%	0%	0%	0%	41%	0.60	112	0.14	119
113	Florida International	-1.04	-1.21	115	-0.68	100	5.4	3.6	4%	2%	0%	0%	0%	45%	0.36	128	0.22	109
114	Utah State	-1.10	-0.93	106	-1.07	114	4.4	2.6	1%	1%	0%	0%	0%	23%	0.63	106	0.38	91
115	North Texas	-1.15	-0.50	93	-1.56	122	4.5	3.3	4%	2%	0%	0%	0%	27%	0.38	127	0.11	120
116	South Alabama	-1.21	-1.29	120	-0.77	106	4.2	2.2	1%	0%	0%	0%	0%	17%	0.72	100	0.59	76
117	Charlotte	-1.21	-0.31	84	-1.81	126	4.7	3.1	2%	1%	0%	0%	0%	31%	0.18	130	0.11	121
118	Kansas	-1.23	-1.30	121	-0.83	108	1.9	0.8	-	0%	0%	0%	0%	0%	2.08	13	1.91	5
119	New Mexico	-1.23	-0.75	101	-1.44	119	4.5	2.3	0%	0%	0%	0%	0%	23%	0.88	83	0.51	78
120	Vanderbilt	-1.27	-0.99	108	-1.13	116	2.9	1.0	0%	0%	0%	0%	0%	2%	1.34	60	1.29	45
121	Texas State	-1.30	-0.90	105	-1.41	118	3.6	2.2	1%	0%	0%	0%	0%	8%	0.63	107	0.50	80
122	UNLV	-1.51	-1.00	110	-1.51	121	2.7	1.8	0%	0%	0%	0%	0%	2%	0.87	86	0.29	101
123	Old Dominion	-1.51	-1.94	128	-0.67	99	3.7	2.7	1%	0%	0%	0%	0%	10%	0.44	124	0.16	114
124	UL Monroe	-1.57	-0.87	104	-1.68	125	2.4	1.6	0%	0%	0%	0%	0%	1%	1.18	69	0.68	71
125	Akron	-1.97	-2.00	129	-1.45	120	1.9	1.1	0%	0%	0%	0%	0%	0%	1.31	61	0.39	89
126	UTEP	-2.06	-1.53	123	-2.11	127	3.0	1.6	0%	0%	0%	0%	0%	4%	0.43	125	0.20	110
127	Connecticut	-2.09	-1.57	124	-2.14	128	2.4	-	-	-	0%	0%	0%	1%	1.14	73	0.00	
128	Bowling Green	-2.22	-2.24	130	-1.58	123	1.8	1.0	0%	0%	0%	0%	0%	0%	0.62	108	0.29	102
129	New Mexico State	-2.39	-1.89	127	-2.17	129	2.1	-	-	-	0%	0%	0%	0%	1.13	74	0.00	
130	Massachusetts	-2.73	-1.76	126	-3.07	130	1.5	-	-	-	0%	0%	0%	0%	0.66	105	0.00	

FO Rookie Projections

Over the years, Football Outsiders has developed a number of methods for forecasting the NFL success of highly drafted players at various positions. Here is a rundown of those methods and what they say about players drafted in 2021.

Quarterbacks: QBASE

This year, we introduced a new version of the QBASE (Quarterback Adjusted Stats and Experience) system which combines the original work done by Andrew Healy with the functional mobility model developed by Jeremy Rosen and Alexandre Olbrecht.

QBASE v2.0 analyzes all rookie quarterbacks chosen among the top 100 picks of the NFL draft since 2004. It uses regression analysis to determine which factors helped predict their career TDYAR/A, or total DYAR per attempt. This combines both passing and rushing value divided by total passes plus runs.

QBASE generates adjusted college performance as a composite of three college statistics: completion rate, rushing yards per attempt, and passing touchdowns per completion. Statistics are adjusted based on strength of schedule and strength of teammates. The latter element gives credit based on the draft-pick value of offensive linemen and receivers drafted in the quarterback's draft year as well as the projected draft position of younger teammates in 2022. However, the usual strength of schedule adjustment was not included in 2021 due to the lack of interconnectivity between conferences in the COVID-affected 2020 college football schedule.

The measurement of past performance is then combined with two other factors: college experience and draft position. The latter factor accounts for what scouts will see but a statistical projection system will not, including personality, leadership, and projection of physical attributes to the next level.

QBASE also looks at the past performance of quarterbacks compared to their projection and, using 50,000 simulations, produces a range of potential outcomes for each prospect: Elite quarterback (over 1.5 TDYAR/A, or roughly 900 or more DYAR in an average 16-game season); Upper Tier quarterback (0.75 to 1.5 TDYAR/A); Adequate Starter (0.0 to 0.75 TDYAR/A); or Bust (less than 0.0 TDYAR/A).

Here are QBASE projections for quarterbacks chosen in the top 100 picks of the 2021 NFL draft:

Player	School	Tm	Rd	Pick	TDYAR/A	Elite	Upper	Adequate	Bust
Trevor Lawrence	Clemson	JAX	1	1	0.68	23%	25%	26%	27%
Zach Wilson	BYU	NYJ	1	2	0.67	22%	25%	26%	27%
Trey Lance	North Dakota St.	SF	1	3	0.43	17%	22%	27%	35%
Justin Fields	Ohio State	CHI	1	11	0.29	13%	20%	27%	40%
Mac Jones	Alabama	NE	1	15	0.04	9%	17%	26%	48%
Kyle Trask	Stanford	TB	2	64	-0.95	2%	5%	13%	80%
Kellen Mond	Florida	MIN	3	66	-0.51	3%	9%	19%	68%
Davis Mills	Texas A&M	HOU	3	67	-0.88	2%	5%	14%	79%

Projections are slightly different from those posted on our website in April because they have been adjusted for the actual draft position of each player and his offensive teammates instead of the projected draft position.

Running Backs: BackCAST

BackCAST is Football Outsiders' metric for projecting the likelihood of success for running back prospects in the NFL draft. Historically, a college running back is more likely to succeed at the NFL level if he has a good size/speed combination, gained a high average yards per carry, and represented a large percentage of his college team's running attack. Criteria measured include:

- Weight and 40-yard dash time at the NFL combine. BackCAST uses pro day measurements for prospects that did not run at the combine (including all 2021 prospects).
- Average yards per rush attempt, with an adjustment for running backs who had fewer career carries than an average drafted running back.
- A measurement of how much each prospect's team used him in the running game during his career relative to an average drafted running back in the same year of eligibility.
- Prospect's receiving yards per game in his college career.

BackCAST considers these factors and projects the degree to which the running back will exceed the NFL production of an "average" drafted running back during his first five years in the NFL. For example, a running back with a 50% BackCAST is projected to gain 50% more yards than the "average" drafted running back. BackCAST also lists each running back's "RecIndex," measuring whether the player is likely to be a ground-and-pound two-down back, more of a receiving back, or something in between. The higher the RecIndex, the better the back is as a receiver.

Here are the BackCAST numbers for running backs drafted in the first four rounds of the 2021 draft, along with the top three later-round picks and the top undrafted free agent.

Player	School	Team	Rd	Pick	BackCAST	RecIndex
Najee Harris	Alabama	PIT	1	24	72.2%	-0.02
Travis Etienne	Clemson	JAX	1	25	124.2%	0.33
Javonte Williams	North Carolina	DEN	2	35	5.9%	0.15
Trey Sermon	Ohio State	SF	3	88	-11.2%	-0.08
Michael Carter	North Carolina	NYJ	4	107	10.1%	0.21
Kene Nwangwu	Iowa St.	MIN	4	119	-60.2%	-0.42
Rhamondre Stevenson	Oklahoma	NE	4	120	14.2%	-0.02
Chuba Hubbard	Oklahoma St.	CAR	4	126	52.9%	0.11
Jermar Jefferson	Oregon St.	DET	7	257	36.3%	0.01
Kenneth Gainwell	Memphis	PHI	5	150	36.1%	1.09
Elijah Mitchell	Louisiana	SF	6	194	31.9%	0.18
Stevie Scott	Indiana	NO	UDFA		27.4%	-0.10

Edge Rushers: SackSEER

SackSEER is a method that projects sacks for edge rushers, including both 3-4 outside linebackers and 4-3 defensive ends, using the following criteria:

- An "explosion index" that measures the prospect's scores in the 40-yard dash, the vertical jump, and the broad jump in pre-draft workouts.
- Sacks per game, adjusted for factors such as early entry in the NFL draft and position switches during college.
- Passes defensed per game.

SackSEER outputs two numbers. The first, SackSEER Rating, solely measures how high the prospect scores compared to players of the past. The second, SackSEER Projection, represents a forecast of sacks for the player's first five years in the NFL. It synthesizes metrics with conventional wisdom by adjusting based on the player's expected draft position (interestingly, not his actual draft position) based on pre-draft analysis by ESPN's Scouts Inc.

Here are the SackSEER numbers for edge rushers drafted in the first three rounds of the 2021 draft, along with the top three later-round picks and the top undrafted free agent.

Name	School	Team	Rd	Pick	SackSEER Projection	SackSEER Rating
Jaelan Phillips	Miami	MIA	1	18	30.5	97.0%
Kwity Paye	Michigan	IND	1	21	21.7	55.6%
Payton Turner	Houston	NO	1	28	15.7	73.9%
Gregory Rousseau	Miami	BUF	1	30	21.3	59.3%
Odafe Oweh	Penn St.	BAL	1	31	24.5	90.9%
Joe Tryon	Washington	TB	1	32	17.4	45.0%
Azeez Ojulari	Georgia	NYG	2	50	18.7	62.1%
Dayo Odeyingbo	Vanderbilt	IND	2	54	6.6	25.9%
Carlos Basham	Wake Forest	BUF	2	61	20.7	88.8%
Joseph Ossai	Texas	CIN	3	69	19.7	89.2%
Malcolm Koonce	Buffalo	LV	3	79	0.2	19.0%
Chauncey Golston	Iowa	DAL	3	84	7.2	29.1%
Patrick Jones	Pittsburgh	MIN	3	90	10.6	13.6%
Ronnie Perkins	Oklahoma	NE	3	96	1.9	38.4%
Elerson Smith	Northern Iowa	NYG	4	116	13.9	95.5%
Shaka Toney	Penn St.	WAS	7	246	12.8	80.0%
Patrick Johnson	Tulsa	PHI	7	234	6.5	59.1%
Hamilcar Rashed	Oregon St.	NYJ	UDFA		11.1	58.4%

Wide Receivers: Playmaker Score

Playmaker Score projects success for NFL wide receivers using the following criteria:

- The wide receiver's peak season for receiving yards per team attempt and receiving touchdowns per team attempt.
- Differences between this prospect's peak season and most recent season, to adjust for players who declined in their final college year.
- Rushing attempts per game.
- A binary variable that rewards players who enter the draft as underclassmen.
- A factor that gives a bonus to wideouts who played on the same college team as other receivers who are projected to be drafted.

Like SackSEER, Playmaker Score outputs two numbers. The first, Playmaker Score, represents a forecast of average receiving yards per year in the player's first five seasons, synthesizing metrics with conventional wisdom by adjusting based on the player's expected draft position. The second, Playmaker Rating, solely measures how high the prospect scores compared to players of the past.

Here are the Playmaker Score numbers for players drafted in the first three rounds of the 2021 draft, along with three later-round picks and two undrafted free agents with high Playmaker Ratings.

Name	School	Team	Rd	Pick	Playmaker Score	Playmaker Rating
Ja'Marr Chase	LSU	CIN	1	5	719	97.9%
Jaylen Waddle	Alabama	MIA	1	6	556	75.5%
DeVonta Smith	Alabama	PHI	1	10	777	99.4%
Kadarius Toney	Florida	NYG	1	20	497	51.6%
Rashod Bateman	Minnesota	BAL	1	27	498	91.1%
Elijah Moore	Ole Miss	NYJ	2	34	616	96.3%
Rondale Moore	Purdue	ARI	2	49	418	75.5%
D'Wayne Eskridge	Western Michigan	SEA	2	56	489	97.9%
Tutu Atwell	Louisville	LAR	2	57	602	98.2%
Terrace Marshall	LSU	CAR	2	59	513	84.0%
Josh Palmer	Tennessee	LAC	3	77	105	8.7%
Dyami Brown	North Carolina	WAS	3	82	197	84.7%
Amari Rodgers	Clemson	GB	3	85	68	19.7%
Nico Collins	Michigan	HOU	3	89	222	6.0%
Anthony Schwartz	Auburn	CLE	3	91	67	49.4%
Jaelon Darden	North Texas	TB	4	129	252	93.9%
Dax Milne	BYU	WAS	7	258	224	89.0%
Amon-Ra St. Brown	USC	DET	4	112	175	82.4%
Tamorrion Terry	Florida State	SEA		UDFA	270	71.6%
Sage Surratt	Wake Forest	DET		UDFA	355	71.0%

Top 25 Prospects

Every year, Football Outsiders puts together a list of the NFL's best and brightest young players ... who have barely played. Eighty percent of draft-day discussion is about first-round picks, and 10% is about the players who should have been first-round picks but instead went in the second round. Particularly if they were quarterbacks.

This list is about that last 10%. It's a stab in the dark at players who may just come out of the woodwork and surprise you this year.

Everybody knows that Trevor Lawrence and Kyle Pitts are good. There's a cottage industry around the idea of hyping every draft's No. 1 quarterback as a potential superstar. But players don't stop being promising just because they don't make waves in their rookie seasons. This is a list of players who have a real chance to make an impact in the NFL despite their lack of draft stock and the fact that they weren't immediate NFL starters.

Previous editions of the list have hyped players such as Geno Atkins, Grady Jarrett, Chris Godwin, Tyreek Hill, and Jamaal Charles before they blew up. Last year's list was thoroughly owned by the pandemic—which kept many young players around the league from getting a real offseason to challenge for a job—but still managed to single out Jamel Dean, Dre'Mont Jones, and Chase Winovich as key contributors.

Most of these lists are heavily dependent on the depth of incoming draft classes. For instance, this year's list doesn't have many running backs outside of the No. 1 slot, because most of the eligible players either played right away or didn't have the requisite talent. Last year's list was packed with cornerbacks. This year is heavier on offensive linemen and wideouts after a 2020 draft class that was quite strong on both of them.

This is the 15th anniversary of the list. We're still relying on the same things we always do: scouting, statistics, measurables, context, ceiling, expected role, and what we hear from other sources. The goal is to bring attention to players who are still developing in their second and third seasons, even after the draftniks have forgotten them. It's important to note that this list is not strictly about fantasy football (otherwise, there would be no offensive linemen on it) and career potential matters. It's not just a list for the 2021 season.

Here's our full criteria:

- Drafted in the third round or later, or signed as an undrafted free agent.
- Entered the NFL between 2018 and 2020.
- Fewer than 500 career offensive or defensive snaps (except running backs, who are allowed just 300 offensive snaps).
- Have not signed a contract extension (players who have bounced around the league looking for the right spot, however, still qualify for the list).
- •Age 26 or younger as of September 1, 2021.

1 Damien Harris, RB, New England; Age 24
Drafted 2019, pick 87 | 251 offensive snaps

It was extremely hard to find anybody talking down Harris, an Alabama back who showcased an advanced skill set in college and came to the Crimson Tide as the No. 1 running back recruit in the nation. Harris was made to split time with Josh Jacobs—you may remember him from places such as the first round of the 2019 draft—and still averaged 6.4 yards per carry and rolled in 23 touchdowns in his four-year career.

Harris is not likely to be a three-down, win-your-fantasy-PPR-league guy. He's a between-the-tackles bruiser, and that's why he lasted until the third round. He's built to pound the rock. He did that successfully last year for the Patriots to the tune of a 9.9% DVOA, and the only reason he didn't surpass eligibility for this list on snaps is because the Patriots had problems sustaining that kind of game plan.

We don't think Harris is going to be a superstar, but we can't rule out that he'll continue to take steps to improve. Bill Belichick noticed, saying of Harris in OTAs: "Damien works extremely hard, all phases and all aspects of his game. Conditioning, training, passing game, protection, route-running. Hardworking kid who tries to do anything he can to help the team." The dreamer comp is Derrick Henry. That might be a little too aspirational, but if Harris can trend towards being similar to the back he split time with in his senior year at Alabama, Jacobs, that would be a nice return on a third-round pick.

2 Adam Trautman, TE, New Orleans; Age 24
Drafted 2020, pick 105 | 393 offensive snaps

After finishing fifth in FCS with 14 touchdowns for Dayton in the 2019 college season, Trautman was looked at as a huge middle-of-the-field target who was going to have to deal with questions about his ability to transition against tougher competition. Running a 6.78s 3-cone drill at the NFL combine—a 97th percentile result among tight ends—caught eyes, and the Saints traded up for him at the last pick in the third round.

While Trautman wasn't a superstar in his first season, he produced at a high efficiency when he was actually targeted. Among tight ends with 10 to 24 targets, Trautman finished with the No. 1 DVOA (39.7%) and the highest catch rate (94%), and was second in DYAR (50). While that all sounds good and Saints-y, take a minute to remember that Trautman wasn't playing with in-his-prime Drew Brees. In fact, he was targeted seven times by Taysom Hill instead of Brees. And he still roasted defenders out of the backfield and provided solid blocking.

With Jared Cook released in a salary cap move and Josh Hill retired, the position is wide open for Trautman this year. Nick Vannett was signed but is more of a blocking tight end. Other than Michael Thomas, the Saints don't really have an established wide receiver either, which creates a big target void. If Trautman steps into it with production anywhere near what we saw last year, he could explode early.

3 Justin Madubuike, DL, Baltimore; Age 23
Drafted 2020, pick 71 | 260 defensive snaps

If you read the intro to our piece, you'll know that one of the most successful brands on the Football Outsiders top prospects list is the undersized defensive tackle. Few draftniks cited Madubuile due to his relative lack of size, which was a tacit admission that this kind of player has been successful and shouldn't be as overlooked as they have been in the past. Madubuike didn't quite hit the Geno Atkins benchmarks as far as athletic ability, but had plenty of overall potential blended with 11 sacks and 23 tackles for loss over his last two years at Texas A&M.

Madubuike was a healthy scratch for the first four weeks of the season, but a key rotational cog from Week 5 onwards, only missing two games for COVID protocols during Baltimore's December COVID scare. Madubuike came alive with a sack, two tackles for loss, and a pass defensed in Baltimore's playoff game against the Titans. The Ravens will probably want to see some development from him as a pass-rusher this offseason, but he plugged the run fairly well.

The interior line in Baltimore is by far the oldest part of the team. Calais Campbell is 35, Derek Wolfe 31, and Brandon Williams 32. Madubuike was going to figure to get some extra playing time anyway with Jihad Ward off to Jacksonville, but as the draft came and went with no extra investment, it became clear he's a huge part of Baltimore's plans going forward. "He played well last year, and I do think he's taken a big step," John Harbaugh said at OTAs. "He dropped to the third round for whatever reason, and we were very, very fortunate and blessed to get him there. The way he played last year to where he is right now is very encouraging. So, I'm excited about him. I can tell you the defensive line is excited about him, too. I saw Derek Wolfe over there celebrating with him a couple times on some things he did well. So, yes—we're fired up about Madubuike."

4 Logan Wilson, LB, Cincinnati; Age 25
Drafted 2020, pick 65 | 343 defensive snaps

The very first pick of the third round of the draft in 2020, Wilson started seeing heavy snaps in Week 5 but was knocked out of action by a high ankle sprain over the last three weeks of the season. The combination of the slow start and the injury is the only reason he's still eligible for the list. Wilson showcased some intriguing blitz skills and paired a solid athletic profile with a great year as a run defender for Wyoming in 2019.

"Bengals middle linebacker" feels like a position that has been up for grabs since Rey Maualuga retired and Vontaze Burfict finally stopped getting second chances. Letting Nick Vigil walk in free agency opened up yet another void, and Wilson and Akeem Davis-Gaither were drafted into it without much help. Of the two, Wilson has the skill set to help on run downs more, but the blitzing and coverage skills are solid selling points for Wilson as well.

Cincinnati defensive coordinator Lou Anarumo was cagey when asked about Wilson entrenching a starting spot in May, but with Josh Bynes gone, it's hard to not read the tea leaves

as looking that way. The Bengals barely even have veteran help in camp; the oldest player on the entire linebacker unit is 26-year-old Jordan Evans, a 2017 draftee. Wilson figures to be the best linebacker on the field this year for Cincinnati, with a chance of developing into something between Nick Kwiatkoski and a smaller Dont'a Hightower.

5 Alex Highsmith, ER, Pittsburgh; Age 24
Drafted 2020, pick 102 | 437 defensive snaps

Pittsburgh took a bet on Highsmith's ridiculous 2019 season at Charlotte, where he improved from three sacks as a junior to 15 as a senior. Running a 4.7s 40-yard dash at 248 pounds at the combine, Highsmith was a bit light for the NFL, but he had the combine metrics we look for. SackSEER, our edge rusher projection system, had Highsmith with a top-10 "explosion index"—its ranking of a player's athleticism—in the 2020 class.

Playing behind Bud Dupree and learning for a year was the plan for Highsmith, but when Dupree tore his ACL in Week 12, Highsmith immediately became an almost-every-down player for Pittsburgh. He notched five quarterback hits and a sack in those final five games of the season but was noticeably absent from the playoff game once the Browns created a massive game-script advantage. He wasn't trusted against the run just yet.

Dupree is now with the Titans, so Highsmith's closest competition on the edge is journeyman Cassius Marsh. "I didn't start my first couple of years in college and then ended up starting," Highsmith told reporters in May. "I took advantage of that opportunity. I feel like my opportunity is presented to me, I'm going to take advantage of it. It's exciting. I'm ready for the challenge." Last year wasn't a dominant pass-rushing display for Highsmith—the NFL isn't Gardner-Webb, it turns out—but he'll have every chance to put one on this year.

6 Kevin Dotson, G, Pittsburgh; Age 24
Drafted 2020, pick 135 | 360 offensive snaps

The first non-combine invitee to be drafted in 2020, Dotson nevertheless had an incredibly successful senior year at Louisiana. He was a small-school standout for a run-heavy offense, and NFL questions persisted around moving up with the competition and his ability to pass set because of a lack of experience there.

Well, it was one season—and an abbreviated one at that—but in four starts, Dotson allowed zero sacks and blew zero pass blocks. David DeCastro missed time with an ankle injury in 2020, and the Steelers didn't have the great offensive line you remember creating lanes for Willie Parker. They were abysmal last year, and change was naturally coming.

So they are turning over the entire interior line, essentially handing Dotson a starting job at left guard without a real competition. That speaks to the level of belief they have in him. "The offensive lines of any teams I've been on, we've been able to plug people in and still get the job done. We're going to miss the leadership of Pouncey, but we have to adjust," Dotson told reporters at OTAs. They're going to need him to be a leader in a hurry.

7 Jordan Elliott, DT, Cleveland; Age 23
Drafted 2020, pick 88 | 307 defensive snaps

We're weighting a lot of disruption over actual sacks in putting Elliott this high on the list. Elliott had just 5.5 college sacks and 16.5 tackles for loss, but he consistently disrupted timing and put pressure on the quarterback by showing lateral quickness and gap-shooting ability. That was the trait that got him in front of everyone's eyes and moved him up draft boards.

The Browns gave Elliott some small roles in packages last season behind Sheldon Richardson. He played more than 40% of the snaps just once all year, and that was in a 38-6 blowout in Week 1. The numbers in and of themselves weren't very encouraging; he had just two hurries and one defeat, but it says a lot that the Browns believed in him all season and didn't hand his job over to someone else.

Both Richardson and Larry Ogunjobi moved on this offseason, leaving Cleveland's interior line in a state of flux. Malik Jackson and Andrew Billings are each coming off of COVID opt-outs, and the only player coming back who played a major role last year is Elliott. "I don't want to be that guy to sit here and sound super excited about everybody," Chris Kiffin, the Browns' defensive line coach, said in a recent interview on Cleveland Browns Daily, "but I'm just telling you, the guy I'm most excited about is Jordan Elliott."

8 Matt Hennessy, C, Atlanta; Age 23
Drafted 2020, pick 78 | 225 offensive snaps

Hennessy was an NFL combine darling. He was 69th percentile or better in basically every agility metric in the combine—3-cone, 20-yard shuttle, 40-yard dash—as well as the explosion measured by vertical jump and broad jump. The question with Hennessy was more about how his weight and playing strength would translate to the NFL, as he's fairly scrawny and does not have the meat-hook arm length that line coaches prefer in the trenches.

In two starts last year, Hennessy did little to silence those doubters. He was called for four penalties and allowed six blown pass blocks and a sack. Of course, most of his extensive playing time was against the Chiefs and Bucs in Weeks 16 and 17. That meant he was dealing with Ndamukong Suh and Chris Jones. While that's not Aaron Donald, it's not exactly the easy transition you're hoping a rookie to get.

With Alex Mack off to the 49ers in free agency, the Falcons haven't provided much in the way of competition for Hennessy this offseason. They spent a fourth-round pick on rookie Drew Dalman. OTA talk was promising, with tackle Jake Matthews saying that Hennessy almost communicates too much now. There's no reason why Hennessy can't take the job and run with it.

9 Drue Tranquill, LB, Los Angeles Chargers; Age 26
Drafted 2019, pick 130 | 385 defensive snaps

Tranquill was 13th on our list last year for the exact same reason he is ninth this year: he profiles to be a modern coverage linebacker. He was the PFWA All-Rookie non-returner/kicker special teams player and finished second on the Chargers in special teams tackles. He allowed just two passes during the entirety of the 2019 season that went more than 15 yards, and one of them had him covering Tyreek Hill downfield for reasons that he all but called stupid vis-à-vis old defensive coordinator Gus Bradley.

What happened last season was: Tranquill took five snaps and was immediately lost for the season with a broken ankle. He was rehabbing with an eye towards coming back in the playoffs had the Chargers reached them, but alas, they did no such thing.

With Nick Vigil off the roster and the development of Kenneth Murray as the first-round pick last season, things are pretty simple for the Chargers. Tranquill and Kyzir White are the other two linebackers on the roster with experience, and Tranquill profiles to stay on the field in nickel. If he can springboard this to a healthy season in Brandon Staley's defense, he's got a chance to skyrocket his perceived value across the NFL.

10 Tyler Biadasz, C, Dallas; Age 23
Drafted 2020, pick 146 | 427 offensive snaps

Coming out of Wisconsin, Biadasz was seen as a no-frills center prospect. He didn't work out at the combine or at the Badgers' pro day due to injury, but he flashed all over the tape. You may remember Jonathan Taylor's 2,000-yard seasons—Biadasz was calling the signals for those, and he did an excellent job on doubles and keeping his mitts on his defenders.

The Cowboys suffered through some unfortunate times on the offensive line last year. Zack Martin was hurt. La'el Collins was hurt. Tyron Smith was hurt. Most importantly for Biadasz, long-time center Travis Frederick was dealing with Guillain-Barre syndrome. That turnover meant that Biadasz played 99% of the snaps from Weeks 5 to 8 before a hamstring injury claimed him as well. Biadasz allowed a sack and demonstrated that he's got some pass-protection adjustments to make in the NFL in those five games.

Cowboys players and coaches were raving about Biadasz at OTAs. "He has just figured out everything that he needs to know being the center of the offensive line—making the calls. He's speaking with more confidence. He's asking the questions that you want a center to ask against certain different things, adjustments, and everything like that, what to do," Collins told reporters. With Joe Looney gone and Frederick retired, there's little on the roster to provide competition for the starting center spot. It's fair to say that the Cowboys are counting on Biadasz.

11 Quintez Cephus, WR, Detroit; Age 23
Drafted 2020, pick 166 | 365 offensive snaps

A throwback, Cephus is a true outside power receiver. Cephus slipped in the draft partially because of a 4.73s 40-yard dash, but he also has an outside build at 6-foot-1, 202 pounds, and he put up 23 bench press reps at the combine. It's very easy to understand this type of player—it's what DK Metcalf would be without game-changing speed. The other factor in Cephus' draft-day drop were rape charges of which he was acquitted in college at Wisconsin.

Cephus actually started the first game of Detroit's season last year and posted a respectable 10.6% DVOA over the season despite getting inconsistent playing time. When Kenny Golladay was healthy enough to play, Cephus was an afterthought. But that didn't happen all that often in 2020, and it was a big reason why Golladay was allowed to leave in free agency. Golladay and Marvin Jones both fleeing left a gaping target void.

Detroit's depth chart at wideout is the major reason Cephus is this high on this list. Breshad Perriman and Tyrell Williams are the presumed one-two punch here. Williams was released by the Raiders, and Perriman is on his fourth team in four seasons. New Lions head coach Dan Campbell praised Cephus at OTAs, saying "We all see it. We feel like he's growing right in front of us. That's what you want these guys to do during this time." The opportunity is in front of Cephus to find 100 targets this year.

12 Bryan Edwards, WR, Las Vegas; Age 22
Drafted 2020, pick 81 | 259 offensive snaps

A big outside receiver prospect, Edwards was available in the third round despite good speed and an obscenely large target share at South Carolina, mainly on account of drops. Drops are at an interesting point in the NFL analytics spectrum. Obviously, it's bad when a drop happens, but for a receiver to make a drop he has to get to the ball, and Edwards made it to a ton of balls. He also made a number of contested catches that showed that maybe he was worth a second-round pick. That's not how it shook out after the NCAA produced another stellar group of wideouts.

Edwards started the first three games of the season and was a bit player in the overall direction of the Raiders' offense, then saw an ankle injury take him off the field. When he got healthy, he was mostly phased out of the offense. Despite the injury and getting yanked around by Gruden, Edwards finished third among all wideouts with 10 to 49 targets with a 36.6% DVOA.

The major concern for Edwards as a prospect is the lesson learned from Ravens wideout Miles Boykin last year: you can be good, but if you aren't a directed part of the offense, it doesn't matter. Raiders wideouts were targeted on a league-low 43.4% of their pass attempts last year, and even with Nelson Agholor gone, John Brown and Henry Ruggs figure to get plenty of outside snaps. Edwards has a good pedigree and showed good results in his small sample of first-year targets. He feels more like a WR4 on this group than someone guaranteed playing time, and that's the major reason he's not higher on this list.

13 Josh Jones, OL, Arizona; Age 24
Drafted 2020, pick 72 | 55 offensive snaps

While he wasn't considered part of the headlining group of offensive tackles in last year's class, Jones was a very common No. 5 behind Andrew Thomas, Tristan Wirfs, Mekhi Becton, and Jedrick Wills. He was the second highest-rated player on Daniel Jeremiah's 2020 big board that qualified for our top 25. When we compile this list internally, one thing we

rely on is looking at who is highest on a player, but that was almost impossible for Jones because everybody loved him. He came out at Houston as a terrific pass-setter who was regarded to have had some inconsistencies in a few games.

And then he joined the Cardinals, who feel set at left tackle with D.J. Humphries. They also had long-time starter Kelvin Beachum win the right tackle job. Jones played only as a sixth lineman or patch swing tackle last year, and both starters were retained. There's not really an easy projection for Jones to play tackle unless one of those two gets hurt.

Jones is part of a competition with Max Garcia and Brian Winters at guard going into training camp. The optimism is still there from the Cardinals. Steve Keim said at OTAs that "Josh has the ability, in my opinion—and I know Sean Kugler, our O-line coach, is high on him just from what he has seen this year—to be able to play not only guard or tackle. We have some positional flexibility there. He has grown a lot over this past season. He has gotten bigger, stronger, which he needed to do. I think he has a really bright future." This ranking reflects the chances that he can be a starting NFL tackle. But it feels weird to send a player with pass sets this good to guard.

14 Zack Baun, LB, New Orleans; Age 24
Drafted 2020, pick 74 | 82 defensive snaps

Baun was by far the most highly thought-of player on this year's list in the minds of draftniks when the 2020 draft process was happening. He drew Kyle Van Noy stylistic comps as a college player who had success as both an edge rusher and a traditional linebacker. But he's only 238 pounds, and Sack-SEER saw him as more of a linebacker than a true edge player. SackSEER gave Baun a projection of just 12.6 sacks through his fifth season, citing his injury history, lack of production outside of his redshirt senior season, and subpar jumps at the combine.

Sure enough, that's kind of unfolding with the Saints. New Orleans traded up to take Baun and turned him into a linebacker, and he spent the 2020 season mostly as a special-teamer. He did start the meaningless finale for the Saints against Carolina, but otherwise had no more than 13 defensive snaps in any one game last year. The Saints traded for Kwon Alexander at the deadline last year to further lock Baun out of playing time.

But with both Alexander and long-time coverage linebacker Alex Anzalone departed, the depth chart is pretty simple for Baun. He needs to beat out Florida State second-rounder Pete Werner to become the linebacker next to Demario Davis. "He's someone that has picked things up and, man, you came away from the season feeling real positive about what you're starting to see with a few of those guys, and he's one of them," said coach Sean Payton at OTAs. Certainly you can understand projecting Baun into that role, but he'll have to hold off Werner.

15 Deonte Harris, WR, New Orleans; Age 23
Undrafted in 2019 | 235 offensive snaps

Most players that make this list have a ton of pre-draft coverage that makes them easy to understand as prospects. Harris, out of Division II Assumption College, is not most prospects.

There weren't many publicly available scouting reports for him. What is out there is some grainy video of him returning punts around a bunch of slow college kids and winning out of the slot as a deep-ball receiver. He also has a physical profile that makes you question whether he can hold up. 5-foot-6 is hard to tackle, but when it gets tackled, bad things usually happen.

As an all-purpose weapon for the Saints, Harris has taken quite a few end arounds for big gains. He was an All-Pro returner in 2019 and was quite good in that area in 2020 as well. As a wideout, Harris was almost exclusively used on quick outs, screens, or underneath routes to try to take advantage of how slippery he is. He proved exceptional there, racking up 13 missed tackles last season. While we don't have a ton of reps of him getting vertical on the route tree, there was some promise there at Assumption and he does a good job coming back for the ball and tracking it.

As we noted above with Adam Trautman, there's not a lot of receiving production returning for the Saints this year outside of Michael Thomas. The target void created may enable us to see a little more of Harris as an outside receiver. That doesn't mean he's going to go Tyreek Hill on the NFL—very few receivers do—but the opportunity is there and he has certainly shown he can be a productive part of an NFL offense already. If he's able to take it one more notch up, he can be the spiritual successor to the Robert Meachems and Devery Hendersons that popped up on deep shots for the Saints for years. Only, you know, much smaller.

16 Julian Okwara, ER, Detroit; Age 23
Drafted 2020, pick 67 | 69 defensive snaps

Okwara led all edge rusher prospects in 2020's draft with an explosion index of 1.4 per our SackSEER system. Coming off a broken leg in 2019, he missed the combine and then Notre Dame's pro day was cancelled, so those numbers have to be taken with a bit of a grain of salt because we are using hand-timed numbers from Okwara's own personal pro day. ("Your own/Personal/Pro day," as Depeche Mode once sang.) Okwara ran a 4.6s 40-yard dash there, and said he ran a 4.53 before the injury. He had eight sacks and 12.5 tackles for loss in 13 games in his junior year.

Okwara played the nicest number of snaps last year after going back on IR for another leg injury suffered against the Jaguars in Week 6. He did factor in as a rotational edge player for the last two games of the season, notching a season-best 26% of the snap share in Week 16 against Tampa Bay. There's not a whole lot else to say about his rookie year; it was a shame that it was wasted on the trainer's table.

Okwara's older brother Romeo re-upped with the Lions this offseason and the two have a plan to be bookmark ends. "So I definitely see myself getting double-digit sacks, my brother the same thing. I think that's something that hasn't been done," the younger Okwara told reporters in May. Well, a little someone named Trey Flowers might have something to say about that, but Okwara absolutely has the raw talent to live up to double-digit sacks. Health and opportunity? That we're not so sure about yet.

17 Ashtyn Davis, S, New York Jets; Age 24
Drafted 2020, pick 68 | 402 defensive snaps

Davis is someone who shined on scouts' boards but also had some health concerns coming out of college, sitting out a bowl game with a groin injury and drawing the vague "medical red flag" from some teams. Davis was a difference-maker at overhang safety with six picks and nine additional passes defensed in his last two years at Cal, showcasing track speed and athleticism. Cal's pro day was canceled and Davis did not work out at the combine, but the skills were obvious enough to get him picked near the top of the third round anyway.

Davis took some time to take over at safety but would become a 99%-snaps player from Weeks 8 to 12 before—you guessed it—injury struck. A foot injury sent Davis to IR and he was lost for the rest of the season. Davis was used in a role that perhaps wasn't the best fit for him, with Marcus Maye entrenched at free safety. Davis defensed just one pass and had the lowest success rate in coverage of any Jets defensive back.

A new coaching staff is in town and that could mean big things for Davis, because Robert Saleh has a pretty stellar recent history as a defensive coordinator. However, Davis didn't show at OTAs or minicamps while recovering from the foot injury, and the team signed LaMarcus Joyner as insurance at safety. There's still a lot of upside here, and we can weigh that against how disappointing last year was, but the history of new coaches working with the previous administration's underused draft picks is not promising.

18 David Long, CB, Los Angeles Rams; Age 23
Drafted 2019, pick 79 | 225 defensive snaps

A second returning player on the list, Long's 2020 opportunity for playing time was swallowed whole by an impressive run from Darious Williams. Not only did Williams take the third corner job, he ran away with it, getting a huge payday in the process. Long started just one game, a 28-17 loss to the Dolphins in Week 8, and allowed a three-yard touchdown to Devante Parker. Still, winning a ball from Parker in tight coverage isn't easy for anybody, and Long was not kept off the field by schlubs—the Rams had one of the best pass defenses in the NFL last year.

On pedigree, Long came out of Michigan as a true outside corner with his most ridiculous calling card being the 6.45s 3-cone time at the 2019 combine. Long had three picks and 12 passes defensed in two years with the Wolverines, with Big Ten quarterbacks all but avoiding him if they could.

Troy Hill fled to the Browns in free agency, and the Rams didn't make any real stabs at replacing him beyond using a fourth-rounder on Central Arkansas corner Robert Rochell. "He has done a great job," Sean McVay said in May. "I think he's really done a nice job elevating his game at the outside location. He has been a guy with some position flex inside, but I think he's really, really done a nice job of growing. He has gotten a lot of really valuable, beneficial reps where you've seen him tangibly improve throughout the course of the offseason because the one thing that we have done full-speed is seven-on-seven. He's taken to Coach [Ejiro] Evero, Coach [Jonathan] Cooley, and Coach [Raheem] Morris' teaching progression, understanding concepts better and I've been really pleased with David and he's a guy we're going to count on and we're expecting him to be a big-time contributor for us." Long certainly appears to have the inside track on playing time this year.

19 Donovan Peoples-Jones, WR, Cleveland; Age 22
Drafted 2020, pick 187 | 268 offensive snaps

Those of you who like raw athletes will very much enjoy the Peoples-Jones experience. At 6-foot-2, 212 pounds, Peoples-Jones profiles as an outside receiver. He ran a 4.48s 40-yard dash on that frame and added 99th-percentile results among wideouts in the vertical jump (44½ inches) and the broad jump (139 inches) at the combine. He was regarded as an excellent return prospect. As for his skills as a wide receiver, well, he never had more than 612 receiving yards for a run-focused Michigan team and scouts dinged his ability to separate.

Peoples-Jones had a fairly successful rookie season, finishing second among wideouts with 10 to 49 targets with a 51.9% DVOA on a 70% catch rate. He surged a bit towards the end of the season as well, finishing with 55 or more yards in three of his last four games. It's easy to understand why the Browns would be excited about what he showed in 2020, but with Odell Beckham back, it's also fairly hard to see a clean fit for him in the starting lineup. The Browns received solid work from KhaDarel Hodge last year, Rashard Higgins and Baker Mayfield seem to have a great connection, and they also drafted Anthony Schwartz in the third round. Peoples-Jones may be a returner first this year if everyone is healthy. But he's also so physically talented that it may be hard for the Browns to leave him out of the receiver rotation.

20 Matt Peart, OT, New York Giants; Age 24
Drafted 2020, pick 99 | 150 offensive snaps

Somewhat of an afterthought in a tackle-rich class, Peart got hit with a critique of "why is a guy this physically talented rated a two-star recruit and sent to Connecticut?" Well, because he's from Jamaica and didn't play football until high school. Peart is a physical dream, with a 6-foot-7 frame and 36⅝-inch arm length that is built to be an obstacle. He ran a 5.06s 40-yard dash with that physique, which would be impressive for any offensive tackle.

The Giants had an interesting offensive line situation last year, right down to firing line coach Marc Colombo after a verbal spat with head coach Joe Judge. They got players such as Peart and Shane Lemieux involved, but also drafted and watched Andrew Thomas struggle. With Kevin Zeitler released and Cameron Fleming not re-signed, there is suddenly a big opening for snaps on the line. Peart had some issues in pass-protection last year but was better than expected as a run-blocker.

The reason Peart is so low? We can't say from our publishing deadline if he'll win a fair battle against Thomas and COVID opt-out Nate Solder. Both of those guys have massive incentives to play if they are retained. Solder publicly said, "who cares who starts?" after Peart was the first-string tackle

at OTAs. It certainly would make sense for the Giants to see what they have, as Solder wasn't exactly great in 2019 anyway. But there are more questions here than there are at the top of our list.

21 Devin Duvernay, WR, Baltimore; Age 23
Drafted 2020, pick 92 | 347 offensive snaps

What Duvernay showed at the University of Texas is the ability to be a gadget wideout around the line of scrimmage. He came out with a strong 1,392-yard season in 2019 after Lil'Jordan Humphrey moved on to the NFL. Some of that was an extension of the running game, and that's definitely Duvernay's calling card. But he also won deep balls, showed NFL-caliber releases, and stacked corners fairly easily in college. A 4.39s 40-yard dash hinted at the upper-echelon speed he could put on the field.

In his first season with the Ravens, Duvernay peaked at about 80% usage as the team dealt with a horrific COVID shortage in early December. Most of the damage he provided was as a kick returner—his lone touchdown came against the Chiefs in Week 3 on a kickoff. Otherwise he only had three targets deep and was mostly a screen and quick-move receiver. Duvernay did not break many tackles in space, but it was a small sample of targets and he has shown the ability to do that in the past.

Unfortunately for Duvernay, the Ravens reinforced wideout pretty heavily this offseason. Sammy Watkins came on as a reclamation project, and the team also drafted Rashod Bateman in the first round. It's hard to see Duvernay growing much out of his 2020 role in 2021 because there are people in front of him. But he does have a little more talent than the 2020 flash might have shown you, and if the Ravens can't get Lamar Jackson a little more focused on the sidelines, Duvernay does profile to be in Jackson's high-usage target areas frequently.

22 Marcus Epps, S, Philadelphia; Age 25
Drafted 2019, pick 191 | 474 defensive snaps

There are two kinds of prospects that tend to hit the end of this list. There are the ones who have the pedigree but haven't done much yet, and there are the ones without the pedigree who have been showing out whenever they get on the field. Epps is in the latter camp. Yet another Wyoming product, Epps got a priority free-agent grade from NFL.com's Lance Zierlein. He was Mel Kiper's 50th-ranked … safety. Epps ran a 4.55s 40-yard dash at his pro day, showing off a nice 6.7s 3-cone time as well. He picked off nine balls in four seasons at Wyoming, adding 22 passes defensed and five forced fumbles. But at 6-foot-even and just 191 pounds, size was a major factor in forcing him out of the NFL's upper rounds.

Drafted by the Vikings, Epps was claimed by the Eagles on waivers and used at free safety in December of 2019. Rodney McLeod was ahead of Epps on the depth chart last year, but after a torn ACL in December, Epps grabbed a major share of the snaps yet again by getting at least 56% of the snaps in each of Philadelphia's last four games. Epps picked off two passes and defensed four more. And while we wouldn't expect this to last at his size, Epps had the best run stop rate of any Eagles secondary player last year at 64%.

The Eagles had themselves a Vikings import offseason on defense. They brought in former Minnesota defensive backs coach Jonathan Gannon as defensive coordinator, and they added Anthony Harris to the safety equation on a one-year deal. Epps will be battling a 31-year-old McLeod and 2020 fourth-rounder K'Von Wallace for playing time, but he outplayed Wallace last year and has shown the ability to be a versatile middle-of-the-field defender. Don't sleep on his chances of yet again bubbling up to the surface in 2021.

23 Amik Robertson, CB, Las Vegas; Age 22
Drafted 2020, pick 148 | 35 defensive snaps

Hell is figuring out the Raiders cornerback depth chart, a place where everyone seems to play poorly and when Jon Gruden just decides he doesn't like you, you're gone. "The best guys are going to play," Gruden said at OTAs. "I don't care if it's Nate Hobbs or Amik Robertson. I don't care what round they came in. We're going to play the best four or five guys and players will decide that." It was a not-so-veiled message, aimed like a dodgeball at Damon Arnette's head. The former first-rounder has disappointed so far.

We can't write about Hobbs here because he's a rookie, but Robertson is an interesting player. Compared to Chris Harris by draftniks, Robertson measured in at 5-foot-8, 187 pounds at the combine. He played strictly nickelback in college because of his size but finished his collegiate career with 14 picks and 48 passes defensed. That's a hard combination of anticipation and ball skills to downplay considering he only played three years.

Buried on the depth chart in 2020, Robertson provided 23 of his 35 snaps in Weeks 4 and 5 before being a healthy scratch towards the end of the year. New defensive coordinator Gus Bradley is also reportedly high on Robertson, and as we have learned in the Gruden Vegas era, the depth chart is always up for grabs with one bad impression. Robertson has the talent to stick if he gets the chance to play next to Casey Hayward and Trayvon Mullen.

24 Lucas Niang, OT, Kansas City; Age 23
Drafted 2020, pick 96 | 0 offensive snaps

Coming out of TCU, Niang was regarded as pro-ready and a "help-now" right tackle prospect by NFL.com's Lance Zierlein. Niang didn't work out at the combine but had 75th percentile or better rankings at 6-foot-6 with 34¼-inch arm length and 10½-inch meathooks. He didn't do any draft workouts after surgery to repair a torn hip labrum but was still considered a top-100 pick and roughly a back-of-the-top-10 tackle by most draftniks.

Certainly you remember what happened to the Chiefs in the Super Bowl. Niang was drafted to deal with a potential injury to Eric Fisher or Mitchell Schwartz. But he opted out of the season under the league's COVID plan, something that was rare from players on rookie contracts and particularly so among players who hadn't played an NFL snap yet.

Niang comes back this year, along with Laurent Duvernay-Tardif, to a team that has gone hog-wild on offensive line this offseason. We know that Orlando Brown and Joe Thuney are starting, and Niang is likely battling with Kyle Long and Mike Remmers at right tackle. Chiefs head coach Andy Reid complemented Niang at OTAs by saying "he has these beautiful feet. I look forward to getting him back in the pads at training camp and moving around and doing what offensive linemen do, the real football part of it." There's a lot of missed time to make up for, but Niang has the talent to emerge as a starter from that group.

25 Jon Greenard, ER, Houston; Age 24
Drafted 2020, pick 90 | 265 defensive snaps

Greenard transferred from Louisville to Florida and led the SEC in sacks in his senior year under former Cardinals defensive leader Todd Grantham. What Greenard lacked in explosion in college, he made up for in heady play. He was perceived by draftniks to have a good grasp of line play, pass-rush moves, and angles. That elevated him to the Texans in the third round even though his subpar jump numbers left him with a SackSEER explosion index score of -0.8, tied for fourthworst in the class.

The Texans refused to acknowledge the concept of rookies last year as they dug into their nice little resting place at the bottom of the division, with Greenard only seeing elevated playing time in the game at Jacksonville that Whitney Mercilus and Jacob Martin missed due to COVID protocols. Naturally, the Texans won that game, which meant the answer was to go right back to the other outside linebackers on the roster. Greenard only received extended playing time again in Weeks 16 and 17 with the season all but over.

What the Texans have done is created a roster so full of mediocre edge rushers that we're really not sure who they'll pick to play. That's the major reason Greenard is so low. He's not a high-ceiling superstar, but Greenard could develop into a positive second- or third-banana edge player with playing time. Do we have any faith that he'll get that playing time on the team that signed Jordan Jenkins and wants to fit Charles Omenihu, Mercilus, and Martin into roles? Not a ton. But he deserves the run. Someone on this roster has to be a long-term piece, right?

Honorable Mention
Hunter Bryant, TE, Detroit
Blake Cashman, LB, New York Jets
Akeem Davis-Gaither, LB, Cincinnati
Deejay Dallas, RB, Seattle
Jacob Eason, QB, Indianapolis
Harrison Hand, CB, Minnesota
Jalen Hurd, WR, San Francisco
Tyler Johnson, WR, Tampa Bay
Terrell Lewis, ER, Los Angeles Rams
Albert Okwuegbunam, TE, Denver

Rivers McCown

Fantasy Projections

Here are the top 270 players according to the KUBIAK projection system, ranked by projected fantasy value (**FANT**) in 2021. We've used the following generic scoring system:

- 1 point for each 10 yards rushing, 10 yards receiving, or 25 yards passing
- 6 points for each rushing or receiving TD, 4 points for each passing TD
- -2 points for each interception or fumble lost
- Kickers: 1 point for each extra point, 3 points for each field goal
- Team defense: 2 points for a fumble recovery, interception, or safety, 1 point for a sack, and 6 points for a touchdown.

These totals are then adjusted based on each player's listed **Risk** for 2021:

- Green: Standard risk, no change
- Yellow: Higher than normal risk, value dropped by 5%
- Red: Highest risk, value dropped by 10%
- Blue: Stronger chance of breakout, value increased by 5%

Note that fantasy totals may not exactly equal these calculations, because each touchdown projection is not necessarily a round number. (For example, a quarterback listed with 2 rushing touchdowns may actually be projected with 2.4 rushing touchdowns, which will add 14 fantasy points to the player's total rather than 12.) Fantasy value does not include adjustments for week-to-week consistency.

The projections listed below for quarterbacks differ from those found in the quarterbacks section earlier in the book because they incorporate the possibility of injury and represent 15-16 games started rather than representing 17 games started. This puts the quarterback projections in line with the other projections which also incorporate the possibility of injury.

Players are ranked in order based on marginal value of each player, the idea that you draft based on how many more points a player will score compared to the worst starting player at that position, not how many points a player scores overall. We've ranked players in five league configurations:

- Flex Rk: 12 teams, starts 1 QB, 2 RB, 2 WR, 1 FLEX (RB/WR), 1 TE, 1 K, and 1 D.
- 3WR Rk: 12 teams, starts 1 QB, 2 RB, 3 WR, 1 TE, 1 K, and 1 D.
- PPR Rk: 12 teams, starts 1 QB, 2 RB, 2 WR, 1 FLEX (RB/WR), 1 TE, 1 K, and 1 D. Also adds one point per reception to scoring.
- 10-3WR Rk: same as 3WR, but with only 10 teams.
- 10-PPR Rk: same as PPR, but with only 10 teams.

These rankings also reduce the value of kickers and defenses to reflect the general drafting habits of fantasy football players. (We estimated five bench players for each team; for each additional bench spot in your league, move kickers and defenses down 10-12 spots.) We urge you to draft using common sense, not a strict reading of these rankings.

The online KUBIAK application featuring these projections is also available at FootballOutsiders.com as part of an FO+ subscription. These projections can be customized to the rules of any specific league with the ability to save multiple league set-ups. The online KUBIAK application is updated based on injuries and changing forecasts of playing time during the preseason, and also has a version which includes individual defensive players.

Player	Team	Bye	Pos	Age	PaYd	PaTD	INT	Ru	RuYd	RuTD	Rec	RcYd	RcTD	FL	Fant	Risk	Flex Rk	3WR Rk	PPR Rk	10-3WR Rk	10-PPR Rk
Dalvin Cook	MIN	7	RB	26				313	1443	14	53	434	2	2	276	Green	1	1	2	1	2
Derrick Henry	TEN	13	RB	27				348	1696	12	20	143	1	1	245	Yellow	2	2	12	2	12
Christian McCaffrey	CAR	13	RB	25				262	1120	10	76	564	3	1	234	Yellow	3	3	3	3	3
Travis Kelce	KC	12	TE	32							109	1372	10	0	196	Green	4	4	1	4	1
Ezekiel Elliott	DAL	7	RB	26				262	1159	12	46	328	2	2	223	Green	5	5	8	5	9
Jonathan Taylor	IND	14	RB	22				270	1257	11	34	259	1	1	222	Green	6	6	15	6	17
Cam Akers	LAR	11	RB	22				266	1150	9	40	335	2	1	214	Green	7	7	17	7	19
Nick Chubb	CLE	13	RB	26				248	1265	9	24	199	1	1	208	Green	8	8	30	8	33
Patrick Mahomes	KC	12	QB	26	5058	35	8	60	287	3				3	367	Green	9	9	19	10	14
Aaron Jones	GB	13	RB	27				206	1027	8	52	398	2	1	203	Green	10	11	16	9	18
Josh Allen	BUF	7	QB	25	4473	30	10	109	513	8				5	365	Green	11	10	21	13	16
Alvin Kamara	NO	6	RB	26				181	836	8	74	626	2	1	196	Yellow	12	15	9	12	10
Saquon Barkley	NYG	10	RB	24				247	1029	10	47	346	2	1	192	Yellow	13	16	27	15	30
Joe Mixon	CIN	10	RB	25				263	997	9	54	384	3	1	192	Yellow	14	17	24	16	24
Tyreek Hill	KC	12	WR	27				5	38	0	89	1304	9	0	191	Green	15	12	6	11	6

Player	Team	Bye	Pos	Age	PaYd	PaTD	INT	Ru	RuYd	RuTD	Rec	RcYd	RcTD	FL	Fant	Risk	Flex Rk	3WR Rk	PPR Rk	10-3WR Rk	10-PPR Rk
J.K. Dobbins	BAL	8	RB	23				224	1190	8	25	211	1	1	191	Green	16	18	43	17	47
D'Andre Swift	DET	9	RB	22				220	959	9	48	363	2	1	191	Green	17	19	26	18	29
Stefon Diggs	BUF	7	WR	28				0	0	0	109	1393	8	0	189	Green	18	13	4	14	4
Justin Herbert	LAC	7	QB	23	4755	35	10	64	268	3				3	347	Green	19	21	31	22	25
Kyler Murray	ARI	12	QB	24	4171	27	11	99	596	7				3	347	Green	20	22	32	23	26
Davante Adams	GB	13	WR	29				0	0	0	104	1254	12	0	184	Yellow	21	14	5	19	5
Darren Waller	LV	8	TE	29							89	1005	8	1	145	Green	22	25	11	21	7
Calvin Ridley	ATL	6	WR	27				3	12	0	98	1314	7	0	177	Green	23	20	7	20	8
Lamar Jackson	BAL	8	QB	24	3150	25	10	158	1020	7				5	337	Green	24	28	40	32	34
Josh Jacobs	LV	8	RB	23				233	928	9	34	252	1	1	175	Green	25	29	47	24	51
Austin Ekeler	LAC	7	RB	26				171	735	5	82	632	3	1	172	Yellow	26	31	20	29	21
DK Metcalf	SEA	9	WR	24				0	0	0	78	1164	9	0	168	Green	27	23	23	25	23
Dak Prescott	DAL	7	QB	28	4794	28	12	68	354	7				4	330	Yellow	28	33	45	39	38
Najee Harris	PIT	7	RB	23				237	955	8	31	211	1	1	168	Green	29	35	57	31	58
Russell Wilson	SEA	9	QB	33	4075	32	11	83	502	3				3	329	Green	30	34	46	42	41
Miles Sanders	PHI	14	RB	24				208	994	8	26	207	1	1	167	Green	31	36	61	33	63
A.J. Brown	TEN	13	WR	24				0	0	0	81	1177	8	0	167	Green	32	24	22	26	22
Michael Thomas	NO	6	WR	28				0	0	0	100	1222	7	0	166	Green	33	26	10	27	11
Justin Jefferson	MIN	7	WR	22				0	0	0	85	1208	8	0	166	Green	34	27	18	28	20
Chris Carson	SEA	9	RB	27				194	869	6	39	298	3	1	166	Green	35	38	50	35	52
Antonio Gibson	WAS	9	RB	23				206	947	8	26	184	1	0	165	Green	36	39	64	36	66
Clyde Edwards-Helaire	KC	12	RB	22				199	862	7	38	294	1	0	163	Green	37	42	54	37	57
Keenan Allen	LAC	7	WR	29				0	0	0	96	1088	9	1	162	Green	38	30	14	30	15
Aaron Rodgers	GB	13	QB	38	4381	37	7	46	179	3				2	324	Yellow	39	41	48	47	44
David Montgomery	CHI	10	RB	24				221	879	8	26	196	1	0	161	Green	40	44	67	38	71
Mike Davis	ATL	6	RB	28				224	857	9	43	278	1	1	160	Yellow	41	46	53	41	56
DeAndre Hopkins	ARI	12	WR	29				0	0	0	104	1221	7	1	160	Green	42	32	13	34	13
George Kittle	SF	6	TE	28							75	918	7	0	125	Yellow	43	47	36	44	27
Julio Jones	TEN	13	WR	32				0	0	0	80	1146	7	0	155	Green	44	37	29	40	32
Ryan Tannehill	TEN	13	QB	33	4076	28	9	57	308	6				3	317	Green	45	52	55	52	50
Tyler Lockett	SEA	9	WR	29				0	0	0	86	1040	8	0	153	Green	46	40	25	43	28
Robert Woods	LAR	11	WR	29				19	116	1	80	955	6	0	150	Green	47	43	34	45	36
Chase Claypool	PIT	7	WR	23				8	20	1	74	965	8	1	149	Green	48	45	38	46	40
CeeDee Lamb	DAL	7	WR	22				8	62	1	76	1025	6	0	146	Green	49	48	39	48	42
Cooper Kupp	LAR	11	WR	28				2	10	0	90	1058	7	0	146	Green	50	49	28	49	31
Amari Cooper	DAL	7	WR	27				2	7	0	84	1088	6	0	145	Green	51	50	33	50	35
Ja'Marr Chase	CIN	10	WR	21				2	6	0	83	1079	6	0	145	Green	52	51	35	51	37
Logan Thomas	WAS	9	TE	30							63	671	7	0	106	Green	53	61	56	59	49
T.J. Hockenson	DET	9	TE	24							69	749	5	0	105	Green	54	64	49	60	45
Tom Brady	TB	9	QB	44	4621	35	12	32	27	3				2	299	Yellow	55	63	69	69	64
Terry McLaurin	WAS	9	WR	25				0	0	0	82	1063	5	0	137	Green	56	53	41	53	43
James Conner	ARI	12	RB	26				182	739	7	26	183	1	1	137	Green	57	65	96	61	129
Diontae Johnson	PIT	7	WR	25				2	6	0	86	958	7	0	137	Green	58	54	37	54	39
Mike Evans	TB	9	WR	28				0	0	0	62	909	7	0	135	Green	59	55	58	55	59
Kenny Golladay	NYG	10	WR	28				0	0	0	64	1030	7	0	135	Yellow	60	56	59	56	60
Chris Godwin	TB	9	WR	25				0	0	0	70	933	7	0	134	Green	61	57	51	57	53
Allen Robinson	CHI	10	WR	28				0	0	0	83	1001	6	0	133	Green	62	58	42	58	46
Matthew Stafford	LAR	11	QB	33	4642	29	11	36	134	1				2	295	Green	63	67	73	74	69
Myles Gaskin	MIA	14	RB	24				183	733	7	34	279	1	1	132	Red	64	71	97	66	82
Noah Fant	DEN	11	TE	24							62	697	5	0	99	Green	65	70	62	65	54
Adam Thielen	MIN	7	WR	31				3	14	0	67	881	8	0	130	Yellow	66	59	60	62	62
Mark Andrews	BAL	8	TE	26							55	648	6	1	98	Green	67	73	70	67	61
Chase Edmonds	ARI	12	RB	25				147	659	4	44	320	3	1	128	Yellow	68	75	80	71	95
DeVonta Smith	PHI	14	WR	23				2	10	0	64	867	7	0	127	Green	69	60	63	63	65
JuJu Smith-Schuster	PIT	7	WR	25				0	0	0	88	881	7	1	127	Green	70	62	44	64	48
Gus Edwards	BAL	8	RB	26				162	807	6	10	90	0	1	126	Green	71	77	122	84	134
Joe Burrow	CIN	10	QB	25	4327	26	9	63	271	5				6	287	Yellow	72	76	78	82	74
Curtis Samuel	WAS	9	WR	25				30	151	2	65	761	4	0	124	Green	73	66	65	68	67
Kenyan Drake	LV	8	RB	27				138	566	6	41	286	1	1	124	Green	74	85	89	85	111
Kyle Pitts	ATL	6	TE	21							55	618	5	0	91	Green	75	83	75	75	68
Kareem Hunt	CLE	13	RB	26				116	493	4	36	290	2	0	123	Blue	76	86	101	87	85
Melvin Gordon	DEN	11	RB	28				190	815	6	27	159	1	1	123	Red	77	87	140	88	97
Damien Harris	NE	14	RB	24				170	802	5	13	103	1	1	123	Green	78	88	124	90	135
Tyler Boyd	CIN	10	WR	27				2	17	0	81	900	5	0	122	Green	79	68	52	70	55
David Johnson	HOU	10	RB	30				148	629	6	30	269	1	1	123	Yellow	80	78	126	92	93

Player	Team	Bye	Pos	Age	PaYd	PaTD	INT	Ru	RuYd	RuTD	Rec	RcYd	RcTD	FL	Fant	Risk	Flex Rk	3WR Rk	PPR Rk	10-3WR Rk	10-PPR Rk
Derek Carr	LV	8	QB	30	4366	26	10	44	160	3				5	283	Green	81	89	81	96	80
Raheem Mostert	SF	6	RB	29				159	794	5	23	198	1	1	121	Red	82	82	164	93	113
Will Fuller	MIA	14	WR	27				0	0	0	67	910	6	0	120	Yellow	83	69	68	72	72
Matt Ryan	ATL	6	QB	36	4466	27	13	37	137	2				3	282	Green	84	94	84	100	81
Robert Tonyan	GB	13	TE	27							45	497	6	0	88	Green	85	98	95	77	83
Kirk Cousins	MIN	7	QB	33	4130	30	11	42	168	2				4	282	Green	86	95	86	101	84
Tee Higgins	CIN	10	WR	22				2	12	0	69	872	5	0	120	Green	87	72	66	73	70
AJ Dillon	GB	13	RB	23				140	634	4	24	183	1	1	117	Blue	88	91	108	99	114
Mike Gesicki	MIA	14	TE	26							49	577	5	0	86	Green	89	101	87	79	77
Leonard Fournette	TB	9	RB	26				159	643	6	20	140	1	0	114	Green	90	96	127	102	137
James Robinson	JAX	7	RB	23				168	714	4	26	185	1	1	114	Yellow	91	97	114	103	125
D.J. Moore	CAR	13	WR	24				0	0	0	63	932	4	0	116	Green	92	74	72	76	75
Daniel Jones	NYG	10	QB	24	3996	23	11	74	460	2				6	278	Green	93	106	98	115	89
Devin Singletary	BUF	7	RB	24				138	596	4	32	233	1	1	109	Green	94	103	109	113	119
Ronald Jones	TB	9	RB	24				148	662	5	13	98	0	0	107	Green	95	105	158	116	150
Mike Williams	LAC	7	WR	27				0	0	0	57	842	6	0	113	Yellow	96	79	82	78	98
Dallas Goedert	PHI	14	TE	26							58	640	4	0	81	Yellow	97	113	83	97	76
Michael Carter	NYJ	6	RB	22				131	563	4	26	197	1	1	105	Green	98	107	130	118	140
Breshad Perriman	DET	9	WR	28				0	0	0	55	928	4	0	113	Yellow	99	80	93	80	117
Jarvis Landry	CLE	13	WR	29				2	5	0	68	830	5	0	113	Green	100	81	71	81	73
DeVante Parker	MIA	14	WR	28				0	0	0	64	827	5	0	112	Green	101	84	76	82	79
Tua Tagovailoa	MIA	14	QB	23	4164	28	13	65	232	3				3	274	Yellow	102	115	102	134	99
Travis Etienne	JAX	7	RB	22				114	505	4	35	237	1	1	102	Green	103	110	120	128	131
Tevin Coleman	NYJ	6	RB	28				134	552	5	28	235	1	0	102	Red	104	111	139	129	142
Zack Moss	BUF	7	RB	24				134	548	5	20	144	1	0	102	Green	105	112	151	130	148
Jalen Hurts	PHI	14	QB	23	3561	24	12	104	583	5				7	273	Yellow	106	117	103	139	104
Irv Smith	MIN	7	TE	23							46	506	5	0	78	Green	107	121	106	106	100
DJ Chark	JAX	7	WR	25				0	0	0	65	842	5	0	111	Yellow	108	90	77	86	87
Rashaad Penny	SEA	9	RB	25				126	578	4	21	157	1	0	100	Yellow	109	114	162	135	151
Eric Ebron	PIT	7	TE	28							52	527	4	0	78	Green	110	122	100	107	86
Christian Kirk	ARI	12	WR	25				0	0	0	67	806	5	0	110	Green	111	92	74	89	78
Bucs D	TB	9	D											0	95	Green	112	125	110	104	88
Michael Gallup	DAL	7	WR	25				0	0	0	52	840	4	0	110	Green	113	93	99	91	136
Odell Beckham	CLE	13	WR	29				3	56	0	62	841	5	0	109	Red	114	99	92	94	116
Jerry Jeudy	DEN	11	WR	22				0	0	0	57	821	5	0	109	Green	115	100	88	95	109
Washington D	WAS	9	D											0	93	Green	116	127	115	109	90
Younghoe Koo	ATL	6	K	27										0	132	Green	117	128	117	112	92
Steelers D	PIT	7	D											0	93	Green	118	129	119	111	91
Ryan Fitzpatrick	WAS	9	QB	39	4058	24	14	52	260	3				3	270	Green	119	126	111	152	130
Nyheim Hines	IND	14	RB	25				72	321	3	46	349	2	0	94	Green	120	124	112	148	123
Harrison Butker	KC	12	K	26										0	130	Green	121	131	125	114	96
Brandon Aiyuk	SF	6	WR	23				4	47	0	59	753	5	0	107	Green	122	102	85	98	106
Hunter Henry	NE	14	TE	27							48	516	4	0	74	Green	123	133	116	119	121
Greg Zuerlein	DAL	7	K	34										0	129	Green	124	139	128	120	101
Jared Goff	DET	9	QB	27	4309	24	12	50	105	4				3	268	Green	125	134	121	159	138
Marquise Brown	BAL	8	WR	24				2	7	0	52	704	6	0	105	Green	126	104	104	105	143
Jason Sanders	MIA	14	K	26										0	128	Green	127	142	129	123	102
Trevor Lawrence	JAX	7	QB	22	3676	24	11	62	342	4				4	267	Green	128	135	123	160	139
Javonte Williams	DEN	11	RB	21				120	521	4	18	118	1	0	89	Green	129	130	169	155	159
Dolphins D	MIA	14	D											0	89	Green	130	145	132	125	103
Eagles D	PHI	14	D											0	89	Green	131	146	133	126	105
Rams D	LAR	11	D											0	89	Green	132	148	134	127	107
Cole Beasley	BUF	7	WR	32				0	0	0	65	771	5	0	104	Green	133	108	79	108	94
Daniel Carlson	LV	8	K	26										0	127	Green	134	149	135	133	110
Jared Cook	LAC	7	TE	34							36	454	5	0	72	Green	135	147	168	136	155
Brandin Cooks	HOU	10	WR	28				0	0	0	60	807	4	0	104	Green	136	109	94	110	122
Giants D	NYG	10	D											0	89	Green	137	151	136	131	108
Justin Tucker	BAL	8	K	32										0	126	Green	138	154	142	137	118
Trey Sermon	SF	6	RB	22				116	500	4	12	96	1	0	85	Green	139	136	180	161	174
Mason Crosby	GB	13	K	37										0	126	Green	140	155	143	138	120
Sony Michel	NE	14	RB	26				109	485	4	11	95	1	0	85	Blue	141	137	182	162	176
Jamaal Williams	DET	9	RB	26				98	403	4	18	137	1	0	84	Blue	142	140	175	164	167
Jason Myers	SEA	9	K	30										0	125	Green	143	159	146	140	124
Ryan Succop	TB	9	K	35										0	125	Yellow	144	161	148	141	126
Tyler Higbee	LAR	11	TE	28							44	482	4	0	70	Green	145	160	156	144	147

Player	Tm	Bye	Pos	Age	PaYd	PaTD	INT	Ru	RuYd	RuTD	Rec	RcYd	RcTD	FL	Fant	Risk	Flex Rk	3WR Rk	PPR Rk	10-3WR Rk	10-PPR Rk
Tyler Bass	BUF	7	K	24										0	125	Green	146	162	149	142	127
Tony Pollard	DAL	7	RB	24				98	424	3	23	162	1	0	82	Blue	147	144	171	166	161
Ben Roethlisberger	PIT	7	QB	39	4380	31	13	30	43	1				3	263	Yellow	148	158	137	174	145
Robby Anderson	CAR	13	WR	28				3	13	0	64	783	4	0	101	Green	149	116	90	117	112
Broncos D	DEN	11	D											0	86	Green	150	166	150	143	128
Packers D	GB	13	D											0	85	Green	151	168	152	145	132
Russell Gage	ATL	6	WR	25				0	0	0	64	747	4	0	101	Green	152	118	91	121	115
Darrell Henderson	LAR	11	RB	24				80	350	3	22	174	1	0	80	Blue	153	153	174	172	166
Matt Gay	LAR	11	K	27										0	124	Green	154	169	154	215	188
Rob Gronkowski	TB	9	TE	32							34	435	4	0	68	Green	155	167	178	149	170
Patriots D	NE	14	D											0	85	Green	156	170	155	146	133
Laviska Shenault	JAX	7	WR	23				21	105	0	56	619	4	0	100	Green	157	119	105	122	146
Courtland Sutton	DEN	11	WR	26				0	0	0	55	791	5	0	100	Yellow	158	120	118	124	153
Bills D	BUF	7	D											0	85	Green	159	173	157	216	189
Saints D	NO	6	D											0	84	Yellow	160	174	159	219	191
Brandon McManus	DEN	11	K	30										0	123	Green	161	175	160	225	194
Evan Engram	NYG	10	TE	27							49	514	3	0	68	Green	162	171	141	151	141
James White	NE	14	RB	29				50	198	2	47	373	2	0	78	Green	163	156	175	144	144
Blake Jarwin	DAL	7	TE	27							45	489	4	0	67	Yellow	164	172	165	153	154
Deebo Samuel	SF	6	WR	25				14	98	1	57	697	4	0	99	Yellow	165	123	113	132	152
Phillip Lindsay	HOU	10	RB	27				96	414	3	15	130	0	0	72	Green	166	176	193	181	182
Alexander Mattison	MIN	7	RB	23				77	331	3	18	148	1	0	70	Blue	167	178	190	183	179
Tyrell Williams	DET	9	WR	29				2	7	0	52	718	4	0	95	Green	168	132	138	147	160
Will Dissly	SEA	9	TE	25							40	417	4	0	63	Green	169	189	177	169	168
Adam Trautman	NO	6	TE	24							39	428	3	0	63	Green	170	190	179	170	171
Darrel Williams	KC	12	RB	26				85	370	3	17	121	1	0	68	Green	171	180	195	186	183
Anthony Firkser	TEN	13	TE	26							38	414	4	0	62	Green	172	191	183	171	173
Sterling Shepard	NYG	10	WR	28				3	29	0	64	700	4	0	94	Yellow	173	138	107	150	149
Justin Jackson	LAC	7	RB	25				79	370	2	25	181	1	0	67	Yellow	174	181	189	188	178
Qadree Ollison	ATL	6	RB	25				91	356	4	12	84	0	0	67	Green	175	182	201	190	197
Henry Ruggs	LV	8	WR	22				8	43	0	42	663	4	1	94	Green	176	141	172	154	186
Latavius Murray	NO	6	RB	31				80	338	2	16	138	1	0	66	Blue	177	184	197	191	187
Wayne Gallman	SF	6	RB	27				73	322	3	16	139	1	0	66	Green	178	185	199	192	190
J.D. McKissic	WAS	9	RB	28				43	183	1	46	337	1	0	66	Green	179	186	166	193	156
Jaylen Waddle	MIA	14	WR	23				3	19	0	56	642	4	0	93	Green	180	143	131	156	157
Carson Wentz	IND	14	QB	29	3946	24	11	53	258	4				5	255	Yellow	181	195	167	197	158
Joshua Kelley	LAC	7	RB	24				88	346	3	15	104	0	0	64	Green	182	188	202	195	198
Jonnu Smith	NE	14	TE	26							35	393	4	0	60	Green	183	199	196	176	181
Antonio Brown	TB	9	WR	33				2	12	0	60	686	6	0	92	Red	184	150	147	157	163
Corey Davis	NYJ	6	WR	26				0	0	0	52	718	4	0	92	Green	185	152	153	158	169
Hayden Hurst	ATL	6	TE	28							37	386	4	0	59	Green	186	200	194	178	180
Malcolm Brown	MIA	14	RB	28				77	306	3	14	110	0	0	61	Green	187	194	205	198	206
Mecole Hardman	KC	12	WR	23				3	36	0	43	606	5	0	91	Green	188	157	176	163	193
Baker Mayfield	CLE	13	QB	26	3798	26	11	53	173	2				3	253	Green	189	201	170	203	164
Cole Kmet	CHI	10	TE	22							41	405	3	0	58	Green	190	202	187	180	177
Michael Pittman	IND	14	WR	24				2	12	0	56	716	4	0	90	Yellow	191	163	161	165	172
Giovani Bernard	TB	9	RB	30				31	128	1	44	317	2	0	59	Green	192	198	173	200	165
Jamison Crowder	NYJ	6	WR	28				0	0	0	64	736	4	0	90	Red	193	164	144	167	162
Hunter Renfrow	LV	8	WR	26				0	0	0	53	663	4	0	90	Green	194	165	163	168	175
Austin Hooper	CLE	13	TE	27							39	384	4	0	57	Yellow	195	204	198	185	184
Allen Lazard	GB	13	WR	26				0	0	0	44	615	4	0	88	Green	196	177	181	173	204
John Brown	LV	8	WR	31				0	0	0	48	665	4	0	86	Yellow	197	179	184	177	207
Gerald Everett	SEA	9	TE	27							37	367	3	0	54	Green	198	208	203	196	199
Jalen Reagor	PHI	14	WR	22				2	12	0	44	586	4	0	85	Green	199	183	188	179	214
Mark Ingram	HOU	10	RB	32				60	247	2	12	92	0	0	49	Green	200	206	229	211	227
KJ Hamler	DEN	11	WR	22				8	38	0	46	570	4	0	84	Green	201	187	185	182	209
O.J. Howard	TB	9	TE	27							28	381	3	0	52	Yellow	202	213	247	199	238
T.Y. Hilton	IND	14	WR	32				0	0	0	49	653	4	0	83	Yellow	203	192	186	184	212
Carlos Hyde	JAX	7	RB	31				55	228	2	14	96	0	0	45	Green	204	209	235	217	232
Tarik Cohen	CHI	10	RB	26				32	137	1	26	191	2	0	45	Yellow	205	210	210	218	215
Marquez Valdes-Scantling	GB	13	WR	27				2	5	0	34	598	4	0	83	Green	206	193	222	187	247
Zach Ertz	PHI	14	TE	31							40	419	2	0	50	Red	207	221	217	204	216
Gabriel Davis	BUF	7	WR	22				0	0	0	35	578	4	0	82	Blue	208	196	211	189	243
Damien Williams	CHI	10	RB	29				45	192	2	10	76	1	0	42	Blue	209	214	243	223	237
Benny Snell	PIT	7	RB	23				51	200	3	11	66	0	0	42	Green	210	216	242	224	236

Player	Team	Bye	Pos	Age	PaYd	PaTD	INT	Ru	RuYd	RuTD	Rec	RcYd	RcTD	FL	Fant	Risk	Flex Rk	3WR Rk	PPR Rk	10-3WR Rk	10-PPR Rk
Tre'Quan Smith	NO	6	WR	25				0	0	0	40	564	4	0	81	Green	211	197	204	194	234
Zach Wilson	NYJ	6	QB	22	3584	21	14	57	269	4				4	243	Green	212	222	192	239	185
La'Mical Perine	NYJ	6	RB	23				64	251	2	11	86	0	0	41	Red	213	218	246	228	240
Jordan Akins	HOU	10	TE	29							33	359	2	0	49	Green	214	226	237	206	230
Samaje Perine	CIN	10	RB	26				37	154	1	20	138	1	0	41	Green	215	219	230	229	228
Dalton Schultz	DAL	7	TE	25							31	317	3	0	49	Blue	216	227	239	207	233
Boston Scott	PHI	14	RB	26				52	228	2	9	70	0	0	40	Green	217	220	248	232	242
Dan Arnold	CAR	13	TE	26							28	338	3	0	48	Green	218	228	250	208	241
Marlon Mack	IND	14	RB	25				46	203	2	9	66	0	0	36	Yellow	219	223	252	243	248
Larry Rountree III	LAC	7	RB	23				47	203	2	7	55	0	0	36	Green	220	224	254	244	250
Mike Boone	DEN	11	RB	26				41	194	2	7	46	0	0	36	Green	221	225	255	245	252
Jimmy Graham	CHI	10	TE	35							29	302	3	0	46	Green	222	238	251	214	245
Falcons D	ATL	6	D											0	84	Green	223	245	207	221	192
Matt Prater	ARI	12	K	37										0	123	Green	224	246	208	227	196
Darnell Mooney	CHI	10	WR	24				5	29	0	52	582	3	0	78	Yellow	225	203	191	201	222
Kyle Juszczyk	SF	6	RB	30				12	46	1	18	164	1	0	34	Green	226	229	244	248	239
A.J. Green	ARI	12	WR	33				0	0	0	48	643	4	0	77	Red	227	205	206	202	235
49ers D	SF	6	D											0	84	Blue	228	249	209	226	195
Chuba Hubbard	CAR	13	RB	22				40	165	1	9	70	0	0	32	Green	229	230	257	251	253
Salvon Ahmed	MIA	14	RB	23				44	183	2	4	30	0	0	32	Green	230	231	265	252	260
Ravens D	BAL	8	D											0	83	Green	231	251	214	230	200
Devontae Booker	NYG	10	RB	29				37	158	1	12	82	0	0	31	Green	232	234	253	255	249
Seahawks D	SEA	9	D											0	83	Green	233	252	215	233	201
Dawson Knox	BUF	7	TE	25							24	272	3	0	44	Yellow	234	247	270	220	266
Darrynton Evans	TEN	13	RB	23				37	161	1	7	48	0	0	31	Green	235	235	264	256	259
Jack Doyle	IND	14	TE	31							27	299	3	0	44	Yellow	236	248	266	222	261
Cowboys D	DAL	7	D											0	83	Green	237	254	216	234	202
Chargers D	LAC	7	D											0	83	Blue	238	255	218	235	203
Marvin Jones	JAX	7	WR	31				0	0	0	43	530	4	0	76	Green	239	207	212	205	244
Jerick McKinnon	KC	12	RB	29				34	153	1	10	75	0	0	30	Yellow	240	239	259	258	256
Chiefs D	KC	12	D											0	83	Green	241	256	220	237	205
Graham Gano	NYG	10	K	34										0	121	Green	242	257	221	246	210
Chris Boswell	PIT	7	K	30										0	121	Green	243	258	223	247	211
Kerryon Johnson	PHI	14	RB	24				38	151	1	4	37	0	0	28	Green	244	240	267	262	262
Browns D	CLE	13	D											0	82	Green	245	259	224	242	208
Darren Fells	DET	9	TE	35							25	287	2	0	42	Green	246	253	269	231	264
Wil Lutz	NO	6	K	27										0	121	Green	247	260	225	249	213
Kalen Ballage	PIT	7	RB	26				30	102	1	13	76	0	0	27	Green	248	241	260	263	257
Kenneth Gainwell	PHI	14	RB	22				23	97	1	13	104	1	0	27	Green	249	243	258	264	255
Peyton Barber	WAS	9	RB	27				43	134	2	3	23	0	0	27	Green	250	244	268	265	265
Parris Campbell	IND	14	WR	24				0	0	0	56	584	4	0	74	Red	251	211	200	209	231
Terrace Marshall Jr.	CAR	13	WR	21				0	0	0	41	563	3	0	73	Green	252	212	228	210	254
Demarcus Robinson	KC	12	WR	27				0	0	0	40	486	4	0	73	Blue	253	215	227	212	251
Brian Hill	TEN	13	RB	26				21	94	1	14	99	1	0	25	Green	254	250	261	268	258
Josh Lambo	JAX	7	K	31										0	120	Green	255	262	231	257	219
Emmanuel Sanders	BUF	7	WR	34				0	0	0	44	523	3	0	73	Green	256	217	219	213	246
Cardinals D	ARI	12	D											0	81	Green	257	263	232	253	217
Randy Bullock	DET	9	K	32										0	120	Green	258	264	233	259	220
Jets D	NYJ	6	D											0	81	Green	259	265	234	254	218
Sam Darnold	CAR	13	QB	24	3896	21	13	50	244	3				4	234	Yellow	260	261	213	269	224
Robbie Gould	SF	6	K	39										0	119	Green	261	267	236	261	223
Panthers D	CAR	13	D											0	81	Green	262	268	238	260	221
Bears D	CHI	10	D											0	80	Green	263	269	240	266	225
Colts D	IND	14	D											0	80	Green	264	270	241	267	226
Drew Lock	DEN	11	QB	25	3969	25	18	59	231	4				4	231	Red	265	266	226	270	229
Rondale Moore	ARI	12	WR	21				6	32	0	40	464	3	0	68	Green	266	232	249	236	267
Nelson Agholor	NE	14	WR	28				0	0	0	37	516	3	0	68	Green	267	233	256	238	268
Deonte Harris	NO	6	WR	24				7	48	0	36	437	3	0	67	Green	268	236	263	240	270
Sammy Watkins	BAL	8	WR	28				0	0	0	38	492	4	0	67	Yellow	269	237	262	241	269
Randall Cobb	HOU	10	WR	31				0	0	0	45	497	3	0	65	Green	270	242	245	250	263

Statistical Appendix

Broken Tackles by Team, Offense

Rk	Team	Plays	Plays w/ BTkl	BT/Play	Total BTkl
1	CAR	944	121	14.9%	141
2	CLE	977	115	14.6%	143
3	MIN	974	117	14.3%	139
4	BUF	979	119	14.2%	139
5	BAL	945	115	14.1%	133
6	KC	1015	121	13.9%	141
7	CHI	995	114	13.5%	134
8	NO	995	109	13.2%	131
9	LV	995	116	12.8%	127
10	LAR	1044	112	12.5%	130
11	LAC	1078	115	12.3%	133
12	JAX	948	94	12.2%	116
13	SF	997	101	12.1%	121
14	MIA	969	91	11.8%	114
15	PIT	1008	103	11.7%	118
16	GB	944	96	11.7%	110
17	DEN	984	93	11.4%	112
18	WAS	986	97	11.3%	111
19	TEN	992	90	11.0%	109
20	ATL	1024	95	10.7%	110
21	ARI	1036	96	10.4%	108
22	HOU	878	77	10.4%	91
23	NE	928	86	10.3%	96
24	DAL	1061	89	10.2%	108
25	PHI	995	93	10.2%	101
26	SEA	956	82	9.9%	95
27	CIN	982	84	9.6%	94
28	IND	986	78	9.0%	89
29	NYJ	895	72	8.6%	77
30	TB	967	74	8.6%	83
31	DET	935	74	8.3%	78
32	NYG	896	67	8.3%	74

Play total includes Defensive Pass Interference.

Broken Tackles by Team, Defense

Rk	Team	Plays	Plays w/ BTkl	BT/Play	Total BTkl
1	SEA	1051	80	8.5%	89
2	TEN	1048	88	9.7%	102
3	WAS	942	84	10.1%	95
4	DAL	1008	95	10.1%	102
5	NO	937	86	10.1%	95
6	IND	940	85	10.3%	97
7	NE	941	88	10.6%	100
8	LAR	926	90	10.9%	101
9	MIN	991	97	11.1%	110
10	CLE	981	98	11.2%	110
11	SF	945	96	11.2%	106
12	LAC	956	88	11.3%	108
13	CIN	987	97	11.8%	116
14	CHI	966	95	11.9%	115
15	NYG	991	100	11.9%	118
16	CAR	970	103	12.0%	116
17	BUF	981	105	12.1%	119
18	DEN	986	99	12.2%	120
19	MIA	942	94	12.5%	118
20	ARI	994	107	12.6%	125
21	NYJ	1025	113	12.7%	130
22	TB	964	110	12.9%	124
23	ATL	987	114	12.9%	127
24	PIT	932	100	13.0%	121
25	BAL	970	109	13.1%	127
26	JAX	1021	119	13.2%	135
27	GB	928	104	13.5%	125
28	DET	1019	119	13.5%	138
29	KC	976	115	13.6%	133
30	PHI	987	111	14.0%	138
31	HOU	1014	123	14.0%	142
32	LV	1002	127	14.9%	149

Play total includes Defensive Pass Interference.

Most Broken Tackles, Defenders

Rk	Player	Team	BTkl	Rk	Player	Team	BTkl	Rk	Player	Team	BTkl
1	Z.Cunningham	HOU	21	5	M.Ojemudia	DEN	17	11	L.David	TB	16
2	K.Fuller	CHI	18	5	J.Schobert	JAX	17	11	C.Davis	TB	16
2	T.Hill	LAR	18	5	A.Terrell	ATL	17	11	N.Hewitt	NYJ	16
2	P.Queen	BAL	18	5	D.White	TB	17	11	Ju.Reid	HOU	16
5	J.Abram	LV	17	11	J.Bates	CIN	16	11	D.Sorensen	KC	16
5	J.Gladney	MIN	17	11	J.Bynes	CIN	16	18	Nine tied with		15

Top 20 Defenders, Broken Tackle Rate

Rk	Player	Team	BTkl	Tkl	Rate
1	L.Joyner	LV	3	50	5.7%
2	E.Kendricks	MIN	4	59	6.3%
3	K.Byard	TEN	5	69	6.8%
4	J.Brown	TEN	3	41	6.8%
5	R.Evans	TEN	4	50	7.4%
6	M.Lattimore	NO	4	49	7.5%
7	D.Davis	NO	6	73	7.6%
8	J.Ward	SF	4	45	8.2%
9	B.J.Goodson	CLE	5	55	8.3%
10	A.Williamson	2TM	6	65	8.5%
11	C.Holcomb	WAS	4	43	8.5%
12	V.Bell	CIN	6	64	8.6%
12	J.Jewell	DEN	6	64	8.6%
14	K.Willis	IND	5	53	8.6%
15	R.Darby	WAS	4	42	8.7%
16	Sq.Griffin	SEA	5	52	8.8%
17	S.Barrett	TB	4	41	8.9%
18	D.Slay	PHI	5	50	9.1%
19	B.Wagner	SEA	8	79	9.2%
20	T.Diggs	DAL	5	48	9.4%

Broken Tackles divided by Broken Tackles + Solo Tackles.
Special teams not included; min. 40 Solo Tackles

Bottom 20 Defenders, Broken Tackle Rate

Rk	Player	Team	BTkl	Tkl	Rate
1	K.Fuller	CHI	18	49	26.9%
2	T.Hill	LAR	18	52	25.7%
3	J.Bynes	CIN	16	48	25.0%
3	E.Harris	LV	15	45	25.0%
3	A.Sendejo	CLE	14	42	25.0%
6	J.Bradberry	NYG	14	43	24.6%
6	A.J.Klein	BUF	14	43	24.6%
8	C.Davis	TB	16	50	24.2%
9	M.Ojemudia	DEN	17	54	23.9%
10	K.Van Noy	MIA	13	42	23.6%
11	J.Gladney	MIN	17	57	23.0%
12	Ju.Reid	HOU	16	54	22.9%
13	M.Peters	BAL	13	44	22.8%
14	A.Terrell	ATL	17	58	22.7%
15	P.Queen	BAL	18	62	22.5%
16	C.Gardner-Johnson	NO	15	52	22.4%
17	J.Abram	LV	17	59	22.4%
18	T.Mullen	LV	15	54	21.7%
19	B.Murphy	ARI	11	40	21.6%
19	J.Wilson	JAX	11	40	21.6%

Broken Tackles divided by Broken Tackles + Solo Tackles.
Special teams not included; min. 40 Solo Tackles

Most Broken Tackles, Running Backs

Rk	Player	Team	BTkl
1	D.Cook	MIN	71
2	D.Montgomery	CHI	70
3	D.Henry	TEN	61
4	A.Kamara	NO	59
5	N.Chubb	CLE	56
5	M.Davis	CAR	56
7	J.Robinson	JAX	55
8	M.Gordon	DEN	51
9	K.Hunt	CLE	50
9	J.Jacobs	LV	50
11	A.Jones	GB	49
12	D.Singletary	BUF	45
13	E.Elliott	DAL	42
14	C.Edwards-Helaire	KC	41
15	A.Gibson	WAS	40
16	J.Conner	PIT	39
16	A.Ekeler	LAC	39
18	J.Taylor	IND	38
19	T.Gurley	ATL	35
20	J.K.Dobbins	BAL	32
20	M.Sanders	PHI	32

Most Broken Tackles, WR/TE

Rk	Player	Team	BTkl
1	D.Hopkins	ARI	26
1	T.Kelce	KC	26
3	C.Kupp	LAR	24
3	L.Shenault	JAX	24
5	S.Diggs	BUF	23
6	A.J.Brown	TEN	21
6	T.Hill	KC	21
8	D.Johnson	PIT	17
9	K.Allen	LAC	16
9	J.Grant	MIA	16
9	DK Metcalf	SEA	16
12	J.Jefferson	MIN	15
12	C.Ridley	ATL	15
12	C.Samuel	CAR	15
12	R.Woods	LAR	15
16	J.Landry	CLE	14
16	B.Aiyuk	SF	14
16	R.Anderson	CAR	14
16	T.McLaurin	WAS	14
16	D.Mooney	CHI	14
16	H.Renfrow	LV	14

Most Broken Tackles, Quarterbacks

Rk	Player	Team	Behind LOS	Beyond LOS	BTkl		Rk	Player	Team	Behind LOS	Beyond LOS	BTkl
1	L.Jackson	BAL	1	36	37		7	T.Bridgewater	CAR	1	12	13
2	K.Murray	ARI	1	26	27		8	S.Darnold	NYJ	4	8	12
3	J.Allen	BUF	3	19	22		9	T.Hill	NO	0	11	11
4	D.Watson	HOU	4	15	19		10	J.Burrow	CIN	1	6	7
5	C.Wentz	PHI	3	15	18		10	D.Jones	NYG	3	4	7
6	C.Newton	NE	1	16	17		10	R.Wilson	SEA	0	7	7

Best Broken Tackle Rate, Offensive Players (min. 80 touches)

Rk	Player	Team	BTkl	Touch	Rate
1	N.Chubb	CLE	56	206	27.2%
2	M.Davis	CAR	56	224	25.0%
2	C.Kupp	LAR	24	96	25.0%
4	T.Kelce	KC	26	105	24.8%
5	D.Montgomery	CHI	70	301	23.3%
6	D.Singletary	BUF	45	194	23.2%
7	A.Ekeler	LAC	39	170	22.9%
8	A.Mattison	MIN	25	109	22.9%
9	D.Hopkins	ARI	26	116	22.4%
10	A.Kamara	NO	59	270	21.9%
11	L.Bell	2TM	21	98	21.4%
12	K.Hunt	CLE	50	236	21.2%
13	J.K.Dobbins	BAL	32	152	21.1%
14	T.Hill	KC	21	100	21.0%
15	T.Pollard	DAL	27	129	20.9%
15	M.Gordon	DEN	51	247	20.6%
17	D.Cook	MIN	71	356	19.9%
18	S.Michel	NE	17	86	19.8%
19	A.Jones	GB	49	248	19.8%
20	A.Gibson	WAS	40	206	19.4%

Best Yards After Contract (min. 100 carries)

Rk	Player	Team	YafC
1	N.Chubb	CLE	3.69
2	D.Henry	TEN	3.61
3	R.Jones	TB	3.35
4	A.Jones	GB	3.30
5	T.Pollard	DAL	3.04
6	G.Edwards	BAL	2.98
7	J.Wilson	SF	2.97
8	J.K.Dobbins	BAL	2.90
9	D.Singletary	BUF	2.85
10	J.Robinson	JAX	2.84

Worst Yards After Contract (min. 100 carries)

Rk	Player	Team	YafC
1	M.Brown	LAR	1.53
2	J.Kelley	LAC	1.64
3	A.Gibson	WAS	1.95
4	K.Drake	ARI	1.97
5	G.Bernard	CIN	2.01
6	B.Hill	ATL	2.05
7	J.Mixon	CIN	2.06
8	B.Snell	PIT	2.08
9	F.Gore	NYJ	2.10
10	D.Swift	DET	2.11

Top 20 Defenders, Passes Defensed

Rk	Player	Team	PD
1	X.Howard	MIA	20
2	J.Bradberry	NYG	18
2	C.Davis	TB	18
2	D.Ward	CLE	18
5	R.Darby	WAS	16
6	J.Bates	CIN	15
6	J.Johnson	CHI	15
8	M.Butler	TEN	14
8	M.Davis	LAC	14
8	T.Diggs	DAL	14
8	J.C.Jackson	NE	14
8	T.Mullen	LV	14
8	D.Williams	LAR	14
14	J.Alexander	GB	13
14	C.Gardner-Johnson	NO	13
14	T.Mitchell	CLE	13
14	K.Moore	IND	13
18	Sq.Griffin	SEA	12
18	J.Haden	PIT	12
18	J.Jenkins	NO	12
18	D.Phillips	CIN	12
18	X.Rhodes	IND	12
18	D.Savage	GB	12

Top 20 Defenders, Defeats

Rk	Player	Team	Dfts
1	R.Smith	CHI	33
1	D.White	TB	33
3	T.J.Watt	PIT	31
4	L.David	TB	29
5	H.Reddick	ARI	28
6	J.Adams	SEA	27
6	M.Jack	JAX	27
6	B.Martinez	NYG	27
9	B.Baker	ARI	26
9	D.Jones	ATL	26
11	D.Lawrence	DAL	25
11	F.Oluokun	ATL	25
13	A.Donald	LAR	24
14	J.Bostic	WAS	23
14	K.Mack	CHI	23
14	J.Peppers	NYG	23
14	J.J.Watt	HOU	23
18	M.Hilton	PIT	22
18	J.Pierre-Paul	TB	22
18	Z.Smith	GB	22

Top 20 Defenders, Quarterback Hits

Rk	Player	Team	Hits
1	C.Lawson	CIN	27
1	T.J.Watt	PIT	27
3	C.Jones	KC	24
4	J.Bosa	LAC	20
5	W.Gholston	TB	19
5	L.Williams	NYG	19
7	A.Hicks	CHI	18
7	G.Jarrett	ATL	18
9	D.Buckner	IND	17
10	A.Donald	LAR	16
10	C.Heyward	PIT	16
10	S.Lawson	MIA	16
13	B.Burns	CAR	15
13	M.Golden	2TM	15
13	M.Judon	BAL	15
13	N.Suh	TB	15
17	E.Ogbah	MIA	14
18	T.Bowser	BAL	13
18	T.Hendrickson	NO	13
18	P.McPhee	BAL	13
18	J.Tillery	LAC	13
18	S.Tuitt	PIT	13
18	J.J.Watt	HOU	13

Includes plays nullified by penalty.

Top 20 Defenders, QB Knockdowns (Sacks + Hits)

Rk	Defender	Team	KD
1	T.J.Watt	PIT	42
2	C.Lawson	CIN	34
3	C.Jones	KC	32
4	L.Williams	NYG	31
5	A.Donald	LAR	30
6	J.Bosa	LAC	29
7	D.Buckner	IND	28
7	T.Hendrickson	NO	28
9	B.Burns	CAR	25
9	E.Ogbah	MIA	25
9	S.Tuitt	PIT	25
12	G.Jarrett	ATL	24
12	Z.Smith	GB	24
14	M.Judon	BAL	23
15	M.Garrett	CLE	22
15	W.Gholston	TB	22
15	A.Hicks	CHI	22
15	N.Suh	TB	22
15	M.Sweat	WAS	22
20	L.Floyd	LAR	21
20	M.Golden	2TM	21
20	C.Heyward	PIT	21

Full credit for whole and half sacks; includes sacks cancelled by penalty. Does not include strip sacks.

Top 20 Defenders, Hurries

Rk	Defender	Team	Hur
1	S.Barrett	TB	48
2	A.Donald	LAR	44
3	C.Jones	KC	41
4	E.Ogbah	MIA	40
5	K.Hyder	SF	39
5	C.Winovich	NE	39
7	H.Landry	TEN	37
7	D.Lawrence	DAL	37
7	A.Smith	DAL	37
10	L.Floyd	LAR	34
11	C.Heyward	PIT	33
12	B.Burns	CAR	32
12	M.Crosby	LV	32
12	M.Golden	2TM	32
12	M.Sweat	WAS	32
12	T.J.Watt	PIT	32
17	J.Hughes	BUF	31
17	C.Jordan	NO	31
19	D.Buckner	IND	30
19	Z.Smith	GB	30
19	L.Williams	NYG	30

Top 20 Quarterbacks, QB Knockdowns (Sacks + Hits)

Rk	Player	Team	KD
1	K.Cousins	MIN	123
2	R.Wilson	SEA	122
3	M.Ryan	ATL	121
4	C.Wentz	PHI	118
5	J.Herbert	LAC	110
5	D.Jones	NYG	110
7	D.Watson	HOU	98
8	R.Tannehill	TEN	90
9	P.Mahomes	KC	87
10	M.Stafford	DET	85
11	T.Brady	TB	84
12	J.Burrow	CIN	81
13	J.Allen	BUF	80
13	N.Mullens	SF	80
15	J.Goff	LAR	78
16	T.Bridgewater	CAR	75
17	S.Darnold	NYJ	73
18	B.Roethlisberger	PIT	72
19	D.Lock	DEN	68
20	C.Newton	NE	65

Includes sacks cancelled by penalties
Does not include strip sacks or "self sacks" with no defender listed.

Top 20 Quarterbacks, QB Hits

Rk	Player	Team	Hits
1	K.Cousins	MIN	85
2	M.Ryan	ATL	79
3	J.Herbert	LAC	76
4	R.Wilson	SEA	73
5	C.Wentz	PHI	67
6	D.Jones	NYG	65
6	R.Tannehill	TEN	65
8	P.Mahomes	KC	64
9	N.Mullens	SF	62
10	T.Brady	TB	61
11	B.Roethlisberger	PIT	58
12	J.Allen	BUF	56
12	J.Goff	LAR	56
14	D.Lock	DEN	50
15	J.Burrow	CIN	48
15	D.Watson	HOU	48
17	P.Rivers	IND	45
18	T.Bridgewater	CAR	44
18	N.Foles	CHI	44
20	M.Stafford	DET	43

Includes plays nullified by penalty.

Top 10 Quarterbacks, Knockdowns per Pass

Rk	Player	Team	KD	Pct
1	C.Wentz	PHI	118	23.0%
2	N.Mullens	SF	80	22.2%
3	D.Jones	NYG	110	21.0%
4	K.Cousins	MIN	123	21.0%
5	R.Wilson	SEA	122	19.2%
6	N.Foles	CHI	63	18.4%
7	J.Burrow	CIN	81	17.9%
8	S.Darnold	NYJ	73	17.6%
9	M.Ryan	ATL	121	17.3%
10	R.Tannehill	TEN	90	16.9%

Min. 200 passes; includes passes cancelled by penalty

Bottom 10 Quarterbacks in Knockdowns per Pass

Rk	Player	Team	KD	Pct
1	K.Murray	ARI	52	8.5%
2	A.Rodgers	GB	57	9.9%
3	B.Mayfield	CLE	53	9.9%
4	D.Carr	LV	57	9.9%
5	T.Tagovailoa	MIA	33	10.2%
6	P.Rivers	IND	63	10.6%
7	B.Roethlisberger	PIT	72	10.9%
8	D.Prescott	DAL	26	11.0%
9	M.Trubisky	CHI	37	11.5%
10	D.Brees	NO	48	11.5%

Min. 200 passes; includes passes cancelled by penalty

Top 10 Most Passes Tipped at Line, Quarterbacks

Rk	Player	Team	Total
1	B.Roethlisberger	PIT	23
2	K.Murray	ARI	18
3	J.Herbert	LAC	15
3	C.Newton	NE	15
5	P.Rivers	IND	14
6	J.Goff	LAR	13
7	J.Allen	BUF	12
7	T.Brady	TB	12
7	L.Jackson	BAL	12
7	N.Mullens	SF	12
7	M.Ryan	ATL	12

Top 10 Tipped at the Line, Defenders

Rk	Player	Team	Total
1	J.J.Watt	HOU	8
2	S.Harris	DEN	7
3	C.Campbell	BAL	6
3	J.Simmons	TEN	6
3	M.Sweat	WAS	6
3	D.Tomlinson	NYG	6
7	M.Addison	BUF	5
7	T.Alualu	PIT	5
7	C.Dunlap	2TM	5
7	C.Jones	KC	5
7	T.J.Watt	PIT	5

2020 Quarterbacks with and without Pass Pressure

Rank	Player	Team	Plays	Pct Pressure	DVOA with Pressure	Yds with Pressure	DVOA w/o Pressure	Yds w/o Pressure	DVOA Dif	Rank
1	B.Roethlisberger	PIT	643	14.3%	-40.7%	4.4	21.7%	6.6	-62.4%	4
2	T.Brady	TB	654	15.0%	-108.3%	2.3	61.8%	8.4	-170.0%	34
3	D.Brees	NO	408	16.4%	-96.1%	3.5	47.5%	7.9	-143.6%	26
4	P.Rivers	IND	573	18.0%	-40.8%	5.0	30.5%	7.9	-71.3%	5
5	D.Haskins	WAS	270	19.3%	-174.2%	0.1	-6.4%	6.3	-167.8%	32
6	M.Stafford	DET	584	20.4%	-47.2%	3.8	34.7%	7.8	-81.9%	12
7	R.Tannehill	TEN	535	21.5%	-90.8%	2.5	76.3%	8.7	-167.1%	31
8	D.Carr	LV	572	21.9%	-76.5%	3.8	48.8%	8.6	-125.3%	23
9	A.Rodgers	GB	576	22.0%	-36.5%	3.2	77.3%	8.9	-113.8%	20
10	M.Trubisky	CHI	335	22.4%	-70.7%	3.5	29.9%	7.2	-100.6%	16
11	J.Burrow	CIN	453	23.2%	-131.1%	0.9	42.5%	7.2	-173.6%	35
12	A.Dalton	DAL	378	23.3%	-83.7%	2.3	12.6%	6.8	-96.4%	15
13	J.Goff	LAR	600	23.3%	-126.8%	1.6	55.8%	8.1	-182.5%	36
14	R.Fitzpatrick	MIA	306	23.5%	11.2%	7.6	29.2%	7.5	-18.0%	1
15	T.Tagovailoa	MIA	332	24.1%	-44.7%	3.3	15.9%	6.3	-60.6%	3
16	B.Mayfield	CLE	538	24.5%	-81.8%	2.5	53.4%	8.0	-135.2%	24
17	T.Bridgewater	CAR	566	24.6%	-62.5%	3.2	47.4%	8.1	-109.9%	18
18	C.Newton	NE	418	24.6%	-132.4%	2.4	33.5%	7.6	-165.9%	30
19	K.Murray	ARI	637	24.6%	-47.4%	4.3	34.8%	7.6	-82.2%	13
20	D.Prescott	DAL	241	25.3%	-62.9%	5.2	51.0%	8.6	-113.9%	21
21	A.Smith	WAS	279	25.4%	-153.6%	1.1	1.7%	6.7	-155.3%	29
22	M.Ryan	ATL	691	25.9%	-39.4%	4.0	34.1%	7.4	-73.6%	7
23	J.Herbert	LAC	655	26.9%	-14.4%	4.4	45.0%	7.6	-59.4%	2
24	G.Minshew	JAX	384	27.1%	-75.7%	2.9	35.7%	7.3	-111.3%	19
25	D.Lock	DEN	491	27.3%	-96.8%	3.1	23.7%	7.3	-120.5%	22
26	P.Mahomes	KC	653	29.6%	-2.1%	5.2	72.3%	8.6	-74.4%	8
27	C.Wentz	PHI	519	29.9%	-114.6%	1.5	22.3%	6.8	-136.9%	25
28	D.Watson	HOU	659	30.0%	-31.4%	5.1	48.2%	8.8	-79.6%	11
29	D.Jones	NYG	520	30.2%	-108.5%	2.0	36.7%	7.1	-145.1%	27
30	N.Foles	CHI	337	30.3%	-56.4%	3.9	15.5%	6.0	-71.9%	6
31	R.Wilson	SEA	666	30.5%	-40.0%	3.8	61.6%	8.1	-101.5%	17
32	N.Mullens	SF	352	30.7%	-119.3%	3.4	48.6%	8.3	-167.8%	33
33	L.Jackson	BAL	454	30.8%	-40.5%	4.3	45.2%	7.7	-85.7%	14
34	J.Allen	BUF	635	30.9%	-10.0%	5.0	65.1%	8.7	-75.1%	9
35	K.Cousins	MIN	577	31.7%	-84.1%	3.3	67.5%	9.3	-151.5%	28
36	S.Darnold	NYJ	430	33.0%	-70.8%	3.3	7.2%	6.5	-78.1%	10

Includes scrambles and Defensive Pass Interference. Does not include aborted snaps.
Minimum: 200 passes.

WR: Highest Slot/Wide Ratio of Targets

Rk	Player	Team	Slot	Wide	Slot%
1	L.Fitzgerald	ARI	70	3	96%
2	C.Beasley	BUF	99	6	94%
3	G.Ward	PHI	75	5	94%
4	C.Lamb	DAL	104	7	94%
5	H.Renfrow	LV	73	5	94%
6	T.Boyd	CIN	101	10	91%
7	A.Miller	CHI	68	7	91%
8	K.Cole	JAX	84	9	90%
9	D.Amendola	DET	62	7	90%
10	C.Kupp	LAR	111	13	90%
11	G.Tate	NYG	47	6	89%
12	C.Samuel	CAR	77	10	89%
13	KJ Hamler	DEN	50	7	88%
14	J.Smith-Schuster	PIT	114	16	88%
15	J.Meyers	NE	68	12	85%
16	Z.Pascal	IND	59	11	84%
17	J.Crowder	NYJ	74	14	84%
18	C.Godwin	TB	70	15	82%
19	R.Woods	LAR	106	23	82%
20	B.Berrios	NYJ	38	9	81%

Min. 50 passes. Slot includes lined up tight.

WR: Highest Wide/Slot Ratio of Targets

Rk	Player	Team	Slot	Wide	Wide%
1	M.Gallup	DAL	25	85	83%
2	A.J.Green	CIN	26	82	81%
3	C.Kirk	ARI	21	59	81%
4	D.Slayton	NYG	26	70	79%
5	D.Johnson	PIT	40	107	79%
6	M.Williams	LAC	24	63	78%
7	D.Byrd	NE	22	56	75%
8	D.Hopkins	ARI	47	117	73%
9	DK Metcalf	SEA	39	92	72%
10	R.Higgins	CLE	18	36	71%
11	D.Parker	MIA	37	73	70%
12	DJ Chark	JAX	32	61	68%
13	J.Washington	PIT	21	39	67%
14	C.Ridley	ATL	53	92	66%
15	S.Miller	TB	21	35	66%
16	J.Reagor	PHI	21	34	66%
17	M.Evans	TB	46	72	65%
18	T.Hilton	IND	40	60	65%
19	T.Fulgham	PHI	28	42	63%
20	J.Brown	BUF	22	32	60%

Min. 50 passes. Slot includes lined up tight.

Top 10 WR Better Lined Up Wide

Rk	Player	Team	Slot	Wide	Slot	Wide	Dif
1	G.Davis	BUF	33	30	-13.9%	38.4%	52.3%
2	D.Robinson	KC	24	34	-21.1%	26.3%	47.3%
3	D.J.Moore	CAR	63	55	-8.3%	29.0%	37.3%
4	J.Brown	BUF	22	32	-9.4%	25.4%	34.8%
5	S.Watkins	KC	30	26	-14.6%	16.7%	31.3%
6	DJ Chark	JAX	32	61	-26.3%	1.3%	27.5%
7	S.Shepard	NYG	48	42	-21.1%	5.4%	26.5%
8	J.Washington	PIT	21	39	-26.2%	0.3%	26.5%
9	A.Brown	TEN	49	62	10.1%	36.3%	26.2%
10	J.Jones	ATL	39	30	21.0%	46.3%	25.3%

Min. 20 targets from each position

Top 10 WR Better Lined Up Slot

Rk	Player	Team	Slot	Wide	Slot	Wide	Dif
1	J.Guyton	LAC	30	27	22.5%	-33.2%	55.7%
2	B.Perriman	NYJ	38	26	14.8%	-30.5%	45.3%
3	R.Gage	ATL	85	25	7.3%	-34.5%	41.8%
4	M.Valdes-Scantling	GB	36	30	28.1%	-10.4%	38.5%
5	J.Grant	MIA	29	26	5.3%	-32.0%	37.3%
6	M.Evans	TB	46	72	46.2%	12.1%	34.1%
7	J.Reynolds	LAR	40	41	2.5%	-27.2%	29.7%
8	M.Pittman	IND	31	31	7.1%	-18.5%	25.7%
9	B.Aiyuk	SF	58	41	10.9%	-13.9%	24.7%
10	M.Jones	DET	80	40	20.0%	-4.8%	24.7%

Min. 20 targets from each position

Top 10 TE Highest Rate of Targets from WR Positions (Slot/Wide)

Rk	Player	Team	Tight	Slot	Wide	Back	WR%
1	J.Cook	NO	11	41	9	0	82%
2	M.Gesicki	MIA	17	70	2	0	81%
3	G.Olsen	SEA	8	29	1	0	79%
4	A.Firkser	TEN	13	40	1	0	76%
5	Z.Ertz	PHI	18	52	1	0	75%
6	J.Reed	SF	11	31	3	1	74%
7	T.Kelce	KC	44	93	10	0	70%
8	J.Graham	CHI	23	42	11	0	70%
9	L.Thomas	WAS	32	75	2	2	69%
10	M.Andrews	BAL	26	60	1	2	69%

Min. 25 passes

Top 10 TE Lowest Rate of Targets from WR Positions (Slot/Wide)

Rk	Player	Team	Tight	Slot	Wide	Back	WR%
1	T.Conklin	MIN	22	2	0	1	8%
2	K.Rudolph	MIN	34	3	0	0	8%
3	W.Dissly	SEA	25	3	1	0	14%
4	R.Gronkowski	TB	69	10	2	0	15%
5	N.Fant	DEN	75	15	3	0	19%
5	R.Rodgers	PHI	25	6	0	0	19%
7	C.Herndon	NYJ	34	8	2	2	22%
8	R.Dwelley	SF	19	6	0	0	24%
9	J.Akins	HOU	33	10	2	4	24%
10	J.Doyle	IND	24	9	0	0	27%

Min. 25 passes

Top 10 RB Highest Rate of Targets from WR Positions (Slot/Wide)

Rk	Player	Team	Back	Slot	Wide	Tight	WR%
1	J.D.McKissic	WAS	59	33	17	1	45%
2	C.Edmonds	ARI	41	18	8	0	39%
3	N.Hines	IND	49	12	14	0	35%
4	T.Pollard	DAL	27	5	8	0	33%
5	J.Wilson	SF	18	4	4	0	31%
6	Du.Johnson	HOU	26	4	6	0	28%
7	J.Williams	GB	26	4	5	0	26%
8	M.Brown	LAR	25	6	2	0	24%
9	G.Bernard	CIN	44	8	6	1	24%
10	J.McKinnon	SF	35	7	4	1	23%

Min. 25 passes

Top 10 Teams, Pct Passes Dropped

Rk	Team	Passes	Drops	Pct
1	ARI	521	16	3.1%
2	CHI	581	18	3.1%
3	MIN	468	18	3.8%
4	BUF	554	22	4.0%
5	JAX	567	24	4.2%
6	HOU	514	22	4.3%
7	CIN	547	25	4.6%
8	LAR	539	25	4.6%
9	IND	516	24	4.7%
10	WAS	558	26	4.7%

Adjusted for passes tipped/thrown away.

Bottom 10 Teams, Pct Passes Dropped

Rk	Team	Passes	Drops	Pct
23	DAL	594	36	6.1%
24	KC	595	37	6.2%
25	NO	497	31	6.2%
26	TB	590	38	6.4%
27	PHI	537	35	6.5%
28	DET	550	36	6.5%
29	BAL	377	27	7.2%
30	SF	532	39	7.3%
31	PIT	627	47	7.5%
32	DEN	516	39	7.6%

Adjusted for passes tipped/thrown away.

Top 20 Players, Passes Dropped

Rk	Player	Team	Total
1	D.Johnson	PIT	15
2	J.Jeudy	DEN	13
3	T.Hill	KC	10
3	A.Kamara	NO	10
5	M.Brown	BAL	9
5	E.Engram	NYG	9
5	E.Elliott	DAL	9
5	R.Gage	ATL	9
5	DK Metcalf	SEA	9
10	N.Agholor	LV	8
10	G.Kittle	SF	8
10	C.Lamb	DAL	8
10	M.Sanders	PHI	8
14	C.Claypool	PIT	7
14	M.Evans	TB	7
14	G.Everett	LAR	7
14	M.Hardman	KC	7
14	T.Higgins	CIN	7
14	T.Lockett	SEA	7
14	D.J.Moore	CAR	7
14	D.Parker	MIA	7
14	M.Valdes-Scantling	GB	7

Top 20 Players, Pct. Passes Dropped

Rk	Player	Team	Drops	Passes	Pct
1	J.Dobbins	BAL	4	24	16.7%
2	M.Sanders	PHI	8	52	15.4%
3	J.Wilson	SF	4	28	14.3%
4	L.Fournette	TB	6	47	12.8%
5	G.Kittle	SF	8	63	12.7%
6	E.Elliott	DAL	9	71	12.7%
7	M.Hall	DET	4	32	12.5%
8	R.Jones	TB	5	42	11.9%
8	K.Hunt	CLE	6	51	11.8%
10	J.Jeudy	DEN	13	113	11.5%
11	T.Gurley	ATL	4	35	11.4%
12	G.Everett	LAR	7	62	11.3%
12	M.Hardman	KC	7	62	11.3%
13	M.Valdes-Scantling	GB	7	63	11.1%
15	J.Guyton	LAC	6	55	10.9%
16	A.Lazard	GB	5	46	10.9%
17	S.Sims	WAS	4	37	10.8%
18	KJ Hamler	DEN	6	56	10.7%
19	D.Johnson	PIT	15	144	10.4%
20	J.Hollister	SEA	4	40	10.0%
20	T.Pollard	DAL	4	40	10.0%

Min. four drops

Top 20 Yards Lost to Drops by Quarterbacks

Rk	Player	Team	Drops	Yds
1	P.Mahomes	KC	36	360
2	D.Lock	DEN	29	352
3	R.Wilson	SEA	31	301
4	B.Roethlisberger	PIT	44	291
5	M.Stafford	DET	32	281
6	T.Brady	TB	37	279
7	A.Rodgers	GB	26	274
8	M.Ryan	ATL	31	260
9	D.Carr	LV	24	245
10	K.Murray	ARI	16	229
11	L.Jackson	BAL	26	225
12	D.Watson	HOU	22	217
13	C.Wentz	PHI	27	208
14	D.Haskins	WAS	13	193
15	D.Jones	NYG	26	187
16	T.Tagovailoa	MIA	15	179
17	R.Tannehill	TEN	22	167
18	J.Goff	LAR	23	166
19	P.Rivers	IND	23	164
20	J.Burrow	CIN	16	155

Based on yardage in the air, no possible YAC included.

Top 20 Intended Receivers on Interceptions

Rk	Player	Team	Total
1	D.J.Moore	CAR	9
2	E.Engram	NYG	6
2	J.Jeudy	DEN	6
4	K.Allen	LAC	5
4	DJ Chark	JAX	5
4	J.Hightower	PHI	5
4	C.Ridley	ATL	5
4	A.Robinson	CHI	5
4	J.Smith-Schuster	PIT	5
4	R.Woods	LAR	5
11	14 tied with		4

Top 10 Completion Percentage Over Expected

Rk	Player	Team	CPOE
1	D.Watson	HOU	5.5%
2	A.Rodgers	GB	5.3%
3	J.Allen	BUF	4.6%
4	K.Cousins	MIN	4.6%
5	R.Wilson	SEA	3.9%
6	K.Murray	ARI	3.9%
7	T.Bridgewater	CAR	3.4%
8	D.Carr	LV	2.1%
9	R.Fitzpatrick	MIA	1.7%
10	B.Mayfield	CLE	1.4%

Min. 200 passes; CPOE adjusted for passes tipped/thrown away.

Bottom 10 Completion Percentage Over Expected

Rk	Player	Team	CPOE
1	D.Haskins	WAS	-6.8%
2	C.Wentz	PHI	-6.5%
3	D.Lock	DEN	-6.3%
4	D.Jones	NYG	-4.2%
5	T.Tagovailoa	MIA	-3.5%
6	S.Darnold	NYJ	-3.5%
7	A.Smith	WAS	-3.0%
8	B.Roethlisberger	PIT	-2.3%
9	N.Mullens	SF	-1.9%
10	A.Dalton	DAL	-1.5%

Min. 200 passes; CPOE adjusted for passes tipped/thrown away.

Top 10 Plus/Minus for Wide Receivers

Rk	Player	Team	Pass	+/-
1	S.Diggs	BUF	166	+17.4
2	D.Adams	GB	149	+13.6
3	C.Samuel	CAR	97	+11.4
4	T.Lockett	SEA	132	+9.8
5	C.Beasley	BUF	107	+9.7
6	C.Godwin	TB	84	+9.7
7	J.Jefferson	MIN	125	+9.1
8	D.Hopkins	ARI	160	+9.1
9	J.Jones	ATL	68	+8.0
10	C.Ridley	ATL	143	+8.0

Min. 50 passes; plus/minus adjusted for passes tipped/thrown away.

Bottom 10 Plus/Minus for Wide Receivers

Rk	Player	Team	Pass	+/-
1	J.Jeudy	DEN	113	-13.3
2	A.J.Green	CIN	104	-11.1
3	D.Johnson	PIT	144	-7.9
4	D.Slayton	NYG	96	-6.6
5	KJ Hamler	DEN	56	-6.5
6	M.Gallup	DAL	105	-5.1
7	D.J.Moore	CAR	118	-4.5
8	D.Byrd	NE	77	-4.3
9	J.Guyton	LAC	55	-4.0
10	N.Harry	NE	57	-4.0

Min. 50 passes; plus/minus adjusted for passes tipped/thrown away.

Top 10 Plus/Minus for Tight Ends

Rk	Player	Team	Pass	+/-
1	R.Tonyan	GB	59	+12.6
2	T.Kelce	KC	145	+8.9
3	D.Waller	LV	145	+8.5
4	R.Rodgers	PHI	31	+5.9
5	M.Alie-Cox	IND	39	+5.0
6	D.Smythe	MIA	29	+4.0
7	D.Arnold	ARI	45	+3.9
8	C.Brate	TB	34	+3.8
9	J.Akins	HOU	49	+3.4
10	T.Higbee	LAR	60	+3.4

Min. 25 passes; plus/minus adjusted for passes tipped/thrown away.

Bottom 10 Plus/Minus for Tight Ends

Rk	Player	Team	Pass	+/-
1	E.Engram	NYG	109	-11.4
2	Z.Ertz	PHI	72	-10.1
3	D.Knox	BUF	44	-6.7
4	E.Ebron	PIT	91	-6.5
5	J.Smith	TEN	65	-5.3
6	H.Hurst	ATL	88	-4.2
7	N.Fant	DEN	93	-3.9
8	J.Reed	SF	46	-3.6
9	C.Kmet	CHI	44	-3.2
10	J.Graham	CHI	76	-3.1

Min. 25 passes; plus/minus adjusted for passes tipped/thrown away.

Top 10 Plus/Minus for Running Backs

Rk	Player	Team	Pass	+/-
1	J.Taylor	IND	39	+3.4
2	A.Ekeler	LAC	65	+3.2
3	M.Davis	CAR	70	+2.2
4	J.Williams	GB	35	+2.2
5	J.White	NE	62	+2.1
6	M.Gaskin	MIA	47	+1.8
7	B.Hill	ATL	30	+1.8
8	J.Mixon	CIN	26	+1.6
9	D.Montgomery	CHI	68	+1.3
10	Du.Johnson	HOU	35	+1.2

Min. 25 passes; plus/minus adjusted for passes tipped/thrown away.

Bottom 10 Plus/Minus for Running Backs

Rk	Player	Team	Pass	+/-
1	M.Sanders	PHI	52	-13.1
2	J.D.McKissic	WAS	110	-7.6
3	J.Wilson	SF	28	-6.4
4	R.Jones	TB	42	-5.5
5	D.Lewis	NYG	30	-4.5
6	M.Gordon	DEN	44	-4.2
7	D.Williams	KC	26	-4.2
8	C.Edwards-Helaire	KC	54	-4.2
9	T.Pollard	DAL	40	-4.2
10	D.Henry	TEN	31	-4.1

Min. 25 passes; plus/minus adjusted for passes tipped/thrown away.

Top 10 Quarterbacks, Yards Gained on Defensive Pass Interference

Rk	Player	Team	Pen	Yds
1	T.Brady	TB	23	395
2	B.Roethlisberger	PIT	19	351
3	D.Carr	LV	10	244
4	C.Wentz	PHI	11	232
5	R.Wilson	SEA	8	198
6	P.Rivers	IND	13	176
7	J.Allen	BUF	8	170
8	R.Tannehill	TEN	10	169
9	A.Rodgers	GB	9	159
10	M.Stafford	DET	9	152

Top 10 Receivers, Yards Gained on Defensive Pass Interference

Rk	Player	Team	Pen	Yds
1	C.Claypool	PIT	8	185
2	M.Evans	TB	9	171
3	N.Agholor	LV	5	155
4	S.Miller	TB	4	116
5	A.Brown	TEN	5	101
6	T.Hilton	IND	7	98
7	M.Jones	DET	5	95
8	D.Hopkins	ARI	6	93
9	B.Perriman	NYJ	5	91
10	T.Fulgham	PHI	4	90

Top 10 Defenders, Yards Allowed on Defensive Pass Interference

Rk	Player	Team	Pen	Yds
1	M.Humphrey	BAL	7	111
2	M.Williams	NO	3	93
3	J.Ramsey	LAR	5	92
4	P.Peterson	ARI	4	86
5	J.Jenkins	NO	6	83
6	C.Ward	KC	3	81
6	R.Ya-Sin	IND	4	81
8	J.Lewis	DAL	4	75
9	C.Davis	TB	5	72
10	J.Johnson	CHI	4	71

Top 20 First Downs/Touchdowns Allowed, Coverage

Rk	Player	Team	Yards	Rk	Player	Team	Yards
1	V.Hargreaves	HOU	45	12	T.Mitchell	CLE	34
2	M.Butler	TEN	44	13	M.Humphrey	BAL	33
3	D.Slay	PHI	40	14	J.Jenkins	NO	32
4	D.Kirkpatrick	ARI	39	14	T.Mullen	LV	32
5	J.Gladney	MIN	38	16	T.Diggs	DAL	31
5	A.Terrell	ATL	38	16	R.Douglas	CAR	31
7	C.Davis	TB	37	16	T.Herndon	JAX	31
7	M.Davis	LAC	37	16	M.Lattimore	NO	31
7	L.Sims	CIN	37	20	J.C.Jackson	NE	30
10	Sq.Griffin	SEA	35	20	P.Peterson	ARI	30
10	A.Oruwariye	DET	35				

Includes Defensive Pass Interference.

Top 20 Passing Yards Allowed, Coverage

Rk	Player	Team	Yards	Rk	Player	Team	Yards
1	M.Butler	TEN	829	11	I.Oliver	ATL	621
2	V.Hargreaves	HOU	776	12	J.Gladney	MIN	615
3	A.Oruwariye	DET	720	13	C.Hayward	LAC	594
4	A.Terrell	ATL	707	13	M.Lattimore	NO	594
5	T.Mitchell	CLE	690	15	R.Darby	WAS	593
6	D.Slay	PHI	680	16	J.C.Jackson	NE	591
7	C.Davis	TB	662	16	L.Sims	CIN	591
8	M.Ojemudia	DEN	655	18	Sq.Griffin	SEA	589
9	M.Davis	LAC	650	19	P.Peterson	ARI	579
10	T.Diggs	DAL	636	20	R.Douglas	CAR	578

Includes Defensive Pass Interference.

Fewest Yards After Catch Allowed, Coverage by Cornerbacks

Rk	Player	Team	YAC
1	B.Callahan	DEN	0.9
2	D.Phillips	CIN	1.1
3	B.Roby	HOU	1.4
4	D.Reed	SEA	1.7
5	J.Dean	TB	2.0
6	M.Davis	LAC	2.1
7	K.Fuller	CHI	2.1
8	R.Darby	WAS	2.2
9	C.Dantzler	MIN	2.3
10	D.Jackson	CAR	2.4
11	J.Alexander	GB	2.4
12	J.Haden	PIT	2.5
13	J.Ramsey	LAR	2.5
14	M.Butler	TEN	2.6
15	J.Verrett	SF	2.6
16	C.Davis	TB	2.7
17	Sq.Griffin	SEA	2.7
18	J.Bradberry	NYG	2.8
19	M.Humphrey	BAL	2.8
20	D.Ward	CLE	2.9

Min. 50 passes or 8 games started.

Most Yards After Catch Allowed, Coverage by Cornerbacks

Rk	Player	Team	YAC
1	C.Harris	LAC	7.0
2	J.C.Jackson	NE	7.0
3	N.Needham	MIA	6.1
4	B.Breeland	KC	6.0
5	A.Oruwariye	DET	5.8
6	I.Oliver	ATL	5.7
7	By.Jones	MIA	5.5
8	K.Sheffield	ATL	5.1
9	M.Alexander	CIN	5.0
10	I.Yiadom	NYG	5.0
11	C.Henderson	JAX	4.9
12	J.Johnson	CHI	4.8
13	D.Williams	LAR	4.6
14	C.Ward	KC	4.5
15	V.Hargreaves	HOU	4.4
16	T.Diggs	DAL	4.4
17	M.Ojemudia	DEN	4.3
17	W.Jackson	CIN	4.3
19	S.Nelson	PIT	4.2
20	S.Murphy-Bunting	TB	4.2

Min. 50 passes or 8 games started.

Top 20 Defenders, Run Tackles for Loss

Rk	Player	Team	TFL
1	T.J.Watt	PIT	12
2	J.J.Watt	HOU	10
2	V.Williams	PIT	10
4	M.Crosby	LV	9
4	J.Hicks	ARI	9
4	D.Lawrence	DAL	9
4	R.Smith	CHI	9
8	L.David	TB	8
8	T.Edwards	PHI	8
8	F.Fatukasi	NYJ	8
8	B.Graham	PHI	8
8	G.Jarrett	ATL	8
8	E.Oliver	BUF	8
8	A.Phillips	NE	8
8	E.Roberts	MIA	8
8	J.Schobert	JAX	8
8	D.White	TB	8
8	Q.Williams	NYJ	8
8	D.Wolfe	BAL	8
20	7 tied with		7

Includes both tackles and assists.

Fewest Avg Yards on Run Tackle, Defensive Line or Edge Rusher

Rk	Player	Team	Tkl	Avg
1	T.J.Watt	PIT	34	0.6
2	A.Donald	LAR	28	1.2
3	F.Fatukasi	NYJ	39	1.3
4	Q.Williams	NYJ	42	1.3
5	D.Onyemata	NO	32	1.3
6	M.Crosby	LV	29	1.4
7	D.Lawrence	DAL	47	1.5
8	J.J.Watt	HOU	45	1.5
9	O.Vernon	CLE	27	1.6
10	C.Young	WAS	28	1.6
11	C.Jordan	NO	41	1.7
12	J.Bosa	LAC	30	1.7
12	B.Graham	PHI	36	1.7
14	T.Alualu	PIT	33	1.7
15	F.Cox	PHI	30	1.7
16	D.Tomlinson	NYG	44	1.7
17	H.Anderson	NYJ	40	1.7
18	D.Brown	CAR	28	1.8
19	K.Mack	CHI	38	1.8
20	Z.Sieler	MIA	41	1.8

Min. 25 run tackles

Fewest Avg Yards on Run Tackle, LB

Rk	Player	Team	Tkl	Avg
1	W.Gay	KC	27	1.9
2	V.Williams	PIT	46	2.3
2	D.Long	TEN	28	2.8
4	B.McKinney	HOU	29	2.8
5	E.Roberts	MIA	47	2.9
6	K.Wright	SEA	34	2.9
7	D.Perryman	LAC	29	2.9
8	K.Alexander	2TM	34	2.9
9	B.Okereke	IND	30	3.0
10	C.Littleton	LV	42	3.1
11	T.Whitehead	CAR	33	3.1
12	L.David	TB	55	3.1
13	M.Kiser	LAR	49	3.2
14	T.Edwards	PHI	47	3.2
15	J.Schobert	JAX	87	3.2
16	D.White	TB	61	3.3
17	D.Davis	NO	71	3.3
17	A.J.Klein	BUF	37	3.3
19	C.Holcomb	WAS	38	3.4
20	T.Reeder	LAR	38	3.4

Min. 25 run tackles

Fewest Avg Yards on Run Tackle, DB

Rk	Player	Team	Tkl	Avg
1	J.Adams	SEA	33	3.0
2	K.Moore	IND	21	3.3
3	I.Oliver	ATL	20	3.6
4	L.Collins	WAS	27	3.6
4	C.Gardner-Johnson	NO	27	3.6
6	J.Lewis	DAL	26	3.7
7	M.Hilton	PIT	23	3.7
8	M.Davis	LAC	22	3.8
9	K.Dugger	NE	29	3.9
10	K.Curl	WAS	41	4.1
11	T.Johnson	BUF	38	4.1
12	T.White	BUF	21	4.2
13	J.Whitehead	TB	39	4.3
13	J.Kearse	DET	35	4.4
15	L.Joyner	LV	28	4.5
16	A.Wingard	JAX	26	4.5
17	J.Peppers	NYG	40	4.6
17	J.Gladney	MIN	30	4.6
19	B.Skrine	CHI	21	4.8
20	A.Phillips	NE	63	4.8

Min. 20 run tackles

Top 20 Offensive Tackles, Blown Blocks

Rk	Player	Pos	Team	Sacks	All Pass	All Run	Total
1	C.Robinson	LT	JAX	7.0	32	10	42
1	J.Taylor	RT	JAX	8.0	37	5	42
1	A.Thomas	LT	NYG	9.0	37	5	42
4	E.Fisher	LT	KC	4.0	32	5	37
4	T.Steele	RT	DAL	9.0	33	4	37
6	M.McGlinchey	RT	SF	5.5	26	8	34
7	D.Dawkins	LT	BUF	4.5	27	6	33
8	A.Jackson	LT	MIA	2.5	23	8	31
9	K.McGary	RT	ATL	1.5	20	9	30
10	B.Knight	LT	DAL	7.0	21	8	29
11	B.Hart	RT	CIN	4.5	23	5	28
11	M.Moses	RT	WAS	1.5	24	4	28
13	D.Smith	LT	TB	4.0	22	5	27
13	S.Tevi	LT	LAC	1.5	20	7	27
15	C.Fleming	RT	NYG	4.0	22	4	26
15	A.Villanueva	LT	PIT	1.5	21	5	26
17	T.Howard	RT	HOU	1.5	19	6	25
17	D.Kelly	RT	TEN	1.0	15	10	25
17	B.Turner	OT/RG	GB	2.5	11	14	25
20	J.Mailata	LT	PHI	5.0	19	5	24
20	J.Matthews	LT	ATL	2.5	16	8	24

Top 20 Offensive Tackles in Snaps per Blown Block

Rk	Player	Pos	Team	Sacks	All Pass	All Run	Total	Snaps	Snaps per BB
1	D.Bakhtiari	LT	GB	1.5	4	0	4	758	189.5
2	A.Whitworth	LT	LAR	1.0	3	1	4	599	149.8
3	G.Bolles	LT	DEN	0.0	7	2	9	1014	112.7
4	D.Brown	LT	SEA	1.0	8	4	12	1048	87.3
5	L.Johnson	RT	PHI	0.5	3	1	5	404	80.8
6	T.Decker	LT	DET	1.0	12	3	15	1049	69.9
7	R.Ramczyk	RT	NO	2.0	11	3	15	1038	69.2
8	C.Okorafor	RT	PIT	3.0	9	6	15	1033	68.9
9	O.Brown	LT/RT	BAL	2.5	12	3	15	1027	68.5
10	B.Shell	RT	SEA	1.0	6	4	10	673	67.3
11	T.Wirfs	RT	TB	1.0	12	4	16	1074	67.1
12	C.Lucas	LT	WAS	1.5	7	1	8	536	67.0
13	M.Onwenu	RT/RG	NE	2.0	6	7	14	926	66.1
14	T.Moton	RT	CAR	2.0	10	6	16	1034	64.6
15	D.Dotson	RT	DEN	0.5	4	3	7	451	64.4
16	A.Castonzo	LT	IND	2.0	9	3	12	749	62.4
17	D.Williams	RT	BUF	2.5	12	5	17	1048	61.6
18	R.Wagner	RT	GB	0.5	6	4	10	611	61.1
19	B.Smith	RT	IND	0.0	8	8	16	938	58.6
20	I.Wynn	LT	NE	3.0	9	2	11	640	58.2

Minimum: 400 snaps

Top 20 Interior Linemen, Blown Blocks

Rk	Player	Pos	Team	Sacks	All Pass	All Run	Total
1	G.Bradbury	C	MIN	2.5	15	20	36
2	F.Lamp	LG	LAC	1.0	21	14	35
3	L.Cushenberry	C	DEN	5.0	18	15	34
4	D.Feeney	C	LAC	2.5	14	16	30
5	D.Lewis	RG	SEA	3.0	17	12	29
6	D.Brunskill	C/RG	SF	2.5	16	12	28
6	L.Tomlinson	LG	SF	4.0	19	9	28
6	C.Williams	LG	DAL	3.5	17	11	28
9	A.Wylie	RG	KC	2.5	18	9	27
10	J.Jackson	LG	DET	1.5	17	8	26
10	M.Paradis	C	CAR	3.5	11	14	26
10	M.Pryor	RG	PHI	4.0	22	4	26
13	D.Dozier	LG	MIN	3.0	16	9	25
14	N.Davis	RG	TEN	1.0	11	13	24
15	C.Lindstrom	RG	ATL	3.5	14	9	23
15	A.Blythe	C	LAR	2.5	12	11	23
15	J.Davis	RG/OT	MIA	1.0	13	10	23
15	M.Glowinski	RG	IND	2.5	17	6	23
15	G.Jackson	RG	LV	1.0	13	10	23
15	S.Lemieux	LG	NYG	3.0	16	7	23
15	A.Mack	C	ATL	0.5	14	8	23
15	D.Risner	LG	DEN	0.0	16	7	23
15	B.Winters	RG	BUF	2.0	18	5	23

Top 20 Interior Linemen in Snaps per Blown Block

Rk	Player	Pos	Team	Sacks	All Pass	All Run	Total	Snaps	Snaps per BB
1	B.Linder	C	JAX	0.0	0	1	1	530	530.0
2	Z.Martin	RG	DAL	0.5	3	0	3	618	206.0
3	A.Reiter	C	KC	0.0	4	1	5	867	173.4
4	B.Powers	RG	BAL	1.0	3	0	3	513	171.0
5	C.Linsley	C	GB	0.0	1	4	5	735	147.0
6	M.Pouncey	C	PIT	0.0	4	3	7	863	123.3
7	J.Thuney	LG	NE	1.0	6	3	9	979	108.8
8	E.McCoy	C	NO	1.0	5	5	10	1073	107.3
9	D.DeCastro	RG	PIT	0.0	5	3	8	845	105.6
10	J.Kelce	C	PHI	1.5	5	6	11	1124	102.2
11	K.Zeitler	RG	NYG	2.0	6	4	10	1001	100.1
12	J.Simmons	LG	SEA	2.0	6	0	6	593	98.8
13	A.Marpet	LG	TB	0.0	6	3	9	850	94.4
14	T.Hopkins	C	CIN	1.5	3	7	10	937	93.7
15	F.Ragnow	C	DET	0.0	4	6	10	931	93.1
16	C.Whitehair	C	CHI	1.0	7	3	10	893	89.3
17	O.Aboushi	RG	DET	1.0	3	4	7	622	88.9
18	J.Bitonio	LG	CLE	1.5	5	7	12	1061	88.4
19	J.Pugh	LG	ARI	0.5	7	4	11	958	87.1
20	T.Biadasz	C	DAL	1.0	4	1	5	426	85.2

Minimum: 400 snaps

Top 20 Tight Ends, Blown Blocks

Rk	Player	Team	Sacks	All Pass	All Run	Total		Rk	Player	Team	Sacks	All Pass	All Run	Total
1	T.Higbee	LAR	1.0	3	10	13		11	T.Conklin	MIN	0.5	2	4	7
2	L.Stocker	ATL	0.0	9	3	12		11	R.Dwelley	SF	1.0	3	4	7
3	N.Fant	DEN	1.0	4	7	11		11	E.Engram	NYG	0.0	1	6	7
3	R.Izzo	NE	1.0	5	6	11		11	G.Everett	LAR	1.0	4	3	7
5	D.Schultz	DAL	1.0	1	9	10		11	R.Gronkowski	TB	0.5	1	6	7
6	J.Smith	TEN	0.0	2	7	9		11	H.Henry	LAC	1.0	5	2	7
6	D.Waller	LV	2.0	3	6	9		11	T.J.Hockenson	DET	1.0	3	4	7
8	D.Sample	CIN	2.0	3	5	8		11	J.O'Shaughnessy	JAX	0.0	1	6	7
8	D.Smythe	MIA	0.0	2	6	8		19	8 tied with					6
8	J.Witten	LV	0.0	2	6	8								

Most Penalties, Offense

Rk	Player	Team	Pen	Yds
1	D.Lewis	SEA	11	75
1	D.Smith	TB	11	80
1	J.Wills	CLE	11	70
4	D.Dozier	MIN	9	74
4	D.J.Fluker	BAL	9	50
4	T.Howard	HOU	9	62
4	J.Pugh	ARI	9	58
4	T.Williams	SF	9	65
9	Q.Nelson	IND	8	55
9	B.O'Neill	MIN	8	45
9	M.Pittman	IND	8	60
9	D.Williams	BUF	8	30
13	12 tied with		7	

Includes declined and offsetting, but not penalties on special teams, turnover returns, or kneeldowns.

Most Penalties, Defense

Rk	Player	Team	Pen	Yds
1	P.Peterson	ARI	12	108
2	A.Hicks	CHI	10	62
2	M.Judon	BAL	10	72
2	M.Sweat	WAS	10	80
2	C.Ward	KC	10	101
6	D.Brown	CAR	9	47
6	C.Davis	TB	9	50
6	D.Kirkpatrick	ARI	9	72
6	M.Lattimore	NO	9	106
10	B.Austin	NYJ	8	65
10	S.Barrett	TB	8	45
10	R.Evans	TEN	8	79
10	C.Gardner-Johnson	NO	8	74
10	M.Humphrey	BAL	8	116
10	M.Jackson	PHI	8	57
10	J.Jenkins	NO	8	83
10	C.Jones	KC	8	66
10	J.Lewis	DAL	8	105
10	M.Peters	BAL	8	81
10	J.Smith	DAL	8	82
10	Z.Smith	GB	8	50

Includes declined and offsetting, but not penalties on special teams, turnover returns, or kneeldowns.

Top 10 Kickers, Gross Kickoff Value over Average

Rk	Player	Team	Kick Pts+	Net Pts+	Kicks
1	J.Tucker	BAL	+4.7	+6.4	95
2	D.Hopkins	WAS	+4.1	+1.7	73
3	T.Bass	BUF	+3.5	+10.0	101
4	J.Myers	SEA	+3.1	+6.3	88
5	J.Slye	CAR	+2.7	+5.0	78
6	J.Elliott	PHI	+2.5	+3.8	69
7	J.Bailey	NE	+2.3	+5.3	71
8	B.Mann	NYJ	+1.4	+0.1	28
9	H.Butker	KC	+1.1	-4.3	93
10	A.Seibert	2TM	+1.1	-1.4	20

Min. 20 kickoffs; squibs and onside not included

Bottom 10 Kickers, Gross Kickoff Value over Average

Rk	Player	Team	Kick Pts+	Net Pts+	Kicks
1	J.Fox	DET	-5.0	-4.1	58
2	R.Sanchez	IND	-3.0	+1.8	74
3	L.Cooke	JAX	-2.9	-1.0	45
4	Y.Koo	ATL	-2.6	-2.6	64
5	K.Fairbairn	HOU	-2.3	+1.4	83
6	S.Gostkowski	TEN	-2.0	+0.1	84
7	D.Bailey	MIN	-2.0	-9.7	76
8	S.Sloman	2TM	-1.6	-2.9	44
9	Z.Gonzalez	ARI	-1.5	2.5	62
10	G.Gano	NYG	-1.1	-7.1	69

Min. 20 kickoffs; squibs and onside not included

Top 10 Punters, Gross Punt Value over Average

Rk	Player	Team	Punt Pts+	Net Pts+	Punts
1	J.Bailey	NE	+16.6	+18.9	55
2	T.Way	WAS	+12.2	+17.9	73
3	M.Dickson	SEA	+11.7	+13.9	61
4	J.Fox	DET	+9.1	+12.2	59
5	S.Koch	BAL	+3.8	+10.1	51
6	J.Berry	PIT	+3.7	+0.4	57
7	J.Charlton	CAR	+3.5	+2.6	45
8	B.Kern	TEN	+3.3	+2.9	37
9	K.Huber	CIN	+3.3	+7.6	71
10	P.O'Donnell	CHI	+3.3	-1.8	64

Min. 20 punts

Bottom 10 Punters, Gross Punt Value over Average

Rk	Player	Team	Punt Pts+	Net Pts+	Punts
1	T.Long	LAC	-13.5	-37.8	60
2	B.Colquitt	MIN	-13.2	-13.7	56
3	B.Mann	NYJ	-8.4	-12.8	82
4	S.Hofrichter	ATL	-7.8	-2.1	56
5	T.Morstead	NO	-4.0	+8.3	62
6	D.Colquitt	2TM	-3.4	-0.9	26
7	S.Martin	DEN	-3.3	-4.5	66
8	C.Johnston	PHI	-3.0	-0.8	72
9	J.Gillan	CLE	-2.9	-1.7	51
10	R.Sanchez	IND	-2.7	-0.1	43

Min. 20 punts

Top 10 Kick Returners, Value over Average

Rk	Player	Team	Pts+	Returns
1	C.Patterson	CHI	+9.1	35
2	D.Duvernay	BAL	+8.7	21
3	A.Roberts	BUF	+7.4	32
4	I.Rodgers	IND	+7.4	24
5	B.Pringle	KC	+7.0	10
6	B.Wilson	CIN	+6.7	24
6	J.Agnew	DET	+5.1	28
8	N.Adderley	LAC	+4.1	11
8	T.Cannon	CAR	+3.6	10
10	D.Johnson	CLE	+1.6	14

Min. eight returns

Bottom 10 Kick Returners, Value over Average

Rk	Player	Team	Pts+	Returns
1	B.Powell	ATL	-4.5	17
2	D.Spencer	DEN	-4.3	15
3	K.Raymond	TEN	-4.1	15
4	B.Scott	PHI	-3.7	28
5	D.Lewis	NYG	-2.6	24
6	C.Claybrooks	JAX	-2.0	15
7	D.Shepherd	GB	-2.0	11
8	M.Taylor	GB	-1.9	9
9	G.Olszewski	NE	-1.7	18
10	D.Peoples-Jones	CLE	-1.7	18

Min. eight returns

Top 10 Punt Returners, Value over Average

Rk	Player	Team	Pts+	Returns
1	G.Olszewski	NE	+15.2	20
2	D.Spencer	DEN	+7.2	16
3	K.Cole	JAX	+6.9	9
4	J.Grant	MIA	+5.3	29
5	N.Hines	IND	+4.2	30
6	J.Agnew	DET	+4.0	14
7	J.Peppers	NYG	+4.0	15
8	D.Harris	NO	+3.7	17
9	H.Renfrow	LV	+2.9	23
10	R.McCloud	PIT	+1.9	29

Min. eight returns

Bottom 10 Punt Returners, Value over Average

Rk	Player	Team	Pts+	Returns
1	S.Sims	WAS	-6.7	24
2	N.Webster	LAR	-5.7	25
3	C.Beebe	MIN	-3.7	9
4	P.Cooper	CAR	-3.7	20
5	D.Peoples-Jones	CLE	-3.0	18
6	G.Ward	PHI	-2.9	21
7	C.Kupp	LAR	-2.5	9
7	K.Hill	LAC	-2.1	12
9	D.Carter	2TM	-2.0	15
10	C.Lamb	DAL	-1.9	24

Min. eight returns

Top 20 Special Teams Plays

Rk	Player	Team	Plays	Rk	Player	Team	Plays
1	G.Odum	IND	20	13	R.Ford	PHI	11
2	C.Barton	SEA	16	13	S.McManis	CHI	11
3	N.Bellore	SEA	14	13	J.Tuioti-Mariner	ATL	11
3	J.Bethel	NE	14	16	O.Burks	GB	10
5	N.Dzubnar	TEN	13	16	C.Ballentine	NYG	10
5	E.Turner	ARI	13	16	C.Carter	CIN	10
7	M.Killebrew	DET	12	16	K.Crossen	HOU	10
7	J.Layne	PIT	12	16	J.Dangerfield	PIT	10
7	E.Robinson	ATL	12	16	T.Matakevich	BUF	10
7	T.Summers	GB	12	16	T.Thomas	CLE	10
7	S.Takitaki	CLE	12	16	T.Vallejo	ARI	10
7	N.Webster	LAR	12				

Plays = tackles + assists; does not include onside or end-half squib kicks.

Top 10 Offenses, 3-and-out per drive

Rk	Team	Pct
1	IND	11.7%
2	CAR	12.3%
3	BUF	13.8%
4	KC	14.2%
5	LV	14.5%
6	DAL	15.3%
7	CLE	15.7%
8	TEN	16.3%
9	MIN	16.8%
10	GB	17.0%

Top 10 Defenses, 3-and-out per drive

Rk	Team	Pct
1	LAR	28.2%
2	PIT	27.4%
3	SF	22.7%
4	PHI	22.3%
5	WAS	22.0%
6	NO	21.5%
7	DEN	21.1%
8	SEA	20.9%
9	CHI	20.8%
10	BUF	20.7%

Bottom 10 Offenses, 3-and-out per drive

Rk	Team	Pct
23	CHI	20.3%
24	NO	20.8%
25	ATL	20.8%
26	LAR	22.2%
27	PHI	23.5%
28	WAS	25.8%
29	MIA	26.6%
30	NYJ	26.6%
31	PIT	26.7%
32	CIN	26.7%

Bottom 10 Defenses, 3-and-out per drive

Rk	Team	Pct
23	HOU	17.0%
24	NYJ	17.0%
25	CLE	16.9%
26	ATL	16.6%
27	DAL	16.1%
28	JAX	15.9%
29	TEN	13.0%
30	DET	12.8%
31	CAR	12.3%
32	MIN	12.1%

Top 10 Offenses, Yards per drive

Rk	Team	Yds/Dr
1	KC	43.60
2	GB	40.93
3	TEN	40.61
4	BUF	40.33
5	LV	38.41
6	HOU	37.74
7	IND	37.49
8	CAR	36.88
9	TB	36.84
10	LAC	36.84

Top 10 Defenses, Yards per drive

Rk	Team	Yds/Dr
1	LAR	24.96
2	PIT	26.33
3	WAS	27.07
4	SF	29.17
5	TB	30.56
6	NO	31.13
7	PHI	31.43
8	CHI	32.29
9	BAL	33.13
10	LAC	33.13

Bottom 10 Offenses, Yards per drive

Rk	Team	Yds/Dr
23	MIA	31.83
24	CHI	31.81
25	PIT	31.47
26	JAX	30.70
27	NYG	30.47
28	PHI	30.35
29	DEN	30.22
30	CIN	29.77
31	WAS	29.02
32	NYJ	26.53

Bottom 10 Defenses, Yards per drive

Rk	Team	Yds/Dr
23	NYJ	37.58
24	NE	37.61
25	CAR	37.78
26	MIN	37.98
27	ATL	38.38
28	JAX	39.95
29	LV	40.10
30	TEN	40.19
31	HOU	41.88
32	DET	41.89

Top 10 Offenses, avg LOS to start drive

Rk	Team	LOS
1	NO	31.9
2	BAL	31.7
3	TB	30.9
4	SEA	30.9
5	IND	30.6
6	PIT	30.5
7	CHI	30.5
8	BUF	30.4
9	LV	29.7
10	MIA	29.6

Top 10 Defenses, avg LOS to start drive

Rk	Team	LOS
1	NE	24.5
2	SEA	25.2
3	IND	25.4
4	BAL	25.4
5	KC	25.9
6	MIA	26.3
7	BUF	26.4
8	NO	27.1
9	HOU	27.5
10	TEN	27.6

Bottom 10 Offenses, avg LOS to start drive

Rk	Team	LOS
23	SF	27.3
24	KC	27.2
25	LAR	27.2
26	DEN	26.7
27	LAC	26.7
28	PHI	26.7
29	JAX	26.6
30	NYJ	26.5
31	HOU	26.5
32	MIN	26.0

Bottom 10 Defenses, avg LOS to start drive

Rk	Team	LOS
23	LAR	29.3
24	NYJ	30.3
25	SF	30.4
26	CLE	30.4
27	JAX	30.5
28	PHI	30.6
29	DAL	30.9
30	DEN	31.6
31	LAC	31.7
32	MIN	32.7

Top 10 Offenses, Points per drive

Rk	Team	Pts/Dr
1	GB	3.22
2	TEN	2.98
3	BUF	2.98
4	KC	2.86
5	TB	2.74
6	NO	2.73
7	SEA	2.66
8	LV	2.63
9	BAL	2.61
10	MIN	2.47

Top 10 Defenses, Points per drive

Rk	Team	Pts/Dr
1	LAR	1.48
2	PIT	1.65
3	WAS	1.74
4	BAL	1.75
5	MIA	1.80
6	TB	1.92
7	NO	1.96
8	SF	2.02
9	ARI	2.04
10	CHI	2.06

Bottom 10 Offenses, Points per drive

Rk	Team	Pts/Dr
23	SF	2.06
24	NE	2.00
25	LAR	1.94
26	CIN	1.77
27	WAS	1.75
28	DEN	1.72
29	NYG	1.69
30	JAX	1.68
31	PHI	1.67
32	NYJ	1.36

Bottom 10 Defenses, Points per drive

Rk	Team	Pts/Dr
23	CLE	2.52
24	NYJ	2.54
25	DAL	2.57
26	CAR	2.57
27	TEN	2.67
28	MIN	2.68
29	JAX	2.77
30	HOU	2.85
31	LV	2.86
32	DET	3.04

Top 10 Offenses, Better DVOA with Shotgun

Rk	Team	% Plays Shotgun	DVOA Shot	DVOA Not	Yd/Play Shot	Yd/Play Not	DVOA Dif
1	BUF	71%	27.7%	-8.3%	6.8	5.5	36.0%
2	PIT	83%	1.8%	-29.1%	5.9	3.6	30.9%
3	LV	59%	11.4%	-9.9%	7.1	4.8	21.4%
4	TEN	42%	31.5%	10.2%	6.2	6.4	21.3%
5	MIA	81%	2.9%	-18.1%	6.0	3.5	21.0%
6	ATL	54%	4.9%	-10.9%	5.9	5.2	15.8%
7	SF	58%	4.4%	-10.4%	6.1	5.3	14.7%
8	GB	60%	35.2%	20.7%	7.0	5.8	14.5%
9	CIN	77%	-14.4%	-28.7%	5.0	4.8	14.3%
10	KC	81%	26.9%	12.9%	6.6	5.5	13.9%

Bottom 10 Offenses, Better DVOA with Shotgun

Rk	Team	% Plays Shotgun	DVOA Shot	DVOA Not	Yd/Play Shot	Yd/Play Not	DVOA Dif
23	IND	75%	3.5%	0.9%	6.4	5.1	2.5%
24	PHI	82%	-16.7%	-17.9%	5.4	4.5	1.2%
25	SEA	70%	13.8%	13.5%	5.9	6.0	0.2%
26	CHI	65%	-11.6%	-9.1%	5.3	5.1	-2.5%
27	DEN	66%	-21.3%	-17.9%	5.7	4.7	-3.4%
28	TB	59%	17.5%	22.6%	6.5	6.4	-5.1%
29	DAL	66%	-10.9%	-4.5%	5.7	4.9	-6.4%
30	NE	53%	-11.2%	-3.6%	5.3	5.5	-7.7%
31	MIN	38%	-1.8%	10.4%	6.3	6.2	-12.2%
32	NO	55%	3.8%	18.3%	6.1	5.7	-14.5%

Top 10 Offenses, Better DVOA with Play-Action

Rk	Team	% PA	DVOA PA	DVOA No PA	Yd/Play PA	Yd/Play No PA	DVOA Dif
1	TB	20%	69.3%	27.7%	10.0	6.9	41.6%
2	DET	24%	41.4%	4.3%	9.1	6.1	37.0%
3	JAX	19%	20.6%	-16.2%	7.0	5.4	36.7%
4	ATL	26%	36.4%	7.1%	8.4	5.9	29.3%
5	DEN	24%	7.9%	-20.4%	6.7	5.7	28.3%
6	CHI	31%	17.0%	-6.6%	7.0	5.4	23.6%
7	HOU	22%	41.7%	18.1%	8.8	7.3	23.6%
8	GB	36%	65.9%	42.3%	7.7	7.6	23.5%
9	ARI	32%	27.4%	8.2%	8.1	6.1	19.2%
10	BAL	34%	24.9%	6.2%	7.4	6.0	18.6%

Bottom 10 Offenses, Better DVOA with Play-Action

Rk	Team	% PA	DVOA PA	DVOA No PA	Yd/Play PA	Yd/Play No PA	DVOA Dif
23	CIN	24%	-7.8%	-3.7%	6.5	5.3	-4.2%
24	NYJ	24%	-16.3%	-11.2%	6.6	5.2	-5.1%
25	PHI	27%	-20.4%	-8.5%	5.6	5.5	-11.9%
26	LV	26%	12.6%	24.8%	6.4	7.9	-12.2%
27	NYG	27%	-19.7%	-7.6%	5.7	5.4	-12.2%
28	TEN	36%	30.8%	45.1%	9.1	6.4	-14.2%
29	KC	35%	37.4%	56.1%	7.9	7.2	-18.6%
30	CAR	22%	-2.2%	17.0%	6.2	6.9	-19.2%
31	IND	25%	-5.0%	21.6%	7.4	7.2	-26.6%
32	PIT	12%	-15.4%	15.8%	5.5	6.4	-31.2%

Top 10 Defenses, Better DVOA vs. Shotgun

Rk	Team	% Plays Shotgun	DVOA Shot	DVOA Not	Yd/Play Shot	Yd/Play Not	DVOA Dif
1	MIN	58%	-7.5%	16.7%	6.1	6.4	-24.2%
2	NE	69%	1.0%	22.2%	5.9	6.0	-21.3%
3	NO	67%	-25.6%	-8.0%	5.4	5.1	-17.6%
4	TEN	73%	10.6%	13.7%	6.0	6.1	-3.1%
5	MIA	69%	-4.3%	-1.3%	6.4	5.4	-3.0%
6	WAS	66%	-19.0%	-17.3%	4.9	5.0	-1.7%
7	DAL	61%	5.4%	6.7%	6.1	5.9	-1.3%
8	BUF	66%	-2.6%	-1.6%	5.9	5.2	-1.1%
9	DEN	65%	0.1%	-0.7%	5.9	5.6	0.8%
10	BAL	71%	-6.4%	-8.1%	5.5	5.1	1.7%

Bottom 10 Defenses, Better DVOA vs. Shotgun

Rk	Team	% Plays Shotgun	DVOA Shot	DVOA Not	Yd/Play Shot	Yd/Play Not	DVOA Dif
23	DET	59%	22.1%	11.9%	6.9	6.1	10.3%
24	PIT	73%	-17.0%	-27.3%	5.2	4.5	10.3%
25	LAC	66%	8.4%	-2.3%	6.0	4.9	10.7%
26	JAX	58%	21.5%	7.5%	7.1	6.1	14.0%
27	CHI	58%	0.7%	-17.5%	6.0	5.0	18.2%
28	CAR	62%	15.5%	-4.1%	6.1	5.3	19.6%
29	NYG	70%	10.7%	-10.1%	6.0	4.2	20.8%
30	HOU	60%	23.4%	2.3%	6.7	6.1	21.1%
31	CIN	73%	17.1%	-10.4%	6.6	5.3	27.5%
32	SEA	68%	12.3%	-21.1%	6.1	4.4	33.4%

Top 10 Defenses, Better DVOA vs. Play-Action

Rk	Team	% PA	DVOA PA	DVOA No PA	Yd/Play PA	Yd/Play No PA	DVOA Dif
1	PIT	18%	-42.2%	-13.9%	6.3	5.4	-28.3%
2	CLE	25%	-2.4%	24.0%	6.7	6.4	-26.4%
3	CAR	26%	-3.3%	23.0%	6.2	6.5	-26.4%
4	SEA	28%	-5.8%	20.4%	5.8	6.6	-26.2%
5	JAX	32%	19.8%	35.6%	8.1	8.0	-15.8%
6	CIN	27%	8.6%	22.8%	7.4	6.9	-14.2%
7	GB	24%	0.9%	6.4%	7.3	5.9	-5.5%
8	SF	28%	-7.2%	-1.7%	6.1	6.1	-5.5%
9	HOU	32%	23.2%	26.3%	7.9	6.8	-3.1%
10	DET	30%	30.8%	33.4%	8.7	7.7	-2.6%

Bottom 10 Defenses, Better DVOA vs. Play-Action

Rk	Team	% PA	DVOA PA	DVOA No PA	Yd/Play PA	Yd/Play No PA	DVOA Dif
23	DEN	27%	13.6%	-5.0%	7.5	6.2	18.6%
24	WAS	28%	-2.3%	-25.1%	6.3	5.1	22.8%
25	MIA	29%	14.2%	-12.0%	8.3	6.4	26.2%
26	BUF	28%	22.5%	-6.2%	7.4	5.9	28.7%
27	DAL	32%	32.3%	2.8%	8.1	6.2	29.5%
28	NO	27%	7.1%	-24.5%	7.5	5.7	31.6%
29	MIN	31%	27.3%	-6.7%	8.9	6.7	33.9%
30	LAR	22%	20.4%	-22.5%	7.7	4.7	42.9%
31	NE	28%	40.0%	-3.9%	8.6	6.4	44.0%
32	TEN	24%	62.4%	11.0%	9.6	6.0	51.4%

2019 Defenses with and without Pass Pressure

Rank	Team	Plays	Pct Pressure	DVOA with Pressure	Yds with Pressure	DVOA w/o Pressure	Yds w/o Pressure	DVOA Dif	Rank
1	PIT	611	30.4%	-105.7%	1.8	17.8%	7.2	-123.4%	26
2	LAR	635	30.2%	-78.4%	3.1	13.8%	6.4	-92.2%	12
3	NO	638	30.1%	-72.9%	3.0	9.6%	7.6	-82.5%	8
4	KC	630	29.8%	-56.9%	4.1	31.3%	7.6	-88.2%	10
5	MIA	613	29.4%	-92.9%	3.2	33.9%	8.5	-126.8%	29
6	PHI	605	29.3%	-86.1%	2.8	55.6%	8.4	-141.7%	31
7	TB	693	29.0%	-88.8%	3.2	27.8%	7.3	-116.6%	21
8	NE	560	28.9%	-64.0%	3.2	37.7%	8.6	-101.7%	15
9	WAS	607	27.7%	-110.7%	1.5	17.0%	7.0	-127.7%	30
10	DAL	588	27.0%	-73.5%	4.0	43.9%	7.9	-117.4%	23
11	BAL	667	26.7%	-78.7%	3.2	27.7%	6.8	-106.4%	17
12	SF	611	26.5%	-51.2%	3.4	13.5%	7.1	-64.7%	4
13	NYJ	653	25.6%	-70.6%	3.4	53.4%	8.4	-124.0%	27
14	ARI	664	25.5%	-89.7%	1.7	30.9%	7.7	-120.6%	24
14	NYG	650	25.1%	-70.8%	2.0	41.8%	7.6	-112.6%	18
14	BUF	649	25.3%	-36.5%	4.7	15.7%	6.9	-52.2%	1
17	CAR	639	24.9%	-58.2%	4.0	37.6%	7.2	-95.9%	14
18	ATL	689	24.7%	-73.9%	4.3	39.9%	8.5	-113.9%	19
19	DEN	642	24.0%	-45.2%	4.0	15.5%	7.3	-60.7%	2
20	IND	638	24.0%	-56.3%	4.3	13.8%	7.4	-70.2%	6
21	CLE	648	23.9%	-75.5%	2.8	45.4%	7.7	-120.9%	25
22	SEA	758	23.9%	-84.8%	2.6	41.3%	7.6	-126.1%	28
23	LAC	603	23.1%	-71.8%	3.0	32.9%	7.4	-104.7%	16
24	TEN	683	23.0%	-38.8%	3.9	44.1%	7.8	-82.9%	9
25	GB	613	22.8%	-110.6%	2.5	37.1%	7.3	-147.7%	32
26	LV	635	22.8%	-53.2%	4.4	37.1%	8.0	-90.2%	11
27	CHI	619	22.8%	-66.5%	3.5	26.1%	7.4	-92.6%	13
28	DET	610	21.0%	-61.1%	4.2	56.2%	9.0	-117.3%	22
29	JAX	595	20.2%	-32.5%	4.6	45.4%	8.9	-77.9%	7
30	HOU	600	20.0%	-66.8%	2.1	47.7%	8.4	-114.5%	20
31	CIN	592	19.9%	-31.3%	5.7	30.9%	7.4	-62.3%	3
32	MIN	592	18.9%	-50.4%	4.1	17.2%	8.1	-67.6%	5
NFL AVERAGE		**632**	**25.2%**	**-70.1%**	**3.3**	**32.7%**	**7.7**	**-102.7%**	

Includes scrambles and Defensive Pass Interference. Does not include aborted snaps.

Author Bios

Editor-in-Chief and NFL Statistician

Aaron Schatz is the creator of FootballOutsiders.com and the proprietary NFL statistics within *Football Outsiders Almanac*, including DVOA, DYAR, and adjusted line yards. He is also responsible each year for producing the Football Outsiders NFL team projections. He writes regularly for ESPN+ and ESPN Chalk and has done custom research for a number of NFL teams. *The New York Times Magazine* referred to him as "the Bill James of football." Readers should feel free to blame everything in this book on the fact that he went to high school six miles from Gillette Stadium before detouring through Brown University and eventually landing in Auburn, Massachusetts. He promises that someday Bill Belichick will retire, the Patriots will be awful, and he will write very mean and nasty things about them. Based on what we saw last year, it may not even take Belichick retiring.

Layout and Design

Vincent Verhei has been a writer and editor for Football Outsiders since 2007. In addition to writing for *Football Outsiders Almanac 2021*, he did all layout and design on the book. During the season, he writes the Quick Reads column covering the best and worst players of each week according to Football Outsiders metrics. His writings have also appeared in *ESPN The Magazine* and in Maple Street Press publications, and he has done layout on a number of other books for Football Outsiders and Prospectus Entertainment Ventures. His other night job is as a podcast host for pro wrestling/MMA website Figurefouronline.com. He is a graduate of Western Washington University.

Fantasy Football Statistician

Scott Spratt is responsible for the KUBIAK fantasy football projections in this book as well as the weekly fantasy projections available on FootballOutsiders.com. He got into analytics through his baseball work for Sports Info Solutions and writing for ESPN and FanGraphs, but he loves football analytics because of the intricacies of the sport. He is a Sloan Analytics Research Paper Competition and Fantasy Sports Writers Association award winner and was a 2018 finalist for FSWA Football Writer of the Year for his writing for Pro Football Focus. He is an elusive native Charlottean and has the Jimmy Clausen-given scars to prove it.

College Football Statisticians

Parker Fleming is an independent college football analyst from Fort Worth, Texas, responsible for the college football EPA numbers in this book. He hosts a podcast and writes the "Purple Theory" newsletter covering TCU, the Big 12, and college football.

Brian Fremeau has been analyzing college football drive stats for Football Outsiders since 2006. A lifelong Fighting Irish fan, Brian can be found every home football Saturday in Notre Dame Stadium. He can be found there every day, in fact, due to his campus facility operations responsibilities. He lives in South Bend, Indiana, with his wife and two daughters.

Contributors

Thomas Bassinger has been writing for the *Football Outsiders Almanac* since 2019. After nearly 15 years in Tampa—six covering the NFL and the Buccaneers—he recently returned home to Philadelphia, mainly for the pretzels but also to join the *Inquirer*. He's the proud father of a singer/flutist and an electric guitarist/kickball superstar.

Ian Boyd covers Texas and Big 12 football on InsideTexas.com and is the author of *Flyover Football: How the Big 12 Became the Frontier for Modern Offense*.

Derrik Klassen is from the Central Valley of California, though he grew up near Tampa Bay, Florida. Covering the NFL draft gave him his start but studying the NFL itself has taken precedence. He has been published at NBC Sports Edge, SB Nation, and Bleacher Report, and has worked for Optimum Scouting, doing charting and scouting reports for their NFL Draft Guide.

Bryan Knowles has been covering the NFL since 2010 with his work appearing on ESPN, Bleacher Report and Fansided. He has been with Football Outsiders since 2016, handling Scramble for the Ball, offseason stat articles, and the various bric-a-brac that comes from a lifetime of staring at spreadsheets and willing them to make some sort of sense. He continues to hold out hope that the Dayton Triangles will one day reform and win their first national championship.

Rivers McCown has written for ESPN.com, Bleacher Report, *USA Today*, and Athlon, among other places. He has edited for Football Outsiders, *Rookie Scouting Portfolio*, and *Pre-Snap Reads Quarterback Catalogue*. He lives in Houston, Texas, with his wife, under the control of two cats and three birds. He has covered the Houston Texans for The Athletic and on his own personal website, RiversMcCown.com, since 2018. He has also appeared in every *Football Outsiders Almanac* since 2011 and can't tell you how old the idea of that makes him feel.

Dan Pizzuta has previously written for Bleacher Report, numberFire, and Big Blue View. He got into football analytics after hearing Aaron Schatz on a podcast once and now he's here. He's currently a writer and editor for Sharp Football Analysis.

Andrew Potter blames Mega Drive classics John Madden Football and Joe Montana Sports Talk Football for his Transatlantic love of the gridiron game. He joined Football Outsiders in 2013 to help with the infamous Twitter Audibles experiment and still compiles Audibles at the Line to this day. He also authors the weekly Injury Aftermath report and co-authors Scramble for the Ball with Bryan Knowles. Though outwardly a fan of the New Orleans Saints, inwardly the Angus resident still yearns for his first gridiron love: NFL Europe's Scottish Claymores.

Mike Tanier is Football Outsiders' latest full-time addition as a Senior Analyst. He has also been contributing to *Football Outsiders Almanac* since 2005. It's a temporal paradox! You may also be familiar with his work from Bleacher Report, *The New York Times*, Sports on Earth, Fansided, and many other outlets. Mike is now a Big Ten dad, or at least a Rutgers dad, as well as a JV tennis and marching band dad. Finally, Mike is the author of *Long Snapper's Blues*, the coming-of-age football-themed romcom book his own mother called "too depressing to finish."

Robert Weintraub is the author of the newly released *The Divine Miss Marble* as well as *The Victory Season, The House That Ruth Built,* and the *New York Times* bestseller *No Better Friend: One Man, One Dog, and their Extraordinary Story of Courage and Survival in WWII*. He has also been a regular contributor to Sports on Earth, Slate, Grantland, *Columbia Journalism Review*, and *The New York Times*.

Carl Yedor was born and raised in Seattle, Washington, and his first vivid football memory was "We want the ball, and we're going to score." In spite of that, he has remained a Seahawks fan to this day, which certainly paid off right around the time he began interning with Football Outsiders in February of 2014. As an undergrad at Georgetown University, he worked with the varsity football team (yes, Georgetown does have a football team) to implement football research into their strategy and game-planning, drawing on his coursework in statistics and his high school experience as an undersized offensive guard and inside linebacker to make recommendations. He lives in Arlington, Virginia, and started his career as an analytics consultant before transitioning to an internal-facing data science role with a credit union.

Acknowledgements

We want to thank all the Football Outsiders readers, all the people in the media who have helped to spread the word about our website and books, and all the people in the NFL who have shown interest in our work. This is our 17th annual book as part of the *Pro Football Prospectus* or *Football Outsiders Almanac* series. We couldn't do this if we were just one guy, or without the help and/or support from all these people:

- The entire staff at EdjSports, especially Tamela Triplett, Anthony Jones, Casey Ramage, Matt Noskow, and our website technical lead Aram Bojadžjan.
- Erik Orr for cover design.
- Cale Clinton, responsible for compiling both The Week in Quotes on our website and The Year in Quotes in this book.
- Mike Harris for help with the season simulation.
- Excel macro master John Argentiero.
- Jim Armstrong, who compiles our drive and pace stats.
- Abe vander Bent, who handles our data parser.
- Our offensive line guru Ben Muth and injury guru Zach Binney.
- Nathan Forster, creator of SackSEER and BackCAST, who is also responsible for improvements on Playmaker Score (originally created by Vincent Verhei).
- Jason McKinley, creator of Offensive Line Continuity Score.
- Jeremy Snyder, our incredibly prolific transcriber of old play-by-play gamebooks.
- Roland Beech, formerly of TwoMinuteWarning.com, who came up with the original ideas behind our individual defensive stats.
- Our editors at ESPN.com, in particular Tim Kavanagh.
- Our friends at Sports Info Solutions who have really expanded what we can do with game charting, particularly Dan Foehrenbach and Matt Manocherian.
- All the friends we've made on coaching staffs and in front offices across the National Football League, who generally don't want to be mentioned by name. You know who you are.

- Our comrades in the revolution: Bill Barnwell (our long-lost brother), Brian Burke and the guys from ESPN Stats & Information, Mina Kimes, Ben Baldwin, Neil Paine, Robert Mays, Danny Kelly, Kevin Clark, and K.C. Joyner, plus everyone at Pro Football Reference, the football guys from footballguys.com, and all of the young analysts doing awesome work with NFLscrapR all over Twitter.
- Also, our scouting buddies, including Andy Benoit, Chris Brown, Greg Cosell, Doug Farrar, Russ Lande, and Matt Waldman.

As always, thanks to our family and friends for putting up with this nonsense.

Aaron Schatz

Football Outsiders Multimedia

Football Outsiders broadcasts on Twitch at 1 p.m. Eastern time every Monday through Friday during the season and every Thursday during the offseason. You can check out those streams at www.twitch.tv/fboutsiders.

You can also find our Twitch broadcasts from Tuesday, Thursday, and Friday as podcasts on the Football Outsiders Podcast Network. Look for those wherever you get your podcasts or go to https://www.footballoutsiders.com/podcasts.

Follow Football Outsiders on Twitter

Follow the official account announcing new Football Outsiders articles and publishing infographics at **@fboutsiders**. You can follow other FO and *FOA 2021* writers at these Twitter handles:

Thomas Bassinger: **@tometrics**
Dave Bernreuther: **@bernreuther**
Zachary Binney: **@binney_z**
Ian Boyd: **@Ian_A_Boyd**
Parker Fleming: **@statsowar**
Brian Fremeau: **@bcfremeau**
Tom Gower: **@ThomasGower**
Derrik Klassen: **@QBKlass**
Bryan Knowles: **@BryKno**
Rivers McCown: **@RiversMcCown**
Ben Muth: **@FO_WordofMuth**
Dan Pizzuta: **@DanPizzuta**
Andrew Potter: **@bighairyandy**
Aaron Schatz: **@FO_ASchatz**
Scott Spratt: **@Scott_Spratt**
Mike Tanier: **@MikeTanier**
Vince Verhei: **@FO_VVerhei**
Robert Weintraub: **@robwein**
Carl Yedor: **@CarlYedor61**

Follow Football Outsiders on Facebook

https://www.facebook.com/footballoutsiders

Follow Football Outsiders on Instagram

https://www.instagram.com/fboutsiders/

MORE FROM

Like what you read? There are plenty of ways to get more of our content.

BLOG:
SPORTSINFOSOLUTIONSBLOG.COM

 **OFF THE CHARTS PODCAST**
APPLE PODCASTS, SPOTIFY, ANCHOR, AND MORE

TWITTER:
@SPORTSINFO_SIS

 **SISDATAHUB.COM**
ADVANCED NFL STATS AND LEADERBOARDS

NEWSLETTER:
SPORTSINFOSOLUTIONS.COM